AMERICA
THE
VIOLENT

AMERICA
THE
VIOLENT

by Ovid Demaris

COWLES BOOK COMPANY, INC.
NEW YORK

To Peace

Copyright 1970 by Ovid Demaris

SBN 402-12241-0

Library of Congress Catalog Card Number 70-87078

Cowles Book Company, Inc.
A subsidiary of Cowles Communications, Inc.

Published simultaneously in Canada by
General Publishing Company, Ltd., 30 Lesmill Road,
Don Mills, Toronto, Ontario

Printed in the United States of America

First Edition

CONTENTS

17414

Author's Note

To the authors listed in the bibliography, I offer my grateful thanks. I am equally grateful to George H. and Jane Smith for their invaluable assistance in researching and preparing the manuscript, and to my editor, Charles N. Heckelmann, who conceived the idea for this book and guided it to conclusion.

Preface

By some grisly coincidence, on the morning I began this preface the headlines of newspapers across the nation were written in blood. Actress Sharon Tate, the pregnant wife of Director Roman Polanski, and four others were found murdered in her fashionable Bel-Air home; according to one detective, all five had died "a horrible, vicious death."

Winnie Ruth Judd, the infamous "trunk murderess" of the nineteen-thirties, was undergoing an extradition hearing to determine whether or not she should be returned to Arizona where she had been confined to a mental institution until her escape seven years ago. *The Free Press,* an underground newspaper in the Los Angeles area, was being sued for $15 million by eighty narcotics agents. Their lives and the safety of their families, they claimed, had been endangered by incitement to violence on the part of the paper when it published their names and addresses. And in Saigon, eight Green Berets were being held for the murder of a Vietnamese double agent.

Two days later, two more murders, described by police as "copy-cat" killings, were discovered in Los Angeles. A man was found, stabbed to death with a meat-carving fork, the word "WAR" and the letters "xxx" cut into his flesh; and as in the Sharon Tate killings, "Death to Pigs" was scrawled in blood at the scene. Either a knife or a whip had slashed to ribbons the back of his female companion.

That same day in Melbourne Beach, Florida, two teen-agers were brutally murdered. The girl had been shot seventeen times. Her boyfriend, his hands and feet tied, was forced to watch and then shot in the head three times.

In San Jose, California, a youth with a blood-spattered white van was being questioned by police about the gory slaying of two other teen-age girls.

In Los Angeles, three members of US, a militant black-power group, were on trial for the shooting deaths of two Black Panther leaders in a UCLA schoolroom.

In New York, a college English teacher described his arrest during the People's Park riot in Berkeley, California, and how he had been clubbed and abused while held for nearly eighteen hours by police.

In Vallejo, California, several San Francisco newspapers received a coded letter claiming that the writer had committed several murders in the area and threatening that he would kill again. Decoded, the unpunctuated message read:

> I like kill people because it is so much fun it is more fun than killing wild game in the forest because man is the most dangerous animal of all to kill something gives me the most thrilling experience the best part of it is that when I die I will be reborn in paradise and all I have killed will become my slaves I will not give you my name because you will try to slow down or stop my collecting of slaves for my afterlife.

On the same day, the nude body of a strangled fifteen-year-old baby-sitter was found in Palmdale; and William Lennon, father of the singing Lennon sisters, was shot down on a golf course at Marina del Rey.

"She was so good. What kind of country? What kind of people?" sobbed Roman Polanski at his wife's burial.

What kind of country? What kind of people? The answer can be found in our history, but not in the ordinary history books one reads in school. Those history books are the products of another national failing, "historical amnesia."

Violence in America, the Report to the National Commission on the Causes and Prevention of Violence, tells how we have managed to ignore the strain of violence in American history. It is the result of "selective recollection," the report says . . . a rephrasing of what psychologists have long called 'screen memories.' As we look back at our lives we screen out the memories that are too unpleasant or for other reasons don't fit our self-image, and we retain what we like to linger on."

This book then is a case study of this amnesiac gap in our history, with selective recollection thrown in reverse. The end result is *America the Violent*—not a pretty picture, but the truth seldom is.

OVID DEMARIS

Santa Barbara, California
September, 1969

Prologue

The record of America's violence goes back to the fog-shrouded sagas of the vikings, the wild and wooly sea rovers whose great dragon-ships were the first to sight our shores. For it was the vikings—Eric the Red with hair and beard the color of fire; his son Leif the Lucky; Thorfinn Karselfni, whose son Snorro was the first white child born in America; and their fierce pirate bands—who brought us our first war and our first murderess.

Leif Ericson arrived first, landing somewhere on the New England coast about A.D. 1000, and his brother, Thorwald, set out for the New World a few years later. Upon landing, Thorwald and his crew discovered three skin canoes drawn up on the beach with three Indians (or *Skraelings*, as they called them) under each. With a single-minded ferocity that would have done credit to later explorers, they immediately seized all but one of the Indians and slaughtered them in cold blood.

But the vikings had met their match at last, for from that brutal moment on, the nomadic hunters who lived so peacefully on the bountiful continent they had discovered in their wanderings were their sworn enemies. The vikings fought with heavy swords and iron axes. The Indians used arrows, which they shot from behind the protection of trees. This kind of warfare proved to be more than the vikings could withstand.

1

They left the land once and for all, and America continued to be—for a time—what one historian has called "the biggest secret" in the world.

First, however, the Amazonian Freydis, Leif's bastard half-sister, would make an even bloodier visit, during which she would raise her ax in America's first mass murder.

Her expedition had barely reached land before trouble broke out between the two groups. Freydis refused to permit Helgi and Finnbogi, two brothers who had sailed with her and Thorward, her husband, to share Leif's house and forced them to build a hut to live in. That was only the beginning. As winter set in, Freydis' band and that of Helgi and Finnbogi began to quarrel until finally the two groups lived in total isolation from each other.

Apparently Freydis had been planning from the beginning the grim events that were to follow. One morning early in spring she arose while her husband was still sleeping and walked barefooted to the hut occupied by the brothers, where she woke Finnbogi and told him she wished to exchange ships with him. He readily agreed, and she returned to Leif's house and got back into bed with Thorward, being careful to place her cold, wet feet against his back. Naturally he woke up and asked what was going on.

"I have been to the brothers," Freydis said, "to try to buy their ship, for I wished to have a larger vessel, but they received my overtures so ill, that they struck me, and handled me very roughly."

Poor Thorward was no match for the schemes of his wife. He arose from bed and called on his men to arm themselves. Then he proceeded to the hut and, catching the brothers and all their men asleep, he disarmed and bound them. They were led from the hut one at a time and as they came out Freydis ordered them killed. In but a few minutes the dew-wet grass was red with blood. But Freydis' men rebelled and refused to kill the five women from the group.

"Hand me an ax!" Freydis ordered.

Ax in hand, she set upon the five women, striking right and left, ignoring their screams and pleas. Finally all five lay hacked to pieces at her feet.

Her bare legs and skirt covered with the women's blood, Freydis turned to her followers and, combining threats with promises, prevailed upon them to keep her murder rampage secret. Shortly afterward she had the ship that had belonged to the brothers loaded with the products of the land they had collected, and set sail for Greenland. Reaching home, all the party told the story they had agreed on—that they had left the others to live in Vinland.

Thus America got off to a bloody start. And it was to get worse. More white men would explore the continent in search of wealth and bring violence with them—this time on a much larger scale and over a longer period.

In April of 1539 Hernando de Soto sailed for Florida with 720 men and 237 horses in search of the gold of the fabled Seven Cities. He was, as novelist and critic Bernard De Voto has stated in *The Course of Empire,* extraordinarily "fond of killing Indians."

His guns and horses terrified them, and he proved that he was "a child of the sun" by the godlike way in which he killed and tortured. His line of march—through Georgia, into parts of the Carolinas, into Tennessee, across Alabama almost to the Gulf, and northwest into Mississippi—was marked by burned villages, destroyed crops, and slaughtered natives. The Spanish of that day killed and maimed their foes with huge dogs of a wolfhound breed that could rip a man to pieces in a few minutes' time.

The Indians battled for their homes and hunting grounds. And after each victory there was reprisal. Whole villages were destroyed to avenge the dead Spaniards—men, women, and children died by sword, dog, and flame. Others were enslaved to act as porters for the conquerors.

3

The land over which the governor [de Soto] had marched lay wasted and was without maize," a chronicler tells us. "The governor ordered one of them to be burned . . . Many dashing into the flaming houses were smothered and, heaped upon one another, burned to death . . . Two the governor commanded to be slain with arrows and the remaining one, his hands having first been cut off, was sent to the cacique [chief] . . . The governor sent six to the cacique, their right hands and their noses cut off . . . Many were allowed to get away badly wounded, that they might strike terror into those who were absent."

They eventually turned back, still killing as they went, but de Soto's lust for gold was cooling and with it his will to live. He died on the banks of the Mississippi River, leaving the remnants of his army to struggle back to their starting point.

The Spanish conquerors—Balboa, León, Pineda, Urijalva, Pizarro, Coronado—instructed the Indian in the white man's ways in the South and Southwest; and the French, in the Northwest. The English did little better in New England and Virginia, where they surpassed all their predecessors—depending on one's point of view—with the first legal execution in the territory of what later became the United States of America.

When Raleigh's Roanoke colony disappeared without a trace, the inhabitants were assumed to have been killed or carried off by Indians. A colony at Jamestown was established shortly thereafter. At first John Smith succeeded in maintaining fairly amicable relationships with the natives.

The colonists, however, weren't so peaceful among themselves; there was almost constant warfare between Smith and his fellow settlers. In fact, Smith was brought ashore under arrest and set free only after sealed orders from the London Company revealed that he had been selected along with six others to form the colony's governing council.

Unfortunately, Smith could not always be on hand at Jamestown. One of his duties was to explore the countryside. He returned from one trip to find the colony in dire straits, with one dead and seventeen wounded by an Indian attack provoked by the president of the council, a most ambitious man named Wingate.

Smith's return, plus the firing of cannon from the ship that still remained off the coast, saved the settlement; but then Wingate plotted to seize Smith and ship him back to England to face trial on trumped-up charges. Smith insisted on an immediate trial in Jamestown and was acquitted, and Wingate was fined for being a troublemaker.

Off again into the wilderness to obtain food from the Indians, Smith returned to find more trouble flaring up among his own people. A group of them were about to sail for England and maroon the remaining settlers.

Taking swift command, Smith trained a cannon on them and threatened to sink the mutineers if they refused to come ashore and surrender. They chose surrender, and the ringleader was tried and sentenced to death.

If the first meeting of the English and the Indians was less violent than later encounters, it probably was because of the forbearance of the Indians toward the invaders of their lands.

"At almost any time during the first decade the Indians could have exterminated the whites simply by leaving them alone," Marion Starkey wrote in *Land Where Our Fathers Died*. "It was years before the latter raised enough corn to meet their needs . . . Without the Indians' willingness to barter their own by no means abundant store, Jamestown would have followed Roanoke Island into limbo."

During one of the "starving times" from which the colonists suffered, there was even an outbreak of cannibalism during which, it was reported, one man "powdered" his wife and ate her.

The English laid the groundwork for racial violence in Virginia, and in 1567 the French and Spanish in Florida brought with them another form of violence that has plagued the country through much of its history—religious bigotry.

Because of religious strife in France between Catholics

and Huguenots, the latter had come to fear for their lives, and it had occurred to some of their leaders, especially Admiral Gaspard de Coligny, that there might be need for a Protestant refuge in the New World. De Coligny still had considerable influence with the king and managed to win him over to the scheme. Two ships were sent to explore the coast of North America in search of a good site for a colony. The explorers settled in northern Florida near a river they called the River of May.

In August, 1565, a fleet commanded by Pedro Menéndez de Avilés, Adelantado of Florida, came in sight of the River of May. De Avilés had an *asiento,* or contract, issued by King Philip II of Spain that called for the liquidation of the Protestant foothold in what Philip considered part of his dominions.

De Avilés, a fanatic Catholic and determined to strike a blow against the growth of the Protestant heresy, was a good choice for the mission. His contract (it was not too dissimilar from the Mafia contracts of today) expressly stated that if he completely exterminated the French he would receive as a reward the governorship of Florida.

Fanaticism and cupidity were allied in the man who was to perpetrate one of the most vicious massacres of whites by other whites that stained the early history of America. Before he set about killing the Huguenots, Menéndez was kind enough to explain why they were being massacred. "I do this not unto Frenchmen with whom my king is at peace but unto heretics." The Spanish celebrated the capture of the fort by tearing out the eyes of the dead and slaughtering the wounded.

So violence from religious bigotry had come to America as had violence from racial bigotry. Both were to remain, to be compounded by the smug self-satisfaction of the Pilgrims—the "only true Christians in all the world," as their Reverend John Smyth described them.

But in the words of Gustavus Meyers in his *History of Bigotry in the United States,* they took with them to America "Old World ideas of proscription by force of which the estab-

6

lished religion or creed aimed to enforce its code of doctrines and assure its supremacy."

Of the 102 passengers cramped on board the *Mayflower*, only forty-one were Pilgrims in any sense of the word. The great majority were "strangers," mostly members in more or less good standing of the Church of England who were going to the New World not to practice their religion but simply to make better lives for themselves.

In the opinion of Christopher Martin, the Pilgrims were a "forwarde & waspish, discontented people. . . ." The opinion of the crew of the *Mayflower* was unprintable. They had come to hate the Pilgrims so much that they were "cursing them dayly with greevous execrations." Only the kindliness of the captain and the first mate and the courage of the other officers seem to have kept the crew from attacking the "saints" bodily.

Mutiny broke out on the *Mayflower* when the "strangers" came to understand that the contracts they had signed placed them under the rule of the "saints"; and that the Pilgrims determined to, as Willison puts it in *Saints and Strangers*, "impose their religious views upon the majority whether the latter chose to accept the Holy Discipline or not."

The Mayflower Compact has been hailed as a cornerstone of American freedom but it was actually intended, Willison points out, to "maintain the status quo on the *Mayflower*, to show inferiors in general and servants in particular their place and keep them where they belonged—i.e., under the thumbs of their masters."

"American democracy was not born in the cabin of the *Mayflower*," says historian Samuel Eliot Morison.

Violence broke out soon after the first landing at Plymouth when the Pilgrims desecrated Indian burial grounds, stole their buried grain and other food supplies and, led by Captain Myles Standish, also known as "Captain Shrimpe," chased a group of six Indians through the woods.

While a large part of the Pilgrim band was off exploring,

looting, and exchanging volleys with the Indians, back on
the *Mayflower* another first in the history of violence in
America took place. This time it was suicide.

The victim was Dorothy, the wife of William Bradford, a
Pilgrim leader who would later become the second governor of
Plymouth Colony.

The Pilgrims were barely settled before they were involved
in still more violence. Two ships arrived loaded with sixty
men who intended to found a colony nearby at the site of
the present-day Weymouth. This group immediately incurred
the Pilgrims' disfavor, for they were not Puritans and even
immoral in the eyes of the "saints." Some of them were
"keeping Indian women."

The Pilgrims did everything they could to make trouble
for their new neighbors, but the newcomers hardly needed
any help in that respect for they neglected their crops and
stole from the Indians. When whippings and sentences to
the pillory didn't stop the thievery, in an effort to placate the
Indians one of the worst offenders was sentenced to die.

However, the condemned man, being young and healthy,
was too important to the colony to be sacrificed and was
replaced on the gallows by a feeble old man. The specter of
capital punishment had first come to America in Jamestown
and now it had arrived in New England, with its evil compounded by the execution of an innocent man as a scapegoat
for the guilty one.

Meanwhile the local tribes were becoming more and more
restive. News of an intended attack on them from the latest
intruders and "Captain Shrimpe's" bullying added fuel to
their growing anger.

Bradford, Standish, and a man named Allerton, who were
chosen by the Pilgrims to deal with the situation, came up with
a plan to rid the colony of two menaces at once. They would
"liquidate" the new colony and slaughter the Indian leaders.
He was to pretend friendship for the Indians so that he "could

take them in such traps as they lay for others." Actually he planned to kill their sachem, cut off his head, and bring it back to Plymouth as a "warning and terror to all of that disposition."

Standish invited the chief, his eighteen-year-old brother, and two others to a feast at his headquarters. The Indians, whose code made much of honor and the proper treatment of guests, thought they would be safe. They soon learned differently.

The doors were locked the second they entered. Standish personally sliced one Indian to pieces with a knife while his men hacked the chief and the other brave to death with their swords. Only the eighteen-year-old boy was left alive. Standish spared his life so that he could be taken out and hanged publicly.

The Pilgrims then fell upon all the Indians they could find in the area. The women, whom they spared, were taken prisoner. Still not satisfied, Standish marched his forces out of town to hunt down a band of the Massachusets and chase them into the swamps.

Then Standish served his ultimatum on the neighboring town to abandon the settlement and leave the area. The frightened men boarded their pinnace and sailed for Maine, hoping to get passage for England in the fleet of fishing ships operating off that coast.

Standish brought the Indian chief's head triumphantly back to Plymouth and was "received with joy." He nailed the head to a spike on the Pilgrims' stockade, where it remained for many years as one of the "sights of Plymouth."

Such violence, cloaked in the guise of law and order, spread in America. The Puritans of Massachusetts made the death penalty legal for treason, murder, witchcraft, adultery, rape, sodomy, and arson. They enacted laws to punish the newly arrived Quakers, whom they denounced as a "cursed sect of heretics lately risen up in the world," and proceeded to hang them, too.

Their continuing need for more and more land, destruction of hunting grounds, and general mistreatment of the Indians finally provoked King Philip's War, the last serious attempt of the Indian to drive the foe into the sea from whence he came.

Philip was captured, but not before six hundred Englishmen had been killed in the fighting, thirteen towns destroyed, and more than a thousand buildings burned.

A Captain Benjamin Church ordered Philip's head and hands cut off and his body chopped up and left for the wolves. The hands were taken to Boston, and the head carried in triumph to Plymouth where it was placed on a spike and displayed for more than twenty years before Increase Mather, father of witch-hunter Cotton Mather, took the jawbone as a trophy. A minister obtained one of the hands, preserved it in rum, and toted it up and down the countryside for years as a prop for his preaching.

The Puritans, almost out of Indians to kill, now turned to hanging witches. The phenomenon started in Salem with a group of young girls and a West Indian slave woman, Tituba, who was fond of telling ghost stories. Before it was over, nineteen people had been hanged, one "witch" pressed to death, and some two hundred thrown into jail.

Previously New England and the rest of the colonies had been singularly free of the witchcraft mania that was sweeping Old England and all of Europe. But in 1681 a group of clergymen led by Increase Mather had taken it upon themselves to combat the danger to religion with proof of the supernatural. So they gathered and set down every instance they could discover of "divine judgments, tempests, floods, earthquakes, thunders as are unusual, strange apparitions, or what ever else shall happen that is prodigious, witchcrafts, diabolical possessions, remarkable judgments upon noted sinners, eminent deliverances and answers to prayer.

"Hangman, do your duty!" was an everyday verdict, and another witch was duly carted off and hanged.

The trials and hangings might have gone on indefinitely if the accusers had not made a mistake or two. They accused the wife of one of the most virulent of the witch-hunters, the Reverend John Hale, of being a witch. The minister suddenly changed his mind about the whole matter and denounced the trials as nothing but superstition.

In the ensuing Second Hundred Years' War England and France squared off in a worldwide struggle that always involved America sooner or later. In Europe wars were fought politely and with as little harm to civilians as possible. Those in America were bloody encounters involving ambush and massacre.

The Indians were used as shock troops by both sides. The Iroquois, urged on by English colonists, massacred the inhabitants of Lachine, near Montreal, in 1689, and according to Bernard DeVoto in *The Course of Empire*, ". . . a band of French militia and Christian Iroquois slaughtered many people at Schenectady, while other bodies of militia and Abenaki Indians raided and killed in New Hampshire and Maine. In 1704, another French and Indian raiding party surprised the sleeping village of Deerfield, Massachusetts, killed fifty-three persons and carried off one hundred and eleven others to captivity in Canada."

Captivity usually meant torture or burning at the stake, a practice that may have been introduced to the Indians by the Spaniards who learned it from the Inquisition.

Pierre Esprit Radisson was captured by the Mohawk and tortured but escaped and wrote of it later: "They burned a frenchwoman; they pulled out her breasts and took a child out of her belly, which they broyled and made the mother eat of it; so in short (she) died."

These are the Huron at work, as quoted by Daniel P. Mannix in *The History of Torture:*

> They often stopped him at the ends of the lodge, breaking
> first his fingers and then his arms, piercing his ears with

11

sticks, tying his hands and then twisting the cords to cut circulation. If he stopped, he was made to sit on the hot coals. On the seventh round, he collapsed so they dragged him onto the coals and put their torches into his crotch. Then the chief interfered, saying that he'd die before the public entertainment in the morning . . . The smoke issuing from his roasting flesh was terrible . . . anger did not appear on the faces of those torturing him but rather gentleness and humanity. Their words expressed only good-natured raillery.

At dawn he was taken outside to a platform with a tree trunk laid across it. He was tied to the tree but given enough rope so he could move about. Now he was burned everywhere as he ran back and forth from one man to another. One torch was down his throat while at the same time another was stuck up his fundament. His eyes were burned out. Burning torches were hung around his neck which he could not remove as his fingers were gone. If he fell down, men under the platform held up their torches and forced him to his feet. They stopped several times to revive him but at last he could no longer move. They then disemboweled him in an effort to make him sit up. Finally they ate the body.

In King William's War, the French and their Indian allies raided the border settlements of New England and New York. They killed, scalped, and burned all the way. When, in the end, they were defeated, the Iroquois changed sides!

Queen Anne's War brought the terror back. The so-called Christian Indians—Caunawaugha, Abenaki, Micmac—raided the English colonies over a period of ten years. With French support they raged through Maine, New Hampshire, and western Massachusetts, and struck so close to Boston that townspeople could smell the smoke of buildings burning twenty miles away. But the French failed and their Indian allies were decimated.

Pontiac's Rebellion followed and again the frontier trembled at the sound of war cries and the smell of burning flesh and buildings.

Our nation was conceived and born in violence—in the violence of the Sons of Liberty and the Patriots of the American port cities of the 1760s and 1770s," says *Violence in America*, the Report to the National Commission on the Causes and Prevention of Violence.

The Sons of Liberty seem to have anticipated the Students for a Democratic Society, for when the British Government passed the American Revenue Act in 1764 and then the Stamp Act in 1765 (in order to pay the debts incurred in the defense of the North American colonies during the French and Indian War) the attempt to collect such revenue led almost at once to fierce rioting on the part of the colonists.

Effigies of Andrew Oliver, the secretary of the Massachusetts Bay Province and stamp distributor, were hung from a huge elm known as the Great Tree. A large crowd gathered around the effigies, which were labeled "The Stamp Officer" and "The Devil." The crowd was entertained by spur-of-the-moment orations and then, led by six men carrying the images on a bier, paraded to the building that was to be the office of the stamp master. Forty of the leading Whigs in the city, disguised as mechanics, headed the march, and cries of "Liberty! No stamps!" echoed everywhere as the office was demolished and not a brick left standing.

Carrying off lumber from the ruined building, the mob built a bonfire on Fort Hill and burned the two effigies. Then they marched to Oliver's home, where they smashed the windows, poured inside, and broke up the furniture. The walls were defaced with various writings. Outside, the rest of the mob was tearing down the fencing and barn and rooting up the garden.

The mob struck again on August 26. This time every record and paper in the office of the registrar of the Vice Admiralty Court was carried into the streets and set on fire.

The Boston Massacre of 1770 began on March 2, when a

group of Boston rope makers took to antagonizing British troops stationed in the city. They cursed and threw rocks and generally made it impossible for the sentries to march their posts or for other troops to come and go.

This went on until March 5, when a Negro sailor, Crispus Attucks, goaded the crowd into pelting the sentries with snowballs and stones and "reviled them with scurrilous language." Others moved in closer and began to hit at the soldiers with clubs, beating their muskets down or trying to pull them out of their hands.

The day ended with five men dead and six wounded and the whole town in an uproar.

The American Revolution that followed was like the wars and riots that preceded it, with Indian raids, massacres, and atrocities on both sides. Not only was the language of violence augmented by a certain Colonel Lynch, ardent practitioner of the method that now bears his name, but according to *Violence in America:*

> . . . the meanest and most squalid sort of violence was from the very beginning to the very last put to the service of the Revolutionary ideals and objectives. The operational philosophy that the end justifies the means became the keynote of Revolutionary violence. Thus given sanctification by the Revolution, Americans have never been loath to employ the most unremitting violence in the interest of any cause deemed to be a good one.

All of the terrorism, however, wasn't on one side. The revolution was also a civil war between Patriot and Tory, and Tories who fell into American hands were sometimes treated as traitors rather than as prisoners of war. Tories living peacefully in their homes were subject to abuse, destruction of property, and violent death.

The most famous atrocity story of the revolution is the so-called Paoli Massacre in which the British supposedly bayoneted defenseless Americans who were trying to surrender. There is some doubt that this incident, which has been blamed on British General Gray, actually took place at all. The story may be based on a letter supposedly written by a Hessian soldier who said he took part in it.

One of the worst cases of pure savagery took place in what was to be the last engagement of the war in the North. A mixed force of British, Hessian, and Loyalist troops led by Benedict Arnold (who as a reward for his treason had been made a British brigadier general) landed near New London on the Connecticut shore. The town was defeated by two forts, Trumbull and Griswold.

At Fort Griswold about one hundred and forty militia under Lieutenant Colonel William Ledyard put up a brisk defense when Lieutenant Colonel Eyre led the attack against them. Eyre was mortally wounded and his men driven back. A second attack was also repulsed but the third was successful, and the British poured into the fort to find the Americans still stoutly resisting.

Several British officers and many of the troops had been killed before Ledyard offered to surrender. He extended his sword to Lieutenant Colonel Van Buskirt of the New Jersey Volunteers, a Tory regiment, and the man took it and then instantly plunged it into Ledyard. The rest of the Tories then began to massacre the defenders and the British and Hessians joined in.

While his men were slaughtering the garrison of Fort Griswold, Arnold was busy ravaging the nearby villages of his home state. At New London he burned the courthouse, the jail, churches, stores, shops, houses, wharves, shipyards, and a dozen ships of various sizes. The nearby town of Groton was also burned to the ground. More than one hundred and forty buildings went up in flames in both towns.

Apparently the American Revolution, was the beginning of a new age in which the old ways of war were to disappear, and in the passions of the times, things were done that would have horrified the professional soldiers of an earlier age when wars were fought by set rules and with as little bloodletting as possible.

As America became engaged in other wars in its by no means uniquely bloody history, the combatants involved, the number of casualties, and the sheer brutality were to increase until in future wars hundreds of thousands of civilians could be slaughtered from the air without causing any particular public outcry.

1 | New Nation, New Violence, 1788-1804

The period following the American Revolution was one of the uneasiest in the history of the nation. A new country was settling down to live with itself and the process was often riotous and bloody.

The first of many riots that rocked New York over the next hundred years took place April 13-14, 1788, and was aimed at an unusual target—the doctors of the city. What had the medical men done to arouse such ire? They were robbing graves—body snatching, as it was called then.

The anatomy classes of King's College (later to become Columbia University) needed cadavers for dissection. There was no provision under the law for obtaining bodies legally. Accordingly, the medical school had made it a class admission practice for each student to supply his own cadaver. The easiest place to get a corpse was from either Potter's Field or the Negro burial ground, where most bodies were buried in common graves without coffins. This body stealing caused little comment until a group of students grew so bold as to remove a body from the graveyard of Trinity Church.

The city's two weekly newspapers took notice and criticized the students severely, reminding their readers of the epidemic of grave robbing that had swept England and Scotland. Despite the outcry, the students continued their reckless activities. Public indignation grew but probably could have been held in check except for an unfortunate incident that took place on the afternoon of Sunday, April 13.

Dr. Richard Bayley was directing several medical students and physicians in the dissection of a cadaver in the laboratory of the New York Hospital. It was a warm, sunny day and the windows were open to let out the fumes from the freshly painted room and the odor of formaldehyde in which the bodies had been preserved. A group of small boys was playing on the lawn outside, and one of them suddenly spotted the ladders the painters had used, set it against the wall, and climbed it to look through the window of the laboratory.

What he saw left him staring, his mouth open. The students were dissecting a female cadaver, and one of them happened to look up and see the boy peering in the window. There is some confusion as to what actually happened then. One story says the student was merely hanging a severed arm up to dry; another, that he waved it at the boy in a spirit of grisly humor; and still a third, that a Dr. Hicks brandished the arm and shouted at the boy, "This is your mother's arm; get off the ladder or I'll hit you with it!"

The terrified boy slid down the ladder, ran home, and told his father. By a grim and almost unbelievable coincidence the boy's mother had died only a short time before. The father was so upset by his son's tale that he asked some friends to go with him to his wife's grave and there they found the casket had been opened and the body was gone.

Horrified and outraged, the men gathered together a group of their fellow stonemasons, armed themselves with clubs, axes, and crowbars, and marched on the hospital. As the story spread, traveling like wildfire and gathering gruesome details, more and more people joined the mob moving up Broadway.

Most of the doctors and students had fled the building by

18

the time the crowd smashed in the locked door of the wing where the laboratory was located. First they wrecked Dr. Bayley's museum of specimens, which was the best in the country; then they broke into the dissecting rooms. They "seized upon the fragments, heads, legs, arms and trunks and exposed them from the windows and doors to public view." The crowd outside roared for vengeance on the doctors, and their fury grew as several cartloads of body pieces were brought out and carried away for reburial.

Four students were discovered hiding in one of the rooms but, before the mob could harm them, Mayor James Duane arrived with Sheriff Robert Boyd and several well-known citizens. The sheriff placed the students under protective custody and had them escorted through the howling crowd to the jail in City Hall Park. Before the day was over, most of the medical students and doctors in New York had taken refuge in jail along with the original four.

It was just as well because the rioting had only begun. The next morning the size of the mob had almost doubled and now included a rougher element of loafers, criminals, and ne'er-do-wells. They assembled at the hospital and determined to search the houses of all twenty-five doctors who practiced in the city.

Mayor Duane, now thoroughly alarmed, called on Governor George Clinton. They faced the mob together and had the Riot Act read. When that didn't disperse the crowd, they appealed to them personally, promising that an official investigation would be made and the guilty punished. This pacified some people and they left, but the main body of the mob was not satisfied and set off to find the missing bodies.

The governor and the mayor went with them, still trying to reason with them and head off violence. A search of the medical rooms of King's College turned up nothing and neither did the searches of the doctors' houses. Gradually, then, the groups got tired and broke up.

But that afternoon about four hundred people began milling around the city jail, threatening the doctors and students inside and vowing to tear down the building if the bodies weren't turned over to them. Inside, the doctors, students, and ordinary criminals barricaded the doors and armed themselves with whatever they could find while Sheriff Boyd tried unsuccessfully to quiet the crowd.

The time had come to call out the troops since the police force wasn't big enough to cope with the situation. Still the mayor and the governor were reluctant to call out the militia, so they sent two small bodies of soldiers to make a demonstration, which they hoped would dispel the mob. The crowd threw dirt and stones at them, jeering and laughing until the soldiers wheeled about and marched away.

Emboldened by their easy victory and reinforced to the point where their number amounted to almost five thousand individuals, the mob rushed the jail and began to batter at the doors. When this didn't work, they smashed windows and tried to climb inside but were beaten back by the small force of defenders.

The governor then issued a call for the militia but only fifty men responded. The rest of the citizen soldiers were part of the mob. A call was sent out for experienced soldiers and for volunteers whose prominence might impress the unruly crowd.

There was a good response to this appeal and among the notables who turned out were John Jay, Alexander Hamilton, and Baron Friedrich Von Steuben, the former German officer who had trained Washington's army. Armed with swords and clubs and with the fifty militiamen as a nucleus, they marched against the mob.

Instead of scattering in the face of the military unit, the crowd screeched its defiance, and rained a hail of rocks and bricks down on the volunteers. John Jay, who was to become the first chief justice of the United States, was struck on the head by a brick and suffered a concussion that kept him in bed for ten days. Hamilton, later Secretary of the Treasury, was hit by a stone. Mayor Duane was knocked to the ground and trampled by the mob. Baron Von Steuben had urged the governor not to put down the riot with firearms but, when he was struck on the forehead by a paving stone, he changed his mind and shouted at Clinton to fire before they were all murdered.

The militia poured two volleys into the crowd and five rioters fell dead while others were wounded. Fire also came from the windows of the jail, but even that wasn't enough to keep the mob from pushing the militia and volunteers back down Broadway as far as St. Paul's Church. There the militia rallied, fixed bayonets, and charged.

Cold steel finally succeeded where musketry failed. The crowd turned and ran from the gleaming bayonets, and by the time help arrived from out-of-town units the next day, the riot was over. At its next session, the New York State Legislature passed laws making a legal supply of cadavers available and setting penalties for grave robbing.

While New Yorkers were rioting, other Americans were rebelling. Among the economic consequences of the revolution and the founding of the new nation were serious agrarian problems. The farmers were caught in a price squeeze between what they could get for their products and what they had to pay for things they bought. Many were heavily in debt and being sued by their creditors. In Massachusetts in 1786, this led to an uprising known as Shays' Rebellion.

During the early months of 1786, mobs had prevented the courts from sitting in Massachusetts. Accordingly, in November, Governor Bowdoin called out three regiments of infantry and three companies of artillery to assure peaceful and undisturbed sessions of the State Supreme Court in Cambridge. Insurgents from Berkshire, Middlesex, Hampshire, and

Worcester counties had gathered near Worcester to march on Cambridge because they believed, as Samuel Ely, one of their leaders and a former clergyman, put it:

> "We must throw up our constitution . . . the constitution is broke already, the Governor has too much salary, the Judges of the Superior Court have too much salary, we can get men that will ride the circuit for half the money . . . the General Court should not sit; we will pay no more respect to them than to puppies."

The militia prevented the proposed march on Cambridge but 350 of the insurgents did seize the courthouse in Worcester. The leader of the rebellion was Daniel Shays, a veteran of the revolution who had since been elected to various local offices.

Finding the way to Cambridge blocked, he led his followers westward toward the arsenal at Springfield. Shays arrived there on January 25, 1787, with a force of twelve hundred men, but found General Shepard waiting for them with companies of artillery. As the rabble advanced, Shepard ordered a "few whiffs of grape," and Shays' army broke ranks and faded away. They continued to retreat through Pelham to Petersham and finally dispersed completely. Shays' Rebellion was over. Governor Bowdoin's impressive show of firmness in the face of attack had saved the day.

A few years later, in 1791, Secretary of the Treasury Hamilton placed a tax on distilled liquor and thereby inadvertently precipitated another and larger rebellion known as the Whisky Insurrection.

The tax was anything but popular with the farmers of Pennsylvania, Virginia, and North Carolina. Their reaction has been described by Dale Van Every in *Ark of Empire:*

> On the frontier direct action was always a first impulse. Physical resistance to the federal impost was instant and vigorous. Mass meetings were held, committees of corre-

spondence organized, protests and memorials drafted. Violence was not at first publicly recommended but was from the first practiced.

A principal response was a popular and spontaneous program of intimidation. Roving gangs of night riders, commonly known as "Tom the Tinker's Boys," destroyed the stills of whisky makers who paid the tax. Federal officials were whipped, tarred and feathered, robbed and burned with heated irons. Inhabitants who admitted federal sympathies were threatened. A people accustomed to bear arms was up in arms.

Since the only troops in the army of the new nation were engaged in a campaign against the Indians under "Mad" Anthony Wayne, the government of President Washington was in a quandary.

The tension and trouble in the West was greatly increased by the influence of the French Revolution. Van Every tells us:

> A series of mass meetings led to the organization of "associations" pledged to mutual resistance to every manifestation of the national government's authority. The movement drew more of its inspiration from the contemporary extravagances of the French Revolution than from the earlier attitudes of the American Revolution. The incipient insurrection took on more and more of the aspects of a class war. Liberty poles were erected, tricolored badges flaunted, Jacobin slogans shouted.

Faced with near-revolution on its frontiers, the government knew it must take action. But that was easier said than done. John Neville, the excise inspector for western Pennsylvania, and United States Marshal David Lenox were fired on when they attempted to serve warrants, and local militia surrounded Neville's home and demanded that all warrants and tax records by destroyed. Neville had taken the precaution of arming his servants and they opened fire

23

when the house was attacked, killing one and wounding five of the insurrectionists.

Neville asked for protection from the nearest civil authorities. When this was refused, he called for Federal troops. Eleven men under the command of Major Abraham Kirkpatrick came from Pittsburgh to defend the house while Neville himself went into hiding.

The next day the rebels were joined by fresh detachments of militia from other districts until they numbered more than five hundred men. They all knew that an attack on Federal troops constituted rebellion against the United States. "The responsibility was accepted and the prospect welcomed."

The militia demanded that the troops inside the house surrender, and when refused, attacked the house. Men on both sides were wounded, and James McFarlane, a militia field commander was killed. The rebels set fire to the outbuildings and when flames threatened the main house, the defenders had to surrender. Lenox was beaten, and the house looted and burned.

The victorious insurgents sent a demand to Pittsburgh that Neville resign and all tax processes and warrants be destroyed. With no help in the offing, Neville and the other Federal officers and sympathizers fled down the Ohio River as five thousand rebel militia marched on Pittsburgh. That town was thought to be pro-government in sympathy, and the invaders intended to loot and burn it. But upon arriving there, they were greeted with hospitality instead of resistance and contented themselves with only minor looting.

Next the rebels began seizing and opening the United States mail. David Bradford, a local lawyer and politician and one of the leaders of the insurrection, seems to have had two reasons for this: first, the apprehension of Federal sympathizers; second, bringing the revolution to a head. A referendum was held to show backing for the actions of the rebels, but since the vote was not secret it was easy for the militants to make sure the more timid voted to their satisfaction.

If Bradford hoped to bring the matter to a head, he succeeded. On August 4, 1794, Justice James Wilson of the Supreme Court certified the western counties to be in a state of insurrection. President Washington then issued a call for the militias of Pennsylvania, New Jersey, Maryland, and Virginia to rally to the colors.

Since a great part of the Pennsylvania militia was in the field with the rebels, only those in the eastern section of the state reported for duty at Carlisle where they were joined by troops from New Jersey. The militia of Maryland and Virginia mustered at Cumberland, where they were placed under the command of Washington's old cavalry commander, "Light Horse" Harry Lee. Washington himself took command of the northern column.

Washington and Lee then led their columns into the territory of the rebellion. Faced by 12,950 soldiers of the "Army of the Constitution," the rebellion collapsed, dissolving almost as fast as it had started.

Meanwhile, an event had taken place farther to the west that would have ended the insurrection, anyway, by making it possible for Wayne to return with his well-trained "legion" to put it down.

Wayne had been placed in command by Washington after American forces had suffered two stunning defeats at the hands of the Indians. General Harmar, in 1790, had conducted a blundering campaign with ill-trained militia and a few regulars in the vicinity of what is now Fort Wayne, Indiana, and had allowed his forces to be cut up piecemeal.

The Revolutionary War General Arthur St. Clair had taken a force of six hundred regulars, eight hundred "levies," and six hundred militia to fight the Indians, and pushing west from Cincinnati, reached the Wabash River. There they were set upon by about a thousand Indians. The poorly trained, poorly led troops had become panic-stricken almost at once.

St. Clair and a few of his men managed to fight their way back to Cincinnati but 637 were killed and 263 wounded in what was probably the heaviest loss ever suffered by American troops at the hands of the Indian, far outdoing the disasters of Braddock and Custer.

It was at that point that President Washington had turned the problem of dealing with the Indians over to Wayne. This he succeeded in doing most effectively. After a careful and steady advance through the wilderness, Wayne's Legion came in sight of the British post of Fort Miami, where several thousand Indians had decided to make a stand.

At the Battle of Fallen Timbers, named for trees uprooted by a storm, he defeated the Indians and had the satisfaction of seeing the British, who had been stirring them up against American settlements, close the doors of the fort in the faces of those who sought shelter there. The Western tribes, their resistance broken, ceded their lands in Ohio to the United States by the Treaty of Greenville on August 3, 1795.

Even when there was no open warfare or rebellion along the Western frontier, it was still bloody enough. Much of the violence was perpetrated by renegade whites who preyed on travelers and settlers with far more ferocity than the Indians.

One of the most notorious of these men was Simon Girty, who had been involved in violence most of his life. He had seen his father killed by an Indian in a drunken brawl; and later he and his brothers were captured and taken to a Delaware village, where they saw their stepfather and an English woman tortured and burned at the stake. The orphaned children were distributed among various tribes, Simon going to the Wyandottes where he learned several Indian dialects and developed proficiency as a scout.

During Lord Dunmore's War, which was brought on by the murder of the great Chief Logan's family by pioneers, Girty served as a scout and messenger for the Colonial forces.

He is reported to have been very much impressed by a speech Logan made and which he transmitted to Dunmore:

> I appeal to any white man to say if ever he entered Logan's cabin hungry and I gave him not meat; if ever he came cold or naked and I gave him not clothing!
>
> During the course of the last long and bloody war, Logan remained in his tent, an advocate of peace. Nay, such was my love for the whites that those of my own country pointed at me as they passed and said, "Logan is the friend of the white man." I had even thought to live with you, but for the injuries of one man.
>
> Colonel Cresap, the last spring, in cold blood and unprovoked, cut off all the relatives of Logan, not sparing even women and children. There runs not a drop of my blood in the veins of any creature. This called on me for revenge. I have sought it. I have killed many. I have fully glutted my vengeance. For my country I rejoice at the beams of peace. Yet do not harbor the thought that mine is the joy of fear. Logan never felt fear. He will not turn on his heel to save his life. Who is there to mourn for Logan? Not one.

Whether this speech convinced Girty of the wrongs done the redman and turned him against the colonists—or whether his later actions were motivated by the fact that he is known to have regarded himself as a British subject—it is a matter of record that he sided with the Loyalists in the American Revolution and led his Indian allies in numerous raids against American settlements.

He led the Mingo Indians in raids against the villages around Fort Pitt during the Revolution and on his return had two scalps hanging from his belt. After an expedition into Kentucky, it was reported he carried enough scalps to decorate the front door of his cabin. He also had a captive woman whom he eventually turned over to the squaws for burning.

He wiped out a group of seventy Americans who were keel-boating up from New Orleans with military supplies from Fort Pitt, killing forty-two and capturing the rest for torture. He was in command of the Indians at the capture of Ruddle's Station, and although he had agreed that the British should have charge of all prisoners, when the gates swung open, he let the Indians run wild and massacre all who were inside. In another instance, he was present but took no part while a prisoner a day was burned for nine days. Girty talked the Indians into freeing the tenth prisoner to carry word of what had happened back to the settlements.

After the defeat and capture of Colonel William Crawford, who had been a friend of Girty's, the renegade is said to have looked on calmly while twenty-three charges of powder were fired into Crawford's body, his ears cut off and pieces of flesh gouged out of his body. When Crawford called to Girty to shoot him, Simon is supposed to have said that he didn't have a gun. Then he watched while the Mingo scalped the tortured man and poured hot coals over his skull before he died.

In the Indian Wars that followed the Revolution, Simon was back in action, leading his warriors in 1790 in an attack on Dunlap's Station in Kentucky. Failing to take the fort, he seized young Abner Hunt and attempted to bring about the surrender of those inside by burning the youth to death, forcing the defenders to listen to his agonized cries throughout the day. When the boy could no longer be heard and the fort still had not fallen, Girty was furious. Whether he did it himself or merely gave his consent is not clear, but someone took a flaming stick from the fire and shoved it into the rectum of the captive.

Girty was present at both Harmar's and St. Clair's defeats but was absent from the Battle of Fallen Timbers, and also from the Battle of the Thames where the Indians were defeated by General Harrison during the War of 1812. Maybe that accounts for the fact that he lived to a great age and died in bed in the middle of February, 1818.

While Simon Girty and his Indians were making things hot for settlers on the Northern frontier, other hard types were terrorizing settlers and travelers along the Wilderness Road, the Natchez Trace, and on the Ohio and Mississippi rivers.

Two early sociopaths of American history were the Harpe brothers—"Big Harpe," whose given name was Micajah, and "Little Harpe," or Wiley. They were born in North Carolina, two years apart. In 1795 they headed west with two sisters —Susan and Betsey Roberts. Susan, the elder of the two, claimed to be Big Harpe's legal wife, and Betsey was mistress to both men.

When they reached the Knoxville, Tennessee area, the Harpes acted like honest settlers for awhile. Little Harpe fell in love with Sally Rice, the daughter of a minister, and after a courtship of several months, her father performed the wedding ceremony. But normal living wasn't enough for the two brothers and they gradually drifted into cattle and horse stealing. They were arrested for the latter but managed to escape from the posse and vanish into the forest.

Shortly after that they committed the first of their many murders. A man named Johnson was found dead, floating in the Holston River. His belly had been ripped open, the entrails removed, and the cavity filled with stones. A second victim was found a few days later, south of Barboursville on the north branch of the Wilderness Road. He was an old pack-peddler named Peyton and he had been tomahawked. Farther on in the wilderness two more bodies were found, travelers named Paca and Bates on their way from Maryland to Nashville. Bates had been shot in the back and Paca's head had been split with a tomahawk.

About a month later a young man from Virginia, Stephen Langford, made the mistake of inviting two strange men and their three female companions to have breakfast with him at a roadside inn and displaying a "well-filled" wallet when he paid for it. A week later Langford's body was found tomahawked, stripped, and robbed. The Harpes had committed their fifth murder. A posse led by Captain Joseph Ballenger pursued them and found them with their small harem. All three women were pregnant.

Although special measures were taken to secure them in jail at Danville, Tennessee, the brothers escaped, leaving the women behind to give birth on county hospitality.

The Harpes had now become so infamous that posses meeting them on the trail turned away rather than try to capture them. Henry Scraggs, a famous "Kentucky Long Hunter," had two groups of men simply melt away from him in fear of the pair but he went on with his pursuit of them alone. He stopped to see an old friend, Colonel Trabue, hoping to get him to join the chase, and the two men were together when they found the body of Trabue's son after the Harpes had finished with him.

"Apparently the Harpes, famished and frenzied by the dangerous chase, had exploded in a very ecstasy of passion. Young Traboe had been shot, kicked, tomahawked, pummeled. His body was macerated by their blows, almost dismembered by their knives," Robert M. Coates says in *The Outlaw Years*.

And all the booty they got from the boy was a sack of beans and a bushel of flour. Scraggs and Trabue, both expert woodsmen, searched for days but found no trace of the Harpes. In the meantime, the three women had slipped out of Danville with their new-born offspring to meet their husbands at a pre-arranged rendezvous.

The massacre of the Trisword family was probably the most infamous of all the Harpes' crimes. A small caravan made up of the two Trisword brothers, their wives, "several children, and a few black servants" had made camp at a place called the point of Clay Lick woods.

The Harpes sneaked up on the sleeping camp at daybreak and opened fire. One Trisword brother and his wife were killed instantly and a child was mortally wounded. With wild yells the Harpes then bounded into the middle of the camp to complete their slaughter. The remaining Trisword brother thought it was an Indian raid and raced off "quite in his undress" to get help. When a rescue party reached the scene, they found "the ground covered for a space with the bodies of men, women, and children, white and black. Some of them dreadfully mangled; and some stripped to the skin."

The next morning Big Harpe committed still another murder—his own infant daughter.

The Harpes came to their ends separately. Big Harpe died at the hands of Moses Stegall whose wife and baby the brothers had murdered. Shot off his horse by another settler named Samuel Leiper, Micajah Harpe lay dying. Stegal came to bend over him and aimed his gun at the outlaw's head. Harpe tried to move his head away and Stegall laughed.

"I wouldn't shoot you in the head, anyway," Robert M. Coates quotes him as saying. "I want that head. I told you I was going to cut it off."

"Stegall took Harpe's own butcher knife, which Leiper compelled him to deliver up, and taking Harpe by the hair of the head, drew the knife slowly across the back of his neck, cutting to the bone; Harpe staring him full in the face, with a grim and fiendish countenance, and exclaiming, 'You are a God Damned rough butcher, but cut on and be damned!'

"Stegall then passed the knife around his neck, cutting to the bone; and then wrung off his head, in the same manner a butcher would of a hog. . . ."

The head was carried by the posse to a place called Robertson's Lick, where they wedged it into the fork of a tree and nailed it. The spot is still called "Harpes Head," and the grisly trophy hung there for many years until an old woman took it down to use in her conjuring.

Little Harpe survived his brother by about five years, during which time he joined the murderous Hole in the Rock gang and was thrown out of it because his cruelty turned even their strong stomachs. He was finally hanged on February 8, 1804.

When the hangman asked if he had any last words to say, Wiley Harpe yelled defiantly, "You can all go to hell, where I'm going!"

All the people of the Natchez Trace were hearty and violent, and even those who did not lead lives of crime fought with almost incredible brutality.

Next to the Harpes, the most famous of the killers of the Natchez Trace was Captain Samuel Mason. He had been a hero during the American Revolution, and the first forty-three years of his life were normal and law-abiding. Then he discovered his seventeen-year-old daughter had been seduced by a rascal he did business with—Ben "The Claw" Kuykendahl. He killed Kuykendahl and then the constable who was pursuing him for the murder. From then on Mason and his sons were wanted men and they took over Kuykendahl's gang of river pirates.

For the next ten years he terrorized both land and river parties traversing the Natchez Trace from New Orleans to Knoxville, piling up a million dollars in loot and four hundred victims murdered in cold blood. Mason was an expert with the Bowie knife and lived by the code, "Show no mercy and leave no witnesses."

He was finally murdered himself by Little Harpe and a man named George Mays. The pair knifed Mason, then cut off his head and took it to Natchez to claim the five-thousand-dollar reward that had been posted for the person who could bring the river pirate to justice. That trip to town resulted in Wiley Harpe's arrest and his subsequent hanging.

2 | The Mob Era, 1834-1861

During the period from the 1830s until the Civil War, the streets of the cities of America were filled with mobs—anti-Catholic mobs, anti-abolitionist mobs, anti-Negro mobs, anti-English-actor mobs, just plain criminal mobs, and even mobs of policemen fighting each other in New York.

Violence in America says of this era:

> The pattern of the urban immigrant slum as a matrix of poverty, vice, crime, and violence was set by Five Points in lower Manhattan before the Civil War. Ulcerating slums along the lines of Five Points and severe ethnic and religious strife stemming from the confrontation between burgeoning immigrant groups and the native American element made the 1830's, the 1840's, and 1850's a period of sustained urban rioting, particularly in the great cities of the Northeast. It may have been the era of the greatest urban violence that America has ever experienced.

The rioting resulting from the influx of Catholics, mainly Irish nationals, into the United States was the most active and vicious of the mob era. Thousands of poor Irish immigrants poured into the country, bringing their religion with them. Previously, the Catholic population of most states had been small and hostility against them took the form of laws denying them the vote or forbidding them to hold public office. But as their numbers increased, most of the laws were repealed and hate and resentment burst loose in the form of riots, especially in places where Protestants were stirred up by lurid accounts of a supposed Irish Catholic take-over of the country, storing of arms, and sexual orgies in convents.

When Catholic leaders objected to Bible teaching in the schools, preferring their own Douay version, the nativists chose to interpret this as an anti-Bible move and formed the American Bible Society that spread anti-Catholic literature all over the nation.

Memories of the Gunpowder Plot in which Guy Fawkes and a handful of fellow Catholics had attempted to blow up the English Parliament and King James I way back on November 6, 1605, were revived, and while Guy Fawkes Day was celebrated in England, America commemorated the event with a No Pope Day on which the pontiff was burned or hanged in effigy. On some occasions, rival groups of bigots would each have their own "Pope" and would battle in the streets for the honor of hanging it in the public square.

"To make matters worse," J. P. Chaplin says in *Rumor, Fear and the Madness of Crowds,* "vicious anti-Catholic propaganda began streaming in from abroad. The very titles of these works—*Master Key to Popery, Jesuit Juggling, Forty Popish Frauds Detected and Disclosed, Female Convents,* with the sub-title: *Secrets of Nunneries Disclosed* —insured the widespread popularity of the books and, at the same time, fanned the fires of prejudice and hate. The book on *Female Convents* was typical of the lot. It was a kind of latter-day *Decameron* purportedly written by Scipio de Ricci, an ex-priest. Filled with allegations of debauchery on the part of nuns and priests, it told of the discovery of infant bodies in hidden vaults under European convents. . . ."

The result of all this agitating and propagandizing was violence. In 1829, it struck Boston. Nativist gangs raged through the Irish section of town, burning and looting.

By August, 1834, the anti-Catholic campaign had stirred up the citizens of Charlestown, across the bay from Boston. Fourteen years earlier a small convent had been built there by the Ursuline sisters. In 1834 it had a staff of ten nuns and three domestics and a female student body of fifty-four girls, most of whom were the daughters of well-to-do Protestant families. The sisters were considered excellent teachers, and the convent had assumed some of the attributes of a modern finishing school.

But this good reputation didn't help the convent when a young woman named Rebecca Reed ran away from the institution and claimed to have been held there in captivity. Her flight was almost immediately followed by the publication of a book about her supposed adventures, *Six Months in a Convent*. With its tales of immorality and cruelty, the book was an instant success.

Soon afterward a fight broke out between some Irish workmen employed by the convent and workers in a nearby brickyard. The brickyard men began circulating rumors that threw doubt on the "moral purity of the convent inmates."

Another event added to the smoldering fires of hate. One of the teaching nuns, Elizabeth Harrison, suffering from an apparent nervous breakdown, left the convent, and went to the home of friends, claiming she had "escaped."

Posters now appeared in the streets calling for action.

Go Ahead! To Arms! To Arms! Ye brave and free the avenging Sword unshield!! Leave not one stone upon another of that curst Nunnery that prostitutes female virtue and liberty under garb of holy Religion. When Bonaparte opened the Nunneries in Europe he found cords of Infant skulls!

After she had calmed down a little, Elizabeth Harrison decided to return to the convent, and this started a new flood of rumors through the area.

A denial by Bishop Fenwick of Boston did nothing to stop the rumor that Elizabeth Harrison was being held prisoner in a secret dungeon of the convent. To silence the stories that were growing more and more lurid, the selectmen of Charlestown, who had been bombarded with placards that threatened, ". . . the truckmen of Boston will demolish the nunnery Thursday night—August 14," went to the convent on August 10 and requested permission to search the building.

They were shown around by Miss Harrison herself, who assured them she not only was not being held a prisoner but had returned of her own free will.

The selectmen published a statement the next day saying they had found nothing objectionable, but the report didn't get into the papers until after the convent had been burned to the ground.

On the night of Monday, August 11, a mob of three thousand gathered outside the Convent of the Ursulines. Some of the men were dressed and painted as Indians, others wore women's clothes as a disguise, but all were angry and demanding that the "secreted" nun be released. One of the selectmen tried to calm the crowd, telling them that there were fifty children and a sick woman inside the convent besides the nuns.

The selectman was brushed aside, and the mob pressed forward, shouting that the convent must be destroyed. Windows were smashed, doors battered down, and furniture flung outside. The library was wrecked, valuables stolen, musical instruments broken. Religious books and holy objects were piled in the middle of the reception room and set afire.

The terrified nuns herded their charges out a back exit and down into a garden out of sight of the mob until the whole area was lit up by the burning building. Fortunately, the father of one of the students, a Mr. Cutter and some of his neighbors tore the pickets from the fence and led the refugees to safety before the screeching mob found them.

Firemen from Charlestown arrived but were unable to put out the fire when their hoses were cut and they were threatened by the mob.

The burning of the Convent of the Ursulines brought a strong reaction in the Boston area. Even the Reverend Lyman Beecher, who had much to do with stirring up the mob, denounced their actions. Several of the rioters were brought to trial but none was ever convicted except a seventeen-year-old boy, Marvin Marcy; he was freed after seven months as the result of a petition signed by Bishop Fenwick, the nuns, and six thousand lay Catholics.

The next important flare-up of anti-Catholic rioting took place in St. Louis, Missouri. It was brought about by rumors that the Catholics of the city had "secret arsenals hidden away in the cellars" of their churches. By the time Election Day came around, the stories were so thick that men went to the polls armed. It wasn't long before rumors were flying that an Irish Catholic had stabbed a member of the Native American party in the back. Mobs gathered quickly, ransacking steamboats at the wharf and looting and destroying houses that belonged to Catholics.

"For forty-eight hours the city has been the scene of one of the most appalling riots that has ever taken place in this country," one of the city's papers reported. "Men have been butchered like cattle, property destroyed and anarchy rules supreme."

Ten men were killed in the St. Louis riot, thirty seriously injured, and an uncounted number wounded less severely. No arms were found in the vaults of any Catholic church.

On May 3, 1844, the Native Americans tried to hold a street meeting in the heavily Irish Kensington district of Philadelphia. The sight of several thousand implacable enemies of their religion and nationality demonstrating in their section of the city enraged and frightened the Irish. They broke up the meeting but three days later, the Nativists returned to the same place and again organized a meeting. A fight started and gunfire issued from the roofs, windows, and doors of nearby houses. The Nativists returned the fire with stones and bricks and pistols.

Then, in the words of Gustavus Myers in *History of Bigotry in the United States,* ". . . Irish men, women and lads rushed out of their abodes carrying firearms or clubs and bludgeons. Irish women fought by the sides of their husbands, directing them where to fire or whom to strike, and even the small Irish boys took a conspicuous hand in the affray. . . ."

One member of the Nativists was killed and he became the martyr of the rioters in the days that followed, just as Horst Wessel became the martyr-hero of the Nazi street fighters in another time and place.

Later that night the Nativists returned and attempted to burn a Catholic school. The Irish, however, had set up a guard composed of their volunteer military unit—the Hibernian Greens—and they fired a volley into the mob, killing two and wounding several others.

The arrival of a brigade of citizen volunteers and the First City Troop of cavalry ended the violence temporarily. However, it was resumed the next day when the Native Americans paraded through the streets carrying an American flag and a sign bearing the message: "This is the flag that was trampled by the Irish papists."

They marched defiantly through the Irish section, gathering around the station house of an Irish fire company. Gunfire broke out and several of the attackers were killed and wounded before they broke in the door, dragged out the fire engine, and destroyed it. After being driven off by volunteers and police, the mob returned that afternoon and burned the firehouse and the homes of more than thirty Irish citizens.

Brigadier General Cadwallader arrived on the scene with a force of militia and restored order but that didn't last long.

The Native Americans issued a call for their supporters to gather at the State House at 3:00 P.M. on May 7 and all were advised to be "prepared for defence."

The mob showed up armed with everything from knives and clubs to pistols and muskets. Mayor Scott tried to avoid further trouble by circulating through the crowd and ordering the arrest of those who carried visible weapons.

The Nativists listened to a speech by the Rev. Mr. Perry denouncing the Irish for murder and for attempting to prevent Bible reading in the schools. Then they moved in a body to the corner of Second and Master Streets in the Kensington district and fighting began again. The market house and twenty-nine private homes were burned. Eight rioters were killed and fourteen men and two boys wounded before the return of General Cadwallader and his militia ended the fighting for another day.

The morning of the next day, May 8, was calm because of the presence of the troops, but a rumor soon spread that they had been ordered not to fire on the crowd. At 2:00 P.M. the mob returned. A row of houses where the Irish had taken refuge at Ninth and Poplar Streets was set on fire. Another crowd burned St. Michael's Church, the pastor's house, and a nearby convent. The fire spread from there to two rows of houses because the mob wouldn't permit fire companies to get through.

The Irish had been ordered by their bishop not to try to defend the churches in the face of the overwhelming numbers of the mob, and a small group of police assigned by Mayor Scott to protect St. Augustine on Fourth Street was driven off by a shower of rocks, bricks, and other missiles. Then the mob set fire to the church. When the fire enveloped the base of the cupola, the mob cheered and when the cross fell into the street, they screeched with delight.

Then they turned to plundering the adjoining schoolhouse, throwing the books from its valuable library into the street, and kicking them into a huge bonfire. The school building and the priest's rectory were set ablaze. About this time the splendidly uniformed and mounted gentlemen of the First City Troop galloped to the scene, but did little beyond protecting the fire companies while they prevented the conflagration from spreading to nearby houses.

The mob moved on to the corner of Second and Phoenix Streets where it burned a Catholic school, fifteen frame houses and looted Irish stores in the vicinity, throwing their goods into the street.

Additional cavalry and artillery were hurried into action. The cavalry scattered the mob at Second and Phoenix, and General Cadwallader took personal command of his troops before the Cathedral of St. John. He declared martial law and gave the mob five minutes to disperse or be fired upon. The mob gave way. A company of U.S. Marines gathered from the naval yard and ships in port defended St. Mary's Church on South Fourth Street by charging with fixed bayonets. Peace returned to the city for almost two months, but it was an uneasy peace enforced by the military.

On July 4, rumors spread that the Irish had been permitted to store arms at the Church of St. Philip de Neri on Queen Street. A crowd gathered and besieged the church, driving off the small force of Hibernia Greens who were defending it. They in turn were driven off by the arrival of a militia unit but returned with cannon they had stolen from ships at the wharves. General Cadwallader brought his whole brigade to the scene, accompanied by Colonel Pleasanton, of the first regiment of artillery, and a battery of guns. A pitched battle ensued.

"General Cadwallader had scarcely taken possession of the church," Major General Patterson who had assumed overall command of the troops in the city reported to Governor Porter, "when his troops were attacked by showers of missiles from a savage and infuriated mob. Self-preservation, if nothing else, rendered necessary that the soldiers should fire.

The first fire caused the insurgents to recoil; but they soon rallied and returned a scattering fire from small arms and field pieces."

One of the two cannon possessed by the mob failed to function and they soon ran out of ammunition for the other, but they loaded it with bolts, chains, and spikes and blasted away. The troops, surrounded and being fired upon from all sides, used their own two cannon loaded with grape shot to drive back the mob. But by 10:00 P.M. they were running out of ammunition, and the arrival of Brigadier General Poumfort with fresh supplies was very welcome. The troops took the mob's remaining cannon at the point of the bayonet, and the insurgents broke and scattered.

The rioting was over but the bigotry that had caused it still existed. A city investigating committee blamed the riots on the Irish, claiming they had "broken up a peaceful procession of American citizens." The grand jury also blamed the Irish because of their "efforts to exclude the Bible from our public schools."

The Know-Nothings took up the cause of the Native Americans in the late 1840s and 1850s with more violence and bloodshed. Ralph Volney Harlow in *The Growth of the United States* says: "A secret political party, known officially as the 'Order of the Star-Spangled Banner,' unofficially as the Know-Nothings, had been organized about 1850. The force back of it was hostility to the growing influence of the Irish Roman Catholics in politics. . . ."

On May 28, 1854, a street preacher named West led a march on New York's City Hall and assaulted a man "who looked to be Irish." A week later there was a riot in Brooklyn led by another New York preacher. The Irish fought back and the police were unable to quell the disturbance. Finally the militia had to be called and they put down the rioting but not before many had been injured.

In Brooklyn on June 11, 1854, a Know-Nothing mob led by J. S. Orr, who called himself "Angel Gabriel," demonstrated at Atlantic Avenue near Hoyt Street. Irish bystanders began to pelt them with paving stones. A riot followed in which many police, Irishmen, and Know-Nothings were injured. The Fourteenth Regiment was sent for and twenty-three arrests were made.

In Buffalo on July 13, there was rioting between a Know-Nothing mob led by a Protestant minister and the Irish of the city. In Lawrence, Massachusetts, on July 11, Know-Nothing mobs fought Irish citizens and wrecked twenty of their houses.

The power of the Know-Nothings was increasing all over the country. They formed a front group called the American party and "elected governors in nine states, and filled legislatures and Congress with Know-Nothing adherents. A clear majority of thirty-three thousand was reaped in Massachusetts. In Congress, eight of the sixty-two members of the Senate were avowed members of this party, and 104 of the 234 members of the House of Representatives. Many other Congressmen were too timid to oppose Know-Nothingism," Gustavus Myers says.

One politician who wasn't too timid to oppose this "wave of the future" was Abraham Lincoln. In a letter written from Springfield, Illinois, on August 24, 1855, he denounced them to a fellow opponent of slavery who had expressed himself favorable to Know-Nothings.

> . . . How can anyone who abhors the oppression of Negroes be in favor of degrading classes of white people . . . As a nation we began by declaring that "all men are created equal." We now practically read it, "all men are created equal except Negroes." When the Know-Nothings obtain control, it will read: "All men are created equal except Negroes, foreigners and Catholics. . . ."

But the Know-Nothings weren't interested in such comments. They preferred violence. In Louisville, Kentucky, Election Day was marked by another riot. In Sidney, Ohio, a

42

Catholic church was blown up, and in Ellsworth, Maine, a Catholic priest, the Reverend John Bapst, was tarred and feathered and ridden out of town on a rail.

To add fuel to the flame, books such as the *Awful Disclosures of Maria Monk, As Exhibited in a Narrative of Her Sufferings, During a Residence of Five Years as a Novice and During Two Years as a Black Nun, in the Hotel Dieu Nunnery at Montreal* swept the country.

"In Mobile, Alabama, the result," David J. Jacobson in *The Affairs of Dame Rumor* says, "was an election bonfire of Catholic homes and the loss of twenty-two lives."

The terror was at its worst in Baltimore where the usually Democratic city government had been taken over by Know-Nothings in the last election.

For awhile it seemed as if these proponents of bigotry would gain control of the Federal Government as well as that of several states, but the tide was beginning to turn. The issue of slavery was starting to override all other issues, and the American people seemed to be growing a little tired of Know-Nothing violence.

In the election of 1856, the Know-Nothings nominated former President Millard Filmore for President but he trailed both Democratic candidate Buchanan and Republican Fremont.

Ralph Volney Harlow tells us: "The Know-Nothing party went to pieces during the campaign of 1856, even more rapidly than it had arisen. The northern and southern wings could not agree on slavery, and the northern members went out in groups to the Republicans."

So the Know-Nothing violence gave way to antiabolitionist and antislavery violence. This sometimes took the form of attacks on Negroes as well as on whites. J. W. Schulte Nordholt notes in *The People That Walk in Darkness:*

> In Philadelphia, the town of brotherly love, a Negress was stoned to death by three white women in 1819. A group

43

of white people forced their way into the Negro district in Cincinnati in 1829, breaking and tearing everything to pieces. There were similar incidents in New York (1834 and 1839) and Philadelphia (1834 and 1842) as well as many in the smaller towns.

A dialogue of violence was also building up during this period. Wendell Phillips, "abolition's golden trumpet," added his share. He advocated that the soil of Massachusetts be made so "hot that a slave-holder would sooner go down to his birthplace in hell" than to go there and try to recapture escaped slaves.

Replying for the proslavery forces, Congressman Hammon of South Carolina said, "I warn the abolitionists, ignorant and infatuated barbarians as they are, that if chance shall throw any of them into our hands, they may expect a felon's death."

The Negro attitude in the North was generally summarized by the words of Henry Highland Garnet speaking before the National Convention of Colored Citizens in 1843:

> However much all of us may desire it, there is not much hope of redemption without the shedding of blood. If you must bleed, let it all come at once—rather die freemen than live to be slaves . . . Brethren, arise, arise! Strike for your lives and liberties. Now is the day and the hour. Let every slave throughout the land do this, and the days of slavery are numbered. You cannot be more oppressed than you have been—you cannot suffer greater cruelty than you have already . . . In the name of God, we ask, are you men? . . . Awake, awake; millions of voices are calling you! . . . Let your motto be resistance! resistance! resistance! No oppressed people have ever secured their liberty without resistance.

A mob of Tammany Hall supporters attacked the Chatham Street Chapel in 1833 to break up a meeting of the New

York Anti-Slavery Society. When they couldn't get into the meeting, they contented themselves with capturing an old Negro, forcing him to dance for their entertainment, and then beating him savagely.

On July 4 of the same year, another mob celebrated Independence Day by running wild in New York, destroying homes, and wrecking stores that belonged to or served Negroes. On July 10, another mob barricaded the streets to hold off mounted police and cavalry and then demolished a minister's home and church to punish him for the crime of advocating the freedom of the slaves. Other disturbances occurred in 1833 with mobs marching through Newark, New Jersey, and Norwich, Connecticut, attacking abolitionists and Negroes.

The worst riot took place in Philadelphia in August. For three days and nights mobs raged through the streets. Forty-four Negro homes were destroyed, one Negro was murdered, and another forced into the river and drowned. Large numbers of blacks were beaten and seriously injured.

Proslavery mobs attacked Negroes and abolitionists in various localities in New York State. New Bedford, Pawtucket, and Worcester were among the New England towns rocked by violence. The rioting spread to Portland, Maine, where Stephen Foster was among those who had to be rescued from mobs. Pennsylvania Hall, a building constructed by the citizens of Philadelphia as a forum for the discussion of civil rights, was burned to the ground by arsonists, and shortly thereafter, the Shelter for Colored Orphans and a Negro church met the same fate.

Elijah Lovejoy, an abolitionist publisher, was shot to death in Alton, Illinois, in 1837 as he tried to defend his printing press from a mob. In the South, those who advocated freedom for the slaves were either killed or driven out.

Arthur Tappan, an abolitionist businessman of New York, received thousands of threatening letters and small hangman's nooses through the mail, and finally opened one parcel to find that the severed ear of a Negro had been sent as a warning.

The build-up of violence to the crescendo we know as the Civil War was shaking America, but there were other types of civil disorder during this period also. A great deal of it was concentrated in New York City, particularly in the Five Points area of what was known as the Bloody Ould Sixth Ward, bounded by Broadway, Canal Street, the Bowery, and Park Row.

In this area "great brawling, thieving" gangs, some containing as many as a thousand members, were identified by such colorful sobriquets as the Dead Rabbits, Bowery Boys, Eastmans, Gophers, Chichesters, Roach Guards, Plug Uglies, Shirt Tails, and Kerryonians.

Newly immigrant Irish made up the vast majority of the population of Five Points and they lived in total squalor.

One street in the area called Cow Bay was a *cul de sac* about thirty feet wide at the entrance and narrowing to a point a hundred feet farther on. It was lined with rickety, clapboarded tenements from one to five stories high, many of them connected by underground passages used by murderers and thieves as escape routes.

Asbury goes on to quote from an 1854 book called *Hot Corn:*

> If you would see Cow Bay, saturate your handkerchief with camphor, so that you can endure the horrid stench, and enter. Grope your way through the long, narrow passage—turn to the right, up the dark and dangerous stairs; be careful where you place your foot around the lower step, or in the corners of the broad stairs, for it is more than shoe-mouth deep with steaming filth.
>
> Be careful, too, or you may meet someone, perhaps a man, perhaps a woman, who in their drunken frenzy may thrust you, for the very hatred of your better clothes, or the fear that you have come to rescue them from their

crazy love dens of death, down, headlong down, those filthy stairs. Up, up, winding up, five stories high, now you are under the black smoky roof; turn to your left—take care and not upset that seething pot of butcher's offal soup that is cooking upon a little furnace at the head of the stairs—open that door—go in, if you can get in.

Look: here is a Negro and his wife sitting upon the floor —where else could they sit, for there is no chair—eating their supper off the bottom of a pail. A broken brown earthen jug holds water—perhaps not all water. Another Negro and his wife occupy another corner; a third sits in the window monopolizing all the air astir. In another corner, what do we see? A Negro man and a stout, hearty, rather good-looking young white woman. Not sleeping together? No, not exactly that—there is no bed in the room —no chair—no table—no nothing—but rags, and dirt, and vermin, and degraded, rum-degraded human beings.

It is not much of a surprise that people living under such circumstances should turn to crime and organize themselves into brawling gangs.

"The Old Brewery was the heart of the Five Points, and was the most celebrated tenement building in the history of the city," Asbury says.

The building had been divided up into rooms and apartments in 1837 when it could no longer serve its original purpose. One large room, called the Den of Thieves, was inhabited by more than seventy-five men, women, and children of all races and color, living without furniture or toilet facilities. Many of the women were prostitutes and serviced their customers right there in the great common room, presumably with the rest of the residents looking on. Around the building was a passageway known as Murderers' Alley and is said to have lived up to its name.

"The cellars of the Old Brewery," Asbury tells us, "were divided into some twenty rooms, which had previously been used for the machinery of the brewing plant, and there were about seventy-five other chambers above-ground, arranged in double rows along Murderers' Alley and the passage leading to the Den of Thieves."

At one time more than a thousand persons of Irish and Negro descent lived in the building. Those in the cellar existed under the worst conditions.

Those who lived in the Old Brewery and similar places struck back at society in the only way they knew. There were innumerable fights and drunken orgies were a constant day-and-night occurrence. Historians of the time estimate that for better than a dozen years the Old Brewery and the Cow Bay tenements were the scene of nightly murders that defied the feeble attempts of the police to apprehend the culprits.

The gangs grew out of these appalling conditions. The Forty Thieves, one of the earlier groups, was formed in Rosanna Peers' grocery store, where their leader, Edward Coleman, received reports from his marauders. The Kerryonians—all natives of County Kerry, Ireland—also hung out at Rosanna's grocery store. This latter group, however, spent most of its time in anti-English activities, doing little street fighting.

The Chichesters, Roach Guards, Plug Uglies, Shirt Tails, and Dead Rabbits also used grocery stores as their head-quarters. The Shirt Tails derived their name from the habit of wearing their shirts outside their pants like modern teen-agers. The Plug Uglies, mostly big Irishmen, got theirs from their huge plug hats, which they filled with wool and leather to protect their heads from their opponents' blows.

The Dead Rabbits, perhaps the most famous of the gangs, were so called because they adopted as their standard a dead rabbit impaled on a pike. The Dead Rabbits and the Roach Guards were deadly enemies and fought up and down the streets of Five Points, but when outsiders came from the Bowery and the waterfront, they joined forces to battle them.

The gangs also had female adherents who fought with the men in the streets. The most famous of these was called Hell-

Cat Maggie, who is said to have filed her front teeth to points so she could rip the throats of enemies. On her fingers she wore long artificial nails made of brass.

Encounters between these rowdy groups were marked by incredible brutality. Eye-gouging, kicking, and stamping were accepted as proper means of combat. The police, most of the time greatly outnumbered by the gangs, were constantly forced to summon assistance from National Guard units and the Regular Army.

The Native Americans and later the Know-Nothings had the allegiance of non-Irish gangs such as the Bowery group who called themselves the American Guards and prided themselves on being native born. These frequently fought with Tammany Hall supporters such as the O'Connell Guards.

On June 21, 1835, these two gangs fought it out in a battle that raged all through the Five Points, involving other groups until rioting became general. The mayor and the sheriff managed to get enough men together to put down the trouble without calling out the troops, but not before a noted surgeon, Dr. W. M. Caffrey, was killed and Justice Olin M. Lowndes was seriously wounded.

On July 7, 1834, mobs attacked the Chatham Street Chapel and the Bowery Theater, where Edwin Forrest was playing. When they were driven away from there, they roared into a residential street and wrecked the house of Lewis Tappan, a well-known abolitionist. Four days later, Five Points gangs sacked a dozen buildings in the Paradise Square area. After setting those on fire, they did the same to five houses of prostitution and carried off the shady ladies whom they divided among themselves and "shamefully mistreated."

One of the most infamous dives in the city at that time was called the Hole-in-the-Wall, and the bouncer was a six-foot-tall Englishwoman called Gallus Mag. She stalked about the dive with a huge bludgeon in one hand and a pistol stuck in her belt.

After knocking a misbehaving customer to the floor, it was

her custom to sink her teeth into his ear and drag him out of the bar in that fashion. If he protested, she would bite the ear off and deposit it in a jar of alcohol behind the bar. Even the police shuddered at her savagery. The Hole-in-the-Wall was finally shut down by the police after seven murders were committed there in less than two months.

The New York police in those days were almost as violent as the gang members they confronted. Captain George W. Walling organized the First Strong Arm Squad in 1853 to suppress the so-called Honeymoon gang. The latter had stationed a member at each corner of Madison Avenue and Twenty-Ninth Street and these men spent their evenings "knocking down and robbing every well-dressed man who appeared."

The Honeymooners left the area almost immediately and moved into the Bowery. The same tactics were used against two groups of brawlers who lived on opposite sides of Twenty-Second Street and were known only as the English and the Irish.

Prior to Captain Walling's appearance on the scene, the inhabitants of these slums swarmed into the street every evening and fought it out. When police entered at all it was in groups of three or more. Walling, however, stationed his whole force around the corner, and when fighting broke out, the policemen rushed in and used their clubs on English and Irish indiscriminately. In no time at all Twenty-Second Street was quiet and peaceful.

By 1855 it was estimated that the gangs had a total membership of thirty thousand individuals. Most of these took part in the riots that rocked the city during the mayoralty election of 1856. Fernando Wood was running for re-election and he had the allegiance of the Dead Rabbits as well as other Five Points gangs. The Bowery Boys and their cohorts supported the Native Americans and the Know-Nothings.

The night before election the mayor sent most of the police

away on furlough and ordered the Dead Rabbits to guard the polls to see that only the right people voted. The Bowery gangs attacked the polling place and scattered the Dead Rabbits but soon the Dead Rabbits surged back armed with clubs, knives, axes, brickbats, and pistols. They defeated the Bowery Boys, and the few police on hand could do nothing but barricade themselves in an empty house and fire an occasional bullet at both sides.

The Dead Rabbits remained in control of the polls, and their candidate won by 34,860 votes to 25,209 for Isaac O. Barker, the Know-Nothing man.

In 1857 the police themselves rioted. The State Legislature had passed several bills abolishing Mayor Wood's corrupt Municipal Police and setting up a Metropolitan Police District that included Manhattan, Brooklyn, and other nearby areas. Wood refused to accept the dissolution of his police department, and when warrants were served on him by members of the Metropolitan force, they were attacked by three hundred Municipal Police.

For almost an hour the battle between the two forces went on all over the confines of City Hall. Fists and clubs were wielded with wild abandon but in the end the Municipal Police succeeded in routing the Metropolitans. The sheriff arrived soon afterward with his staff of office in hand and a sword strapped to his side and attempted to arrest the mayor.

Well protected by his own police, the mayor refused to submit to arrest. Just about that time the Seventh Regiment was marching down Broadway on its way to take a boat for Boston, where it was to be entertained by a Massachusetts regiment. As the regiment came in sight of city Hall, with flags flying and drums beating, the sheriff and members of the Metropolitan Police Board went out to meet the commander, Major General Charles Sandford, and convinced him that the peace and dignity of the city were threatened. The soldiers were deployed to surround City Hall, and the general,

51

with drawn sword and surrounded by a platoon of infantry with fixed bayonets strode into the building and arrested the mayor.

But that didn't end the battle between the Municipals and the Metropolitans. The feud went on for some time with very odd results, as described by Asbury:

> Whenever a Metropolitan arrested a criminal, a Municipal came along and released him, and the thug went about his business while the policemen fought . . . In consequence of this situation the gangsters and other criminals ran wild throughout the city, revelling in an orgy of loot, murder and disorder. Respectable citizens were held up and robbed in broad daylight on Broadway and other principal streets, while Municipal and Metropolitan policemen belabored each other with clubs.

One of the worst riots in the city's history took place while the divided police were at each other's throats. The Dead Rabbits, the Plug Uglies and other Five Points gangs celebrated the Fourth of July by attacking the building at No. 42 Bowery that the Bowery Boys and the Atlantic Guards used as a club house. The Dead Rabbits and friends were driven off but returned to attack another hangout known as the Green Dragon. They caught the Bowery Boys and their allies by surprise, soundly thrashed them, and added insult to injury by drinking up every drop of liquor in the place.

This final insult enraged the Bowery Boys and they swarmed out of their hideaways and attacked with bludgeons, knives, brass knuckles, and guns. The battle raged up and down Bayard Street. The few policemen who could be spared from their own feuding were driven off.

The "Boys" might have been fighting yet if the Eighth and Seventy-first regiments hadn't been turned out to overwhelm the gangs and end the rioting.

Shortly thereafter the Municipal police were dissolved and the Metropolitan force took over. It was fortunate they did because within a few years the city was almost destroyed by the gangs as they joined wholeheartedly in the great Draft Riots of 1863.

3 | A Curse on the Land, 1619-1861

On a day in 1619, a ship came to Jamestown and brought with it the makings of a curse of violence that rests heavily on America to this day. The coming of the ship was little noted at the time, but its arrival loomed larger in the history of violence in America than any other single event. John Rolfe recorded the event in his journal as though it were a matter of little importance.

> About the last of August came in a Dutch man of warre that sold us twenty negars.

The colonists needed those slaves and at first treated them more as bond servants with a chance to gain freedom by working off their "indentures" in the same way open to white bond servants. The blacks were needed because the Indians refused to be enslaved and the "gentlemen adventurers" who made up so large a part of the Jamestown contingent considered manual labor beneath them. Indeed, part of the reason for the numerous "starving times" the colony endured was this disinclination to put hand to plow.

At one point this led to a "no work, no eat" edict by

John Smith, and in 1610 to the organization of the entire settlement into a work force that was, according to Saunders Redding, "marched to their daily work in squads and companies, under officers, and severest penalties. . . ."

However, free-born, if lazy, Englishmen were not going to put up with that kind of treatment for long, and they rejoiced in the arrival of the twenty blacks, which seemed to them to open up an inexhaustible source of free labor. The first twenty were soon followed by many more, and as their numbers increased, the concept of their place in Colonial society changed.

They were no longer looked upon as indentured servants but as slaves for life. This system grew even though there was no legal sanction for it in the colony's charter or in English law. Indeed, as Robert Goldston points out in *The Negro Revolution,* slavery in British territory was illegal at that time. But the law was ignored and eventually changed to suit the new social system that grew up around slavery. And the attitude that evolved with that system became the blackest stain on American life, conducive to more violence than any other of our institutions.

"The Christian precepts of kindness, charity and human dealing need not apply to them (the slaves) . . . was not intended to apply to them, for they were a heathen breed, demonstrably inferior," Saunders says. "Thus began in North America the rationalization of race caste. Before long its knotty, insidious tendrils, seeming to uphold what they would pull down, were clinging to every fissure in the national frame.

"In literal terms, what happened was that a twisted body of moral and ethnic assumptions grew up around and fed upon a body of expedient practices. Once this process got fairly started—and it had by mid-century—the Negro was thoroughly enslaved. . . ."

A central fact of violence in America is racial bigotry. It

was less prevalent in the early days because the Elizabethans and even some of the later colonials thought of the Indian not so much by his race as by the fact that he was a "savage." Parenthetically, it didn't matter how charitably most of the coastal Indians behaved toward their uninvited visitors. To the European, they were savages. But it wasn't a racial matter.

The racial division grew up as a rationale for slavery, probably a Christian rationale at that. If one accepted Biblical teachings, one could hardly treat fellow human beings as the black slaves were treated, but if one could convince one's self that they were subhuman or even animals, then all the theological problems were solved. In Jefferson's time this was still a weighty question, but by the 1830s or 40s many learned divines had solved everything for the slaveholder by pronouncing the Negro an animal and therefore without a soul.

This was what made slavery in America more degrading and vicious than that of the ancient world. Slavery in Rome was mainly a matter of bad luck. It had no racial overtones. Slaves were black or white and so were the masters. In Rome and the rest of the ancient world, slavery was a military and economic matter, the consequences of defeat in battle or of being on the bottom of the wage scale.

Not that it was any more pleasant than slavery in America. Since slaves were so cheap, their physical lot may have been worse, but they were never less than human in their master's mind or in their own. Each slave was regarded as a man or a woman, not referred to as a "buck" or a "bitch." More practically, the freed slave carried no stigma with him. The class distinctions were bad enough, but there was not the sick mythology the white man's guilt-ridden mind made up concerning race.

In America, no matter how successful, rich, attractive, polite, or intelligent a Negro might be, he was still considered the same in the white's mind. He was an animal without a soul whose processes of thought were different and inferior and whose hypersexuality was a menace to every white woman in the land.

Being a slave for life was a humiliating, soul-stifling business; being a slave owner was a brutalizing and enervating one. In the early days after the revolution this was recognized by many. George Washington and John Randolph freed their slaves in their wills, and Jefferson intended to but his monetary affairs were in such a state that he was unable to.

Jefferson called slavery "a perpetual exercise of the most boisterous passions, the most unremitting despotism on the one part and the degrading submission on the other." He pointed out that white children raised under these circumstances were being turned into tyrants patterned after their slave-owning fathers. Owning slaves destroyed the morals and the will to work of the whites, and the very act was a violation of a gift of God. "Indeed, I tremble for my country when I reflect that God is just; that His justice cannot sleep forever. . . ."

For a brief time there were economic and idealistic reasons to hope that slavery might die out in America. It had become such a bad proposition economically that John Randolph suggested that soon instead of seeing ads in the papers for "fugitive slaves," one might see ads for "fugitive masters" who had taken to their heels to escape the burden.

But unfortunately slavery didn't fade away. Indeed, with the invention of the cotton gin and, oddly enough, the ending of the slave trade in 1808, the price of slaves began to skyrocket. A Negro who sold for five hundred dollars in 1800 went up to one thousand dollars in 1820 and to eighteen hundred dollars in 1860. Instead of talking about freeing their chattels or about the disadvantages of slavery, plantation owners were breeding slaves, opening up new fields and passing a code of laws that made those of the Draconian code seem mild by comparison.

In *The People That Walk in Darkness*, J. W. Schulte Nordholt tells us about this code:

The more the system was extended, the more rigorous the legislation became. Slaves could not leave their plantations without a pass, they could not own, buy or sell anything, their testimony was invalid . . . Conversely, the law gave them no protection. In South Carolina in 1740 the killing of a slave was punishable by a fine of 700 pounds, but if this had been performed accidentally "in sudden heat and passion," the fine was only 350 pounds. This law was withdrawn in 1821. Much could happen accidentally: in Georgia the murdering of a slave was not punishable at all if "death should happen by accident in giving such slave moderate correction." The slaves were not allowed to visit the houses of white people or of free Negroes, or to receive them in their cabins. They could not own firearms, of course.

There were the heaviest of punishments for minor offenses, usually whipping or branding. Imprisonment or the death penalty were not applied often, for these meant a loss to the masters, although there were regulations for compensation in such cases. A list showing compensation cases between 1780 and 1864 has been preserved in Virginia. It shows a total of 1,418 death sentences and deportation cases, of which 402 were for murder, attempted murder or poisoning and ninety-one for revolt or conspiracy . . .

Ulrich B. Phillips in *American Negro Slavery* adds more evidence of the repressiveness of the slave codes:

Laws were passed forbidding ". . . all but servants in livery to wear any but coarse clothing . . . No slaves were to be sold liquors without their masters' approval; none were to be taught to write. . . . no houses or lands were to be rented to slaves, and no slaves were to be kept on any plantation where no white person was resident. . . . Slave marriages, furthermore, were declared void of all civil effect; and jurisdiction over slave crimes was transferred to courts of inferior grade and informal procedure."

Sometimes the courts were so informal that they were little

more than drum head affairs that verged on lynch mobs. The law fell hard not only on the slave but also on the free black and even upon those whose Negro blood was barely discernible. Phillips continues his grim account:

> In general, the letter of the law in slaveholding states at the middle of the nineteenth century presumed all persons with a palpable strain of Negro blood to be slaves unless they could prove the contrary, and regarded the possession of them by masters as presumptive evidence of legal ownership.

Saunders Redding gives us additional evidence in *They Came in Chains:*

> A master could whip his slaves at will, cut their rations, crop their ears, brand them, pillory them, or inflict upon them any other punishment that seemed in his judgment, "right." Slaves could not leave their masters' premises without a pass. They had no right of assembly. They could not own property and therefore could not buy or sell or trade. Arms were forbidden them. Dogs were taboo. Slaves could not sue or be sued, prosecute for a battery, nor enter a civil suit. They could not give evidence against a white person. Not even in self-defense could they lift their hands against a "Christian" white, and in Virginia until 1788 it was legally impossible for a white man to murder a slave. The death of a slave under punishment was either accidental homicide or manslaughter, neither of which made white men liable to prosecution.

The only restraint placed on the white in his relations with the Negro was that of the protection of property. A white who killed another man's slave could be sued for damages just as he could be if he killed another man's cow or horse. The Constitutional Court of South Carolina in a far-reaching decision upheld these tyrannical laws in 1847:

A slave can invoke neither Magna Charta nor common law . . . In the very nature of things he is subject to despotism. Law to him is only a compact between his rulers, and the questions which concern him are matters agitated between them. The various acts concerning slaves contemplate throughout the subordination of the servile class to every free white person and enforce the stern policy which the relation of master and slave necessarily requires. Any conduct of a slave inconsistent with due subordination contravenes the purpose of these acts.

What these laws produced was not so much safety for the masters which those who passed them sought, but a violent tinge to society that has come down to us today. In slave times it produced a society not unlike that of totalitarian dictatorship.

That the violent laws were violently enforced can be seen from old court records, newspaper accounts and the narrations of old ex-slaves remembering how things were.

In 1838, Micajah Ricks of North Carolina advertised to find a runaway female slave.

> . . . the woman is tall and black. A few days before she ran away I branded her with a hot iron on the left side of her face. I tried to mark her with the letter M, and she kept a cloth over her head and face, and a fly bonnet on her head so as to cover the burn.

A Kentucky owner described his missing slave as "a sprightly mulatto wench, with branding marks . . . on her forehead, cheek and chest."

A North Carolina planter offered a reward of ten dollars for the capture of his slave, or twenty dollars for the man's head and no questions asked.

From court records in Baldwin County, Georgia, between 1812 and 1832, come the following notations of punishments meted out to Negro slaves:

1812   Major convicted of rape and hanged.

1815   Tom convicted of murdering a fellow slave sentenced to branding on each cheek with the letter M and to thirty-nine lashes on his bare back on each of three successive days.

1816   John, a slave of William McGeehee, convicted of theft of a $100 bill was sentenced to whipping in a similar fashion.

1818   Aleck, found guilty of assault. Received fifty lashes on three days in succession.

1819   Rodney: Sentenced to death by hanging for arson.

1822   John, convicted of burglary but recommended to mercy. Sentenced to be branded with a T on the right cheek and to receive three times thirty-nine lashes.
        The same John on the same day was sentenced to death for assaulting a white man.

1825   John Ponder's George convicted of burglary. Jury recommended mercy but the death sentence was passed anyway.

1826   Elleck, convicted of assault received the death sentence.

An old slave woman is quoted in *The People That Walk in Darkness* on the type of treatment she received from her master:

He ties me to the stake, and every half-hour for four hours they lay ten lashes on my back. For the first couple of hours the pain am awful. I'se never forgot it. Then I'se stood so much pain I not feel so much, and when they take me loose, I'se just 'bout half dead. I lays in the bunk two days, gitting over that whipping, gitting over it in the body but not the heart. No, sir. I has that in the heart till this day.

Also quoted on page 47 of the same book are the remarks of an escaped slave, William Grimes, speaking in 1825:

61

> If it were not for the stripes on my back which were made
> while I was a slave, I would, in my will, leave my skin a
> legacy to the government, desiring that it be taken off and
> made into parchment and then bind the Constitution of
> glorious, happy, and free America. Let the skin of an Amer-
> ican slave bind the charter of American liberty!

That fine bit of irony throws a special light on the theory
that slaves were treated well and that in their simple way
loved old Massa and Missus. So do the records of slave attacks
on their masters and slave insurrections. The Negro was
thought of as a simple-minded soul with no desire for freedom
and no hatred for those who oppressed him. That kind of
rationalizing may have been necessary in order for the owners
to sleep at night, but it was far from the truth as the records
show. There were innumerable instances of slaves attacking,
killing, poisoning their masters as well as many cases of arson.
These were not the actions of simple-minded people content
with their lot and neither were the following as recorded in
They Came in Chains:

> Female slaves murdered masters, mistresses and children.
> They wiped out whole families, as did Cicely, a slave
> woman in Mississippi, who killed her master, his wife and
> two children with a broad axe; or Sallie, who knocked her
> master unconscious and roasted his head in the fireplace
> . . . the slave nurse who dragged the mistress' baby from
> her black breast and dashed its brains out against a
> stone . . . .

Statistics tell the story of the hate and violence slavery
produced. In *American Negro Slavery,* Ulrich B. Phillips
gives us the record of conviction for serious crimes among
slaves in Virginia from 1780 to 1864.

> The gross number of convictions was 1,418, all but 91
> of which were of males. For arson there were 90 slaves

convicted, including 29 women. For burglary there were 277, with but one woman among them. The highway robbers numbered 15, the horse thieves 20 and the thieves of other sorts 24.

It might be noted that since the records are based on a series of vouchers issued by the state to pay the masters of convicted slaves for the loss of the slave who was either executed or deported, lesser crimes are not covered.

For murder there were 346, discriminated as having been committed upon the master 56, the mistress 11, the overseer 11; upon other white persons 120; upon free negros 7; upon slaves 85, including 12 children all of whom were killed by their own mothers; and upon persons not described 60. Of the murderers 307 were men and 39 women. For poisoning and attempts to poison, including the administering of ground glass, 40 men and 16 women were convicted.

None of these statistics give any support to the idealized Old South image where slaves worked cheerfully in the fields and Ole Massa sipped his mint julep without ever giving a thought to whether some slave might have slipped ground glass into it.

And if murder and arson were common on the part of the blacks against the white, so was organized revolt. The picture drawn by some writers of a docile, contented slave population fades before the reality of the struggle for freedom against impossible odds.

David Walker, a free Negro who lived in Boston, expressed the feelings of the blacks in a pamphlet he called, *Walker's Appeal, in Four Articles,* published in 1829:

Never make an attempt to gain our freedom, or natural rights . . . until your way is clear—when that hour arrives and you move, be not afraid or dismayed, for be you assured that Jesus Christ the King of Heaven, and of Earth who is the God of Justice and armies will go before you. And those who have for hundreds of years stolen our rights, and kept us ignorant of Him and His divine worship, He will remove . . .

Let twelve good black men get armed for battle and they will kill and put to flight fifty whites . . . If you commence, make sure work, don't trifle, for they will not trifle with you. Kill or be killed. Had you rather not be killed than be a slave to a tyrant who takes the life of your wife and children? Look upon your wife and children and mother and answer God Almighty, and believe this that it is no more harm to kill a man who is trying to kill you than to take a drink of water when you are thirsty.

The South was incensed and terrified by this "Appeal," and several slave states petitioned Massachusetts to suppress it, but Massachusetts didn't choose to do so. With foolhardy courage, Walker went to Richmond, Virginia, and passed out his pamphlet himself. Most of the copies were seized by the police and Walker was arrested. He disappeared into the darkness of the Richmond jail, never to be seen again.

Long before Walker put the idea of revolt into words, the actuality was taking place. Herbert Aptheker estimates there were a total of 250 revolts or attempted revolts. Robert Goldston in *The Negro Revolution* says that more than "four slave uprisings took place between 1750 and 1850. Most of them were of minor importance, involving a handful of slaves maddened by harsh treatment who would rise up, burn the plantation houses, and murder their masters' families."

The first recorded attempted revolt took place in Gloucester County, Virginia, in 1663. A group of indentured white servants and black slaves plotted to revolt but were betrayed by one of the servants to the colonial assembly. Another plot was discovered in 1687 in the "Northern Neck" section of Virginia. And in 1709 a plot in Isle of Wight County, Virginia, resulted in three slaves being given thirty-nine lashes, and a free Negro being lashed fifty times while the two ring-leaders were bound over for trial by the governor and another slave was proclaimed an outlaw.

In 1712, a group composed of "Coromantee and Paw Paw Negroes" plotted to revolt in New York. It was believed they had been stirred up by whites at a mission school opened by Elias Neau, an agent of the Society for the Propagation of the Gospel. They were also said to have obtained the services of a conjurer to protect them against the weapons of their white antagonists.

Armed with guns, hatchets, knives, and swords, the rebels struck one dark night in April, setting fire to a house to lure the whites to the scene. Then they opened fire and set upon the whites with their other weapons. Troops were rushed from the Battery and managed to stop the slaughter but not before nine whites had been killed and others wounded. Rather than face the brutal vengeance of the whites, six of the slaves killed themselves before capture but many others were seized.

The punishment meted out to the slaves who fell into the hands of the authorities was in keeping with the customary savagery of the law in these cases. More than a dozen were hanged; one poor unfortunate was broken on the wheel; still another was sentenced to be burned with a slow fire.

South Carolina saw the next uprising in 1720, and it was put down after some of the rebels were hanged, others banished and the rest burned at the stake. Then things were quiet until 1729 when a group of about twenty Angola blacks, led by a man named Jonny, rebelled. They broke into an arms store, took what they needed and set out to march toward Florida, where they had been told freedom awaited.

It is reported they marched in military formation with drums beating, killing any whites they encountered and attracting recruits as they proceeded. They paused, however, to plunder some stores of rum and were attacked by a party of hastily summoned militia. Several rebels were killed and others captured. Most of them scattered and hid. However, ten stalwart souls fought their way south for thirty more miles and then finding themselves surrounded held out to the last man. Twenty-one whites and forty-four blacks died in "Jonny's" rebellion.

In 1741 in New York another plot was uncovered, only it seemed more imaginary than real in the end. Margaret Kerry, a young white prostitute in a house run by John Hughson for Negro slaves, testified that her employer was the head of a conspiracy of slaves who were planning a general revolt. Hughson, his wife and the girl were all hanged and so was John Ury, who was convicted of being a Catholic priest as well as a conspirator. Twenty-nine Negroes were also hanged or burned at the stake.

The most important uprising of early times was that of Gabriel Prosser. It was the most carefully planned of all, and if it had succeeded might have changed the whole course of history in the South. Gabriel belonged to Thomas H. Prosser of Henrico County, Virginia, and like many slaves took the surname of his master. At the time he was about 24 years of age, an extraordinary young man of giant physique, great courage, high intellect and with some of the magnetic appeal and dynamism that characterizes a spiritual leader. Gabriel, in fact, thought of himself as a prophet destined to unshackle the chains of his people.

He began to plan his rebellion as early as June, 1800. His wife, his brothers, and Jack Bowler, another giant Negro, were his chief lieutenants. Together they recruited over a thousand other slaves from Henrico and Carolina Counties, Goochland and Petersburg. Some accounts say he had pledges from as many as ten thousand slaves to rise when he gave the word.

Gabriel's plan was simple. On August 20 his recruits would gather, murder all the whites in the area, and then advance on Richmond in three columns under designated officers. One column was to seize the penitentiary, which also served as the state arsenal, another was to take the powder magazine in another part of town, while the third was to attack the townspeople and stir the city blacks to rebellion. Gabriel planned to offer whites a chance to surrender but those who did not would be massacred except for Quakers, Methodists, and Frenchmen.

Once in command of the city with the state treasury and arsenal in his hands, the Negro leader was confident he could hold out against all comers.

Actually, they were pitifully under-armed. Their weapons included a little more than a hundred handmade swords, a peck of hand-cast bullets and ten pounds of gunpowder. Axes, shovels, hoes, scythes, clubs and rocks constituted the rest of their arsenal and they counted on gaining additional and better arms from the whites they subdued and killed.

Many of the slaves in Gabriel's "army" had been soldiers in the American Revolution and had an elementary knowledge of military tactics. Slaves had been offered their freedom if they helped fight the British, but once the war was over the promise was conveniently forgotten and many were again enslaved. There can be little wonder that many of these flocked to Gabriel's flag, which was to bear the legend *Liberty or Death*.

Gabriel had spent his Sundays for months reconnoitering the city of Richmond, planning where fires could be set and how the arsenal and State House were to be captured. He even toyed with the idea of an alliance with the Catawba Indians and of stealing horses for part of his men. He picked a time when the crops would be ready for harvest and the cattle ready for slaughter so that his forces could live off the land.

His planning turned out to be better than the execution of it. Two slaves, Tom and Pharaoh, who belonged to Moseley Sheppard, informed their master of the plot on the day the rebellion was to start. Sheppard sent couriers to warn

Richmond. Governor Monroe called out the militia and sent units of cavalry to patrol the roads while guards were posted at the State House and arsenal.

Almost a thousand of Gabriel's followers made good their pledge and kept the planned rendezvous at Old Brook Swamp, six miles from Richmond. Then the rain that had been falling lightly throughout the afternoon turned into a cloudburst that washed away bridges and turned the roads into impassable bogs. Under those conditions it was impossible to reach the city so the rebels had to scatter with the intention of carrying out their plans later.

By the time the storm ended it was already too late. The whole state was aroused and the whites struck quickly. Martial law was declared and scores of Negroes were arrested, including thirty-five of Gabriel's lieutenants. Gabriel managed to elude capture at first, stowing away on the schooner *Mary,* which had sailed from Richmond to Norfolk. But he was again betrayed by one of his own people, dragged out of the ship's hold, and returned to Richmond for trial.

Gabriel was hanged on October 7, 1800, before a wildly cheering crowd. Five of his closest friends from the Prosser plantation were also hanged as were nineteen more belonging to other masters. Ten others were sentenced to be transported overseas.

Not a single white had died and all of Gabriel's planning had come to naught. Nevertheless, his abortive rebellion sent such a chill of fear throughout the state and much of the rest of the South that it was used as an excuse for the passage of increasingly repressive legislation.

The next few years were marked by panicky behavior on the part of the whites at any hint of slave rebellion. The militia was called out in July, 1804, at Savannah, Georgia, and at Columbia, South Carolina, in 1805. Night patrols were instructed to pick up every stray Negro they saw. One over-zealous patrolman shot a slave who was "peacefully following his own master, and was indicted next day for murder."

Another abortive rebellion took place in 1816 in Spottsylvania and Louisa Counties, Virginia, led by George Boxley, the white proprietor of a country store and a kind of early-day John Brown. Boxley was friendly with the Negroes and attended their religious gatherings, telling them that "a little white bird had brought him a holy message to deliver his fellowmen from bondage."

The plot was betrayed by a slave woman and several of Boxley's followers were arrested. In a brave but foolish attempt to rescue them, he marched with a few blacks to attack the jail. The slaves, however, lost heart on the way and deserted him, and after a period of hiding out, Boxley surrendered. Six of the Negroes were hanged and six others transported. Boxley managed to break out of jail and escape.

Denmark Vesey was a lucky man. Brought from Africa in his youth and sold into slavery, he had won fifteen hundred dollars in a lottery and used part of it to buy his freedom and become an artisan. Somehow he managed to get an education and was said to be able to speak several languages. He had been a slave long enough to know he hated the institution and those who had conceived it. He planned for four years to bring his plot to maturity. He read extensively all available accounts of antislavery sentiment and activities overseas and up North and used this information to stir up Negro friends and others who were connected with the African Church.

One of Vesey's lieutenants was a conjurer or witch doctor named Gullah Jack who bestowed charmed crabs' claws upon the more superstititious members of the conspiracy to make them invulnerable. By the spring of 1822 all was ready for the outbreak.

Different types of slaves had been organized into separate commands. Angolas, Eboes and the Carolina-born groups each had their own leaders, and arrangements had been made for plantation slaves in nearby areas to rise at the same time those in Charleston did. The Negro cook on a ship bound for San Domingo carried letters from Vesey to leaders there requesting assistance or at least a place of refuge if the revolt should fail. The revolt itself was scheduled for Sunday, June 16.

But just as in the case of Gabriel's rebellion and Boxley's plot, there was betrayal. On May 30, George, the body servant of a Mr. Wilson, sought out his master with the news. Two of Vesey's followers, Mingo Harth and Peter Poyas, were arrested and questioned. When they denied any knowledge of the plot, they were released with "confidential slaves" appointed to watch them. Another body slave, William, was arrested and after he had been held in solitary confinement for a week he betrayed the full nature of the plot and the date it was to come to fruition.

The military was called out and arrests began. Vesey, Peter Poyas, and Gullah Jack, along with 121 slaves, including nine freedmen and four whites, were soon in jail. Thirty-five of the blacks were hanged with Denmark Vesey reportedly counseling his followers to "Die silent as you will see me do." Thirty-four others were deported, and the four whites—a Scotchman, a Spaniard, a German peddler, and a Charlestonian —were sentenced to jail for terms ranging from three to twelve months for sympathizing with the rebellion.

Nat Turner didn't bother with any of the careful planning Denmark Vesey and Gabriel Prosser had indulged in. However, because of his indomitable will his revolt was a more successful and far more bloody affair.

The rebellion began in Southampton County, Virginia, in 1831 and lasted for just forty-eight hours but those two days were among the most violent in the history of slavery in America.

Nat Turner was 31 years old and had been taught to read. His reading, however, was confined almost entirely to the Bible and somehow he came to believe he had been chosen by God to free his people. In fact, he claimed that he had had a vision commanding him to take up the fight for freedom for his people.

Nat, foreman of a small plantation and a Baptist exhorter, gathered a small group of eight Negroes around him on Sunday, August 21, and, without any definite plan of operations, attacked his master's family armed with a hatchet and a broad axe. Five whites, including a baby, succumbed to the sudden assault.

Armed with a few guns, the group started on a murdering crusade over the countryside, during which they were joined by fifty or sixty more escaped slaves. They moved from plantation to plantation killing all whites they came across.

"I took my station in the rear," Nat said in his confession, "and it was my object to carry terror and devastation wherever we went. I placed fifteen or twenty of the best-armed and most to be relied on in front, who generally approached the houses as fast as their horses could run. This was for two purposes—to prevent their escape, and strike terror to the inhabitants . . . I sometimes got in sight to see the work of death completed; viewed the mangled bodies as they lay, in silent satisfaction, and immediately started in quest of other victims. . . ."

The slaughter went on through the night, the next day and the next night as men, women and children were beaten and hacked to death.

Turner, however, has been quoted as saying that ". . . indiscriminate massacre was not their intention after they obtained foothold, and was resorted to in the first instance to strike terror and alarm. Women and children would afterwards have been spared, and men, too, who ceased to resist."

Mary Berkeley Minor Blackford, the wife of a planter, recorded in her diary how many slaves either saved or attempted to save their owners when the rebels appeared:

A few minutes after the negroes were seen riding up the lane leading to the house . . . they were in the house and had commenced their work of slaughter. The Mother of the family, who had always enjoyed the affection of her negroes, was among the first killed. Her own servants had nothing to do with the insurrection; on the contrary (as will be seen), did all they could to protect the family at the risk of their own lives.

A little girl clung to her Mistress and begged for her life until her own was threatened. She then fled and hid under the bed. An old negro named Wallace vainly entreated for the life of his Mistress. After murdering the good old lady, they threatened to kill him. He told them to do it as he cared not to live now she was dead.

The youngest of the daughters happened to be a little way from the house in some very high corn, which concealed her, and might have escaped, but losing all presence of mind (on hearing what was going on) screamed loudly in spite of the entreaties of a young negro girl who was with her; drawn by her screams, the murderers rushed upon her. Aggy, the girl with her, endeavored to shield her young mistress at the risk of her own life, but was torn from her with such force as to tear the strong Virginia cloth dress she had on from her shoulders and thrown to the ground where she expected to be killed herself, but they contented themselves with the murder of her young mistress.

The rebellion ended as it had begun—in bloodshed. Marching toward the town of Jerusalem, the county seat, the outlaws came to the plantation of a wealthy planter named Parker. According to Herbert Aptheker in *Nat Turner's Slave Rebellion,* "Some of the Negroes wished to recruit his slaves." Turner was against this but the others prevailed and the party split up with Nat and about nine others remaining at the gate to the plantation. Those who went to the Parker house found plentiful supplies of cider and other liquors and began drinking.

Turner went to find them and during his absence a group of eighteen white volunteers attacked and dispersed his men with fowling pieces and birdshot ammunition. When Turner and the rest of his men returned, the whites were driven off but then they were reinforced by a company of militia which scattered the slaves.

Turner and about twenty of his men got together again and attacked a farmhouse but were driven off by the fire of the five men and boys inside aided by "slave auxiliaries." The militia came quickly and all the rebels except Nat were either killed or taken prisoner. He escaped and eluded capture for two months by hiding out in the swamps.

The vengeance of the whites was as bloody as that of the slaves had been. And in the grim, frenzied search of the countryside that followed many innocent blacks were shot down along with members of the rebel band. Perhaps as many as a hundred innocent Negroes were slaughtered in return for the fifty or so whites who died, and of the forty-seven captured, Nat Turner and eighteen others were hanged.

The rebellion produced another flood of repressive laws and heated talk about enslaving all free Negroes and/or transporting them. It added to the fear and the brutality of the whites and made it impossible for anyone to speak in favor of abolition without being accused of stirring up the slaves to revolt. Very few Southern whites would have taken the point of view expressed by Mary Berkeley Minor Blackford in her diary, parts of which were printed in *The Plantation South*, edited by Katharine M. Jones.

Following her account of how many lives were saved by the Negroes, she says that this was "notwithstanding that as a people they have so many wrongs . . . And I am sure that with a hundredth part of the wrongs they suffer we white people would have risen in arms fifty times. . . ."

4 | The Years of Blood, 1850-1868

They called it Bleeding Kansas and the name fitted. It was a wound from which the lifeblood of a nation was draining. It could only be cured by the dreadful surgery of war.

Immigrants were pouring into the new territory of Kansas from both the South and the Northwest. The violation of the Missouri Compromise and the introduction of squatter sovereignty under the Kansas-Nebraska Act brought about the trouble. The act said that either Kansas or Nebraska might become a state "with or without slavery, as their constitutions may prescribe at the time of admission." Advocates of slavery and those opposed to it immediately began to move toward making sure that Kansas came into the Union with a constitution that suited their particular beliefs.

Emigrant aid societies sprang up in New England and the Northwest. Bands of so-called border ruffians who supported slavery crossed into Kansas to vote and to fight. The first voting and the first fighting went against the antislavery forces because of the superior armament of the proslavery group and the proximity of the Missouri border across which they could make their forays.

David R. Atchison, the proslavery Democratic leader in Missouri, bluntly expressed their purpose. "There are eleven hundred coming over from Platte County to vote, and if that ain't enough we can send five thousand—enough to kill every God-damned abolitionist in the Territory."

The legislature elected by these outsiders promptly set to work drawing up a constitution for Kansas that would not only make a slave state of the territory but would also introduce the police state system that was used in the Southern States to enforce slavery.

To allow Kansas to become a state under such a constitution was abhorrent to the free soil forces. On September 5, a "Free State Convention" assembled in Big Springs and attacked the proslavery forces, declaring that the legislature had warped and defiled the powers of Congress, made a mockery of the Declaration of Independence, and violated the constitutional bill of rights.

The delegates then proclaimed that they owed no obedience to the acts of the "spurious legislature" and would defy it, peaceably if possible, but to a "bloody issue" if necessary. Meeting again at Topeka, the free soil forces produced the Topeka Constitution, which forbade slavery after July 4, 1857, and forwarded it to Washington.

The so-called Wakarusa War followed shortly thereafter. The Wakarusa was a little stream that flowed into Kansas not far from Lawrence and was merely the scene for a show of force by both proslavery and free soil advocates.

Believing that the Free State group had a secret organization to resist the laws and attack Southern settlers, the slavery men organized what they called a Law and Order party that they meant to use to overawe and intimidate the abolitionists.

But the invaders didn't find Lawrence as unprepared as they expected. Six hundred men had gathered there and more were pouring in all the time. Trenches were dug and barricades set up across the streets.

Both sides were spoiling for a fight and were being further stirred up by reports of violence by the other. Proslavery people listened to rumors that the Free Staters were burning down the houses and driving the families of Southern sympathizers out into the cold and snow. Abolitionists accused the Missourians of killing or raping Free State women.

A direct clash at that time might have produced a casualty list that would have shocked the nation and perhaps brought on the Civil War years early. But it didn't take place. The governor managed to intervene and talk both groups into disbanding temporarily.

While the Kansans fought each other, their partisans in the East and South were sending men and arms into the fray.

Sharp's rifles were becoming the chief export from New England to the West. They cost twenty-five dollars each but abolitionist leaders were determined that as many free soilers as possible must have them. Eli Thayer, speaking before a meeting at Worcester, Massachusetts, said he was a man of peace but that he would buy ten rifles out of his own pocket if the townspeople would contribute another ninety. The response was enthusiastic and twenty-three were subscribed for on the spot.

Atchison called on the South to send its young men and to "let them come well armed!" Colonel Jefferson Buford of Alabama sold his slaves to raise money to bring men to Kansas to fight for slavery. A battalion of three hundred men gathered at Montgomery. They mustered at one of the churches there and a Methodist minister prayed for divine guidance, while a Baptist minister presented Colonel Buford and each of his men with a Bible to take with them.

In the North, Henry Ward Beecher sent twenty-five Bibles and twenty-five Sharp's rifles to a group leaving for Kansas. Beecher's remark that the guns would be of more use in Kansas than the Bibles led to the rifles being called "Beecher's Bibles."

As winter ended in Kansas, the fighting began again. E. P. Brown, a free-soil man, was waylaid by "ruffians" near Leavenworth. He was set upon with knives and a hatchet and fatally wounded. Then horsemen dumped him, dying, at the door of his cabin. With a shout of "Here's Brown!" they rode off. His horrified wife went insane from the shock. A short time afterward a man named Phillips who was a believer in squatter sovereignty was also murdered by proslavery men.

"Blood for Blood!" screamed a proslavery paper. "But for each drop spilled, we shall require one hundred fold! . . . Let us purge ourselves of all abolition emissaries . . . and give distinct notice that all who do not leave immediately for the East, *will leave for eternity!*"

And it seemed as though that was just what the proslavery forces set out to do on May 20. An armed group composed of the Lecompton Guards, the Doniphan Tigers, Buford's troop, and the Platte County Rifles under Atchison descended on the town of Lawrence. Antislavery leaders were seized and although the citizens did not resist several were shot and two killed. The invaders raised a blood-red flag over the free-soil newspaper *Herald of Freedom*. In the center of one side of the banner was a lone star and on the other side were the words "Southern Rights." Then that paper and the *Free-State* were invaded, their presses smashed and tossed into the river, and all books and papers burned.

The mob brought up three cannon and blasted the Free State Hotel. When they couldn't batter it down, they ransacked and looted it and then burned it to the ground. After that they set fire to Governor Robinson's house and pillaged a number of other houses and shops.

Back in Washington there was more violence over the territory. Senator Charles Sumner in a speech entitled "The Crime Against Kansas" so incensed the proslavery members of Congress that one of them set out to take a "gentleman's" revenge on him. Congressman Preston S. Brooks of Edgefield, South Carolina, armed with a gutta-percha cane and followed by other Southern representatives, invaded the Senate chamber where Sumner sat at his desk writing.

The first inkling Sumner had that something was wrong was when he heard his name spoken as Brooks set upon him.

The Southerner rained blows on Sumner's bare head with the heavy cane. Stunned and almost blinded, the older man struggled to get to his feet, knocking over his desk and lurching forward until he fell to the floor some distance beyond it.

Representative Morgan of New York and several others tried to rush to the senator's assistance but were held back by Senator Toombs of Georgia and Representatives Edmundson of Virginia and Keitt of South Carolina. Only after Sumner lay bleeding and unconscious on the floor was anyone permitted to go near him.

Sumner was so seriously injured that he did not recover for several years. The North was incensed over the cowardly attack but the South was ecstatic.

The *Richmond Examiner* said Sumner was a foul-mouthed poltroon who "when caned for cowardly vituperation, falls to the floor an insensate lump of incarnate cowardice."

Others viewed it differently. They could see that the shortness of tempers on both sides was leading inevitably toward a blood bath.

"Violence reigns in the streets of Washington," William Cullen Bryant wrote, ". . . violence has now found its way into the Senate chamber. Violence lies in wait on all the navigable rivers and all the railways of Missouri, to obstruct those who pass from the Free States into Kansas."

Some weeks after the attack on Sumner, a friend called on the injured senator and was introduced to a John Brown of Osawatomie, Kansas.

"It was the first time I had ever seen John Brown," the friend recalled later. "They were speaking of the assault by Preston Brooks. and Mr. Sumner said, 'The coat I had on at that time is hanging in that closet. Its collar is stiff with blood. You can see it, if you please, Captain.' John Brown arose, went to the closet, slowly opened the door, carefully took down the coat, and looked at it for a few minutes with the reverence with which a Roman Catholic regards the relics of a saint."

A short time later John Brown answered the attack on Lawrence and the beating of Sumner at a place called Pottawatomie Creek. He answered it in blood.

Many modern historians believe Brown was a madman. His mother and grandmother had died insane and other members of his family were similarly afflicted.

At Pottawatomie the madness was most in evidence. Brown had gathered eight men together for a raid against proslavery elements without telling them his true intentions. One of the eight made a "confession" in 1876 and told what happened when they paused a half mile from the first house to be attacked.

"We are soldiers of the Lord," Brown told his followers. "The Lord has ordered us to destroy with our cutlasses these families of the devil living in this valley. We will kill all the men, every one of them."

Brown's men stared at him in consternation, and his son spoke up. "You mean, father, murdering all those men?"

"The Lord has spoken," Brown answered.

Henry Williams objected. "If the Lord wants them killed, let Him kill them."

Brown flew into an insane rage. He drew the cutlass he had brought all the way from New England and struck Williams on the head with it, splitting his skull and killing him instantly. The others stood staring in horror and fear.

"Onward, soldiers of the Lord, onward to Victory!"

None dared hold back then, but followed Brown to the home of Jim Doyle, a local proslavery leader. Doyle came to the door and stood staring at the eight men with bared cutlasses. He started to dart back in and close the door. Brown's cutlass lashed out and split his skull in two.

"Come out, all of you!" Brown shouted to those who remained inside. "Come out in the name of the army of the Lord!"

Doyle's two older sons came running from the house. Brown cut down Drury Boyle and one of his men killed William.

Screeching in a high-pitched voice, Brown used his cutlass to hack Drury's arms from his body. Next he cut off the head and finally, with blood-curdling shrieks, picked up a severed arm and sliced the fingers from the hand one by one.

They rode on to the next house on Brown's list. The scene was repeated several times more. How many died . . . five, eight, or twelve . . . it depends upon which account you believe, but John Brown's cutlass drank blood that night. Shortly thereafter the fighting in Kansas became general.

"WAR! WAR!" screamed the Westport, Missouri, *Border Times* as it told of Brown's massacre.

Free-soil men in Leavenworth had to be rescued from lynch mobs. Shannon's Sharp Shooters marched on Osawatomie in search of John Brown, burning and looting as they went. They killed a free-soil settler named Cantrell and captured two of Brown's sons. Brown counterattacked and captured twenty-three proslavery men.

There was an engagement at Palmyra that lasted three hours, and Franklin was attacked by proslavery forces. A horde of border ruffians descended on Lawrence and more of them flooded into Kansas from the river area. Alarmed by reports of invasion, Free State men gathered together and began drilling for defense, leaving their wives and children to take care of the farms. In certain areas groups of from five to ten men worked the land together, keeping their weapons within easy reach.

A proslavery mob in control of Leavenworth made up a list of fifty business and professional men they considered Free Staters and ordered them to leave the territory in three days. Many of them did. Osawatomie was raided again on June 7. The houses were looted, the horses run off, and several Free State men murdered. Colonel Sumner of the First U.S. Dragoons had taken the field but his forces were too few and too slow of movement to stop the spreading guerrilla warfare.

In the South "a body of higher-law abolitionists" was accused of having set the prairies afire. In the North the pro-slavery forces were blamed. They were both right.

Free-soil Rangers attacked Franklin. They found some of Buford's Southern recruits with a brass six-pounder and lots of ammunition. The fighting was heavy but the casualties totaled only one killed and several wounded when the pro-slavery forces retreated with the loss of their cannon.

"General" John W. Reid went to Osawatomie with 250 pro-slavery men to search for "Old Brown." They killed one of his sons as they rode into the village. (Another son had gone insane after hearing of the massacre at Pottawatomie and a third had been killed by a "possie" while "trying to escape.") With forty riflemen, Brown opened fire from the underbrush and held the Missourians at bay for awhile. Eventually a charge swept them from the field, twelve men died, and the town was burned.

Three men were killed and several wounded when free soilers attacked Fort Titus. Only the arrival of the governor prevented them from lynching the prisoners taken when the fort surrendered.

A pitched battle was prevented when Colonel P. St. George Cooke threw his small force of U.S. Dragoons between two large forces and by persuasion and threats managed to send them both home without bloodshed.

The "madness of the hour" may have been stayed, but more madness was on the way. Even the new governor, John White Geary, managed to bring only temporary peace by arresting leaders and disarming followers on both sides.

John Brown left Kansas and headed east. He had bigger things in mind—freeing the slaves and fomenting a full-scale revolution. His next act did more to bring on the Civil War than any single act of any other man. He knew only too well what would enrage the South to blind, unreasoning action. Slave owners feared nothing so much as a slave uprising. In their minds this was a danger not only to their property and families but to the whole social fabric, and they would go to any lengths to keep such a thing from happening.

Brown called upon the abolitionist businessmen and preachers of the East to help finance his scheme to seize the Federal arsenal at Harpers Ferry and to rouse the slaves to rebellion.

Frederick Douglass, a former slave and now an abolitionist leader, was one person who saw the insanity of Brown's plan. He met with Brown and listened to him describe how he intended to seize the arsenal at Harpers Ferry, capture leading citizens who lived there, and hold them as hostages. Douglass was astonished and dismayed and tried to talk the old man out of his foolhardiness.

Douglass argued with Brown all night, trying to point out that the scheme might end in a general massacre of his people instead of gaining their freedom. Brown wouldn't listen. He was determined on his course. When Douglass said it was hopeless to attack both the state of Virginia and the Federal Government with twenty men, Brown replied, "If God be for us, who can be against us?"

White abolitionists weren't as wise as Douglass. Many sent money and promised arms. Thomas Wentworth Higginson, a minister, replied to a request for money, "I am always ready to invest money in treason, but at present have none to invest."

Four thousand dollars were raised from such people as Dr. Samuel Gridley Howe and Gerrit Smith, and John Brown led eighteen men, four of them black, into Virginia.

Ralph Volney Harlow describes Brown's raid in his book *The Growth of the United States:*

> On Sunday night, October 16, with a force of eighteen men, he made his attack. By way of warning at the start, he told his followers not to take life unnecessarily, but not to hesitate in defending themselves. His men then cut the telegraph wires, seized the bridge of the Potomac, and captured the federal arsenal at Harpers Ferry. By mid-

night Brown was in full possession of the town, government property and all. Then he sent out a party to begin freeing the slaves and to seize white citizens for hostages.

Among the hostages was Colonel Lewis W. Washington, grandnephew of George Washington. Several citizens, including the mayor, were shot down in the street. However, the first to die at the hands of Brown's freedom fighters was a black man—Shepard Heyward, a freedman—shot down when a train was held up at the station.

By morning the militia was swarming in the fields like angry bees and Brown and his men were trapped in the arsenal, still expecting the slaves to rise and rush to their assistance. None came, and the fifty or so slaves his men had rounded up showed no inclination to fight in such a hopeless cause. One by one Brown's men were hunted down and killed.

Again the first to die was a Negro, a man named Newby who had followed Brown in the hope of freeing his wife and seven children who were still slaves. Newby and two others had been placed to guard the railroad bridge. The Jefferson Guards charged the bridge and Brown's men ran for it. The two whites made it but Newby didn't. He was hit in the throat by a man who had run out of ammunition and had used a spike as a missile. Fired from a rifle, the spike ripped Newby's throat open and he died in the gutter while the townspeople—many of whom were drunk—cheered.

"The brave drunks rushed upon the corpse, cutting off the ears and prodding it with sticks. The sober men, sensible enough to remain under cover, sickened at the sight," Laurence Greene states in *The Raid*.

Twice Brown sent out men with flags of truce, hoping to use his prisoners as bargaining material. The first man he sent out was seized by militiamen. The second one was accompanied by Brown's son, Watson. Both of them were shot down. Watson managed to drag himself back to the arsenal but he was mortally wounded and in great pain all that night.

Billy Leeman, a twenty-year-old who had been with Brown since Kansas, tried to escape by swimming the Potomac. He was shot by a townsman when he pulled himself up on a shoal halfway across the river to rest. Two others of Brown's men did escape, and he was trapped with about half-a-dozen followers in the engine house of the arsenal. Still the militia was reluctant to attack them. They preferred to build up their courage with liquor.

Finally a train arrived from Washington bringing marines commanded by Robert E. Lee and J. E. B. Stuart. Carrying a demand from Lee for Brown's surrender, Stuart went to the roundhouse. When Brown refused, Stuart dodged to one side and waved his plumed hat for the marines to come in with bayonets. They moved in quickly, battering down the doors with axes and a steel ladder used as a ram.

As the marines burst through the opening, Colonel Washington pointed Brown out to them. The old man was kneeling, trying to cock a carbine. A marine struck at him with a sword, slashing him about the head and arms. Brown went down, bleeding but not mortally injured.

One of the marines was killed as he tried to enter but others poured into the room. Jeremiah Anderson, crying, "I surrender!" was struck with such force by a bayonet that he was pinned to the wall. The body hung suspended while the dying man made gurgling sounds in his throat, then it slowly began to revolve until finally it came to rest, head downward.

Another of Brown's men was also bayoneted. Only Brown and two others were taken prisoner.

Brown had wanted martyrdom. The State of Virginia was quick to accommodate him with a hanging despite pleas from men such as Stonewall Jackson who asked clemency for the old man. On December 2, 1859, shortly before he died, he made a statement that was to be long remembered.

"I, John Brown, am now quite *certain* that the crimes of this *guilty* land will never be purged *away* but with blood."

Church bells tolled in the North and Emerson wrote of him, "That new saint, than whom none purer or more brave was ever led by love of man into conflict and death—that new saint who will make the gallows glorious like the Cross."

War would come now. It had been inevitable for a long time but now both sides seemed to rush toward it with an eagerness only a few men tried to stop. Lincoln was elected President in 1860, and almost at once the slave states began to make preparations to secede from the Union. And this despite the fact that the election had shown the majority of the people were opposed to secession.

The planter aristocracy, however, was determined to take any steps needed to preserve their "peculiar institution." The near police state that had ruled the South since the days of Nat Turner's rebellion made it possible for the few to drag the many into war. South Carolina went first, followed by Mississippi, Florida, Alabama, Georgia, Louisiana, and Texas.

In Georgia, those opposed to secession tried to stop the break but were shoved aside by the rebels. North Carolina, Arkansas, and Tennessee had all called special elections, with most people voting against secession but going along because the planters wanted it. Virginia held out until the last, with most of her people opposed to leaving the Union. A vote wasn't allowed until secession was a *fait accompli*.

Thus the millions in the South who were not slave owners would be permitted to fight and die for the right of a few to keep slaves.

Fort Sumter in the harbor of Charleston, South Carolina, was fired upon on April 12, 1861, and shortly thereafter President Lincoln issued a call to the states for troops to put down the rebellion. The small regular army of some sixteen thousand men was scattered all over the western frontier and troops were needed to protect Washington itself.

85

The first violence of the war came in the streets of Baltimore as to the relief of Washington the Sixth Massachusetts marched through the city.

Maryland was a slave state but there was a large pro-Union population in its western sections. Baltimore, however, was in the hands of proslavery mobs headed by the police marshal and a secessionist city council and abetted by a vacillating mayor. Since there was no direct railroad connection between the North and Washington, all trains had to pass·through Baltimore and troops were forced to detrain and march from one station to another. Determined that no troops would pass, the secessionist leaders sent their mobs into the streets to block the passage of the Sixth Massachusetts.

The police were sent to the Camden Street station, a mile from the real danger area. The troops were loaded into cars drawn by horses and proceeded slowly along the tracks on Pratt Street. The mob set upon the cars, hurling stones and tearing up the tracks. Eventually most of the regiment had to get out of the cars and walk while the crowd continued to pelt them with rocks and stones. A gun was fired and then another and, before the incident was over, four infantrymen had been killed, several people in the mob had died, and many were seriously injured.

The Sixth Massachusetts did reach Washington, but the Baltimore mobs, aided by police, turned back eight hundred unarmed Philadelphians trying to get to the capital to offer their services. The police marshal, George P. Kane, a strong slavery man, decided that the best way to prevent Northern troops from getting through was to destroy the railroad bridges that connected Baltimore with the North. Accordingly, he sent out gangs and they demolished the short Canton span and the long bridges over Gunpowder and Bush creeks. Then they traveled fifteen miles north of Baltimore and destroyed two wooden bridges at Couckeysville.

This very effectively isolated Washington. From April 19 on, the Federal Government was cut off from the states that supported it. The mob ran the city of Baltimore April 20 and 21. The President Street station was shut down, Unionists were forcibly induced to take down their flags, and Union soldiers were hunted down in the streets. Kane telegraphed a Maryland congressman, telling him to send men through Virginia and Maryland to arouse and hurry riflemen to Baltimore. Then on April 21 the wires were cut and it was no longer possible for Washington to get in touch with the North except by the hazardous Harpers Ferry route.

The reign of terror against Union sympathizers continued until April 24. Hundreds were beaten and driven from the city while Kane's police stood by and watched and the mayor and governor wrung their hands helplessly.

In Washington, General Winfield Scott, the ancient but still doughty hero of the War of 1812 and the Mexican War, feared the rebels would be on the city at any moment to seize the President, the Cabinet, and the Treasury. He gathered what local troops he could and rallied his few regulars and marines. He decided that if the city was attacked, he'd make the Treasury Building the focus of his defense. His intention was to hide the President and the Cabinet in the basement and concentrate the troops in Lafayette Square.

Union troops were on their way but Baltimore was still blocking them. The Seventh New York, Eighth Massachusetts, and First New York Zouaves were all held up outside the city. Orders could have been given for them to fight their way through or even to bombard the city, but it was feared that would drive Maryland into the Confederacy, so the orders were withheld.

Reviewing the Sixth Massachusetts, which alone had reached the capital, Lincoln expressed his despair. "I don't believe there is any North. The Seventh Regiment is a myth. Rhode Island is not known in our geography any longer. You are the only Northern realities."

But the next morning the city was saved. General Ben Butler of the Massachusetts state troops came up with a plan to bypass Baltimore and its mobs by way of Annapolis. With his Eighth Massachusetts and the New York Seventh, he repaired a rusty, rickety single-track railroad from Annapolis and sent the Seventh on to the capital.

Ben Butler then turned his attention to doing something about Baltimore. The central and western sections of Maryland had risen for the Union, but the city itself was in almost a state of seige with its arrogant mobs burning Union flags and chivying Union sympathizers. Butler moved with his Massachusetts troops to restore the city to the Union.

He reinforced Fort McHenry, had Fort Morris garrisoned, and set gangs of men to rebuilding the railway bridges. The troops occupied Relay House on May 5, and the next day the Northern Central Railroad was in business again. On May 12, Butler took a thousand men and a battery and occupied Federal Hill, which commanded the city. He also seized a store of arms about to be shipped to the South.

It only remained for Butler to arrest Ross Winan, one of the richest men in the county, on charges of supplying arms to the rebels. Butler's remark that hanging a man worth $15 million ought to teach traitors a lesson had a salutary effect on Winan and other secessionists in the city.

In the West also there were mobs and blood running in the streets. Missouri, like Maryland, was tottering on the brink of leaving the Union. Although Missourians had done most of the fighting to turn Kansas into a slave state, with the advent of war there had been a reaction there in favor of the Union—a movement joined by some of the proslavery people.

"One of the baffling factors in the Missouri situation was the fact that its Unionists included both conservative proslavery men and zealous abolitionists, who distrusted one another about as much as they distrusted the secessionists," Bruce Catton says in *The Coming Fury*.

Ignoring the fact that a clear majority of the state's people favored the Union, Governor Claiborne Jackson plotted to carry it over into the Confederacy, and wrote to President Jefferson Davis, to request cannon to be used in seizing the United States arsenal at St. Louis where there were 60,000 muskets, 90,000 pounds of powder, and 1,500,000 ball cartridges.

As part of his plot, Jackson called out the state militia, composed mainly of the proslavery planter class, and had them encamp on hills overlooking the arsenal to wait for the arrival of the cannon from the South.

But the Union forces were not asleep. Captain Lyon, in command of the arsenal, had received orders from the War Department "instructing him to arm loyal citizens, protect the public property, and muster into service four regiments of Missourians."

The loyal population of the state was largely made up of German refugees who had fled from terror in their native land and knew its face when they saw it again in America. They had been formed in guard units and they rallied to the Union cause and were armed with part of the muskets in the armory. The rest of the muskets were shipped into Illinois.

The Union forces under Captain Lyon and a man named Frank Blair then proceeded to take care of the secessionist miltia. With two companies of regulars and about four thousand German home guards (whom the proslavery people had taken to calling Hessians) they marched on the militia at Camp Jackson. The commander of the state forces, General Frost, protested ". . . surely no United States officer would attack law-abiding citizens who were carrying out their Constitutional function of organizing and instructing a body of state militia?"

The fact that the militia had been gathered for the unconstitutional function of attacking the U.S. arsenal seemingly escaped the gentleman's mind. He was reminded of it when he found his camp surrounded by regulars and home guardsmen who demanded his surrender. The proslavery general offered his sword, and his 50 officers, 639 men, 3 siege guns,

1 mortar, 6 brass field pieces, and 1200 rifled muskets fell into Federal hands.

Proslavery mobs poured into the streets of St. Louis as the militia was marched back into town. They waved Southern flags, cheered for Jefferson Davis, and jostled and cursed the troops. The regulars in the lead fixed bayonets and leveled them at the mob. It melted away before the gleaming steel but formed again around the Germans, who lacked the regulars' training and discipline.

A woman screamed suddenly and ran up to one of the guards and spat on him. Angered, the man turned and chased her with bayonet leveled, forgetting all he'd ever heard about the sanctity of Southern womanhood. A man with a revolver tried to break through to the prisoners, and when he was pushed away, fired and wounded an officer. The Germans fired in retaliation.

At first the shots were aimed in the air but as the mob continued to pelt them with rocks and fire pistols in their faces, the troops leveled their muskets and fired in earnest.

Twenty-eight of the mob were killed and wounded but innocent civilians and soldiers also died in the blood-soaked streets. A baby was killed as its mother held it. Captain Constantine Blandovski was mortally wounded while his Third Volunteer regiment was standing at rest. Shouts and screams were mixed with sharp commands. Death struck from out of the blue and those who were present never forgot the terror of that day.

But that was only the beginning. For four more years Missouri was torn by violence and bitter internal strife. And the violence began that very night.

Secessionist mobs swept through the city, shouting and brandishing weapons, tearing down and burning the Union flag wherever they found it. The police who had been heavily infiltrated on the governor's orders by proslavery men stood by and watched while pro-Union citizens were beaten and their homes burned. Union sympathizers turned out, organized into armed bands, and fought with the secessionists.

Federal troops restored order, but the next day there was more fighting when an armed mob attacked one of the German regiments that was marching from the arsenal to its mustering place. The troops fought their way through, killing twelve members of the mob and suffering some losses themselves.

War swept over the land. Untrained militia in fancy uniforms fought each other at Bull Run, and the South staggered to victory in that first pitched battle on the principle that the "mob which fled last was the winner." The U.S. Navy blockaded the ports of the South and hundreds of thousands of men flocked to the colors on both sides. The casualty lists grew.

The magnitude of the conflict is indicated by Lynn Montross in *War Through the Ages:*

> As measured by anything in Europe's past, the American Civil War is astronomical in its statistics. The theater of operations embraced an area so vast that a single flanking movement covered a distance of 800 miles. More t an 2,000 combats took place, of which 149 were engagements of enough importance to be called battles. Half a million soldiers gave their lives, either on the battlefield or as a direct consequence of the campaigns. The cost in money to the North alone amounted to nearly five billion dollars; and the South did not admit defeat until every resource, both moral and material, had been exhausted.

General Winfield Scott had warned the North that it would take an army of well-trained regulars to win the war and had predicted that it would take three years of hard fighting to put down the rebellion. The politicians had laughed at the old general and whispered that he was in an advanced stage of senility. Union statesmen, generally, were of the opinion that the South could be defeated in a matter of a few months.

If Scott had been younger (he was 75 at the time) and able to bring the military ability that had won in 1812 to bear on the problem, or if the politicians had been wiser, four years of bloodshed might have been replaced by a few quick months of pacification. But that wasn't to be.

On April 6, 1862, what were in effect two armed mobs of civilians staggered together at a place that forever after would be known as Bloody Shiloh. Thirty-three thousand inexperienced Northern troops were surprised by forty thousand equally green rebels. They pounded each other for two days, "suffering casualties which would have appalled regulars."

The rebel general, A. S. Johnston, was among those killed, and Grant's army, after being reinforced, managed to push the Confederates from the field. At dusk on April 7 when it began to sleet, about twenty thousand dead and wounded lay on the ground. Confederate casualties ran to 22 percent, while Union losses amounted to approximately a third.

In the savage Seven Days' Battle, Lee led 87,000 men against McClellan's 109,000 but managed to defeat the latter, with losses on each side of at least 15,000 men. Following up their victory, the Confederates ran into entrenched Union riflemen at Malvern Hill who shot down 6,000 rebels in a few hours.

Lee learned a lesson from that setback that European generals didn't learn throughout the entire First World War. Sending troops to attack trenches manned by men with breech-loading Sharp rifles or Spencer repeating carbines was sending them to their death. Thus he defeated General Pope at the Second Battle of Bull Run by the use of riflemen in trenches and inflicted 14,000 casualties for a loss of 9,000.

At Antietam, McClellan with a vastly superior army failed to annihilate Lee's 40,000 plus troops and suffered 12,000 casualties to 10,000 for the Southern forces. General Burnside fought 79,000 Confederates at Fredericksburg with 122,000 Union troops and came off second best with the loss of 12,650 dead and wounded.

A few weeks after this horror, an even greater slaughter took place in Tennessee. An army of 43,000, under the command of General William Rosecrans, clashed with 37,000 of Braxton Bragg's men. A desperate battle ensued at Murfreesboro on December 31, 1862, and the Union forces suffered 13,250 losses and the Confederates, 9,865. Neither side won and a few days later Bragg finally retreated, but the remnants of Rosecrans' army were too worn out to pursue.

At Chancellorsville, there were 120,000 Union troops and 55,000 rebels, under the respective commands of "Fighting Joe" Hooker and Robert E. Lee. When the battle was over, the Federal loss was 16,000 as opposed to 12,000 suffered by the Confederates.

In June of 1863, Lee decided to invade the North and marched to a place of little importance in Pennsylvania called Gettysburg. In attempting to drive out the few regiments of Federal cavalry defending Gettysburg, the Confederate commander on the field called in reinforcements. Before long most of Lee's army was committed against the increasing numbers of Union troops. Despite their top generals, the Union forces had managed to pick an ideal defensive position and nothing Lee's army could do succeeded in dislodging them. Lee's genius seems to have slept that day. After failing to crush either Union flank, he hurled the 15,000 men of Pickett's corps against the strongly held center.

Statistics can best sum up the appalling result of that charge. People who have made a study of war say that losses of more than 30 percent will usually stop an assault, but of the 4,500 men in Pickett's division, 3,393 were casualties. This was a loss of 75 percent. One regiment lost all but a tenth of its numbers, and all 18 brigade and regimental commanders were killed or wounded.

The most important battle of the war ended after 23,000

Union and 30,000 rebel casualties. Lee was forced to retreat and Northern territory never again was threatened.

The heavy casualties on the battlefield forced both sides to turn to conscription to maintain their armies. This resulted in more violence.

In the South it was widespread and can be partly accounted for by a great deal of pro-Union sentiment among the poorer classes of people. The German sections of Texas, the swamps of Florida, and the mountains of the Ozarks became favorite hiding places for deserters from the Confederate Army. Recruiting officers and provost marshals dared not enter these places without an army escort.

When the conscription law in the Confederacy exempted men who owned twenty slaves or more, resentment flared.

W. W. Holden, editor of the Raleigh *Standard,* led the movement and some people thought his editorials were close to treason. A detachment of Georgia troops passing through Raleigh on September 9, 1863, attacked the *Standard*'s office. The next day a pro-Confederate paper was destroyed by a Unionist mob. Holden ran against Governor Vance as a peace candidate in 1864, and those who voted for him in pro-Confederate areas were frequently subjected to what was euphemistically termed "violent unpopularity."

In December of 1862, at Industry, Texas, which is in Austin County, draftees attacked a Confederate officer. They drove him off and then organized armed bands for the purpose of defending themselves. These were German settlers but they threatened to destroy fellow Germans who remained loyal to the Confederacy.

In Randolph County, in northern Alabama, civilians defied the Conscription Act. An armed mob, led by the Peace Society, raided the county jail and freed deserters who had been arrested.

There was opposition to the draft in the North, too, and this along with the work of southern agents and intense anti-

Negro feelings on the part of the Irish population led to the worst riot in the history of the nation.

Particularly distasteful to many of the poor in the North was the fact that the Conscription Act had a clause that permitted well-to-do men to buy a substitute for three hundred dollars if their names were drawn. When the drawing began in New York City, rioting followed.

Southern sympathizers and Confederate agents had been active in the city for weeks and they had great influence among the rowdy gangs of Five Points and elsewhere. The draft was in reality nothing but the spark that set off the powder keg that was the gang-infested city. The Draft Riot of July, 1863, was nothing more than the largest in a series that had rocked the city since the eighteen-thirties.

The riots started as a treasonable insurrection against the United States Government, then became a destructive attack against the well-to-do, and finally a race riot with Negroes as targets. Scores of separate incidents were "equal in fury to many full scale riots," says Willard A. Heaps in *Riots U.S.A.*

There is some evidence that the riots were carefully planned by Copperheads and that cadres of Southern saboteurs may have infiltrated the city. Irving Werstein in *July 1863* supports this theory with a description of a group of Southerners gathered in a warehouse at the foot of Fourth Street on the East River planning to burn the city:

> Some had come to the city by way of Canada, others had been smuggled in on merchant ships. A few had arrived by train, by wagon, even on foot, assuming various disguises and identities. Now the time for concealment was ending. The waiting was over. Arms caches were dragged from secret storerooms.
>
> By morning, two hundred well-armed dedicated men would be on the move, following a master plan to burn ships at their moorings, important buildings and other ob-

jectives. During the confusion of an apparently spontaneous mass uprising against the draft, certain of these infiltrators had been selected to kill or capture the leading officials of the city and other prominent men, and to take power in New York.

At one point during the riots, there was an attack on the Union Steam Works, possibly an attempt to steal the large supplies of arms stored there. The fighting was heavy, and police battling the mob noticed that the leaders of the attack were a one-armed giant, with a huge bludgeon that he used as a flail, and a slender young man in dirty overalls armed with a knife and club.

Both men were killed, the giant by gunshot and the young man by having his throat pierced by a picket of an iron railing he fell against when hit on the head. A policeman removed the body from the railing and was surprised to see that under the dirty overalls were cashmere pants, a linen shirt, and a rich vest. The young man's features were described as aristocratic and he had fair, white skin and well-cared-for hands. Although dressed on the outside like a working man, he had obviously never done day labor in his life. Unfortunately, no one ever learned his identity, for his body disappeared when the fighting was over, carried off by the rioters.

As many as fifty thousand rioters may have taken part in the four days of fighting. The Colored Orphans Asylum was attacked by a mob. A handful of police managed to hold them off long enough for the three hundred children to be spirited out by the superintendent. Then the building was looted and burned. Immediately afterward the mob launched an assault on the arsenal and gun factory at Second Avenue and Twenty-First Street.

The police defending the building fought desperately but were driven out the back way. Part of the mob surged into the building searching for arms. Police reinforcements attacked those who were still outside and some of the rioters threw torches into the building. It burst into flames, trapping dozens of rioters inside.

No one knows how many died but Asbury says that "after the riots had subsided and workmen began to clear away the debris, more than fifty baskets and barrels of human bones were carted from the ruins and buried in Potter's Field."

The mob attacked Negroes at every opportunity. Three black men were hanged on the first day of fighting, and after that an average of three a day were discovered who had been slashed and/or beaten and then hanged. Some were burned by women who poured oil into wounds already inflicted by rioters and set fire to them, dancing and singing obscenely while the human torches were reduced to charred skeletons.

But it wasn't only Negroes who suffered at the hands of the mob. Colonel O'Brien, who had rendered yeoman service as a commander of militia against the mob, was set upon outside his home. Irving Werstein records the attack:

> He was kicked and beaten, and then a rope was twisted about his ankles and he was dragged back and forth over the cobblestones. A Catholic priest interfered long enough to administer the last rites of the church, and then departed, leaving Colonel O'Brien to the tender mercies of the infuriated rioters.

Troops poured into the city, some of them called directly from the field of Gettysburg. The mob fought the troops with unbelievable fury. Cannon were used in the narrow streets. Troops charged mobs who were hanging Negroes.

Marching into Eighth Avenue, soldiers found a gang of women gathered about three Negroes hanging from lamp-posts. While a mob of men yelled and cheered, the women hacked savagely at the dangling bodies.

Colonel Mott spurred into their midst and cut down one of the Negroes. A rioter tried to drag him from his horse and he ran him through with his sword.

The mob tried to march to Wall Street to sack the financial

district but were turned back by police. They attacked Horace Greeley's *New York Tribune* time after time, finally being turned back by Gatling guns brought ashore from warships and mounted on the building.

The rioting had started on Monday. It didn't really end until Thursday when the streets were filled with troops and the police were ruthlessly hunting down rioters and beating them to death with their heavy locust clubs or driving them off the tops of buildings to their deaths.

The riots ended but the war went on. Grant took Vicksburg after battles in which thousands died on each side and the city was reduced to near starvation. In a terrible battle at Chickamauga, General George Thomas earned the title of the "Rock of Chickamauga" when he saved the Union Army from disaster in a battle in which twenty-one thousand Confederates and sixteen thousand Union soldiers were killed or wounded.

Four bloody battles were fought between May 5 and June 3, 1864—the Wilderness, Spottsylvania, North Anna, and Cold Harbor. In the Battle of the Wilderness, the wounded died screaming when the tangled underbrush caught fire. At Spottsylvania they fought for thirteen days with the battle reaching its height around the so-called Bloody Angle. At Cold Harbor the Union troops were hurled against entrenched rebels and driven back with the loss of six thousand dead and wounded. The fighting ended with Lee seeming to have had the better of it but falling back with his army decimated, having lost thirty-two thousand men to Federal casualties of fifty thousand.

In the fighting around Petersburg, trench systems and barbed wire were used. In a huge mine explosion the Union troops destroyed part of the Confederate line and killed and buried alive hundreds of rebels. But then, as their assault wave passed through the huge 150-foot crater the mine had left in the enemy lines, they were counterattacked and driven back. The crater was so large that it can still be seen near Petersburg where seven thousand men died.

Sherman marched to the sea, fighting Johnston most of the way in skirmish and pitched battle. The Federal Army suffered a bloody repulse at Kenesaw Mountain and during May and June, Sherman absorbed seventeen thousand casualties and inflicted about as many. Sherman captured Atlanta after defeating John H. Hood in three hard-fought battles during which Hood hurled his men against entrenched riflemen time after time and was hit with heavy losses.

The Union forces marched on, wreaking devastation that is still remembered in story and song. Sherman's sixty thousand men traveled three hundred miles, leaving a devastated swath sixty miles wide through the granary of the Confederacy.

Meanwhile, Grant's cavalry commander, Phil Sheridan, rode through much of Virginia, destroying the rich farming country.

Sherman captured Savannah and Thomas annihilated Hood's army at Nashville. Then Grant, Sherman, and Sheridan closed in on Lee. On April 2, 1865, Grant broke through the Petersburg lines and drove the Confederates back into Richmond. Lee had only 28,356 men left out of his Army of North Virginia, which had numbered 55,000 three months before. In a desperate attempt to break out of Richmond, he was blocked by Sheridan's cavalry on April 9, and the war ended with his surrender at Appomattox.

In the West there was still some fighting, led by the former slave trader and future KKK head, Nathan Bedford Forrest. Forrest had achieved quite a reputation as a leader of irregular cavalry, whom he called his "hoss critters." He became one of the great heroes of the South but his reputation in the North was that of a bloodthirsty monster after his troops captured Fort Pillow.

After taking the fort, his men massacred the Negro prisoners. They were beaten to death with muskets, bayoneted, burned alive, and even crucified.

Frederick Douglass protested to President Lincoln over the incident and suggested that the United States do the same to Confederate prisoners. Lincoln, however, thought this too strong a measure to take.

Many Southern-oriented histories have either underplayed the Fort Pillow massacre or have gone so far as to claim that it didn't take place. That it did is clear from all unprejudiced accounts and also from the specific orders issued by Jefferson Davis saying that any Northern officer taken while commanding Negro troops should be executed and any former Negro slaves captured in battle should be turned over to their home states and tried for rebellion. The penalty for rebellion, of course, was death.

Forrest was given to psychotic rages that made his men more afraid of him than they were of the enemy. When in such a rage, he was likely to do anything. Only his ancient mother could calm him at such times, and she could hardly be present on the field of battle.

An even more violent character to come out of the Civil War was the guerrilla leader William C. Quantrill, who has been called the "Bloodiest Man in American History."

Quantrill was born in Canal Dover, Ohio, and moved in the eighteen-fifties to Kansas where he taught school for some time. He also seems to have been engaged in more dubious activities such as slave selling and horse stealing, but it took the Civil War to bring him into prominence. He embraced, or pretended to embrace, the Southern cause and gathered around him a band of gunmen and cutthroats that included Jesse James and the Younger Brothers. Although they occasionally operated in concert with Confederate troops, Quantrill and his men spent most of their time running off horses, robbing banks, and shooting down defenseless civilians.

On August 21, 1863, Quantrill and his band seized Lawrence, Kansas. Although there was no resistance they slaughtered every man in the town. It is variously estimated that from 140 to 200 unarmed civilians were shot down by Quantrill, Frank and Jesse James, and Cole Younger and his brothers. The town was then set afire and 185 buildings burned, the bank looted, and large numbers of horses run off.

Federal cavalry rode in pursuit of Quantrill almost at once. Many of his men were hunted down and shot on the spot. Others were hanged. The Union officer in command reported that his men had killed twenty-one in one day and a total of eighty during the hunt. He also informed his superiors that because of the bestiality of the crimes at Lawrence no prisoners had been taken and none would be.

Houses of guerrilla sympathizers were searched and when goods known to have been looted from Lawrence were found, the houses were burned, as were those of known guerrillas. Quantrill escaped with some of the most murderous members of his gang—Bloody Bill Angerson, Arch Clements, Alexander Franklin James, his younger brother Jesse, Cole Younger, and two of his brothers.

Quantrill was to find, however, that the raid had made a marked man of him, and that many of his Southern supporters now saw through his pose as a Confederate leader and began to refer to him as "Butcher" Quantrill. Guerrillas came to be so savagely hated that some were scalped and others had their ears cut off when they fell into the hands of local residents. The scalping may have been partly in revenge for their own use of this tactic. Andy Blunt, Bill Anderson, and a couple of others scalped four North Missouri militiamen, and in an old account one raider describes his companions this way:

> The bridles of the horses the Guerrillas rode were adorned with scalps. One huge, red-bearded Guerrilla, six feet and over, girdled about the waist with an armory of revolvers, had dangled from every conceivable angle a profuse array of these ghastly trophies.

The Quantrill gang re-formed after the retreat from Lawrence and conducted many more raids that resulted in clashes with Federal troops. Among the exploits credited to Jesse James during this period were the murder of several unarmed Union soldiers on leave and an affair where he disguised himself as a woman to gain admission into a house of prostitution in order to kill militiamen he knew were being entertained there.

With the Civil War coming to an end, Quantrill made repeated efforts to ingratiate himself with Confederate leaders, hoping he would be included in the general surrender and expecting amnesty for those who had fought for the Southern cause. His efforts failed to produce the commission he wanted. Even the fact that regular Confederate officers like General Sterling Price had used his bloody services and were thus at least morally implicated in his crimes didn't convince Confederate authorities that he should have the right to call himself a soldier. He was a bandit and in the end he died like one.

The guerrillas were hunted down by well-trained companies of marksmen armed with repeating carbines. Bloody Bill Anderson and William Smith, commanding several hundred men, found they could do nothing against Federal cavalry using Spencer carbines and infantry with rifles. Smith was struck by five balls and Anderson by three, including a minie ball in the heart. Frank and Jesse James managed to escape the manhunt—Frank going to Kentucky and Jesse heading for Texas.

Quantrill gathered a body of forty men whom he disguised as Union soldiers in the hope of fleeing south. They met at the farm of Mrs. Duprez. In a horse-stealing foray, they killed a Major Houston and were recognized despite their stolen uniforms. Pursued up the Salt River, the handful that remained took refuge at the farm of Jim Wakefield.

Federal troops found them there and shot them down almost to a man. Only three managed to escape, and Quantrill wasn't among them. Running on foot, he got about three-quarters of a mile from the house before he was hit in the spine by a bullet and fell in the Wakefield pasture. He was taken to a hospital in Louisville where he lingered for six weeks with his legs paralyzed before dying.

Quantrill is regarded by many authorities as the father of the western outlaws. Many of those who rode with him showed up later with gangs of their own, looting and killing without the excuse of the Civil War. Jesse James was one of them.

The son of a Baptist preacher, he spent his childhood, according to one biographer, burying small animals alive. Jesse claimed he had been mistreated because the Government hadn't granted him amnesty as it did other Confederates, and he used this as the excuse for his outlaw raids. Stories, poems, and plays written many years after his career came to an end have tended to glorify him and suggest he was regarded as a kind of Robin Hood by the people of his time.

Accounts of old-timers who knew him or lived in the area give the lie to this. Ed V. Burkholder in an article entitled "Who Killed Jesse James?" says of one such man, "Gilmore laughed at these stories."

People in those days thought Jesse and Frank were just plain wild and had no justification for their lives of crime. Gilmore said that Jesse, "when sober, was a sullen, mean, sadistic killer, shooting men without so much as blinking an eye," but when drunk was good-natured and given to Bible-thumping. Frank, on the other hand, was mean only when drunk. Sober, he became so disgusted with Jesse's murderous ways that he tried to quit the gang several times.

Jesse left a trail of killings across the West, including three Pinkerton detectives, one of whom he butchered and left by the side of the trail as an example to other law officers. On September 7, 1879, the James gang and the Youngers invaded

103

Northfield, Minnesota, and held up the First National Bank. In a drunken rage, Frank shot the cashier and brought the whole town down on them.

Rifles appeared at every window and six-guns fired from every door. Two of the escaping outlaws were shot down in the street and most of the rest were wounded. Only the James brothers made good their escape. The Youngers were run down and taken in the woods. When they surrendered, Cole had eleven wounds, Jim had nine, and Bob's right arm was shattered. The three were sent to prison, and Bob eventually died there. Cole and Jim served twenty-five year sentences and were released.

Frank James finally gave himself up for his crimes in Missouri but a jury of Southern sympathizers refused to convict him and later he received a full pardon from the governor. Jesse went into hiding but when a ten-thousand-dollar reward was posted for him, dead or alive, two members of his gang, Bob and Charley Ford, tracked him down.

The story usually told is that Jesse was shot in the back by Bob Ford as he stood on a chair to hang up a sampler that said "Home Sweet Home." But Burkholder's informant, who was the first person on the scene except for Jesse's wife, said he was shot from the front. Although he was only fourteen at the time, Al Gilmore remembered that the body was in the middle of the room, not near any chair. The bullet was a soft-nosed one and had hit Jesse below the eye, "taking the eye, a part of the ear and the temple with it."

The story about the shot in the back first appeared in a play called *The Outlaws of Missouri* because something was needed to pep up the action. Jesse's publicity since his death has been very favorable. Ballads, plays, and motion pictures have glorified him clear down to the present. One such film in 1938 was viewed by Jesse's granddaughter and her comment was, "About the only connection it had with fact was that there was once a man named James and he did ride a horse."

The end of the Youngers and the Jameses left the field open for the so-called Wild Bunch who used as a hideout a barren basin surrounded by mountains located in Northern Wyoming called the Hole in the Wall. The leader of this crew was Butch Cassidy, a calm, calculating character who could keep such vicious and quarrelsome killers as Kid Curry and the Sundance Kid from shooting each other and turn them, instead, to the profitable business of robbing banks and railroads.

Cassidy's original specialty had been horse stealing but he moved into the big time when he formed the Train Robbers Syndicate. He ran afoul of the Pinkerton Detective Agency, however, and they took up the chase.

Hounded out of America, Cassidy moved to another frontier area—Argentina. There he resumed his career of bank robbery with the help of Harry Longbaugh, the Sundance Kid, and a schoolteacher named Etta Place. The Pinkertons were still on Cassidy's trail, and when a series of robberies occurred in the Argentine, all staged by two Gringo men and a woman, Agent Frank Dimaio tracked them down. Etta Place returned to the States, and the Sundance Kid and Cassidy tried their luck in Bolivia before going to Mexico where they were shot down by Government troops.

Billy the Kid was another legend of the West and supposedly ran up a record of killing twenty-one men in the twenty-one years of his life. His first victim was an unarmed blacksmith, E. P. Cahill, whom he killed in a quarrel on August 17, 1877. Billy was then 17. Most of the rest of his victims were also unarmed or shot in the back. His contemporaries considered him "a dirty little killer." He was, in fact, a homicidal neurotic who killed for the fun of it.

Born in New York City, the Kid was taken west by his mother while still a child. His real name was Henry McCarty but he assumed the name of William H. Bonney when his thieving ways got him into trouble with the law. It was also convenient in avoiding arrest for the murder of Cahill.

His mother died when he was 16, and less than a year later Billy was arrested for the first time. He was put in jail for stealing clothes from two Chinese men, but he escaped and got out of town. From then on he turned to horse stealing and finally to the job of hired killer during the famous Lincoln County war where he fought on the side of the large ranchers against a group of cattlemen whose investment in cows and land was relatively small.

The Kid and five of his cohorts lay in wait behind a plank gate in Lincoln one morning and shot down the sheriff and one of his deputies. Later, Bonney and nine other gunmen who called themselves the Regulators killed a man named "Buckshot" Roberts at Blazer's Mills. The Kid blamed Roberts for the death of John Tunstall, his friend and employer.

After a pitched battle in which the cavalry intervened, Billy rode off with a few followers. Then he killed a young Indian agent, Morris J. Bernstein, and became a Federal fugitive. A little later, Billy and his friends shot a lawyer named Chapman, soaked him in whiskey and set him afire. Bonney tried to cop out by offering to turn state's evidence against the others but the deal fell through. Billy the Kid was finally killed by Sheriff Pat Garrett, a man who had once befriended him.

Another of the legendary heroes of the West was Wild Bill Hickok, and his reputation doesn't hold up under close scrutiny any more than the others. His original nickname was "Duck Bill" in reference to a deformed upper lip which he later hid under a flowing mustache. Those who feared him as a gunman called him "Dutch Bill" and later this evolved into "Wild Bill."

His fearsome reputation seems to have been based mainly on his boast of having killed six members of the McCandles clan in Kansas in 1861. The way Hickok told the story, the McCandles were desperate outlaws and secessionists and he shot it out with them single-handed, killing them in a desperate battle. There is another side to the story, however, and it is supported by an article in the *Nebraska History Magazine,* by the recent publication *Violence in America,* and by the book *The Hero in America* by Dixon Wecter.

This version gives the name of those killed as McCanles rather than McCandles and says Hickok killed only two men and a boy and that all three were unarmed. Hickok is said to have fired from behind a curtain in the Russell Majors and Waddel station to kill David McCanles, his hired hand and a 12-year-old son who had come to collect a debt. Still other versions place the incident in Nebraska and list only McCanles as having been shot through the head from ambush.

Other accounts of Hickok's life say he killed only three men all told, and that he often shot his victims out of nervous cowardice. As sheriff of Ellis County, Kansas, he was credited with killing a man named Phil Coe as well as (by mistake) his own deputy.

In 1876, while playing poker in a Deadwood saloon, he was shot. Since he was holding a pair of aces and a pair of eights at the time, that combination was forever afterward known in the West as "the dead man's hand." Fittingly, Hickok was shot in the back by a young man who was looking for a reputation as a gunman. When the youth testified that Hickok had killed his brother, he was freed by the jury, but later when the story was discovered to be a lie, he was retried and hanged.

Buffalo Bill Cody who was more of a showman than a real western badman often bragged of his many wounds—137. His wife, in her old age, however, reported that he had suffered only one wound, a creased scalp in a brush with the Sioux, and that instead of numerous Indians she could remember only one he had killed. Apparently that one was the young chief Yellow Hand because that deed was witnessed by a cavalry patrol. Cody described what happened after the killing in his autobiography:

"Jerking his war-bonnet off, I scientifically scalped him in about five seconds and shouted, 'The first scalp for Custer!'"

Presumably that made the shade of George Custer, who had that same year lost his yellow locks and two hundred and sixty-five of his men at the Little Big Horn, rest more easily.

It wasn't only the well-known gunmen of the West who were violent. The whole frontier tradition was one of violence. Ranchers fought squatters and sheep herders, and everyone killed Indians.

The Sand Creek massacre was probably one of the most vicious in the long series of such crimes that the white man perpetrated against the Indians. On November 28, 1864, a large number of Cheyenne and Arapaho Indians had gathered to surrender after having been on the warpath. A Colorado regiment of militia under the command of Colonel J. M. Chivington left Fort Lyon, Colorado. They had marched three hundred miles to surround the followers of Chief Black Kettle at Sand Creek.

"Scalps are what we're after," Chivington told his men. "I long to be wading in gore! Kill and scalp all Indians—big ones and little ones! Nits make lice!"

And that was what the cold, dirty, ill-trained militia did despite Black Kettle's offer to surrender and his raising of first an American and then a white flag. One old chief, White Antelope, was shot down as he stood unarmed, singing the death song of the Cheyenne in front of his lodge. Women clutching babies to their breasts were killed and their bodies mutilated. A soldier seized a squaw by the hair and cut out her heart and carried it around on a stick. Old braves were beaten to the ground and scalped while still alive. Terrified squaws rushed up to the militiamen, screaming, "We are women!" They were riddled with bullets along with the rest.

Most of the Indians were without arms because Black Kettle had given up more than half the tribe's weapons as proof of his peaceful intentions. Those who were armed fought back, and the militia suffered nine men killed and thirty-eight wounded. After the battle was over, Chivington and his officers amused themselves by blowing out the brains of the children who had been captured. More than three hundred Cheyenne were murdered and all their ponies driven off. Black Kettle himself escaped only to die in another attack by whites at a later date.

Many settlers in the area were lavish in their praise of Chivington and his men, but at least one man denounced the massacre. It was Kit Carson, the old scout. He denounced Chivington and called him a dog. Asking who was really civilized, the white man or the red, Carson said, "I don't like a hostile Redskin and when they're hostile, I've fought 'em as hard as any man. But I never yet drew a bead on a squaw or her papoose and I loathe and hate the man that would . . . no one but a coward or a dog would do it . . . when we white men do such awful things, these poor critters don't know no better than to follow suit."

A Congressional commission investigated the Sands Creek affair in 1868 and agreed with Carson. A report was issued condemning the affair in strong words:

> It scarcely has its parallel in the records of Indian barbarity . . . men, fleeing women and infants were tortured and mutilated in a way which would have put to shame the savages of interior Africa. . . .

Chief Black Kettle was killed at the battle of Washita when George Custer's Seventh Cavalry attacked the village. Despite Black Kettle's reluctance to take the warpath, many of his braves had been out seeking revenge for Sands Creek and had killed many settlers during the autumn of 1868. White captives and scalps were in the camp on the Washita River when Custer's cavalrymen attacked. Black Kettle and his wife were both killed. Other Indian women also died. One was deliberately shot by a trooper when he saw her drag a little white boy out of one of the lodges and stab him. A white woman captive was killed by a stray bullet as she lay hidden in a tepee. Black Kettle's 14-year-old son refused to surrender and fired at Captain Fred Benteen. When the fourth bullet hit him, the captain shot the boy to death. Fourteen of Custer's men were killed, mostly because of his usual lack of strategic sense and poor scouting which was to lead to the bloody massacre at the Little Big Horn on June 26, 1876, during which Custer and the Seventh Cavalry were decimated by an overwhelming coalition of Sioux and Cheyenne warriors.

Whites also slaughtered each other. One of the most famous incidents happened in Utah territory. In September, 1857, one hundred and forty immigrants were passing through Mormon areas on their way to California. They were attacked at Mountain Meadows by the Mormons who promised to let them live if they surrendered, and then proceeded to shoot down the one hundred and twenty men and women, sparing only the seventeen children.

The brutal activities of the many desperados that roamed the frontier brought its own retaliatory viciousness on the part of official and unofficial bodies of individuals in all the western territories. Lynch law and vigilantism—frequently manifested in mining camps—became a way of life and in many towns and cities they became the only effective method of coping with law-breaking.

"Beginning with the first significant outbreak in the gold-rush metropolis of San Francisco in 1849 and continuing for 53 years down to 1902 there were at least 210 vigilante movements in the West," says Richard Maxwell Brown in *Violence in America*. He records 729 "known" victims. It would be hard for anyone to estimate how many unknown victims there were but it must have run well into the thousands.

Law in the West took another turn in its "hanging" judges such as Parker and Bean. Judge Isaac C. Parker operated his notorious Federal court at Fort Smith, Arkansas, and piled up a record second to none. In the 25-year period that he sat on the bench, 344 persons were tried for offenses punishable by death. Of these, 174 were convicted and 168 sentenced to hang. Eighty-eight were hanged and 6 others died either in prison or while attempting to escape.

That this tradition of violence on the Western frontier has come down to us in the twentieth century is amply proven by newspaper headlines of "shoot-outs" between police and outlaws, or between armed citizens who still behave in the tradition of Hickok or Billy the Kid.

5 | Klan and Lynch Mob, 1865-1934

The Ku Klux Klan started as a joke among a group of college students who had been officers in the Confederate Army and it has been a violent thread running through American history ever since. Organized in December, 1865, at Pulaski, Tennessee, it was at first more of a social group than a terrorist organization. Originally the members planned on naming themselves Knights of the Circle but were concerned that they might be confused with an older organization known as Knights of the Golden Circle. Someone then suggested Knights of the Kuklos since *kuklos* is the Greek word for "circle." This was agreed on and later was shortened to Kuklos Klan, which eventually became Ku Klux Klan.

The first Grand Wizard of the Klan was a Confederate cavalryman, General Nathan Bedford Forrest. He was a pre-war slave trader and the perpetrator of the massacre of Negro soldiers and their dependents at Fort Pillow. Pursuant to the orders of Jefferson Davis that all Negroes taken prisoner while fighting for the North should be killed, Forrest had murdered 229 of the 262 Negro defenders of the garrison, burning some of them at the stake. Burning was to become a favorite tactic of the KKK.

The Klan's greatest period of expansion was in 1867 when,

as a result of the Black Codes and several race riots, the Reconstruction Acts were passed and an attempt was made to implement the Thirteenth and Fourteenth amendments to the Constitution by allowing the Negro to take his proper place in society. To the Southern aristocrats who controlled the Klan and to the red-necked poor whites who made up its ranks, that was a threat to the Southern way of life, particularly to that flower of plantation culture—the white woman of Dixie. Such a threat could be answered in only one way—insensate, consistent violence.

By 1868, the Klan reportedly had more than 500,000 members and its terrorist acts numbered in the millions. Local law enforcement bodies simply ignored its activities, and if Federal authorities apprehended Klan members, the local courts refused to indict.

"Klansmen rode the highways and country lanes, burning houses and farms, whipping and flogging Federal sympathizers and massacring Negroes," say the authors of *Inside Ku Klux Klan*. "If a black man was believed to be guilty of having seduced a white woman, he was castrated, tarred and feathered, then lynched. Likewise, if a white woman was believed to have encouraged the sexual advances of a black man, she was murdered—usually only after she had been shaven bald and made to parade through the streets nude, the words 'nigger-lover' painted across (or carved by pen-knife into) her chest and back."

The Klan burned down schools as fast as the Government could build them. If a Negro had a prosperous farm, the farm was burned and he was lynched. The Klan broke into jails, dragged out Negro prisoners and "smashed their skulls, broke their necks and threw them into the river." Thirteen volumes of a Congressional Investigating Committee's report were printed documenting the atrocities of this group. The wave of terror became so sickening that even General Forrest couldn't stand it and he dissolved the Klan in 1869. The action was futile. The Klan went right on riding.

J. W. Schulte Nordholt details some of the atrocities committed by the Klan in his book, *The People That Walk in Darkness:*

> Thirty-five men were murdered in six months in South Carolina, while 262 people were flogged. In Texas there were 905 murders in two years. In Livingston, Alabama, a little girl of nine was whipped to such an extent that she died a week later. In South Carolina the crippled Baptist clergyman, Elias Hill, was assaulted by a group of masked men and left lying out in the cold night . . .
>
> Fortunately, the poor victims occasionally fought back. A Negro from Tuscaloosa, Alabama, who lived with a white woman, was visited by the Ku Klux Klan because of this insult to the white race. He shot at them when they arrived and killed one of them, but he himself was killed immediately afterward. The dead white man was a boy from a good family who (once more proving the two-sided morals of the South) was himself living with a Negro girl.

The governor of North Carolina, a former Unionist, antisecessionist Democrat who had come to power during Reconstruction, raised a militia of tough hill men to fight the Klan, but in most states the Klan rode roughshod over everyone as soon as the backs of the Federal troops were turned.

In Meridian, Mississippi, in 1871, the Klan led a riot. A group of Negro leaders had been jailed for political activities and other Negroes had gathered outside the jail in hopes of protecting them. Led by hooded Klansmen, armed whites set upon the unarmed Negroes, scattering them and killing several. Then the jailed leaders were taken out and hanged.

The atrocities were accomplishing the specific purposes of the Klan. Negroes were being kept away from the voting booth and denied an education and the means of earning a decent living. This forced them back into a peonage hardly superior, except in name, to the state of slavery from which they had so recently been freed.

114

In Louisiana, in the few weeks preceding the election of 1867, as many as two thousand persons were killed, wounded, or otherwise injured. Congress then moved to brand the Klan as "a fearful conspiracy against society . . . it has demoralized society, and held men silent by the terror of its acts and by its powers for evil." And in 1875 the Klan took the extreme step of murdering Negro Senator Charles Caldwell of Mississippi.

The original Klan disappeared after Rutherford B. Hayes became President. Actually Samuel J. Tilden was elected but the Hayes forces made a deal to withdraw Federal troops from the South if the votes of the disputed states were thrown to their candidate. The bargain was struck, with Southern radicals estimating that the Klan was no longer needed to "defend the honor of the South."

Approximately five thousand Negroes were lynched by white mobs between 1865 and 1955. This does not include unreported murders, legal lynchings, or actions taken by "kangaroo courts." It was a common occurrence in early post-slavery days for the homes and schools of black people to be burned. In race riots alone over five hundred blacks were killed between 1865 and 1940, and many others were abused and injured. Comparatively few whites were killed in the same disturbances. Eventually all of this persecution, pillage, and intimidation led to the civil-rights movement of the 1950s and the vicious retaliation against all people—white or black—who took part in or supported that movement.

Lynching, however, goes back much further than 1865, and there has always been much speculation as to how the term originated. Some sources say lynch law was first put into operation in America in South Carolina during the years 1767 to 1769. Later during the Revolutionary War it was used against Tories near what is now the city of Lynchburg, Virginia. Here it was supposedly started by Colonel Charles Lynch and took its name from him. Other authorities credit it to a James Lynch of Piedmont, Virginia, whose neighbors chose him to pass sentence on law breakers because they were so far away from town and a court of law. There is even one theory that it goes back to a James Lynch Fitz-Stephen, who was warden of Galway in 1526, and is said to have sentenced his own son to death for murder.

However it got its name, the practice of lynching in America goes back at least to 1711 when rumors spread through the city of New York, alleging that Negroes were making sexual assaults on white women. White mobs were soon raging through the streets, beating and murdering Negroes. Before it was over, fourteen black men had been burned at the stake and eighteen hanged. A year later there was another series of lynchings in the same city based on the same type of rumor.

The charge of sexual interest in white women was long to remain the most deadly that could be made against a Negro man. Time after time, on little or no evidence, Negroes were hanged or burned for this "crime." Some examples of this have been preserved in newspaper clippings and other sources.

Columbus, Georgia *Sentinel,* August 12, 1851

Our community has just been made to witness the most high-handed and humiliating act of violence that it has ever been our duty to chronicle . . . At the May term of the Superior Court a negro man was tried and condemned on the charge of having attempted to commit rape upon a little white girl in this county. His trial was a fair one, his counsel was the best our bar afforded, his jury was one of the most intelligent that sat upon the criminal side of our court, and on patient and honest hearing he was found guilty and sentenced to be hung on Tuesday, the 12th inst. This by the way, was the second conviction. The negro had been tried and convicted before, but his counsel had moved and obtained a new trial, which we have seen resulted like the first in a conviction.

Notwithstanding his conviction, it was believed by some

that the negro was innocent. Those who believed him innocent, in a spirit of mercy, undertook a short time since to procure his pardon; and a petition to that effect was circulated among our citizens and, we believe, very numerously signed. This we think was a great error . . . The petition was sent to Governor Towns, and on Monday evening last the messenger returned with a full and free pardon to the criminal.

In the meantime the people had begun to flock in from the country to witness the execution; and when it was announced that a pardon had been received, the excitement which immediately pervaded the streets was indescribable. Monday night passed without any important demonstration.

Tuesday morning the crowd in the streets increased, and the excitement with it. A large and excited multitude gathered early in the morning at the market house, and after numerous violent harangues a leader was chosen, and resolutions passed to the effect that the mob should demand the prisoner at four o'clock in the afternoon, and if he should not be given up he was to be taken by force and executed.

After this decision the mob dispersed, and early in the afternoon upon the ringing of the market bell, it reassembled and proceeded to the jail. The sheriff of the county of course refused to surrender the negro, when he was overpowered, the prison doors broken open, and the unfortunate culprit dragged forth and hung.

Of course, there was never any question of punishment for lynch mobs or their leaders, but since slaves were valuable property there is one case on record in White County, Tennessee, in 1858, where an owner brought suit against the members of a mob who had lynched his slave. The fact that an owner could sue for damage to his property when a slave was killed may have accounted for lynching not being as popular before the Civil War as it was afterward. The record is more complete after the turn of the century.

The casual brutality of many of the early twentieth century lynchings and killings of Negroes is excmplified by the following newspaper accounts:

New York *Tribune*, March 17, 1901

Nashville, Tenn., March 16—Miss Ballie Crutchfield, a colored woman, met death at the hands of a mob of several hundred about midnight last night. They stormed the home, hauled her out of bed and dragged her through the dirt-and-gravel streets leading to Round Lick Creek, on the outskirts of town. There they tied her hands with hemp behind her bloodied, gravel-pitted back; knotted a burlap sack over her head and took turns raping her; then shot her through the head and dumped her lifeless body into the creek. The mob was looking for William Crutchfield, brother of the victim, in connection with the theft of a purse. Unable to find him, they lynched Ballie Crutchfield instead.

Vicksburg *Evening Post*, February 8, 1904

An eye-witness to the lynching of Luther Holbert and his wife, negroes, which took place in Doddsville yesterday, today gave the *Evening Post* the following details concerning retribution exacted from the couple before they were burned at the stake:

When the two negroes were captured, they were tied to trees and, while the funeral pyres were being prepared, they were forced to hold out their hands while one finger at a time was chopped off. The fingers were distributed as souvenirs. The ears of the murderers were cut off. Holbert was beaten severely, his skull fractured and one of his eyes, knocked out with a stick, hung by a shred from the socket.

Some of the mob used a large corkscrew to bore into the flesh of the man and the woman. It was applied to their arms, legs and body, then pulled out. . . .

New York *Tribune,* March 20, 1906

Knoxville, Mar. 19—Ed Johnson, the negro convicted of rape, was lynched tonight after word was received that the United States Supreme Court had granted him an appeal.

Most victims of the mobs were Negroes but sometimes they were whites who opposed the activities of the Klan and other racist groups. In August, 1922, Watt Daniels and Thomas F. Richards of Mer Rouge, Louisiana, died because of their opposition to the Klan. Together with three other men, they were kidnapped, but unlike the other three they were not released after being beaten. It wasn't until December that their bodies were found, wired and weighted and sunk in the sixty-foot depths of Lake LaFourche. Part of the testimony given at an investigation was printed in the New Orleans *Times-Picayune:*

Charles W. Duval, professor of pathology at Tulane University:

"I would say that the hands and feet had been chopped or mashed off. The bones at these extremities were jagged and protruding. In the bodies we found striking injuries, especially in the long bones in the arms and legs. Each of the twelve bones of the arms and legs were broken in three places, at the lower, middle and upper. The same was found on the opposite side.

"In the legs we found that the thighs had the same sort of injury fracture at the upper, middle and lower parts. These breaks were always three in number and were equally distant from one another. The breaks were very striking because of the marked similarity. There is very good evidence that these bones were fractured before death. . . .

"On removing the clothes there was noted an entire absence of all the external genitalia. Close inspection shows these organs were removed with some sharp cutting instrument, as evidenced by the relatively smooth remaining skin edges in the area and the inner sides of the thighs and perineum."

"Was the cutting done before or after death?" Judge Coco asked.

"It was our opinion that the organs were removed before death. The alterations we found could not have been done after death. There was evidence that much blood had flowed."

The head, Dr. Duval said, was nothing but "loose skin and a few bones. . . ." Dr. Duval said that the nature of the head wounds suggested crushing rather than blows and suggested some special device had been used. Any one of the injuries the two young men had suffered would have resulted in death.

"Were these injuries inflicted simultaneously or at different times?" Judge Coco asked.

"That would depend on whether the men were tortured."

"Tortured? What is your opinion on that?"

"I believe the bodies were most inhumanely tortured."

One would expect that an outraged community would have insisted that the torturer-killers be found and brought to justice. No such thing happened. In a courtroom guarded by National Guard machine guns and rifles, two grand juries listened to witness after witness identify the Klansmen who had kidnapped the men and point to their leaders, Captain J. K. Skipworth, the Exalted Cyclops, and Dr. B. M. McKoin. Neither grand jury could bring itself to produce indictments and the Klansmen were acquitted.

That there is a psycho-sexual element in many lynchings is a matter of record. Believing their own myths of the superior sexual power of the Negro, lynch mobs took particular pleasure in mutilating blacks. This is borne out by hundreds of newspaper accounts of the first three decades of our present century. The cases listed in this chapter are little more than a random sampling of the atrocities committed against the members of an ethnic minority in a land dedicated to the principles of freedom and equality for all men. One can't help thinking that there is a curse on the land. A curse of violence and death that came with that first shipload of slaves. Violence caused by the pathological hatred of the white man for the blacks he has wronged.

6 | The Red Summers, 1900-1919

In his study of racial tensions, Professor Allen Grimshaw of Indiana University identified thirty-three major interracial disturbances in the United States between 1900 and 1949. Eighteen of these occurred between 1915 and the so-called "Red Summer" of 1919. Five major riots took place between 1940 and 1944 but only that in Detroit in 1943 was on a scale comparable to those of earlier periods.

The lynch mob was the weapon of white rural America against the Negro, and race riot was the weapon of white urban America during the period from 1900 to 1943.

Not that lynching had died out. With the revival of the Klan in 1915, it came back into its own, and while city streets were filled with rioting mobs, night riders roamed the countryside.

The NAACP made a study of lynching which it issued in 1919. It was entitled *Thirty Years of Lynching in the United States, 1889–1918* and listed 3,324 lynchings. Sixty-one of those victims were women.

J. W. Schulte Nordholt in *The People That Walk In Darkness* gives numbers for the period between 1918 and 1930:

> The high figures of the nineties were fortunately not reached again, although the years immediately following

the war showed a large increase. In 1918 there were 64 cases, 4 of which were white people; in 1919, 83, including 7 whites; in 1920, 61 and 8 whites; in 1921, 64 and 5 whites; in 1922, 57 and 6 whites. After that, there was a decline to 16 cases in 1924 and 10 in 1929, but in 1930 there were again 21 cases.

Many of the lynch mobs assumed a size equal to or larger than those engaged in rioting in the cities as can be seen from the following incidents mentioned by Nordholt:

> At least 75,000 people were present at the twenty-one lynchings which took place in 1930. A classic example of such atrocities was a lynching in Ocilla, Georgia, in January, 1930. A Negro, James Irwin, was accused (probably justly so) of assaulting and murdering a white girl. Despite anything the sheriff could do, a crowd took him to the place of the crime and killed him. For more than an hour Irwin was tortured, his fingers and toes being cut off one by one. The rest of the gruesome treatment to which he was subjected was of a nature better left undescribed. (A doctor who was a member of the investigation committee said that even de Sade would never have been able to invent anything so terrible.) Finally, he was strung up to a tree by his hands and slowly burnt.

Lynched in the back country, Negroes fled to the cities to escape the bestiality of their fellowmen and were met with the horror of the race riot.

On August 15, 1900, mobs in New York set out to get the most famous Negro entertainers in the city. They swept through the streets from one theater to another searching for Ernest Hogan, Williams and Walker, and Coke and Johnson. Fortunately they didn't find them, but Walker just barely escaped and Hogan had to barricade himself in his dressing room at the Winter Garden Theater in Times Square and spend the night in the locked building.

Robbed of their prey, the rioters went wild. Several thousand strong, the mob stormed through the streets, pulling Negro men and women out of hacks and off streetcars and beating them brutally. And there was no help for the blacks from policemen. They were out for revenge themselves since one of their number had been knifed by a Negro and died from the wound. The beatings they administered were every bit as vicious as the ones the mob was carrying out.

Negroes who complained to the authorities that they had been beaten by the police were treated like criminals.

In Georgia things were even worse. In a hotly contested campaign for governor in 1906, the Populist leaders Hoke Smith and Tom Watson accused Clark Howell and the Democrats of wanting political equality for the Negro. This was duly reported in the newspapers of Atlanta.

All through the summer the papers carried stories of Negro assaults on white women. Every one of them was later proved to be without foundation, but that didn't seem to matter. Nor did it alter the effect they had on whites who read them. Three alleged rape stories were published in May, another in July and two in August.

Then on September 22, extras flooded the streets of Atlanta. The *Evening News,* a new paper in town, brought out four extras in six hours. TWO ASSAULTS! screamed eight-inch high headlines, and the next extra, THIRD ASSAULT! Then the Atlanta *Journal* in its second extra of that Saturday afternoon declared: ANGRY CITIZENS IN PURSUIT OF BLACK BRUTE WHO ATTEMPTED ASSAULT ON MRS. CHAPIN RESCUED FROM FIEND BY PASSING NEIGHBOR.

There may have been a real Mrs. Chapin but there was not a real attacker.

By evening the overstoked furnace of fear and hate exploded. Mobs formed and raged through the streets, hunting down and attacking anyone with a black skin, regardless of sex or age. In Peachtree Street there was a barbershop owned by a Negro that catered to whites only. The mob beat the

125

barbers, wrecked the shop and stomped the lame Negro bootblack to death.

As the rioters progressed, they broke into hardware stores and pawnshops and armed themselves. Negroes were taken from cars and streetcars, and the maddened whites murdered them with their bare hands in some instances, tearing them limb from limb. Other blacks were forced to jump from viaducts to the railroad tracks some forty feet below. One Negro man was castrated and another disemboweled. Before the night was over, thousands of blacks had fled for protection to the white people who employed them. And most of them received it, for not every white in town had gone mad.

The rioting died down on Sunday but broke out anew on Monday with city police and sheriff's deputies as part of the mob. They invaded the Brownsville section and the area around the Negro Clark College and the Gammon Theological Seminary. This was a decent neighborhood where people lived in neat houses and had built with their own money the only public school.

There is disagreement among the accounts of the Atlanta rioting as to just how many Negroes died. Saunders Redding says, "No one knows the total number of injuries, permanent cripplings and deaths . . ." Jacobson states there were ten Negroes murdered, among whom were two women, and "the count of wounded, some permanently disabled and others disfigured, was sixty Negroes."

There is general agreement, however, that the repeated rumors of attacks on white women by Negroes set off the rioting and that the Negroes killed were innocent of any wrong doing.

The all-white investigating committee made that clear in its report:

> Among the victims of the mob there was not a single vagrant. They were earning wages in useful work up to the

time of the riot. They were supporting themselves and their families or dependent relatives . . . About seventy persons were wounded, and among these there was an immense amount of suffering . . . Many . . . are disfigured, and several are permanently disabled . . .

It is clear that several hundred murderers and would be murderers are at large in this community. Events have demonstrated that the slaughter of innocents does not deter the criminal classes from committing more crimes . . . The crimes of the mob included robbery as well as murder . . . the property of innocent and unoffending people was taken . . . victims, both men and women, were treated with unspeakable brutality . . . All this sorrow has come to people who are absolutely innocent of wrongdoing.

There is little wonder that the Negroes of America were horrified and angered by the ease with which they could be murdered in the street. William E. B. DuBois, then a professor at the Negro University of Atlanta, expressed the shock and anger in his Litany of Atlanta:

Bewildered we are, and, passion-tossed, mad with the madness of a mobbed and mocked and murdered people . . . We bow our heads and harken soft to the sobbing of women and little children. We beseech Thee to hear us, good Lord! Our voices sink in silence and night. Hear us, good Lord! In night, O God of a godless land! Amen.

God may have been listening to Professor DuBois but his fellow Americans were not, for two years later in Springfield, Illinois, rioting flared again.

A white woman, Mrs. Mabel Hallam, had been having an illicit love affair and one night her lover beat her, leaving visible bruises. Terrified when questioned by her husband as to the origin of the marks, she claimed to have been set upon and raped by a Negro—a George Richardson who was a native of the town. Luckily for Richardson, he was spirited out of town before the lynch mob came looking for him.

Unable to vent their rage on the man accused, the mob turned on other Negroes. A barber named Burton was mutilated and burned and his shop was completely demolished. Then the mob, led by a white woman who was an indicted criminal and out on bond, raged through the city attacking and beating every Negro they could find and plundering their homes.

With the police either unable or unwilling to protect them, the Negroes were forced to protect themselves. This they did with guns and whatever other weapons they could find. For the first time in history, a race riot resulted in more whites than blacks being killed as four of the howling, looting mob were shot down.

After twenty-four hours of unchecked rioting, the state militia arrived and quelled the disturbance—but not before the mob had lynched another Negro. This time it was eighty-four-year-old William Donegan. His crime? Thirty years earlier he had married a white woman.

As a result of having defended themselves from the white mob, more than fifty employees of the city were fired, although "it was acknowledged that their efficiency and fidelity were not questioned." The state discharged others who worked for it in Springfield, and the Illinois *State Journal* editorialized that "it was not the fact of the whites' hatred toward the Negroes but of the Negroes' own misconduct, general inferiority, or unfitness for free institutions that were at fault."

More than a thousand Negroes, many respected and substantial citizens among them, left the city to settle elsewhere.

There was one beneficial result of the Springfield rioting —the eventual founding of the NAACP. The journalist William English Walling was in Chicago when the rioting started in Springfield and he hurried there and was an eye-witness to many actions of the mob. Having recently returned from

Czarist Russia where the citizens were engaged in one of their periodic pogroms against the Jews, Walling was no stranger to violence.

He wrote that he had seen nothing in that benighted land that was any worse than what occurred in Springfield and called for a "large and powerful body of citizens" to organize and help the Negroes. He said he was afraid that if something of the sort was not done, every hope of political democracy would be destroyed "in the North as in the South," and that "American civilization would have either a rapid degeneration or another profounder and more revolutionary civil war. . . ."

The call for help was answered by Mary White Ovington, a wealthy white social worker of New York, and Dr. Henry Moskowitz, a well-to-do member of the New York Jewish community. They were joined by W. E. B. DuBois, John Dewey, Jane Addams, and others, and formed the National Negro Committee in May, 1909. This was incorporated in 1910 as the National Association for the Advancement of Colored People.

During the next few years there was a marked increase in the number of Negroes leaving the South, and that section that had previously welcomed their departure now began to worry about a labor shortage, some people going so far as to urge better treatment for the blacks.

A half-hearted attempt to bring justice to the Negro was made in the South but before long a return was made to more violent methods in an effort to stop emigration. Labor agents who were hiring Negroes for work in the North were hounded and often arrested. In one case, the agent was jailed and the two hundred Negroes he had recruited were dragged from the northbound train and beaten. After awhile it became difficult for Negroes to buy train tickets to Northern cities. White plantation owners came to rely more and more on the whip to keep their Negroes in line. There was an increase in lynching and general terrorism as Negroes redoubled their frantic attempts to escape their bondage by fleeing northward.

And Nordholt says:

> The curious phenomenon of a mass exodus of Southern Negroes to the North began in approximately 1915; away from the exhausted earth, the dilapidated cabins and the lynching whites, to the land of freedom and equality. Two large waves can be distinguished, the first from 1916 to 1918 and the second in 1922 and 1923. The extent of this movement becomes clear from the following figures: in 1910 the population of the South was 29.8 per cent Negro; in 1920, 26.9 per cent; in 1930, 24.7 per cent. In 1910, 1,027,674 Negroes lived in the North; in 1920, 1,472,309; in 1930, 2,402,219. Between 1920 and 1930, the Negro population in the South increased by 5 per cent, in the West by 51 per cent and in the North by 63.6 per cent. Thus the Negro became a town-dweller. In 1900, only 22.7 per cent of the Negroes lived in towns; in 1910, 27.4 per cent; in 1920, 34 per cent; in 1940, 52 per cent. This brought terrific problems, for the Negro was not as welcome as he had imagined.

The rate of growth has accelerated in more recent times. Over the past 16 years, about 98 percent of the rise in Negro population has been in the central city, and the projection is that it will grow at an average of 484,000 a year and reach a total of 30.7 million by 1985.

And having moved to the cities, what kind of welcome did the Negro actually receive? Not a very cordial one. The war years of 1917 to 1919 were known as the period of the "Red Summers." While Negro soldiers were fighting for democracy in France, their fellows were being lynched and killed in race riots at home.

East St. Louis, Illinois, on July 2, 1917 saw the beginning of the worst race riot of the twentieth century. This city which lies across the Mississippi River from St. Louis, Missouri, was then a railroad and industrial center. In addition to twenty-seven rail lines crossing through or terminating in the city, there were stockyards, meat packing plants and the works of the Aluminum Ore Company and the American Steel Company.

More than six thousand Negroes had been lured there in the three years before the riot by the need for workers. When a strike broke out in the packing plants in 1916 and in the aluminum plant in 1917, many Negroes were employed as strike breakers, causing intense resentment among white workers.

On May 28, 1917, during a meeting of workers with the City Council, a rumor was circulated that a Negro had shot a white man in a holdup. Then more stories spread about white girls having been attacked by blacks, and it wasn't long before a mob of three thousand surged into the downtown area and began to attack any Negro unfortunate enough to be on the streets. Saloons and businesses patronized by Negroes were wrecked, scores of Negroes were beaten and several shot but none were killed that first day.

Several companies of the Illinois National Guard arrived the next day at the request of the mayor and an uneasy peace was restored. But the police force proved to be anti-Negro and the beating of blacks continued all through June. The thing that touched off the rioting again was another rumor. Among the whites it was said that the Negroes were just waiting until July 4 to strike back at their tormenters, and in the Negro community, the rumor was reversed to say the whites were planning an attack.

Such an atmosphere of distrust and suspicion was bound to lead to trouble. On the night of July 1 a Negro shot a white man who attacked him. In retaliation a number of whites in a Ford sped through the Negro section, firing into homes. On their second trip, the fire was returned. A police car, also a Ford, was sent to investigate, and the Negroes fired at it thinking it was the raider car again. One detec-

131

tive was killed instantly and the other wounded so badly that he died the next day.

On July 2, the bullet-riddled, blood-stained car was placed on display outside the main police station. A crowd gathered and was harangued by speakers who called for "all worthy citizens" to arm themselves for action. That afternoon the mob entered the downtown area and shot the first Negro they came across.

Watched by hundreds of white shoppers, the rioters began to assault every Negro they could find. Breaking up into small bands, they spread a path of terror as they advanced on the Negro district. Stoning and clubbing any dark-skinned person, regardless of age or sex, they left the unconscious victims strewn along the sidewalks. Groups of white women set upon Negro women and beat them with fists, feet, stones, and sticks. Someone even went along behind the rioters and shot the wounded still lying dazed in the street.

When the mob got to the shacks of the poorer Negro district, they set the houses on fire and then began the diabolical game of shooting the residents as they tried to escape from the smoke and flame.

While this was going on, police and guardsmen made no move to interfere. The mob took full advantage of this license to kill. The hoses of fire engines were cut by axes and more fires set. Seriously wounded Negro men and children were picked up bodily and hurled into the flames.

A young Russian Jew who was visiting in the city compared the terror with that of the pogroms in his native land and came to the conclusion that the Russian bigots could have taken some lessons from those of East St. Louis.

A sixteen-block area was completely burned out, and the official figure for buildings totally destroyed was set at 312. The arrival of more troops finally brought the violence under control, but not before the mob's bloody work was done.

100 NEGROES SHOT, BURNED, CLUBBED TO DEATH IN E. ST. LOUIS RACE WAR, read the head-

lines of the St. Louis *Globe-Democrat* on July 3. But the state's attorney blandly stated that he could prosecute no one because he was unable to find a single person who had witnessed anyone committing violence on July 2.

Perhaps the uproar that swept the country over the riot changed the minds of the authorities because eighty-two whites and twenty-three Negroes were ultimately indicted by a grand jury. However, even here the Negro was discriminated against since only four whites were tried for murder, while eleven Negroes were sentenced for the killing of the two detectives.

There was no exact count of how many died in that East St. Louis blood bath. The police estimated that eight whites and thirty-nine Negroes had been killed but a Congressional investigating committee reported that the mob had "deliberately murdered by shooting, burning and hanging between one hundred and two hundred beings who were black." In addition, hundreds of Negroes were injured and hundreds more driven from the city.

The year 1917 also saw riots in Chester, Pennsylvania, and Philadelphia and a soldiers' riot in Houston, Texas. In a typical piece of bureaucratic blundering, thousands of Negroes who flocked to the colors to fight the Kaiser were stationed in the South where they were not wanted and were sure to be ill treated. The bigoted police were overly enthusiastic in enforcing the segregation laws on streetcars and too free with the term "nigger" around Northern Negroes who resented it.

The situation came to a head in September near Houston where the Twenty-fourth Infantry was stationed when a white policeman roughed up a Negro woman in front of a Negro soldier. The soldier went to her aid and was beaten insensible. An unarmed Negro M.P. was shot at and pistol-whipped when he inquired why the soldier had been attacked.

Previously the weapons of the Twenty-fourth had been taken away "to avoid trouble," the official record said. Now, about a hundred soldiers overrode that decision and broke into the armory and got their rifles. Then they marched on the police station, shooting as they went. Before the affair was over, seventeen persons lay dead.

In marked contrast to the mild punishment meted out to white rioters, the Negro soldiers were speedily tried, thirteen sentenced to death and hanged and forty sentenced to life imprisonment.

The year 1919 produced the prototype of what we have come to know as a "long hot summer." There were riots in Longview, Texas; Knoxville, Tennessee; Omaha, Nebraska; Elaine, Arkansas; Chicago, Illinois, and Washington, D.C.

During the summer of 1919 there were eight major clashes between the races. Chester, Pennsylvania, was lucky. If the mob of whites swarming into a Negro section of town had been met by an equal number of blacks, the number of lives lost could have soared into the hundreds. As it was, seven Negroes and five whites were killed.

A riot started in Longview, Texas, and lasted for several days after a black man was punished for reporting a lynching. One white and two Negroes were dead when the riot was over and damage to property ran to sixty thousand dollars. Elaine, Arkansas, and Knoxville, Tennessee, also had riots. And in Washington, D.C., a series of beatings of Negroes resulted in four white men being shot and killed.

Arthur I. Waskow in *From Race Riot to Sit-In* also speaks of it:

> What an official of the National Association for the Advancement of Colored People called the "Red Summer" of 1919 began early and ended late. Estimates of the number of "race riots" have run as high as twenty-five, and any such count would have to include an affray in Berkeley, Georgia, on February 28 and another in Bogalusa, Louisiana, on November 23.
>
> But not all of these twenty-five can qualify as riots— some were expanding lynchings, others brief clashes of sullen crowds which quickly dispersed—and many made

little impact . . . But even by reducing the number of "riots" to the seven that seem most important because they evoked a national response, the "Red Summer" must be reckoned to have lasted from May 10, when Charleston, South Carolina, had its riot, to September 30, when Phillips County, Arkansas, had its. Between these dates came major explosions in Longview, Texas; Washington, D.C.; Chicago; Knoxville; and Omaha.

Charleston's riot was between local Negroes and white sailors from a nearby naval training base. The trouble started with a fight between a Negro and two sailors on Saturday night liberty. When the Negro was shot and killed, other Negroes attacked the sailors who, in turn, were joined by other sailors. Both sides were battling with clubs and guns, and although the original two sailors were arrested, the fighting spread until hundreds of sailors were marching toward the Negro district. As they went, they invaded shooting galleries and stole rifles and ammunition, beat up and shot any Negroes they came across and broke into Negro-owned shops and stores.

Marines were called in to help control the sailors, and the streets were cleared. Two Negroes had been killed and seventeen wounded. Seven sailors and one white policeman had also been wounded. The quick work of the Charleston police and the military authorities had avoided a much worse outbreak. Six sailors were ordered held for general court-martial on charges of "conduct to the prejudice of good order and discipline" and "manslaughter" and were convicted.

Trouble came in Longview, Texas, over a story carried in the Chicago Negro magazine the *Defender*. The story concerned a lynching near Longview several months earlier. The Negro had been lynched after being accused of raping a white woman. The *Defender* said it had learned from the young woman herself that she had not been raped, had in fact been in love with the Negro and was "prostrated" by his death.

Infuriated by the story, a group of whites went to the Negro section to find the man they believed to have written the piece, a Negro schoolteacher named Samuel L. Jones. When they found him, Waskow says, they "beat him with iron rods and gun butts, and ordered him to leave Longview. The police did not interfere."

Not content with that, a larger group of whites invaded the Negro section "to look up the professor and see what condition he was in." The Negroes fired on them and four were wounded. The whites retreated, gathered recruits and returned. On finding the Negro area deserted, they set fire to Jones' house, several other homes and Negro shops as well as an office used as a lodge hall by the Negro Business Men's League.

The police arrested half-a-dozen Negroes, charged them with rioting and began a search of the countryside for the missing Jones and another Negro leader. They ordered all undisturbed copies of the *Defender* burned and banned its future circulation in the town.

National Guardsmen and Texas Rangers arrived and restored order by disarming both sides and imposing a curfew on all townspeople. The Rangers arrested twenty-three whites and charged them with arson and assault with intent to commit murder. Twenty Negroes were also arrested but they were removed to a jail in Austin to avoid mob violence. All the whites were released on bail, and a short time later the Negroes were also released although some were forbidden to return to Longview.

Increasing segregation of Negro workers in Washington, D.C., was one of the root causes of the riot that shook the nation's capital. Racial tension had also been stirred up by the Washington *Post,* then published by Ned McLean who was bitterly opposed to the way the police force operated. His paper began the creation of an artificial "crime wave" by playing up every minor infraction of the law and sensationalizing the ordinary assault and robbery cases. The Negroes were assigned most of the blame for the "crime wave."

NEGROES ATTACK GIRL . . . WHITE MEN VAINLY PURSUE, the *Post* headlined on Saturday, July 19. The story itself described the "attack" as two Negroes jostling a secretary on her way home and trying to seize her umbrella. When she resisted, they fled. The girl's name was given and it was stated that she was the wife of a man in the naval aviation department.

Washington, of course, was full of marines and sailors, and the evening of the day the story appeared, several hundred of them set out to avenge the "attack." Marching into southwest Washington, they stopped any Negroes they met and beat them, making no distinction between men or women. White civilians joined the servicemen and the resulting mob chased one Negro couple to their home and tried to break in.

District and military police dispersed the mob. Eight Negroes were arrested and "held for investigation." Two whites were also taken into custody. Shortly afterwards three more Negroes were stopped by the police and one of them opened fire and wounded an officer. The next morning, the NAACP asked the Secretary of the Navy to cancel the leaves of all marines and sailors who were leading the rioting. Nothing was done, however, because the Secretary of the Navy thought the Negroes were largely to blame.

That Sunday night at about 10:00 P.M., the situation got completely out of hand when the police arrested a Negro on a minor charge and a milling crowd of whites snatched him away and beat him over the head before the police could recover him. A few minutes later fighting broke out between Negro civilians and white servicemen. Three Negroes were badly injured.

A mob of sailors and soldiers surged up Pennsylvania Avenue, shouting and waving heavy belts and weighted neckerchiefs. They chased and beat Negroes, even pulling some of them off streetcars to do so. Outnumbered, most Negroes fled but some fought back, and fifteen men of both races were arrested during this part of the rioting. The leaves of the servicemen were up at midnight and they had to return to their bases, but a civilian mob took over and there were more clashes with Negroes at several points in the city. The few police were aided by patrols from the provost marshal's office and made some headway as the night progressed, and there was hope the next morning that the worst might be over.

The Washington *Post* made sure it wasn't by printing the following paragraph at the end of its coverage of the rioting:

> It was learned that a mobilization of every available serviceman stationed in or near Washington or on leave here has been ordered for tomorrow evening near the Knights of Columbus hut on Pennsylvania Avenue between Seventh and Eighth Streets. The hour of assembly is 9 o'clock and the purpose is a "clean up" that will cause the events of the last two evenings to pale into insignificance.

Exactly who had given the "orders" was not clear. A strong condemnation of the notice was issued by Negro community leaders and by District officials. But this didn't stop alarmed Negroes from arming themselves. Guns were bought, and Negro veterans took out their rifles and prepared to defend themselves.

The rioting now reached its most dangerous level with the provoked blacks striking back. A group of twenty or thirty boarded a streetcar and beat up the motorman and conductors. Speeding automobiles filled with armed Negroes fanned out through the city to fire on sailors and soldiers.

Monday night blood ran in the streets of the capital. Four men were killed, eleven others mortally or seriously wounded. Six white policemen, one white marine, three white civilians, and five Negro civilians were among the casualties. More than three hundred persons were arrested.

The rioting got out of hand because of newspaper provocation and also because of the lack of enthusiasm on the part of the District police in protecting Negroes. In addition, the forces available were too small to deal with the problem. As late as Tuesday morning, there were only seven hundred Washington police and a provost guard of four hundred soldiers, sailors and marines to control fighting that had spread over most of the city. Now, however, most of the servicemen who had engaged in the early phases were confined to their bases and it was mainly civilians who were involved.

A mob of more than a thousand whites made repeated attempts to fight their way into the Negro area and were turned back only by the timely arrival of cavalry which had to charge several times to break up the attacking crowd.

Negroes all over town were fighting back. Some opened fire with pistols when attacked. In Negro districts, they beat stray whites who wandered in and fired at passing streetcars and automobiles. At least eight carloads of armed Negroes raced through white residential districts, their occupants firing at random into houses or at passersby. White gunmen used the same tactic, and there was at least one reported running battle between such carloads of whites and blacks.

It was finally decided to bring large numbers of troops into the city to restore order. Major General William G. Haan was placed in command, and he moved troops in from Camp Meade, marines from Quantico and sailors from two ships lying in the Potomac. He also took a much more important step. He silenced the newspapers on the theory that much of the riot was "merely a newspaper war." Later he wrote a brother officer, "When I got them [the newspapers] to agree to say approximately what I wanted them to say, which was the truth, then soon everything was over."

The combination of silenced newspapers and heavy concentration of troops brought peace to the capital but there were still repercussions. The NAACP pleaded with Attorney General A. Mitchell Palmer to proceed against the Washington *Post* for inciting the riot by its "mobilization notice" but the action was refused. Several newspapers called for laws on the sale of firearms and others demanded increased police powers. W. E. B. DuBois pointed out that the bias of the Washington police in dealing with Negroes had much to do with making the riot worse.

An even worse riot erupted in Chicago on Sunday, July 27, when a Negro boy swimming in Lake Michigan was carried by the tide past an imaginary line that separated white from black areas. Whites began stoning the boy and he was carried farther and farther out into the lake until he drowned. A white policeman refused to arrest those responsible for the stoning. However, he arrested a Negro for a minor infraction and Negroes standing nearby attacked him. General fighting broke out between whites and blacks and soon spread to other areas of the city.

While the stoning was the specific incident that set off the fighting, the racial situation in the city had been tense for many months. The Negro population of Chicago had more than doubled in two years, causing an overcrowded condition in the established Negro residence area. When Negroes who had lived in the city for a long time tried to move into traditionally white sections, the whites showed their resentment and fear by a series of bombings on those who had dared leave the "Black Belt."

There had been many warnings of impending trouble but these had been ignored by Mayor William H. (Big Bill) Thompson. He was known as a "spoils politician" and had little to do with the "socially conscious" men who were worried about race relations, and the Negroes he appointed to office somehow failed to warn him that racial tension was near the breaking point.

As news of the fighting along the lake shore spread, both whites and Negroes began gathering into gangs. The whites were organized around so-called athletic clubs composed of teen-agers and youths connected with neighborhood politicians. The Negro gangs were spur-of-the-moment groups, less well organized and far less numerous. That Sunday night the whites attacked first and beat twenty-seven Negroes, stabbed seven and shot four. The Negroes retaliated by beating four whites, stabbing five and shooting one. Monday morning things quieted as both races reported for work, but as workers began to return home in the afternoon, gangs of youthful whites set upon the Negroes. They dragged them off streetcars and beat and gagged them. Four blacks were beaten to death and one white was stabbed by a Negro he was trying to murder.

The governor of Illinois ordered the National Guard to its armories but Mayor Thompson refused to ask that they intervene in the riot. He insisted the police could handle the situation.

On Tuesday a mob of white soldiers, sailors, and civilians flooded into the Loop area of downtown Chicago and hunted down and killed two Negroes while horrified shoppers and theater goers looked on. Another Negro was killed in the Italian district on the West side. Since most of the city's thirty-five hundred policemen had been stationed in the "Black Belt" to control Negro rioting, the whites downtown had a free hand.

Rumors on both sides inflamed the participants. "Negro women of the stockyard district had had their breasts hacked off after being subjected to sexual violence." "Negroes were being soaked in gasoline, set afire, and made to run like living torches until the flames overcame them." "Gangs of Negroes were raping white women." "Negroes were firing the houses of white people." These were only a few of the wild stories circulated.

Despite the fact that 229 citizens had been injured on Monday and 139 on Tuesday, "Big Bill" still refused to ask for the waiting National Guard to be sent into the streets.

Wednesday brought fresh clashes although a steady rain kept many people indoors. Two Negroes and two whites were killed and forty-two of both races injured. Political supporters of Mayor Thompson finally persuaded him that the police were failing to protect Negroes and that the Guard should be called in. At 10:00 P.M. Wednesday night he made his request and six thousand troops were deployed through the city before morning.

The aftermath of the rioting brought evidence of prejudice on the part of white officials. The state's attorney, Maclay Hoyne, brought in a list of indictments to the grand jury that was entirely Negro. One newspaper reported that those accused were "all the shades of black and chocolate and tan, but . . . no sign of white."

The grand jury threatened to resign in protest. Finally, seventeen whites and fifty Negroes were indicted, although the larger number of Negroes killed during the rioting would indicate that more whites had used violence.

The last important riot of 1919 was the only one that took place in a rural setting. In Phillips County, Arkansas, the Negro sharecroppers were being held in virtual peonage. After months of labor they would sell their crops and find that instead of having money coming, they were in debt to the white landlords who had sold them seed and rented them the land. In hope of getting justice, they formed an organization called the Progressive Farmers and Household Union of America. The whites charged that the group had been set up as part of a plot to massacre the white people in the nearby town of Elaine and reported that the town was "almost completely surrounded by blacks heavily armed."

The Negroes had been meeting at a church at Hoop Spur discussing the problems of hiring a lawyer when whites arrived and started firing into the church, killing a number of those inside. The few blacks who were armed returned the fire, and one deputy was killed and another wounded.

Then the whole district became the scene of an all-out hunt for Negroes. No one knows exactly how many victims there were, but it has been estimated the total exceeded two hundred.

Prisoners were gathered together by the hundreds and penned up in enclosures. Then the whites came and inspected them like cattle. They were sorted into two groups: the ones who had not belonged to the Union being considered "good niggers" and the others "bad niggers." The latter were forced to agree to work without pay until they had wiped out the terrible guilt of having belonged to a union. Seventy-nine refused to do so and were then charged with murder and rioting. When the legal proceedings were over, twelve were sentenced to death and sixty-seven given terms in jail ranging from twenty years to life.

Action by the NAACP and other agencies reinforced by public opinion brought about a change in the minds of the people of the county and most of the Negroes were freed after some years, while the twelve sentenced to death were saved by the Supreme Court.

The long hot summer of 1919 was drawing to a close but it left a mark on American life that remains today.

7 | Roaring Twenties, Striking Thirties, 1919-1939

In all the world, no nation has had a bloodier or more violent labor history than the United States. Practically no industry, no geographical location, has been exempt from labor violence. It is not confined to any particular labor groups, but it does seem to happen more frequently in some industries. No matter what their race, color, or national origin, workers have consistently tried to keep strikebreakers from taking their jobs. In other instances, they themselves have been attacked.

Labor violence in America usually erupted when a dispute was already in progress between labor and management. Sometimes it was sparked by pickets and their sympathizers trying to keep a struck plant from being run by strikebreakers; at other times trouble flared up as a result of the actions of company guards or police in trying to keep the plant open. The roles of aggressors and victims have shifted back and forth between employers and employees at different times in different places.

The goals of union violence were usually limited: Prevent strikebreakers or raw materials from entering a struck plant, and keep the finished product from leaving the premises. In some of the more serious clashes, casualties were high, but it wasn't often that labor violence spread to other parts of the community.

While most trade unions emphasized from their beginnings the desire for peaceful labor relations and saw violence as a self-defeating tactic, a few groups looked at it differently and saw violence as a creative force, advocating "propaganda by the deed."

There was some attempt in the eighteen-eighties to carry this attitude over into the formation of armed groups to be used in labor disputes. As early as 1875 an education and defense organization (*Lehr und Wehr Vereine*) was formed in Chicago and soon spread to other cities. Workers, mostly of foreign origin, met regularly and drilled with weapons.

A conference of social revolutionaries which met in Chicago in 1881 adopted a resolution recognizing "the armed organizations of workingmen who stand ready with gun to resist encroachment upon their rights, and recommend the formation of like organizations in all States."

Another convention held in Pittsburgh in 1883 came up with the pronouncement that since all institutions of the state are aligned against the working man, he had a right to arm himself for self-defense and offense. The convention members also felt that since no ruling class had ever surrendered its privileges, working men had to work for the overthrow of the system by force.

Anarchists played a considerable role in the early days of the union movement in America, and Albert Parsons, August Spies, and Samuel Fielden were all defendants in the notorious Haymarket trial. The German anarchist, Johann Most, published a treatise, *Revolutionary War Science,* on the use of arms and the making of what are known today as Molotov cocktails.

There is little evidence, however, that any of this early drilling or the various proclamations and publications ever led to any actual violence. The anarchists had little support even at the height of their influence. The belief was widely held that these armed groups were merely playing a game and represented no threat to anyone. Violence in labor disputes did not arise because the participants believed in "propaganda by the deed." Even many of the exponents of that doctrine came to see that it was self-defeating. Experience probably did much to convince them of this. Terrorist methods were met with savage repression on the part of governments. Consequently, examples of anarchist violence in the United States are very few.

One was the attack on Henry Frick during the Homestead steel strike, and that boomeranged, making him a folk hero when he fought off the attacker after being wounded. The assassination of President McKinley is another example since Czolgosz claimed to be an anarchist. But labor violence was another thing entirely and cannot be traced to the thinking of such people.

Violence usually came because of the refusal of factory owners to recognize unions and because of their attempts to replace striking workers with strikebreakers, or "scabs" as they came to be known. The attitude of most businessmen during the early days of the labor movement can best be summarized in the words of one mine operator, George F. Baer:

> The rights and interests of laboring men will be protected and cared for—not by labor agitators, but by the Christian men to whom God in His infinite wisdom has given the control of the property interests of the country, and upon successful management on which so much depends . . . Pray earnestly that right may triumph, always remembering that the Lord God Omnipotent still reigns, and that His reign is one of law and order, and not one of violence and crime.

The New York Times felt that Baer's words were inclined to "verge very close upon unconscious blasphemy," and the New York *American* remarked, "The pious pirate is a new thing. Baer and his relations between a just God and the thieving trusts must be left to the pulpit for adequate treatment."

Religious papers were equally vehement in their denunciation of Mr. Baer's attitudes toward God and the workingman. The *Churchman* called his statement a "ghastly blasphemy." The Baptist publication, the *Watchman,* said: "The divine rights of kings was bad enough, but not so intolerable as the doctrine of the divine rights of plutocrats to administer things in general with the presumption that what it pleases them to do is the will of God."

The workingmen of America can perhaps be forgiven if they were unwilling to accept the rule of George F. Baer and his peers.

There had been violence in American labor relations long before the days of Baer and before a labor movement as such existed. The Molly Maguires were more of an ethnic-based secret society than a labor union, but their activities in connection with the anthracite coal regions set standards for violence that have seldom if ever been equaled. Made up of Irish-Americans the Molly Maguires had numerous branches in the hard coal regions of Pennsylvania, dating from 1854 to 1877 and perhaps later.

In Ireland, the name had been used by one of the Ribbon societies that were known for their devotion to threatening and beating up process servers and the agents of landlords. In Pennsylvania, a lawless element took over control of the organization and created an inner order for the purpose, one gathers, of intimidating miners of other national origin, particularly the Welsh, English, and Germans. They also wanted to rid the area of mine superintendents, bosses, and police who offended any member of the order in any way.

All a member had to do was lodge a formal complaint against such a person with his "body master," and that individual would confer with his fellow officers in the neighboring districts and make arrangements to have the objectionable official removed. In this way the crime was always committed by a stranger to the area.

The society grew in strength during the Civil War and by 1875 it completely dominated coal miners by means of its reign of terror. The power of the Molly Maguires was finally broken through the efforts of James McParlan, an Irish-Catholic Pinkerton detective, who infiltrated one of their lodges and obtained evidence that led to the arrest and conviction of many members during the 1876-1877 period.

Violence directed against labor resulted in what has come to be called the Haymarket Riot of May 4, 1886. It began with a strike at the McCormick works in Chicago on May 3. Several strikers were killed by police, and a meeting was called for the next day at a square on Randolph Street called the Haymarket.

A large crowd gathered at the appointed time and was addressed by labor leaders and others, some of whom were anarchists. When police moved in to disperse the meeting, a bomb was thrown by an unknown hand. Seven policemen were killed and many more wounded.

In retaliation, seven anarchists were arrested and charged with the murders because they were "morally conspirators and accomplices in the killing, because they had repeatedly and publicly advocated such acts against the servants of government." They were convicted and sentenced to death. Four were hanged, one committed suicide and two had their death sentences commuted to life imprisonment.

The year 1877 was particularly violent. Strikes and riots swept unexpectedly across the United States, beginning in Martinsburg, West Virginia, after a wage cut was announced by the Baltimore and Ohio Railroad. This was the second cut in a short period of time, and the men walked off the trains and chased anyone who tried to take their places.

Federal troops were sent in almost at once and succeeded in calming the area but there were new flare-ups all over the country. Troops had to be sent to Philadelphia, and in Pittsburgh a mob forced a company of militia to retreat. Again Federal troops restored order.

In Pennsylvania, New York, and New Jersey, railroads were almost completely disrupted. On July 24, strikes against the Erie, New York Central, the Delaware Lackawanna Western, and the Canada Southern operating in New York, Pennsylvania, and Ohio, idled approximately one hundred thousand persons. Rioting was suppressed by Federal and state troops, and at times the latter were actually responsible for the violence. Thirteen persons were killed and forty-three wounded in Reading, Pennsylvania, when citizens and militia clashed. A coroner's jury said the troops were guilty of an unjustified attack upon peaceful citizens.

The trouble reached Chicago and work on all railroads entering that city was stopped. On July 26 there was an attempt by police to clear the streets that brought on a clash resulting in the death of nineteen people and the wounding of more than one hundred when police and militia charged a crowd.

Railroad strikes followed in 1885–86 in several western states. The Knights of Labor attempted to obtain the restoration of a wage cut and were refused. A strike was called and troops were sent into the Parsons, Kansas area after several workers were reportedly killed by strikers. In East St. Louis there was fighting between a group of deputies and a mob. Six men and a woman were killed "and it was later established that the deputies had fired rifle shots into a crowd and then escaped to St. Louis."

On April 9, an attempt to move a coal train through East St. Louis resulted in more violence when a posse directed a mob to disperse and tried to arrest a man who was blocking the train.

The mob then began pelting the deputies with stones, and one of the officers raised his rifle and fired. A man in the crowd fell. The rain of stones continued to fall on the deputies and pistol shots seemed to come from all directions. The deputies returned the fire and since they were better armed, the effect was deadly. The firing continued until the crossing was clear, people scattering in a panic and seeking protection in nearby houses.

The workers struck back with incendiaries and over forty railroad cars were burned. The militia was required to restore order.

Also in 1886 a peaceful strike in the Lehigh region of Pennsylvania resulted in an attack on the strikers by company police. "Throughout the Lehigh region there were no mobs . . . These men were not a mob. They obeyed the law. They simply declined to work for shriveled wages . . . During the whole of the strike serious violence was incited by the company rather than the men," reported a committee from the United States House of Representatives.

The steel lockout in Homestead, Pennsylvania, in July, 1892, was not peaceful and is an example of how far both sides will sometimes go in an effort to destroy the other. It has been called, "one of the great battles for worker's rights," and "a battle which for bloodthirstiness and boldness could not be excelled in actual warfare."

At that time, the Carnegie Steel Company (later to become the United States Steel Corporation) had its largest plant at Homestead, a town seven miles east of Pittsburgh on the Monongahela River. It employed 3,800 of the town's 11,000 population and operated twenty-four hours a day.

A steelworker's lot was not a happy one in those days. He worked a twelve-hour shift, seven days a week in temperatures that soared to 130 degrees. There was no time allowed out for meals, no place to wash up and there was no compensation for the frequent accidents. That the work was hazardous can be deduced from the fact that three hundred men were killed and two thousand hurt on the job in various mills in the Pittsburgh area during the year before the strike.

Henry Clay Frick, in charge of company labor policy, hated the unions. When he had his own company before joining Carnegie, he had always crushed any such movements by calling in deputy sheriffs, state militia, and/or Pinkerton detectives. His antagonism toward the Amalgamated Association of Iron and Steel Workers, to which about seven hundred Homestead workers belonged, was intensified when he had to make concessions in settling a strike in 1889. Accordingly, when the three-year contract neared expiration in June, 1892, a showdown was bound to occur.

Union representatives asked for a small wage increase, basing their request on increased prices and profits since the old contract was drawn up. Frick refused and issued an ultimatum saying his terms had to be accepted by June 24. Since Andrew Carnegie, the owner of the company, was vacationing in Scotland, there was no one else to whom an appeal could be made.

A strike was called for July 2, and the fight was on. Determined to break the union, Frick began shutting down the plant when the contract deadline was not met. He had already signed up skilled workers from other mills and hired three hundred Pinkerton detectives to protect company property and the scabs. Recruited from New York and Chicago, these armed men were scheduled to meet at Ashtabula, Ohio, and go from there to Youngstown by train. The final stage of the trip would be made by boat up the Monongahela. All ammunition and guns were to be shipped separately and the men armed only after they came within the boundaries of the state of Pennsylvania.

Two barges were prepared to transport the Pinkertons, one fixed up as a dormitory and the other as a dining room. Tugs would tow the barges, and as soon as the men were landed on Carnegie property, they would be deputized. Each was to receive five dollars per day. Armed with two hundred and fifty Winchester rifles, three hundred pistols, and plenty of ammunition, their task was to guard the company premises. They were dressed in dark blue trousers with lighter blue stripes, and wore slouch hats decorated with colorful bands.

By June 30 the plant was shut down and the workers locked out. Then a solid board wall, fifteen feet high, was erected all around the mill, extending on the river side clear down to the water's edge. Barbed wire was strung on top and holes drilled at eye level for the guards who would patrol its three-mile length.

The strikers had learned of Frick's plans for the Pinkerton squad and had stationed a lookout at Pittsburgh to warn them of the approach of the barges. When the pilot on the tug sounded the required whistle for the landing, people from all over Homestead rushed to the river banks. The strikers were armed and they fired into the inky blackness that cloaked the river. They were so enraged that they knocked down the new fence blocking the approach to the river and rushed to the landing. There the two opposing groups came face to face. The townspeople numbered close to ten thousand and were armed with rifles, pistols, revolvers, sticks, clubs and stones.

The Pinkerton leader shouted that his men were coming ashore. As soon as a gangplank was put into place, the strikers tried to dislodge it but failed. There were jeers and stones for the disembarking men at first, then they were shot at. One was killed and five wounded. The Pinkertons fired back, killing two and injuring thirty.

There was a lull in the fighting then, the would-be company guards retreating below deck while the strikers erected barricades at the top of the embankment. The wounded and dead were removed and the women banished from the line of fire. The tug departed for Pittsburgh under a hail of bullets.

Toward dawn the strikers ordered the Pinkerton men to surrender, but the answer came back, "If you don't withdraw, we will mow every one of you down."

Another landing was attempted around eight o'clock in the

morning and the battle raged for two hours, leaving more dead on both sides.

The strikers tried throwing dynamite sticks at the barges in an effort to force the men ashore, but they couldn't get close enough to do much damage. Even Civil War cannon fired from both sides of the river were ineffective.

The next maneuver of the strikers was to raid the plant's oil tanks, pour it on the water's surface and set it ablaze. Then they ignited a raft of greasy rags, hoping it would drift into the barges. When neither of these gambits worked, they loaded eleven barrels of oil on a small car and sent it crashing down the bank. It missed its target, going off course before it hit the water. During this time both sides maintained a steady fusillade of gunfire.

All afternoon union leaders tried to reason with the mob, telling them that further violence would only cause more bloodshed and gain them nothing. About five o'clock the repeated pleas began to show results and arrangements were made for the surrender of the Pinkertons.

The prisoners were promised safe passage to the Homestead railroad station, but when they were all ashore, their barges were burned and the mob attacked them. Forty were beaten unconscious and nearly every one was injured before they were herded into the downtown theater and held under guard until the midnight train left for Pittsburgh. The grim toll of the day's fighting was thirty-five dead and four hundred injured.

Frick appealed to Governor Pattison for help and, on July 12, eight thousand National Guardsmen marched into Homestead and put the city under martial law. Frick brought in scabs, forced the strikers off company property, and filed charges against their leaders for the attack on the Pinkertons.

The troops stayed until October, giving Frick time to get into full production with nonunion men. By November the union treasury was empty and the strike was broken. Union members were never rehired. Frick had done what he set out to do and it wasn't until 1935 that the steelworkers were effectively organized again, and then it was done by the CIO.

In 1894, the Pullman strike began as a protest against a wage cut and layoff of workers. Although the company said this was caused by the depression of 1893, the workers took note of the fact that dividends were not cut and neither were the salaries of officers and managers. Consequently, in May of 1894, an employee committee requested that the old wage scale be reinstated. This was refused and three members of the committee were discharged as "chronic troublemakers." The Pullman workmen in Chicago went on strike in protest on May 11 and asked the American Railway Union for support. In retaliation, the company laid off all nonunion workers and closed the plant.

The day after the ARU's boycott went into effect was the day trouble started. In an effort to keep trains from entering or leaving Chicago, engines were uncoupled from their cars, and single cars were used to obstruct the main tracks. Switches were thrown that shunted trains to dead-end sidings, and scab firemen and engineers were bodily removed from trains and the conductors threatened.

Within the city limits, however, activities were limited to stone throwing and hissing and booing the scab workers. Chicago police prevented the gathering of groups large enough to cause violence. But in outlying communities there were outbreaks, and at Blue Island a mob got out of control and completely halted operations of the Rock Island Railroad.

At the request of the General Railway Managers' Association, between fifteen hundred and two thousand men were recruited and sworn in as United States deputy marshals. Since the railroads were paying their salaries, these United States peace officers were also company employees. And the minute these men were brought in, trouble began in earnest. Passenger and freight service was halted as cars were overturned, derailed, or burned. All twenty-four railroads in the city were put out of commission. Supplies couldn't reach their destinations, meat was ruined by the heat or stolen from the idle trains. Even the mail was tied up.

Attorney General Richard Olney, a railroad lawyer and member of the board of several lines, felt that vigorous action in Chicago would keep the strike from spreading across the country. As a result, the first Federal injunction to halt a labor dispute was issued.

On July 2, Federal judges in Chicago issued injunctions ordering "all persons to refrain from interfering or stopping any of the business of any of the railroads in Chicago engaged as common carriers."

But the injunctions apparently acted as a spur to the strikers rather than a checkrein. Federal agents arriving at Blue Island to serve the injunction were greeted by a crowd of from two to three thousand people who drowned out the reading of the injunction with shouts of, "To hell with the government! To hell with the court!"

Some members of the mob surged forward and threw themselves in front of an engine trying to move through the yards. Deputy marshals opened fire and were set upon by the crowd. One marshal was stabbed and several others beaten.

The fighting resulted in President Cleveland's ordering five hundred Federal troops to the scene. The action was apparently taken at the urging of Attorney General Olney without any consultation with either the mayor of Chicago or the governor of Illinois.

The arrival of the troops on July 4 did little to cool the situation. Gangs of youths sometimes accompanied by female allies, swarmed into the railroad yards intent on doing as much damage as possible. The arriving troops were forced to push their way through the mob with bayonets. But as they moved along the railroad right of way, the crowd closed in behind them and went right on with their disruptive activities. Pullman cars were sidetracked and freight cars derailed and set on fire.

155

The scattered nature of the railroad yards made it almost impossible for troops and police to protect all the rolling stock. As soon as troops would hurry to one area, the roaming mobs would turn up in another to burn and loot. More manpower was needed so Mayor John Hopkins called on Governor John Altgeld to send in the Illinois National Guard. Two thousand state troops were hurried to the city and were soon followed by two thousand more.

Even the arrival of these reinforcements had little effect on the mobs which now numbered at least ten thousand individuals. Troops charging with bayonets fixed dispersed different groups but others formed almost immediately. A fire of incendiary origin destroyed seven buildings of the 1892 World Columbian Exposition. It was never established whether the fires were set by the strikers but the press laid the blame at their door.

On Friday, July 6, mobs again roamed through the rail yards doing $340,000 worth of damage. Hundreds of freight cars had been coupled together in order to make it easier for the troops and police to guard them. This proved to be a mistake because it made it easier for members of the mob to sneak between them and start fires. A brisk breeze spread the fire from car to car, and since little fire equipment was available it was impossible to stop the conflagration. At the Panhandle yards at Fiftieth Street in South Chicago, seven hundred cars were looted and then set afire.

The worst violence came on July 7 when a company of the Illinois National Guard was attacked by the mob. Thousands of people were following the train and some of them became bolder as they went along, encouraged by the sheer numbers behind them. The train halted near Loomis Street so that crewmen could right an overturned flat car. Jeers and curses came from the crowd as well as a hail of stones and bricks. A few shots were also fired. The commander warned the crowd to disperse. When they failed to comply with the order, he directed his men to load their guns. Some of the women and children left then, but the mood of the rioters turned uglier and they continued to hurl rocks at the troops.

The commander next ordered a bayonet charge, which resulted in injuries to a number of people. Temporarily the railroad right of way was cleared. The crowd returned, however, determined to halt the train. Some of the people rushed to upset the car that had just been replaced on the tracks while others threw anything they could get their hands on at the soldiers. Those in the crowd who were armed began firing their guns. The lieutenant was struck on the head by a stone, and four of his men were severely wounded. Caught in such a desperate situation, the commander ordered his men to fire at will and to make sure every shot counted.

Screams and curses echoed in the streets as the volley of rifle fire poured into the midst of the rioters. When the smoke cleared, the crowd had scattered but there were four dead and twenty wounded, including several women.

The violence at Loomis Street marked the beginning of the end of the rioting. On July 8, President Cleveland issued a proclamation warning against "taking part with a riotous mob in forcibly resisting and obstructing the execution of the laws," and saying that the rioters ". . . cannot be regarded otherwise than as public enemies."

There were now more than fourteen thousand men (police, militia, and Army regulars) in the Chicago area and these were supported by five thousand Federal marshals. This overwhelming force plus the President's proclamation brought the strike to an end with most of the strikers returning to work. Thirteen had been killed, fifty-three seriously injured, and several hundred arrested.

The United States Strike Commission investigated the claims of both sides and recommended that the Pullman company make many of the changes demanded by the workers. The recommendations were ignored.

That same year, 1894, coal strikes brought more violence. Miners on strike in Slope, Alabama, were ordered to vacate the company town, and Negro strikebreakers were brought in. On May 7, a band of armed men invaded the Price mine and blew up boilers, burned supplies and destroyed other property. On July 16, a gunfight broke out at Slope, five miles from Birmingham, and three Negro strikebreakers and a deputy were killed. Troops were ordered in by the governor and peace restored.

In April, 1899, there was a riot at Coeur d'Alene, Idaho, among lead miners. Several years of effort by the International Workers of the World, commonly called the Wobblies, to organize workers at the mines of the district had been accompanied by increasing violence. Nonunion workers had been beaten and their lives threatened. There had been bombings and sabotage, and Federal troops had been called in from time to time. On July 11, 1892, armed union men attacked company guards and nonunion workers. Several of the latter were killed. In 1894, forty masked men shot and killed the Government witness against the union gunmen. An attempt was made to blow up a mine at Wardner and a mine superintendent was kidnapped.

During this time, all but one mine became unionized. This was the one called the Bunker Hill and Sullivan Company at Wadner. Because of their refusal to recognize the union, trouble erupted. A mob of union men seized a train, loaded it with eighty kegs of dynamite and moved in on the mine. When the train reached Wadner, the men swarmed off it and raced toward the home of the superintendent whom they intended to kill. He had been warned and fled the town, so the miners burned his house and other company buildings. Then a ton and a half of dynamite was spread through the mine. The resulting explosion wrecked the mine and the concentrator. Then the company boarding house and bunkhouse were burned to the ground.

Bloodshed resulted when two groups of invading miners mistook each other for company guards and opened fire. A man named Smythe was killed and several others wounded. Further violence occurred when the union men were leaving the blasted mill and came on two of its employees. Both men were badly beaten and one received a bullet wound that later led to his death.

Many of the union men were hunted down and arrested. Supported by the governor, the mine owners smashed the union, forcing all those reemployed to foreswear union activities. The support he gave the mine owners led to Governor Steunenberg's death when the union hired a professional assassin to kill him with a thrown bomb.

Much of this violence was felt in the anthracite coal fields of Pennsylvania. In 1897, a peaceful group of strikers, marching from Hazleton to Latimer were set upon by the sheriff and his deputies. They opened fire on the unarmed men, killing eighteen and seriously wounding forty. Most of those killed were shot in the back, but when the sheriff and several deputies were tried for murder, they were acquitted.

A strike staged by the United Mine Workers in 1900 resulted in a clash that killed one strikebreaker. On July 1, 1902, a colliery at Old Forge was attacked and one striker was killed. The next day another was killed at Duryea. As the strike went on, assaults and shootings took place more frequently. Toward the end of July, two regiments were ordered to Shenandoah, which had fallen into the hands of rioters. It was here that a storekeeper was beaten to death for providing ammunition for deputies, and strikebreakers and deputies were constantly assaulted.

In Carbon County a coal and iron policeman killed a striker and troops were ordered in on August 18. The violence continued with bridges and trestles being dynamited and attacks made on those who wouldn't join the strikers.

In September the governor ordered troops into the three anthracite counties. One striker was killed on September 28, and later that same day, the Lehigh Valley Coal Company's office at Mount Carmel was attacked and demolished by seven hundred strikers who also took control of the roads which led to the colliery.

The New York *Tribune* reported that by the end of September the strike had resulted in fourteen persons being killed, sixteen shot from ambush, and forty-two seriously wounded. Sixty-seven aggravated assaults had been committed. One house and four bridges had been dynamited while sixteen houses, ten buildings, three washrooms, and three stockades had been burned. Of fifteen attempts to wreck trains, six had succeeded. And in fourteen schools students refused to attend classes taught by persons who had fathers or brothers working in the mines during the strike.

The activities of the coal and iron police were particularly conducive to violence during this period. A former Scotland Yard detective, Thomas Beet, who investigated them reported that their techniques resembled those of a feudal system of warfare where private interests could employ mercenaries to wage war on command.

A Congressional investigating committee looked into the activities of these private armies during the strike in July, 1909, led by the IWW against the Pressed Steel Car Company of McKee's Rock, Pennsylvania. They found that workers had been forcibly kept in stockades and compelled to work by armed guards.

> There was an armed guard at each end of the car, and [passengers were] not allowed to leave the train, and when they got in the camp they were forced to work there by the deputies of the car companies, the car companies being authorized by the sheriff to appoint whatever deputies they chose.

The state constabulary didn't behave much better. During a strike at the Bethlehem Steel Co. at South Bethlehem, Pennsylvania, in February, 1910, they arrived on the scene and immediately went into action. They "assaulted a number of people standing peaceably on the street . . . and they shot down an innocent man . . . who was standing in the Majestic Hotel when one of the troopers rode up to the pavement of the hotel door and fired two shots into the barroom," a Congressional report states.

In 1912, during a copper workers' strike in Michigan, the operatives of Waddell Private Detective Agency spread a rumor that their men had been fired on from a particular house. Supported by deputies, they surrounded the building and opened fire. There were fifteen people inside, including two women and four children. One man was killed instantly and another was mortally wounded, shot down while sitting at a table eating his dinner. A baby was also hit but survived. The deputies then gathered up large stones and broken bottles and scattered them around the house in an attempt to prove they had been attacked from inside. The district attorney didn't believe their story and labeled their action "wanton murder" and asked for second degree murder charges against both detectives and deputies.

The Illinois Central Shopmen's strike of June, 1911, resulted in assorted mayhem, and there were attacks in various parts of the country on strikebreakers. In McComb, Mississippi, two hundred and fifty armed men opened fire on a carload of strikebreakers. Several men were killed and a number of railroad cars burned. On January 17, 1912, in the same area, five Negroes working for the railroad were attacked and three killed. The railroad shops at Water Valley, Mississippi, were attacked and there was violence in New Orleans.

In California, then as now, farm workers were trying to organize. At the Durst Brothers ranch in Wheatland, living conditions for migrant workers were very poor. There was no housing for many hundreds and the campsites were unsanitary. Toilet facilities were inadequate, and the workers were charged a fee for drinking water. All of this made the migrants feel so dissatisfied that they elected a committee to

161

negotiate with the Dursts. What they decided to ask for was an increase in the price of picking and improved sanitation.

Headed by Richard Ford and Herman Suhr, a member of the IWW, the committee met with one of the Durst brothers. Durst turned down the demands and slapped Ford in the face with his glove. A constable then tried to arrest Ford. When a warrant was insisted on, he left but quickly returned with several deputy sheriffs and the district attorney of the county.

Again they tried to arrest Ford and this time the argument resulted in a shoot-out. Two hop pickers were killed plus a deputy sheriff and the district attorney. Militia arrived the next day but wasn't needed since order had already been restored. Four members of the committee were arrested and tried for murder, Ford and Suhr among them, and it was these two who were convicted and sentenced to prison.

A Michigan copper strike in 1913 led to the killing of two strikers by company guards and the death of seventy-two women and children during a union Christmas party when a panic was deliberately started by shouts of fire.

One of the bloodiest strikes in history was that of the United Mine Workers against the Colorado coal industry—the so-called Ludlow War. Even before the strike started a union organizer was shot by a detective hired by the Colorado Fuel Iron Company, and a marshal working for the company was killed in return.

On October 7, 1913, guards attacked the camp into which the strikers had moved after being ejected from the company town, killing a man and wounding a boy. Three strikers were shot and one killed several days later when guards fired into a miners' meeting. A guard was killed the next day in a shoot-out between miners and guards. An armored train, nicknamed the "Death Special," was on its way to Ludlow when strikers opened fire, killing the engineer.

Order was restored temporarily when the National Guard arrived, but the Guard was withdrawn except for one company under a Lieutenant K. E. Linderfelt who was violently prejudiced against the strikers and whose men, for the most part, were company guards in uniform. On April 20, 1914, Linderfelt led his troops in a surprise foray on the strikers' camp at Ludlow. Five men and a boy were killed by machine-gun fire. Linderfelt then had the strikers' tents set afire, and eleven children and two women who were sheltering in them were suffocated or burned to death.

The enraged strikers struck back. They attacked mine after mine, burning buildings and killing any guards they couldn't drive off. Two hundred armed strikers attacked the mines at Forges and before they were finished, nine guards and one strikebreaker were dead and the buildings in flames.

"During the ten days of fighting, at least fifty persons had lost their lives, including twenty-one killed at Ludlow," says a report to the U.S. Commission on Industrial Relations. *Violence in America* estimates that a total of seventy-four were killed during the period of the strike.

The war years brought more labor violence and with it the persecution and virtual destruction of the IWW, which openly opposed the war. On July 22, 1916, a bomb killed many people marching in a Preparedness Day parade in San Francisco. IWW leaders Thomas Mooney and Warren K. Bellings were indicted, tried, and sentenced to death on evidence that has since come to be considered completely fraudulent. Mooney served many years in jail before being freed by Governor Olson of California.

In another violent episode, a fight broke out between IWW workers and a "citizens committee" at Everett, Washington, on November 6, 1916. The Industrial Workers of the World had set up a union hall in Everett but were driven out of town by vigilantes and the sheriff. When forty-one IWW men returned, they were surrounded and disarmed by several hundred vigilantes and forced to run the gauntlet between two rows of men who beat them with clubs.

At Centralia, Washington, an IWW hall had been set up

in 1916 and wrecked during a Red Cross parade shortly thereafter. The IWW opened another hall, and during the Armistice Day celebration in 1919, the members barricaded themselves there. The hall was attacked by marchers from the Armistice parade, and the Wobblies opened fire, killing three members of the American Legion and mortally wounding another. That night Wesley Everest, a veteran and member of the IWW, was lynched by a mob of citizens in revenge for the shootings.

Beginning in 1917 and lasting until 1920, the nation struggled in the throes of a Red scare. The IWW, which stated in its constitution that "the working class and the employing class have nothing in common," and said that "between these two classes a struggle must go on until the workers of the world organize as a class and take possession of the earth and the machinery of production and abolish the wage system," found itself the chief target of the forces referred to as law and order.

"More than one thousand members were imprisoned in the course of two years," says Dwight L. Drummond in *America in Our Time,* "many being given long-term sentences, and others being deported. The nature of the suppression may be judged from the fact that indictments were drawn up against men who had been dead for years."

Another indication of the nature of the suppression was that one man was sentenced to five years in prison "for impeding a train by word of mouth."

The Wobblies as an effective organization were destroyed by the persecution during and after the war, but they still maintain an office in Chicago and their membership is estimated at around two thousand with about ten thousand sympathizers. They still sing their songs and talk about the old days.

The present leader of the IWW is Carl Keller, its general secretary, who in an interview in 1967 said that some of today's college rebels were joining his group. "This is true, even among the sick kids, the ones who want to legalize pot and LSD," he said. "Even among the kookie ones who wear buttons saying: 'I Hate the State.' " Keller thinks the "sick kids are immature rebels who carry the natural rebellion of a child into the adult world, and seem to want to remain children." Keller was a migrant worker when he joined the IWW and is puzzled by the present day college rebels. "You know," he said, "some of them have never seen a pick and shovel."

One of the great watershed events in labor violence was the police strike in Boston in 1919.

"There is no right to strike against the public safety by anybody, any time, anywhere," Governor Calvin Coolidge said in answer to a plea by Samuel Gompers, President of the American Federation of Labor, that the striking policemen be reinstated instead of dismissed out of hand as Police Commissioner Edwin Curtis insisted on doing.

This strike was unique in American history. At no time, before or since, has a U.S. city been deprived of police protection to such an extent that a mob could take it over. The rioters looted, robbed, and destroyed simply because there was no one to stop them. They had no sympathy for the striking policemen; they just took advantage of the opportunity to run wild when it was presented.

The strike was no surprise. For a long time, the police had been unhappy over low pay, unsanitary and crowded station houses, promotions based on favoritism instead of merit and an inadequate pension system. When they asked Commissioner Curtis to do something about the situation, he made no secret of the fact that he thought them rebellious troublemakers. They formed a local unit of the AFL, and Curtis declared their officers guilty of disobedience. The union said if the men were fired, they'd strike. The men were suspended on September 8, and on September 9, about eleven hundred of the 1,459 patrolmen turned in their revolvers. billy clubs, locker keys and badges and walked out of the nineteen precincts. The city of Boston was then defenseless against any and all crimes.

Word that 90 percent of the police force was not reporting for duty swept through the city rapidly, terrifying ordinary citizens but delighting those who had little regard for law. Gangs of juveniles began smashing windows, sabotaging trolley cars, stealing automobiles and turning in false fire alarms.

Then the adults joined in. Thousands of persons jammed into Scollay Square in downtown Boston where only ten of the usual 129 policemen were on duty. They broke into theaters, smashed plate glass windows and carried off whatever struck their fancy from the stores of the area. People loaded down with stolen goods traded it openly as they made their way along Washington Street. Men shot craps and played dice in Boston Common.

When details of the night's violence hit the papers next morning, the authorities blamed the striking police for it; they, in turn, said it was Commissioner Curtis' fault; that he had been warned ahead of time and had assured the public that an emergency force would take over.

Mayor Peters called out the State Guard, personally took charge of the Police Department, and told Coolidge he needed three thousand more guardsmen. That night cavalry patrolled Scollay Square. Pistols were used and guardsmen had to make a bayonet charge to disperse the unruly mob. Many were injured when they fell and were trampled by the stampeding crowd.

The scene was the same in South Boston. A mob of 10,000 rampaged up and down West Broadway, robbing and looting. Some people were armed and shot at the soldiers using rifles and bayonets. By midnight the guardsmen had endured enough harassment from the rioters and fired directly into the crowd. Two men were killed and nine wounded, but the crowd dispersed and order was restored.

Thursday morning Governor Coolidge called out additional guardsmen. It took seventy-five hundred to maintain control, and some of them were on duty until almost Christmas. By that time Commissioner Curtis had rebuilt his police force, introducing, ironically enough, the changes for which the ex-members had sacrificed their jobs.

During 1923 and 1924, railroad strikes resulted in much violence. E. C. McGregor, a strike leader, was seized by a mob in Harrison, Arkansas, and lynched. Other strikers were driven out of town by vigilantes. Strikers themselves also resorted to violence, and twenty persons were killed by them in various parts of the country. The National Guard had to be called to duty in several states to restore order.

As union membership increased, however, labor violence decreased. The period between 1923 and 1932 was singularly free of violence except in one or two areas. Harlan County, Kentucky, was one of these. So numerous were the killings there over a twenty-year period it became known as "Bloody Harlan." The trouble ended in 1941 when the mine operators recognized the United Mine Workers of America, headed by John L. Lewis.

The coming of the New Deal in 1933 saw the passage of laws regulating labor relations, with the result that there was a further easing of labor violence. The famous sit-down strikes of the thirties were practically bloodless, producing little more than a few black eyes and cuts from flying glass or thrown bricks. In 1940 there were seven deaths due to labor disputes, but they occurred in scattered locations.

New laws and a new generation of labor and business leaders have almost ended violence in labor disputes. In recent years strikes are usually settled by collective bargaining or resorting to the National Labor Relations Board rather than to guns and dynamite.

8 | Criminal Violence, 1919-1969

A few days before he was to testify before a grand jury, Police Chief Peter Hennessey was cut down by shotgun blasts at the door of his home. He lived long enough to identify his attackers as "the dagoes."

The grand jury presentment read in part:

> The extended range of our researchers has developed the existence of the secret organization styled "Mafia." The evidence comes from several sources fully competent in themselves to attest its truth, while the fact is supported by the long record of blood-curdling crimes, it being almost impossible to discover the perpetrators or to secure witnesses.
>
> As if to guard against exposure, the dagger or the stiletto is selected as the deadly weapon to plunge into the breast or back of the victim and silently do its work. Revenge was their motive . . . The officers of the Mafia and many of its members are known. Among them are men born in this city of Italian parentage, using their power for the basest purposes, be it said to their eternal disgrace. The larger number of the Society is composed of Italians or Sicilians who have left their native land, in most instances under assumed names to avoid conviction for crimes they

committed; and others were escaped convicts and bandits, outlawed in their own land, seeking the city of New Orleans for the congenial companionship of their own class . . . Today there is recorded in the office of the Italian consul the names of some 1100 Italians and Sicilians landed here during several years past, showing the official record of their criminality in Italy and Sicily.

Sound familiar? It was actually written in 1890!

Even then Italians were far from being the originators of organized crime. The partnership between politician and criminal (the foundation of organized crime) goes back at least a century, long before Italians were recruited by American business as a cheap labor force. The "King of Chicago gamblers" following the Civil War was Michael Cassius McDonald, who created the city's first real political machine—it was made up of gamblers, saloonkeepers and whoremasters. Called "Mike McDonald's Democrats," the machine and its philosophy have survived to this day.

Shortly before his death in 1907, the Chicago *Daily News* reminisced:

> Mike McDonald is dying. When the city had a scant half million this man ruled it from his saloon and gambling house by virtue of his political power. During many succeeding years he had a controlling influence in the public affairs of this community . . . Bad government was accepted as a matter of course. Vice sat in the seats of power and patronized virtue with a large and kindly tolerance, asking only that it remain sufficiently humble and not too obtrusive. Gambling was a leading industry.

The Irish, the Jews, and other ethnic groups had their fling at organized crime long before the Italians were on the scene. But by the turn of the century, the struggle for rackets and troops (not ethnic domination) was the source of most of the underworld violence. The death of Police Chief Hen-

169

nessey in New Orleans resulted from his attempt to investigate a series of brutal murders resulting from a power struggle between two Sicilian gangs for control of the New Orleans waterfront. Tribute was received for all cargo moving on or off the docks, making it a lucrative racket.

Following the death of Hennessey, indictments were returned against nineteen Mafia members. In a pattern that has grown all too familiar through the years, the best criminal lawyers in the country were hired by the mafiosi, and all but three of the defendants were freed by the jury. Then something extraordinary happened. A mob of several thousand enraged citizens broke into the prison and killed eleven of the racketeers—two were hung from lamp posts and nine were lined up against a wall and executed by a makeshift firing squad.

But once the Mafia hoodlum was on the scene, violence increased. At first the growth was mostly intramural. For example, of the forty-one gangland slayings in Los Angeles from 1906 to 1934, thirty-four victims were Sicilians and Italians, four were Jews, and three were Irish.

One of the early Mafia dons in New York was Ignazio "Lupo the Wolf" Saietta, who had escaped from Sicily in 1899 after murdering a man. Settling in East Harlem, Lupo the Wolf joined his brother-in-law, Giuseppe Morello, in running the Italian lottery and pushing dope. Later they branched out with a protection racket that extorted tribute from artichoke dealers, olive oil and cheese peddlers, and small store owners.

In ten years, these crimes against their own countrymen had made them rich and powerful leaders in the Mafia. Letters demanding tribute carried the crude imprimatur of a black hand, bringing to America a practice that had terrorized Sicilians for more than a century in the old country. (From time to time, the Italian Government has declared war on the Mafia, sending troops into Sicily to round up hundreds of mafiosi. Although sensationalized in the press, results have not been any more promising there than here. *Omertà*, the Mafia code of silence, is effective in both countries.)

Black Hand extortionists were so brazen in Chicago that they used to tack imprimatured notices with the names of the intended victims (to accommodate prospective widows) on a nearby "death tree." Forty-three executions were thus advertised in one eighteen-month period. In New York City, Black Hand extortion became so menacing that a special squad, headed by Lieutenant Joseph Petrosino, was organized to fight it. Like Hennessey before him, Petrosino became too enthusiastic: while in Sicily in 1909 to check police files of suspected criminals, he was killed by a shot in the back.

Lupo the Wolf missed the bonanza of Prohibition. He branched out too quickly during World War I and got thirty years for counterfeiting. Ciro Terranova, known as the "Artichoke King," became the new uptown boss. But there was a lot of territory left, and with every mob fully aware of the enormous profits to be made from bootlegging, all hell broke loose in the underworld. Every mob in the city and in the country was out to gain as much control as possible. New mobs sprang up overnight.

Some of the mobs in New York and New Jersey were led by Joe "The Boss" Masseria (his *caporegimes* or lieutenants included such incipient mob luminaries as Charley "Lucky" Luciano, Vito Genovese, Willie Moretti, Joseph "Joe Adonis" Doto, and Frank Costello). Other mobs were led by "Legs" Diamond, Arthur "Dutch Schultz" Flegenheimer, Louis "Lepke" Buchalter, Jacob "Gurrah" Shapiro, Benjamin "Bugsy" Siegel and Meyer Lansky (who formed the Bug-Meyer mob), "Mad Dog" Vincent Coll, Waxy Gordon, Abner "Longie" Zwillman, Arnold Rothstein, Frank "Frankie Yale" Uale, George Uffner, Salvatore Maranzano, Owney Madden, William "Big Bill" Dwyer, and Anthony "Li'l Augie Pisano" Carfano. There were countless others, many of whom never made it past their first month of operation.

If competition for the booze dollar was lively in New York,

it was strictly murder in Chicago. Big Jim Colosimo, dead on the eve of the decade, was the harbinger of it all. His was the classic bogus "rags to riches" epic of the poor immigrant boy in the new land: the flashy dresser with the diamond rings, diamond stickpins, diamond-studded garters and diamond-adorned watch fob; the "legit" cafe proprietor and genial host to politicians and college boys; the whoremonger with the morals and temper of a spider; the wealthy sportsman with a gentlemanly interest in the sport of kings; the carefree gambler and gay playboy; the manipulator, the king maker, and the vote buyer; the corrupter of society; the extortioner and murderer.

Big Jim was also a lover. First he married a madam with a couple of dollar houses on the levee. At about the same time Hinky Dinky Kenna and Bathhouse John Coughlin, bosses of the First Ward (it includes the Loop), made him a precinct captain in charge of getting out the Italian vote. An aggressive thug, Colosimo became the overlord of vice on the levee in relatively short order.

At the peak of his career, he divorced the madam and on April 20, 1920, he married Dale Winters, a singer in his cafe (just like in the movies). Three weeks later, someone walked up behind him in his cafe and emptied a gun into his head. The rumor was that Johnny Torrio, imported from New York by Colosimo, had himself imported Frankie Yale to do the job.

Torrio buried his boss in the grand manner that was to become underworld fashion. Honorary pall bearers included judges, congressmen, state legislators, aldermen and committeemen.

If any doubt had existed before that funeral of the tangible power of the vicelords, it was quickly and irrevocably eased. The city—from Mayor Big Bill Thompson, who owed his election to boodle aldermen, to the police chief, who took his orders directly from the mayor and party bosses—owed allegiance to the underworld. The explanation was not to be found in the evils of Prohibition, for it had been in effect barely four months. The evil was to be found in the genes and chromosomes of a parasitic political system.

Now there was not only Prohibition but prosperity as well. There were plenty of dollars to fight for. Gangs sprang up from every direction except from out of the lake—gangs that numbered such notorious hoodlums as Roger Touhy, Dion O'Bannion, "Nails" Morton, "Bugs" Moran, the "Terrible" Gennas, Duke Cooney, Vince "The Schemer" Drucci, the Sheltons, "Dago" Lawrence Mangano and "Terrible Terry" Druggan, Hymie Weiss, Murry "The Camel" Humphreys, Jake "Greasy Thumb" Guzik, and Joe Aiello, who lived with the dream of one day eliminating Big Al Capone because he resented seeing a Neopolitan bossing Sicilians. The dream ended on a Chicago street in 1930; the coroner extracted 62 machine-gun slugs from Aiello's body.

The gangs manufactured booze, imported it, distributed it, hijacked truckloads of it—and peddled it in twenty thousand speakeasies to millions of Chicagoans who were fervently against sin, gambling, prostitution, graft, corruption, murder, violence of any kind, drunken driving, and most certainly bootlegging.

The gangs paid the cop, they elected the judge, they sponsored the politician, they intimidated the reformer, they cajoled the press, they waylaid the squealer, and they waged total warfare against all competitors. The icepick, the rope, the snub-nosed automatic, the sawed-off shotgun, the Thompson submachine gun, and the pineapple were the tools of the trade. The one-way ride, the cement overcoat, the racketeer, the bootlegger, the speakeasy, the gangster, the massacre, the gang war, the Black Sox, Teapot Dome, the flapper, the hip flask, the Charleston, and the racoon coat were the symbols of the decade. Babe Ruth, Jack Dempsey, Rudolph Valentino, Charles Lindbergh, and Al Capone were equally its heroes.

With Colosimo laid away in his splendid sepulcher, Torrio

decided that he, too, needed a bodyguard and summoned a young, ruthless thug from Brooklyn who went by the alias of Al Brown (newspapers in the early period—1920 to 1924 —refer to this alias instead of the real name, Alphonse Capone).

In those days Torrio's headquarters were located in a building called the Four Deuces, at 2222 South Wabash Avenue. Its four stories were dedicated to the three most popular vices known to man: drinking, gambling, and fornication. Naturally, it was a busy place, frequented by the aristocracy of crime as well as of politics and business. An even dozen unsolved murders were committed in the Four Deuces, but, considering what was taking place off the premises, it was probably the safest place in town.

In the twelve years (1920 to 1931) that Mr. Brown was in town, six hundred and twenty-nine gang slayings went unsolved within the city limits, not counting the more than five thousand homicides not classified as gang killings. Policemen and politicians were shot or bombed as readily as hoodlums. Mayhem was the order of the day. Not only did the gangs fight for the gambling, prostitution and bootlegging millions, they fought for control of labor unions. At least fourteen buildings were bombed and two policemen were killed as a result of the Building Trades war.

Not all the violence, however, was Capone-inspired.

Honest policemen who fought it out with gangsters more often than not ended up dead and disgraced: Early one rainy morning in 1925 four detectives (Michael J. Conway, Charles B. Walsh, Harold F. Olson, and William Sweeney) found an automobile belonging to Bugs Moran, riddled with bullets and abandoned. A few minutes later, a big black sedan came skidding and twisting up Western Avenue.

"It's Mike Genna," Sweeney said to Olson, who was at the wheel. "After that car."

It was public knowledge that the "Terrible" Genna brothers (Angelo, Jim, Mike, Pete, Sam, and Tony) and Bugs Moran were at war over the spoils of the North Side. Within three blocks both cars were traveling at better than seventy miles an hour on the wet pavement. Suddenly, the inevitable truck was driven into the path of the chase. With angry squeals of brakes, both cars spun out of control, the Genna sedan smashing down a lamppost and the squad car careening in a wild skid before heading straight for the Genna car.

The four gangsters (Mike Genna, John Scalici, Albert Anselmi, and one never identified) were struggling out of the wreckage as the police jumped out to face them.

"Didn't you hear the gong?" Olson demanded angrily.

Seconds later Olson and Walsh were dead with a dozen bullet wounds. Conway dropped to the street with his jaw shot away. Hiding behind the squad car, Sweeney emptied his revolver at the fleeing gangsters, and then grabbing the two guns dropped by the dead officers, he took after Genna. One of his bullets severed an artery in Genna's leg. Moments later, huddled in a cellar into which he had plunged, Mike Genna fired one last shot and died. Anselmi and Scalisi were apprehended in a neighborhood store in the act of purchasing two caps. The fourth gangster got away.

With minor variations, the legal antics that followed were typical of the era. The day after the crime, Sweeney began receiving telephoned death threats and skull-marked warnings in his mail. Just before the trial was to start a bomb blew away the front of his home.

The Genna gang, almost decimated in recent months, was convinced that its status depended on "springing" its two gunmen. A vast defense fund was gathered from storekeepers and alcohol cookers who were persuaded at gun point to "defend the good name of Sicily."

One hundred thousand dollars was raised in a few days, but the maniacal Gennas demanded more, increasing the pressure on their hirelings. The first to be murdered was Henry Spingola, a brother-in-law of the Gennas. He had originally contributed ten thousand dollars but balked when pressed for another donation, explaining that he did not know the defendants very well. His real problem was that he did not know his in-laws well enough.

Two suppliers of yeast to the gang reluctantly put up four thousand dollars for the second defense fund, but committed Spingola's fatal error. They warned the collector that it was the last money he could expect from them. Within a week they were dead.

Samoots Amatuna, a middleweight in the underworld, got possession of the first list of contributors and went around telling them that the Gennas should make certain changes in their approach to the case; or otherwise there was no sense in continuing with the donations. He was halfway through the list when a bullet passed through his head. Vito Bascone, a wealthy wine dealer, refused to make a third payment "for the honor of Sicily" and followed the others in sudden death. And three lazy collectors followed him: Orrazio "The Scrouge" Tropea, Little Joe Calabriese and Edward "The Eagle" Bardello.

Meanwhile, State Attorney Robert E. Crowe was assuring the press that "these men will go straight to the gallows." However, when the trial started the desired outcome did not appear too promising. The first panel of 238 veniremen provided just four jurors.

O. W. Payne, a dropout venireman, provided the answer: "It wouldn't be healthy to bring in a verdict of guilty. Pressure is brought to bear on our families. I'd have to carry a gun the rest of my life if I served and found these two men guilty."

After months of delays, the case finally came to trial. Michael Ahearn, one of many defense counsels, advanced a popular theory: "If a police officer detains you even for a moment, against your will, and you kill him, you are not guilty of murder. It's just manslaughter. If the policeman uses force of arms, you may kill him in self-defense and the law cannot harm you."

This theory, though legally false, was technically correct in Chicago. Officers Olson and Walsh were the fourth and fifth policemen killed that week.

The jury was apparently impressed by this theory for it found the defendants guilty of manslaughter in the death of Walsh and they were sentenced to fourteen years in prison. Months later in a trial for the murder of Olson they were acquitted. The Illinois Supreme Court granted them a new trial in the Walsh case and they were subsequently acquitted.

At one point during the first trial, when the death penalty seemed a certainty, Defense Attorney Patrick O'Donnel had waved a small book before the jury. "I have here," he roared, "the names of policemen Mike Genna paid by the month. Two hundred of these policemen belong at the Maxwell Street station, two squads came from the central office and one from the State's Attorney's office. This outfit got more than $8,000 monthly." After lengthy denials on one side and threats of publishing the names on the other, the notebook was never referred to again.

No man lives forever, especially a Chicago gunman on a losing team. Four years later Scalisi, Anselmi, and one Joe Ginta, got a fast one-way ride courtesy of Bugs Moran. He thought it only fair since four thugs had knocked off seven of his men in a garage on North Clark Street on St. Valentine's Day. Chicago newspapers, incidentally, seldom fail to note the anniversary of this momentous event.

Beer vans rumbled through Chicago streets night and day in long convoys, and high-powered black limousines swept in deftly disconnected caravans to Canada and New York and Florida and New Orleans. The deluge of money was breathtaking. Capone, who was not in the habit of tossing figures about recklessly, admitted paying thirty million dollars a year for protection in Chicago.

Torrio lasted four years, his bodyguard always at his side, which was less than half as long as Colosimo had lasted. One day while riding along in his nice big black sedan another big black sedan pulled up alongside and opened fire with sawed-off shotguns. The chauffeur and a dog beside him on the front seat were killed instantly. Torrio stared incredulously at the two holes in his derby.

Two days later as he and his wife were tiptoeing from their car on a street directly behind their home, intending to sneak through their own backyard, a big black sedan (a popular model) roared down the street, spewing lead from two machine guns. Fifty slugs—"poisoned in garlic" (Italian style)—riddled the buildings and trees about them, three of the shots finding their mark.

After a month in the hospital "wavering between life and death," Johnny Torrio decided it was time to visit the old country and booked passage on the first available steamship bound for Italy. He returned to New York City years later and became one of the leaders in the Mafia. By 1931, the year Capone was sentenced to eleven years in Federal prison for tax evasion, only one gang of importance was left in Chicago—his own—which was taken over by his cousin, Frank "The Enforcer" Nitti.

When violence was cooling off in Chicago, New York was in the midst of the Castellammarese War, so named because the leader of one of the warring factions, Salvatore Maranzano, was from the Sicilian town of Castellammarese del Golfo. The "enemy," Joe Masseria, was a stubborn man, an old Mustache Pete who refused to listen to the advice of his top aides: Luciano, Genovese, and Costello. His Gargantuan ego and his years of absolute power made him easy prey to deceit in his own ranks.

Tired of a war which had cost some sixty lives, Luciano and Genovese made a deal with Maranzano: they would have Masseria killed and Maranzano would stop the war and grant amnesty to all soldiers. Masseria was invited to dine with Luciano at a Coney Island restaurant, and while Luciano was washing his hands in the men's room, three assassins came in and sprayed twenty slugs (five found their mark) around the dining room.

Years later (during the Murder, Inc., investigation) Abe "Kid Twist" Reles identified the three as Albert Anastasia (boss of Murder, Inc.), Joe Adonis, and Bugsy Siegel. If true, it was an imposing trio, worthy of the supreme stature of The Boss. The inclusion of Siegel was further demonstration of the new era of co-operation dawning in the underworld.

Less than six months later (September 10, 1931), four of Luciano's men, posing as police officers, walked into Maranzano's office at 230 Park Avenue and methodically disposed of him (four gunshot and six stab wounds) while a dozen or so thugs and customers faced the wall in the outer office. It has been estimated that some forty Mustache Petes (known also as the Greaser Crowd) were slain in coordinated raids across the country within forty-eight hours of Maranzano's death.

In his testimony before the Permanent Subcommittee on Investigations chaired by Senator John L. McClellan, Joseph Valachi, the first mafioso to ever so testify, credited Maranzano with organizing the Mafia (he called it *La Cosa Nostra,* Our Thing) into family units, each with its own geographical boundaries, which would determine the size of a family. Each would have a *capo,* boss; a *sottocapo,* underboss; a *consiglieri,* counselor or adviser, and any number of *caporegimes,* lieutenants, who supervised crews of soldiers, or "button" men. The code of *omertà* (honor and silence) prevailed. And all of it would fall under the domain of the *Capo di Tutti Capi*—Boss of All Bosses—namely Maranzano.

After his death, Luciano and other bosses formed a national *commissione* made up of nine to twelve bosses of the largest families. The *commissione's* function is roughly analogous to the board of directors of a large conglomerate —it sets guidelines and policies, acts as a court of last resort, settles jurisdictional disputes, and its approval is mandatory for all high-level assassinations.

Only New York and Chicago have been selected as examples, but gang violence afflicted every major city (and some minor ones) during Prohibition. Repeal in 1933 hit the underworld hard, but not any harder than the Depression. The eternal search is for the dollar, whether it be from booze, gambling, prostitution, narcotics, extortion, loan sharking, union racketeering, or legitimate business.

When prison doors closed behind Capone, gangster headlines vanished with him. Masseria, Maranzano, and Luciano did not possess enough color to appeal to tabloid writers. But out on the prairie a phenomenon as strange as the Depression itself suddenly captured the imagination of the American people.

Bold men with strong American names and colorful sobriquets were prowling the length and breadth of the land, sacking a bank here, killing a cop there, kidnapping a rich man whenever one could be found in a country hovering perilously on the brink of economic disaster. The outlaw gangs of the Wild West had long since become legend. Fast horses and rough trails had made crime possible and profitable in those frontier days; bad roads and fast cars were making it possible now.

The Thompson submachine gun had replaced the six-shooter. Bank robberies were occurring at the rate of two a day. Gun battles were an almost daily news item. Of two thousand hardened felons, a dozen or so big names crowded the headlines: Francis Keating, Thomas Holden, Frank Nash, Alvin Karpis, Verne Miller, "Pretty Boy" Floyd, "Machinegun" Kelly, Ma Barker, Bonnie and Clyde, Harvey Bailey, Earl Christman, Ray Terrill, "Baby Face" Nelson, and Johnnie Dillinger, *numero uno* on the G-men's most-wanted list.

One year—from a minor drugstore holdup after his parole in 1933 to his death on a Chicago street in 1934—was long enough to make Dillinger a legend in his own time. Whatever else he represented, it was daring, it was action, it was living—which was more than most Americans could say for their own condition at that desperate moment in history.

The FBI had fallen on evil times before Dillinger appeared on the scene. J. Edgar Hoover was working hard at regilding the bureau's image, tarnished during the Harding administration, and he was under constant fire from Congress for having used eavesdropping methods and mail drops on several senators and congressmen who had been critics of the bureau. To add insult to injury, the G-men got involved in several inept episodes with Dillinger, the most painful of which took place at Little Bohemia Lodge.

Having been tipped on Dillinger's whereabouts, the G-men had no sooner surrounded the lodge before three innocent customers came dashing out and were cut down by the agents' machine-gun fire. While this was going on in the front, the gang was slipping out the back way.

The attack on the lodge lasted an hour; then sixteen agents, armed with machine guns, automatic rifles, shotguns, tear gas equipment and steel vests, waited twelve hours before making their next move. Melvin Purvis, the agent in charge, began the final stage of the attack at daybreak the next morning with a barrage of tear gas bombs.

Moments later a small voice was heard from within the house: "We'll come out if you'll stop firing."

"Come out and bring everyone with you—with your hands up," Purvis ordered.

Four gun molls came out, followed by the owner and his wife. (For many years Little Bohemia was the greatest tourist attraction in the Midwest, and for a while Dillinger's father was one of the guides.)

J. Edgar Hoover's order after Little Bohemia was to "act

first, talk afterward. Shoot straight and get the right man."

Attorney General Cummings was more explicit: "Shoot to kill—then count to ten."

At the end, Melvin Purvis was there for the kill. When Dillinger came out of the Biograph with Anna Sage, the "woman in red," on one arm and Polly Hamilton Keele on the other, Purvis tried to light a cigar (the signal for his men to close in) but his hands were shaking so violently it became impossible. But the sign was caught and two agents sidled up to Purvis as he moved directly behind Dillinger.

What transpired next is open to speculation. Purvis claims he shouted, "Stick 'em up, Johnnie!" and that Dillinger broke into a run, heading for an alley, his right hand tugging frantically at his trouser pocket. Purvis said he tore the buttons off his coat trying to beat him to the draw. This account is disputed by several witnesses.

A Mrs. Esther Gousinow, who lived in a second-floor apartment across the street from the Biograph, told reporters: "Then I saw a young man walk out of the theater, accompanied by two girls. They were only about ten feet away from the alley when I saw three men walk up behind them. I heard two shots—there may have been more—and the man with the two girls fell to the sidewalk. I thought at first that it was a holdup and that the victim was killed."

Dillinger was struck by four bullets, all in the back. The fatal one, fired virtually at point-blank rage, entered at the base of the skull and exited through the left cheekbone. He fell on his face, with his own gun still in his pocket. Like vultures with carrion, people dipped handkerchiefs and pieces of paper in his blood as souvenirs. Hoover shared this morbid fascination to a degree: a white plaster death mask of Dillinger, along with his straw hat, .38 automatic and other memorabilia, lie under glass next to the director's office in the Justice Department, a trophy of a celebrated hunt.

Evelyn Frechette, one of Dillinger's girl friends, toured the country with a carnival sideshow to tell wide-eyed audiences of her life with Johnnie. His favorite songs, she said, were *Happy Days Are Here Again* and *The Last Roundup*. Unconsciously, Johnnie had bridged the gap. There have been thousands of outlaws, but only one Jesse James and one John Dillinger. Separated by much more history than years, they were nevertheless brothers under the skin. Though ruthless and violent men, they had that touch of magic that somehow transcends evil in the public imagination.

Whatever it was that Dillinger had, the others were a different breed. Many were little more than psychopathic killers, more interested in shooting than robbing. "Baby Face" Nelson's final encounter began with a wrong look. Late on the afternoon of November 27, 1934 (four months after Dillinger's death), he was driving toward Chicago with his wife and John Paul Chase when he spotted a sedan with two special agents going in the opposite direction.

"I don't like the way those guys looked at me," he said, swinging the car around to give chase. "Let 'em have it."

There was an exchange of lead and Nelson turned down a side road, only to find himself being chased by another police car, manned by Special Agent Ed Hollis and Inspector Sam Cowley. Nelson braked to a stop and, before the agents could bring their own car under control, Nelson with a chopper and Chase with an automatic rifle began firing. When it was over, the agents lay dead and Nelson near death with seventeen bullet wounds. His body, nude and blood-spattered, was found the next morning abandoned beside a cemetery wall.

Clyde Barrow and Bonnie Parker, immortalized by Hollywood as star-crossed lovers, were probably the least attractive outlaws of the thirties. Barrow's love of guns was pathological. He never went anywhere without the back seat of the car piled high with assorted weapons. In two years of roving through the Southwest, this pair, with the help of an occasional confederate, robbed gas stations, grocery stores, and small banks. Unlike Dillinger and Nelson, they never attempted a large-scale bank job, but in their criminal wanderings, they killed thirteen times before they died in a hail of police bullets.

Almost all the desperadoes ended up on slabs, struck down by lawmen's lead. They did not enjoy the political immunity of gangsters. The more imaginative ones considered themselves the spiritual descendants of the Western outlaw. They liked the attention they attracted. If the gangsters looked upon them with contempt, they returned the compliment with their own stiff-necked pride.

Alvin Karpis objected to being addressed as a hoodlum by J. Edgar Hoover. "I'm no hood," he said. "And I don't like being called a hood. I'm a thief." Then he explained the difference: "A thief is anybody who gets out and works for his living, like robbing a bank, or breaking into a place and stealing stuff, or kidnapping somebody. He really gives some effort to it. A hoodlum is a pretty lousy sort of scum. He works for gangsters and bumps off guys after they have been put on the spot. Why, after I'd made my rep, some of the Chicago Syndicate wanted me to work for them as a hood—you know, handling a machine gun. They offered me two hundred and fifty dollars a week and all the protection I needed. I was on the lam at the time and not able to work at my regular line. But I wouldn't consider it. 'I'm a thief,' I said, 'I'm no lousy hoodlum.' "

Karpis, Dillinger and others of their ilk would not have cared to work with the new type of killer who was coming on the scene. They were the gang killers who evolved to replace the shoot-'em-up boys of the Prohibition era. Murder, Inc., left a bloody record, but its founding was part of the more businesslike image the crime lords were seeking to establish. And its operation may have contributed to a lower crime rate among the captains and troops who served the Mafia.

There were numerous gang slayings between 1930 and 1940. "The killing, though, was not then and is not now done for fun, for passion or for robbery; it is solely for the preservation and improvement of the vast business interest: the rackets," Burton B. Turkus explained in his book *Murder, Inc.* (written with Sid Feder).

As an assistant district attorney in Brooklyn, Turkus, with the help of a handful of investigators, had singlehandedly cracked the execution arm of the Syndicate (Luciano's new confederation of mobs) in New York, and won convictions and death sentences for seven members, including Louis "Lepke" Buchalter, the only gang boss ever legally executed.

Although each family had its own killers, it was thought safer and more mobile to use an outside squad of experts. If there was a job (mostly, the killing of defectors) that needed doing in another city, word would go out and a team from the Extermination Department would be dispatched forthwith. They would be in and out of town before anyone was even aware that a job had been done.

Harry Strauss liked being known as the Beau Brummel of the Brownsville (hometown of Murder, Inc.) underworld. He was ambitious and worked hard to get ahead.

"Like a ballplayer, that's me," he would say. "I figure I get seasoning doing these jobs here. Somebody from one of the big mobs spots me. Then, up to the big leagues." He was so eager to advance that he volunteered for "contracts" and was credited with more than thirty murders in more than a dozen cities.

In addition to veteran assassins called "troops" and group leaders called "troop bosses," Murder, Inc. sponsored a group of apprentices called "punks" who did odd jobs like stealing cars for hits or disposing of bodies. Sometimes punks worked their way up into the higher echelons of the organization and became fully accredited troops.

The troops were particular about doing a nice clean job, making sure of the kill and leaving as few clues as possible. They used guns, ropes, and icepicks. Some victims were taken for gang-style rides; others were shot down on lonely streets. Quite a few were dropped into quicklime pits, some were buried alive or cremated.

The straw boss of the operation was Abe "Kid Twist" Reles and he became Turkus' star witness. In the first twelve days of "singing," he exhausted a battery of stenographers. His rapid-fire tattling filled twenty-five notebooks with names, places, facts, minute details, interesting sidelights, personal impressions of one murder after another.

"I can tell you about fifty guys that got hit; I was on the inside," he told Turkus at the beginning of his bloody aria.

Besides having a fantastic memory, he had a thorough understanding of the law of corroboration. Before turning informer, he had made a deal with Turkus' boss, Brooklyn District Attorney William O'Dwyer.

"I can make you the biggest man in the country," he told O'Dwyer. "But I've got to make a deal first."

"Name it," O'Dwyer said.

"I want to walk out clean."

O'Dwyer nodded. "We'll let you plead guilty to second degree murder, and ask the court for consideration for you."

Reles, who had personally executed a dozen contracts and had directed countless others, shook his head and pounded the desk. "Nothing doing," he said. "No plea to murder two, or any other kind of murder. I walk out clean and that's it."

"Listen, O'Dwyer said, "we've got enough stuff on you right now to send you to the chair."

Reles laughed. "You ain't got no corroboration. But I'm the guy who can tell you where to get it."

The deal was made.

Reles' confession shattered Murder, Inc. beyond repair. The first to fall under his verbal guillotine were Harry Strauss and Bugsy Goldstein. Next came Happy Maione and Dasher Abbandando. All four went to the chair. Lepke was next.

"We had connections," Reles explained. "It wasn't easy at first. But now we got an in with the Purple Mob, we work with Bugsy Siegel in California, and with Lepke and the troops he's got. We are with Charley Lucky. With the Jersey troops, too, and Chicago and Cleveland, Miami, New Orleans, Havana, Kansas City, Denver. Hell, everywhere."

"What was in it for you?" he was asked.

"Me and my partners was in shylocking, the restaurant business, the unions and strike business, the trucking business, the moving-van business, the garment industry—with Lepke, you know—crap games, slot machines, bookmaking, payrolls on a few bookies, some whorehouses."

Before his song ended, Reles gave the details to some eighty-five murders in Brooklyn, and admitted knowledge to hundreds of unsolved killings across the country, permitting police to clear up many old unsolved murders.

The underworld was in a panic. Elimination of witnesses, in and out of custody, became the first order of business. All were ordered to search their souls and come up with lists of eligible hits—the law of corroboration became the law of the jungle.

Bugsy Siegel was recalled from California and placed in charge of all executions. But everybody was issuing contracts. Sometimes a contract from Siegel for a lesser hoodlum coincided with that hoodlum's contract for a hireling. The confusion made for chaos and terror.

Gunmen roamed the streets in carloads like Gestapo agents, breaking down doors in the night to empty revolvers in the heads of whimpering victims. Lammisters huddled in dirty little rooms in strange cities, frantically trying to remember if they had ever overheard anything that might make ganglang nervous.

It was no longer a question of loyalty. The question now was whether a contract had already been issued. Soon terrified hoodlums were running to the law instead of for cover. The mob had overplayed its hand. Vicious killers like Allie Tick Tock, "Blue Jaw" Magoon and Sholem Bernstein sang right along with Reles, their eager voices blending in a farewell dirge for Lepke, Mendy Weiss, and Louis Capone.

In the course of Reles' confession, Turkus had interrupted to ask how he could have committed murder so casually. Reles countered with a question: "How did you feel when you tried your first law case?"

"I was rather nervous," Turkus admitted.

"And how about your second case?"

"It wasn't so bad, but I was still a little nervous."

"And after that?"

"Oh, after that, I was all right, I was used to it."

"You answered your own question," Reles replied. "It's the same with murder. I got used to it."

A big problem, Reles admitted, was disposing of bodies. Rivers and lakes were particularly bad. No matter how the corpses were weighted down, they always seemed to rise to the surface in a few weeks. Then the killers had tried fire, soaking the body with gasoline and touching a match to it. This was not foolproof either, since it required a completely deserted place.

The wave of reform that brought seven hoodlums to the death house in 1940 had begun early in 1935 with a campaign for law and order and the appointment of Thomas E. Dewey as a special prosecutor. Dewey went for the top man, Luciano, and paraded sixty-eight witnesses (forty prostitutes, twelve pimps and sixteen ordinary citizens—bellhops, maids, waiters, anyone who could testify to Luciano's movements and associates) to the stand. Luciano and eight accomplices were convicted on sixty-two counts each of extortion and racketeering. Luciano received the stiffest penalty: thirty to fifty years in prison.

The trial made Dewey governor of New York and nearly President of the United States. Turkus' prosecution of Murder, Inc. made O'Dwyer mayor of New York City. (Nine years later Dewey agreed to parole and exile Luciano to Italy, on the reported claim that the prisoner had made a contribution to the war effort.)

The postwar period brought some changes. The age of Capone and Murder, Inc. was past, and people tended to disbelieve the existence of organized crime, particularly anything as fanciful as the Mafia. When Senator Estes Kefauver took his Crime Investigating Committee on a tour of big cities in 1950 many citizens saw on television real hoodlums for the first time. The committee's report attested to the underworld's existence:

> There is a nation-wide crime syndicate known as the Mafia, whose tentacles are found in many large cities. It has international ramifications which appear most clearly in connection with the narcotics traffic. The domination of the Mafia is based fundamentally on "muscle" and "murder." The Mafia is a secret conspiracy against law and order which will ruthlessly eliminate anyone who stands in the way of its success in any criminal enterprise in which it is interested. It will destroy anyone who betrays its secrets. It will use any means available—political influence, bribery, intimidation, etc. to defeat any attempt on the part of law-enforcement to touch its top figures or interfere with its operations.

Members of a Senate subcommittee had this point brought home to them in 1963 when then Attorney General Robert F. Kennedy testified that the physical protection of witnesses who had cooperated with the Federal Government in organized crime cases "often required that those witnesses change their appearance, change their names, or even leave the country."

The Crime Commission Report concluded that a nation "unable to protect its friends from its enemies by means less extreme than obliterating their identities surely is being seriously challenged, if not threatened."

Yet many private citizens still deny the Mafia's existence,

and some in public life belittle the efforts of persons working toward its exposure and eradication. When *Look* magazine (September 23, 1969) accused San Francisco Mayor Joseph L. Alioto of being "enmeshed in a web of alliances with at least six leaders of La Cosa Nostra," the mayor took to television to deny the charges, stating in effect that he had been assured by top law enforcement officials that there was no such thing as *La Cosa Nostra* in California—an act of faith comparable to saying that there are no Birchers in Orange County.

Former Governor Pat Brown also took to television to affirm his faith in Alioto's integrity, going him one better: "Because a man is convicted of a few crimes does not mean he's a member of some secret crime organization . . . *Look* published this story solely to boost its circulation!"

All six men named in the story were high-level mafiosi, including Jimmy Lanza, identified by the Justice Department as the boss of the San Francisco family, and Jimmy "The Weasel" Fratianno, identified in 1957 before the California State Assembly Rackets Investigating Subcommittee by Captain James E. Hamilson, head of the Los Angeles Police Intelligence Unit, as "the chief executioner for the Mafia on the West Coast. I have heard as high as sixteen deaths attributed to him."

Fratianno's arrest record included rape, armed robbery, fraud, bookmaking—his most recent prison sentence, 1954 to 1960, was for extortion, and he was out on bail at this writing on a one-to-three year prison sentence, again for extortion.

Of course, none of this is relevant if one chooses to deny the Mafia's existence. After all, it does hover on fantasy that men would secretly join in concert to commit crimes that would endow them with immense wealth (President Nixon estimated crime's annual gross at $50 billion), vast political power, and godlike imperium over life and death.

Nevertheless, through the years certain events have called

attention to this probability. The "summit" crime conclave at Apalachin in 1957, where some seventy-odd Italians and Sicilians (from every corner of the nation—many with criminal records relating to the kind of offense associated with organized crime) were discovered enjoying a little barbecue on a nice Sunday afternoon, converted some doubters in certain police circles, but not J. Edgar Hoover—not then, at least. It took an attorney general with a brother in the White House to convince the director of the error of his stubbornness.

Robert Kennedy had great expertise in organized crime, much of it gained in the years he served as chief counsel for the Senate rackets (McClellan) committee. In 1959 he lashed out at the Justice Department and the FBI:

> The department still hasn't learned what it is dealing with. They're over there shuffling papers and handing out press releases. They have to do more investigating. They should use the FBI to find out who these racketeers are, whom they meet, where they go, what businesses they're in, how they operate . . . The FBI has to be ordered into this job.

One of Kennedy's first moves as Attorney General was to create the Organized Crime and Racketeering Section, a special group of crime fighters assigned exclusively to this problem and assisted by a reluctant FBI.

At the outset of the Valachi hearings in 1963, Kennedy assessed organized crime as "one of the biggest businesses in America," dealing in murder, gambling, narcotics, extortion, bribery, blackmail, prostitution, loan sharking, counterfeiting, hijacking bootlegging and particularly legitimate business.

"The racketeer is not someone dressed in a black shirt, white tie, and diamond stickpin, whose activities affect only a remote underworld circle. He is more likely to be outfitted in a gray flannel suit and his influence is more likely to be as far-reaching as that of an important industrialist." Despite increased law enforcement efforts, Kennedy said, "organized crime has not diminished, but has become an even more urgent national problem."

There were doubters even in his own organization. William Hundley, chief of the new section on organized crime and racketeering, told writer Peter Maas that "before Valachi came along, we had no tangible evidence that anything like this actually existed. He's the first to talk openly and specifically about the organization. In the past we've heard that so-and-so was a 'Syndicate man' and that was all. Frankly, I always thought it was a lot of hogwash."

Regardless of this peculiar resistance to face hard, cold facts in certain quarters, the government's viewpoint has changed drastically in the past nine years since Kennedy forced Hoover into the battle. To quote the director a few years later: "The FBI is dedicated to the destruction of the organized underworld. The battle is joined."

Whether the FBI can destroy organized crime remains to be seen. So far the progress has been the other way. Investment in legitimate business, presently the most active phase of the operation, is not a recent phenomenon. It has been in evolution a half-century, going back to the day when the hoodlum graduated from his role as a ward tough and the tool of political bosses (who in turn were tools of the robber barons) and became a bona fide gangster and the master of his own rackets. Today legitimate income is perhaps even greater than the return from rackets. The investigative problem is staggering.

"Look at it this way," an IRS official confided after examining a report on a suspected front corporation which had built a $30 million apartment complex on Chicago's Lake Shore Drive. "I'd venture to say it's impossible to stand on a street corner in any large city in this country and not be able to point at something they own. But when you talk of checking out a single front, you're talking about man-years, not man-hours—ten men, two to three years, and then what have we got? It's not a crime to invest in business, not even for the underworld's overworld. This overworld is so fantastic, so huge and complex, and so far ahead of us, we're lucky just to know how little we do know."

With billions to invest, mob fronts are forced to concentrate on quantity. In Miami Beach, according to Mayor Elliot Roosevelt, "the mob doesn't run this town, it owns it." The same applies, in varying degrees, nationwide.

In Tucson, a former Chicago paving contractor with close Mafia ties has built thousands of new homes and several retirement havens. Near Carlsbad, California, the former owners (oldtime Cleveland mobsters) of a popular Las Vegas hostelry, along with other notable businessmen, have built a $300 million residential playground described in brochures as the Riviera of the Pacific.

In Beverly Hills, California, a mob-owned bank channels money to fronts with a device called a "takeout letter" which does not become part of the loan file. Instead it is kept in the personal vault of the bank president, away from the prying eyes of Federal auditors.

Three hundred miles to the north, in San Jose, millionaire Joe Cerrito fronted his own enterprises (restaurants, a cheese company, auto agencies, a used car lot, vending machines, coin operated games, bakeries, orchards and dry-cleaning plants) in anonymity until the Justice Department identified him in 1967 as one of twenty-four national Mafia bosses.

"A study of its investments," the IRS official continued, "gives an insight into the flexibility of its power structure. I know of about eight or nine major investors, fronts, in Chicago who represent fairly prominent segments of the mob. Now, these people are connected with, I'd say, thousands —not directly certainly in all cases—of subfronts. They have their captains and lieutenants, who in turn have theirs, and so on down the line. One large corporation may have fronts from three or four big ones in Chicago, another from New Orleans, a half dozen from the New York-New Jersey area,

Miami, and from other places. They're all in this thing together. It's like Vegas—it's open to all accredited representatives.

"I know of one international hotel chain that has representatives from just about every significant family in the country, and some not so significant. I tell you, trying to knock them out of the box is like fighting a multi-headed snake with your bare hands. You may grab one or two heads, but the others will surely poison you."

The wave of gangland murders in the Greater Boston area in the mid-sixties was reminiscent of an earlier period. Chicago has seen over a thousand unsolved gangland slayings since Colosimo's elegant funeral. In Jackson Township, New Jersey, in March 1967, the FBI uncovered what they called a Cosa Nostra murder farm containing the hidden graves of two victims. An informant hinted that as many as twenty victims might have been buried there.

Harold "Kayo" Konisberg, convicted extortionist and Mafia soldier, admitted involvement in twenty-nine gang murders. He told agents that he carried out twelve of the Mafia contracts himself. He swore that all the victims had been buried on the farm. If they were gone, then someone had removed them. Four witnesses who had talked to police in Miami in 1967 were later murdered and dumped into surrounding bodies of water, one apparently while still alive. Gerald Covelli, a small-time hood who testified against two mafiosi in Chicago, later fled to Los Angeles with a new identity. However, on June 18, 1967, a time bomb planted under the driver's seat of his car exploded, killing him instantly.

The stories of violence are endless. But this should not surprise anyone. Murder, after all, is the only discipline available to the underworld. There are no prisons for wayward colleagues.

9 | Racial Violence, 1943-1969

World War II was in full swing. On battlefronts around the world, Americans of all races were fighting Fascism, but back home in America they were fighting and killing each other.

Los Angeles was filled with servicemen in June, 1943, plus many thousands of war workers. Then, as now, the city also had a large Mexican-American population. Trouble began between the servicemen and the Mexican-Americans as the result of rumor.

A group of eleven sailors got into an altercation with some Mexican youths on a street corner near the latter's home base. The sailors later claimed they were set upon by a gang of *pachucos* wearing zoot-suits. The fight didn't amount to much, but most of the sailors suffered cuts and bruises and no one was injured seriously.

Police were dispatched to the area but made no arrests. It wasn't long before rumors began to spread through nearby military bases. Zoot-suiters had had the nerve to attack United States sailors. The Navy's honor had to be avenged.

Two hundred sailors gathered for just that purpose. They hired twenty taxicabs and cruised through downtown Los Angeles looking for *pachucos*. A Mexican boy was spotted, and sailors poured out of the cabs and beat him insensible.

They set upon three more and injured them so badly they had to be hospitalized. The Shore Patrol arrested several servicemen but failed to stop the violence.

Then rumors of the rape of a sailor's wife and of the killing of a marine spread through camps and bases. The first attacks had been staged strictly by sailors but now marines and soldiers were urged to join the fray.

"SAILOR TASK FORCE HITS L.A. ZOOTERS! ZOOT-SUIT GANGSTERS FLEE FROM MIDDIES!" newspaper headlines shrieked with more enthusiasm than accuracy.

On June 5, a uniformed mob descended on the city and, before the day was over, more than forty-four Mexicans were in the hospital with serious injuries. Even more violent events followed on June 7 and 8. Rumors spread like wildfire, encouraged and embellished by the newspapers.

"ZOOT-SUIT CHIEFS GIRDING FOR WAR ON NAVY!" read one headline while another took the opposite tack: "ZOOT-SUITERS LEARN LESSON IN FIGHT WITH SERVICEMEN."

Downtown Los Angeles was taken over by the serviceman mob, swollen now by inflamed civilians, that swarmed through the streets taking vengeance for imagined wrongs. They beat and mauled every boy or man they found wearing a zoot-suit; they broke into theaters and dragged out those who looked to be of Mexican descent, stripping them of their clothes and pounding them until they lay bleeding on the sidewalks. They stopped streetcars, boarded them and hauled off anyone with a dark complexion. By this time, it didn't matter if the person seemed Mexican or not. Negroes and Filipinos were given the same treatment. Through it all, crowds of citizens cheered and laughed to show their appreciation.

In almost every instance, the police stood by and watched until the rioters had finished their work, and then arrested . . . the victims. The Los Angeles City Council acted quickly, adopting a resolution declaring that the wearing of zoot-suits in the city was a misdemeanor.

With the city authorities either unable or unwilling to act, the military moved in. Los Angeles was declared off limits and servicemen were confined to their bases. Naval personnel as far away as San Diego, where large numbers of sailors had been gathering for a march on Los Angeles, were forbidden to go north on leave. That ended the rioting on the West Coast, but a more serious confrontation was building up in the Middle West.

Detroit had been on the verge of an outbreak for months. Lured by the prospect of work in the motor capital's war industries, approximately 50,000 Negroes and even more Southern whites had poured into the city. A climate of hate grew up that was carefully nurtured by spokesmen for pro-Nazi and racists groups. Gerald L. K. Smith, Frank J. Norris, and Father Coughlin had all been active in and around the city.

John Roy Carlson, a writer who infiltrated many of these groups during the war period, tells in his book, *Under Cover,* of contacts with various leaders. He quotes one labor organizer, identified as Tony, who was attempting to win workers away from the CIO and into a Fascist-front group called the National Workers League:

> We don't need many guys. We just send one or two in a shop . . . Our men talk to the right kind of a guy, den dis man gets a friend to come in with him . . . You begins your woik by talking against the Jews and the nigger. The Jew got us into the war. You tell 'em that. The Jew is keeping labor down by controlling the money. It's the Jew who hires niggers and gives them low wages. There is angles, see; there is angles. When a guy in a shop gets up and talks against the kikes, and some other guy in the shop don't like it, we call on this second guy . . . There is angles. You gotta loin 'em. You ties in the niggers with the

Jew, den you call the Jews Communists. That gets 'em.
Catch on, kid?

In Carlson's opinion the city was being deliberately set on
fire. He felt that Hitler would not overlook the key industrial
city of the United States in his quest to rule the world.
Every resource the Nazis could spare, whether money or
brain power, was being used in Detroit to accomplish one
purpose—to harm the American war effort by stirring up
trouble in the ranks of labor.

One need not agree that Adolf Hitler had taken a personal
interest in stirring up racial hatred in Detroit to believe that
the activities of racist and pro-Fascist groups helped to increase the tensions. Carlson was writing about events that
preceded the riot but as he left the city he sensed it coming:
"I could not stifle the feeling that Detroit was dynamite."

The Federal Government was also aware that Detroit was
like a keg of dynamite waiting to explode. Report 109 of
the Office of War Information's bureau of intelligence spoke
of the situation on March 15, 1943:

> In Detroit, the situation is not good. Unless it is carefully
> handled you can have trouble there any day, and when it
> bursts out it will require harsh treatment, not in subduing
> the Negroes, but the whites.

The trouble came three months and five days later, on
June 20, 1943. It started on a hot, sticky day (as so many
riots do). The heat had sent thousands of people to Belle
Isle, a park island in the Detroit River. Crowds poured across
the bridge from the city on one side and from Grand Boule-
vard on the other. Among the crowds were a considerable
number of Negroes, and the racial tension that had been
building for so long erupted first in an argument and then
a fist fight between a white man and a Negro on the bridge.
The conflict spread to others of both races but order was
restored by the police before it got too serious. Then a group

of Negro teen-agers attacked several white men and trouble flared anew.

Rumor did the rest. In the white sections, a rumor circulated that a white woman had been raped on the park bridge by a Negro. As the story spread, it grew in scope. The next version said she had been killed after being raped. The one after that indicated she had been carrying a baby, and her Negro assailant had thrown the baby into the river before attacking the mother and then tossing her after the child.

By the time the story reached the tough, working-class neighborhoods of Detroit, two white women who had been raped and a least that many babies had had their heads smashed on the bridge's railing before being tossed into the river.

From bar to bar, from pool hall to pool hall, the rumors flew and in their wake left a rising tide of hate, punctuated by a fierce desire for revenge. Shirt-sleeved men carrying pool cues, clubs, and bottles poured into the streets and headed toward Belle Isle.

In the meantime, in Paradise Valley, one of the two packed Negro districts, rumors were also being spread. In a smoky nightclub where blazing jazz almost drowned out thought, there was a sudden silence when a Negro youth grabbed up a microphone and yelled into it, "Come on and take care of a bunch of whites who have killed a colored woman and her baby at Belle Isle Park!"

Until that moment no one had been killed or even seriously injured but, as both sides heard the same inflammatory rumor, real violence broke out. Paradise Valley erupted. Negroes poured into the streets with makeshift weapons. They stoned passing cars that carried whites and burned white-owned business establishments.

On Belle Isle mass fighting was going on, with two hundred white sailors joining in. Negroes swarming out from Paradise Valley met mobs surging from the white working-class neighborhoods. By midnight a dozen sections of the city were torn by looting and fighting. White mobs laid in wait outside movie houses and ambushed Negroes as they came out. When Negroes pleaded with police for protection, they were told, "See the chief!"

Negroes were beaten to death in the streets while white women and children stood by and cheered. Other blacks were shot down by police while attempting to defend themselves. Cars were burned, sometimes with the owner still inside. It is interesting to note that the only neighborhoods in the central city that remained calm were those that were integrated.

Rioting continued all through the next day with whites hunting down and beating any Negro they came across. Toward evening four white teen-agers shot and killed a middle-aged Negro, Moses Kiska, "because we didn't have anything to do." Most of the twenty-five Negro fatalities, however, were at the hands of the police. While they used tear gas and rubber truncheons against white rioters, they employed revolvers, shotguns, and machine guns against Negroes.

Because the police were actually part of the riot, Federal troops were sent into the city. The troops behaved well, as did most of the personnel who accompanied them. One soldier when asked why he and his buddies were protecting the blacks is quoted by J. W. Schulte Nordholt as saying, "I'm helping the Negroes because we had a Negro with us [in the war] who saved a lot of our lives."

Order was restored and the damage assessed. Nine whites and twenty-five Negroes were dead, and the value of property destroyed ran into several hundreds of thousands of dollars, though in some quarters estimates ran as high as two million. Of course, there was no way of calculating the legacy of fear and hate that became part of the city's heritage.

The blame for the whole bloody affair was placed completely on the Negroes. The mayor announced that he was "rapidly losing patience with those Negro leaders who insisted that their people did not and will not trust policemen and the Police Department."

"After what happened," Mayor Jeffries continued, "I am certain that some of these leaders are more vocal in their caustic criticism of the Police Department than they are in educating their own people to their responsibilities as citizens."

The reactions of others were similar. One person said that Mrs. Roosevelt was to blame because "she backs up the colored race all over the South."

"Factory jobs," said another. "You put too many Negroes close to whites and the whites don't like it."

"Northerners don't understand the Negro," Southerners stated.

"I think they've got the scum of the country here, and neither one likes the smell of the other," a Detroiter told a Gallup Poll representative.

There was yet another riot in 1943. This time Harlem was the scene of the trouble. It started when a white policeman tried to arrest a Negro woman. A black soldier came to the woman's defense, and before long rioting became general. But this was no person-to-person clash with whites. Cars were stoned and set on fire and white-owned stores were looted. Bricks were thrown at police, but the major emphasis was on looting and burning. Six persons were killed, mostly victims of police gunfire, and five hundred were injured. A hundred rioters were jailed.

The post-war years saw fresh racial violence. In August, 1947, a disabled Negro veteran and music student named Lloyd Curtis Jones was sitting with a group of friends at the Columbus Circle entrance to Central Park in New York City. A police officer, Patrolman Francis Le Maire, objected to their impromptu musicale and ordered them to "move on." He emphasized his order by poking Jones in the stomach with his nightstick. The disabled veteran objected and was promptly struck over the head with such force that the nightstick shattered. Jones threw up his arms to ward off further blows, and Le Maire then drew his gun and fired three bullets into the Negro's stomach, wounding him seriously. Le Maire was cleared of any blame in the case.

In Rochester, New York, in November of the same year, there was another killing. Roland T. Price, a Negro veteran, complained that he had been short-changed by the cashier of a restaurant. The manager, who had strongly objected to serving Price in the first place, called the police. The officers who answered the call sided with the manager and began to push Price around. When he protested, the officers shot and killed him. They claimed he had attempted to draw a gun, but it was later revealed that Price had been unarmed. This did not prevent the all-white coroner's jury from exonerating the killers.

In June of 1948, a 15-year-old Negro boy, Leon Moseley, was brutally manhandled and then shot to death by two white police officers. His crime was driving without lights.

In August, 1949, a mob of two thousand whites besieged the house of a Negro family who had moved into a white neighborhood. Windows were broken and attempts made to burn the house down. The family moved.

Racial violence in the South was more widespread and far more bloody. Isaac Woodward had served his country in the Navy for four years, fifteen months of which had been spent aboard ship in the Pacific war zone. He came home and was discharged in Georgia. Catching a bus for his home in South Carolina, Woodward got into an argument with the bus driver for refusing to comply with the order, "Go to the back of the bus."

The driver called police. Woodward was arrested and locked up in the local jail. There he was beaten and finally blinded by having a rubber truncheon thrust into one eye and then the other. The guard who committed the barbaric act was not arrested because he had acted "in self-defense."

The postwar period also saw the third revival of the Ku

Klux Klan. A nationwide phenomenon in the twenties, the Klan had died because of its own bestialities and because of scandals and thievery among its leadership. The third coming of the Klan immediately added to the quota of mayhem in the South.

Fifteen hooded Klansmen headed by "Parson" Jack Johnston pushed their way into a Phenix City, Alabama courtroom and staged a demonstration in the jury box. A Klan mob of 189 burned a 10-foot cross on the lawn of the Emmanuel County Courthouse while Grand Dragon Green attacked President Truman and warned his listeners that integration wouldn't end "at the bedroom door." As always the preoccupation of the white racist with sex in regard to the Negro came through. "We rededicate our lives to the protection of white womanhood."

A hooded group of Klansmen attacked the home of the one-armed mayor of Iron City, Georgia. A long-time Klan opponent, C. L. Drake filled so many of the Klansmen with buckshot that they gave up their plot to kidnap him because he had criticized Governor Herman Talmadge.

On the morning of February 25, 1946, in Columbia, Tennessee, James C. Stephenson, a 19-year-old Negro veteran of the Navy, went with his mother to pick up a radio from a repair shop. Mrs. Stephenson paid the $13.00 bill, then discovered that the radio still wasn't working.

"Thirteen dollars and the radio not playing," Mrs. Stephenson said.

The white repair man, William Fleming, considered this an insult and charged from behind his counter and started shoving the Stephensons out of the shop. He was joined by one of his workers who attacked Jones from behind as Fleming kicked Mrs. Stephenson and knocked her down. The young veteran broke away from his attacker to rescue his mother and knocked Fleming through his plate glass window.

A grocer dashed from a neighboring store, yelling the white Southerner's battle cry. "Kill the black bastards!"

A crowd gathered quickly and joined the chorus. "Lynch them! Lynch them!"

Policemen arrived to protect the white mob from their Negro assailants. One of the representatives of law and order raised his billy club to strike James Stephenson. His mother cried out, "Don't hit my boy!"

The officer complied with her request and beat her over the head instead. The Stephensons were arrested and taken before a local judge.

"Were you fighting?" the judge demanded, and when the Stephensons attempted to explain, brushed their words aside and said, "Guilty. Fifty dollars."

A warrant was then sworn out by C. Hayes Denton, a local magistrate, charging the Stephensons with "attempting to commit murder by use of a dangerous instrument, to-wit, pieces of glass," and bail was set at $3,500 each.

A mob gathered outside the jail, and the sheriff hastily phoned a Negro businessman and told him to make bond and get the mother and son out or they'd be lynched. Julius Blair did as instructed and managed to spirit the Stephensons out of town.

But the mob was still milling around the jail. About a hundred men armed with rifles, shotguns and pistols spent the time drinking and talking, trying to work up enough courage to invade the Negro section, called Mink Slide, and "get those niggers." But the mob really wasn't ready for that in spite of the amount of whisky consumed when they heard rumors that Negro war veterans armed with German and Japanese trophy guns were preparing to meet any attack.

In Mink Slide, Negro leaders were urging people to remain inside and avoid trouble. The war veterans had only a few shotguns, a couple of target rifles and a few pistols. At nightfall, they blacked out Mink Slide, locking their doors and pulling down the shades. The streets were deserted except for an occasional Negro patrol car, the children were hidden and the whole area was silent and tense.

Shortly after dark, carloads of whites began sporadic raids into the outskirts of Mink Slide, firing at random into the unlighted buildings. When a police car hurried to the scene, it was mistaken for one of the raider cars since it was without distinguishing markings. A shotgun let loose a blast and peppered the policemen with bird shot. The car turned and went back to town, and the mayor called Nashville and asked for the National Guard.

Governor McCord dispatched five hundred heavily armed guardsmen, including a machine gun company, to Columbia. In command was Brigadier General Jacob Dickinson. The troops were joined by seventy-five highway patrolmen under the command of Lynn Bomar, state director of public safety.

Ignoring the white mob that was gathered for another attack on Mink Slide, General Dickinson formed a cordon around Mink Slide and announced to the press, "The nigra rebels are surrounded."

At dawn the invasion of Mink Slide began. State highway patrolmen armed with tommy-guns, automatic rifles, and carbines moved in first, firing into houses as they went. The steel-helmeted militia followed with fixed bayonets. The homes of Negroes were riddled with countless rounds of ammunition.

The state director of public safety took personal charge as police broke into Negro-owned shops and restaurants, wrecking furniture and hurling supplies and equipment into the streets. Not content with that, they shattered mirrors, windows, and pictures, and smashed cash registers, helping themselves to the money therein. Then they invaded private residences, breaking down the doors and hustling the people into the street.

Every man, woman, and child in Mink Slide was driven outside, beaten with rifle butts and billy clubs and made to stand with their hands over their heads. It was at this point that the first fatality occurred: a Negro man resisted and was shot and killed by a blast of submachine-gun fire.

In a long procession, Negroes were marched through the streets of the city like prisoners of war and lodged in the town jail and other makeshift places of imprisonment.

Governor McCord arrived, conferred with city authorities and decided to ignore publicly that there had been an attempted lynching or an unprovoked attack on Mink Slide by white gunmen. He simply announced that "an armed Negro uprising" had been forestalled in the nick of time by the judicious use of force.

The Columbia *Daily Herald* agreed with him, making its position clear in an editorial:

> The Negro has not a chance of gaining supremacy over a sovereign people, and the sooner the better elements of the Negro race realize this the better off the race will be . . .

With complete disregard for facts, the national press picked up the story and headlined it across the country as a "Negro Riot" or "Negro Rebellion."

Seventy of the Negroes rounded up were charged with various crimes, mostly an attempt to commit murder. Bail was set at $5,000 each, a total of $350,000 which the Negro community couldn't possibly raise.

Inside the jail, a deliberately terroristic process of obtaining confessions was begun. One at a time the prisoners were led down corridors lined with armed men and pushed into an empty room for interrogation. They were told that if they talked and revealed details of the revolutionary plot, they would be treated leniently. Third-degree methods, bribery, and threats all proved useless. There was nothing to confess and no one did.

On February 28, more vigorous methods were used to produce confessions. William Gordon, James Johnson, and Napoleon Stewart were taken into the interrogation room together and worked over for several hours. When they still failed to give "satisfactory answers," they were taken into another office by deputy sheriffs and state troopers.

A few minutes later there was a burst of machine-gun fire and screams.

Gordon and Johnson were carried out, bodies riddled by bullets, bleeding to death. They were taken to King's Daughters Hospital where blood plasma was administered but were refused admission or further treatment because this was a "white only hospital." They died as they were being transported to Nashville.

An all-white grand jury investigated the case for two months but could find "no violation of civil rights," and said the officers acted in self-defense. Any talk of attempted lynching or attacks by whites on Mink Slide was blamed on "inflammatory articles in the Communist press . . ."

The violence at Columbia had been official, but the unofficial kind was also prevalent.

A white taxi driver was stabbed to death in Greenville, South Carolina, and a Negro youth, Willie Earle, was arrested and charged with the crime. *Life* reported:

> Early next morning, a lynch mob driving cabs took Earle from the jail at nearby Pickens, beat him, kicked him, pounded him with the butt of a shotgun, then stabbed him five times, gouged a huge piece of flesh from his thigh and finally blew off most of his head with three blasts from the shotgun.

Twenty-six of the lynch mob confessed and were tried in an atmosphere that "frequently took on the informal aspect of a family picnic," and the verdict was "not guilty."

R. C. Hunt, who had shot off the victim's head, threw a party to celebrate, saying, "Justice has been done on both sides."

Another of the lynch mob, Duran Keenan, said, "It's the best thing that ever happened to this country."

In February, 1947, a Negro minister, Reverend A. C. Epps, was warned by whites to move out of a white neighborhood. Two weeks later his home was bombed and wrecked. The perpetrators of the outrage were seen joking with the police who were supposedly investigating the bombing.

At Sardis, Georgia, in May, a 23-year-old Negro veteran studying at Temple University under the GI Bill was shot to death by a white man whom he failed to address as "sir." The matter was considered too trivial to merit a trial.

An 83-year-old Negro, William Brown, was caught hunting squirrels near Lettworth, Louisiana, in July. The game warden took Brown to the edge of the woods and shot him in the head. Then he went to a nearby white sharecropper and told him, "I just shot a nigger; let his folks know."

The Klan had a busy year in 1951. In Springdale, Alabama, the Exalted Cyclops of the local KKK den, Joe Pritchett, led a group of his terrorists in a particularly brutal attack. Because as Pritchett later said, "We just wanted some nigger at random," they dragged Judge Aaron, a housepainter, from his girl's front porch and took him to a deserted shack. There they castrated him with razor blades and then poured turpentine into the wound.

The Klan got more than they bargained for when they decided to terrorize a group of Lumbee Indians in Robeson County, North Carolina. The Indians got word of the Klan's intentions and struck first. While a group of seventy-five armed Kluxers were burning a twelve-foot cross, they suddenly found themselves surrounded by three hundred and fifty armed and war-whooping Lumbees. The Indians shot out the electric lights that had been rigged up for the gathering, peppered the Klan cars with gunfire and slashed tires, ripped apart the KKK microphones and public address system and scattered the hooded heroes into the underbrush. Then they proudly carried off the white Klan banner with its red letters KKK to hang in their recreation room at the reservation. Considerable self-restraint on the part of the Lumbees saved the scalps of the Klansmen from joining the captured banner.

Meanwhile, the civil rights movement was beginning in the

South, and the reaction to it was an increase in violence. Medgar Evers, 37-year-old leader of the Mississippi Negro civil rights drive, was shot down by a hidden gunman as he stepped from his car in the driveway of his Jackson home. Evers was hit in the back by a .30 caliber bullet, and the rifle that fired it was found in a honeysuckle thicket near the scene. There were fingerprints on the gun but Jackson police were unable to find the killer.

The FBI arrested 42-year-old Byron de la Beckwith, a member of the Mississippi White Citizens Council. Beckwith was tried twice for the murder but won mistrials in both instances when the jury failed to agree on a verdict.

In 1967, Beckwith decided to translate his popularity over the killing into political office. He said, "In announcing my candidacy for the office of lieutenant governor I wish to express my heartfelt gratitude to the fine Christian people of Mississippi for the manner in which they have sustained and sheltered me in times past. It is as a popular candidate that I will campaign, and it is as a popular official that I will serve. The people of Mississippi will determine their proper choice."

Denise McNair, 11 years old, and Carol Robertson, Cynthia Wesley and Addie Collins, all 14, died on Sunday, September 15, 1963, when the 15th Avenue Baptist Church in Birmingham, Alabama, was bombed during Sunday School. Eighteen others were injured by the blast. One girl, Sarah Jean Collins, 12, was almost totally blinded.

When angry Negroes poured into the streets after the bombing, two more were killed by police, one of them a 16-year-old boy. That night a 9-year-old Negro boy was murdered by two white youths riding on a motor scooter. One of the three men arrested by state police in this case was convicted on a misdemeanor charge for possession of dynamite. He was sentenced to six months in jail and fined $100.

Racial strife flared in Jacksonville, Florida, on March 2, 1964, after attempts to integrate bars and restaurants. Ten gasoline bombs exploded in hotels and bars in the Negro section, and Mrs. Johnnie Mae Chappell, a 36-year-old Negro woman, was shot and killed as she walked along US 1, north of the city. The shots came from a passing automobile. A white man was shot in front of a bar and another was tied to a tree and slashed with razors as the blacks struck back.

Mayor Burns announced on the radio that no more attempts at integration would be tolerated since Negroes had no right to "force their presence at certain hotels, restaurants and other businesses." He neglected to mention Mrs. Chappell's murder or the ten fire bombs.

Three civil rights workers disappeared on June 21, 1964, outside Philadelphia, Mississippi. Two were young white men from New York—Michael Schwerner and Andrew Goodman —and the third was a Negro youth, James Chaney, from Meridian, Mississippi. Although it was later learned that they had been detained illegally by deputy sheriffs and then turned over to a mob that murdered them and hid the bodies on a nearby farm, local officials at first professed to believe that nothing had happened to the young men and insinuated they had gone into hiding or left the state.

Local police and state officers refused to cooperate with the FBI. In one instance, FBI agents dragging a river for the bodies reported that state highway patrolmen stood on the river bank laughing and shouting taunts at them.

"If you want to find that damn nigger, just float a relief check out there," one of them yelled. "That black bastard will reach up and grab it."

William Bradford Huie characterized the attitude of white Mississippi for the *New York Herald Tribune:* "It was all a hoax . . . And, if there had been a crime, it wasn't really a crime because the victims were the guilty parties: They had 'asked for it.'"

Eventually, eighteen men, including the sheriff, one of his deputies and a minister associated with the KKK were arrested for the murders as the result of an intensive investigation by the FBI. But US Commissioner Esther Carter, a

210

politically appointed, Mississippi-born spinster without any legal training, freed the defendants without a hearing. The State of Mississippi refused to indict them, but a Federal grand jury did bring indictments under an 1870 law against the infringement of civil rights.

Klan gunmen murdered Mrs. Viola Liuzzo, a white Detroit housewife, on March 25, 1965, as she helped drive Negro and white marchers from the scene of the Selma-to-Montgomery civil rights march. Despite the fact that an FBI informer and the young Negro man who was riding with Mrs. Liuzzo when she was killed gave eye-witness testimony, and Alabama Attorney General Flowers prosecuted the case with vigor, a Lowndes County jury freed the accused killers.

Later jury members expressed themselves as shocked and concerned over the reaction to their verdict throughout the country and blamed it on the Communist-inspired Negro revolution that was in the making.

"If Mrs. Liuzzo hadn't been down here where she had no business being, doing something she shouldn't have been doing, she wouldn't have been killed," said Lewis H. McCurdy, foreman of the jury and former member of the White Citizens Council.

Attempts to integrate schools in the South led to several incidents of violence. In Little Rock, Arkansas, Governor Orville Faubus engraved his name forever in the annals of bigotry when he blocked school integration by use of the National Guard and by closing the schools. Wild rioting broke out at the University of Mississippi when James Meredith was admitted as a law student. Mobs of students and outsiders repeatedly attacked Federal marshals, and General Edwin A. Walker called for armed volunteers from all over the country to flock to Mississippi to aid Governor Barnett in resisting integration. The mob killed two bystanders, one a French newsman, and was not dispersed until Federal troops arrived on the scene.

The Montgomery bus boycott led to the rise of the late Reverend Martin Luther King, Jr. and to the development of his nonviolent philosophy, based on tenets espoused by Mahatma Gandhi. Despite King's peaceful beliefs, he and his followers were often the victims of mayhem. King's home was bombed, and so were those of his associate, Reverend Ralph Abernathy, and of King's brother. Stoned, arrested, and manhandled, King was in constant danger of his life.

His closest brush with death in those early years came while he was on tour in the North to publicize his book *Stride Toward Freedom*. The incident occurred in Blumstein's department store in Harlem on September 20, 1958.

Throughout his trip King had been under attack by black nationalists. He was called an "Uncle Tom" and contemptuously referred to as "d'Lawd" by fanatics. Even this early in his career, they had spotted King as one of the few individuals who was really working to bind up the nation's wounds rather than seeking to destroy it. Earlier that September day, King had denounced black nationalists to their faces and had been booed when he stated, "Black supremacy is as bad as white supremacy."

Busily autographing copies of *Stride Toward Freedom*, shaking hands and chatting with customers, King did not notice the dark-skinned, heavy-set woman with dangling gold earrings as she pushed her way rudely to the front of the line.

"Are you Martin Luther King?" she demanded when she was face to face with him.

"Yes, I am," King said, smiling at her.

The woman burst into a stream of curses, drew an eight-inch Japanese letter opener from her dress and plunged it into his chest. Then she beat at him with her fists, screeching incoherently. She was pulled away by the people in line behind her. King was rushed to the hospital with the letter opener still in his chest. Doctors told him later that the blade had been within a few millimeters of the aorta. A sneeze, a cough, a sudden twist of the body could have punctured that artery and brought about his death.

On his release from the hospital, King made a prophetic statement concerning death and violence in America. Seated in a wheelchair, he spoke to a few friends and well-wishers on September 30, 1958:

"The pathetic aspect of this experience is not the injury to one individual. It demonstrates that a climate of hatred and bitterness so permeates areas of our nation that inevitably deeds of extreme violence must erupt. Today it was I. Tomorrow it could be another leader or any man, woman or child who will be the victim of lawlessness and brutality."

During the years of civil rights struggle in the South, frustrations had been building among ghetto dwellers in the North and West. These frustrations began to produce trouble in the summer of 1964. On July 16, in New York City, several young Negroes returning home from summer school classes became involved in an altercation with a white building superintendent. When an off-duty police lieutenant intervened, one of the boys, a 15-year-old, allegedly attacked him with a knife. The officer shot and killed the boy.

Almost at once a crowd of black teen-agers gathered and began smashing store windows and shouting taunts at police. Reinforcements were needed before order could be restored.

The following day agitators, including those of the Marxist-Leninist Progressive Labor Party, were active in the area passing out inflammatory leaflets that charged the police with brutality.

On July 18, a rally called by CORE to protest the murder of civil rights workers in Mississippi was converted into a march of protest against alleged police brutality in Harlem. When the crowd reached the precinct station, there was a clash with police; one marcher was killed and twelve officers and nineteen marchers injured.

For the next several days, Harlem in Manhattan and Bedford Stuyvesant in Brooklyn were swept by rioting. Molotov cocktails were thrown into stores owned by whites. Policemen were pelted with bricks and stones, and fired their revolvers in return. Thousands of dollars worth of damage and scores of injuries were reported.

A week later rioting erupted in Rochester when police tried to arrest an intoxicated Negro youth at a street dance. The trouble lasted for two days and resulted in the National Guard being summoned. During the next two weeks there were disturbances in three other New Jersey cities—Jersey City, Elizabeth and Patterson. Minor violence occurred in Chicago and Philadelphia following clashes between police and Negroes.

On August 11, 1965, events in Watts, California, set the pattern for riots over the next several years. As usual the riot was touched off by what should have been a minor incident. A highway patrol car stopped two young Negro men for speeding. A crowd gathered and was at first peaceful, listening with amusement to the half-jovial exchange between the officers and the young men, who had been drinking but apparently weren't drunk.

Then several misunderstandings resulted when the mother of the young men, Rena Frye, arrived on the scene. Additional officers had also arrived, and the crowd became restless. When all the Fryes were arrested with what the bystanders claimed was unnecessary brutality, there was open defiance. The arrest of a young lady barber, Joyce Anne Gaines, incensed the crowd even more. Accused of spitting on a police officer, she was still wearing her barber's smock when taken into custody.

The crowd mistook the smock for a maternity dress and rumors spread that a pregnant "soul sister" had been arrested and was being brutalized by police. A rain of stones and bottles was soon falling on police in the area. They reacted slowly, first withdrawing from the area and then returning in full force. By that time a near insurrection was under way.

Crowds of Negro youths began bombarding passing white motorists with rocks along Imperial Highway and other arterial routes running through the area. Negro social workers and ministers who tried to warn away incoming whites were stopped by police.

When a group of community leaders set up road blocks in an attempt to save whites from violence, police insisted they be removed because they constituted a traffic hazard. Dozens of unsuspecting motorists ventured into the riot area and were attacked. Some cars were burned and several whites were badly beaten by young blacks before being rescued by older Negroes and sheltered in their homes or taken out of the area.

The rioting spread and attention was focused on white-owned businesses. Grocery stores, liquor stores, and pawn shops were looted and burned. Fire engines, answering alarms, were pelted with rocks and fire hoses were cut.

In one fantastic incident, a mob that had been harassing firemen as they tried to put out a blaze suddenly rushed to their aid when they were trapped by falling walls. In the space of a few seconds they turned from throwing stones to tearing at the smoldering debris with their bare hands to rescue the men they had been tormenting.

The behavior of city officials left much to be desired. Mayor Sam Yorty had spent much of his first term in office embroiled in fights with the City Council and had ignored all warnings that trouble was brewing in Watts, including one from the Civil Rights Commission. Once the rioting began, Yorty's actions were even less helpful and were described by *Newsweek* as "curiously episodic throughout the disorders."

After the rioting was over, *Newsweek* pointed out, Yorty "blamed, in turn, the state police (for the arrest that triggered the riot), the Communists (for agitating over police

215

brutality) and poverty chief Sargent Shriver (for holding up the city's anti-poverty money)." Still later, Yorty was to blame then-Governor Pat Brown for being on vacation out of the state when the riot occurred and the local Negro leaders for not being in closer contact with the people of Watts.

Los Angeles Police Chief William Parker, though an honest and efficient officer in many ways, had long been at odds with the Negro community. He had done away with a hopeful attempt at police-community understanding when he became chief. He now reacted typically. "One person threw a rock . . . then, like monkeys in a zoo, others started throwing rocks."

The National Guard was finally ordered in by Lieutenant Governor Glenn Anderson and order was restored. The guard was inexperienced and in a few instances listened to the urging of local police and used their guns more freely than guard officers thought necessary. In several accidental shootings innocent motorists or bystanders were killed. On the whole, however, the guard behaved well and its arrival was welcomed by a large majority of the black community.

Thirty-six hours after the guard arrived, the trouble had terminated. The riot proved to be extremely costly—the worst, in fact, since the Detroit riot of 1943. Thirty-six people died, 1,032 were injured, and 3,952 were arrested. Property damage was estimated at more than $40 million. Another brief flare-up in Watts the following year resulted in the loss of three lives, including two whites.

Chicago's turn came in July, 1966, and was triggered by an even more trivial incident than that which had precipitated the trouble in Watts. Again the weather was sweltering, and a Negro youth turned on fire hydrants so children could play in the water and cool off. When policemen turned off the hydrants, the entire West Side exploded. The few dollars saved in the city's water bill resulted in three deaths, millions of dollars in property loss and many injuries and arrests.

The conditions under which the 350,000 Negroes of Chicago's West Side live are revealed in a story told to D. J. R. Bruckner, chief of the Los Angeles *Times* Chicago bureau, and carried in the July 24, 1966, issue of that paper:

> At 3 a.m. July 14, in the midst of the riot, a reporter was attacked by a large rat on a West Side street corner. Two teen-aged Negro boys, returning, they said, from a riot foray, beat off this beast with a baseball bat and a board, explaining they were happy enough to fight rats which were, on the whole, worse than white newsmen. . . . rats are the manifest evidence of the inhumanity out there. They are everywhere, along with the debris of demolished buildings, the dirt in the streets, the cheap bars. People grow up among the rats and live with them.

In Chicago, too, the mayor accepted no blame for the rioting but sought to lay it on the doorstep of those who were trying to alleviate the problems that caused it.

On Friday, July 15, Mayor Richard J. Daley accused persons working with Dr. Martin Luther King, Jr. and the Southern Christian Leadership Conference of "training youths in the methods and aims of violence."

Dr. King said the mayor's charges were "false and absurd." King explained that his staff had been exhibiting films of the Watts riot to show the adverse effects of violence and that Dr. James Bevel had been "lecturing on violence throughout the Negro ghetto, asking persons not to use violence, but to rely on Dr. King's nonviolent movement."

King went into the streets in an effort to calm the rioters but found his influence and doctrine meant little. Young toughs laughed at his pleas and one youth labeled him a "hit-and-run messiah."

Newspapers accused King of losing prestige, and stated that Black Power advocates were winning the people to their views. Leaders on both sides suggested King get out of Chicago, and he did leave. In a few weeks he was back to lead a series of open-housing marches that were resisted by mobs

217

of swastika-waving hoodlums. The following are typical of the shouts and taunts hurled at King's cohorts:

"Two, four, six, eight! We don't want to integrate!"

"I wish I were an Alabama trooper, that is really what I'd like to be; for if I were an Alabama trooper; then I could kill a nigger legally!"

A hail of rocks, bottles, and firecrackers fell on the marching column as the mob yelled its hate. "Kill the nigger-loving cops! Wallace for President!"

"Did you see those nuns?" a woman asked. "Did you see the nuns marching with the niggers? I was never so shocked. They should have hit them with rocks . . . and I'm a good Catholic."

Some of the marchers were hit by rocks. Albert C. Raby was hit by four bricks and fell to his knees. On August 6, King himself was struck by a rock almost the instant he got out of his car in Marquette Park. Raby was hit again and so was Franciscan nun, Sister Mary Angelica.

The mob was made up mostly of Polish-Lithuanian-Irish ethnic groups and they filled the air with their hate.

"You can buy guns cheap in Indiana," a girl told those around her. "After you use them, throw them away—the police will never tie you to them."

"This is a terrible thing," Dr. King said later. "I have been in the civil rights movement for many years all through the South, but I have never seen—not in Alabama or Louisiana—mobs as hostile and hateful as this crowd."

Teen-agers mounted on motorcycles decorated with Confederate flags and anti-Negro slogans roared around the fringes of the march. THE ONLY WAY TO STOP NIGGERS IS TO EXTERMINATE THEM, read one sign. Another said, GET RED KING OUT OF HERE.

Dr. King said, "We intended to go over there and bring the evil out into the open and it came out in the open. We shall march again . . . we shall keep marching until we find justice in this city."

218

On August 15, there were three marches and 3,000 whites attended a Nazi-organized meeting where middle-aged white women screamed at marching priests, "Nigger lovers! Look at them! Someone should boil the skin off you scum!"

On August 17, there were twenty marches, and Nazi thugs headed by their Midwest secretary, Ericka Himmler, a 21-year-old Chicago woman, passed out hate leaflets. On August 22, nearly two thousand Nazis gathered for a meeting addressed by leaders of the American Nazi party and the Ku Klux Klan. When it was over, white mobs stoned two groups of freedom marchers.

Dr. King denied that the marches were stirring up hatred: "They have revealed hatred that already existed."

A break finally came with an agreement by Mayor Daley to support open housing and the marches ended in at least partial victory.

Less than a week after Chicago, the Hough section of Cleveland exploded. For the first time there was some evidence that Negro extremists—although they didn't instigate the rioting—exploited and enlarged it. Four Negroes, including one young woman, were killed and many others were injured.

"Law enforcement officers were responsible for two of the deaths, a white man firing from a car for a third, and a group of young white vigilantes for the fourth," says the *U.S. Riot Commission Report*.

Rioting came to Cincinnati on June 12. Tension had built up over the arrest, trial and conviction of a Negro jazz musician named Posteal Laskey for a series of assaults on middle-aged white women, several of which resulted in death. The "Cincinnati Strangler" case aroused Negro resentment because they felt Laskey didn't get a fair trial in spite of the fact that two of the principal witnesses against him were black. Then a cousin of Laskey, Peter Frakes, was arrested for carrying a sandwich-board reading "Cincinnati Guilty —Laskey Innocent." An anti-loitering ordinance which blacks believe was used mainly against them added to the tensions.

Rioting and looting began with the use of Molotov cocktails and stoning of cars. A white motorist, who died three weeks later, and a Negro suffered gunshot wounds. Quick use was made of the National Guard, which used considerable restraint in the use of its weapons. Within a period of two hours the streets were quiet. Damage, fortunately, was kept to a minimum.

Atlanta burst into flames as Cincinnati quieted. On June 17, a minor police matter set it off. The black militant Stokely Carmichael was on hand to turn what might have remained trivial into something more dangerous. Moderate Negroes had to contend with Carmichael and H. Rapp Brown in their efforts to calm their people. SNCC leaders said that a group of young Negroes who volunteered for a community patrol were "selling their black brothers out," and should be treated as "Black Traitors." Carmichael reportedly stated, "It's not a question of law and order. We are not concerned with peace. We are concerned with the liberation of black people. We have to build a revolution."

A series of disorders resulted in the death of one man and serious injury to a boy at the hands of police. A petition was drawn up by a group of moderate Negro leaders "demanding that Stokely Carmichael get out of the community and allow the people to handle their own affairs. It was signed by more than 1,000 persons in the Dixie Hills area," according to the *Riot Commission Report*.

In Newark, New Jersey, tension had been rising steadily between black residents and the city administration, particularly where one hundred and fifty acres in the heart of the Central Ward were concerned. The Planning Board wanted the land as the site for a new state medical and dental college, but some Negroes contended this was an effort to weaken the political power of the blacks by moving out large numbers of them.

In addition, there were cries of "Brutality!" against members of the mainly Italian police force. As in most such cases, enough officers did abuse their power to lend credibility to such charges.

On July 12, the alleged beating of a Negro cab driver was the direct spark that led to one of the major riots of the year. He was taken to the Fourth Precinct Police Station, and within minutes rumors were spreading by word of mouth and by cab radio. Descriptions of Smith's beating and injuries became more and more exaggerated. Despite efforts by Negro community leaders to disperse the crowds that had gathered, rioting broke out and was followed by the usual looting and arson. Guns were stolen from stores, and a Negro boy was wounded. After a couple of days of turmoil, state police and the National Guard were sent in and apparently both groups behaved badly.

In one incident, police opened fire on looters going in and out of a furniture store on Springfield Avenue. One bullet smashed the window in the kitchen of a Mrs. D. J.'s apartment. She heard a cry and her three-year-old daughter came running from the bedroom, blood streaming down from her left eye where the bullet had entered. After two months in the hospital, the little girl lost the sight in her left eye and became deaf in her left ear.

Meanwhile, down in the street, Horace W. Morris came out of the building intending to get into a car and drive to Newark Airport. An associate director of the Urban League in Washington, D.C., he had been visiting relatives in Newark. His two brothers and his 73-year-old stepfather were with him. All along the street people were standing watching the looting, and just as the police arrived, several looters cut across in front of one group of onlookers.

The police fired and bullets struck the spectators. Isaac Harrison, the elderly stepfather, started back toward the building where he lived but had his legs kicked from under him by a bullet. Horace Morris tried to help him to his feet, and when he fell again, one of the brothers stooped over to pick him up. As he did, bullets hit him in the right arm and left leg. Horace and the other brother finally got the two wounded men to safety in the vestibule of the building where more than fifty angry, frightened people were already jammed.

In the same vicinity, about 5:00 P.M., a small caliber bullet killed a police detective. Later on in the riot, a fireman was hit and killed by a .30 caliber bullet. Both deaths were attributed to snipers.

One family decided to go out to dinner around 8:00. Mrs. L. M., her husband, four sons and her brother-in-law got into the car and drove to a restaurant. On the way home, her husband was driving and he panicked when they came to a National Guard roadblock. He slowed, then swerved out and around it. One guardsman fired after them. When they reached home and got out to go in the house, they found ten-year-old Eddie dead. A bullet had hit him in the head.

Most of the looting and burning had ended by nightfall but reports of sniper fire continued to increase. Later the New Jersey National Guard labeled those reports as "deliberately or otherwise inaccurate." Their chief of staff, Major General James F. Cantwell, testifying before the Armed Services Subcommittee of the House of Representatives, said there was too much firing against snipers to begin with because the guard was thinking of it as a military action.

Boys throwing firecrackers from the roof of a building resulted in police and guardsmen firing into the Hayes Housing Project.

Eloise Spellman, mother of several children, fell with a bullet through her neck in her tenth floor apartment.

Across the street, people were standing at a window watching the firing when several troopers turned and fired in their direction. A grandmother, Mrs. Hattie Gainer, was hit.

The 2-year-old daughter of Rebecca Brown was standing at the window a block away. Mrs. Brown went to pull her away and was struck in the back by a bullet.

All three women died.

During the riot there were two hundred and fifty fire alarms but many were false and only thirteen were considered by the city to be "serious." Damage was estimated at $10,251,000. Twenty-three persons were killed—a white detective, a white fireman and twenty-one Negroes.

In Jersey City a few fires were set and rocks thrown and mass arrests made. There was one fatality. A Negro passenger in a cab was killed when a Negro boy threw a Molotov cocktail into the vehicle.

Minor rioting took place in Elizabeth, Englewood, and Plainfield, New Jersey, at approximately the same time as that in Newark and Jersey City. A white police officer was beaten to death by Negro youths in Plainfield. State police and National Guardsmen restored order.

"TANKS IN DETROIT. RIOTING SPREADS UNCONTROLLED," read the headlines on July 24, 1967, as the worst riot in America since the New York draft riots flared in the motor city.

According to the *Riot Commission Report*, "police brutality was a recurrent theme in Detroit."

In one of a series of raids on "blind pigs" (after-hours drinking and gambling clubs), the police arrested eighty-two people. The weather was hot and humid and the crowd that gathered quickly turned angry and began looting stores along Twelfth Street.

When a seventeen-man police commando unit tried to make the first sweep about 7:50 A.M., approximately three thousand people were out on Twelfth Street. They didn't resist: they simply gave way on one side, letting the police move down the street, and then closed in behind them.

A shoe store was set on fire at 8:25 but firemen were permitted to extinguish the blaze. However, the situation was deteriorating rapidly.

By the middle of the morning, it was estimated that a

fourth of the police department had reported for duty. Of the 1,122 force, 540 were in or near the area of the rioting. A group of 108 officers was trying to form a cordon around the six blocks involved. No one attempted to stop the looters, and there was no use of force by the men in the police cars.

Police Commissioner Girardin said later, "If we had started shooting in there . . . not one of our policemen would have come out alive. I am convinced it would have turned into a race riot in the conventional sense."

It was what sociologists are now coming to call a commodity riot, a riot in which, instead of attacking white people, the deprived blacks attack the symbols of the white man's economic stranglehold on the ghetto—white-owned stores, shops, and other businesses. This has been the pattern of all the riots of the "long hot summers."

At first the monetary loss in the riot was estimated as high as $500 million. Those estimates have since been scaled down drastically to somewhere between $40 and $50 million.

One of the grimmest stories to come out of the Detroit riot was that of the killings at the Algiers Motel. Police raided the motel after National Guardsmen reported sniper fire coming from the buildings. No weapons were found but several young Negro men and two white girls were rounded up and the youths were beaten. Later the bodies of three Negro youths were found inside the motel. The Detroit *News* investigation located witnesses who reported that the victims —Aubrey Pollard, 19; Carl Cooper, 17, and Fred Temple, 18 —had been killed by police.

"Everyone they shot, they shot for no reason at all," said Roderick D. Davis, a 20-year-old rock 'n' roll singer who was staying at the motel. He told the Associated Press that sixteen or seventeen policemen and guardsmen stormed into the motel annex at 1:00 A.M. after seven or eight shots were heard. The officers smashed in doors and rounded up five or six Negro youths and two white girls. Cursing and waving shot-

224

guns, they forced the young people to stand against a wall. Then, Davis said, a Detroit policeman took a knife from his pocket and dropped it on the floor.

"He told the boy [an unidentified Negro] to pick the knife up," Davis related. "He [the Negro youth] said he wasn't going to do it. The policeman said, 'If you don't, we're going to kill you.'

"So the boy reached down slowly against the wall and picked the knife up and the police told him to stab him [the officer] with it.

"The boy started crying and said no and dropped the knife.

"And that's when another policeman hit me in the head and told me to keep my face toward the wall and then in the next second I heard a shot. I heard somebody fall to the floor."

The case against the officers indicted for these murders was seriously compromised by pretrial publicity, including a book dealing exclusively with the subject. The trial judge sharply criticized those responsible for the publicity and granted a change of venue and a long delay. The case against Ronald August, a suspended white policeman who admitted killing one of the youths, came to trial in June, 1969, after two years of delay. It was held in Mason, Michigan, before an all-white jury. Avery Weisvrasser, assistant Wayne County prosecutor, called the killing "cold-blooded murder" and "lynch law."

The defense challenged the credibility of several prosecution witnesses and argued that the prosecution had failed to prove premeditation and malice. Testifying in his own defense, August claimed he killed Pollard in self-defense. He said he took Pollard into another room to question him and to save him from further beating by other officers. There, he said, Pollard attempted to grab his shotgun and it went off, killing the youth.

Circuit Judge William Beer ordered the jury to either find August guilty of first degree murder or acquit him. He did

225

not comment on his reasons for ruling out a verdict of second-degree murder or manslaughter. The jury deliberated for about three hours before returning to announce it had found August innocent.

Reporters asked August what his plans were after his acquittal and he said, "I'm going to pray."

No other cases had been brought to trial at this writing.

In the spring of 1968 Martin Luther King, Jr. was assassinated. Rioting in Chicago, Washington, D.C., and Baltimore followed. Federal troops had to be used in all three cities and again they proved far more capable of lowering the level of violence than police and National Guard units.

The nation was shocked by the sight of looting and burning in the very shadow of the Capitol and by the seemingly endless repetition of the riots. On all sides there were dire predictions of fresh outbreaks on a much larger scale and of guerrilla warfare in the cities. Some blacks seem to think a civil war between blacks and whites is inevitable, but the feeling is apparently less prevalent in the Negro community than among those who would like to use it as a means to grab power. Contrary to expectations, the summer of 1968 proved to be relatively "cool" and so did that of 1969.

10 | Political Violence, 1958-1969

Two foreigners have perhaps best expressed the attitudes toward violence of the far left and the far right in America. The words have so similar a sound to them that one even wonders while remembering that any study of totalitarianism will show the similarity of the extremes.

"Violence is a cleansing force," Frantz Fanon* says. "It frees the native of his inferiority complex and from his despair and inaction; it makes him fearless and restores his self-respect . . . Violence alone, violence committed by the people, violence organized and educated by its leaders, makes it possible for the masses to understand social truth."

Benito Mussolini could have been speaking for the right when he compared the "creative violence" of the Fascist to other kinds. There is, he claimed, "a violence that liberates, and a violence that enslaves . . . a violence that is moral and a violence that is immoral."

Strangely enough, violence on the part of the armed and militant right in this country in recent years has been mainly confined to rhetoric. Despite extensive armories that include antitank guns, machine guns, rifles, and thousands of tons

---

* Frantz Fanon was a black psychiatrist from Martinique who worked with the Algerian rebels against the French. He has lately become one of the heroes of the New Left and the black militants.

of ammunition, the radical right has done astonishingly little shooting in its self-proclaimed war to save America from itself.

If one actually believed in the invading hordes and ravaging mobs that are conjured up in the imaginations of the Minutemen and their ilk, one might be tempted to indict them for negligence of duty in defending the state. Quite frankly, the John Birch Society, the Minutemen, the California Rangers, and the National Renaissance Party combined have resorted to less violence than a single Klavern of the KKK or, to go further back in history, a single Know-Nothing chapter.

When one contemplates the terrible danger the right sees on all sides, one can only wonder why their gun hands hang limply at their sides.

Here are some of the nightmares envisioned by the Birch Society and Minutemen, as reported by then-Senator Thomas H. Kuchel in the July 20, 1963, issue of *The New York Times:*

> 35,000 Communist Chinese troops bearing arms and wearing deceptively dyed powder-blue uniforms are poised on the Mexican border about to invade San Diego; the United States has turned over—or will at any moment—its Army, Navy and Air Force to the command of a Russian colonel in the United Nations; almost every well-known American or free-world leader is, in reality, a top Communist agent; a United States army guerrilla warfare exercise in Georgia, called Water Moccasin III, is actually a United Nations operation preparatory to taking over our country.

With such terrible things going on, wouldn't you expect the Minutemen to have swarmed into the streets with smoking flintlocks? They haven't. Instead, they have talked and planned and polished their guns, occasionally dreaming of blowing up a police station, robbing a bank or perhaps putting poison gas in the ventilator system of the United Nations.

228

In 1958, the right fought the rising tide of Communism by throwing bombs into synagogues. On October 12, 1958, a bomb blasted a Jewish temple in Atlanta, causing $200,000 worth of damage. The police reported that a small group had planned the bombings and that arrests would follow soon. On October 15, a homemade bomb damaged a Jewish temple in Peoria.

Two years later, on January 29, 1960, a bomb smashed fifty-one windows in a new synagogue which earlier in the month had been smeared with swastikas. The police questioned a dozen teen-aged boys who belonged to a group called the Nordic Reich Youth Party. Its members wore Nazi uniforms and swastika armbands and carried daggers with "SS" on them. All but two were released after questioning.

An unidentified assailant threw eggs at Helen Gahagan Douglas, wife of actor Melvyn Douglas and former Congresswoman from California. In Dallas, Lady Bird and Senator Lyndon Johnson were roughed up by a mob wearing red, white, and blue uniforms. On hand in the crowd were such GOP notables as Senate candidate John Tower, Representative Bruce Alger, and Peter O'Donnell, the Dallas County Republican chairman. The incident was later credited with throwing Texas into the Democratic camp and winning the election for John F. Kennedy.

At El Camino College in California, the young editor of a nationally circulated right-wing student paper announced on March 3, 1961, that he had been beaten by a gang of hoods because of his anti-Communist political views. The student told how five men forced their way into his apartment at 3:00 a.m. "They formed a circle with me in the middle and they passed me from man to man. It was like a wolfpack. Everywhere I turned I was slugged or kicked."

According to the Los Angeles *Times*, the police on the scene were of the opinion that the young man "had been worked over by experts."

Insisting that the beating was connected with his recent

political activities, the youthful editor said, "They called me 'Nazi' and 'Fascist' and various unprintable names and warned me I was 'getting off easy' this time."

The attack followed a week-long series of telephone threats warning him not to appear on the Tom Duggan television show Saturday night and to cease his outspoken criticism of Communist-front organizations, he said. Then he talked about his newspaper, the *Student Statesman,* which he said was a venture of Dr. Thomas Wyatt and his Crusade for God and Freedom whose headquarters were in the Embassy Auditorium in downtown Los Angeles.

The incident produced a flurry of editorials in Los Angeles area newspapers deploring the brutal attacks. Television news personality George Putnam stood in front of his flag and emoted over the rising tide of left-wing violence. The American Legion sent off letters to Senator Eastland, chairman of the Senate Judiciary Committee, and to Representative Walters, chairman of the House Un-American Activities Committee, describing the attack. Legion leaders said the student had been beaten by men using "typical Communist terminology" shortly after he had appeared on a television program to outline the anti-Communist policy of his paper.

Meanwhile, the young man was reported as being in "fair" condition at Daniel Freeman Memorial Hospital in Inglewood with his eyes blackened and his lips swollen.

It was then that the police stated it was their opinion the beating was a hoax and that the student editor's injuries had been self-inflicted.

Silence descended on the case.

In December 1961, one of the traveling circuses of the right wing was in Los Angeles. While orators at the Project Alert meetings denounced Communism, Socialism, liberals, and the United Nations, a more active partisan planted a bomb outside the headquarters of the United Nations Association. It failed to go off.

A few weeks later, the terrorists were more efficient. A

bomb exploded at Communist Party headquarters. However, there were no injuries and little damage was inflicted.

On February 2, 1962, there were two more bombings. This time the homes of ministers in the San Fernando valley were the targets. While the Reverend Brooks Miller, pastor of the Emerson Unitarian Church in Canoga Park, and the Reverend John G. Simmons, pastor of the Matthews Lutheran Church in North Hollywood, were engaged in a panel discussion on the subject "The Extreme Right—A Threat to Democracy?" their homes were blasted by bombs.

The Los Angeles *Herald Examiner* quoted an anonymous police officer who hinted darkly that this was the work of Communists who were trying to win sympathy for their cause. Representative Hiestand, a member of the John Birch society, said it was deplorable and went on to attribute it to Communists. Project Alert leaders stated they did not believe in terrorism and that the FBI should investigate and find out why left-wingers were bombing each other's homes.

No one was ever arrested, and Project Alert packed up its three rings, its clowns and menagerie, and moved on to another city.

In April 1962, a retired army officer and his wife returned from the jai alai games at Tijuana to their home on Coronado Island and found their 19-year-old son hanging from the beamed ceiling in the master bedroom.

It was the father's stated opinion that this was a "ritualistic murder by Communists or other subversives to get at me because I am a member of the John Birch Society." He also said his son had recently been appointed editor of a right-wing newspaper published at San Diego State College.

The youth's wrists reportedly were bound together with the palms of the hands facing each other and both hands secured behind the head. "It would have been impossible for him to have hanged himself," the retired officer said and demanded an investigation.

There was noticeable uneasiness among conservative student leaders at San Diego State following the hanging. Miss Billie Lutz, 19, of Pacific Beach said she was quitting the Students for Freedom because she was "in fear of my safety." Another conservative leader, Albert Halterman, 19, announced that a hangman's noose was discovered in his car. District Attorney Don Keller stated there was no proof of any connection between the latter incident and the "ritual" hanging.

"It may have been a prank, but we are investigating," the D.A. said and then informed reporters that Ray Pinker, Los Angeles Police Department crime laboratory specialist, was assisting local authorities in trying to solve the case.

On April 15, Pinker made his findings known. He said the youth's hands had not been tied but had been caught in the strands of rope when the boy apparently reached up to try to relieve the pressure of his weight on the rope.

"There is nothing to show the involvement of any other person," Pinker said. "It would have taken at least three men to hang the boy as he was found, and in such a gang murder the men would have brought their own rope and tied better knots than the clumsy one that was found in the rope."

So much for "ritualistic" murder on "Idiot's Island," as Coronado is sometimes called.

During the 1964 election there was a flutter of right-wing activity. Rockefeller campaign officials in California announced in May that an estimated one hundred and forty anonymous callers had threatened to bomb their campaign offices in Los Angeles County. A "substantial" number of the calls were from women who screamed obscenities at the persons answering the phones, the spokesman said. Workers were also threatened with beatings.

In the San Francisco area Rockefeller-for-President volunteers received phone calls at home threatening them with violence. Jan St. Clair, vice chairman of the Santa Clara County group, received four such calls, one caller threatening,

"The next time I see you with the governor I'm going to shoot."

A bomb threat forced evacuation of the San Jose Rockefeller headquarters but no bomb was found.

Young supporters of Barry Goldwater invaded a Rockefeller meeting. ". . . They came in the kitchen and up the back way, tore down all our posters," Rockefeller said. "There were about five thousand people here. They put stuff in the punch—it may have been acid—to spoil it. They went around with their hands squashing all the sandwiches . . . This doesn't seem like America . . . They were . . . with the Young Republican group in California, the Birch Society, the Minutemen and other organizations of citizens that are highly organized, highly disciplined, highly financed . . . such tactics are very serious as portents for the future."

In Dallas, Adlai Stevenson was hit on the head by a placard wielded by an angry demonstrator and spat upon.

Daniel Burrous, Ku Klux Klan, American Nazi Party and National Renaissance Party member, shot himself with a .32 caliber pistol a few minutes after reading an article in *The New York Times* revealing that he was of Jewish background. Burrous was famous in the Klan and Nazi Party for his advocation that all Jews be killed. Klan members watched as Burrous committed "ritualistic" suicide.

Right-wing extremists were blamed on November 2, 1965, for vandalism at the Valley Peace Center in Sherman Oaks, California. A symbol of an atomic bomb had been painted on the building with the words "Drop it" underneath. Minuteman stickers with the slogan "Fight Communism to the Death" had previously been found on the building. They were posted next to bullet holes in the walls and windows. The headquarters had been damaged by grenades in December 1963 and January 1964.

In New Jersey in January 1966, Robert Goldman, a talk show moderator of station WTTM, was talking to a caller on the telephone when two men walked into the studio and attacked him. The victim had recently interviewed a folk singer with leftist political views on his program. He said he had been threatened with death several times since Joe Frazier, a member of the Chad Mitchell Trio, had appeared on his show and described himself as a member of the W. E. B. DuBois Club.

On Monday, September 5, 1966, an attempt was made to blow up the Communist headquarters in New York. Some damage was done to windows, typewriters, and a radiator but, according to a Los Angeles *Times* dispatch, "Ironically, the bomb caused the most damage across the street from the Communist office. It destroyed 110-year-old stained-glass windows at the Serbian Eastern Orthodox Church of St. Sava. The windows depicted the life of Christ. Ninety percent of the church parishioners are refugees from Communism."

An ex-Minuteman, on November 10, 1966, told of a plan to put cyanide in the air-conditioning system of the UN building in New York. According to Jerry Brooks, the plan (which he admitted originating) had been discussed with Robert Bolivar DePugh and Walter P. Peyson of the Minutemen during a training session in Narbonne, Missouri. The training was in the use of five or six types of machine guns and rifles.

Election year 1968 saw wild violence on the left but only minor violence on the right. George Wallace held up an imaginary rifle and told how to solve the problem of suburban disorder. "Bam, shoot 'em dead on the spot! Shoot to kill if anyone throws a rock at a policeman or a Molotov cocktail. Don't shoot any children, just shoot the adult standing beside the kid that throws the rock. That may not prevent the burning and looting, but it sure will stop it after it starts."

The Los Angeles *Times* reported: "A newsman from New York after listening to Wallace talk about 'skinning heads' and 'poppin' skulls,' turned to another reporter and whispered, 'You know, he's serious!' "

"Some of you anarchists better have your day now because after November fifth, you are through," Wallace told hecklers who yelled, "Nazi!" at him. "Some of you college students who've been raising blood, money and clothes for the Viet Cong—we gonna drag you by the hair and stick you under the jail."

Rival factions of Wallace supporters came to blows at a meeting of the American Independent Party in Bakersfield, California. The Reverend Alvin Mayall, who claimed to be state chairman, blamed the disturbance on William K. Shearer, who also claimed the same post. Shearer, a former leader of the CLEAN anti-pornography drive as well as one of the original organizers of AIP, could not be reached for comment but local members of the party told what had happened.

"Shearer and his group came in uninvited and took over the room that an individual had rented and paid for with his own money," Mr. Mayall said. "There were some blows exchanged. Some blood was shed. We had to call the police and they sent every available officer they had out there."

There was some political violence of another kind in America during 1968 when anti-Castro Cubans bombed pro-Castro Cubans and then bragged about it. Also bombed were consulates, travel agencies, airline and tourist offices of countries that maintained diplomatic or economic relations with the Castro government. Found at the scene of some of the bombings was literature bearing the words "Cuban Power."

The Soviet Embassy in Washington was bombed on February 22, 1968. "The violent explosion, which shattered more than two dozen windows in the area and was felt several blocks away, badly damaged the unoccupied ground floor office of the embassy's No. 2 man," the *Washington Post* reported.

No one was injured, but the Soviets issued a stiff protest and President Johnson and Secretary of State Dean Rusk expressed regret.

All told, right-wing violence in 1968 and 1969 was minimal, and this is especially strange at a time when the far left was practically taking the country apart and threatening not to put it back together again. Draft cards and flags were burned in the streets, political conventions and speeches were disrupted on all sides by young radicals, and the nation was abandoned by the patriotic right. A picture comes to mind of Minutemen huddling in their bunkers, California Rangers running for the hills, and John Birch Society members hiding under their beds while SDS stormtroopers rage across campuses and Black Student Union terrorists chase professors up trees. Of course it could be that the forces of the right are merely regrouping and rearming for *Der Tag*.

Some of them like Robert De Pugh, who was recently arrested for plotting to blow up a police station and knock over all the banks in a small Northwest town (though he pleaded innocent, according to a UPI dispatch of September 13, 1969), may just be holding back while they obtain funds for the cause. Others are striking out individually.

A UPI story from Detroit on May 17, 1968, tells of one such incident:

> An unemployed cab driver who thought the country was "overrun with Communists" was under arrest today for lining three college students up against a wall and shooting them, killing one and critically wounding the others.
>
> Police said Edward Waniolek, 40, vowing to "shoot some Communists," walked into a Socialist Workers Party hall Monday, asked for a book by Lenin and shot the three young men.
>
> Jan Garrett, 22, and Walter Graham, 19, both hospitalized with critical bullet wounds, told police Waniolek lined them up against a wall, screamed "You're all a bunch of Commies—put your money on the floor," and sprayed rifle and pistol bullets at them.

Leo Bernard, 27, a senior biology student at Wayne State University who hadn't enrolled since last September was killed. He was a member of the Socialist Workers Party.

From the sometimes violent, sometimes talkative right, we now turn our attention to the endlessly talkative and often violent left.

The Black Panthers are supposedly a black nationalist organization like the Black Muslims, but their acceptance of Ché Guevara as a saint and their close alliance with Maoist-oriented groups such as the SDS and the Peace and Freedom Party tend to belie this image. While the Muslims have deep roots in the black community and are impervious to white influence of any kind, the Panthers have constantly allowed themselves to be manipulated by white Maoists to the disadvantage of their own presumed ends and of black nationality itself.

The SDS-trained and dedicated anarchists and the equally trained and dedicated Maoists who make up the leadership of the badly splintered student group have consistently used the Panthers and the Black Student Union as cannon fodder in their so-called revolution.

The Panthers' history has been one of violence, but at least part of the time the blacks have been as much victims as perpetrators. The big three of the movement—Huey P. Newton, Bobby Scale, and Eldridge Cleaver—have all engaged in clashes with police, and less prominent Panthers have been killed and wounded in gun battles with officers.

The Panthers' expressed aim is gaining total control for blacks over their own lives. They have, however, allowed themselves to become allied with anti-American forces around the world. In a jail-cell interview printed in the Cuban paper *El Mundo,* Newton said the Panthers consider themselves "an integral part of the army of resistance urged by Guevara to combat American imperialism." He then went on, "We are increasing our resistance and we are taking up our posi-

237

tion beside all other nations to resist the No. 1 criminal of the world—US imperialism."

The goals of the Black Panthers outlined in their party platform are interpreted by the Associated Press this way:

> Freedom for blacks to run their own communities; an end to what they call the robbery of the black community by white merchants and landlords; housing that is fit to live in; the removal of white police from black communities; an educational system that teaches blacks their true history and their role in present society; the release of all blacks from all jails and prisons; exemption from military service and a United Nations supervised plebiscite of black people in America to see how they want themselves governed.

The Panthers' prime motivation, however, has seemed to be aggressiveness toward whites—most especially white police. Eldridge Cleaver has been quoted as saying: "From now on, we niggers have got to stop killing other niggers and start killing police." In his best-selling book *Soul on Ice,* he elaborates on that theme: "We shall have our manhood. We have had it or the earth will be leveled by our attempts to gain it."

The Black Panthers first came to national attention when they marched, guns in hand and bandoliers across chest, into the California State Capitol at Sacramento to protest a bill that would have restricted the carrying of loaded guns within city limits. Like their opposite numbers on the far right, the Panthers and many of their white militant allies are strongly opposed to any attempt to limit the number of guns in the hands of private citizens.

The Panthers have been involved in various incidents with the police. The most famous one resulted in the death of an Oakland police officer John F. Frey, Jr. On October 27, 1967, Huey Newton, the founder of the Black Panthers, and Gene McKinney, another Panther, went out to celebrate the end of a three-year probation period Newton had been serving.

They were in a Volkswagen belonging to Newton's fiancée, Laverne Williams, when Officer Frey spotted them.

After checking out the license number against a list Oakland police carry in their prowl cars, Frey radioed police headquarters, "It's a known Panther vehicle." Then he stopped the car and trouble began.

At his trial nearly a year later, Newton testified that he and his friends were looking for a restaurant where they could buy "soul food," and that when Frey stopped them, the officer called him a "nigger" and roughed him up, then shot him without provocation. Officer Herbert Heanes, who arrived on the scene in time to assist Frey, testified Newton opened fire first. Neither Frey's gun nor the one Newton was alleged to be carrying was found.

"Did you shoot and kill Officer Frey?" Newton's attorney, Charles Garry, asked Heanes.

"No, sir," Heanes answered.

"Isn't it a fact," Garry persisted, "that you shot Officer Frey?"

Garry presented witness after witness who testified that the dead man was a racist who waged a campaign of terror against Negroes in Oakland. A lawyer watching the proceedings was quoted as saying, "You get the impression that the dead man is on trial here because Garry constantly takes swipes at him . . ."

After four days of deliberation, the jury brought in a verdict of guilty of voluntary manslaughter. One jury member told reporters they were impressed by Newton's testimony that he had been called a "nigger" and roughed up.

Faced with a two-to-fifteen year sentence, Newton sent word to his followers to "cool it because the power structure would be looking for an opportunity to move in on the Black Panther party," but there were rumblings of anger among the Panthers and considerable agitation in his behalf among white leftists.

A Negro Episcopal deacon was quoted in a Los Angeles

239

Times story: "The Newton case spelled it out; a black man can't get a fair trial in this country. The jury punished him when they knew in their hearts he should have been acquitted. Because if he shot that cop then he shot him in self-defense."

Apparently some members of the Oakland police force were also dissatisfied with the verdict because a few days after Newton's conviction, two officers drove by Panther headquarters and fired carbines into it. They were said to have been drinking and were charged with firing a gun into an inhabited dwelling and dropped from the force.

Eldridge Cleaver had also been involved in a shoot-out with police in which one Panther was killed and two—including Cleaver—were wounded. Two policemen were also wounded, and a rifle taken from Cleaver. Ordered to jail on charges of violating his parole on a 1958 conviction of assault to commit rape and murder, Cleaver was freed by a San Francisco judge who said the action against him had been political. The judge's decision was later overruled and Cleaver was scheduled to return to jail when he fled the country.

An interesting comparison can be drawn between the tactics of left-wing attorneys and those of the late Klan lawyer Matt Murphy acting in the Liuzzo murder case. Murphy spent more time indicting the victim than defending his clients. "Do you know those big black niggers were driven by the woman, sitting in the back seat? Niggers! One white woman and those niggers . . . Riding right through our county! Communists dominate them niggers . . . the Zionists that run that bunch of niggers . . . and when white people join up to them, they become white niggers. Integration breaks every moral law God ever wrote . . . no white woman can ever marry a descendant of Ham. That's God's law . . . There was a rabbi in that truck. A rabbi. Of course, he stopped and put the nigger in the back. And there they were—rabbi with a nigger . . . white woman . . . nigger man . . . all in there feet to feet . . ."

Panther attorneys and those defending SDS members in the San Francisco area use similar tactics.

"Do you know what an Uncle Tom is?" they demand of Negroes who testify against their clients.

"Do you sleep with a gun under your pillow?" is a thinly veiled threat for those who testify against Panthers.

Panthers have been involved in shootings other than with police. Two of them were shot down in a UCLA classroom, allegedly by gunmen from US, another black nationalist group. Defectors from the Panthers have accused them of using terroristic methods against members of the black community and of engaging in shakedowns.

Other violent left groups among blacks are the Revolutionary Action Movement (RAM) and the Black Student Union (BSU), which startled the nation by taking over a building at Cornell at gun point and so terrorizing the administrators that all their demands were granted.

On March 7, 1969, Timothy Peebles, a 19-year-old member of the BSU at San Francisco State College, and William Pulliam were charged with possession of a bomb, exploding a bomb, and conspiracy. They had allegedly carried a lead pipe filled with gunpowder into the college building and Peebles had attempted to set it off. The device went off in Peebles' face as he was trying to set the timing mechanism. Two other bombs were found in a suitcase nearby. Peebles, a brilliant student, was new to militancy when he joined the BSU. He was blinded by the blast.

BSU chairman Benny Stewart charged that the injuries to Peebles were the fault of Acting President S. I. Hayakawa and Governor Reagan because of the "suppressive atmosphere created on the campus by them."

RAM is a Mao-worshiping revolutionary group whose membership has been estimated as anywhere between 50 and 1,000. In July 1967, twenty-four members were arrested in New York and Philadelphia and "charged with conspiracy to blow up a subway station, set fire to a lumberyard and assassinate two moderate leaders of the civil-rights movement, the NAACP's Roy Wilkins and the Urban League's Whitney Young," according to *Newsweek*.

A machine gun, a dozen rifles, and a thousand rounds of ammunition plus some steel-tipped arrows were seized in the raid. The persons arrested were anything but ghetto dwellers. They included Herman Ferguson, an assistant principal in the New York City school system; Ursula West, the schoolteacher daughter of a distinguished University of Louisville professor; George Samuels, owner of a Queens delicatessen, and Michelle Doswell Kaurouma, a public school teacher.

According to authorities, RAM had adopted the slogan, "Kill, baby, kill!" and was dedicated to arming Negroes in the slums and training them for guerrilla warfare against whites.

It was later revealed that the home of another of the men arrested, Max Stanford, RAM's field chairman, was decorated with Chinese banners and a portrait of Mao Tse-tung. RAM plans were described by Phillip Abbott Luce, a Progressive Labor Party defector, in the following words: "According to the plans of RAM terror will be the major weapon . . . Bombs will be placed in New York's Grand Central Station or other public places; key personalities will be assassinated; snipers will indiscriminately murder innocent citizens; theaters will be fired."

Evidence that RAM and the Citywide Citizens Action Committee of Detroit were being used by white revolutionaries to further their own ends was presented by Negro newspaperman and author Carl T. Rowan in the December 6, 1967, issue of the Los Angeles *Times*. He said the CCAC was being investigated for the part some of its leaders played in the Detroit riot, and that it was rumored that the "Peking-oriented Progressive Labor Party is manipulating and perhaps financing CCAC through its Detroit operatives."

Rowan talked to the CCAC leader, Reverend Albert Cleage,

and asked him about the group's intentions. "Does your group propose that American Negroes resort to guerrilla warfare in urban areas?"

"Guerrilla warfare is the black man's answer to the white man's final solution."

"What does that mean?" Rowan asked.

"The white man in this country has about decided on genocide as the only way to silence the black man's revolt," he explained, "and as Rap Brown put it so eloquently we don't intend to walk meekly to the gas chambers."

Rowan reported that investigators for the Justice Department had discovered "unsettling evidence that black revolutionaries and some white 'colleagues' had well-organized advance plans to exploit and spread the violence in Detroit and Newark" and that "investigators have become intrigued by the activities of several white women who have been active in, or on the fringes of, the most bellicose black nationalist groups. There is evidence that at least some of these women are the conduits for money that is being fed into these revolutionary groups. Yet, the probers want to avoid what could be branded a shameful attempt to tar as 'disloyal' all white women who are working actively for first-class citizenship for Negroes."

Rowan says there is "pretty solid" evidence "Communist China used an elaborate international set of conduits to put a million dollars into Philadelphia for use by the Revolutionary Action Movement . . ."

One of the ironies of our time is that dissidence should be most prevalent in the two most dissimilar segments of our society. The Negro militants usually come from the most downtrodden part of our culture, while those in the university community are the most pampered. An underfed, out-of-work ghetto Negro who riots or joins a revolutionary group is a tragic figure, but the spoiled scion of suburbia rioting on a college campus is simply ludicrous. And it is one of the fantastic irrationalities of American life that the justified black rebellion is in most cases put down with extensive and sometimes excessive force, while the rioting student is handled with kid gloves and pleadings on all sides against "overreaction."

A Presidential Commission ending a three-year study of mental health reported on May 8, 1969, that "among the nation's 90 million boys and girls under age 25, two million are psychotic and in need of immediate care and treatment."

There was cause that spring for the American public to suspect that the entire two million were loose in the universities of the nation.

The SDS (Students for a Democratic Society) is probably responsible for more shattered nerves among college administrators than all other student movements combined. Aside from the money extracted from taxpayers' pockets to pay for broken windowpanes, library books, and an occasional building, however, its place in a history of violence is not terribly significant. Still the sight of a group of SDS stormtroopers swaggering across a college campus must have about the same effect on a timorous administrator as that of a convoy of Hell's Angels motorcyclists on a small-town mayor.

There is, indeed, a closer connection between the violent Hell's Angels and the SDS and other student groups than is generally realized. The connection is through the hippies and so-called street people such as those who call themselves the "Up Against the Wall Mother-Fuckers" of Berkeley. The hippies have been closely allied with the Hell's Angels for several years, and peace groups, which were at first hostile toward the Angels and were attacked by them in one famous incident, have also tended to accept the motorcyclists as allies.

The Angels have left a trail of violence across the face of California and other states and have been adopted by the hippies as their "police." They have been present at most student rebellions in the San Francisco area. Even more important is the fact that their life style has been accepted and adopted by large numbers of SDS and other militant

244

students. The drug culture, the profanity, the childish urge to "blow the minds of the citizens" with outrageous acts, the beards, the long hair, the filthy clothing and above all the tendency to violence are all part of the image of this small group of hoodlums that has become the way of life of the student left.

The SDS, or at least that part of it that is not anarchist, recognizes Herbert Marcuse as its intellectual mentor. Marcuse, a pleasant, intelligent, and seemingly gentle man, is a rather incongruous figure to be accepted as their saint. He is a Marxist only by courtesy, as the Soviet branch of the family has often pointed out. He is actually an elitist. He believes that the elite have the right to deny toleration and even the vote to those who do not qualify for elite status.

Professor Marcuse's theories bear a strong resemblance to those of H. L. Hunt, the ultra-right Texas millionaire, who in his "novel" *Alpaca* recommended a "Cashocracy," where voting power would be proportionate to a person's wealth. In Marcuse's society voting power would be proportionate to one's status in the academic world.

Marcuse would not turn society over to the worker, as Marx preached, or leave it in the hands of the majority, as democracy attempts to do, but give it to the student elite who have not been contaminated by the system. Blacks in Marcuse's opinion have been "so thoroughly colonized" as to render them incapable of "rational" political decisions and would not be permitted to vote.

Presumably, once in power, Marcuse's student elite would re-educate the blacks into proper attitudes and then return their franchise. Or perhaps not—if one considers Marcuse's attitude toward other groups who fail in his estimate to "think rationally." He suggests "withdrawal of toleration of freedom of speech and assembly from groups and movements" which fail to meet his standards.

The SDS and other student groups have been apt pupils of the master in the "withdrawal of toleration of freedom of

245

speech and assembly" of those with whom they disagree, and they disagree with the majority of the student body and with most professors and administrators. Withdrawal of toleration in the case of professors would mean being denied the right to teach or being silenced by goon squads of SDS terrorists. To the students, it would mean being forbidden to take part in student government, to edit student papers, or to take any part in campus life.

America's pacifists during the late 1960's have become fond of a chant which says, "Kill for Peace." Sometimes it has seemed they are willing to do just that. Bombs have been set off in draft boards, recruiters have been beaten and fires set that menaced life. Peace marchers, according to police, attempted to burn down the Century Plaza Hotel with President Johnson inside. Shouting bands of "pacifists" made campaigning a high-risk profession during the 1968 Presidential campaign.

11 | The Phenomenon of the Assassin, 1835-1968

Has America entered a period of its history that will be known as its Day of the Assassin? Since there is reason to fear that our public figures are in daily danger of being struck down by a political opponent or sociopathic killer, this seems a distinct possibility.

How and why did we reach such a deplorable state? Answers vary. Some say there are too many guns, too easily available. Others point out that violence on television is too prevalent and too widely accepted. Still others insist that America is a sick society, its members eaten by the virulent cancer of suspicion and contempt for the opinions and rights of fellow citizens. All these answers are at least partial truths, but other contributing factors must be taken into consideration before a valid conclusion is reached.

The age-old phenomenon of assassination has been used more consistently in some nations and cultures than in others. It flourished in Rome where Julius Caesar and many emperors who followed him died violently because of their political policies or beliefs. It was, and is, a way of life in the Middle East. That area, in fact, gave the political killer his name. As *Time* pointed out in its June 14, 1968, issue, "The word derives from the Arabic *hashshashin*, 'those who use hashish.'

At the time of the Crusades, a secret sect of the Mohammedan Ismailians employed terrorists while they were ritually high on hashish, which is similar to marijuana."

There were periods in European history when assassination flourished. Catherine de 'Medici and her sons were noted for their political murders. William the Silent was assassinated in 1584. Assassination was endemic in Czarist Russia from the time of Ivan the Terrible up to, and even after, the Revolution. Great Britain had a bloody period during the War of the Roses but changed thereafter. The last and only British prime minister to be assassinated was Spencer Perceval who died in 1812 at the hands of a lunatic in the lobby of the House of Commons. Several attempts were made on the life of Queen Victoria but none was successful.

In the twenty years preceding World War I, five chiefs of state and government were assassinated: President M. Sadi-Carnot of France in 1894, Premier Canovas of Spain in 1897, Empress Elizabeth of Austria in 1898, King Humbert of Italy in 1900, and Premier Canalejas of Spain in 1912.

In the Balkans, King Alexander of Serbia and his wife Draga Mashin were murdered by a group of Serbian army officers who later organized the murder group called the Black Hand. The Archduke Franz Ferdinand of Austria-Hungary was assassinated at Sarajevo in 1914, an act that precipitated the outbreak of World War I.

The concept of assassination came to the United States for the first time in the mind of an English housepainter named Richard Lawrence. Lawrence believed that the United States was still part of the British Empire and that he ruled over both as King Richard III. He also believed that the Government owed him a huge sum of money and that Andrew Jackson, President of the United States, was keeping the money from him and had also caused his father's death. Accordingly, on Friday, January 30, 1835, he set out to kill Jackson.

By his own admission he had approached Martin van

Buren and informed him that if he wasn't given the money owed him, he would kill both the Vice President and President Jackson.

Because of his mental condition, Lawrence had ceased to work and spent much of his time brooding about the millions of dollars he was going to get when Jackson no longer stood in the way. He quarreled with his landlady over back rent and threatened to slit her throat or blow her brains out.

Although he gave every indication of being insane, Lawrence moved around Washington with complete freedom, frequently attending sessions of Congress where he listened to long speeches, many of which were wildly critical of President Jackson.

Another of his constant activities was practicing with the two fine pistols he had inherited from his father. He bragged about his ability as a marksman, and he had the pistols with him one day early in January 1835 when he showed up at the White House and asked for an appointment with the President. Aides told him President Jackson was unable to see him that day and suggested he return some other time.

On January 23, Lawrence came back and by some odd circumstance was admitted to the President's office. He found Jackson talking with Representative Sutherland of Pennsylvania, but immediately launched into a long harangue about the money the Government owed him. He demanded that Jackson start paying off this mythical debt by writing him a check for a thousand dollars on the Bank of the United States. Not in the least alarmed by the man's erratic behavior, Jackson put him off with a remark that he was busy and had another caller waiting. Lawrence hesitated for a minute and then departed. He had forgotten to bring his guns with him that day.

Andrew Jackson was a man not easily worried by threats. He had lived on the frontier and was no stranger to violence. He and his beloved Rachel had accidentally married before her divorce from her first husband was final. The mistake was used against Jackson by his enemies who delighted in referring to him as an adulterer.

Captain Lewis Robards, Rachel's first husband, talked about her new marriage insultingly, and Jackson threatened to "cut off his ears and ran his thumb judiciously along the blade of his hunting-knife."

A political foe by the name of Servier who also called himself "Nolichucky Jack," taunted Jackson with running off with another man's wife, and Jackson shouted, "Great God! Do you mention *her* sacred name?"

Then he went for the man with his walking stick and had to be restrained from thoroughly caning him. Jackson challenged the man to a duel, which ended with Servier hiding behind a tree to escape Jackson's well-aimed bullet.

Charles Dickinson, a lawyer who blackened Mrs. Jackson's good name, wasn't lucky enough to find a tree handy and was shot between the eyes by the future President. Jackson had also been involved in a tavern brawl on September 4, 1813, with Thomas Hart Benton, later a senator from Missouri, and Benton's brother Jesse. The affair took place in Nashville, Tennessee, and several bystanders joined in the struggle with such weapons as dirks and sword canes. Jackson was seriously wounded when Jesse Benton shot him in the back.

In 1815, General Jackson had ordered six militiamen shot for desertion, and during his campaign for the Presidency in 1838, this was used against him. A pamphlet called the "Coffin Handbill" pictured six black coffins and, detailing the executions in lurid prose, included the allegation that one of the deserters had not been killed outright but had writhed in agony on top of his coffin where he had knelt to be shot.

Jackson supporters answered the outcry over his alleged harshness to deserters with humor by publishing "Supplement to the Coffin Handbill." This informed "the gentle reader that this monster, this more than cannibal, General Jackson, ate the whole six militia-men at one meal! Yes, my shuddering countrymen, he swallowed them whole, coffins and all, without the slightest attempt at mastication."

The hero of the Battle of New Orleans had also been attacked after becoming President. In ill health when he started a tour of the United States in May, 1833, he found himself recovering rapidly after he was attacked by a naval purser who had been dismissed from the service because of embezzlement. The violence "seem'd to have put his blood in motion."

This incident took place on the steamer *Cygnet* at Alexandria, Virginia. The former naval officer, Robert B. Randolph, walked up to the President, hit him in the face and tried to tweak his nose. He picked on the wrong man. Cane in hand, Jackson went for his assailant, chased him down the gangplank and tried to break down a door to get at him. When finally persuaded to desist, Jackson refused to bring charges against the man. According to his code, if a man attacked you, you either shot him or caned him but you didn't take him to law.

Jackson often received threats of death, and it gave him a certain perverse pleasure to give them to Francis Blair to publish in his paper, *The Globe*.

Worried by thoughts of assassination, Jackson's friends warned him: "You are now the only hope of this nation . . . I pray you take care of yourself, & guard against poison and the dagger. Be always prepared to give yourself a vomit."

No one, however, thought to warn him against Richard Lawrence, who later said he "assumed that everyone knew he intended to kill Andrew Jackson."

After his two earlier attempts, Lawrence waited until January 30, 1835. The President had gone to the Capitol building to attend the funeral of Representative Warren R. Davis of South Carolina, and Lawrence waited patiently outside, not wanting to do anything so unseemly as interrupting the services.

Jackson came out of the Capitol leaning on the arm of

Secretary of the Treasury Levi Woodbury. A procession of congressmen and other officials followed. Lawrence, standing behind one of the Corinthian columns, took his pistols from his pocket and cocked them. Then he stepped out in front of the President, took aim at his heart and pulled the trigger of the pistol in his right hand.

The percussion cap exploded loudly but nothing happened. The gun had failed to fire. Lawrence dropped it, transferred the second pistol to his right hand and lifted it to fire. Jackson had been limping along, leaning on Woodbury's arm and looking old and sick, but now he charged his assailant with upraised cane. Lawrence fired the second pistol with the muzzle pressed almost against the chest of the enraged President. It misfired, too.

A naval officer named Godney grabbed Lawrence by the shoulder, and Woodbury and several congressmen also seized him. By now, the problem was no longer that of protecting the President from a would-be assassin but of protecting Lawrence from the wrathful Andrew Jackson.

Bystanders succeeded in dragging Lawrence away without the sound caning the President would have administered. He was later tried by a court and declared insane. Confined in an asylum, he lived out the rest of his life thinking he was Richard III in the Tower of London.

The two pistols used by Lawrence were examined and found to be in perfect working condition. An expert on small arms estimated that the chance of both misfiring was something like one in 125,000.

Abraham Lincoln was not so lucky on Good Friday, April 14, 1865, as he sat in Ford's Theatre and laughed at a third-rate comedy called *Our American Cousin*. He was killed by a less than third-rate actor, John Wilkes Booth, whose main claim to fame was the fact that he was the brother of the great Edwin Booth. The details of the assassination are too well known to require much elaboration, but a review of the violence that accompanied it may be pertinent.

A fanatic sympathizer of the Southern cause, Booth had gathered a small group of similarly minded men around him in 1864 with the avowed purpose of kidnapping Lincoln and carrying him off to the Confederacy to be used as hostage for the exchange of large numbers of Confederate prisoners. After Lee's surrender at Appomattox, he changed his plan from kidnapping to assassination.

Three of Booth's group were in Washington with him when the assassination decision was made. He assigned to Lewis Paine, the gorillalike son of a Florida minister, and David E. Herold, a slow-witted youth, the task of killing Secretary of State William Seward. George A. Atzerodt, a 33-year-old native of Prussia, was given the task of murdering Vice President Andrew Johnson. Lincoln, Booth claimed for himself. Other than Booth, Paine seems to have been the only one who actually had any real intentions of carrying out the nefarious scheme.

Booth arrived at Ford's Theatre at 9:30 and learned that the guard assigned to Lincoln's box had moved away from the door to a seat from which he could watch the play. Booth had carefully timed his deed so that it would take place when there was only one actor on stage, and he stood listening for the line that was his cue. Henry Hawk said, "Don't know the manners of good society, eh? Well, I guess I know enough to turn you inside out, old gal—you sockdologizing old mantrap."

Booth stepped quickly into the Presidential box, lifted his derringer until it was close to Lincoln's head and pulled the trigger, yelling as he fired, *"Sic semper tyrannis!"*

Major Henry R. Rathbone, fiancé of the daughter of a New York senator, was in the box as a guest of the Lincolns and he turned instantly and grappled with the intruder. Booth dropped the derringer and drew a dagger. He slashed at the major repeatedly, inflicting a deep gash in the young man's arm.

Then he leaped on the balustrade, waved his bloody dagger and shouted, "The South is avenged!" or as some witnesses heard it, "Revenge for the South!"

He jumped to the stage but his spur caught in the Treasury Guard's flag which decorated the Presidential box, throwing him off balance. He landed hard and broke the shinbone of his left leg.

Dashing past the bewildered Henry Hawk and eluding one quick reacting member of the audience who tried to catch him, Booth ran through the back entrance into an alley where a man was holding his horse. He struck the man with the hilt of his dagger, knocking him out of the way, then leaped on the horse and rode at full speed for the Anacostia Bridge. There he was challenged by a sentry but made up a satisfactory excuse and was allowed to leave the city.

In the meantime, Lincoln was examined by a doctor, then removed from the box and carried across the street to the home of William Petersen and placed on the bed in a room that was rented to a young War Department stenographer named William Clark. He died there at 7:22 the next morning.

And while the President lay dying, reports came in of an attack on Secretary of State William Seward. Having broken his jaw in a fall from a horse, Seward was bedridden. Lewis Paine arrived at the house and told the servant who answered the door that he was delivering medicine from Seward's doctor and had to see the Secretary personally to give him instructions about how to take it. The servant refused him entrance but Paine pushed him aside and ran up the stairs to the second floor. There he was stopped by one of the Secretary's sons, Frederick Seward. Paine repeated his story and young Seward glanced into his father's room, saw that his father was asleep and told Paine he couldn't be disturbed.

Paine drew a revolver, smashed it over the son's head and burst into the Secretary's room. There he slashed the male nurse, Sergeant George F. Robinson, across the forehead and leaped on Secretary Seward, groping for his throat and stabbing.

Seward was saved by the steel brace on his broken jaw but was stabbed in the cheek and on both sides of his neck before he could roll off the bed onto the floor. Another of Seward's sons and Robinson wrestled briefly with Paine but the would-be assassin fought them off, stabbed Emerick W. Hansell, a State Department clerk who rushed to their aid, and ran down the stairs screaming, "I'm mad! I'm mad!" He fled the house, leaving five wounded men behind.

Booth had been joined by David Herold somewhere beyond Anacostia Bridge but before they reached Surratt's tavern. It was Herold who went inside to get whisky, spyglasses and a carbine which had previously been hidden there. Then they made their way to the home of Dr. Samuel Mudd, who cut off Booth's boot and splinted the broken leg.

As they continued on their way, they were aided by other Confederate sympathizers. Booth, however, was shocked to read in some newspapers that for the most part the South condemned his deed. He had expected to be hailed as a hero for killing Lincoln.

Booth and Herold fell in with three ex-Confederate soldiers who had served with Mosby's guerrillas. They helped the two fugitives conceal themselves in a big tobacco barn at the farm of Richard H. Garrett. They were found by a detail of twenty-six Union cavalrymen.

Surrounded, Booth refused to surrender. He asked to be given a chance to come out fighting and when this was repeatedly refused and the soldiers threatened to set fire to the barn, he let the frightened Herold leave but refused to come out himself. The cavalrymen thereupon fired the barn and there was some shooting. Booth fell with a bullet behind his right ear. An argument then ensued as to whether he had been shot or shot himself.

A Sergeant Boston Corbett came forward and claimed the

honor of having shot Booth, saying God had told him to do it. He became famous overnight as the man who had revenged Lincoln, but actually the best evidence seems to indicate that Booth shot himself. Corbett was a religious fanatic and later became insane.

Booth lingered for several hours although paralyzed by a bullet which had struck the cervical vertebrae. He was conscious off and on and begged his captors to shoot him. Once he muttered, "Tell Mother I died for my country. I have done what I thought was for the best." Toward the end he asked one of the soldiers to lift his hands so he could see them. "Useless, useless," he said, and a few minutes later was dead.

All that remained was for the living conspirators to be tried. Four of them were hanged—Paine, Herold, Atzerodt, and Mrs. Surratt.

Charles J. Guiteau was an itinerant evangelist who could have served as the model for Sinclair Lewis' Elmer Gantry. He swindled, wenched and politicked his way across the country for years in typical Gantry style . . . but he did one thing Gantry never did—he killed a President.

Guiteau was born in Freeport, Illinois, on September 8, 1841. His father was a man of some substance in the town and a devotee of a cult of Bible communism preached by the Reverend John H. Noyes and practiced at Oneida Community. After he was grown, Charles spent several years at the Oneida colony, and in 1865 set out for New York, telling his father he was taking "the Bible for my textbook and the Holy Ghost for my schoolmaster."

Guiteau worked at being a lawyer off and on but he found it much more agreeable to live off other people. And he never gave up his first love—religion. He published pamphlets and books, mostly cribbed from other people's writings, and preached wherever and whenever he could find

256

someone to listen. He wandered back and forth across the country on trains but seldom paid his fare.

Guiteau might have gone on for the rest of his life as a wandering preacher if he hadn't become interested in politics and thought he had a future in it. He was sincerely devoted to the Republican Party and when it was in danger of being split between the Half-Breeds and the Stalwarts, he became concerned and began to write political pamphlets. One of these was called "Garfield Against Hancock" and in it Guiteau engaged in what was then the favorite Republican tactic of "waving the bloody shirt."

> This is the issue—a solid North against a solid South. The North conquered the South on the field of battle, and now they must do so at the polls in November, or they may have to fight another war. Ye men whose sons perished in the war, what say you to this issue? Shall we have another war? Shall our National Treasury be controlled by ex-rebels and their Northern allies, to the end that millions of dollars of Southern war claims be liquidated? If you want the republic bankrupted, with the prospect of another war, make Hancock President. If you want prosperity and peace, make Garfield President, and the Republic will develop till it becomes the greatest and wealthiest nation on the globe.

The fact that Hancock had been one of the truly authentic Union heroes of the Civil War didn't deter Guiteau from referring to him as an ally of the rebels.

Garfield, of course, was elected, and Charles Guiteau immediately sought political favors on the ground that his pamphlet had won the election. He began to haunt the White House and ask for appointment to the "Paris consulship," sending notes and copies of his pamphlet to Garfield and to Secretary of State Blaine.

Time after time Garfield refused to see him, and no one

else did anything about his preposterous claim. Guiteau eventually came to think of the President as the man who was destroying the Republican Party. In his mind, Garfield was a Half-Breed who wanted to accept the South as equal partner with the North as well as institute civil service reform. Guiteau was a Stalwart and considered Vice President Chester Arthur one too. At his trial he told how the idea that the President must be killed first came to him:

> . . . greatly depressed in mind and spirit from the political situation . . . I had gone to sleep, when an impression came over my mind like a flash that if the President was out of the way, this whole thing would be resolved and everything would go well. That is the first impression I had with reference to removing the President.

The inspiration had come from God, Guiteau thought, but at first he didn't accept it:

> I was kept horrified. Kept throwing it off. Did not want to give the matter any attention at all. Tried to shake it off. But it kept growing upon me, pressing me, goading me, so, as a matter of fact, at the end of two weeks my mind was thoroughly fixed as to the necessity for the President's removal and the divinity of the inspiration. I never had the slightest doubt as to the divinity of the inspiration from the first of June. That was the day my mind became thoroughly fixed as to the necessity for his removal.

God, however, left the details of the killing to Charles Guiteau. On June 6 he bought a gun and started practicing, firing at saplings in a wood close to the White House. He made several abortive attempts to carry out his God-given mission. He considered doing it while Garfield was in church because "I could not think of a more sacred place for removing him than while he was at his devotions." Then he thought of killing the President while he and Mrs. Garfield were leaving the city by train but refrained because Mrs. Garfield was leaning on her husband's arm and looked so frail he didn't have the heart to fire.

On July 1, 1881, he gave up another attempt because ". . . very hot sultry night, and I felt tired and wearied by the heat, so nothing was done about it then."

The next day unfortunately was pleasant and Garfield was leaving that morning for a two-week vacation, so Guiteau decided to go through with his task. He made a few arrangements first. He hired a hack to stand by to take him to jail after he had killed the President, and then he had his shoes shined. In his pocket he had a note addressed to the American people. It read in part:

> The President's nomination was an act of God.
> His election was an act of God.
> His removal is an act of God.

Another letter was addressed to the White House:

> The President's tragic death was a sad necessity, but it will unite the Republican party and save the Republic. Life is a fleeting dream and it matters little when one goes. A human life is of small value . . . I presume the President was a Christian and that he will be happier in Paradise than here. It will be no worse for Mrs. Garfield, dear soul, to part with her husband this way than by natural death. He is liable to go at any time anyway . . . I had no ill-will toward the President . . . I am a lawyer, theologian and politician . . . I am a Stalwart of the Stalwarts . . . I am going to jail.

Then he waited at the Baltimore and Potomac depot at Constitution Avenue and Sixth Street until the President passed through to board his train. When Garfield was about three-quarters of the way across the waiting room, Guiteau stepped out from behind a bench, walked up behind the President and shot him in the back.

"My God, what is this?" Garfield gasped, and Guiteau stepped closer and fired again. As the President collapsed, Guiteau turned to run for the hack but was stopped by a policeman named Patrick Kearney.

"It's all right," the assassin said. "Keep quiet, my friend. I wish to go to the jail. Now Arthur is President of the United States. I am a Stalwart of the Stalwarts."

Garfield died on September 19, and on November 14, 1881, Guiteau declared at his trial: "I come here in the capacity of an agent of the Deity in this matter." He told the jury that if he wasn't freed, "I expect an act of God that will blow this court out of that window if it is necessary."

After his conviction, he shouted, "My blood will be on the heads of that jury, don't you forget it—that is my answer! God will avenge this outrage!"

In 1900, William Goebel, Democratic Governor-elect of Kentucky, was preparing to take office. He had waged a bitter battle against the Republicans and against the railroad interests of the state. As he entered the grounds of the State Capitol on January 30, he was shot down.

At the time Frankfort was filled with thousands of hill people who were vigorously pro-Republican. The oath of office was administered to Goebel as he lay on his deathbed; he died three days later. The Republican Secretary of State, Caleb Powers, and others were arrested, tried and convicted of complicity in the crime. Powers served eight years and three months in jail before he was pardoned and then elected to Congress by his grateful constituents for four terms, 1911-19.

At the time of the murder, the Hearst papers set up a howl about it. They pretended to believe the affair, which was strictly local, had been the official policy of the Republican Party. William McKinley was the head of that party and President of the United States. The Hearst press attacked him with all the vehemence the yellow journalism of the time could muster.

There is no reason to think Leon Czolgosz ever read the attacks in the press, but he did fire the gun that killed President William McKinley. Czolgosz was a slender, baby-faced 28-year-old American of Polish descent who considered himself an anarchist although he had never belonged to an anarchist organization. In fact, the only one he ever tried to join mistook him for an informer and warned the membership against him. He did read anarchist literature, however, and listened to their speeches. He was also inspired by the deeds of overseas anarchists who were quite active at that time.

Anarchists had murdered the Archbishop of Paris, the Czar of Russia, the President of France, the Shah of Persia, the Prime Minister of Spain, the Empress of Austria and the King of Italy. They had tried but failed to murder the Pope, the Emperor of Austria, the Queen of Spain, the German Kaiser, and the Prince of Wales.

Czolgosz thought a lot about those killings, especially that of King Humbert of Italy on July 29, 1900, by a weaver named Gaetano Bresci. Bresci had practiced firing his revolver for months before the deed, in the woods outside Weehawken, New Jersey. Then he had returned to Italy and killed the king. His only reason was that anarchists believed that no government should exist and those who headed governments should die. Czolgosz was so excited by this murder that he cut slippings about it from the papers and read and reread them, even taking them to bed with him. It isn't known if he decided to kill McKinley then or later, but he was beginning to think of killing someone because he spoke of the possibility to a friend.

Visiting the man at his tailor shop, Czolgosz talked with him about how bad things were for the poor and how the rich had all the best of it. Then Czolgosz suddenly blurted out that he thought he'd do something about the situation by killing a priest.

"Why kill a priest?" the tailor asked. "There are so many

priests; they are like flies—a hundred will come to his funeral."

After thinking it over, Czolgosz decided his friend was right. Killing a single priest wouldn't help much. He'd have to kill someone else. And on May 5, he went to a lecture by the famous woman anarchist, Emma Goodman.

"Men living under the galling yoke of government and ecclesiasticism are not free," she said. "We anarchists must lift that yoke! Listen to me, fellow anarchists. Our brave comrades who assassinated the rulers of Europe were inspired by high and noble motives. They could not stand idly by and allow conditions to remain as they were.

"Hear me: Assassination is a natural phenomenon! It has always existed and always will exist as long as we have government. I say to you that killing a king makes people think!"

Perhaps this didn't influence Czolgosz any more than the newspaper attacks did, but people of the time thought it did, and Emma Goldman was arrested and held for several months as a possible conspirator and the Hearst papers were denounced from one end of the land to the other.

Czolgosz went to Buffalo and apparently decided to murder the President when he read in the paper that McKinley was to appear at the Pan American Exposition on September 5. Fifty thousand people listened to William McKinley make his last speech on the exposition grounds. One of them was Czolgosz. Then he got into the long line outside the Palace of Music and waited patiently for his turn to shake the President's hand.

He had his gun in his pocket along with the handkerchief he wrapped around his right hand to conceal the weapon. He moved slowly forward between a big, burly man with a mustache and a six-foot-seven Negro named James Parker. A Secret Service agent named Ireland gave the following eye-witness account:

A few moments before Czolgosz, the assassin, approached,
a man came along with three fingers of his right hand tied

up in a bandage, and he had shaken hands with his left. When Czolgosz came up I noticed he was a boyish-looking fellow, with an innocent face, perfectly calm, and I also noticed that his right hand was wrapped in what appeared to be a bandage. I watched him closely, but was interrupted by the man in front of him, who held on to the President's hand an unusually long time. This man appeared to be an Italian, and wore a heavy black mustache. He was persistent, and it was necessary for me to push him along so that the others could reach the President. Just as he released the President's hand, and as the President was reaching for the hand of the assassin, there were two quick shots.

Startled for a moment, I looked and saw the President draw his right hand up under his coat, straighten up, and, pressing his lips together, give Czolgosz the most scornful and contemptuous look possible to imagine. At the same time I reached for the young man and caught his left arm. The big Negro standing just back of him, and who would have been next to take the President's hand, struck the young man in the neck with one hand, and with the other reached for the revolver, which had been discharged through the handkerchief, and the shots from which had set fire to the linen.

Immediately a dozen men fell upon the assassin and bore him to the floor. While on the floor Czolgosz again tried to discharge the revolver, but before he could point it at the President it was knocked from his hand by the Negro . . . On the way down to the station Czolgosz would not say a word, but seemed greatly agitated.

The President was conscious and his first thought was for his invalid wife. "Be careful about her. Don't let her know," he said. His second thought was for the assassin who was in danger of being killed by the enraged guards and bystanders. "Let no one hurt him!"

A cavalryman's heavy boot had just crashed into Czolgosz' groin, and fists and rifles were beating at him from all sides. James Parker later testified: "We thumped him and slapped his face, and I took a knife out of my pocket and started to cut his throat, but he never flinched. Gamest man I ever saw in my life."

"Stop them!" called the President, who had collapsed into the arms of Secretary George C. Cortelyou. "Clear the hall. Leave that man alone."

The troops cleared the hall, but as news of the shooting spread, a huge crowd gathered outside and there was danger that a riot might break out. The Secret Service agents decided they'd have to spirit Czolgosz out of the Palace of Music or he'd be lynched.

An agent poured a pail of water over Czolgosz. "Get up, you bastard," he said. "I have orders to get you to jail alive."

Unable to rise, Czolgosz was picked up by two soldiers and carried to a side room where he was permitted to wash the blood off his face.

"Why did you shoot the President?" another agent demanded.

"I am an anarchist. I did my duty," Czolgosz answered.

The President had been rushed to the exposition hospital and the first examinations by the doctors produced optimistic statements as to his condition. One bullet had done little damage. The other had passed through both walls of the stomach. The wounds in his stomach were closed at once. Although serious, they were not believed likely to be fatal. For a short time he seemed to improve, and Vice President Roosevelt who had hurried to his side felt confident enough to return to an interrupted vacation. Gangrene set in, however, and McKinley died eight days after the shooting.

Doctors who examined Czolgosz were of the unanimous decision that he was sane and rational and, as he himself believed, a dedicated anarchist.

Two lawyers were assigned to defend him but he refused to talk to them. "I don't believe in courts or courtrooms," he declared. "I don't believe in laws."

In a trial that lasted eight hours and twenty-six minutes, including the time it took to pick a jury, Czolgosz was convicted. His defense consisted mostly of speeches of apology by his lawyers for defending him and concluding with a eulogy of the President. He was sentenced to death in the electric chair.

He was electrocuted at Auburn prison on October 29. After he was pronounced dead, his body was placed in a coffin and a carboy of sulfuric acid poured on it. The assumption was that the body would be consumed in twelve hours. Then all his clothes and effects were burned just as they would have been if he'd been suspected of having the plague.

If Czolgosz did carry a plague, the germ had already spread to a man named John N. Schrank.

On the night after McKinley died, Schrank had a dream in which he found himself standing in the White House staring at an open coffin surrounded by flowers. As he watched, the man in the coffin sat up and pointed a finger at a corner of the room. When Schrank turned and looked, he saw a figure dressed in a monk's habit. The monk was Theodore Roosevelt and the dead man was William McKinley.

"There is my murderer," the late President said to Schrank. "Avenge my death."

Schrank brooded about the dream but did nothing about it for eleven years. He had been born in Munich, Bavaria, in 1876 and brought to the United States by an aunt and uncle. The uncle, Dominick Flammang, purchased a saloon in New York which prospered, and when the older people died, Schrank inherited both the saloon and a tenement building.

A mild, dreamy-looking man, Schrank spent most of his time reading and thinking about politics. He was devoted to the Republican Party and intensely patriotic. His reading led him to the conclusion that the first pillar of American freedom was the concept that no President should serve more

265

than two terms. This along with his conviction that Teddy Roosevelt had somehow connived in the murder of McKinley made him decide to kill Roosevelt in 1912.

Roosevelt had served out McKinley's term and had been elected to a full term of his own. He had then retired and passed on the Presidency to William Howard Taft. Angered over Taft's failure to carry out his policies, Teddy decided to run for the Presidency again. His forces were defeated in the Republican convention, however, and the nomination went to Taft. Roosevelt then formed his own Progressive Party, commonly called the Bull Moose party because of TR's habit of saying he "felt like a bull moose."

Schrank was sitting in his room on the morning of September 14, 1912, the eleventh anniversary of McKinley's death, writing a poem entitled "Be a Man." He felt a touch on his shoulder and looked up into the white face of the late President. "Let not a murderer take the Presidential chair. Avenge my death," McKinley said. That convinced Shrank and he decided to kill Roosevelt to prevent his winning a third term. He bought a revolver and started to follow Roosevelt along his campaign trail.

After several failures to catch up with the fast-moving Bull Moose candidate, Schrank was more successful on the night of October 14 in Milwaukee, Wisconsin. Roosevelt was there to address a crowd at the Milwaukee Auditorium.

Standing outside the Gilpatrick Hotel, Roosevelt was waving to a friendly crowd when Schrank, peering between the heads of two men in front of him, lifted his revolver and fired. Roosevelt was hit in the right breast by a bullet which luckily had to pass through fifty pages of his typewritten speech which he had folded in half and placed in his breast pocket. Nevertheless, the bullet still penetrated four inches into his body.

Schrank didn't get off a second shot. He was tackled by Elbert E. Martin, Roosevelt's stenographer who had played right tackle for Detroit University. The crowd surged around

Schrank, some of them yelling for him to be lynched, but Roosevelt said, "Don't hurt him," and appeared so calm and unhurt that they listened.

Urged to go to the hospital, Roosevelt refused and ordered his driver to take him to the auditorium where he spoke for fifty minutes to a crowd which barely listened. They alternately cheered and pleaded that he get immediate medical attention.

"It takes more than that to kill a Bull Moose," he told them. "I give you my word. I do not care a rap about being shot, not a rap."

Roosevelt recovered without complications, and Schrank was tried for attempted murder and judged insane after a panel of five alienists examined him.

Sentenced to Central State Hospital in Waupun, Wisconsin, he died there on September 15, 1943. Roosevelt carried the bullet in his chest for the rest of his life but it never seemed to bother him.

On the evening of February 15, 1933, Mayor Anton J. Cermak of Chicago was seated on the bandstand in Miami's Bayfront Park when President-elect Franklin D. Roosevelt's motorcade swung into the amphitheater. A crowd of ten thousand cheered as Roosevelt raised himself up and sat on top of the rear seat of the open touring car and delivered a pleasant but brief informal speech. Followed by other dignitaries, Cermak was the first one to reach and shake hands with FDR. They chatted a moment before Cermak stepped away and moved toward the rear of the car. Then it happened. Five rapid shots, which sounded like firecrackers to Roosevelt, rang out in less than fifteen seconds. Cermak and four others near him were simultaneously cut down.

The assassin, Giuseppe Zangara, a 32-year-old Italian immigrant, was immediately apprehended and flung across the trunk rack of one of the limousines and driven to jail with three policemen sitting on top of him. Zangara's asserted

267

motivation for the crime was that he suffered from severe chronic stomach pains and that he blamed capitalists for his physical discomfort.

"Back in Italy," he said, "the capitalists got to be boss to my father, and my father send me to work, and I have no school, and I have trouble with my stomach. And that way, I make my idea to kill the President—kill any President, any king."

Despite this viewpoint, he repeatedly admitted during interrogation that he had no personal grievance against Roosevelt. He had thought, he said, of assassinating President Hoover, but it was cold in Washington that time of year, and since Roosevelt was in Florida, it was more convenient that way. To add to the confusion, he was a registered Republican and opposed to labor unions and radicals.

The full report of the two psychiatrists who examined him ran less than a hundred words:

> The examination of this individual reveals a perverse character willfully wrong, remorseless and expressing contempt for the opinions of others. While his intelligence is not necessarily inferior, his distorted judgment and temperament is incapable of adjustment to the average social standards. He is inherently suspicious and anti-social. Such ill-balanced erratic types are classified as a psychopathic personality. From this class are recruited the criminals and cranks whose pet schemes and morbid emotions run in conflict with the established order of society.

Cermak died on March 6 and Zangara's murder trial took place on March 9. It lasted all of one day. Ten days later he walked unassisted into the death chamber and sat down in the electric chair with a defiant smile.

"See, I no scared of electric chair," he told the guards. "Goodbye, adios to all the world." Moments later, he impatiently shouted, "Go ahead. Push the button." And they did.

United States Senator Huey P. Long was waiting for the special elevator that would take him to the office of the Governor of Louisiana when a small man in a white linen suit stepped through a cordon of bodyguards and pressed a .32 caliber automatic pistol against the Kingfish's abdomen and opened fire. Revolvers and machine guns blazed from all sides and Carl Austin Weiss, a Baton Rouge doctor, fell dead with sixty-one bullets in him, but not before Long had been mortally wounded.

"I wonder why he shot me," Long said in the car as they rushed him to a hospital.

There has been considerable doubt in some minds that Weiss actually killed Long. Schlesinger speaks of this in *The Politics of Upheaval:*

> Some in Louisiana would always wonder whether Long was not killed by his own bodyguards, either accidentally, when they misinterpreted Weiss's desire to hold Long in a moment's conversation, or purposely in revenge for a long history of humiliation, and whether the bodyguards did not then riddle Weiss's body with bullets to cover their error, or crime. "Why," people asked, "was there never an autopsy?"

Evidence that Long may not have been killed by Weiss was presented at the inquest. The doctor who operated on Long before he died gave as his opinion that the bullet which did the fatal damage was of forty-five caliber rather than from a .32 automatic. The pistols and submachine guns of the guards could all have fired forty-five bullets.

They tried to kill Harry Truman on November 1, 1950. The would-be assassins were Oscar Collazo and Griselio Torresola, Puerto Ricans living in New York. They were both members of the Puerto Rican Nationalist movement, a splinter group that believes the island should completely

269

sever its ties with the United States, as opposed to the larger commonwealth or statehood segments of the population.

Oscar Collazo may have been assigned this task by the New York leaders of the party or may have volunteered for it, but Torresola seems to have been a veteran terrorist especially picked by Albizu Campos, the party's leader in San Juan. There wasn't sufficient evidence to link Campos or other party members to the attempted assassination but at the time it was made, there was also an attempt to kill Governor Luis Muñoz Marín of the Commonwealth and an open rebellion in which many Nationalists were killed.

Collazo and Torresola arrived in Washington armed with guns and carrying sixty-nine rounds of ammunition between them. They spent the night in a hotel and after some last minute lessons for Collazo in how to handle a gun, they reconnoitered Blair House where the President was staying while the White House was being renovated. They then separated and, coming from different directions, tried to shoot their way in.

Despite the fact that Blair House was much more exposed and harder to guard than the White House, the enterprise was doomed from the beginning, but it cost two lives. Policeman Leslie Coffelt was mortally wounded by Torresola and he, in turn, killed the gunman. Collazo, a Secret Service agent, and another guard were wounded. Collazo recovered and was tried for murder. He was convicted and sentenced to death but the sentence was commuted to life imprisonment by President Truman.

In another instance of Puerto Rican Nationalist violence, a woman and three men shot up the House of Representatives on March 1, 1954. Lolita Lebron, a 34-year-old sewing machine operator and mother of two children, started the action by waving a red, white, and blue Puerto Rican flag and opening fire with a Luger at the congressmen below. Her companions—Rafael Cancel Miranda, Andres Figueroa Cordero, and Irving Flores Rodriguez—blazed away also.

The one hundred and forty-three congressmen who were present in the chamber scattered in all directions. They dove under tables and hid behind desks or dashed for the doors. Representative Kenneth Roberts of Alabama was hit in the left leg. Clifford Davis of Tennessee was hit in the calf of his right leg. George F. Fallon of Maryland took a shot in the right buttock, and Ben F. Jenson of Iowa was struck in the back. Representative Alvin M. Bentley of Michigan was the most seriously wounded. He was hit by a bullet that struck in the right armpit and went clear through his body, leaving a hole in his lung and diaphragm. He was rendered first aid by Representatives Walter H. Judd of Minnesota and A. L. Miller of Nebraska, both physicians.

The four terrorists were overpowered by bystanders and guards and arrested. The five wounded recovered from their injuries.

On February 21, 1965, a man who had been christened Malcolm Little but renamed himself Malcolm X, stepped onto the stage in the Audubon Ballroom on upper Broadway in New York. Until March of 1964, he had been one of the leaders of the Black Muslims. Then he withdrew and set up his own Muslim Mosque, Inc. and Organization of Afro-American Unity. He was at the Audubon Ballroom to speak to four hundred of his followers. He greeted them with *Assalaam alaikum"* (Peace be unto you) and the audience shouted, *"Wa-alaikum salaam"* (And unto you be peace).

But before Malcolm X could begin to speak, a disturbance broke out in the crowd. "Get your hands off my pockets!" a man shouted. "Don't be mussing with my pockets!"

Malcolm raised his hands. "Now, brothers!" he said. "Be cool, don't get excited . . ."

As though on signal, three men rushed toward the rostrum.

When they were about eight feet from Malcolm, they opened fire. One man used a sawed-off shotgun and the others had pistols. Malcolm was hit at point-blank range by the shotgun. Thirteen shotgun pellets tore into his chest and heart; several pistol slugs struck his thighs and legs.

"There was what sounded like an explosion," a woman witness said. "I looked up at Malcolm, and there was blood running out of his goatee."

The shotgun wielder was hit by a bullet from one of Malcolm's bodyguards and went down. The other two killers escaped temporarily. The enraged onlookers set upon the fallen man and were beating him when he was arrested and dragged off by the police. His name was Thomas Hagan, alias Talmadge Hayer, and he had a long police record.

Malcolm X was dead, and despite the fact that two of the three killers were found to be members of the Black Muslims, many militant blacks believed he was murdered on the orders of the white power structure. Their attitude, though regrettable, can be understood. As Malcolm himself was so fond of saying, "We didn't land on Plymouth Rock. It landed on us."

George Lincoln Rockwell was living in California when he read a copy of *Mein Kampf* written by a recently deceased author named Adolf Hitler.

"I was hypnotized, transfixed," Rockwell said. "Within a year I was an all-out Nazi, worshipping the greatest mind in two thousand years—Adolf Hitler."

Rockwell founded the American Nazi Party in 1958 and embarked on a campaign that he hoped would make him Fuhrer of the United States. "I'm going to completely separate the black and white races and preserve white Christian domination in this country, and I'm going to have the Jew Communists and any other traitors gassed for treason."

Rockwell never made it. A young lieutenant of his, John Patler, had become so bigoted that he called his fellow Nazis "blue-eyed devils" and had to be kicked out of the organization. Shortly thereafter, as Rockwell was backing his car out of a laundromat parking lot, Patler shot him down. He died before he got to see the publication of his latest book, *White Power*, the cover blurb of which promised a program to provide "white men everywhere with a workable inspiring plan for doing on a worldwide basis what Adolf Hitler did for Germany."

The assassination of Malcolm X and Lincoln Rockwell caused barely a stir in the minds of the American people. The assassination of John Fitzgerald Kennedy, Martin Luther King and Robert Francis Kennedy shook the country to its very foundations.

The weather in Dallas on the morning of November 22, 1963, was as sullen as the city's political climate. There had been a threat of rain and clouds lowered over the city most of the morning, but by the time Air Force One touched down at Love Field, the Texas sun had broken through and the day turned as cheerful as the troubled politicians who met the plane were at the prospect of Presidential aid in difficult political problems.

It is said that a secretary named Kennedy warned Abraham Lincoln against going to Ford's Theatre and that a secretary named Lincoln warned Jack Kennedy against going to Dallas. If so, the secretary named Lincoln had more reason to fear for her employer's life in Dallas than did the secretary named Kennedy for President Lincoln's at Ford's Theatre. Dallas was a hotbed of right-wing activity where Adlai Stevenson had been roughed up and spat upon and where even favorite son Lyndon Johnson had been pushed around in a hotel lobby.

Later there was to be a lot of talk about the climate of hate in Dallas, and there isn't any doubt it existed, but whether it played any part in the events of that November day will probably never be known. Certainly the President's arrival was greeted by evidence of hate in a full-page newspaper ad calling him a traitor and asking for his impeachment.

But there was no sign of hate in the crowds that flocked to see him. The population of Dallas seemed to be as glad to see Jack Kennedy as he apparently was to be there. They lined the ten-mile route of the motorcade that was to carry him from Love Airport to the Trade Mart in downtown Dallas. A cheering crowd, estimated at five thousand, greeted the Kennedys as they descended from the plane, and the pleased President made his Secret Service men nervous by going over to the fence to shake hands with people.

The motorcade that was to carry the President through Dallas to the Trade Mart where he was to deliver a luncheon speech was composed of twenty-one cars and buses escorted by a dozen police motorcycles.

Six persons were in the Presidential car: Secret Service Agent William R. Greer was driving. Beside him sat Roy H. Kellerman, the assistant special agent in charge of the White House detail and the President's bodyguard. Behind Kellerman, on the jump seat, was Governor John B. Connally, and on the other jump seat was Mrs. Connally. Mrs. Kennedy, dressed in a pink suit and holding a bouquet of red roses presented to her at the airport, was seated behind Mrs. Connally. Jack Kennedy was on his wife's right, behind the governor.

Clearing weather had led the President to have the bubble top of his Lincoln limousine removed before leaving the airport, and his desire to let the people see him had caused him to ask the Secret Service agents not to ride on the steps or the rear bumper. He also asked the motorcycle police to remain either ahead of or behind the car, not alongside. Whether any of these changes in routine protective measures made any difference in what followed is difficult to know, but if the bubble top had been in place and guards riding the steps beside the President, an already difficult shot might have been made even more so.

The Presidential car was preceded by a pilot car that was

well in advance of the main body of the motorcade, and by a lead car in which rode Jesse E. Curry, the Dallas chief of police; the sheriff, J. E. Decker, and two Secret Service agents, one of whom was Winston G. Lawson, who had made the security preparations in Dallas. Behind the President's car was his escort car followed by Vice President Johnson's car.

The scheduled route took the motorcade from the airport through a Dallas suburb and then along Main Street. It made a right turn onto Houston Street, proceeded along it for a short distance, then made a left turn onto Elm Street, passing a plaza on one corner of which stood the Texas School Book Depository, an old seven-story red brick building.

Pleased by the reception the President was getting, Mrs. Connally turned to him as the car entered Houston Street and saw him smiling and waving to the crowd.

"Mr. President," she said, "you can't say Dallas doesn't love you."

Mrs. Connally said later that the President's smile broadened and he opened his mouth as though to answer her. The words were never uttered. At that moment, approximately 12:30 P.M., there was a sound that Agent Kellerman at first took for the pop of a firecracker.

The President clutched his throat, and the agent thought he heard him say, "My God, I am hit."

Mrs. Kennedy leaned a little toward her husband just as what Kellerman described as "a flurry of shots" rang out. A motorcycle officer said, "His head exploded in blood."

"Oh, my God, they have shot my husband, I have his brains in my hand," Mrs. Kennedy cried, looking down at her blood-splattered pink suit. "I love you, Jack."

Governor Connally had been hit in the back by a bullet that cut through his chest, shattering a rib and collapsing a lung before emerging from the front to shatter a bone in his wrist and lodge in his left thigh.

"Oh no, no, no," Connally moaned. "My God, they're going to kill us all."

He collapsed into his wife's arms as Agent Kellerman yelled to the driver, "Let's get out of here. We are hit."

Kellerman then picked up the phone and called the lead car. "Lawson, this is Kellerman. We are hit. Get us to the hospital immediately."

The lead car notified Parkland Hospital that the President had been shot and was being brought there. The Dallas police chief ordered his men by radio to surround the Texas School Book Depository. Sheriff Decker ordered his men to the railroad yards near the area that has come to be known as the "grassy knoll."

Just before the car picked up speed, Jackie Kennedy, in an apparent state of hysteria, climbed from the rear seat and started to crawl back along the trunk of the Lincoln. Secret Service Agent Clint Hill, who had been riding the left front bumper of the follow-up car, ran toward the Presidential car, pulled himself up onto the trunk and pushed Mrs. Kennedy back into the seat and down out of the line of fire.

The motorcade raced along at speeds up to eighty miles an hour toward Parkland Hospital, four miles from the scene of the shooting. The President's car made the trip in nine minutes, and doctors and nurses had a stretcher waiting to rush the wounded man to "Trauma L," an emergency room.

As soon as the doctors saw the extent of Kennedy's wounds, they knew he couldn't live. In fact, except for a few life signs, he was already dead, but they tried every available technique in a hopeless struggle to save him.

Back at the scene of the shooting there was confusion. Some witnesses reported the shots came from the direction of the grassy knoll that was in front of the Presidential car when the firing took place. Several policemen ran in that direction and one dashed up the hill on his motorcycle. Other witnesses, including Howard Leslie Brennah, a 45-year-old steamfitter, who from his vantage point on a concrete wall across the street from the Book Depository had seen a man in the sixth-floor window fire a rifle at the President's car, pointed toward the red brick building.

The first officer to enter the Book Depository was Marrion L. Baker, a motorcycle patrolman. He had seen frightened pigeons rising from a perch on a window ledge and, with service revolver in hand, had hurried into the building where he was met by Roy Truly, the depository superintendent. Truly led the officer up to the second floor and Baker saw a slim, young man of medium height walking toward the lunchroom. It was Lee Harvey Oswald.

"Come here," the officer shouted at Oswald, waving his gun for emphasis.

Oswald moved toward the officer and Truly. "Do you know this man?" Baker demanded of Truly. "Does he work here?"

Truly replied in the affirmative and Baker dashed on up the stairs.

Oswald apparently continued on his way to the lunchroom, bought a coke and passed through some offices on the second floor still carrying it. Somehow he managed to leave the building that was now crawling with police and, traveling by bus, cab, and on foot, reached his room in the home of Mrs. A. C. Johnson. There he changed into a light-colored jacket and picked up a revolver.

Then he left the house and walked along the street in a seemingly aimless way until a police car pulled up alongside him and Officer J. D. Tippit began to question him. Oswald leaned over with his head in the car window, apparently talking casually with the officer for a few moments. Then he stood up and started to walk away. Tippit got out of the car and started around in front of it as though to question Oswald further. Oswald then allegedly drew his revolver and fired four times, killing Tippit instantly.

Horrified witnesses later reported they saw Oswald hurry off down the street in the direction from which he had come. One testified he was muttering about "poor dumb cop," or "poor damn cop." As he went, he fumbled with the gun, taking out four used cartridges and dropping them in full sight of several witnesses. Then he made his way to the Texas Theater, about six blocks from the shooting of the policeman, and attracted further attention to himself by entering without paying.

Police hurried to the theater. On seeing them, Oswald said, "Well, it's all over now," and drew his revolver and tried to fire it.

It misfired and he was subdued and arrested. He was taken into custody a little after 1:50 p.m. In the two days he was held, he repeatedly denied having killed either the President or Officer Tippit.

Because of rumors that an attempt might be made to harm Oswald, the Dallas police decided to transfer him from police headquarters to the more secure county jail. As some seventy policemen stood guard, Oswald was brought from his cell and paraded before television cameras toward the car that was to carry him to county jail. A short, heavy-set man stepped out of a crowd of reporters and shot Oswald in the abdomen.

As police grappled with the gunman in front of television cameras and millions of watchers, he was heard to shout, "You know me, boys . . . I'm Jack Ruby."

Jack Ruby was the owner of a local tavern. He had a police record and made a habit of hanging around police headquarters. He later said he had visited the Western Union office on the same block and had stepped into the basement out of curiosity at the exact moment of Oswald's transfer; in a sudden rage, and to save Mrs. Kennedy the ordeal of Oswald's trial, he had drawn his gun and fired.

People who knew Ruby testified that he was a great admirer of Kennedy and had been so concerned about the right-wing hatred of him that he had suspected their involvement in the President's assassination.

Tried by a Dallas jury, Ruby was convicted and sentenced

to death. The sentence was never carried out because Ruby died of cancer at Parkland Hospital three years later while awaiting a new trial following the reversal of his conviction by an appellate court.

President Johnson appointed Chief Justice Earl Warren as chairman of a presidential commission to investigate the assassination. Members of the commission were Senators Richard B. Russell and John Sherman Cooper; Representatives Hale Boggs and Gerald Ford; Allen W. Dulles, and John J. McCloy. The report stated that Oswald, a somewhat confused Marxist who had once defected to Russia, married a Russian girl, and then returned to the United States, had acted alone out of motives more personal than political. It also concluded that Ruby had acted alone.

Because Oswald was never brought to trial and because of certain discrepancies in the Warren Report, caused perhaps by its hurried preparation, there has been speculation ever since as to whether the full truth about the assassination is known.

Various theories have been advanced, some charging conspiracy. The theories are based mainly on doubts about the number of shots actually fired, the testimony of witnesses who thought the shots came from the grassy knoll, seeming discrepancies in timing—highlighted by a film of the assassination taken by Abraham Zapruder, a bystander, which shows Kennedy's head jerking backward as he is hit—and by Oswald's allegedly poor marksmanship.

Among the books which attempt to prove these theories are *Who Killed Kennedy?* by Thomas G. Buchanan, which assumes a right-wing conspiracy; *The Second Oswald,* by Richard H. Popkin, which assumes that another man who looked like Oswald did the actual firing and that Lee Harvey was the fall guy; *Rush to Judgment* by Mark Lane, a critique of the Warren Commission's inquiry, and *Inquest* by Edward Jay Epstein, an examination of the methods used by the commission and the evidence it examined.

Another critic of the report, Penn Jones, Jr., a Texas publisher, has put forth a theory of conspiracy that has resulted in a list of thirty-three mysterious deaths of people involved in various ways with the Kennedy tragedy and its aftermath.

Examination of the evidence presented by Jones indicates that most of these deaths were due to natural causes or accidental, but there are a few that are somewhat strange. One of these was Betty MacDonald, who worked for Ruby and was a witness for Darell Ganer when he was accused of murdering Warren Reynolds, one of the witnesses to the Tippit slaying. Miss MacDonald allegedly hung herself in a Dallas jail cell. Then there is Jim Koethe, who was working on a book about the assassination and was killed by a karate chop to the throat. And Bill Hunter who was shot to death by a policeman playing with his gun in a Long Beach, California, police station.

A supporter of the conspiracy theory, District Attorney Jim Garrison of New Orleans attempted to prove that businessman Clay Shaw and an odd character named David W. Ferrie were involved. Ferrie supposedly died of natural causes after leaving two suicide notes. At a trial that attracted nationwide attention, Garrison failed to prove there was any link between Shaw and Oswald or that there was any conspiracy at all. Shaw was freed of the charge by the jury.

The evidence for Oswald as the sole killer as detailed in the Warren Report is that Kennedy was hit twice and Connally once by one of the two bullets that hit the President; that only three shots were fired altogether and those from the sixth-floor window of the Book Depository; that Oswald's mail-order Italian rifle was found near that window with three shell casings nearby; that the bullet fragments found in the car and the intact bullet labeled No. 399 found on the stretcher came from Oswald's gun; that Oswald's palm print was on the rifle and his fingerprints on boxes piled near the window, and that Oswald was seen by at least five people in the building between 12:00 and 12:30.

An assassin struck again at the fabric of American life through the body of another of its great men when Martin Luther King, Jr. was struck down by a high-powered rifle as he stood on the balcony of the Lorraine Motel in Memphis, Tennessee, on April 4, 1968. Dr. King was in Memphis to aid the cause of striking garbage truck operators when he was killed.

The Eastern Airlines jet that carried King from Atlanta to Memphis had been delayed for fifteen minutes before takeoff while luggage was checked for bombs that an anonymous caller had warned were aboard. But King was used to this sort of thing. He had been threatened many times, stabbed once, and had his house bombed. By 1968 he was beyond fear.

"Maybe I've got the advantage over most people," he told his friends shortly before his death. "I've conquered the fear of death."

At other times he spoke of the danger. "It may get me crucified. I may even die. But I want it said even if I die in the struggle that 'he died to make men free!'" And just a few days before the tragedy, he spoke of the possibility again. "Like everybody I would like to live a long life. Longevity has its place. But I'm not concerned about that now. I just want to do God's will . . . I've looked over and I've seen the Promised Land. I may not get there with you, but I want you to know tonight that we as a people will get to the Promised Land."

After a staging session with some of his lieutenants, King had washed up in preparation for leaving for dinner. Then he walked out onto the balcony of his second-floor room to get some air. He leaned on the iron railing while he chatted with friends down below.

"I want you to sing that song *Precious Lord* for me," he said to soul singer Ben Branch who was to perform at the Claiborne Temple rally later that evening. "Sing it real pretty."

Solomon Jones, Dr. King's chauffeur, called up to him to be sure to wear a topcoat because the evening would be chilly. King grinned and nodded. "Okay, I will."

At that moment there was a crack that sounded to one aide like a stick of dynamite going off. A heavy caliber bullet smashed through King's neck, exploded against his lower right jaw, severed his spinal cord and slammed him away from the rail up against the wall.

"Oh, Lord!" moaned one of the other men as he leaned over the fallen leader and saw the extent of his wounds.

Hurriedly the minister's aides wrapped towels around the gaping wound, hoping to slow the bleeding. In a few moments the area was swarming with police who found the murder weapon, a 30.06 Remington pump rifle, a pair of binoculars and a suitcase near the rooming house where the shot had come from. In the bathroom of the rooming house they found a single cartridge casing. The marksman had knelt in the bathtub to fire at King, an easy target just 205 feet away.

King was rushed to St. Joseph's Hospital, one-and-a-half miles away, but it was clear almost at once that his wound was fatal. He was pronounced dead an hour after the shot was fired.

The search for the killer was obscured at first by a mysterious radio report of a white Mustang fleeing with a police car after it, but the evidence left at the scene soon enabled police to identify the man who had registered at the rooming house under the name of John Willard as Eric Starvo Galt and finally as James Earl Ray.

Ray was a small-time criminal who had botched every crime he had attempted to commit in almost comic opera fashion (dropping his Army discharge papers at the scene of one, falling out of his escape car at another, etc.), but now he suddenly began to behave with considerable criminal finesse.

Four days after King's death, Ray crossed the border into Canada, apparently because he was aware how ridiculously easy it is to obtain a Canadian passport. He rented a room from a Mrs. Fela Szpakowsky in Toronto. Ray had previously armed himself with the identities of four Toronto men, all of whom had lived in the suburb of Scarborough and resembled him slightly. They were Eric St. Vincent Galt, John Willard, Paul Bridgman, and Ramon George Sneyd. Exactly how he obtained these aliases is not clear but they served him well both before and after the killing.

On April 16, Ray went to the Kennedy Travel Bureau where arrangements were made for him to be issued a Canadian passport for $8 in the name of Sneyd. All he had to do to get this was sign an affidavit saying he was a Canadian citizen. On April 18, Ray received a phone call and moved to another room in the home of Mrs. Yee Sun Loo, which he had rented in advance. On May 2, he picked up his passport and paid $345 in cash for a return excursion flight to London. Four days later he boarded a plane for England.

He spent six days in London and then flew to Lisbon for some obscure reason, perhaps in the hope of contacting recruiters for mercenary fighters in Africa or, as some have suggested, perhaps for the payoff for the murder of King. In Lisbon he stayed at the Hotel Portugal and obtained a new Canadian passport by pointing out that his surname was misspelled on the one he had.

He flew back to London on May 17 but it is not known where he stayed for the next eleven days. On May 28, he checked into the New Earl's Court Motel. On June 5, he telephoned the London *Daily Telegraph* and inquired how a person could go about joining mercenary forces in Africa. He moved again, this time to the Pax Hotel, and seldom left his room for the next three days. On June 8, Ray was arrested by British police at London's Heathrow Airport as he was boarding a plane for Brussels. He was extradited to the United States and scheduled to stand trial in Memphis on Monday, March 11, 1969.

That is where the story ends. Instead of standing trial,

Ray was persuaded to plead guilty and was given a 99-year sentence for the slaying of Dr. King. In a hearing lasting only 137 minutes, the state presented the *pro forma* evidence and the judge handed down the sentence. His attorney, Percy Forman, said, "I've never had any hope but to save this man's life."

Forman and the prosecution were in agreement that Ray was the gunman and that he had acted alone. The fact that no trial was held has left doubts in many minds that Ray was the only one involved. Ray himself hinted otherwise in his effort to gain a new trial after changing his mind and hiring new lawyers who, incidentally, were KKK-connected.

On the night of June 5, 1968, anguished Americans cried out, "Not again! Oh God, not again!" For that was the night an assassin's bullet struck Robert F. Kennedy as he was celebrating his victory in the California primary. He had just reversed the seemingly unstoppable McCarthy avalanche that had been building since New Hampshire and had crested in Oregon two weeks before. For the first time since his brother's death, the office John had held seemed within Robert's grasp. An assassin's bullet was to deny it to him just as an earlier one had removed his brother from it.

As the returns showed Kennedy had won, he left his fifth-floor suite in the Los Angeles Ambassador Hotel and went down to the crowded Embassy Ballroom to greet his ecstatic followers. After a few preliminary jokes and mock-serious "thank you's" to various campaign aides, he finished his short speech with a hopeful look at the future:

> I think we can end the divisions within the United States . . . What I think is quite clear is that we can work together . . . We are a great country, a selfless . . . and a compassionate country . . . So my thanks to all of you and on to Chicago and let's win.

Then Senator Kennedy moved off to attend a press conference, trailed by a group of his staff. Waiting for him in the serving pantry through which he chose to pass because of the crush in the ballroom was a small, swarthy, bristly-haired young man, dressed all in blue. In his hand he held a 22-caliber Iver-Johnson Cadet revolver concealed in a rolled-up Kennedy campaign poster.

As Kennedy moved through the crowd of cooks, waiters, busboys, and others who wanted to shake hands, the short man with the hidden gun moved closer, a faint smile on his face. The poster was dropped and the gun raised to within a foot or so of the senator's head.

When Martin Luther King, Jr. had been murdered, Robert Kennedy had talked of "this mindless menace of violence which again stains our land." Now it struck him down as Sirhan Sirhan, an embittered Palestinian, coolly pulled the trigger.

"The sonofabitch was standing there with one foot forward and his arm extended like he was on a target range," journalist Pete Hamill described him as the shots rang out.

Mutual Radio network's Andrew West was in the passageway with his tape recorder running when the shooting occurred. "Senator Kennedy has been . . . Senator Kennedy has been shot! Is that possible, ladies and gentlemen? It *is* possible! He has . . . Not only Senator Kennedy! Oh my God! . . . I am right here, and Rafer Johnson has hold of the man who apparently fired the shot. He still has the gun! The gun is pointed at me right this moment! Get the gun! Get the gun! Stay away from that guy! Get his thumb! Break it if you have to! Get the gun, Rafer! Hold him! We don't want another Oswald! Hold him, Rafer! . . . The Senator is on the ground! He's bleeding profusely . . . the ambulance has been called for, and this is a terrible thing! . . . The shock is so great my mouth is dry . . . we are shaking as is everyone else. I do not know if the Senator is dead or alive . . ."

Senator Kennedy's friends and bodyguards, Negro athletes Rafer Johnson and the 6-foot-5, 287-pound Roosevelt Grier, former Los Angeles Ram lineman, together with George Plimpton and several others, wrestled with the gunman as more shots rang out.

Paul Schrade, a United Auto Workers regional director and Kennedy campaign worker, suffered a head wound. William Weisel, an ABC-TV unit manager, was shot in the abdomen. Elizabeth Evans suffered a scalp wound, and a bullet pierced the thigh of Ira Goldstein. Another stray bullet caught Irwin Stroll in the calf.

Kennedy lay on the floor, still conscious but mortally wounded. Sirhan Sirhan had picked his ammunition carefully. They were long, hollow-nosed bullets, the most lethal type that could be used in that kind of gun.

The fatal shot struck the mastoid bone behind Senator Kennedy's right ear at a 45-degree angle and smashed through the posterior fossa—the rear portion of the skull where the brain stem connects the top of the spinal cord to the cerebrum which is the "thinking" part of the brain. Wounds to the brain stem are usually fatal, and the very least they produce is a permanent state of coma.

After what seemed like an endless wait, an ambulance arrived and Kennedy was taken away. The police pushed through the crowd in the ballroom, dragging the gunman toward a waiting car while some of those in the crowd shouted, "Get the bastard! Kill him! Lynch him!"

"I want him alive!" Jesse Unruh shouted to the police. "You're responsible to me! I want him alive!"

On the way to the police station, the still unidentified gunman told Unruh, "I did it for my country."

Unruh, assuming the young man was American, asked, "Why him? Why him? He tried to do so much."

Back at the hotel, the Senator's stunned friends and campaign workers struggled to realize what had happened and tried to comfort each other.

"It was my fault," Roosevelt Grier sobbed. "I should have been in front of him."

Budd Schulberg and others tried to console him. "How do you defend against a man with a hidden revolver? If you're in front, he moves to the side. If you're at his side, he slips in behind . . ."

Charles Evers, whose brother Medgar died at the hands of an assassin, hid his head in his hands. "Oh God, how many have to go, how many more, how many? Will it ever stop?"

The ambulance sped the two-and-a-half miles from the hotel to the Central Receiving Hospital, and the stretcher was rolled into Emergency Room No. 2.

By this time, Kennedy was nearly pulseless and his eyes were fixed and staring. His blood pressure was close to zero. Blood was pouring from his head wound.

"The bullet hit the switchboard," Dr. V. F. Bazilauskas said when he saw him.

A priest arrived and said the last rites, and Bazilauskas was just about ready to pronounce Bobby dead. Instead they went to work, giving him more oxygen, running an "airway" tube down his throat and massaging his chest to help his heart.

They administered adrenalin, albumin and Dextran—a temporary blood substitute—and he started to respond. His blood pressure soared to 150 over 90 and his heart became stronger. Dr. Bazilauskas let Ethel Kennedy listen to the heart beat through his stethoscope.

"She listened, and like a mother hearing a first baby's heartbeat, she was overjoyed," the doctor said.

Back at the Ambassador, the stunned crowd was still milling around. Two girls with Kennedy placards had scrawled the words "God Bless" across his name on their signs. Twenty or so grieving workers were kneeling around the Moorish fountain praying. A well-dressed young black man picked up a chair and tossed it into the fountain cursing. Friends walked him around the lobby to quiet him.

A reporter who worked with Kennedy in San Francisco wrote in his notebook: "They seemed almost to expect it.

There is grief. But more, there is a kind of weird acceptance. Horrible to see. They've been through assassinations before." All over the country people were saying, "I told you so. They got him." The fear that another assassin would strike had hung over the whole campaign. An article in the June 17, 1968 issue of *Newsweek* had reported the following story:

> Once in Oregon, a balloon popped loudly during a surprise party aboard Kennedy's campaign jet; Kennedy's hand rose slowly to his face, the back covering his eyes, the gaiety stopped cold for an agonizingly slow ten-count. Again, as his motorcade toured San Francisco's Chinatown a day before the California primary, firecrackers went off with sharp bursts in a puff of purplish smoke. Bobby's face froze in a little half-smile. A shudder seized his body. His knees seemed almost to buckle.

There had been threats and shouted insults from the crowd, especially at university campuses and in San Francisco. "Fascist pig!" was the taunt they usually yelled at a man whose chief constituency had been the blacks and Mexican-Americans of the state. Kennedy had known the danger but he went on with the campaign. He had mentioned the possibility that some day people would no longer be able to refer to "the Kennedy assassination" without specifying which one.

In 1966 he had responded to a question about his plans by saying, "Six years is so far away, tomorrow is so far away. I don't even know if I'll be alive in six years." But when asked if the threat of assassination didn't deter him, he told reporters, "If anyone wants to kill me, it won't be difficult," and then quoted from historian Edith Hamilton: " 'Men are not made for safe havens.' "

While Kennedy was being rushed from Central Receiving to the better equipped Good Samaritan Hospital, Sirhan Sirhan was enjoying the attention he was getting at police headquarters.

"Sirhan Bishara Sirhan joked and bantered with his captors for hours after his arrest for the fatal shooting of Sen. Robert F. Kennedy at the Ambassador Hotel last June 5, it was disclosed today," the Los Angeles *Herald-Examiner* reported during Sirhan's trial.

He kidded Deputy District Attorney John Howard about his weight and suggested he was inherently lazy, telling him he should go out and exercise. He jokingly demanded that Police Sergeant W. C. Johnson taste coffee given him by police.

After tasting it, the sergeant handed it to him and said, "If anything happens, we go together."

Sirhan laughed. "I'll hold you to that."

Sirhan refused to talk about the shooting of Kennedy but was perfectly willing to talk about everything else. He discussed the recent conviction of Deputy District Attorney Jack Kirschke for killing his wife and her lover and about the Boston Strangler.

When told by Sergeant Johnson that the strangler had choked his victims with a nylon stocking and then made a bow out of it, the young Arab remarked, "That's really cruel. I wonder often . . . what would cause a man to do such a thing." He described Kirschke as "thirsty . . . hungry for blood."

At 1:44 A.M. (P.D.T.) Thursday, twenty-five hours after being wounded, Robert Kennedy died, his wife and his brother, Senator Edward Kennedy, at his side. Later, the entire nation mourned as the funeral train carried his body from New York to Washington, D.C., for burial beside his martyred brother.

A special three-cell suite was prepared for Sirhan Sirhan by the State of California to protect him if he should be convicted and his trial was delayed in order to allow passions to cool.

On January 24, 1969, the selection of a jury of eight men and four women was completed and a fifteen-week trial began. During the trial Sirhan Sirhan admitted killing Senator Kennedy because of the Senator's support of Israel. He told the court that when he heard of Kennedy's advocacy of aid for that nation, he hated him so much that "if he were in front of me, the way I felt then, so help me God, he would have died. Right then and there."

Sirhan was convicted of first degree murder and on April 24, 1969, was sentenced to death. However, there is a long road of appeal and legal maneuvering between the Arab youth and the gas chamber and it seems improbable that he will ever be executed.

The people of America wait and wonder if and when the next assassin will strike.

12 | The Youth Rebellion, 1964-1969

The war between the under-thirty segment of the population and the rest of America may have begun formally in Berkeley, California, in 1964 when Mario Savio stood before a crowd of students and told them:

> There's a time when the operation of the machine becomes so obvious, makes you so sick at heart, that you can't take part, you can't even tacitly take part. And you've got to put your bodies upon the gears and upon the wheels, upon the levers, upon all the apparatus and you've got to make it stop.
>
> And you've got to indicate to the people who run it, to the people who own it, that unless you're free, the machine will be prevented from working at all.

The student rebellion has come a long way from those first confrontations over free speech at Berkeley. At that time the students were struggling for rights they had once possessed but which had been taken away by a short-sighted administrator. Over the years the struggle has changed to a demand for rights never granted before but which the students feel are basic.

It came a long way, through Columbia, Northwestern,

Cornell, San Francisco State and dozens of other colleges, and on the way it changed from rebellion to revolution. The trail is littered with ruined reputations, broken bones and an occasional dead body but, as a new semester begins, the revolution continues with no one able to prediict the final outcome.

As the rebellion spread, more often than not it exploded into violence. At San Jose State in California, a campus demonstration against the Vietnam war turned into rioting on November 21, 1967. Police were called when a crowd of 800 refused to disperse from in front of the college administration building where Dow Chemical recruiters were interviewing job applicants.

After several hours of peaceful demonstration, the dissidents had turned violent. Chairs were thrown through windows, and a chain was stretched across the doors to prevent entry and egress. Previous to this incident students had burned an American flag and an effigy of President Johnson. City police, supported by California highway patrolmen and Santa Clara County sheriff's officers, moved onto the campus. Tear gas was used and police forced their way through the crowd with billy clubs. Some of the rioters kicked police and others shouted taunts.

College Vice President William Dusel said the demonstrators had staged an illegal assault against the college and there would be no dialogue with a mob. College officials, however, later invited members of the Students for a Democratic Society (SDS), the key campus group involved, to meet with them.

Governor Ronald Reagan, who had ridden into office partly on the wave of reaction to the original Berkeley troubles, was quick to react to the San Jose State disturbance. "What has happened today," he said, "is inexcusable. Once it has been established who is to blame, those persons must be punished."

Reagan also told reporters his support of firm action was not political interference in the higher education system, but was necessary to preserve the system.

In April, 1968, trouble broke out at Columbia University. Several hundred students led by SDS and black militants seized five university buildings, held the dean captive for twenty-six hours and demanded complete amnesty for their actions. Their aim in doing this was to gain amnesty for previous outbreaks, to rid the university of its connection with the Institute of Defense Analysis and prevent the building of a gymnasium to which some black leaders were opposed.

After days of negotiations over the student demands, Columbia President Grayson Kirk reluctantly asked New York City police to clear the buildings. Black militants who had broken away from SDS-led white students and set up their own control of Hamilton Hall left peacefully. But the white rebels refused even when more than a thousand police, including many from the Tactical Patrol Force, moved onto campus during the evening of Monday, April 29. At 2:30 A.M. the police went into action. The Low Memorial Library was cleared quickly with only minor scuffles.

The real trouble began at Mathematics and Fayerweather Halls where SDS members and their sympathizers, led by Mark Rudd and Tom Hayden, were barricaded. These rebels had been ejected from Hamilton Hall by the black militants and were determined to hold out here until their demands for amnesty were granted.

"One of the members of the defense committee in Math Hall, when approached by moderate students in opposition to his instruction to the commune that it use clubs and gasoline against the police, retorted, 'You fucking liberals don't understand what the scene's about. It's about power and disruption. The more blood the better,' " two eye-witnesses reported in an article in the May 11, 1968, *New Republic.*

At 4:00 A.M. school officials decided to make one more

effort to talk the rebels into leaving before the police were sent in. One of them moved toward the building carrying a bull horn.

"On behalf of the university trustees, I now request you to leave the building peacefully . . ."

"Bullshit!"

"Drop dead, you creep!"

"Get those goddam fascist cops off the campus!"

"Come and get us, you bastards!"

And then the shout went up, "Up against the wall, you motherfuckers!"

The police moved in. Most of the students either left peacefully (some claimed later that they had been held against their will) or resorted to the nonviolent tactic of going limp and forcing police to carry them out. Others, however, fought bitterly with the policemen.

Soapy water had been sloshed on the marble floor in the hope that police would be unable to maneuver. Students were armed with makeshift clubs, brass knuckles, and pieces of lead pipe. Chairs, desks, and other articles of furniture were hurled from upper windows.

"Violence against the police was on a large scale," Deputy Police Commissioner John F. Walsh reported. "Police were punched, bitten, and kicked, with many attempts to kick policemen in the groin. A pattern was seen in the use of females to bite and kick policemen."

The violence was not all on the side of the students. The police have been accused of brutality by students and by various other witnesses. A pregnant girl was allegedly dragged down a flight of stairs by the hair. Professors who tried to interfere in behalf of students were beaten with nightsticks. Some students were supposedly dragged down steps, leaving a trail of blood.

When the halls were cleared, the police attacked a crowd outside composed mostly of innocent bystanders. There were no serious injuries among the students, but two police officers out of the seventeen injured had to be hospitalized and are troubled by their injuries to this day. One officer was kicked in the chest and suffered a heart attack. Another was seriously injured when a student leaped on his back, feet first, from an overhanging ledge.

Once inside the building, university officials were dismayed at the evidence they found of student activity during the seven-day siege. President Kirk's office had been wrecked. Students had urinated into a wastebasket, broken into his stock of liquor and cigars, rifled and stolen private papers, photographs, files, and books they hoped to make use of later. A manuscript, representing several years' work, was destroyed because the professor who had written it was considered "unprogressive" by the students.

President Kirk exclaimed, "My God, how could human beings do things like this?"

A police officer commented, "These bums had been shacking up in there for days. They had defecated on the rugs and chairs. The girls had nailed their sanitary napkins to the walls with sickening suggestions written under them. God, I've seen some terrible things in my life as a cop, but this was the worst. When Kirk came in, he just stood there swaying, like he was going to die."

Mark Rudd and three other SDS leaders were suspended for their part in the seizure of the buildings. A student strike paralyzed the university for a large part of the semester and, in May, Rudd led another attack on Hamilton Hall. Police were brought in again and cleared the building. Rudd was arrested and charged with inciting to riot, criminal trespass and criminal solicitation. He was held on $2,500 bail, which was paid by his father, a real estate broker.

Rioting broke out again on May 22 when bands of student rebels tore up paving blocks and hurled them through windows and at police. Doors were smashed and fires set in several buildings. Professor Orest Ranum, a liberal professor who considered the SDS a fascist organization and opposed the rebellious activity, was a particular target of the rebels. His office was broken into, and his personal papers, representing years of research, were burned. A further confrontation with police resulted in fifty-one students and sixteen policemen being injured.

The Columbia Law School faculty condemned the actions of the students. They said that using muscles instead of minds to express dissent had no place in the academic setting, and that students were not a privileged class, free to break rules the community at large were obliged to obey.

The law professors also pointed out that ransacking the president's files and burning a professor's work was a violation of the Fourth Amendment to the Constitution which protects Americans against unlawful search and seizure.

Other university professors disagreed. A segment of the university community condones the disruption of classes taught by those who support US policy, and believes that attempts to drive conservative professors from the campus, and other forms of outright violence can be justified by the moral aims and the good conscience of the dissidents.

Violence that is "relevant and meaningful," it is felt, dramatizes just grievances and brings them to public attention. They say no one has the right to utilize a university for "racist, militarist, or imperialist activities."

Following closely on the heels of the Columbia rebellion, trouble started at Northwestern in May, 1968. Blacks seized the business office building and remained encamped there for thirty-eight hours until university officials surrendered to a long list of demands.

James Turner, a graduate student in sociology and head of the Afro-American Student Union on campus, said, "The situation at Northwestern University has been positively resolved. We want to say that the difference in outcome of this situation and that of Columbia University was due to the wisdom, responsibility and willingness to learn on the part of the administrators at Northwestern University. They have generally displayed themselves as men of integrity and sincerity."

Rather than strikes and seizures of buildings, other universities were plagued by bombings and fires.

On July 6, 1968, Stanford was the scene of a fire (the direct result of arson) that caused $300,000 damage. The fire was set in the office of retiring President J. E. Wallace Sterling. His files were rifled, faculty personnel records partially burned, and papers belonging to the Stanford Research Institute were stuffed into a green bag. The aronist apparently intended to carry them off but for some reason dropped them near the door.

The Stanford Research Institute had recently been attacked by campus militants for accepting contracts from the Defense Department. The estimated loss of $300,000 included only the damage to the completely gutted office but not that to Sterling's personal property. His rare book collection was destroyed as were many mementoes gathered over 40 years of teaching. A number of valuable paintings were damaged and one work of art, a Chinese scroll by Chinzan, was destroyed.

This was the third case of arson at Stanford since February when a Navy Reserve Officers Training Corps building was badly damaged. The arsonist returned May 7 to complete the destruction of the ROTC building. A college official called the latest fire "part of the whole picture of protests on campus."

J. Edgar Hoover, in his annual report for 1968, alleged that the Students for a Democratic Society had conducted workshops in sabotage and explosives at their national convention in June held at Michigan State University. He said the participants discussed various devices that might be developed for use in planned attacks on Selective Service facilities and in connection with other forms of violent demonstrations. He also said they explored the use of combustible materials and various types of bombs that could be devised to destroy communications and plumbing systems of strategic buildings. They even discussed the finer points of firing Molotov cocktails from shotguns and similar forms of so-called defense measures that could be used in defiance of police action.

Student militants were blamed for the bombing of a building that housed a Central Intelligence Agency office in Ann Arbor, Michigan, on October 1, 1968. Police Chief Walter Krasny told reporters that three to six sticks of dynamite were used in the blast set off on the front doorstep. Glass was shattered and there was some interior damage. Krasny stated that the explosion looked like the same pattern, the same method of operation as that employed in a series of blasts that occurred during September at Federal and police offices in the Detroit area.

In San Francisco they were having similar problems with antiwar youths. An alleged Army deserter from Fort Ord was arrested by FBI and Oakland police on October 17, 1968, and charged with a series of terror bombings and sabotage in the East Bay Area. Police discovered four and a half sticks of gelamite, an explosive similar to dynamite; two other explosives, fourteen booster charges, and fifty-eight blasting caps in his apartment. They also found a book on explosives and how to use them, and a pink paper upon which were drawn maps of the Berkeley Hills area where several dynamited Pacific Gas and Electric Company transmission towers were located.

Trouble began to stir at San Francisco State College over the actions of black militant George Mason Murray, an instructor of English there. In a speech before students at Fresno State College on October 25, 1968, Murray urged them to seize control of the college by armed force if necessary.

"If the students want to run the college—if the administration won't go for it—then you control it with a gun," he told a thousand students. "We are all slaves. The only way to become free is to kill all slave masters."

Asked to identify the slave masters who should be killed,

Murray replied that he meant members of boards of education, the people in the State House, the White House, the Pentagon, the Supreme Court and the Chase Manhattan Bank.

Later in his speech he referred to the American flag as "a piece of toilet paper."

The month before, State College trustees had demanded that San Francisco State President Robert Smith fire Murray. Smith had refused. The trustees had been angered by a previous Murray statement that every United States soldier killed in Vietnam meant one less racist to worry about at home.

Murray was suspended on November 1, 1968, after urging black students to bring guns on campus. The suspension brought on a strike, called by the Black Student Union, to protest the action and demand a black studies program. Violence between police and students caused the college to be closed by a vote of the faculty.

While trouble was simmering at San Francisco State, it burst into full bloom at San Fernando Valley State when thirty-four persons, fourteen of them women, were seized by black militants and held for four hours. Several of the hostages were threatened with knives and squirted with fire extinguishers. Charges of kidnapping, false imprisonment, robbery, burglary, and assault were brought against twenty-four of those involved. Some of the charges have since been dropped; other defendants are awaiting trial.

President Smith was fired from San Francisco State and Dr. S. I. Hayakawa, the famed semanticist and opponent of New Left militancy, was appointed acting president. He ordered the college opened on Monday, December 2, and announced a policy of keeping it open.

"Police will be available to the fullest extent necessary to maintain and restore peace when school opens," Hayakawa said. "I make this declaration in order to give myself and my associates in the administration the freedom to act quickly and positively in response to whatever contingencies may arise—and we have been warned that dangerous situations may arise."

Minor violence accompanied the opening of the college. Hayakawa waded into a group of some one hundred and fifty student dissidents, mounted a pickup truck belonging to the SDS and urged students to return to classes. When he was refused access to the microphone, Hayakawa pulled the wires loose and said sound equipment was banned on campus.

"You're destroying property; we'll sue you," a student shouted.

"Go ahead and sue me—I'll come out and do this every day!" he said.

When Hayakawa got down from the truck he was surrounded by shouting, cursing students, who were supported by some faculty members, and roughed up. The jaunty tam-o-shanter the slight 62-year-old semanticist was wearing was knocked from his head, and he was pummeled by bearded, long-haired white students who backed the strike by the Black Student Union and the Third World Liberation Front which had joined it.

Hayakawa later gave reporters his views on the causes of the trouble on his campus. He said it stemmed mainly from the "hunger for humiliation" which some white leftists feel. After stating that they will take as revealed truth anything an angry black man says, Hayakawa continued, "They are capable of getting their whole idea of how American Negroes think and feel from listening to a few extremists and black neurotics with an identity problem, and imagine that they are beginning to understand the Negro. They have not had the experience that I have had."

Hayakawa managed to keep the 18,000-student college open for two weeks in the face of constant disruption by a small minority of students backed by some faculty members but was forced to close on December 14, declaring an early Christmas vacation, because of a threatened invasion by militants from other schools. The militants proclaimed the early closing a victory for them and announced they would continue their disruptive tactics when school reopened after Christmas vacation.

While the educational facilities of the nation were being rocked by demonstrations that spread from the universities down into the high schools, the largest confrontation between youthful dissenters and their elders took place in Chicago at the 1968 Democratic party nominating convention. The struggle was well advertised in advance and torrents of words have been written about it ever since.

The groups that planned to protest in the convention city were rather diverse but united by several basic grievances, two of the most important being the Vietnam war and the assumed refusal of the convention to nominate the peace candidate, Eugene McCarthy.

Generally these groups were organized around the National Mobilization Committee to End the War in Vietnam headed by David Dillinger, but other elements such as the SDS were also present, most importantly the Yippies (Youth International Party) headed by Abbie Hoffman, Jerry Rubin, and Paul Krassner, among others.

From the point of view of the Yippies and their allies, it was an almost perfect performance with the Chicago police playing their parts with almost unbelievable faithfulness to the script. The script was one that is always useful in revolutionary or prerevolutionary times—idealistic youth versus brutal police.

Afterward, Hoffman talked about what had happened. "It was groovy. We wanted to fuck up their image on TV. I fight through the jungle of TV, you see . . . It's all in terms of disrupting the image, the image of a democratic society being run peacefully and orderly and everything is according to business."

It started in Lincoln Park, an 11,085-acre strip of land between Chicago's Lake Shore Drive and Oil Town. The demonstrators had been gathering there since August 18, with Yippie and other leaders setting up headquarters at the southern end of the park. Newsmen and television cameras were on hand to record the demonstrators practicing *washoi*, a locked-arm riot tactic developed by Japanese students, and taking lessons in karate and judo. They also learned how to kick and how to use a rolled magazine as a weapon.

The early days passed peacefully as more and more demonstrators—Yippies, National Mobilization people, motorcycle gangs, SDS members, hippies and clean-cut youth for Gene McCarthy—poured in. Jerry Rubin began the street-theater fun by nominating a pig named Pigasus for President.

The Yippies said their candidate's platform was garbage. "Who knows more about garbage than a pig?" and "If our president gets out of line, we'll eat him." Pigasus was eventually seized by the Humane Society, and six persons were arrested.

There was no serious trouble with police until August 25, and then it came over the matter of whether the demonstrators would be permitted to remain in the park after 11:00 P.M. The police had received orders to clear the park at that hour, but the demonstrators planned on spending the night there.

There was an impasse at 5:18 when a large, flat-bed truck flying a Yippie flag arrived and police at first refused to admit it. Abbie Hoffman was discussing the matter with police when the trouble started. About sixty or seventy demonstrators, led by a member of the Headhunters motorcycle gang, had climbed aboard the truck. As an agreement was reached as to where the truck could park and it started to move, the crowd grew angry, thinking it was being sent from the park.

Pressing close around the truck and the police, some of the demonstrators began to shout and scream at the officers. At this point an arrest was made, and the crowd tried to keep the paddy wagon from driving away with the arrested man.

"Sit down in front of the paddy wagon!" one youth shouted. "Get in close! Get their guns!"

When two plainclothes officers moved to arrest the youth doing the yelling, the crowd surged forward.

"Let him alone! Let him alone!" they shouted.

The young man resisted and the crowd tried to help him pull away. As police dragged him off, the crowd followed, yelling, "Kill the pigs!"

The long-haired youth began to scream that he was bleeding and again tried to escape. A heckler was arrested, but the crowd pushed forward so aggressively that the police broke into a run with the demonstrators after them, yelling, "Pig, pig, fascist pig!" and "Kill the pigs!"

The police fled toward Stockton Drive where they were reinforced by seventy-five additional men who formed a double line along the sidewalk. As they loaded the first prisoner into the police van, an 18-year-old girl dashed up, and said she was the arrested man's girlfriend and demanded to be taken along. The police tried to push her away, and she began screaming and striking at them, ripping their clothes. Finally three policemen picked her up bodily and tried to throw her into the paddy wagon. They missed. She hit the back of the vehicle and had to be picked up and thrown in again.

By now the crowd had broken through the police lines and were engaging in a free-swinging fight with the officers. Feeling they were about to be overrun, the police called for help. Additional police officers arrived and used their clubs to force the crowd back.

At 8:30 it was discovered that a number of trash fires had been set in the park. When firemen arrived to put them out, they were abused and the policeman helping them was hit by a thrown bottle. At this time the police announced over a bull horn that a curfew was to go into effect at eleven o'clock and the park would be closed.

Trouble had already broken out near the fieldhouse. Twelve

policemen had been forced back against the wall, the field-house lights making them an ideal target for the demonstrators who were shouting vicious epithets at them.

"The police had not initiated the barrage of abuse, and they were not responding in any way," the Walker Report states.

At first the demonstrators stayed several feet from the cornered police but as their numbers grew, they began to push against them, still yelling and screaming. A lighted cigarette thrown from the roof landed on an officer's bare arm, and others were hit by rocks. This situation continued for about half an hour until the arrival of police reinforcements who lined up with the original twelve.

Then as the crowd continued to press in on them, there was a warning from the police line, "All right, get out of the way!" and the officers charged, swinging their clubs.

A VISTA volunteer reported that he was hit in the stomach and on the back by police who were not wearing badges or nameplates. A medic from Northwestern University later testified as to what he saw:

> When someone would fall, three or four cops would start beating him. One kid was beaten so badly he couldn't get up. He was bleeding profusely from the head. The kids scattered to the street and the police moved about two hundred yards and then regrouped around the building. A couple of dozen Yippies were clubbed. I treated five myself.

The same witness reported seeing another medic being struck by an officer. "Hey, I'm a medic!" the white-coated youth said.

"Excuse me," said the officer and hit him again.

While this was going on, Abbie Hoffman was telling police that he and his followers would not obey the curfew. "We're going to stay here 'til eleven o'clock at night, and at eleven o'clock at night we're going to test our legal right to be in this park and sleep here." The police commander informed him that any who stayed in the park after eleven would be arrested. "Groovy!" Hoffman replied.

At 10:30 a warning, drafted by the United States Attorney and city officials, was broadcast to the crowd. "This is a final warning. The park is closed; all persons now in the park, including representatives of the news media, are in violation of the law and subject to arrest . . . This is a final warning; you are in violation of the law. Move out, NOW!"

The crowd hesitated. Some demonstrators had climbed trees and were using megaphones to urge them to remain while others—their own marshals—urged them to leave.

One Yippie yelled to those around him, "We are here to defend freedom. You people who want to stay in the park, stay in the park. People who want to leave, leave. People who want to grope, grope. But for those of you who want to stay, don't panic if a motorcycle comes near you."

Other demonstrators were yelling at the marshals, "Daley gives orders! Don't give us orders, you fascists!"

At this point, some witnesses felt that the demonstrators were about to attack each other, but as the lights of TV cameras focused more intensely on the scene, those who wished a confrontation began to win out. A 14-year-old boy waving a Viet Cong flag and a Chicago actor standing beside him began to chant, "Stay in the park! Parks belong to the people!" Others took up the shout, drowning out those who favored leaving.

"This is suicide! Suicide!" some of the marshals shouted but they were outshouted by Yippies who called them "authoritarian" and tried to take their microphones away. The crowd milled around, still undecided, waiting for someone to do something dynamic to move them in one direction or the other.

Suddenly the 14-year-old boy leaped on the shoulders of a man standing nearby and waving his Viet Cong flag, shouted, "Follow me! To the streets! To the streets! The streets belong to the people!"

Others quickly took up the cry. "Let's go to the streets!"

About six hundred demonstrators followed the flag-waving boy out into Eugenie Triangle. They were joined by others until they numbered between fifteen hundred and two thousand as they ran south toward the Loop. Among them were many reporters who tried to interview them as they walked or ran.

Chanting was loud but indiscriminate. "Humphrey go!" "Ho, Ho, Ho Chi Minh!" "The street is free!" "The street is ours!" and "Free Huey!"

Two young men were now in the front ranks holding North Vietnamese flags as the block-long mass of people raced down both sides of Clark Street, leaping over fire hydrants and car fenders, dodging around telephone poles and each other.

They surged through traffic, pounding on the fenders and windows of cars, demanding that motorists honk their horns in support. At North Avenue and La Salle, they were met by twenty policemen who blocked their path and tried to direct them out of the street and onto the sidewalk. The crowd was running in all directions, and the arrival of twenty-five additional plainclothes officers and more in uniform didn't keep the police from being forced back about fifty feet, part of the crowd pushing after them.

At that point the police reformed and charged the crowd. Witnesses reported seeing a man with arms folded across his chest pushed down and kicked by police. The crowd screamed, "Police brutality!" but began to disperse, many heading back toward Lincoln Park. Others formed up and marched south on Michigan Avenue, shouting, "Peace now!" and "Ho, Ho, Ho Chi Minh!" and tipping over garbage cans and smashing car headlights and windows.

Back at Lincoln Park the police had begun the process of clearing the area as they had warned. Two United States attorneys who were on hand reported later that they thought the police were now in a "state of excited anger," and said they heard some officers saying they wanted to bust the heads of the demonstrators.

The crowd was told they had thirty seconds to start moving. When they didn't, police began moving in on foot and on motorcycles. News photographers were thick in the crowd taking pictures and, according to police, blinding them with their lights.

The crowd was shouting, "Hell, no, we won't go!" and "The streets belong to the people!" Some simply screeched epithets: "Oinks!" "Pigs!" "Fascists!" and "Shitheads!"

Traffic around the park had come to a halt. The police asked newsmen to leave and, when they refused, pushed them and finally hit them with batons. Several arrests were made. A police lieutenant shouting through a bull horn couldn't make himself heard because so many motorists were honking their horns at the request of a demonstrator crawling over the tops of their cars.

Suddenly eight or ten policemen broke from the line they had formed and charged the demonstrators, swinging nightsticks. The crowd fell back into the northbound lane of Stockton Drive, crawling over and squeezing between vehicles.

Discipline gone, the police were yelling, too. "Get out of the park, you bastards" The crowd yelled back, "Pigs! Oink, oink, oink, pigs, pigs!"

As soon as the police gave up the pursuit, the crowd turned and surged back into the park.

"The thing about this crowd," the Walker Report quotes one witness as saying, "was that it thrived on confrontation. It behaved in a way much different than any crowd I've ever seen. During racial riots, the police would break up the crowd and the crowd would stay broken up. It might regroup in another place but rarely would it head back for direct confrontation with its assailants . . . what it would do . . . regroup and surge back to the police and yell more epithets, as much as saying: 'Do it again.' "

The police commanders were still trying to keep control of their men. They were yelling at them to get back into line and obey orders. In fact, one official used his own baton to block a blow aimed at a photographer.

Tear gas canisters were now being thrown into the crowd and some policemen were shouting: "Kill the Commies!" and "Get the bastards!"

A man standing in the divider strip in the middle of Clark Street threw a bottle at an officer and four police rushed him, knocked him down and then arrested him.

Part of the demonstrators, meanwhile, had been forced onto the sidewalks along Clark Street. This segment of the crowd wasn't violent. They were moving away when they were suddenly attacked by twelve to twenty policemen who broke ranks and started to pummel them with batons. Some were knocked down and beaten. A reporter told of seeing police jab a young blonde girl in the stomach and knock her, screaming, to the sidewalk. Two or three officers caught a fleeing girl, clubbed her to the ground and kicked her. A free-lance photographer who took pictures of the incident had his camera broken.

Monday afternoon the scene shifted to Grant Park across from the Conrad Hilton Hotel where convention headquarters were located. Violence began with a march led by a khaki-clad young woman riding on the shoulders of a giant Negro and carrying a red flag.

The march was headed toward police headquarters to protest the arrest of student leader Tom Hayden. The girl was arrested at Balboa and Michigan as were nine others, and three to four hundred demonstrators turned toward the Conrad Hilton, chanting: "What do we want? Revolution! When do we want it? Now!"

They paused to surround a statue of a Civil War general named Logan and drape it with Viet Cong and red flags. There they were joined by many more demonstrators and began to hurl their usual insults at police.

There is some doubt and confusion as to what happened next but, seemingly, ten or twelve policemen pushed into the crowd and tried to drag the demonstrators off the statue. Most of those who had moved toward the Hilton rushed back toward the statue. The police immediately formed a skirmish line and went to meet them.

It took about ten minutes to clear the statue and the last demonstrator removed was a boy with a red flag, kicking wildly. Five officers were injured in this incident, and the boy received a broken arm and was hit in the groin by a policeman.

Most of the demonstrators returned to Lincoln Park as darkness fell. A large crowd gathered and a heavy concentration of television equipment was in evidence. As soon as the lights came on, the performance started. Two men wearing Nazi helmets waved black flags of anarchy for the benefit of the cameras and another thrust his red flag in front of them. A Viet Cong banner was added to the scene but when the lights picked out an American flag nearby, a shout of "Burn it! Burn it!" went up.

Motorcyclists in German helmets and denim jackets roamed through the crowd tossing firecrackers. Outside the park a group of demonstrators passing a police car with open windows paused and one of them squirted a burning liquid into the eyes of an officer. He was rushed to a hospital but the demonstrators eluded arrest.

At 9:35 an unruly mob headed south on Wells Street. Some of them marched down the middle of the street shouting the usual obscenities. Others broke windows, hurled trash cans into the street and damaged cars. Police attempted to block the way and overreacted again.

At least one innocent bystander was beaten and several news media employees were attacked in various ways since the police were now convinced the newsmen were siding with the demonstrators. Forty-six arrests were made, and five officers were injured in a hail of missiles from the crowd.

At this time police were receiving reports that a thousand or more demonstrators were planning on staying in Lincoln Park that night and were armed with sharpened bamboo spears, razor blades stuck in shoes, a shotgun and ample supplies of bathroom tiles for throwing. They were to be supported by the Headhunters and the Blackstone Rangers, a black youth gang, and were barricaded behind overturned picnic tables.

The Blackstone Rangers never materialized but the barricades were real. When police moved into the park they found them manned by demonstrators with flags flying—two Viet Cong, a black flag of anarchy and a red flag of revolution.

As soon as police appeared, the chants started. "Hell, no, we won't go!" "Kill the pigs!"

They made it quite clear they wouldn't go even if gas was used. Then they began raining bottles, stones, and tiles on the assembled police.

The district commander ordered his men to retire out of range. When the 11:00 o'clock deadline passed, he sent a traffic safety car equipped with a loudspeaker to drive past the barricades and announce: "Anyone remaining in the park from now on is in violation of the law. Please leave the park. This includes the news media. The park is now closed."

The crowd shouted its defiance, and the media representatives remained in place. At 11:45 the warning was repeated and greeted by a hail of rocks from the barricade.

At this point a single police car that had lost its way blundered into the area held by the crowd. As it moved along at ten to fifteen miles an hour shouts went up. "Get the police car! Get the police car!"

The surprised driver threw the car in reverse and tried to escape but the demonstrators crowded around the car, throwing rocks, bottles, and sticks. A bottle smashed the windshield on the driver's side.

The watching police in the lines in front of the barricades began to stir and strain forward.

"They've got the squad car, kill them!" an officer yelled.

"There's a squad car trapped!" another one shouted.

About fifty Task Force officers broke ranks and moved toward the car. The car broke away, and the police were ordered back into line but one was heard to shout, "If we back down here, the whole town goes up tonight!"

Several more officers broke rank and moved toward the barricade. They were greeted with a hail of rocks. One officer was struck and went down as a cheer went up from the barricade. Another officer was hit in the side. He chased the rock thrower but was set upon by three hippies and beaten. His wrist was sprained and he was hit in the chest with a stick, but his assailants got away.

At 12:27 the police began using tear gas and smoke bombs. As the bombs exploded the entire Task Force line moved towards the barricades. They advanced under a hail of bricks and bottles and charged the barricades, shouting, some witnesses said, "Kill, kill, kill, kill!" as they went.

Twenty-five of the defenders of the barricade ran toward the South Pond. Police raced after them. "Into the pond, throw them into the pond!" a policeman yelled.

A young man and his girl reported they were knocked down, dragged along the embankment, and the girl beaten on head, arms, and legs before they were both thrown into the water.

The police commanders were trying to reform their lines, but individual officers were chasing fleeing demonstrators. Two seminary students were attacked. One was smashed over the right eye with a gun butt and the other knocked down and beaten. As the one lay on the ground, several persons in the crowd shouted that the police had killed a priest.

The same kind of overreaction took place a little later when the police cleared Clarke Street and Eugenie Triangle of a crowd of about a thousand people. At least some of those gassed and hit with nightsticks were innocent bystand-ders. Intermittent violence continued into the early morning hours.

Tuesday, August 27, was fairly peaceful during most of the day, both demonstrators and police resting and regrouping their forces. It wasn't until about 4 P.M. that the situation became heated again. A team of police was surrounded in Lincoln Park by shouting demonstrators. A squad of thirty police pushed their way through without using their batons and rescued the trapped officers.

Another attempt to clear Lincoln Park at curfew brought more trouble. When the crowd refused to move, tear gas was thrown and a sanitation truck was used to spray gas from a nozzle. The truck was pelted with rocks, bottles, and bricks. A Task Force officer riding the running board of the truck was struck in the leg and had to take shelter behind the open door. As more missiles pounded at the truck, his helmet was cracked by a large object.

Police claimed that in this confrontation the crowd used sharpened stakes taken from a snow fence, a cork ball with nails driven through it, a knife, an icepick. Their reaction was much the same as before. There were beatings and abuse. A youth was dragged by his long hair, beaten about the head and shoulders, and finally kicked in the head.

All through the week, stink bombs had been set off in the Hilton and the Sheraton-Blackstone hotels. The air in both buildings smelled like vomit during the whole period. Foul-smelling liquid was poured on the lobby rug at the Hilton, and butyric acid, which smells like rotten eggs, had been lib-erally doused over the furniture in both lobbies.

Paper bags containing feces and cans of urine were being rained on police from the windows of the Hilton.

A police lieutenant said a girl approached him and threw human excrement in his face. Other officers claimed they were kicked by demonstrators who had razor blades fixed on

312

their shoes. As the night wore on the police became more nervous and restive. The Walker Report says the seven hundred police around the Hilton were nearly exhausted. Most of the men had been on duty for twelve hours and some for as long as fifteen.

"It was clear that the Chicago police had had it," a Washington *Post* reporter said.

Shortly thereafter National Guard units moved into the Hilton to relieve the exhausted police. When the general in command of the unit tried to address the crowd, he was greeted with shouts of "Sieg Heil! Sieg Heil!" The demonstrators turned on their sound system full blast and drowned him out by singing, "This Land Is Your Land."

A series of antiwar orators now spoke to the troops over the loudspeaker. One was introduced as Mr. Love and referred to the President as "that son-of-a-bitch Johnson," which brought applause from the crowd. A priest followed him to the platform and denounced the war and called on the delegates in the hotel to flash their room lights if they agreed. The lights in about ten or twenty rooms flashed on and off.

"The Guard apparently stood its ground without any significant response—physical or verbal—to the demonstrators, despite a level of abuse that one Guard official calls 'unbelievable,'" the Walker Report says.

As the night wore on, the crowd grew quieter. At one point, Tom Hayden, one of the founders of the SDS, took the microphone and talked. He had, he said, "gone underground to get the pig off my back. Now that the pig is on the collective back of all of us, we are going to find a way to go underground." Then he advised the crowd to get some sleep. By 4:55 all was quiet.

Wednesday, however, proved to be the day of the worst police rioting.

"They were tossing anything they could lay their hands on—heavy chunks of concrete, sticks, cans, bags of what looked like paint," a witness said. "I was hit in the stomach with a large brick and also on the ankle and back of the head with thrown objects. I suffered a large bruise on my right side from a thrown brick."

"At first," a St. Louis newsman wrote, "the police stepped forward in unison, jabbing in an upward motion with their nightsticks with each step and looking like a well-drilled marching unit . . . suddenly they stopped the unison and began flailing with their clubs in all directions . . . People scattered . . . some went down, screaming and cursing and moaning. I saw a number of women . . . literally run over. In the wink of an eye, the police appeared to have lost all control."

The police hit anyone who stood in their path. Men, women, clergymen, newsmen were struck; some of them were hit as they lay on the ground. People were jammed together, trying to run. Others fell and were trampled. One girl said she looked into the face of a policeman and was terrified by his expression, that "it was like he wanted to kill."

The police rioting lasted about twenty minutes and then they withdrew to a grove of trees north and west of the bandshell. The crowd yelled obscenities after them, and someone on the platform shouted, "We won it, baby!"

Thirty policemen were injured in the fighting but there is no accurate count of the number of demonstrators hurt since most were treated at the scene.

Dick Gregory then addressed the crowd, calling Mayor Daley a fat, red-faced hoodlum. David Dillinger urged a march on the Amphitheatre but said that anyone looking for trouble shouldn't join the march but take to the streets on their own. "We don't want violence. So don't come with us."

Another speaker was caught on sound film urging those who wanted violence to "break up in small groups and do your own thing in the Loop." Dillinger returned to the mike and told the crowd there was a group that intended to break out of the park and be violent. He said anyone who wanted to go with them was free to do so but the group he was leading would be nonviolent.

The word that passed through the crowd was, "If you want to do violence, that's your thing; but get away from the group."

The march toward the convention began with about five or six thousand participants. They were halted at Columbus and Balboa Drive by about forty policemen whose senior officer informed David Dillinger that on orders of the Chicago Police Department there would be no march.

The marchers sat down on the sidewalk, and the police told them they were breaking the law but made no arrests. The march leaders then began to negotiate with city officials.

Around the Hilton, more trouble was brewing. Yippies and hippies were engaging in the usual taunting of police, and the women were said to be the worst offenders. An assistant United States Attorney and a policeman were sprayed in the face with oven cleaner as the crowd continued its vicious chanting of obscenities.

A reporter from a Chicago paper noticed a hail of debris from one of the upper floors of the Hilton and testified that he went into the building and up to the fifteenth floor where he discovered the debris was coming from the campaign suite of Senator Eugene McCarthy.

Unable to march toward the convention hall, the crowd with Dillinger joined those in front of the Hilton. The police in the area were now in a violent mood. Witnesses testified that they were now giving in to vicious verbal abuse of the rioters.

Segments of the crowd tried to break through National Guard lines. Tear gas used to control the crowd drifted down on those gathered in Grant Park and out onto Michigan Avenue. One large group of demonstrators poured across a foot bridge onto Michigan Avenue and surrounded the SCLC's Poor People's marchers and their mule train. At first the SCLC people welcomed the demonstrators but later grew worried for their safety in the crush and asked police to help extricate them.

With Viet Cong, red, and black flags flying at their head, the crowd poured out of Grant Park and moved south on Michigan. Four or five policemen reportedly attacked people during this time, and some witnesses thought the parade marshals had lost control of the marchers. Several thousand made their way to a spot opposite the northeast corner of the Hilton. Here they were separated from two to three thousand demonstrators on the east by a police line, and another five hundred were near the east face of the hotel. The police at this time had the feeling of being surrounded.

A police officer was knocked down and surrounded by a group he thought intended to stomp him. He was rescued by fellow officers while the usual obscene insults filled the air.

A band of long-haired demonstrators tore down an American flag from in front of a private club and carried it into the street to burn it. A Vietnam veteran grabbed it from them and was attacked by the crowd. Passersby were also attacked by the crowd. In one instance, five persons charged out of Michigan Avenue onto the sidewalk, knocked a pedestrian down, formed a circle around him and started kicking him viciously. When they'd finished, they unlocked arms and melted back into the crowd.

All during this period the same endlessly repeated abuse was being hurled at policemen and Guardsmen, and the police were replying in kind. A new element was added as college girls and hippies tried sexual provocation as a weapon.

One hippie girl went up to a policeman and lifted her skirt to show him her sexual organs. "I'll bet you haven't had a piece in a long time, have you?" she said.

Another female, a clean-looking blonde in a red miniskirt, made lewd sexual motions in front of police. She was urged on by the crowd in what police thought was an attempt to provoke an arrest and set off more fighting.

An observer from the ACLU said that at that time he felt

this was a violent crowd which had come looking for trouble. People were yelling, firecrackers exploding, horns tooting and loudspeakers blaring. Police microphones added to the uproar with orders no one could hear: "Please gather in the park on the east side of the street. You may have your peaceful demonstrations and speechmaking there."

The crowd made no attempt to move. Several arrests were made and the loudspeakers blared again. "Will any non-demonstrators, anyone who is not a part of this group, any newsmen, please leave the area."

The police car issuing the warnings was surrounded by the mob and its windows were plastered with McCarthy stickers. A rear tire was flattened before the car could move away. Some demonstrators were sitting down in the middle of Michigan Avenue, and their loudspeakers were competing with those of the police, telling the crowd, "You don't have to go! Hell, no, don't go!"

The Walker Report states that the crowd was becoming increasingly ugly. Demonstrators were pushing police, spitting in their faces and pelting them with rocks, bottles, shoes, glass, and other objects.

The events that followed are confused by conflicting reports. The police moved forward and began assaulting the crowd. They said later they were under heavy attack by missiles thrown from the crowd and that individual officers were cut off and beaten. Other witnesses deny this, and film taken at the scene does not show the missiles. The policemen disobeyed orders to stay in ranks and began indiscriminately to attack anyone in their path. Newsmen at the front of the crowd were caught in the first surge. A St. Louis reporter was knocked down, clubbed and his glasses broken. An ACLU representative said police were cursing and shouting, "Kill, kill, kill!" A Chicago *Daily News* reporter also heard this chant.

The police kept coming and the crowd tried to escape. The press was so great that the people caught in the middle couldn't move. A great deal of yelling and screaming resulted. Innocent bystanders and passersby were trapped by the retreating mob, crushed against buildings, and knocked down. Many were beaten by police when they didn't move.

A secretary reported having been trapped up against the Blackstone Hotel. Fearing that she would be crushed, she managed to work her way to the edge of the street and saw police everywhere. She was hit on the head from behind with a billy club. Knocked down onto her hands and knees, she was hit again around the shoulders. When she finally got to her feet again, she noticed that the policemen were not wearing their badges. She eventually made her way into the Blackstone and was taken to a hospital where she received twelve stitches for a head wound.

A Los Angeles Police Department observer first stated that during the week the restraint of the police both as individuals and as an organization was beyond reason but said of this specific occasion that many officers acted without restraint and used force beyond what was needed. He said there was little leadership to prevent such conduct and that officers were not controlled by supervisory personnel.

One witness told the Commission on Violence that only a saint could have swallowed the vile remarks directed at the officers, but he did think they went too far in clubbing the Yippies. He saw them in the park, swatting at boys and girls lying on the grass, and more than once saw two officers pulling at the arms of a Yippie until the arms left their sockets while a third jabbed a riot stick in the youth's groin.

There was more fighting as the crowd moved away from the Hilton. Police attacked demonstrators and bystanders at several points. A well-dressed woman was sprayed with Mace when she protested against the beating of a young man. People were knocked into the plate glass window of the Haymarket Bar and beaten by police despite the fact that many were badly cut. An officer on a motorcycle tried to run people down on the sidewalk. Other demonstrators and bystanders were forced over the rail of an underground garage by policemen on motorcycles.

The level of violence fell off after Wednesday night although minor incidents occurred, among them a raid on McCarthy headquarters after the National Guard complained of being bombarded by objects thrown from the windows of the fifteenth floor of the Hilton.

The casualty list for the week of trouble is somewhat lighter than might be expected. There were no deaths and few serious injuries. The Commission of Violence found that 192 police and 102 demonstrators had been treated by Chicago area hospitals. That list does not include those who were given first aid for the effects of Mace or tear gas or those treated at the scene by the medics accompanying the demonstrators, but it is indicative of the overall total.

While the use of violence by Chicago police may be considered the major victory of the young student activists, there were many more victories and defeats in the colleges throughout the academic year.

San Francisco State reopened after Christmas, and George Murray's suspension was made permanent. He was later jailed for carrying a concealed weapon. There were nine bombings, many fires and other destruction. Tactical Squad police fought with students in struggles that left eighty-five students and forty-two police injured and caused thousands of dollars in damage. A black student studies program was scheduled to open the following fall, but Professor Nathan Hare was dropped as head of it.

At Claremont College a bomb seriously wounded a 20-year-old secretary and student when she picked up a shoebox addressed to Government Professor Lee C. McDonald from his mailbox. Mrs. Mary Ann Keatley's doctors were in doubt as to whether she would regain normal vision or whether the thumb of her right hand could be saved. Her 21-year-old husband said, "Her left eye was ripped open and her right one was penetrated by a fragment, but she can distinguish light." She also lost two fingers on her right hand. No motive for the bombing other than student unrest was forthcoming.

At New York City College, a fire blamed on arsonists destroyed the auditorium on May 8, 1969—an act that CCNY President Buell G. Gallagher said was performed by adventurers in guerrilla tactics who had taken over from the responsible black and Puerto Rican students. A second fire, apparently set at the same time broke out in Wagner Hall. The incident followed a clash between Negro and white students in which seven white students suffered head wounds.

Ten Negroes, including four girls, staged a hit-and-run vandalism attack in one building and disrupted classes. Some classes were canceled, fire alarms went off, and white students wearing red armbands marched about the campus and ran through buildings. Some two hundred protestors faced about two hundred counterdemonstrators but the two groups were kept apart by police.

The confrontation had come about after black and Puerto Rican students had demanded a separate school for black and Hispanic studies and a freshman enrollment reflecting the racial balance of city high schools.

On the same day the ROTC building at Howard University was gutted by fire, a fire truck was set ablaze and cars stoned as a crowd of one thousand persons, many of them teen-agers, from off campus roamed the grounds. At one point the rioters broke into the school of religion yelling, "Let's burn it! Let's burn it!"

The trouble at this largely black school resulted from demands by militants that Howard become more relevant to the black community. One of the leaders of the militants, Ewart Brown, was quoted in *Esquire* as saying, "You put a gun to their head and they still don't believe you until you pull the trigger."

Trouble brought 1,900 National Guardsmen to the campus of the University of Wisconsin at Madison. In support of black student demands, there had been picketing, sit-ins, and a march on the State Capitol. The Guardsmen restored order after thirty-six arrests, three suspensions and six forced withdrawals of students.

At Harvard police were called on campus to quell disturbances. A graduate student was given a one-year jail sentence for assaulting Dean Robert B. Watson during a seizure of University Hall on April 9, 1969. Some one hundred and seventy other students were convicted of trespassing and fined $20 each. The usual black student and ROTC complaints were blamed.

Also in April of 1969, black students at Cornell seized Willard Straight Hall and held it until the university administrators gave in to their demands. A band of one hundred black men and women paraded out afterward, carrying an arsenal of seventeen rifles, shotguns and homemade spears. The surrender of the administrators led to some criticism but they defended themselves by saying if police had been used to clear the building there might have been a blood bath.

The pictures of armed students that appeared in the press were shocking to the American people because of the implication of a new era of armed violence in the schools.

Berkeley was again the scene of violence during the early part of 1969. This was the so-called People's Park confrontation. The "park," a vacant area owned by the university, had been taken over by Berkeley "street people" and decorated with a few potted plants. Complaints from neighbors about "orgies" and drug use led to the university fencing in the area. An attempt to tear down the fence by those who were used to congregating there brought on the trouble. A sweep of police down Telegraph Avenue resulted in rock-throwing and the use of riot guns. A young man on a rooftop was killed and another so seriously wounded that he is suing for the loss of his eyesight.

The National Guard sent in by Governor Reagan used a

helicopter to spray students, hippies and innocent bystanders alike. Ronald Reagan praised the action but others have denounced it.

Various reasons have been offered by experts and the not so expert for the outburst of violence on college campuses. The students blame a lack of relevance in their education, the war and racism, but are not very explicit about the first and sometimes highly subjective as to what constitutes institutional racism. Observers have questioned what the SDS, for instance, would do if they were to win all their demands.

Columnist Max Lerner feels that society has failed to prove its credibility to the young idealist. He says that despite the many gains and advantages of our society, its hypocrisy and blind spots are more glaring than those of less fortunate societies and that the great wealth and creature comforts of America are against it in the minds of idealistic students. ". . . the fact of prosperity and power becomes itself a count against the society and is used both as a source of guilt and self-hatred and as a weapon for revolution," he says in his column of June 30, 1969.

A conservative point of view of the reason for student militancy is expressed by Professor John O. Nelson, who teaches philosophy at the University of Colorado. He believes there has been overemphasis on the necessity for college education and that too many students with no real calling have entered the universities.

He thinks student unrest is an expression of their frustration at not being and doing what they are by nature fitted to be and do. Young people who in former years went into trades and crafts were dealing with the concrete, the real world that they could understand and handle, he believes, but the young people of today who continue in school until 22 or beyond are in direct contact only with symbols or symbols of symbols which have themselves been divorced from reality. This causes the college student to have no tolerance for reality and to become dissatisfied and disoriented.

To escape boredom, students today turn to crusading and finally to something real—violence.

There really is not much difference between the students' contention that their education lacks relevance and Professor Nelson's view that most of them would be happier without a college degree. There is in both viewpoints the suggestion that boredom with the collegiate way of life and disgust with the society that creates it is partly to blame. That boredom can produce violence has long been known by those who have studied the behavior of juvenile gangs.

Harold I. Lief, M.D., pointed out the importance of boredom in his article "Contemporary Forms of Violence" in the symposium *Violence in the Streets*. He pinpoints the importance of violence to a youth's standing in his peer group:

> . . . teen-age violence is characterized by the value attached to the violent act itself, "coolly" carried out with little regard for the victim or to the purpose of the act. It is the violence itself that gives the gang member a sense of his own existence, as well as a sense of belonging to a group. A conformist whose greatest fear is to be left alone, ignored, or rejected by his gang, he has no sense of autonomy, of being able to influence or manipulate his environment in any constructive fashion.

Perhaps the steady rise of juvenile delinquency and crime in the streets that has plagued the United States since the end of World War II can be considered another facet of the rebellion spreading from our colleges to our high schools. It is a war of the young against the over-thirty segment of the population as well as against society. The war's major battles are fought on the college campus and in the political arena by students, but its skirmishes are fought in the streets and alleys by juvenile gangs and "street people."

Teen-age violence has always been a part of our national heritage but its growth in the fifties and sixties has been phenomenal. Los Angeles in the fifties was terrorized by the so-called White Fence gang, and Chicago in the sixties had its Blackstone Rangers. New York teen violence reached one of its peaks in the exploits of a group called the Human Torch gang. Four youths who "got a kick out of seeing blood flow," as one of them expressed it, were charged with beating and kicking one man to death, horsewhipping teenage girls and torturing a vagrant and throwing him into the East River.

Police quoted one of the boys as saying he had "an abstract hatred for bums—I despise them. Last night was a supreme adventure for me."

In 1957, gangs of young toughs terrorized New York by attacking passengers on subways and in parks. On August 5, Acting Police Commissioner James R. Kennedy placed the city's 23,000 police on special alert to block new outbreaks. Prior to this, teen-agers had killed two boys and a man in little more than a week. A few hours after the alert, teen-age toughs wounded two men in Brooklyn with an unprovoked shotgun blast, and police on bicycles broke up a gang fight between two groups in the Bronx who were slugging it out with baseball bats, heavy leather belts, and iron pipes.

These and other incidents of that summer led columnist Robert Ruark to write:

> Thank the Good Lord I don't live in New York but spend the majority of my time in civilized jungles such as Tanganyika or Kenya. For if I lived in New York I would apply for a pistol permit and indulge myself in shooting for sport a great many people who are described as teenagers.

Juvenile arrests in 1957 were up 20 percent for felonious assault, 36 percent for robbery, 15 percent for grand larceny. One out of every ten New Yorkers arrested belonged to the youthful offenders group.

Some individual crimes were of such a shocking nature that they received national attention. BOY, 15, THROWS

CHILD TO DEATH was the headline on an AP story datelined New York, February 12, 1958. The story related how Francis Michael Medalle, who had been expelled from parochial school a month before, had killed the pretty 7-year-old daughter of neighbors by hurling her from the roof of a twelve-story Bronx apartment house.

"I need a strong girl to help me bring a heavy box down from the roof," the boy told Kathleen Hegmann. "If you come up and help me, I'll give you ten cents and a lollipop."

"I put my hands around her neck and choked her a little bit, I don't know why. And then I pushed her off the roof," Francis told police.

Four months later, four members of a youth gang were convicted of slaying Michael Farmer, the polio-crippled son of a New York fireman. Headlines told of rioting Negro teen-agers running wild on an excursion boat between Buffalo and the Crystal Beach Amusement Park in Ontario, Canada. The ship was turned into a "nightmare of flashing knives and sobbing, frightened passengers." Fourteen persons were injured and nine youths arrested.

In Detroit, on January 22, 1960, a man was hospitalized after being found bloody and battered in the lobby of an apartment building. Joan Wierda, a 17-year-old high school student, and four male companions were accused of the robbery-beating. She had carved her initials on the man's back with a knife because "I hate my father and he looks like him."

On that same day, Los Angeles police reported that no section of the city was free of youth gangs. They reported eighty-nine of what they called "hot" gangs and said every race, every social and economic level was represented among the youthful offenders. Those arrested for such crimes as burglary, assault, and auto theft equaled all other age groups combined.

Even areas such as suburban West Valley, North Hollywood, and Hollywood were listed as being infested by gangs

325

of youths, usually consisting of from twenty-five to fifty members, who were constantly floating around the county —often in stolen autos.

The late Drew Pearson took note of the rising juvenile crime rate in June, 1961. His column of June 7 reported that "juvenile violence has exploded into a national disgrace during the past decade. The crime rate for the 10-to-18-year-olds has shot up 175 percent while the number of teen-agers has increased only 35 percent."

Pearson revealed that the Senate Juvenile Delinquency Committee estimate that if the trend were not reversed, 1,000,000 teen-agers would be hauled before the courts in 1965, over 1,400,000 by 1970 for crimes other than traffic offenses. This compared with only 470,000 cases in 1958, the latest year for which records were then complete.

Girl gangs were increasing faster than boy gangs and were equal in ferocity, the Los Angeles *Times* reported on April 23, 1963. There had been incidents of girl gang fights that went far beyond the hair-pulling stage—fights with razors and knives. An exhaustive twenty-eight-month study of the problem had been suggested by the USC Youth Study Center.

In Garnett, Kansas, hundreds of rioting youths fought officers and firemen early on July 2, 1963, when beer halls were closed after thousands of people had gathered for sports car racing. Police Captain Robert C. Cowdin of nearby Ottowa, Kansas, collapsed and died after firing tear gas at rioters who were pelting police with bricks, beer bottles and other articles and had twice tried to storm the jail on City Square to release arrested youths. There were more than a hundred injuries.

By May 4, 1965, columnist David Lawrence was urging the use of troops to police the streets of Washington, D.C. He quoted from a letter by a serviceman whose wife had been attacked twice by Negro youths. "When she screamed for help, he stabbed her four times with some vicious, narrow daggers, almost like icepicks. She died 12 days later in the hospital." The writer then suggested some possible remedies for street crime:

> Would the use of the Marines and troops be possible to stop the crime wave? Should all men be fingerprinted? Should criminals be deported? Surely there must be some solution to save our country. It is more dangerous to walk the streets of Washington, D.C., than anything I faced in World War II and the Korean police action, and I have nine campaign ribbons and lived through it, only to find my wife murdered in front of our home in Washington, D.C.

"WE NEED YOU! DO YOUR PART FOR YOUR COMMUNITY. PROTECT YOUR FAMILY. WE NEED VOLUNTEERS FOR NIGHT PATROL. TWO-WAY RADIO SUPPLIED," read a sign in the window of an empty store at Leffert Street and Kingston Avenue in New York in September 1965. A group of orthodox Jews had formed a vigilante group called the Maccabees.

Police dogs were being used by guards on patrol at the Bronx Zoo because there had been sixteen violent attacks on caged zoo animals by young vandals during a two-month period. New Yorkers were afraid to park their cars on side streets at night for fear every window would be smashed, and seasoned city dwellers refused to enter self-service elevators with anyone they didn't know or recognize because he "might be a stranger with a switchblade."

Young lovers no longer walked in Central Park, and the benches on the Bronx's Grand Concourse were deserted at night. Even the hansom cabs no longer drove through Central Park at night. The police were working in teams known as "Murphy's Marauders."

The FBI "crime clock" for 1966 was a shocker. "An American woman is raped every 12 minutes. A house in the United States is burglarized every 37 seconds. Someone is robbed every 4½ minutes in this nation."

327

By 1967 the *fear* of crime in the streets was becoming more important than the actual crime. All over America the older generation was reacting to the youthful rebellion being fought on the streets. The term juvenile delinquency was appearing less frequently and the code phrase "crime in the streets" with its hint of racial overtones was taking its place.

TERROR IN CITY STREETS ALARMS MIDWEST-ERNERS, the Los Angeles *Times* reported on September 24, 1967. According to the story, the kind of street violence that had plagued New York for years had spread to large and medium-sized cities in the Middle West. There was fear among city officials and citizens that law enforcement was degenerating into a kind of street warfare between police and criminals, with the average citizen both innocent bystander and victim. Violent crime had moved out of the central city and into the suburbs and was constantly increasing.

People were mainly concerned with five types of crime: assaults, armed robbery, gang fights, riots, and organized crime operations. Armed robbery was increasing faster than any other type of crime, and increasing in direct proportion to the number of guns being purchased by citizens for their own defense. Detroit had seen the most "spectacular outbreak" of armed robbery. That particular crime had increased 65 percent in a twelve-month period and was still rising.

In Chicago, in large sections of the South Side, parks were practically unused in the evening for fear of assault. The parking area around the juvenile courthouse in Detroit had become a permanent war zone, and a large northwest section was paralyzed by fear of personal assault to such an extent that one could walk down the streets in the middle of the day without meeting anyone brave enough to venture out.

In Cleveland police were warning reporters to stay off city buses, and Marquette University in Milwaukee had taken to providing escorts for nuns walking from the hospital to their convent a block away. Chicago parents were accompanying their children to and from school to protect them from gangs of young hoodlums who practiced shakedowns and assault. Detroit and Cleveland were also being plagued by gangs of motorcycle outlaws.

In a lead story in its July 11, 1969 issue, *Life* reported on the fear of crime in Baltimore. A full-page picture of a young mother staring out a window from behind a heavy chain link fence topped with barbed wire was captioned: "In a Baltimore ghetto, Mrs. Judy Brookhouser watches from the caged window of her apartment in 'The Compound' —the guarded complex operated by Johns Hopkins for families of staff doctors."

Crime was up all over the United States—robberies 22 percent, beatings 8 percent. In large cities and the suburbs, fear had turned nighttime into a prison. City dwellers were buying dogs, building fences, buying guns and expensive locks in larger numbers than ever before. The training of guard dogs had become big business and private police protection was in growing demand.

Some attempts were made to counter the belief that America was undergoing an unprecedented crime wave. Richard Nixon stressed law and order in the 1968 Presidential campaign, Hubert Humphrey pointed out that the number of homicides was lower than in 1930, and Attorney General Ramsey Clark remarked that the average American's chance of being a victim of a crime of violence was about once in 400 years and if he wanted to improve his chances he should avoid his friends and relatives since statistically they are the most likely to harm him.

However, guns and law-and-order candidates were becoming part of the American way of life. In Minneapolis, a policeman was elected mayor.

Tony Imperiale, a beefy, gun-toting city councilman of Newark, has said, "My guns protect me and my family." At the time he made the statement he headed a vigilante-like group that boasted it kept a secret arsenal and could obtain a tank and two helicopters whenever they became necessary in the defense of the city's whites.

Imperiale and his counterparts in other cities were part of the reaction of older, more conservative people to the youth rebellion. Another part of the reaction was the ever-growing shift to the political right in America. A recent poll taken in California revealed there had been a 10 percent increase in voters who considered themselves conservative in the last year.

Rebellion produces reaction. Reaction could easily bring violent repression. Can the country absorb the shock of the youth rebellion without an overreaction that could prove more harmful than the rebellion itself? Only time will tell.

The Gun and the Sociopath, 1965-1969

GUNS DON'T KILL PEOPLE, PEOPLE KILL PEOPLE

You see that slogan on bumper stickers from one end of the land to the other. The National Rifle Association and its allies must have had them printed by the million, and millions of gun lovers display them proudly. There are others who are not so firmly convinced that guns don't kill people. A lot of them are dead.

In Detroit a man bought a gun to protect his home shortly after the riots. One night he heard footsteps in the hallway and then saw the knob of his bedroom door begin to turn very slowly. He picked up the pistol from the nightstand and fired. He had shot his 3-year-old daughter through the head.

In Paramount, California, a 5-year-old boy discovered a .25 caliber automatic pistol behind a vase on a television set. Thinking it was a toy, he pointed it at a 2-year-old girl and shot her.

In Phoenix, Arizona, a young sailor returning home on leave was shot to death by his father. The father fired a rifle through a door, thinking there was a prowler outside. The son was dead on arrival at the hospital.

In New York, the 22-year-old adopted son of a government official fatally wounded himself with a shot in the head. He was playing Russian roulette—with a single bullet in the gun. He was betting with himself that he could pull the trigger without having the cartridge come under the hammer and fire. He lost.

In San Diego there was a whole series of fatalities from guns . . . and these were guns in the hands of experts—marines.

Two sentries were standing guard duty at the North Island Naval Station. They carried loaded shotguns. One gun went off and one sentry died.

Several weeks earlier a lance corporal was shot in the stomach by a fellow military policeman who said his .45 caliber pistol fired accidentally.

A month prior to that a civilian visitor was fatally wounded when a sentry's rifle fired accidentally.

In San Bernardino, California, a man who had gone out searching for prowlers returned home to reassure his wife he hadn't found any. Not expecting her husband's return so soon, the wife grabbed the family gun, a .38 caliber pistol, when she heard the front door open. She fired four times at the dark figure in the living room just as her husband cried out, "Don't shoot! It's me! It's me! Don't shoot!" The warning came too late. Two bullets struck him in the abdomen. He was taken to the Community Hospital where his condition was reported as fair. The wife was taken to the same hospital in shock.

Time estimates that Americans own "somewhere between 50 million and 200 million pistols and revolvers, shotguns and rifles, as well as uncounted machine guns, hand grenades, bazookas, mortars, even antitank guns. At least 3,000,000 are bought each year, some two-thirds through the mails—'as easily,' in Lyndon Johnson's words, 'as baskets of fruit or cartons of cigarettes.' "

Time also reports some of the ways guns are advertised for eager buyers. A derringer pistol is offered as the "dandy little model that killed two of our country's Presidents— Abraham Lincoln and William McKinley." Another ad was for a "submachine gun for Father's Day," and a third, "For $99.50 a 20 mm antitank gun. Ideal for long-range shots at deer and bear or at cars and trucks or even a tank if you happen to see one."

"There are more guns in Los Angeles than in Saigon," a Negro leader is reported as saying. Supposedly that city alone has more than 3,000,000 guns in the hands of its citizens. And the Blackstone Rangers, a Negro street gang in Chicago, is estimated to be armed with 1,200 hand guns, some of them stored for safekeeping in the church of their friendly pastor.

Americans have guns and they use them. Since the turn of the century, nearly 800,000 people have been killed by privately owned guns. And those are only the reported cases. Many go unreported. Compare that 800,000 to the 630,768 killed in all the nation's wars. Of the 20,000 fatal shootings in 1967, 7,000 were murders and homicides, 3,000 were accidental deaths and 10,000 suicides. Another 100,000 persons were wounded by gunfire.

Arthur M. Schlesinger, Jr., in *Violence: America in the Sixties*, compares the American record with that of other nations:

> Japan, England, and West Germany are, next to the United States, the most heavily industrialized countries in the world. Together they have a population of 214 million people. Among these 214 million, there are 135 gun murders a year. Among the 200 million people of the United States, there are 6,500 gun murders a year— about forty-eight times as many. Philadelphia alone has about the same number of criminal homicides as England, Scotland and Wales combined—as many in a city of two

million (and a city of brotherly love, at that) as in a nation of 45 million.

Time makes this frightening comparison of killings between America and other nations:

> With a rate of 5.6 homicides per 100,000 the U.S. outpaces all of the other industrialized nations which have stringent gun laws. This is true especially in gun deaths. In 1962 there were 29 murders by gunfire in all of England and Wales (with one-fourth the U.S. population), 37 in Japan (with one-half the population), and 4,954 in the U.S. Out of 400,000 criminals arrested in England and also over a recent three year period, only 159 were carrying guns.

The week of June 15 to June 22, 1969, was Murder Week in the United States. A total of 206 people died by guns in that seven-day period, lending credence to the Report to the National Commission on the Causes and Prevention of Violence statement that "Americans are a bloody-minded people both in action and reaction."

Of the 206 deaths, 131 were homicides, 59 suicides and 16 accidental gunshot deaths. "Among the suicides was a New Jersey policeman. Accidental deaths included a soldier of Ft. Carson, Colo., who apparently shot himself while target shooting. Another accidental death was that of a Seattle man who shot himself while showing off for his stepsons and twirling a pistol on his finger."

California, according to an Associated Press release, led the country in homicides, suicides and accidental deaths by gunshot. The Golden State had thirty gunshot deaths—twenty suicides and ten homicides. "Los Angeles County led the state with eight homicides . . ."

Los Angeles had an even bloodier week later in 1969. On Wednesday, August 13, the Los Angeles *Herald Examiner* headlined an article by Dawson Oppenheimer: "L.A. 'UTOPIA' FOR MURDER."

There had been a five-day record of twenty-nine homicides. The coroner's office told the paper it had investigated the deaths of fifty homicide victims in the preceding three weeks and that twenty-nine of these had occurred since Friday night, August 8. Dr. Thomas Noguchi said five forensic pathologists were at work on 16-hour shifts during that violent weekend, compared to the normal number of two working eight-hour shifts. The victims of the five-day murder spree included twenty men and nine women. "All but eight were under 55 years of age, and all but two were 18 years of age or older."

The *Herald Examiner* quoted UCLA psychiatry professor Dr. Charles W. Wahl as calling Los Angeles a "psychological El Dorado" where the chances of being murdered are better than average. He described Los Angeles as a magnet which draws thousands of poorly adjusted malcontents. Other such El Dorados, he said, were San Francisco, Chicago, New York, and New Orleans.

The American people seem convinced of the danger of the weapons culture in which we live. Time after time they have expressed themselves as favoring strong gun controls in their answers to Gallup and other polls.

"Pollster George Gallup," says *Time*, "maintains that in his very first sampling on gun control 34 years ago, 84 percent of the nation favored strong legislation. The figure has remained at or near that level ever since."

The Gallup Poll released on February 7, 1965, showed the following answers to this question: "Would you favor or oppose a law which would require a person to obtain a police permit before he or she could buy a gun?"

Yes 73%
No 23%
No opinion 4%

Even among gun owners, the proposal was favored by 60 percent of the respondents.

The Harris Poll taken in April 1968 showed 71 percent of the public demanded stronger gun controls while 23 percent opposed them.

The public was convinced but the National Rifle Association was not. Time after time it urged its 900,000-odd members to write their congressmen and oppose such laws.

On June 15, 1968, NRA urged "the sportsmen of America" to lay down a barrage of mail in opposition to pending gun-control legislation. "The right of sportsmen in the United States to obtain, own and use firearms for proper lawful purpose is in the greatest jeopardy in the history of our country." Letters poured in. Some of them went to newspapers. Many others went to legislators.

Supporters of the NRA testified before congressional committees. A doctor who had come all the way from Arizona to testify was typical. He claimed arms-control legislation was part of a subversive plot to take over the government. "The Dodd bill represents a further attempt by a subversive power to make us part of one-world socialistic government," he charged.

"The gun is the standard of freedom in the United States of America," another Arizona witness testified. "When there are restrictions placed on the right of the American citizen to keep and bear arms, it is only a matter of time before the Communist takeover."

This endlessly repeated theory that registration of weapons will lead to a takeover of the nation is combined with the notion that the safety of Americans from riots and crime lies in home arsenals. To these two doctrines the NRA adds the one that says a gun in the home is necessary to protect the family from criminals. "Where guns are outlawed, only outlaws will have guns," is one way they phrase it.

Far from protecting the home, a gun more often contributes to the seriousness of violence there. Thirty-eight percent of the murders committed in the country happen within the family. Five psychologists, in a report to the American Psychological Association convention on September 2, 1967, said that "nice guys," that is noncriminals, commit most murders. "Thirty-eight percent are committed within the family and forty percent occur among friends. And abusive parents killed more children in 1962 than were killed by leukemia, cystic fibrosis and muscular dystrophy combined."

A brief scanning of any daily newspaper will serve to prove the point that a wife or husband with a pistol, or a mother or father with a rifle is far more dangerous to most people's safety than a hardened criminal would be.

WIFE, 20, KILLS MATE AS MAKE-UP SPURNED

A pretty 20-year-old mother shot her estranged husband to death yesterday after he kissed another girl in front of her. He slapped her across the face twice and then jeered at her tearful plea for reconciliation. She admittedly fired a single shot into the breast of Leslie Plymire, 24, when he was pinned to the lawn in front of her home by two men who were trying to break up the quarrel.

"When you love a person you just can't stand that kind of treatment," she sobbed after the shooting. "I know what I did but I don't know why . . . I went back to my sister's apartment and got her husband's pistol. He had been showing it around at a party and I knew he kept it in a bedroom closet. I got it and took it to the bathroom to load it."

In the same issue of the same paper is the story of another killing in the family: "A 26-year-old man who killed his former brother-in-law Sunday evening 'because he wised off too much' was captured early today in a South Gate shack where he had been hiding out since the murder."

Here are additional dispatches showing the fatal role of guns in the lives of our nation's men and women:

Los Angeles *Times*, Tuesday, May 8, 1962:

337

WIFE HELD FOR MURDER IN FILM EDITOR DEATH

Mrs. Jeane Sampson, 40, was charged with murder Monday, a few hours after the shooting of her film writer husband as they struggled for a revolver with which she threatened to end her life . . . Sampson was wounded fatally . . . before the terrified eyes of his daughter, Terry, 10, who tried vainly to warn him away from her mother . . . During the evening Mrs. Sampson called Terry into the bathroom and locked the door. The child screamed when she saw Sampson's .38 caliber revolver in her mother's hands, and the father came to the door. "I don't want to tell, daddy," the child replied as Sampson asked what the matter was, then she screamed, "Go away, daddy, or you'll get hurt!" Police said Sampson broke open the door and grappled with his wife for possession of the gun. It fired, the bullet striking Sampson in the abdomen . . .

Los Angeles *Mirror-News*, February 8, 1960:

HUSBAND SLAIN TAUNTING WIFE

A liquor store owner was shot to death by his red-headed wife after he had sneered at her unsuccessful attempt to commit suicide as she sat beside him in their car.

"You're so dumb you don't even know how to fire a gun," Frank Brill, 49, taunted his wife, Teresa, 40, shortly before she turned the gun on him and shot him in the chest.

A child with a gun is just as dangerous as a wife. Here is an Associated Press story dated October 14, 1961:

BOY, 11, KILLS DAD TO PROTECT MOTHER

Schenectady—Can many say they faced a harder decision than that which confronted Paul Berrian, 11? There was his father drunk and pointing a gun at his mother. What decision was Paul to make . . . Berrian carried two 12-gauge shotguns from a bedroom, loaded them, placed one on a table and pointed the other at his wife. He threatened to kill her and the children . . . then Paul picked up

the other gun and made his decision. It was the first time
the boy had ever fired a gun. The charge struck his father
in the back. Death was instantaneous.

An AP story dated March 12, 1962:

BOY, 17, KILLS PARENTS, TWO YOUNGER BROTHERS

Concord, N.H.—A bespectacled youth of 17 admitted to
police Sunday he killed his entire family—parents and two
brothers—to relieve them of their troubles. Police quoted
the boy as saying: "I was thinking about their suffering.
They always have troubles." The boy arrived home from
work at a supermarket Saturday night and found his parents mad at each other. The parents went out shortly afterwards. In their absence, the boy got a Japanese 7.7 caliber
rifle and shot his two younger brothers. He then shot his
mother and father when they returned.

A husband kills his wife because he had seen her kissing
another man and because a gun was lying handy.

A Los Angeles policeman shoots his wife and himself while
his daughter looks on because a reconciliation has failed.

A 61-year-old man kills his wife because "she was too
arrogant."

A daughter kills her father in an argument over an onion
which was the last one in the house.

The list could go on forever. There is only one real connection between any of these people—not one of them was
a criminal up until the moment they killed. In each case
the gun had been bought to protect the home, not with
any criminal intent.

"It would be a tragic mistake to disarm the law-abiding
American people while the criminal elements, revolutionaries
and assassins in our midst remain armed to the teeth. They
can always obtain unlawfully their weapons. And they do
so . . . I agree with the forthright Ronald Reagan that Citizen Joe Doaks is not the correct target for a firearms ban

339

and subsequent registration . . . there is a better way to get the required job done. Just make it tough on criminals," writes George Todt in his syndicated column.

But the idea that the criminal commits most gun violence is a mythical one. The majority of gun deaths occur because there is a gun in the home . . . in a housewife's purse . . . in a child's hand . . . in the hand of a man who has never before performed a criminal act in his life. Not one assassin of an American President could be considered a criminal until he used a gun to kill a President. And those walking time bombs who have so often in recent years splashed blood all over the landscape—the sociopaths—are almost never criminals until they commit mass murder. No drive to get tougher on criminals would stop the sociopath from killing. The only thing that will stop him is if, when his tormented mind finally snapped, no gun is readily available.

On September 6, 1949, Howard Unruh, a quiet, Bible-reading ex-soldier, walked out of his mother's apartment in Camden, New Jersey, and moved calmly through the business section, shooting down strangers with his souvenir Luger. One after the other he shot down a score of people, killing thirteen. When trapped by police in his apartment, he was still calm and quietly answered the telephone when it rang.

"Hello," he said.

"Is this Howard?" Phillip Buxton, editor of the Camden *Courier-Post* asked.

"Yes, this is Howard. What is the last name of the party you want?" the young man asked politely as police bullets tore through the walls of the room where he stood.

"Unruh."

"Who are you and what do you want?"

"I'm a friend," Buxton said. "And I want to know what they're doing to you."

"Well, they haven't done anything to me, yet, but I'm doing plenty to them."

"How many have you killed?"

"I don't know yet—I haven't counted 'em, but it looks like a pretty good score."

"Why are you killing people?"

"I don't know. I can't answer that yet—I am too busy. I'll have to talk to you later."

Shortly afterward when tear gas was lobbed into the apartment, he walked out, still calm, and surrendered.

"What's the matter with you?" someone demanded. "Are you psycho?"

"I'm not psycho," Unruh said. "I have a good mind."

Later while psychiatrists were examining him, he said he had killed because "people were talking about me and making derogatory remarks about my character . . . I would have killed a thousand if I'd had bullets enough."

Howard Unruh was declared insane and is presently in the New Jersey State Mental Hospital at Trenton.

On November 17, 1950, Ernie Ingenito of Vineland, New Jersey, angered because his wife had left him to live with her parents and had forbidden him to see his children, went on a shooting rampage. Loading his small arsenal of three pistols and an Army carbine into his car, he drove to the home of his wife's parents. Invading the house with a gun in each hand, he shot and wounded his wife and killed his father-in-law. Then he followed the mother-in-law to the home of her parents and killed four more of his in-laws and wounded three others. He was sentenced to life in prison.

Charles Starkweather was 19 when he and his girl friend, Carol Ann Fugate, embarked on a path of murder that covered several states. They began by killing three members of the girl's family, then went on a rampage that left eight more dead. Starkweather said he had always wanted to be a criminal and at first took all the blame for the murders but later told police his 14-year-old girlfriend had helped.

Reverend George Kuhn, pastor of some of the victims, blamed the Starkweather family. "I would like to say to the father that, instead of taking him out and making him into

341

a sharpshooter, he should have taken the boy to church and taught him the respect for the soul of man."

"I suppose they'll have the chair ready for me," Starkweather said. They did.

The girl was sentenced to life in prison on Starkweather's testimony: "After I shot her folks and killed her baby sister, Carol sat and watched television while I wrapped the bodies up in rags and newspapers. We lived in her folks' house for three, four days before we ran away. . . ." She had also been his willing accomplice in the other murders.

"I give you my hate," 22-year-old Robert William Jordan said in a note before he killed three fellow employees and wounded a secretary.

An INS story dated September 9, 1954, tells about the Elizabeth City, North Carolina, killings:

> A 22-year-old youth with the fear of Army induction in his heart and a rifle in his hands killed three men and wounded a woman secretary at an Elizabeth City freezer locker plant today. Police said Robert William (Bobby) Jordan surrendered after officers surrounded the freezer plant and threatened to use tear gas.
>
> Chief of Police W. C. Owens said . . . Jordan appeared suddenly at the plant between 7:30 and 8:00 A.M. and began shooting at the fellow employees who he said had laughed at him.

The letter Jordan wrote before going on his shooting spree is interesting because it shows sociopathic thinking. Addressed to Whom It May Concern, the note was found in his rooming-house room.

"I cannot escape my fate, the fate I was created for. I am a sheep among wolves, persecuted at every turn. The world is completely against me but persecution must end somewhere and I am confident it ends with the grave . . . yet, in my short 22 years, I have had a full, complete, and extremely unhappy life . . ."

Jordan expressed his scorn for "unhappiness, war and the problems of conflict of everyday life," and added, "The tears I shed are genuine, for the poor fools that are riding on a big balloon that is headed for a pin cushion . . . The only way to escape one problem is to create another one. It is just as simple as rolling off a log and not half as hard as the ground.

"Well, I guess I better close now. I give you all my hate and hope the balloon bursts."

Jordan had been slated to appear for Army induction that day.

The year 1965 was one in which mass murderers seemed to abound in the land.

Paul Krueger, 17, and John Angles, 16, started out from California to go to Venezuela to start a revolution. They took with them four rifles, a shotgun, two boxes of 30-30 caliber cartridges, a saber, a machete, a bayonet, and other weapons. They didn't reach their goal. Their journey ended on a beach in Texas where they shot down three sports fishermen in cold blood with a high-powered rifle. The reason for the killing, they said, was to obtain a boat to get to Venezuela.

John Angles, when arrested by Texas police, had in his possession a large Nazi flag that had once hung on the wall of his room. He blamed Paul Krueger, his fellow cadet from the Army and Navy Academy in Carlsbad, California.

The parents of the boys argued over who was to blame for the runaways' actions.

"Paul never ran away in his life. He was a most exemplary boy. He loved to shoot, to hunt and to ride," Mrs. Edna Krueger said.

"He is not a wild kid. He never raises his voice. He's very restrained. The other boy [Angles] is sort of a beatnik type. I don't believe that boy's story," said Krueger's father, Dr. Richard Krueger, member of the Orange County Planning Commission and owner of a manufacturing plant.

"We're not just patting him on the back," Mrs. Krueger said, "but he was a good boy, and everyone thought so."

Paul Krueger had been a model cadet, always well groomed and well behaved. He carried his neatness home with him to the luxurious rambling structure with a view of the Pacific. The three dead men left three widows and nine orphans.

Michael Andrew Clark, like Paul Krueger, was a model boy. He was just 16 when he took his father's hunting rifle from a locked case, got into his mother's car and drove north on Route 101 toward Santa Maria, California. There he found a good spot above the highway and began to shoot at passing motorists.

The first car he hit belonged to the Reida family. The husband, William, was wounded, 5-year-old Kevin was mortally wounded and another son injured. Mrs. Reida leaped from the stalled car and ran toward passing cars for help. One of them slowed as she frantically signaled but the driver, Joel W. Kocab, was already dead at the wheel from the boy sniper's well-aimed bullets. Another car slowed down, and Mrs. Reida ran toward it. Charles Christopher Hogan, 21, was fatally wounded beside the driver, Mrs. Kathleen Smith.

Passersby who attempted to flag down cars driving into the danger zone were ignored and those drivers then came under fire. Finally Mrs. Reida managed to push her wounded husband aside and drive out of range just before the highway patrol arrived and returned the sniper's fire. Michael Clark, after killing three people and wounding eleven, turned the rifle on himself. He was dead when police reached the crest of the hill.

Police were unable to discover any motive for the mass attack. Michael's stunned parents could offer no reason for their son's actions, but they could and did talk about what a good boy he had been.

"I think that we will have to review our American moral standards even if it means going back to some of the old ways, because the boy that was involved in this was not the boy Michael was," Mrs. Joyce Clark told Los Angeles *Herald Examiner* staff writers. "I think in terms of the moral values of society there seems to be a relaxation away from the strong religious convictions people should carry in their lives. All this accent on violence and sex: Michael was never in any way prone to ideas of violence—but look what happened. In general, young people must cope with some very adult ideas, and they aren't quite capable. Parents aren't being very wise in allowing children to meet such things.

"We protected Michael, but obviously he must have seen and talked a lot—somewhere, somehow. We don't have a television set in our home because when it broke three years ago we just didn't have it fixed. With just TV, kids are deprived of the full cycle of cultural life . . ."

Michael's father said, "He was a good student. He was church-going since he was 3. He had hobbies such as fishing and camping. He was a Sea Scout. He belonged to no gangs, and was never in trouble with the law, the school or us. Too much pressure. Too much violence in the movies and TV—too much for a quiet boy like Michael. We've got to do something to remove part of the pressure. Something to help boys like Michael . . . The rifle was locked in a cabinet, and he knew where the keys were. It was my deer-hunting rifle, one I'd reworked myself. He's been hunting with me previously . . ."

Dr. Edward J. Stainbrook, USC school of medicine psychiatrist, explained why "good boys go wrong," in referring to the Michael Clark case. "The key is overcontrol," Dr. Stainbrook said in commenting on seemingly inexplicable acts of violence by adolescents, a Los Angeles *Times* story stated.

By overcontrol, he referred to the youngster's self-discipline, not the control exercised by his parents, the doctor was quoted as explaining. He described some children as undercontrolled and others overcontrolled. The overcontrolled

345

get a reputation for being "good boys" but they may be seething with repressed aggressions.

"Referring to a Biblical expression that what 'filleth the heart goeth out through the mouth,' Dr. Stainbrook went on to say, '. . . if the feelings dammed up in the heart do not go out the mouth, they will be acted out in some other way.' "

The nature of the act that resolves the feelings is bound up with the use of guns, the doctor said. "It often appears that a family's conscious or unconscious reasons for sanctioning the presence of guns in the home become intricately bound up with the use that the gun is sometimes put to. . . . whether the youngster eventually acts out his fantasies by shooting and killing or by some less drastic and destructive means depends partly on why the gun was in the house in the first place."

Richard Franklin Speck didn't use a gun to kill the eight young nurses in Chicago on July 14, 1966. He preferred a knife and his bare hands. A sexual psychopath whose release came from the act of killing instead of rape, he probably found a gun too impersonal a weapon. He did, however, use a gun to force his way into the nurses' apartment and to scare them into obedience while he bound their wrists and took them off one at a time to be murdered in another room.

"I'm a fanatic about guns," said Charles A. Whitman, father of Charles Joseph Whitman. "I raised my boys to know how to handle guns."

Charles Joseph Whitman loved guns and collected a sizable armory in his 25 years. On August 1, 1966, he killed his wife and his mother and then loaded his guns into a foot-locker. He had a 6mm Remington bolt-action rifle with a 4-power Leupold telescopic sight, a 35mm Remington rifle, a 9mm Luger pistol, a Galesi-Brescia pistol, a .357 Smith & Wesson Magnum revolver, a machete, a Bowie knife and a hatchet. Three other rifles and two derringers he decided not to take with him.

Then, apparently deciding he didn't have enough weapons, he went to Sears Roebuck and used his credit card to buy a 12-gauge shotgun, the barrel of which he sawed off. Still feeling undergunned, he went to Davis Hardware and purchased a .30 caliber carbine, and at Church's gunshop he bought 30-shot magazines for his latest acquisition.

Then he dragged the whole lot up to the top of the clock tower on the campus of the University of Texas at Austin and opened fire on people walking below. Before he finished, he had killed fifteen persons, wounded thirty-one and achieved the dreadful distinction of becoming the greatest mass murderer in American history. He also contributed a new psychological term—the Whitman syndrome—to the language.

The Whitman syndrome is now the name used by doctors to describe students who display a compulsive desire to be generally destructive or homicidal—a youth whose repressed hate bursts loose in violence.

All of those mentioned in the latter part of this chapter, except Speck, seem to have been victims of this syndrome. So also was Benny Smith, another model, overcontrolled youth, who murdered five women and girls in a beauty parlor in Mesa, Arizona, a few months after Whitman's day of violence.

None of them had anything in common except that they had never before performed a criminal act, they had guns available, and they were driven by overwhelming internal pressures.

In his book, *Must You Conform?* the late psychiatrist Robert Lindner wrote of the sociopathic, or psychopathic, personality in terms that pinpoint much of the violence with which we have dealt in this chapter:

> Under the rubble of Berlin there lies the corpse of one who embodied in his person the forces that can and very likely will undo our civilization. We can only despair that the chancellery that collapsed on him was made of mere

stone, that it could entomb only his flesh and not the spirit he represented—not the plague of which he was a germ. For the menace of world-wide psychopathy did not die with Adolf Hitler.

Lindner describes sociopaths as men and women who are in but not part of our world. They suffer from a total disorder of personality that makes them completely unfit for social living. They are driven by internal pressures that often become so irresistible that they must strike out violently against people around them.

Lindner thought of this type of personality as the carrier of the seeds of violence, and the sociopath may, indeed, be the central fact of violence in our time and our history. Assassins, mass murderers, and many criminals are of this atavistic type. The sociopath not only exists, but his existence as well as his actions spreads the disease.

Everyone has noticed how one murder is often followed by a similar killing. The Sharon Tate killings in Bel-Air, California, were followed two days later by the murder of a couple in the Los Angeles Silver Lake district which bore such a startling resemblance to the first crime that the police first thought they were connected. It was later decided, however, that the second was only a "copy cat" affair, inspired by the first one but not committed by the same person or persons.

Waves of mass killings sweep across the country from time to time as one sociopath imitates the actions of another. A Charles Whitman produces a Benny Smith, and a Starkweather inspires half a dozen imitators. One airline highjacking leads to scores, and a single campus riot sows the seeds for trouble at other universities.

In addition to being influenced by the actions of fellow sociopaths, such a person is affected by the temper of the times. In all times and countries there have been people like the witch hunters of Salem, Simon Girty, John Brown,

348

William Quantrill, Jesse James, Billy the Kid, Lee Harvey Oswald, and Richard Speck. Some were rebels with a cause, others without a cause, but all were sociopaths, carriers of the seeds of violence. And since the taint is in all human beings, it could very well have been us instead of them.

Appearing in all times and all places, sociopaths are most prevalent and most dangerous during periods of revolutionary turmoil. In America they have appeared in the greatest numbers and most violent form in Colonial, Revolutionary, Civil War and perhaps our present revolutionary times. The sociopathic phenomenon was predominant in Hitler's Germany, in Revolutionary France, in Revolutionary Russia and in Rome during the times of Marius and Sulla.

The sociopath influences his era and is influenced by it. The Harpes would probably have been murderers no matter when they lived, but John Brown could have spent his life as a peaceful backwoods preacher without the catalyst of a cause into which he could channel all the fanaticism of which he was capable. Quantrill surely was twisted by something in his childhood that turned him to mass violence. But without the violent *zeitgeist* of the Civil War, he would not have had the horsemen at his back who enabled him to appease his blood lust. Charles Whitman, torn by boyhood hates and twisted by the "gun culture" of his upbringing, might have turned to violence in any case, but it is possible that he was infected by the virus of psychopathy fanned into open flames by our turbulent times.

14 | The Rhetoric of Violence, 1968-1969

The cry for violence, no matter how senseless and bloody, isn't one-sided. The "peaceful" antiwar demonstrators who gathered in front of the Century Plaza Hotel to greet President Johnson on June 23, 1967, proved themselves at least a match for Reverend Dallas Roquemore.

"I believe that Lyndon Johnson is no more human than Hitler," Rap Brown shouted. "Hitler gassed people to death! Lyndon Johnson burns them to death!"

The crowd waved its pro-assassination signs: LEE HARVEY OSWALD, WHERE ARE YOU NOW THAT WE NEED YOU and screeched, "HEY, HEY, LBJ! How many babies did you burn today?"

And then in a particularly vicious thrust the pacifists celebrated the birth of the President's new grandson by hoisting a sign that read: BURN BABY BIRD!

All over the country public figures who have displeased the far right have received letters in the mail with the following cheerful message:

> See the old man at the corner where you buy your paper? He may have a silencer equipped pistol under his coat. That extra fountain pen in the pocket of the insurance

salesman who calls on you might be a cyanide gas gun.
What about your milkman? Arsenic works slow but sure.
Your auto mechanic may stay up nights studying booby
traps. These patriots are not going to let you take their
freedom away from them. They have learned the silent
knife, the strangler's cord, the target rifle that hits the spar-
rows at 200 yards. Traitors beware! Even now the cross
hairs are on the back of your necks.*

"Take ten," has become a catch phrase among black mili-
tants. It means, take ten whites with you when you go, and
Stokely Carmichael is fond of greeting his audiences with,
"How many whites did you kill today?"

Anticipating the defeat of Barry Goldwater in 1964, the
John Birch Society told its members, "Get your guns, boys!"
The following additional advice was passed on:

> If Goldwater is defeated we can expect Americans by the
> tens of thousands will flock to patriotic organizations. The
> biggest danger comes from the fact that the Communists
> expect this to happen and their sympathizers in our Fed-
> eral Government may move quickly to pick up known
> patriots before they can get fully organized . . . seek the
> advice of experienced members [of Minutemen and other
> para-military groups] of how to go about purchasing an
> unregistered gun at the right price . . . For young children
> semi-automatic .22 rifles, older children Garands, Spring-
> fields and Enfields.

The legions of the left must have shaken with fear at
the prospect of swarms of moppets armed with semiauto-
matic .22 rifles, although if the casualty lists of children
killed in gun accidents are to be believed, they would probably have been deadly only to each other. Still, the violent
thought was there.

* The letter was originally published in the March 15, 1963, issue of *On
Target,* the news sheet of the Minutemen. It was later sent in letter form to
twenty congressmen who had voted against an appropriation to the House
Committee on Un-American Activities.

Leaflets signed by an organization calling itself the "Harvard Council for Restoring U.S. Democracy," were distributed in the vicinity of that university in November, 1965.

WHY KILL LBJ?

Because he is responsible for the deaths of thousands of Americans in Vietnam, forced to fight for their own lives in a futile war in which they do not believe. Someone must kill L.B.J. if democracy is to be restored to the U.S.

"Violence is golden when it is used to put down evil," Dick Tracy told us the day after Robert Kennedy died of violence.

"Every society coerces people," says Chip Sills, the Princeton SDS leader. "In order to change the system, we must be prepared and able to coerce back. Force must be met by force. Violence is sometimes not only justified but required."

William F. Buckley, Jr. tells us in his book, *Up From Liberalism,* "Sometimes the minority cannot prevail except by force; then it must determine whether the prevalence of its will is worth the price of using force."

A manifesto published in the *Berkeley Barb* reads as follows:

> We will destroy the university unless it serves the people . . . We will break the power of the landlords . . . We will defend ourselves against law and order . . . We shall abolish the tyranical police forces not chosen by the people . . . We propose a referendum to dissolve the present government, replacing it with one based on the tradition of direct participation of the people.

The Guardian, a New Left newspaper, supports the rightist National Rifle Association and declares its opposition to "restrictions on weapons which would deprive sections of the population of a means of self-defense while the state itself is abundantly armed."

"Americans have buried their last Martin Luther King," Professor Harry Edwards, originator of the black athletes' Olympic boycott, said. "From now on it's going to be a life for a life, a head for a head, a leader for a leader . . . you can forget about nonviolence."

The hymn to violence and mayhem goes on. It rises in power, and voice after voice is added to it until other sounds are drowned out. The pleas of reason fade before the loud excesses of unreason.

"There are those today who would impeach Earl Warren. After reading some 16 or 17 of the decisions handed down by the highest court in the land, I felt that impeachment is not a proper penalty. Rather it appears to me the more deserving punishment would be hanging," said Colonel Mitchell Paige in a speech before Project Alert, a school for anti-Communists held in Los Angeles, prior to Warren's retirement from the Supreme Court. The colonel also issued a call for volunteers to invade Cuba. "There are millions of Americans who would volunteer their services to eliminate that impudent skunk Castro . . ."

"For the SDS, violence means wrecking selective service files—at night, when there is no one there to be hurt. We're not nonviolent; we'd like to take over the city. But we can't. So we'll use long-range political organization. We're ready to use force to achieve a political end . . ."

The threat of black violence has become an excellent tool for Negroes. Yet how do you draw a line between "good" violence and "bad" violence?

Any brand of violence is contagious, as this land of assassination knows. However, since madness now seems to be the country's outstanding aspect, more people may become violent merely to attract attention, merely to be heard. "Just to be taken seriously," as one calm man said.

353

Nora Sayre, New York correspondent for the *New States-man* of London, on special assignment to cover the Chicago convention riot, wrote in the October, 1968 issue of *The Progressive:*

> Many of us are wrestling with evaluations of the fact of force. If violence in the United States could result in peace in Vietnam, then I would support it—with a ravaging disgust at a society which forces one to make such a choice. I haven't the physical courage to fight for peace in the streets, but I bless those who do . . .

Retired Air Force Brigadier General Robert Scott, who wrote *God Is My Co-Pilot*, told an American Legion meeting that a military takeover of the United States by "devious or direct means" may become necessary if the politicians cannot control lawlessness:

> Military takeover is a dirty word in this country but if the professional politicians cannot keep law and order it is time we do so by devious or direct means . . . If there is no law to prevent the Adam Clayton Powells, Stokeley Carmichaels and Rap Browns from burning down the country, what is wrong with us saying, "We will build it up again but we'll bury you first"?

"Ho, Ho, Ho Chi Minh!" chanted the delegates to the SDS convention, "Two-four-six-eight, organize and smash the state!"

William Penn Patrick of San Rafael, California, addressed the United Republicans of California in convention assembled, saying: "I disagree with those who want to impeach Earl Warren, I think we should hang him."

Loud applause came from 200 Republican leaders as he went on to criticize George Romney of Michigan for his handling of the Detroit riots and to say that if he were in a position of authority in such an instance, "I would issue orders to shoot to kill anyone who's going to riot or demonstrate or loot the stores."

This was greeted by a standing ovation from UROC members who later called on Congress to investigate the possibility of impeaching President Johnson for committing treason because of his opposition to the existing government in Rhodesia, his decision to give "aid and comfort" to Communist-dominated countries and his antipoverty program.

Professor Harry Edwards, the San Jose State sociologist and leader of the black boycott of the Olympics, was quoted in *Newsweek* for March 11, 1968, as follows: "I'm for splitting up in twos and threes, killing the mayor, getting the big utilities and poisoning the goddamned water."

Colonel Frank B. Rigg, USA retired, writing in the *National Guardsman*, predicts a coming era of guerrilla war in America's cities. He would:

> . . . demand that guard units be in action for months to years . . .
>
> Require guardsmen to fight one of the nastiest forms of warfare known to mankind—namely, counter-guerrilla warfare in city areas.
>
> Intensify the psychological strain of having to confront fellow Americans with cold steel and perhaps even hot lead . . .
>
> We are fighting a similar war in Vietnam but the swamps, jungles and mountains out there are simple compared with what urban guerrilla warfare could offer in the continental United States.
>
> Here in the old core cities there are skyscrapers—asphalt —sewer jungles that are manmade . . . more formidable than nature's if determined rioters and guerrillas chose to use it properly.

Eldridge Cleaver addressed a group of San Francisco lawyers:

This whole apparatus, this capitalistic system and its institutions and police all need to be assigned to the garbage can of history, and I don't give a fuck who doesn't like it. If we can't have it, nobody's gonna have it. We'd rather provoke a situation . . . that will disrupt cities and the economy so that the enemies of America could come in and pick the gold from the teeth of these Babylonian pigs. . . .

The right to revolution can't be taken from the people. . . . You're all chasing dollars, but there are other people who are chasing dollars to buy guns to kill judges and police and corporation lawyers. We need lawyers today who have a law book in one hand and a gun in the other . . . so that if he goes to court and that don't come out right, he can pull out his gun and start shooting.

You people on the other side, I love you . . . I hope you'll take guns and shoot judges and police.

Robert Franklin Williams, RAM leader who is now a fugitive, says:

The weapons of defense employed by the Afro-American freedom fighters must consist of a poor man's arsenal. Gasoline fire bombs, lye or acid bombs . . . can be used extensively. During the night hours such weapons, thrown from roof tops, will make the streets impossible for racist cops to patrol . . . gas tanks on public vehicles can be choked up with sand . . . long nails driven through boards, and tacks with large heads are effective to slow the movement of traffic on congested roads at night.

Derailing trains causes panic. Explosive booby traps on police telephone boxes can be employed. High-powered sniper rifles are readily available. Armor-piercing bullets will penetrate oil-storage tanks from a distance . . . Flame throwers can be manufactured at home . . . America is a house on fire. FREEDOM NOW, or let it burn down!

Robert Bolivar DePugh, fugitive head of the Minutemen, is quoted by George Thayer in *The Farther Shores of Politics:*

356

'I could kill everyone in the United States except myself if I wanted to . . .' To do this, he said, it would be merely a matter of assembling certain viruses from his own Biolab Corporation laboratories and spreading them throughout the country simply by coughing on enough outbound passengers at a large municipal airport. Of course, he added, he would have to immunize himself, but within two weeks he would be the only person alive in the nation.

Robert Franklin Williams, meet Robert Bolivar DePugh!

15 | The Media and Violence, 1949-1969

Marshall McLuhan, the prophet of the electronic media, has spoken on the subject of television as related to violence. He suggests that it ". . . alters the image that people have of themselves. It changes their relations to others. The gap so created can only be filled by violence. Such violence has no goal except the need to form a new image, to create a new meaning for the individual or the group."

Writing in *The Saturday Review*, Richard L. Tobin reported the results of an eight-hour period spent monitoring the three networks and half a dozen local channels:

> We marked down ninety-three specific incidents involving sadistic brutality, murder, cold-blooded killing, sexual cruelty and related sadism . . . We encountered seven different kinds of pistols and revolvers, three varieties of rifles, three distinct brands of shotgun, half a dozen assorted daggers and stilettos, two types of machete, one butcher's cleaver, a broadaxe, rapiers galore, a posse of sabers, an electric prodder, and a guillotine. Men (and women and even children) were shot by gunpowder, burned at the stake, tortured over live coals, trussed and beaten in relays, dropped into molten sugar, cut to ribbons (in color), repeatedly kneed in the groin, beaten while being held de-

fenseless by other hoodlums, forcibly drowned, whipped with a leather belt . . . By the end of the stint we were quite insensitive, almost immune to the shock of seeing a human being in pain.

When one realizes that a whole generation of children has grown up on this sort of diet and that [the vast majority of children and teen-agers spend hours in front of the boob tube, the influence of television entertainment on violence becomes at least a matter for debate.]

That the emphasis on violence on television is nothing new is clearly shown by a survey taken in 1954 and quoted by Arthur Schlesinger, Jr. in *Violence: America in the Sixties.*

A 1954 survey showed that 23.3 percent of the programs between 4 and 10 p.m. featured violence and crime; in 1961 the proportion had increased by more than a third to 34.2 percent. For "prime time"—7 to 10 p.m.—the proportion had jumped even more spectacularly—from 16.6 percent in 1954 to 50.6 percent in 1961. A 1964 survey showed a "perceptible decline" in the extent to which one network—CBS—went in for violence; but the other networks took up the slack, and the aggregate percentages remained about the same.

Schlesinger also presents evidence from Dr. Wilbur Schramm, director of the Institute of Communication Research at Stanford, that violence on the screen does have some effect on real life behavior.

["Experiments have shown," Dr. Schramm is quoted as saying, "that normal persons who see a violent film subsequently exhibit nearly twice as much violence as persons who have not seen such a film."]

After citing another survey taken in 1968, Schlesinger says that while no one wants to return to a reign of censorship, society has a "certain right of self-defense" and calls upon the media to work out "forms of self-restraint."

A *Christian Science Monitor* survey taken six weeks after the assassination of Robert Kennedy is quoted as an apparent answer to requests for self-restraint by the networks:

> . . . twenty-two staff members [were given] the ghastly assignment of watching 85½ hours of television including prime evening hours and Saturday morning cartoons. In seven evenings of viewing the investigators recorded 81 killings and 210 incidents or threats of violence; an additional 162 incidents were reported on Saturday morning. The most violent evening hours were between 7:30 and 9:00 —at a time when an estimated 26.7 million young people between the ages of two and seventeen are watching television. In these hours violent incidents occurred at an average of once every 16.3 minutes.

In a recent study of violence on television made in October 1967 and repeated in October 1968 and released in July 1969, the Annenberg School of Communications at the University of Pennsylvania came up with results very much like the earlier ones and concluded that television portrays "a largely violent America . . . with a most violent past and a totally violent future."

The study makes the following additional revelations:

> In both years violence prevailed in eight out of 10 prime time or Saturday shows. Half of all the leading characters in the plays committed violence, one in 10 turned killer and one in 20 was killed.
>
> The casualty count of injured and dead was at least 790 for the two weeks . . . one in every 10 acts of violence resulted in a fatality.

The investigators learned that half the killings were done by "good guys" who received no punishment for their acts.

It was also noted that persons of foreign descent and non-whites committed the major portion of the violence and paid with their lives for every life they took while white Americans did not.

Young adult males were the greatest perpetrators of violence, and the majority of those persons killed were over thirty years of age. The most violent were young, unmarried, or middle-aged males. Law officers and criminals accounted for one-third of the disturbances and committed half the killings.

The reviewers saw no sign that any attempt was made to portray the real horror of violence. Instead, it was completely impersonal and without pain. Witnesses to scenes of violence were shown as passive spectators.

The question of whether televised violence leads to real-life violence is not settled, although many prominent people have expressed opinions on the subject. Walter Lippmann has said that, though he believes in freedom of speech and thought, he has no objection to the censorship of mass entertainment of the young. He thinks the risks to our liberties are less doing that than in taking a chance on violence becoming unmanageable. Many psychologists, however, believe there is little relation between witnessed violence and acted-out violence. Some even say that television violence works as a catharsis to relieve tensions and draw off the threat of antisocial activity.

Television, of course, is not the only media that plays up violence. Newspapers display the goriest headlines and pictures, and the comic book industry has long been under attack by psychiatrists such as Frederic Wertham and Gershon Legman.

Writing in 1949, Legman expressed the opinion that most children who were 6 years old in 1938 had absorbed a minimum of 18,000 pictures of beatings, shootings, stranglings, puddles of blood, and torturings-to-death from comic books. And he says these children will have identified with the heroes of the strips, the ones responsible for all the pain and death and bloodshed.

Legman also calls to our attention the difference in the way violence and sex are treated in print in America. Sex is legal, in reality, and murder is a crime. But on paper, just the reverse is true. It is considered a crime to write about sex while writing about murder is perfectly all right.

Admittedly, considerably more freedom is allowed in writing about sex today than twenty years ago, yet it is violence that is regarded by most people as the more fit, or moral, subject matter. And what does this reveal about us as a people? That we are just naturally vicious and bloody-minded? Or perhaps that we all have frustrations, fears, inadequacies, and hangups, whether of a sexual, economic, or personal nature, and that we tend to work them off in a safe, socially acceptable way?

Is this also the reason we flock to see movies such as *Bonnie and Clyde?* One of the most popular movies of our time, it was also a critical success and was praised for its artistic use of violence.

One film student said that *Bonnie and Clyde* captured the true spirit of the American people, the spirit that is pragmatic, rebellious, violent, and joyous. He believes this spirit can either create or kill, and that John Brown had it in full measure. Today, the Black Panthers have it, he says. Not everyone understands it. He feels that doctors, dentists, and real estate salesmen are among those who don't, and that musicians, cab drivers, used-car salesmen, and bus drivers are among those who do understand it.

Apparently newspapers and movie and ad writers across the country also understand it because advertisements for violent films literally drip with blood.

KILLER VS KILLER
These Men Lived Only For
The Split-Second It
Takes To Kill

That headline copy highlighted an ad for a western called *The Last Challenge*. It was accompanied by a picture of one man shooting another sprawled grotesquely across a table in a bar.

Glenn Ford plays in *Heaven With A Gun*, and the blurb tells us: "His name is Jim Gillian—and he can kill as fast as a snake can strike."

The emphasis on violence, horror, and sadism that has marked the promotion and advertising of many movies is mild compared to some of the ways the media has encouraged rather than merely reported violence.

Time in its April 26, 1968 issue described some of these provocations:

> Recently, Los Angeles' KNBC sent a film team to Claremont Men's College to shoot a debate on Viet Nam, and caused a ruckus when the students spotted the newsmen unpacking half a dozen posters with pro and con war slogans. Later, a spokesman for KNBC admitted that the posters were intended as "colorful additions to the set." On other occasions, a TV cameraman induced protesters to burn a city bus, while another persuaded two hippies to attempt to block President Johnson's entrance into a Washington club.

During the so-called People's Park March at Berkeley in March 1969, a top sheriff's officer said that a Hollywood film crew hired "Black Panther types" to join the demonstrations. Thomas L. Houchins, chief of the criminal division, told reporters that the same thing happened during a student strike at the University of California on March 6. He stated that he thought their reason for doing this was that the protest wasn't lively enough for them.

The film crew, it was revealed, was from MGM and was headed by an Italian film director who had been shooting student unrest scenes at another school and had rushed in to get some "real" action shots.

Time says, "The most frequent charge leveled by the critics of it is that television with its vast reach and visual impact is in a sense the germ carrier that spreads the plague of riots across the U.S."

It is possible that television has done more to build up certain militant black leaders than anything they have done themselves. This is certainly the opinion of some of the more moderate black leaders who, after spending a lifetime working for civil rights, suddenly find themselves in a time of turmoil ignored by television which rushes to get the opinion of hitherto almost unknown militants. National Urban League Director Whitney Young expressed himself on this subject when asked how large he estimated Stokely Carmichael's following to be. "About fifty Negroes and about five thousand white newsmen," Young replied.

Network officials have denied they tend to give more time to militants than to moderates. CBS News President Richard Salant has been quoted as saying, "Our test is not whether we approve of the event or agree with the individual, but whether it is legitimate news."

On the morning of Robert Kennedy's death, *Ramparts,* a magazine that has become a spokesman for the extremist left, arrived in the homes of its subscribers. In addition to articles attacking Vice President Humphrey as viciously as it had previously attacked Senator Eugene McCarthy, while singing a paean of praise for the student rioters of Columbia University, this issue contained an advertisement that is probably the most outright incitement to assassination since the infamous full-page ad in Dallas on November 22, 1963.

The *Ramparts* ad was for a number of posters, mostly psychedelic in nature, but containing two that seemed beyond the realm of satire or even human decency. The first, in the upper left-hand corner of Page 57, was a photograph of a T-shirted, bushy-haired young rifleman aiming directly at the camera. The caption was: TRAIN NOW—CAMPAIGN

'68. By some fantastic coincidence, the gunman bore a striking resemblance to Sirhan Bishara Sirhan.

The second poster referred to appeared in the middle of the page and showed a cartoon likeness of then President Johnson and Vice President Humphrey dressed as Batman and Robin. The caption reads: DYNAMIC DUO EXPOSED, and both figures have bull's-eyes painted on their chests, presumably for the edification of assassination-minded readers.

As Robert Kennedy campaigned through California, he encountered as many signs of hatred on the left as his brother had met from the right. Rocks were thrown on at least one occasion, and mobs of hippies shouted, "Fascist!"

It is possible to wonder if their reading matter didn't have something to do with their hatred for a candidate who was a representative of the more moderate left.

The San Francisco *Express Times,* published by Marvin Garson, husband of the author of the fun play *MacBird,* outdid even *Ramparts.* On May 23, 1968, it carried a cartoon, actually a photograph of an open coffin in which lay Robert F. Kennedy, the obvious victim of assassination. The cartoon was in support of the extremist Peace and Freedom Party and was captioned: WHY WASTE YOUR VOTE?

Under the picture, Garson relates what happened to him at an imaginary fund-raising dinner for Kennedy. Going into the bar for a drink, Garson meets the ghost of President Warren G. Harding and asks him what he thinks of Kennedy. The dead man replies that he doesn't see any point in throwing away a vote on a dead man. He says that Kennedy is going to be killed and that, in his opinion, there's not much there to kill. His final word is that he is a lot more alive than Robert Kennedy.

TV's part in fomenting riots has been discussed rather extensively and the network executives have been quite vehement in defending their media against charges of helping to inflame public opinion. In 1967 at the request of the

365

Justice Department, many stations did attempt to prevent the broadcasting of inflammatory material during a period of unrest. This self-censorship is said to have worked quite well during the Detroit, Cincinnati, and Milwaukee riots but apparently it soon broke down because of opposition by networks and other causes.

In Newark, TV coverage was somewhat less than responsible. Newark's police director, Dominick A. Spina, complained that television seemed to have a knack for picking the most volatile people off the street and leading them into making violent statements. Any individual standing on a corner screaming was just as likely to get on camera as a responsible citizen. An administrative assistant to the mayor, Donald Malafronte, said, "They picked on every black face who proclaimed himself a leader. Casuals who had never raised a voice in community affairs all of a sudden were spokesmen on television."

Plainfield, New Jersey officials also attacked the activities of TV.

"They gave the impression that the whole town was going up in flames," Mayor George F. Hetfield told *Time*. "Soon we had busloads of people coming in from Philadelphia and Newark who were professional manipulators."

The newcomers were treated as though they were experts on the town of Plainfield. On NBC, a Negro was introduced as the pastor of the Shiloh Baptist Church. He said the police were prolonging the riots just so they could beat up more blacks. It came out later when Plainfield clergymen complained about the incident that this man had only recently arrived in town and was an assistant in a Bible study course at Shiloh.

When he set up the United States Riot Commission on July 27, 1967, President Johnson charged the members with the task of discovering "what effect do the mass media have on the riots?"

The commission cleared the media of many charges of

slanted and provocative news coverage and came to the following conclusions:

First, that despite incidents of sensationalism, inaccuracies, and distortions, newspapers, radio and television, on the whole, made a real effort to give a balanced, factual account of the 1967 disorders.

Second, despite this effort, the portrayal of the violence that occurred last summer failed to reflect accurately its scale and character. The overall effect was, we believe, an exaggeration of both mood and event.

Third, and ultimately most important, we believe that the media have thus far failed to report adequately on the causes and consequences of civil disorders and the underlying problems of race relations.

The commission commented further:

We have found a significant imbalance between what actually happened in our cities and what the newspaper, radio, and television coverage of the riots told us happened. The commission, in studying last summer's disturbances, visited many of the cities and interviewed participants and observers. We found that the disorders, as serious as they were, were less destructive, less widespread, and less a black-white confrontation than most people believed.

Statistically, the commission discovered that television and newspapers used more soothing than inflammatory items during riot periods. However, several factors were identified which, it was believed, could have created inaccurate and exaggerated impressions as to the magnitude and severity of the disturbances.

There were instances of glaring errors in reportage of the 1967 riots. In some cases the stories didn't support the somewhat frightening headlines under which they appeared. Rumors were reported that had no basis in fact. There were even instances where newsmen, instead of giving an

367

account of what was really happening, went to the extreme of staging riotous events for the television cameras.

Property damage during the Detroit riot was said to be in excess of $500 million. When a careful investigation was made, the true figure turned out to be $40 to $45 million. The Associated Press, however, continued to report damage as exceeding a billion dollars as late as February 9, 1968.

Television coverage, in particular, tended to make the riots sound like confrontations between blacks and whites. Actually, most of the damage, injuries, and deaths took place in all-Negro areas, so they couldn't accurately be called race riots.

The commission did not suggest that the media should tell less than the truth or in any way try to manage the news. In fact, the comment was advanced that it would be unwise if not dangerous to play down what was happening in the hope that this would somehow cut down the incidence of violence. The commission also stated that greater care should be taken in reporting civil disorder. The tendency to handle such events as just another story, was to be avoided as well as the inclination to get a story at any price.

In some cases, it was felt, perhaps knowing what was going on elsewhere or seeing it on television may have lowered inhibitions or stirred the viewer to outrage or a desire for excitement. Ghetto dwellers who were interviewed said they thought this to be true. It also follows that police and officials in other cities must have been conditioned by news reports in their responses to events in their own areas.

At the conference held by the commission at Poughkeepsie, some news media representatives admitted to mistakes. One editor told the conference that his paper used words in their leads and headings during the riot that he wished they could take back because they were wrong. He said they used the words "sniper kings" and "nests of snipers," only to discover later that most of those so designated were the constituted authorities shooting at each other. There was only one verified sniper in the whole eight-day riot. He was drunk and was firing a pistol from a window. Television network representatives admitted that some "live" coverage of disorders might have inflamed the situation and stated that they tried, whenever possible, to edit taped or filmed sequences before they were broadcast. The television people also admitted that the use of live television coverage by helicopter during the Watts riot had been inflammatory.

"Most errors involved the mistakes of fact, exaggeration of events, overplaying of particular stories, or prominently displayed speculation about unfounded rumors of potential," the commission noted. "This is not only a local problem; because of the wire services and networks, it is a national one."

It then goes on to list examples of exaggeration and mistakes that may have contributed to the disorders.

> In Tampa, Florida, a deputy sheriff died in the early stages of the disturbance, and both national wire services immediately bulletined the news that the man had been killed by rioters. About thirty minutes later, reporters discovered that the man had suffered a fatal heart attack.
>
> In Detroit, a radio station broadcast a rumor, based on a telephone tip, that Negroes planned to invade suburbia one night later; if plans existed, they never materialized.

One important and perhaps indicative incident of television irresponsibility that the commission does not deal with because it took place during the Watts riot was not covered by the report. An account of the incident was given in *Rivers of Blood, Years of Darkness,* Robert Conot's excellent account of Watts, and a slightly different, shorter version appears in *Burn, Baby, Burn* by Jerry Cohen and William S. Murphy.

The Los Angeles County Human Relations Commission had called a meeting in Athens Park August 12, 1965. Rioting had broken out in the Watts area the day before and community leaders hoped to cool tempers there and prevent a resumption of the rioting. Several hundred people gathered to listen to speeches and pleas for peace. The speakers included Mrs. Rena Frye, whose arrest along with her son the night before had served as the spark that set off the rioting.

"I am the woman who was arrested last night," Mrs. Frye told the crowd. "I'm here to ask you, please, to help me and to help others in this community to calm the situation down so that we will not have a riot tonight!"

The pleas were well received by the crowd, but there was trouble when a boy of about sixteen grabbed the microphone and began to babble into it.

"It's like this, the way the policemens treat you round here. I'm going to tell you something. It ain't going to be lovely tonight whether you like it or not!"

The crowd tried to shout him down, and the television cameras that were on hand kept grinding away.

"I was down on Avalon last night, and we the Negro people have got completely fed up!" the boy continued. "They not going to fight down here no more. You know where they going? They're after Whiteys! They going to congregate. They don't care! They going out to Inglewood, Playa del Rey, and everywhere else the white man is supposed to stay. They going to do the white man in tonight! And I'm going to tell you . . ."

The audience surged forward and half a dozen youths grabbed the screaming boy away from the microphone. Moderate voices were heard again as ministers, community leaders and even the heads of youth gangs pleaded for peace, but several of the leaders noticed that the television cameramen were already packing up their gear to leave.

Sgt. Vivian Strange of the Community Relations Unit of the Los Angeles Police Department and several others hurried over to the television people and pleaded with them not to show the tirade by the boy . . . who was, after all, hardly anyone of importance. The television crew refused to promise anything.

"Everybody has it," one cameraman said. "We can't say we won't use it, and then have some other station put it on the air."

That night KNXT ran some film footage of the Athens Park meeting. With a sure hand as to what was newsworthy, nothing was shown of the ministers who had counseled peace nor of any of the moderate leaders. But surely Mrs. Frye was newsworthy. No, apparently not. Perhaps because she, too, had called for peace. Nothing from the whole meeting was broadcast except the wild talk by an unknown boy. Only he of all who had been there was newsworthy!

Rioting began shortly after dark that night and soon Watts was burning.

Los Angeles County District Attorney Evelle J. Younger is among those who are less than sanguine about the effect of television on racial peace. In a speech in Las Vegas to the annual convention of the National Association of Defense Lawyers in Criminal Cases, he suggested how a riot might be provoked by the use of television and radio:

"First you get a white man, preferably a Nazi or member of the Ku Klux Klan or some white citizens group to go on a radio or television talk show and relate the rumor that 100 Negro snipers have been imported from some city outside the state to shoot up, not Watts, but Beverly Hills, Glendale or San Marino. The zealot should brandish a firearm—that's why TV is better—and say, 'By God, let them come, I'm ready!'"

According to Younger, the rumor would be repeated on many talk shows as often as possible, with the various callers pretending to have independent knowledge of the threatened attack. Then another call would be made by a person pretending to be a gun dealer and saying he had only five weapons left.

"Every gun in town will, of course, be sold within a matter of hours," Younger said, "and the Negro extremists will react as anticipated."

Then the hypothetical planners of this hypothetical riot would take the most important step of all. They would arrange for a television camera to be brought into the area selected as the site for the arranged riot.

"If you promise them excitement, you get cooperation," Younger said of the television industry.

The television people would take over in the manufacturing of the riot. They would arrange to interview a black nationalist leader and would ask him his reaction to the way the whites were buying up all the guns. The extremist would then scream into the camera: "Whitey is out to exterminate the Negro and the Negro must move first!"

Then a Negro youth must be found and asked if he has heard the rumor that thirty minutes before, in another area of the city, a white policeman shot and killed a Negro teen-ager for stealing a package of cigarettes. The youth would then be put on camera and encouraged to yell, "Burn, baby, burn!" or "Get Whitey!" or something equally inflammatory.

The television people would be careful, Younger observed, to see that the head of the Urban League or the NAACP never got a chance to go on the air to calm people down.

By then things would be moving along fast enough that the cameraman could be filming the first liquor store broken into so that "anyone inclined to stay home will get into the act. He would also be told to concentrate on acts of violence and when a policeman reacts to provocation show the reaction and not the provocation."

It would be helpful, Younger said, to show a policeman with a nightstick and another shot of a Negro child who had fallen and cut his face while running. Then the two shots could be edited to make it appear that the officer was beating the child.

From then on violence would not have to be manufactured.

While this scenario is of an imaginary riot, the actions of some representatives of the media during the Watts and

372

other urban riots, and most particularly during the Chicago convention rioting, seem to fit the pattern very well. Although there is no evidence that the Watts or other urban riots were planned, there certainly is evidence that the media people played their tragic part.

That someone, perhaps with right-wing connections, may have been trying to carry out the first part of Younger's scenario is suggested by a series of rumors that received wide circulation in Los Angeles during late 1966 and early 1967. The rumors first appeared in right-wing publications and were then picked up by newspapers, but they got their most effective boost on radio and television talk shows, just as Younger suggested they could.

The first newspaper account of the coming catastrophe was contained in a column by Bill Schulz in the Los Angeles *Herald-Express* under the heading LEFTISTS PLAN MORE L.A. RIOTS.

Schulz said the Progressive Labor Party was planning a king-size Watts rebellion that would destroy the Los Angeles industrial complex. The plan for this was supposedly contained in a PLP publication called "The Revolt in Watts and the Coming Battle," which Schulz said drove home the point that Los Angeles is "the hub of a mammoth industrial complex. . . . The greatest fear of the imperialist enemy is that the black people in the South Los Angeles ghetto will shut down the factories."

The publication supposedly contained a detailed map on which major factories and industrial centers were pinpointed, including the General Motors assembly plant and the industrial complex of Goodyear Rubber.

Schulz himself admitted that the PLP was an almost completely white organization. At the time of the publication it was generally known that the total membership in the Los Angeles area was some half a dozen fuzzy-haired and fuzzy-minded white youths who later became embroiled in quarrels with black militant groups and were practically run out of the Watts area by the blacks. The credibility of a story that suggested the black community might have followed a PLP plan for revolution is, to say the least, in doubt.

A more detailed and wider circulated version of this plot was contained in an article entitled "The Plan to Burn Los Angeles" written by Gary Allen and first published in the May 1967 issue of *American Opinion,* the house organ of the John Birch Society. The magazine had no sooner dropped into the mail chutes of faithful Birchers than the telephones on every talk show in the city began to jingle and frantic tennis-shoe types began to spread the story all over the air.

Basically, the horror story ran something like this: The first Watts riot had been a carefully staged rehearsal for the plan to take the city over completely at a later date. The riot had been planned and directed by "highly trained Communists" known to the Los Angeles Police Intelligence Division as "The Organization."

According to the article, "The Organization" was composed of forty to fifty Negroes sent by the Communists into Los Angeles from all over the United States. It included Black Muslims, Black Nationalists, members of the Deacons for Defense, the Communist Revolutionary Action Movement (RAM) and professionals from other "militant and Marxist groups."

The article claimed that during the Watts rioting men wearing red armbands and speaking through bull horns directed the mobs. It also stated that the rioters had deliberately stolen large numbers of guns to build up an arsenal for the forthcoming revolution. The takeover would begin when hundreds of police lured into Watts by calls for help were shot down. The Central and Valley Services Divisions, the two main sources of police communications, would be destroyed by bazooka fire or dynamite while off-duty policemen would be hunted down in their homes and killed.

Fires would be set throughout the city and in the surrounding oil fields and foothills. Civic Center and the Wilshire area were to be burned next. Mobs of enraged Communists would then shoot down all white men and children, leaving only the women alive as "rewards for the insurrectionists."

The takeover of Los Angeles was supposed to be followed by outbreaks all over the country.

If ever an article was written that had all the elements needed to inflame already nervous whites and send them scurrying to gun stores, this was it. That it was ridiculous on the face of it and that there was no evidence to substantiate its allegations didn't prevent it from being widely broadcast and, no doubt, believed.

Talk shows that were such an important part of the media at the time were the prime channels of circulation, just as Younger suggested they might be. Apparently the "communicasters" were perfectly willing to let the rumor mongers have their way without bothering to check facts. Since one of the most popular TV talk-show hosts had encouraged a black militant to display a gun on the air during the Watts rioting and had himself produced one to counter it, this was probably to be expected.

The Los Angeles *Times'* Gene Blake, however, did investigate the story. He went directly to the Intelligence Division of the Los Angeles Police Department, where Gary Allen claimed to have gotten his information.

Captain Harold E. Yarnell, Jr., head of the division, said flatly that he had investigated and was sure no one in his department had ever spoken to the writer, identified by the magazine as a "Los Angeles journalist and Stanford graduate."

"If we had such information, we wouldn't talk to a writer," the captain said. "It is not our position that the August 1965 riot was Communist-inspired. We have never been able to isolate any group as being motivating forces or manipulators."

As for the huge supply of arms that had been stolen and put away for the coming bloodbath, Yarnell dismissed that by saying: "The only arsenals we've found have been those of paramilitary right-wing groups."

"I don't know why they print such stuff," Yarnell said. "All it does is give some of these kooks ideas."

The media might well remember that and be more active in searching out the truth as the Los Angeles *Times* did in this instance, rather than airing or publishing unsubstantiated rumors and inflammatory opinions. In an age of violence such as the one we live in, it would seem the least we could ask of media people is to take the utmost care to avoid bringing on upheaval while performing its task of reporting it. Most responsible segments of the communication industry do take that care and the trend seems to be in that direction, but there is still sufficient violence-promoting taking place to constitute a serious problem, especially where television is concerned. [For starting or prolonging a riot, one TV picture is truly worth a hundred thousand words.]

Epilogue

This then is our record. We have tempered Nature at her most savage and made a homeland; shaped a steadfast democracy that has extended itself beyond our shores to defend and assist a whole world of humanity; and developed a wondrous technology that has made real Man's dreams and fantasies of a Space Age.

But the history of "America the Beautiful"—the land of towering mountains, rolling prairies, grassy plains, dense forests, sparkling lakes and rivers, and mighty men—is also that of "America the Violent"—the same nation that massacred the Indian, chained the black, bombed Hiroshima, and perpetrated My Lai.

Are we then, as Arthur Schlesinger, Jr., tells us, "the most frightening people on the planet"? Have our deeds betrayed our goals?

Are we as violent as Mexico? What about India, where millions have died in religious strife? Millions more have died in Russia in a calculated and deliberate policy of mass liquidation conducted by leaders for political expediency. Frenchmen have only to look back a few years to a time when assassinations came by the dozens, when no French-

377

man was safe in the streets or in his home from the plastic bomb and the guns of Fascist and Communist killers, when even Charles de Gaulle was hunted through his own domain by OAS gunmen and saved from numerous assassination attempts only by the excellence of his security forces.

We know about Japan and Germany, and we know that in the Arab States the hangings of political enemies are shown on television, and the bodies of slain kings, presidents, and premiers are dragged through the streets by screeching mobs.

All over the world men are fighting and dying for causes. Contending religious groups slaughter each other in North Ireland. In the Tyrolean Alps, terrorists steadily blow up bridges, power lines, trains, and their fellowmen in the name of Austrian nationalism. In Biafra thousands of blacks (men, women, and children) are dying with the help of whites who have rushed in for obscure political reasons to support one side or the other. Bombs set off by adherents of Welsh nationalism killed a British military policeman and two terrorists during the investiture of Prince Charles as Prince of Wales. In Central America a soccer match led to riots, killings, the breaking of diplomatic ties and finally— *reductio ad absurdum*—to war between two tiny republics.

Does not the human species seem to have a built-in propensity for violence? Is there not in every man a dark corner, a twisted core of amorality as intrinsic as heart, lungs, and brain?

Many of the world's great religious, philosophical, and literary thinkers would have us believe and accept that evil is an inescapable fact of human nature. Goethe, for example, in frank self-ackowledgment, declared that he had never heard of a crime of which he did not feel capable himself. And Russian critic Merezhkovsky explained Dostoevsky's success thusly:

> The reader is aghast at his omniscience, his penetration into the conscience of a stranger. We are confronted by our own secret thoughts, which we would not reveal to a friend, not even to ourselves.

Is man then Martin Luther's "saint and sinner" who must live always in an awareness of his dual nature; and by, let's say, a common-sense dictum for ethics such as that once put forth by Abraham Lincoln?—

> The true rule in determining to embrace or reject anything is not whether it have any evil in it, but whether it have more of evil than of good. There are few things wholly evil or wholly good. Almost everything, especially of government policy, is an inseparable compound policy of the two, so that our best judgment of the preponderance between them is continually demanded.

As the Bible allowed for "the flesh and the devil," so must we. But as moderns who have come such a long way, can we continue to shrug it off?

Are there any cures for the violence that has stained history? Perhaps the first step toward understanding the causes and finding hope for a cure lies in facing the fact of guilt. Richard Maxwell Brown, a professor at the College of William and Mary, speaks of this in a paper reproduced in the Report to the National Commission on the Causes and Prevention of Violence:

> We must recognize that, despite our pious official disclaimers, we have always operated with a heavy dependence upon violence in even our highest and most idealistic endeavors. We must take stock of what we have done rather than what we have said. When that is done, the realization that we have been an incorrigibly violent people is overwhelming.
>
> We must realize that violence has not been the action only of the roughnecks and racists among us but has been the tactic of the most upright and respected of our people. Having gained this self-knowledge, the next problem becomes the ridding of violence, once and for all, from the real (but unacknowledged) American value system. Only then will we begin to solve our social, economic, and po-

litical problems by social, economic, and political means rather than evading them by resort to the dangerous and degrading use of violence.

Having so faced the enemy within, can we determine the reasons for it? Few, if any, books are listed under the heading *Violence* in library card catalogs, and even the new *International Encyclopedia of the Social Sciences* does not contain a single entry in that category.

Lately, however, the matter has become more and more important in the minds of the American people and in the thinking of behavioral scientists, historians, and political leaders. Even today's youth has predicated its near-revolution on its sensitivity to the wrongs of our society. They are sincerely fighting evil tooth and nail—an evil that they believe to be singular to their elders and other members of what they derisively call the Establishment. With an ancient wisdom far beyond their years and experience, they have adopted the catchword, "Love," and emblazon this curious war cry—admittedly along with less savory four-letter words—on their banners and posters.

Konrad Lorenz and other ethnologists interpret their studies of the instinctive behavior of animals to mean that mankind has a "killing imperative," that aggression, and thus violence, is an evolutionary instinct—a drive inherited by man from the lower animals. If Lorenz and those who agree with him are right, modern man is trapped in his violent patterns. Lorenz points out that most carnivores, especially those equipped with lethal teeth and claws like the wolf, have instinctive inhibitions against killing members of their own species.

Man developed no such inhibitions because he was not originally equipped with the natural weapons of other carnivores. Not until his brain developed and he invented weapons was he a danger to his entire species. By then it may have been too late for mankind to develop the inhibitions that

380

carnivores possess. Of all such species, only the rat and man kill their fellows.

Many anthropologists and psychiatrists disagree with this view. In *A Sign for Cain*, Frederic Wertham, M.D., says:

> Human beings have a capacity for violence, which is very different from an instinct in any strict sense. A natural inborn instinct is something positive. Sex and desire for food, for instance, are positive biological instincts . . . Without sex the race would die out; without the desire for food the individual would die. But violence is due to negative factors. Without violence humanity would flourish.

There has also been considerable discussion about the possibility that violence in our society is the result of overcrowding in our cities. Walter Lippmann said in a recent interview with AP:

> I'm worried about the growth of the size of the country, of the population here and in other countries of the world —outrunning man's capacity to govern himself. I think the central and dramatic problem of our time is that the number of people who have to be governed and the number of people who take part in government has increased beyond what anybody expected . . . That is the question which is grinding up from the inside. Crime, racial unrest, student discontent—the readily apparent social problems— are symptoms. They're caused by this fundamental convulsion.

Some observers have suggested that national violence— war and foreign adventures—are responsible for violence on the home front. Norman Cousins, editor of the *Saturday Review*, seems to be one of these:

> Violence in our world is interconnected. It is chain reactive. It runs from the small to the large and back again, from the half-crazed individual with a handgun to space

armadas with explosives that can incinerate whole cities, from men who have contempt for law to nations that refuse to consider the establishment of law in the world . . . The consequences of anarchy in the streets are serious. The consequences of anarchy among nations are catastrophic.

Robert Kennedy, in a speech he made to the young people of South Africa on their Day of Affirmation in 1966, summed it up this way:

> There is discrimination in this world and slavery and slaughter and starvation. Governments repress their people; and millions are trapped in poverty while the nation grows rich; and wealth is lavished on armaments everywhere.
> These are differing evils, but they are the common works of man. They reflect the imperfection of human justice, the inadequacy of human compassion, our lack of sensibility toward the sufferings of our fellows.

Some statistics gathered by the National Commission on the Causes and Prevention of Violence, however, tend to show there is no connection, or at least no direct connection, between national and private violence. For example, crime and violence declined sharply in Britain in 1940 during the height of the blitz and even mental illness was at its lowest peak in years. A decline was also noted in political violence in the United States during the First and Second World War periods, but an increase manifested itself during the Vietnam action. There is undoubtedly some correlation between the populace's belief in the justice or injustice of the war and the incidence of private mayhem.

It would appear that aggression and violence, can even be programmed for political purposes. Anti-Semitism, long a tactic of the right, has now become one of the chief weapons of the far left and black militancy. It is being used by Maoist student leaders and black militants most effectively to stir up hatred among black people against Jews. At first it was disguised by the term anti-Zionism, which has become almost as much of a code word among leftists as law-and-order has on the right. More recently, the appeal to prejudice has become more open and is quite blunt in its advocacy of violence.

> Hey, Jew boy, with that yarmulke
> on your head,
> You pale-faced Jew boy—I wish
> you were dead.

That poem goes on for twenty-four even more violent lines. It was read over a New York radio station by Leslie Campbell, a twenty-nine-year-old black militant leader. Campbell claimed the poem had been written by a sixteen-year-old Harlem girl, and he and Julius Lester, another black militant who runs a panel program on WDAI-FM, agreed that it was "beautiful."

Other blacks who feel the same way have had their pictures in the press, carrying signs reading: JEWS GET OUT OF PALESTINE. IT'S NOT YOUR HOME ANYWAY! MOSES WAS THE FIRST TRAITOR AND HITLER WAS THE MESSIAH.

Further evidence of the intense anti-Semitic activity on the left can be seen in the effort to turn Sirhan Sirhan into a hero of the student movement, and the considerable demand for posters depicting the killer of Bobby Kennedy as a freedom fighter. They feature an idealized picture of Sirhan Sirhan and a drawing of an Arab guerrilla fighter. The assassin's words at the time of the killing, "I have done it for the sake of my country," are prominently displayed. The poster also contains an attack on the late Senator Kennedy as a supporter of Zionism.

Other leftists show their hatred of Jews by active participation in the Arab guerrilla war against Israel. One hundred and forty radical Western students arrived in Jordan in late July, 1969, to form an anti-Zionist foreign legion. Their leaders are reported as saying they were taking up the Arab cause for tactical reasons. "Our movement would wither without a liberation war," one of them said. "With Ché Guevara dead and Vietnam almost over, we need the Palestinians to carry the flag of our cause."

As far back as October 23, 1967, the Anti-Defamation League announced that a study of publications printed by the Student Nonviolent Coordinating Committee and the National States Rights Party showed that both groups used the same Arab source of anti-Semitic hate materials.

On April 21, 1969, B'nai B'rith stated an investigation had revealed that leftist extremists and black militants were both funneling money into Arab guerrilla organizations and spreading their hate literature in the United States. Those accused were the Students for a Democratic Society, the Black Panthers, the Black Muslims, and the Havana-based Organization for Solidarity of Peoples of Africa, Asia, and Latin America.

If violence can be programmed, can it be unprogrammed? Can hate be cured? Is there any evidence of methods that can be used to at least reduce the level of violence?

"The elimination of all violence in a free society is impossible," the Commission on Violence said in January, 1969, "but the better control of illegitimate violence is an urgent imperative, and one within our means to accomplish."

Two men who were the victims of violence had previously expressed their hope for its control.

Robert Kennedy was speaking to a black audience in Indianapolis when he heard the news of Martin Luther King's death. He expressed his shock and grief and then said:

> In this difficult day, in this difficult time for the United States, it is perhaps well to ask what kind of nation we are and what direction we want to move in. For those of you who are black . . . considering the evidence that white

people are responsible for the shooting . . . you can be filled with bitterness, with hatred, and a desire for revenge. We can move in that direction or we can make the effort, as Martin Luther King did, to replace that violence, that state of bloodshed that has spread across the land.

For those of you who are black and tempted to be filled with hatred at the injustice of such an act, I can also feel in my heart the same kind of feeling.

I had a member of my family killed but he was killed by a white man . . . But we have to make an effort in the United States, we have to make an effort to understand . . . What we need . . . is not division; what we need . . . is not hatred; what we need . . . is not violence or lawlessness, but love and wisdom, and compassion toward one another, and feeling justice toward those who still suffer within our country, whether they be white or they be black.

Martin Luther King said following the death of John Kennedy:

> The assassination of President Kennedy killed not only a man but a complex of illusions. It demolished the myth that hate and violence can be confined in an airtight chamber to be employed against but a few. Suddenly the truth is revealed that hate is a contagion; that it grows and spreads as a disease; that no society is so healthy that it can automatically maintain its immunity . . .
>
> We are all involved in the death of John Kennedy. We tolerated hate; we tolerated the stimulation of violence in all walks of life; and we tolerated the differential applications of law, which said a man's life was sacred only if we agreed with his views . . . We mourn a man who had become the pride of a nation, but we grieve as well for ourselves because we know we were sick.

The fact that violence has been with us from the beginning does not necessarily mean it has to be with us forever. Some forms of violence have died out in our country. The religious riots that once rocked our cities have long been gone from our midst. Lynching, the blackest stain of all, has all but disappeared in recent years. We still have racial violence and prospects are for more rather than less in the future. Political violence, which seemed on the decline in America, has increased in the last few years and, as always, we have the sociopath among us.

There are too many guns in too many hands in America for there not to be violence. There is too much hate and too many voices trumpeting that hate. Our forms of entertainment are filled with violence. A boxing match excites the audience into cries of "Kill!" and our motion pictures glorify violence and its perpetrators. If there is a solution to violence in America, it lies in trying to dispel the climate of hate that provides the growing weather for the seeds of psychopathy.

Anton Chekhov said, "If you hang a gun on the wall in the first act, you have to use it by the third."

Too many guns, figuratively and literally, are being hung on too many walls in America, and there is, as Norman Mailer says, "a lust for apocalypse" abroad in the land.

The apocalypse could come in the form of race war. We could have new "red summers" that would make the "long, hot summers" of 1965-68 look like mild springs. The guns that have been placed on the walls must be taken down long before the third act, and the problems that caused them to be placed there must be solved.

"The Legacy Left by Senator Robert F. Kennedy," the eulogy delivered at his funeral services in St. Patrick's Cathedral, New York, June 8, 1968, by his brother, Senator Edward M. Kennedy, concluded with Bobby's own words:

Some men see things as they are and say why. I dream things that never were and say why not.

Indeed, why not?

Bibliography

Adler, Bill, ed., *The Wisdom of Martin Luther King*. New York, Lancer Books, Inc., 1968.

Allen, Frederick Lewis, *Since Yesterday*. New York and London, Harper & Brothers, 1940.

Aptheker, Herbert, *Nat Turner's Slave Rebellion*. New York, Grove Press, Inc., 1966.

Asbury, Herbert, *The Gangs of New York*. New York, Alfred A. Knopf, Inc., 1927.

Bakal, Carl, *The Right To Bear Arms*. New York, Toronto, and London, McGraw-Hill, Inc., 1966.

Bales, William A., *A Tiger in the Streets*. New York, Dodd, Mead and Company, 1962.

Bennett, Lerone, Jr., *What Manner of Man*. New York, Pocket Books, Inc., 1968.

Billington, Ray A., *The Protestant Crusade, 1800–1860*. New York, The Macmillan Company, 1938.

Boland, Charles Michael, *They All Discovered America*. New York, Doubleday, Permaback Edition, 1963.

Bradford, William, *Of Plymouth Plantation, 1628–1647*. Samuel Eliot Morison Ed., New York, Alfred A. Knopf, Inc., 1953.

Carlson, John Roy, *Under Cover*. New York, E. P. Dutton & Co., Inc., 1943.

Carr, William H. A., *JFK: A Complete Biography 1917–1963*. New York, Lancer Books, Inc., 1968.

Catton, Bruce, *The Coming Fury*. New York, Pocket Books, Inc., 1967.
———, *Glory Road*. New York, Pocket Books, Inc., 1964.

Chaplin, J. P., *Rumor, Fear and the Madness of Crowds*. New York, Ballantine Books, Inc., 1959.

Coates, Robert M., *The Outlaw Years*. New York, Pennant Books, Inc., 1954.

Cohen, Jerry, and Murphy, William S. *Burn, Baby, Burn!* New York, Avon Books, 1966.

Conot, Robert, *Rivers of Blood, Years of Darkness.* New York, Bantam Books, Inc., 1967.

Cook, Fred J., *The FBI Nobody Knows.* New York, The Macmillan Company, 1964.

De Ford, Miriam Allen, *Murderers Sane & Mad.* New York, Avon Books, 1966.

Demaris, Ovid, *Captive City: Chicago in Chains.* New York, Lyle Stuart, 1969.

Demaris, Ovid, *Lucky Luciano.* Derby, Conn., Monarch Books, Inc., 1960.

———, *The Dillinger Story.* Derby, Conn., Monarch Books, Inc., 1961.

Demaris, Ovid, and Reid, Ed, *The Green Felt Jungle.* New York, Trident Press, 1963.

American Military History 1607–1953. Department of the Army ROTC Manual No. 145–20, Washington, D.C., U.S. Government Printing Office, 1956.

DeVoto, Bernard, *The Course of Empire,* Boston, Houghton Mifflin Company, 1952.

Donovan, Robert J., *The Assassins.* New York, Popular Library, Inc., 1962.

Dumond, Dwight Lowell, *America in Our Time 1896–1946.* New York. Henry Holt and Company, 1947.

Epstein, Benjamin R., and Forster, Arnold, *The Radical Right.* New York, Vintage Books, A Division of Random House, 1967.

Epstein, Edward Jay, *Inquest.* New York, Bantam Books, 1966.

Fanon, Frantz, *Black Faces, White Masks.* New York, Grove Press, Inc., 1967.

———, *The Wretched of the Earth.* New York, Grove Press, 1968.

Faulkner, Harold Underwood, *American Political and Social History.* New York and London, Appleton-Century-Crofts, 1948.

Gillette, Paul J., and Tillinger, Eugene, *Inside Ku Klux Klan.* New York, Pyramid Press, 1965.

Goldston, Robert, *Satan's Disciples.* New York, Ballantine Books, 1962.

———, *The Negro Revolution.* New York, Signet Books, New American Library, 1968.

Violence in America: Historical and Comparative Perspectives, Vols. I and II. Report to the National Commission on the Causes and Prevention of Violence, Washington, D.C., 1969.

Greene, Laurence, *The Era of Wonderful Nonsense.* Indianapolis-New York, The Bobbs-Merrill Company, Inc., 1939.

Harolow, Ralph Volney, *The Growth of the United States,* Vol. I: The Establishment of the Nation Through the Civil War (Revised Edition). New York, Henry Holt and Company, 1943.

Heaps, Willard A., *Riots U.S.A. 1765–1965.* New York, The Seabury Press, Inc., 1966.

Hernton, Calvin C., *Sex and Racism in America.* New York, Grove Press, 1965.

Hudson, Jan, *The Sex and Savagery of the Hell's Angels.* London, The New English Library Ltd., 1967.

Jacobson, David J., *The Affairs of Dame Rumor.* New York, Rinehart & Company, Inc., 1948.

Jones, Katharine M., *The Plantation South.* Indianapolis-New York, The Bobbs-Merrill Company, Inc., 1957.

Kahn, Albert E., *High Treason.* New York, The Hour Publishers, 1950.

Kefauver, Estes, *Crime in America.* Garden City, N.Y., Doubleday & Company, Inc., 1951.

Kennedy, Robert F., *The Enemy Within.* New York, Harper & Brothers, 1960.

King, Martin Luther, Jr., *Why We Cain't Wait.* New York and Toronto, The New American Library, 1964.

———, *Stride Toward Freedom.* New York, Harper & Row Publishers, 1964.

———, *Where Do We Go From Here: Chaos or Community?* Boston, Beacon Press, 1968.

Lamb, Harold, *New Found World.* Garden City, N.Y., Doubleday & Company, Inc., 1955.

Landesman, Jay Irving, and Legman, Gershon (eds.), *Neurotica.*

Leech, Margaret, *Reveille in Washington 1860–1865.* New York and London, Harper & Brothers, 1941.

Lewis, Anthony, *Portrait of a Decade: The Second American Revolution, 1954–1964.* New York, Random House, Inc., 1964.

Lewis, Lloyd, *Myths After Lincoln*. Editions for the Armed Services, Inc. by arrangement. New York, Harcourt, Brace and Company, 1929.

Lewis, Lloyd, and Smith, Henry Justin, *Chicago: The History of Its Reputation*. New York, Harcourt, Brace and Company, 1920.

Lewis, Norman, *The Honored Society*. New York, G. P. Putnam's Sons, 1964.

Lindner, Robert, *Must You Conform?* New York, Grove Press, Inc. 1956.

Lipton, Dean, *The Truth About Simon Girty*. New York, Adventure Classics (Imprint of Pyramid Press), March 1957.

Louderback, Lew, *The Bad Ones*. New York, A Fawcett Gold Medal Book, 1968.

Maas, Peter, *The Valachi Papers*. New York, G. P. Putnam's Sons, 1968.

Marine, Gene, *The Black Panthers*. New York, The New American Library, Inc., 1969.

Montross, Lynn, *War Through the Ages*. New York and London, Harper & Brothers, 1944, 1946.

Morison, Samuel Eliot, *The Story of the Old Colony of New Plymouth*. New York, Knopf, 1956.

Myers, Gustavus, *History of Bigotry in the United States,* edited and revised by Henry M. Christman. New York, Capricorn Books (Imprint of G. P. Putnam's Sons), 1960.

Nevins, Allan, *Ordeal of the Union: A House Dividing 1852–1857,* Vol. II. New York, Charles Scribner's Sons, 1947.

———, *The Emergence of Lincoln,* Vol. I. New York, Charles Scribner's Sons, 1950.

———, *The Emergence of Lincoln,* Vol. II. New York, Charles Scribner's Sons, 1950.

———, *The War for the Union,* Vols. I and II. New York, Charles Scribner's Sons, 1959 and 1960.

Nordholt, J. W. Schulte, *The People That Walk in Darkness*. New York, Ballantine Books, Inc., first printed in the English language 1960, Burke Publishing Company Ltd.

Parrinder, Geoffrey, *Witchcraft*. Baltimore, Md., Penguin Books, Inc., 1958.

Peterson, Virgil W., *Barbarians in Our Midst*. Boston, Little, Brown and Company, 1952.

Phillips, Ulrich B.,.*American Negro Slavery*. Baton Rouge, Louisiana State University Press, 1966.

Pollard, James E., *The Presidents and the Press*. New York, The Macmillan Company, 1947.

Popkin, Richard H., *The Second Oswald*. New York, Avon Books, 1966.

Porges, Irwin, *The Violent Americans*. Derby, Conn., Monarch Books, Inc. 1963.

Preston, John Hyde, *A Short History of the American Revolution*. New York, Pocket Books, Inc., 1952.

Preston, Richard A., Wise, Sydney F., and Werner, Herman O., *Men in Arms*. New York, Frederick A. Praeger, Inc., 1956.

Redding, Saunders, *They Came in Chains*. Pihladelphia-New York, J. B. Lippincott Co., 1950.

Rudwick, Elliott M., *Race Riot at East St. Louis, July 2, 1917*. Carbondale, Southern Illinois University Press, 1964.

Sandburg, Carl, *The Chicago Race Riot*. New York, Harcourt, Brace and Howe, 1919.

Schlesinger, Arthur M., Jr., *Violence: America in the Sixties*. New York, Signet Books, New American Library, 1968.

————, *The Crisis of the Old Order 1919–1933*. Boston, Houghton Mifflin Company, 1957.

————, *The Politics of Upheaval*. Boston, Houghton Mifflin Company. 1960.

Shapiro, Fred C., and Sullivan, James W., *Race Riots: New York 1964*. New York, Thomas Y. Crowell, 1964.

Shogan, Robert, and Craig, Thomas, *The Detroit Race Riot: A Study in Violence*. Philadelphia, Chilton Book Company, 1964.

Siberman, Charles E., *Crisis in Black and White*. New York, Random House, Inc., 1964.

Ramparts Magazine, Editors of, *In the Shadow of Dallas*. San Francisco, California, 1967.

Skolnick, Jerome H., *The Politics of Protest*. New York, Ballantine Books, Inc., 1969.

Slosson, Preston William, *The Great Crusade and After, 1914–1928*. New York, The Macmillan Company, 1930.

Smith, George H., *Martin Luther King, Jr.: Drum Major for Justice*, Unpublished manuscript to be published by Lancer Books, New York.

391

Sondern, Frederic, Jr., *Brotherhood of Evil: The Mafia.* New York, Farrar Straus and Cudahy, 1959.

Spears, John R., *The American Slave Trade.* New York, Ballantine Books, Inc., 1960.

Starkey, Marion L., *The Devil in Massachusetts.* New York, Alfred A. Knopf, Inc., 1950.

———, *Land Where Our Fathers Died.* Garden City, N.Y., Doubleday & Company, Inc., 1962.

Steiger, Brad, *The Mass Murderer.* New York, Award Books, 1967.

Stern, Philip Van Doren, *The Man Who Killed Lincoln.* New York, Dell Publishing Co., Inc., 1955.

Stone, Irving, *They Also Ran.* Garden City, N.Y., Doubleday, Doran and Company, Inc., 1944.

Sullivan, Mark, *Our Times,* Vol. I, The Turn of the Century. New York-London, Charles Scribner's Sons, 1926.

———, *Our Times,* Vol. II, America Finding Herself. New York-London, Charles Scribner's Sons, 1927.

———, *Our Times.* Vol. III, Pre-War America. Chautauqua, N.Y., Chautauqua Press, 1931.

Summers, Montague, *The History of Witchcraft.* New York, University Books, 1956.

Task Force on Violent Aspects of Protest and Confrontation. Skolnick Report to the National Commission on the Causes and Prevention of Violence. Washington, D.C., Government Printing Office, 1969.

Task Force Report: Organized Crime. President's Commission on Law Enforcement and Administration of Justice, The. Washington D.C., Government Printing Office, 1967.

Thayer, George, *The Farther Shores of Politics.* New York Simon & Schuster, Inc., 1967.

Thompson, Hunter S., *Hell's Angels, A Strange and Terrible Saga.* New York, Random House, Inc., 1967.

Turkus, Burton B., and Feder, Sid., *Murder, Inc.* New York, Farrar, Straus and Young, 1951.

Van Every, Dale, *Ark of Empire.* New York, The New American Library Inc., 1963.

Walker Report. National Commission on the Causes and Prevention of Violence. Submitted by the Director of the Chicago Study Team. Washington, D.C., Government Printing Office, 1969.

Ward, Christopher, *The War of the Revolution,* Vols. I and II. New York, The Macmillan Company, 1952.

Waskow, Arthur I., *From Race Riot to Sit-In: 1919 and the 1960's.* Garden City, N.Y., Doubleday & Company, Inc., 1966.

Watts Report: Violence in the City—An End or a Beginning? Report by the Governor's Commission on the Los Angeles Riots. December 2, 1965.

Wecter, Dixon, *The Hero in America.* Ann Arbor, Michigan, The University of Michigan Press, 1963.

Wellman, Paul I., *Spawn of Evil.* New York, Pyramid Books, 1965.

Wertenbaker, Thomas Jefferson, *The Puritan Oligarchy.* New York, Grosset's Universal Library, Grosset & Dunlap, 1947.

Wertham, Fredric, *A Sign for Cain.* New York, Paperback Library, 1969.

Westin, Alan F. (ed.). *Freedom Now! The Civil Rights Struggle in America.* New York Basic Books, Inc., Publishers, 1964.

Willison, George F., *Saints and Strangers.* New York, Reynal & Hitchcock, 1945.

Wood, W. B., and Edmonds, J. S., *Military History of the Civil War.* New York, G. P. Putnam's Sons, 1937. (Reprinted 1958), Capricorn Edition 1960.

Index

395

King, Martin Luther, Jr., 212-13, 226, 281-84, 384-85
King Philip's War, 10
King William's War, 12
King's College, 17, 19
Kirk, Grayson, 293, 295
Knights of Labor, 149
Know-Nothings, 41-43, 49, 228
Konisberg, Harold "Kayo," 194
Kreuger, Paul, 343-44
Ku Klux Klan, 228, 233
  civil rights movement and, 210-11, 240
  Indians and, 208
  Negroes and, 112-15, 123, 202-3, 208, 210-11, 218

labor (see also names, industries), 144-67
  anarchism, 145-46, 148, 158, 160, 163-65
  Negro, 129, 131, 158, 161, 197
  race riots and, 197 ff.
  strikebreakers, 131, 151-53, 158, 161
  strikes, 131, 146, 148 ff.
  unions, 146, 151, 153, 174
Lanza, Jimmy, 190
Law and Order party, 75
Lawrence (Kans.), 77, 100-1
Lawrence, Richard, 248-49, 251, 252
lead miners, 158-59
Lebron, Lolita, 270-71
left, see radical left; names
Leif Ericson, 1-2
Leif the Lucky, 1-2
Lincoln, Abraham, 42, 87, 100, 252-54, 379
Le Maire, Francis, 201-2
Linderfelt, K. E., 163
Little Big Horn, battle of, 108, 110
Little Rock (Ark.), 211
Liuzzo, Mrs. Viola, 211, 240
Logan, Chief, 26-27
Long, Huey P., 269
Longview (Tex.), 134-36
Look magazine, 190
Lord Dunmore's War, 26
Los Angeles, 195-97, 214-17, 229 ff., 284-90, 302 ff., 333 ff., 369 ff.
Louisiana, 115, 118-19, 208, 269
Lovejoy, Elijah, 45

Luciano, Charley "Lucky," 171, 178-80, 184, 187-89
Ludlow War, 162-63
Lumbee Indians, 208
Lynch, Charles, 14, 115
Lynch, James, 115-16
lynch law, 115-16, 123-24, 164, 167
lynch law
  Negroes and, 113 ff., 123-24, 128, 207-8
  West, 110

Mafia, 168 ff., 178-79, 184 ff., 189-94
Malcolm X., 271-72, 273
Malvern Hill, battle of, 92
Maoism, 237, 241-43, 382
Maranzano, Salvatore, 171, 178-79, 180
Marcuse, Herbert, 245-46
Maryland, 43, 86-88, 226, 329
Mason, Samuel, 32
Massachusetts (see also names, subjects), 6 ff., 21-22, 34-37, 41
Masseria, Joe, 178-79, 180
Mayall, Rev. Alvin, 235
Mayflower, 7-8
McCandles (McCanles), 106-7
McCarthy followers, 301, 315, 319
McClellan, John L., 179, 191
McCord, Gov., 205, 206
McCormick strike, 148
McCurdy, Lewis H., 211
McDonald, Michael Cassius, 169
McKinley, William, 146, 260-65
McKinney, Gene, 238-39
McKoin, Dr. B. M., 120
McLuhan, Marshall, 358
McParlan, James, 148
Meredith, James, 211
Meridian (Miss.), 114
Metropolitans, 51-52
Mexican-Americans, 195-97
Miami (Fla.), 267-68
Miami Beach (Fla.), 193
Michigan (see also Detroit; names, subjects), 161, 162, 298
Michigan State University, 297-98
Middle Atlantic States (see also names, subjects), 22 ff., 149 ff.
Midwest (see also names, subjects), 25 ff., 104, 127 ff., 149, 158, 180 ff., 266-67

399

Office of War Information, 197
Ohio (*see also* names, subjects), 42-43, 219-20
Old Brewery, 47, 48
Olney, Richard, 155
Olson, Harold F., 174-75, 177
open-housing movement, 217-19
Organized Crime and Racketeering Section, 191-92
Orr, J. S., 41-42
Osawatomie (Kans.), 80, 81
Oswald, Lee Harvey, 277-80
outlaws, western, 103-7, 180, 184

Paine, Lewis, 253-56
Palmer, A. Mitchell, 139
Paoli Massacre, 14-15
Parker, Bonnie, 180, 183-84
Parker, Isaac C., 110-11
Parker, William, 216
Patler, John, 272-73
Patterson, Maj. Gen., 40
Peebles, Timothy, 241
Pennsylvania (*see also* names, subjects), 22-25, 37-41, 133, 134, 147 ff., 159 ff.
Permanent Subcommittee on Investigations, 179, 190-91
Petersburg, battle of, 98-99
Petrosino, Joseph, 171
Philadelphia (Miss.), 210-11
Philadelphia (Pa.), 37-41, 43 ff., 133
Philip II, King of Spain, 6
Phillips, Wendell, 44
Pilgrims, 6-9
Pinker, Ray, 232
Pinkerton agents, 105, 147, 151-53
Pittsburgh (Pa.), 24, 150-53
Place, Etta, 105
Plug Uglies, 46, 48, 52
police
  bias, 140, 196, 239
  Black Panthers and, 237-40
  Chicago convention disorders, 302 ff.
  corruption, 172-73, 177-78
  killing of, in self-defense, 176-77
  mobs assisted or unrestrained by, 86, 87, 90-91, 136, 196, 200
  private armies of, 159-60
  riots and feuds of, 50-53
  state, 205-7
  strike, 165-67

violence, 200 ff., 205-7, 212, 221 ff., 223 ff., 237 ff.
politics and crime, 169 ff.
Pontiac's Rebellion, 12-13
Populism, 125
Pottawatomie (Kans.), 79-80, 81
Powers, Caleb, 260
Preparedness Day bombing, 163
Pressed Steel Car Co., 160
Price, Roland T., 202
Price, Sterling, 102
Pritchett, Joe, 207
Progressive Farmers and Household Union of America, 142-43
Progressive Labor Party, 213, 242, 373 ff.
Project Alert, 230-31
Prohibition, 171 ff., 177-78, 180
propaganda (*see also* news media), 350-57
  anti-Catholic, 34, 35, 43
  anti-Semitic, 383-84
  Negro, 44, 63-64
Prosser, Gabriel, 66-68
psychology and violence, 322-23, 337 ff., 377 ff.
Puerto Rican Nationalist Movement, 269-71
Pulliam, William, 241
Pullman strike, 154-57
Puritans, 9-10
Purple Mob, 186-87
Purvis, Melvin, 181, 182
Putnam, George, 230

Quantrill, William C., 100-3
Queen Anne's War, 12

racial bigotry (*see also* places, ethnic groups), 1 ff., 7 ff., 33 ff., 43-45, 54 ff., 113 ff., 123 ff., 147-48, 195 ff., 240
racketeers, 168 ff.
radical left (*see also* names), 145-46, 163-65, 237-44, 350 ff., 364-65, 382 ff.
radical right (*see also* names), 197-98, 218-19, 227-37, 350 ff.
radio programs, 233-34
Radisson, Pierre Esprit, 11
railroads, 148-50, 154-57, 161, 167
Randolph, John, 57

404

Pillsbury

THE COMPLETE BOOK OF BAKING

VIKING

Cherry Squares p. 480

The Complete Book of Baking
Pillsbury Publications
The Pillsbury Company

Publisher: Sally Peters
Publication Manager: Diane B. Anderson
Senior Editor: Jackie Sheehan
Food Editor: Nancy Lilleberg
Associate Food Editors: Sharon Saldin, Grace Wells, Lola Whalen
Test Kitchen Coordinator: Pat Peterson
Contributing Editor: Patricia Miller
Nutrition Information: Pillsbury Technology
Art Direction and Design: Tad Ware & Company, Inc.
Production Coordinator: Michele Warren
Production Assistant: Terri Peterson
Food Stylist: Barb Standal
Text Photography: Studio 3
Cover Photography: Glenn Peterson Inc.

VIKING
Published by the Penguin Group
Penguin Books USA Inc, 375 Hudson Street,
New York, New York 10014, U.S.A.
Penguin Books Ltd, 27 Wrights Lane,
London W8 5TZ, England
Penguin Books Australia Ltd, Ringwood,
Victoria, Australia
Penguin Books Canada Ltd, 10 Alcorn Avenue,
Toronto, Ontario, Canada M4V 3B2
Penguin Books (N.Z.) Ltd, 182–190 Wairau Road,
Auckland 10, New Zealand

Penguin Books Ltd, Registered Offices:
Harmondsworth, Middlesex, England

First Published in 1993 by Viking Penguin,
a division of Penguin Books USA Inc.

10 9 8 7 6 5 4 3 2 1

ISBN 0-670-84768-2
CIP data available.

Printed in the United States of America

CONTENTS

BAKING FROM A TO Z

For years, one of our sayings at Pillsbury has been, "Nothing says lovin' like something from the oven." And there are countless ways to express your love — from golden loaves of fresh-baked bread to still-gooey chocolate chip cookies to luscious fruit-filled pies.

You'll find all those and more on these pages, where we've gathered together our best baking recipes, tips and techniques.

Whether you're a new baker or an old pro, you'll find helpful information in this chapter about baking ingredients, equipment, terms and techniques that will help you turn out delicious results every time.

Pictured: **Chocolate Chunk Cookies** *p. 33*

BAKING FROM A TO Z

When you learn to read, you begin by
mastering the ABCs. Learning to bake is much the
same, but you need to become familiar with the IETTs — Ingredients,
Equipment, Terms and Techniques. Once you feel comfortable
with these baking basics, you'll be confident in the kitchen,
no matter what recipe you choose.

SIX EASY STEPS TO BAKING SUCCESS

1. Read through the entire recipe before
   you begin . . . it takes the surprise factor out
   of baking. You'll know just what ingredients
   and equipment you'll need and how much
   time the recipe will take.

2. Review the techniques you'll be using. If
   something is unfamiliar, refer to this chapter
   for help.

3. Set out and measure the ingredients in
   advance. Set out the equipment you'll
   need, too.

4. Clean up as you go. It's confusing to bake
   in chaos. So put ingredient containers away,
   wipe up spills and place dirty dishes in the
   sink.

5. Keep distractions to a minimum so that
   you won't accidentally skip a step or leave
   out an ingredient.

6. Relax! Baking is a pleasure, not a chore.
   So take your time, enjoy what you're doing
   and let your creativity flow.

INGREDIENTS

*Begin with the best ingredients and you will be
off to a good start. Fresh ingredients will help
ensure that the final product is a success. Here's a
reference list of the most common baking
ingredients:*

BAKING POWDER

Double-acting is the most popular kind of
baking powder. It reacts first with liquids
and then with heat during baking. Because
baking powder, over time, loses its ability to
leaven baked goods, use it before the
expiration date on the can.

• You can substitute ½ teaspoon of cream of
  tartar and ¼ teaspoon of baking soda for
  1 teaspoon of baking powder.

• To determine if baking powder is still active,
  add 1 teaspoon to ⅓ cup of hot water. If it
  bubbles vigorously, it's still active and will
  give good baking results.

BAKING SODA

Baking soda reacts instantly with liquids and
acidic ingredients such as molasses, sour
cream and buttermilk. Baked goods with
baking soda should be baked as soon after the
liquid is added as possible. When an acid isn't
included in the recipe, cream of tartar is sometimes used.

BUTTER - SEE FATS

CHOCOLATE

Chocolate and cocoa products come from cocoa beans.

Chocolate should be wrapped tightly in foil or resealable plastic bags and stored in a cool, dry place for up to 9 months. The best storage conditions are between 60° and 78°F., with less than 50% relative humidity.

A grayish coating or "bloom" may form on chocolate when it is stored in a too-warm place because the cocoa butter rises to the surface. Bloom does not affect the flavor or quality. When used in a recipe, the chocolate will regain its original color.

Chocolate comes in countless forms and varieties — all of them delicious. Because they differ in flavor and performance, be sure to use the type specified in the recipe.

- **Chips:** For best results use real chocolate chips, not chocolate-flavored ones. Chips are available in sizes from mini to chunks and in several flavors: semi-sweet, milk, mint and vanilla milk. Vanilla milk chips are similar to a white baking bar and melt well for glazes and fillings.

- **Chocolate syrup:** This syrup is a combination of cocoa, corn syrup and flavoring.

- **Milk:** This is sweet chocolate with milk added. It is available in bars, chips and other shapes.

- **Semi-sweet:** This is unsweetened chocolate with sugar, additional cocoa butter and flavorings added. It may be molded into blocks, chips or bars.

- **Sweet baking or cooking:** Also called German sweet chocolate, it's similar to semi-sweet, but has a higher sugar content. It is available in bars.

- **Unsweetened:** This is the basic type from which all others are made. It is molded into 1 or 2-ounce blocks and packed 4 to 8 in a package.

- **Unsweetened cocoa:** This is pure chocolate powder with no ingredients added. Powdered drink mixes containing cocoa powder, sugar, flavoring and sometimes milk solids, should not be used as a substitute for unsweetened cocoa.

- **White:** White chocolate isn't really chocolate at all. It's a blend of cocoa butter, sugar, milk and flavorings and is available in blocks, bars and other shapes. White baking bars contain the greatest amount of cocoa butter. Vanilla-flavored candy coating, also known as almond bark, contains more sugar than white baking bars.

COCONUT

- Coconut is the white, sweet meat of the fresh coconut. Ready-to-use forms are available in cans or plastic bags. **Flaked** coconut (longer and moister pieces) or **shredded** coconut (shorter and drier pieces) can be used interchangeably in recipes unless otherwise specified.

EGGS

Eggs provide structure and volume and can bind ingredients together.

Use large eggs in recipes for baked goods unless another size is specified.

Use clean, fresh eggs with no cracks for baking. Fresh eggs have yolks that are firm and rounded and whites that are thick and clear.

Eggs should be stored in the refrigerator to preserve their freshness and quality and to prevent the growth of bacteria.

When separating eggs, wash your hands and the shells first before you begin. See p. 23.

Egg whites can be frozen in a freezer container for later use. Thaw them before using.

Fat-free and cholesterol-free egg products are available in the supermarket refrigerator and freezer cases. They are made using egg whites and, depending on the brand, contain no fat or less fat than whole eggs. All are cholesterol-free. Egg products can replace whole eggs in many recipes. Use ¼ cup thawed egg product for each egg called for in the recipe. Do not substitute egg products for eggs in cream puffs or popovers because they won't puff or pop.

FATS

Fats tenderize, provide flavor, help bind ingredients together and produce browning in baked goods. The main types of fats used in baking are:

- **Butter:** Sweet flavored and made from cream, butter is available salted or unsalted in 1-pound blocks, quarter-pound (½-cup) sticks and whipped in tubs. Butter is interchangeable with margarine in most recipes, but is recommended for candy, puff pastry, and croissants. If whipped butter is used, it should be measured by weight, not volume; 8 ounces of whipped butter equals 1 cup.

- **Butter-margarine blends:** These blends of 60% margarine and 40% butter are available in sticks and tubs.

- **Margarine:** This is made from a variety of vegetable oils including corn and soybean. Margarine is available in sticks, in tubs and whipped. Because whipped and tub margarines are softer and contain a higher percentage of air, only stick margarine should be used in baking. Margarine is interchangeable with butter in most recipes.

- **Lard:** Lard is pork fat that has been processed and refined. It is softer and oilier than butter or margarine and creates a flaky texture in biscuits and pie crusts.

- **Reduced-calorie or lowfat butter or margarine:** These products contain at least 20% less fat than regular butter or margarine and have water and air added. THEY SHOULD NOT BE USED FOR BAKING.

- **Vegetable oils:** These oils are low in saturated fat, contain no cholesterol and are pressed from a variety of seeds or kernels such as canola, corn, safflower, sunflower and soybean. They are referred to as "oil" in our recipes and are interchangeable. Olive oil should not be used in baking unless specified in the recipe.

- **Vegetable shortening:** This solid fat is made from vegetable oils that have been processed with air. Shortening is practically flavorless. It also is available in butter flavor. Our recipes call for "shortening."

FLAVORINGS

For best results, extracts, flavors and liqueurs should be added to ingredients at room temperature, or once a dish (such as custard or frosting) has been removed from the heat.

- **Extracts and flavors:** There are scores of extracts and flavors that can be added to baked goods, such as almond, lemon, mint, rum and orange. These extracts or flavors may be used in place of liqueurs, although the flavors may not be as true or intense. The most popular extract is vanilla. Pure vanilla extract is made from vanilla beans and alcohol. Imitation vanilla is made of synthetic flavors and coloring; it is about half as expensive as vanilla extract and may leave an unpleasant aftertaste.

- **Liqueurs:** These alcohol-based beverages may be used to add chocolate, fruit, mint, nut or coffee flavors to baked goods.

FLOUR

Flour provides the structure for baked goods. It is the finely ground meal produced during the grinding of various edible grains. The most common flours are made from hard and soft wheat, blended during milling to produce different kinds of flour.

Flour is enriched to restore the natural iron and B vitamins that are lost during milling. Enrichment causes no change in the flour's taste, color, texture, quality or caloric value.

Flour may be bleached or unbleached. Bleached flour goes through an aging process which improves its baking performance and whitens the flour. Unbleached flour is allowed to age naturally, and is creamy-white in color. Bleaching does not affect the nutritional value of flour.

Today's flour is pre-sifted more than 100 times during milling, so it is no longer necessary to sift it before measuring.

Store flour in an airtight container in a cool, dry place. It also may be kept in the refrigerator or freezer — just let it warm to room temperature before using. All purpose and bread flours should be used within 18 to 24 months of purchase; self rising flour should be used within 12 to 18 months. Because whole grain flours contain fat from the wheat germ, they become rancid more quickly and are best stored in the refrigerator or freezer. Use them within 1 year.

There are a number of different types of flour. Be sure to use the type specified in the recipe.

• **All purpose:** Milled from the inner part of the wheat kernel, it contains a blend of hard and soft wheat. This versatile flour is appropriate for all uses and is available bleached or unbleached. Our recipes have been developed with bleached all purpose flour but unbleached flour can be used instead.

• **Bread:** Especially milled for baking with yeast, this flour contains more protein which gives the bread structure and increases the elasticity of the dough, resulting in loaves with higher volume. See p. 421.

• **Cake:** Made from soft wheat, it produces tender, delicate cakes.

• **Cracked wheat:** In this flour, wheat kernels are fractured but not finely ground during milling. The flour contains "chunks" of the cracked kernel, giving baked products a coarser, crunchier texture.

• **Rye:** It is available in medium (the most common) light and dark rye flour. Because rye flour has less baking strength than all purpose or bread flour, it should be used in combination with them in baking.

• **Self rising:** Baking powder, which makes baked goods rise, and salt are added during milling. One cup contains 1½ teaspoons baking powder and ½ teaspoon salt. It is especially suited for biscuits, muffins, light cakes and pastries. It is not recommended for popovers, egg-leavened cakes, chocolate recipes, rich bar cookies or yeast breads. It is available bleached or unbleached.

• **Whole wheat or graham:** Milled from the entire wheat kernel, it has a higher nutritional value and contains more fiber than other flours. Baked products have a heavier, more compact texture. Because whole wheat flour has less baking strength than all purpose flour, it should be used in combination with all-purpose or bread flour.

FRUIT

Fruit is available fresh, frozen, canned, candied or dried.

Select fresh fruit that is ripe, full of flavor and free of blemishes. All fresh fruit should be washed before using.

See p. 211 for Dessert Garnishes made with fruit.

Some of the most popular fruits and the varieties best for baking are:

• **Apples:** Choose apples for baking that have tart flavor and firm texture: Jonathan, McIntosh, Winesap, Granny Smith, Rhode Island, Greening, Rome Beauty and Northern Spy. One pound of apples is equivalent to 3 medium apples or 3 cups of sliced apples.

• **Apricots:** Fresh, canned or dried may be used for baking. One pound of apricots is equivalent to 8 to 12 whole apricots or 2½ cups of sliced apricots.

• **Berries:** Strawberries, raspberries, blueberries, blackberries, gooseberries and boysenberries are available fresh or frozen. For fresh, wash just before using. To freeze berries, wash and drain on paper towels; arrange on baking sheet and freeze until solid. Transfer frozen berries to freezer bags. Frozen berries are available in the supermarket freezer case with or without sugar or syrup added. Use thawed or frozen as specified in the recipe.

- **Bananas:** Bananas can be used for baking and cooking at different stages of ripeness. Use green-tipped in cooked desserts, full-yellow in uncooked desserts or pies and, brown-speckled for breads and cookies. One pound of bananas is equivalent to 3 bananas. One sliced banana equals 2/3 cup; 3 mashed bananas equal 1 cup.

- **Cherries:** Choose tart, firm varieties for baking like Montmorency, Early Richmond and English Morella. Popular sweet varieties are Bing, Queen Anne and Tartarian. One pound of cherries is equivalent to 2 1/3 cups of pitted cherries.

- **Cranberries:** Choose plump, firm, brightly colored berries. Store in the refrigerator or freezer. One 12-oz. pkg. fresh cranberries is equal to 3 cups.

- **Dates:** Available dried year-round and fresh from late summer through the winter. Dried and fresh are interchangeable in most recipes. Use scissors to cut dates. One pound dates is equal to 2 3/4 cups pitted and chopped dates.

- **Peaches:** Peaches are classified as freestone, meaning the pit separates easily from the flesh, or clingstone, meaning the fruit clings to the pit. Clingstone peaches are used for commercial products; freestone are more commonly found in the marketplace and are easiest to use for eating and baking. One pound of peaches is equivalent to 3 medium peaches or 3 cups of sliced peaches.

- **Pears:** Choose Bartlett for poaching, Bosc, Anjou and Comice for baking (when still firm). One pound of pears is equivalent to 3 medium pears or 3 1/2 cups of sliced pears.

- **Prunes:** High in fiber and sugar, prunes are dried plums. One pound dried pitted prunes is equal to 2 1/4 cups.

- **Pumpkin:** Canned pumpkin comes in 2 types: pumpkin (puree only) and pumpkin pie filling (sugar and seasonings added). Fresh pumpkin may replace canned pumpkin in recipes. A 5-pound pumpkin yields about 4 1/2 cups of cooked puree.

- **Raisins:** Available year-round, they are dark brown or golden in color. One pound of raisins equals 3 cups.

- **Rhubarb:** Choose crisp, plump, medium-sized stalks. Rhubarb leaves are poisonous and should not be eaten. One pound rhubarb is equal to 2 cups chopped and cooked rhubarb.

GRAINS

In addition to being milled for flour, grain derivatives are used as ingredients in recipes. Some types are:

- **Bulgur:** This is cracked, partially cooked wheat, which gives bread a chewy texture and nutty flavor. It is nutritionally identical to whole wheat. Use as is or as specified in recipe.

- **Oats:** A whole grain high in fiber; its bran may help lower cholesterol levels. Rolled oats are available in 3 varieties: old-fashioned, quick-cooking and instant. Old-fashioned and quick-cooking oats are interchangeable in recipes, unless otherwise specified. Instant oats are used primarily for breakfast cereal. Oat bran may be used in muffins or quick breads as an added ingredient or as a substitute for part of the flour or rolled oats. See Cook's Note p. 458.

- **Wheat germ:** These are flakes made from the sprouting part of the wheat kernel that are high in nutritional value and fiber. They may be used as a cereal or stirred into baked goods to add texture, vitamins and minerals. Due to its high fat content, wheat germ should be stored in the refrigerator or freezer. See Cook's Note p. 448.

HERBS – see SPICES, HERBS AND SEEDS

MILK

Milk is a common liquid used in baking to moisten ingredients. It affects the consistency of the batter or dough. Use only the freshest milk and dairy products.

There are a number of milk products. Be sure to use the type specified in the recipe.

- **Buttermilk:** Despite its name, buttermilk contains no "butter." It is skim milk that has had bacteria cultures added to thicken it and give it a tangy flavor.

- **Evaporated:** This is whole milk that has been cooked to reduce the water content and is available in cans. It can be used as is, or re-constituted by adding ½ cup water to ½ cup evaporated milk to make 1 cup. It also is available as evaporated skimmed milk.

- **Half-and-half:** This is milk that contains 12% butterfat.

- **Regular:** This includes whole, 2%, 1% and skim. Milk containing differing percentages of butterfat may be used interchangeably in most recipes.

- **Sour cream:** Dairy sour cream is 18 to 20% fat, although low (light) and nonfat options now are available. Always use the type specified in the recipe. The milk has been treated with a lactic acid culture, which gives sour cream its characteristic tang and thick texture. Sour cream will curdle if it becomes too hot. Always add sour cream at the end of the cooking time and heat it only until it is warm, not hot. Never boil dairy sour cream.

- **Sweetened condensed:** This is milk that has been cooked to reduce the water content and has sugar added. This process makes the milk very sweet and thick. Do not substitute it for evaporated milk.

- **Whipping cream:** This is milk that contains from 32% (light) to 40% (heavy) butterfat. The high butterfat content allows it to be whipped, doubling in volume. Sugar is often added to whipped cream when it is used as a dessert topping. See p. 23.

- **Yogurt:** Yogurt is made from milk ranging from skim to half-and-half, which affects its fat content. The milk is treated with a bacteria culture which gives yogurt its tangy taste and thick texture. Yogurt is commercially available in a wide range of flavors, and also may be made at home with a yogurt maker. Yogurt adds flavor and moistness to recipes.

NUTS

All nuts are a good source of protein, contain no cholesterol but are high in fat and calories.

Store nuts in an airtight container in a cool, dry place or freeze them for up to 6 months. Unshelled nuts keep longer than shelled.

Each variety of nut has its own special characteristics, distinctive taste, aroma and use. Some of the most popular for baking are:

- **Almonds:** First cousin to the peach, almonds are flat, oval-shaped nuts with a brown skin that can be removed through blanching. Almond paste is made of ground blanched almonds, sugar and a liquid. Marzipan also is made of almonds, but is sweeter and finer-textured than almond paste. Almonds are available whole (shelled or in the shell), blanched, sliced or slivered.

- **Hazelnuts or filberts:** These are small, round, buttery nuts available whole (shelled or in the shell).

- **Macadamia:** Grown in Hawaii, these creamy, round nuts are especially popular in combination with coconut and pineapple. They are available shelled in jars or cans.

- **Peanuts:** Peanuts are actually a legume similar to garden peas. Peanuts are available in the shell or shelled, salted or unsalted, raw or roasted, and honey roasted.

- **Peanut butter:** Peanut butter is available in creamy and chunky varieties. Natural and old-fashioned peanut butters contain peanuts and peanut oil with no added sugar. The peanut oil separates out and must be stirred back in. To prevent separation, store these peanut butters in the refrigerator.

- **Pecans:** Grown primarily in the southern U.S., pecans are rich, buttery and have the highest fat content of any nut. They're versatile and available in the shell, shelled, halved and chopped.

- **Walnuts:** The most popular varieties of walnuts are English and black. English walnuts, the most common, are mild flavored and available year-round. Black walnuts have a stronger, richer flavor, are difficult to shell and are available only seasonally. Walnuts are available in the shell, shelled, halved and chopped.

SALT

Salt provides flavor, and in yeast breads, it controls the rate of growth of the yeast. The 2 most common types are:

- **Kosher salt:** A coarse-grained, additive-free salt sometimes used in baking. In our recipes, we refer to this as coarse salt.

- **Table salt:** A fine-grained salt used in cooking and at the table as a seasoning. Iodine is often added to table salt for dietary needs.

SPICES, HERBS AND SEEDS

Spices, herbs and seeds add that just-right touch of seasoning to baked goods. Store dried herbs, spices and seeds in a cool, dark, dry area in airtight containers. Seasonings lose flavor when exposed to heat and light, such as when stored over or near your kitchen range or in a countertop spice rack. Herbs and spices should be replaced annually. Store fresh herbs with cut stems in water in the refrigerator.

Herbs can be used either fresh or dried. One tablespoon of fresh herbs is equivalent to 1 teaspoon crushed or ½ teaspoon ground herbs. Here are some of the most popular for baking:

SPICES

- **Allspice:** This is called "4 spices" by the French because it tastes like a blend of cinnamon, cloves, nutmeg and juniper berry. It is available whole or ground.

- **Cardamom:** This is a 3-sided, creamy white pithy pod which contains 17 to 20 seeds. The seeds are pungent yet sweet. It is available in the pod, as shelled seeds or as ground seeds.

- **Cinnamon:** This is a mild, sweet spice which comes from the bark of a tree. It is available in stick, ground or as an oil.

- **Cloves:** Grown in Madagascar and Zanzibar, this pungent, oily spice is available whole, ground or as an oil.

- **Ginger:** This sweet yet slightly tangy spice comes from the root of a lily. Ginger is available fresh, ground and candied.

- **Nutmeg:** Nutmeg is the sweet, hard kernel of a fruit. Mace is from the same fruit and similar in flavor. Nutmeg is usually available in ground form but can be purchased whole.

- **Pumpkin pie spice:** This is a blend of cinnamon, ginger and nutmeg. To make your own, combine 4 teaspoons cinnamon, 1 teaspoon ginger, ½ teaspoon allspice, ½ teaspoon nutmeg and ½ teaspoon cloves.

- **Saffron:** Harvested from the autumn crocus, this golden-yellow spice is rare, costly, has a strong flavor and must be used sparingly. It imparts a yellow color to food.

HERBS

- **Basil:** This is a versatile, savory herb that is available in a wide range of varieties: Italian, lemon, spicy globe, cinnamon and opal.

- **Dill:** This is a member of the parsley family and has a tart, lemony flavor. It is available as dill weed and dill seed.

- **Mint:** This is usually used fresh in beverages or as a garnish.

- **Oregano:** This is a pungent herb that gives Italian food its distinctive flavor.

- **Parsley:** There are about 37 varieties of parsley. It's crisp, sharp flavor is often used in combination with other herbs.

- **Rosemary:** The leaves of this shrub-like herb have a strong, piney flavor and should be used sparingly.

- **Sage:** Sage is commonly used in poultry stuffing, but also works well in breads.

- **Thyme:** French and lemon are the most popular varieties of this pungent, aromatic herb.

SEEDS

- **Anise:** This is a comma-shaped seed that imparts a sweet licorice flavor.

- **Dill:** This is a flat seed from the dill plant. It adds a tart, lemony flavor.

- **Caraway:** This is an aromatic seed with a sharp, distinctive flavor.

- **Poppy:** This is a slate-blue, tiny seed from a variety of non-opium poppy grown in Holland.

- **Sesame:** This is a nutty-flavored seed used especially for topping baked goods.

- **Sunflower:** When cracked open, this seed contains a sweet, grayish, oval-shaped nut that adds crunch to baked goods.

SUGAR AND SWEETENERS

Sugar and sweeteners flavor and tenderize baked goods and give them a golden brown crust.

Sugar is processed from either sugar cane or sugar beets. There is no difference in quality or performance between cane or beet sugar.

Sugar should be stored in an airtight, moisture-proof container to prevent lumping.

There are a number of types of sugars and sweeteners. Be sure to use the type specified in the recipe.

- **Brown sugar:** This contains some molasses making it moist and firm. Both light and dark brown sugar are available. Dark brown sugar has a slightly stronger flavor because it contains more molasses. Brown sugar should be stored in a tightly sealed glass or plastic container in a cool, dry place to prevent it from drying out. To soften brown sugar that has dried out, add a piece of apple (placed in an open plastic bag) to the storage container. Seal tightly; remove the apple after 2 days.

- **Corn syrup:** This is a thick, sweet syrup available in 2 forms: light or dark. Dark corn syrup has a stronger flavor and is dark in color.

- **Granulated sugar:** This is a refined, white, all purpose sugar from which all the molasses has been removed.

- **Honey:** This is a very sweet, thick liquid made by bees from flower nectar. It contributes sweetness, moisture and a distinct flavor to baked goods. Use regular honey, not whipped, in recipes. If honey crystallizes, place the open jar in a pan of hot water until the honey turns liquid again.

- **Molasses:** This is a by-product of the sugar refining process and is available in 3 forms: light, dark and blackstrap. Light molasses is lightest in color and flavor; dark has a rich flavor; and blackstrap has a bitter flavor unsuitable for baking.

- **Powdered sugar:** Also known as confectioners' sugar, it is finely ground sugar which contains cornstarch for ease of mixing and blending. It may need to be sifted to remove lumps.

- **Superfine sugar:** This is sugar that is granulated to the finest crystals. It is ideal for making meringues and cakes.

YEAST

Yeast is bacteria that is activated by warm liquid and sugar. Because yeast is a living plant, accurate liquid temperatures are necessary for baking success and a thermometer offers the most accurate temperature control. Heat the liquid to the temperature specified in the recipe. The action of the bacteria produces gas bubbles which cause baked goods to rise. See p. 418 for Secrets for Baking with Yeast. One envelope of active dry yeast equals $2\frac{1}{4}$ teaspoons of bulk active dry yeast or $\frac{1}{3}$ of a 2-ounce cake of compressed fresh yeast.

- **Active dry yeast (or regular):** These dehydrated granules are the most popular form of yeast. Active dry yeast is available in packets or jars.

- **Compressed fresh yeast:** This moist form of yeast is available in the refrigerator section of the grocery store. It must be stored in the refrigerator and used within 2 weeks.

- **Fast-acting (or quick-rising yeast):** These dehydrated granules reduce the rising time for dough by about half. Use this form interchangeably with regular yeast, and remember to reduce the rising time. Fast-acting yeast is available in packets or jars.

EMERGENCY SUBSTITUTIONS

For best results, use the ingredients called for in the recipe. But, if you run out of or run short of an ingredient, here are some substitutes that can fill in those gaps. Some substitutions may cause a change in texture or flavor, therefore, use these substitutions only when necessary.

EMERGENCY SUBSTITUTIONS

Ingredient	Substitute
Active dry yeast, 1 package	$2\frac{1}{4}$ teaspoons dry or $\frac{1}{3}$ cake compressed yeast, crumbled
Baking powder, 1 teaspoon	$\frac{1}{4}$ teaspoon baking soda plus $\frac{1}{2}$ teaspoon cream of tartar
Buttermilk, 1 cup	1 tablespoon vinegar or lemon juice plus enough milk to make 1 cup
Cake flour, 1 cup	1 cup all purpose flour minus 2 tablespoons
Cornstarch, 1 tablespoon	2 tablespoons flour
Dairy sour cream, 1 cup	1 cup plain yogurt
Flour (for thickening), 1 tablespoon	$1\frac{1}{2}$ teaspoons cornstarch
Half-and-half, 1 cup	$\frac{7}{8}$ cup ($\frac{3}{4}$ cup plus 2 tablespoons) milk plus 3 tablespoons margarine or butter
Honey, 1 cup	$1\frac{1}{4}$ cups sugar plus $\frac{1}{4}$ cup liquid
Lemon, 1 medium (fresh juice)	2 to 3 tablespoons bottled lemon juice
Orange, 1 medium (fresh juice)	$\frac{1}{4}$ to $\frac{1}{3}$ cup orange juice
Yogurt (plain), 1 cup	1 cup dairy sour cream
Self rising flour, 1 cup	1 cup all purpose flour plus $1\frac{1}{2}$ teaspoons baking powder and $\frac{1}{2}$ teaspoon salt
Semi-sweet chocolate, 1 ounce	1 ounce unsweetened chocolate plus 1 tablespoon sugar OR 3 tablespoons semi-sweet chocolate chips
Semi-sweet chocolate chips, (for melting) $\frac{1}{2}$ cup	3 ounces semi-sweet chocolate
Unsweetened chocolate, 1 ounce	3 tablespoons unsweetened cocoa plus 1 tablespoon shortening or margarine

EQUIPMENT

Having a well-equipped kitchen will add to your baking enjoyment and success. You don't need to have a lot of equipment, or the most expensive, but a few basic, versatile and good-quality tools will allow you to create just about any recipe. Basic tools of the baking trade are:

- **Baking pans:** For best results, choose shiny metal ones. Aluminum and tin are the best metals for baking pans. However, insulated, dark-surfaced and nonstick pans are becoming increasingly popular. Foods baked in insulated pans require more baking time and take longer to brown. Foods baked in dark-surfaced pans require a shorter baking time and brown more quickly.

Pans come in standard sizes. It is essential to use the correct size of pan so that your baked goods will turn out well. The types and sizes of pans called for most often in this book are:

> 8-inch square pan
> 8 or 9-inch round cake pan
> 8x4-inch loaf pan
> 9x5-inch loaf pan
> 9-inch pie pan
> 9 or 10-inch springform pan
> 10-inch tart pan
> 10-inch tube pan
> 12-cup Bundt® pan*
> 13x9-inch pan
> 15x10x1-inch baking (or jelly roll) pan
> casserole or souffle dishes of
>   assorted sizes
> cookie sheets of assorted sizes
> muffin pans of assorted sizes

If the recipe calls for a pan you don't have, you can generally use what you do have, however, changing pan sizes will alter baking times. This chart will help you make practical pan-size substitutions:

PAN SUBSTITUTIONS

Recipe calls for:	Substitute:
8x4-inch loaf pan	Two 5½x3¼-inch loaf pans
9x5-inch loaf pan	Two 7½x3¾-inch loaf pans OR three 5½x3½-inch loaf pans
One 9-inch round cake pan	One 8-inch square pan
Two 9-inch round cake pans	Three 8-inch round cake pans
12-cup Bundt® pan	One 10-inch tube pan OR two 9x5-inch loaf pans
13x9-inch	Two 9-inch round cake pans OR two 8-inch round cake pans OR two 8-inch square pans

- **Blender, food processor:** A blender or food processor can speed some preparation steps by chopping, grinding and mixing. Choose one with variable speeds and parts that are easy to clean.

- **Bowls:** Choose a set of 4 nesting glass, stainless steel, plastic, or pottery bowls. Some sets are available with spouts for pouring. Plastic bowls may retain food odors, colors and oils.

- **Bread machine:** A nice-to-have, but not-necessary piece of equipment that mixes and bakes bread all in the same machine.

- **Custard cups:** These small glass cups may be used in the oven for baking single-serving desserts and custards. They also are handy for separating eggs, coloring small amounts of frosting and other baking uses.

- **Decorating bag:** This is also referred to as a pastry bag and is a waxed cloth, plastic or paper bag which comes with a variety of screw-on tips for decorating with frostings and icings. See Decorating Tips and Designs p. 185.

- **Eggbeater:** This is a hand-held rotary eggbeater that can be used in place of a wire whisk or electric mixer.

---

*Bundt® is a registered trademark of Northland Aluminum Products, Inc., Minneapolis, MN.

- **Electric mixer:** This appliance is used for mixing and whipping ingredients. A portable, hand-held mixer is great for light jobs. A free-standing electric mixer works best for bigger quantities and longer mixing times. Many freestanding mixers also come with bread dough hooks for making yeast bread.

- **Grater:** A utensil that has surfaces to produce fine to coarse shreds. It is available in plastic or metal.

- **Juicer:** This is a glass, metal or ceramic utensil for removing the juice from citrus fruits. Choose a juicer with holes for straining the juice from the pulp, a spout for pouring and a handle. Some juicers have a rim for placing over a measuring cup or bowl.

- **Knives:** An assortment of sharp, serrated and plain-edged knives, in sizes ranging from paring to butcher, will fit all your baking needs.

- **Measuring cups:** You will need 2 kinds: a glass measuring cup, which holds 1, 2 or 4 cups, for measuring all liquids, and a set of metal or plastic ¼, ⅓, ½ and 1 cup measuring cups for dry ingredients.

- **Measuring spoons:** Measuring spoons for ¼, ½, and 1 teaspoon and 1 tablespoon are available in metal or plastic for measuring small amounts of both dry and liquid ingredients.

- **Metal spatula:** These are used for leveling off ingredients. Rounded end spatulas are used for frosting cakes.

- **Mixing spoons:** Whether you prefer plastic, wood, or metal, have several mixing spoons of varying sizes on hand.

- **Pancake turner:** This is used to remove cookies from baking sheets or bars from pans. One with a short, wide blade works best.

- **Pastry brush:** Use these to spread glazes and grease pans. Choose brushes with soft natural or synthetic bristles that won't tear or mark dough.

- **Pastry cloth:** A sturdy, washable, canvas-like cloth to help prevent rolled doughs from sticking to countertops or tables.

- **Rolling pin:** This is used for rolling out doughs. Choose a smooth, non-porous finish, either wood, marble or plastic. Wooden rolling pins are lightweight, inexpensive and readily available. However, they can become permeated with oils and flour if the surface is nicked or damaged. To keep doughs from sticking, cover the rolling pin with a rolling pin cover. Marble rolling pins are heavy, and roll dough evenly and quickly. When chilled, dough does not stick to them.

- **Rolling pin cover:** This is also referred to as a stockinette cover. Made of a tube-knit cotton, it is stretched over a rolling pin. The cloth is then lightly floured and helps prevent rolled doughs from sticking.

- **Rubber scraper:** Choose a wide, slightly stiff blade and a strong handle for scraping the sides of the bowl during mixing. Keep one just for baking so that it won't pick up strong odors from other savory foods such as onions.

- **Strainer:** This is necessary for draining liquids and for rinsing fruit and is available in plastic or wire mesh.

- **Timer:** This is important for accurate baking times and is available in a number of styles. Choose one with a loud tone.

- **Wire racks:** For cooling baked goods, racks allow air to circulate around the food and keep crusts from getting soggy. They are available in several sizes.

- **Wire whisk:** This is used for mixing, beating egg whites and whipping cream and is available in a variety of sizes. Larger whisks are appropriate for bigger quantities and heavier mixtures.

HOW TO MEASURE INGREDIENTS

Knowing how to measure ingredients, and then measuring carefully, will help ensure that your baked goods will turn out just right.

Measuring liquids: Use a clear, standard liquid measuring cup with a pouring spout. This cup has measuring marks for ¼, ⅓, ½, ⅔, ¾ and 1 cup, as well as fluid ounces and milliliters. Place the measuring cup on a level surface and fill to the desired mark. Read the measurement at eye level for accuracy.

Measuring dry ingredients: Use standard dry measuring cups that come in sets of ¼, ⅓, ½ and 1 cup. Lightly spoon the ingredient into the measuring cup. Level it off with the straight edge of a spatula or knife.

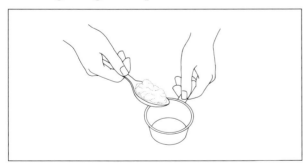

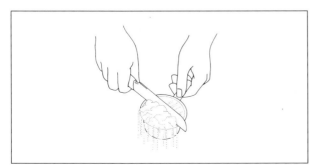

Measuring solid fats and brown sugar: Use standard dry measuring cups. Firmly press the ingredient into the cup and level it off with a spatula or knife.

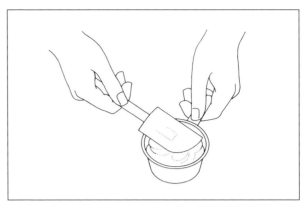

Measuring margarine or butter: The wrappers on stick butter or margarine are printed with measuring marks for each tablespoon, ¼ cup, ⅓ cup and ½ cup. Use a knife to cut the margarine or butter at the desired mark.

Here are some additional measures for margarine or butter:

⅛ stick = 1 tablespoon = ½ ounce
¼ stick = 2 tablespoons = 1 ounce
½ stick = 4 tablespoons = 2 ounces
1 stick = ½ cup = 4 ounces
2 sticks = 1 cup = 8 ounces
4 sticks = 2 cups = 16 ounces

Measuring dairy sour cream and yogurt: Use standard dry measuring cups. Spoon the ingredient into the cup and level it off with a spatula or knife.

Measuring small amounts of ingredients: Use standard measuring spoons for all ingredients. These spoons generally come in sets of ¼, ½, and 1 teaspoon and 1 tablespoon. For dry ingredients, fill the spoon and then level it off with a spatula or knife. For liquid ingredients, fill the spoon full.

EQUIVALENTS

Use these measuring equivalents if you halve or double a recipe:

> 3 teaspoons = 1 tablespoon
> 4 tablespoons = ¼ cup
> 5 tablespoons + 1 teaspoon = ⅓ cup
> 8 tablespoons = ½ cup
> 16 tablespoons = 1 cup
> 2 cups = 1 pint
> 2 pints = 1 quart
> 4 quarts = 1 gallon

TERMS

The language of baking clarifies what techniques and methods are needed for each recipe. Once you learn this language, you're on your way to mastering any recipe.

Bake: To cook in an oven with dry heat. The oven should always be heated for 10 to 15 minutes before baking.

Batter: A mixture of flour, liquid and other ingredients that is thin enough to pour.

Beat: To thoroughly combine ingredients and incorporate air with a rapid, circular motion. This may be done with a wooden spoon, wire whisk, rotary eggbeater, electric mixer or food processor.

Blanch: To partially cook food by plunging it into boiling water for a brief period, then into cold water to stop the cooking process.

Blend: To thoroughly combine 2 or more ingredients.

Boil: To heat a liquid until bubbles rise continually to the surface and break.

Caramelize: To heat sugar until it is melted and brown. Caramelizing sugar gives it a distinctive flavor.

Chop: To cut into small pieces using a sharp knife, appliance or scissors.

Coats spoon: When a thin, even film covers a metal spoon after it has been dipped into a cooked mixture and allowed to drain.

Combine: To stir together 2 or more ingredients until mixed.

Cool: To come to room temperature.

Cream: To beat 1 or more ingredients, usually margarine or butter, sugar and/or eggs, until the mixture is smooth and fluffy.

Crimp: To seal the edges of 2 layers of dough with the tines of a fork or your fingertips.

Cut in: To distribute solid fat throughout the dry ingredients using a pastry blender, fork or 2 knives in a scissors motion.

Dash: A measurement less than ⅛ teaspoon.

Dough: A soft, thick mixture of flour, liquids, fat and other ingredients.

Dot: To distribute small amounts of margarine or butter evenly over the surface of pie filling or dough.

Drizzle: To drip a glaze or icing over food from the tines of a fork or the end of a spoon.

Dust: To sprinkle lightly with sugar, flour or cocoa.

Flute: To make or press a decorative pattern into the raised edge of pastry.

Fold in: To gently combine a heavier mixture with a more delicate substance such as beaten egg whites or whipped cream without causing a loss of air. See p. 22.

Glaze: To coat with a liquid, thin icing or jelly before or after the food is cooked.

Grate: To shred with a hand-held grater or food processor.

Grease: To rub fat on the surface of a pan or dish to prevent sticking.

Grind: To produce small particles of food by forcing food through a grinder.

Knead: To fold, push and turn dough or other mixture to produce a smooth, elastic texture.

Lukewarm: A temperature of about 95°F. that feels neither hot nor cold.

Mix: To stir together 2 or more ingredients until they are thoroughly combined.

Mix until just moistened: To combine dry ingredients with liquid ingredients until the dry ingredients are thoroughly moistened, but the mixture is still slightly lumpy.

Partially set: To refrigerate a gelatin mixture until it thickens to the consistency of unbeaten egg whites.

Peel: To remove the skin of a fruit or vegetable by hand or with a knife or peeler. This also refers to the skin or outer covering of a fruit or vegetable.

Proof: To allow yeast dough to rise before baking. Or, to dissolve yeast in a warm liquid and set it in a warm place for 5 to 10 minutes until it expands and becomes bubbly.

Refrigerate: To chill in the refrigerator until a mixture is cool or a dough is firm.

Rind: The skin or outer coating of foods such as citrus fruit or cheese.

Rolling boil: To cook a mixture until the surface billows rather than bubbles.

Rounded teaspoon: To mound dough slightly in a measuring teaspoon.

Scald: To heat a mixture or liquid to just below the boiling point.

Score: To cut slits in food with a knife, cutting part way through the outer surface.

Softened: Margarine, butter, ice cream or cream cheese that is in a state soft enough for easy blending, but not melted.

Shred: To cut food into narrow strips using a grater or food processor fitted with a shredding disk.

Soft peaks: To beat egg whites or whipping cream to the stage where the mixture forms soft, rounded peaks when the beaters are removed.

Steam: To cook food on a rack or in a wire basket over boiling water.

Stiff peaks: To beat egg whites to the stage where the mixture will hold stiff, pointed peaks when the beaters are removed.

Stir: To combine ingredients with a spoon or whisk using a circular motion.

Toss: To mix lightly with a lifting motion, using 2 forks or spoons.

Whip: To beat rapidly with a wire whisk or electric mixer to incorporate air into a mixture in order to lighten and increase the volume of the mixture.

Zest: The colored outer peel of citrus fruit which is used to add flavor. The zest is often referred to as grated peel in recipes.

TECHNIQUES

You've become familiar with Ingredients, Equipment, How to Measure and Terms. Now it's time to brush up on Techniques. These are the methods or "how-tos" that will make your baking experience a success.

ADDING EGG YOLKS TO A HOT MIXTURE

Egg yolks will cook too quickly if added all at once to a hot mixture. This must be done gradually. To add egg yolks to a hot mixture:

1. Stir a spoonful of the hot mixture into the beaten egg yolks to condition them to the temperature of the hot mixture.

2. Add the egg yolk mixture to the remaining hot mixture and continue to stir over low heat until it thickens to the desired consistency.

BEATING EGG WHITES

Beaten egg whites incorporate air into baked goods or are used for meringues. They can be beaten with an electric mixer, hand-held rotary eggbeater or whisk. Bring egg whites to room temperature for best volume. (Use them within 30 minutes.) Be sure that both the bowl and beaters are clean and dry. Even a small amount of grease or oil, including specks of yolk, will prevent the whites from whipping properly. To beat egg whites:

1. Begin beating slowly, gradually increasing the speed as the egg whites begin to foam.

2. Beat the egg whites until they hold the desired shape, either soft or stiff peaks.

BROWNING BUTTER

Browned butter adds a rich, distinctive flavor to baked goods and frostings. To brown butter:

1. Place butter in a heavy saucepan over medium heat.

2. Melt butter, stirring occasionally. As the butter heats, it will foam.

3. Continue heating until butter becomes a rich caramel color, stirring frequently. Remove from heat.

FOLDING IN INGREDIENTS

Beaten egg whites or whipped cream are common ingredients that are folded into batters and other mixtures. They both contain air in the form of small bubbles, so folding, rather than mixing, is done to retain the air in the mixture. The egg whites and whipping cream are fragile, so use a light touch. To fold in egg whites or whipped cream:

1. Start with a large bowl containing the heavier mixture and place half of the egg whites or whipped cream on top of the mixture.

2. Using a circular motion with a rubber scraper, cut through the center of the mixture across the bottom of the bowl, gently lifting up and over.

3. After each fold, rotate the bowl slightly in order to incorporate the ingredients evenly.

4. Fold in the remaining egg whites or whipped cream until both mixtures are uniformly combined and no streaks remain.

HEATING THE OVEN

To help ensure accurate baking times, it is necessary to heat the oven for 10 to 15 minutes before baking.

KNEADING DOUGH

Kneading dough evenly distributes the ingredients, develops structure and makes the dough elastic so that it will rise and stay risen as the yeast works. Use a press, fold and turn motion. To knead dough:

1. Flatten the ball of dough with your hands and fold it in half toward you.

2. Press and push the dough away with the heels of your hands.

3. Rotate the dough a quarter turn and repeat these steps for 5 to 10 minutes or until the dough is smooth and elastic.

PREPARING THE PAN

Most recipes for baked goods call for the pan to be greased, or greased and floured. Prepare the pan before you begin making the recipe.

To grease a pan:

1. Use a solid vegetable shortening because it won't brown or add flavor to your baked goods. The recipes in this book have been tested with shortening unless otherwise specified.

2. With a paper towel or pastry brush, apply a thin, even layer of shortening to the pan. Grease generously, if specified in recipe, to ensure easy removal of baked items from the pan.

To grease and flour a pan:

1. Grease the pan. Then add a tablespoonful of flour to the pan and shake the pan so that flour sticks to all greased areas.

2. Turn the pan upside down and tap the bottom to remove excess flour.

OR

1. In a small bowl, blend ¼ cup shortening and ¼ cup all purpose flour until well mixed.

2. To grease and flour a pan, apply a thin, even layer of the shortening-flour mixture with a paper towel or pastry brush. (Store remaining mixture in an airtight container in the refrigerator.)

To paper-line a pan:

1. Line the pan with parchment paper or waxed paper cut to the appropriate size.

2. Grease the paper if specified in the recipe.

SEPARATING EGGS

A number of recipes call for the whites and yolks of eggs to be separated. Before you begin, wash your hands and the egg shells. You'll also need a bowl and 2 cups. To separate eggs:

1. Tap the side of the egg on the edge of a bowl or cup to crack the shell. Tip the egg so that the majority of its contents are in 1 half; pull the 2 halves of the shell apart.

2. Pass the yolk from shell half to shell half several times, allowing the white to slip off into a cup. Place the yolk in another cup.

3. Inspect the white for small amounts of yolk. If any yolk is present in the white, remove it with a spoon. Any yolk in the white will prevent the whites from beating into peaks.

4. Transfer the white to the bowl.

TOASTING NUTS AND COCONUT

Toasting nuts or coconut until golden brown adds a warm, rich flavor to these ingredients.

To toast nuts:

1. Heat the oven to 350°F. Spread nuts in a single layer on a cookie sheet. Bake for 5 to 10 minutes or until light golden brown to golden brown, stirring occasionally. (The baking time will vary, depending on the type of nut.) Watch them closely to avoid over-browning.

2. To toast in the microwave oven, spread nuts in a microwave-safe pan. Microwave on HIGH for 4 to 8 minutes or until light golden brown, stirring frequently.

To toast coconut:

1. Heat the oven to 350°F. Spread coconut evenly on a cookie sheet. Bake for 7 to 8 minutes or until light golden brown, stirring occasionally. Watch closely to avoid overbrowning.

2. To toast in the microwave oven, spread coconut in a microwave-safe pan. Microwave on HIGH for 4½ to 8 minutes, tossing the coconut with a fork after each minute.

WHIPPING CREAM

Whipped cream is used as an ingredient and as a topping in numerous recipes. Cream can be whipped with an electric mixer, hand-held rotary eggbeater or wire whisk. Before beginning, the cream, bowl and beaters should be very cold; chill them in the refrigerator or freezer for a few minutes. Whipping cream will double in volume when whipped. To whip cream:

1. Begin beating slowly to avoid splatters, then gradually increase speed as the cream thickens.

2. Beat until soft peaks form. Don't overbeat, or you'll end up with butter! If you whip cream too far ahead of time, it may separate. If this happens, stir it briefly with a wire whisk.

3. To sweeten whipped cream, gradually beat in 2 tablespoons of powdered sugar for each cup of whipping cream.

HIGH ALTITUDE BAKING

Baking at high altitudes, 3,500 feet above sea level or more, can be a challenge. For best results, follow the high altitude directions when they're included in the recipe. In addition, here are some general guidelines:

• Because there is generally lower humidity at high altitudes, flour tends to dry out more quickly and may absorb more liquid in a recipe. Store flour in an airtight container.

• At any altitude above sea level, the air pressure is lower. This lower air pressure allows baked foods to rise faster. Leavening agents such as yeast, baking powder and baking soda create larger gas bubbles that expand rapidly. The larger bubbles can weaken the structure of baked goods and cause cakes and breads to collapse unless recipe adjustments are made. In addition, too much sugar can weaken the structure of baked goods.

• Water boils at a lower temperature than at sea level (as elevation increases, the boiling point is reduced 2 degrees per 1,000 foot increase) so foods take longer to cook. Liquids evaporate faster at high altitudes so foods such as cooked frostings and candies will become harder more rapidly.

If no high altitude adjustments are given in a recipe, here are some suggestions to try:

• In cakes made with fats or oil, reduce the sugar called for in the recipe by 3 tablespoons per cup. If given a choice, use the largest pan size suggested.

• In cake or bar-type cookies, reduce the sugar called for in the recipe by 3 tablespoons per cup. If given a choice, use the largest pan size suggested.

• In yeast breads, use slightly less flour since flour is drier at high altitudes. Yeast breads will require a shorter rising time and should rise only until double in size to prevent them from collapsing during baking.

• Quick breads often need 2 to 4 tablespoons additional flour and a higher baking temperature.

FREEZING BAKED GOODS

It's wonderful to have a pie, dessert, cookies or cake baked and stored in the freezer for your family or unexpected guests. Many baked goods freeze and thaw beautifully. When freezing baked goods, note the following:

• The freezer temperature should be 0°F. or less.

• Use moisture-proof, vapor-proof wraps or containers such as plastic containers with tight-fitting lids, heavy-duty foil, freezer bags and freezer paper.

• Be sure that there's room for expansion when filling containers. When wrapping foods, press the air out and seal tightly.

Follow these guidelines to ensure that your baked goods retain their freshness and flavor in the freezer:

FREEZING GUIDELINES

Food	Special Tips	Storage Time	Thawing Hints
Breads: Yeast Breads, coffee cakes, muffins and quick breads.	Cool completely; do not frost or decorate. Place coffee cakes on foil-wrapped cardboard before freezing.	Up to 1 month	Unwrap slightly and thaw at room temperature for 2 to 3 hours. Serve at room temperature or reheat, wrapped in foil, at 350°F. for 15 to 20 minutes.
Cakes: Frosted or unfrosted. (Buttercream frosting freezes best; egg-white frostings and custard fillings do not freeze well.)	Cool cakes completely; place frosted cakes in the freezer to harden the frosting before covering. Place layer cakes in a cake container to prevent crushing. Angel and chiffon cakes are best left in the pan or placed in rigid containers to avoid crushing them. Cakes may be filled or frosted with whipped cream or whipped topping before freezing.	Unfrosted: Up to 6 months Frosted: Up to 3 months	Unfrosted: Thaw covered at room temperature for 2 to 3 hours. Frost or serve according to the recipe. Frosted: Thaw loosely covered overnight in the refrigerator.
Cheesecakes	If baked, cool completely before wrapping.	Up to 5 months	Thaw wrapped in the refrigerator for 4 to 6 hours.
Cookies	Package cookies in containers with tight-fitting lids. If cookies have been frosted before freezing, freeze them on a cookie sheet, then package the frozen cookies between layers of waxed paper in a rigid container.	Unfrosted: Up to 12 months Frosted: Up to 2 months	Thaw in the container at room temperature. If cookies should be crisp when thawed, remove them from the container before thawing.
Pies: Baked pumpkin or pecan pies and either baked or unbaked fruit pies.	Cool baked pies quickly. For unbaked pie, brush the bottom pastry with egg white before filling to prevent it from becoming soggy. Do not slit the top pastry. Cover pies with an inverted foil or paper plate and then wrap.	Baked: Up to 4 months Unbaked: Up to 3 months	Baked: Unwrap and heat at 325°F. for 45 minutes or until warm or room temperature. Unbaked: Unwrap, cut slits in the top pastry and bake at 425°F. for 15 minutes, then bake at 375°F. for 30 to 45 minutes or until the center is bubbly.
Pies: Chiffon. (Custard pies, cream pies and pies with meringue topping do not freeze well.)	Do not top with whipped cream or whipped topping. Refrigerate to set, then wrap as you would a fruit pie.	Up to 2 months	Unwrap and thaw in the refrigerator 2 to 3 hours. Top as desired.

COOKIES

Cookies! They're America's favorite sweet treat — ideal with a mug of cold milk, a cup of hot coffee, a tall glass of lemonade or just by themselves.

In this chapter, you'll find easy-to-make drop cookies, tender cutouts for melt-in-your-mouth appeal, intriguing shapes of all sorts and special cookies to celebrate the seasons of the year. You'll also find bars from elegant to hearty that can be toted anywhere from a wedding shower to a backyard barbecue.

Pictured: **Fudgy Brownies** *p. 98,* **Oatmeal Coconut Fun Chippers** *p. 36,* **Salted Peanut Chews** *p. 88*

COOKIES

Cookies are a wonderful way to learn about baking
or to become reacquainted with the joys of making treats from scratch.
Choose a recipe to suit a special occasion or one just right for everyday
snacking. The basics are easy and the results are delightful.

KINDS OF COOKIES

*Although cookies come in all shapes, sizes and
flavors, there are just six basic kinds. The recipes
in this chapter are grouped by these kinds:*

BAR

Bar cookies are made from a soft dough that is
spread in a pan. They can be layered or filled,
chewy or crisp. (Recipes begin on p. 83.)

BROWNIES

Brownies are probably the most popular bar
cookie. Soft and chewy, they can be made
in a wide variety of flavors. (Recipes begin
on p. 98.)

CUT-OUT

Made from a stiff dough, these cookies are
rolled into a thin or thick sheet. The rolled
dough can be cut into just about any shape
with a cookie cutter or with a sharp knife and
pattern. (Recipes begin on p. 72.)

DROP

One of the easiest cookies to make, drop
cookies are made from a softer dough that is
dropped from a spoon in mounds onto a
cookie sheet. (Recipes begin on p. 33.)

MOLDED, SHAPED AND PRESSED

To make these cookies, a stiff dough is molded
into shapes such as crescents, logs or balls.
They can be pressed flat with a fork or the
bottom of a glass. Cookies can also be made
using a cookie press or gun. (Recipes begin
on p. 53.)

SLICED

Also known as refrigerator cookies, these are
made from a stiff dough that is shaped into a
long, smooth roll and chilled. To bake, slices
are cut from the roll. These cookies can be
either thin and crisp or thick and crunchy.
(Recipes begin on p. 47.)

SECRETS TO SUCCESSFUL COOKIES

*Every batch of cookies you bake will be a success
once you learn these few simple secrets!*

SECRETS FOR ANY COOKIES

**Use either margarine or butter inter-
changeably in most recipes.** They give cookies
good flavor and crisp texture. Solid vegetable
shortening, used in some recipes, makes a
crunchier cookie. Tub, soft, whipped, liquid or
reduced-fat or -calorie butters or margarines
should not be used because the additional air
and water in them may result in thin, flat
cookies.

Measure accurately with standard measuring cups and spoons. The correct amount of ingredients will help ensure that cookies and bars aren't dry, crumbly or so soft that they spread too much during baking.

Heat the oven for 10 to 15 minutes before baking cookies.

Use shiny aluminum pans and cookie sheets. They will brown cookies lightly and evenly. Dark cookie sheets may absorb heat and cause cookies to overbrown on the bottom. If you use insulated cookie sheets, remember that cookies will not brown as much on the bottom and they may take slightly longer to bake.

Grease pans and cookie sheets with shortening. If the recipe calls for the pans or sheets to be greased, shortening works best. Butter tends to brown too quickly, and oils or spray-on coatings can sometimes cause sticking.

Place dough on cool cookie sheets. This will prevent the dough from melting and spreading before baking. Space them carefully to avoid unattractive run-together cookies.

Leave at least 2 inches around all sides of the cookie sheets or pans in the oven. This space allows the hot air to circulate properly. For best results, bake only 1 sheet or pan of cookies at a time on the center rack of the oven.

Cool cookies or pans of bars on wire racks. Place cookies in a single layer so that air can circulate around them. Steam from the cooling cookies evaporates and prevents them from becoming soggy.

SECRETS FOR BAR COOKIES AND BROWNIES

Use the proper size of pan. Bars or brownies baked in a pan that is too large can be dry and overbaked; if it's too small, they might be underbaked.

Bake bars in a foil-lined pan for easy removal and freezing. Line the pan with foil so that it extends up the sides and over the edges of the

pan. When the recipe calls for a greased pan, grease the foil. After baking and cooling, lift the bars from the pan using the extended foil edges. With a long knife, cut into bars; or wrap with additional foil and freeze.

Cool bars in the pan before cutting. Cutting when cool prevents the bars or brownies from crumbling. However, some recipes may call for cutting bars while warm.

Cut bars into decorative shapes. Cut bars on the diagonal to form diamonds (see diagram) or cut with a cookie cutter, such as a heart or star shape. Bar scraps can be cut into small cubes and layered with pudding or ice cream in dessert dishes.

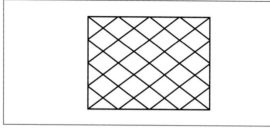

Cutting Bars into Diamonds

Remove the corner bar first. Removal of the remaining bars or brownies will be easier.

SECRETS FOR CUT-OUT COOKIES

Dust rolling pin and smooth surface with flour. This will prevent dough from sticking. If you use a rolling pin cover on the rolling pin and a pastry cloth, rub a small amount of flour into them. Too much flour will make cookies tough and dry. See p. 80.

Roll only part of the chilled dough at a time. Keep the remaining dough in the refrigerator.

Roll the dough to the appropriate thickness. Thinner dough makes a crisper cookie; thicker dough makes a softer, chewier cookie.

Check the thickness with a ruler. Cookies will bake evenly when the dough is rolled to a uniform thickness.

Use a pancake turner to transfer cookies. This will prevent unbaked cookies from stretching and tearing and baked cookies from breaking.

SECRETS FOR DROP COOKIES

Use the same amount of dough for each cookie. You can use either a teaspoon or tablespoon, depending on what size cookie you want.

Drop the dough onto the cookie sheet by pushing it from a teaspoon with a rubber scraper or another teaspoon. See p. 32.

Space the cookies carefully. This prevents the cookies from baking together. If you're trying a new recipe, you may want to "test bake" 2 or 3 cookies to see how much they spread.

SECRETS FOR SLICED COOKIES

Mold the dough into rolls as specified in the recipe.

Wrap the rolls of cookie dough in waxed paper, foil or plastic wrap. Twist the ends to seal them tightly. Refrigerate the dough until it is firm.

Use a thin sharp knife for slicing cookies. Remove the storage wrap before slicing.

Refrigerate rolls up to 1 week. You can also wrap them in foil and freeze for up to 6 months.

SECRETS FOR MOLDED, SHAPED AND PRESSED COOKIES

Refrigerate dough before shaping if necessary for easier handling.

Dust hands lightly with flour. This prevents the dough from sticking to your hands. Roll each cookie smoothly between your palms. Take time when molding fancy shapes so that all the cookies look the same.

Flatten cookies with your thumb, a fork or the bottom of a glass. Dip them in either flour or sugar to prevent sticking.

Using a Cookie Press

When making pressed cookies . . .
- Use room-temperature margarine or butter.
- Test for consistency by pressing a small amount of dough through the press. If the dough is too soft, refrigerate it briefly or add 1 to 2 tablespoons of flour. If the dough is too stiff, add 1 egg yolk.
- Use a cool, ungreased cookie sheet.
- Hold the cookie press so that it rests on the cookie sheet. Force the dough onto the sheet until the dough appears at the edge of the mold. Lift the press when you've completely formed the shape.
- If you don't own a cookie press, dough can be pressed through a decorating bag fitted with a ¼ to ½-inch diameter star tip.

HOW TO TELL WHEN COOKIES ARE DONE

Cookies are best when they've been baked just the right time — not too long and not too short. Here are some easy ways to tell when cookies are done.

Check cookies at the minimum baking time. Even 1 minute can make a difference! Continue checking them every minute until done. Immediately remove cookies from the sheets with a pancake turner, unless the recipe calls for them to cool on the sheet. If cookies stick to the sheet, they may have cooled too long. Return them to the oven briefly.

Cookies are done when . . . they are firmly set or browned according to recipe directions. When you touch them lightly with your finger, almost no imprint will remain. Bake cookies according to recipe directions for the correct amount of browning.

Bake brownies according to recipe directions.
- Cake-like brownies are done when they just begin to pull away from the sides of the pan, when a toothpick inserted in the center comes out clean, or when they are set in the center.
- Fudgy brownies do not have a specific done-ness test. Bake the brownies within the time range stated in the recipe. Baking at the minimum time will produce very moist brownies. Baking at the maximum time will produce a moist brownie, but one that is not as "wet" as the one baked at the minimum time. Experiment to obtain the results that you prefer. Our recipes carry a DO NOT OVERBAKE statement. Overbaking brownies (baking beyond the maximum time) can result in dry, hard brownies, especially around the pan edges.

KEEPING COOKIES FRESH AND FLAVORFUL

If cookies last long enough to take them off the cooling rack, here are some tips for keeping them at their fresh-from-the-oven best.

Store different kinds of cookies in separate containers.

Cookie jars are only for short-term storage.

Store soft cookies in a container with a tight-fitting cover. Place sheets of waxed paper between layers so cookies won't stick together. Frosted or filled cookies should be stored in a single layer.

Store crisp cookies in a container with a loose-fitting cover. However, if you live in a humid climate, containers should be tightly covered. If crisp cookies soften, place them on a cookie sheet and warm them in a 300°F. oven for 3 to 5 minutes.

Store bars and brownies in the baking pan. Cover the pan tightly with plastic wrap or foil or slip it into a plastic bag and seal with a twist tie. Some frostings or fillings may require refrigeration.

Line cardboard containers with foil or plastic wrap. This will prevent the cookies from absorbing any cardboard flavor or aroma.

MAILING COOKIES

When sending cookies to loved ones far away, a few simple packing precautions will help keep the cookies from becoming crumbs.

Choose cookies that can withstand the trip. Bars, drop cookies and soft, moist cookies travel well.

Use a cardboard box or metal container. Line the container with plastic wrap, waxed paper or foil to preserve flavors.

Wrap fragile cookies in bottom-to-bottom pairs. Use foil, waxed paper or plastic wrap.

Cushion cookies with crumpled waxed paper. Place it on the top and bottom of the container and between each layer of cookies. Pack cookies tightly enough to avoid shifting.

Place the cookie container in a sturdy box. The shipping box should be slightly larger so that bubble wrap, foam pellets, shredded paper or crumpled newspaper can be packed around the cookie container. Don't use popcorn or cereal for cushioning because it may attract insects or rodents and absorb odors during shipping.

Mark the box "perishable" to encourage careful handling. You may also want to send cookies first class to ensure priority handling and prompt delivery.

NUTRITION IN THIS CHAPTER

Nutrition per serving means the calculation was done on 1 cookie or 1 bar.

How to Make Drop Cookies

STEP 1. Beat brown sugar, sugar, margarine and shortening until light and fluffy. Blend in vanilla and egg. Mix in flour, baking soda and salt.

STEP 2. By hand, stir in coarsely chopped chocolate and nuts until evenly distributed.

STEP 3. Drop mounds of dough onto ungreased cookie sheets, placing dough about 2 inches apart to allow for spreading during baking.

CHOCOLATE CHIP COOKIES

¾ **cup firmly packed brown sugar**
½ **cup sugar**
½ **cup margarine or butter, softened**
½ **cup shortening**
1½ **teaspoons vanilla**
1 **egg**
1¾ **cups all purpose flour**
1 **teaspoon baking soda**
½ **teaspoon salt**
1 **(6-oz.) pkg. (1 cup) semi-sweet chocolate chips**
½ **cup chopped nuts or shelled sunflower seeds, if desired**

Heat oven to 375°F. In large bowl, combine brown sugar, sugar, margarine and shortening; beat until light and fluffy. Add vanilla and egg; blend well. Stir in flour, baking soda and salt; mix well. Stir in chocolate chips and nuts. Drop dough by teaspoonfuls 2 inches apart onto ungreased cookie sheets. Bake at 375°F. for 8 to 10 minutes or until light golden brown. Cool 1 minute; remove from cookie sheets.
Yield: 4 dozen cookies.

HIGH ALTITUDE:
Above 3500 Feet: No change.

NUTRITION PER SERVING:
Calories 100; Protein 1g; Carbohydrate 11g; Fat 6g; Sodium 70mg.

VARIATIONS:

CHOCOLATE CHIP COOKIE BARS: Prepare dough as directed in recipe. Spread in ungreased 13x9-inch pan. Bake at 375°F. for 15 to 25 minutes or until light golden brown. Cool completely. Cut into bars.
Yield: 36 bars.

CHOCOLATE CHUNK COOKIES: Prepare dough as directed in recipe, substituting 8 oz. coarsely chopped semi-sweet chocolate for chocolate chips. Drop dough by tablespoonfuls 3 inches apart onto ungreased cookie sheets. Bake at 375°F. for 9 to 12 minutes or until light golden brown. Immediately remove from cookie sheets.
Yield: 3 dozen cookies.

(Recipe continued on next page.)

Chocolate Chunk Cookies

(Recipe continued from previous page.)

CHOCOLATE CHIP ICE CREAM COOKIE-WICHES: Prepare dough as directed in recipe. Drop by heaping teaspoonfuls 3 inches apart onto ungreased cookie sheets. Bake at 375°F. for 9 to 14 minutes or until light golden brown. Cool 1 minute; remove from cookie sheets. Cool completely. To assemble each cookie-wich, place scoop of favorite flavor ice cream on bottom side of 1 cookie; flatten ice cream slightly. Place another cookie, bottom side down, on top of ice cream. Gently press cookies together in center to form ice cream sandwich. Quickly wrap in foil. Freeze.
Yield: 12 cookie-wiches.

CHOCOLATE CHOCOLATE CHIP COOKIES: Prepare dough as directed in recipe, substituting 1 cup margarine or butter, softened, for the ½ cup margarine and ½ cup shortening. Decrease vanilla to 1 teaspoon. Add ¼ cup unsweetened cocoa with flour. Drop dough by teaspoonfuls 2 inches apart onto ungreased cookie sheets. Bake at 375°F. for 7 to 11 minutes or until set.
Yield: 4 dozen cookies.

JUMBO CANDY COOKIES: Prepare dough as directed in recipe, omitting ½ cup sugar, 1 cup semi-sweet chocolate chips and ½ cup chopped nuts. Increase vanilla to 2 teaspoons. Stir 1 cup candy-coated chocolate pieces and ½ cup shelled sunflower seeds into dough. Refrigerate if necessary for easier handling. Shape dough into 2-inch balls. Place 4 inches apart on ungreased cookie sheets. Press an additional ½ cup candy-coated chocolate pieces into balls to decorate tops of cookies. Bake at 350°F. for 15 to 20 minutes or until light golden brown. Cool 2 minutes; remove from cookie sheets.
Yield: 14 cookies.

MAXI CHIPPERS: Prepare dough as directed in recipe. For each cookie, use ⅓ cup of dough; place 4 inches apart on ungreased cookie sheets. Bake at 375°F. for 12 to 18 minutes or until light golden brown. Cool 1 minute; remove from cookie sheets.
Yield: 10 cookies.

MINI CHIPPERS: Prepare dough as directed in recipe. Drop dough by ½ teaspoonfuls 1 inch apart onto ungreased cookie sheets. Bake at 375°F. for 5 to 7 minutes or until light golden brown. Immediately remove from cookie sheets.
Yield: 12½ dozen cookies.

SOFT AND CHEWY CHOCOLATE CHIP COOKIES

Try this big batch recipe for soft and chewy cookies. For extra chocolaty cookies, use the larger amount of chocolate chips.

1¼ **cups sugar**
1¼ **cups firmly packed brown sugar**
1½ **cups margarine or butter, softened**
2 **teaspoons vanilla**
3 **eggs**
4¼ **cups all purpose flour**
2 **teaspoons baking soda**
½ **teaspoon salt**
1 **to 2 (12-oz.) pkg. semi-sweet chocolate chips***

Heat oven to 375°F. In large bowl, beat sugar, brown sugar and margarine until light and fluffy. Add vanilla and eggs; blend well. Add flour, baking soda and salt; mix well. Stir in chocolate chips.** Drop dough by rounded tablespoonfuls 2 inches apart onto ungreased cookie sheets.

Bake at 375°F. for 8 to 10 minutes or until light golden brown.
Yield: 6 dozen cookies.

TIPS:
* If desired, half of the dough can be made with butterscotch, peanut butter, vanilla milk or mint chocolate chips instead of semi-sweet chocolate chips.
**At this point, dough can be frozen. Wrap tightly and freeze up to 2 months. To bake, thaw at room temperature for 1 to 2 hours. Bake as directed above.

HIGH ALTITUDE:
Above 3500 Feet: Decrease sugar, brown sugar and margarine to 1 cup each. Bake as directed above.

NUTRITION PER SERVING:
Calories 110; Protein 1g; Carbohydrate 16g; Fat 5g; Sodium 95mg.

CHOCOLATE CHIP COOKIES SUPREME

We've created a new, contemporary recipe for chocolate chip cookies. You'll enjoy the combination of rum extract and white chocolate in these chewy, moist cookies.

- 1 cup sugar
- 1 cup firmly packed brown sugar
- 1½ cups margarine or butter, softened
- 2 teaspoons vanilla
- ½ teaspoon rum extract
- 2 eggs
- 3 cups all purpose flour
- 1½ cups oat bran
- 1 teaspoon baking powder
- 1 teaspoon baking soda
- ¼ teaspoon salt
- 1 (6-oz.) pkg. (1 cup) semi-sweet chocolate chips
- 1 (6-oz.) pkg. white baking bars, chopped, or 1 cup vanilla milk chips
- 1 cup chopped walnuts or pecans

Heat oven to 375°F. In large bowl, beat sugar, brown sugar and margarine until light and fluffy. Add vanilla, rum extract and eggs; blend well. Stir in flour, oat bran, baking powder, baking soda and salt; mix well. Stir in chocolate chips, white baking bar and walnuts. (Dough will be stiff.) Drop dough by rounded tablespoonfuls 2 inches apart onto ungreased cookie sheets.

Bake at 375°F. for 9 to 15 minutes or until light golden brown. Cool 1 minute; remove from cookie sheets.

Yield: 4 dozen cookies.

HIGH ALTITUDE:
Above 3500 Feet: Decrease granulated sugar to ½ cup; increase flour to 3½ cups. Bake as directed above.

NUTRITION PER SERVING:
Calories 180; Protein 2g; Carbohydrate 21g; Fat 10g; Sodium 115mg.

SUPREME CHOCOLATE MINT CHIP COOKIES

Cocoa flavors the dough and mint chocolate chips are the surprise in these easy drop cookies.

COOKIES
- 4 cups all purpose flour
- 1 cup unsweetened cocoa
- 1 teaspoon baking soda
- ½ teaspoon salt
- 1½ cups sugar
- 1 cup firmly packed brown sugar
- 1½ cups margarine or butter, softened
- 3 eggs
- 1 (10-oz.) pkg. (1½ cups) mint chocolate chips

GLAZE
- 2 cups sugar
- ½ cup unsweetened cocoa
- ½ cup margarine or butter
- ½ cup milk
- 1 teaspoon vanilla

Heat oven to 350°F. Lightly grease cookie sheets. In large bowl, combine flour, 1 cup cocoa, baking soda and salt. In another large bowl, beat sugar, brown sugar and margarine until light and fluffy. Add eggs; blend well. Stir in flour mixture; mix well. Stir in mint chips. Drop dough by tablespoonfuls 3 inches apart onto greased cookie sheets; flatten slightly.

Bake at 350°F. for 8 to 10 minutes or until set. Cool 1 minute; remove from cookie sheets. Cool completely.

In medium saucepan, combine all glaze ingredients except vanilla. Bring to a boil; boil 1 minute. Stir in vanilla; cool slightly.* Beat until smooth and of glaze consistency. Spread glaze on cooled cookies. Let stand until glaze is set.

Yield: 6 dozen cookies.

TIP:
* To cool frosting quickly, place saucepan on ice in large bowl. If glaze becomes too thick, reheat slightly for spreading consistency.

HIGH ALTITUDE:
Above 3500 Feet: Increase flour to 4 cups plus 2 tablespoons. Bake as directed above.

NUTRITION PER SERVING:
Calories 150; Protein 2g; Carbohydrate 21g; Fat 7g; Sodium 105mg.

OATMEAL COCONUT FUN CHIPPERS

This thick, chewy oatmeal cookie can be made with quick-cooking or old-fashioned rolled oats. Cookies made with old-fashioned rolled oats have a moister, coarser texture.

1½ cups firmly packed brown sugar
1 cup margarine or butter, softened
1 tablespoon milk
1 tablespoon vanilla
2 eggs
2¼ cups all purpose flour
2 teaspoons baking powder
1 teaspoon baking soda
½ teaspoon salt
2 cups rolled oats
1 cup coconut
1 (10-oz.) pkg. multi-colored candy-coated chocolate chips or 1½ cups semi-sweet chocolate chips

Heat oven to 375°F. In large bowl, beat brown sugar and margarine until light and fluffy. Add milk, vanilla and eggs; blend well. Stir in flour, baking powder, baking soda and salt; mix well. Stir in oats, coconut and chocolate chips. Drop dough by rounded tablespoonfuls 2 inches apart onto ungreased cookie sheets.

Bake at 375°F. for 9 to 13 minutes or until light golden brown. Cool 1 minute; remove from cookie sheets. Cool completely.
Yield: 4 dozen cookies.

HIGH ALTITUDE:
Above 3500 Feet: Decrease brown sugar to 1¼ cups; increase flour to 2½ cups. Bake as directed above.

NUTRITION PER SERVING:
Calories 130; Protein 2g; Carbohydrate 18g; Fat 6g; Sodium 110mg.

OATMEAL RAISIN COOKIES

Every mouth-watering bite of these crispy-chewy oatmeal cookies is full of good tasting nuts and raisins.

¾ cup sugar
¼ cup firmly packed brown sugar
½ cup margarine or butter, softened
½ teaspoon vanilla
1 egg
¾ cup all purpose flour
½ teaspoon baking soda
½ teaspoon cinnamon
¼ teaspoon salt
1½ cups quick-cooking rolled oats
½ cup raisins
½ cup chopped nuts

Heat oven to 375°F. Grease cookie sheets. In large bowl, beat sugar, brown sugar and margarine until light and fluffy. Add vanilla and egg; blend well. Stir in flour, baking soda, cinnamon and salt; mix well. Stir in rolled oats, raisins and nuts. Drop dough by rounded teaspoonfuls 2 inches apart onto greased cookie sheets.

Bake at 375°F. for 7 to 10 minutes or until edges are light golden brown. Cool 1 minute; remove from cookie sheets.
Yield: 3½ dozen cookies.

HIGH ALTITUDE:
Above 3500 Feet: Increase flour to 1 cup. Bake as directed above.

NUTRITION PER SERVING:
Calories 70; Protein 1g; Carbohydrate 10g; Fat 3g; Sodium 55mg.

CHEWY DATE DROPS

Dates have always been recognized as a good high-energy food because of their carbohydrate, iron and protein content. Store dates tightly covered at room temperature or in the refrigerator for longer storage.

- 2 **cups chopped dates**
- ½ **cup sugar**
- ½ **cup water**
- 1 **cup sugar**
- 1 **cup margarine or butter, softened**
- 1 **teaspoon vanilla**
- 3 **eggs**
- 4 **cups all purpose flour**
- 1 **teaspoon baking soda**
- 1 **teaspoon salt**
- 1 **cup chopped walnuts or pecans**

In medium saucepan, combine dates, ½ cup sugar and water. Cook over medium heat until thickened, stirring occasionally. Cool.

Heat oven to 375°F. Grease cookie sheets. In large bowl, beat brown sugar, ½ cup sugar and margarine until light and fluffy. Add vanilla and eggs; blend well. Stir in flour, baking soda and salt; mix well. Stir in date mixture and nuts. Drop dough by rounded teaspoonfuls 2 inches apart onto greased cookie sheets.

Bake at 375°F. for 8 to 10 minutes or until light golden brown. Immediately remove from cookie sheets.

Yield: 6 dozen cookies.

HIGH ALTITUDE:
Above 3500 Feet: Decrease sugar beaten with margarine to ¼ cup. Bake as directed above.

NUTRITION PER SERVING:
Calories 100; Protein 1g; Carbohydrate 15g; Fat 4g; Sodium 80mg.

COCONUT MACAROONS

Coconut macaroons are a delicious, chewy variation of the classic almond macaroon cookie. The combination of few ingredients and the drop cookie method makes them a snap to prepare.

- 2 **egg whites**
- ⅓ **cup sugar**
- 2 **tablespoons all purpose flour**
  Dash salt
- ¼ **teaspoon almond extract**
- 2 **cups coconut**

Heat oven to 325°F. Grease and lightly flour cookie sheet. In medium bowl, beat egg whites lightly. Add sugar, flour, salt and almond extract; blend well. Stir in coconut. Drop dough by tablespoonfuls 2 inches apart onto greased and floured cookie sheet.

Bake at 325°F. for 13 to 17 minutes or until set and lightly browned. Immediately remove from cookie sheet.

Yield: 1 dozen cookies.

HIGH ALTITUDE:
Above 3500 Feet: No change.

NUTRITION PER SERVING:
Calories 90; Protein 1g; Carbohydrate 12g; Fat 4g; Sodium 20mg.

COOK'S NOTE

MACAROONS

Macaroons originated in Italy and can be traced to a monastery where they have been made since 1791. Brought to France in the 16th century, the macaroons of many French towns are famous, including the best known ones made in Nancy. During the 17th century, macaroons were baked by the Carmelite nuns who followed the principle: "Almonds are good for girls who do not eat meat." During the Revolution, two nuns who hid in the town of Nancy made and sold macaroons. They became known as the "Macaroon Sisters," and in 1952 the street on which they had operated was named after them.

Chocolate Cherry Surprise Cookies

~

For chocolate and cherry lovers, this is a delicious adaptation of the famous German Black Forest torte.

COOKIES
- ¾ **cup sugar**
- ¼ **cup firmly packed brown sugar**
- ½ **cup margarine or butter, softened**
- ½ **teaspoon almond extract**
- 1 **egg**
- 1¾ **cups all purpose flour**
- ½ **cup unsweetened cocoa**
- ½ **teaspoon baking soda**
- ¼ **teaspoon salt**
- ½ **cup milk**
- ½ **cup chopped walnuts or pecans**
- 18 **to 20 maraschino cherries, halved, drained**
- 18 **to 20 large marshmallows, halved**

FROSTING
- 3 **cups powdered sugar**
- 3 **tablespoons margarine or butter, melted**
- ½ **teaspoon vanilla**
- 3 **oz. semi-sweet chocolate, melted**
- 5 **to 6 tablespoons water**

Heat oven to 375°F. In large bowl, combine sugar, brown sugar, ½ cup margarine, almond extract and egg; blend well. In small bowl, combine flour, cocoa, baking soda and salt; blend well. Add to sugar mixture alternately with milk, mixing well after each addition. Stir in walnuts. Drop dough by rounded tablespoonfuls 2 inches apart onto ungreased cookie sheets. Firmly press cherry half, cut side down, into top of each cookie.

Bake at 375°F. for 6 to 8 minutes. Firmly press marshmallow half, cut side down, over cherry on top of each hot cookie. Bake an additional 2 minutes or until marshmallows are puffed. Cool 1 minute; remove from cookie sheets. Cool completely.

In small bowl, combine all frosting ingredients, adding enough water for desired spreading consistency. Blend until smooth. Frost top of each cookie with about 2 teaspoonfuls frosting, covering marshmallow completely. Garnish if desired.
Yield: 3 dozen cookies.

HIGH ALTITUDE:
Above 3500 Feet: Increase flour to 2 cups. Bake as directed above.

NUTRITION PER SERVING:
Calories 150; Protein 2g; Carbohydrate 25g; Fat 6g; Sodium 85mg.

Texan-Sized Almond Crunch Cookies

~

Big, tender, crunchy cookies to tempt young and old, this recipe was a finalist in the 30th Pillsbury BAKE-OFF® Contest.

- 1 **cup sugar**
- 1 **cup powdered sugar**
- 1 **cup margarine or butter, softened**
- 1 **cup oil**
- 1 **teaspoon almond extract**
- 2 **eggs**
- 3½ **cups all purpose flour**
- 1 **cup whole wheat flour**
- 1 **teaspoon baking soda**
- 1 **teaspoon cream of tartar**
- 1 **teaspoon salt**
- 2 **cups coarsely chopped almonds**
- 1 **(6-oz.) pkg. almond brickle baking chips**
  Sugar

Heat oven to 350°F. In large bowl, beat 1 cup sugar, powdered sugar, margarine and oil until well blended. Add almond extract and eggs; blend well. Add all purpose flour, whole wheat flour, baking soda, cream of tartar and salt; mix well. Stir in almonds and brickle chips. If necessary, cover with plastic wrap and refrigerate dough about 30 minutes for easier handling.

Shape large tablespoonfuls of dough into balls. Roll in sugar. Place 5 inches apart on ungreased cookie sheets. With fork dipped in sugar, flatten each in crisscross pattern.

Bake at 350°F. for 12 to 18 minutes or until light golden brown around edges. Cool 1 minute; remove from cookie sheets.
Yield: 3½ dozen (4-inch) cookies.

HIGH ALTITUDE:
Above 3500 Feet: No change.

NUTRITION PER SERVING:
Calories 230; Protein 3g; Carbohydrate 22g; Fat 15g; Sodium 130mg.

CHOCOLATE-GLAZED FLORENTINES

Although the name implies that these cookies originated in Florence, Italy, and the candied fruit and almonds are typical of Italian cooking, Austrian bakers also claim to have invented them.

COOKIES
- ⅓ **cup margarine or butter**
- ⅓ **cup honey**
- ¼ **cup sugar**
- 2 **tablespoons milk**
- ¼ **cup all purpose flour**
- ⅓ **cup finely chopped candied orange peel**
- ⅓ **cup chopped candied cherries**
- ⅓ **cup slivered almonds**

GLAZE
- 4 **oz. semi-sweet chocolate**
- 1 **teaspoon shortening**

Heat oven to 325°F. Generously grease and flour cookie sheets. Melt margarine in medium saucepan over medium heat; remove from heat. Stir in honey, sugar and milk; stir in flour. Cook over medium heat for 3 to 6 minutes or until slightly thickened, stirring constantly. Remove from heat; stir in candied peel, cherries and almonds. Drop mixture by teaspoonfuls 3 inches apart onto greased and floured cookie sheets.

Bake at 325°F. for 8 to 13 minutes or until edges are light golden brown. (Edges will spread and centers will remain soft.) Cool 1 minute; carefully remove from cookie sheets. (If cookies harden on cookie sheet, return to oven for 30 to 60 seconds to warm.) Cool completely.

Line large cookie sheet with waxed paper. Turn cookies upside down on waxed paper-lined cookie sheet. In small saucepan, melt glaze ingredients; stir to blend. Spread over flat surface of each cookie to within ¼ inch of edge. When set but not hard, use fork to make wavy lines in chocolate, if desired. Let stand until set. Store between sheets of waxed paper in airtight container in refrigerator.

Yield: 2½ dozen cookies.

NUTRITION PER SERVING:
Calories 80; Protein 1g; Carbohydrate 11g; Fat 4g; Sodium 30mg.

GERMAN CHOCOLATE CAKE MIX COOKIES

These easy-to-make chewy chocolate cookies are on our list of most requested recipes. The cookies puff during baking and then settle when removed from the oven, forming a pretty crinkled top.

- 1 **(18.25-oz.) pkg. pudding-included German chocolate cake mix**
- 1 **(6-oz.) pkg. (1 cup) semi-sweet chocolate chips**
- ½ **cup rolled oats**
- ½ **cup raisins**
- ½ **cup oil**
- 2 **eggs, slightly beaten**

Heat oven to 350°F. In large bowl, combine all ingredients; blend well. Drop dough by rounded teaspoonfuls 2 inches apart onto ungreased cookie sheets.

Bake at 350°F. for 8 to 10 minutes or until set. Cool 1 minute; remove from cookie sheets.

Yield: 4½ dozen cookies.

HIGH ALTITUDE:
Above 3500 Feet: Add ¼ cup flour to dry cake mix. Bake as directed above.

NUTRITION PER SERVING:
Calories 80; Protein 1g; Carbohydrate 11g; Fat 4g; Sodium 60mg.

COOK'S NOTE

GIVING COOKIES AS GIFTS

Try some of these packaging ideas for sharing homemade cookies with relatives and friends.

- Use decorative paper sacks or freezer bags and tie them with colorful ribbons.
- Decorate coffee or shortening cans with wrapping paper or colorful adhesive paper.
- Pack cookies in a wide-mouth canning jar. Cover the lid with fabric and secure it by screwing on the outer ring.
- Weave ribbons through fruit or vegetable baskets lined with colored cellophane or plastic wrap for a more festive look.
- Purchase decorated tins.

Brown Sugar Shortbread Puffs

These rich, buttery cookies can be made large or small.

- 1 **cup firmly packed brown sugar**
- 1¼ **cups margarine or butter, softened**
- 1 **teaspoon vanilla**
- 1 **egg yolk**
- 2¼ **cups all purpose flour**

Heat oven to 350°F. In large bowl, beat brown sugar and margarine until light and fluffy. Add vanilla and egg yolk; blend well. Add flour; stir until mixture forms a smooth dough. Drop dough by rounded teaspoonfuls 2 inches apart onto ungreased cookie sheets.

Bake at 350°F. for 10 to 15 minutes or until lightly browned and set.

Yield: 4 dozen cookies.

TIP:
To make larger puffs, drop dough from a ¼-cup ice cream scoop. Bake until lightly browned and set.

HIGH ALTITUDE:
Above 3500 Feet: No change.

NUTRITION PER SERVING:
Calories 80; Protein 1g; Carbohydrate 9g; Fat 5g; Sodium 50mg.

Pumpkin Cookies with Penuche Frosting

For easy shaping of these spice cookies, try a small ice cream scoop with a release bar. A number 80 or 90 scoop works well, yielding about 1 rounded teaspoonful of dough for each cookie.

COOKIES
- ½ **cup sugar**
- ½ **cup firmly packed brown sugar**
- 1 **cup margarine or butter, softened**
- 1 **cup canned pumpkin**
- 1 **teaspoon vanilla**
- 1 **egg**
- 2 **cups all purpose flour**
- 1 **teaspoon baking powder**
- 1 **teaspoon baking soda**
- 1 **teaspoon cinnamon**
- ¼ **teaspoon salt**
- ¾ **cup chopped walnuts or pecans**

PENUCHE FROSTING
- 3 **tablespoons margarine or butter**
- ½ **cup firmly packed brown sugar**
- ¼ **cup milk**
- 1½ **to 2 cups powdered sugar**

Heat oven to 350°F. In large bowl, beat sugar, ½ cup brown sugar and 1 cup margarine until light and fluffy. Add pumpkin, vanilla and egg; blend well. Add flour, baking powder, baking soda, cinnamon and salt; mix well. Stir in walnuts. Drop dough by rounded teaspoonfuls 2 inches apart onto ungreased cookie sheets.

Bake at 350°F. for 10 to 12 minutes or until light golden brown around edges. Immediately remove from cookie sheets. Cool completely.

In medium saucepan, combine 3 tablespoons margarine and ½ cup brown sugar. Bring to a boil. Cook over medium heat 1 minute or until slightly thickened, stirring constantly. Cool 10 minutes. Add milk; beat until smooth. Beat in enough powdered sugar for desired spreading consistency. Frost cooled cookies. Let stand until frosting is set.

Yield: 5 dozen cookies.

HIGH ALTITUDE:
Above 3500 Feet: No change.

NUTRITION PER SERVING:
Calories 100; Protein 1g; Carbohydrate 12g; Fat 5g; Sodium 75mg.

Pumpkin Cookies with Penuche Frosting

PEANUT AND CANDY JUMBLES

Children will enjoy helping with these chunky, chewy cookies and munching on the extra candy and peanuts!

1	cup firmly packed brown sugar
1/2	cup margarine or butter, softened
1/2	cup creamy peanut butter
1	tablespoon vanilla
1	egg
1	cup all purpose flour
1/2	cup whole wheat flour
1	teaspoon baking soda
3/4	cup salted peanuts
3/4	cup candy-coated chocolate pieces

Heat oven to 375°F. In large bowl, beat brown sugar, margarine and peanut butter until light and fluffy. Add vanilla and egg; blend well. Stir in all purpose flour, whole wheat flour and baking soda; mix well. Stir in peanuts and candy-coated chocolate pieces. Drop dough by rounded tablespoonfuls 2 inches apart onto ungreased cookie sheets.

Bake at 375°F. for 6 to 10 minutes or until light golden brown. Immediately remove from cookie sheets. Cool completely.

Yield: 3 dozen cookies.

HIGH ALTITUDE:
Above 3500 Feet: Decrease brown sugar to 3/4 cup. Bake as directed above.

NUTRITION PER SERVING:
Calories 130; Protein 3g; Carbohydrate 14g; Fat 7g; Sodium 105mg.

SPANISH PEANUT COOKIES

One of many peanut varieties, Spanish peanuts are generally used with their edible red skins. The peanuts add unique flavor and crunch to these easy-to-make cookies.

1	cup firmly packed brown sugar
3/4	cup margarine or butter, softened
1/4	cup creamy peanut butter
2	teaspoons vanilla
1	egg
1 3/4	cups all purpose flour
1	teaspoon baking soda
	Dash salt
1	cup Spanish peanuts

Heat oven to 375°F. In large bowl, beat brown sugar, margarine and peanut butter until light and fluffy. Add vanilla and egg; blend well. Stir in flour, baking soda and salt; mix well. Stir in peanuts. Drop dough by heaping teaspoonfuls 2 inches apart onto ungreased cookie sheets.

Bake at 375°F. for 8 to 12 minutes or until light golden brown. Cool 1 minute; remove from cookie sheets.

Yield: 3 1/2 dozen cookies.

HIGH ALTITUDE:
Above 3500 Feet: Decrease brown sugar to 3/4 cup; increase flour to 1 3/4 cups plus 2 tablespoons. Bake as directed above.

NUTRITION PER SERVING:
Calories 100; Protein 2g; Carbohydrate 10g; Fat 6g; Sodium 95mg.

FROSTED CASHEW COOKIES

"Beurre noisette" is the French term for "brown butter." Using medium heat and browning the butter just until it's a light hazelnut color will add the desired rich flavor to these special cookies.

COOKIES
- 1 cup firmly packed brown sugar
- ½ cup butter or margarine, softened
- ½ teaspoon vanilla
- 1 egg
- 2 cups all purpose flour
- ¾ teaspoon baking powder
- ¾ teaspoon baking soda
- ⅓ cup dairy sour cream
- ¾ cup coarsely chopped salted cashews

BROWN BUTTER FROSTING
- ½ cup butter (do not substitute margarine)
- 2 cups powdered sugar
- 3 tablespoons half-and-half or milk
- ½ teaspoon vanilla

Heat oven to 375°F. Lightly grease cookie sheets. In large bowl, beat brown sugar and ½ cup butter until light and fluffy. Add ½ teaspoon vanilla and egg; blend well. Add flour, baking powder, baking soda and sour cream; mix well. Stir in cashews. Drop dough by rounded teaspoonfuls 2 inches apart onto greased cookie sheets.

Bake at 375°F. for 8 to 10 minutes or until golden brown. Immediately remove from cookie sheets. Cool completely.

Heat ½ cup butter in medium saucepan over medium heat until light golden brown. Remove from heat. Stir in powdered sugar, half-and-half and ½ teaspoon vanilla; beat until smooth. Frost cooled cookies.

Yield: 4 dozen cookies.

HIGH ALTITUDE:
Above 3500 Feet: No change.

NUTRITION PER SERVING:
Calories 100; Protein 1g; Carbohydrate 13g; Fat 5g; Sodium 70mg.

CHERRY POPPY SEED TWINKS

Just drop the dough onto the cookie sheet for this easy, filled thumbprint cookie.

- 1 cup powdered sugar
- 1 cup margarine or butter, softened
- 1 teaspoon vanilla
- 1 egg
- 2 cups all purpose flour
- 2 tablespoons poppy seed
- ½ teaspoon salt
- ½ cup cherry preserves

Heat oven to 300°F. In large bowl, beat powdered sugar and margarine until light and fluffy. Add vanilla and egg; blend well. Stir in flour, poppy seed and salt; mix well. Drop dough by rounded teaspoonfuls 1 inch apart onto ungreased cookie sheets. With finger, make indentation in center of each cookie. Fill each with about ½ teaspoon of the preserves.

Bake at 300°F. for 20 to 25 minutes or until edges are light golden brown. Immediately remove from cookie sheets.

Yield: 2½ dozen cookies.

HIGH ALTITUDE:
Above 3500 Feet: No change.

NUTRITION PER SERVING:
Calories 120; Protein 1g; Carbohydrate 14g; Fat 7g; Sodium 110mg.

COCOA-MALLOW COOKIE-WICHES

Marshmallow creme is a thick whipped mixture that is available in jars. No melting is necessary to make the creamy filling in these yummy chocolate sandwich cookies.

COOKIES
- 1 cup sugar
- ½ cup margarine or butter, softened
- 1 teaspoon vanilla
- 1 egg
- 1 cup milk
- 2 cups all purpose flour
- ½ cup unsweetened cocoa
- 1½ teaspoons baking soda
- ½ teaspoon baking powder
- ½ teaspoon salt

FILLING
- 2 cups powdered sugar
- 1 cup marshmallow creme
- ¼ cup margarine or butter, softened
- ¼ cup shortening
- 3 to 4 teaspoons milk
- 1 teaspoon vanilla

Heat oven to 375°F. Grease cookie sheets. In large bowl, combine sugar, ½ cup margarine, 1 teaspoon vanilla and egg; blend well. Stir in 1 cup milk. Add remaining cookie ingredients; mix well. Drop dough by rounded teaspoonfuls 2 inches apart onto greased cookie sheets.

Bake at 375°F. for 7 to 9 minutes or until edges appear set. Cool 1 minute; remove from cookie sheets. Cool completely.

In large bowl, combine all filling ingredients; beat until light and fluffy, about 2 minutes. Place flat sides of 2 cookies together with 1 tablespoon filling, sandwich-style. Store in tightly covered container.
Yield: 30 sandwich cookies.

HIGH ALTITUDE:
Above 3500 Feet: No change.

NUTRITION PER SERVING:
Calories 170; Protein 2g; Carbohydrate 24g; Fat 7g; Sodium 170mg.

HEAVENLY CHOCOLATE BROWNIE COOKIES

One of the best little cookies you'll ever eat. This recipe requires the use of parchment paper which is readily available at a supermarket or specialty food store.

- 4 oz. semi-sweet chocolate, chopped
- 2 oz. unsweetened chocolate, chopped
- ⅓ cup margarine or butter
- ¾ cup sugar
- 1½ teaspoons instant coffee granules or crystals
- 2 eggs
- ½ cup all purpose flour
- ¼ teaspoon baking powder
- ¼ teaspoon salt
- ¾ cup milk chocolate chips
- ¾ cup chopped walnuts or pecans

In small saucepan over low heat, melt semi-sweet chocolate, unsweetened chocolate and margarine, stirring constantly until smooth. Remove from heat; cool.

Heat oven to 350°F. Cover cookie sheets with parchment paper. In large bowl, beat sugar, instant coffee and eggs at high speed for 2 to 3 minutes. Blend in melted chocolate. Stir in flour, baking powder and salt; mix well. Stir in milk chocolate chips and walnuts. Drop dough by teaspoonfuls 2 inches apart onto parchment-lined cookie sheets.

Bake at 350°F. for 7 to 11 minutes or until tops of cookies are cracked. DO NOT OVERBAKE. Cool 1 minute; remove from parchment paper.
Yield: 3 dozen cookies.

HIGH ALTITUDE:
Above 3500 Feet: No change.

NUTRITION PER SERVING:
Calories 110; Protein 1g; Carbohydrate 10g; Fat 7g; Sodium 40mg.

CHOCOLATE RAISIN SMILE COOKIES

To make the frosting faces, place the frosting in a resealable plastic freezer bag and snip off a corner to make a very small hole. Squeeze the frosting gently through the opening.

COOKIES
1½ cups sugar
1 cup firmly packed brown sugar
1½ cups margarine or butter, softened
2 teaspoons vanilla
3 eggs
3 cups all purpose flour
1 cup unsweetened cocoa
1 teaspoon baking soda
¼ teaspoon salt
2 cups raisins

FROSTING
1 cup powdered sugar
1 drop red food color
2 drops yellow food color
2 to 4 teaspoons milk

Heat oven to 350°F. In large bowl, beat sugar, brown sugar and margarine until light and fluffy. Add vanilla and eggs; blend well. Stir in flour, cocoa, baking soda and salt; mix well. Stir in raisins. Drop dough by rounded tablespoonfuls 2 inches apart onto ungreased cookie sheets.

Bake at 350°F. for 10 to 14 minutes or until slightly set. Cool 1 minute; remove from cookie sheets.

In medium bowl, combine all frosting ingredients, adding enough milk for desired decorating consistency. Using decorating bag, decorating bottle, plastic bag or small spoon, make smiling faces on cookies.
Yield: 5 dozen cookies.

HIGH ALTITUDE:
Above 3500 Feet: Decrease sugar to 1¼ cups; decrease brown sugar to ¾ cup. Increase flour to 3½ cups. Bake as directed above.

NUTRITION PER SERVING:
Calories 130; Protein 1g; Carbohydrate 20g; Fat 5g; Sodium 95mg.

VARIATION:

GIANT COOKIE SMILES: Prepare cookie dough as directed above. For each cookie, place ¼ cup of dough 3 inches apart on ungreased cookie sheets. Bake at 350°F. for 10 to 14 minutes or until slightly set. Continue as directed above.
Yield: 2½ dozen cookies.

CANDIED FRUIT DROPS

Candied fruit is available in the baking section of large supermarkets.

¾ cup firmly packed brown sugar
1 cup margarine or butter, softened
1 egg
1¾ cups all purpose flour
½ teaspoon baking soda
½ teaspoon salt
1 (8-oz.) pkg. (1½ cups) chopped dates
1 cup chopped green candied pineapple
1 cup chopped red candied cherries
1½ cups chopped pecans or walnuts

Heat oven to 350°F. In large bowl, beat brown sugar and margarine until light and fluffy. Add egg; blend well. Add flour, baking soda and salt; mix well. Stir in dates, candied fruit and pecans. Drop dough by teaspoonfuls 2 inches apart onto ungreased cookie sheets.

Bake at 350°F. for 10 to 12 minutes. Cool 1 minute; remove from cookie sheets. Cool completely.
Yield: 7 dozen cookies.

HIGH ALTITUDE:
Above 3500 Feet: Increase flour to 2 cups. Bake as directed above.

NUTRITION PER SERVING:
Calories 70; Protein 1g; Carbohydrate 9g; Fat 4g; Sodium 45mg.

CHEWY GRANOLA COOKIES

Granola is a mixture containing various combinations of grains, nuts and dried fruits. We've included a variety of these ingredients to create healthful, tasty cookies.

- 1½ **cups all purpose flour**
- 3 **cups rolled oats**
- 1 **cup wheat germ**
- 1 **teaspoon baking powder**
- ½ **teaspoon salt**
- 1 **cup firmly packed brown sugar**
- 1 **cup margarine or butter, softened**
- ½ **cup honey**
- 1½ **teaspoons vanilla**
- 2 **eggs**
- ½ **cup raisins**
- ½ **cup chopped almonds**
- ¼ **cup sesame seeds**
- ¼ **cup shelled sunflower seeds**

Heat oven to 375°F. Lightly grease cookie sheets. In medium bowl, combine flour, oats, wheat germ, baking powder and salt; mix well. In large bowl, beat brown sugar, margarine and honey until light and fluffy. Add vanilla and eggs; blend well. Add flour mixture; mix well. Stir in remaining ingredients. Drop dough by rounded teaspoonfuls 2 inches apart onto greased cookie sheets.

Bake at 375°F. for 7 to 8 minutes or until edges are light golden brown. Immediately remove from cookie sheets.

Yield: 5 dozen cookies.

TIP:

For large-sized cookies, place ¼ cup of dough 4 inches apart on greased cookie sheets. Using metal spoon, flatten into 3-inch circles. Bake at 375°F. for 12 to 14 minutes.

Yield: 2½ dozen cookies.

HIGH ALTITUDE:
Above 3500 Feet: No change.

NUTRITION PER SERVING:
Calories 100; Protein 2g; Carbohydrate 13g; Fat 5g; Sodium 65mg.

GRANOLA APPLE COOKIES

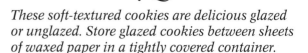

These soft-textured cookies are delicious glazed or unglazed. Store glazed cookies between sheets of waxed paper in a tightly covered container.

COOKIES
- 1½ **cups firmly packed brown sugar**
- ½ **cup margarine or butter, softened**
- ¼ **cup milk**
- 1 **tablespoon lemon juice**
- 1 **teaspoon grated lemon peel**
- 1 **egg**
- 1½ **cups all purpose flour**
- 1 **cup whole wheat flour**
- 1 **teaspoon baking soda**
- 1 **teaspoon cinnamon or nutmeg**
- ¼ **teaspoon salt**
- 1½ **cups finely chopped apples**
- 1 **cup granola**

GLAZE
- ¾ **cup powdered sugar**
- 2 **to 3 teaspoons lemon juice**

Heat oven to 375°F. In large bowl, beat brown sugar and margarine until light and fluffy. Add milk, 1 tablespoon lemon juice, lemon peel and egg; blend well. Stir in all purpose flour, whole wheat flour, baking soda, cinnamon and salt; mix well. Stir in apples and granola. Drop dough by heaping teaspoonfuls 2 inches apart onto ungreased cookie sheets.

Bake at 375°F. for 9 to 13 minutes or until light golden brown. Immediately remove from cookie sheets. Cool completely.

In small bowl, combine glaze ingredients, adding enough lemon juice for desired drizzling consistency. Drizzle over cooled cookies.

Yield: 3 dozen cookies.

HIGH ALTITUDE:
Above 3500 Feet: Decrease brown sugar to 1 cup. Bake as directed above.

NUTRITION PER SERVING:
Calories 140; Protein 2g; Carbohydrate 21g; Fat 6g; Sodium 80mg.

BASIC REFRIGERATOR COOKIES

Sometimes called icebox cookies, these golden cookies are formed into a log, wrapped and refrigerated. They are sliced into rounds just before baking.

- ¾ **cup sugar**
- ¾ **cup firmly packed brown sugar**
- 1 **cup margarine or butter, softened**
- 1½ **teaspoons vanilla**
- 2 **eggs**
- 3 **cups all purpose flour**
- 1½ **teaspoons baking powder**
- ¾ **teaspoon salt**
- 1 **cup finely chopped nuts**

In large bowl, combine sugar, brown sugar, margarine, vanilla and eggs; beat well. Stir in flour, baking powder and salt; blend well. Stir in nuts. Divide dough into 3 equal parts. Shape each into roll 1½ inches in diameter. Wrap each roll in plastic wrap; refrigerate at least 2 hours or until firm.

Heat oven to 425°F. Cut dough into ¼-inch slices. Place 1 inch apart on ungreased cookie sheets. Bake at 425°F. for 5 to 7 minutes or until light golden brown. Immediately remove from cookie sheets. Cool completely.

Yield: 7½ dozen cookies.

TIP:
Cookie dough can be kept up to 2 weeks in refrigerator or up to 6 weeks in freezer. Slice and bake frozen dough as directed above.

HIGH ALTITUDE:
Above 3500 Feet: Add 3 tablespoons milk with sugar mixture. Bake as directed above.

NUTRITION PER SERVING:
Calories 60; Protein 1g; Carbohydrate 7g; Fat 3g; Sodium 50mg.

VARIATIONS:

COCONUT REFRIGERATOR COOKIES:
Add 1 cup coconut with nuts.

LEMON REFRIGERATOR COOKIES:
Add 1 tablespoon grated lemon peel with flour.

ORANGE REFRIGERATOR COOKIES:
Add 1 tablespoon grated orange peel with flour.

SPICE REFRIGERATOR COOKIES:
Add 1 teaspoon cinnamon, ½ teaspoon nutmeg and ¼ to ½ teaspoon cloves with flour.

OATMEAL REFRIGERATOR COOKIES

The answer to fresh cookies on a moment's notice. Mix, shape, wrap and refrigerate up to 2 weeks, then slice and bake as needed.

- 1 **cup sugar**
- 1 **cup firmly packed brown sugar**
- 1 **cup margarine or butter, softened**
- 2 **eggs**
- 2 **cups all purpose flour**
- 1 **teaspoon baking powder**
- 1 **teaspoon baking soda**
- 1 **teaspoon salt**
- 2 **cups quick-cooking rolled oats**
- 1 **cup coconut**
- ½ **to 1 cup chopped nuts**

In large bowl, combine sugar, brown sugar, margarine and eggs; beat well. Add flour, baking powder, baking soda and salt; mix well. Stir in oats, coconut and nuts. Divide dough in half. Shape each half into roll 2 inches in diameter. Wrap each roll in plastic wrap; refrigerate at least 2 hours or until firm.

Heat oven to 375°F. Cut dough into ¼-inch slices. Place 2 inches apart on ungreased cookie sheets. Bake at 375°F. for 8 to 11 minutes or until golden brown. Immediately remove from cookie sheets. Cool completely.

Yield: 6 dozen cookies.

HIGH ALTITUDE:
Above 3500 Feet: No change.

NUTRITION PER SERVING:
Calories 80; Protein 1g; Carbohydrate 11g; Fat 4g; Sodium 80mg.

PINWHEEL DATE COOKIES

These mouth-watering cookies with their marvelous date filling have long been favorites of all the "kids" who raid cookie jars.

FILLING
- ¾ cup finely chopped dates
- ¼ cup sugar
- ⅓ cup water
- 2 tablespoons finely chopped nuts

COOKIES
- 1 cup firmly packed brown sugar
- ½ cup margarine or butter, softened
- 1 egg
- 1½ cups all purpose flour
- 1½ teaspoons baking powder
- ¼ teaspoon salt

In small saucepan, combine dates, sugar and water. Bring to a boil. Reduce heat; cover and simmer 5 minutes or until thick. Stir in nuts. Cool.

In large bowl, beat brown sugar, margarine and egg until light and fluffy. Stir in flour, baking powder and salt; mix at low speed until dough forms. Cover with plastic wrap; refrigerate 1 hour for easier handling.

On lightly floured surface, roll dough into 16x8-inch rectangle; carefully spread with date filling. Starting with 16-inch side, roll up jelly-roll fashion; cut in half to form two 8-inch rolls. Wrap each roll in plastic wrap; refrigerate at least 2 hours.

Heat oven to 375°F. Cut dough into ¼-inch slices. Place 2 inches apart on ungreased cookie sheets. Bake at 375°F. for 6 to 9 minutes or until light golden brown. Immediately remove from cookie sheets. Cool completely.
Yield: 4½ to 5 dozen cookies.

HIGH ALTITUDE:
Above 3500 Feet: Increase flour to 1½ cups plus 2 tablespoons. Bake as directed above.

NUTRITION PER SERVING:
Calories 50; Protein 1g; Carbohydrate 8g; Fat 2g; Sodium 35mg.

CRANBERRY AND ORANGE PINWHEELS

This refrigerator cookie dough features a pretty swirl of cranberry filling.

FILLING
- 1 tablespoon cornstarch
- ¾ cup whole berry cranberry sauce
- ¼ cup orange marmalade

COOKIES
- ¾ cup firmly packed brown sugar
- ½ cup margarine or butter, softened
- 1 egg
- 1¾ cups all purpose flour
- 1 teaspoon baking powder
- 1 teaspoon grated orange peel
- ¼ teaspoon salt
- ¼ teaspoon allspice

In small saucepan, combine all filling ingredients. Bring to a boil over medium heat, stirring constantly. Refrigerate until thoroughly chilled.

In large bowl, beat brown sugar, margarine and egg until light and fluffy. Stir in remaining ingredients; mix well. Cover with plastic wrap; refrigerate 1 hour for easier handling.

On lightly floured surface, roll dough into 16x8-inch rectangle. Spoon and spread cooled filling evenly over dough to within ½ inch of edges. Starting with 16-inch side, roll up jelly-roll fashion; cut in half to form two 8-inch rolls. Wrap each roll in plastic wrap; refrigerate at least 2 hours.

Heat oven to 375°F. Generously grease cookie sheets. Using sharp knife, cut dough into ½-inch slices. Place 2 inches apart on greased cookie sheets. Bake at 375°F. for 9 to 13 minutes or until light golden brown. Immediately remove from cookie sheets. Cool completely.
Yield: 3 dozen cookies.

HIGH ALTITUDE:
Above 3500 Feet: Increase flour to 2 cups. Bake as directed above.

NUTRITION PER SERVING:
Calories 80; Protein 1g; Carbohydrate 13g; Fat 3g; Sodium 60mg.

Cranberry and Orange Pinwheels,
Granola Apple Cookies p. 46

SPICED WHOLE WHEAT REFRIGERATOR COOKIES

Because of its firm chewy texture, this traditional icebox cookie is ideal for mailing. Pack the cookies snugly in rows in a sturdy box or metal container. If necessary, cushion cookies with crumpled waxed paper.

- ½ cup sugar
- ½ cup firmly packed brown sugar
- ½ cup margarine or butter, softened
- 2 tablespoons water
- 2 teaspoons vanilla
- 1 egg
- 1¾ cups whole wheat flour
- 1 teaspoon baking powder
- 1 teaspoon cinnamon
- ½ teaspoon baking soda
- ¼ teaspoon salt
- ¼ teaspoon cloves
- ½ cup finely chopped pecans or walnuts

In large bowl, beat sugar, brown sugar and margarine until light and fluffy. Add water, vanilla and egg; blend well. Add whole wheat flour, baking powder, cinnamon, baking soda, salt and cloves; mix well. Stir in pecans. Shape dough into two 6-inch long rolls. Wrap each roll in plastic wrap; refrigerate at least 2 hours or until firm.

Heat oven to 375°F. Using sharp knife, cut dough into ¼-inch slices. Place 2 inches apart on ungreased cookie sheets. Bake at 375°F. for 6 to 8 minutes or until set. Cool 1 minute; remove from cookie sheets. Cool completely.
Yield: 3½ dozen cookies.

HIGH ALTITUDE:
Above 3500 Feet: Decrease sugar to ⅓ cup; decrease brown sugar to ⅓ cup. Increase flour to 2 cups. Bake as directed above.

NUTRITION PER SERVING:
Calories 70; Protein 1g; Carbohydrate 9g; Fat 3g; Sodium 60mg.

CRISP AND CHEWY MOLASSES COOKIES

Store this cookie dough in the refrigerator for up to 5 days and bake cookies as desired. Either light or dark molasses can be used to make this favorite cookie.

- ¾ cup sugar
- ½ cup margarine or butter, softened
- ½ cup molasses
- 1 egg
- 2 cups all purpose flour
- 1½ teaspoons baking soda
- ½ teaspoon cinnamon
- ¼ teaspoon cloves
- ¼ teaspoon nutmeg
- ¼ teaspoon ginger

In large bowl, beat sugar and margarine until light and fluffy. Add molasses and egg; blend well. Stir in remaining ingredients; mix well. Cover with plastic wrap; refrigerate 30 minutes for easier handling. Shape dough into roll 9½ inches long. Wrap roll in plastic wrap; refrigerate at least 6 hours or up to 5 days.

Heat oven to 375°F. Cut dough into ½-inch slices; cut each slice into fourths. Place 2 inches apart on ungreased cookie sheets. Bake at 375°F. for 6 to 10 minutes or until set. Immediately remove from cookie sheets. Cool completely.
Yield: 5 dozen cookies.

HIGH ALTITUDE:
Above 3500 Feet: Decrease sugar to ½ cup; decrease molasses to ¼ cup. Bake as directed above.

NUTRITION PER SERVING:
Calories 45; Protein 1g; Carbohydrate 7g; Fat 2g; Sodium 50mg.

PEANUT BUTTER COOKIES

Easily prepared and always familiar because of the forked pattern, peanut butter cookies are delicious anytime.

- ½ **cup sugar**
- ½ **cup firmly packed brown sugar**
- ½ **cup margarine or butter, softened**
- ½ **cup peanut butter**
- 2 **tablespoons milk**
- 1 **teaspoon vanilla**
- 1 **egg**
- 1¾ **cups all purpose flour**
- 1 **teaspoon baking soda**
- ½ **teaspoon salt**
  Sugar

Heat oven to 375°F. In large bowl, beat sugar, brown sugar, and margarine until light and fluffy. Add peanut butter, milk, vanilla and egg; blend well. Stir in flour, baking soda and salt; mix well. Shape dough into 1-inch balls. Place 2 inches apart on ungreased cookie sheets. Flatten in crisscross pattern with fork dipped in sugar.

Bake at 375°F. for 10 to 12 minutes or until golden brown. Immediately remove from cookie sheets. Cool completely.

Yield: 3½ dozen cookies.

HIGH ALTITUDE:
Above 3500 Feet: No change.

NUTRITION PER SERVING:
Calories 80; Protein 1g; Carbohydrate 10g; Fat 4g; Sodium 95mg.

BUTTERSCOTCH CHIP PEANUT BUTTER COOKIES

Butterscotch chips add a unique flavor to these peanut butter cookies. They're a great addition to lunch boxes.

- ½ **cup sugar**
- ½ **cup firmly packed brown sugar**
- ¾ **cup margarine or butter, softened**
- ½ **cup chunky peanut butter**
- 1 **teaspoon vanilla**
- 1 **egg**
- 1¾ **cups all purpose flour**
- 1 **teaspoon baking soda**
- ½ **teaspoon salt**
- 1 **cup butterscotch chips**

Heat oven to 375°F. In large bowl, beat sugar, brown sugar, margarine and peanut butter until light and fluffy. Add vanilla and egg; blend well. Stir in flour, baking soda and salt; mix well. Stir in butterscotch chips. Shape dough into 1-inch balls. Place 2 inches apart on ungreased cookie sheets. Flatten slightly with fork dipped in flour or sugar.

Bake at 375°F. for 6 to 10 minutes or until golden brown. Immediately remove from cookie sheets. Cool completely.

Yield: 4 to 5 dozen cookies.

HIGH ALTITUDE:
Above 3500 Feet: Increase flour to 2 cups. Bake as directed above.

NUTRITION PER SERVING:
Calories 80; Protein 1g; Carbohydrate 8g; Fat 4g; Sodium 75mg.

PEANUT BLOSSOMS

Sometimes called Brown-Eyed Susans, these cookies crowned with a chocolate kiss are from the 9th Pillsbury Grand National Baking Contest, the early name of the BAKE-OFF® Contest.

1¾   cups all purpose flour
½   cup sugar
½   cup firmly packed brown sugar
1   teaspoon baking soda
½   teaspoon salt
½   cup shortening
½   cup peanut butter
2   tablespoons milk
1   teaspoon vanilla
1   egg
    Sugar
48   milk chocolate candy kisses

Heat oven to 375°F. In large bowl, combine flour, ½ cup sugar, brown sugar, baking soda, salt, shortening, peanut butter, milk, vanilla and egg; blend at low speed until stiff dough forms. Shape into 1-inch balls; roll in sugar. Place 2 inches apart on ungreased cookie sheets.

Bake at 375°F. for 10 to 12 minutes or until golden brown. Immediately top each cookie with a candy kiss, pressing down firmly so cookie cracks around edge; remove from cookie sheets. Cool completely.
Yield: 4 dozen cookies.

HIGH ALTITUDE:
Above 3500 Feet: No change.

NUTRITION PER SERVING:
Calories 100; Protein 2g; Carbohydrate 12g; Fat 5g; Sodium 65mg.

HAWAIIAN COOKIE TARTS

These melt-in-your-mouth cookies are perfect for party trays. They are like miniature pineapple pies.

COOKIES
1¾   cups all purpose flour
½   cup powdered sugar
2   tablespoons cornstarch
1   cup margarine or butter, softened
1   teaspoon vanilla

FILLING
1   cup pineapple preserves
½   cup sugar
1   egg
1½   cups coconut
    Powdered sugar

Heat oven to 350°F. In large bowl, combine flour, ½ cup powdered sugar and cornstarch; blend well. Add margarine and vanilla. By hand, blend until a soft dough forms. Shape dough into 1-inch balls. Place 1 ball in each of 36 ungreased miniature muffin cups; press in bottom and up sides of each cup.*

Spoon 1 teaspoon pineapple preserves into each dough-lined cup. In small bowl, combine sugar and egg. Using fork, beat until well blended. Stir in coconut until well coated with egg mixture. Spoon 1 teaspoon coconut mixture over pineapple preserves in each cup.

Bake at 350°F. for 23 to 33 minutes or until crusts are very light golden brown. Cool 20 minutes. To release cookies from cups, hold muffin pan upside down at an angle over wire rack. Using handle of table knife, firmly tap bottom of each cup until cookie releases. Cool completely. Just before serving, sprinkle with powdered sugar.
Yield: 3 dozen cookies.

TIP:
* If only 1 muffin pan is available, keep remaining cookie dough refrigerated until ready to bake.

NUTRITION PER SERVING:
Calories 130; Protein 1g; Carbohydrate 17g; Fat 6g; Sodium 55mg.

Peanut Blossoms

CHOCOLATY SHORTBREAD COOKIES

Store these tender chocolate cookies in a single layer, tightly covered.

- ¾ **cup sugar**
- ½ **cup margarine or butter, softened**
- ½ **cup shortening**
- 1 **teaspoon vanilla**
- 1 **egg**
- 2¼ **cups all purpose flour**
- ¼ **cup unsweetened cocoa**
- ½ **teaspoon baking powder**
  Sugar

Heat oven to 325°F. In large bowl, beat ¾ cup sugar, margarine and shortening until light and fluffy. Add vanilla and egg; blend well. Stir in flour, cocoa and baking powder; mix well. Shape dough into 1-inch balls. Place 2 inches apart on ungreased cookie sheets. Flatten slightly with bottom of glass dipped in sugar.

Bake at 325°F. for 8 to 13 minutes or until set. Cool 1 minute; remove from cookie sheets.
Yield: 3 dozen cookies.

HIGH ALTITUDE:
Above 3500 Feet: Increase flour to 2½ cups. Bake as directed above.

NUTRITION PER SERVING:
Calories 100; Protein 1g; Carbohydrate 10g; Fat 6g; Sodium 40mg.

ORANGE BUTTER COOKIES IN CHOCOLATE

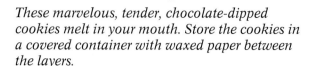

These marvelous, tender, chocolate-dipped cookies melt in your mouth. Store the cookies in a covered container with waxed paper between the layers.

COOKIES
- 1 **cup sugar**
- ¾ **cup butter or margarine, softened**
- 1 **teaspoon vanilla**
- 1 **egg**
- 2 **cups all purpose flour**
- 1 **teaspoon baking powder**
- ¾ **teaspoon salt**
- 2 **tablespoons grated orange peel**

GLAZE
- 1 **(6-oz.) pkg. (1 cup) semi-sweet chocolate chips**
- ¼ **cup shortening**
- 3 **tablespoons light corn syrup**

Heat oven to 375°F. In large bowl, beat sugar and butter until light and fluffy. Add vanilla and egg; blend well. Stir in flour, baking powder, salt and orange peel. Shape dough into 1-inch balls. Place 2 inches apart on ungreased cookie sheets. Flatten to ⅛ to ¼-inch thickness with bottom of glass dipped in sugar.

Bake at 375°F. for 6 to 8 minutes or until edges are lightly browned. Cool 1 minute; remove from cookie sheets.

Line cookie sheets with waxed paper. In small saucepan, combine glaze ingredients. Cook over low heat, stirring constantly until smooth. Remove from heat. Pour glaze into glass measuring cup; set in pan of hot water. Dip half of each cookie into glaze; shake off excess chocolate. Place dipped cookies on waxed paper-lined cookie sheets. Refrigerate until glaze is set, about 10 minutes.
Yield: 6 dozen cookies.

HIGH ALTITUDE:
Above 3500 Feet: No change.

NUTRITION PER SERVING:
Calories 70; Protein 1g; Carbohydrate 7g; Fat 4g; Sodium 50mg.

No-Roll Sugar Cookies

What an easy way to make a large batch of sugar cookies! For variety, try the variations.

- 1 cup sugar
- 1 cup powdered sugar
- 1 cup margarine or butter, softened
- 1 cup oil
- 1 teaspoon vanilla
- 2 eggs
- 4¼ cups all purpose flour
- 1 teaspoon baking soda
- 1 teaspoon cream of tartar
- 1 teaspoon salt

In large bowl, beat sugar, powdered sugar and margarine until light and fluffy. Add oil, vanilla and eggs; blend well. Stir in flour, baking soda, cream of tartar and salt; mix well. Cover with plastic wrap; refrigerate at least 2 hours or overnight for easier handling.

Heat oven to 375°F. Shape dough into 1-inch balls. Place 2 inches apart on ungreased cookie sheets. Flatten with bottom of glass dipped in sugar. Bake at 375°F. for 5 to 8 minutes or until set but not brown. Immediately remove from cookie sheets. Cool completely.

Yield: 9 to 10 dozen cookies.

HIGH ALTITUDE:
Above 3500 Feet: No change.

NUTRITION PER SERVING:
Calories 60; Protein 1g; Carbohydrate 6g; Fat 3g; Sodium 45mg.

VARIATIONS:

ALMOND SUGAR COOKIES: Add 1 teaspoon almond extract with the vanilla.

ORANGE SUGAR COOKIES: Add 2 teaspoons grated orange peel and 1 teaspoon cinnamon with the dry ingredients.

Whole Wheat Sugar Cookies

Whole wheat flour and nutmeg add new flavor to the all-time favorite sugar cookie. Just shape the dough into balls, roll them in the sugar-cinnamon mixture and bake.

- 1 cup sugar
- ½ cup margarine or butter, softened
- 2 tablespoons milk
- 1 teaspoon grated lemon peel
- 1 teaspoon vanilla
- 1 egg
- 2 cups whole wheat flour
- 1 teaspoon baking powder
- ½ teaspoon baking soda
- ½ teaspoon salt
- ½ teaspoon nutmeg
- 2 tablespoons sugar
- ½ teaspoon cinnamon

In large bowl, beat 1 cup sugar and margarine until light and fluffy. Add milk, lemon peel, vanilla and egg; blend well. Add flour, baking powder, baking soda, salt and nutmeg; mix well. Cover with plastic wrap; refrigerate 1 hour for easier handling.

Heat oven to 375°F. In small bowl, combine 2 tablespoons sugar and cinnamon. Shape dough into 1-inch balls; roll in sugar-cinnamon mixture. Place 2 inches apart on ungreased cookie sheets.

Bake at 375°F. for 8 to 10 minutes or until light golden brown. Cool 1 minute; remove from cookie sheets. Cool completely.

Yield: 2 to 3 dozen cookies.

HIGH ALTITUDE:
Above 3500 Feet: No change.

NUTRITION PER SERVING:
Calories 70; Protein 1g; Carbohydrate 11g; Fat 3g; Sodium 85mg.

CARAMEL CREAM SANDWICH COOKIES

These rich butter cookies with delicate caramel flavor are a prizewinning recipe from the 6th Pillsbury BAKE-OFF® Contest held in 1955.

COOKIES
- ¾ **cup firmly packed brown sugar**
- 1 **cup butter or margarine, softened**
- 1 **egg yolk**
- 2 **cups all purpose flour**

FROSTING
- 2 **tablespoons butter (do not substitute margarine)**
- 1¼ **cups powdered sugar**
- ½ **teaspoon vanilla**
- 4 **to 5 teaspoons milk**

In large bowl, beat brown sugar and 1 cup butter until light and fluffy. Add egg yolk; blend well. Stir in flour; mix well. Cover with plastic wrap; refrigerate 15 minutes for easier handling.

Heat oven to 325°F. Shape dough into 1-inch balls. Place 2 inches apart on ungreased cookie sheets. Flatten to 1½-inch circles with fork dipped in flour. Bake at 325°F. for 10 to 14 minutes or until light golden brown. Immediately remove from cookie sheets. Cool completely.

Heat 2 tablespoons butter in medium saucepan over medium heat until light golden brown. Remove from heat. Stir in remaining frosting ingredients, adding enough milk for desired spreading consistency; blend until smooth. Spread 1 teaspoon frosting between 2 cooled cookies. Repeat with remaining frosting and cookies.*
Yield: 2½ dozen sandwich cookies.

TIP:

* If frosting becomes too stiff as it cools, add enough additional milk for desired spreading consistency.

HIGH ALTITUDE:
Above 3500 Feet: No change.

NUTRITION PER SERVING:
Calories 130; Protein 1g; Carbohydrate 16g; Fat 7g; Sodium 70mg.

NUTMEG COOKIE LOGS

Nutmeg is found in the fruit of a tropical evergreen called a nutmeg tree.

COOKIES
- ¾ **cup sugar**
- 1 **cup margarine or butter, softened**
- 2 **teaspoons vanilla**
- 2 **teaspoons rum extract**
- 1 **egg**
- 3 **cups all purpose flour**
- 1 **teaspoon nutmeg**

FROSTING
- 2 **cups powdered sugar**
- 3 **tablespoons margarine or butter, softened**
- ¾ **teaspoon rum extract**
- ¼ **teaspoon vanilla**
- 2 **to 3 tablespoons half-and-half or milk Nutmeg**

In large bowl, beat sugar, 1 cup margarine, 2 teaspoons vanilla, 2 teaspoons rum extract and egg until light and fluffy. Stir in flour and 1 teaspoon nutmeg; mix well. Cover with plastic wrap; refrigerate 30 to 45 minutes for easier handling.

Heat oven to 350°F. Divide dough into 6 pieces. On lightly floured surface, shape each piece of dough into long rope, ½ inch in diameter. Cut into 3-inch lengths; place on ungreased cookie sheets. Bake at 350°F. for 12 to 15 minutes or until light golden brown. Immediately remove from cookie sheets. Cool completely.

In small bowl, combine all frosting ingredients except nutmeg, adding enough half-and-half for desired spreading consistency. Spread on top and sides of cookies. If desired, mark frosting with tines of fork to resemble bark. Sprinkle lightly with nutmeg. Let stand until frosting is set. Store in tightly covered container.
Yield: 4½ to 5 dozen cookies.

HIGH ALTITUDE:
Above 3500 Feet: No change.

NUTRITION PER SERVING:
Calories 80; Protein 1g; Carbohydrate 11g; Fat 4g; Sodium 40mg.

Caramel Cream Sandwich Cookies

MERINGUE MUSHROOMS

These delightful, airy little cookies are wonderful to eat or use as a garnish for other desserts.

 2 egg whites, room temperature
 ¼ teaspoon cream of tartar
 ½ cup sugar
 1 to 2 tablespoons unsweetened cocoa
 2 oz. semi-sweet chocolate

Heat oven to 200°F. Line 2 cookie sheets with foil or parchment paper. In small bowl, beat egg whites and cream of tartar at medium speed until soft peaks form. Add sugar 1 tablespoon at a time, beating at high speed until stiff glossy peaks form and sugar is dissolved. Spoon meringue into decorating bag with ¼-inch plain decorating tip (No. 10, 11 or 12). For mushroom caps, pipe about fifty 1-inch mounds on one foil-lined cookie sheet. Lightly sift cocoa over caps.

Bake at 200°F. for 45 to 60 minutes or until firm and very lightly browned. Remove from oven. Immediately turn caps over; with finger, make indentation in center of each cap. Cool completely. Brush off any excess cocoa.

On second foil-lined cookie sheet, pipe remaining meringue into 50 upright stems, about ¾-inch tall. Bake at 200°F. for 40 to 45 minutes or until firm. Immediately remove from cookie sheet; cool completely.

Melt chocolate in small saucepan over low heat, stirring constantly. To assemble each mushroom, spread a small amount of melted chocolate in indentation of cap; insert pointed end of stem into chocolate. Let stand until dry. Store loosely covered at room temperature.
Yield: 4 to 5 dozen cookies.

NUTRITION PER SERVING:
Calories 12; Protein 0g; Carbohydrate 2g; Fat 0g; Sodium 0mg.

VARIATION:

MINT WREATHS: *Omit cocoa and chocolate.* Add ¼ teaspoon mint extract and a few drops of green food color, if desired, to egg whites when adding last tablespoon of sugar. Spoon meringue into decorating bag with ¼-inch plain decorating tip. Pipe two 1½-inch circles of meringue, one on top of the other, on foil-lined cookie sheet. Repeat for remaining wreaths. Decorate with bits of red and green candied cherries. Bake at 200°F. for 45 minutes. Turn oven off; leave meringues in oven an additional 1 hour to dry. Carefully peel from foil. Cool completely.
Yield: 3 dozen cookies.

MEXICAN WEDDING CAKES

These buttery shortbread cookies can be shaped either into balls or crescents.

 ½ cup powdered sugar
 1 cup butter or margarine, softened
 2 teaspoons vanilla
 2 cups all purpose flour
 1 cup finely chopped or ground almonds or pecans
 ¼ teaspoon salt
  Powdered sugar

Heat oven to 325°F. In large bowl, beat ½ cup powdered sugar, butter and vanilla until light and fluffy. Stir in flour, almonds and salt; mix until dough forms. Shape into 1-inch balls. Place 1 inch apart on ungreased cookie sheets.

Bake at 325°F. for 15 to 20 minutes or until set but not brown. Immediately remove from cookie sheets. Cool slightly; roll in powdered sugar. Cool completely. Reroll in powdered sugar.
Yield: 5 dozen cookies.

HIGH ALTITUDE :
Above 3500 Feet: No change.

NUTRITION PER SERVING:
Calories 60; Protein 1g; Carbohydrate 6g; Fat 4g; Sodium 40mg.

COOK'S NOTE

A COOKIE WITH MANY NAMES

Swedish Tea Cakes or Butterballs, Russian Tea Cakes, Mexican Wedding Cakes . . . many different names describe this favorite holiday cookie. The shape may be in a crescent, a log or a ball. Cookies may be plain, dipped in melted chocolate or rolled in powdered sugar. For a variation, substitute 1 cup miniature semi-sweet chocolate chips for 1 cup finely chopped nuts.

Chocolate Almond Bonbons,
Mexican Wedding Cakes

CHOCOLATE ALMOND BONBONS

This Pillsbury BAKE-OFF® Contest finalist prepared her delicious chocolate cookies in the Grand Ballroom of the Waldorf-Astoria Hotel in December, 1952, along with 99 other finalists.

   4 **oz. sweet baking chocolate**
   2 **tablespoons milk**
  ¼ **cup sugar**
  ¾ **cup margarine or butter, softened**
   2 **teaspoons vanilla**
   2 **cups all purpose flour**
  ¼ **teaspoon salt**
   1 **(3½-oz.) tube almond paste**
      Sugar

Heat oven to 350°F. In small saucepan over low heat, melt chocolate in milk, stirring occasionally until smooth. In large bowl, beat ¼ cup sugar and margarine until light and fluffy. Blend in chocolate mixture and vanilla. Stir in flour and salt; mix well. Using rounded teaspoonfuls of dough, shape into balls. Place 2 inches apart on ungreased cookie sheets. Make an indentation in center of each cookie. Fill each with scant ¼ teaspoon almond paste; press dough around filling to cover.

Bake at 350°F. for 9 to 11 minutes or until set. Remove from cookie sheets; roll in sugar. Cool completely.
Yield: 4 dozen cookies.

HIGH ALTITUDE:
Above 3500 Feet: No change.

NUTRITION PER SERVING:
Calories 70; Protein 1g; Carbohydrate 8g; Fat 4g; Sodium 45mg.

SNICKERDOODLES

The whimsical name of this favorite cookie, which originated in New England, is simply a nineteenth century nonsense word for a quickly made confection.

1½ cups sugar
½ cup margarine or butter, softened
1 teaspoon vanilla
2 eggs
2¾ cups all purpose flour
1 teaspoon cream of tartar
½ teaspoon baking soda
¼ teaspoon salt
2 tablespoons sugar
2 teaspoons cinnamon

Heat oven to 400°F. In large bowl, beat 1½ cups sugar and margarine until light and fluffy. Add vanilla and eggs; blend well. Add flour, cream of tartar, baking soda and salt; mix well. In small bowl, combine 2 tablespoons sugar and cinnamon. Shape dough into 1-inch balls; roll balls in sugar-cinnamon mixture. Place 2 inches apart on ungreased cookie sheets.

Bake at 400°F. for 8 to 10 minutes or until set. Immediately remove from cookie sheets. Cool completely.
Yield: 4 dozen cookies.

HIGH ALTITUDE:
Above 3500 Feet: No change.

NUTRITION PER SERVING:
Calories 70; Protein 1g; Carbohydrate 12g; Fat 2g; Sodium 50mg.

VARIATION:

WHOLE WHEAT SNICKERDOODLES:
Use 1¾ cups all purpose flour and 1 cup whole wheat flour.

CHOCOLATE PIXIES

When melting chocolate, constant stirring is needed to keep the mixture smooth and to prevent scorching.

¼ cup margarine or butter
4 oz. unsweetened chocolate
2 cups all purpose flour
2 cups sugar
½ cup chopped walnuts or pecans
2 teaspoons baking powder
½ teaspoon salt
4 eggs
Powdered sugar

In large saucepan over low heat, melt margarine and chocolate, stirring constantly until smooth. Remove from heat; cool slightly. Stir in remaining ingredients except powdered sugar; mix well. Cover with plastic wrap; refrigerate at least 1 hour for easier handling.

Heat oven to 300°F. Shape dough into 1-inch balls; roll each in powdered sugar, coating heavily. Place 2 inches apart on ungreased cookie sheets. Bake at 300°F. for 13 to 18 minutes or until set. Immediately remove from cookie sheets. Cool completely.
Yield: 4 dozen cookies.

HIGH ALTITUDE:
Above 3500 Feet: Increase flour to 2¼ cups. Bake as directed above.

NUTRITION PER SERVING:
Calories 80; Protein 1g; Carbohydrate 12g; Fat 3g; Sodium 50mg.

COOK'S NOTE

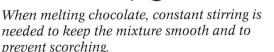

COOKIE HISTORY

The first cookies were created quite by accident. Cooks used a small amount of cake batter to test their oven temperature before baking a large cake. These little test cakes were called "koekje," meaning "little cake" in Dutch.

CARAMEL PECAN STICKY BUN COOKIES

~

The title says it all! These buttery rich cookies would be a great addition to any cookie tray. The recipe will be requested often.

COOKIES
- 1 cup margarine or butter, softened
- ½ cup sugar
- ½ cup dark corn syrup
- 2 egg yolks
- 2½ cups all purpose flour

FILLING
- ½ cup powdered sugar
- ¼ cup margarine or butter
- 3 tablespoons dark corn syrup
- ½ cup coarsely chopped pecans, toasted, p. 23
- 1 egg white, slightly beaten

In large bowl, beat 1 cup margarine and sugar until light and fluffy. Add ½ cup corn syrup and egg yolks; blend well. Stir in flour; mix well. Cover with plastic wrap; refrigerate 1 hour for easier handling.

In small saucepan, combine powdered sugar, ¼ cup margarine and 3 tablespoons corn syrup; bring to a boil. Remove from heat. Stir in pecans. Refrigerate at least 10 minutes.

Heat oven to 375°F. Lightly grease cookie sheets. Shape dough into 1½-inch balls. Place 2 inches apart on greased cookie sheets. Bake at 375°F. for 5 minutes. Remove from oven. Brush dough lightly with egg white. With spoon, carefully make deep indentation in center of each cookie; fill each with ½ teaspoon filling. Return to oven and bake an additional 6 to 9 minutes or until light golden brown. Cool 1 to 2 minutes; remove from cookie sheets. Cool completely.

Yield: 3 dozen cookies.

HIGH ALTITUDE:
Above 3500 Feet: Decrease margarine in cookies to ¾ cup; decrease dark corn syrup in cookies to ⅓ cup. Bake as directed above on *ungreased* cookie sheets.

NUTRITION PER SERVING:
Calories 140; Protein 1g; Carbohydrate 16g; Fat 8g; Sodium 80mg.

CHERRY WINKS

~

Maraschino cherries are available in the canned fruit section of grocery stores. Purchase cherries without stems for this 1950 Pillsbury BAKE-OFF® Contest winning favorite.

- 1 cup sugar
- ¾ cup shortening
- 2 tablespoons milk
- 1 teaspoon vanilla
- 2 eggs
- 2¼ cups all purpose flour
- 1 teaspoon baking powder
- ½ teaspoon baking soda
- ½ teaspoon salt
- 1 cup chopped pecans or walnuts
- 1 cup chopped dates
- ⅓ cup chopped maraschino cherries, well drained
- 1½ cups coarsely crushed cornflakes cereal
- 15 maraschino cherries, quartered, drained

Heat oven to 375°F. Grease cookie sheets. In large bowl, combine sugar, shortening, milk, vanilla and eggs; beat well. Stir in flour, baking powder, baking soda, salt, pecans, dates and ⅓ cup chopped cherries; mix well. Cover dough with plastic wrap and refrigerate for easier handling.

Drop dough by rounded teaspoonfuls into cereal; thoroughly coat. Form into balls; place 2 inches apart on greased cookie sheets. Lightly press maraschino cherry piece into top of each ball. Bake at 375°F. for 10 to 15 minutes or until light golden brown.

Yield: 5 dozen cookies.

HIGH ALTITUDE:
Above 3500 Feet: No change.

NUTRITION PER SERVING:
Calories 90; Protein 1g; Carbohydrate 12g; Fat 4g; Sodium 55mg.

LEMON BUTTER COOKIES

These lemony morsels are more tender when made with butter, but margarine is an acceptable alternative.

- ½ cup sugar
- ½ cup powdered sugar
- ¾ cup butter or margarine, softened
- ¼ cup oil
- 1 tablespoon grated lemon peel
- 1 tablespoon lemon juice
- 1 egg
- 2½ cups all purpose flour
- ½ teaspoon cream of tartar
- ½ teaspoon baking soda
- ¼ teaspoon salt
  Yellow decorator sugar

In large bowl, beat sugar, powdered sugar, butter and oil until light and fluffy. Add lemon peel, lemon juice and egg; blend well. Stir in flour, cream of tartar, baking soda and salt; mix well. Cover with plastic wrap; refrigerate 1 hour for easier handling.

Heat oven to 350°F. Shape dough into 1-inch balls; roll in decorator sugar. Place 2 inches apart on ungreased cookie sheets. Bake at 350°F. for 7 to 12 minutes or until set. Immediately remove from cookie sheets.

Yield: 3½ dozen cookies.

HIGH ALTITUDE:
Above 3500 Feet: Decrease sugar to ⅓ cup; increase flour to 2¾ cups. Bake as directed above.

NUTRITION PER SERVING:
Calories 90; Protein 1g; Carbohydrate 11g; Fat 5g; Sodium 60mg.

WHITE-CAPPED MOCHA COOKIES

Use your choice of candy coating or white baking bar to create these delectable candy-filled party cookies.

COOKIES
- ½ cup firmly packed brown sugar
- ¼ cup sugar
- ½ cup margarine or butter, softened
- 1 (8-oz.) pkg. cream cheese, softened, reserving 2 oz. for frosting
- 2 teaspoons instant coffee granules or crystals
- 2 teaspoons hot water
- 1 egg
- 2 cups all purpose flour
- ¼ cup unsweetened cocoa
- 1 teaspoon baking powder
- 2 to 3 oz. vanilla-flavored candy coating or white baking bar, cut into small pieces (about ¼-inch cubes)

FROSTING
- 1 cup powdered sugar
  Reserved 2 oz. cream cheese
- 2 to 3 teaspoons milk

Heat oven to 350°F. In large bowl, beat brown sugar, sugar, margarine and 6 oz. of the cream cheese until light and fluffy. In small bowl, dissolve instant coffee in hot water. Add dissolved coffee and egg; blend well. Stir in flour, cocoa and baking powder; mix well. Shape level tablespoonfuls of dough around each piece of candy coating, covering completely. Place 2 inches apart on ungreased cookie sheets.

Bake at 350°F. for 8 to 11 minutes or until set. Cool 1 minute; remove from cookie sheets. Cool completely.

In small bowl, combine all frosting ingredients, adding enough milk for desired spreading consistency. Frost cooled cookies.

Yield: 4½ dozen cookies.

HIGH ALTITUDE:
Above 3500 Feet: Decrease baking powder to ½ teaspoon. Bake as directed above.

NUTRITION PER SERVING:
Calories 80; Protein 1g; Carbohydrate 10g; Fat 4g; Sodium 45mg.

GINGER SNAPS

Ginger cookies with a crackly sugar topping are a long-standing favorite cookie jar cookie. For chewy cookies, bake just until set. For crisper cookies, bake 2 to 3 minutes longer.

- 1 cup sugar
- ¾ cup margarine or butter, softened
- ¼ cup molasses
- 1 egg
- 2¼ cups all purpose flour
- 2 teaspoons baking soda
- 1 teaspoon cinnamon
- ½ teaspoon salt
- ½ teaspoon ginger
- ½ teaspoon cloves
- ¼ teaspoon nutmeg
- ¼ cup sugar

In large bowl, beat 1 cup sugar, margarine, molasses and egg until light and fluffy. Stir in remaining ingredients except ¼ cup sugar; mix well. Cover with plastic wrap; refrigerate 1 hour for easier handling.

Heat oven to 350°F. Shape dough into 1-inch balls; roll in ¼ cup sugar. Place 2 inches apart on ungreased cookie sheets. Bake at 350°F. for 8 to 12 minutes or until set. (Cookies will puff up and then flatten during baking.) Cool 1 minute; remove from cookie sheets. Cool completely.
Yield: 4½ to 5 dozen cookies.

HIGH ALTITUDE:
Above 3500 Feet: Decrease baking soda to 1½ teaspoons. Bake as directed above.

NUTRITION PER SERVING:
Calories 60; Protein 1g; Carbohydrate 9g; Fat 2g; Sodium 85mg.

CRISP CHOCOLATE SNAPS

Chocolate lovers will find this eye-catching version of a cookie classic irresistible. Smaller-sized snaps can be made for holiday cookie trays.

- 2 cups sugar
- 1 cup firmly packed brown sugar
- 1½ cups margarine or butter, softened
- 2 teaspoons vanilla
- 3 eggs
- 6 oz. unsweetened chocolate, melted, cooled
- ½ teaspoon red food color, if desired
- 4 cups all purpose flour
- 2 teaspoons baking soda
- 1 teaspoon salt
  Sugar

In large bowl, beat sugar, brown sugar and margarine until light and fluffy. Add vanilla, eggs, unsweetened chocolate and food color; blend well. Stir in flour, baking soda and salt; mix well. Cover with plastic wrap; refrigerate 1 to 2 hours for easier handling.

Heat oven to 350°F. Lightly grease cookie sheets. Shape dough into 1½-inch balls; roll in sugar. Place 3 inches apart on greased cookie sheets. Bake at 350°F. for 8 to 12 minutes or until set. (Cookies will puff up and then flatten during baking.) Cool 1 minute; remove from cookie sheets. Cool completely.
Yield: 6 dozen cookies.

HIGH ALTITUDE:
Above 3500 Feet: No change.

NUTRITION PER SERVING:
Calories 110; Protein 1g; Carbohydrate 15g; Fat 5g; Sodium 110mg.

Triple Chocolate Strip Cookies

~

Make dozens of chocolate cookies in minutes by baking the rich chocolate dough in logs and then cutting them into strips.

COOKIES
- 2 cups all purpose flour
- ½ cup unsweetened cocoa
- ½ teaspoon baking soda
- ¼ teaspoon salt
- ¾ cup sugar
- ½ cup firmly packed brown sugar
- ¾ cup margarine or butter, softened
- 2 eggs
- 1 (12-oz.) pkg. (2 cups) semi-sweet chocolate chips

WHITE CHOCOLATE GLAZE
- 2 oz. white chocolate or vanilla-flavored candy coating

CHOCOLATE GLAZE
- 2 oz. semi-sweet chocolate, cut into pieces
- ½ teaspoon margarine or butter

Heat oven to 350°F. Lightly grease 2 cookie sheets. In medium bowl, combine flour, cocoa, baking soda and salt. In large bowl, beat sugar, brown sugar and ¾ cup margarine until light and fluffy. Add eggs; blend well. Stir in flour mixture; mix well. Stir in chocolate chips. Divide dough into 4 equal portions. Shape each portion into a 12-inch roll. Place 2 rolls 2 inches apart on each greased cookie sheet.

Bake at 350°F. for 14 to 18 minutes or until toothpick inserted in center of each roll comes out almost clean. Remove from cookie sheets; cool on wire racks 10 minutes.

In small heavy saucepan over low heat, melt white chocolate. Drizzle over 2 rolls. In same saucepan, melt semi-sweet chocolate and ½ teaspoon margarine. Drizzle over remaining 2 rolls. Let stand until glazes are set. Cut rolls diagonally into 1-inch strips.

Yield: 4 dozen cookies.

HIGH ALTITUDE:
Above 3500 Feet: No change.

NUTRITION PER SERVING:
Calories 130; Protein 1g; Carbohydrate 15g; Fat 7g; Sodium 65mg.

Split Seconds

~

You'll enjoy this unique method for making delicious shortbread cookies. Choose your favorite flavor of jelly or preserves to make this 1954 Pillsbury BAKE-OFF® Contest classic.

- ¾ cup margarine or butter, softened
- ⅔ cup sugar
- 2 teaspoons vanilla
- 1 egg
- 2 cups all purpose flour
- ½ teaspoon baking powder
- ½ cup red jelly or preserves

Heat oven to 350°F. In large bowl, beat margarine and sugar until light and fluffy. Add vanilla and egg; blend well. Stir in flour and baking powder; mix well. Divide dough into 4 equal parts. On lightly floured surface, shape each part into 12x¾-inch roll; place on ungreased cookie sheets. Using handle of wooden spoon or finger, make depression about ½ inch wide and ¼ inch deep lengthwise down center of each roll. Fill each roll with 2 tablespoons jelly.

Bake at 350°F. for 15 to 20 minutes or until light golden brown. Cool slightly; cut diagonally into strips. Cool completely on wire racks.

Yield: 4 dozen cookies.

HIGH ALTITUDE:
Above 3500 Feet: No change.

NUTRITION PER SERVING:
Calories 70; Protein 1g; Carbohydrate 9g; Fat 3g; Sodium 40mg.

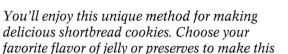

Split Seconds

APRICOT SNOWCAPS

A drizzle of white chocolate adds a special touch to these thumbprint-style cookies.

COOKIES
- ½ **cup sugar**
- ½ **cup firmly packed brown sugar**
- ¼ **cup margarine or butter, softened**
- ¼ **cup shortening**
- ½ **teaspoon vanilla**
- 1 **egg**
- 1 **cup all purpose flour**
- ½ **teaspoon baking powder**
- ½ **teaspoon baking soda**
- ½ **teaspoon salt**
- 1 **cup quick-cooking rolled oats**
- ½ **cup prepared apricot filling**

GLAZE
- 1 **(6-oz.) pkg. white baking bars, chopped**
- 2 **tablespoons shortening**

Heat oven to 350°F. In large bowl, beat sugar, brown sugar, margarine and ¼ cup shortening until light and fluffy. Add vanilla and egg; blend well. Add flour, baking powder, baking soda and salt; mix well. Stir in rolled oats. Shape dough into 1-inch balls; place 2 inches apart on ungreased cookie sheets. Make a small indentation in each cookie; fill with ½ teaspoon apricot filling.

Bake at 350°F. for 9 to 13 minutes or until light golden brown. Cool 1 minute; remove from cookie sheets. Meanwhile, in small saucepan over very low heat, melt glaze ingredients. Spoon or drizzle over warm cookies. Cool completely.

Yield: 3 dozen cookies.

HIGH ALTITUDE:
Above 3500 Feet: Decrease sugar to ⅓ cup; increase flour to 1⅓ cups. Bake as directed above.

NUTRITION PER SERVING:
Calories 110; Protein 1g; Carbohydrate 14g; Fat 5g; Sodium 70mg.

ALMOND KISS COOKIES

For a special occasion, these pretty cookies can be made ahead and frozen. Place the cookies between sheets of waxed paper in a tightly covered container and freeze them for up to 6 months.

COOKIES
- ½ **cup sugar**
- ½ **cup firmly packed brown sugar**
- ½ **cup margarine or butter, softened**
- ½ **cup shortening**
- 1 **teaspoon almond extract**
- 1 **egg**
- 2 **cups all purpose flour**
- 1 **teaspoon baking soda**
- ¼ **teaspoon salt**
-   **Sugar**
- 48 **almond-filled milk chocolate candy kisses**

GLAZE
- ¼ **cup seedless raspberry preserves or red currant jelly**
- ¼ **teaspoon almond extract**

In large bowl, beat sugar, brown sugar, margarine and shortening until light and fluffy. Add 1 teaspoon almond extract and egg; blend well. Stir in flour, baking soda and salt; mix well. Cover with plastic wrap; refrigerate 1 hour for easier handling.

Heat oven to 325°F. Shape dough into 1-inch balls; roll in sugar. Place 2 inches apart on ungreased cookie sheets. Bake at 325°F. for 7 to 12 minutes or until light golden brown. Immediately top each cookie with a candy kiss, pressing down gently. Remove from cookie sheets.

In small bowl, combine glaze ingredients; blend well. Drizzle over cookies. Cool completely.

Yield: 4 dozen cookies.

HIGH ALTITUDE:
Above 3500 Feet: No change.

NUTRITION PER SERVING:
Calories 110; Protein 1g; Carbohydrate 13g; Fat 6g; Sodium 65mg.

LEBKUCHEN

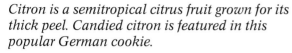

Citron is a semitropical citrus fruit grown for its thick peel. Candied citron is featured in this popular German cookie.

COOKIES
- 1 **cup honey**
- ¾ **cup firmly packed brown sugar**
- 1 **tablespoon grated lemon peel**
- 1 **egg, beaten**
- 2½ **cups all purpose flour**
- ½ **teaspoon baking soda**
- ½ **teaspoon salt**
- 1 **teaspoon cinnamon**
- 1 **teaspoon nutmeg**
- 1 **teaspoon ginger**
- ½ **to 1 teaspoon cloves**
- ½ **teaspoon allspice**
- ¼ **cup chopped candied orange peel**
- ¼ **cup chopped candied citron**
- ⅓ **cup chopped almonds**
  Sliced almonds

GLAZE
- ½ **cup powdered sugar**
- ⅛ **teaspoon almond extract**
- 2 **to 4 tablespoons water**

Heat honey in medium saucepan over medium heat just until it begins to bubble; do not boil. Remove from heat; cool. Stir in brown sugar, lemon peel and egg. In large bowl, combine flour and remaining cookie ingredients except sliced almonds. Add honey mixture; mix well. Cover with plastic wrap; refrigerate 1 to 2 hours for easier handling.

Heat oven to 400°F. Grease cookie sheets. In small bowl, combine glaze ingredients, adding enough water for desired glaze consistency; blend until smooth. Cover; set aside.

Shape dough into 1-inch balls. Place 2 inches apart on greased cookie sheets. Gently press balls to ¼-inch thickness with glass dipped in cool water. Gently press 1 almond slice in center of each cookie.

Bake at 400°F. for 5 to 9 minutes or until set. Immediately remove from cookie sheets. Immediately brush cookies with glaze. Cool completely.
Yield: 5 dozen cookies.

TIP:
For softer cookies, store with a slice of apple in a tightly covered container. Replace apple slice frequently.

HIGH ALTITUDE:
Above 3500 Feet: Decrease brown sugar to ½ cup; increase flour to 2½ cups plus 2 tablespoons. Bake as directed above.

NUTRITION PER SERVING:
Calories 60; Protein 1g; Carbohydrate 14g; Fat 1g; Sodium 35mg.

MOLASSES SPRITZ COOKIES

The delightful aroma of these cookies while baking will conjure up memories of Christmases past. This spicy cookie is a delicious variation of the traditional butter spritz cookie.

- ½ **cup sugar**
- ½ **cup margarine or butter, softened**
- ½ **cup molasses**
- 4 **teaspoons boiling water**
- 1¾ **cups all purpose flour**
- 1 **teaspoon baking soda**
- 1½ **teaspoons ginger**

In large bowl, beat sugar and margarine until light and fluffy. Add molasses and water; blend well. Stir in flour, baking soda and ginger; mix well. Cover with plastic wrap; refrigerate 1 hour for easier handling.

Heat oven to 375°F. Fill cookie press; using star tip, form cookies in 2 to 3-inch "S" shapes 1 inch apart on ungreased cookie sheets. Bake at 375°F. for 5 to 7 minutes or until set. Cool 1 minute; remove from cookie sheets. Cool completely.
Yield: 5 to 6 dozen cookies.

HIGH ALTITUDE:
Above 3500 Feet: Decrease sugar to ¼ cup; increase flour to 2 cups. Bake as directed above.

NUTRITION PER SERVING:
Calories 35; Protein 0g; Carbohydrate 5g; Fat 1g; Sodium 30mg.

THUMBPRINTS

Only a few ingredients are needed to make these tasty cookies.

- ½ **cup sugar**
- 1 **cup margarine or butter, softened**
- 1 **teaspoon vanilla**
- 2 **egg yolks**
- 2¼ **cups all purpose flour**
- 1 **teaspoon baking powder**
- ¼ **cup any flavor jam or preserves**

In medium bowl, beat sugar, margarine, vanilla and egg yolks until light and fluffy. Gradually add flour and baking powder; mix well. Cover with plastic wrap; refrigerate 30 minutes for easier handling.

Heat oven to 350°F. Shape dough into 1-inch balls; place 2 inches apart on ungreased cookie sheets. With thumb, make imprint in center of each cookie. Bake at 350°F. for 11 to 14 minutes or until light golden brown around edges. Spoon about ¼ teaspoon jam into each baked cookie. Cool completely.

Yield: 3½ dozen cookies.

HIGH ALTITUDE:
Above 3500 Feet: No change.

NUTRITION PER SERVING:
Calories 80; Protein 1g; Carbohydrate 9g; Fat 5g; Sodium 60mg.

VARIATIONS:

CUSTARD-FILLED THUMBPRINTS: Prepare and shape cookie dough as directed above; do not bake. In small saucepan, combine 1 tablespoon sugar, 1 tablespoon flour and ¼ teaspoon almond extract. Gradually add ½ cup whipping cream or half-and-half; cook over low heat until smooth and thickened, stirring constantly. In small bowl, blend 2 tablespoons hot mixture into 1 slightly beaten egg yolk. Return to saucepan; blend well. Cook just until mixture bubbles, stirring constantly. Cool. Spoon ½ teaspoon filling into each *unbaked* cookie. Bake as directed above. Omit jam. Store cookies in refrigerator.

LEMON-FILLED THUMBPRINTS: Prepare and bake cookies as directed above. Omit jam. In medium saucepan, combine 1 beaten egg, ⅔ cup sugar, 2 to 3 teaspoons grated lemon peel, 1 teaspoon cornstarch, ¼ teaspoon salt, 3 tablespoons lemon juice and 1 tablespoon margarine or butter. Cook over low heat until smooth and thickened, stirring constantly. Cool filling slightly. Spoon ¼ teaspoon filling into each *baked* cookie. Sprinkle with powdered sugar or coconut. Store cookies in refrigerator.

SPRITZ

Spritz are delightful Scandinavian cookies formed into fanciful shapes by forcing dough through a cookie press. The name comes from "spritzen," which is German for "to squirt or spray."

- 1 **cup powdered sugar**
- 1 **cup margarine or butter, softened**
- ½ **teaspoon vanilla**
- 1 **egg**
- 2⅓ **cups all purpose flour**
- ¼ **teaspoon salt**

Heat oven to 400°F. In large bowl, beat powdered sugar, margarine, vanilla and egg until light and fluffy. Stir in flour and salt; blend well. Fit cookie press with desired plate. Fill cookie press; press dough onto ungreased cookie sheets.

Bake at 400°F. for 5 to 7 minutes or until lightly browned on edges. Immediately remove from cookie sheets. Cool completely.

Yield: 5 dozen cookies.

HIGH ALTITUDE:
Above 3500 Feet: No change.

NUTRITION PER SERVING:
Calories 50; Protein 1g; Carbohydrate 5g; Fat 3g; Sodium 45mg.

VARIATIONS:

CHOCOLATE SPRITZ: Add 2 oz. melted unsweetened chocolate to powdered sugar mixture.

EGGNOG SPRITZ: Substitute 1 teaspoon rum flavoring for vanilla. Add ¼ teaspoon nutmeg with dry ingredients.

ORANGE SPRITZ: Add 1 tablespoon grated orange peel with dry ingredients.

Spritz

Molasses Jack-O'-Lantern Cookies

~

A great recipe for a children's party.

COOKIES
- 1 cup sugar
- ½ cup margarine or butter, softened
- ⅓ cup molasses
- 1 egg
- 2 cups all purpose flour
- 2 teaspoons grated orange peel
- 1½ teaspoons baking soda
- 1 teaspoon cinnamon
- ½ teaspoon ginger
- ¼ teaspoon salt
- ¼ teaspoon cloves

ICING
- 1 recipe Buttery Decorator Icing p. 184
- 3 drops red food color
- 6 drops yellow food color
- 4 drops green food color
  Miniature chocolate chips
  Candy corn
  Gumdrops

In large bowl, beat sugar and margarine until light and fluffy. Add molasses and egg; blend well. Stir in flour and remaining cookie ingredients; mix well. Cover with plastic wrap; refrigerate 1 to 3 hours for easier handling.

Heat oven to 350°F. On well-floured surface, roll half of dough at a time to ⅛-inch thickness. Keep remaining dough refrigerated. Cut with floured 3-inch pumpkin-shaped or round cookie cutter. Place 1 inch apart on ungreased cookie sheets. Bake at 350°F. for 6 to 9 minutes or until set. Immediately remove from cookie sheets.

In small bowl, combine half of Buttery Decorator Icing, 3 drops red food color and 3 drops of the yellow food color; blend well to make orange icing. Divide remaining icing mixture in half; place in 2 small bowls. Add 4 drops green food color to 1 bowl and remaining 3 drops yellow food color to second bowl; blend each well. To decorate cookies, frost each cookie with orange-colored icing. Use green and yellow icings, chocolate chips, candy corn and gumdrops to make faces on frosted cookies.
Yield: 24 cookies.

Molasses Jack-O'-Lantern Cookies

HIGH ALTITUDE:
Above 3500 Feet: Decrease sugar to ⅔ cup; increase flour to 2½ cups. Bake as directed above.

NUTRITION PER SERVING:
Calories 220; Protein 1g; Carbohydrate 35g; Fat 9g; Sodium 160mg.

Linzer Stars

~

Red jelly is sandwiched between tender cookies.

- ½ cup sugar
- ½ cup margarine or butter, softened
- 1 tablespoon milk
- 1 teaspoon vanilla
- 1 egg
- 1¼ cups all purpose flour
- 1 teaspoon cream of tartar
- ½ teaspoon baking soda
- ¼ teaspoon salt
  Powdered sugar
- ½ cup cherry or red currant jelly

In large bowl, beat sugar and margarine until light and fluffy. Add milk, vanilla and egg; blend well. Stir in flour, cream of tartar, baking soda and salt; mix well. Cover with plastic wrap; refrigerate 3 hours for easier handling.

Heat oven to 425°F. Using cloth-covered rolling pin and well-floured pastry cloth, roll out ⅓ of dough at a time to ⅛-inch thickness. Keep remaining dough refrigerated. Cut with floured 3-inch star-shaped cookie cutter. Using 1-inch round cookie cutter, cut out center of half of dough stars to form cookie tops. Place stars 1 inch apart on ungreased cookie sheets. Return dough centers to remaining dough for rerolling.

Bake at 425°F. for 3 to 5 minutes or until edges are light golden brown. Cool 1 minute; remove from cookie sheets. Cool completely. To assemble cookies, sprinkle powdered sugar over tops of cut-out cookies. Spread ½ teaspoon jelly over bottom side of each whole cookie. Place sugar-topped cookie over jelly.
Yield: 4 dozen sandwich cookies.

HIGH ALTITUDE:
Above 3500 Feet: Increase flour to 1¼ cups plus 2 tablespoons. Bake as directed above.

NUTRITION PER SERVING:
Calories 50; Protein 1g; Carbohydrate 7g; Fat 2g; Sodium 45mg.

Grandma's Date-Filled Cookies

GRANDMA'S DATE-FILLED COOKIES

~

Only a few ingredients combine to create a soft, old-fashioned filled cookie. For the filling, chop up whole pitted dates or purchase chopped dates.

COOKIES
1½ cups firmly packed brown sugar
 1 cup margarine or butter, softened
 1 teaspoon vanilla
 3 eggs
3½ cups all purpose flour
 1 teaspoon baking soda

FILLING
 2 cups chopped dates
 1 cup sugar
 1 cup water

In large bowl, beat brown sugar and margarine until light and fluffy. Add vanilla and eggs; beat well. Stir in flour and baking soda; mix well. Cover with plastic wrap; refrigerate at least 2 hours for easier handling.

Meanwhile, in medium saucepan combine all filling ingredients. Bring to a boil; reduce heat and simmer 10 minutes, stirring frequently. Refrigerate until ready to use. (Mixture will thicken as it cools.)

Heat oven to 375°F. On well-floured surface, roll out ⅓ of dough at a time to ⅛-inch thickness. Keep remaining dough refrigerated. Cut with floured 2½-inch round cookie cutter. In half of cookies, cut and remove 1-inch round hole or desired shape from center.* Place whole cookies on ungreased cookie sheet. Spoon 1 teaspoon cooled filling onto center of each. Top with dough ring. Using finger-tips or fork, press edges of dough to seal. Repeat with remaining dough and filling. Bake at 375°F. for 7 to 10 minutes or until light golden brown.
Yield: 3½ dozen cookies.

TIP:
* The center of a doughnut cutter or canape cutters can be used.

HIGH ALTITUDE:
Above 3500 Feet: No change.

NUTRITION PER SERVING:
Calories 150; Protein 2g; Carbohydrate 27g; Fat 5g;
Sodium 90mg.

OLD-FASHIONED SUGAR COOKIES

This sensational cookie recipe of German origin is a Christmas Eve tradition in many families. Crushed caraway seed combined with tiny candy sprinkles add a wonderfully unique flavor.

COOKIES

- 3 cups all purpose flour
- 1 teaspoon baking powder
- 1 teaspoon baking soda
- 1/8 teaspoon salt
- 1 cup margarine or butter
- 2 eggs
- 1 1/2 cups sugar
- 1 teaspoon vanilla
- 1/2 teaspoon lemon extract

FROSTING

- 2 cups powdered sugar
- 1/3 cup margarine or butter, softened
- 1/2 teaspoon vanilla
- 1 to 2 tablespoons half-and-half or milk

TOPPING

- 1/4 cup multi-colored candy sprinkles or chocolate sprinkles
- 1/2 to 1 teaspoon crushed caraway seed

In large bowl, combine flour, baking powder, baking soda and salt; mix well. Using fork or pastry blender, cut in 1 cup margarine until mixture is crumbly.

In small bowl, beat eggs. Gradually add sugar, 1 teaspoon vanilla and lemon extract, beating until light. Add to flour mixture in large bowl. Stir by hand until dough forms. (If necessary, knead dough with hands to mix in dry ingredients.) Cover with plastic wrap; refrigerate 1 hour for easier handling.

Heat oven to 375°F. On lightly floured surface, roll out 1/3 of dough at a time to 1/8-inch thickness. Keep remaining dough refrigerated. Cut with 2 1/2 to 3-inch floured cookie cutters. Place 1 inch apart on ungreased cookie sheets.

Bake at 375°F. for 6 to 11 minutes or until edges are light golden brown. Immediately remove from cookie sheets. Cool completely.

In small bowl, combine all frosting ingredients, adding enough half-and-half for desired piping consistency; blend until smooth. In shallow bowl, combine topping ingredients. Using decorating bag fitted with large writing tip or small star tip, pipe several 1/4 to 1/2-inch dollops of frosting on each cookie. Sprinkle immediately with topping to coat frosting dollops. Let stand until set.
Yield: 4 to 5 dozen cookies.

HIGH ALTITUDE:
Above 3500 Feet: Increase flour to 3 1/4 cups; decrease sugar to 1 1/4 cups. Bake as directed above.

NUTRITION PER SERVING:
Calories 100; Protein 1g; Carbohydrate 13g; Fat 4g; Sodium 75mg.

LEMON BLACK-EYED SUSAN COOKIES

- 1 cup sugar
- 1 cup margarine or butter, softened
- 3 tablespoons lemon juice
- 1 egg
- 3 cups all purpose flour
- 1 1/2 teaspoons baking powder
- 1/4 teaspoon salt
- 1 egg yolk
- 1 teaspoon water
  Few drops yellow food color
- 3/4 cup semi-sweet chocolate chips

In large bowl, beat sugar and margarine until light and fluffy. Add lemon juice and egg; blend well. Stir in flour, baking powder and salt; mix well. Cover with plastic wrap; refrigerate 1 hour for easier handling.

Heat oven to 400°F. On lightly floured surface, roll half of dough at a time to 1/4-inch thickness. Keep remaining dough refrigerated. Cut with floured 2 to 3-inch flower-shaped cookie cutter. Place 1 inch apart on ungreased cookie sheets. In small bowl, combine egg yolk and water; blend well. Stir in food color. Brush tops of cookies with egg yolk mixture.

Bake at 400°F. for 5 to 7 minutes or until edges are light golden brown. Immediately place chocolate chip in center of each cookie. Remove from cookie sheets.
Yield: 5 1/2 dozen cookies.

HIGH ALTITUDE:
Above 3500 Feet: No change.

NUTRITION PER SERVING:
Calories 70; Protein 1g; Carbohydrate 9g; Fat 4g; Sodium 50mg.

CHOCOLATE VALENTINE COOKIES

Bake a batch of these special heart-shaped cookies for that special Valentine's Day party. A creamy cherry filling is sandwiched between chocolate cookies.

COOKIES
- 1 cup sugar
- 1 cup margarine or butter, softened
- 1/4 cup milk
- 1 teaspoon vanilla
- 1 egg
- 2 3/4 cups all purpose flour
- 1/2 cup unsweetened cocoa
- 3/4 teaspoon baking powder
- 1/4 teaspoon baking soda

FROSTING
- 2 cups powdered sugar
- 1/2 cup margarine or butter, softened
  Red food color
- 2 to 3 tablespoons maraschino cherry liquid or milk

In large bowl, beat sugar and 1 cup margarine until light and fluffy. Add milk, vanilla and egg; blend well. Stir in flour, cocoa, baking powder and baking soda; mix well. Cover with plastic wrap; refrigerate 1 hour for easier handling.

Heat oven to 350°F. On floured surface, roll out 1/3 of dough at a time to 1/8-inch thickness. Keep remaining dough refrigerated. Cut with floured 2 1/2-inch heart-shaped cookie cutter. Place half of the hearts 1 inch apart on ungreased cookie sheets. Cut a 1-inch heart-shape from the centers of remaining hearts. Place cut-out hearts on cookie sheets. Return small hearts to remaining dough for rerolling.

Bake at 350°F. for 9 to 11 minutes or until set. Immediately remove from cookie sheets; cool completely.

In small bowl, combine all frosting ingredients, adding enough cherry liquid for desired spreading consistency; blend until smooth. Frost bottom side of whole cookies. Place cut-out cookies over frosting.
Yield: 4 dozen sandwich cookies.

HIGH ALTITUDE:
Above 3500 Feet: Decrease baking powder to 1/4 teaspoon. Bake as directed above.

NUTRITION PER SERVING:
Calories 110; Protein 1g; Carbohydrate 14g; Fat 6g; Sodium 85mg.

SANDWICHED MINT SURPRISES

You'll notice that these cookies have no sugar in the dough. The sweetness comes from dipping the cookies in sugar and from the mints baked in the center.

- 2 cups all purpose flour
- 1 cup margarine or butter, softened
- 1/3 cup half-and-half
- 3 tablespoons unsweetened cocoa
- 1/2 teaspoon vanilla
  Sugar
- 36 thin pastel mint wafers

In large bowl, beat flour, margarine, half-and-half, cocoa and vanilla until well blended. Cover with plastic wrap; refrigerate 30 minutes for easier handling.

Heat oven to 375°F. Lightly grease cookie sheets. On lightly floured surface, roll half of dough to 1/8-inch thickness. Keep remaining dough refrigerated. Cut with lightly floured 2-inch round cookie cutter. Dip 1 side of each dough round in sugar. Place half of dough rounds, sugared side down, on greased cookie sheets. Place mint wafer in center of each dough round. Top each with second dough round, sugared side up. Press fork firmly around edges of each to seal.

Bake at 375°F. for 8 to 10 minutes or until set. Cool 1 minute; remove from cookie sheets.
Yield: 3 dozen cookies.

HIGH ALTITUDE:
Above 3500 Feet: No change.

NUTRITION PER SERVING:
Calories 100; Protein 1g; Carbohydrate 11g; Fat 6g; Sodium 75mg.

POPPY SEED SUGAR COOKIES

Orange and almond flavors and a poppy seed glaze combine to create a new version of the rolled sugar cookie. Cut them large for the cookie jar or small and dainty for parties.

COOKIES

1¼ cups sugar
⅔ cup margarine or butter, softened
1 teaspoon almond extract
1 teaspoon vanilla
1 teaspoon butter flavor, if desired
1 tablespoon orange juice
2 eggs
3 cups all purpose flour
2 tablespoons poppy seed
2 teaspoons baking powder
½ to 1 teaspoon salt

GLAZE

⅓ cup sugar
¼ teaspoon poppy seed
2 tablespoons orange juice
¼ teaspoon almond extract
¼ teaspoon vanilla
1 teaspoon butter flavor, if desired

In large bowl, beat 1¼ cups sugar, margarine, 1 teaspoon almond extract, 1 teaspoon vanilla and 1 teaspoon butter flavor until light and fluffy. Add 1 tablespoon orange juice and eggs; blend well. By hand, stir in flour, 2 tablespoons poppy seed, baking powder and salt until well blended. If necessary, refrigerate dough for easier handling or stir in small amount of flour until no longer sticky.

Heat oven to 350°F. On lightly floured surface, roll out ⅓ of dough at a time to ⅛ to ¼-inch thickness. Keep remaining dough refrigerated. Cut with 2½ to 3-inch cookie cutter of desired shape. Place 2 inches apart on ungreased cookie sheets.

Bake at 350°F. for 9 to 12 minutes or until light golden brown. While cookies are baking, combine all glaze ingredients; mix well. Immediately brush baked cookies with glaze, stirring glaze occasionally. Cool 1 minute; remove from cookie sheets. Let stand until glaze is set.
Yield: 2½ to 3 dozen cookies.

HIGH ALTITUDE:
Above 3500 Feet: No change.

NUTRITION PER SERVING:
Calories 110; Protein 2g; Carbohydrate 17g; Fat 4g; Sodium 120mg.

BROWN SUGAR CUTOUTS

These caramel-flavored cookies are wonderful just as they are; however, for a holiday cookie tray you may wish to decorate them with a simple vanilla icing.

1 cup margarine or butter, softened
1 cup firmly packed brown sugar
1 teaspoon vanilla
1 egg
2½ cups all purpose flour
½ teaspoon baking soda

In large bowl, beat margarine and brown sugar until light and fluffy. Add vanilla and egg; blend well. Stir in flour and baking soda; mix well. Cover with plastic wrap; refrigerate 1 to 2 hours for easier handling.

Heat oven to 375°F. On floured surface, roll out ⅓ of dough at a time to ⅛-inch thickness. Keep remaining dough refrigerated. Cut with floured 1¾ to 2-inch cookie cutter. Place 1 inch apart on ungreased cookie sheets.

Bake at 375°F. for 5 to 8 minutes or until light golden brown. Immediately remove from cookie sheets.
Yield: 4 dozen cookies.

HIGH ALTITUDE:
Above 3500 Feet: Increase flour to 3 cups. Bake as directed above.

NUTRITION PER SERVING:
Calories 80; Protein 1g; Carbohydrate 9g; Fat 4g; Sodium 60mg.

STEP-BY-STEP FEATURE ～
How to Make Cut-Out Cookies

STEP 1. Dust a rolling pin and flat, smooth surface with flour. Use just enough flour to prevent sticking. Shape a portion of dough into a flattened ball.

STEP 2. With light strokes, roll from the center of the dough to the edges. Repeat until dough is of uniform desired thickness.

STEP 3. Cut out dough with floured cookie cutter, cutting shapes close together. Transfer cookies to an ungreased cookie sheet using a pancake turner.

WHOLE WHEAT GINGERBREAD BOYS AND GIRLS

Create a variety of gingerbread folks using various sized cookie cutters. Let imaginations run wild as children help to decorate them with frosting and small candies.

COOKIES

1½ **cups sugar**
1 **cup margarine or butter, softened**
⅓ **cup molasses**
1 **egg**
2¼ **cups all purpose flour**
1 **cup whole wheat flour**
2 **teaspoons baking soda**
½ **teaspoon salt**
2 **teaspoons ginger**
2 **teaspoons cinnamon**

FROSTING AND DECORATIONS

2 **cups powdered sugar**
⅓ **cup margarine or butter, softened**
½ **teaspoon vanilla**
1 **to 2 tablespoons half-and-half or milk**
   Assorted small candies, if desired

In large bowl, beat sugar and 1 cup margarine until light and fluffy. Add molasses and egg; blend well. Stir in all purpose and whole wheat flour, baking soda, salt, ginger and cinnamon; mix well. If necessary, cover with plastic wrap and refrigerate 1 hour for easier handling.

Heat oven to 350°F. On lightly floured surface, roll out ¼ of dough at a time to ⅛-inch thickness. Keep remaining dough refrigerated. Cut with floured 5-inch (or desired size) gingerbread boy and girl cookie cutters. Place 1 inch apart on ungreased cookie sheets. If desired, move arms and legs of unbaked cookies for different poses. Cut scraps of dough into hats, scarves, etc.; place on cookie sheet against or slightly overlapping cookies.

Bake at 350°F. for 6 to 9 minutes or until set. Cool 1 minute. Remove from cookie sheets. Cool completely.

(Recipe continued on next page.)

Whole Wheat Gingerbread Boys and Girls

(Recipe continued from previous page.)

In medium bowl, combine powdered sugar, ⅓ cup margarine, vanilla and enough half-and-half for desired spreading or piping consistency; blend until smooth. Frost and decorate as desired. Let stand until frosting is set. Store in loosely covered container.

Yield: 2½ dozen cookies.

HIGH ALTITUDE:
Above 3500 Feet: Decrease sugar to 1 cup; increase all purpose flour to 2¾ cups. Bake as directed above.

NUTRITION PER SERVING:
Calories 210; Protein 2g; Carbohydrate 33g; Fat 9g; Sodium 210mg.

FROSTED GINGERBREAD CUTOUTS

Cinnamon, ginger, cardamom and cloves flavor these cookies.

COOKIES

1½ **cups sugar**
  1 **cup margarine or butter, softened**
  3 **tablespoons molasses**
  1 **egg**
  2 **tablespoons water or milk**
3¼ **cups all purpose flour**
  2 **teaspoons baking soda**
  ½ **teaspoon salt**
  2 **teaspoons cinnamon**
1½ **teaspoons ginger**
  ½ **teaspoon cardamom**
  ½ **teaspoon cloves**

FROSTING

  ¾ **cup water**
  1 **envelope unflavored gelatin**
  ¾ **cup sugar**
  ¾ **cup powdered sugar**
  1 **teaspoon baking powder**
  1 **teaspoon vanilla**

In large bowl, beat 1½ cups sugar, margarine and molasses until light and fluffy. Add egg and 2 tablespoons water; blend well. Stir in flour, baking soda, salt, cinnamon, ginger, cardamom and cloves; mix well to form a smooth dough. Cover with plastic wrap; refrigerate 1 hour for easier handling.

Heat oven to 350°F. On floured surface, roll out ⅓ of dough to ⅛-inch thickness. Keep remaining dough refrigerated. Cut with floured 2½-inch cookie cutters. Place 1 inch apart on ungreased cookie sheets. Repeat with remaining dough. Bake at 350°F. for 9 to 11 minutes or until set. Immediately remove from cookie sheets. Cool completely.

In 2-quart saucepan, combine ¾ cup water and gelatin; let stand 5 minutes. Stir in ¾ cup sugar; bring to a boil. Reduce heat; simmer 10 minutes. Stir in powdered sugar; beat until foamy. Stir in baking powder and vanilla; beat at highest speed until thick, about 10 minutes. Spread frosting on cooled cookies or pipe frosting following outline of cookies. Allow frosting to set for several hours before storing.

Yield: 8 to 10 dozen cookies.

HIGH ALTITUDE :
Above 3500 Feet: No change.

NUTRITION PER SERVING:
Calories 45; Protein 1g; Carbohydrate 7g; Fat 2g; Sodium 50mg.

COOK'S NOTE

GINGERBREAD HISTORY

Stories about gingerbread have appeared since the beginning of written history. The earliest gingerbread was made from bread crumbs, honey and spices; gradually the crumbs and honey were replaced by flour and molasses.

Ginger, the predominant spice in gingerbread, was used during the Middle Ages both as a preservative and as a medicine for a variety of ills. Because gingerbread did not spoil as quickly as other baked goods did in those days, it was thought to be somewhat magical.

For hundreds of years in Europe, cookies were made by pressing gingerbread into molds before baking. Spicy little figures of people and animals, sometimes decorated with edible gold paint, were sold at medieval fairs. In the 17th century, gingerbread baking was a profession in itself and gingerbread bakers alone had the right to make it, except at Christmas time, when everyone could make it.

DATE MAPLE CREAM BARS

Cooking the filling for this luscious bar softens the dates and thickens the mixture. These bars have delicious old-fashioned flavor and will remind you of the date bars that your grandma used to make.

FILLING
- ¾ **cup firmly packed brown sugar**
- 1 **tablespoon cornstarch**
- 1½ **cups finely chopped dates**
- 1½ **cups dairy sour cream**
- 1 **teaspoon maple extract**
- 3 **egg yolks**

BASE AND TOPPING
- 1¼ **cups all purpose flour**
- 2 **cups quick-cooking rolled oats**
- ¾ **cup firmly packed brown sugar**
- ½ **teaspoon baking soda**
- ¾ **cup margarine or butter**

Heat oven to 350°F. Grease 13x9-inch pan. In medium saucepan, combine all filling ingredients. Cook over medium heat until slightly thickened, stirring constantly. Cool slightly.

In medium bowl, combine flour, rolled oats, ¾ cup brown sugar and baking soda; mix well. With pastry blender or fork, cut in margarine until mixture is crumbly. Reserve 1½ cups oat mixture for topping. Press remaining oat mixture evenly in bottom of greased pan.

Bake at 350°F. for 10 minutes. Spoon filling evenly over base. Sprinkle with reserved oat mixture. Return to oven and bake an additional 20 to 30 minutes or until light golden brown and set. Cool completely. Cut into bars.
Yield: 36 bars.

HIGH ALTITUDE:
Above 3500 Feet: No change.

NUTRITION PER SERVING:
Calories 150; Protein 2g; Carbohydrate 21g; Fat 7g; Sodium 70mg.

KWIK-KRUMB RAISIN BARS

This yummy bar, filled with the goodness of raisins and applesauce, is perfect with a hot cup of coffee or tea.

FILLING
- 2½ **cups raisins**
- 1 **cup water**
- 1 **cup applesauce**
- 1 **teaspoon lemon juice**
- ¼ **teaspoon cinnamon**

BASE AND TOPPING
- 2 **cups rolled oats**
- 1 **cup all purpose flour**
- ½ **cup sugar**
- ½ **cup coconut**
- ¾ **cup margarine or butter**

In medium saucepan, bring raisins and water to a boil. Reduce heat; simmer 15 minutes. Drain; stir in applesauce, lemon juice and cinnamon. Set aside.

Heat oven to 350°F. In large bowl, combine oats, flour, sugar and coconut. Using pastry blender or fork, cut in margarine until mixture resembles coarse crumbs. Reserve 2½ cups of crumb mixture for topping. Press remaining crumb mixture firmly in bottom of ungreased 13x9-inch pan. Spread evenly with filling. Sprinkle with reserved crumb mixture; press lightly.

Bake at 350°F. for 30 to 40 minutes or until light golden brown. Cool completely. Cut into bars.
Yield: 36 bars.

HIGH ALTITUDE:
Above 3500 Feet: No change.

NUTRITION PER SERVING:
Calories 120; Protein 1g; Carbohydrate 18g; Fat 5g; Sodium 45mg.

APRICOT ALMOND SQUARES

Delicate fruit flavor and a streusel topping make this bar a luscious choice for a party tray.

BASE
- 1 (18.5-oz.) pkg. pudding-included yellow or white cake mix
- ½ cup margarine or butter, melted
- ½ cup finely chopped almonds
- 1 cup apricot preserves

FILLING
- 1 (8-oz.) pkg. cream cheese, softened
- ¼ cup sugar
- 2 tablespoons all purpose flour
- ⅛ teaspoon salt
- 1 teaspoon vanilla
- 1 egg
- ⅓ cup apricot preserves
- ½ cup coconut

Heat oven to 350°F. Generously grease 13x9-inch pan. In large bowl, combine cake mix and margarine; mix at low speed until crumbly. Stir in almonds. Reserve 1 cup base mixture for filling. Press remaining mixture in bottom of greased pan. Carefully spread 1 cup preserves over base.*

In same bowl, beat cream cheese, sugar, flour, salt, vanilla and egg until well blended. Stir in ⅓ cup preserves at low speed. Carefully spread filling mixture over base. Combine reserved 1 cup base mixture and coconut; sprinkle over filling.

Bake at 350°F. for 30 to 40 minutes or until golden brown and center is set. Cool completely. Cut into bars. Store in refrigerator.

Yield: 36 bars.

TIP:
* For ease in spreading, preserves can be warmed slightly.

HIGH ALTITUDE:
Above 3500 Feet: No change.

NUTRITION PER SERVING:
Calories 160; Protein 2g; Carbohydrate 22g; Fat 8g; Sodium 150mg.

CARAMEL APPLE BARS

This is the perfect recipe when apples are plentiful. Caramel ice cream topping combines with apples and nuts for rich, moist bars.

CRUST
- 2 cups all purpose flour
- 2 cups quick-cooking rolled oats
- 1½ cups firmly packed brown sugar
- 1 teaspoon baking soda
- 1¼ cups margarine or butter, melted

FILLING
- 1½ cups caramel ice cream topping
- ½ cup all purpose flour
- 2 cups coarsely chopped apples
- ½ cup chopped walnuts or pecans

Heat oven to 350°F. Grease 15x10x1-inch baking pan. In large bowl, combine all crust ingredients; mix at low speed until crumbly. Press half of crumb mixture, about 2½ cups, in greased pan. Reserve remaining crumb mixture for topping. Bake at 350°F. for 8 minutes.

In small saucepan over medium heat, combine caramel topping and ½ cup flour. Bring to a boil, stirring constantly. Boil 3 to 5 minutes or until mixture thickens slightly, stirring constantly. Sprinkle apples and nuts onto warm base. Pour caramel mixture evenly over top. Sprinkle with reserved crumbs.

Return to oven and bake 20 to 25 minutes or until golden brown. Cool completely. Cut into bars.* Store in tightly covered container.

Yield: 48 bars.

TIP:
* For ease in cutting, refrigerate bars.

HIGH ALTITUDE:
Above 3500 Feet: Bake at 375°F. as directed above.

NUTRITION PER SERVING:
Calories 150; Protein 2g; Carbohydrate 22g; Fat 6g; Sodium 135mg.

OATMEAL CARMELITAS

This time-tested favorite is an often-requested recipe that is easy to make and delicious to eat. Prepare it for your next potluck or bake sale.

CRUST
- 2 cups all purpose flour
- 2 cups quick-cooking rolled oats
- 1½ cups firmly packed brown sugar
- 1 teaspoon baking soda
- ½ teaspoon salt
- 1¼ cups margarine or butter, softened

FILLING
- 1 (12.5-oz.) jar (1 cup) caramel ice cream topping
- 3 tablespoons all purpose flour
- 1 (6-oz.) pkg. (1 cup) semi-sweet chocolate chips
- ½ cup chopped nuts

Heat oven to 350°F. Grease 13x9-inch pan. In large bowl, blend all crust ingredients at low speed until crumbly. Press half of crumb mixture, about 3 cups, in bottom of greased pan. Reserve remaining crumb mixture for topping. Bake at 350°F. for 10 minutes. Meanwhile, in small bowl combine caramel topping and 3 tablespoons flour; set aside. Sprinkle warm crust with chocolate chips and nuts. Drizzle evenly with caramel mixture; sprinkle with reserved crumb mixture.

Return to oven and bake an additional 18 to 22 minutes or until golden brown. Cool completely. Refrigerate 1 to 2 hours or until filling is set. Cut into bars.

Yield: 36 bars.

HIGH ALTITUDE:
Above 3500 Feet: No change.

NUTRITION PER SERVING:
Calories 200; Protein 3g; Carbohydrate 27g; Fat 9g; Sodium 160mg.

OATMEAL CHOCOLATE CHIP BARS

Healthful oats help give these lunch box bars their chewy cookie texture.

- 1½ cups firmly packed brown sugar
- 1 cup shortening
- 2 tablespoons molasses
- 2 teaspoons vanilla
- 2 eggs
- 3 cups quick-cooking rolled oats
- 1 cup all purpose flour
- 1 teaspoon baking soda
- 1 teaspoon salt
- ¾ cup chopped nuts
- 1 (12-oz.) pkg. (2 cups) semi-sweet chocolate chips

Heat oven to 350°F. Grease 15x10x1 or 13x9-inch pan. In large bowl, beat brown sugar and shortening until light and fluffy. Add molasses, vanilla and eggs; blend well. Stir in oats, flour, baking soda and salt; blend well. Stir in nuts and chocolate chips. Spread in greased pan.

Bake at 350°F. for 20 to 25 minutes or until light golden brown and center is set. Cool slightly. Cut into bars. Serve warm or cool.

Yield: 48 bars.

HIGH ALTITUDE:
Above 3500 Feet: No change.

NUTRITION PER SERVING:
Calories 140; Protein 2g; Carbohydrate 17g; Fat 8g; Sodium 75mg.

COOK'S NOTE

BAKING BARS IN JELLY ROLL PANS

Follow specific recipe directions for pan sizes. Standard jelly roll pans are 15x10x1-inch. Using a jelly roll pan that does not have 1-inch sides may result in the recipe spilling out of the pan during baking.

Poppy Seed Squares

Delicate crumb layers that melt in your mouth surround a marvelous poppy seed filling. It's no wonder these bars were a favorite of our taste panel.

FILLING
- ⅓ cup poppy seed, ground*
- ⅓ cup almonds, ground*
- ⅓ cup sugar
- ⅓ cup milk
- 2 tablespoons margarine or butter
- ½ teaspoon almond extract
- 1 egg white

BASE
- 1¾ cups all purpose flour
- ¾ cup powdered sugar
- ⅓ cup ground almonds
- 1 teaspoon baking powder
- ¾ cup margarine or butter
- 1 teaspoon almond extract
- 1 egg yolk

To prepare filling, in small saucepan combine poppy seed, almonds, sugar and milk. Cook over medium heat 10 to 15 minutes or until thick and milk is absorbed. Cool 15 minutes. Stir in 2 tablespoons margarine, ½ teaspoon almond extract and egg white; blend well. Cool.

Heat oven to 350°F. In medium bowl, combine flour, powdered sugar, ⅓ cup ground almonds and baking powder. Using pastry blender or fork, cut in ¾ cup margarine until mixture resembles coarse crumbs. With fork, stir in 1 teaspoon almond extract and egg yolk. Press half of crumb mixture firmly in bottom of ungreased 9-inch square pan. Carefully spread with filling mixture. Sprinkle with remaining crumb mixture; pat lightly.

Bake at 350°F. for 25 to 33 minutes or until light golden brown. Cool completely. Cut into bars.
Yield: 25 bars.

TIP:
* Poppy seed and almonds can be ground together in blender at medium speed for 1 minute, scraping sides once.

HIGH ALTITUDE:
Above 3500 Feet: No change.

NUTRITION PER SERVING:
Calories 150; Protein 2g; Carbohydrate 14g; Fat 9g; Sodium 90mg.

Sunburst Lemon Bars

These home-baked lemon bars, with a delicate crumb crust and mouth-watering lemon filling, have been a favorite for generations, particularly for family gatherings and potlucks.

CRUST
- 2 cups all purpose flour
- ½ cup powdered sugar
- 1 cup margarine or butter, softened

FILLING
- 4 eggs, slightly beaten
- 2 cups sugar
- ¼ cup all purpose flour
- 1 teaspoon baking powder
- ¼ cup lemon juice

FROSTING
- 1 cup powdered sugar
- 2 to 3 tablespoons lemon juice

Heat oven to 350°F. In large bowl, combine all crust ingredients at low speed until crumbly. Press mixture evenly in bottom of ungreased 13x9-inch pan. Bake at 350°F. for 20 to 30 minutes or until light golden brown.

Meanwhile, in large bowl combine all filling ingredients except lemon juice; blend well. Stir in ¼ cup lemon juice. Pour mixture over warm crust.

Return to oven and bake an additional 25 to 30 minutes or until top is light golden brown. Cool completely.

In small bowl, combine 1 cup powdered sugar and enough lemon juice for desired spreading consistency; blend until smooth. Spread over cooled bars. Cut into bars.
Yield: 36 bars.

HIGH ALTITUDE:
Above 3500 Feet: No change.

NUTRITION PER SERVING:
Calories 140; Protein 2g; Carbohydrate 22g; Fat 6g; Sodium 75mg.

Sunburst Lemon Bars

GINGERBREAD BARS

Enjoy these not-too-sweet bars with hot apple cider on a crisp autumn day. Store them tightly covered.

- ½ cup sugar
- ½ cup oil
- ½ cup molasses
- 1 egg
- 1½ cups all purpose flour
- ¾ teaspoon baking soda
- ½ teaspoon cinnamon
- ¼ teaspoon salt
- ¼ teaspoon nutmeg
- ¼ teaspoon cloves
- ¼ cup boiling water
- ½ cup granola
- ½ cup raisins
  Powdered sugar, if desired

Heat oven to 350°F. Grease 13x9-inch pan. In large bowl, beat sugar, oil and molasses until well blended. Add egg; blend well. Add flour, baking soda, cinnamon, salt, nutmeg and cloves; mix well. Add boiling water; blend well. Stir in granola and raisins. Spread in greased pan.

Bake at 350°F. for 20 to 30 minutes or until toothpick inserted in center comes out clean. Cool completely. Sprinkle with powdered sugar. Cut into bars.

Yield: 36 bars.

HIGH ALTITUDE:
Above 3500 Feet: Increase flour to 2 cups; increase boiling water to ½ cup. Bake as directed above.

NUTRITION PER SERVING:
Calories 80; Protein 1g; Carbohydrate 12g; Fat 4g; Sodium 45mg.

SALTED PEANUT CHEWS

Reminiscent of a popular candy bar, these are sure to be a favorite with everyone.

CRUST
- 1½ cups all purpose flour
- ⅔ cup firmly packed brown sugar
- ½ teaspoon baking powder
- ½ teaspoon salt
- ¼ teaspoon baking soda
- ½ cup margarine or butter, softened
- 1 teaspoon vanilla
- 2 egg yolks
- 3 cups miniature marshmallows

TOPPING
- ⅔ cup corn syrup
- ¼ cup margarine or butter
- 2 teaspoons vanilla
- 1 (12-oz.) pkg. (2 cups) peanut butter chips
- 2 cups crisp rice cereal
- 2 cups salted peanuts

Heat oven to 350°F. In large bowl, combine all crust ingredients except marshmallows at low speed until crumbly. Press firmly in bottom of ungreased 13x9-inch pan.

Bake at 350°F. for 12 to 15 minutes or until light golden brown. Remove from oven. Immediately sprinkle with marshmallows. Return to oven and bake an additional 1 to 2 minutes or until marshmallows just begin to puff. Cool while preparing topping.

In large saucepan, combine all topping ingredients except cereal and peanuts; heat just until chips are melted and mixture is smooth, stirring constantly. Remove from heat; stir in cereal and peanuts. Immediately spoon warm topping over marshmallows; spread to cover. Refrigerate until firm. Cut into bars.

Yield: 36 bars.

HIGH ALTITUDE:
Above 3500 Feet: No change.

NUTRITION PER SERVING:
Calories 210; Protein 5g; Carbohydrate 23g; Fat 11g; Sodium 200mg.

AUSTRIAN CREAM CHEESE BARS

When the occasion is special, you'll enjoy this layered candy-like bar.

CRUST

1½ **cups all purpose flour**
1 **cup firmly packed brown sugar**
½ **teaspoon cinnamon**
⅔ **cup margarine or butter, softened**

TOPPING

1 **(8-oz.) pkg. cream cheese, softened**
¾ **cup sugar**
2 **tablespoons all purpose flour**
2 **eggs**
1 **(6-oz.) pkg. (1 cup) semi-sweet chocolate chips**

GLAZE

1 **(6-oz.) pkg. (1 cup) semi-sweet chocolate chips**
½ **to ¾ cup chopped pecans or walnuts, toasted, p. 23**

Heat oven to 350°F. In large bowl, combine all crust ingredients. Beat at medium speed about 2 minutes or until crumbly and well blended. Press mixture into ungreased 13x9-inch pan. Bake at 350°F. for 12 minutes. Remove from oven.

In small bowl, beat cream cheese, sugar, 2 tablespoons flour and eggs at medium speed until smooth, about 2 minutes. Stir in 1 cup chocolate chips. Pour over partially baked crust.

Return to oven and bake an additional 15 to 20 minutes or until topping is almost set. Remove from oven; immediately sprinkle 1 cup chocolate chips over top. Return to oven for 1 minute to melt chips. Gently spread melted chips over top. Sprinkle with pecans; lightly press into glaze. Refrigerate 1 hour. Cut into bars. Store in refrigerator.

Yield: 36 bars.

HIGH ALTITUDE:

Above 3500 Feet: Increase flour in crust to 1¾ cups. Bake as directed above.

NUTRITION PER SERVING:
Calories 190; Protein 2g; Carbohydrate 21g; Fat 11g; Sodium 60mg.

ROCKY ROAD CRESCENT BARS

Marshmallows, peanuts and chocolate chips top a creamy peanut butter filling and bake into a tempting sweet treat.

1 **(8-oz.) can refrigerated crescent dinner rolls**
½ **cup sugar**
¾ **cup peanut butter**
1 **(8-oz.) pkg. cream cheese, softened**
½ **cup corn syrup**
1 **teaspoon vanilla**
1 **egg**
1½ **cups miniature marshmallows**
¾ **cup salted peanuts or other nuts, chopped**
1 **(6-oz.) pkg. (1 cup) semi-sweet chocolate chips**

Heat oven to 375°F. Unroll dough into 2 long rectangles. Place in ungreased 13x9-inch pan; press over bottom to form crust. Firmly press perforations to seal. Bake at 375°F. for 5 minutes.

In medium bowl, combine sugar, peanut butter and cream cheese; blend until smooth. Stir in corn syrup, vanilla and egg; mix well. Pour mixture over partially baked crust; spread evenly. Sprinkle with marshmallows, peanuts and chocolate chips.

Return to oven and bake an additional 25 to 30 minutes or until filling is firm to touch. Cool completely. Refrigerate 1 to 2 hours. Cut into bars. Store in refrigerator.

Yield: 36 bars.

NUTRITION PER SERVING:
Calories 150; Protein 3g; Carbohydrate 15g; Fat 9g; Sodium 125mg.

CHEWY APPLESAUCE BARS

Muesli cereal is a blend of grains, fruits and nuts that has been a tradition in many parts of Europe for centuries. It adds texture, flavor and whole grain goodness to these breakfast bars.

BARS
- 1 cup firmly packed brown sugar
- ½ cup margarine or butter, softened
- 1 cup applesauce
- 1 egg
- 1½ cups all purpose flour
- 1 teaspoon baking soda
- 1 teaspoon cinnamon
- ¼ teaspoon salt
- ¼ teaspoon cloves
- ¼ teaspoon nutmeg
- 2 cups muesli cereal

GLAZE
- 2 tablespoons margarine or butter
- ¼ cup firmly packed brown sugar
- 1 teaspoon powdered sugar

Heat oven to 350°F. Grease and flour 13x9-inch pan. In large bowl, beat 1 cup brown sugar and ½ cup margarine until light and fluffy. Add applesauce and egg; blend well. Stir in flour, baking soda, cinnamon, salt, cloves and nutmeg; mix well. Stir in cereal. Spread mixture in greased and floured pan.

Bake at 350°F. for 25 to 30 minutes or until toothpick inserted in center comes out clean.

To prepare glaze, melt 2 tablespoons margarine in small saucepan over low heat. Stir in ¼ cup brown sugar. Cook about 1 minute or until mixture bubbles, stirring constantly. Remove from heat. Stir in powdered sugar. Quickly drizzle glaze over top of warm bars. Cool completely. Cut into bars.

Yield: 24 to 36 bars.

HIGH ALTITUDE:
Above 3500 Feet: No change.

NUTRITION PER SERVING:
Calories 100; Protein 1g; Carbohydrate 16g; Fat 4g; Sodium 100mg.

CHOCOLATY CARAMEL PECAN BARS

These indulgent candy-like bars won rave reviews from our taste panel of home economists. A buttery, tender crust is topped with caramel, pecans and chocolate. What could be more inviting?

CRUST
- ½ cup powdered sugar
- ½ cup margarine or butter, softened
- 1 tablespoon whipping cream
- 1 cup all purpose flour

FILLING
- 24 vanilla caramels, unwrapped
- ⅓ cup whipping cream
- 2 cups pecan halves

TOPPING
- 1 teaspoon margarine or butter
- ½ cup milk chocolate chips
- 2 tablespoons whipping cream

Heat oven to 325°F. Grease 9-inch square pan. In medium bowl, combine powdered sugar, ½ cup margarine and 1 tablespoon whipping cream; blend well. Add flour; mix until crumbly. With floured hands, press evenly in greased pan. Bake at 325°F. for 15 to 20 minutes or until firm to touch.

Meanwhile, in medium saucepan combine caramels and ⅓ cup whipping cream. Cook over low heat until caramels are melted and mixture is smooth, stirring occasionally. Remove from heat. Add pecans; stir well to coat. Immediately spoon over baked crust; spread carefully to cover.

In small saucepan over low heat, melt 1 teaspoon margarine and chocolate chips, stirring constantly. Stir in 2 tablespoons whipping cream. Drizzle over filling. Refrigerate 1 hour or until filling is firm. Cut into bars.

Yield: 24 bars.

NUTRITION PER SERVING:
Calories 200; Protein 2g; Carbohydrate 18g; Fat 14g; Sodium 75mg.

RASPBERRY-FILLED WHITE CHOCOLATE BARS

There is no sugar added to spreadable fruit. You'll find it in the jam and jelly section of most large grocery stores. It's delicious baked in these special occasion bars.

- ½ cup margarine or butter
- 1 (12-oz.) pkg. (2 cups) vanilla milk chips or 2 (6-oz.) pkg. white baking bars, chopped
- 2 eggs
- ½ cup sugar
- 1 cup all purpose flour
- ½ teaspoon salt
- 1 teaspoon amaretto liqueur or almond extract
- ½ cup raspberry spreadable fruit or jam
- ¼ cup sliced almonds, toasted, p. 23

Heat oven to 325°F. Grease and flour 9-inch square pan or 8-inch square baking dish. Melt margarine in small saucepan over low heat. Remove from heat. Add 1 cup of the vanilla milk chips. Let stand; do not stir.

In large bowl, beat eggs until foamy. Gradually add sugar, beating at high speed until lemon-colored. Stir in vanilla milk chip mixture. Add flour, salt and amaretto; mix at low speed until just combined. Spread half of batter (about 1 cup) in greased and floured pan. Bake at 325°F. for 15 to 20 minutes or until light golden brown.

Stir remaining 1 cup vanilla milk chips into remaining half of batter; set aside. Melt spreadable fruit in small saucepan over low heat. Spread evenly over warm, partially baked crust. Gently spoon teaspoonfuls of remaining batter over fruit spread. (Some fruit spread may show through batter.) Sprinkle with almonds.

Return to oven and bake an additional 25 to 35 minutes or until toothpick inserted in center comes out clean. Cool completely. Cut into bars.
Yield: 16 to 24 bars.

HIGH ALTITUDE:
Above 3500 Feet: No change.

NUTRITION PER SERVING:
Calories 170; Protein 2g; Carbohydrate 21g; Fat 9g; Sodium 100mg.

WHITE CHOCOLATE ALMOND BARS

For ease in preparation, the batter is mixed in the same saucepan used to melt the white baking bar.

- 2 oz. white baking bar, chopped
- ½ cup margarine or butter
- ¾ cup sugar
- 2 eggs
- 1 teaspoon almond extract
- ⅔ cup all purpose flour
- ½ teaspoon baking powder
- ¼ teaspoon salt
- ½ cup chopped almonds
- 1 tablespoon powdered sugar

Heat oven to 350°F. Grease and lightly flour bottom only of 8 or 9-inch square pan. Melt white baking bar in medium saucepan over very low heat, stirring constantly until smooth. Add margarine; stir until melted. Remove from heat; stir in sugar. Beat in eggs 1 at a time. Add almond extract. Add flour, baking powder, salt and almonds to chocolate mixture; mix well. Spread in greased and floured pan.

Bake at 350°F. for 25 to 35 minutes or until golden brown and center is set. Cool completely. Sprinkle with powdered sugar. Cut into bars.
Yield: 24 bars.

TIPS:
White baking bar melts slower than regular chocolate.
A wire whisk works well when blending the chocolate and margarine.

HIGH ALTITUDE:
Above 3500 Feet: Decrease sugar to ⅔ cup; increase flour to ¾ cup. Bake as directed above.

NUTRITION PER SERVING:
Calories 110; Protein 2g; Carbohydrate 11g; Fat 6g; Sodium 80mg.

Peanut Brittle Bars

You'll enjoy the contrast between salty and sweet in these easy-to-make bars. The surprise is the nut-like flavor the whole wheat flour contributes to the crust.

BASE

1½	**cups all purpose flour**
½	**cup whole wheat flour**
1	**cup firmly packed brown sugar**
1	**teaspoon baking soda**
¼	**teaspoon salt**
1	**cup margarine or butter**

TOPPING

2	**cups salted peanuts**
1	**cup milk chocolate chips**
1	**(12.5-oz.) jar (1 cup) caramel ice cream topping**
3	**tablespoons all purpose flour**

Heat oven to 350°F. Grease 15x10x1-inch baking pan. In large bowl, combine all base ingredients except margarine; mix well. Using pastry blender or fork, cut in margarine until crumbly. Press evenly in greased pan. Bake at 350°F. for 8 to 14 minutes or until golden brown.

Sprinkle peanuts and chocolate chips over warm base. In small bowl, combine caramel topping and 3 tablespoons flour; blend well. Drizzle evenly over chocolate chips and peanuts. Return to oven and bake an additional 12 to 18 minutes or until topping is set and golden brown. Cool completely. Cut into bars.

Yield: 48 bars.

HIGH ALTITUDE:
Above 3500 Feet: No change.

NUTRITION PER SERVING:
Calories 150; Protein 3g; Carbohydrate 17g; Fat 8g; Sodium 150mg.

Pumpkin Bars

Deliciously spiced and topped with cream cheese frosting, these traditional bars are great teamed with a mug of hot apple cider.

BARS

2	**cups all purpose flour**
2	**cups sugar**
2	**teaspoons baking powder**
1	**teaspoon baking soda**
1	**teaspoon cinnamon**
1	**teaspoon nutmeg**
½	**teaspoon salt**
½	**teaspoon cloves**
1	**cup oil**
1	**(16-oz.) can (2 cups) pumpkin**
4	**eggs**
½	**cup chopped nuts**
½	**cup raisins**

FROSTING

2	**cups powdered sugar**
⅓	**cup margarine or butter, softened**
1	**(3-oz.) pkg. cream cheese, softened**
1	**tablespoon milk**
1	**teaspoon vanilla**

Heat oven to 350°F. Grease 15x10x1-inch baking pan. In large bowl, combine all bar ingredients except nuts and raisins; beat at low speed until moistened. Beat 2 minutes at medium speed. Stir in nuts and raisins. Pour into greased pan.

Bake at 350°F. for 25 to 30 minutes or until toothpick inserted in center comes out clean. Cool completely.

In small bowl, combine all frosting ingredients; beat until smooth. Frost cooled bars. Cut into bars. Store in refrigerator.

Yield: 48 bars.

HIGH ALTITUDE:
Above 3500 Feet: Decrease baking soda to ½ teaspoon. Bake at 375°F. for 30 to 35 minutes.

NUTRITION PER SERVING:
Calories 150; Protein 2g; Carbohydrate 20g; Fat 8g; Sodium 85mg.

Light and Spicy Pumpkin Bars

LIGHT AND SPICY PUMPKIN BARS

The combination of whole wheat flour, brown sugar and sweet spices gives these pumpkin bars a delicious rich flavor.

BARS
- 1 **cup all purpose flour**
- 1 **cup whole wheat flour**
- 1½ **cups firmly packed brown sugar**
- 2 **teaspoons baking powder**
- 1 **teaspoon baking soda**
- 1 **teaspoon cinnamon**
- ½ **teaspoon nutmeg**
- ½ **teaspoon cloves**
- ¼ **teaspoon salt**
- ½ **cup oil**
- ½ **cup apple juice**
- 1 **(16-oz.) can (2 cups) pumpkin**
- 2 **eggs**

FROSTING
- 1½ **cups powdered sugar**
- 2 **tablespoons margarine or butter, softened**
- ½ **teaspoon vanilla**
- 2 **to 3 tablespoons plain yogurt**

Heat oven to 350°F. Grease and flour 15x10x1-inch baking pan. In large bowl, beat all bar ingredients at low speed until moistened. Beat 2 minutes at medium speed. Spread in greased and floured pan.

Bake at 350°F. for 20 to 30 minutes or until tooth-pick inserted in center comes out clean. Cool completely.

In medium bowl, combine all frosting ingredients, adding enough yogurt for desired spreading consistency; beat until smooth. Frost cooled bars; sprinkle with nutmeg, if desired. Refrigerate to set frosting. Cut into bars.

Yield: 48 bars.

HIGH ALTITUDE:
Above 3500 Feet: Increase all purpose flour to 1⅓ cups; decrease baking powder to 1 teaspoon. Bake as directed above.

NUTRITION PER SERVING:
Calories 90; Protein 1g; Carbohydrate 15g; Fat 3g; Sodium 60mg.

GLAZED FRUITCAKE SQUARES

This fruitcake-like bar is festive, easy and delicious.

BARS
- 2 cups powdered sugar
- ½ cup margarine or butter, softened
- ¼ cup brandy*
- 2 eggs
- 2 cups all purpose flour
- 3 teaspoons baking powder
- 1 teaspoon salt
- 2 cups chopped candied fruit
- 1 cup coarsely chopped walnuts

GLAZE
- 1 cup powdered sugar
- 1 tablespoon margarine or butter, softened
- 1 to 2 tablespoons brandy**

Heat oven to 375°F. Grease 15x10x1-inch baking pan. In large bowl, combine powdered sugar, ½ cup margarine, ¼ cup brandy and eggs; mix well. By hand, stir in remaining bar ingredients; press in greased pan.

Bake at 375°F. for 15 to 25 minutes or until light golden brown. Cool. In small bowl, combine all glaze ingredients, adding enough brandy for desired drizzling consistency; beat until smooth. Drizzle glaze over top. When glaze is set, cut into bars.

Yield: 48 bars.

TIPS:
* To substitute for brandy in bars, use ¼ cup water or orange juice and 1 teaspoon brandy extract.
** To substitute for brandy in glaze, combine 1 to 2 tablespoons water with ½ teaspoon brandy extract.

HIGH ALTITUDE:
Above 3500 Feet: No change.

NUTRITION PER SERVING:
Calories 110; Protein 1g; Carbohydrate 16g; Fat 4g; Sodium 110mg.

WHOLE WHEAT ZUCCHINI BARS

When zucchini is plentiful, you can shred and freeze it in amounts just right for these wholesome bars.

BARS
- 3 eggs
- 1½ cups sugar
- 1 cup oil
- 1½ cups whole wheat flour
- ½ cup all purpose flour
- 1 teaspoon baking powder
- ½ teaspoon salt
- 1 teaspoon cinnamon
- 2 cups shredded zucchini
- 1 cup dried currants or raisins

GLAZE
- 1 cup powdered sugar
- ¼ teaspoon cinnamon
- 2 tablespoons margarine or butter, melted
- 2 tablespoons milk

Heat oven to 350°F. Grease 13x9-inch pan. In large bowl, beat eggs. Add sugar and oil; beat well. In medium bowl, combine whole wheat flour, all purpose flour, baking powder, salt and 1 teaspoon cinnamon. Add flour mixture to egg mixture; mix well. Stir in zucchini and currants. Spread in greased pan.

Bake at 350°F. for 40 to 50 minutes or until toothpick inserted in center comes out clean. Cool completely.

In small bowl, combine all glaze ingredients until smooth. Spread evenly over cooled bars. Cut into bars.

Yield: 36 bars.

HIGH ALTITUDE:
Above 3500 Feet: No change.

NUTRITION PER SERVING:
Calories 130; Protein 1g; Carbohydrate 17g; Fat 7g; Sodium 50mg.

THREE LAYER BARS

No flour is used to make these rich, delicious bars. They boast a chewy crust full of nuts and coconut and a creamy pudding filling that's lightly glazed with milk chocolate.

CRUST
- ½ **cup margarine or butter**
- ¼ **cup unsweetened cocoa**
- 2 **teaspoons vanilla**
- 1 **egg, slightly beaten**
- 2 **cups graham cracker crumbs**
- ½ **cup powdered sugar**
- ½ **cup shredded coconut**
- ½ **cup chopped nuts**

FILLING
- ½ **cup margarine or butter**
- ½ **cup milk**
- 1 **(3-oz.) pkg. vanilla pudding and pie filling mix (not instant)**
- 3 **cups powdered sugar**

TOPPING
- 1 **(8-oz.) bar milk chocolate, cut up**
- 1 **tablespoon graham cracker crumbs**

Heat oven to 350°F. Grease 13x9-inch pan. In medium saucepan, combine ½ cup margarine and cocoa. Cook over low heat until melted. Remove from heat. Add vanilla and egg; mix well. Stir in remaining crust ingredients; mix well. Press mixture in bottom of greased pan. Bake at 350°F. for 10 minutes. Cool.

Melt ½ cup margarine in medium saucepan over low heat. Blend in milk and pudding mix; cook until mixture thickens slightly, about 5 minutes, stirring constantly. Remove from heat. Beat in 3 cups powdered sugar until smooth. Spread over crust. Refrigerate 20 to 30 minutes or until set.

Melt chocolate in small saucepan over low heat, stirring constantly. Spread evenly over filling. Sprinkle with 1 tablespoon graham cracker crumbs. Refrigerate 10 to 15 minutes to set chocolate. Cut into bars. Store in refrigerator.

Yield: 36 bars.

NUTRITION PER SERVING:
Calories 170; Protein 2g; Carbohydrate 22g; Fat 9g; Sodium 120mg.

PEANUT BUTTER RIBBON BARS

Brownie mix helps to make these special bars easy to make. They have a creamy peanut butter flavor.

FILLING
- 1 **(3-oz.) pkg. cream cheese, softened**
- ⅓ **cup peanut butter**
- ¼ **cup sugar**
- 1 **teaspoon vanilla**
- 1 **egg**

BARS
- 1 **(21½-oz.) pkg. fudge brownie mix**
- ⅓ **cup water**
- ⅓ **cup oil**
- 1 **egg**

GLAZE
- 1 **oz. semi-sweet chocolate, cut into pieces**
- 2 **teaspoons shortening**

Heat oven to 350°F. Generously grease bottom of 13x9-inch pan. In small bowl, combine all filling ingredients; beat at medium speed until smooth. Set aside.

In large bowl, combine all bar ingredients; beat 50 strokes with spoon. Spread half of batter in greased pan. Drop filling by tablespoonfuls over batter. Spoon remaining batter over filling. Marble by pulling knife through batter in wide curves. Bake at 350°F. for 30 to 35 minutes or until set.

In small saucepan over low heat, melt chocolate and shortening, stirring constantly. Drizzle glaze over bars. Refrigerate at least 1 hour. Cut into bars. Store in refrigerator.

Yield: 36 bars.

HIGH ALTITUDE:
Above 3500 Feet: Add ¼ cup flour to dry brownie mix. Bake as directed above.

NUTRITION PER SERVING:
Calories 120; Protein 2g; Carbohydrate 16g; Fat 6g; Sodium 80mg.

CHARMIN' CHERRY BARS

Scarlet cherries, coconut and walnuts top a buttery crust in this 1951 Junior Winner from the 3rd Pillsbury BAKE-OFF® Contest.

CRUST
   1 **cup all purpose flour**
   ¼ **cup powdered sugar**
   ½ **cup margarine or butter, softened**

FILLING
   ¼ **cup all purpose flour**
   ¾ **cup sugar**
   ½ **teaspoon baking powder**
   ¼ **teaspoon salt**
   2 **eggs**
   ½ **cup maraschino cherries, well drained, chopped**
   ½ **cup coconut**
   ½ **cup chopped walnuts**

Heat oven to 350°F. In small bowl, combine 1 cup flour and powdered sugar. Using fork or pastry blender, cut in margarine until mixture resembles coarse crumbs. Press crumb mixture firmly in bottom of ungreased 9-inch square pan. Bake at 350°F. for 10 minutes.

Meanwhile, in same small bowl combine ¼ cup flour, sugar, baking powder and salt. Add eggs; beat well. Stir in cherries, coconut and walnuts. Spread over partially baked crust.

Return to oven and bake an additional 25 to 30 minutes or until golden brown. Cool completely. Cut into bars.
Yield: 25 bars.

HIGH ALTITUDE:
Above 3500 Feet: No change.

NUTRITION PER SERVING:
Calories 120; Protein 2g; Carbohydrate 14g; Fat 6g; Sodium 75mg.

SO-EASY SUGAR COOKIES

The name says it all — and they're so good, they'll become a family favorite! Instead of rolling out the dough, it's baked in a pan, then cut into squares.

   ¾ **cup sugar**
   ⅓ **cup margarine or butter, softened, or shortening**
   ⅓ **cup oil**
   1 **tablespoon milk**
   1 **to 2 teaspoons almond extract**
   1 **egg**
   1½ **cups all purpose flour**
   1½ **teaspoons baking powder**
   ¼ **teaspoon salt**
   1 **tablespoon sugar**

Heat oven to 375°F. In large bowl, beat ¾ cup sugar, margarine, oil, milk, almond extract and egg until light and fluffy. Stir in flour, baking powder and salt; blend well. Spread evenly in ungreased 15x10x1-inch baking pan; sprinkle with 1 tablespoon sugar.

Bake at 375°F. for 10 to 12 minutes or until light golden brown. Cool 5 minutes. Cut into bars.
Yield: 48 bar cookies.

FOOD PROCESSOR DIRECTIONS:
Place ¾ cup sugar, margarine, oil, milk, almond extract and egg in food processor bowl with metal blade. Cover; process until light and fluffy. Add flour, baking powder and salt. Cover; process using on/off turns just until flour is well blended. (Do not overprocess or cookies will be tough.) Continue as directed above.

HIGH ALTITUDE:
Above 3500 Feet: Decrease baking powder to 1 teaspoon. Bake as directed above.

NUTRITION PER SERVING:
Calories 50; Protein 1g; Carbohydrate 6g; Fat 3g; Sodium 35mg.

So-Easy Sugar Cookies

FUDGY BROWNIES

The ultimate in fudgy brownies!

BROWNIES
- 4 oz. unsweetened chocolate
- ½ cup margarine or butter
- 2 cups sugar
- 4 eggs
- 2 teaspoons vanilla
- 1 cup all purpose flour
- ¼ teaspoon salt

GLAZE
- 2 oz. white baking bar, chopped, ⅓ cup vanilla milk chips, or ⅓ cup semi-sweet chocolate chips
- 3 teaspoons oil

Heat oven to 350°F. Grease 13x9-inch pan. In small saucepan over low heat, melt chocolate and margarine, stirring constantly until smooth. Remove from heat; cool slightly.

In medium bowl, beat sugar, eggs and vanilla until light and fluffy. Add flour, salt and chocolate mixture; blend well. Spread in greased pan. Bake at 350°F. for 30 to 38 minutes. DO NOT OVERBAKE. Cool completely.

In small saucepan, melt glaze ingredients over low heat, stirring constantly until smooth. Drizzle glaze over brownies. Let stand until glaze is set. Cut into bars.

Yield: 36 bars.

HIGH ALTITUDE:
Above 3500 Feet: No change.

NUTRITION PER SERVING:
Calories 110; Protein 2g; Carbohydrate 16g; Fat 6g; Sodium 55mg.

CHOCO-LITE BROWNIES

- ⅔ cup all purpose flour
- ¾ cup sugar
- ⅓ cup unsweetened cocoa
- ¼ teaspoon baking powder
- ¼ teaspoon salt
- ⅓ cup margarine or butter, melted
- 2 teaspoons vanilla
- 2 eggs, slightly beaten
  Powdered sugar

Heat oven to 350°F. Grease and flour bottom only of 8-inch square pan. In large bowl, combine flour, sugar, cocoa, baking powder and salt; blend well. Add margarine, vanilla and eggs; stir just to combine. Pour into greased and floured pan.

Bake at 350°F. for 18 to 23 minutes or until set. DO NOT OVERBAKE. Sprinkle with powdered sugar. Cool completely. Cut into bars.

Yield: 24 bars.

HIGH ALTITUDE:
Above 3500 Feet: Increase flour to ¾ cup. Bake as directed above.

NUTRITION PER SERVING:
Calories 70; Protein 1g; Carbohydrate 10g; Fat 3g; Sodium 70mg.

CHOCOLATE CHUNK PECAN BROWNIES

This culinary inspiration was developed for chocoholics. It's a moist, nut-textured, intensely flavored brownie to satisfy that chocolate craving.

- 1 cup margarine or butter
- 2 cups sugar
- 2 teaspoons vanilla
- 4 eggs, slightly beaten
- 1 cup all purpose flour
- ½ cup unsweetened cocoa
- ½ teaspoon salt
- 8 oz. semi-sweet chocolate, coarsely chopped
- 1 cup chopped pecans

Heat oven to 350°F. Grease 13x9-inch pan. In medium saucepan over low heat, melt margarine. Add sugar, vanilla and eggs; blend well. Stir in flour, cocoa and salt; mix well. Add chocolate and pecans. Pour into greased pan.

Bake at 350°F. for 30 to 40 minutes or until set. Cool completely. Cut into bars.

Yield: 36 bars.

HIGH ALTITUDE:
Above 3500 Feet: No change.

NUTRITION PER SERVING:
Calories 160; Protein 2g; Carbohydrate 19g; Fat 10g; Sodium 105mg.

CHOCOLATE SYRUP BROWNIES

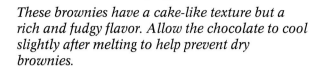

These brownies are baked in a square pan. It's the perfect size for smaller households.

BROWNIES
- ½ **cup margarine or butter, softened**
- ½ **cup sugar**
- 2 **eggs**
- ½ **cup chocolate syrup**
- 2 **teaspoons vanilla**
- ¾ **cup all purpose flour**
- ¼ **teaspoon salt**

FROSTING
- 1 **cup powdered sugar**
- 2 **tablespoons chocolate syrup**
- 1 **tablespoon margarine or butter, softened**
- 2 **to 4 teaspoons milk**

Heat oven to 350°F. Grease 8-inch square pan. In large bowl, combine ½ cup margarine and sugar; beat until light and fluffy. Add eggs, ½ cup chocolate syrup and vanilla; beat well. Stir in flour and salt. Pour into greased pan.

Bake at 350°F. for 25 to 30 minutes or until toothpick inserted in center comes out clean. Cool completely.

In small bowl, combine all frosting ingredients, adding enough milk for desired spreading consistency; beat until smooth. Spread over cooled brownies. Cut into bars.

MICROWAVE DIRECTIONS:
Grease 10x6-inch (1½-quart) microwave-safe dish. Prepare brownies as directed above. Pour into greased dish. Microwave on MEDIUM for 8 minutes, rotating dish ½ turn halfway through cooking. Microwave on HIGH for 2 to 3 minutes or until center is set. Cool completely on flat surface.

Prepare frosting and frost as directed above. Cut into bars.
Yield: 12 to 16 bars.

HIGH ALTITUDE:
Above 3500 Feet: Increase flour to 1 cup. Bake as directed above. For microwave, cook in greased 9-inch round microwave-safe dish. Microwave on MEDIUM for 8 minutes, rotating dish every 2 minutes. Microwave on HIGH for 1 to 2 minutes or until center is set.

NUTRITION PER SERVING:
Calories 170; Protein 2g; Carbohydrate 24g; Fat 7g; Sodium 130mg.

FAVORITE FUDGE BROWNIES

These brownies have a cake-like texture but a rich and fudgy flavor. Allow the chocolate to cool slightly after melting to help prevent dry brownies.

BROWNIES
- 5 **oz. unsweetened chocolate, cut into pieces**
- ¾ **cup margarine or butter**
- 1 **tablespoon vanilla**
- 2¼ **cups sugar**
- 4 **eggs**
- 1⅓ **cups all purpose flour**
- 1½ **cups coarsely chopped nuts**

FROSTING
- 1½ **cups powdered sugar**
- 2 **tablespoons unsweetened cocoa**
- ¼ **cup margarine or butter, softened**
- 2 **tablespoons milk**
- ½ **teaspoon vanilla**
  Pecan or walnut halves, if desired

Heat oven to 375°F. Grease 13x9-inch pan. In small saucepan over low heat, melt chocolate and ¾ cup margarine, stirring constantly until smooth. Remove from heat. Stir in 1 tablespoon vanilla; set aside.

In large bowl, combine sugar and eggs; beat about 7 minutes or until sugar is dissolved. Add flour, chocolate mixture and nuts to egg mixture; stir just until blended. Pour batter into greased pan.

Bake at 375°F. for 25 to 35 minutes. DO NOT OVERBAKE. Cool completely.

In small bowl, combine all frosting ingredients except pecans; blend until smooth. Frost cooled bars; refrigerate 1 hour. Cut into bars; garnish each bar with a pecan half.
Yield: 24 bars.

HIGH ALTITUDE:
Above 3500 Feet: No change.

NUTRITION PER SERVING:
Calories 280; Protein 4g; Carbohydrate 34g; Fat 17g; Sodium 95mg.

GOURMET MINT BROWNIES

A mint-flavored cream cheese filling is swirled through a chocolate brownie.

FILLING
- 1 (8-oz.) pkg. cream cheese, softened
- 1/4 cup sugar
- 1 egg
- 1 teaspoon mint extract
- 4 drops green food color

BROWNIES
- 1 cup margarine or butter
- 4 oz. unsweetened chocolate, cut into pieces
- 2 cups sugar
- 2 teaspoons vanilla
- 4 eggs
- 1 cup all purpose flour

FROSTING
- 2 tablespoons margarine or butter
- 2 tablespoons corn syrup
- 2 tablespoons water
- 2 oz. unsweetened chocolate, cut into pieces
- 1 teaspoon vanilla
- 1 cup powdered sugar

Heat oven to 350°F. Grease and flour 13x9-inch pan. In small bowl, beat cream cheese and 1/4 cup sugar until smooth. Add 1 egg, mint extract and food color; mix well. Set aside.

In large saucepan, melt 1 cup margarine and 4 oz. chocolate over very low heat, stirring constantly. Remove from heat; cool slightly. Stir in 2 cups sugar and 2 teaspoons vanilla. Add 4 eggs 1 at a time, beating well after each addition. Stir in flour; mix well. Spread in greased and floured pan. Carefully spoon filling over brownie mixture. Lightly swirl filling into brownie mixture.

Bake at 350°F. for 45 to 50 minutes or until set. Cool completely.

In heavy saucepan, bring 2 tablespoons margarine, corn syrup and water to a rolling boil. Remove from heat. Add 2 oz. chocolate; stir until melted. Stir in 1 teaspoon vanilla and powdered sugar; beat until smooth. Frost cooled bars. Cut into bars. Store in refrigerator.
Yield: 36 bars.

HIGH ALTITUDE:
Above 3500 Feet: No change.

NUTRITION PER SERVING:
Calories 180; Protein 2g; Carbohydrate 20g; Fat 11g; Sodium 95mg.

PECAN BLONDIES

The term "blondie" refers to a brownie containing no chocolate. Our version of blond brownies is moist and chewy, with a rich melt-in-your-mouth flavor.

- 1 1/2 cups firmly packed brown sugar
- 1/2 cup margarine or butter, softened
- 2 teaspoons vanilla
- 2 eggs
- 1 1/2 cups all purpose flour
- 1 teaspoon baking powder
- 1/2 teaspoon nutmeg
- 1/4 teaspoon salt
- 1/2 cup chopped pecans
- 1 tablespoon powdered sugar

Heat oven to 350°F. Grease 13x9-inch pan. In large bowl, beat brown sugar and margarine until light and fluffy. Add vanilla and eggs; blend well. Add flour, baking powder, nutmeg and salt; mix well. Spread in greased pan. Sprinkle with pecans.

Bake at 350°F. for 18 to 28 minutes or until set and golden brown. Cool completely. Sprinkle with powdered sugar; cut into bars.
Yield: 36 bars.

HIGH ALTITUDE:
Above 3500 Feet: Increase flour to 1 3/4 cups. Bake as directed above.

NUTRITION PER SERVING:
Calories 90; Protein 1g; Carbohydrate 13g; Fat 4g; Sodium 60mg.

VARIATION:

DATE PECAN BLONDIES: Stir 1 cup chopped dates into batter before spreading in pan.

CHEWY BUTTERSCOTCH BROWNIES

The marvelous coconut-pecan base adds special appeal to these luscious change-of-pace brownies. They are sure to satisfy a sweet tooth.

BASE
- ¼ cup margarine or butter
- 1 cup flaked coconut
- ½ cup firmly packed brown sugar
- ½ cup chopped pecans

BROWNIES
- 1 cup firmly packed brown sugar
- ½ cup margarine or butter, softened
- ½ teaspoon vanilla
- 1 egg
- 1½ cups all purpose flour
- ½ teaspoon baking soda
- ¼ teaspoon salt
- ½ cup miniature marshmallows
- ½ cup chopped pecans
- 1 cup miniature marshmallows, if desired

GLAZE
- 1 tablespoon margarine or butter
- ½ cup powdered sugar
- ¼ cup firmly packed brown sugar
- 2 to 4 teaspoons milk

Heat oven to 350°F. Grease 13x9-inch pan. In small saucepan, melt ¼ cup margarine. Stir in remaining base ingredients. Press mixture in bottom of greased pan.

In large bowl, beat 1 cup brown sugar and ½ cup margarine until light and fluffy. Add vanilla and egg; blend well. Stir in flour, baking soda and salt; mix well. Add ½ cup marshmallows and ½ cup pecans; blend well. Spoon brownie mixture over base; gently spread with wet hands.

Bake at 350°F. for 20 to 27 minutes or until golden brown. Sprinkle with 1 cup marshmallows. Bake an additional 2 minutes. Cool completely.

In small saucepan, melt 1 tablespoon margarine. Stir in powdered sugar, ¼ cup brown sugar and enough milk for desired drizzling consistency. Drizzle glaze over brownies. Cut into bars.
Yield: 48 bars.

HIGH ALTITUDE:
Above 3500 Feet: Decrease brown sugar in brownies to ¾ cup.

NUTRITION PER SERVING:
Calories 110; Protein 1g; Carbohydrate 14g; Fat 5g; Sodium 65mg.

ZEBRA BROWNIES

These rich brownies with their creamy filling have been an all-time favorite.

FILLING
- 2 (3-oz.) pkg. cream cheese, softened
- ¼ cup sugar
- ½ teaspoon vanilla
- 1 egg

BROWNIES
- 1 (21.5-oz.) pkg. fudge brownie mix
- ⅓ cup water
- ⅓ cup oil
- 1 egg

Heat oven to 350°F. Grease bottom of 13x9-inch pan. In small bowl, combine all filling ingredients; beat until smooth. Set aside.

In large bowl, combine all brownie ingredients; beat 50 strokes with spoon. Spread half of brownie batter in greased pan. Pour filling mixture over brownie batter, spreading to cover. Top with spoonfuls of remaining brownie batter. To marble, pull knife through batter in wide curves; turn pan and repeat.

Bake at 350°F. for 30 to 35 minutes or until set. DO NOT OVERBAKE. Cool completely. Refrigerate at least 1 hour. Cut into bars. Store in refrigerator.
Yield: 36 bars.

HIGH ALTITUDE:
Above 3500 Feet: See package for directions.

NUTRITION PER SERVING:
Calories 110; Protein 1g; Carbohydrate 16g; Fat 5g; Sodium 70mg.

PUMPKIN PATCH BROWNIES

———— ❧ ————

This whimsical special occasion treat is especially easy to make with fudge brownie mix and ready-to-spread frosting. The piped frosting can be easily done using a resealable plastic freezer bag with a corner snipped off to make a small hole.

BROWNIES
- 1 (21.5-oz.) pkg. fudge brownie mix
- 1 teaspoon cinnamon
- ½ cup water
- ½ cup oil
- 1 egg

FROSTING
- 1 can ready-to-spread chocolate fudge frosting
- 1 cup ready-to-spread vanilla frosting
- 3 to 4 drops green food color
- 24 candy pumpkins

Heat oven to 350°F. Line 13x9-inch pan with foil, leaving enough foil on sides to lift brownies out of pan. Grease foil. In large bowl, combine all brownie ingredients; beat 50 strokes by hand. Spread in foil-lined pan.

Bake at 350°F. for 28 to 35 minutes. DO NOT OVERBAKE. Cool completely. Remove brownies from pan by lifting foil edges. Invert onto serving plate, tray or heavy cardboard covered with foil. Remove foil from brownies. Frost sides and top with chocolate fudge frosting. With knife, score frosting into 24 bars.

In small bowl, combine vanilla frosting and green food color; blend well. Using decorating bag, decorating bottle, or resealable plastic bag with a small hole cut in one corner, pipe green frosting to make vine and leaf design on each bar. Place 1 candy pumpkin on each bar. Refrigerate 1 to 2 hours or until frosting is firm; cut into bars.
Yield: 24 bars.

HIGH ALTITUDE:
Above 3500 Feet: See package for directions.

NUTRITION PER SERVING:
Calories 340; Protein 2g; Carbohydrate 54g; Fat 13g; Sodium 190mg.

VARIATION:

PUMPKIN FIELD BROWNIES: Prepare brownies and frost with chocolate fudge frosting as directed above. Do not score. Prepare green frosting as directed above. Pipe vines and leaves randomly over chocolate fudge frosting. Place desired number of candy pumpkins randomly among leaves and vines.

FRUITCAKE FANTASY BROWNIES

———— ❧ ————

Whether you like fruitcake or not, we think you will enjoy these fudgy, fruit-filled brownies.

- ½ cup margarine or butter
- 4 oz. semi-sweet chocolate
- 1 (14-oz.) can sweetened condensed milk (not evaporated)
- ½ teaspoon rum extract
- 2 eggs
- 1¼ cups all purpose flour
- ¾ teaspoon baking powder
- ¼ teaspoon salt
- 2 cups candied fruitcake mixture
- 1 cup chopped pecans or walnuts

Heat oven to 350°F. Grease 13x9-inch pan. In large saucepan, melt margarine and chocolate over low heat, stirring constantly. Remove from heat. Add sweetened condensed milk and rum extract; blend well. Add eggs 1 at a time, beating well after each addition. Add flour, baking powder and salt; mix well. Stir in candied fruit and pecans. Spread in greased pan.

Bake at 350°F. for 28 to 36 minutes or until toothpick inserted in center comes out clean. Cool completely. Cut into bars.
Yield: 36 bars.

HIGH ALTITUDE:
Above 3500 Feet: Increase flour to 1½ cups. Bake as directed above.

NUTRITION PER SERVING:
Calories 140; Protein 2g; Carbohydrate 20g; Fat 7g; Sodium 85mg.

White Chocolate Chunk Brownie Wedges

These elegant brownie wedges are loaded with chunks of semi-sweet chocolate. Cover the pan tightly with foil to maintain freshness.

BROWNIES
- ½ **cup margarine or butter**
- 4 **oz. white baking bars, cut into pieces**
- 2 **eggs**
- ⅛ **teaspoon salt**
- ½ **cup sugar**
- 1½ **teaspoons vanilla**
- 1¼ **cups all purpose flour**
- 2 **oz. semi-sweet chocolate, cut into pieces**

GLAZE
- 1 **oz. semi-sweet chocolate**
- 2 **teaspoons margarine or butter**

Heat oven to 350°F. Grease and flour 9-inch round cake pan. In small saucepan, melt ½ cup margarine and 2 oz. of the white baking bar over low heat, stirring constantly until melted. Remove from heat; set aside.

In small bowl, combine eggs and salt; beat until frothy. Add sugar and continue beating for about 3 minutes or until light in color and thickened. Add melted chocolate mixture and vanilla; blend well. Stir in flour; mix well. Fold in remaining white chocolate pieces and semi-sweet chocolate pieces. Spread in greased and floured pan.

Bake at 350°F. for 23 to 28 minutes or until toothpick inserted in center comes out clean. Cool on wire rack.

In small saucepan, melt glaze ingredients until smooth, stirring constantly. Drizzle glaze over brownies. Let stand until set. Cut into wedges.
Yield: 12 wedges.

HIGH ALTITUDE:
Above 3500 Feet: Increase flour to 1⅓ cups. Bake as directed above.

NUTRITION PER SERVING:
Calories 260; Protein 3g; Carbohydrate 28g; Fat 15g; Sodium 140mg.

Fudgy Orange Hazelnut Brownies

Delicate orange frosting complements these dense brownies. Hazelnuts, also known as filberts, add a distinctive flavor.

BROWNIES
- 1 **cup sugar**
- ½ **cup margarine or butter, softened**
- ⅓ **cup unsweetened cocoa**
- 1 **tablespoon grated orange peel**
- 2 **eggs**
- 1 **cup all purpose flour**
- ½ **teaspoon baking soda**
- ¼ **teaspoon salt**
- 1 **cup coarsely chopped hazelnuts (filberts)**

FROSTING
- 1 **cup powdered sugar**
- 1 **teaspoon grated orange peel**
- 1 **to 2 tablespoons milk**

Heat oven to 350°F. Grease 9-inch square pan. In large bowl, beat sugar and margarine until light and fluffy. Add cocoa, 1 tablespoon orange peel and eggs; blend well. Add flour, baking soda and salt; mix well. Stir in hazelnuts. Spread in greased pan.

Bake at 350°F. for 23 to 33 minutes or until firm to touch. DO NOT OVERBAKE. Cool completely.

In small bowl, combine powdered sugar, 1 teaspoon orange peel and enough milk for desired spreading consistency; blend until smooth. Spread over cooled brownies. Let stand until set. Cut into bars.
Yield: 24 bars.

HIGH ALTITUDE:
Above 3500 Feet: Increase flour to 1¼ cups. Bake as directed above.

NUTRITION PER SERVING:
Calories 140; Protein 2g; Carbohydrate 19g; Fat 8g; Sodium 105mg.

GLAZED CHEESECAKE BROWNIES

Two favorites, brownies and cheesecake, are combined in this unique bar. They cut beautifully and will make an attractive addition to your holiday cookie tray.

TOPPING
- 1 (8-oz.) pkg. cream cheese, softened
- 2 tablespoons margarine or butter, softened
- ½ cup sugar
- 1 teaspoon vanilla
- 2 eggs

BROWNIES
- 4 oz. semi-sweet chocolate, cut into pieces
- 3 tablespoons margarine or butter
- ½ cup sugar
- 1 teaspoon vanilla
- 2 eggs
- ½ cup all purpose flour
- ½ teaspoon baking powder
- ¼ teaspoon salt

GLAZE
- 1 oz. semi-sweet chocolate, cut into pieces
- 2 teaspoons margarine or butter

Heat oven to 350°F. Grease and flour 9-inch square pan. In small bowl, combine all topping ingredients; blend well. Set aside.

In medium saucepan, melt 4 oz. chocolate and 3 tablespoons margarine over low heat, stirring constantly until smooth. Remove from heat; cool. Add ½ cup sugar and vanilla; blend well. Beat in 2 eggs 1 at a time, blending well after each addition. Add flour, baking powder and salt to chocolate mixture; stir just until blended. Pour into greased and floured pan. Pour topping over batter.

Bake at 350°F. for 40 to 50 minutes or until toothpick inserted in center comes out clean. Cool on wire rack.

In small saucepan, melt glaze ingredients until smooth, stirring constantly. Drizzle over brownies. Refrigerate at least 4 hours. Cut into bars. Store in refrigerator.
Yield: 24 bars.

HIGH ALTITUDE:
Above 3500 Feet: Increase flour to ½ cup plus 2 tablespoons. Bake as directed above.

NUTRITION PER SERVING:
Calories 140; Protein 2g; Carbohydrate 14g; Fat 9g; Sodium 100mg.

BRAZIL NUT BROWNIES

What could be more delicious than white chocolate frosting atop fudgy brownies?

BROWNIES
- 1 (21.5-oz.) pkg. fudge brownie mix
- ½ cup oil
- ¼ cup water
- ¼ cup coffee-flavored liqueur or strong coffee
- 1 egg
- 1 cup coarsely chopped brazil nuts

FROSTING
- 2 tablespoons margarine or butter, melted
- 1 cup powdered sugar
- 2 tablespoons coffee-flavored liqueur or strong coffee
- 1 tablespoon water
- 3 oz. white baking bars, chopped, or ½ cup vanilla milk chips
- 1 tablespoon oil

Heat oven to 350°F. Grease 13x9-inch pan. In large bowl, combine all brownie ingredients except nuts; beat 50 strokes by hand. Stir in brazil nuts. Spread in greased pan. Bake at 350°F. for 28 to 35 minutes. DO NOT OVERBAKE. Cool completely.

In medium bowl, combine margarine, powdered sugar, 2 tablespoons liqueur and 1 tablespoon water; blend well. In small saucepan over low heat, melt white baking bar and 1 tablespoon oil, stirring constantly. Add to powdered sugar mixture; beat until smooth. Spread over cooled brownies. Let stand until set. Cut into bars.
Yield: 36 bars.

HIGH ALTITUDE:
Above 3500 Feet: See package for directions.

NUTRITION PER SERVING:
Calories 170; Protein 2g; Carbohydrate 20g; Fat 9g; Sodium 70mg.

CAKES

A cake is something special! Traditionally, cakes mark the occasions of our lives, including showers, weddings, birthdays, graduations and anniversaries.

Whether you choose a layer cake topped with creamy frosting, a moist sheet cake laden with raisins and spices, or a feather-light angel food cake, we've outlined the techniques for making them all. And, we've provided tips for adding festive finishing touches like garnishes and glazes.

Pictured: **Apple Pecan Layer Cake** *p. 115,* **Black Bottom Cups** *p. 144*

CAKES

~

Draw ooohs and aaahs
from family and friends by baking a cake!
A snack cake takes no longer than stirring up a mix, or with some
extra time and attention, you can create an elaborate
"company's coming" cake to rival any bakery's.

KINDS OF CAKES

There are 2 main types of cakes — butter and foam cakes. Butter cakes are those made with solid shortenings and foam cakes are those made with a large number of eggs or egg whites.

BUTTER

Even though these cakes also may be made with solid shortening or margarine, most people still call them "butter" cakes. They're moist, light, tender and fine-textured. (Recipes begin on p. 113.)

FOAM

Foam cakes contain a large number of eggs or egg whites. Their light, fluffy texture comes from the air beaten into the eggs and from steam that forms in the batter during baking. The 3 types of foam cakes are angel food, chiffon and sponge. Angel food cakes contain no shortening or oil and use only egg whites. Chiffon cakes contain oil and use egg yolks and whites. Sponge cakes contain no shortening or oil and use egg yolks and whites. (Recipes begin on p. 181.)

SECRETS TO SUCCESSFUL CAKES

From a snack cake to a multi-layered birthday cake, some basic secrets will help make every cake a success!

SECERETS FOR ANY CAKES

Use shiny metal pans. Shiny aluminum pans reflect heat away from the cake and give it a tender, light-brown crust. Dark pans can cause a thick, dark crust. Insulated pans require a longer baking time.

Use the proper size of pan. When checking the size, measure from inside edge to inside edge. A cake made in a pan that is too large can be flat and overbaked, while one made in a pan that is too small may overflow during baking or take longer to bake.

Prepare the pan according to recipe directions. Pans for butter cakes are usually greased and floured. Pans for foam cakes are usually not.

Heat the oven 10 to 15 minutes before baking.

Measure ingredients accurately. Be sure to add them in the order and manner specified in the recipe.

Don't overbeat or underbeat the batter. Underbeating or overbeating will affect the texture and volume of the cake. These recipes have been tested using an electric mixer, which produces the highest volume, but they also may be mixed by hand. One minute of beating time with a mixer equals 150 strokes by hand.

Fill pans half full. This will ensure that the cake bakes evenly, and that the batter doesn't overflow the pan during baking. If you're using a special-shaped pan like a heart or Christmas tree, measure how much batter it will hold by filling it with water. Measure the amount of water and use half that amount of batter. Extra batter can be used for cupcakes.

Carefully space pans in the oven. Place single pans in the middle of the center rack. For more than 1 pan, leave at least 1 inch between the pans and the sides of the oven for good air circulation. If necessary, stagger the pans on 2 oven racks so one is not directly above the other and the air flows evenly around them.

Cool cakes completely before filling, frosting or glazing them.

Know the number of servings per cake. If you're baking for a group, here's a handy guide for knowing what size cake will serve the whole crowd:

Size of cake	Serves
8 or 9-inch layer cake	12 to 16
8 or 9-inch square cake	6 to 9
13x9-inch rectangular cake	12 to 16
10x4-inch tube cake	16 to 20
12-cup bundt cake	16 to 20

SECRETS FOR BUTTER CAKES

Use butter, margarine or solid shortening. Don't substitute oil, even if the recipe calls for the shortening to be melted.

Use solid shortening to prepare the pan. Grease the bottom and sides of the pan with about 1 tablespoon of solid vegetable shortening (butter, margarine and oil don't coat as evenly) for each 8 or 9-inch round cake pan. Use a paper towel or pastry brush to spread the shortening. Then dust the greased pan with about 2 tablespoons of flour, shaking it until the bottom and sides are well coated. (If you're baking a chocolate cake, you can use cocoa instead of flour.) Tap out the excess flour. For nonstick pans, follow the manufacturer's instructions.

Instead of greasing and flouring pans, you also may use pan inserts made of parchment paper. The inserts are available at many cooking specialty stores. Use paper or foil baking cups to line cupcake pans.

Make a hollow. After filling the pans with batter, make a slight hollow in the center of the batter with the back of a spoon or spatula. This will give the cake a nicely rounded, rather than humped, top.

Cool cake in the pan. Cool cake on a wire rack for 5 to 20 minutes before removing it from the pan. To remove a cake, carefully run a knife along the edge to loosen it from the pan. Place another wire rack on top of the pan. With the pan sandwiched between the 2 racks, turn it over. Carefully lift the pan from the cake. So that the top of the cake will be facing up, once again sandwich the cake between 2 racks and turn it over. Remove the top rack.

If the cake sticks to the pan, return it to the oven and heat for 1 minute. Remove it from the pan.

Cut the cake with a thin, sharp knife. Use a sawing, back-and-forth motion. If the frosting sticks, dip the knife in hot water and wipe it with a damp towel after cutting each slice. An electric knife also works well for cutting most layer cakes.

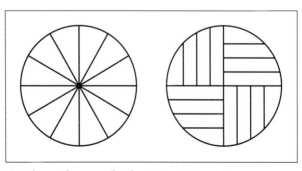

Cutting a layer cake for 12 or 16 servings

SECRETS FOR FOAM CAKES

Do not grease or flour the tube pan. During baking, the batter must be able to cling to the sides of the pan and the center tube in order to rise properly.

Beat eggs at room temperature. For the highest volume, bring egg whites to room temperature before beating them. Be sure that no egg yolk remains in the whites, and that the bowl, beaters and rubber scraper are clean and free from any oil or shortening. Even a little bit of grease will prevent the whites from beating properly.

Break bubbles in the batter. So that the cake will have an even texture, cut through the batter with a knife before baking to break large air bubbles and to seal the batter against the sides of the pan and center tube.

Bake on the bottom rack. In some ovens, cakes in tube pans bake better on the bottom rack, preventing the top from getting too brown. You may need to remove the top oven rack to leave adequate room for the pan or for the cake to expand.

Cool cake in the pan. To prevent this delicate type of cake from collapsing after baking, turn the tube or Bundt® pan upside down on a wire rack, heat-proof funnel or the neck of a bottle so the cake doesn't touch the counter.

Remove it carefully from the pan. To remove the cake, use a thin-bladed knife and, with a sawing motion, run it between the cake and the pan. Place the serving plate on top of the pan and turn it upside down. Rap one side of the pan with the flat side of the knife blade, and carefully lift the pan from the cake.

Cut it with a serrated knife. Use a smooth, gentle sawing motion. Or, use an electric knife.

Freeze leftover egg whites. If you have leftover egg whites, lightly beat them, place them in a freezer container and freeze. Thaw them in the refrigerator and use them like fresh egg whites in foam cakes, meringues and cooked frostings. One egg white equals 2 tablespoons.

How to Tell
When Cakes Are Done

Underbaked cakes are soggy, pale and raw-tasting; overbaked cakes are dry, too brown and may stick in the pan. To be sure that your cake is done just right, follow these simple steps.

Check for doneness at the minimum baking time. Then check at 1-minute intervals until the cake is done.

Butter cakes are done when . . .
- A toothpick inserted in the center comes out clean.
- The top is rounded, smooth and springs back when lightly touched in the center.

Foam cakes are done when . . .
- The top springs back when touched.
- The cracks on top look and feel dry. (If the cake is underbaked, it will pull away from the sides and tube and/or fall out of the pan when inverted).

Keeping Cakes
Fresh and Flavorful

To keep cakes at the peak of their flavor and quality:

Store when completely cooled. Cakes with frostings or fillings containing dairy products should be refrigerated.

Store under cake cover or large bowl. If a cake has a fluffy cooked frosting, insert a knife handle under an edge of the cake cover so it isn't airtight. The frosting can be totally absorbed by the cake when stored in an airtight container. If you don't have a cake cover, cakes with creamy frostings also can be covered lightly with foil, plastic wrap or waxed paper. To keep the frosting from sticking to the protective covering, insert several toothpicks halfway into the cake around the edges and in the center to support the covering.

Freeze unfrosted cakes. For unfrosted butter cakes, cool completely, wrap in heavy-duty foil and freeze. Foam cakes may be frozen in the pan to prevent crushing. Cover tightly and freeze. Unfrosted cakes may be stored in the freezer up to 6 months.

Freeze cakes with buttercream frosting. Frosted cakes can be frozen in a tightly covered plastic container. Or, place cake in freezer until frosting is frozen. Then wrap tightly in plastic wrap or foil and freeze up to 3 months. Cooked, boiled or fruit frostings and fillings don't freeze as well. Place layer cakes in a box or cake container to prevent crushing, then wrap the box in foil or plastic wrap before freezing. Foam cakes may be filled or frosted with whipped cream or whipped topping before freezing. Frosted cakes may be stored in the freezer up to 3 months.

Thaw cakes at room temperature. Thaw unfrosted cakes covered and frosted cakes loosely covered for 2 to 3 hours at room temperature.

SECRETS FOR SUCCESSFUL FROSTINGS, GARNISHES AND DECORATIONS

Easy or elaborate, frosting, garnishes, and other decorations add the crowning touch to your cake creation. (Recipes for frostings begin on p. 184.)

Create the right consistency. Frosting should have a smooth consistency that is firm enough to hold swirls and other patterns and yet soft enough to spread. Glazes should be thin enough to pour or drizzle but not so thin they run off the cake.

Make frosting patterns. Decorate a cake as you frost it by making swirls, crisscrosses, zigzags or spirals with a spatula, knife or the tines of a fork.

Tint frosting with food color. Mix enough of each color before you begin frosting or decorating. The color will darken as the frosting dries.

Add easy garnishes. A cake can be made extra-special by adding a garnish. See p. 210 for **Dessert Garnishes.** Here are just a few things that can be arranged on or sprinkled over a cake:
- Animal crackers
- Chocolate or butterscotch chips, nuts, raisins
- Coconut, colored sprinkles, sugar
- Candies such as mint wafers, jelly beans, gumdrops, peppermints or licorice strings
- Candied, fresh or dried fruit
- Fresh or artificial flowers. When using fresh flowers, choose nontoxic chemical-free blossoms such as nasturtiums, violets, roses or pansies.

Add easy decorations. Try these easy decorating ideas:
- Drizzle melted chocolate around the top edge of the cake for a border effect. Or dip a toothpick in melted chocolate to create marble or spiderweb designs.
- Sift powdered sugar or cocoa onto an unfrosted cake. For a lacy pattern, use a paper doily. Lay the doily on top of the cake. Carefully sift an even layer of powdered sugar or cocoa over it. Lift the doily straight up, leaving a pattern on the cake.
- Use a cookie cutter to mark a design on the frosting of a cake or cupcake. Fill in the design with colored sugar, sprinkles or chopped nuts.

Simple Decorating Bag
A resealable plastic freezer bag can be used as a simple decorating bag. Fill the bag with frosting and seal it. For a writing tip effect, snip off 1 corner, making a very small hole; squeeze the frosting gently through the opening. If you want to use decorative tips, snip off ¼ inch of 1 corner. Place the desired tip in the corner of the bag, fill it with frosting, seal and decorate.

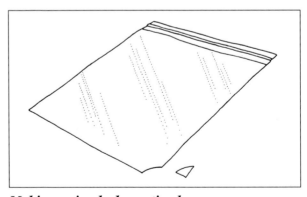

Making a simple decorating bag

NUTRITION IN THIS CHAPTER
Nutrition per serving means the calculation was done on 1 serving, 1 cupcake, 1 petits fours or 1/12 of the frosting recipe.

STEP-BY-STEP FEATURE ～
How to Frost a Two-Layer Cake

STEP 1. Cool cake layers completely on wire racks. When cooled, brush off the crumbs with a pastry brush or your fingers.

STEP 2. Place one layer, top side down, on plate. Place strips of waxed paper under cake edge. Spread with frosting; add second layer, top side up.

STEP 3. Frost sides of cake then top of cake, blending the frosting at the edges. Carefully remove waxed paper strips.

BASIC YELLOW CAKE

This cake is rich, moist and delicious. We suggest frosting it with **Chocolate Buttercream Frosting** *p. 184.*

2½	cups all purpose flour
3	teaspoons baking powder
¼	teaspoon salt
1¼	cups sugar
¾	cup margarine or butter, softened
1	teaspoon vanilla
3	eggs
1	cup milk

Heat oven to 350°F. Grease and flour two 8 or 9-inch round cake pans. In medium bowl, combine flour, baking powder and salt. In large bowl, beat sugar and margarine until light and fluffy. Add vanilla and eggs; blend well. Alternately add dry ingredients and milk, beating well after each addition. Spread batter evenly in greased and floured pans.

Bake at 350°F. for 27 to 35 minutes or until toothpick inserted in center comes out clean. Cool 10 minutes; remove from pans. Cool completely. Fill and frost as desired.
Yield: 12 servings.

TIP:
Cake can be baked in greased and floured 13x9-inch pan. Prepare as directed above. Bake at 350°F. for 33 to 40 minutes. Cool completely. Frost or top as desired.

HIGH ALTITUDE:
Above 3500 Feet: Decrease sugar to 1 cup. Bake as directed above.

NUTRITION PER SERVING:
Calories 310; Protein 5g; Carbohydrate 42g; Fat 13g; Sodium 280mg.

Basic Yellow Cake,
Chocolate Buttercream Frosting p. 184

SIMPLY WHITE CAKE

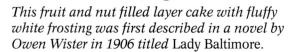

*This lovely white cake can be used anytime a basic white cake is desired. Try it with **Chocolate Cream Frosting**, p. 184, or prepare it for **Lady Baltimore Cake** (this page).*

  2 cups all purpose flour
1½ cups sugar
  3 teaspoons baking powder
½ teaspoon salt
  1 cup milk
½ cup shortening
  1 teaspoon vanilla or ½ teaspoon almond
      extract
  5 egg whites

Heat oven to 350°F. Grease and flour two 9-inch round cake pans. In large bowl, blend flour, sugar, baking powder, salt, milk and shortening at low speed until moistened; beat 2 minutes at medium speed. Add vanilla and egg whites; continue beating an additional 2 minutes. Pour into greased and floured pans.

Bake at 350°F. for 27 to 35 minutes or until toothpick inserted in center comes out clean. Cool 10 minutes; remove from pans. Cool completely. Fill and frost as desired.
Yield: 12 servings.

TIP:
Cake can be baked in 13x9-inch pan. Grease and flour bottom only. Bake at 350°F. for 33 to 40 minutes or until toothpick inserted in center comes out clean. Cool completely. Frost or top as desired.

HIGH ALTITUDE:
Above 3500 Feet: Decrease sugar to 1¼ cups. Bake as directed above.

NUTRITION PER SERVING:
Calories 260; Protein 4g; Carbohydrate 42g; Fat 9g; Sodium 200mg.

VARIATIONS:

COCONUT CAKE: Stir 1 cup flaked coconut into batter before pouring into greased and floured pans. Sprinkle additional coconut over frosting.

POPPY SEED CAKE: Combine ¼ cup poppy seed with an additional ¼ cup milk; allow to stand 30 minutes. Add to batter with egg whites and vanilla.

LADY BALTIMORE CAKE

This fruit and nut filled layer cake with fluffy white frosting was first described in a novel by Owen Wister in 1906 titled Lady Baltimore.

LADY BALTIMORE FILLING
⅓ cup golden or dark raisins
⅓ cup chopped pitted dates or dried figs
⅓ cup chopped pecans
  2 tablespoons cream sherry
  1 cup White Cloud Frosting p. 188

CAKE
    Simply White Cake (this page), or 18.5-oz.
    pkg. pudding-included white cake mix

FROSTING
    White Cloud Frosting p. 188

In small bowl, combine raisins, dates, pecans and sherry; mix well. Cover; let stand at least 1 hour at room temperature to blend flavors, stirring occasionally.

Meanwhile, prepare and bake cake as directed in recipe or on package using two 8 or 9-inch round cake pans. Cool completely.

Prepare frosting as directed in recipe. Add 1 cup of the frosting to raisin mixture; stir until combined. Spread raisin filling between cake layers. Spread remaining frosting on sides and top of cake.
Yield: 12 servings.

HIGH ALTITUDE:
Above 3500 Feet: See recipe or package for directions.

NUTRITION PER SERVING:
Calories 390; Protein 5g; Carbohydrate 69g; Fat 11g; Sodium 280mg.

VARIATION:

LORD BALTIMORE CAKE: Omit Lady Baltimore Filling. Prepare and bake cake as directed above. Prepare White Cloud Frosting substituting ¼ cup firmly packed brown sugar for the ¼ cup sugar.

To prepare Lord Baltimore Filling, place 1 cup of the frosting in small bowl. Add ½ cup chopped pecans, ½ cup crumbled soft macaroon cookies and ¼ cup chopped candied cherries; mix well. Spread filling between cake layers. Spread remaining frosting on sides and top of cake.

APPLE PECAN LAYER CAKE

This layered apple cake is topped with a browned butter frosting.

CAKE
2½ **cups all purpose flour**
2 **cups sugar**
1 **teaspoon baking powder**
1 **teaspoon baking soda**
1 **teaspoon salt**
1 **teaspoon cinnamon**
1½ **cups applesauce**
¾ **cup oil**
2 **eggs**
½ **cup chopped pecans**

APPLE BROWN BUTTER FROSTING
½ **cup butter (do not use margarine)**
4½ **cups powdered sugar**
6 **to 8 tablespoons apple juice**

Heat oven to 350°F. Grease and flour two 9-inch round cake pans. In large bowl, combine flour, sugar, baking powder, baking soda, salt and cinnamon. Add applesauce, oil and eggs; blend at low speed until moistened. Beat 2 minutes at high speed. Stir in pecans. Pour batter into greased and floured pans.

Bake at 350°F. for 30 to 40 minutes or until toothpick inserted in center comes out clean. Cool 10 minutes; remove from pans. Cool completely.

In small heavy saucepan over medium heat, brown butter until light golden brown, stirring constantly. Remove from heat; cool completely. In large bowl, combine browned butter, powdered sugar and 4 tablespoons of the apple juice; blend at low speed until moistened. Continue beating until well blended, adding additional apple juice for desired spreading consistency.

To assemble cake, place 1 cake layer, top side down, on serving plate; spread evenly with about ¼ of frosting. Top with remaining cake layer, top side up. Spread sides and top of cake with remaining frosting. Garnish as desired.
Yield: 12 servings.

HIGH ALTITUDE:
Above 3500 Feet: Decrease sugar to 1¾ cups. Bake at 375°F. for 25 to 35 minutes.

NUTRITION PER SERVING:
Calories 650; Protein 4g; Carbohydrate 104g; Fat 26g; Sodium 390mg.

BLACK FOREST CAKE

Black Forest torte originated in Germany and traditionally is chocolate cake layered with cherries, kirsch and whipped cream. **Basic Chocolate Cake** *p. 116 can be used to make the cake, if desired.*

CAKE
1 **(18.25-oz.) pkg. pudding-included dark chocolate cake mix**
 Water
 Oil
 Eggs

FILLING
1 **(21-oz.) can cherry fruit pie filling**
½ **teaspoon almond extract**

FROSTING
1 **pint (2 cups) whipping cream**
½ **cup powdered sugar**
2 **tablespoons brandy**
 Chocolate Curls p. 210

Heat oven to 350°F. Grease and flour two 8 or 9-inch round cake pans. Prepare and bake cake mix according to package directions. Cool completely.

In small bowl, combine filling ingredients. In medium bowl, beat whipping cream at highest speed until slightly thickened. Gradually add powdered sugar, beating until stiff peaks form. Fold in brandy.

Place 1 cake layer on serving plate; spread 1 cup filling to within 1 inch of edge. Top with second cake layer. Frost top and sides with whipped cream. Spoon remaining filling in center of top of cake; garnish with chocolate curls. Refrigerate until serving time. Store in refrigerator.
Yield: 12 servings.

HIGH ALTITUDE:
Above 3500 Feet: See package for directions.

NUTRITION PER SERVING:
Calories 500; Protein 5g; Carbohydrate 61g; Fat 27g; Sodium 360mg.

BASIC CHOCOLATE CAKE

This traditional cake is rich, chocolaty and dense.

CAKE
  2 cups all purpose flour
1¼ teaspoons baking soda
  ½ teaspoon salt
1½ cups sugar
  ½ cup margarine or butter, softened
  1 teaspoon vanilla
  2 eggs
  4 oz. unsweetened chocolate, melted
  1 cup milk

FROSTING
  1 cup whipping cream, whipped
  2 tablespoons powdered sugar

Heat oven to 350°F. Grease and flour two 8 or 9-inch round cake pans. In medium bowl, combine flour, baking powder and salt. In large bowl, beat sugar and margarine until light and fluffy. Beat in vanilla and eggs. Stir in chocolate. Alternately add dry ingredients and milk, beating well after each addition. Spread batter evenly in greased and floured pans.

Bake at 350°F. for 27 to 35 minutes or until toothpick inserted in center comes out clean. Cool 10 minutes; remove from pans. Cool completely.

In small bowl, beat cream until soft peaks form. Blend in powdered sugar; beat until stiff peaks form. Fill and frost cake with whipped cream.
Yield: 12 servings.

TIP:
Cake can be baked in greased and floured 13x9-inch pan. Prepare as directed above. Bake at 350°F. for 33 to 40 minutes. Cool completely.

HIGH ALTITUDE:
Above 3500 Feet: Decrease sugar to 1¼ cups. Bake as directed above.

NUTRITION PER SERVING:
Calories 380; Protein 5g; Carbohydrate 48g; Fat 19g; Sodium 320mg.

CHOCOLATE CAKE MAKE-OVER

We've developed this cake especially for those who desire a moist cake with fewer calories and less fat.

CAKE
1¾ cups all purpose flour
  ½ cup unsweetened cocoa
1¼ teaspoons baking soda
  ½ teaspoon salt
1¼ cups sugar
  ½ cup margarine or butter, softened
  1 teaspoon vanilla
  4 egg whites
  1 cup lowfat buttermilk

FROSTING
  2 cups light frozen whipped topping, thawed

Heat oven to 350°F. Grease and flour two 8 or 9-inch round cake pans. In medium bowl, combine flour, cocoa, baking soda and salt. In large bowl, beat sugar and margarine until light and fluffy. Beat in vanilla and egg whites. Alternately add dry ingredients and buttermilk, beating well after each addition. Spread batter evenly in greased and floured pans.

Bake at 350°F. for 27 to 35 minutes or until toothpick inserted in center comes out clean. Cool 10 minutes; remove from pans. Cool completely. Fill and frost with whipped topping. Garnish as desired.
Yield: 12 servings.

TIP:
Cake can be baked in greased and floured 13x9-inch pan. Prepare as directed above. Bake at 350°F. for 33 to 40 minutes. Cool completely.

HIGH ALTITUDE:
Above 3500 Feet: Decrease sugar to 1 cup. Bake as directed above.

NUTRITION PER SERVING:
Calories 260; Protein 5g; Carbohydrate 40g; Fat 10g; Sodium 370mg.

Chocolate Cake Make-Over

Brown Butter Apricot Cake

This orange-flavored cake is filled with apricot preserves and topped with a frosting. It was a winner in the 32nd Pillsbury BAKE-OFF® Contest in 1986.

CAKE
- 1 (18.5-oz.) pkg. pudding-included white cake mix
- 1¼ cups water
- ⅓ cup oil
- 1 tablespoon grated orange peel
- 1 teaspoon orange extract
- 3 egg whites

FROSTING AND FILLING
- ½ cup butter (do not use margarine)
- 3 to 4 cups powdered sugar
- ⅓ cup orange juice
- ⅔ cup apricot preserves
- ⅓ cup chopped walnuts or pecans

Heat oven to 350°F. Grease and flour two 8 or 9-inch round cake pans. In large bowl, combine all cake ingredients at low speed until moistened. Beat 2 minutes at high speed. Pour batter into greased and floured pans.

Bake at 350°F. for 20 to 30 minutes or until toothpick inserted in center comes out clean. Cool 15 minutes; remove from pans. Cool completely.

Meanwhile, in small heavy saucepan over medium heat, brown butter until light golden brown, stirring constantly. Remove from heat; cool completely. In large bowl, combine browned butter, 3 cups powdered sugar and orange juice at low speed until moistened. Beat 2 minutes at medium speed or until smooth and well blended. Beat in up to 1 cup additional powdered sugar if necessary for desired spreading consistency.

To assemble cake, slice each cake layer in half horizontally; remove top half from each layer. Spread ⅓ cup of the preserves on bottom half of each layer; replace top half. Place 1 filled layer, top side down, on serving plate; spread with ½ cup of frosting. Top with second filled layer, top side up. Frost sides and top of cake with remaining frosting. Sprinkle walnuts over cake. Refrigerate until serving time. Store in refrigerator.
Yield: 12 servings.

HIGH ALTITUDE:
Above 3500 Feet: Add ¼ cup flour to dry cake mix; increase water to 1⅓ cups. Bake at 375°F. for 20 to 30 minutes.

NUTRITION PER SERVING:
Calories 500; Protein 3g; Carbohydrate 81g; Fat 20g; Sodium 360mg.

Chocolate Praline Layer Cake

This recipe won $25,000 in the 33rd Pillsbury BAKE-OFF® Contest and is one of Pillsbury's most requested recipes. It is spectacular to serve and marvelous to eat!

CAKE
- ½ cup butter or margarine
- ¼ cup whipping cream
- 1 cup firmly packed brown sugar
- ¾ cup coarsely chopped pecans
- 1 (18.25-oz.) pkg. pudding-included devil's food cake mix
- 1¼ cups water
- ⅓ cup oil
- 3 eggs

TOPPING
- 1¾ cups whipping cream
- ¼ cup powdered sugar
- ¼ teaspoon vanilla
  Pecan halves, if desired
  Chocolate Curls, if desired, p. 210

Heat oven to 325°F. In small saucepan, combine butter, ¼ cup whipping cream and brown sugar. Cook over low heat just until butter is melted, stirring occasionally. DO NOT OVERCOOK. Pour into two ungreased 9 or 8-inch round cake pans; sprinkle evenly with chopped pecans.

In large bowl, combine remaining cake ingredients at low speed until moistened. Beat 2 minutes at high speed. Carefully spoon ¼ of batter over pecan mixture around edge of one pan; fill center of pan with ¼ of batter. Repeat with remaining batter and pan.

Bake at 325°F. for 35 to 45 minutes or until top springs back when touched lightly in center. Cool 3 minutes; remove from pans. Cool completely.

In small bowl, beat 1¾ cups whipping cream until soft peaks form. Gradually add powdered sugar and vanilla; beat until stiff peaks form. To assemble cake, place 1 layer, praline side up, on serving plate. Spread top with half of whipped cream mixture. Top with remaining layer, praline side up. Spread top with remaining whipped cream. Garnish with pecans and chocolate curls. Refrigerate until serving time. Store in refrigerator.

Yield: 12 servings.

HIGH ALTITUDE:

Above 3500 Feet: Add 2 tablespoons flour to dry cake mix; increase water to 1⅓ cups. Bake at 350°F. for 30 to 35 minutes. Immediately remove from pans.

NUTRITION PER SERVING:

Calories 610; Protein 5g; Carbohydrate 56g; Fat 41g; Sodium 470mg.

STARLIGHT DOUBLE-DELIGHT CAKE

In 1951, the $25,000 First Prize in the Pillsbury BAKE-OFF® Contest was awarded to the contestant who entered this inventive chocolate cake. First you make the frosting and then you use part of it in the cake batter.

FROSTING

    2 (3-oz.) pkg. cream cheese, softened
    ½ cup margarine or butter, softened
    ½ teaspoon vanilla
    ½ teaspoon peppermint extract
    6 cups (1½ lb.) powdered sugar
    ¼ cup hot water
    4 oz. semi-sweet chocolate, melted

CAKE

    2 cups frosting, prepared as directed
    ¼ cup margarine or butter, softened
    3 eggs
    2 cups all purpose flour
 1½ teaspoons baking soda
    1 teaspoon salt
    ¾ cup milk

Heat oven to 350°F. Grease and flour two 9-inch round cake pans. In large bowl, combine cream cheese, ½ cup margarine, vanilla and peppermint extract; blend until smooth. Add powdered sugar alternately with hot water, beating until smooth. Blend in chocolate.

In another large bowl, combine 2 cups of the frosting mixture and ¼ cup margarine; blend well. Beat in eggs 1 at a time, beating well after each addition. Add flour, baking soda, salt and milk; beat until smooth. Pour batter evenly into greased and floured pans.

Bake at 350°F. for 30 to 40 minutes or until toothpick inserted in center comes out clean. Cool 5 minutes; remove from pans. Cool completely.

To assemble cake, place 1 layer, top side down, on serving plate; spread with about ¼ of frosting. Top with second layer, top side up. Spread sides and top of cake with remaining frosting.

Yield: 12 servings.

HIGH ALTITUDE:

Above 3500 Feet: Increase flour to 2½ cups and use 1½ cups of frosting mixture in cake. Bake as directed above.

NUTRITION PER SERVING:

Calories 520; Protein 6g; Carbohydrate 79g; Fat 21g; Sodium 520mg.

COOK'S NOTE

SOFTENING CREAM CHEESE

Cream cheese can be softened in the microwave oven for ease in spreading or blending it with other ingredients. Remove the cream cheese from its foil package and place it on a microwave-safe plate. Microwave 8 oz. of cream cheese on MEDIUM for 1 to 1½ minutes or until it has softened.

German Chocolate Cake with Coconut Pecan Frosting

Sweet baking chocolate is a blend of unsweetened chocolate, sugar and cocoa butter. It adds a light, mild flavor to this classic cake.

CAKE
    4 oz. sweet baking chocolate, cut into pieces
    ½ cup water
    2 cups sugar
    1 cup margarine or butter, softened
    4 eggs
  2½ cups all purpose flour
    1 teaspoon baking soda
    ½ teaspoon salt
    1 cup buttermilk
    1 teaspoon vanilla

COCONUT PECAN FROSTING
    1 cup sugar
    1 cup evaporated milk
    ½ cup margarine or butter
    3 eggs, beaten
  1⅓ cups flaked coconut
    1 cup chopped pecans or walnuts
    1 teaspoon vanilla

Heat oven to 350°F. Grease and lightly flour three 9-inch round cake pans. In small saucepan over low heat, melt chocolate with water; cool. In large bowl, beat 2 cups sugar and 1 cup margarine until light and fluffy. Add 4 eggs 1 at a time, beating well after each addition. Stir in chocolate mixture. Add flour and remaining cake ingredients; blend at low speed until well combined. Pour batter into greased and floured pans.

Bake at 350°F. for 35 to 45 minutes or until toothpick inserted in center comes out clean. Cool 5 minutes; remove from pans. Cool completely.

In medium saucepan, combine 1 cup sugar, evaporated milk, ½ cup margarine and 3 eggs. Cook over medium heat until mixture starts to bubble, stirring constantly. Stir in coconut, pecans and 1 teaspoon vanilla. Cool to room temperature. Spread frosting between cake layers and on top, leaving sides unfrosted.
Yield: 12 servings.

HIGH ALTITUDE:
Above 3500 Feet: Decrease sugar in cake to 1¾ cups; decrease baking soda to ¾ teaspoon. Bake at 375°F. for 25 to 30 minutes.
NUTRITION PER SERVING:
Calories 730; Protein 10g; Carbohydrate 85g; Fat 39g; Sodium 540mg.

Toasted Butter Pecan Cake

This yellow cake has a subtle pecan flavor in both the cake and buttery frosting. It may take a little more time to prepare, but it's worth the effort!

    ¼ cup butter, melted (do not substitute margarine)
    2 cups chopped pecans
  2¾ cups all purpose flour
    2 teaspoons baking powder
    ½ teaspoon salt
    2 cups sugar
    1 cup butter or margarine, softened
    4 eggs
    1 cup milk
    2 teaspoons vanilla

FROSTING
    ¼ cup butter or margarine, softened
    4 cups powdered sugar
    1 teaspoon vanilla
    4 to 6 tablespoons half-and-half or milk

Heat oven to 350°F. Grease and flour three 8 or 9-inch round cake pans. Combine ¼ cup butter and pecans in shallow pan. Bake at 350°F. for 20 to 25 minutes or until toasted, stirring occasionally. Cool slightly.

In small bowl, combine flour, baking powder and salt. In large bowl, beat sugar and 1 cup butter until light and fluffy. Add eggs 1 at a time, beating well after each addition. Alternately add dry ingredients and milk to sugar mixture, beating well after each addition. Stir in 2 teaspoons vanilla and 1⅓ cups of the toasted pecans. Pour into greased and floured pans.

Bake at 350°F. for 20 to 30 minutes or until cake springs back when touched lightly in center. Cool 10 minutes; remove from pans. Cool completely.

In small bowl, beat ¼ cup butter until light and fluffy. Gradually add powdered sugar, 1 teaspoon vanilla and enough half-and-half for desired spreading consistency. Stir in remaining pecans. Spread frosting between cake layers and on top.
Yield: 16 servings.

HIGH ALTITUDE:
Above 3500 Feet: Decrease sugar to 1¾ cups. Bake at 375°F. for 20 to 30 minutes.

NUTRITION PER SERVING:
Calories 570; Protein 6g; Carbohydrate 70g; Fat 30g; Sodium 310mg.

WHIPPED CREAM ORANGE MARMALADE CAKE

For the best volume, chill the bowl and beaters before beating the cream.

CAKE
- ¼ **cup frozen orange juice concentrate, thawed**
- 1¼ **cups whipping cream**
- 3 **eggs**
- 1 **teaspoon vanilla**
- 1¾ **cups all purpose flour**
- 1¼ **cups sugar**
- 2 **teaspoons baking powder**
- 2 **teaspoons grated orange peel**
- ½ **teaspoon salt**

FROSTING
- 1 **cup whipping cream**
- ¼ **cup powdered sugar**
- 1 **teaspoon orange-flavored liqueur or orange juice**

FILLING
- 2 **to 4 tablespoons orange-flavored liqueur or orange juice**
- 1 **to 1½ cups orange marmalade**

Heat oven to 350°F. Grease and flour two 9 or 8-inch round cake pans. In large bowl, gradually add ¼ cup orange juice concentrate to 1¼ cups whipping cream; beat at high speed until stiff peaks form. Set aside.

In small bowl, beat eggs and vanilla on high speed until thick and lemon-colored, about 5 to 7 minutes. Fold into whipped cream mixture.

In medium bowl, combine flour and remaining cake ingredients. Fold into whipped cream mixture until well blended. Spread batter evenly in greased and floured pans.

Bake at 350°F. for 23 to 28 minutes or until golden brown and toothpick inserted in center comes out clean. Cool 10 minutes; remove from pans. Cool completely.

In medium bowl, beat all frosting ingredients at medium speed until stiff peaks form. Set aside.

To assemble cake, place 1 layer on serving plate. Sprinkle 1 to 2 tablespoons orange-flavored liqueur evenly over top. Spread with half of the orange marmalade. Top with second layer. Sprinkle remaining 1 to 2 tablespoons of the orange-flavored liqueur over top. Spread with remaining orange marmalade. Frost sides of cake with frosting. Refrigerate 2 hours before serving. Store in refrigerator.
Yield: 12 to 16 servings.

HIGH ALTITUDE:
Above 3500 Feet: Increase flour to 2 cups. Bake as directed above.

NUTRITION PER SERVING:
Calories 350; Protein 4g; Carbohydrate 55g; Fat 13g; Sodium 135mg.

COOK'S NOTE

WHIPPED CREAM AS A FROSTING

Whipped cream can be an easy, delicious frosting for any type of cake. To make 2½ cups of whipped cream (for a 2-layer or 13x9-inch cake), begin with 1¼ cups of chilled whipping cream. Beat the whipping cream at medium speed in a chilled deep bowl with chilled beaters. Beat until soft peaks form; beat in 2 tablespoons powdered sugar. DO NOT OVERBEAT. The whipping cream can be flavored with ½ teaspoon of vanilla, ¼ teaspoon of cinnamon or 1 to 2 tablespoons of brandy, rum or flavored liqueur. Add the flavoring with the powdered sugar. Cakes frosted with whipped cream need to be stored in the refrigerator.

COOKIES 'N CREAM CAKE

Because this cake has been so popular, we've provided a tip that allows you to prepare it as a 13x9-inch sheet cake.

CAKE
- 1 (18.5-oz.) pkg. pudding-included white cake mix
- 1¼ cups water
- ⅓ cup oil
- 3 egg whites
- 1 cup coarsely crushed creme-filled chocolate sandwich cookies

FROSTING
- 3 cups powdered sugar
- ¾ cup shortening
- ¼ cup milk
- 1 teaspoon vanilla

Heat oven to 350°F. Grease and flour two 9 or 8-inch round cake pans. In large bowl, combine all cake ingredients except crushed cookies at low speed until moistened; beat 2 minutes at high speed. By hand, stir in cookies. Pour batter into greased and floured pans.

Bake at 350°F. for 25 to 35 minutes or until toothpick inserted in center comes out clean. Cool 15 minutes; remove from pans. Cool completely.

In small bowl, combine all frosting ingredients; beat until smooth. To assemble cake, place 1 cake layer, top side down, on serving plate; spread evenly with about ¼ of frosting. Top with remaining cake layer, top side up. Spread sides and top of cake with remaining frosting. Garnish as desired.

Yield: 12 servings.

TIP:
Cake can be prepared in greased and floured 13x9-inch pan. Bake at 350°F. for 30 to 40 minutes. Cool completely.

HIGH ALTITUDE:
Above 3500 Feet: Add 3 tablespoons flour to dry cake mix; increase water to 1⅓ cups. Bake at 375°F. for 20 to 30 minutes.

NUTRITION PER SERVING:
Calories 520; Protein 3g; Carbohydrate 72g; Fat 25g; Sodium 350mg.

Cookies 'n Cream Cake

CHOCOLATE SOUR CREAM CAKE

A much requested recipe.

CAKE
- 2 cups all purpose flour
- 2 cups sugar
- 1¼ teaspoons baking soda
- 1 teaspoon salt
- ½ teaspoon baking powder
- 1 cup water
- ¾ cup dairy sour cream
- ¼ cup shortening
- 1 teaspoon vanilla
- 2 eggs
- 4 oz. unsweetened chocolate, cut into pieces, melted, cooled

SOUR CREAM CHOCOLATE FROSTING
- 3 cups powdered sugar
- ¼ cup dairy sour cream
- ¼ cup margarine or butter, softened
- 3 tablespoons milk
- 1 teaspoon vanilla
- 3 oz. unsweetened chocolate, cut into pieces, melted, cooled

Heat oven to 350°F. Grease and flour two 8 or 9-inch round cake pans; line bottom of pans with waxed paper. In medium bowl, combine flour, sugar, baking soda, salt and baking powder; blend well. In large bowl, combine remaining cake ingredients; add dry ingredients. Blend at low speed until moistened; beat 3 minutes at high speed. Pour batter into greased, floured and lined pans.

Bake at 350°F. for 30 to 40 minutes or until toothpick inserted in center comes out clean. Cool 10 minutes; remove from pans. Cool completely.

In small bowl, combine all frosting ingredients at low speed until moistened; beat at high speed until smooth and creamy. To assemble cake, place 1 cake layer, top side down, on serving plate; spread evenly with about ¼ of frosting. Top with remaining cake layer, top side up. Spread sides and top of cake with remaining frosting.

Yield: 12 servings.

HIGH ALTITUDE:
Above 3500 Feet: Decrease sugar in cake to 1¾ cups; omit baking powder. Bake at 375°F. for 25 to 35 minutes.

NUTRITION PER SERVING:
Calories 540; Protein 6g; Carbohydrate 80g; Fat 22g; Sodium 400mg.

MARDI GRAS PARTY CAKE

Brown sugar whipped cream surrounds the sides of this delicate cake. It is topped and layered with a coconutty filling.

CAKE
- ⅔ cup butterscotch chips
- ¼ cup water
- 2¼ cups all purpose flour
- 1¼ cups sugar
- 1 teaspoon baking soda
- 1 teaspoon salt
- ½ teaspoon baking powder
- 1 cup buttermilk
- ½ cup shortening
- 3 eggs

FILLING
- ½ cup sugar
- 1 tablespoon cornstarch
- ½ cup half-and-half or evaporated milk
- ⅓ cup water
- ⅓ cup butterscotch chips
- 1 egg, slightly beaten
- 2 tablespoons margarine or butter
- 1 cup coconut
- 1 cup chopped nuts

SEAFOAM CREAM
- 1 cup whipping cream
- ¼ cup firmly packed brown sugar
- ½ teaspoon vanilla

Heat oven to 350°F. Generously grease and flour two 9-inch round cake pans. In small saucepan over low heat, melt ⅔ cup butterscotch chips in ¼ cup water, stirring until smooth. Cool slightly. In large bowl, combine flour, remaining cake ingredients and cooled butterscotch mixture at low speed until moistened; beat 3 minutes at medium speed. Pour batter into greased and floured pans.

Bake at 350°F. for 20 to 30 minutes or until toothpick inserted in center comes out clean. Cool 10 minutes; remove from pans. Cool completely.

In medium saucepan, combine ½ cup sugar and cornstarch; stir in half-and-half, ⅓ cup water, ⅓ cup butterscotch chips and 1 egg. Cook over medium heat until mixture thickens, stirring constantly. Remove from heat. Stir in margarine, coconut and nuts; cool slightly.

In small bowl, beat whipping cream until soft peaks form. Gradually add brown sugar and vanilla, beating until stiff peaks form.

To assemble cake, place 1 cake layer, top side down, on serving plate. Spread with half of filling mixture. Top with second layer, top side up; spread remaining filling on top to within ½ inch of edge. Frost sides and top edge of cake with seafoam cream. Refrigerate at least 1 hour before serving. Store in refrigerator.

Yield: 16 servings.

TIP:
Cake can be baked in 13x9-inch pan. Grease bottom only of pan. Bake at 350°F. for 30 to 35 minutes or until toothpick inserted in center comes out clean. Cool completely. Spread top of cooled cake with filling mixture. Serve topped with seafoam cream.

HIGH ALTITUDE:
Above 3500 Feet: Bake at 350°F. for 30 to 35 minutes. Cool 7 minutes; remove from pans. Cool completely.

NUTRITION PER SERVING:
Calories 460; Protein 6g; Carbohydrate 51g; Fat 27g; Sodium 270mg.

PRINCESS PARTY CAKE

This is an old-fashioned layer cake delicately flavored with pineapple-orange juice, pecans and coconut.

CAKE
- 3 cups all purpose flour
- 1½ cups sugar
- 4 teaspoons baking powder
- 1 teaspoon salt
- 1 cup milk
- ¾ cup shortening
- 5 eggs, reserving 3 egg whites for frosting
- ⅓ cup frozen pineapple-orange juice concentrate, thawed
- 1 teaspoon vanilla

FROSTING
- 1 cup sugar
- ¼ teaspoon cream of tartar
- ¼ teaspoon salt
- ⅓ cup light corn syrup
- ¼ cup frozen pineapple-orange juice concentrate, thawed

FILLING
- ¼ cup coconut
- ¼ cup chopped pecans
- ½ cup crushed pineapple, well drained

Heat oven to 350°F. Generously grease and flour three 8 or 9-inch round cake pans. In large bowl, combine flour, 1½ cups sugar, baking powder, 1 teaspoon salt, milk and shortening; beat at low speed for 1½ minutes. Add 2 eggs and 3 egg yolks 1 at a time, beating well after each addition. Blend in ⅓ cup juice concentrate and vanilla; beat 1½ minutes at low speed. Pour into greased and floured pans.

Bake at 350°F. for 20 to 25 minutes or until toothpick inserted in center comes out clean. Cool 10 minutes; remove from pans. Cool completely.

In top of double boiler, combine reserved egg whites and all frosting ingredients. Place over rapidly boiling water (water should not touch bottom of pan). Cook frosting, beating constantly at highest speed, about 7 minutes or until stiff peaks form. Remove from heat; continue beating until of spreading consistency. To prepare filling, combine ⅓ of frosting with coconut, pecans and pineapple; mix well.

To assemble cake, place 1 cake layer on serving plate; spread with half of filling. Place second layer over filling; spread with remaining filling. Top with remaining cake layer; frost sides and top of cake with remaining frosting.

Yield: 16 servings.

HIGH ALTITUDE:
Above 3500 Feet: Increase flour to 3 cups plus 3 tablespoons. Bake as directed above.

NUTRITION PER SERVING:
Calories 390; Protein 5g; Carbohydrate 61g; Fat 14g; Sodium 280mg.

COOK'S NOTE

MAKING FLUFFY COOKED FROSTINGS

- An electric mixer is necessary to achieve a fluffy cooked frosting. If you do not have a portable mixer, use the head from your standard mixer.
- The presence of fat will reduce the "foaming" action when beating cooked frosting containing egg whites, so make sure the whites contain no specks of yolk and the bowl and beaters are free of any oil or fat residue. Avoid using plastic bowls because they tend to retain fat.
- On damp humid days, slightly less water can be used to make the frosting because it will absorb moisture from the air.
- Beat frosting until stiff peaks form. DO NOT UNDERBEAT.
- When spreading a cooked frosting, use a wet spatula for a smoother appearance.

DARK CHOCOLATE SACHER TORTE

This Viennese classic is made with layers of chocolate cake filled with apricot jam and covered with a creamy chocolate glaze. Serve it with billows of whipped cream.

CAKE
- ½ **cup finely chopped dried apricots**
- ½ **cup rum***
- 1 **(18.25-oz.) pkg. pudding-included devil's food or dark chocolate cake mix**
- ¾ **cup water**
- ⅓ **cup oil**
- 3 **eggs**

GLAZE
- 2 **(10-oz.) jars apricot preserves**
- 2 **tablespoons rum****

FROSTING
- 1 **(6-oz.) pkg. (1 cup) semi-sweet chocolate chips**
- ¾ **cup margarine or butter**
- ½ **to 1 cup sliced almonds**

Heat oven to 350°F. Grease and flour two 9 or 8-inch round cake pans. In small bowl, combine apricots and ½ cup rum; let stand 10 minutes. In large bowl, combine apricot-rum mixture and remaining cake ingredients at low speed until moistened; beat 2 minutes at high speed. Pour into greased and floured pans.

Bake at 350°F. Bake 9-inch layers 25 to 35 minutes; bake 8-inch layers 35 to 45 minutes or until toothpick inserted in center comes out clean. Cool 15 minutes; remove from pans. Cool completely.

In small saucepan over low heat, melt glaze ingredients; strain to remove large apricot pieces. To assemble torte, carefully slice each layer in half horizontally to make 4 layers. Place 1 layer on serving plate; spread with ¼ cup glaze. Repeat with remaining layers and glaze, ending with cake layer. Spread remaining ¼ cup glaze over top of torte, allowing some to run down sides. Refrigerate 1 hour or until glaze is set.

In small saucepan over low heat, melt chocolate chips and margarine, stirring constantly until smooth. Refrigerate 30 minutes or until slightly thickened, stirring occasionally. Spread frosting over sides and top of cake. Arrange almond slices on sides of cake. Refrigerate at least 1 hour before serving. Garnish as desired. Store in refrigerator.
Yield: 16 servings.

TIPS:
* To substitute for ½ cup rum in cake, use 2 teaspoons rum extract plus water to make ½ cup.
** To substitute for 2 tablespoons rum in glaze, use 1 teaspoon rum extract plus water to make 2 tablespoons.

HIGH ALTITUDE:
Above 3500 Feet: Add 3 tablespoons flour to dry cake mix. Bake at 375°F. for 30 to 40 minutes.

NUTRITION PER SERVING:
Calories 470; Protein 5g; Carbohydrate 57g; Fat 23g; Sodium 340mg.

BANANA TORTE

Here's a moist sour cream banana cake filled with a rich vanilla custard and topped with sweetened whipped cream. One taste and you'll know it's homemade.

CAKE
- 1 **cup sugar**
- ½ **cup margarine or butter, softened**
- ¾ **cup mashed ripe bananas**
- 1 **teaspoon vanilla**
- 2 **eggs**
- 2 **cups all purpose flour**
- 1 **teaspoon baking soda**
- 1 **teaspoon baking powder**
- ½ **teaspoon salt**
- ½ **cup dairy sour cream**
- ½ **cup chopped nuts**

FILLING
- 1 **cup milk**
- ½ **cup sugar**
- 3 **tablespoons all purpose flour**
- ¼ **teaspoon salt**
- 2 **egg yolks**
- 1 **teaspoon vanilla**

TOPPING
- **Powdered sugar**
- **Whipping cream, whipped, sweetened***

Heat oven to 350°F. Grease and flour 9-inch square pan. In large bowl, beat 1 cup sugar and margarine until light and fluffy. Add bananas, 1 teaspoon vanilla and 2 eggs; mix well. Gradually add 2 cups flour, baking soda, baking powder and ½ teaspoon salt; mix well. Blend in sour cream; stir in nuts. Pour batter into greased and floured pan.

Bake at 350°F. for 40 to 45 minutes or until tooth-pick inserted in center comes out clean. Cool 5 minutes; remove from pan. Cool completely.

Meanwhile, in medium saucepan heat milk until very hot; do not boil. In medium bowl, combine ½ cup sugar, 3 tablespoons flour and ¼ teaspoon salt. Stir in hot milk; mix well. Return mixture to saucepan; cook over medium heat until mixture boils and thickens, about 4 to 5 minutes, stirring constantly. In small bowl, beat 2 egg yolks; gradually blend ¼ of hot milk mixture into yolks. Add egg yolk mixture to saucepan; cook 2 to 3 minutes, stirring constantly. Remove from heat; stir in 1 teaspoon vanilla. Cool.

To assemble cake, slice cooled cake horizontally into 2 layers; spread filling between layers. Sprinkle powdered sugar over top layer. Serve topped with sweetened whipped cream. Store in refrigerator.
Yield: 9 servings.

TIP:
* To prepare sweetened whipped cream, for each cup of whipping cream gradually add 2 to 4 tablespoons sugar or powdered sugar during beating.

HIGH ALTITUDE:
Above 3500 Feet: No change.

NUTRITION PER SERVING:
Calories 510; Protein 8g; Carbohydrate 65g; Fat 25g; Sodium 500mg.

MOCHA CREAM CHOCOLATE TORTE

Inspired by a Belgian dessert, this buttercream-layered torte from the 1986 BAKE-OFF® Contest is a perfect ending for a special meal. It is surprisingly easy to make.

CAKE
- 1 (18.25-oz.) pkg. pudding-included German chocolate cake mix
  Water
  Oil
  Eggs

FROSTING
- ½ cup sugar
- ¼ cup cornstarch
- 2 tablespoons instant coffee granules or crystals
- 1¼ cups milk
- 1 cup margarine or butter, softened
- ¼ cup powdered sugar
  Chocolate sprinkles, if desired
  Whole blanched almonds, if desired

Heat oven to 350°F. Grease and flour 13x9-inch pan. Prepare and bake cake mix according to package directions. Cool 15 minutes; remove from pan. Cool completely.

Meanwhile, in medium saucepan combine sugar, cornstarch and instant coffee; blend well. Gradually stir in milk. Cook over medium heat until mixture thickens and boils, stirring constantly. Remove from heat; cover with plastic wrap. Refrigerate 30 minutes or until cool. (Mixture will be very thick.) In large bowl, beat margarine and powdered sugar until well blended. Gradually add cooled coffee mixture; beat until light and fluffy.

To assemble torte, cut cooled cake in half length-wise. Slice each half in half horizontally to make 4 layers. Place 1 layer on serving tray. Spread top with about ⅓ cup frosting. Repeat with remaining layers and frosting. Frost sides and top of cake. Sprinkle top of torte with chocolate sprinkles; garnish with almonds. Store in refrigerator.
Yield: 12 servings.

HIGH ALTITUDE:
Above 3500 Feet: See package for directions.

NUTRITION PER SERVING:
Calories 460; Protein 5g; Carbohydrate 49g; Fat 28g; Sodium 460mg.

CARROT CAKE WITH CREAMY COCONUT FROSTING

Pineapple not only adds an interesting flavor to this classic cake, it also helps to keep it moist. It's easy to make and is perfect for any occasion.

CAKE
2½ **cups all purpose flour**
2 **teaspoons baking soda**
1 **teaspoon salt**
1 **teaspoon cinnamon, if desired**
2 **cups sugar**
1 **cup oil**
2 **teaspoons vanilla**
2 **eggs**
2 **cups shredded carrots**
1 **(8-oz.) can crushed pineapple, well drained**
½ **cup raisins**
½ **cup chopped nuts**

CREAMY COCONUT FROSTING
1 **(8¼-oz.) pkg. cream cheese, softened**
2½ **cups powdered sugar**
6 **tablespoons margarine or butter, softened**
2 **teaspoons vanilla**
1 **cup coconut**
½ **cup chopped nuts**

Heat oven to 350°F. Grease and flour 13x9-inch pan. In medium bowl, combine flour, baking soda, salt and cinnamon; set aside. In large bowl, combine sugar, oil, 2 teaspoons vanilla and eggs; beat well. Stir in flour mixture; mix well. Stir in carrots, pineapple, raisins and ½ cup nuts. Pour batter into greased and floured pan.

Bake at 350°F. for 50 to 60 minutes or until cake springs back when touched lightly in center. Cool completely.

In large bowl, combine cream cheese, powdered sugar, margarine and 2 teaspoons vanilla; beat until smooth. Stir in coconut and ½ cup nuts. Spread over cooled cake.
Yield: 16 servings.

HIGH ALTITUDE:
Above 3500 Feet: Increase flour to 2¾ cups; decrease sugar to 1½ cups. Bake as directed above.

NUTRITION PER SERVING:
Calories 560; Protein 6g; Carbohydrate 66g; Fat 30g; Sodium 380mg.

GOLDEN CARROT PINEAPPLE CAKE

We've substantially reduced the fat and calories.

CAKE
1½ **cups all purpose flour**
1 **cup whole wheat flour**
2 **teaspoons baking soda**
1 **teaspoon cinnamon**
½ **teaspoon salt**
1 **cup sugar**
⅔ **cup oil**
1 **(8-oz.) can crushed pineapple in its own juice, undrained**
½ **cup frozen cholesterol-free egg product, thawed**
2 **teaspoons vanilla**
2 **cups shredded carrots**
½ **cup raisins**

LIGHT CREAMY FROSTING
4 **oz. light cream cheese, softened**
2 **tablespoons margarine, softened**
1 **cup powdered sugar**
1 **teaspoon vanilla**

Heat oven to 350°F. Grease and flour 13x9-inch pan. In medium bowl, combine all purpose flour, whole wheat flour, baking soda, cinnamon and salt; set aside. In large bowl, combine sugar, oil, pineapple, egg product and 2 teaspoons vanilla; beat well. Stir in flour mixture; mix well. Stir in carrots and raisins. Pour batter into greased and floured pan.

Bake at 350°F. for 30 to 40 minutes or until top springs back when touched lightly in center. Cool completely.

In small bowl, combine cream cheese and margarine; beat until smooth. Gradually beat in powdered sugar and vanilla. Spread over cooled cake.
Yield: 16 servings.

HIGH ALTITUDE:
Above 3500 Feet: Decrease sugar to ¾ cup. Bake as directed above.

NUTRITION PER SERVING:
Calories 290; Protein 4g; Carbohydrate 41g; Fat 12g; Sodium 280mg.

Golden Carrot Pineapple Cake

Pineapple Upside-Down Cake

~

*This pretty cake is welcome for dessert anytime —
it's a small cake so there are few leftovers.*

- ½ **cup firmly packed brown sugar**
- ¼ **cup margarine or butter, melted**
- 6 **canned pineapple slices, drained**
- 6 **maraschino cherries**
- 2 **eggs, separated**
- ½ **cup sugar**
- ¾ **cup all purpose flour**
- ½ **teaspoon baking powder**
- ¼ **teaspoon salt**
- ¼ **cup pineapple juice**
  Whipped cream

Heat oven to 350°F. In small bowl, combine brown
sugar and margarine; blend well. Spread in bottom
of ungreased 9-inch round cake pan. Arrange
pineapple slices and maraschino cherries over
brown sugar mixture. Set aside.

In small bowl, beat egg yolks until thick and lemon
colored. Gradually add sugar; beat well. Add flour,
baking powder, salt and pineapple juice to egg yolk
mixture; mix well. In another small bowl, beat egg
whites until stiff peaks form; fold into batter. Pour
batter evenly over pineapple slices and cherries.

Bake at 350°F. for 30 to 35 minutes or until toothpick inserted in center comes out clean. Cool
upright in pan 2 minutes; invert onto serving plate.
Serve warm with whipped cream.
Yield: 6 servings.

HIGH ALTITUDE:
Above 3500 Feet: Increase flour to ¾ cup plus
3 tablespoons. Bake at 375°F. for 30 to 35 minutes.

NUTRITION PER SERVING:
Calories 340; Protein 4g; Carbohydrate 55g; Fat 13g;
Sodium 230mg.

Cranberry Upside-Down Cake

~

*Crimson cranberries almost glow when this
dessert is turned out of the pan. Serve it warm or
cool, with cream or whipped cream.*

- ⅔ **cup sugar**
- 2 **cups fresh or frozen cranberries (do not
  thaw)**

CAKE
- 1¼ **cups all purpose flour**
- 1 **cup sugar**
- 1½ **teaspoons baking powder**
- ½ **teaspoon salt**
- 1 **teaspoon grated lemon peel**
- ⅔ **cup milk**
- ¼ **cup shortening**
- ¼ **teaspoon vanilla**
- 1 **egg**

Heat oven to 350°F. Grease 8-inch square pan.
Sprinkle ⅓ cup of the sugar in pan. Arrange cranberries over sugar; sprinkle with remaining ⅓ cup
sugar. Cover with foil. Bake at 350°F. for 30 minutes. Remove foil; cool.

In large bowl, combine all cake ingredients; blend
at low speed until moistened. Beat 2 minutes at
medium speed. Pour batter evenly over cranberries.

Bake at 350°F. for 40 to 50 minutes or until toothpick inserted in center comes out clean. For easy
removal, run knife around edge of pan. Invert onto
serving plate, leaving pan over cake for 2 minutes;
remove pan. Serve warm or cold.
Yield: 9 servings.

HIGH ALTITUDE:
Above 3500 Feet: Decrease sugar in cake to ¾ cup.
Bake as directed above.

NUTRITION PER SERVING:
Calories 290; Protein 3g; Carbohydrate 54g; Fat 7g;
Sodium 190mg.

FROSTED BANANA SNACK CAKE

Well-ripened bananas are the flavor secret of this yummy cake. To hasten ripening, place bananas in a paper or plastic bag or fruit-ripening bowl.

CAKE
- 3/4 cup sugar
- 1/3 cup margarine or butter, softened
- 3/4 cup mashed ripe bananas
- 1/4 cup buttermilk
- 1 teaspoon vanilla
- 1 egg
- 1 1/4 cups all purpose flour
- 1 teaspoon baking powder
- 1/2 teaspoon baking soda
- 1/2 teaspoon salt
- 1/2 teaspoon cinnamon
- 1/8 teaspoon cloves
- 1/8 teaspoon nutmeg
- 1/4 cup chopped walnuts or pecans

FROSTING
- 2 cups powdered sugar
- 1 (3-oz.) pkg. cream cheese, softened
- 2 tablespoons margarine or butter, softened
- 1 tablespoon milk
- 1/2 teaspoon vanilla

Heat oven to 350°F. Grease and flour 8 or 9-inch square pan. In large bowl, beat sugar and 1/3 cup margarine until light and fluffy. Add bananas, buttermilk, vanilla and egg; mix well. Add remaining ingredients except nuts; mix well. Stir in nuts. Spread batter in greased and floured pan.

Bake at 350°F. for 25 to 30 minutes or until golden brown and toothpick inserted in center comes out clean. Cool completely.

In medium bowl, combine all frosting ingredients; beat until smooth and creamy. Spread over cooled cake. Store in refrigerator.
Yield: 9 servings.

HIGH ALTITUDE:
Above 3500 Feet: Decrease sugar to 1/2 cup. Bake as directed above.

NUTRITION PER SERVING:
Calories 390; Protein 4g; Carbohydrate 58g; Fat 16g; Sodium 370mg.

BANANA SNACK CAKE

This cake is perfect for after school snacking or toting to a picnic.

- 1 cup sugar
- 1 cup margarine or butter, softened
- 2 eggs
- 1/2 cup buttermilk
- 1 cup mashed ripe bananas
- 1 teaspoon vanilla
- 2 cups all purpose flour
- 1 cup quick-cooking rolled oats
- 1 1/2 teaspoons baking soda
- 1/2 teaspoon salt
- 1 (6-oz.) pkg. (1 cup) semi-sweet chocolate chips
- 1/2 cup chopped nuts

Heat oven to 350°F. Grease 13x9-inch pan. In large bowl, combine sugar, margarine and eggs; mix well. Stir in buttermilk, bananas and vanilla; blend well. Stir in flour, oats, baking soda and salt; mix well. Stir in chocolate chips. Spread batter in greased pan. Sprinkle nuts evenly over top.

Bake at 350°F. for 30 to 35 minutes or until toothpick inserted in center comes out clean.
Yield: 16 servings.

HIGH ALTITUDE:
Above 3500 Feet: No change.

NUTRITION PER SERVING:
Calories 340; Protein 5g; Carbohydrate 38g; Fat 19g; Sodium 320mg.

Chocolate Fudge Snack Cake

Serve this rich, chocolaty cake warm with vanilla ice cream.

CAKE
- ½ cup margarine or butter
- 1 (11.75-oz.) jar hot fudge ice cream topping
- 1½ cups all purpose flour
- 1½ cups sugar
- 1 cup mashed potato flakes
- 1 teaspoon baking soda
- ¾ cup buttermilk
- 1 teaspoon vanilla
- 2 eggs
- 1 cup finely chopped walnuts
- 1 (6-oz.) pkg. (1 cup) semi-sweet chocolate chips

GLAZE
- ½ cup sugar
- ¼ cup buttermilk
- ¼ cup margarine or butter
- 1½ teaspoons light corn syrup or water
- ¼ teaspoon baking soda
- ½ teaspoon vanilla
- 2 tablespoons chopped walnuts

Heat oven to 350°F. Grease and flour 13x9-inch pan. In small saucepan over low heat, melt ½ cup margarine and fudge topping, stirring constantly until smooth. In large bowl, combine flour and remaining cake ingredients except 1 cup walnuts and chocolate chips; beat at low speed until well blended. Add fudge mixture; beat 2 minutes at medium speed. By hand, stir in 1 cup walnuts and chocolate chips. Pour batter into greased and floured pan.

Bake at 350°F. for 40 to 45 minutes or until toothpick inserted in center comes out clean.

In small saucepan, combine all glaze ingredients except vanilla and 2 tablespoons walnuts. Bring to a boil over medium heat. Reduce heat; simmer for 5 minutes or until light golden brown, stirring constantly. Remove from heat; stir in vanilla. Pour warm glaze over warm cake, spreading to cover. Sprinkle with 2 tablespoons walnuts. Serve warm or cool.
Yield: 16 servings.

HIGH ALTITUDE:
Above 3500 Feet: Increase flour to 1¾ cups; decrease sugar in cake to 1 cup. Bake as directed above. Increase simmering time for glaze to 8 minutes.

NUTRITION PER SERVING:
Calories 450; Protein 6g; Carbohydrate 57g; Fat 22g; Sodium 220mg.

Chocolate Cherry Bars

Cake mix and cherry pie filling combine to create a moist cake rich in chocolate flavor with cherries throughout.

CAKE BARS
- 1 (18.25-oz.) pkg. pudding-included devil's food cake mix
- 1 (21-oz.) can cherry fruit pie filling
- 1 teaspoon almond extract
- 2 eggs, beaten

FROSTING
- 1 cup sugar
- ⅓ cup milk
- 5 tablespoons margarine or butter
- 1 (6-oz.) pkg. (1 cup) semi-sweet chocolate chips

Heat oven to 350°F. Grease and flour 15x10x1-inch baking pan or 13x9-inch pan. In large bowl, combine all bar ingredients; stir until well blended. Pour into greased and floured pan.

Bake at 350°F. in 15x10x1-inch pan for 20 to 30 minutes or in 13x9-inch pan for 25 to 30 minutes or until toothpick inserted in center comes out clean.

In small saucepan, combine sugar, milk and margarine. Bring to a boil; boil 1 minute, stirring constantly. Remove from heat; stir in chocolate chips until smooth. Pour and spread over warm cake. Cool completely. Cut into squares. Garnish as desired.
Yield: 36 to 48 servings.

HIGH ALTITUDE:
Above 3500 Feet: Bake at 375°F. in 15x10x1-inch pan for 20 to 30 minutes or in 13x9-inch pan for 25 to 30 minutes.

NUTRITION PER SERVING:
Calories 120; Protein 1g; Carbohydrate 20g; Fat 4g; Sodium 95mg.

S'MORE SNACK CAKE

Graham crackers, chocolate chips and marshmallow creme are among the ingredients in this delightful cake, inspired by the popular picnic treat of the same name. You can be sure everyone will be back for more.

- 1 cup all purpose flour
- 2 cups graham cracker crumbs
- 1 teaspoon baking powder
- ½ teaspoon baking soda
- ½ teaspoon salt
- 1 cup firmly packed brown sugar
- ½ cup shortening
- 3 eggs
- 1 cup milk
- 1 cup miniature semi-sweet chocolate chips
- 1 (7-oz.) jar (1½ cups) marshmallow creme

Heat oven to 350°F. Grease and flour 13x9-inch pan. In medium bowl, combine flour, graham cracker crumbs, baking powder, baking soda and salt; mix well. Set aside.

In large bowl, beat brown sugar, shortening and eggs until well blended. Add dry ingredients and milk; mix at low speed until well blended. Beat at medium speed 1 minute. Stir in ⅔ cup of the chocolate chips. Spread batter evenly in greased and floured pan.

Bake at 350°F. for 25 to 35 minutes until toothpick inserted in center comes out clean. Cool 15 minutes.

Meanwhile, melt remaining ⅓ cup chocolate chips in small saucepan over low heat. Spoon teaspoonfuls of marshmallow creme onto top of warm cake; carefully spread with knife dipped in hot water. Drizzle with melted chocolate and swirl chocolate through marshmallow creme to marble. Cool completely.

Yield: 16 servings.

HIGH ALTITUDE:
Above 3500 Feet: Increase flour to 1 cup plus 2 tablespoons. Bake at 375°F. for 20 to 30 minutes.

NUTRITION PER SERVING:
Calories 290; Protein 4g; Carbohydrate 44g; Fat 12g; Sodium 220mg.

DOUBLE CHOCOLATE CREAM CHEESE CAKE

A meringue-like topping forms on this dense chocolate cake.

CAKE
- 3 cups all purpose flour
- 2 cups sugar
- ½ cup unsweetened cocoa
- 2 teaspoons baking soda
- ½ teaspoon salt
- 2 cups hot coffee
- ⅔ cup oil
- 2 tablespoons vinegar
- 2 teaspoons vanilla
- 2 eggs

TOPPING
- ⅓ cup sugar
- 1 (8-oz.) pkg. cream cheese, softened
- ½ teaspoon vanilla
- 1 egg
- 1 (6-oz.) pkg. (1 cup) semi-sweet chocolate chips
- 1 cup finely chopped nuts
- ¼ cup sugar

Heat oven to 350°F. Grease and flour bottom only of 13x9-inch pan. In large bowl, combine all cake ingredients at low speed until moistened; beat 1 minute at medium speed (batter will be thin). Pour batter into greased and floured pan.

In small bowl, beat ⅓ cup sugar, cream cheese, ½ teaspoon vanilla and 1 egg until fluffy; stir in chocolate chips and nuts. Spoon teaspoonfuls of topping evenly over batter; sprinkle with ¼ cup sugar.

Bake at 350°F. for 45 to 60 minutes or until toothpick inserted in cake portion comes out clean. Cool completely. Store in refrigerator.

Yield: 16 servings.

HIGH ALTITUDE:
Above 3500 Feet: Decrease baking soda to 1½ teaspoons. Bake at 375°F. for 60 to 70 minutes.

NUTRITION PER SERVING:
Calories 480; Protein 7g; Carbohydrate 59g; Fat 24g; Sodium 280mg.

Apricot Gooey Cake

This easy-to-make snack cake is just the right size for smaller families. An apricot and coconut topping makes it special.

½ **cup dried apricots**
1½ **cups water**

CAKE
1¾ **cups all purpose flour**
½ **teaspoon baking powder**
½ **teaspoon baking soda**
½ **teaspoon salt**
1 **cup sugar**
⅓ **cup margarine or butter, softened**
½ **teaspoon vanilla**
¼ **teaspoon lemon extract**
1 **egg**
⅔ **cup water**

FROSTING
¼ **cup firmly packed brown sugar**
2 **tablespoons margarine or butter**
   Reserved pureed apricots
½ **cup coconut**

In small saucepan, combine apricots and 1½ cups water. Cook over medium heat 15 to 20 minutes or until apricots are tender, stirring occasionally. Drain; puree apricots. Set aside.

Heat oven to 350°F. Grease and flour 9-inch square pan. In small bowl, combine flour, baking powder, baking soda and salt. In large bowl, beat sugar and ⅓ cup margarine until light and fluffy. Add vanilla, lemon extract and egg; beat well. Alternately add dry ingredients and ⅔ cup water to sugar mixture, beating well after each addition. Stir in 2 tablespoons of the pureed apricots. Pour batter into greased and floured pan.

Bake at 350°F. for 25 to 35 minutes or until toothpick inserted in center comes out clean. Cool slightly.

In small saucepan, combine brown sugar, 2 tablespoons margarine and remaining pureed apricots. Bring to a boil over medium heat; boil 1 minute, stirring constantly. Remove from heat; stir in coconut. Immediately spread over warm cake. Cool completely.
Yield: 9 servings.

HIGH ALTITUDE:
Above 3500 Feet: Bake at 375°F. for 25 to 35 minutes.

NUTRITION PER SERVING:
Calories 330; Protein 4g; Carbohydrate 53g; Fat 12g; Sodium 320mg.

Macaroon Cookie Cake

In this recipe, a quick-to-mix chocolate cake is baked with a coconut topping. It's like eating a candy bar!

CAKE
1¾ **cups all purpose flour**
1¼ **cups sugar**
1½ **teaspoons baking powder**
1 **teaspoon salt**
½ **teaspoon baking soda**
½ **cup margarine or butter, softened**
1 **cup buttermilk**
1 **teaspoon vanilla**
3 **eggs**
3 **oz. unsweetened chocolate, melted**

TOPPING
1 **(14-oz.) can sweetened condensed milk (not evaporated)**
1 **(7-oz.) pkg. (2⅔ cups) coconut**
1 **teaspoon vanilla**

Heat oven to 350°F. Grease and flour 13x9-inch pan. In large bowl, combine all cake ingredients at low speed until moistened; beat 3 minutes at medium speed. Pour batter into greased and floured pan. In small bowl, combine all topping ingredients; mix well. Carefully drop by teaspoonfuls over batter.

Bake at 350°F. for 30 to 40 minutes or until top springs back when touched lightly in center. Cool completely.
Yield: 15 servings.

HIGH ALTITUDE:
Above 3500 Feet: Increase flour to 2 cups; decrease sugar to 1 cup. Bake at 375°F. for 30 to 40 minutes.

NUTRITION PER SERVING:
Calories 370; Protein 7g; Carbohydrate 50g; Fat 17g; Sodium 350mg.

Pumpkin Gingerbread with Caramel Sauce

Although this old-time favorite is best served warm, it can be made several hours ahead and served at room temperature.

GINGERBREAD
2¼   cups all purpose flour
½   cup sugar
⅔   cup margarine or butter
¾   cup coarsely chopped pecans
1   teaspoon baking soda
1½   teaspoons ginger
½   teaspoon cinnamon
¼   teaspoon salt
¼   teaspoon cloves
¾   cup buttermilk
½   cup light molasses
½   cup canned pumpkin
1   egg

CARAMEL SAUCE
½   cup margarine or butter
1¼   cups firmly packed brown sugar
2   tablespoons light corn syrup
½   cup whipping cream

Heat oven to 350°F. In large bowl, combine flour and sugar. Using pastry blender or fork, cut in ⅔ cup margarine until mixture resembles fine crumbs. Stir in pecans. Press 1¼ cups of crumb mixture into bottom of ungreased 9-inch square pan. To remaining crumb mixture, add remaining gingerbread ingredients; mix well. Pour evenly in crust-lined pan.

Bake at 350°F. for 40 to 50 minutes or until toothpick inserted in center comes out clean.

In medium saucepan, melt ½ cup margarine; stir in brown sugar and corn syrup. Bring to a boil; cook until sugar dissolves, about 1 minute, stirring constantly. Stir in whipping cream; return to a boil. Remove from heat. Serve sauce over warm gingerbread topped with a scoop of ice cream. Garnish with chopped pecans, if desired.

Yield: 12 servings.

MICROWAVE DIRECTIONS:
To prepare sauce in microwave, place margarine in 4-cup microwave-safe measuring cup. Microwave on HIGH for 1 minute or until melted. Stir in brown sugar and corn syrup. Microwave on HIGH for 2 to 3 minutes or until sugar dissolves, stirring once halfway through cooking. Stir in whipping cream. Microwave on HIGH for 45 to 60 seconds or until mixture boils, stirring once halfway through cooking.

HIGH ALTITUDE:
Above 3500 Feet: Add 3 tablespoons flour to remaining crumb mixture. Bake as directed above.

NUTRITION PER SERVING:
Calories 510; Protein 5g; Carbohydrate 63g; Fat 27g; Sodium 360mg.

Toffee Bar Cake

You'll love this brown sugar cake with a crunchy candy bar topping.

2   cups all purpose flour
2   cups firmly packed brown sugar
½   cup shortening
1   teaspoon baking soda
½   teaspoon salt
1   cup milk
1   teaspoon vanilla
1   egg
½   cup chopped nuts
6   (1.4-oz.) chocolate covered toffee bars, broken into small pieces

Heat oven to 350°F. Grease 13x9-inch pan. In large bowl, combine flour, brown sugar and shortening until crumbly; reserve 1 cup for topping. Add baking soda, salt, milk, vanilla and egg to remaining crumb mixture; beat 3 minutes. Pour into greased pan. Sprinkle with reserved crumb mixture, nuts and toffee bars.

Bake at 350°F. for 30 to 40 minutes or until toothpick inserted in center comes out clean. Cool completely. Serve with whipped cream, if desired. 12 servings.

HIGH ALTITUDE:
Above 3500 Feet: Decrease brown sugar to 1¾ cups. Reserve ¾ cup mixture for topping. Increase eggs to 2. Bake at 375°F. for 30 to 40 minutes.

NUTRITION PER SERVING:
Calories 440; Protein 5g; Carbohydrate 58g; Fat 21g; Sodium 245mg.

GINGERBREAD WITH RASPBERRY PEAR SAUCE

Gingerbread — classic, yet classy! Experience this unique flavor combination of red raspberries and pears served over wedges of traditional gingerbread.

GINGERBREAD

1⅓ cups all purpose flour
½ cup firmly packed brown sugar
½ teaspoon baking powder
½ teaspoon baking soda
¼ teaspoon salt
¾ teaspoon cinnamon
½ teaspoon ginger
½ cup shortening or margarine
½ cup boiling water
½ cup molasses
1 egg, slightly beaten

RASPBERRY PEAR SAUCE

1 (10-oz.) pkg. frozen raspberries, thawed
¼ cup sugar
1 tablespoon lemon juice
3 firm pears, peeled, cut into bite-size pieces (about 3 cups)

Heat oven to 350°F. Grease bottom only of 9-inch round pan. In large bowl, combine flour, brown sugar, baking powder, baking soda, salt, cinnamon and ginger; mix well. Add remaining gingerbread ingredients; blend well. Pour into greased pan.

Bake at 350°F. for 25 to 35 minutes or until toothpick inserted in center comes out clean.

Drain raspberries, reserving ¼ cup liquid. In blender container or food processor bowl with metal blade, blend raspberries and reserved ¼ cup liquid at highest speed until smooth. Press through large strainer to remove seeds; discard seeds. In large skillet, combine raspberry puree, sugar, lemon juice and pears. Bring to a boil. Reduce heat; simmer until pears are tender. Serve sauce warm or cool over wedges of gingerbread. Garnish each serving with sweetened whipped cream, if desired.
Yield: 8 servings.

MICROWAVE DIRECTIONS:

To prepare gingerbread, prepare batter as directed above. Pour into ungreased 8-inch (1½-quart) round microwave-safe dish. Microwave on HIGH for 5 to 7 minutes or until toothpick inserted in center comes out clean. Cool directly on counter for 10 minutes.

To prepare sauce, prepare raspberry puree as directed above. In medium microwave-safe bowl or 8-cup microwave-safe measuring cup, combine raspberry puree with sugar, lemon juice and pears. Microwave on HIGH for 5 to 6 minutes or until pears are tender, stirring twice during cooking. Serve as directed above.

HIGH ALTITUDE:

Above 3500 Feet: Increase flour to 1⅔ cups; decrease brown sugar to ¼ cup. Bake or microwave as directed above.

NUTRITION PER SERVING:

Calories 410; Protein 3g; Carbohydrate 67g; Fat 14g; Sodium 170mg.

COOK'S NOTE

PEARS

Pears come in many varieties. The Bartlett variety is best for fresh snacks, salads and poaching. Bosc, Anjou and Comice varieties are good when firm for baking and when fully ripened for snacks and salads. Since pears must be picked before they're ripe, allow them to ripen at room temperature in a paper bag or a loosely covered bowl. When ripe, pears yield to a gentle pressure of the hand.

Gingerbread with Raspberry Pear Sauce

Chocolate Chip Zucchini Cake

Sheet cakes are perfect for any occasion and they're quick and easy to make. This one is great unfrosted, or can be frosted with your favorite chocolate frosting. Choose small, firm zucchini to use in this recipe.

1½   cups sugar
½   cup margarine or butter, softened
¼   cup oil
1   teaspoon vanilla
2   eggs
2½   cups all purpose flour
¼   cup unsweetened cocoa
1   teaspoon baking soda
½   cup buttermilk
2   cups shredded zucchini
½   to 1 cup semi-sweet chocolate chips
½   cup chopped nuts

Heat oven to 350°F. Grease and flour 13x9-inch pan. In large bowl, combine sugar, margarine, oil, vanilla and eggs; beat well. Add flour, cocoa, baking soda and buttermilk; blend well. Fold in zucchini, chocolate chips and nuts. Spread in greased and floured pan.

Bake at 350°F. for 35 to 45 minutes or until toothpick inserted in center comes out clean. Cool completely. Frost as desired.

Yield: 16 servings.

HIGH ALTITUDE:
Above 3500 Feet: Bake at 375°F. for 30 to 40 minutes.

NUTRITION PER SERVING:
Calories 330; Protein 4g; Carbohydrate 42g; Fat 17g; Sodium 160mg.

Caramel Apple Cake

Brown sugar gives this cake its great caramel flavor. Raisins and apples add an interesting texture. Refer to p. 11 for suggestions on varieties of apples to use when baking.

CAKE
1¾   cups all purpose flour
1½   cups firmly packed brown sugar
1½   teaspoons cinnamon
½   teaspoon salt
½   teaspoon baking powder
½   teaspoon baking soda
1   teaspoon vanilla
¾   cup margarine or butter, softened
3   eggs
1½   cups finely chopped peeled apples
½   to 1 cup chopped nuts
½   cup raisins, if desired

FROSTING
2   cups powdered sugar
¼   teaspoon cinnamon
¼   cup margarine or butter, melted
½   teaspoon vanilla
4   to 5 teaspoons milk

Heat oven to 350°F. Grease and flour 13x9-inch pan. In large bowl, combine flour, brown sugar, cinnamon, salt, baking powder, baking soda, vanilla, margarine and eggs; beat 3 minutes at medium speed. Stir in apples, nuts and raisins. Pour into greased and floured pan.

Bake at 350°F. for 30 to 40 minutes or until toothpick inserted in center comes out clean. Cool completely.

In small bowl, blend all frosting ingredients, adding enough milk for desired spreading consistency. Spread over cooled cake.

Yield: 15 servings.

HIGH ALTITUDE:
Above 3500 Feet: Decrease brown sugar to 1 cup. Bake at 375°F. for 25 to 35 minutes.

NUTRITION PER SERVING:
Calories 390; Protein 4g; Carbohydrate 53g; Fat 18g; Sodium 280mg.

DIXIE SPICE CAKE WITH CARAMEL FROSTING

This delicious old-fashioned cake is rich with traditional spice cake flavor.

CAKE
2¼ cups all purpose flour
1¼ cups firmly packed brown sugar
½ cup sugar
1 teaspoon baking soda
½ teaspoon salt
½ teaspoon nutmeg
½ teaspoon allspice
1 cup buttermilk
⅔ cup shortening
1 teaspoon vanilla
3 eggs
1 cup chopped walnuts or pecans

CARAMEL FROSTING
½ cup margarine or butter
1 cup firmly packed brown sugar
¼ cup milk
3 cups powdered sugar
½ teaspoon vanilla

Heat oven to 350°F. Generously grease and flour bottom only of 13x9-inch pan. In large bowl, combine all cake ingredients except nuts at low speed until moistened; beat 3 minutes at medium speed. Stir in nuts. Pour batter into greased and floured pan.

Bake at 350°F. for 40 to 45 minutes or until top springs back when touched lightly in center. Cool completely.

In medium saucepan, melt margarine; add brown sugar. Cook over low heat 2 minutes, stirring constantly. Add milk; continue cooking until mixture comes to a rolling boil. Remove from heat. Gradually add powdered sugar and vanilla; mix well. If needed, add a few drops of milk for desired spreading consistency. Spread over cooled cake.
Yield: 12 servings.

HIGH ALTITUDE:
Above 3500 Feet: Increase flour to 2¼ cups plus 3 tablespoons; decrease brown sugar in cake to 1 cup. Bake at 375°F. for 35 to 40 minutes.

NUTRITION PER SERVING:
Calories 640; Protein 6g; Carbohydrate 94g; Fat 27g; Sodium 330mg.

BUTTER CRUMSHUS CAKE

Softened cream cheese adds moistness to this quick cake. The topping is baked on.

CAKE
⅓ cup butter or margarine, softened
1 (3-oz.) pkg. cream cheese, softened
1 cup all purpose flour
⅔ cup sugar
1 teaspoon baking powder
¼ teaspoon baking soda
¼ teaspoon salt
½ teaspoon vanilla
¼ cup milk
1 egg

TOPPING
¼ cup firmly packed brown sugar
3 tablespoons all purpose flour
1 tablespoon butter or margarine

Heat oven to 350°F. Generously grease and flour bottom only of 8-inch square pan. In large bowl, beat ⅓ cup butter and cream cheese until light and fluffy. Add flour and remaining cake ingredients. Blend at low speed until well combined; beat 2 minutes at medium speed. Spread batter evenly in greased and floured pan.

In small bowl, combine all topping ingredients until crumbly. Sprinkle topping evenly over batter.

Bake at 350°F. for 30 to 40 minutes or until toothpick inserted in center comes out clean. Serve warm or cool.
Yield: 6 to 8 servings.

HIGH ALTITUDE:
Above 3500 Feet: Decrease sugar to ½ cup. Bake as directed above.

NUTRITION PER SERVING:
Calories 280; Protein 4g; Carbohydrate 38g; Fat 13g; Sodium 280mg.

Orange Kiss-Me Cake

At the 1950 Pillsbury BAKE-OFF® Contest, this fresh orange cake won the $25,000 Grand Prize. For the freshest flavor, use a sweet, juicy, thin-skinned orange.

CAKE
- 1 orange
- 1 cup raisins
- ⅓ cup walnuts
- 2 cups all purpose flour
- 1 cup sugar
- 1 teaspoon baking soda
- 1 teaspoon salt
- 1 cup milk
- ½ cup margarine, softened, or shortening
- 2 eggs

TOPPING
- Reserved ⅓ cup orange juice
- ⅓ cup sugar
- 1 teaspoon cinnamon
- ¼ cup finely chopped walnuts

Heat oven to 350°F. Grease and flour 13x9-inch pan. Squeeze orange, reserving ⅓ cup juice for topping. In blender container, food processor bowl with metal blade or food mill, grind together orange peel and pulp, raisins and ⅓ cup walnuts; set aside.

In large bowl, combine flour and remaining cake ingredients at low speed until moistened; beat 3 minutes at medium speed. Stir in orange-raisin mixture. Pour batter into greased and floured pan.

Bake at 350°F. for 35 to 45 minutes or until tooth-pick inserted in center comes out clean. Drizzle reserved ⅓ cup orange juice over warm cake in pan. In small bowl, combine ⅓ cup sugar and cinnamon; mix well. Stir in ¼ cup walnuts; sprinkle over cake. Cool completely.

Yield: 12 to 16 servings.

HIGH ALTITUDE:
Above 3500 Feet: Increase flour to 2 cups plus 2 tablespoons. Bake at 375°F. for 35 to 40 minutes.

NUTRITION PER SERVING:
Calories 250; Protein 4g; Carbohydrate 39g; Fat 10g; Sodium 290mg.

Old-Fashioned Oatmeal Cake with Broiled Topping

Serve this cake for brunch, dessert or a snack.

CAKE
- 1½ cups quick-cooking rolled oats
- 1¼ cups boiling water
- 1 cup sugar
- 1 cup firmly packed brown sugar
- ½ cup margarine or butter, softened
- 1 teaspoon vanilla
- 3 eggs
- 1½ cups all purpose flour
- 1 teaspoon baking soda
- ½ teaspoon baking powder
- ½ teaspoon salt
- 1½ teaspoons cinnamon
- ½ teaspoon nutmeg

TOPPING
- ⅔ cup firmly packed brown sugar
- ¼ cup margarine or butter, melted
- 3 tablespoons half-and-half or milk
- 1 cup coconut
- ½ cup chopped nuts

Grease and flour 13x9-inch pan. In small bowl, combine rolled oats and boiling water; let stand 20 minutes.

Heat oven to 350°F. In large bowl, beat sugar, 1 cup brown sugar and ½ cup margarine until light and fluffy. Add vanilla and eggs; beat well. Add oatmeal and remaining cake ingredients; mix well. Pour batter into greased and floured pan.

Bake at 350°F. for 35 to 45 minutes or until tooth-pick inserted in center comes out clean.

Heat broiler. In small bowl, combine ⅔ cup brown sugar, ¼ cup margarine and half-and-half; beat at highest speed until smooth. Stir in coconut and nuts. Spoon over warm cake; spread to cover. Broil 4 to 6 inches from heat for 1 to 2 minutes or until bubbly and light golden brown. Cool completely.

Yield: 16 servings.

HIGH ALTITUDE:
Above 3500 Feet: Decrease brown sugar in cake to ¾ cup; increase flour to 1½ cups plus 3 table-spoons. Bake at 375°F. for 30 to 40 minutes.

NUTRITION PER SERVING:
Calories 360; Protein 4g; Carbohydrate 52g; Fat 15g; Sodium 270mg.

WHOLE WHEAT WALNUT CRUMB CAKE

～

This lightly spiced cake can be baked in cake layer pans or in a 13x9-inch pan. It's great for picnics.

STREUSEL
1 cup chopped walnuts or pecans
⅓ cup firmly packed brown sugar
1 teaspoon cinnamon

CAKE
2 cups whole wheat flour
1 cup sugar
3 teaspoons baking powder
½ teaspoon salt
1 cup milk
⅓ cup margarine or butter, softened
1 egg

GLAZE
¾ cup powdered sugar
1 to 2 tablespoons water

Heat oven to 350°F. Grease and flour two 8 or 9-inch round cake pans. In small bowl, mix all streusel ingredients until well blended; set aside.

In large bowl, combine all cake ingredients at low speed until moistened; beat 2 minutes at medium speed. Spread about ¾ cup of batter in each greased and floured pan; sprinkle ¼ of streusel mixture evenly over batter in each pan. Carefully spread remaining batter over streusel in each pan; sprinkle with remaining streusel mixture.

Bake at 350°F. for 20 to 30 minutes or until toothpick inserted in center comes out clean. Cool slightly. In small bowl, combine powdered sugar and enough water for desired drizzling consistency; blend until smooth. Drizzle over warm cakes.
Yield: 2 cakes; 6 to 8 servings each.

TIP:
Cake can be baked in 13x9-inch pan. Spread half of batter in greased and floured pan; sprinkle half of streusel mixture evenly over batter. Carefully spread remaining batter over streusel; sprinkle with remaining streusel mixture. Bake at 350°F. for 25 to 35 minutes or until toothpick inserted in center comes out clean.

HIGH ALTITUDE:
Above 3500 Feet: Increase flour to 2¼ cups. Bake at 375°F. for 20 to 30 minutes.

NUTRITION PER SERVING:
Calories 220; Protein 4g; Carbohydrate 33g; Fat 9g; Sodium 180mg.

BRAN CAKE

～

This cake is especially delicious served warm from the oven. The batter can be prepared several hours ahead, refrigerated, then baked just before serving.

CAKE
1½ cups all purpose flour
1½ cups bran flakes cereal with raisins
½ cup sugar
1 teaspoon baking powder
½ teaspoon baking soda
½ teaspoon salt
1 cup buttermilk
¼ cup margarine or butter, melted
1 egg, slightly beaten

TOPPING
2 tablespoons sugar
½ teaspoon cinnamon

Heat oven to 400°F. Grease bottom only of 8-inch square or 9-inch round pan. In large bowl, combine all cake ingredients; stir just until ingredients are moistened. Spread batter in greased pan. Combine topping ingredients; sprinkle over batter.*

Bake at 400°F. for 30 to 40 minutes or until toothpick inserted in center comes out clean.
Serve warm.
Yield: 9 servings.

TIP:
* If desired, cover pan with plastic wrap and store in refrigerator up to 12 hours. Bake as directed above.

HIGH ALTITUDE:
Above 3500 Feet: Increase flour to 1½ cups plus 3 tablespoons. Bake at 400°F. for 20 to 30 minutes.

NUTRITION PER SERVING:
Calories 220; Protein 5g; Carbohydrate 37g; Fat 6g; Sodium 360mg.

BLACK BOTTOM CUPS

These unique cupcakes boast a filling of cream cheese and chocolate chips — delicious!

  2 (3-oz.) pkg. cream cheese, softened
  1/3 cup sugar
  1 egg
  1 (6-oz.) pkg. (1 cup) semi-sweet chocolate chips
  1½ cups all purpose flour
  1 cup sugar
  ¼ cup unsweetened cocoa
  1 teaspoon baking soda
  ½ teaspoon salt
  1 cup water
  1/3 cup oil
  1 tablespoon vinegar
  1 teaspoon vanilla
  ½ cup chopped almonds, if desired
  2 tablespoons sugar, if desired

Heat oven to 350°F. Line 18 muffin cups with paper baking cups. In small bowl, combine cream cheese, 1/3 cup sugar and egg; mix well. Stir in chocolate chips; set aside.

In large bowl, combine flour, 1 cup sugar, cocoa, baking soda and salt. Add water, oil, vinegar and vanilla; beat 2 minutes at medium speed. Fill paper-lined muffin cups half full. Top each with 1 tablespoonful cream cheese mixture. Combine almonds and 2 tablespoons sugar; sprinkle evenly over cream cheese mixture.

Bake at 350°F. for 20 to 30 minutes or until cream cheese mixture is light golden brown. Cool 15 minutes; remove from pans. Cool completely. Store in refrigerator.
Yield: 18 cupcakes.

HIGH ALTITUDE:
Above 3500 Feet: No change.

NUTRITION PER SERVING:
Calories 250; Protein 3g; Carbohydrate 31g; Fat 13g; Sodium 160mg.

DOUBLE CHOCOLATE CHUNK CUPCAKES

These are great to pack in lunches.

  2 cups all purpose flour
  ½ cup firmly packed brown sugar
  ¼ cup unsweetened cocoa
  1 teaspoon baking soda
  ¼ teaspoon salt
  1 cup buttermilk
  ½ cup margarine or butter, melted
  ½ teaspoon almond extract
  1 egg
  ½ cup vanilla milk chips or 3 oz. white baking bars, chopped
  ½ cup milk chocolate chips
  ¼ cup chopped slivered almonds

Heat oven to 375°F. Grease 18 muffin cups. In large bowl, combine flour, brown sugar, cocoa, baking soda and salt; blend well. Add buttermilk, margarine, almond extract and egg; blend just until dry ingredients are moistened. Fold in vanilla and milk chocolate chips and almonds. Fill greased muffin cups ¾ full.

Bake at 375°F. for 15 to 20 minutes or until toothpick inserted in center comes out clean. Cool 3 minutes; remove from pan. Serve warm or cool.
Yield: 18 cupcakes.

HIGH ALTITUDE:
Above 3500 Feet: No change.

NUTRITION PER SERVING:
Calories 200; Protein 4g; Carbohydrate 24g; Fat 10g; Sodium 190mg.

COOK'S NOTE

CUPCAKES

Most cake batters can be baked in paper-lined muffin cups for cupcakes. A one-layer cake recipe yields 12 to 15 cupcakes; a two-layer cake recipe yields 24 to 30 cupcakes. Fill cups ⅔ full and bake at 350°F. for 15 to 20 minutes or until tops spring back when lightly touched. Immediately remove cupcakes from pan; cool. Cupcakes can be frosted by dipping the top of each cupcake in frosting; turn slightly and remove.

Peanut Butter Cups

PEANUT BUTTER CUPS

Creamy or chunky peanut butter can be used for these irresistible treat-filled cupcakes.

1¾ **cups all purpose flour**
1¼ **cups firmly packed brown sugar**
  3 **teaspoons baking powder**
  1 **teaspoon salt**
  1 **cup milk**
 ⅓ **cup shortening**
 ⅓ **cup peanut butter**
  1 **teaspoon vanilla**
  2 **eggs**
24 **miniature milk chocolate-covered peanut butter cups, unwrapped**

Heat oven to 350°F. Line 24 muffin cups with paper baking cups. In large bowl, combine all ingredients except peanut butter cups at low speed until moistened; beat 2 minutes at medium speed. Fill paper-lined muffin cups ⅔ full. Press a peanut butter cup into batter until top edge is even with batter.

Bake at 350°F. for 18 to 28 minutes or until tops spring back when touched lightly in center. Serve warm or cool.

Yield: 24 cupcakes.

HIGH ALTITUDE:
Above 3500 Feet: No change.

NUTRITION PER SERVING:
Calories 170; Protein 4g; Carbohydrate 23g; Fat 7g; Sodium 185mg.

COCONUT MACAROON CAKES

When you have leftover egg whites, lightly beat the whites, place them in a freezer container or screw-top jar and freeze. When you've collected enough for these simple but special cupcakes, thaw the whites in the refrigerator and use them like fresh egg whites.

- ¾ **cup all purpose flour**
- 1⅓ **cups sugar**
- ½ **teaspoon baking powder**
- ¼ **teaspoon salt**
- 6 **egg whites**
- ½ **teaspoon cream of tartar**
- 1 **teaspoon almond extract**
- 1 **cup coconut**

Heat oven to 350°F. Line 18 muffin cups with paper baking cups. In medium bowl, combine flour, 1 cup of the sugar, baking powder and salt; set aside.

In large bowl, beat egg whites, cream of tartar and almond extract until foamy; gradually add remaining ⅓ cup sugar, beating until stiff peaks form. Gradually fold flour mixture into egg whites. Gently fold in coconut. Fill paper-lined muffin cups ⅔ full.

Bake at 350°F. for 25 to 35 minutes or until light golden brown and top crust is dry. Cool completely.

Yield: 18 cupcakes.

HIGH ALTITUDE:
Above 3500 Feet: Increase flour to ¾ cup plus 2 tablespoons. When beating egg white-sugar mixture, beat only until soft peaks form. Bake at 375°F. for 20 to 25 minutes. 21 cupcakes.

NUTRITION PER SERVING:
Calories 100; Protein 2g; Carbohydrate 20g; Fat 1g; Sodium 55mg.

RUM CROWN CAKES

These little cakes have a sponge-like texture.

SYRUP
- 1 **cup sugar**
- ¾ **cup water**
- ¼ **cup orange juice**
- 2 **tablespoons rum**

GLAZE
- ½ **cup apricot preserves**
- 2 **tablespoons rum**
- 1 **tablespoon orange juice**

CUPCAKES
- ⅔ **cup sugar**
- ½ **cup margarine or butter, softened**
- 4 **eggs**
- ¾ **cup all purpose flour**
- ½ **cup cornstarch**
- 2 **teaspoons baking powder**
- ¼ **teaspoon salt**

In small saucepan, combine 1 cup sugar and water; bring to a boil, stirring until sugar dissolves. Remove from heat. Add ¼ cup orange juice and 2 tablespoons rum; set aside. In small bowl, combine all glaze ingredients; blend well. Set aside.

Heat oven to 350°F. Grease and flour 18 fluted muffin cups.* In large bowl, beat ⅔ cup sugar and margarine until light and fluffy. Add eggs 1 at a time, beating well after each addition. In small bowl, combine flour, cornstarch, baking powder and salt. Gradually add flour mixture to sugar mixture; blend well. Spoon batter into greased and floured muffin cups, filling ⅔ full.

Bake at 350°F. for 15 to 20 minutes or until toothpick inserted in center comes out clean. With long-tined fork, immediately pierce each cake 3 times; spoon syrup over cakes in pan. Remove from pan immediately by inverting onto wire rack. Brush tops with glaze. If desired, decorate cakes with whipped cream using decorating bag.

Yield: 18 cakes.

TIP:
* Standard muffin cups can be used in place of fluted muffin cups.

HIGH ALTITUDE:
Above 3500 Feet: Bake at 375°F. for 15 to 20 minutes.

NUTRITION PER SERVING:
Calories 200; Protein 2g; Carbohydrate 32g; Fat 6g; Sodium 140mg.

Chocolate Pound Cake

A chocolate delight!

CAKE
- 3 cups sugar
- 1 cup margarine or butter, softened
- ½ cup shortening
- 1 teaspoon vanilla
- 5 eggs
- 3 cups all purpose flour
- ¼ cup unsweetened cocoa
- ½ teaspoon baking powder
- ½ teaspoon salt
- 1 cup milk

GLAZE
- 2 tablespoons unsweetened cocoa
- 1 tablespoon water
- 1 tablespoon light corn syrup
- 2 tablespoons margarine or butter
- ¼ teaspoon vanilla
- ½ cup powdered sugar

Heat oven to 350°F. Grease and flour 10-inch tube pan. In large bowl, combine sugar, 1 cup margarine, shortening and 1 teaspoon vanilla; beat until light and fluffy. Add eggs 1 at a time, beating well after each addition. In medium bowl, combine flour, ¼ cup cocoa, baking powder and salt. Alternately add flour mixture and milk to sugar mixture, beginning and ending with flour mixture and beating well after each addition. Pour batter into greased and floured pan.

Bake at 350°F. for 70 to 85 minutes or until toothpick inserted in center comes out clean. Cool upright in pan 25 minutes; invert onto serving plate. Cool completely.

In small saucepan, combine 2 tablespoons cocoa, water, corn syrup and 2 tablespoons margarine. Cook over low heat until mixture thickens, stirring constantly. Remove from heat. Stir in ¼ teaspoon vanilla and powdered sugar; beat until smooth. Spread glaze over top of cooled cake, allowing some to run down sides.

Yield: 16 servings.

HIGH ALTITUDE:
Above 3500 Feet: Increase flour to 3¼ cups. Bake at 375°F. for 70 to 80 minutes.

NUTRITION PER SERVING:
Calories 450; Protein 5g; Carbohydrate 62g; Fat 22g; Sodium 270mg.

Orange Currant Pound Cake

Raisins can be substituted for currants in this recipe.

CAKE
- 3 cups all purpose flour
- ½ teaspoon baking powder
- ½ teaspoon salt
- 1 tablespoon grated orange peel
- 2¾ cups sugar
- 1½ cups margarine or butter, softened
- 1 teaspoon vanilla
- 6 eggs
- 1 cup dairy sour cream
- 1 cup currants

SAUCE
- ¼ cup sugar
- 1 tablespoon cornstarch
- ¾ cup orange juice
- 1 to 2 tablespoons orange liqueur

Heat oven to 350°F. Generously grease and flour 12-cup Bundt® pan. In large bowl, combine flour, baking powder, salt and orange peel; set aside. In large bowl, beat sugar and margarine until light and fluffy. Add vanilla and 1 egg at a time, beating well after each addition. Alternately add dry ingredients and sour cream to sugar mixture, beating well after each addition. Stir in currants. Pour batter into greased and floured pan.

Bake at 350°F. for 55 to 65 minutes or until toothpick inserted in center comes out clean. Cool 15 minutes; invert onto serving plate. Cool completely.

To prepare sauce, combine sugar and cornstarch in small saucepan. Stir in orange juice. Cook over medium heat until mixture boils and thickens, stirring constantly. Stir in liqueur. Serve cake with warm orange sauce.

Yield: 16 servings.

HIGH ALTITUDE:
Above 3500 Feet: Bake at 375°F. for 50 to 60 minutes.

NUTRITION PER SERVING:
Calories 480; Protein 6g; Carbohydrate 66g; Fat 22g; Sodium 310mg.

BUTTER PECAN POUND CAKE

A buttery glaze tops this rich cake.

CAKE
- 2 tablespoons ground pecans
- 1½ cups butter, softened (do not use margarine)
- 1 (3-oz.) pkg. cream cheese, softened
- 2 cups firmly packed brown sugar
- 1 cup sugar
- 5 eggs
- 3 cups all purpose flour
- ½ teaspoon baking powder
- ¼ teaspoon salt
- 1 teaspoon vanilla
- 1 teaspoon maple extract
- ¾ cup milk
- 1 cup chopped pecans, toasted, p. 23

GLAZE
- 2 tablespoons butter or margarine
- 2 tablespoons firmly packed brown sugar
- ½ cup powdered sugar
- 1 teaspoon vanilla
- 1 to 2 tablespoons hot water

Heat oven to 350°F. Grease 10-inch tube pan. Sprinkle with ground pecans, coating bottom and sides of pan. In large bowl, beat 1½ cups butter, cream cheese, 2 cups brown sugar and sugar until light and fluffy. Add eggs 1 at a time, beating well after each addition. In small bowl, combine flour, baking powder and salt; mix well. Add vanilla and maple extract to milk. Add flour mixture to butter mixture alternately with milk, beginning and ending with flour mixture. Fold in pecans. Pour batter into greased and coated pan.

Bake at 350°F. for 65 to 80 minutes or until toothpick inserted in center comes out clean. Do not open oven door for first hour of baking. Cool upright in pan 10 minutes; invert onto cooling rack. Cool completely.

In small saucepan, melt 2 tablespoons butter with 2 tablespoons brown sugar. Bring to a boil; boil until thickened, stirring constantly. Remove from heat; stir in remaining glaze ingredients, adding enough water for desired glaze consistency. Spoon over cake.
Yield: 16 to 20 servings.

HIGH ALTITUDE:
Above 3500 Feet: Decrease brown sugar in cake to 1½ cups; increase flour to 3⅓ cups. Bake as directed above.

NUTRITION PER SERVING:
Calories 420; Protein 5g; Carbohydrate 52g; Fat 22g; Sodium 230mg.

LEMON DELIGHT POUND CAKE

You'll enjoy this lemon-flavored cake — and it's so easy to make!

CAKE
- 2½ cups all purpose flour
- 1½ cups sugar
- 3 teaspoons baking powder
- ½ teaspoon salt
- ¾ cup apricot nectar or orange juice
- ¾ cup oil
- 2 teaspoons lemon extract
- 4 eggs

GLAZE
- 1½ cups powdered sugar
- ½ cup lemon juice

Heat oven to 325°F. Generously grease and flour 12-cup Bundt® pan. In large bowl, combine all cake ingredients. Blend at low speed until moistened; beat 3 minutes at medium speed. Pour batter into greased and floured pan.

Bake at 325°F. for 40 to 50 minutes or until toothpick inserted near center comes out clean. Remove cake from oven. With long-tined fork, poke deep holes every inch. In small bowl, blend glaze ingredients until smooth. Spoon half of glaze over hot cake in pan. Let stand upright in pan 10 minutes; invert onto serving plate. Spoon remaining glaze over cake. Cool completely.
Yield: 16 servings.

HIGH ALTITUDE:
Above 3500 Feet: Decrease baking powder to 2½ teaspoons. Bake at 350°F. for 40 to 50 minutes.

NUTRITION PER SERVING:
Calories 300; Protein 4g; Carbohydrate 45g; Fat 12g; Sodium 140mg.

CRANBERRY ORANGE POUND CAKE

Pound cakes were so named because the ingredients traditionally were measured by the pound. This sensational version, studded with cranberries, is a perfect buffet dessert for a party.

CAKE

2¾ cups sugar
1½ cups butter or margarine, softened
1 teaspoon vanilla
1 teaspoon grated orange peel
6 eggs
3 cups all purpose flour
1 teaspoon baking powder
½ teaspoon salt
1 (8-oz.) container dairy sour cream
1½ cups chopped fresh or frozen cranberries (do not thaw)

BUTTER RUM SAUCE

1 cup sugar
1 tablespoon all purpose flour
½ cup half-and-half
½ cup butter
4 teaspoons light rum or ¼ teaspoon rum extract

Heat oven to 350°F. Generously grease and lightly flour 12-cup Bundt® pan. In large bowl, beat 2¾ cups sugar and 1½ cups butter until light and fluffy. Add vanilla and orange peel. Add eggs 1 at a time, beating well after each addition. In medium bowl, combine 3 cups flour, baking powder and salt; add alternately with sour cream, beating well after each addition. Gently stir in cranberries. Pour batter into greased and floured pan.

Bake at 350°F. for 65 to 75 minutes or until toothpick inserted in center comes out clean. Cool 15 minutes; remove from pan.

Meanwhile, in small saucepan combine 1 cup sugar and 1 tablespoon flour. Stir in half-and-half and ½ cup butter. Cook over medium heat until thickened and bubbly, stirring constantly. Remove from heat; stir in rum. Serve warm sauce over cake.
Yield: 16 servings.

TIP:

To prepare butter rum sauce in microwave, combine sugar and flour in 2-cup microwave-safe measuring cup. Stir in half-and-half and butter. Microwave on MEDIUM for 3 to 4 minutes or until thickened, stirring once halfway through cooking. Stir in rum.

HIGH ALTITUDE:

Above 3500 Feet: Decrease sugar in cake to 2½ cups. Bake as directed above.

NUTRITION PER SERVING:

Calories 550; Protein 6g; Carbohydrate 67g; Fat 29g; Sodium 360mg.

SOUR CREAM POUND CAKE

Flavored with orange peel and vanilla, this dense pound cake needs no frosting. Serve it with a dusting of powdered sugar, if desired.

2¾ cups sugar
1½ cups butter or margarine, softened
1 teaspoon vanilla
6 eggs
3 cups all purpose flour
1 teaspoon grated orange or lemon peel
½ teaspoon baking powder
½ teaspoon salt
1 cup dairy sour cream

Heat oven to 350°F. Generously grease and flour 12-cup Bundt® pan. In large bowl, beat sugar and butter until light and fluffy. Add vanilla; add eggs 1 at a time, beating well after each addition. In medium bowl, combine flour, orange peel, baking powder and salt. Add dry ingredients alternately with sour cream, beating well after each addition. Pour batter into greased and floured pan.

Bake at 350°F. for 55 to 65 minutes or until toothpick inserted in center comes out clean. Cool 15 minutes; invert onto serving plate. Cool completely.
Yield: 16 servings.

HIGH ALTITUDE:

Above 3500 Feet: Decrease sugar to 2½ cups. Bake at 375°F. for 55 to 65 minutes.

NUTRITION PER SERVING:

Calories 440; Protein 5g; Carbohydrate 53g; Fat 23g; Sodium 290mg.

Pumpkin Pound Cake with Walnut Sauce

~

CAKE

2¾ cups sugar
1½ cups butter or margarine, softened
1 teaspoon vanilla
6 eggs
3 cups all purpose flour
½ teaspoon baking powder
½ teaspoon salt
¾ teaspoon cinnamon
½ teaspoon ginger
¼ teaspoon cloves
1 cup canned pumpkin

SAUCE

1 cup firmly packed brown sugar
¼ cup dark corn syrup
½ cup whipping cream
2 tablespoons butter or margarine
  Dash salt
½ teaspoon vanilla
½ cup chopped walnuts or walnut halves

Heat oven to 350°F. Generously grease and lightly flour 12-cup Bundt® pan. In large bowl, beat sugar and 1½ cups butter until light and fluffy. Add 1 teaspoon vanilla; add eggs 1 at a time, beating well after each addition. In small bowl, combine flour, baking powder, ½ teaspoon salt, cinnamon, ginger and cloves; mix well. Alternately add dry ingredients and pumpkin to butter mixture, beating well after each addition. Pour batter into greased and floured pan.

Bake at 350°F. for 60 to 70 minutes or until toothpick inserted in center comes out clean. Cool 15 minutes; invert onto serving plate. Cool completely.

In medium saucepan, combine brown sugar, corn syrup, whipping cream, 2 tablespoons butter and dash of salt. Bring to a boil over medium heat, stirring constantly. Reduce heat to low; simmer 5 minutes, stirring constantly. Remove from heat; stir in ½ teaspoon vanilla and walnuts. Serve warm sauce over cake. Refrigerate any remaining sauce.
Yield: 16 servings.

TIP:
Cake can be baked in two greased and floured 9x5-inch loaf pans. Bake as directed above.

Pumpkin Pound Cake with Walnut Sauce

HIGH ALTITUDE:
Above 3500 Feet: Decrease sugar to 2½ cups. Bake at 375°F. for 50 to 60 minutes.

NUTRITION PER SERVING:
Calories 530; Protein 6g; Carbohydrate 71g; Fat 26g; Sodium 310mg.

Toffee Pound Cake

~

Almond brickle baking chips are available in the baking section of the grocery store.

CAKE

2½ cups all purpose flour
1½ cups sugar
1 teaspoon baking soda
½ teaspoon salt
1½ cups buttermilk
½ cup margarine or butter, softened
¼ cup shortening
1½ teaspoons vanilla
3 eggs
1 (6-oz.) pkg. almond brickle baking chips

GLAZE

⅓ cup margarine or butter
2 cups powdered sugar
1 teaspoon vanilla
2 to 3 tablespoons water

Heat oven to 350°F. Grease and flour 12-cup Bundt® or 10-inch tube pan. In large bowl, combine all cake ingredients except brickle chips at low speed until moistened; beat 3 minutes at medium speed. By hand, stir in brickle chips. Pour batter into greased and floured pan.

Bake at 350°F. for 50 to 60 minutes or until toothpick inserted in center comes out clean. Cool upright in pan 10 minutes; invert onto serving plate. Cool completely.

In medium saucepan, heat ⅓ cup margarine until light golden brown; remove from heat. Blend in powdered sugar and 1 teaspoon vanilla. Add water until glaze is smooth and of drizzling consistency. Immediately spoon over top of cooled cake, allowing some to run down sides.
Yield: 16 servings.

HIGH ALTITUDE:
Above 3500 Feet: No change.

NUTRITION PER SERVING:
Calories 400; Protein 4g; Carbohydrate 55g; Fat 19g; Sodium 295mg.

LEMON POPPY SEED CAKE

~

A lemon glaze tops this cake.

CAKE
- 1 (18.25-oz.) pkg. pudding-included lemon cake mix
- 1 cup water
- 1/3 cup oil
- 3 eggs
- 2 tablespoons poppy seed

GLAZE
- 1 cup powdered sugar
- 1 tablespoon lemon juice
- 1 tablespoon milk
- 1 tablespoon margarine or butter, softened
- 2 to 3 drops yellow food color, if desired
  Poppy seed, if desired

Heat oven to 350°F. Grease and flour 10-inch tube or 12-cup Bundt® pan. In large bowl, combine all cake ingredients at low speed until moistened; beat 2 minutes at highest speed. Pour batter into greased and floured pan.

Bake at 350°F. for 35 to 45 minutes or until toothpick inserted in center comes out clean. Cool upright in pan 25 minutes; invert onto serving plate. Cool completely.

In small bowl, blend all glaze ingredients except poppy seed until smooth and of drizzling consistency. If needed, add a few drops of milk for desired drizzling consistency. Drizzle over cooled cake. Sprinkle poppy seed over top.
Yield: 16 servings.

MICROWAVE DIRECTIONS:
Grease and sugar 12-cup microwave-safe Bundt® pan. Prepare cake batter as directed above. Pour batter into greased and sugared pan. Microwave on HIGH for 11 to 12 minutes or until cake surface is no longer doughy and cake pulls away from sides of pan, rotating pan 1/4 turn every 3 minutes. Cool upright in pan 10 minutes; invert onto serving plate. Cool completely. Glaze as directed above.

HIGH ALTITUDE:
Above 3500 Feet: Add 3 tablespoons flour to dry cake mix. Bake at 375°F. for 35 to 45 minutes.

NUTRITION PER SERVING:
Calories 230; Protein 3g; Carbohydrate 32g; Fat 10g; Sodium 230mg.

TUNNEL OF FUDGE CAKE

~

This cake features a tunnel of fudgy goodness.

CAKE
- 1¾ cups sugar
- 1¾ cups margarine or butter, softened
- 6 eggs
- 2 cups powdered sugar
- 2¼ cups all purpose flour
- ¾ cup unsweetened cocoa
- 2 cups chopped walnuts*

GLAZE
- ¾ cup powdered sugar
- ¼ cup unsweetened cocoa
- 4 to 6 teaspoons milk

Heat oven to 350°F. Grease and flour 12-cup Bundt® pan or 10-inch tube pan. In large bowl, combine sugar and margarine; beat until light and fluffy. Add eggs 1 at a time, beating well after each addition. Gradually add 2 cups powdered sugar; blend well. By hand, stir in flour and remaining cake ingredients until well blended. Spoon batter into greased and floured pan; spread evenly.

Bake at 350°F. for 58 to 62 minutes.** Cool upright in pan on wire rack 1 hour; invert onto serving plate. Cool completely.

In small bowl, combine all glaze ingredients, adding enough milk for desired drizzling consistency. Spoon over top of cake, allowing some to run down sides. Store tightly covered.
Yield: 16 servings.

TIPS:
* Nuts are essential for the success of this recipe.
** Since this cake has a soft filling, an ordinary doneness test cannot be used. Accurate oven temperature and baking times are essential.

HIGH ALTITUDE:
Above 3500 Feet: Increase flour to 2¼ cups plus 3 tablespoons. Bake as directed above.

NUTRITION PER SERVING:
Calories 550; Protein 8g; Carbohydrate 58g; Fat 32g; Sodium 300mg.

CHOCOLATE ALMOND HEAVEN CAKE

In its original form, chocolate is quite bitter. Semi-sweet chocolate has added sugar, lecithin and vanilla to improve the flavor and texture. A generous amount of semi-sweet chocolate is used here to create a rich chocolate fantasy, especially for chocolate lovers!

CAKE
- 1¼ cups margarine or butter
- 10 oz. semi-sweet chocolate or 1⅔ cups semi-sweet chocolate chips
- 8 eggs, separated
- 2 cups sugar
- 1 cup all purpose flour
- ¾ cup ground almonds

FROSTING
- 4 oz. semi-sweet chocolate or ⅔ cup semi-sweet chocolate chips
- ½ cup margarine or butter
- ⅓ cup chopped almonds
- Sliced almonds

Heat oven to 350°F. Grease and flour 10-inch tube pan. In medium saucepan over low heat, melt 1¼ cups margarine and 10 oz. chocolate, stirring constantly. Set aside.

In large bowl, beat egg whites until soft peaks form; set aside. In another large bowl, beat egg yolks at highest speed, gradually adding sugar. Beat until thick and lemon colored, about 5 minutes. Gently stir chocolate mixture into yolks until blended. Gently stir flour and ¾ cup ground almonds into chocolate mixture. (Mixture will be very thick and heavy.) Fold ⅓ of beaten egg whites into chocolate mixture. Gradually fold in remaining egg whites until well blended and no large lumps remain. Pour batter into greased and floured pan.

Bake at 350°F. for 60 to 70 minutes or until toothpick inserted in center comes out clean and edges are brown. Cool upright in pan 15 minutes; invert onto wire rack. Cool completely.

In small saucepan over low heat, melt 4 oz. chocolate and ½ cup margarine, stirring constantly. Cool 30 minutes. Place cake on serving plate, flat side up. Spread frosting over top and sides of cake. Sprinkle chopped almonds over top of cake; garnish sides with sliced almonds.
Yield: 20 servings.

HIGH ALTITUDE:
Above 3500 Feet: Decrease sugar to 1¾ cups. Bake at 375°F. for 50 to 60 minutes.

NUTRITION PER SERVING:
Calories 420; Protein 5g; Carbohydrate 37g; Fat 28g; Sodium 220mg.

CHOCOLATE CHIP CAKE

It is important to grease the Bundt® pan well, including the creases, so the cake doesn't stick.

CAKE
- ½ cup margarine or butter, softened
- 1 (8-oz.) pkg. cream cheese, softened
- 1 cup sugar
- 1 teaspoon vanilla
- 2 eggs
- 2 cups all purpose flour
- 1 teaspoon baking powder
- ½ teaspoon baking soda
- ¼ teaspoon salt
- ¼ cup milk
- 1 cup miniature semi-sweet chocolate chips

GLAZE
- ⅓ cup ready-to-spread chocolate frosting, melted, or Chocolate Glaze p. 186

Heat oven to 350°F. Grease 12-cup Bundt® pan. In large bowl, beat margarine, cream cheese and sugar until light and fluffy. Add vanilla; add eggs 1 at a time, beating well after each addition. Add flour, baking powder, baking soda and salt; mix well. Stir in milk and chocolate chips. Mixture will be very thick. Spread in greased pan.

Bake at 350°F. for 30 to 40 minutes or until toothpick inserted in center comes out clean. Cool upright in pan 15 minutes; invert onto serving plate. In small saucepan over low heat, melt frosting; drizzle over cooled cake.
Yield: 16 servings.

HIGH ALTITUDE:
Above 3500 Feet: No change.

NUTRITION PER SERVING:
Calories 310; Protein 4g; Carbohydrate 36g; Fat 17g; Sodium 220mg.

ALMOND LEGEND CAKE

Legend has it that whoever finds the whole almond in this tasty cake is assured of good luck!

CAKE
- ½ cup chopped almonds
- 1 (18.5-oz.) pkg. pudding-included yellow cake mix
- ½ cup orange juice
- ½ cup water
- ⅓ cup oil
- ½ teaspoon almond extract
- 3 eggs
- 1 whole almond

GLAZE
- ½ cup apricot preserves
- 2 to 3 teaspoons orange juice

Heat oven to 350°F. Generously grease 12-cup Bundt® or 10-inch tube pan. Gently press ½ cup chopped almonds in bottom and half way up sides of pan. In large bowl, combine remaining ingredients except whole almond at low speed until moistened; beat 2 minutes at high speed. Stir in whole almond. Carefully pour batter into greased and nut-lined pan.

Bake at 350°F. for 35 to 45 minutes or until toothpick inserted near center comes out clean. Cool upright in pan 10 minutes; invert onto serving plate.

In small bowl, combine glaze ingredients, adding enough orange juice for desired glaze consistency. Spoon over warm cake. Cool completely.

Yield: 16 servings.

HIGH ALTITUDE:
Above 3500 Feet: Add ¼ cup flour to dry cake mix. Bake at 375°F. for 35 to 45 minutes.

NUTRITION PER SERVING:
Calories 250; Protein 3g; Carbohydrate 34g; Fat 11g; Sodium 220mg.

ALMOND MOCHA CAKE

"It melts in your mouth" describes the texture of this brownie-like chocolate cake. Coffee and amaretto enhance its deep dark chocolate flavor.

- ½ cup chopped almonds
- 1¼ cups strong coffee*
- ½ cup margarine or butter
- 1 (12-oz.) pkg. (2 cups) semi-sweet chocolate chips
- 1 cup sugar
- ¼ cup amaretto or 2 teaspoons almond extract*
- 2 cups all purpose flour
- 1 teaspoon baking soda
- 1 teaspoon vanilla
- 2 eggs
- Powdered sugar

Heat oven to 325°F. Generously grease 12-cup Bundt® or 10-inch tube pan. Gently press almonds in bottom and half way up sides of greased pan. In medium saucepan over low heat, warm coffee. Add margarine and chocolate chips; cook until mixture is smooth, stirring constantly. Remove from heat; stir in sugar and amaretto. Place in large bowl; cool 5 minutes.

At low speed, gradually blend flour and baking soda into chocolate mixture until moistened. Add vanilla and eggs; beat at medium speed about 30 seconds or just until well blended. Pour into greased and nut-lined pan.

Bake at 325°F. for 60 to 75 minutes or until toothpick inserted in center comes out clean. Cool upright in pan 25 minutes; invert onto serving plate. Cool completely; sprinkle with powdered sugar.

Yield: 16 servings.

TIP:
* If using almond extract for amaretto, increase coffee to 1½ cups.

HIGH ALTITUDE:
Above 3500 Feet: No change.

NUTRITION PER SERVING:
Calories 320; Protein 4g; Carbohydrate 41g; Fat 16g; Sodium 150mg.

Chocolate 'Tato Cake

CHOCOLATE 'TATO CAKE

Moist and rich describe this sweet chocolate cake made with sour cream.

CAKE
- 4 **oz. sweet baking chocolate**
- 1 **cup mashed potato flakes**
- 1 **cup boiling water**
- 1½ **cups all purpose flour**
- 1¼ **cups sugar**
- 1¼ **teaspoons baking soda**
- 1 **teaspoon salt**
- 1 **teaspoon vanilla**
- ½ **cup margarine, softened, or shortening**
- ½ **cup dairy sour cream**
- 3 **eggs**
- ½ **cup chopped pecans, if desired**

GLAZE
- 2 **oz. sweet baking chocolate**
- 1 **tablespoon water**
- 1 **tablespoon margarine or butter**
- ½ **cup powdered sugar**
- ¼ **teaspoon vanilla**
  Dash salt

Heat oven to 350°F. Generously grease 12-cup Bundt® or 10-inch tube pan. Break 4 oz. chocolate into pieces; place in large bowl. Add potato flakes; pour boiling water over flakes and chocolate. Let stand 5 minutes or until potato flakes are softened and chocolate is melted; stir to combine. Add flour and remaining cake ingredients except pecans. Blend at low speed until moistened; beat 3 minutes at medium speed. Stir in pecans. Pour batter into greased pan.

Bake at 350°F. for 45 to 60 minutes or until tooth-pick inserted near center comes out clean. Cool upright in pan 30 minutes; invert onto serving plate. Cool completely.

In small saucepan over low heat, melt 2 oz. chocolate with water and margarine. Remove from heat; add powdered sugar, ¼ teaspoon vanilla and dash salt, beating until smooth. Stir in additional water, a few drops at a time, if needed for desired glaze consistency. Immediately spoon glaze over cooled cake, allowing some to run down sides.
Yield: 20 servings.

HIGH ALTITUDE:
Above 3500 Feet: Decrease sugar to 1 cup. Bake as directed above.

NUTRITION PER SERVING:
Calories 240; Protein 3g; Carbohydrate 30g; Fat 12g; Sodium 260mg.

Jelly Bean Confetti Cake

Jelly beans are available in many flavors and colors. Choose your favorites to make this whimsical cake. Tossing the jelly beans with a small amount of flour keeps them from sinking in the batter.

- ¾ **cup miniature jelly beans, cut in half**
- 2 **cups all purpose flour**
- 1¼ **cups sugar**
- 1 **cup margarine or butter, softened**
- 1 **(8-oz.) pkg. cream cheese, softened**
- 1 **teaspoon vanilla**
- 3 **eggs**
- 1½ **teaspoons baking powder**
- ¼ **teaspoon salt**
  Powdered sugar

Heat oven to 325°F. Generously grease and flour 12-cup Bundt® pan. In small bowl, toss jelly beans with 2 tablespoons of the flour; set aside.

In large bowl, beat sugar, margarine, cream cheese and vanilla until well blended. Add eggs 1 at a time, beating well after each addition. Add remaining flour, baking powder and salt; blend well. Spoon 1 cup batter evenly over bottom of greased and floured pan. Stir jelly beans into remaining batter; spoon over batter in pan.

Bake at 325°F. for 50 to 60 minutes or until toothpick inserted in center comes out clean. Cool upright in pan 10 minutes; invert onto serving plate. Cool completely. Sprinkle with powdered sugar.

Yield: 16 servings.

HIGH ALTITUDE:
Above 3500 Feet: Decrease sugar to 1 cup. Bake at 350°F. for 50 to 60 minutes.

NUTRITION PER SERVING:
Calories 320; Protein 4g; Carbohydrate 39g; Fat 18g; Sodium 250mg.

Rum Ring Cake

French savarins are rich yeast cakes soaked with rum-flavored syrup and then filled with pastry cream or fresh fruit. This recipe is a simple but equally delicious version of this classic dessert.

CAKE
- 2 **cups all purpose flour**
- 1 **cup sugar**
- 4 **teaspoons baking powder**
- ¼ **teaspoon salt**
- ½ **cup milk**
- ¼ **cup margarine or butter, melted**
- 1 **teaspoon vanilla**
- 4 **eggs**

SYRUP
- 1 **cup sugar**
- 1 **cup water**
- ¼ **cup rum or orange juice**

GLAZE AND FRUIT
- ½ **cup apricot preserves**
- 2 **cups cut-up fresh fruit**

Heat oven to 350°F. Generously grease 12-cup Bundt® pan or 8-cup ring mold. In large bowl, combine all cake ingredients at low speed until moistened; beat 2 minutes at medium speed. Pour into greased pan.

Bake at 350°F. for 30 to 40 minutes or until toothpick inserted in center comes out clean.

While cake is baking, prepare syrup. In medium saucepan, combine 1 cup sugar and water. Bring to a boil, stirring constantly until sugar dissolves. Remove from heat; add rum. Cool slightly. Using a long-tined fork, pierce hot cake in pan at 1-inch intervals; immediately pour syrup over cake. Cool cake in pan 15 minutes; invert onto serving plate. Cool completely.

In small saucepan, heat apricot preserves. Strain or sieve to remove large apricot pieces; drizzle over cooled cake. To serve, fill center of cake with cut-up fresh fruit.

Yield: 16 servings.

HIGH ALTITUDE:
Above 3500 Feet: Increase flour to 2 cups plus 3 tablespoons. Bake at 375°F. for 25 to 35 minutes.

NUTRITION PER SERVING:
Calories 250; Protein 4g; Carbohydrate 47g; Fat 5g; Sodium 160mg.

SPICY RAISIN BRUNCH CAKE

Brunch traditionally is a combination of breakfast and lunch, usually eaten between 11 a.m. and 3 p.m. It gained popularity in England around 1900. Try this nut and spice filled cake for your next brunch.

CAKE
- 2 cups all purpose flour
- ½ cup raisins
- ½ cup chopped walnuts
- ½ teaspoon baking soda
- 1½ teaspoons pumpkin pie spice
- ¼ to ½ teaspoon cloves
- 1 cup firmly packed brown sugar
- ½ cup apricot preserves
- ½ cup margarine or butter, softened
- 2 tablespoons rum or ½ teaspoon rum extract
- 4 eggs
- ⅔ cup buttermilk

GLAZE
- 1 cup powdered sugar
- 1 teaspoon margarine or butter, softened
- ½ teaspoon rum, if desired
- 5 to 6 teaspoons milk

Heat oven to 350°F. Grease and flour 12-cup Bundt® pan. In medium bowl, combine flour, raisins, walnuts, baking soda, pumpkin pie spice and cloves; set aside. In large bowl, combine brown sugar, preserves, margarine, rum and eggs; beat well. Alternately add flour mixture and buttermilk to sugar mixture, beating well after each addition. Pour batter into greased and floured pan.

Bake at 350°F. for 40 to 50 minutes or until toothpick inserted in center comes out clean. Cool upright in pan for 45 minutes. Invert onto serving plate.

In small bowl, combine all glaze ingredients until smooth; drizzle over cake. Store frosted cake loosely covered.
Yield: 16 servings.

HIGH ALTITUDE:
Above 3500 Feet: No change.

NUTRITION PER SERVING:
Calories 280; Protein 4g; Carbohydrate 44g; Fat 10g; Sodium 140mg.

WHOLE WHEAT APPLE RING CAKE

Cinnamon adds a spicy accent.

CAKE
- 3 cups whole wheat flour
- 2 teaspoons baking powder
- 1 teaspoon cinnamon
- ½ teaspoon salt
- 2 cups firmly packed brown sugar
- 1¼ cups oil
- 2 teaspoons vanilla
- 4 eggs
- 2 cups shredded peeled apples

GLAZE
- ½ cup firmly packed brown sugar
- 1 tablespoon light corn syrup
- 1 tablespoon margarine or butter
- 1 tablespoon milk

Heat oven to 350°F. Grease and flour 12-cup Bundt® pan. In medium bowl, combine whole wheat flour, baking powder, cinnamon and salt; set aside. In large bowl, combine brown sugar, oil, vanilla and eggs; beat well. Add flour mixture; blend well. Fold in apples. Spoon batter into greased and floured pan.

Bake at 350°F. for 45 to 55 minutes or until toothpick inserted in center comes out clean. Cool upright in pan 10 minutes; invert onto serving plate. Cool completely.

In small saucepan, combine all glaze ingredients. Bring to a boil; boil 1 minute, stirring constantly. Cool 5 to 10 minutes or until of desired drizzling consistency. Drizzle glaze over cooled cake.
Yield: 16 servings.

HIGH ALTITUDE:
Above 3500 Feet: Decrease brown sugar in cake to 1¾ cups. Bake at 375°F. for 35 to 45 minutes.

NUTRITION PER SERVING:
Calories 390; Protein 5g; Carbohydrate 53g; Fat 20g; Sodium 140mg.

EGGNOG CAKE WITH FRUIT SAUCE

There is no eggnog in this finely textured whipped cream cake, but you'll find it captures the flavor of the holiday beverage. The fruit sauce is a delicious change of pace and makes this cake very special!

CAKE
2¾ **cups all purpose flour**
1⅔ **cups sugar**
2 **teaspoons baking powder**
1 **teaspoon salt**
1 **teaspoon nutmeg**
1 **pint (2 cups) whipping cream (do not substitute)**
2 **to 3 teaspoons rum extract**
4 **eggs**

FRUIT SAUCE
⅓ **cup firmly packed brown sugar**
1 **tablespoon cornstarch**
1 **(30-oz.) can fruit cocktail or apricot halves, drained, reserving liquid**
¼ **cup margarine or butter**
¼ **teaspoon almond extract**

Heat oven to 325°F. Grease and flour 12-cup Bundt® pan. In large bowl, combine all cake ingredients at low speed until moistened; beat 3 minutes at medium speed (portable mixer at highest speed). Pour batter into greased and floured pan.

Bake at 325°F. for 60 to 70 minutes or until toothpick inserted in center comes out clean. Cool upright in pan 25 minutes; invert onto serving plate. Cool completely.

In medium saucepan, combine brown sugar and cornstarch. Stir in reserved fruit liquid, margarine and almond extract. Cook over medium heat until mixture comes to a boil, stirring constantly; boil 1 minute. Remove from heat; stir in fruit. Serve fruit sauce warm or cool over cake slices.
Yield: 16 servings.

HIGH ALTITUDE:
Above 3500 Feet: Decrease sugar to 1½ cups. Bake at 350°F. for 50 to 60 minutes.

NUTRITION PER SERVING:
Calories 370; Protein 5g; Carbohydrate 53g; Fat 16g; Sodium 240mg.

APPLESAUCE FRUIT CAKE

Chockfull of spices, nuts and fruit!

1½ **cups sugar**
1 **cup shortening**
2 **eggs**
3¼ **cups all purpose flour**
1½ **teaspoons baking soda**
2 **teaspoons cinnamon**
1 **teaspoon allspice**
1 **teaspoon cloves**
½ **teaspoon salt**
1½ **cups chopped nuts**
1½ **cups raisins**
1½ **cups coarsely chopped dates**
½ **cup coarsely chopped red maraschino cherries, drained, or candied cherries**
2 **cups applesauce**
6 **red maraschino cherries, halved and drained, or candied cherries**
6 **pecan halves**

Heat oven to 325°F. Grease 10-inch tube pan; line bottom with waxed paper or foil and grease again. In large bowl, beat sugar and shortening until light and fluffy. Add eggs; blend well. Reserve ½ cup flour. Add remaining 2¾ cups flour, baking soda, cinnamon, allspice, cloves and salt to egg mixture. Blend at low speed until moistened; beat 2 minutes at medium speed.

In another large bowl, combine ½ cup reserved flour with nuts, raisins, dates and ½ cup cherries; stir until nuts and fruit are lightly coated. By hand, stir nut-fruit mixture and applesauce into batter; mix well. Pour batter into greased and waxed paper-lined pan; top with cherry halves and pecans.

Bake at 325°F. for 1¼ to 1¾ hours or until toothpick inserted in center comes out clean. Cool upright in pan 5 minutes. Remove from pan; remove waxed paper. Turn upright onto wire rack. Cool completely. Wrap cooled cake in plastic wrap or foil to keep moist. Store in refrigerator.
Yield: 20 servings.

HIGH ALTITUDE:
Above 3500 Feet: No change.

NUTRITION PER SERVING:
Calories 380; Protein 5g; Carbohydrate 58g; Fat 17g; Sodium 150mg.

Applesauce Fruit Cake

GOLDEN LEMON CAKE ROLL

The lemon filling is superb.

CAKE
- Powdered sugar
- 3/4 cup all purpose flour
- 1/2 cup sugar
- 1 1/2 teaspoons baking powder
- 1/2 teaspoon salt
- 9 egg yolks
- 1/2 cup sugar
- 1/2 cup cold water
- 1/2 teaspoon lemon extract

FILLING
- 1/2 cup sugar
- 1/8 teaspoon salt
- 3 tablespoons lemon juice
- 2 tablespoons margarine or butter
- 3 egg yolks
- 1 teaspoon grated lemon peel
- 1/2 cup whipping cream, whipped

Heat oven to 375°F. Lightly sprinkle clean towel with powdered sugar; set aside. Grease bottom only of 15x10x1-inch baking pan; line pan with waxed paper and grease again. In medium bowl, combine flour, 1/2 cup sugar, baking powder and 1/2 teaspoon salt; mix well.

In large bowl, beat 9 egg yolks at high speed until light lemon colored. Gradually add 1/2 cup sugar, beating until thickened. Add water and lemon extract; blend well. By hand, gently fold dry ingredients into egg mixture; blend well. Spread batter in greased and paper-lined baking pan.

Bake at 375°F. for 15 to 18 minutes or until top springs back when touched lightly in center. Immediately invert cake onto sugared side of towel. Quickly remove waxed paper. Starting with shortest end, roll up cake in towel; cool completely on wire rack.

In small saucepan, combine 1/2 cup sugar, 1/8 teaspoon salt, lemon juice, margarine and 3 egg yolks; blend well. Cook over low heat until thickened, stirring constantly. Remove from heat; stir in lemon peel. Cool to room temperature. Fold whipped cream into cooled filling mixture. Unroll cooled cake; spread filling mixture over cake. Roll up again. Cover; refrigerate 1 to 2 hours before serving. Store in refrigerator.
Yield: 12 servings.

HIGH ALTITUDE:
Above 3500 Feet: No change.

NUTRITION PER SERVING:
Calories 250; Protein 4g; Carbohydrate 34g; Fat 11g; Sodium 180mg.

JELLY ROLL

The British name for jelly roll is Swiss roll. Whatever we call it, it is traditionally a light, airy cake that is rolled with a variety of fillings. We've left the choice of fillings up to you in this recipe, but any flavor of jam or jelly is delicious!

- Powdered sugar
- 4 eggs
- 3/4 cup sugar
- 1/4 cup cold water
- 1 teaspoon vanilla
- 1 cup all purpose flour
- 1 teaspoon baking powder
- 1/4 teaspoon salt
- 3/4 cup favorite jelly or preserves

Heat oven to 375°F. Lightly sprinkle clean towel with powdered sugar; set aside. Generously grease and lightly flour 15x10x1-inch baking pan. In large bowl, beat eggs at highest speed until thick and lemon-colored, about 5 minutes. Gradually add sugar, beating until light and fluffy. Stir in water and vanilla. Add flour, baking powder and salt; blend at low speed just until dry ingredients are moistened. Spread batter evenly in greased and floured pan.

Bake at 375°F. for 8 to 12 minutes or until top springs back when touched lightly in center. Loosen edges; immediately invert onto sugared side of towel. Starting with shortest end, roll up cake in towel; cool completely on wire rack.

When cake is cooled, unroll; remove towel. Spread cake with jelly; roll up again, rolling loosely to incorporate filling. Wrap in foil or waxed paper. Store in refrigerator. If desired, serve sprinkled with additional powdered sugar.
Yield: 8 to 10 servings.

HIGH ALTITUDE:
Above 3500 Feet: No change.

NUTRITION PER SERVING:
Not possible to calculate because of recipe variables.

Jelly Roll

Harvest Pumpkin Cake Roll

This delicate pumpkin-flavored cake roll is filled with a complementary raisin filling and frosted with rich cream cheese frosting.

FILLING
- ³/₄ **cup firmly packed brown sugar**
- 3 **tablespoons cornstarch**
- ¹/₄ **teaspoon salt**
- ¹/₄ **teaspoon cinnamon**
- ¹/₈ **teaspoon nutmeg**
- 1 **cup water**
- 1 **cup raisins**
- 1 **tablespoon margarine or butter**
- 1¹/₂ **teaspoons lemon juice**

CAKE
- **Powdered sugar**
- ³/₄ **cup all purpose flour**
- 1 **teaspoon baking powder**
- 2 **teaspoons cinnamon**
- ¹/₂ **teaspoon salt**
- ¹/₄ **teaspoon cloves**
- ¹/₄ **teaspoon ginger**
- ¹/₄ **teaspoon nutmeg**
- 4 **eggs**
- ³/₄ **cup sugar**
- ¹/₂ **cup canned pumpkin**

FROSTING
- ¹/₂ **cup margarine or butter, softened**
- 1 **(3-oz.) pkg. cream cheese, softened**
- ¹/₂ **teaspoon vanilla**
- 2 **cups powdered sugar**

To prepare filling, in medium saucepan combine brown sugar, cornstarch, ¹/₄ teaspoon salt, ¹/₄ teaspoon cinnamon and ¹/₈ teaspoon nutmeg. Gradually stir in water. Add raisins. Cook over medium heat until mixture boils and thickens, stirring constantly. Boil 1 minute; remove from heat. Stir in 1 tablespoon margarine and lemon juice. Refrigerate until cool.

Heat oven to 375°F. Lightly sprinkle clean towel with powdered sugar; set aside. Generously grease bottom only of 15x10x1-inch baking pan; line with waxed paper and grease again. In small bowl, combine flour, baking powder, 2 teaspoons cinnamon, ¹/₂ teaspoon salt, cloves, ginger and ¹/₄ teaspoon nutmeg; set aside. In large bowl, beat eggs on highest speed for 5 minutes or until thick and lemon colored. Gradually beat in sugar. Stir in pumpkin. Fold flour mixture into pumpkin mixture. Spread batter evenly in greased and paper-lined pan.

Bake at 375°F. for 12 to 20 minutes or until top springs back when touched lightly in center. DO NOT OVERBAKE. Immediately invert cake onto towel; carefully remove waxed paper. Starting with shorter end, roll up hot cake in towel. Cool 30 minutes.

To prepare frosting, in small bowl combine ¹/₂ cup margarine, cream cheese and vanilla. Add powdered sugar; beat until smooth. To assemble cake roll, carefully unroll cake; remove towel. Spread evenly with raisin filling. Roll cake up again (cake may crack slightly). Place on serving plate, seam side down. Spread with frosting. If desired, garnish with additional raisins or chopped nuts. Refrigerate until serving time. Store in refrigerator.

Yield: 12 servings.

TIP:
Recipe can be made ahead and frozen. Thaw before serving.

HIGH ALTITUDE:
Above 3500 Feet: No change.

NUTRITION PER SERVING:
Calories 370; Protein 4g; Carbohydrate 61g; Fat 13g; Sodium 310mg.

Heavenly Hawaiian Cake Roll

It is important that the baking pan used in this recipe be at least 1 inch deep to prevent the batter from overflowing. Some 15x10-inch pans are not this deep.

FILLING
- ⅓ cup margarine or margarine, melted
- ½ cup firmly packed brown sugar
- 1 cup coconut
- 2 tablespoons chopped maraschino cherries
- 1 (8-oz.) can crushed pineapple in its own juice, well drained, reserving ½ cup liquid

CAKE
- Powdered sugar
- 3 eggs
- 1 cup sugar
- Reserved ½ cup pineapple liquid
- 1 cup all purpose flour
- 1 teaspoon baking powder
- ¼ teaspoon salt

TOPPING
- ½ cup whipping cream
- 2 tablespoons powdered sugar
- ½ teaspoon vanilla
- ¼ cup chopped macadamia nuts, toasted, p. 23

Heat oven to 375°F. Line 15x10x1-inch baking pan with foil. Spread margarine evenly in bottom of pan; sprinkle with brown sugar. Sprinkle coconut, maraschino cherries and pineapple evenly over brown sugar; lightly press down. Set aside.

Lightly sprinkle clean towel with powdered sugar; set aside. In small bowl, beat eggs at high speed until thick and lemon colored, about 5 minutes. Gradually add sugar; beat well. If necessary, add enough water to reserved pineapple liquid to measure ½ cup. At low speed, add reserved pineapple liquid; blend well. Add flour, baking powder and salt; beat until smooth. Spread evenly over filling mixture in pan.

Bake at 375°F. for 13 to 18 minutes or until top springs back when touched lightly in center. Invert cake onto sugared side of towel. Gently lift sides of foil from cake; carefully remove foil. Starting with shorter end and using towel to guide cake, roll up. (Do not roll towel into cake.) Wrap towel around rolled cake; cool completely on wire rack.

In small bowl, combine whipping cream, powdered sugar and vanilla; beat until stiff peaks form. Place cake roll on serving plate, seam side down. Spread topping over sides and top of cake roll; sprinkle with nuts. Store in refrigerator.

Yield: 12 servings.

TIP:
Chopped, toasted almonds or pecans can be substituted for macadamia nuts.

HIGH ALTITUDE:
Above 3500 Feet: No change.

NUTRITION PER SERVING:
Calories 300; Protein 3g; Carbohydrate 41g; Fat 14g; Sodium 140mg.

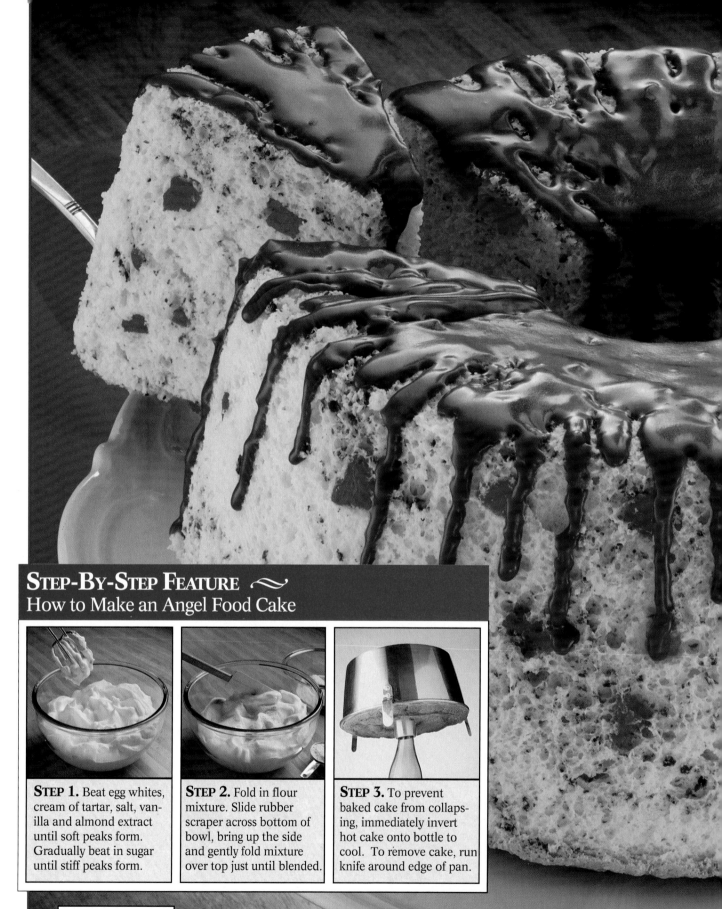

How to Make an Angel Food Cake

STEP 1. Beat egg whites, cream of tartar, salt, vanilla and almond extract until soft peaks form. Gradually beat in sugar until stiff peaks form.

STEP 2. Fold in flour mixture. Slide rubber scraper across bottom of bowl, bring up the side and gently fold mixture over top just until blended.

STEP 3. To prevent baked cake from collapsing, immediately invert hot cake onto bottle to cool. To remove cake, run knife around edge of pan.

ANGEL FOOD CAKE

¾ **cup all purpose flour**
¾ **cup sugar**
1½ **cups (about 12) egg whites, room**
    temperature
1½ **teaspoons cream of tartar**
¼ **teaspoon salt**
1½ **teaspoons vanilla**
½ **teaspoon almond extract**
¾ **cup sugar**

Place oven rack at lowest position. Heat oven to 375°F. In small bowl, combine flour and ¾ cup sugar. In large bowl, beat egg whites, cream of tartar, salt, vanilla and almond extract until mixture forms soft peaks. Gradually add ¾ cup sugar, beating on highest speed until stiff peaks form. Spoon flour-sugar mixture ¼ cup at a time over beaten egg whites; fold in gently just until blended. Pour batter into ungreased 10-inch tube pan. With knife, cut gently through batter to remove large air bubbles.

Bake at 375°F. on lowest oven rack for 30 to 40 minutes or until crust is golden brown and cracks are very dry. Immediately invert cake onto funnel or soft drink bottle; let hang until completely cool. Remove cooled cake from pan.

Yield: 12 servings.

TIP:
To make loaves, bake in 2 ungreased 9x5-inch loaf pans for 25 to 30 minutes.

HIGH ALTITUDE:
Above 3500 Feet: Increase flour to 1 cup; increase egg whites to 1¾ cups (about 13). Bake at 400°F. for 30 to 35 minutes.

NUTRITION PER SERVING:
Calories 140; Protein 4g; Carbohydrate 31g; Fat 0g; Sodium 90mg.

VARIATION:

CHOCOLATE-CHERRY ANGEL FOOD CAKE:
Fold ⅓ cup well-drained, chopped maraschino cherries and 1 oz. grated semi-sweet chocolate into batter. Bake as directed above. In small saucepan over low heat, melt 2 tablespoons margarine or butter and 1 oz. semi-sweet chocolate with 1 tablespoon corn syrup. Stir in 1 cup powdered sugar and 2 to 3 tablespoons maraschino cherry liquid until smooth and of desired drizzling consistency. Immediately drizzle over cooled cake.

Chocolate-Cherry Angel Food Cake

CHIFFON CAKE

Chiffon cake is a foam cake that has oil added to it.

2	cups all purpose flour
1½	cups sugar
3	teaspoons baking powder
¼	teaspoon salt
¾	cup cold water
½	cup oil
7	egg yolks
½	teaspoon vanilla
4	teaspoons finely grated lemon peel
7	egg whites
½	teaspoon cream of tartar

Heat oven to 325°F. In large mixing bowl, combine flour, sugar, baking powder and salt. Add water, oil, egg yolks and vanilla. Beat on low speed until moistened; beat on high speed 5 minutes or until very smooth, scraping sides of bowl occasionally. Fold in lemon peel. Transfer to another large bowl. Thoroughly wash mixing bowl and beaters.

In large mixing bowl, beat egg whites and cream of tartar until stiff peaks form, about 3 minutes. Gradually add egg yolk mixture to egg whites, folding gently to combine. Pour into ungreased 10-inch tube pan.

Bake at 325°F. for 60 to 75 minutes or until top springs back when lightly touched. Immediately invert cake onto funnel or soft drink bottle; let hang until completely cool. To remove cake from pan, run edge of knife around outer edge of pan and tube. Remove cooled cake from pan. Glaze with **Lemon Glaze** p. 186, if desired.
Yield: 12 servings.

HIGH ALTITUDE:
Above 3500 Feet: Bake at 350°F. for 55 to 60 minutes.

NUTRITION PER SERVING:
Calories 300; Protein 6g; Carbohydrate 41g; Fat 12g; Sodium 160mg.

SPONGE CAKE

Sponge cakes do not contain shortening of any kind. They include whole eggs, as opposed to angel food cakes, which use only egg whites.

6	eggs
¾	teaspoon cream of tartar
¾	cup sugar
1½	cups all purpose flour
¾	cup sugar
1	tablespoon grated orange peel
1	teaspoon baking powder
½	teaspoon salt
½	cup apricot nectar or water
1	teaspoon rum extract or vanilla

Heat oven to 350°F. Separate eggs, placing whites in large bowl and yolks in small bowl. Add cream of tartar to egg whites; beat until mixture forms soft peaks. Gradually add ¾ cup sugar, beating at highest speed until stiff peaks form. Add flour and remaining ingredients to egg yolks. Blend at low speed until moistened; beat 1 minute at medium speed. Pour over egg whites; fold in gently just until blended. Pour batter into ungreased 10-inch tube pan.

Bake at 350°F. for 35 to 45 minutes or until top springs back when touched lightly in center. Immediately invert cake on funnel or soft drink bottle; let hang until completely cool. Remove cooled cake from pan.
Yield: 12 servings.

HIGH ALTITUDE:
Above 3500 Feet: Decrease total sugar to 1¼ cups. Bake at 375°F. for 35 to 45 minutes.

NUTRITION PER SERVING:
Calories 200; Protein 5g; Carbohydrate 39g; Fat 3g; Sodium 150mg.

LEMON PLATINUM CAKE

This luscious cake deserves a special occasion! Layered with lemon cream filling and frosted with billows of whipped cream, it guarantees a grand entrance.

CAKE
- 8 egg whites
- 1 teaspoon cream of tartar
- ½ teaspoon salt
- 1 cup sugar
- 7 egg yolks
- 1 cup all purpose flour
- ⅓ cup lemon juice
- 2 teaspoons grated lemon peel

FILLING
- 1 cup sugar
- ¼ cup cornstarch
- Dash salt
- 1¼ cups water
- 2 egg yolks
- 3 tablespoons lemon juice
- 1 tablespoon margarine or butter
- 2 teaspoons grated lemon peel

TOPPING
- 2 cups whipping cream
- 3 to 4 drops yellow food color, if desired
- 2 kiwifruit, peeled, sliced, if desired

Heat oven to 325°F. In large bowl, beat egg whites until foamy. Add cream of tartar and ½ teaspoon salt; beat until soft peaks form. Gradually add ½ cup of the sugar, beating until stiff peaks form. Set aside.

In small bowl, beat 7 egg yolks until lemon colored, about 2 minutes. Gradually add remaining ½ cup sugar, beating until thick and light lemon colored. Add flour, ⅓ cup lemon juice and 2 teaspoons lemon peel to egg yolk mixture; beat at low speed for 1 minute. By hand, gently fold egg yolk mixture into egg white mixture. Pour batter into ungreased 10-inch tube pan.

Bake at 325°F. for 40 to 55 minutes or until top springs back when touched lightly in center. Immediately invert cake onto funnel or soft drink bottle; let hang until completely cool. Remove from pan.

In small saucepan, combine 1 cup sugar, cornstarch and dash salt; mix well. Gradually stir in water. Cook over medium heat until mixture thickens and boils, stirring constantly; remove from heat. In small bowl, beat 2 egg yolks; gradually blend small amount of hot mixture into egg yolks. Add egg yolk mixture to saucepan; cook over low heat 2 to 3 minutes or until thickened, stirring constantly. Remove from heat; stir in 3 tablespoons lemon juice, margarine and 2 teaspoons lemon peel. Cool.

In small bowl, beat whipping cream until slightly thickened. Add ½ cup of the cooled filling mixture and food color; beat until thickened, about 30 seconds. DO NOT OVERBEAT.

To assemble cake, slice cake horizontally to make 3 layers. Place bottom layer on serving plate; spread with half (about ½ cup) of remaining filling mixture. Place middle layer on top; spread with remaining filling. Top with third layer, cut side down. Spread sides, center and top of cake with topping. Refrigerate at least 1 hour before serving. Just before serving, cut kiwifruit slices in half and arrange on cake or garnish individual servings as desired. Store in refrigerator.

Yield: 12 to 16 servings.

HIGH ALTITUDE:
Above 3500 Feet: No change.

NUTRITION PER SERVING:
Calories 290; Protein 5g; Carbohydrate 36g; Fat 15g; Sodium 130mg.

COOK'S NOTE

SPLITTING CAKE OR CAKE LAYERS
Using toothpicks as a cutting guideline and a long-bladed sharp knife, slice cake or cake layers horizontally. Hold the top of the cake or layer with the other hand to prevent shifting of the layers as you cut. The top layer of the cake should be placed with the cut side against the filling and the smooth side up.

BUTTERCREAM FROSTING

For the very creamiest results, be sure to use butter. Do not substitute margarine.

²/₃ **cup butter, softened**
4 **cups powdered sugar**
1 **teaspoon vanilla**
2 **to 4 tablespoons half-and-half or milk**

In large bowl, beat butter until light and fluffy. Gradually add powdered sugar, beating well. Beat in vanilla and half-and-half, adding enough half-and-half for desired spreading consistency.
Yield: Frosts 2-layer or 13x9-inch cake.

NUTRITION PER SERVING:
Calories 250; Protein 0g; Carbohydrate 40g; Fat 11g; Sodium 105mg.

VARIATIONS:

BROWNED BUTTER FROSTING: In large saucepan over medium heat, brown butter until light golden brown, stirring constantly. Blend in remaining ingredients; beat until smooth.

CHOCOLATE BUTTERCREAM FROSTING: Blend into butter ¹/₃ cup unsweetened cocoa, or 2 envelopes premelted unsweetened chocolate baking flavor, or 2 oz. unsweetened chocolate, melted.

CHOCOLATE-CHERRY BUTTERCREAM FROSTING: Blend 3 tablespoons drained chopped maraschino cherries into Chocolate Buttercream Frosting.

COFFEE BUTTERCREAM FROSTING: Dissolve 1¹/₂ teaspoons instant coffee granules or crystals in 2 tablespoons of the half-and-half.

LEMON BUTTERCREAM FROSTING: Substitute 2 to 4 tablespoons lemon juice for the half-and-half and 1 teaspoon grated lemon peel for the vanilla.

NUT BUTTERCREAM FROSTING: Stir in ¹/₄ cup chopped nuts.

ORANGE BUTTERCREAM FROSTING: Substitute 2 to 4 tablespoons orange juice for the half-and-half and 1 teaspoon grated orange peel for the vanilla.

PEANUT BUTTER FROSTING: Add 3 tablespoons peanut butter to the butter.

BUTTERY DECORATOR ICING

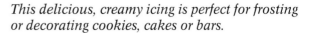

This delicious, creamy icing is perfect for frosting or decorating cookies, cakes or bars.

¹/₂ **cup butter or margarine, softened**
¹/₄ **cup shortening**
1 **teaspoon vanilla**
¹/₈ **teaspoon salt**
4 **cups powdered sugar**
2 **to 4 tablespoons milk**

In large bowl, beat butter and shortening until light and fluffy. Add vanilla and salt. Beat in powdered sugar 1 cup at a time, scraping down sides of bowl. Add 2 tablespoons milk; beat at high speed until light and fluffy. Add enough additional milk for desired spreading consistency.
Yield: 3 cups.

TIP:
This icing can be made up to 2 weeks in advance and stored in an airtight container in the refrigerator. Bring to room temperature and beat before using.

NUTRITION PER SERVING:
Calories 220; Protein 0g; Carbohydrate 40g; Fat 8g; Sodium 105mg.

CHOCOLATE CREAM FROSTING

Whipped cream frostings such as this are always better when served immediately.

1 **cup whipping cream**
¹/₃ **cup chocolate syrup**

In small bowl, beat whipping cream at highest speed just until it begins to thicken. Gradually add chocolate-flavored syrup and continue beating until soft peaks form. Frost cake and serve immediately; store in refrigerator.
Yield: Frosts 2-layer or 13x9-inch cake.

NUTRITION PER SERVING:
Calories 90; Protein 1g; Carbohydrate 6g; Fat 8g; Sodium 10mg.

Decorating Tips and Designs

Simple to elaborate decorations can be made using a decorating bag and tips. Either whipped cream or frosting can be used to make designs on cakes and desserts. For whipped cream decorations, use a larger decorating bag and tips. After decorating, refrigerate the cake or dessert until serving time.

To decorate with frosting, use recipe for **Buttery Decorator Icing** p. 184. The following suggestions will be helpful as you begin to decorate.

- Sift the powdered sugar used in frostings. Small lumps present in unsifted powdered sugar may clog a tip.

- A frosting must be the right consistency for decorations to hold their shape. Adjust the consistency with a small amount of powdered sugar or water.

- When tinting frosting, always mix enough of each color before decorating. Frosting will darken slightly as it dries.

- Cover the frosting bowl with a damp cloth to prevent drying.

- Pack frosting to the bottom of the bag to prevent air bubbles. Squeeze out a little frosting before starting to decorate.

- Make sure the frosted surface upon which decorations will be made is smooth and even.

- Draw the design on the cake with a toothpick before beginning to decorate.

- Frosting made with butter or margarine may soften during decorating due to the heat of your hand. If frosting becomes too soft, chill for a few minutes.

- Parchment paper can be used to make a disposable decorating bag.

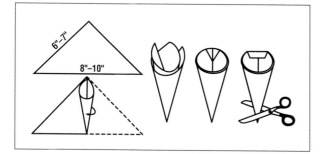

Making a Paper Decorating Bag

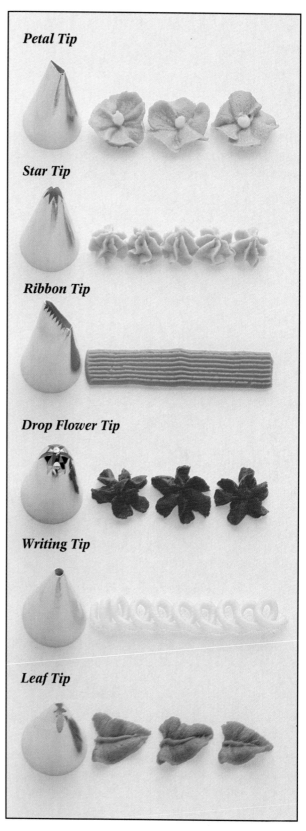

Petal Tip

Star Tip

Ribbon Tip

Drop Flower Tip

Writing Tip

Leaf Tip

Basic Powdered Sugar Glaze

For a nice even glaze, use a small plastic decorator bottle filled with the glaze to frost the cake. Or, place the frosting in a resealable plastic freezer bag and snip off 1 corner, making a very small hole. Squeeze the glaze gently through the opening.

- 2 cups powdered sugar
- 2 tablespoons margarine or butter, softened
- 1 teaspoon vanilla
- 3 to 4 tablespoons milk or half-and-half

In medium bowl, combine all ingredients, adding enough milk for desired glaze consistency. Use to glaze cakes, coffee cakes or pastries.

Yield: 1½ cups.

NUTRITION PER SERVING:
Calories 100; Protein 0g; Carbohydrate 20g; Fat 2g; Sodium 25mg.

VARIATIONS:

CHOCOLATE GLAZE: Add 2 oz. unsweetened chocolate, melted, or 2 envelopes premelted unsweetened chocolate baking flavor.

COFFEE GLAZE: Substitute hot water for milk. Dissolve 1 teaspoon instant coffee granules or crystals in the hot water.

LEMON GLAZE: Substitute 2 tablespoons lemon juice for part of milk and add 1 teaspoon grated lemon peel.

MAPLE GLAZE: Add ½ teaspoon maple extract.

ORANGE GLAZE: Substitute orange juice for milk and add 1 teaspoon grated orange peel.

SPICE GLAZE: Combine ¼ teaspoon cinnamon and ⅛ teaspoon nutmeg with powdered sugar.

Coconut Pecan Frosting

A classic frosting.

- 1 cup sugar
- 1 cup evaporated milk
- ½ cup margarine or butter
- 3 eggs, beaten
- 1⅓ cups flaked coconut
- 1 cup chopped pecans or almonds
- 1 teaspoon vanilla

In medium saucepan, combine sugar, milk, margarine and eggs. Cook over medium heat until mixture starts to bubble, stirring constantly. Stir in remaining ingredients. Cool until of desired spreading consistency.

Yield: Frosts 2-layer or 13x9-inch cake.

NUTRITION PER SERVING:
Calories 317; Protein 5g; Carbohydrate 23g; Fat 24g; Sodium 135mg.

Broiled Coconut Topping

We suggest using this topping on spice, carrot or yellow cake. It's quick and easy.

- ¼ cup margarine or butter
- 1 cup flaked or shredded coconut
- ⅔ cup firmly packed brown sugar
- ½ cup chopped nuts
- 3 tablespoons half-and-half or milk

Heat broiler. In small saucepan, melt margarine. Stir in remaining ingredients. Spread on warm cake. Broil 4 to 6 inches from heat for 1 to 2 minutes or until bubbly and light golden brown. (Watch carefully, mixture burns easily.)

Yield: Tops 13x9-inch cake.

NUTRITION PER SERVING:
Calories 150; Protein 1g; Carbohydrate 16g; Fat 10g; Sodium 50mg.

CREAM CHEESE FROSTING

Soften cream cheese at room temperature or in the microwave. To soften cream cheese in the microwave, remove it from the wrapper and microwave it on MEDIUM for 1 to 1½ minutes.

- 3 cups powdered sugar
- 1 (8-oz.) pkg. cream cheese, softened
- 2 tablespoons margarine or butter, melted
- 1 teaspoon vanilla

In large bowl, combine all ingredients; beat until smooth.

Yield: Frosts 2-layer or 13x9-inch cake.

NUTRITION PER SERVING:
Calories 180; Protein 1g; Carbohydrate 25g; Fat 8g; Sodium 80mg.

CHOCOLATE CREAM CHEESE FROSTING

Use low heat and stir constantly when melting chocolate chips.

- 1 (3-oz.) pkg. cream cheese, softened
- 2 cups powdered sugar
- 1 (6-oz.) pkg. (1 cup) semi-sweet chocolate chips, melted, cooled
- 3 tablespoons milk
- 1 teaspoon vanilla

In small bowl, combine cream cheese and powdered sugar; beat at medium speed until light and fluffy. Blend in melted chocolate, milk and vanilla at low speed until smooth. If necessary, add additional milk 1 teaspoon at a time for desired spreading consistency.

Yield: Frosts 2-layer or 13x9-inch cake.

NUTRITION PER SERVING:
Calories 170; Protein 1g; Carbohydrate 29g; Fat 7g; Sodium 25mg.

ALMOND BARK BUTTERCREAM FROSTING

Using low heat to melt the almond bark is the secret to making this frosting smooth and creamy. We like the frosting on chocolate cake, but it's delicious on other cake flavors too.

- 6 oz. almond bark or vanilla-flavored candy coating, cut into pieces
- 3 to 4 tablespoons chocolate-flavored liqueur
- ¾ cup butter, softened
- ¼ cup powdered sugar

In small saucepan over low heat, melt almond bark, stirring constantly. Remove from heat; stir in chocolate liqueur. Cool 30 minutes.

In small bowl, beat butter and powdered sugar until light and fluffy. Gradually beat in cooled almond bark mixture until smooth.

Yield: Frosts 2-layer or 13x9-inch cake.

NUTRITION PER SERVING:
Calories 200; Protein 1g; Carbohydrate 10g; Fat 19g; Sodium 115mg.

COOK'S NOTE

MELTING CHOCOLATE

Chocolate should be melted over low heat and stirred constantly to prevent scorching. Small amounts of water may cause it to "seize" or become thick, lumpy and grainy, so use utensils and equipment that are dry. Chocolate can sometimes be returned to melting consistancy by adding 1 teaspoon of solid shortening for every 2 ounces of chocolate and reheating it.

SEVEN-MINUTE FROSTING

This traditional frosting is fluffy, white and almost meringue-like in texture. It's easy to make, but takes 7 minutes to cook.

- 1½ cups sugar
- ¼ teaspoon cream of tartar
- ¼ teaspoon salt
- ⅓ cup water
- 2 teaspoons light corn syrup
- 2 egg whites
- 1 teaspoon vanilla

In top of double boiler, combine all ingredients except vanilla. Place over rapidly boiling water (water should not touch bottom of pan); beat at highest speed until mixture stands in peaks, about 7 minutes. DO NOT OVERCOOK. Remove from heat; add vanilla. Continue beating until frosting holds deep swirls, about 2 minutes.

Yield: Frosts 2-layer or 13x9-inch cake.

NUTRITION PER SERVING:
Calories 102; Protein 0g; Carbohydrate 26g; Fat 0g; Sodium 54mg.

VARIATIONS:

CHERRY FROSTING: Substitute ⅓ cup maraschino cherry liquid for water. Fold ⅓ cup drained chopped maraschino cherries into finished frosting.

CHOCOLATE REVEL FROSTING: Add ⅓ cup semi-sweet chocolate chips to finished frosting. Let stand 1 to 2 minutes. Chocolate will swirl through frosting when spread on cake.

LEMON FROSTING: Fold 3 teaspoons grated lemon peel into finished frosting.

MAPLE FROSTING: Substitute ½ to 1 teaspoon maple extract for vanilla.

NESSELRODE FROSTING: Substitute 1 teaspoon rum extract for vanilla. Place 1 cup frosting in small bowl; stir in ½ cup chopped mixed candied fruit and ½ cup toasted coconut. Spread between layers. Frost sides and top with remaining plain frosting.

ORANGE FROSTING: Fold 3 teaspoons grated orange peel into finished frosting.

PEPPERMINT FROSTING: Substitute 3 to 5 drops peppermint extract for vanilla. Fold ½ cup crushed hard peppermint candy into finished frosting.

WHITE CLOUD FROSTING

This delicate, airy frosting is a classic. Try it on any chocolate or white cake.

- 2 egg whites
- ¼ teaspoon salt
- 1 teaspoon vanilla
- ¼ cup sugar
- ¾ cup light corn syrup

In small deep bowl, beat egg whites, salt and vanilla at medium speed until foamy. Gradually add sugar 1 tablespoon at a time, beating at highest speed until soft peaks form and sugar is dissolved. In small saucepan over medium heat, bring corn syrup just to a boil. Pour in thin stream over egg whites, beating at highest speed until mixture forms stiff peaks.

Yield: Frosts 2-layer or 13x9-inch cake.

NUTRITION PER SERVING:
Calories 80; Protein 1g; Carbohydrate 20g; Fat 0g; Sodium 70mg.

GANACHE

Ganache (gahn-AHSH) is a rich combination of chocolate and cream that ranges in consistency from fudgy to light and airy, depending on the proportion of whipping cream to chocolate. This recipe makes enough ganache to frost a layer cake.

- 12 oz. semi-sweet chocolate, chopped, or 1 cup semi-sweet chocolate chips
- 1 cup whipping cream
- 2 tablespoons butter or margarine

In small saucepan, combine chocolate and whipping cream; heat over low heat until chocolate is melted and mixture is smooth and creamy, stirring constantly. Remove from heat; stir in butter. Refrigerate 30 to 45 minutes or until cold, stirring occasionally.

With wooden spoon or hand mixer, beat chilled mixture until thick and creamy and of desired spreading consistency.

Yield: Frosts 2-layer or 13x9-inch cake.

NUTRITION PER SERVING:
Calories 220; Protein 2g; Carbohydrate 19g; Fat 18g; Sodium 30mg.

COOK'S NOTE

GANACHE

Ganache is a rich mixture of chocolate and whipping cream that's used as a frosting or piped onto a dessert as a garnish. The mixture is heated over low heat until the chocolate is melted. Then it is chilled and beaten with a wire whisk or electric beater until it is thick enough to spread. Ganache sets up rather quickly, so stop and check the consistency frequently. DO NOT OVER-BEAT ganache; it will thicken and resemble fudge. If ganache becomes too thick to spread, stir in 1 tablespoon of warm cream, or warm it slightly over hot water or in the microwave on LOW. The mixture will not be as glossy, but it will be spreadable.

To pipe the ganache decoratively, beat the mixture until it holds its shape when mounded. Spoon it into a decorating bag fitted with the desired tip. Pipe it directly onto the dessert.

FUDGE FROSTING

This fudgy frosting is delicious on almost any flavor of cake!

- 2 cups sugar
- ¾ cup half-and-half
- 2 oz. unsweetened chocolate or 2 envelopes premelted unsweetened chocolate baking flavor
- 2 tablespoons light corn syrup
- ⅛ teaspoon salt
- 2 tablespoons margarine or butter
- 1 teaspoon vanilla

In large saucepan, combine sugar, half-and-half, chocolate, corn syrup and salt. Cook over low heat, stirring just until sugar is dissolved. Cover; cook over medium heat for 2 minutes. Uncover; cook until candy thermometer reaches soft ball stage (234°F.), about 5 minutes. Do not stir while cooking. Remove from heat; add margarine. Cool to lukewarm (110°F.). Additional cooling may cause frosting to harden too soon.

Add vanilla; beat until frosting begins to thicken and loses its gloss. If necessary, thin with a few drops of half-and-half.

Yield: Frosts 2-layer or 13x9-inch cake.

NUTRITION PER SERVING:
Calories 210; Protein 0g; Carbohydrate 38g; Fat 7g; Sodium 55mg.

VARIATIONS:

MARSHMALLOW NUT FUDGE FROSTING:
Add 1 cup miniature marshmallows and ½ cup chopped nuts to frosting just before spreading.

PEANUT BUTTER FUDGE FROSTING: Add ¼ cup creamy peanut butter with margarine.

DESSERTS

~

Dessert adds that sweet touch to the end of a meal or the end of a day. There's a dessert that's perfect for every occasion and in this chapter you'll find the dessert that fits yours to a "T."

The collection starts with down-home family favorites — cobblers, crisps and deep dish pies — and moves on to delicious dessert squares, creamy cheesecakes, elegant tortes . . . and more! A special section offers secrets for successful desserts, including easy tips for sensational finishing touches.

Pictured: **Chocolate Toffee Cloud** *p. 249,* **Ruby Razz Crunch** *p. 212*

DESSERTS

Dessert adds a finishing touch to any meal,
whether it is a made-in-minutes fruit cobbler or a masterpiece of many layers.
Because desserts are so versatile, you'll find ones that not only complement
your meal, but also fit your level of baking expertise.

KINDS OF DESSERTS

Desserts fall into several main categories:

BAKED AND STEAMED PUDDINGS

These moist, hearty, old-fashioned desserts are either baked in a pan, cooked in the micro-wave or steamed in a mold on the stovetop. (Recipes begin on p. 240.)

CHEESECAKES

Cheesecakes do contain cheese — most often it's cream, Neufchatel, cottage or ricotta cheese. Sometimes yogurt cheese is used. Rich and dense, cheesecakes have many flavor, crust and topping variations. (Recipes begin on p. 222.)

CRISPS, COBBLERS, BUCKLES AND PANDOWDIES

Fruit is the hallmark of these traditional desserts. They are usually topped with a pastry crust, streusel or biscuit topping. (Recipes begin on p. 196.)

CUSTARDS, FLANS AND SOUFFLES

Eggs are the main ingredient in all of these desserts. Custards and flans are baked until delicately firm and are sometimes topped with caramel or fruit. A souffle is a puffy, feather-light dessert with a reputation for elegance. (Recipes begin on p. 237.)

MERINGUES

A hard meringue is a confection of beaten egg whites, sugar and sometimes flavorings, which is shaped and then baked. These crisp, airy shells can be topped with custard, mousse, fruit or other fillings. A soft meringue is used to top desserts such as Baked Alaska. (Recipes begin on p. 248.)

SHORTCAKES

Shortcakes are drop or rolled biscuits, sponge cakes or pound cakes topped with fruit. (Recipes begin on p. 206.)

TORTES

Tortes can be made in several ways. They can be multi-layered desserts with a variety of fillings and toppings or dense confections baked in a springform pan. (Recipes begin on p. 254.)

SECRETS FOR SUCCESSFUL DESSERTS

Desserts incorporate a few basic baking techniques that will help you approach even the most elaborate confection with confidence.

SECRETS FOR STEAMED PUDDINGS

Use molds with tight-fitting lids for steamed puddings. Grease the inside of the mold with shortening and then sprinkle it with sugar.

Place molds on a wire rack or trivet in a Dutch oven. Choose a Dutch oven that is large enough to allow steam to circulate completely around the molds. Bring 1 inch of water to a boil, add the molds and cover the Dutch oven tightly. Cook at high heat until steam begins to escape, then reduce the heat to low.

Remove the mold lid after steaming. This allows the pudding to "rest," allows excess steam to escape and minimizes cracking when the pudding is unmolded.

Run a knife between the mold and the pudding to loosen the pudding for unmolding. Invert a plate over the mold. Hold the plate firmly against the mold and turn the mold upside down. The pudding should slip from the mold.

SECRETS FOR CHEESECAKES

Make the cheesecake 24 to 36 hours before serving it. This allows the cheesecake to cool and firm up completely, and allows flavors to blend and mellow. Cool the cheesecake to room temperature and then store it in the refrigerator.

Use the pan size called for in the recipe.

Have eggs and cream cheese at room temperature before mixing the batter.

Follow these tips to help prevent cracks in cheesecakes:

- **Use an electric mixer or food processor to beat the filling.** Beat at medium speed just until smooth. Overbeating or mixing at high speed can cause cracks to form in the cheesecake as it bakes.

- **Place a shallow pan half full of water on the lower rack in the oven.** The water will help minimize cracking in the top of the cheesecake.

- **Let the cheesecake "rest" after baking.** Unless other directions are specified in the recipe, when the cheesecake is done, turn off the oven and open the door. Allow the cheese-

cake to rest for 30 minutes, then transfer it to a cooling rack in a draft-free spot until it reaches room temperature. When completely cool, remove the sides of the pan and then refrigerate.

- **Do not jar the cheesecake while it is baking or cooling.**

Cut cheesecakes using a wet knife or a piece of dental floss. Dip the knife in water before each cut. To use dental floss, stretch it tightly between your hands and press firmly through the cheesecake.

SECRETS FOR CUSTARDS

Avoid overbaking custards. Because custards are made with eggs, they can curdle or become rubbery and watery if overbaked. To protect the protein in the eggs from excessive heat, bake custard in cups placed on a rack or folded towel set in a pan of hot water (about 1 inch deep).

SECRETS FOR SOUFFLES

Heat the oven 10 to 15 minutes before baking. A hot oven will allow the souffle to begin rising immediately.

Beat egg whites just until they form stiff peaks. Overbeaten egg whites will prevent the souffle from rising. Fold them gently into the batter.

Handle with care! A souffle is a delicate dessert supported by the air incorporated into the egg whites. Gently spoon the batter into the baking dish, and avoid jarring it as it is placed in or removed from the oven. Also, close and open the oven door carefully.

Serve immediately. A souffle will only hold its shape a few minutes after it's removed from the oven. As the steam escapes, it will begin to fall. Because of this, you'll want to carefully plan for the serving time.

SECRETS FOR HARD MERINGUES

Avoid making meringues on hot, humid days. High humidity will prevent meringues from reaching their full volume, and they will "weep" (beads of moisture will form on the meringue) and become sticky after baking.

Use beaters, utensils and bowls that are clean and free from grease. Even a small amount of grease (or speck of egg yolk) will prevent beaten egg whites from reaching their full volume. Use glass or stainless steel bowls rather than plastic, because plastic bowls tend to retain fat.

Egg whites should come from clean, fresh eggs with no cracks.

Bring egg whites to room temperature before beating them. Set the bowl of egg whites in a large bowl of very warm water and stir them gently for a few minutes.

Begin beating the egg whites slowly, gradually increasing speed as the egg whites begin to foam.

Beat the egg whites until they hold the desired shape, either soft or stiff peaks.

Add sugar gradually while beating. This will ensure that the sugar dissolves completely and that stiff glossy peaks will form.

Bake meringues for a long time at a low temperature. This gives meringues their crisp, melt-in-your-mouth texture. Cool completely.

Fill or top meringues just before serving to prevent them from becoming soggy.

HOW TO TELL WHEN DESSERTS ARE DONE

Just an extra minute in the oven can make a dessert overbaked. Here are some tips for telling when desserts are done:

Read the description in the recipe. The recipe provides a specific description of what a dessert looks like when it's done. It may say the top will be golden brown or cracked, or that the dessert will begin pulling away from the sides of the pan or that the filling will be bubbly around the edges.

Two common descriptions for rich, moist desserts are:

- **". . . until almost set."** About a 3-inch diameter circle in the center will be soft and will jiggle when the dessert is moved slightly. The edges of the dessert will be set and have a dry appearance. As the dessert cools, the center will become firm.

- **". . . until set."** The center of the dessert will be soft when touched lightly, but will not jiggle when moved. The center will become more firm as the dessert cools.

Check desserts at the minimum baking time. If the dessert isn't quite done, check at 1-minute increments until it meets the description in the recipe.

Baked and steamed puddings are done when . . . they are set and firm.

Baked custards and flans are done when . . . a knife inserted halfway between the center and the edge of the custard comes out clean. The center of the custard may look soft, but as it cools, it will become firm. An overbaked custard will have a porous, rubbery texture and liquid will seep from it when cut with a spoon.

A souffle is done when . . . it has doubled in volume and is firm, and the top is golden brown.

KEEPING DESSERTS FRESH AND FLAVORFUL

Many desserts have a very short lifespan — and not just because they get gobbled up! Souffles, for example, must be baked and served immediately. Hard meringues, once they're filled, will become soggy. However, other desserts such as cheesecakes, cobblers and squares can be stored or frozen with great success. Here are some tips for keeping desserts at their peak:

Store unfilled meringues, puffs and eclairs in an airtight, moisture-proof container. Meringues should be stored in a tin or other container with a tight-fitting lid in a cool, dry place to keep them crisp and to prevent droplets of moisture from forming, also known as weeping. Store up to 2 days at room temperature, or freeze them for up to 1 month. Puffs or eclairs should be stored in the refrigerator. Limit storage time to overnight. For longer storage, place unfilled puffs in an airtight container and freeze them for up to 3 months.

Store egg- or milk-based desserts in the refrigerator. Custards and flans are at their best served the day they are prepared. Baked puddings can be served warm from the oven or covered and stored in the refrigerator. They should not be frozen. Add whipped cream just before serving.

Store cobblers, dumplings and cheesecakes in the refrigerator. Cover them tightly with foil or plastic wrap. These desserts also freeze well. To freeze: allow to cool completely after baking; wrap tightly in moisture- and vapor-proof covering and freeze for 4 to 5 months. Fruit-filled dumplings may be frozen baked or unbaked. When freezing an unbaked dumpling, brush the bottom crust with egg white before filling it to prevent it from becoming soggy. Fill and shape it, but do not cut air vents in the crust. Wrap tightly and freeze. Bake the dumplings according to the recipe after thawing them at room temperature. For baked dumplings, cool completely, wrap and freeze.

SERVING DESSERTS WITH A FLAIR

One of the joys of serving a dessert is making it look pretty. Here are a few easy ideas for dressing up simple or sensational desserts.

Drizzle or pipe chocolate sauce on an individual plate before placing a wedge of cheesecake or a hard meringue on it. See diagram for Plate Painting.

Plate Painting

Dust a serving plate or individual plate with cocoa or powdered sugar before placing the dessert on it.

Line the serving plate with a paper doily.

Make an arrangement of mint sprigs and/or edible flowers such as roses on top of the dessert or on the serving plate at the base of the dessert.

NUTRITION IN THIS CHAPTER

Nutrition per serving means the calculation was done on 1 cream puff, 1 meringue shell or 1 serving.

APPLE CRISP

A crisp is a fruit dessert that is baked with a top layer of buttered crumbs, which forms a crisp, crumbly crust as it bakes. Try the flavor variations we offer.

FRUIT MIXTURE
- 6 **cups sliced peeled apples**
- 1 **teaspoon cinnamon, if desired**
- 1 **tablespoon water**
- 1 **teaspoon lemon juice**

TOPPING
- 1 **cup rolled oats**
- ¾ **cup all purpose flour**
- ¾ **cup firmly packed brown sugar**
- ½ **cup margarine or butter, softened**

Heat oven to 375°F. Place apples in ungreased 2-quart casserole or 8-inch square (1½-quart) baking dish. Sprinkle with cinnamon, water and lemon juice. In large bowl, combine all topping ingredients; mix until crumbly. Sprinkle crumb mixture evenly over apples. Bake at 375°F. for 25 to 35 minutes or until fruit is tender and topping is golden brown. Serve warm with cream, ice cream or whipped cream, if desired.
Yield: 12 (½-cup) servings.

MICROWAVE DIRECTIONS:
Using 8-inch square (1½-quart) microwave-safe dish, prepare apple crisp as directed above. Microwave on HIGH for 12 to 14 minutes or until fruit is tender, rotating dish ¼ turn once during cooking.

NUTRITION PER SERVING:
Calories 210; Protein 2g; Carbohydrate 32g; Fat 8g; Sodium 95mg.

VARIATIONS:

APPLE CHEESE CRISP: Top baked crisp with 2 oz. (½ cup) shredded Cheddar cheese; bake an additional 2 to 3 minutes or until cheese melts.

BLUEBERRY CRISP: Substitute blueberries for the apples.

PEACH CRISP: Substitute sliced peeled peaches for the apples.

PEAR CRANBERRY CRISP: Substitute 5 cups sliced peeled pears, 1½ cups fresh or frozen cranberries, 1 cup sugar, 2 tablespoons flour and 2 teaspoons grated orange peel for fruit mixture.

PEACH BERRY CRUMBLE

This colorful fruit-laden cobbler is the perfect ending for a meal or is great for a coffee break.

TOPPING
- 1 **cup all purpose flour**
- ¾ **cup sugar**
- ¼ **cup margarine or butter, softened**
- 1 **egg, slightly beaten**

FRUIT MIXTURE
- 1 **cup sugar**
- 3 **tablespoons cornstarch**
- 1 **cup water**
- ¼ **teaspoon almond extract**
- 1 **(16-oz.) pkg. frozen sliced peaches, thawed**
- 1 **cup fresh or frozen cranberries (do not thaw)**
- 1 **cup fresh or frozen blackberries (do not thaw)**

Heat oven to 400°F. In medium bowl, combine flour and ¾ cup sugar. Using pastry blender or fork, cut in margarine until crumbly. Stir in egg; mix well. Set aside.

In small saucepan, combine 1 cup sugar and cornstarch; add water. Cook over medium heat until mixture boils and thickens, stirring constantly. Stir in almond extract. In ungreased 8-inch square (1½-quart) baking dish, combine peaches, cranberries and blackberries; stir in hot cornstarch mixture. Sprinkle topping over fruit mixture.

Bake at 400°F. for 40 to 45 minutes or until topping is golden brown. Serve warm. If desired, serve with sweetened sour cream, whipped cream or ice cream.
Yield: 9 servings.

NUTRITION PER SERVING:
Calories 330; Protein 3g; Carbohydrate 67g; Fat 6g; Sodium 70mg.

SIMPLE FRUIT CRISP

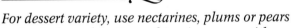

Select your favorite flavor of fruit filling to make this easy-to-prepare crisp.

- 1 (21-oz.) can fruit pie filling (cherry, blueberry, raspberry, apricot or apple)
- 1 cup all purpose flour
- ½ cup firmly packed brown sugar
- ½ teaspoon cinnamon, if desired
- ½ teaspoon nutmeg, if desired
- ⅓ cup margarine or butter, softened

Heat oven to 375°F. Spread pie filling in ungreased 8-inch square (1½-quart) baking dish. In medium bowl, combine all remaining ingredients until crumbly; sprinkle over filling. Bake at 375°F. for 25 to 30 minutes or until golden brown. If desired, serve warm with ice cream or whipped topping.
Yield: 6 to 8 servings.

NUTRITION PER SERVING:
Calories 310; Protein 2g; Carbohydrate 59g; Fat 8g; Sodium 95mg.

INDIVIDUAL PEACH CRISP

For dessert variety, use nectarines, plums or pears instead of peaches. Serve this crisp warm with cream or ice cream.

- 1½ cups (2 medium) sliced peeled peaches
- 3 tablespoons all purpose flour
- 3 tablespoons brown sugar
- 3 tablespoons rolled oats
- 3 tablespoons chopped walnuts, if desired
- ⅛ teaspoon cinnamon
- 2 tablespoons margarine or butter

Heat oven to 350°F. Spoon peaches evenly into 3 ungreased 10-oz. custard cups. In small bowl, combine all remaining ingredients; blend with fork until crumbly. Sprinkle crumb mixture evenly over peaches. Bake at 350°F for 25 to 30 minutes or until fruit is tender and topping is golden brown. Serve warm.
Yield: 3 servings.

MICROWAVE DIRECTIONS:
Prepare peach crisp as directed above using 3 ungreased 6-oz. custard cups. Microwave on HIGH for 2½ to 4½ minutes or until peaches are tender, rearranging custard cups once during cooking. Serve warm.

NUTRITION PER SERVING:
Calories 260; Protein 3g; Carbohydrate 34g; Fat 13g; Sodium 95mg.

FRESH PLUM CRUMB

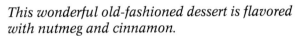

This wonderful old-fashioned dessert is flavored with nutmeg and cinnamon.

FRUIT MIXTURE
- 5 cups chopped, pitted plums
- 2 tablespoons quick-cooking tapioca
- 3 eggs
- 1½ cups sugar
- ¼ cup all purpose flour
- ½ teaspoon nutmeg
- 3 tablespoons milk

TOPPING
- ¾ cup rolled oats
- ¾ cup firmly packed brown sugar
- ½ teaspoon cinnamon
- ¼ teaspoon salt
- ¼ cup margarine or butter, melted

Heat oven to 375°F. Lightly grease 13x9-inch pan. In medium bowl, combine plums and tapioca; set aside. In large bowl, lightly beat eggs; stir in sugar, flour, nutmeg and milk. Gently fold in plum mixture. Pour into greased pan. In medium bowl, combine rolled oats, brown sugar, cinnamon and salt; mix well. Stir in margarine; sprinkle over plum mixture.

Bake at 375°F. for 40 to 45 minutes or until golden brown. Serve warm.
Yield: 16 to 20 servings.

NUTRITION PER SERVING:
Calories 170; Protein 2g; Carbohydrate 32g; Fat 4g; Sodium 95mg.

Blueberry Plum Crunch Cups

Dessert warm from the oven is a welcome surprise on a cool day.

FRUIT MIXTURE
2½ **cups purple plums, pitted, sliced***
2½ **cups blueberries***
¼ **cup firmly packed brown sugar**

TOPPING
1 **cup all purpose flour**
⅓ **cup sugar**
⅓ **cup firmly packed brown sugar**
½ **teaspoon salt**
¼ **teaspoon nutmeg**
1 **egg**
1 **tablespoon margarine or butter, melted**

Heat oven to 375°F. Grease six 6-oz. custard cups; place on cookie sheet. In medium bowl, gently combine plums, blueberries and ¼ cup brown sugar. Spoon about ½ cup fruit mixture into each greased cup.

In medium bowl, combine flour, sugar, ⅓ cup brown sugar, salt and nutmeg; mix well. Add egg; mix until crumbly. Sprinkle about ¼ cup flour mixture over each cup of fruit; drizzle each with about ½ teaspoon melted margarine. Bake at 375°F. for 25 to 30 minutes or until topping is golden brown. Serve warm with ice cream, if desired.
Yield: 6 servings.

TIP:
* Two 16-oz. cans purple plums, drained, pitted and sliced, and 2½ cups frozen blueberries, thawed and drained, can be substituted for the fresh fruit.

NUTRITION PER SERVING:
Calories 310; Protein 4g; Carbohydrate 65g; Fat 4g; Sodium 220mg.

Chocolate Cherry Crunch

Cherries are layered between a chocolate shortbread mixture, forming what is known as a "crunch" in this easy recipe.

CRUST AND TOPPING
1 **cups all purpose flour**
¾ **cup firmly packed brown sugar**
¾ **cup quick-cooking rolled oats**
¼ **cup unsweetened cocoa**
¼ **teaspoon salt**
½ **cup margarine or butter, softened**

FRUIT MIXTURE
1 **(21-oz.) can cherry fruit pie filling**
1 **teaspoon brandy extract, if desired**

Heat oven to 350°F. In large bowl, combine flour, brown sugar, oats, cocoa, and salt; mix well. Using pastry blender or fork, cut in margarine until crumbly. Press 1 cup crumb mixture into bottom of ungreased 8 or 9-inch square pan. In medium bowl, combine pie filling and brandy extract; spoon evenly over crust. Sprinkle remaining crumb mixture evenly over cherry filling; press lightly into filling.

Bake at 350°F. for 25 to 30 minutes or until light golden brown. Serve with ice cream or whipped cream, if desired.
Yield: 6 to 8 servings.

HIGH ALTITUDE:
Above 3500 Feet: No change.

NUTRITION PER SERVING:
Calories 410; Protein 4g; Carbohydrate 72g; Fat 13g; Sodium 230mg.

PEACHY PINEAPPLE DESSERT

Butterscotch chips add a unique richness to this deliciously sweet, quick and easy fruit cobbler.

- ¼ **cup margarine or butter, melted**
- 1 **(21-oz.) can peach fruit pie filling**
- 1 **(15.25 or 20-oz.) can crushed pineapple, undrained**
- 1 **(6-oz.) pkg. (1 cup) butterscotch chips**
- 1 **(10-oz.) can refrigerated flaky biscuits**
- ⅓ **cup chopped nuts**
  Whipped topping or ice cream, if desired

Heat oven to 400°F. In medium saucepan, combine 2 tablespoons of the melted margarine, peach filling, pineapple and butterscotch chips; heat until hot and bubbly.* Pour hot fruit mixture into ungreased 12x8-inch (2-quart) baking dish. Separate dough into 10 biscuits; cut each into 4 pieces. Dip biscuit pieces into remaining melted margarine; arrange over hot fruit mixture. Sprinkle with nuts.

Bake at 400°F. for 15 to 18 minutes or until golden brown. Serve warm or cool topped with whipped topping or ice cream.

Yield: 10 servings.

TIP:

* Fruit mixture can be heated in baking dish; heat at 400°F. for 20 minutes or until hot and bubbly. Top with biscuit pieces and nuts; bake as directed above.

NUTRITION PER SERVING:
Calories 380; Protein 3g; Carbohydrate 46g; Fat 20g; Sodium 350mg.

BLUEBERRY BUCKLE RING

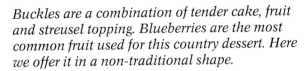

Buckles are a combination of tender cake, fruit and streusel topping. Blueberries are the most common fruit used for this country dessert. Here we offer it in a non-traditional shape.

CAKE
- 1½ **cups all purpose flour**
- 2 **teaspoons baking powder**
- ¼ **teaspoon salt**
- ¾ **cup sugar**
- ¼ **cup margarine or butter, softened**
- 1 **egg**
- ½ **cup milk**
- 3 **cups fresh or frozen blueberries (do not thaw)**

TOPPING
- ⅓ **cup all purpose flour**
- ½ **cup firmly packed brown sugar**
- ½ **teaspoon cinnamon**
- ¼ **cup margarine or butter**
- ¼ **cup chopped walnuts**

Heat oven to 350°F. Grease and flour 10-inch tube pan. In medium bowl, combine 1½ cups flour, baking powder and salt; set aside. In large bowl, beat sugar and ¼ cup margarine until light and fluffy. Add egg; beat well. Alternately add dry ingredients and milk to sugar mixture, beating well after each addition. Spread ⅔ of batter into greased and floured pan; top with blueberries. Carefully spread with remaining batter.

In medium bowl, combine ⅓ cup flour, brown sugar and cinnamon. Using pastry blender or fork, cut in ¼ cup margarine until mixture is crumbly. Stir in nuts. Sprinkle over batter. Bake at 350°F. for 55 to 65 minutes or until cake is deep golden brown. Cool 10 minutes; remove from pan. Serve warm with cream, if desired.

Yield: 8 servings.

HIGH ALTITUDE:
Above 3500 Feet: No change.

NUTRITION PER SERVING:
Calories 410; Protein 5g; Carbohydrate 63g; Fat 15g; Sodium 300mg.

Blueberry Buckle Ring

BLUEBERRY PEACH COBBLER

Tender sugar-crusted biscuits sit atop a tasty blend of fruit. This cobbler is delicious warm from the oven.

FRUIT MIXTURE
- 1/3 cup sugar
- 1 tablespoon cornstarch
- 3/4 cup unsweetened orange juice
- 1 1/2 cups fresh or frozen blueberries (do not thaw)
- 1 cup fresh or frozen peach slices, cut into 1-inch pieces (do not thaw)
- 1 teaspoon grated orange peel

BISCUITS
- 1 cup all purpose flour
- 1 tablespoon sugar
- 1 teaspoon baking powder
- 1/4 teaspoon baking soda
- 1/2 cup buttermilk
- 3 tablespoons oil
- 1 tablespoon sugar

In medium saucepan, combine 1/3 cup sugar and cornstarch. Gradually stir in orange juice. Cook over medium heat until mixture comes to a boil and is slightly thickened and clear, stirring constantly. Stir in blueberries and peach pieces; cook until fruit is hot. Stir in orange peel; set aside.

Heat oven to 375°F. In medium bowl, combine flour, 1 tablespoon sugar, baking powder and baking soda; mix well. Stir in buttermilk and oil just until dry ingredients are moistened. Pour hot fruit mixture into ungreased 1 1/2-quart casserole. Drop dough by tablespoonfuls over fruit mixture. Sprinkle dough with 1 tablespoon sugar. Bake at 375°F. for 20 to 25 minutes or until biscuits are light golden brown.
Yield: 8 servings.

HIGH ALTITUDE:
Above 3500 Feet: No change.

NUTRITION PER SERVING:
Calories 220; Protein 3g; Carbohydrate 39g; Fat 6g; Sodium 90mg.

CALIFORNIA FRUIT COBBLER

Cobblers are fruits baked with a crust. Slices of refrigerated crescent dough form the crust for this cobbler, which calls for fresh summer fruits. The fruit can be either peeled or unpeeled.

- 3/4 cup sugar
- 1/4 cup cornstarch
- 2 cups sliced nectarines, cut 1/2 inch thick
- 2 cups sliced pears, cut 1/2 inch thick
- 2 cups sliced plums, cut 1/2 inch thick
- 1 (8-oz.) can refrigerated crescent dinner rolls
- 2 tablespoons honey
- 1 tablespoon margarine or butter, softened

TOPPING
- 1/2 cup dairy sour cream
- 1 tablespoon brown sugar

Heat oven to 375°F. In large saucepan, combine sugar, cornstarch and fruit. Cook over medium heat until mixture is hot and bubbly, stirring occasionally. Pour into ungreased 12x8-inch (2-quart) baking dish.

Remove dough from can in rolled sections; DO NOT UNROLL. Cut each roll into 3 slices; cut each slice in half. Arrange around edge of baking dish, placing cut side toward edge of baking dish to form a scalloped appearance.

Bake at 375°F. for 20 to 25 minutes or until crescents are deep golden brown and mixture is bubbly. In small bowl, combine honey and margarine; brush over crescents. In small bowl, combine topping ingredients. Spoon over cobbler to serve.
Yield: 6 servings.

NUTRITION PER SERVING:
Calories 440; Protein 4g; Carbohydrate 75g; Fat 14g; Sodium 340mg.

APPLE BERRY COBBLER

Refrigerated biscuits make this recipe especially quick to prepare.

¼ **cup sugar**
4 **teaspoons cornstarch**
1 **(10-oz.) pkg. frozen whole berries, thawed, drained, reserving ½ cup liquid**
2 **medium thinly sliced peeled apples**
1 **egg, separated**
1 **tablespoon water**
1 **(10-oz.) can refrigerated flaky biscuits**
2 **to 4 tablespoons sugar**

Heat oven to 400°F. In medium saucepan, combine ¼ cup sugar and cornstarch. Stir in reserved liquid. Cook over medium heat until thickened, stirring constantly. Stir in berries and apples; cook 3 to 5 minutes or until apples are just tender, stirring occasionally. Pour into ungreased 12x8-inch (2-quart) baking dish.

Beat egg yolk with water. Separate dough into 10 biscuits. Dip tops of biscuits in beaten yolk mixture; arrange, dipped side up, on top of hot fruit mixture. Bake at 400°F. for 10 to 15 minutes or until biscuits are golden brown.

Meanwhile, beat egg white until foamy; gradually add 2 to 4 tablespoons sugar, beating until stiff peaks form. Spoon meringue on top of each baked biscuit. Return to oven and bake an additional 5 to 6 minutes or until meringue is light golden brown. Serve warm. Store in refrigerator.

Yield: 10 servings.

NUTRITION PER SERVING:
Calories 170; Protein 3g; Carbohydrate 30g; Fat 4g; Sodium 300mg.

RASPBERRY PEACH COBBLER

Biscuits, made tender and moist with sour cream, top a sensational combination of raspberries and peaches. Serve it with half-and-half for a rich taste treat.

BISCUITS
1 **cup all purpose flour**
½ **cup sugar**
1 **teaspoon baking powder**
¼ **teaspoon salt**
¾ **cup dairy sour cream**
2 **tablespoons margarine or butter, melted**
1 **egg**

FRUIT MIXTURE
¾ **cup sugar**
3 **tablespoons cornstarch**
1 **(10-oz.) pkg. frozen raspberries with syrup, thawed, drained, reserving liquid**
1 **(16-oz.) pkg. frozen sliced peaches without syrup, thawed, drained**
1 **tablespoon sugar**

Heat oven to 375°F. In medium bowl, combine flour, ½ cup sugar, baking powder and salt; mix well. Stir in remaining biscuit ingredients; set aside.

In medium saucepan, combine ¾ cup sugar, cornstarch and reserved raspberry liquid. Cook over medium heat until mixture boils; boil 1 minute, stirring constantly. Add raspberries and peaches; cook 1 minute. Pour into ungreased 2-quart casserole. Spoon biscuit mixture over hot fruit mixture, forming 9 biscuits around edge of casserole. Sprinkle biscuits with 1 tablespoon sugar.

Bake at 375°F. for 35 to 45 minutes or until biscuits are golden brown. Serve warm.

Yield: 9 servings.

HIGH ALTITUDE:
Above 3500 Feet: No change.

NUTRITION PER SERVING:
Calories 330; Protein 3g; Carbohydrate 63g; Fat 8g; Sodium 140mg.

OLD-FASHIONED BERRY COBBLER

Use a heart-shaped cookie cutter to cut out the dough to top this cobbler.

FRUIT MIXTURE
- 4 cups frozen raspberries, blackberries or loganberries (do not thaw)
- ½ cup seedless raspberry jam
- 2 tablespoons quick-cooking tapioca*
- 2 tablespoons sugar
- 2 tablespoons margarine or butter

TOPPING
- 1 cup all purpose flour
- 2 tablespoons sugar
- 2 teaspoons baking powder
- ¼ teaspoon salt
- ¼ cup margarine or butter
- 2 to 4 tablespoons milk
- 1 egg
- ½ teaspoon sugar

Heat oven to 425°F. Grease 10x6-inch (1½-quart) baking dish or 1½-quart casserole. In large bowl, combine berries, jam, tapioca and 2 tablespoons sugar; mix gently. Spread in greased dish. Dot with 2 tablespoons margarine. Bake at 425°F. for 15 to 20 minutes or until mixture begins to bubble; stir.

In large bowl, combine flour, 2 tablespoons sugar, baking powder and salt; mix well. With pastry blender or fork, cut in ¼ cup margarine until crumbly. In small bowl, beat 2 tablespoons milk and egg until blended. Stir into flour mixture until blended, adding additional milk if necessary to form stiff dough. On lightly floured surface, roll out dough to ½-inch thickness. With 2-inch cookie cutter, cut out hearts, circles or diamonds. Place on top of hot fruit mixture; sprinkle with ½ teaspoon sugar.

Bake at 425°F. for 10 to 20 minutes or until fruit bubbles around edges and biscuits are light golden brown. Serve warm with cream or ice cream, if desired.
Yield: 6 to 8 servings.

TIP:
* Cornstarch can be substituted for tapioca; the fruit mixture will not be as clear.

HIGH ALTITUDE:
Above 3500 Feet: No change.

NUTRITION PER SERVING:
Calories 280; Protein 4g; Carbohydrate 45g; Fat 10g; Sodium 260mg.

WINTER FRUIT DEEP-DISH PIE

Sprinkle the pastry with sugar before baking.

FILLING
- 1 (29-oz.) can sliced peaches, undrained
- 1 (16-oz.) can purple plums, drained, pitted and quartered
- ½ cup coarsely chopped nuts
- ½ cup dark or golden raisins
- ½ cup firmly packed brown sugar
- 2 tablespoons cornstarch
- ¼ teaspoon cinnamon
- ¼ teaspoon nutmeg

BISCUIT PASTRY
- 2 cups all purpose flour
- 1 tablespoon sugar
- 3 teaspoons baking powder
- 1 teaspoon salt
- ⅓ cup shortening
- 1 cup dairy sour cream
  Milk
  Sugar

Heat oven to 400°F. In 2½-quart shallow oval or round baking dish or casserole, combine all filling ingredients.

In medium bowl, combine flour, sugar, baking powder and salt. Using pastry blender or fork, cut in shortening until mixture resembles coarse crumbs. Stir in sour cream until blended. On floured surface, toss dough lightly to coat with flour. Knead 8 to 10 times. Roll lightly into oval slightly smaller than casserole, about ½ inch thick. Trim edges. Flute edge, if desired. Using biscuit cutter, cut 1 or 2-inch circle in center of pastry or cut a decorative design using small cookie cutters. Top fruit mixture with pastry. (Edge of pastry should not touch sides of casserole.) Brush pastry lightly with milk; sprinkle with sugar.

Bake at 400°F. for 35 to 45 minutes or until pastry is dark golden brown. Cool at least 20 to 30 minutes before serving. If desired, serve with cream or ice cream.
Yield: 8 servings.

HIGH ALTITUDE:
Above 3500 Feet: Bake at 400°F. for 30 to 40 minutes.

NUTRITION PER SERVING:
Calories 490; Protein 7g; Carbohydrate 72g; Fat 20g; Sodium 410mg.

PEAR PANDOWDY

The biscuit topping will bake best if it is placed over a hot filling.

FILLING
- 4 cups sliced peeled pears (about 4 pears)
- ¼ cup firmly packed brown sugar
- ¼ teaspoon cinnamon
- ¼ teaspoon nutmeg
- 3 tablespoons margarine or butter
- 1 tablespoon lemon juice

TOPPING
- 1 cup all purpose flour
- ¼ cup sugar
- 1 teaspoon baking powder
- ¼ teaspoon salt
- ½ cup margarine or butter
- ¼ cup water
- 1 teaspoon sugar
- 2 cups whipped cream or ice cream, if desired

Heat oven to 375°F. Grease 8-inch square (1½-quart) baking dish or 2-quart casserole. In medium saucepan, combine all filling ingredients. Cook over medium heat until mixture is hot, stirring occasionally.

In small bowl, combine flour, ¼ cup sugar, baking powder and salt; mix well. Using pastry blender or fork, cut in ½ cup margarine until mixture forms coarse crumbs. Add water, stirring just until dry ingredients are moistened. Pour hot filling into greased baking dish. Drop topping by rounded tablespoonfuls onto hot filling. Sprinkle with 1 teaspoon sugar. Bake at 375°F. for 30 to 40 minutes or until golden brown. Serve warm with whipped cream.
Yield: 9 servings.

HIGH ALTITUDE:
Above 3500 Feet: No change.

NUTRITION PER SERVING:
Calories 360; Protein 2g; Carbohydrate 35g; Fat 24g; Sodium 270mg.

APPLE BROWN BETTY

Apple Brown Betty is the most traditional of betties, dating back to colonial America. A betty is a baked pudding made of layers of sugared, spiced fruit and buttered bread crumbs.

- 5 cups (5 medium) sliced peeled apples
- ½ cup firmly packed brown sugar
- 1 teaspoon grated lemon peel
- ¼ teaspoon nutmeg
- 1 tablespoon lemon juice
- 1 cup dry bread crumbs
- ½ cup margarine or butter, melted
  Whipping cream

Heat oven to 375°F. Grease 8-inch square (1½-quart) baking dish. In large bowl, combine apples, brown sugar, lemon peel, nutmeg and lemon juice; mix well. In medium bowl, combine bread crumbs and margarine; sprinkle ½ cup bread crumb mixture in greased baking dish. Spoon apple mixture over crumb mixture; top with remaining bread crumb mixture.

Cover; bake at 375°F. for 45 to 50 minutes or until apples are almost tender. Uncover; bake an additional 15 to 20 minutes or until top is crisp and golden brown. Serve warm with cream.
Yield: 8 (½-cup) servings.

NUTRITION PER SERVING:
Calories 250; Protein 2g; Carbohydrate 33g; Fat 12g; Sodium 230mg.

COOK'S NOTE

PANDOWDY

Pandowdies were first made in the 1600s. Similar to a cobbler, a pandowdy is a fruit mixture covered with a layer of soft biscuit dough. It was customary for the server to "dowdy the pan," or cut into the dessert with a spoon and stir the top and bottom together a bit before serving.

STRAWBERRY SHORTCAKE

Enjoy this classic dessert of summer — tender shortcake, warm from the oven, piled high with fresh strawberries and whipped cream.

SHORTCAKE
- 2 **cups all purpose flour**
- ½ **cup sugar**
- 3 **teaspoons baking powder**
- ½ **teaspoon salt**
- ½ **cup margarine or butter**
- ¾ **cup milk**
- 2 **eggs, slightly beaten**
- 4 **cups sliced strawberries**
- ½ **cup sugar**

TOPPING
- 1 **cup whipping cream**
- 2 **tablespoons powdered sugar**
- ½ **teaspoon vanilla**

Heat oven to 375°F. Grease and flour 8 or 9-inch round cake pan. In large bowl, combine flour, sugar, powder and salt. Using pastry blender or fork, cut in margarine until mixture resembles coarse crumbs. Add milk and eggs, stirring just until dry ingredients are moistened. Spoon into greased and floured pan.

Bake at 375°F. for 25 to 30 minutes or until tooth-pick inserted in center comes out clean. Cool 10 minutes; invert onto serving platter. Split layer in half, if desired.

Meanwhile, in medium bowl combine strawberries and sugar; mix well. Refrigerate 30 minutes or until serving time.

Just before serving, prepare topping. In small bowl, beat whipping cream until soft peaks form. Add powdered sugar and vanilla; beat until stiff peaks form. Serve with shortcake and sweetened straw-berries. Store in refrigerator.
Yield: 8 servings.

HIGH ALTITUDE:
Above 3500 Feet: Increase flour to 2 cups plus 2 tablespoons; decrease baking powder to 2½ teaspoons. Bake at 375°F. for 30 to 35 minutes.

NUTRITION PER SERVING:
Calories 490; Protein 7g; Carbohydrate 62g; Fat 25g; Sodium 420mg.

STRAWBERRY SHORTCAKE MAKE-OVER

We've cut 200 calories and 18 grams of fat!

SHORTCAKE
- 1⅔ **cups all purpose flour**
- ⅓ **cup sugar**
- 3 **teaspoons baking powder**
- ½ **teaspoon salt**
- ½ **cup evaporated skim milk**
- ¼ **cup margarine, melted**
- 2 **teaspoons vanilla**
- 1 **egg, slightly beaten, or ¼ cup frozen cholesterol-free egg product, thawed**
- 4 **cups sliced strawberries**
- ¼ **cup sugar**

TOPPING
- ⅔ **cup evaporated skim milk**
- 3 **tablespoons powdered sugar**
- 1 **teaspoon vanilla**

Heat oven to 350°F. Grease and flour 8 or 9-inch round cake pan. In large bowl, combine flour, sugar, baking powder and salt. Add ½ cup evapo-rated skim milk, margarine, 2 teaspoons vanilla and egg, stirring just until dry ingredients are moistened. Spoon into greased and floured pan.

Bake at 350°F. for 17 to 24 minutes or until tooth-pick inserted in center comes out clean. Cool 10 minutes; invert onto serving platter. Split layer in half, if desired.

Meanwhile, in medium bowl combine strawberries and sugar; mix well. Refrigerate 30 minutes or until serving time.

To prepare topping, place small bowl and beaters in refrigerator to chill. Pour ⅔ cup evaporated skim milk into freezer container. Freeze until slushy, about 50 minutes.

Just before serving, spoon into small chilled bowl. Beat with chilled beaters until fluffy. Add powdered sugar and 1 teaspoon vanilla; beat until soft peaks form, scraping bowl occasionally. Serve immediate-ly with shortcake and sweetened strawberries.* Store in refrigerator.
Yield: 8 servings.

Strawberry Shortcake Make-Over

TIP:
* Topping can be held in freezer for up to 20 minutes or in refrigerator for 10 minutes.

HIGH ALTITUDE:
Above 3500 Feet: Increase flour to 1¾ cups; decrease baking powder to 2 teaspoons. Bake at 375°F. for 18 to 25 minutes.

NUTRITION PER SERVING:
Calories 290; Protein 7g; Carbohydrate 50g; Fat 7g; Sodium 360mg.

COOK'S NOTE

LEFTOVER WHIPPED CREAM

Drop dollops of any leftover whipped cream onto a sheet of foil and freeze them uncovered until firm. Then, transfer them to an airtight freezer container and freeze for later use to top desserts. The dollops will thaw on the servings in a matter of minutes.

CHOCOLATE STRAWBERRY SHORTCAKE

Old-fashioned strawberry shortcake has been updated to become a chocolate lover's delight.

SHORTCAKE
- 2 cups all purpose flour
- ½ cup sugar
- ⅓ cup unsweetened cocoa
- 3 teaspoons baking powder
- ¼ teaspoon salt
- ½ cup margarine or butter
- 1 cup milk
- 2 tablespoons sugar

FILLING
- 4 to 5 cups strawberries
- ¼ cup sugar
- 1 cup whipping cream, whipped, sweetened p. 23
- Fudge sauce, if desired

Heat oven to 400°F. Grease two 9 or 8-inch round cake pans. In large bowl, combine flour, ½ cup sugar, cocoa, baking powder and salt. Using pastry blender or fork, cut in margarine until mixture resembles coarse crumbs. Stir in milk just until moistened. Spread in greased pans. Sprinkle 2 tablespoons sugar over dough.

Bake at 400°F. for 15 to 20 minutes or until cake begins to pull away from sides of pans. Cool 15 minutes; remove from pans. Cool completely.

Reserve 5 whole strawberries for garnish. Halve remaining strawberries lengthwise. In large bowl, combine halved strawberries and ¼ cup sugar.

Place 1 shortcake, bottom side up, on serving plate. Top with half of strawberries and half of whipped cream. Place remaining shortcake on top, right side up. Top with remaining strawberries and whipped cream. Garnish with remaining whole strawberries. Drizzle with fudge sauce. Store in refrigerator.
Yield: 12 servings.

HIGH ALTITUDE:
Above 3500 Feet: No change.

NUTRITION PER SERVING:
Calories 370; Protein 5g; Carbohydrate 49g; Fat 19g; Sodium 250mg.

APRICOT AND CREAM SHORTCAKE

Shortcakes are usually as seasonal as the fruits that dress them.

- 1 (18.5-oz.) pkg. pudding-included yellow cake mix
- 1 (3-oz.) pkg. apricot flavor gelatin
- ⅓ cup water
- 1 (8-oz.) container vanilla or apricot yogurt
- 3 eggs
- 1 cup water
- 1 (4-oz.) container (1¾ cups) frozen whipped topping, thawed
- Apricot slices

Heat oven to 350°F. Grease 13x9-inch pan. In large bowl, combine cake mix, 2 tablespoons of the gelatin, ⅓ cup water, yogurt and eggs at low speed until moistened. Beat 2 minutes at high speed. Pour into greased pan.

Bake at 350°F. for 30 to 40 minutes or until toothpick inserted in center comes out clean. Cool cake in pan on cooling rack 15 minutes. Meanwhile, heat 1 cup water in small saucepan. Add remaining gelatin; stir to dissolve. Using long-tined fork, prick cake at ½-inch intervals. Pour gelatin mixture evenly over cake; refrigerate. Serve with whipped topping and apricot slices. Store in refrigerator.
Yield: 12 servings.

HIGH ALTITUDE:
Above 3500 Feet: Add 2 tablespoons flour to dry cake mix; increase water in cake to ½ cup. Bake at 375°F. for 25 to 30 minutes.

NUTRITION PER SERVING:
Calories 280; Protein 5g; Carbohydrate 47g; Fat 9g; Sodium 320mg.

VARIATION:

PEACHES AND CREAM SHORTCAKE: Substitute peach flavor gelatin, peach yogurt and peach slices for apricot.

PLANTATION PEACH SHORTCAKE

—〜—

This version of shortcake was a Pillsbury BAKE-OFF® Contest finalist in l952. The biscuit-like shortcake has brown sugar and nuts baked right in the layers. It's topped off with luscious peaches and whipped cream.

1¾ **cups all purpose flour**
¼ **cup firmly packed brown sugar**
3 **teaspoons baking powder**
½ **teaspoon salt**
½ **cup margarine or butter**
½ **cup chopped pecans**
⅔ **cup half-and-half or milk**
1 **egg, slightly beaten**
3 **medium peaches, peeled, sliced**
1 **cup whipping cream, whipped, sweetened p. 23**

Heat oven to 450°F. Generously grease two 8-inch round cake pans.* In large bowl, combine flour, brown sugar, baking powder and salt. Using pastry blender or fork, cut in margarine until mixture resembles coarse crumbs. Add pecans, half-and-half and egg; stir just until soft dough forms. Spread dough evenly in greased pans.

Bake at 450°F. for 10 to 12 minutes or until light golden brown. Remove from pans. Cool. To serve, spoon peaches and whipped cream between layers and on top. Store in refrigerator.

Yield: 8 servings.

TIP:

* For individual shortcakes, turn out dough onto well floured surface; knead gently 5 or 6 times. Roll dough to ½-inch thickness. Cut with floured 3-inch cutter. Place on ungreased cookie sheet. Bake at 450°F. for 8 to 10 minutes. To serve, split short-cakes; spoon peaches and whipped cream between layers and on top.

HIGH ALTITUDE:
Above 3500 Feet: No change.

NUTRITION PER SERVING:
Calories 470; Protein 6g; Carbohydrate 41g; Fat 31g; Sodium 410mg.

NECTARINE-BERRY SHORTCAKE

—〜—

Refrigerated biscuits are baked in a circle in this easy shortcake. Try other fresh fruits, too.

¼ **cup sugar**
1 **teaspoon cinnamon**
1 **(10-oz.) can refrigerated flaky biscuits**
2 **tablespoons margarine or butter, melted**
3 **to 4 nectarines or peaches, sliced**
1 **cup blueberries**
½ **cup sugar**
1 **(8-oz.) container (3½ cups) frozen whipped topping, thawed**

Heat oven to 375°F. Lightly grease large cookie sheet. In small bowl, combine ¼ cup sugar and cinnamon. Separate dough into 10 biscuits; separate each biscuit into 2 layers. Dip 1 side of each biscuit piece in margarine, then in sugar-cinnamon mixture. On greased cookie sheet, arrange 9 biscuit pieces, sugared side up, in a 6-inch diameter ring, overlapping edges. Place 1 biscuit piece in center of ring. Repeat with remaining biscuit pieces to form second circle.

Bake at 375°F. for 11 to 14 minutes or until biscuits are golden brown. Cool 1 minute; remove from cookie sheet.

While biscuits are baking, combine nectarines, blueberries and ½ cup sugar. To assemble short-cake, place 1 biscuit circle on serving plate; spoon half of nectarine-blueberry mixture over biscuit layer. Top with half of the whipped topping. Repeat layers with remaining biscuit circle, fruit and whipped topping. Store in refrigerator.

Yield: 8 to 10 servings.

NUTRITION PER SERVING:
Calories 270; Protein 2g; Carbohydrate 41g; Fat 12g; Sodium 330mg.

CHOCOLATE FILIGREES

Chocolate Filigree Hearts: Trace heart pattern on white paper. Cut twelve 3x3-inch squares of waxed paper. In small saucepan over low heat, melt ¼ cup semi-sweet chocolate chips or 2 oz. semi-sweet chocolate cut into small pieces with 1½ teaspoons shortening, stirring until

melted. Pour melted chocolate into a decorating bag fitted with a small writing tip or into a small plastic freezer bag with small tip cut from 1 corner. Place a waxed paper square over the heart pattern. Pipe chocolate over the heart design, outlining heart. Carefully slip out pattern piece. Repeat, making 12 hearts. Refrigerate 5 to 10 minutes or until set.

Carefully remove from waxed paper. (For Two-Tone Chocolate Filigree Hearts continue as directed below.) Arrange on dessert as desired.

Two-Tone Chocolate Filigree Hearts: To make Two-tone Chocolate Filigree Hearts, prepare the Chocolate Filigree Hearts as

directed above. Melt vanilla-flavored candy coating or flavored chips such as butterscotch or peanut butter. Pour contrasting color/flavor of melted chips into another decorating bag. Pipe desired filigree design inside each Chocolate Filigree Heart. Refrigerate 5 to 10 minutes or until set. Carefully remove from waxed paper and arrange on dessert.

Filigree Shamrocks: Trace shamrock pattern on white paper. Melt 1 oz. white baking bar or almond bark. Stir in a small amount of

green paste food color; cool slightly. Pour mixture into a decorating bag fitted with a small writing tip, or into a small plastic freezer bag with small tip cut from 1 corner.

Cut twelve 3x3-inch squares of waxed paper. Place a square over the shamrock pattern. Pipe mixture over the shamrock outlining the shamrock. Carefully slip out pattern piece. Repeat, making 12 shamrocks. Refrigerate 5 to 10 minutes or until set. Carefully remove from waxed paper. Arrange on dessert as desired.

CHOCOLATE CURLS

Small Chocolate Curls: Place 1 to 2 oz. of semi-sweet chocolate on a piece of foil. Let stand in warm place (80 to 85°F.) for 5 to 10 minutes or until slightly softened. With a vegetable peeler and using long strokes, shave chocolate from the bottom of the square. Transfer curls to dessert using a toothpick. Milk chocolate curls can be made using a thick milk chocolate bar and this method.

Large Chocolate Curls: Melt 4 oz. semi-sweet chocolate. With spatula, spread melted chocolate in thin layer on 2 inverted cookie sheets. Refrigerate until just firm but not brittle, about 10 minutes. Using metal spatula or pancake turner, scrape chocolate from pan, making curls. The width of the spatula will determine the width of the curls. Transfer curls to dessert using a toothpick.

CHOCOLATE CUTOUTS

Melt semi-sweet or sweet baking chocolate. Pour onto waxed paper-lined cookie sheet. Spread evenly to ⅛ to ¼ inch thickness. Refrigerate until slightly hardened, about 10 minutes. Press canape or small cookie cutters firmly into chocolate. Lift gently from waxed paper with spatula. Scraps of chocolate can be remelted or chopped for an easy dessert topping.

CHOCOLATE LEAVES

Melt unsweetened, semi-sweet or sweet baking chocolate, or vanilla-flavored candy coating. Brush melted chocolate evenly on underside of washed and dried nontoxic leaves (ivy, mint, lemon or rose leaves). Wipe off any chocolate that may have dripped to top side of leaf. Refrigerate leaves about 10 minutes or until chocolate is set. Apply second layer of chocolate over first layer. Refrigerate until chocolate is set. Carefully peel leaf away from chocolate. Store in refrigerator or freezer until ready to use.

CHOCOLATE-DIPPED FRUIT

Choose perfect fruits; wash and pat dry. Dip ½ to ⅔ of each fruit in melted white baking bar or dark chocolate. (One-fourth cup semi-sweet chocolate chips melted with 1 teaspoon oil will coat enough fruit to garnish most desserts.) Place on waxed paper-lined trays; refrigerate until set. Store in refrigerator.

GRATED CHOCOLATE

Let bar of chocolate (any type) stand in warm place (80 to 85°F.) until slightly softened, about 10 minutes. Using hand grater, rub bar of chocolate back and forth across grater. Clean surface frequently to prevent clogging. Sprinkle grated chocolate on dessert.

CITRUS STRIPS (ZEST)

With a lemon zester, remove strips of peel from an orange, lemon or lime. Sprinkle the strips (or zest) over the dessert. If a lemon zester is not available, remove long strips of peel with a vegetable peeler, making sure to remove only the colored part. Cut these pieces into thin julienne strips.

CITRUS TWISTS

With a sharp knife, cut an orange, lemon or lime into ⅛-inch-thick slices. On each slice, make 1 cut from the outside edge to the center. Twist the ends in opposite directions to form a twist. Or, use half of a slice and twist.

STRAWBERRY FANS

To make strawberry fans, select firm berries with stems or caps and symmetrical tips. Starting at the tip and cutting almost to the stem, cut each berry into thin slices. Gently spread the slices to form open fans.

PEANUT CHOCOLATE PARFAIT DESSERT

This peanut butter and chocolate lovers' dessert made a 1986 Pillsbury BAKE-OFF® Contest finalist $15,000 richer.

CRUST
- 1 (18.25-oz.) pkg. pudding-included devil's food cake mix
- ½ cup margarine or butter, melted
- ¼ cup milk
- 1 egg
- ¾ cup peanuts

FILLING
- ¾ cup peanut butter
- 1½ cups powdered sugar
- 1 (8-oz.) pkg. cream cheese, softened
- 2½ cups milk
- 1 (8-oz.) container (3½ cups) frozen whipped topping, thawed
- 1 (5.25-oz.) pkg. instant vanilla pudding and pie filling mix

TOPPING
- ½ cup peanuts
- 1 (1.45-oz.) bar milk chocolate, chilled, grated

Heat oven to 350°F. Grease and flour bottom only of 13x9-inch pan. In large bowl, combine all crust ingredients at medium speed until well blended. Spread evenly in greased and floured pan. Bake at 350°F. for 20 to 25 minutes. DO NOT OVERBAKE. Cool.

In small bowl, combine peanut butter and powdered sugar at low speed until crumbly; set aside. In large bowl, beat cream cheese until smooth. Add milk, whipped topping and pudding mix; beat at low speed 2 minutes until well blended.

Pour half of cream cheese mixture over cooled, baked crust. Sprinkle with half of peanut butter mixture. Repeat with remaining cream cheese and peanut butter mixtures. Sprinkle with ½ cup peanuts; gently press into filling. Sprinkle with grated chocolate. Cover; refrigerate or freeze until serving time. Store in refrigerator or freezer.
Yield: 16 servings.

HIGH ALTITUDE:
Above 3500 Feet: No change.

NUTRITION PER SERVING:
Calories 530; Protein 10g; Carbohydrate 55g; Fat 31g; Sodium 650mg.

PUMPKIN PIE SQUARES

Butterscotch pudding flavors the crust in these hard-to-resist dessert squares.

CRUST
- ¾ cup all purpose flour
- ¾ cup rolled oats
- ½ to 1 cup chopped nuts
- ½ cup margarine or butter, softened
- 1 (3.63-oz.) pkg. butterscotch pudding and pie filling mix (not instant)

FILLING
- 1 cup coconut, if desired
- 1½ teaspoons pumpkin pie spice
- 1 (16-oz.) can (2 cups) pumpkin
- 1 (12-oz.) can sweetened condensed milk (not evaporated)
- 2 eggs

Heat oven to 350°F. In large bowl, combine all crust ingredients; mix well. Press in bottom of ungreased 13x9-inch pan. In same bowl, combine filling ingredients; blend well. Pour over crust.

Bake at 350°F. for 35 to 45 minutes or until knife inserted in center comes out clean. Cool. Cut into squares. Serve topped with whipped cream or ice cream, if desired. Store in refrigerator.

Yield: 12 to 15 squares.

NUTRITION PER SERVING:
Calories 300; Protein 6g; Carbohydrate 34g; Fat 16g; Sodium 130mg.

LEMON PIE SQUARES

A soft meringue covers this lemon lovers' delight.

CRUST
- 1 (18.25-oz.) pkg. pudding-included lemon cake mix
- ¼ cup margarine or butter, softened
- 3 egg yolks
- 1 cup coconut

MERINGUE
- 3 egg whites
- ½ cup sugar

FILLING
- 1 (22-oz.) can lemon pie filling

Heat oven to 350°F. In large bowl, combine all crust ingredients at low speed until crumbly. Press in bottom of ungreased 13x9-inch pan. Bake at 350°F. for 10 minutes.

Meanwhile, in small bowl beat egg whites at medium speed until soft peaks form. Gradually add sugar 1 tablespoon at a time, beating at high speed until stiff glossy peaks form and sugar is dissolved. Spread lemon filling over partially baked crust; spread meringue over lemon filling.

Bake an additional 15 to 25 minutes or until meringue is light golden brown. Cool completely; cut into squares. Garnish with **Citrus Twists** p. 211 or as desired.

Yield: 12 servings.

HIGH ALTITUDE:
Above 3500 Feet: No change.

NUTRITION PER SERVING:
Calories 370; Protein 3g; Carbohydrate 66g; Fat 11g; Sodium 390mg.

Lemon Pie Squares

APRICOT DATE DESSERT

Yogurt adds a nice tang to this quick and easy dessert.

CRUST
- 1 (18.5-oz.) pkg. pudding-included yellow cake mix
- ¼ cup margarine or butter, softened
- 2 egg yolks
- 1 (8-oz.) container apricot, orange or plain yogurt

FILLING
- 1 cup chopped dates
- ½ cup chopped nuts
- ½ cup flaked coconut

TOPPING
- 2 egg whites
- 2 tablespoons sugar
- ½ cup apricot preserves
- ½ cup chopped nuts
- ½ cup flaked coconut

Heat oven to 350°F. Grease 13x9-inch pan. In large bowl, combine cake mix, margarine, egg yolks and ¼ cup of the yogurt at low speed until crumbly. Press in bottom of greased pan. Bake at 350°F. for 15 to 20 minutes or until light golden brown.

Meanwhile, in same bowl combine remaining yogurt and all filling ingredients until well blended. Spoon evenly over baked crust. In small bowl, beat egg whites until foamy. Gradually add sugar; beat until stiff peaks form. Fold in apricot preserves; spread over filling. Sprinkle with ½ cup nuts and ½ cup coconut. Bake an additional 15 to 20 minutes or until light golden brown. Cool completely.

Yield: 12 to 15 servings.

HIGH ALTITUDE:
Above 3500 Feet: No change.

NUTRITION PER SERVING:
Calories 330; Protein 4g; Carbohydrate 53g; Fat 13g; Sodium 260mg.

APPLE CUSTARD DESSERT

Look for firm, bright-colored apples for baking.

CRUST
- 2 cups all purpose flour
- 2 tablespoons sugar
- ⅛ teaspoon salt
- ¾ cup margarine or butter

FILLING
- 6 cups thinly sliced peeled apples
- 1 cup sugar
- ½ teaspoon cinnamon
- 2 tablespoons sugar
- 2 tablespoons cornstarch
- 3 egg yolks
- 2 cups half-and-half

MERINGUE
- 3 egg whites
- ¼ teaspoon cream of tartar
- ½ cup sugar

Heat oven to 350°F. In large bowl, combine flour, 2 tablespoons sugar and salt. Using pastry blender or fork, cut in margarine until crumbly. Press in bottom of ungreased 13x9-inch pan. Bake at 350°F. for 15 minutes. In large bowl, combine apples, 1 cup sugar and cinnamon; spread over partially baked crust. Bake an additional 50 to 60 minutes or until apples are tender. Cool.

Meanwhile, in medium saucepan combine 2 tablespoons sugar and cornstarch. Stir in egg yolks and half-and-half; blend well. Cook over medium heat until mixture boils and thickens, stirring constantly. Remove from heat. Place plastic wrap or waxed paper on hot filling to prevent film from forming; cool slightly while preparing meringue.

In small bowl, beat egg whites and cream of tartar until soft peaks form, about 1 minute. Add ½ cup sugar, 1 tablespoon at a time, beating at high speed until stiff glossy peaks form. Pour half-and-half mixture over baked apples, spreading evenly. Spoon meringue over filling, spreading to edges of pan. Bake at 350°F. for 20 to 25 minutes or until light golden brown. Cool completely. Store in refrigerator.

Yield: 12 servings.

NUTRITION PER SERVING:
Calories 400; Protein 5g; Carbohydrate 56g; Fat 18g; Sodium 170mg.

Festive Apple Cheese Squares

A light dusting of powdered sugar tops these pretty dessert squares.

1 (8-oz.) pkg. cream cheese, softened
1¾ cups sugar
2 teaspoons vanilla
5 eggs
1 cup margarine or butter, softened
3 cups all purpose flour
1½ teaspoons baking powder
½ teaspoon salt
1 (21-oz.) can apple fruit pie filling
12 maraschino cherries, halved, drained
Powdered sugar

In small bowl, beat cream cheese and ¼ cup of the sugar until smooth and creamy. Add 1 teaspoon of the vanilla and 1 egg; blend well. Set aside.

Heat oven to 350°F. Grease 15x10x1-inch baking pan. In large bowl, beat margarine and remaining 1½ cups sugar until light and fluffy. Add remaining 1 teaspoon vanilla and 4 eggs; blend well. Stir in flour, baking powder and salt; mix well. Spread mixture in greased pan. Spread apple filling to within 1 inch of edge. Spoon teaspoonfuls of cream cheese mixture onto apple filling, in 4 rows of 6 dollops, dividing dessert into 24 servings. DO NOT SPREAD. Place cherry half on top of each dollop of cream cheese mixture.

Bake at 350°F. for 35 to 45 minutes or until golden brown. Cool completely; sprinkle with powdered sugar.
Yield: 24 servings.

HIGH ALTITUDE:
Above 3500 Feet: Decrease 1½ cups sugar to 1¼ cups. Bake as directed above.

NUTRITION PER SERVING:
Calories 270; Protein 4g; Carbohydrate 35g; Fat 13g; Sodium 200mg.

Sour Cream Apple Squares

Withstanding the test of time, this proven favorite comes to us from the 26th Pillsbury BAKE-OFF® Contest held in 1975.

2 cups all purpose flour
2 cups firmly packed brown sugar
½ cup margarine or butter, softened
1 cup chopped nuts
1 to 2 teaspoons cinnamon
1 teaspoon baking soda
½ teaspoon salt
1 cup dairy sour cream
1 teaspoon vanilla
1 egg
2 cups finely chopped peeled apples

Heat oven to 350°F. In large bowl, combine flour, brown sugar and margarine; beat at low speed until crumbly. Stir in nuts. Press 2¾ cups of crumb mixture in bottom of ungreased 13x9-inch pan. To remaining mixture, add cinnamon, baking soda, salt, sour cream, vanilla and egg; mix well. Stir in apples. Spoon evenly over base.

Bake at 350°F. for 30 to 40 minutes or until toothpick inserted in center comes out clean. Cut into squares. Serve with whipped cream or ice cream, if desired.
Yield: 12 servings.

HIGH ALTITUDE:
Above 3500 Feet: Bake at 375°F. for 25 to 35 minutes.

NUTRITION PER SERVING:
Calories 410; Protein 5g; Carbohydrate 57g; Fat 19g; Sodium 300mg.

RASPBERRY PRETZEL DELIGHT

This is a perfect dessert to make for a party.

CRUST
1½ **cups crushed pretzels**
¼ **cup sugar**
½ **cup margarine or butter, melted**

FILLING
1 **(12-oz.) can sweetened condensed milk (not evaporated)**
½ **cup water**
1 **(3.4-oz.) pkg. instant vanilla pudding and pie filling mix**
1 **(4-oz.) container (1¾ cups) frozen whipped topping, thawed**

TOPPING
1 **(21-oz.) can raspberry fruit pie filling**

Heat oven to 350°F. In large bowl, combine all crust ingredients; mix well. Press in bottom of ungreased 13x9-inch pan. Bake at 350°F. for 8 minutes; cool.

In same large bowl, combine condensed milk and water; blend well. Add pudding mix; beat 2 minutes. Refrigerate 5 minutes. Fold in whipped topping. Spread on cooled, baked crust. Refrigerate until filling is firm, about 1 hour.

Spoon topping over filling. Cover; refrigerate until serving time. Garnish with frozen whipped topping, fresh raspberries and mint leaves, if desired. Store in refrigerator.
Yield: 16 servings.

NUTRITION PER SERVING:
Calories 250; Protein 3g; Carbohydrate 38g; Fat 10g; Sodium 290mg.

VARIATIONS:

BLUEBERRY PRETZEL DELIGHT: Substitute 21-oz. can blueberry fruit pie filling for raspberry fruit pie filling.

CHERRY PRETZEL DELIGHT: Substitute 21-oz. can cherry fruit pie filling for raspberry fruit pie filling.

REFRIGERATOR PISTACHIO DESSERT

This attractive dessert can be made a day ahead of time.

CRUST
1¼ **cups all purpose flour**
½ **cup margarine or butter, softened**
½ **cup finely chopped pistachios**

FILLING
1 **(8-oz.) pkg. cream cheese, softened**
1 **cup powdered sugar**
1 **(8-oz.) container (3½ cups) frozen whipped topping, thawed**
2 **(3.75-oz.) pkg. instant pistachio pudding and pie filling mix**
3 **cups milk**

Heat oven to 350°F. Grease 13x9-inch pan. In small bowl, combine flour and margarine at low speed until crumbly. Stir in pistachios; press in bottom of greased pan. Bake at 350°F. for 18 to 22 minutes or until light golden brown; cool.

In small bowl, combine cream cheese and powdered sugar until smooth and creamy. Fold in half of the whipped topping; spread over cooled, baked crust. In large bowl, beat pudding mix and milk at medium speed until thickened, about 5 minutes. Pour mixture carefully over cheese layer. Spread with remaining whipped topping. Refrigerate several hours or overnight.
Yield: 12 servings.

TIP:
Recipe can be halved; use 9-inch square pan.

NUTRITION PER SERVING:
Calories 420; Protein 6g; Carbohydrate 45g; Fat 25g; Sodium 240mg.

Raspberry Pretzel Delight

STRAWBERRIES AND CREAM SQUARES

A moist and chewy macaroon-like base is topped with a fluffy whipped cream and strawberry mixture.

BASE
- 1 cup walnuts
- 16 saltine crackers
- 3 egg whites
- ¼ teaspoon cream of tartar
- 1 cup sugar
- ½ teaspoon baking powder
- ½ teaspoon almond extract

TOPPING
- 1 cup whipping cream
- 2 tablespoons powdered sugar
- ½ teaspoon almond extract
- 2 cups sliced strawberries

GARNISH
- **Whole strawberries, if desired**

Heat oven to 300°F. Grease 8-inch square pan. In food processor bowl with metal blade or blender container, combine walnuts and crackers; process until mixture resembles coarse crumbs. In large bowl, beat egg whites and cream of tartar until foamy. Gradually add sugar, baking powder and ½ teaspoon almond extract, beating continuously at high speed until sugar is dissolved and stiff peaks form. Fold in crumb mixture. Spoon into greased pan, spreading evenly. Bake at 300°F. for 30 minutes or until set. Cool completely.

In small bowl, beat whipping cream until soft peaks form. Add powdered sugar and ½ teaspoon almond extract; beat until stiff peaks form. Fold in 2 cups strawberries. Spoon over cooled crust. Refrigerate until serving time. Garnish with whole strawberries.
Yield: 9 servings.

HIGH ALTITUDE:
Above 3500 Feet: Increase saltine crackers to 20. Bake as directed above.

NUTRITION PER SERVING:
Calories 330; Protein 5g; Carbohydrate 36g; Fat 19g; Sodium 100mg.

ALMOND FRUIT PIZZA SQUARES

Celebrate summer with this colorful and delicious dessert, made easily with refrigerated dough.

- 2 (8-oz.) cans refrigerated crescent dinner rolls
- 1 tablespoon sugar
- 1 (8-oz.) pkg. cream cheese, softened
- 1 (3½-oz.) tube almond paste
- ½ teaspoon almond extract
- 2 tablespoons sugar
- 2 cups strawberries, halved
- 1 cup raspberries
- 1 cup seedless green grapes, halved
- 1 (11-oz.) can mandarin orange segments, drained
- 2 kiwifruit, peeled, sliced, quartered
- ½ cup apricot preserves
- ¼ cup slivered almonds, toasted, p. 23

Heat oven to 375°F. Separate dough into 4 long rectangles. Place rectangles crosswise in ungreased 15x10x1-inch baking pan; press over bottom and 1 inch up sides to form crust. Firmly press perforations to seal. Sprinkle with 1 tablespoon sugar. Bake at 375°F. for 14 to 19 minutes or until golden brown. Cool completely.

In food processor bowl with metal blade or blender container, combine cream cheese, almond paste, almond extract and 2 tablespoons sugar; process until smooth. Spread evenly over cooled crust; top with strawberries, raspberries, grapes, orange segments and kiwifruit. Heat preserves in small saucepan until melted; brush over fruit. Sprinkle with almonds. Cover; store in refrigerator.
Yield: 15 servings.

TIP:
Other fruits can be substituted. If using fruits such as bananas, apples, pears or peaches, toss with orange or lemon juice to prevent discoloration and serve within 4 hours.

NUTRITION PER SERVING:
Calories 270; Protein 5g; Carbohydrate 33g; Fat 14g; Sodium 300mg.

Streusel Pecan Pie Squares

Your turn to host the family get-together? Serve up these rich dessert squares. They're an easy version of southern pecan pie.

CRUST
- 3 cups all purpose flour
- ¾ cup firmly packed brown sugar
- 1½ cups margarine or butter, softened

FILLING
- ¾ cup firmly packed brown sugar
- 1½ cups corn syrup or maple-flavored syrup
- 1 cup milk
- ⅓ cup margarine or butter, melted
- 1 teaspoon vanilla
- 4 eggs
- 1½ cups chopped pecans

Heat oven to 400°F. In large bowl, combine all crust ingredients at low speed until crumbly. Reserve 2 cups crumb mixture for filling and topping. Press remaining crumb mixture in bottom and ¾ inch up sides of ungreased 15x10x1-inch baking pan. Bake at 400°F. for 10 minutes.

In large bowl, combine ¼ cup reserved crumb mixture and all filling ingredients except pecans; mix well. Stir in pecans. Pour over partially baked crust. Bake an additional 10 minutes.

Reduce oven temperature to 350°F. Sprinkle remaining 1¾ cups reserved crumb mixture over filling. Bake at 350°F. for 20 to 25 minutes or until filling is set and crumb topping is golden brown. Serve with whipped cream or ice cream, if desired.
Yield: 15 servings.

NUTRITION PER SERVING:
Calories 570; Protein 6g; Carbohydrate 69g; Fat 32g; Sodium 320mg.

Streusel Rhubarb Dessert Squares

Here's a wonderful fruit dessert. Serve it warm, topped with whipped cream.

CRUST
- 1 cup all purpose flour
- ⅓ cup powdered sugar
- ⅓ cup margarine or butter

FILLING
- 1¼ cups sugar
- ¼ cup all purpose flour
- ½ teaspoon salt
- 2 eggs, slightly beaten
- 3 cups sliced fresh or frozen rhubarb (do not thaw)

TOPPING
- ¾ cup all purpose flour
- ½ cup sugar
- ¼ teaspoon cinnamon
- ⅓ cup margarine or butter

Heat oven to 350°F. In medium bowl, combine 1 cup flour and powdered sugar. Using pastry blender or fork, cut in ⅓ cup margarine until crumbly. Press in bottom of ungreased 9-inch square pan. Bake at 350°F. for 15 minutes.

In medium bowl, combine all filling ingredients; mix well. Pour over partially baked crust. In medium bowl, combine all topping ingredients except ⅓ cup margarine. Using pastry blender or fork, cut in ⅓ cup margarine until crumbly. Sprinkle over filling. Bake an additional 45 to 55 minutes or until topping is light golden brown and rhubarb is tender.
Yield: 6 to 8 servings.

NUTRITION PER SERVING:
Calories 470; Protein 5g; Carbohydrate 74g; Fat 17g; Sodium 330mg.

CHEESECAKE

Top with fresh fruit or chocolate sauce.

CRUST
- 2 cups graham cracker crumbs (about 32 squares)
- ½ cup margarine or butter, melted

FILLING
- 3 eggs
- 2 (8-oz.) pkg. cream cheese, softened
- 1 cup sugar
- ¼ teaspoon salt
- 2 teaspoons vanilla
- 3 cups dairy sour cream

Heat oven to 350°F. In medium bowl, combine crust ingredients; press over bottom and 1½ inches up sides of ungreased 10-inch springform pan. In large bowl, beat eggs. Add cream cheese, sugar, salt and vanilla; beat until smooth. Add sour cream; blend well. Pour into crust-lined pan.

Bake at 350°F. for 60 to 70 minutes or until edges are set. Center of cheesecake will be soft. Cool in pan 5 minutes; remove sides of pan. Cool completely. Store in refrigerator.

Yield: 16 servings.

NUTRITION PER SERVING:
Calories 360; Protein 6g; Carbohydrate 23g; Fat 27g; Sodium 290mg.

COOK'S NOTE

CREAM CHEESE

Cream cheese is a soft, white spreadable cheese made from cow's milk. Regular cream cheese is available in 3 and 8-ounce packages. Other forms of cream cheese include soft and whipped varieties and light cream cheese. Always use regular cream cheese in recipes (do not substitute tub varieties) unless another form is specified.

COOKIES 'N CREAM CHEESECAKE

Cookies and cream is one of the newest cheesecake flavors. Our version features chunks of chocolate sandwich cookies.

CRUST
- 1½ cups crushed creme-filled chocolate sandwich cookies (about 15 cookies)
- 2 tablespoons margarine or butter, softened

FILLING
- 3 (8-oz.) pkg. cream cheese, softened
- 1 cup sugar
- 3 eggs
- 1 cup whipping cream
- 2 tablespoons margarine or butter, melted
- 2 teaspoons vanilla
- 1 cup coarsely chopped creme-filled chocolate sandwich cookies (about 10 cookies)

GARNISH
- Whipped cream
- Crushed creme-filled chocolate sandwich cookies

Heat oven to 325°F. In medium bowl, combine crust ingredients; mix well. Press in bottom and up sides of ungreased 10-inch springform pan. Refrigerate 15 minutes.

In large bowl, beat cream cheese at medium speed until smooth and creamy. Gradually add sugar, beating until smooth. At low speed, add eggs 1 at a time, beating just until blended. Add whipping cream, 2 tablespoons margarine and vanilla; beat until smooth. Stir in 1 cup chopped cookies. Pour into crust-lined pan.

Bake at 325°F. for 50 to 60 minutes or until edges are set. Turn oven off; with door open at least 4 inches, let cake stand in oven for 30 minutes or until center is set. Remove from oven; cool to room temperature on wire rack. Remove sides of pan. Refrigerate overnight. To garnish, top with whipped cream; sprinkle with crushed cookies. Store in refrigerator.

Yield: 16 servings.

NUTRITION PER SERVING:
Calories 410; Protein 6g; Carbohydrate 27g; Fat 31g; Sodium 270mg.

FRUIT JEWEL CHEESECAKE

This creamy cheesecake crowned with glazed fruit makes a spectacular dessert.

CRUST

1½ cups graham cracker crumbs (about 24 squares)

¼ cup margarine or butter, melted

FILLING

3 (8-oz.) pkg. cream cheese, softened

1 cup sugar

4 eggs

1½ cups dairy sour cream

2 teaspoons grated lemon peel

CITRUS GLAZE

1 tablespoon sugar

2 teaspoons cornstarch

½ cup orange juice

¼ cup water

1 tablespoon lemon juice

¼ teaspoon grated lemon peel

TOPPING

1 pint (2 cups) strawberries, sliced

2 cups fresh or canned pineapple chunks, well drained

1 cup blueberries

Heat oven to 350°F. In medium bowl, combine crust ingredients; press in bottom of ungreased 10-inch springform pan. In large bowl, beat cream cheese and 1 cup sugar at medium speed until smooth and creamy. At low speed, add eggs 1 at a time, beating just until blended. Add sour cream and 2 teaspoons lemon peel; blend well. Pour into crust-lined pan. Bake at 350°F. for 50 to 60 minutes or until center is set. Cool. Refrigerate for several hours or overnight.

In small saucepan, combine 1 tablespoon sugar and cornstarch. Gradually add orange juice and water. Bring to a boil over medium heat, stirring constantly. Stir in lemon juice and ¼ teaspoon grated lemon peel. Cool. Just before serving, carefully remove sides of pan. Arrange fruit over cheesecake. Spoon or brush glaze over fruit. Store in refrigerator.

Yield: 16 servings.

NUTRITION PER SERVING:
Calories 360; Protein 6g; Carbohydrate 28g; Fat 25g; Sodium 240mg.

APPLESAUCE CHEESECAKE

Delicate apple flavor laced with a hint of cinnamon is a winning combination.

CRUST

1¼ cups graham cracker crumbs (about 20 squares)

½ cup chopped pecans, toasted, p. 23

¼ cup firmly packed brown sugar

¼ cup margarine or butter, melted

FILLING

3 (8-oz.) pkg. cream cheese, softened

1 cup sugar

2 tablespoons all purpose flour

3 eggs

1 cup applesauce

½ teaspoon cinnamon

⅛ teaspoon nutmeg

Heat oven to 350°F. In medium bowl, combine all crust ingredients; mix well. Press in bottom of ungreased 10-inch springform pan.

In large bowl, beat cream cheese and sugar at medium speed until smooth and creamy. Add flour; blend well. At low speed, add eggs 1 at a time, beating just until blended. Add remaining ingredients; beat until well blended. Pour into crust-lined pan.

Bake at 350°F. for 50 to 60 minutes or until center is set. Cool. Refrigerate several hours or overnight. Just before serving, carefully remove sides of pan. Store in refrigerator.

Yield: 16 servings.

NUTRITION PER SERVING:
Calories 320; Protein 5g; Carbohydrate 27g; Fat 22g; Sodium 220mg.

STEP-BY-STEP FEATURE ❧
How to Make a Decorative Cheesecake

STEP 1. Spoon chocolate batter by teaspoonfuls onto batter in pan, forming 9 drops around outside and 5 drops in center, using all the batter.

STEP 2. Starting in center of 1 outer drop, run knife through centers of outer drops; run knife through inner drops, forming 2 circles of hearts.

STEP 3. Place a shallow pan half full of water on bottom rack of oven when baking the cheesecake to help minimize cracks in the cheesecake.

CHOCOLATE ORANGE CHEESECAKE

~

Make this cheesecake for your sweetheart.

- ⅓ **cup graham cracker crumbs (about 5 to 6 squares)**
- 4 **(8-oz.) pkg. cream cheese, softened**
- 1⅓ **cups sugar**
- 4 **eggs**
- 2 **tablespoons orange-flavored liqueur or orange juice**
- 1 **teaspoon grated orange peel**
- 3 **oz. semi-sweet chocolate, melted**

Heat oven to 325°F. Lightly grease bottom and sides of 9-inch springform pan. Sprinkle graham cracker crumbs over bottom and sides of pan. In large bowl, beat cream cheese at medium speed until smooth and creamy. Gradually add sugar, beating until smooth. At low speed, add eggs 1 at a time, beating just until blended. Add liqueur and orange peel; beat 2 minutes at medium speed, scraping sides of bowl occasionally.

In small bowl, reserve 1½ cups of batter. Pour remaining batter into crumb-lined pan. Slowly blend melted chocolate into reserved batter. Drop spoonfuls of chocolate batter onto batter in pan. Using a table knife, swirl chocolate batter through light batter to marble.

Bake at 325°F. for 1 hour or until set. Cool for 10 minutes; remove sides of pan. Refrigerate several hours or overnight. Store in refrigerator.
Yield: 16 servings.

NUTRITION PER SERVING:
Calories 330; Protein 6g; Carbohydrate 24g; Fat 23g; Sodium 200mg.

VARIATION:

HEARTS-TO-YOU CHEESECAKE: To form heart design in top of cheesecake, spoon chocolate batter by teaspoonfuls onto batter in pan, forming a circle of 9 drops around outside and a circle of 5 drops in center; continue to spoon batter onto drops using all of chocolate batter. Starting in center of 1 outer drop, run knife through centers of outer drops; run knife through centers of inner drops, forming 2 separate rings of connected hearts.

Hearts-To-You Cheesecake

CHOCOLATE CHIP CHEESECAKE

Drizzle the chocolate glaze in a fancy design over the top for a special finishing touch.

CRUST
- 2 cups crushed creme-filled chocolate sandwich cookies (20 cookies)
- 2 tablespoons margarine or butter, melted

FILLING
- 3 eggs
- 2 (8-oz.) pkg. cream cheese, softened
- ¾ cup sugar
- 1 teaspoon vanilla
- ½ cup whipping cream
- 1 cup miniature semi-sweet chocolate chips

GLAZE
- ¼ cup miniature semi-sweet chocolate chips
- 1 teaspoon shortening

Heat oven to 325°F. In medium bowl, combine crust ingredients; press in bottom and 1 inch up sides of ungreased 10-inch springform pan.

Beat eggs in large bowl. Add cream cheese, sugar and vanilla; beat until smooth. Add whipping cream; blend well. Stir in 1 cup chocolate chips. Pour into crust-lined pan. Bake at 325°F. for 60 to 75 minutes or until center is set. Cool.

In small saucepan over low heat, melt glaze ingredients, stirring constantly. Drizzle over cooled cheesecake. Refrigerate several hours or overnight. Carefully remove sides of pan before serving.
Yield: 12 servings.

NUTRITION PER SERVING:
Calories 450; Protein 6g; Carbohydrate 36g; Fat 31g; Sodium 240mg.

ROYAL MARBLE CHEESECAKE

Ribbons of dark chocolate are swirled throughout the filling to create this pretty cheesecake.

CRUST
- ¾ cup all purpose flour
- 2 tablespoons sugar
  Dash salt
- ¼ cup margarine or butter
- 1 (6-oz.) pkg. (1 cup) semi-sweet chocolate chips, melted

FILLING
- 3 (8-oz.) pkg. cream cheese, softened
- 1 cup sugar
- ¼ cup all purpose flour
- 2 teaspoons vanilla
- 6 eggs
- 1 cup dairy sour cream

Heat oven to 400°F. In small bowl, combine ¾ cup flour, 2 tablespoons sugar and salt. Using pastry blender or fork, cut in margarine until mixture resembles coarse crumbs. Stir in 2 tablespoons of the melted chocolate. Reserve remaining chocolate for filling. Press in bottom of ungreased 9-inch springform pan.

Bake at 400°F. for 10 minutes or until very light brown. Remove from oven. Reduce oven temperature to 325°F.

In large bowl, beat cream cheese and 1 cup sugar until light and fluffy. Add ¼ cup flour and vanilla; blend well. At low speed, add eggs 1 at a time, beating just until blended. Add sour cream; mix well. Place 1¾ cups filling mixture in medium bowl; stir in reserved melted chocolate. Pour half of plain filling over crust. Top with spoonfuls of half of the chocolate filling. Cover with remaining plain filling, then with spoonfuls of remaining chocolate filling. Using table knife, swirl chocolate filling through plain filling.

Bake at 325°F. for 60 to 75 minutes or until center is almost set. Cool 10 minutes; remove sides of pan. Cool 2 to 3 hours. Refrigerate 8 hours or overnight before serving. Store in refrigerator.
Yield: 16 servings.

NUTRITION PER SERVING:
Calories 370; Protein 7g; Carbohydrate 28g; Fat 26g; Sodium 200mg.

CRANBERRY LEMON CHEESECAKE TART

This sweet dessert has a tart cranberry topping. It can be made ahead of time and refrigerated or frozen using the directions in the tip below.

CRUST
Pastry for One-Crust Pie p. 268

TOPPING
3 tablespoons sugar
1 tablespoon cornstarch
1½ cups fresh or frozen cranberries
¾ cup sugar
⅓ cup water

FILLING
1 (8-oz.) pkg. cream cheese, softened
½ cup whipping cream
⅓ cup sugar
1 teaspoon grated lemon peel

GARNISH
½ cup whipping cream, whipped

Prepare and bake pastry for Baked Pie Shell using 10-inch tart pan with removable bottom or 9-inch pie pan.

In small bowl, combine 3 tablespoons sugar and cornstarch. In medium saucepan over medium heat, combine cranberries, ¾ cup sugar and water. Bring to a boil, stirring until sugar is dissolved; boil 2 minutes, stirring constantly. Stir cornstarch mixture into cranberry mixture. Bring to a boil; boil 1 minute, stirring constantly. Cool to room temperature.

In small bowl, beat all filling ingredients until light and fluffy. Spoon evenly into cooled, baked tart shell. Carefully spoon topping over filling. Refrigerate until serving time. Garnish with whipped cream. Store in refrigerator.
Yield: 10 servings.

TIP:
Tart can be covered and frozen without topping. Let stand at room temperature about 10 minutes before serving. Spoon topping over filling. Garnish with whipped cream.

NUTRITION PER SERVING:
Calories 360; Protein 3g; Carbohydrate 39g; Fat 23g; Sodium 150mg.

LEMON CHEESECAKE PIE

This light, refreshing pie garnished with lemon **Citrus Twists** *p. 211 is a real beauty. No one will guess it is low in calories too.*

1¼ cups graham cracker crumbs
(about 20 squares)
3 tablespoons margarine or butter, melted
1 (3-oz.) pkg. lemon flavor gelatin
1 cup boiling water
2 cups lowfat cottage cheese
1 to 2 teaspoons grated lemon peel

Heat oven to 350°F. In medium bowl, combine graham cracker crumbs and margarine; press in bottom and up sides of 9-inch pie pan. Bake at 350°F. for 4 to 5 minutes. Cool.

In small bowl, dissolve gelatin in boiling water. Cool to lukewarm. In blender container, blend cottage cheese and lemon peel until smooth. Slowly blend in gelatin mixture; pour into cooled baked crust. Refrigerate until set, about 2 hours. Garnish as desired. Store in refrigerator.
Yield: 8 servings.

NUTRITION PER SERVING:
Calories 180; Protein 10g; Carbohydrate 21g; Fat 7g; Sodium 400mg.

Peppermint Marble Cheesecake

PEPPERMINT MARBLE CHEESECAKE

CRUST
- 2 tablespoons margarine or butter, melted
- 1 cup crushed creme-filled chocolate sandwich cookies (about 10 cookies)
- 2 tablespoons sugar

FILLING
- 2 (8-oz.) pkg. cream cheese, softened
- 3/4 cup sugar
- 3 eggs
- 1/2 cup whipping cream
- 1 teaspoon vanilla
  Dash salt
- 9 oz. white baking bars, melted, cooled slightly
- 1/4 teaspoon peppermint extract
- 2 to 4 drops green food color

GARNISH
- Filigree Shamrocks or Chocolate Cutouts p. 210, if desired
- 1/2 cup whipping cream, whipped, if desired

Heat oven to 325°F. Brush bottom and sides of 9-inch springform pan with melted margarine. In small bowl, combine remaining margarine and crust ingredients; mix well. Press evenly into bottom of greased pan. Bake at 325°F. for 8 minutes. Cool.

In large bowl, beat cream cheese at medium speed until smooth and creamy. Gradually beat in 3/4 cup sugar. At low speed, add eggs 1 at a time, beating just until blended. Add whipping cream, vanilla and salt; beat until smooth. Add white baking bars; beat just until blended. Reserve 1 cup cheesecake batter; pour remaining batter over crust. Add extract and food color to reserved 1 cup batter; blend well. Drop tablespoonfuls of peppermint batter onto batter in pan, forming 5 to 6 spots. Using a table knife, swirl peppermint batter through light batter to marble.

Bake at 325°F. for 40 to 50 minutes or until edges are set and center is almost set. Turn oven off; let cheesecake stand in oven 30 minutes with door open at least 4 inches. Remove from oven. Run sharp knife around sides of pan. Cool to room temperature on wire rack. Cover; refrigerate at least 24 hours before serving.

To serve, remove sides of pan. Garnish with Filigree Shamrocks or Chocolate Cutouts and whipped cream. Store in refrigerator.
Yield: 12 servings.

NUTRITION PER SERVING:
Calories 460; Protein 7g; Carbohydrate 37g; Fat 33g; Sodium 230mg.

MINIATURE CHEESECAKES

These tasty little cheesecakes can be served as a dessert or as part of a cookie assortment.

CHEESECAKES
- 2 (3-oz.) pkg. cream cheese, softened
- ¼ cup sugar
- 1 egg
- ½ teaspoon almond extract

TOPPING
- ¾ cup dairy sour cream
- 3 tablespoons sugar
- ¼ teaspoon almond extract

GARNISH
- ⅓ cup raspberry jam or other red jam or preserves

Heat oven to 350°F. Line 24 miniature muffin cups with paper baking cups. In medium bowl, beat cream cheese and ¼ cup sugar until smooth and creamy. Add egg and ½ teaspoon almond extract; beat until smooth. Fill paper-lined muffin cups ¾ full.

Bake at 350°F. for 15 minutes or until set. DO NOT OVERBAKE. Meanwhile, in small bowl combine all topping ingredients; blend well. Top each cheesecake with 1 heaping teaspoon topping. Bake an additional 5 to 8 minutes or until set. Cool 15 to 20 minutes.*

Spoon about ½ teaspoon jam onto each cheesecake. Refrigerate until serving time. Store in refrigerator.
Yield: 24 miniature cheesecakes.

TIP:
* At this point, cheesecakes can be covered and frozen up to 1 month. Thaw in refrigerator. Garnish just before serving.

NUTRITION PER SERVING:
Calories 70; Protein 1g; Carbohydrate 7g; Fat 4g; Sodium 30mg.

CHERRY CRESCENT CHEESECAKE CUPS

Colorful and delicious cherry-topped cheesecakes are made easily with refrigerated crescent roll dough.

FILLING
- 1 (8-oz.) pkg. cream cheese, softened
- 1 egg
- 1 cup powdered sugar
- ¼ cup chopped almonds
- ½ to 1 teaspoon almond extract

CRUST
- 1 (8-oz.) can refrigerated crescent dinner rolls

TOPPING
- 1 cup cherry fruit pie filling
- 1 to 2 tablespoons amaretto or cherry-flavored brandy, if desired
- 1 tablespoon margarine or butter

Heat oven to 350°F. Grease 8 muffin cups. In medium bowl, combine cream cheese and egg until smooth. Add powdered sugar, almonds and extract; mix well.

Separate dough into 4 rectangles; firmly press perforations to seal. Press or roll each rectangle into an 8x4-inch rectangle. Cut each in half crosswise to form 8 squares. Press each square into bottom of greased muffin cup, leaving corners of each square extended over sides of cup. Place about ¼ cup cream cheese mixture into each cup. Bring 4 corners of each square together in center of cup and firmly press points together to seal.

Bake at 350°F. for 18 to 23 minutes or until golden brown. Immediately remove from muffin cups. In small saucepan, combine all topping ingredients; cook over low heat until bubbly and margarine melts. Serve over warm desserts. Store in refrigerator.
Yield: 8 servings.

TIP:
To reheat, wrap loosely in foil; heat at 350°F. for 20 to 25 minutes.

NUTRITION PER SERVING:
Calories 370; Protein 6g; Carbohydrate 41g; Fat 20g; Sodium 340mg.

CRESCENT CHEESECAKE TART

There's no need for a special tart pan in this recipe.

- 1 (8-oz.) can refrigerated crescent dinner rolls
- 1 egg white
- 1 teaspoon water
- 1 to 2 cups assorted fresh fruit (kiwifruit slices, raspberries, blueberries)

FILLING
- 2 (3-oz.) pkg. cream cheese, softened
- 2 tablespoons sugar
- 1 egg yolk
- ¼ teaspoon almond extract

Heat oven to 350°F. Separate dough into 2 long rectangles; firmly press perforations to seal. Place 1 rectangle on ungreased cookie sheet. In small bowl, combine egg white and water; brush over rectangle. Cut two 1-inch strips of dough from short side of the remaining rectangle. Cut remaining dough lengthwise into 4 long 1-inch strips. Place 1 long strip evenly on each long edge of rectangle. Place short strips on each short edge. Place remaining strips on top of first long strips. (See diagram.) Brush with remaining egg white. Bake at 350°F. for 15 minutes.

In small bowl, combine all filling ingredients; beat until smooth. Spread over crust. Bake an additional 12 to 15 minutes or until crust is deep golden brown and filling is set. Cool on wire rack. Garnish with fruit. Store in refrigerator.

Yield: 8 servings.

NUTRITION PER SERVING:
Calories 220; Protein 4g; Carbohydrate 19g; Fat 14g; Sodium 300mg.

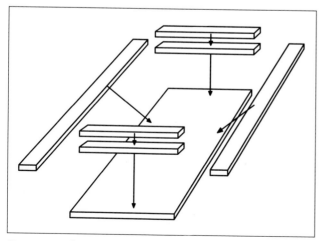

Crescent Cheesecake Tart

BLUEBERRY LEMON CHEESECAKE PIE

This all-American pie features red strawberry fans over blueberries and white cream cheese filling.

PASTRY
- Pastry for Two-Crust Pie p. 268
- 2 tablespoons sugar
- 2 tablespoons margarine or butter, melted
- 2 teaspoons lemon peel
- Dash nutmeg

FILLING
- 1 (8-oz.) pkg. cream cheese, softened
- ⅓ cup sugar
- 1 to 2 teaspoons grated lemon peel
- ½ cup whipping cream, whipped

TOPPING
- 1 (21-oz.) can blueberry fruit pie filling
- Strawberry Fans p. 211
- Whipping cream, whipped, sweetened p. 23

Heat oven to 450°F. Prepare pastry for Two-Crust Pie. Roll out one circle of pastry and place in 9-inch pie pan. Bake as directed for Baked Pie Shell.

Roll out remaining pastry; cut stars from pastry using a 2 to 3-inch star-shaped cookie cutter. Transfer stars to cookie sheet. In small bowl, combine 2 tablespoons sugar, margarine, 2 teaspoons grated lemon peel and nutmeg. Brush over stars just to edges. Bake at 450°F. for 6 to 8 minutes or until light golden brown. Transfer stars to wire rack.

In small bowl, beat cream cheese, ⅓ cup sugar and 1 to 2 teaspoons lemon peel until smooth and creamy. Fold in whipped cream. Spoon evenly into cooled pie shell. Spoon blueberry filling evenly over lemon filling. Refrigerate at least 1 hour before serving. Garnish with star cutouts, strawberry fans and whipped cream. Store in refrigerator.

Yield: 8 servings.

NUTRITION PER SERVING:
Calories 600; Protein 4g; Carbohydrate 61g; Fat 38g; Sodium 420mg.

Orange Cheesecake

This featherweight cheesecake is a refreshing ending for any meal.

CRUST
- 1 cup vanilla wafer crumbs (about 20 wafers)
- 2 tablespoons margarine or butter, melted

FILLING
- 2 envelopes unflavored gelatin
- 1/3 cup sugar
- 3/4 cup orange juice
- 1 (15-oz.) container light ricotta cheese
- 1 (16-oz.) container nonfat vanilla yogurt
- 2 tablespoons orange-flavored liqueur or orange juice, if desired
- 1 (11-oz.) can mandarin orange segments, well drained

Heat oven to 375°F. In small bowl, combine crust ingredients; press in bottom of ungreased 9 or 10-inch springform pan. Bake at 375°F. for 8 to 10 minutes or until light golden brown. Cool.

In small saucepan, combine gelatin, sugar and orange juice; let stand 1 minute. Stir over medium heat until dissolved. In blender container or food processor bowl with metal blade, process ricotta cheese until smooth. Add yogurt, gelatin mixture and liqueur; blend well. Stir in orange segments.

Pour into cooled, baked crust. Cover; refrigerate several hours or until firm. Before serving, carefully remove sides of pan. Garnish as desired. Store in refrigerator.

Yield: 12 servings.

NUTRITION PER SERVING:
Calories 160; Protein 7g; Carbohydrate 23g; Fat 5g; Sodium 100mg.

Glazed Almond Amaretto Cheesecake

A topping of glazed almonds adds a beautiful touch to this dessert.

TOPPING
- 1/2 cup sugar
- 1/4 cup water
- 1 cup sliced almonds
- 1 teaspoon amaretto

CRUST
- 2 cups graham cracker crumbs (about 32 squares)
- 1/4 cup finely chopped almonds
- 1/3 cup margarine or butter, melted

FILLING
- 2 (8-oz.) pkg. cream cheese, softened
- 1 cup sugar
- 3 eggs
- 1 cup dairy sour cream
- 1/2 cup whipping cream
- 1/4 cup amaretto
- 1/2 teaspoon almond extract

In small saucepan, combine 1/2 cup sugar and water. Bring to a boil. Boil 2 minutes; remove from heat. Stir in sliced almonds and 1 teaspoon amaretto. With slotted spoon, transfer almonds to waxed paper; separate with fork. Cool.

Heat oven to 350°F. In medium bowl, combine all crust ingredients; press in bottom and 1 1/2 inches up sides of ungreased 10-inch springform pan. In large bowl, beat cream cheese and 1 cup sugar at medium speed until smooth and creamy. At low speed, add eggs 1 at a time, beating just until blended. Add sour cream, whipping cream, 1/4 cup amaretto and almond extract; blend well. Pour into crust-lined pan.

Bake at 350°F. for 60 to 75 minutes or until center is set. Arrange sliced almonds in 2-inch wide circle around outer edge of cheesecake during last 15 minutes of baking time. Cool 15 minutes; carefully remove sides of pan. Cool completely. Refrigerate several hours or overnight before serving. Store in refrigerator.

Yield: 16 servings.

NUTRITION PER SERVING:
Calories 390; Protein 6g; Carbohydrate 33g; Fat 26g; Sodium 220mg.

CREAMY CHOCOLATE LACE CHEESECAKE

A chocolate lover's fantasy! This cheesecake features a pretty topping.

CRUST

1½ cups chocolate wafer crumbs (about 24 wafers)
½ cup finely chopped almonds
¼ cup margarine or butter, melted

FILLING

2 (8-oz.) pkg. cream cheese, softened
⅔ cup sugar
3 eggs
1 (12-oz.) pkg. (2 cups) semi-sweet chocolate chips, melted, cooled
1 cup whipping cream
2 tablespoons margarine or butter, melted
1 teaspoon vanilla

TOPPING

1 cup dairy sour cream
1½ teaspoons vanilla
1 teaspoon sugar
½ oz. unsweetened chocolate, melted

Heat oven to 325°F. Butter or grease 9-inch springform pan. In large bowl, combine crust ingredients; mix well. Press in bottom and up sides of buttered pan; refrigerate.

In large bowl, beat cream cheese and ⅔ cup sugar at medium speed until smooth and creamy. At low speed, add eggs 1 at a time, beating just until blended. Add melted chocolate chips; beat well. Add whipping cream, 2 tablespoons margarine and 1 teaspoon vanilla; beat until smooth. Pour into crust-lined pan. Bake at 325°F. for 55 to 65 minutes or until edges are set. Center of cheesecake will be soft. Cool in pan 5 minutes; carefully remove sides of pan. Cool completely.

In small bowl, combine sour cream, 1½ teaspoons vanilla and 1 teaspoon sugar; stir until smooth. Spread over cooled cheesecake. Drizzle with ½ oz. melted chocolate in lace pattern. Refrigerate several hours or overnight before serving. Garnish as desired. Store in refrigerator.

Yield: 16 servings.

NUTRITION PER SERVING:
Calories 470; Protein 7g; Carbohydrate 31g; Fat 36g; Sodium 180mg.

EASY FRUIT CHEESECAKES

These scrumptious individual cheesecakes can be made ahead and frozen.

24 vanilla wafers
3 (8-oz.) pkg. cream cheese, softened
1 cup sugar
¼ teaspoon nutmeg
1 teaspoon vanilla
3 eggs
½ cup apricot preserves
3 kiwifruit, peeled, sliced

Heat oven to 325°F. Line 24 muffin cups with paper or foil baking cups. Place 1 vanilla wafer in bottom of each cup. In large bowl, beat cream cheese, sugar, nutmeg, vanilla and eggs until smooth, scraping sides of bowl occasionally. Pour mixture into paper-lined muffin cups, filling ⅔ full. Bake at 325°F. for 20 to 25 minutes or until set.*

Meanwhile, melt apricot preserves in small saucepan over low heat. Place 1 slice of kiwifruit on each cheesecake. Carefully spoon 1 teaspoon melted apricot preserves over top. Cover; refrigerate overnight. Store in refrigerator.

Yield: 24 cheesecakes.

TIPS:

* At this point, cheesecakes can be covered and frozen up to 1 month. Thaw in refrigerator. Garnish just before serving.

Other fruits, such as sliced strawberries, can be substituted for kiwifruit.

NUTRITION PER SERVING:
Calories 180; Protein 3g; Carbohydrate 18g; Fat 11g; Sodium 105mg.

Praline Cheesecake

PRALINE CHEESECAKE

~

Pecan halves can be pressed into the praline topping of this rich, creamy cheesecake while the topping is still warm.

CRUST
  1 **cup graham cracker crumbs (about 16 squares)**
  ¼ **cup chopped pecans**
  ¼ **cup butter or margarine, melted**

FILLING
  3 **(8-oz.) pkg. cream cheese, softened**
  1 **cup firmly packed brown sugar**
  3 **eggs**
  1 **cup whipping cream**
  2 **teaspoons vanilla**

TOPPING
  ½ **cup firmly packed brown sugar**
  ¼ **cup butter or margarine**

GARNISH
  Pecan halves, if desired

Heat oven to 450°F. In small bowl, combine crust ingredients; press firmly in bottom of ungreased 9-inch springform pan.

In large bowl, beat cream cheese at medium speed until smooth and creamy. Gradually beat in 1 cup brown sugar. At low speed, add eggs 1 at a time, beating just until blended. Add whipping cream and vanilla; beat until smooth. Pour into crust-lined pan. Bake at 450°F. for 10 minutes. Reduce oven temperature to 250°F.; bake an additional 65 to 75 minutes or until center is set. Cool 10 minutes; carefully remove sides of pan. Cool completely.

In small saucepan, combine topping ingredients. Cook over medium heat until thick and well blended, stirring constantly. Spread evenly over top of cooled cheesecake. Garnish with pecan halves. Refrigerate at least 2 hours before serving. Store in refrigerator.
Yield: 12 to 16 servings.

FOOD PROCESSOR DIRECTIONS:
Prepare crust as directed above. To prepare filling, place cream cheese in food processor bowl with metal blade. Process until smooth. Add brown sugar and eggs; process until well combined. With machine running, pour whipping cream and vanilla through feed tube; process until mixture is smooth and creamy. Pour into crust-lined pan; continue as directed above.

NUTRITION PER SERVING:
Calories 380; Protein 5g; Carbohydrate 26g; Fat 29g; Sodium 240mg.

Pumpkin Cheesecake with Praline Sauce

This pumpkin cheesecake could compete with traditional pumpkin pie as a new holiday favorite.

CRUST
  1 tablespoon butter or margarine, softened
1¼ cups finely chopped pecans
 ¼ cup fine dry bread crumbs
  2 tablespoons sugar
  2 tablespoons butter or margarine, melted

FILLING
  4 (8-oz.) pkg. cream cheese, softened
  1 cup firmly packed brown sugar
 ⅔ cup sugar
  5 eggs
 ¼ cup all purpose flour
  2 teaspoons pumpkin pie spice
  2 tablespoons brandy, if desired
  1 (16-oz.) can (2 cups) pumpkin

PRALINE SAUCE
 ½ cup firmly packed brown sugar
 ¼ cup water
 ¼ cup butter (do not substitute margarine)
  1 egg, beaten
 ¼ cup chopped pecans
 ½ teaspoon vanilla

Heat oven to 350°F. Butter 9-inch springform pan using 1 tablespoon butter. In medium bowl, combine 1¼ cups pecans, bread crumbs and 2 tablespoons sugar. Drizzle melted butter over pecan mixture; toss to combine. Press into bottom and up sides of buttered pan; refrigerate.

In large bowl, beat cream cheese at medium speed until smooth and creamy. Gradually beat in 1 cup brown sugar and ⅔ cup sugar until smooth. At low speed, add 5 eggs 1 at a time, beating just until blended. In small bowl, combine flour, pumpkin pie spice, brandy and pumpkin; mix well. Gradually add to cream cheese mixture; beat until smooth. Pour into crust-lined pan.

Bake at 350°F. for 1 hour 20 minutes to 1 hour 30 minutes or until center is set. Turn oven off; let cake stand in oven 30 minutes with door open at least 4 inches. Remove from oven. Run sharp knife around sides of pan. Cool to room temperature on wire rack. Cover; refrigerate overnight.

In small saucepan over medium heat, combine ½ cup brown sugar, water and ¼ cup butter. Bring to a boil; boil 2 minutes. Gradually blend small amount of hot syrup into beaten egg. Return egg mixture to saucepan; cook over low heat 1 minute, stirring constantly. Remove from heat; stir in ¼ cup pecans and vanilla. Remove sides of pan from cheesecake. Serve sauce slightly warm over wedges of cheesecake. Store in refrigerator.

Yield: 16 servings.

MICROWAVE DIRECTIONS:
Prepare cheesecake as directed above. To prepare sauce, place ¼ cup butter in 4-cup microwave-safe measuring cup. Microwave on HIGH for 45 seconds to 1 minute or until melted. Stir in ½ cup brown sugar and water. Microwave on HIGH for 1 to 1½ minutes or until boiling. Boil 1 minute. Gradually blend small amount of hot syrup into beaten egg. Return egg mixture to measuring cup; blend well. Microwave on MEDIUM for 30 seconds or until slightly thickened. Stir in ¼ cup pecans and vanilla. Serve slightly warm over wedges of cheesecake.

HIGH ALTITUDE:
Above 3500 Feet: In filling, increase flour to ¼ cup plus 1 tablespoon. Bake at 350°F. for 1 hour 15 minutes to 1 hour 25 minutes.

NUTRITION PER SERVING:
Calories 500; Protein 8g; Carbohydrate 39g; Fat 35g; Sodium 260mg.

Cook's Note

SPRINGFORM PAN

A springform pan is a round pan with straight sides 2½ to 3 inches in height. They are available in a number of sizes, 9 and 10-inch diameter pans being the most common. The side of the pan has a spring or clamp, which allows expansion and removal of the side from the bottom of the pan. Cheesecakes or tortes baked in this type of pan can be served easily once the side of the pan is removed.

Creme De Menthe Cheesecake Squares

This dessert has a chocolate wafer base topped with a mint-flavored cheesecake and is frosted with rich semi-sweet chocolate. The 13x9-inch pan makes enough to serve 20 guests.

CRUST
- 1 (8½-oz.) pkg. chocolate wafers, crushed (1¾ cups)
- ½ cup margarine or butter, melted

FILLING
- 2 (8-oz.) pkg. cream cheese, softened
- ½ cup dairy sour cream
- 4 eggs
- ⅔ cup sugar
- ½ cup creme de menthe syrup or liqueur
- ¼ teaspoon mint extract

TOPPING
- 4 oz. semi-sweet chocolate, chopped
- ½ cup dairy sour cream

Heat oven to 350°F. In medium bowl, combine crust ingredients; mix well. Press in bottom and 1 inch up sides of ungreased 13x9-inch pan. Freeze crust while preparing filling.

In large bowl, combine all filling ingredients; beat on low speed until smooth. Pour into crust-lined pan. Bake at 350°F. for 30 to 35 minutes or until knife inserted in center comes out clean. Cool on wire rack.

Melt chocolate in small saucepan over low heat, stirring constantly. Cool 5 minutes; beat in sour cream. Spread over warm cheesecake. Refrigerate 3 hours or until firm. Cut into squares. Store in refrigerator.

Yield: 20 servings.

NUTRITION PER SERVING:
Calories 300; Protein 4g; Carbohydrate 23g; Fat 20g; Sodium 160mg.

Fudge-Glazed Cheesecake with Caramel Sauce

This cheesecake is baked in a round cake pan.

CRUST
- 1 cup crushed creme-filled chocolate sandwich cookies (about 10 cookies)*
- ¼ cup chopped pecans
- 1 tablespoon margarine or butter, melted

CHEESECAKE
- 2 (8-oz.) pkg. cream cheese, softened
- ½ cup sugar
- ¼ cup whipping cream
- 2 eggs

FUDGE GLAZE
- 2 oz. semi-sweet chocolate, chopped
- 2 tablespoons whipping cream

CARAMEL SAUCE
- 1 cup caramel ice cream topping
- ½ cup pecan halves, toasted, p. 23

Heat oven to 325°F. Line 8 or 9-inch round cake pan with foil so that foil extends over sides of pan. In large bowl, combine all crust ingredients; mix well. Press into foil-lined pan. Bake at 325°F. for 8 minutes.

In large bowl, beat cream cheese at medium speed until smooth and creamy. Gradually beat in sugar and whipping cream. At low speed, add eggs 1 at a time, beating just until blended. Pour over crust. Bake at 325°F. for 35 to 45 minutes or until center is set. Cool to room temperature on wire rack.

In small saucepan, melt chocolate with 2 tablespoons whipping cream over very low heat, stirring constantly. Spread over cheesecake. Cover; refrigerate 4 hours or overnight.

In small bowl, combine caramel topping and pecans; mix well. To serve, lift foil-lined cheesecake from pan; remove foil. Place cheesecake on serving plate; cut into wedges. Serve with caramel sauce. Store in refrigerator.

Yield: 12 to 16 servings.

TIP:
* Cookies can be crushed in food processor bowl with metal blade by processing broken cookies until uniform fine crumbs form. Or, place cookies in plastic bag; seal. Crush with rolling pin until uniform fine crumbs form.

NUTRITION PER SERVING:
Calories 310; Protein 5g; Carbohydrate 28g; Fat 20g; Sodium 180mg.

BAKED PEAR CUSTARD WITH CARAMEL SAUCE

Choose any variety of pear for this caramel-topped custard. Ripe pears should feel firm but yield to gentle pressure.

CUSTARD
- 4 pears, peeled, quartered
- ¾ cup all purpose flour
- ¾ cup sugar
- 4 eggs
- 2 cups half-and-half
- 2 tablespoons sugar

CARAMEL SAUCE
- 1 cup firmly packed brown sugar
- ¼ cup dark corn syrup
- ½ cup half-and-half
- 2 tablespoons butter or margarine
  Dash salt
- ½ teaspoon vanilla

Heat oven to 375°F. Grease 2½-quart shallow casserole. Arrange pears in greased casserole. In large bowl, combine flour and ¾ cup sugar. Add eggs; beat well. Gradually stir in 2 cups half-and-half. Pour over pears; sprinkle with 2 tablespoons sugar.

Bake at 375°F. for 40 to 50 minutes or until knife inserted near center comes out clean.

In medium saucepan, combine all sauce ingredients except vanilla. Cook over medium heat until mixture boils, stirring constantly. Reduce heat to low; simmer 5 minutes, stirring constantly. Stir in vanilla. Serve caramel sauce over warm pear custard. Store in refrigerator.

Yield: 8 to 10 servings.

NUTRITION PER SERVING:
Calories 380; Protein 5g; Carbohydrate 63g; Fat 12g; Sodium 100mg.

BAKED CUSTARD

Baked custard is done when it appears set but still jiggles slightly. The custard will firm up as it cools.

- 3 eggs, slightly beaten
- ¼ cup sugar
- ⅛ teaspoon salt
- 1 teaspoon vanilla
- 2½ cups milk
  Dash nutmeg

Heat oven to 350°F. In large bowl, combine eggs, sugar, salt and vanilla; blend well. Gradually stir in milk. Pour into 6 ungreased 6-oz. custard cups. Sprinkle with nutmeg. Place custard cups in 13x9-inch pan. Pour boiling water into pan around custard cups to a depth of 1 inch.

Bake at 350°F. for 45 to 55 minutes or until knife inserted near center comes out clean. Serve warm or cold. Store in refrigerator.

Yield: 6 servings.

TIP:
If desired, pour mixture into 1 to 1½-quart casserole. Place in 13x9-inch pan; pour boiling water into pan around casserole to a depth of 1 inch. Bake at 350°F. for 50 to 60 minutes.

NUTRITION PER SERVING:
Calories 120; Protein 7g; Carbohydrate 13g; Fat 4g; Sodium 125mg.

CUSTARD WITH RASPBERRY PUREE

For a colorful presentation, top this cholesterol-reduced custard with fresh fruit and mint leaves.

CUSTARD
- 2 tablespoons brown sugar
- 1/8 teaspoon salt
- 1 cup evaporated skim milk
- 1/2 cup frozen cholesterol-free egg product, thawed
- 1/2 teaspoon vanilla
  Nutmeg

RASPBERRY PUREE
- 1 (10-oz.) pkg. frozen raspberries with syrup, thawed

GARNISH
- Fresh fruit, if desired
- Mint leaves, if desired

Heat oven to 325°F. In 2-cup measuring cup, combine brown sugar, salt, milk, egg product and vanilla; blend well. Place 4 ungreased 5-oz. custard cups in 9-inch square pan on oven rack. Pour custard mixture into custard cups. Pour boiling water into pan around custard cups to a depth of 1 inch.

Bake at 325°F. for 30 to 35 minutes or until knife inserted in center comes out clean. To unmold, loosen edges with knife. Invert dessert plate on top of each custard cup. Quickly invert to release hot custard onto plate. Sprinkle with nutmeg.

Pour raspberries into food processor bowl with metal blade or blender container. Cover; process until smooth. Strain to remove seeds. Spoon 2 tablespoons sauce on each plate around warm custard. Garnish with fresh fruit and mint leaves. Serve with additional sauce. Store in refrigerator.
Yield: 4 servings.

NUTRITION PER SERVING:
Calories 210; Protein 9g; Carbohydrate 34g; Fat 4g; Sodium 200mg.

CARAMEL FLAN

Serve fresh fruit in the center of this custard dessert ring.

- 1/2 cup sugar
- 5 eggs
- 2 1/2 cups milk
- 1/2 cup sugar
- 1 teaspoon vanilla
- 3 cups fresh fruit (strawberry halves or slices, seedless grapes, pineapple cubes or peeled and sliced kiwifruit)

In small heavy skillet over medium heat, caramelize 1/2 cup sugar, stirring constantly until sugar melts and turns rich golden brown. Pour into 8-inch ring mold; holding pan with pot holders, swirl so sugar coats bottom and sides.

Heat oven to 325°F. In large bowl, slightly beat eggs. Stir in milk, 1/2 cup sugar and vanilla. Place caramel-coated ring mold in shallow baking pan on oven rack. Pour egg mixture over caramel in mold. Pour hot water into pan around mold to a depth of 1 inch.

Bake at 325°F. for 55 to 60 minutes or until a knife inserted halfway between center and edge comes out clean. Remove mold from hot water; cool on wire rack. Refrigerate at least 3 1/2 hours.

To unmold, loosen edges with spatula. Invert mold onto serving plate. Spoon any caramel that remains in mold over custard. Serve with fruit. Store in refrigerator.
Yield: 8 servings.

NUTRITION PER SERVING:
Calories 210; Protein 7g; Carbohydrate 34g; Fat 5g; Sodium 80mg.

CARAMEL-TOPPED CHOCOLATE FLAN

The caramel runs down the sides of the custard forming a sauce when unmolded. It's wonderful warm or cold.

CARAMEL
- ⅓ cup sugar
- 2 tablespoons water
- ⅛ teaspoon cream of tartar

FLAN
- 1⅓ cups half-and-half
- 3 oz. sweet baking chocolate, chopped
- 2 tablespoons sugar
- 3 eggs
- ½ teaspoon vanilla

In small heavy saucepan over medium heat, combine ⅓ cup sugar, water and cream of tartar until mixture comes to a boil, stirring constantly. Let boil without stirring until mixture begins to caramelize, about 10 to 12 minutes. If it darkens in one spot, swirl pan around gently. Stir until mixture is a medium caramel color. Immediately pour caramel into bottom of 6 ungreased 6-oz. custard cups; set aside.

In small saucepan over low heat, combine half-and-half, chocolate and 2 tablespoons sugar, stirring constantly until smooth. Remove from heat. In small bowl, beat eggs and vanilla until light and lemon colored. Gradually add chocolate mixture; blend well. Carefully pour custard over caramel in custard cups. Place cups in 13x9-inch pan. Pour very hot water into pan to within ½-inch of tops of custard cups. Bake at 325°F. for 50 minutes or until knife inserted in center comes out clean. Unmold and serve warm or refrigerate in custard cups and serve cold. Garnish with whipped cream and fresh fruit, if desired. Store in refrigerator.

Yield: 6 servings.

NUTRITION PER SERVING:
Calories 300; Protein 6g; Carbohydrate 31g; Fat 17g; Sodium 65mg.

CHOCOLATE SOUFFLE

Always bake a souffle on the middle oven rack in a preheated oven. Do not open the oven door for at least the first 25 minutes of baking or the souffle may fall.

- ½ cup sugar
- 2 tablespoons cornstarch
- ¼ teaspoon salt
- ¾ cup milk
- 2 oz. unsweetened chocolate or 2 envelopes premelted unsweetened chocolate baking flavor
- 3 tablespoons margarine or butter
- 1 teaspoon vanilla
- 4 eggs, separated
- ¼ teaspoon cream of tartar
  Whipped cream or topping, if desired

Heat oven to 350°F. Prepare 4 to 5-cup souffle dish or casserole with foil band by cutting 3-inch strip of foil to go around top of dish. Lightly grease dish and strip of foil. With greased side toward inside of dish, secure foil band around top of dish, letting it extend 2 inches above edge of dish.

In medium saucepan, combine sugar, cornstarch and salt; stir in milk. Cook over medium heat until mixture boils and thickens, stirring constantly. Remove from heat; stir in chocolate and margarine until melted. Stir in vanilla. Add egg yolks 1 at a time, beating well after each addition. In large bowl, beat egg whites with cream of tartar until soft peaks form. Gently fold in chocolate mixture. Pour into greased souffle dish.*

Bake at 350°F. for 45 to 50 minutes or until knife inserted near center comes out clean. Remove foil band; immediately serve souffle with whipped cream or topping.

Yield: 10 servings.

TIP:
* Souffle can stand at room temperature, loosely covered, up to 1 hour before baking.

NUTRITION PER SERVING:
Calories 170; Protein 4g; Carbohydrate 15g; Fat 11g; Sodium 130mg.

APRICOT SOUFFLE

This delicate, melt-in-your-mouth souffle is enhanced with a luscious apricot sauce.

- 2 tablespoons cornstarch
- 2 tablespoons sugar
- ¾ cup evaporated skim milk
- ¼ cup apricot preserves
- 3 tablespoons apricot nectar
- 1 teaspoon vanilla
- 6 egg whites
- ½ teaspoon cream of tartar

SAUCE
- ⅓ cup apricot preserves
- 2 tablespoons apricot nectar

Spray 2½-quart souffle dish with nonstick cooking spray. In small saucepan, combine cornstarch and sugar. Add milk, ¼ cup apricot preserves and 3 tablespoons apricot nectar. Cook over medium heat until mixture boils and thickens, stirring constantly. Pour into large bowl; stir in vanilla. Cover surface with plastic wrap; set aside. Cool to room temperature.

Heat oven to 425°F. In large bowl, beat egg whites and cream of tartar until stiff peaks form, about 2 to 3 minutes. Gently fold egg white mixture into cooled apricot mixture. Spoon into spray-coated souffle dish. Place souffle dish in 13x9-inch pan. Pour boiling water into pan around souffle dish to a depth of 1 inch. Place in 425°F. oven. Immediately reduce heat to 350°F.; bake 25 minutes or until puffy, set and golden brown.

Meanwhile, in small saucepan combine sauce ingredients. Cook over medium heat until thoroughly heated. Serve souffle immediately with sauce.

Yield: 6 to 8 servings.

HIGH ALTITUDE:
Above 3500 Feet: No change.

NUTRITION PER SERVING:
Calories 120; Protein 4g; Carbohydrate 25g; Fat 0g; Sodium 70mg.

GRANDMA'S RICE PUDDING

Short-grain rice works well in cooked puddings. The pudding will set up slightly when cool.

- ½ cup uncooked white rice (not instant)
- ½ cup sugar
- 2 cups milk
- 1 tablespoon margarine or butter
  Cinnamon, nutmeg or raisins, if desired

Heat oven to 300°F. Grease 1½-quart casserole. In greased casserole, combine rice, sugar and milk; dot with margarine. Bake at 300°F. for 1¾ to 2 hours until rice is tender and pudding is creamy, stirring occasionally. Cool; sprinkle each serving with cinnamon. Store in refrigerator.

Yield: 4 (½-cup) servings.

NUTRITION PER SERVING:
Calories 270; Protein 6g; Carbohydrate 49g; Fat 5g; Sodium 95mg.

QUICK RICE PUDDING

This recipe starts with cooked rice.

- 2 cups milk
- 1½ cups cooked white rice
- ½ cup raisins, if desired
- ⅓ cup sugar
- 1 teaspoon cinnamon
- 1 teaspoon vanilla
- 2 eggs, beaten

Heat oven to 350°F. In medium saucepan, heat milk to very warm. DO NOT BOIL. Remove from heat; add remaining ingredients; mix well. Pour into ungreased 1½-quart casserole. Place casserole in 13x9-inch pan. Pour boiling water in pan around casserole to a depth of 1 inch. Bake at 350°F. for 30 minutes. Carefully stir pudding; bake an additional 15 to 20 minutes or until knife inserted near center comes out clean. Serve warm or cold with cream, if desired.

Yield: 12 (½-cup) servings.

NUTRITION PER SERVING:
Calories 100; Protein 3g; Carbohydrate 19g; Fat 2g; Sodium 35mg.

CREAM CHEESE BREAD PUDDINGS WITH RUM SAUCE

Bread pudding has graduated from "the poor man's dessert" of years past. This exceptional microwave version is served warm with a marvelous buttery rum sauce.

BREAD PUDDINGS
- 1/3 cup raisins
- 2 tablespoons water
- 1 (3-oz.) pkg. cream cheese, softened
- 1/4 cup sugar
- 2 eggs
- 1 1/2 cups milk
- 1 teaspoon vanilla
- 5 (1-oz.) slices oatmeal bread or whole wheat bread, cut into 1/2-inch cubes

RUM SAUCE
- 1/4 cup butter or margarine
- 1/2 cup firmly packed brown sugar
- 2 tablespoons milk
- 1 tablespoon dark rum or 1/2 teaspoon rum extract
- Nutmeg or cinnamon

MICROWAVE DIRECTIONS:
In large microwave-safe bowl, combine raisins and water; microwave on HIGH for 1 to 1 1/2 minutes or until mixture boils. Set aside.

Butter four 1-cup souffle dishes or 10-oz. custard cups. In small bowl, beat cream cheese and sugar until smooth. Add eggs 1 at a time, beating well after each addition. Slowly beat in 1 1/2 cups milk and vanilla. Add bread to raisins; stir. Pour milk mixture over bread, stirring well. Spoon mixture evenly into buttered dishes.

Arrange dishes in circle in microwave oven. Cover with waxed paper; microwave on MEDIUM for 10 to 14 minutes or until knife inserted near center comes out clean, rotating dishes once halfway through cooking. Let stand while preparing sauce.

To prepare sauce, in 4-cup microwave-safe measuring cup, microwave butter on HIGH for 45 to 60 seconds or until melted. Stir in brown sugar and 2 tablespoons milk. Microwave on HIGH for 1 to 1 1/2 minutes or until boiling; stir. Microwave on HIGH an additional minute; stir in rum. To serve, sprinkle nutmeg over puddings; serve with sauce.
Yield: 4 servings; 2/3 cup sauce.

NUTRITION PER SERVING:
Calories 550; Protein 12g; Carbohydrate 72g; Fat 25g; Sodium 450mg.

FRUIT AND RICE PUDDING

This is an old favorite tastefully tailored for healthier eating. Fruit bits are added for a new flavor twist.

- 1 1/2 cups skim milk
- 2 cups cooked brown rice
- 1/2 cup dried fruit bits
- 1/4 cup firmly packed brown sugar
- 1/4 teaspoon cinnamon
- 1/2 cup frozen cholesterol-free egg product, thawed
- 1 teaspoon vanilla

Heat milk in small saucepan until very warm. Heat oven to 350°F. In ungreased 1 1/2-quart casserole, combine all ingredients. Place casserole in 13x9-inch pan. Pour boiling water into pan around casserole to a depth of 1 inch.

Bake at 350°F. for 35 to 45 minutes. Carefully stir pudding; bake an additional 15 to 25 minutes or until knife inserted in center comes out clean. Serve warm.
Yield: 6 servings.

NUTRITION PER SERVING:
Calories 190; Protein 6g; Carbohydrate 36g; Fat 3g; Sodium 75mg.

CRANBERRY PUDDING WITH BUTTER SAUCE

The perfect holiday dessert for a small gathering.

PUDDING
1½ **cups finely crushed dry bread crumbs**
1 **cup sugar**
1 **tablespoon all purpose flour**
1½ **teaspoons baking powder**
¼ **teaspoon salt**
¼ **teaspoon ginger**
¼ **teaspoon cinnamon**
⅛ **to ¼ teaspoon allspice**
⅓ **cup butter or margarine, melted**
⅓ **cup milk**
1 **cup coarsely chopped fresh or frozen cranberries (do not thaw)**
1 **egg, slightly beaten**

BUTTER SAUCE
½ **cup sugar**
1 **teaspoon cornstarch**
½ **cup whipping cream**
¼ **cup butter or margarine, melted**
½ **teaspoon vanilla**

MICROWAVE DIRECTIONS:
Grease bottom only of 4-cup microwave-safe measuring cup; line bottom with microwave-safe waxed paper and grease again. In large bowl, combine bread crumbs, 1 cup sugar, flour, baking powder, salt, ginger, cinnamon and allspice. Stir in ⅓ cup butter, milk, cranberries and egg; mix well. (Batter will be stiff.) Spoon batter into greased and lined measuring cup; press down slightly. Cover tightly with microwave-safe plastic wrap. Microwave on MEDIUM for 11 to 14 minutes, rotating measuring cup ½ turn halfway through cooking. Pudding is done when it starts to pull away from sides of measuring cup. Uncover; let stand on flat surface 5 minutes. Loosen pudding from sides of measuring cup; invert onto serving plate. Remove waxed paper; cool slightly.

In 4-cup microwave-safe measuring cup, combine ½ cup sugar and cornstarch. Stir in whipping cream and ¼ cup butter. Microwave on HIGH for 1½ to 2 minutes or until mixture boils, stirring once during cooking. Microwave on HIGH for 1 minute.

Stir in vanilla. Cut pudding into wedges. Serve warm sauce over warm pudding.
Yield: 6 servings; 1 cup sauce.

HIGH ALTITUDE:
Above 3500 Feet: No change.

NUTRITION PER SERVING:
Calories 490; Protein 4g; Carbohydrate 62g; Fat 27g; Sodium 450mg.

STEAMED PLUM PUDDING

This moist pudding has been England's traditional Christmas dessert for nearly 300 years.

1 **cup all purpose flour**
3 **tablespoons brown sugar**
1 **teaspoon cinnamon**
½ **teaspoon baking powder**
½ **teaspoon allspice**
½ **teaspoon cloves**
¼ **teaspoon baking soda**
½ **cup milk**
3 **tablespoons oil**
2 **tablespoons molasses**
1 **egg**
1 **cup candied fruit**
½ **cup raisins**
½ **cup chopped nuts**

Using solid shortening, generously grease 1-quart mold or casserole. In medium bowl, combine all ingredients except fruit, raisins and nuts. Mix until dry ingredients are moistened. Fold in fruit, raisins and nuts. Spoon into greased mold. Cover with lid or foil. Place on wire rack in large steamer or Dutch oven. Pour boiling water, 3 to 4 inches deep, into steamer; cover. Keep water boiling gently over low heat. If necessary, add water to maintain steam.

Steam 1½ to 2 hours or until pudding springs back when touched lightly in center. Cut into slices. If desired, serve hot with **Rum Hard Sauce** p. 245.
Yield: 6 to 8 servings.

HIGH ALTITUDE:
Above 3500 Feet: No change.

NUTRITION PER SERVING:
Calories 290; Protein 4g; Carbohydrate 47g; Fat 11g; Sodium 105mg.

Cranberry Pudding with Butter Sauce

Hot Fudge Pudding Cake

Bring back memories of grandma's kitchen with this homey dessert. It's cake and sauce all in one. Serve it with whipped cream or ice cream.

- 1¼ **cups all purpose flour**
- ¾ **cup sugar**
- 2 **tablespoons unsweetened cocoa**
- 1½ **teaspoons baking powder**
- ½ **teaspoon salt**
- ½ **cup milk**
- 2 **tablespoons margarine or butter, melted**
- 1 **teaspoon vanilla**
- 1 **cup sugar**
- 2 **tablespoons unsweetened cocoa**
  Dash salt
- 1⅓ **cups water, heated to 120 to 130°F.**

Heat oven to 350°F. In small bowl, combine flour, ¾ cup sugar, 2 tablespoons cocoa, baking powder and ½ teaspoon salt. Stir in milk, margarine and vanilla; blend well. Spread batter in ungreased 9-inch round or square pan.

In small bowl, combine 1 cup sugar, 2 tablespoons cocoa and dash salt; mix well. Sprinkle evenly over cake batter. Pour hot water over sugar mixture. Bake at 350°F. for 35 to 45 minutes or until center is set and firm to the touch. Serve warm.
Yield: 8 servings.

HIGH ALTITUDE:
Above 3500 Feet: No change.

NUTRITION PER SERVING:
Calories 280; Protein 3g; Carbohydrate 60g; Fat 4g; Sodium 270mg.

Lemon Pudding Cake

Magically, as this dessert bakes, a lemony cake rises to the top, leaving a delicious sauce on the bottom. This reduced-calorie version uses skim milk, but whole milk can be substituted.

- 3 **eggs, separated**
- ½ **cup skim or lowfat milk**
- ¼ **cup lemon juice**
- 1 **teaspoon grated lemon peel**
- ½ **cup sugar**
- ⅓ **cup all purpose flour**
- ⅛ **teaspoon salt**

Heat oven to 350°F. Grease 1-quart casserole. In small bowl, beat egg yolks; stir in milk, lemon juice and lemon peel. Add sugar, flour and salt; beat until smooth. In another small bowl, beat egg whites until stiff peaks form. Gently fold yolk mixture into beaten egg whites. DO NOT OVER-BLEND. Pour into greased casserole. Place casserole in 13x9-inch pan. Pour boiling water into pan around casserole to a depth of 1 inch.

Bake at 350°F. for 25 to 35 minutes or until light golden brown. Serve warm or cool.
Yield: 6 (½-cup) servings.

NUTRITION PER SERVING:
Calories 140; Protein 5g; Carbohydrate 24g; Fat 3g; Sodium 90mg.

Sour Cream Raisin Pudding Cake

Serve this pudding cake warm from the oven with a cup of flavored coffee.

CAKE
- 1 **cup all purpose flour**
- ⅔ **cup sugar**
- 2 **teaspoons baking powder**
- ¼ **teaspoon salt**
- ¾ **cup dairy sour cream**
- 2 **tablespoons oil**
- 1 **cup raisins**
- ½ **cup chopped nuts**
- ¾ **cup firmly packed brown sugar**
- 1½ **cups water, heated to 120 to 130°F.**

TOPPING
- ½ **cup whipping cream, whipped**
- ½ **cup dairy sour cream**

Heat oven to 350°F. In large bowl, combine flour, sugar, baking powder, salt, ¾ cup sour cream and oil; mix well. Stir in raisins and nuts. Spread evenly in ungreased 8 or 9-inch square pan. In small bowl, combine brown sugar and hot water; pour over batter.

Bake at 350°F. for 50 to 60 minutes or until cake is golden brown and toothpick inserted in cake comes out clean. In small bowl, fold together whipped cream and ½ cup sour cream; refrigerate. Serve pudding cake warm topped with cream topping. Store in refrigerator.
Yield: 9 servings.

Above 3500 Feet: Bake at 350°F. for 45 to
55 minutes.

NUTRITION PER SERVING:
Calories 410; Protein 4g; Carbohydrate 59g; Fat 19g;
Sodium 150mg.

BANANA BREAD PUDDING WITH RUM HARD SAUCE

*In England, hard sauce is known as brandy
butter. In this recipe, a delicious rum-flavored
hard sauce tops a memorable, sweetly spiced
pudding.*

BREAD PUDDING
  4 **cups raisin bread cubes**
  3 **medium, firm ripe bananas, sliced**
  ½ **cup coconut**
  ½ **cup firmly packed brown sugar**
  1 **teaspoon cinnamon**
  ⅛ **teaspoon nutmeg**
  ½ **teaspoon vanilla**
  1¾ **cups milk**
  2 **eggs, beaten**

RUM HARD SAUCE
  1 **cup powdered sugar**
  ¼ **cup butter or margarine, softened**
  1 **tablespoon rum or ½ to 1 teaspoon rum
       extract**
  1½ **teaspoons hot water**

Heat oven to 350°F. Grease 10x6-inch (1½-quart)
baking dish. Place 2 cups bread cubes in greased
dish; top with banana slices, coconut and remaining bread cubes. In medium bowl, combine brown
sugar, cinnamon, nutmeg, vanilla, milk and eggs;
blend well. Pour over bread cubes. With back of
spoon, press bread cubes down slightly. Let stand
10 minutes. Bake at 350°F. for 45 to 50 minutes or
until center is set.

In small bowl, combine all hard sauce ingredients.
Beat at high speed until well blended. Cover; refrigerate until serving time. Serve sauce with warm
pudding. Store any remaining bread pudding and
sauce in refrigerator.

Yield: 8 to 10 servings; ¾ cup sauce.

NUTRITION PER SERVING:
Calories 410; Protein 5g; Carbohydrate 79g; Fat 8g;
Sodium 95mg.

APPLE BREAD PUDDING WITH VANILLA SAUCE

*Enjoy fall's abundance of apples in this
wonderful down-home dessert.*

BREAD PUDDING
  4 **cups soft whole wheat or white bread cubes**
  2 **cups thinly sliced peeled apples**
  ¼ **cup raisins**
  1 **cup firmly packed brown sugar**
  1¾ **cups milk**
  ¼ **cup margarine or butter**
  1 **teaspoon cinnamon**
  ½ **teaspoon vanilla**
  2 **eggs, beaten**

VANILLA SAUCE
  ½ **cup sugar**
  ½ **cup firmly packed brown sugar**
  ½ **cup whipping cream**
  ½ **cup margarine or butter**
  1 **teaspoon vanilla**

Heat oven to 350°F. Grease 10x6-inch (1½-quart)
baking dish. In large bowl, combine bread, apples
and raisins. In small saucepan, combine 1 cup
brown sugar, milk and ¼ cup margarine. Cook
over medium heat until margarine is melted; pour
over bread mixture in bowl. Let stand 10 minutes.
Stir in cinnamon, ½ teaspoon vanilla and eggs.
Pour into greased baking dish.

Bake at 350°F. for 40 to 50 minutes or until center
is set and apples are tender.

In small saucepan, combine sugar, ½ cup brown
sugar, whipping cream and ½ cup margarine. Cook
over medium heat until mixture boils, stirring
occasionally. Stir in vanilla. Serve warm sauce over
pudding. Store any remaining bread pudding and
sauce in refrigerator.

Yield: 8 servings; 1½ cups sauce.

NUTRITION PER SERVING:
Calories 550; Protein 6g; Carbohydrate 74g; Fat 26g;
Sodium 380mg.

Chocolate Bread Pudding with Cherry Raspberry Sauce

This spectacular souffle-like bread pudding is a chocolate lover's fantasy.

BREAD PUDDING
- 1 (6-oz.) pkg. (1 cup) semi-sweet chocolate chips
- 1 cup whipping cream
- ⅔ cup firmly packed brown sugar
- 5 eggs, separated
- ½ cup margarine or butter, cut into pieces
- 1 teaspoon vanilla
- 4 cups soft bread cubes

CHERRY RASPBERRY SAUCE
- 2 tablespoons sugar
- 4 teaspoons cornstarch
- 1 (16-oz.) can pitted dark sweet cherries, drained, reserving liquid
- 1 (10-oz.) pkg. frozen raspberries in syrup, thawed, drained, reserving liquid

Heat oven to 350°F. Grease 12x8-inch (2-quart) baking dish. In large saucepan, combine chocolate chips and whipping cream. Heat over medium-low heat until chips are melted, stirring occasionally. Stir in ⅓ cup of the brown sugar. Add egg yolks 1 at a time, blending well after each addition. Continue cooking until slightly thickened, stirring constantly. Add margarine and vanilla; stir until smooth. Remove from heat; stir in bread cubes.

In large bowl, beat egg whites at medium speed until soft peaks form. Gradually add remaining ⅓ cup brown sugar, beating at high speed until stiff peaks form. Fold egg white mixture into chocolate mixture. Pour into greased baking dish. Place baking dish in 13x9-inch or larger pan. Pour boiling water into pan around baking dish to a depth of 1 inch. Bake at 350°F. for 35 to 40 minutes or until center is set.

In medium saucepan, combine sugar and cornstarch. Gradually stir in reserved liquids from fruits. Cook over medium-high heat until mixture boils and thickens, stirring constantly. Cool slightly; stir in fruit. Serve over warm bread pudding. Store any remaining bread pudding and sauce in refrigerator.

Yield: 10 to 12 servings; 1⅓ cups sauce.

NUTRITION PER SERVING:
Calories 390; Protein 6g; Carbohydrate 45g; Fat 22g; Sodium 220mg.

Old-Fashioned Bread Pudding with Brandy Hard Sauce

Bread pudding, a simple, thrifty pudding of the past, has been rediscovered today as a delicious custard embellished with raisins and nuts and served with hard sauce.

BREAD PUDDING
- 2½ cups white and whole wheat bread cubes
- 1¼ cups warm milk
- ¼ cup sugar
- ½ teaspoon cinnamon
- ½ teaspoon nutmeg
- ½ teaspoon vanilla
- 2 eggs, beaten
- ½ cup raisins
- ¼ cup chopped nuts, if desired

BRANDY HARD SAUCE
- 1 cup powdered sugar
- ¼ cup butter or margarine, softened
- 2 teaspoons hot water
- 1 tablespoon brandy or bourbon or 1 teaspoon brandy extract

Heat oven to 350°F. Grease 1-quart casserole. In greased casserole, combine bread cubes and milk. In medium bowl, combine sugar, cinnamon, nutmeg, vanilla and eggs; mix well. Stir in raisins and nuts. Add egg mixture to bread cube mixture; mix well. Bake at 350°F. for 45 to 50 minutes or until pudding is set.

In small bowl, combine all hard sauce ingredients. Beat at high speed until well blended. Cover; refrigerate until serving time. Serve sauce with warm pudding. Store any remaining bread pudding and sauce in refrigerator.

Yield: 4 to 5 servings; ¾ cup sauce.

NUTRITION PER SERVING:
Calories 370; Protein 6g; Carbohydrate 55g; Fat 14g; Sodium 250mg.

Old-Fashioned Bread Pudding with Brandy Hard Sauce

LIGHT AND EASY BAKED ALASKA

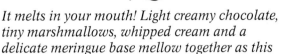

This impressive looking dessert is low in fat and calories.

1½ **pints (3 cups) any flavor frozen yogurt, softened**
1 **pint (2 cups) vanilla frozen yogurt, softened**
1 **loaf angel food cake (approximately 8x4 inches)**
MERINGUE
3 **egg whites**
¼ **teaspoon cream of tartar**
¼ **teaspoon salt**
⅔ **cup sugar**

Line 1½-quart freezer-safe bowl with foil; place in freezer until well chilled. Using back of spoon, press 1½ pints flavored yogurt in bottom and up sides of foil-lined, chilled bowl. Freeze 30 minutes. Spoon vanilla yogurt into center; press down firmly and level off. Freeze 30 minutes.

Slice cake in half horizontally to form 2 layers. Place both cake layers side by side to cover frozen yogurt in bowl. With sharp knife, trim cake around edge of bowl, making sure cake fits snugly against side of bowl. Cover; freeze several hours or overnight.

Heat oven to 450°F. Invert cake and yogurt onto ungreased cookie sheet. Carefully remove foil. Return cake and yogurt to freezer. In small bowl, beat egg whites, cream of tartar and salt until foamy. Gradually add sugar, beating continuously at high speed until sugar is dissolved and stiff peaks form. Frost yogurt and cake with meringue mixture, covering completely and sealing to cookie sheet. Immediately bake at 450°F. for 4 minutes or until lightly browned. Cut into slices; serve immediately.
Yield: 12 servings.

NUTRITION PER SERVING:
Calories 180; Protein 4g; Carbohydrate 34g; Fat 3g; Sodium 160mg.

CHOCOLATE MERINGUE DESSERT

It melts in your mouth! Light creamy chocolate, tiny marshmallows, whipped cream and a delicate meringue base mellow together as this dessert chills.

MERINGUE
6 **egg whites**
½ **teaspoon cream of tartar**
¼ **teaspoon salt**
1½ **cups sugar**

FILLING
2 **(3-oz.) pkg. cream cheese, softened**
⅔ **cup chocolate syrup**
1 **pint (2 cups) whipping cream**
1 **cup miniature marshmallows**
½ **cup sliced almonds**
⅓ **cup chocolate syrup**

Heat oven to 450°F. Grease 13x9-inch pan. In large bowl, beat egg whites, cream of tartar and salt at medium speed until soft peaks form. Gradually add sugar 2 tablespoons at a time, beating at high speed until stiff glossy peaks form and sugar is almost dissolved, about 10 minutes. Spread in greased pan. Place in 450°F. oven; turn oven off. Leave in closed oven several hours or overnight. (Inside of meringue will still be soft.)

In small bowl, beat cream cheese and ⅔ cup chocolate syrup until smooth. In large bowl, beat whipping cream until stiff peaks form. Fold chocolate mixture and marshmallows into whipped cream. Spread over meringue. Sprinkle with almonds. Refrigerate at least 4 hours. To serve, cut into squares; place on plates. Drizzle each serving with about 1 teaspoon of chocolate syrup. Store in refrigerator.
Yield: 16 servings.

NUTRITION PER SERVING:
Calories 290; Protein 4g; Carbohydrate 34g; Fat 16g; Sodium 115mg.

SUMMER SNOWBALLS

~

Any combination of jam and ice cream could be used for this spectacular dessert. Marshmallow creme makes the meringue easy to prepare and foolproof.

- 2 tablespoons orange marmalade
- 1 teaspoon orange juice
- 4 individual sponge cake cups
- 1 pint (2 cups) orange sherbet
- 3 egg whites
- 1 (7-oz.) jar (1½ cups) marshmallow creme

In small bowl, combine marmalade and orange juice. Place sponge cake cups 3 inches apart on cookie sheet. Brush with marmalade mixture. Place 1 scoop sherbet on each sponge cake cup. Freeze until firm.

In large bowl, beat egg whites until soft peaks form. Gradually add marshmallow creme, beating until stiff peaks form. Spread meringue evenly over sherbet and sponge cake cups, covering completely. Freeze.

To serve, heat oven to 500°F. Remove snowballs from freezer; bake at 500°F. for 3 to 4 minutes or until lightly browned. Serve immediately.

Yield: 4 servings.

NUTRITION PER SERVING:
Calories 450; Protein 7g; Carbohydrate 98g; Fat 4g; Sodium 180mg.

COOK'S NOTE

~

CUTTING DESSERTS

Desserts featuring soft creamy fillings between layers can be easily cut with an electric knife. No pressure is required when cutting with an electric knife, so the filling is not pressed out between the layers.

CHOCOLATE TOFFEE CLOUD

~

When preparing meringue, add the sugar about a tablespoon at a time when beating egg whites.

MERINGUES
- 6 egg whites
- ½ teaspoon cream of tartar
  Dash salt
- 2 cups sugar

FILLING AND TOPPING
- 1 pint (2 cups) whipping cream
- ½ cup powdered sugar
- ⅓ cup unsweetened cocoa
- ½ cup coarsely crushed chocolate-covered toffee candy bars, reserving 3 tablespoons for garnish

Heat oven to 275°F. Line 2 cookie sheets with parchment or brown paper. In large bowl, beat egg whites, cream of tartar and salt at medium speed until soft peaks form. Gradually add sugar 1 tablespoon at a time, beating at high speed until stiff glossy peaks form and sugar is almost dissolved. Spread half of meringue into an 8-inch circle on paper-lined cookie sheet; repeat with remaining mixture on other cookie sheet.

Bake at 275°F. for 50 to 60 minutes or until crisp and dry. (Meringue may crack slightly.) Turn oven off; keep door closed for 2 hours. Remove meringues from oven; cool completely. Carefully remove meringues from paper.

In medium bowl, combine whipping cream, powdered sugar and cocoa. Beat at high speed until stiff peaks form. Fold in crushed candy. Place 1 meringue on serving plate. Spread with half of filling. Repeat layers. Sprinkle with reserved crushed candy. Garnish with **Chocolate Curls** p. 210, if desired. Refrigerate several hours before serving. Store in refrigerator.

Yield: 12 to 16 servings.

NUTRITION PER SERVING:
Calories 340; Protein 3g; Carbohydrate 38g; Fat 21g; Sodium 90mg.

STEP-BY-STEP FEATURE ∽
How to Make Meringue Shells (Tartlets)

STEP 1. Begin with egg whites that contain no specks of yolk. Beat until soft peaks form. Soft peaks will curl down when the beaters are lifted.

STEP 2. Gradually add sugar, 1 tablespoon at a time, beating until the sugar is almost dissolved. Continue beating until stiff peaks form.

STEP 3. Line a cookie sheet with parchment paper or foil. Pipe meringue onto paper-lined cookie sheet in spirals.

LEMON STRAWBERRY PIE TORTE

A perfect dessert for a summer luncheon.

CRUST
- ⅔ cup all purpose flour
- 3 tablespoons finely chopped nuts
- 2 tablespoons brown sugar
- ⅓ cup margarine or butter, softened

FILLING
- 1 (8-oz.) pkg. cream cheese, softened
- 1⅓ cups milk
- 1 (3.75-oz.) pkg. instant lemon pudding and pie filling mix
- 3 to 4 cups halved or whole strawberries, reserving 1 large whole berry for garnish

TOPPING
- 1 (3-oz.) pkg. strawberry flavor gelatin
- ¾ cup boiling water
- ¾ cup cold water

Heat oven to 350°F. In medium bowl, combine flour, nuts and brown sugar. Using pastry blender or fork, cut in margarine until crumbly. Press in bottom of ungreased 9 or 10-inch springform pan. Bake at 350°F. for 15 to 22 minutes or until light golden brown. Cool completely.

In small bowl, beat cream cheese at medium speed until smooth and creamy. Gradually blend in milk until smooth. Add pudding mix; beat at low speed 1 minute or until thickened. Pour over cooled, baked crust. Arrange strawberry halves, cut side up and pointing outward, on top of filling in circular pattern, starting at outside edge of pie. (Whole berries can be set pointed end up in circular pattern, starting at outside edge of pie.) Place reserved strawberry in center of pie. Refrigerate pie while preparing topping.

In small bowl, dissolve gelatin in boiling water. Stir in cold water. Refrigerate until mixture is cooled, about 15 minutes. Slowly pour gelatin mixture over strawberries. (Berries may not be completely covered.) Refrigerate at least 3 hours or until set.

Just before serving, run knife, dipped in hot water, around edge of pan to loosen. Carefully remove sides of pan.

Yield: 10 servings.

NUTRITION PER SERVING:
Calories 310; Protein 6g; Carbohydrate 33g; Fat 17g; Sodium 220mg.

STREAMLINED HUNGARIAN TORTE

This pastry torte is a Pillsbury BAKE-OFF® Contest classic. Feathery-light meringue tops flaky pastry layers filled with nuts and apricot preserves. It is not as time-consuming as you might think.

- 1 pkg. active dry yeast
- ¼ cup warm water
- 1⅓ cups margarine or butter
- 3½ cups all purpose flour
- ½ cup dairy sour cream
- 4 eggs, separated
- 1¾ cups chopped walnuts
- ¾ cup sugar
- 1 teaspoon cinnamon
- 1 (10-oz.) jar (¾ cup) apricot preserves*
- ½ cup sugar

Heat oven to 350°F. Grease 13x9-inch pan. In small bowl, dissolve yeast in warm water (105 to 115°F.). In large bowl, using pastry blender or fork cut margarine into flour until mixture resembles coarse crumbs. Stir in sour cream, egg yolks and dissolved yeast just until soft dough forms.

Shape dough into a ball; divide into 3 equal parts. On well floured surface, roll each part to 13x9-inch rectangle. Place 1 rectangle in bottom of greased pan. Reserve ¼ cup of the walnuts. Combine remaining walnuts, ¾ cup sugar and cinnamon; sprinkle over dough in pan. Top with second dough rectangle; spread evenly with preserves. Top with remaining dough rectangle. Bake at 350°F. for 40 to 50 minutes or until light golden brown.

In large bowl, beat egg whites until foamy. Gradually add ½ cup sugar, 1 tablespoon at a time, beating until stiff peaks form, about 3 minutes. Cover baked pastry with egg white mixture; sprinkle with reserved walnuts. Bake an additional 10 to 15 minutes or until golden brown. Cool.

Yield: 16 servings.

TIP:
* Other flavors of preserves can be substituted.

HIGH ALTITUDE:
Above 3500 Feet: No change.

NUTRITION PER SERVING:
Calories 460; Protein 7g; Carbohydrate 50g; Fat 26g; Sodium 200mg.

PIES AND
PASTRIES

❦

Pie. It's an all-time favorite that even defines the spirit of our country: "As American as apple pie." Whether topped with streusel or baked in a deep dish, then crowned with a scoop of ice cream or dollop of whipped cream, it's little wonder Americans love their pie.

In this chapter, choose from glorious fruit pies, sumptuous cream pies or light meringues. Or indulge in the art of making pastries — cream-filled puffs, fruit tarts, strudels, puff pastry confections and more.

Pictured: **Eclairs** p. 333, **Lemon Meringue Pie** p. 314, **Winter Fruit Phyllo Tarts** p. 325

PIES AND PASTRIES

Flaky-crusted pies have always been prized by pie lovers and
pie bakers, not just because they're the perfect complement to a steaming
cup of coffee, but because they're a yardstick by which a pie baker's skill is measured.
In this chapter, you'll learn how to make flaky pie crust,
as well as pastries and delectable fillings.

KINDS OF PIES AND PASTRIES

*Although the fillings are countless, there are only
a few main types of pies and pastries:*

FRUIT PIES

These are made with 1 or 2 crusts; the top crust
can be plain or decorative, such as a lattice.
Use fresh, frozen, canned or dried fruit for
fillings or use canned pie filling when time's
short. (Recipes begin on p. 271.)

CUSTARD PIES

These are 1-crust pies that have a filling made
with milk and egg which bakes with the pastry.
This type includes pecan and pumpkin pies.
(Recipes begin on p. 288.)

CREAM PIES

This category includes 1-crust (pastry or
crumb) pies filled with custard or pudding and
crowned with meringue or whipped topping.
The crust is baked first and then the filling and
toppings are added. (Recipes begin on p. 300.)

MERINGUE PIES

Meringue pies are 1-crust custard or cream pies
topped with a soft meringue. (Recipes begin on
p. 314.)

TARTS

These are 1-crust or crumb-crust shallow or
miniature pies. They may be fruit, custard or
cream-filled and are crowned with toppings

such as whipped cream, streusel or meringue.
(Recipes begin on p. 317.)

PASTRIES

This category includes a wide range of desserts
made with different kinds of pastry, such as
buttery dough, flaky phyllo (FEE-low) and airy
puff pastry. The pastries can be filled with fruit
and/or nuts, custard or whipped cream. (Recipes begin on p. 333.)

CREAM PUFFS AND ECLAIRS

These egg-rich crisp, hollow pastries are filled
with whipped cream, pudding or custard.
(Recipes are on p. 333.)

SECRETS FOR SUCCESSFUL PIES AND PASTRIES

*Pies and pastries require a light touch and a bit of
patience, but the results are well worth the effort!
Here are some secrets for making your pies and
pastries a success:*

SECRETS FOR ANY PIES

**Use only the ingredients called for in the
recipe.** Do not substitute oil, butter or margarine when shortening is called for. Shortening
refers to solid vegetable shortening. In the
past, lard was commonly used for pie crust.
Lard makes a tender, flaky crust, has a
distinctive flavor and can be substituted for
the shortening.

Measure and blend ingredients carefully. Careful measurement and thorough blending will yield the highest quality pastries and fillings.

Stir flour and salt together thoroughly. Then add the shortening and liquid.

Use a pastry blender or fork to cut in the shortening. Using a pastry blender or fork will distribute the shortening evenly to give the pastry its flaky texture.

Use ice-cold water. Cold water contributes to a flaky crust. Add an ice cube to the water, removing it before adding the water to the flour/shortening mixture.

Avoid overmixing. Overmixing can toughen the pastry. Use a light touch.

Refrigerate the dough before rolling. For easier handling, the dough can be refrigerated for 30 minutes before rolling it out.

Flour the surface for rolling. A floured surface is essential for rolling out dough without sticking, but the less flour used, the flakier the pastry will be. For best results, roll dough on a lightly floured pastry cloth using a cloth-covered rolling pin. Rub the flour into the pastry cloth and cloth-covered rolling pin. You can anchor the corners of the cloth with tape to a flat surface. OR, chilled dough can be placed between 2 large sheets of waxed paper or plastic wrap before rolling it out.

Choose dull-finished aluminum or glass pie pans. Shiny pie pans can give your pie a soggy bottom. Nine-inch pie pans are the standard size used in the recipes in this chapter.

Do not grease the pie pan. Because of the high proportion of fat in pastry dough, there is no need to grease the pan before baking, unless it is specified in the recipe.

When placing the pastry in the pan:
- Fold the pastry in half or quarters and place it in the pie pan. Unfold it gently.

- Firmly press the dough against the sides and bottom without stretching it. If the dough is stretched, the crust will shrink as it bakes.

- Mend any cracks by lightly wetting your fingers and pressing the edges together.

- With a kitchen shears or knife, trim uneven edges of dough that may be hanging over the pan, then flute or decorate the edges.

- For 2-crust pies, trim the bottom pastry even with the pan edge. Add filling and cover with top pastry, allowing a 1-inch overlap of top pastry around the edge. Press edges well to seal. Form a standing rim of pastry and flute. For other finishing touches see p. 266.

Prick an unfilled pastry shell before baking. If the pastry shell is to be baked before it's filled, prick the bottom and sides with a fork to keep it from puffing during baking. If it does begin to puff, reprick the crust. Don't prick the bottom of an unbaked pastry before you pour in the filling, or the filling will seep under the pastry.

If you're making a 2-crust pie, try:
- Brush the top pastry with a slightly beaten egg white to make it shiny. If desired, sprinkle it with sugar.

- Brush the top pastry with milk, cream, or a mixture of 1 egg yolk and 1 tablespoon water to make the crust golden brown. If desired, sprinkle it with sugar.

Cut vents in the top crust of a 2-crust pie. Vents allow the steam that forms during baking to escape and minimize bubbling over of the filling. They can be cut before or after the pastry is placed over the filling, and can be plain or fancy.

If the crust is baking unevenly:
- If the edges are browning before the center is done, cover those edges with 2-inch-wide strips of foil. Gently fold the strips over the edges.

- If the whole top is getting too brown, loosely drape a sheet of foil over the pie.

- For more information, see the Cook's Note on p. 281 to learn how to make a special foil cover.

If you're making a crumb crust (see chart p. 269):
- Finely crush the crumbs using a food processor, or place broken cookies or crackers in a plastic bag and crush them with a rolling pin.

- Press the crumbs evenly over the bottom and up the sides of the pan, then press another pie pan of the same size firmly into the crust to make it smooth.

- If the crust is baked, it will release from the pan easily when the pie is cut. If the crust has been chilled to set it, press a warm towel around the outside of the pan to soften the margarine and make cutting and serving easier.

If time is extra short . . . In this cookbook, all pie recipes call for homemade crusts, but if time is short, you can use convenience products such as refrigerated rolled-out pie crusts, sticks of pie crust dough, frozen unbaked pie crusts or purchased crumb crusts.

If you have some extra time . . . Make 2 pies at the same time. Freeze the extra pie for a future use.

SECRETS FOR MERINGUE PIES

Place soft meringue over a hot filling. When topping a pie, spread the meringue over the pie until it touches the crust. This will create a tight seal and prevent shrinkage during baking.

Cool the pie completely after baking and before refrigerating it.

Dip a knife in water before making each cut when slicing the finished pie.

SECRETS FOR PASTRIES

Two popular types of pastry dough are phyllo and puff pastry. Here are tips for using them successfully:

Phyllo (filo)
- Phyllo dough is a delicate, thinly rolled wheat dough used as a wrapper for a variety of fillings. It's used frequently in Greek and Middle Eastern pastries. The paper-thin dough can be found in the freezer section of the supermarket. A 1-pound box usually contains about 22 pastry sheets, each about 18x14 inches.

- Thaw phyllo dough in the refrigerator for 8 to 12 hours before using it.

- Have all other ingredients ready before opening the phyllo package. Cover the sheets with plastic wrap to prevent them from drying out.

- Brush the phyllo sheets with either margarine or butter to produce the characteristic flakiness and to help prevent sticking. See our Step-By-Step Feature on p. 336.

Puff pastry
- Elegant and airy, puff pastry is used for special desserts such as palmiers. Because the technique involved with making puff pastry requires some skill and time, you may choose to purchase already-made puff pastry. You'll find it in the freezer section of your supermarket. See our Cook's Note on Making Puff Pastry on p. 334.

- Purchase the freshest pastry dough.

- Store pastry in the freezer for several months or in the refrigerator for 1 week.

- Thaw puff pastry in the refrigerator so that it remains cold.

- Keep the pastry cold during preparation of the recipe. The colder the pastry, the better it will rise, puff and separate into layers.

- Lightly flour the rolling pin and rolling surface.

- After cutting and shaping, refrigerate the dough to chill it before baking.

- Heat the oven for 10 to 15 minutes before baking.

SECRETS FOR CREAM PUFFS

Heat the oven 10 to 15 minutes before baking. The oven must be hot so that the pastry puffs up immediately. Puffs will double in size.

Bake until properly done. Cream puffs that have been baked to the proper doneness (golden brown and firm to the touch) will retain their shape and won't collapse.

Cut a slit in the side of each puff after baking. The slit lets the steam escape, allowing the inside of the puff to dry so that it won't become soggy.

Fill puffs as close to serving time as possible. This will prevent the puffs from becoming soggy.

HOW TO TELL WHEN PIES AND PASTRIES ARE DONE

As with any baked good, knowing when a pie or pastry is done is key to the success of your baking experience.

A pie crust is done when . . . it is evenly light golden brown.

Fruit pies are done when . . . the crust is golden brown and the filling is bubbly.

Custard pies are done when . . . a knife inserted in the center comes out clean.

Meringue pies are done when . . . the meringue has a golden glow and the tips of the meringue are light golden brown.

Puffs and eclairs are done when . . . they are golden brown and firm to the touch.

KEEPING PIES AND PASTRIES FRESH AND FLAVORFUL

Pies and pastries can be refrigerated or frozen to keep them at their just-baked best. See Freezing Guidelines p. 25.

Refrigerate pies containing dairy products or eggs. Pies made with eggs, milk, dairy sour cream, whipped cream, whipped topping, yogurt or cream cheese should be refrigerated as soon as possible after they've been prepared. Custard and cream pies, or pies with meringue topping do not freeze well.

Store fruit pies at room temperature, in the refrigerator or freezer. A fruit pie can be stored at room temperature for up to 2 days. If the room is very warm, the pie should be refrigerated. Fruit pies can be frozen baked or unbaked.

Refrigerate or freeze pumpkin and pecan pies. Pumpkin and pecan pies keep well in the refrigerator, or can be frozen after they are baked.

Freeze pie dough or unbaked shells. Keeping pie dough or unbaked pie shells in the freezer will give you a jump on pie baking when time is short. To freeze dough, form it into a flattened ball and wrap it tightly in moisture- and vapor-proof wrap. Freeze shells in the pan (a disposable foil pie pan works well for freezing). If freezing more than 1 shell, stack them and then wrap tightly.

Store baked puff pastries in the freezer. They don't hold up well in the refrigerator, so wrap puff pastries tightly in moisture- and vapor-proof wrap and freeze.

Store unfilled puffs and eclairs in an airtight, moisture-proof container. Puffs and eclairs should be kept in a container with a tight-fitting lid and stored in the refrigerator. Limit storage time to overnight. For longer storage, place unfilled puffs in an airtight container and freeze for up to 3 months.

NUTRITION IN THIS CHAPTER

Nutrition per serving means calculation was done on 1 serving, 1 cream puff/pastry, 1 individual tart or 1 dumpling.

PASTRY FOR PIES AND TARTS

ONE-CRUST PIE
- 1 cup all purpose flour
- ½ teaspoon salt
- ⅓ cup shortening
- 2 to 4 tablespoons ice water

In medium bowl, combine flour and salt. Using pastry blender or fork, cut shortening into flour until mixture resembles coarse crumbs. Sprinkle flour mixture with water 1 tablespoon at a time, while tossing and mixing lightly with fork. Add water until dough is just moist enough to form a ball when lightly pressed together. (Too much water causes dough to become sticky and tough; too little water causes edges to crack and pastry to tear easily while rolling.)

Shape dough into ball. Flatten ball to ½-inch thickness, rounding and smoothing edges. On floured surface, roll lightly from center to edge into 11-inch circle. Fold pastry in half; place in 9-inch pie pan or 9 or 10-inch tart pan. Unfold; gently press in bottom and up sides of pan. Do not stretch.

If using pie pan, fold edge under to form a standing rim; flute edges. If using tart pan, trim pastry edges if necessary.

- **For Filled One-crust Pie**: Fill and bake as directed in recipe.
- **For Baked Pie Shell (Unfilled)**: Prick bottom and sides of pastry generously with fork. Bake at 450°F. for 9 to 12 minutes or until light golden brown; cool. Continue as directed in recipe.

Yield: One-Crust pastry.

TIPS:
See Variations in next column; use half of the ingredient amounts specified.

See p. 273 for food processor directions.

NUTRITION PER SERVING:
Calories 130; Protein 2g; Carbohydrate 12g; Fat 8g; Sodium 130mg.

TWO-CRUST PIE
- 2 cups all purpose flour
- 1 teaspoon salt
- ⅔ cup shortening
- 5 to 7 tablespoons ice water

In medium bowl, combine flour and salt. Using pastry blender or fork, cut shortening into flour until mixture resembles coarse crumbs. Sprinkle flour mixture with water 1 tablespoon at a time, while tossing and mixing lightly with fork. Add water until dough is just moist enough to form a ball when lightly pressed together. (Too much water causes dough to become sticky and tough; too little water causes edges to crack and pastry to tear easily while rolling.)

Shape dough into 2 balls. Flatten 1 ball to ½-inch thickness, rounding and smoothing edges. On lightly floured surface, roll from center to edge into 11-inch circle. Fold pastry in half; place in 9-inch pie pan, or 9 or 10-inch tart pan. Unfold; gently press in bottom and up sides of pan. Do not stretch.

Trim pastry even with pan edge. Roll out remaining pastry; set aside. Continue as directed in recipe.
Yield: Two-crust pastry.

TIP:
See p. 273 for food processor directions.

NUTRITION PER SERVING:
Calories 260; Protein 3g; Carbohydrate 24g; Fat 17g; Sodium 270mg.

VARIATIONS:

CHEESE PASTRY: Add ½ to 1 cup shredded Cheddar or American cheese to flour. Omit salt.

EXTRA FLAKY PASTRY: Add 2 teaspoons sugar with flour and 2 teaspoons vinegar with water.

WHOLE WHEAT PASTRY: Substitute up to 1 cup whole wheat flour for all purpose flour. Additional water may be necessary.

Press-in-the-Pan Oil Pastry

If you have avoided making pies because you do not like to roll out pastry, try this easy recipe.

1¾ **cups all purpose flour**
1 **teaspoon sugar**
1 **teaspoon salt**
½ **cup oil**
¼ **cup milk**

Heat oven to 425°F. In medium bowl, combine flour, sugar and salt. In small bowl, combine oil and milk; pour over flour mixture. Stir with fork until well mixed. Press in bottom and up sides of 9-inch pie pan; flute edge. If desired, crust can be rolled out between 2 sheets of waxed paper.

Prick bottom and sides of pastry generously with fork. Bake at 425°F. for 12 to 17 minutes or until light golden brown. Cool completely. Fill with desired filling.
Yield: 9-inch baked pie shell.

MICROWAVE DIRECTIONS:
Prepare pastry as directed above using 9-inch microwave-safe pie pan; flute edge. Prick bottom and sides of pastry generously with fork. Microwave on HIGH for 6 to 8 minutes, rotating pan ½ turn every 2 minutes. Crust is done when surface appears dry and flaky. Cool completely.

NUTRITION PER SERVING:
Calories 230; Protein 3g; Carbohydrate 22g; Fat 14g; Sodium 270mg.

Crumb Pie Crusts

Cookie crumb crusts are easy because there is no rolling of dough.
Fill these crusts with ice cream or creamy pudding fillings.
See the easy directions below.

Kind of Cookie	Amounts of Crumbs	Sugar	Margarine or Butter, Melted
Chocolate Wafer	1¼ cups (20 wafers)	¼ cup	¼ cup
Creme-Filled Choco/Vanilla Cookie	1½ cups (15 cookies)	none	¼ cup
Crisp Macaroon Cookie	1½ cups	none	¼ cup
Gingersnap Cookie	1½ cups	none	¼ cup
Graham Cracker*	1½ cups (24 squares)	¼ cup	⅓ cup
Granola (coarsely crushed)	1½ cups	none	¼ cup
Pretzel**	1¼ cups	¼ cup	½ cup
Vanilla Wafer	1½ cups (30 wafers)	none	¼ cup

Heat oven to 375°F. In medium bowl, combine crumbs, sugar and melted margarine; blend well. Press mixture firmly in bottom and up sides of 8- or 9-inch pie pan or in bottom of 9-inch springform pan. Bake at 375°F. for 8 to 10 minutes. Cool; fill with ice cream or pudding. Freeze or refrigerate.

TIPS:
* One-half teaspoon cinnamon can be added, if desired.
** For easier serving, butter pan before preparing crust.

STEP-BY-STEP FEATURE ∼
How to Make and Roll Out Pastry

STEP 1. After shortening is cut evenly into flour, add ice water 1 tablespoon at a time; toss lightly with a fork until dough forms.

STEP 2. With light strokes, roll pastry into an 11-inch circle. Fold dough in half or quarters; transfer to pan and unfold without stretching.

STEP 3. For two-crust pie, trim bottom pastry even with pan edge; add filling. Cover with top pastry, allowing 1-inch overlap; fold over. Seal and flute.

RASPBERRY CHERRY PIE

Adding another fruit to a can of prepared fruit pie filling makes a filling that is doubly delicious.

CRUST
>**Pastry for Two-Crust Pie p. 268**

FILLING
- 2 **cups fresh or frozen whole raspberries (do not thaw)**
- ¼ **to ½ cup sugar**
- 1 **tablespoon all purpose flour**
- 1 **(21-oz.) can cherry fruit pie filling**

Prepare pastry for Two-Crust Pie using 9-inch pie pan.

Heat oven to 400°F. In large bowl, combine all filling ingredients; stir gently. Spoon into pastry-lined pan. Top with remaining pastry; fold edge of top pastry under bottom pastry.* Press together to seal; flute edge. Cut slits or shapes in several places in top pastry.

Bake at 400°F. for 40 to 45 minutes or until crust is golden brown and filling is bubbly. (Place foil or cookie sheet on lowest oven rack during baking to guard against spills.)

Yield: 8 servings.

TIP:
* If desired, top with lattice crust p. 267.

NUTRITION PER SERVING:
Calories 440; Protein 3g; Carbohydrate 74g; Fat 15g; Sodium 200mg.

COOK'S NOTE

BAKING FRUIT PIES

When baking a fruit pie, a cookie sheet or baking pan can be placed under the pie to catch any juice that might otherwise over-flow onto the bottom of the oven.

Raspberry Cherry Pie

Perfect Apple Pie

Tart apples, such as Granny Smith and Pippin, make the best pie. This delicious apple pie, a Pillsbury favorite, has stood the test of time.

CRUST
  Pastry for Two-Crust Pie p. 268

FILLING*
  6 **cups thinly sliced peeled apples**
  ¾ **cup sugar**
  2 **tablespoons all purpose flour**
  ¾ **teaspoon cinnamon**
  ¼ **teaspoon salt**
  ⅛ **teaspoon nutmeg**
  1 **tablespoon lemon juice**

Prepare pastry for Two-Crust Pie using 9-inch pie pan.

Heat oven to 425°F. In large bowl, combine all filling ingredients; toss lightly. Spoon into pastry-lined pan. Top with remaining pastry; fold edge of top pastry under bottom pastry. Press together to seal; flute edge. Cut slits or shapes in several places in top pastry.

Bake at 425°F. for 40 to 45 minutes or until apples are tender and crust is golden brown.
Yield: 8 servings.

TIP:
* Two 21-oz. cans apple fruit pie filling can be substituted for filling.

NUTRITION PER SERVING:
Calories 370; Protein 2g; Carbohydrate 57g; Fat 15g; Sodium 270mg.

VARIATIONS:

CARAMEL PECAN APPLE PIE: Immediately after removing pie from oven, drizzle with ⅓ cup caramel ice cream topping. Sprinkle with 2 to 4 tablespoons chopped pecans.

CHEESE CRUST APPLE PIE: Substitute Cheese Pastry p. 268 for Pastry for Two-Crust Pie.

Apple Cobblestone Pie

Coconut adds texture to this pie topping.

CRUST
  Pastry for Filled One-Crust Pie p. 268

FILLING
  6 **to 10 medium apples, peeled, quartered**
  ½ **cup sugar**
  3 **tablespoons all purpose flour**
  ½ **teaspoon cinnamon**
  ¼ **teaspoon nutmeg**
  1 **tablespoon lemon juice**

TOPPING
  ⅔ **cup coconut**
  ¼ **cup all purpose flour**
  ¼ **cup sugar**
  2 **tablespoons margarine or butter, softened**

Prepare pastry for Filled One-Crust Pie using 9-inch pie pan.

Heat oven to 375°F. In large bowl, combine all filling ingredients until apples are well coated. Arrange apples, rounded side up, in pastry-lined pan, placing close together to resemble cobblestones. Sprinkle any remaining sugar mixture over apples.

In medium bowl, combine all topping ingredients until crumbly; sprinkle over apples. Bake at 375°F. for 40 to 50 minutes or until apples are tender.
Yield: 8 servings.

TIP:
Large apples can be substituted for medium apples; cut each into 6 pieces.

NUTRITION PER SERVING:
Calories 390; Protein 3g; Carbohydrate 62g; Fat 15g; Sodium 170mg.

Cook's Note

BAKING APPLES

Apple varieties good for baking and cooking have tart flavor and firm texture. For successful results, choose Jonathan, McIntosh, Winesap, Granny Smith, Rhode Island Greening, Rome Beauty or Northern Spy varieties. One pound of apples is equivalent to 3 medium apples and yields 3 cups of sliced apples.

WHOLE WHEAT APPLE MINCEMEAT PIE

Old-time mincemeat included ground meat in the mixture. Modern versions do not contain meat but are combinations of spicy chopped fruit. Prepared mincemeat is available in most large supermarkets.

CRUST
- 1 **cup all purpose flour**
- 1 **cup whole wheat flour**
- 2 **tablespoons sugar**
- ½ **teaspoon salt**
- ½ **cup shortening**
- ½ **cup cold water**

FILLING
- 4 **cups sliced peeled apples**
- 1⅓ **cups prepared mincemeat**
- ½ **cup sugar**
- 2 **tablespoons all purpose flour**
- ½ **teaspoon grated lemon peel**
- 1 **tablespoon lemon juice**

TOPPING
- 1 **egg white**
- 2 **tablespoons water**
- 1 **to 2 teaspoons sugar**

Heat oven to 375°F. In medium bowl, combine 1 cup all purpose flour, whole wheat flour, 2 tablespoons sugar and salt; blend well. Using pastry blender or fork, cut in shortening until mixture resembles coarse crumbs. Sprinkle flour mixture with cold water 1 tablespoon at a time, while tossing and mixing lightly with fork. Add water until dough is just moist enough to form a ball when lightly pressed together.

Shape dough into 2 balls. Flatten balls; smooth edges. Roll 1 ball lightly on floured surface from center to edge into 10 ½-inch circle. Fold dough in half; place in 9-inch pie pan. Unfold; fit evenly in pan. Do not stretch. Trim bottom pastry even with pan edge. Roll out remaining dough; set aside.

In large bowl, combine all filling ingredients; spoon into pastry-lined pan. Top with remaining pastry; fold edge of top pastry under bottom pastry. Flute edge. Cut slits in several places in top pastry. Combine egg white and 2 tablespoons water; brush over top. Sprinkle lightly with 1 to 2 teaspoons sugar.

Bake at 375°F. for 40 to 50 minutes or until apples are tender.
Yield: 8 servings.

NUTRITION PER SERVING:
Calories 430; Protein 5g; Carbohydrate 72g; Fat 14g; Sodium 140mg.

COOK'S NOTE

MIXING PASTRY WITH A FOOD PROCESSOR

If you have a food processor, you can try using it to mix pastry dough. It's easy and reliable and makes a high-quality crust. To mix pastry dough:

- Place the dry ingredients in the food processor and process for 20 seconds.

- Mix all liquid ingredients together. You can place the mixture in the refrigerator or add an ice cube to chill it thoroughly.

- Cut the margarine or butter into small pieces and distribute it evenly over the top of the dry ingredients. Or drop spoonfuls of shortening evenly over the dry ingredients. Process for 15 to 20 seconds or until the mixture looks like coarse crumbs.

- Take the liquid mixture out of the refrigerator or remove the ice cube. Add the liquid in a slow, steady stream to the flour/shortening mixture as the food processor is running. Process until the liquid is just distributed throughout the dough and the dough holds together. Pinch a marble-sized piece of dough between your thumb and index finger. If it doesn't hold together, add more liquid.

EASY APPLE PIE FOLDOVER

Smaller families will enjoy this easy version of apple pie.

FILLING
1½ cups (2 medium) thinly sliced peeled apples
¼ cup firmly packed brown sugar
1 tablespoon water
1 teaspoon lemon juice
1 tablespoon all purpose flour
1 tablespoon sugar
¼ teaspoon salt
½ teaspoon vanilla
1 tablespoon margarine or butter

CRUST
Pastry for One-Crust Pie p. 268
1 tablespoon water
1 egg

In medium saucepan, combine apples, brown sugar, 1 tablespoon water and lemon juice. Cook over medium heat until bubbly, stirring occasionally. Reduce heat to low; cover and cook 6 to 8 minutes or until apples are tender, stirring occasionally. In small bowl, combine flour, sugar and salt; stir into apple mixture. Cook until mixture thickens, stirring constantly. Remove from heat; stir in vanilla and margarine. Cool 15 to 20 minutes.

Meanwhile, prepare pastry for One-Crust Pie. Heat oven to 375°F. Place circle of pastry on ungreased cookie sheet. Spoon fruit mixture evenly on half of pastry to within ½ inch of edge. In small bowl, beat 1 tablespoon water and egg; brush over edges of pastry. Fold remaining side of pastry over fruit, turnover fashion; press edges to seal firmly.* Flute edge; cut small slits in top of pastry. Brush surface with egg mixture.

Bake at 375°F. for 25 to 35 minutes or until crust is golden brown.
Yield: 4 servings.

TIP:
* If desired, cut out decorative shapes from remaining side of pastry before folding pastry over fruit. Omit slits.

NUTRITION PER SERVING:
Calories 380; Protein 4g; Carbohydrate 48g; Fat 19g; Sodium 370mg.

TOPSY TURVY APPLE PIE

This fun-to-serve upside-down pie features traditional apple filling baked between two flaky pie crusts and topped with a rich pecan glaze.

GLAZE
¼ cup firmly packed brown sugar
1 tablespoon margarine or butter, melted
1 tablespoon corn syrup
¼ cup pecan halves

CRUST
Pastry for Two-Crust Pie p. 268

FILLING
⅔ cup sugar
2 tablespoons all purpose flour
½ teaspoon cinnamon
4 cups sliced peeled apples

GARNISH
Whipped cream or ice cream, if desired

In 9-inch pie pan, combine brown sugar, margarine and corn syrup; mix well. Spread mixture evenly in bottom of pan; arrange pecans over mixture. Prepare pastry for Two-Crust Pie. Place bottom pastry over mixture in pan, gently pressing pastry to fit pan.

Heat oven to 425°F. In small bowl, combine sugar, flour and cinnamon; mix well. Arrange half of apple slices in pastry-lined pan; sprinkle with half of sugar mixture. Repeat with remaining apple slices and sugar mixture. Top with remaining pastry; fold edge of top pastry under bottom pastry. Press together to seal and flute edge. Cut slits in several places in top pastry.

Bake at 425°F. for 8 minutes. Reduce oven temperature to 325°F.; bake an additional 25 to 35 minutes or until apples are tender and crust is golden brown. (Place pan on foil or cookie sheet during last 15 minutes of baking to guard against spills.)

Loosen edge of pie; carefully invert onto serving plate. Serve warm or cold with whipped cream or ice cream.
Yield: 8 servings.

NUTRITION PER SERVING:
Calories 440; Protein 2g; Carbohydrate 59g; Fat 22g; Sodium 350mg.

Topsy Turvy Apple Pie

CHERRY PIE

This versatile recipe gives you the option of using canned tart cherries, fresh tart cherries or cherry fruit pie filling.

CRUST
>   **Pastry for Two-Crust Pie p. 268**

FILLING*
>   2 **(16-oz.) cans pitted red tart cherries, drained****
> 1¼ **cups sugar**
> ¼ **cup all purpose flour**
>   2 **tablespoons margarine or butter**

Prepare pastry for Two-Crust Pie using 9-inch pie pan.

Heat oven to 425°F. In large bowl, combine cherries, sugar and flour; toss lightly to mix. Spoon into pastry-lined pan. Dot with margarine. Top with remaining pastry.*** Fold edge of top pastry under bottom pastry. Press together to seal; flute edge. Cut slits in several places in top pastry.

Bake at 425°F. for 35 to 45 minutes or until juice begins to bubble through slits in crust.
Yield: 8 servings.

TIPS:
* Two 21-oz. cans cherry fruit pie filling can be substituted for filling.
** Four cups pitted fresh red tart cherries can be substituted for canned cherries. If desired, sprinkle cherries with ¼ teaspoon almond extract before dotting with margarine.
*** If desired, top with lattice crust p. 267; brush with beaten egg white and sprinkle with sugar.

NUTRITION PER SERVING:
Calories 470; Protein 5g; Carbohydrate 68g; Fat 20g; Sodium 310mg.

FRESH RASPBERRY LATTICE PIE

*For an elegant presentation, garnish this lattice-topped pie with **Chocolate Leaves** p. 211.*

FILLING
> 4½ **cups raspberries***
> 1¼ **cups sugar**
>   5 **tablespoons cornstarch**
>   **Dash salt**
>   1 **tablespoon margarine or butter**

CRUST
>   **Pastry for Two-Crust Pie p. 268**

GARNISH
>   **Powdered sugar**
>   **Chocolate Leaves p. 211, if desired**

In medium saucepan, combine raspberries, sugar, cornstarch and salt. Cook over medium heat, stirring constantly until mixture boils and thickens, about 15 minutes. Refrigerate for 1 hour or until mixture comes to room temperature.

Prepare pastry for Two-Crust Pie using 9-inch pie pan. Heat oven to 425°F. Pour filling into pastry-lined pan; dot with margarine.

To make lattice top, cut remaining pastry into ½-inch-wide strips. Arrange strips in lattice design over filling as shown on p. 267. Trim edges and flute. With any remaining pastry, form small pea-sized balls and place over the crossings in lattice pattern.

Bake at 425°F. for 35 to 45 minutes or until golden brown. Sprinkle with powdered sugar before serving. Garnish with Chocolate Leaves.
Yield: 6 to 8 servings.

TIP:
* Frozen whole raspberries, thawed and well drained, can be substituted for fresh raspberries.

NUTRITION PER SERVING:
Calories 480; Protein 2g; Carbohydrate 72g; Fat 20g; Sodium 360mg.

FRESH BLUEBERRY PIE

Fresh blueberries make this succulent fruit pie extra special.

CRUST
Pastry for Two-Crust Pie p. 268

FILLING
4 **cups fresh or frozen blueberries, thawed, well drained**
¾ **cup sugar**
¼ **cup all purpose flour**
¼ **teaspoon cinnamon**
2 **teaspoons lemon juice**
2 **tablespoons margarine or butter**

TOPPING
Milk
Sugar
Cinnamon
Cinnamon ice cream, if desired

Prepare pastry for Two-Crust Pie using 9-inch pie pan.

Heat oven to 425°F. In large bowl, combine blueberries, ¾ cup sugar, flour, ¼ teaspoon cinnamon and lemon juice; mix lightly. Spoon into pastry-lined pan. Dot with margarine. Top with remaining pastry; fold edge of top pastry under bottom pastry. Press together to seal; flute edge. Cut slits in several places in top pastry. Brush pastry with milk; sprinkle with sugar and cinnamon.

Bake at 425°F. for 45 to 55 minutes or until golden brown. Serve warm or cool with cinnamon ice cream.
Yield: 6 to 8 servings.

NUTRITION PER SERVING:
Calories 460; Protein 3g; Carbohydrate 63g; Fat 22g; Sodium 390mg.

CRUNCHY CRUST BLUEBERRY SWIRL PIE

This delicious Pillsbury BAKE-OFF® Contest recipe features a press-in-the-pan pie crust of nuts and rolled oats with a blueberry-lemon filling that is swirled with sour cream.

CRUST
¾ **cup all purpose flour**
½ **cup rolled oats**
½ **cup chopped nuts**
2 **tablespoons sugar**
½ **cup margarine or butter, melted**

FILLING
1 **(3-oz.) pkg. lemon flavor gelatin**
½ **cup boiling water**
1 **(21-oz.) can blueberry fruit pie filling**
½ **cup dairy sour cream**

Heat oven to 400°F. Grease 9-inch pie pan. In medium bowl, combine flour, rolled oats, nuts and sugar. Add melted margarine; mix well. Press mixture evenly in bottom and up to top edge of greased 9-inch pie pan.

Bake at 400°F. for 11 to 14 minutes or until golden brown. Cool.

In medium bowl, dissolve gelatin in boiling water; stir in pie filling. Refrigerate until thickened. Pour into cooled, baked crust. Spoon sour cream by teaspoonfuls onto filling. With spatula, swirl sour cream into filling. Refrigerate until serving time. If desired, top with whipped cream. Store in refrigerator.
Yield: 8 servings.

NUTRITION PER SERVING:
Calories 390; Protein 5g; Carbohydrate 50g; Fat 21g; Sodium 180mg.

Fresh Strawberry Pie

Use the recipe and variations below to make wonderful fresh fruit pies when your favorite fruit is at its peak.

CRUST
> **Pastry for One-Crust Pie p. 268**

FILLING
- 3 pints (6 cups) strawberries
- 1 cup sugar
- 3 tablespoons cornstarch
- ½ cup water
- 4 to 5 drops red food color, if desired

TOPPING
> **Whipped cream**

Prepare and bake pastry as directed for Baked Pie Shell using 9-inch pie pan.

In small bowl, crush enough strawberries to make 1 cup. In medium saucepan, combine sugar and cornstarch. Add crushed strawberries and water. Cook until mixture boils and thickens, stirring constantly; stir in food color. Cool.

Spoon remaining whole or sliced strawberries into cooled, baked pie shell; pour cooked strawberry mixture over top. Refrigerate 3 hours or until set. To serve, top with whipped cream. Store in refrigerator.
Yield: 6 to 8 servings.

NUTRITION PER SERVING:
Calories 300; Protein 2g; Carbohydrate 47g; Fat 12g; Sodium 139mg.

VARIATIONS:

FRESH PEACH PIE: Substitute sliced peaches for strawberries. Omit red food color.

FRESH RASPBERRY PIE: Substitute raspberries for strawberries.

Fresh Strawberry Rhubarb Pie

You'll enjoy this version of a midwestern favorite. It's wonderful served with whipped cream or vanilla ice cream.

CRUST
> **Pastry for Two-Crust Pie p. 268**

FILLING
- 1 pint (2 cups) strawberries
- 3 cups chopped rhubarb*
- 1 cup sugar
- ¼ cup cornstarch

Prepare pastry for Two-Crust Pie using 9-inch pie pan.

Heat oven to 400°F. In large bowl, combine all filling ingredients; mix lightly. Spoon into pastry-lined pan; top with remaining pastry. Fold edge of top pastry under bottom pastry. Press together to seal; flute edge. Cut slits in several places in top pastry.

Bake at 400°F. for 45 to 60 minutes or until golden brown. (Place pan on foil or cookie sheet during last 15 minutes of baking to guard against spills.) If desired, serve with whipped cream and additional strawberries.
Yield: 8 servings.

TIP:
* One 16-oz. pkg. frozen sliced rhubarb, thawed and well drained, can be substituted for fresh rhubarb.

NUTRITION PER SERVING:
Calories 380; Protein 2g; Carbohydrate 57g; Fat 16g; Sodium 330mg.

Cook's Note

RHUBARB

There are two types of rhubarb: outdoor (garden) and indoor (hothouse). Outdoor rhubarb becomes available in spring and lasts until fall. Hothouse rhubarb is available January through June. When buying rhubarb, look for crisp, plump, medium-sized stalks. The stalks will vary in color from green tinged with pink to pink or red. If there are any leaves, they should be fresh looking, not wilted or damaged.

Old-Fashioned Pineapple Rhubarb Pie

Fresh rhubarb can be stored, unwashed, in the crisper section of the refrigerator for up to a week. Wash it just before using.

CRUST
    Pastry for Filled One-Crust Pie p. 268

FILLING
    3 **cups chopped fresh rhubarb or 16-oz. pkg. frozen sliced rhubarb**
    ¾ **cup sugar**
    ¼ **cup all purpose flour**
    1 **(8 ¼-oz.) can crushed pineapple, drained**

TOPPING
    ½ **cup all purpose flour**
    ½ **cup sugar**
    ¼ **cup margarine or butter**

Prepare pastry for Filled One-Crust Pie using 9-inch pie pan.

Heat oven to 425°F. In large bowl, combine all filling ingredients; toss to combine. Spoon into pastry-lined pan. In small bowl, combine all topping ingredients until crumbly; sprinkle over fruit mixture.

Bake at 425°F. for 15 minutes. Reduce oven temperature to 400°F.; bake an additional 25 minutes or until filling is hot and bubbly.
Yield: 8 servings.

NUTRITION PER SERVING:
Calories 350; Protein 3g; Carbohydrate 57g; Fat 13g; Sodium 170mg.

Fireside Fruit Pie

A beautiful medley of apricots, apples and dates.

CRUST
    Pastry for Two-Crust Pie p. 268

FILLING
    1 **(17-oz.) can apricot halves, drained, reserving liquid**
    ½ **cup sugar**
    2 **tablespoons cornstarch**
    3 **cups chopped peeled tart apples**
    1 **cup chopped dates**
    1 **tablespoon lemon juice**

Prepare pastry for Two-Crust Pie using 9-inch pie pan.

Heat oven to 425°F. In large saucepan, combine reserved apricot liquid, sugar, cornstarch, apples, dates and lemon juice. Cover; cook gently until apples are soft, stirring occasionally. Remove from heat; fold in apricot halves. Spoon into pastry-lined pan.

To make decorative top crust, use canape cutter (about 1 inch) to cut out center of dough. Repeat cutouts in an evenly spaced pattern, working from center to within 1½ inches of edge. Arrange pastry over filling; fold edge of top pastry under bottom pastry. Press together to seal; flute edge.

Bake at 425°F. for 25 to 35 minutes or until crust is golden brown and filling bubbles.
Yield: 8 servings.

NUTRITION PER SERVING:
Calories 450; Protein 2g; Carbohydrate 74g; Fat 16g; Sodium 330mg.

Cook's Note

MAKING A FOIL COVER FOR A PIE CRUST EDGE

- Using 12-inch-wide foil, cut a piece 4 inches longer than the diameter of the pie pan.
- Cut a circle from the center of the foil that is 2 inches smaller than the diameter of the pie pan.
- Center the foil over the partially baked pie after about 15 to 20 minutes of baking and gently fold it around the fluted edge.
- Another idea for making a foil cover is to cut a 7-inch-diameter circle from the center of a 12-inch disposable foil pizza pan. It can be reused over and over again!

STREUSEL-TOP PEACH PIE

Fresh peaches grown in the United States are available from May through October.

CRUST
> **Pastry for Filled One-Crust Pie p. 268**

FILLING
- 4 **cups sliced peeled peaches***
- ½ **cup powdered sugar**
- ⅓ **cup all purpose flour**
- ½ **teaspoon cinnamon**

TOPPING
- ¾ **cup all purpose flour**
- ½ **cup firmly packed brown sugar**
- ½ **teaspoon cinnamon**
- ⅓ **cup margarine or butter**

Prepare pastry for Filled One-Crust Pie using 9-inch pie pan.

Heat oven to 375°F. In large bowl, combine all filling ingredients; toss gently. Spoon into pastry-lined pan. In medium bowl, combine all topping ingredients until crumbly; sprinkle over filling.

Bake at 375°F. for 40 to 45 minutes or until peaches are tender and topping is golden brown. **Yield: 8 servings.**

TIP:
* Two 29-oz. cans peach slices, well drained, or 4 cups frozen sliced peaches, thawed and well drained, can be substituted for the fresh peaches.

NUTRITION PER SERVING:
Calories 370; Protein 3g; Carbohydrate 53g; Fat 15g; Sodium 190mg.

VARIATIONS:

STREUSEL-TOP APRICOT PIE: Substitute 4 cups fresh apricot halves or 2 (29-oz.) cans apricot halves, well drained, for the peaches.

STREUSEL-TOP BLUEBERRY PIE: Substitute 4 cups fresh or unsweetened frozen blueberries, partially thawed and drained, for the peaches. Well drained, canned blueberries can also be used.

STREUSEL-TOP PEACH BLUEBERRY PIE: Substitute 1 cup blueberries for 1 cup of the peaches.

STREUSEL-TOP PEACH RASPBERRY PIE: Substitute 1 cup raspberries for 1 cup of the peaches.

GEORGIA PEACH 'N PECAN PIE

Native Georgian pecans paired with homegrown peaches make this pie a matchless creation.

CRUST
> **Pastry for Filled One-Crust Pie p. 268**

FILLING
- ¼ **cup sugar**
- 3 **tablespoons all purpose flour**
- ¼ **teaspoon nutmeg**
  Dash salt
- ½ **cup light corn syrup**
- 3 **eggs**
- 3 **cups cubed peeled peaches***
- ¼ **cup margarine or butter, melted**

TOPPING
- ½ **cup coarsely chopped pecans**
- ¼ **cup all purpose flour**
- ¼ **cup firmly packed brown sugar**
- 2 **tablespoons margarine or butter, softened**

Prepare pastry for Filled One-Crust Pie using 9-inch pie pan.

Heat oven to 400°F. In large bowl, combine sugar, 3 tablespoons flour, nutmeg, salt, corn syrup and eggs; beat at medium speed 1 minute. Stir in peaches and ¼ cup margarine. Spoon into pastry-lined pan.

In small bowl, combine all topping ingredients; mix well. Sprinkle over peach filling.

Bake at 400°F. for 35 to 45 minutes or until center is set. Serve warm or cool with whipped cream, if desired.

Yield: 8 servings.

TIP:
* One 29-oz. can peach slices, well drained and cubed, can be substituted for the fresh peaches.

NUTRITION PER SERVING:
Calories 450; Protein 5g; Carbohydrate 53g; Fat 24g; Sodium 325mg.

Georgia Peach 'n Pecan Pie,
Streusel-Top Peach Blueberry Pie

DUTCH PEACH CREAM PIE

This pie features a rich crust made with margarine and sour cream.

CRUST AND TOPPING*
- 2 cups all purpose flour
- 1 cup margarine or butter
- 3 tablespoons dairy sour cream
- 1/4 cup firmly packed brown sugar

FILLING
- 1/3 cup firmly packed brown sugar
- 1/4 teaspoon ginger
- 1/4 teaspoon nutmeg
- 1 cup dairy sour cream
- 1 egg, beaten
- 4 medium peaches, peeled, thickly sliced or halved (2 cups)**

Heat oven to 375°F. In medium bowl, combine flour and margarine. Using pastry blender or fork, cut margarine into flour until mixture resembles coarse crumbs. Reserve 1 cup mixture. Add 3 tablespoons sour cream to remaining flour mixture; toss with fork until dough forms. Shape dough into ball. With floured fingers, press dough evenly in bottom and up to top edge of 9-inch pie pan or 10-inch tart pan with removable bottom. Flute edge. Bake at 375°F. for 20 to 25 minutes or until lightly browned; cool.

Meanwhile, in small bowl combine reserved crumb mixture with   cup brown sugar; set aside. In medium bowl, combine 1/3 cup brown sugar, ginger, nutmeg, 1 cup sour cream and egg; mix well. Pour half of filling mixture into cooled, baked pie shell. Arrange peaches on filling. Pour remaining filling over peaches. Sprinkle with reserved crumb mixture.

Bake at 375°F. for 25 to 35 minutes or until center is set and topping is golden brown. Serve warm or cool. Store in refrigerator.

Yield: 8 servings.

TIPS:

* To prepare pastry in food processor, place _3/4 cup margarine_ or _butter_ and flour in food processor bowl with metal blade. Process until crumbly. Reserve 1 cup mixture. Add 3 tablespoons sour cream; process 4 to 5 seconds or until mixture is well blended. Continue as directed above.

** One 16-oz. can peach slices or 29-oz. can peach halves, well drained, can be substituted for fresh peaches.

NUTRITION PER SERVING:
Calories 480; Protein 6g; Carbohydrate 45g; Fat 31g; Sodium 310mg.

CRANBERRY BLUEBERRY PIE

Blueberries and cranberries are native American berries. The sweet blueberries and tart cranberries form a delicious flavor combination in this sensational pie.

FILLING
- 2 cups sugar
- 1/4 cup cornstarch
- 2 cups fresh or frozen cranberries
- 2 tablespoons lemon juice
- 1 (16-oz.) pkg. frozen blueberries

CRUST
- Pastry for Two-Crust Pie p. 268
- 1/2 teaspoon powdered sugar, if desired

In large saucepan, combine all filling ingredients. Cook over medium-high heat until mixture boils, stirring constantly. Reduce heat; simmer until cranberries pop and mixture is very thick. Cool 15 minutes.

Prepare pastry for Two-Crust Pie using 9-inch pie pan.

Heat oven to 425°F. Pour filling into pastry-lined pan. To make lattice top, cut remaining pastry into 1/2-inch-wide strips. Arrange strips in lattice design over filling. Trim edges and flute.

Bake at 425°F. for 25 to 35 minutes or until golden brown. Cool 2 to 3 hours before serving. Sprinkle with powdered sugar just before serving.

Yield: 8 servings.

NUTRITION PER SERVING:
Calories 490; Protein 2g; Carbohydrate 89g; Fat 15g; Sodium 200mg.

FRESH PEACH 'N BLUEBERRY PIE

Tapioca or cornstarch thickened pies will be clearer than those thickened with flour. In this pie, we've combined favorite summer fruits.

CRUST
> **Pastry for Two-Crust Pie p. 268**

FILLING
- 5 to 5½ cups sliced peeled peaches*
- 1 cup blueberries*
- 1 tablespoon lemon juice
- 1 cup sugar
- 3 tablespoons quick-cooking tapioca or cornstarch
- ¼ teaspoon salt
- 2 tablespoons margarine or butter

TOPPING
> **Whipped cream, if desired**

Prepare pastry for Two-Crust Pie using 9-inch pie pan.

Heat oven to 425°F. In large bowl, combine peaches, blueberries and lemon juice. Add sugar, tapioca and salt; toss gently. Spoon fruit mixture into pastry-lined pan. Dot with margarine. Top with remaining pastry; fold edge of top pastry under bottom pastry. Press together to seal; flute edge. Cut slits in several places in top pastry.

Bake at 425°F. for 40 to 50 minutes or until golden brown. Serve warm or cool garnished with whipped cream.
Yield: 8 servings.

TIP:
* One 16-oz. pkg. frozen peaches and 1 cup frozen blueberries, thawed and drained, can be substituted for fresh fruit.

NUTRITION PER SERVING:
Calories 470; Protein 3g; Carbohydrate 66g; Fat 22g; Sodium 420mg.

COOK'S NOTE

PIE TOPPINGS

Select from these topppings when you want to add a little something special to your fruit pie.

Sweetened Whipped Cream: In small bowl, beat 1 cup whipping cream until soft peaks form. Blend in 2 tablespoons powdered sugar and ½ teaspoon vanilla; beat until stiff peaks form.
Yield: 2 cups.

Spicy Whipped Cream: In small bowl, beat 1 cup whipping cream until soft peaks form. Blend in 2 tablespoons powdered sugar, ¼ teaspoon cinnamon (or ⅛ teaspoon cinnamon and ⅛ teaspoon nutmeg) and ½ teaspoon vanilla; beat until stiff peaks form.
Yield: 2 cups.

Sweetened Sour Cream Topping: In small bowl, combine 1 cup dairy sour cream, 2 tablespoons brown sugar and 1 tablespoon grated orange peel until well blended. Gradually stir in 1 to 2 teaspoons orange-flavored liqueur or orange juice. Cover; refrigerate until serving time. Stir before serving.
Yield: 1 cup.

Easy Creme Fraiche: In small bowl, sprinkle 2 tablespoons brown sugar and dash salt over 1 cup dairy sour cream; let stand 2 minutes. Gently fold in ½ cup whipping cream 1 tablespoon at a time, until thoroughly blended. Cover; refrigerate until serving time.
Yield: 1½ cups.

Orange Whipped Cream Cheese: In small bowl, beat 1 (8-oz.) pkg. cream cheese, softened, with 3 to 4 tablespoons half-and-half or milk until of a fluffy consistency. Stir in ½ teaspoon grated orange peel.
Yield: 1¼ cups.

SLICES OF LEMON PIE

This tart and tangy lemon pie is an updated version of an old Shaker favorite.

CRUST
Pastry for Two-Crust Pie p. 268

FILLING
  2 **cups sugar**
  ⅓ **cup all purpose flour**
  ¼ **teaspoon salt**
  ⅔ **cup water**
  2 **tablespoons margarine or butter, softened**
  2 **to 3 teaspoons grated orange peel**
  3 **eggs**
  1 **to 2 lemons, peeled, sliced ⅛ inch thick**

Prepare pastry for Two-Crust Pie using 9-inch pie pan.

Heat oven to 400°F. In large bowl, combine sugar, flour and salt. Add water, margarine, orange peel and eggs; beat until well blended. Stir in lemon slices. Pour into pastry-lined pan. Top with remaining pastry; fold edge of top pastry under bottom pastry. Press together to seal; flute edges. Cut slits in several places in top pastry.

Bake at 400°F. for 35 to 45 minutes until golden brown. Cool completely. Store in refrigerator.
Yield: 8 servings.

NUTRITION PER SERVING:
Calories 510; Protein 5g; Carbohydrate 80g; Fat 19g; Sodium 320mg.

COOK'S NOTE

DRIED FRUIT

Dried fruit is fruit that has been dehydrated (50 to 75 percent of the water is removed) by exposure to the sun or by mechanical heating methods. Dried fruit is very sweet and has a chewy texture. Follow recipes directions when dried fruit is used. Some recipes call for the dried fruit as is; some recipes call for reconstituting the dried fruit in a liquid.

HARVEST MOON FRUIT PIE

Fall brings abundant supplies of fresh apples and cranberries. They are extra special when combined with dried apricots in this 2-crust pie.

CRUST
Pastry for Two-Crust Pie p. 268

FILLING
  4 **cups sliced peeled apples**
  ¾ **cup fresh or frozen cranberries, ground***
  ½ **cup dried apricots, ground***
1¼ **cups sugar**
  2 **tablespoons all purpose flour**
  ½ **teaspoon cinnamon**
  ¼ **teaspoon nutmeg**
  ¼ **teaspoon salt**
  1 **tablespoon margarine or butter**

Prepare pastry for Two-Crust Pie using 9-inch pie pan.

Heat oven to 375°F. In large bowl, combine all filling ingredients except margarine; mix well. Pour into pastry-lined pan. Dot with margarine. Top with remaining pastry; fold edge of top pastry under bottom pastry. Press together to seal; flute edge. Cut slits in several places in top pastry.

Bake at 375°F. for 40 to 50 minutes or until golden brown.
Yield: 8 servings.

TIP:
* Cranberries and apricots can be ground at the same time in food processor bowl with metal blade or in blender container.

NUTRITION PER SERVING:
Calories 470; Protein 4g; Carbohydrate 71g; Fat 19g; Sodium 350mg.

ORANGE PEAR-FECT MINCE PIE

This scrumptious pie is topped with a creamy caramel sauce spiked with orange liqueur.

CRUST
>**Pastry for Two-Crust Pie p. 268**

FILLING
- 1 **large orange**
- 1 **(27-oz.) jar (2⅔ cups) prepared mincemeat**
- 1 **pear, peeled, sliced into 3/8-inch thick wedges**

CARAMEL SAUCE
- 1 **cup firmly packed brown sugar**
- 2 **teaspoons cornstarch**
- 1 **cup half-and-half**
- 2 **tablespoons margarine or butter, cut in small pieces**
- 1 **tablespoon orange-flavored liqueur, if desired**

Prepare pastry for Two-Crust Pie. Heat oven to 425°F. Place 1 circle of pastry on ungreased cookie sheet.

Grate peel from orange; place in medium bowl. Pare off and discard remaining peel and pith from orange; seed and cut orange flesh into chunks. Add orange chunks and mincemeat to peel in bowl; gently combine. Spoon half of mixture on center of pastry; spread to within 1½ inches of edge. Layer pear wedges over mincemeat mixture; top with remaining mincemeat mixture. Place remaining pastry over filling. Fold edge of bottom pastry over top pastry; pinch and flute edges to seal. Cut slits in several places in top pastry.

Bake at 425°F. for 30 to 40 minutes or until crust is golden brown.

In medium saucepan, combine brown sugar and cornstarch. Stir in half-and-half and margarine. Cook over medium heat until mixture boils, stirring constantly. Reduce heat; simmer 8 to 10 minutes or until mixture thickens, stirring occasionally. Stir in liqueur. Serve warm over wedges of pie.

Yield: 8 to 10 servings.

NUTRITION PER SERVING:
Calories 520; Protein 3g; Carbohydrate 85g; Fat 19g; Sodium 510mg.

GLAZED PINEAPPLE PIE

A golden pineapple filling bakes inside a flaky double crust. A powdered sugar glaze makes it extra special.

CRUST
>**Pastry for Two-Crust Pie p. 268**
- ¾ **cup coconut**

FILLING
- 1 **cup sugar**
- ¼ **cup all purpose flour**
- ¼ **teaspoon salt**
- 1 **tablespoon lemon juice**
- 1 **tablespoon margarine or butter, melted**
- 1 **(20-oz.) can crushed pineapple in its own juice, drained, reserving liquid for glaze**

GLAZE
- ½ **cup powdered sugar**
- ¼ **teaspoon rum extract**
- 1 **to 2 tablespoons reserved pineapple liquid**

Prepare pastry for Two-Crust Pie using 9-inch pie pan. Sprinkle coconut over bottom of pastry-lined pan.

Heat oven to 400°F. In medium bowl, combine all filling ingredients; mix well. Spoon filling mixture over coconut, spreading evenly. Top with remaining pastry; fold edge of top pastry under bottom pastry. Press together to seal; flute edge. Cut slits in several places in top pastry.

Bake at 400°F. for 35 to 40 minutes or until golden brown. Cool slightly.

In small bowl, combine all glaze ingredients, adding enough pineapple liquid for desired spreading consistency; stir until smooth. Drizzle or spread over slightly warm pie. Serve warm or cool.

Yield: 6 to 8 servings.

NUTRITION PER SERVING:
Calories 450; Protein 3g; Carbohydrate 66g; Fat 19g; Sodium 350mg.

CUSTARD PIE

It's best to eat custard pie soon after it's baked. Always store it in the refrigerator.

CRUST
Pastry for Filled One-Crust Pie p. 268

FILLING
3 eggs
¾ cup sugar
¼ teaspoon salt
¼ teaspoon nutmeg or cinnamon
1 teaspoon vanilla
2½ cups hot milk

Prepare pastry for Filled One-Crust Pie using 9-inch pie pan.

Heat oven to 400°F. In large bowl, beat eggs. Add sugar, salt, nutmeg and vanilla; mix well. Blend in hot milk. Pour into pastry-lined pan. Bake at 400°F. for 25 to 30 minutes or until knife inserted near center comes out clean. Cool. Serve slightly warm or chilled. Store in refrigerator.
Yield: 8 servings.

NUTRITION PER SERVING:
Calories 270; Protein 6g; Carbohydrate 34g; Fat 12g; Sodium 260mg.

PINEAPPLE CHESS PIE

In chess or transparent pies, layers form in the filling as the pie bakes. In this pie a transparent bottom layer is topped with a crunchy coconut layer.

CRUST
Pastry for Filled One-Crust Pie p. 268

FILLING
3 eggs
1 cup firmly packed brown sugar
¼ cup margarine or butter, melted
1 teaspoon vanilla
½ cup coconut
½ cup rolled oats
1 (8-oz.) can crushed pineapple, undrained

TOPPING
Ice milk, ice cream or whipped topping, if desired

Prepare pastry for Filled One-Crust Pie using 9-inch pie pan.

Heat oven to 350°F. In large bowl, beat eggs at high speed until thick and lemon colored. Gradually beat in brown sugar. Blend in margarine and vanilla. Stir in remaining ingredients except ice milk. Pour pineapple mixture into pastry-lined pan.

Bake at 350°F. for 40 to 50 minutes or until center is set. Serve warm or cool with ice milk.
Yield: 8 servings.

NUTRITION PER SERVING:
Calories 400; Protein 4g; Carbohydrate 50g; Fat 20g; Sodium 320mg.

EGGNOG CUSTARD PIE

This pie is flavored with nutmeg and brandy.

CRUST
Pastry for Filled One-Crust Pie p. 268

FILLING
3 eggs
⅓ cup sugar
⅛ teaspoon salt
⅛ to ¼ teaspoon nutmeg
2 cups dairy eggnog (not canned)
2 tablespoons brandy or rum
1 teaspoon vanilla

TOPPING
1 cup whipping cream
3 tablespoons powdered sugar
1 to 2 teaspoons brandy or rum
Nutmeg

Prepare pastry for Filled One-Crust Pie using 9-inch pie pan.

Heat oven to 350°F. In large bowl, beat eggs. Add remaining filling ingredients; blend well. Pour into pastry-lined pan. Cover with foil; bake at 350°F. for 25 minutes. Remove foil; bake an additional 30 to 40 minutes or until knife inserted in center comes out clean. Cool completely.

In small bowl, beat whipping cream until soft peaks form. Add powdered sugar and 1 to 2 teaspoons brandy; beat until stiff peaks form. Garnish pie with whipped cream topping; sprinkle with nutmeg. Store in refrigerator.
Yield: 6 to 8 servings.

NUTRITION PER SERVING:
Calories 390; Protein 6g; Carbohydrate 33g; Fat 25g; Sodium 200mg.

DANISH RAISIN CUSTARD PIE

This European-style pie has a rich butter cookie crust and is baked in a layer cake pan. It's delicious!

CRUST
1¼ cups all purpose flour
 ⅓ cup powdered sugar
 1 teaspoon grated lemon peel
 ½ cup margarine or butter
 2 egg yolks, slightly beaten

FILLING
 1 cup raisins
 2 tablespoons sugar
 3 tablespoons water
 2 tablespoons orange juice
 2 eggs
 2 tablespoons sugar
 1 teaspoon vanilla
1½ cups half-and-half

Heat oven to 375°F. Grease 9-inch round cake pan. In medium bowl, combine flour, powdered sugar and lemon peel; blend well. Using pastry blender or fork, cut in margarine until mixture resembles coarse crumbs. Add egg yolks; toss with fork until crumbly. Press in bottom and up sides of greased pan.

Bake at 375°F. for 13 to 18 minutes or until light golden brown around edges. Remove from oven. Increase oven temperature to 400°F.

In small saucepan, combine raisins, 2 tablespoons sugar, water and orange juice. Bring to a boil. Reduce heat; simmer uncovered 3 to 8 minutes or until liquid is absorbed. In medium bowl, slightly beat eggs. Stir in 2 tablespoons sugar and vanilla; blend well. In another small saucepan over low heat, heat half-and-half until warm. Gradually add to egg mixture, beating constantly with wire whisk. Spoon raisin mixture into partially baked crust, spreading evenly. Pour egg mixture over raisin mixture.

Bake at 400°F. for 19 to 24 minutes or until custard is set and knife inserted near center comes out clean. Store in refrigerator.
Yield: 8 servings.

NUTRITION PER SERVING:
Calories 370; Protein 6g; Carbohydrate 43g; Fat 20g; Sodium 170mg.

BLACK BOTTOM PIE

Three heavenly layers.

CRUST
Pastry for Filled One-Crust Pie p. 268

CHOCOLATE LAYER
 ½ cup sugar
 ⅓ cup unsweetened cocoa
 ½ cup light corn syrup
 1 teaspoon vanilla
 3 eggs
 ¼ cup margarine or butter, melted

CUSTARD LAYER
 ⅓ cup sugar
 2 tablespoons cornstarch
    Dash salt
 2 cups milk
 4 eggs, well beaten
 ½ teaspoon vanilla
 2 teaspoons rum extract*

TOPPING
 1 cup whipping cream, whipped
    Chocolate Curls, if desired, p. 210

Prepare pastry for Filled One-Crust Pie using 9-inch pie pan.

Heat oven to 350°F. In large bowl, combine ½ cup sugar and cocoa. Add corn syrup, 1 teaspoon vanilla and 3 eggs; beat well. Stir in margarine. Pour into pastry-lined pan. Bake at 350°F. for 30 to 40 minutes or until center is set. (Chocolate layer will be puffy when removed from oven.) Cool completely.

In small saucepan over medium heat, combine ⅓ cup sugar, cornstarch, salt, milk and 4 eggs; mix well. Cook over medium heat, stirring constantly, until mixture boils and thickens. Remove from heat; stir in rum extract. Cover with plastic wrap; cool.

Spoon cooled custard over cooled chocolate layer. Refrigerate at least 1 hour before serving. Top with whipped cream; garnish with Chocolate Curls. Store in refrigerator.
Yield: 10 servings.

TIP:
* If desired, substitute 2 to 4 tablespoons light rum, bourbon, brandy or Irish whiskey for rum extract.

NUTRITION PER SERVING:
Calories 450; Protein 8g; Carbohydrate 46g; Fat 26g; Sodium 310mg.

CHOCOLATE SILK PECAN PIE

Sink your teeth into a chocolate layer that's as smooth as silk, followed by a sweetened, crunchy pecan layer.

CRUST
    Pastry for Filled One-Crust Pie p. 268

PECAN FILLING
  1/3 **cup sugar**
  1/2 **cup dark corn syrup**
   3 **tablespoons margarine or butter, melted**
  1/8 **teaspoon salt, if desired**
   2 **eggs**
  1/2 **cup chopped pecans**

CHOCOLATE FILLING
   1 **cup hot milk**
  1/4 **teaspoon vanilla**
 1 1/3 **cups semi-sweet chocolate chips**

TOPPING
   1 **cup whipping cream**
   2 **tablespoons powdered sugar**
  1/4 **teaspoon vanilla**
    Chocolate Curls, if desired, p. 210

Prepare pastry for Filled One-Crust Pie using 9-inch pie pan.

Heat oven to 350°F. In small bowl, combine sugar, corn syrup, margarine, salt and eggs; beat 1 minute at medium speed. Stir in pecans. Pour into pastry-lined pan.

Bake at 350°F. for 40 to 55 minutes or until center of pie is puffed and golden brown. Cool 1 hour.

While filled crust is cooling, combine all chocolate filling ingredients in blender container or food processor bowl with metal blade; blend 1 minute or until smooth. Refrigerate about 1½ hours or until mixture is slightly thickened but not set. Gently stir; pour into cooled, filled crust. Refrigerate until firm, about 1 hour.

In small bowl, beat whipping cream, powdered sugar and 1/4 teaspoon vanilla until stiff peaks form. Spoon or pipe over filling. Garnish with Chocolate Curls. Store in refrigerator.
Yield: 8 to 10 servings.

NUTRITION PER SERVING:
Calories 490; Protein 5g; Carbohydrate 46g; Fat 32g; Sodium 240mg.

CHOCOLATE PECAN PIE

This rich chocolate version of pecan pie is topped with whipped cream and chocolate-dipped nuts.

CRUST
    Pastry for Filled One-Crust Pie p. 268

FILLING
   1 **cup light corn syrup**
  1/2 **cup sugar**
  1/4 **cup margarine or butter, melted**
   1 **teaspoon vanilla**
   3 **eggs**
   1 **(6-oz.) pkg. (1 cup) semi-sweet chocolate chips**
 1 1/2 **cups pecan halves**

TOPPING
   2 **tablespoons reserved semi-sweet chocolate chips**
  10 **pecan halves**
    Whipped cream

Prepare pastry for Filled One-Crust Pie using 9-inch pie pan.

Heat oven to 325°F. In large bowl, combine corn syrup, sugar, margarine, vanilla and eggs; beat well. Reserve 2 tablespoons chocolate chips for topping. Stir in remaining chocolate chips and 1½ cups pecans. Spread evenly in pastry-lined pan.

Bake at 325°F. for 55 to 65 minutes or until deep golden brown and filling is set. Cool completely.

Line cookie sheet with waxed paper. Melt 2 tablespoons reserved chocolate chips in small saucepan over low heat. Dip each of 10 pecan halves into chocolate. Place on paper-lined cookie sheet. Refrigerate 15 to 20 minutes or until chocolate is set.

Garnish pie with whipped cream and chocolate-dipped nuts. Store in refrigerator.
Yield: 10 servings.

NUTRITION PER SERVING:
Calories 570; Protein 5g; Carbohydrate 60g; Fat 34g; Sodium 180mg.

Chocolate Pecan Pie

Texas Osgood Pecan Pie

A thin, crisp meringue forms during the baking of this rich pecan pie, a traditional pie in Texas.

CRUST
    Pastry for Filled One-Crust Pie p. 268

FILLING
  1 **cup sugar**
  ½ **cup margarine or butter, softened**
  ¼ **teaspoon cinnamon**
  ¼ **teaspoon cloves**
  1 **teaspoon vinegar**
  1 **teaspoon vanilla**
  4 **eggs, separated**
  1 **cup chopped pecans**
  1 **cup raisins or chopped dates**

TOPPING
  ¾ **cup whipping cream, whipped**

Prepare pastry for Filled One-Crust Pie using 9-inch pie pan.

Heat oven to 325°F. In large bowl, beat sugar and margarine at medium speed until light and fluffy. Add cinnamon, cloves, vinegar, vanilla and egg yolks; blend well. Stir in pecans and raisins.

In small bowl, beat egg whites until stiff peaks form; fold into pecan-raisin mixture. Spoon into pastry-lined pan.

Cooks Note

CANDIED ORANGE PEEL

To prepare candied orange peel, use a vegetable peeler to remove the colored outer peel of 2 oranges. Cut the peel into thin strips. In small saucepan, combine ¾ cup sugar, ½ cup water and orange peel. Bring to a boil; reduce heat, cover and simmer for 15 minutes. Drain. Spread orange peel on waxed paper; cool 10 minutes. Roll pieces of peel in 3 tablespoons of sugar until well coated. Let dry overnight. Store in an airtight container in the refrigerator up to 3 months. Use the peel as a garnish for desserts.

Bake at 325°F. for 35 to 45 minutes or until golden brown and center is set. Cool. Serve with whipped cream.
Yield: 8 servings.

NUTRITION PER SERVING:
Calories 580; Protein 6g; Carbohydrate 56g; Fat 39g; Sodium 270mg.

Golden Pecan Pie

Even the most ardent calorie watchers find it hard to resist the sweet seduction of pecan pie.

CRUST
    Pastry for Filled One-Crust Pie p. 268

FILLING
  ⅓ **cup firmly packed brown sugar**
  1½ **teaspoons all purpose flour**
  1¼ **cups light corn syrup**
  1¼ **teaspoons vanilla**
  3 **eggs**
  1½ **cups pecan halves or broken pecans**
  2 **tablespoons margarine or butter, melted**

Prepare pastry for Filled One-Crust Pie using 9-inch pie pan.

Heat oven to 375°F. In large bowl, combine brown sugar, flour, corn syrup, vanilla and eggs; beat well. Stir in pecans and margarine. Pour into pastry-lined pan.

Bake at 375°F. for 40 to 50 minutes or until center of pie is puffed and golden brown. Cool.
Yield: 8 servings.

NUTRITION PER SERVING:
Calories 490; Protein 5g; Carbohydrate 64g; Fat 25g; Sodium 190mg.

VARIATION:

ORANGE PECAN PIE: Add ½ teaspoon grated orange peel to filling. Garnish with candied orange peel, if desired.

FUDGY BROWNIE PIE

You'll love this brownie in a crust! It has an indulgent whipped cream topping that's irresistible.

CRUST
    Pastry for Filled One-Crust Pie p. 268

FILLING
- ½ **cup sugar**
- ⅓ **cup unsweetened cocoa**
- ½ **cup light corn syrup**
- 1 **teaspoon vanilla**
- 3 **eggs**
- ¾ **cup chopped nuts**
- ¼ **cup margarine or butter, melted**

TOPPING
- 1 **cup whipping cream**
- 2 **tablespoons powdered sugar**
- 1½ **teaspoons orange extract**
- 2 **tablespoons orange marmalade**
- 1 **to 2 teaspoons orange juice or water**

Prepare pastry for Filled One-Crust Pie using 9-inch pie pan.

Heat oven to 350°F. In large bowl, combine sugar and cocoa. Add corn syrup, vanilla and eggs; beat well using wire whisk or rotary beater. Stir in nuts and margarine. Pour into pastry-lined pan. Bake at 350°F. for 30 to 40 minutes or until center is set. Cool completely.

In small bowl, beat whipping cream until soft peaks form. Add powdered sugar and orange extract; beat until stiff peaks form. Spread or pipe over cooled filling. In small bowl, combine orange marmalade and enough orange juice for drizzling consistency. Drizzle marmalade mixture over whipped cream. Refrigerate at least 30 minutes before serving. Store in refrigerator.

Yield: 8 servings.

NUTRITION PER SERVING:
Calories 540; Protein 6g; Carbohydrate 50g; Fat 35g; Sodium 280mg.

SWEET CHOCOLATE PIE

A wire whisk works well to mix ingredients in this recipe.

CRUST
    Pastry for Filled One-Crust Pie p. 268

FILLING
- 1 **cup sugar**
- ⅓ **cup margarine or butter**
- 4 **oz. sweet baking chocolate, chopped**
- ½ **cup evaporated milk or half-and-half**
- 1 **teaspoon vanilla**
- 4 **eggs**
- 1 **cup coconut**
- ½ **cup chopped pecans or walnuts**

TOPPING
    Whipped cream, if desired

Prepare pastry for Filled One-Crust Pie using 9-inch pie pan.

Heat oven to 350°F. In medium saucepan, combine sugar, margarine and chocolate. Cook over low heat, stirring constantly until smooth. Remove from heat; cool 5 minutes. Add evaporated milk, vanilla and eggs; beat until well blended. Sprinkle coconut and pecans in bottom of pastry-lined pan; slowly pour chocolate mixture over coconut and pecans.

Bake at 350°F. for 35 to 45 minutes or until center is set. Cool completely. Serve with whipped cream.

Yield: 8 to 10 servings.

NUTRITION PER SERVING:
Calories 450; Protein 5g; Carbohydrate 42g; Fat 29g; Sodium 250mg.

Peanut Butter Lovers' Pie

Use either chunky or creamy peanut butter for the baked filling. The pie is sumptuous when topped with hot fudge sauce and a sprinkling of chopped peanuts.

CRUST
> **Pastry for Filled One-Crust Pie p. 268**

FILLING
- 2 **eggs, separated, at room temperature**
- ½ **cup firmly packed brown sugar**
- ¾ **cup peanut butter**
- ¼ **cup dark corn syrup**
- 1 **(5-oz.) can (⅔ cup) evaporated milk or milk**
- 1 **teaspoon vanilla**

Prepare pastry for Filled One-Crust Pie using 9-inch pie pan.

Heat oven to 350°F. In small bowl, beat egg whites until stiff peaks form. In large bowl, beat egg yolks and brown sugar until mixture is light in color and thickened. Blend in peanut butter and corn syrup. Gradually beat in milk and vanilla. Fold egg whites into peanut butter mixture. Pour into pastry-lined pan.

Bake at 350°F. for 30 to 35 minutes or until filling is set. Serve warm or at room temperature. Store in refrigerator.

Yield: 8 to 10 servings.

NUTRITION PER SERVING:
Calories 320; Protein 9g; Carbohydrate 31g; Fat 18g; Sodium 240mg.

Apricot Delight Pie

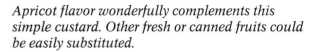

Apricot flavor wonderfully complements this simple custard. Other fresh or canned fruits could be easily substituted.

CRUST
> **Pastry for Filled One-Crust Pie p. 268**

FILLING
- 1 **(14-oz.) can sweetened condensed milk (not evaporated)**
- ½ **cup dairy sour cream**
- 1 **egg**
- 1 **(17-oz.) can apricot halves, well drained**
- ¼ **cup apricot preserves, melted**

Prepare pastry for Filled One-Crust Pie using 9-inch pie pan.

Heat oven to 375°F. In small bowl, combine sweetened condensed milk, sour cream and egg; mix well. Pour into pastry-lined pan.

Bake at 375°F. for 25 to 35 minutes or until just set. Cool 10 minutes.

Arrange well-drained apricot halves over cooled filling. Brush with apricot preserves. Refrigerate until serving time. Store in refrigerator.

Yield: 8 servings.

MICROWAVE DIRECTIONS:
Prepare pastry for One-Crust Pie using 9-inch microwave-safe pie pan. Prick crust generously with fork. Microwave on HIGH for 6 to 8 minutes, rotating pan ½ turn every 2 minutes. Crust is done when surface appears dry and flaky. In 4-cup microwave-safe measuring cup, combine sweetened condensed milk, sour cream and egg; mix well. Microwave on HIGH for 2½ to 3 minutes, stirring with wire whisk once during cooking. Cook until mixture starts to thicken. Pour into cooked crust. Microwave on MEDIUM for 3 to 4 minutes or until just set in center. Cool 10 minutes. Continue as directed above.

NUTRITION PER SERVING:
Calories 370; Protein 7g; Carbohydrate 50g; Fat 17g; Sodium 220mg.

Praline Creme Pumpkin Pie

Praline and creamy orange-flavored layers top this sensational pumpkin pie.

CRUST
>   **Pastry for Filled One-Crust Pie p. 268**

FILLING
- ½ **cup sugar**
- 1½ **teaspoons pumpkin pie spice**
- ¼ **teaspoon salt**
- 1 **(16-oz.) can (2 cups) pumpkin**
- 1 **(12-oz.) can (1½ cups) evaporated milk**
- 2 **eggs, slightly beaten**

PRALINE LAYER
- ¼ **cup firmly packed brown sugar**
- 2 **tablespoons all purpose flour**
- ¼ **cup margarine or butter**
- ½ **cup chopped pecans**

TOPPING
- 1 **(3-oz.) pkg. cream cheese, softened**
- 2 **teaspoons milk**
- 1 **teaspoon grated orange peel**
- 1 **(8-oz.) container (3½ cups) frozen whipped topping, thawed**

Prepare pastry for Filled One-Crust Pie using 9-inch pie pan.

Heat oven to 425°F. In large bowl, combine all filling ingredients; beat until well blended. Pour into pastry-lined pan. Bake at 425°F. for 15 minutes.

Meanwhile, in small bowl combine brown sugar and flour. Using pastry blender or fork, cut in margarine until mixture resembles coarse crumbs. Stir in pecans. Sprinkle pecan mixture over pumpkin filling. Reduce oven temperature to 350°F.; bake an additional 30 to 35 minutes or until knife inserted near center comes out clean. Cool completely.

In small bowl, combine cream cheese, milk and orange peel; mix until smooth. Gently fold whipped topping into cream cheese mixture. Spoon over cooled pie. Refrigerate until serving time. Store in refrigerator.

Yield: 10 to 12 servings.

NUTRITION PER SERVING:
Calories 340; Protein 6g; Carbohydrate 34g; Fat 21g; Sodium 270mg.

Old-Fashioned Pumpkin Pie

For lovers of this traditional Thanksgiving dessert, all the familiar flavors and smooth creamy texture are here.

CRUST
>   **Pastry for Filled One-Crust Pie p. 268**

FILLING
- ¾ **cup sugar**
- 1½ **teaspoons pumpkin pie spice**
- ½ **teaspoon salt**
- 1 **(16-oz.) can (2 cups) pumpkin**
- 1 **(12-oz.) can (1½ cups) evaporated milk**
- 2 **eggs, beaten**

TOPPING
- ½ **cup whipping cream, whipped**

Prepare pastry for Filled One-Crust Pie using 9-inch pie pan.

Heat oven to 425°F. In large bowl, combine all filling ingredients; blend well. Pour into pastry-lined pan. Bake at 425°F. for 15 minutes. Reduce oven temperature to 350°F.; bake an additional 40 to 50 minutes or until knife inserted near center comes out clean. Cool; refrigerate until serving time. Serve with whipped cream. Store in refrigerator.

Yield: 8 servings.

NUTRITION PER SERVING:
Calories 320; Protein 7g; Carbohydrate 42g; Fat 14g; Sodium 310mg.

VARIATION:

MAPLE PUMPKIN PIE: Substitute ½ cup maple-flavored syrup for ½ cup of the evaporated milk.

Cook's Note

PUMPKIN PIE SPICE

To make pumpkin pie spice, combine 4 teaspoons cinnamon, 1 teaspoon ginger, ½ teaspoon allspice, ½ teaspoon nutmeg and ½ teaspoon cloves. Store in a tightly sealed container in a cool, dark place.

Old-Fashioned Pumpkin Pie

Honey Pumpkin Pie

You'll enjoy the honey flavor in this classic holiday pie.

CRUST
Pastry for Filled One-Crust Pie p. 268

FILLING
- 1 (16-oz.) can (2 cups) pumpkin
- ¾ cup honey
- ½ teaspoon salt
- 1¼ teaspoons cinnamon
- ½ teaspoon ginger
- ¼ teaspoon cloves
- ¼ teaspoon nutmeg
- 3 eggs, slightly beaten
- 1 (12-oz.) can (1½ cups) evaporated milk

Prepare pastry for Filled One-Crust Pie using 9-inch pie pan.

Heat oven to 425°F. In large bowl, combine pumpkin, honey, salt, cinnamon, ginger, cloves and nutmeg; mix well. Add eggs; blend well. Gradually add milk, beating at low speed until well blended. Pour into pastry-lined pan.

Bake at 425°F. for 15 minutes. Reduce oven temperature to 350°F.; bake an additional 45 to 55 minutes or until knife inserted near center comes out clean. Cool completely before serving. Store in refrigerator.

Yield: 8 servings.

NUTRITION PER SERVING:
Calories 290; Protein 6g; Carbohydrate 48g; Fat 9g; Sodium 360mg.

Sweet Potato Pie

Dry sherry adds a smooth sweet taste to this traditional southern pie.

CRUST
Pastry for Filled One-Crust Pie p. 268

FILLING
- 1½ cups mashed canned sweet potatoes
- ⅔ cup firmly packed brown sugar
- 1 cup half-and-half
- 1 teaspoon cinnamon
- ½ teaspoon allspice
- 1 tablespoon dry sherry or lemon juice
- 2 eggs, beaten

TOPPING
- 1 cup whipping cream
- 2 tablespoons sugar
- 1 teaspoon vanilla
  Pecan halves

Prepare pastry for Filled One-Crust Pie using 9-inch pie pan.

Heat oven to 425°F. In blender container or food processor bowl with metal blade, combine all filling ingredients; blend well. Pour into pastry-lined pan.

Bake at 425°F. for 15 minutes. Reduce oven temperature to 350°F.; bake an additional 30 to 40 minutes or until pie is set in center. Cool completely.

In small bowl, beat whipping cream, sugar and vanilla until soft peaks form. Garnish pie with whipped cream and pecan halves. Store in refrigerator.

Yield: 6 to 8 servings.

NUTRITION PER SERVING:
Calories 450; Protein 5g; Carbohydrate 53g; Fat 24g; Sodium 190mg.

Cook's Note

PUMPKIN

Pumpkin, a member of the squash family, is rich in vitamin A and contains a fair amount of vitamins B and C. It also provides such minerals as calcium, iron, potassium, and phosphorus.

There are 2 types of canned pumpkin available. Read the label carefully to make certain you are buying the type of canned pumpkin that is called for in your recipe. *Canned pumpkin* contains unseasoned pumpkin puree. It is used in most pumpkin recipes. *Canned pumpkin pie filling* has sugar and seasonings added to the pulp during processing. Usually only eggs and milk are necessary to complete this pie filling.

French Silk Chocolate Pie

FRENCH SILK CHOCOLATE PIE

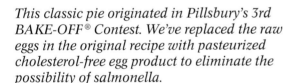

This classic pie originated in Pillsbury's 3rd BAKE-OFF® Contest. We've replaced the raw eggs in the original recipe with pasteurized cholesterol-free egg product to eliminate the possibility of salmonella.

CRUST
  Pastry for One-Crust Pie p. 268

FILLING
  3 oz. unsweetened chocolate, chopped
  ¾ cup butter, softened (do not substitute margarine)
  1 cup sugar
  ½ teaspoon vanilla
  ¾ cup frozen cholesterol-free egg product, thawed

TOPPING
  ½ cup sweetened whipped cream
    Chocolate Curls, if desired, p. 210

Prepare and bake pastry as directed for Baked Pie Shell using 9-inch pie pan; cool.

Melt chocolate in small saucepan over low heat; cool. In small bowl, beat butter until fluffy; add sugar gradually, beating until light and fluffy. Blend in cooled chocolate and vanilla. Add egg product ¼ cup at a time, beating at high speed 2 minutes after each addition. Beat until mixture is smooth and fluffy. Pour into cooled, baked pie shell. Refrigerate at least 2 hours before serving. Garnish with whipped cream and Chocolate Curls. Store in refrigerator.
Yield: 8 to 10 servings.

NUTRITION PER SERVING:
Calories 400; Protein 5g; Carbohydrate 34g; Fat 28g; Sodium 270mg.

VARIATION:

FRENCH SILK CHOCOLATE TARTLETS:
Prepare and roll pastry for Two-Crust Pie. Cut pastry into 8 quarters. Place 1 quarter of pastry in bottom and up sides of each of 8 tartlet pans. Trim edges. Generously prick crust with fork. Bake at 450°F. for 8 to 10 minutes until lightly browned; cool. Divide filling evenly into cooled, baked crusts.
Yield: 8 tartlets.

VANILLA CREAM PIE

This basic cream pie can be flavored in many ways. Choose from the variations below.

CRUST
Pastry for One-Crust Pie p. 268

FILLING
3/4 **cup sugar**
1/4 **cup cornstarch**
1/4 **teaspoon salt**
3 **cups milk**
3 **egg yolks, slightly beaten**
2 **tablespoons margarine or butter**
2 **teaspoons vanilla**

Prepare and bake pastry as directed for Baked Pie Shell using 9-inch pie pan; cool.

In medium saucepan, combine sugar, cornstarch and salt; mix well. Stir in milk, blending until smooth. Cook over medium heat until mixture boils and thickens, stirring constantly. Boil 2 minutes; remove from heat. Blend a small amount of hot mixture into egg yolks. Add yolk mixture to hot mixture, blending well. Cook until mixture just begins to bubble, stirring constantly. Remove from heat; stir in margarine and vanilla. Pour into cooled, baked pie shell. Refrigerate 3 hours or until set. If desired, serve with whipped cream. Store in refrigerator.
Yield: 8 servings.

NUTRITION PER SERVING:
Calories 330; Protein 6g; Carbohydrate 38g; Fat 17g; Sodium 290mg.

VARIATIONS:

BANANA CREAM PIE: Cool filling in saucepan to lukewarm. Slice 2 or 3 bananas into cooled, baked pie shell; pour filling over bananas.

BUTTERSCOTCH CREAM PIE: Substitute firmly packed brown sugar for sugar.

CHOCOLATE CREAM PIE: Increase sugar to 1 cup and add 2 oz. unsweetened chocolate to filling mixture before cooking.

COCONUT CREAM PIE: Stir 1 cup coconut into cooked filling with margarine and vanilla.

CHOCOLATE DATE CREAM PIE

Free yourself from last-minute preparations with this delightful do-ahead dessert.

CRUST
1 1/4 **cups chocolate wafer cookie crumbs (about 22 cookies)**
1/4 **cup sugar**
1/3 **cup margarine or butter, melted**

FILLING
1 **cup dates, cut up**
1 **cup water**
1 **cup miniature marshmallows**
1/2 **cup chopped walnuts**
1/4 **cup miniature chocolate chips**
1 **cup whipping cream**
2 **tablespoons powdered sugar**
1/2 **teaspoon vanilla**

TOPPING
Sweetened whipped cream, if desired
Walnut halves dipped in chocolate, if desired

Heat oven to 375°F. In medium bowl, combine all crust ingredients; blend well. Reserve 2 tablespoons of crumb mixture for garnish. Press remaining mixture in 9-inch pie pan to form crust. Bake at 375°F. for 5 minutes. Cool completely.

In medium saucepan, combine dates and water. Bring to a boil. Reduce heat; simmer 6 to 8 minutes or until thickened, stirring occasionally. Remove from heat. Add marshmallows; stir until melted. Cool to room temperature. Stir in chopped walnuts and chocolate chips.

In small bowl, beat 1 cup whipping cream, powdered sugar and vanilla until stiff peaks form. Spread date mixture in cooled crust. Spread whipped cream over top; sprinkle with reserved crumb mixture. Refrigerate until firm, at least 2 hours or overnight. Garnish with dollops of whipped cream and walnut halves. Store in refrigerator.
Yield: 8 servings.

NUTRITION PER SERVING:
Calories 450; Protein 4g; Carbohydrate 46g; Fat 28g; Sodium 125mg.

Bavarian Chocolate Ripple Cream Pie

Our taste panel was crazy about this pie. It has a tasty macaroon crust with rippled layers of chocolate and whipped cream.

CRUST
- 1 cup finely crushed crisp coconut macaroon cookies
- ½ cup finely chopped almonds
- ⅓ cup firmly packed brown sugar
- ¼ cup all purpose flour
- ⅓ cup margarine or butter, melted

FILLING
- 1 envelope unflavored gelatin
- 1¾ cups milk
- ¾ cup sugar
- 2 oz. semi-sweet chocolate, chopped
- 2 tablespoons margarine or butter
- 1 teaspoon vanilla
- 1 cup whipping cream, whipped

TOPPING
- Grated Chocolate p. 210

Heat oven to 350°F. In small bowl, combine all crust ingredients. Press in bottom and up sides of 9-inch pie pan. Bake at 350°F. for 15 minutes; cool.

Soften gelatin in 1 cup of the milk for 5 minutes. In small saucepan over medium heat, combine gelatin mixture, sugar and chocolate; stir constantly just until mixture begins to boil and chocolate is melted. Remove from heat; stir in 2 tablespoons margarine until smooth. Add remaining ¾ cup milk and vanilla; mix well. Refrigerate until almost set.

Alternately layer chocolate mixture and whipped cream in cooled, baked crust forming 4 layers and ending with whipped cream. With spatula, gently swirl through the top 2 layers to marble. Refrigerate at least 2 hours before serving. Garnish with Grated Chocolate. Store in refrigerator.

Yield: 8 servings.

NUTRITION PER SERVING:
Calories 500; Protein 6g; Carbohydrate 48g; Fat 32g; Sodium 170mg.

Black Forest Cream Pie

Dinner guests will be impressed by this chocolate and cherry favorite. It can be made early in the day and refrigerated until serving time.

CRUST
- Pastry for One-Crust Pie p. 268

FILLING
- 6 oz. semi-sweet chocolate, chopped
- 2 tablespoons margarine or butter
- ¼ cup powdered sugar
- 1 (8-oz.) pkg. cream cheese, softened
- 1 (21-oz.) can cherry fruit pie filling

TOPPING
- 1 cup whipping cream, whipped
- Grated Chocolate p. 210

Prepare and bake pastry as directed for Baked Pie Shell using 9-inch pie pan or 10-inch tart pan with removable bottom; cool.

In small saucepan, melt 6 oz. chocolate and margarine over low heat, stirring constantly; remove from heat. In small bowl, beat powdered sugar and cream cheese. Stir in melted chocolate mixture; beat until smooth. Fold in 1 cup of the cherry pie filling. Set aside remaining pie filling. Spread mixture evenly into cooled, baked pie shell. Refrigerate 1 hour.

In small bowl, combine topping ingredients. Spread evenly over cooled chocolate layer. Spoon remaining cherry pie filling in a band around outer edge of pie. Refrigerate until serving time. Garnish with Grated Chocolate, if desired. Store in refrigerator.

Yield: 12 servings.

NUTRITION PER SERVING:
Calories 430; Protein 3g; Carbohydrate 43g; Fat 27g; Sodium 160mg.

Maple Banana Cream Pie

A unique crust treatment and complementary maple flavor transform ordinary banana cream pie into something special.

FILLING
 1 (3-oz.) pkg. vanilla pudding and pie filling mix (not instant)
 1½ cups milk
 ½ cup maple-flavored syrup
 2 medium bananas, sliced

CRUST
  Pastry for Two-Crust Pie p. 268

TOPPING
 1 cup whipping cream
 2 tablespoons maple-flavored syrup
  Maple leaf cutouts, if desired*

Prepare pudding according to package directions using 1½ cups milk and ½ cup syrup. Cover surface with plastic wrap; cool 1 hour.

Prepare and bake half of pastry as directed in One-Crust Pie recipe for Baked Pie Shell, using 9-inch pie pan; cool. Meanwhile, roll out remaining pastry; place on ungreased cookie sheet. Cut pastry into 8-inch circle, reserving scraps for cutouts.* Generously prick circle with fork. Bake at 450°F. for 8 minutes or until lightly browned; cool completely.

Arrange banana slices over bottom of cooled, baked pie shell. Spoon half of cooled filling over bananas; top with cooled 8-inch crust. Spoon remaining filling over crust. Refrigerate 5 hours or until set.

In small bowl, combine whipping cream and 2 tablespoons syrup; beat until soft peaks form. Pipe or spoon over pie. Garnish with maple leaf cutouts.
Yield: 8 servings.

TIP:
* To make cutouts, use maple leaf-shaped cookie cutter or desired shape. Cut shapes from pastry; transfer to cookie sheet. Sprinkle with sugar. Bake at 450°F. for 6 to 8 minutes or until lightly browned. Cool on wire rack.

NUTRITION PER SERVING:
Calories 500; Protein 4g; Carbohydrate 61g; Fat 27g; Sodium 280mg.

Strawberries and Cream Pie

Neufchatel cheese, a reduced-fat cream cheese, can be substituted for the cream cheese in this luscious pie.

CRUST
  Pastry for One-Crust Pie p. 268

FILLING
 1 (8-oz.) pkg. cream cheese, softened
 ⅓ cup sugar
 ¼ to ½ teaspoon almond extract
 1 cup whipping cream, whipped
 4 cups strawberries

TOPPING
 ½ cup semi-sweet chocolate chips
 1 tablespoon shortening

Prepare and bake pastry as directed for Baked Pie Shell using 9-inch pie pan or 10-inch tart pan with removable bottom; cool.

In large bowl, beat cream cheese until fluffy. Gradually add sugar and almond extract; blend well. Fold in whipped cream. Spoon into cooled, baked pie shell. Arrange strawberries, points up, over filling. Refrigerate.

In small saucepan over low heat, melt chocolate chips and shortening, stirring constantly until smooth. Drizzle over strawberries and filling. Refrigerate until set. Store in refrigerator.
Yield: 10 to 12 servings.

NUTRITION PER SERVING:
Calories 290; Protein 3g; Carbohydrate 23g; Fat 22g; Sodium 150mg.

Cook's Note

BRAIDED CRUST

To prepare braided edge, place the pastry in the pan; trim pastry even with edge of pan. Brush edge of crust with egg white. Using second crust, cut crust into twelve ¼ to ⅜-inch strips. Braid 3 strips together and place on edge of crust, pressing lightly to secure. Repeat with remaining strips.

Strawberries and Cream Pie

RASPBERRY ANGEL CREAM PIE

Walnuts are pressed into the crust before baking.

CRUST
> **Pastry for One-Crust Pie p. 268**
- ¼ cup chopped walnuts or pecans

FILLING
- 25 large marshmallows
- ½ cup milk
- 1 cup whipping cream, whipped

TOPPING
- ⅓ cup sugar
- 2 tablespoons cornstarch
- ¾ cup water
- 1 teaspoon lemon juice
- 1 teaspoon orange-flavored liqueur, if desired
- 1 teaspoon red food color, if desired
- 2 cups fresh or frozen whole raspberries, thawed, drained

GARNISH
> **Whipped cream**
> **Whole raspberries**

Heat oven to 450°F. Prepare pastry for One-Crust Pie using 9-inch pie pan. Press walnuts into bottom of pastry-lined pan. Generously prick pastry with fork. Bake at 450°F. for 9 to 12 minutes or until light golden brown. Cool completely.

In large saucepan, combine marshmallows and milk. Cook over medium heat until marshmallows are melted, stirring constantly. Cover; refrigerate until thickened but not set, 35 to 45 minutes. (Mixture may separate as it cools.)

Fold in whipped cream. Spread over bottom of cooled, baked crust. Refrigerate until thoroughly chilled, about 1 hour.

In medium saucepan, combine sugar and cornstarch; mix well. Gradually stir in water, lemon juice, liqueur and food color. Cook over medium heat 10 minutes, stirring occasionally. Stir in 1 cup of the raspberries. Continue cooking until thickened and clear, stirring constantly. Cover surface with plastic wrap. Refrigerate until just cool, about 1 hour.

Fold in remaining 1 cup raspberries. Spoon evenly over cooled filling. Refrigerate 1 to 2 hours or until set. Garnish with whipped cream and whole raspberries. Store in refrigerator.
Yield: 8 servings.

NUTRITION PER SERVING:
Calories 400; Protein 3g; Carbohydrate 44g; Fat 24g; Sodium 160mg.

QUICK HAWAIIAN CREAM PIE

Favorite flavors of the tropics, banana, pineapple and coconut, are highlighted in this cream pie.

CRUST
> **Pastry for One-Crust Pie p. 268**

FILLING
- 1 cup whipping cream
- ½ cup milk
- 1 tablespoon rum or 1 teaspoon rum extract
- 1 (3.4-oz.) pkg. instant vanilla pudding and pie filling mix
- ½ cup whipping cream, whipped
- ⅓ cup (1 small) mashed ripe banana
- 1 (8-oz.) can crushed pineapple, well drained

TOPPING
- ½ cup coconut
- ¼ to ½ cup chopped pecans, toasted, p. 23

Prepare and bake pastry as directed for Baked Pie Shell using 9-inch pie pan; cool.

In small bowl, combine 1 cup whipping cream, milk, rum and pudding mix; beat at high speed until thick. Fold in whipped cream, banana and pineapple. Spoon into cooled, baked pie shell. Top with coconut and pecans. Refrigerate about 3 hours or until set. Store in refrigerator.
Yield: 8 servings.

NUTRITION PER SERVING:
Calories 420; Protein 3g; Carbohydrate 32g; Fat 31g; Sodium 340mg.

ORANGE KIST COCONUT CREAM PIE

This light, creamy pie from the 1990 Pillsbury BAKE-OFF® Contest has a mild orange flavor and is topped with almonds and coconut.

CRUST
> **Pastry for One-Crust Pie p. 268**

FILLING
- 1 cup sugar
- 3 tablespoons cornstarch
- 1 cup water
- ¼ cup orange juice
- ¼ cup margarine or butter
- 1 tablespoon grated orange peel
- 3 egg yolks
- ½ cup coconut, toasted, p. 23
- ½ cup dairy sour cream
- ½ cup whipping cream, whipped

TOPPING
- ½ cup whipping cream
- 2 tablespoons powdered sugar
- ¼ cup coconut, toasted, p. 23
- 2 tablespoons sliced almonds, toasted, p. 23

Prepare and bake pastry as directed for Baked Pie Shell using 9-inch pie pan; cool.

In medium saucepan, combine sugar and cornstarch; mix well. Stir in water, orange juice, margarine, orange peel and egg yolks. Cook over medium heat until mixture thickens and boils, about 5 minutes, stirring constantly. Cover surface with plastic wrap. Refrigerate until just cool, about 1 hour. Stir in ½ cup toasted coconut and sour cream. Fold in whipped cream. Spoon into cooled, baked pie shell.

In small bowl, beat ½ cup whipping cream and powdered sugar until stiff peaks form. Spread over filling. Garnish with ¼ cup toasted coconut and almonds. Refrigerate 1 to 2 hours. Store in refrigerator.

Yield: 8 servings.

NUTRITION PER SERVING:
Calories 490; Protein 4g; Carbohydrate 46g; Fat 32g; Sodium 220mg.

CRANBERRY CREAM PIE

Creme de cassis, a black currant liqueur, is the flavoring in the topping of this quick and easy pie.

CRUST
> **Pastry for One-Crust Pie p. 268**

FILLING
- 1 (3-oz.) pkg. raspberry flavor gelatin
- ¾ cup boiling water
- 1 (16-oz.) can whole berry cranberry sauce
- 1 (3.4-oz.) pkg. vanilla instant pudding and pie filling mix
- ¾ cup milk
- 1 (8-oz.) container (3½ cups) frozen whipped topping, thawed
- 1 tablespoon creme de cassis, if desired

Prepare and bake pastry as directed for Baked Pie Shell using 9-inch pie pan; cool.

In medium bowl, combine gelatin and boiling water; stir to dissolve. Stir in cranberry sauce. Refrigerate just until cool, 10 to 15 minutes.

In large bowl, prepare pudding mix with ¾ cup milk as directed on package; let stand about 2 minutes. Blend in gelatin mixture. Fold in 2½ cups of the whipped topping. Spoon into cooled, baked pie shell. Refrigerate until set, about 2 hours.

In small bowl, fold creme de cassis into remaining 1 cup whipped topping. Pipe or spoon dollops on top of pie. Garnish as desired. Store in refrigerator.

Yield: 10 servings.

NUTRITION PER SERVING:
Calories 220; Protein 8g; Carbohydrate 33g; Fat 6g; Sodium 170mg.

CANTALOUPE CREAM PIE

This refreshing dessert is best served the same day and is an excellent source of vitamins A and C.

CRUST
> **Pastry for One-Crust Pie p. 268**

FILLING
- 1 **envelope unflavored gelatin**
- ½ **cup orange juice**
- 1 **large (1½ lb.) cantaloupe, halved, seeded**
- ¼ **cup sugar**
- 2 **teaspoons grated orange peel**
- 1 **cup whipping cream**

TOPPING
- ⅓ **cup apricot jam**
- 2 **tablespoons orange-flavored liqueur or orange juice**

Prepare and bake pastry as directed for Baked Pie Shell using 9-inch pie pan; cool.

In small saucepan, combine gelatin and orange juice; let stand 1 minute. Cook and stir over low heat until gelatin is dissolved. Scoop melon into balls (about 2 cups); reserve. Remove remaining melon from rind; cut into pieces. In blender container or food processor bowl with metal blade, puree melon pieces, sugar and orange peel until smooth. Add gelatin mixture and whipping cream; blend well. Refrigerate until slightly thickened, about 10 minutes. Pour into cooled, baked pie shell; spread evenly. Refrigerate until set, 45 to 60 minutes. Top with melon balls. Refrigerate 1 hour or until set.

Just before serving, heat jam in small saucepan until melted; stir in liqueur. Spoon over pie.
Yield: 8 servings.

NUTRITION PER SERVING:
Calories 330; Protein 3g; Carbohydrate 38g; Fat 19g; Sodium 125mg.

LEMON FUDGE RIBBON PIE

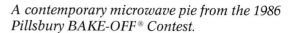

A contemporary microwave pie from the 1986 Pillsbury BAKE-OFF® Contest.

CRUST
> **Pastry for One-Crust Pie p. 268**
- ½ **teaspoon unsweetened cocoa**

FILLING
- 1 **(8-oz.) pkg. cream cheese, cut into 2 pieces**
- 1 **cup sugar**
- ¼ **cup lemon juice**
- 1 **teaspoon vanilla**
- 3 **eggs, beaten**
- ½ **oz. unsweetened chocolate or 1 oz. semi-sweet chocolate**

TOPPING
- 1 **cup whipping cream**
- 1 **tablespoon powdered sugar**
  Grated Chocolate, if desired, p. 210

MICROWAVE DIRECTIONS:
Prepare pastry for One-Crust Pie using 9-inch microwave-safe pie pan. Prick crust generously with fork. Sprinkle edge of pastry with cocoa; rub in gently with finger tips before fluting. Microwave on HIGH for 6 to 8 minutes, rotating pan ½ turn every 2 minutes. Crust is done when surface appears dry and flaky. Cool completely.

In medium microwave-safe bowl, microwave cream cheese on HIGH for 1 to 1½ minutes to soften. Stir in sugar until smooth. Add lemon juice, vanilla and eggs; blend well. Microwave on HIGH for 2 minutes; stir. Microwave on HIGH for an additional 3 to 5 minutes, stirring every 2 minutes, until smooth and thickened.

In small microwave-safe bowl, microwave unsweetened chocolate on HIGH for 2 minutes or until melted; blend in ½ cup of the lemon filling. Pour into cooled, baked crust; spread evenly. Carefully spread remaining lemon filling over chocolate filling. Cover with waxed paper; refrigerate 3 to 4 hours or until firm.

In small bowl, beat whipping cream until soft peaks form. Blend in powdered sugar; beat until stiff peaks form. Spoon or pipe over filling. Garnish with Grated Chocolate. Store in refrigerator.
Yield: 8 servings.

NUTRITION PER SERVING:
Calories 490; Protein 6g; Carbohydrate 43g; Fat 33g; Sodium 290mg.

SOUR CREAM RAISIN PIE

In this rich pie, plump raisins are surrounded by a spicy sour cream filling.

CRUST
  Pastry for One-Crust Pie p. 268

FILLING
1½ **cups raisins**
 ¾ **cup sugar**
 ¼ **cup cornstarch**
 ½ **teaspoon cinnamon**
 ¼ **teaspoon salt**
 ¼ **teaspoon nutmeg**
 2 **cups milk**
 3 **egg yolks, beaten**
 1 **cup dairy sour cream**
 1 **tablespoon lemon juice**
 1 **cup whipping cream, whipped**

Prepare and bake pastry as directed for Baked Pie Shell using 9-inch pie pan; cool.

In medium saucepan, combine raisins, sugar, cornstarch, cinnamon, salt and nutmeg; mix well. Stir in milk, blending until smooth. Cook over medium heat until mixture boils, stirring constantly. Boil 1 minute; remove from heat. Blend small amount of hot raisin mixture into egg yolks; add yolk mixture to hot mixture. Add sour cream; mix well. Cook just until mixture starts to bubble, stirring constantly. Remove from heat; stir in lemon juice. Cool slightly; pour into cooled, baked pie shell. Refrigerate 2 hours or until set. Top with whipped cream. Store in refrigerator.

Yield: 8 servings.

NUTRITION PER SERVING:
Calories 530; Protein 7g; Carbohydrate 61g; Fat 29g; Sodium 260mg.

VARIATION:

SOUR CREAM RAISIN MERINGUE PIE: Heat oven to 350°F. Substitute meringue for 1 cup whipping cream. In small bowl, beat 3 egg whites and ¼ teaspoon cream of tartar at medium speed until soft peaks form, about 1 minute. Gradually add ¼ cup sugar, 1 tablespoon at a time, beating at highest speed until stiff peaks form and sugar is dissolved. Spoon meringue over filling. Seal to edge of crust. Bake at 350°F. for 10 to 15 minutes or until lightly browned. Cool completely. Store in refrigerator.

SWEET CHERRITY PIE

In this pie from the 1976 Pillsbury BAKE-OFF® Contest, a cream cheese layer is topped with a pink fluffy cherry layer. It's best when refrigerated overnight before serving.

CRUST
 1 **cup all purpose flour**
 ½ **to 1 cup finely chopped nuts**
 ¼ **cup firmly packed brown sugar**
 ½ **cup margarine or butter, softened**

FILLING
 1 **(8-oz.) pkg. cream cheese, softened**
 ½ **teaspoon almond extract**
 1 **cup powdered sugar**
 1 **cup whipping cream***
 1 **(21-oz.) can cherry fruit pie filling**

Heat oven to 375°F. In ungreased 13x9-inch pan, combine all crust ingredients; mix well. Bake at 375°F. for 15 to 20 minutes or until golden brown, stirring once during baking. Reserve ½ cup of the crumb mixture for topping. Firmly press remaining warm crumb mixture in bottom and up sides of ungreased 9 or 10-inch pie pan. Refrigerate 15 minutes.

In small bowl, combine cream cheese, almond extract and powdered sugar; blend until smooth. Spread over cooled, baked crust. In medium bowl, beat whipping cream until stiff peaks form. Fold in pie filling. Spoon over cream cheese layer. Sprinkle with reserved ½ cup crumb mixture. Refrigerate 2 to 3 hours or until thoroughly chilled before serving. Store in refrigerator.

Yield: 8 to 10 servings.

TIP:
* Do not use frozen whipped topping; a curdled appearance will result.

NUTRITION PER SERVING:
Calories 540; Protein 6g; Carbohydrate 57g; Fat 34g; Sodium 190mg.

BLUEBERRY LEMON MOUSSE PIE

A layer of spiced, glazed blueberries tucked under a blanket of chilled lemon chiffon makes this pie cool and refreshing.

CRUST
- Pastry for One-Crust Pie p. 268

FILLING
- 1 (16½-oz.) can blueberries
- ¼ cup sugar
- 2 tablespoons cornstarch
- 1 teaspoon grated lemon peel
- ½ teaspoon nutmeg
- ⅛ teaspoon ground cardamom, if desired
- 1 tablespoon margarine or butter

TOPPING
- 1 (3-oz.) pkg. lemon flavor gelatin
- 1 cup boiling water
- ½ cup cold water
- 1 teaspoon grated lemon peel
- 1 cup whipping cream, whipped

Prepare and bake pastry as directed for Baked Pie Shell using 9-inch pie pan; cool.

Drain blueberries, reserving ½ cup liquid. In small saucepan, combine sugar and cornstarch; stir in blueberry liquid. Cook over medium heat until mixture boils and thickens, stirring constantly. Boil slowly 1 minute; remove from heat. Stir in blueberries and remaining filling ingredients. Set aside to cool while preparing topping.

In large bowl, dissolve gelatin in boiling water. Stir in cold water and lemon peel. Refrigerate until mixture begins to thicken and is of syrupy consistency, about 30 to 45 minutes. Beat thickened gelatin at highest speed about 3 to 4 minutes or until light and fluffy; gelatin should about double in volume. Fold whipped cream thoroughly into gelatin. Pour blueberry filling into cooled, baked pie shell; spoon lemon topping over cooled filling. Refrigerate at least 1 hour before serving. Store in refrigerator.
Yield: 8 servings.

NUTRITION PER SERVING:
Calories 390; Protein 4g; Carbohydrate 46g; Fat 21g; Sodium 195mg

WHITE CHOCOLATE PECAN MOUSSE PIE

This light and fluffy mousse pie flavored with buttered pecans will melt in your mouth! It's best served well chilled.

CRUST
- Pastry for One-Crust Pie p. 268

FILLING
- 2 tablespoons butter
- 2 cups chopped pecans
- 1 cup vanilla milk chips or 6-oz. pkg. white baking bars, chopped
- ¼ cup milk
- 2 cups whipping cream
- ⅓ cup sugar
- 1 teaspoon vanilla

GARNISH
- 1 tablespoon Grated Chocolate p. 210, or ¼ cup chocolate syrup, if desired

Heat oven to 450°F. Prepare pastry for One-Crust Pie using 10-inch springform pan or 9-inch pie pan. Place pastry in pan; press in bottom and up sides of pan. With fork dipped in flour, press top edge of pastry to sides of pan. Generously prick pastry with fork. Bake at 450°F. for 9 to 11 minutes or until light golden brown. Cool completely.

Melt butter in 10-inch skillet over medium heat. Stir in pecans. Cook until pecans are golden brown, about 6 minutes, stirring constantly. Cool at room temperature 1 hour.

In small saucepan over low heat, melt vanilla milk chips with milk, stirring constantly with wire whisk. Cool at room temperature 1 hour.

In large bowl, beat whipping cream until stiff peaks form. Fold in sugar, vanilla, pecans and melted vanilla milk chips. Spoon into cooled, baked crust. Refrigerate 4 hours before serving. Just before serving, garnish with Grated chocolate. Store in refrigerator.
Yield: 10 to 12 servings.

TIP:
Pie can be frozen. Let stand at room temperature 30 to 45 minutes before serving.

NUTRITION PER SERVING:
Calories 470; Protein 4g; Carbohydrate 27g; Fat 39g; Sodium 140mg.

Chocolate Caramel Mousse Pie

Candy fans will love the classic flavors of caramel, pecans and chocolate in a pie from the 1992 Pillsbury BAKE-OFF® Contest.

CRUST
> **Pastry for One-Crust Pie p. 268**

FILLING
- 1 **cup evaporated milk**
- 6 **oz. semi-sweet chocolate, chopped**
- 1 **envelope unflavored gelatin**
- 3 **tablespoons water**
- 1 **cup powdered sugar**
- 1 **teaspoon vanilla**
- 1 **(14-oz.) pkg. caramels, unwrapped**
- 1/3 **cup evaporated milk**
- 1 **cup chopped pecans**

TOPPING
- 1 **cup whipping cream**
- 2 **tablespoons powdered sugar**
- 1/2 **teaspoon vanilla**
- 1/3 **cup pecan halves**

Prepare and bake pastry as directed for Baked Pie Shell using 9-inch pie pan or 10-inch tart pan with removable bottom; cool.

In heavy saucepan, combine 1 cup evaporated milk and chocolate. Cook over medium heat until chocolate melts, stirring constantly. In small bowl, dissolve gelatin in water. Add to chocolate mixture; beat until well blended. Add 1 cup powdered sugar and 1 teaspoon vanilla; beat until mixture is smooth. Refrigerate until mixture is slightly thickened, 15 to 20 minutes.

In medium saucepan, combine caramels and 1/3 cup evaporated milk. Cook over medium heat until caramels are melted, stirring constantly. Reserve 1/3 cup of the caramel mixture; set aside. Spread remaining caramel mixture over bottom of cooled, baked pie shell. Sprinkle with 1 cup chopped pecans.

In small bowl, beat whipping cream, 2 tablespoons powdered sugar and 1/2 teaspoon vanilla until stiff peaks form. Beat chilled chocolate mixture on high speed until mixture is light in color, about 2 minutes. Fold in 1 cup of the whipped cream, reserving remaining whipped cream for garnish. Refrigerate chocolate mixture for 15 to 30 minutes or until thickened. Spoon and spread chocolate mixture over chopped pecans. Pipe or spoon reserved whipped cream around edge of pie. If necessary, slightly heat reserved 1/3 cup caramel mixture. Drizzle over pie; garnish with pecan halves. Refrigerate 2 hours or until set. Store in refrigerator.
Yield: 8 to 10 servings.

NUTRITION PER SERVING:
Calories 630; Protein 8g; Carbohydrate 71g; Fat 38g; Sodium 220mg.

Cook's Note

MOUSSE

The term mousse refers to a light airy mixture that can be either sweet or savory. The characteristic light fluffy texture of mousse is made by folding beaten egg whites or whipped cream into a gelatin or custard mixture. Dessert mousses are often flavored with chocolate or pureed fruit.

LEMON LUSCIOUS PIE

Garnish this velvety smooth sour cream lemon pie with whipped cream and walnuts.

CRUST
Pastry for One-Crust Pie p. 268

FILLING
  1 **cup sugar**
  3 **tablespoons cornstarch**
  1 **cup milk**
  ¼ **cup lemon juice**
  3 **egg yolks, slightly beaten**
  ¼ **cup margarine or butter**
  1 **tablespoon grated lemon peel**
  1 **cup dairy sour cream**

Prepare and bake pastry as directed for Baked Pie Shell using 9-inch pie pan; cool.

In medium saucepan, combine sugar and cornstarch; mix well. Stir in milk, lemon juice and egg yolks; cook over medium heat until thick, stirring constantly. Remove from heat; stir in margarine and lemon peel. Cool. Fold in sour cream. Spoon into cooled, baked pie shell. Refrigerate at least 2 hours or until set. Store in refrigerator.
Yield: 8 servings.

NUTRITION PER SERVING:
Calories 430; Protein 4g; Carbohydrate 44g; Fat 27g; Sodium 270mg.

LEMON TRUFFLE PIE

White chocolate and lemon are featured in this heavenly pie.

CRUST
Pastry for One-Crust Pie p. 268

FILLING
  1 **cup sugar**
  2 **tablespoons cornstarch**
  2 **tablespoons all purpose flour**
  1 **cup water**
  2 **egg yolks, beaten**
  1 **tablespoon margarine or butter**
  ½ **teaspoon grated lemon peel**
  ¼ **cup lemon juice**
  1 **cup vanilla milk chips or 6-oz. pkg. white baking bars, chopped**
  1 **(8-oz.) pkg. light cream cheese (Neufchatel), softened**
  ½ **cup whipping cream**
  1 **tablespoon sliced almonds, toasted, p. 23**

Prepare and bake pastry as directed for Baked Pie Shell using 9-inch pie pan; cool.

In medium saucepan, combine sugar, cornstarch and flour; mix well. Gradually stir in water until smooth. Cook over medium heat until mixture thickens and boils, stirring constantly. Reduce heat; cook 2 minutes, stirring constantly. Remove from heat. Blend about ¼ cup of hot mixture into egg yolks. Gradually stir yolk mixture into hot mixture in saucepan. Cook over low heat until mixture comes to a boil, stirring constantly. Cook 2 minutes, stirring constantly. Remove from heat; stir in margarine, lemon peel and lemon juice. Place ⅓ cup of hot lemon mixture in small saucepan; cool remaining mixture 15 minutes. Add vanilla milk chips to hot lemon mixture in small saucepan. Stir over low heat just until chips are melted.

In small bowl, beat cream cheese until fluffy. Add vanilla milk chip mixture; beat until well blended. Spread over bottom of cooled, baked pie shell. Spoon remaining lemon mixture over cream cheese layer. Refrigerate 2 to 3 hours or until set.

In small bowl, beat whipping cream until stiff peaks form. Pipe or spoon over pie. Garnish with toasted almonds. Store in refrigerator.
Yield: 8 to 10 servings.

NUTRITION PER SERVING:
Calories 400; Protein 5g; Carbohydrate 44g; Fat 23g; Sodium 230mg.

Lemon Truffle Pie, Apricot Tea Tart p. 321

Mocha Frappe Pie

For tender flaky pie crust, add just enough cold water to moisten the flour mixture, tossing it gently with a fork. Once the mixture is moistened, stop mixing.

CRUST
- 1 cup all purpose flour
- 2 tablespoons sugar
- ½ teaspoon salt
- ⅓ cup shortening
- 1 egg yolk
- 2 to 3 tablespoons water

FILLING
- 4¼ cups miniature marshmallows
- ¼ cup sugar
- 1 (5-oz.) can (⅔ cup) evaporated milk
- 2 teaspoons instant coffee granules or crystals
- 1 (6-oz.) pkg. (1 cup) semi-sweet chocolate chips
- 1 cup whipping cream, whipped

TOPPING
- Chocolate Curls, if desired, p. 210

Heat oven to 375°F. In medium bowl, combine flour, 2 tablespoons sugar and salt; mix well. Using pastry blender or fork, cut in shortening until mixture resembles coarse crumbs. In small bowl, combine egg yolk and 2 tablespoons water. Stir egg yolk mixture into flour mixture with fork until mixture forms a ball. Add additional water, if necessary, until dough is moist enough to hold together.

Shape dough into a ball. Flatten ball; smooth edges. On lightly floured surface, roll ball lightly from center to edge to form a 10½-inch circle. Fold pastry in half; place in 9-inch pie pan. Unfold; fit evenly in pan. Do not stretch. Fold edge under to form standing rim; flute. Prick bottom and sides of crust with fork. Bake at 375°F. for 12 to 17 minutes or until light golden brown. Cool completely.

In large saucepan over low heat, melt marshmallows, ¼ cup sugar, milk and coffee until mixture is smooth, stirring occasionally. Stir in chocolate chips until melted. Cool slightly. Spread ¾ cup of chocolate mixture in bottom of cooled, baked pie shell. Refrigerate remaining chocolate mixture until thoroughly cooled, about 15 minutes. Fold whipped cream into remaining chocolate mixture. Spoon over chocolate layer; spread evenly.

Refrigerate 2 to 3 hours. Garnish with Chocolate Curls. Store in refrigerator.
Yield: 8 servings.

NUTRITION PER SERVING:
Calories 490; Protein 5g; Carbohydrate 55g; Fat 28g; Sodium 180mg

White Christmas Pie

This creamy white filling in a chocolate crust is topped with bright red raspberry sauce. It's a treat for your eyes as well as your taste buds.

CRUST
- 1 cup all purpose flour
- ¼ cup firmly packed brown sugar
- 2 tablespoons unsweetened cocoa
- ¼ teaspoon salt
- ⅓ cup shortening
- 3 to 4 tablespoons cold water

FILLING
- ¼ cup sugar
- ¼ cup cornstarch
- 1½ cups milk
- 1 (6-oz.) pkg. white baking bars, chopped, or 1 cup vanilla milk chips
- 1 teaspoon vanilla
- ¾ cup whipping cream
- 2 tablespoons powdered sugar

RASPBERRY SAUCE AND GARNISH
- 1 (10-oz.) pkg. frozen raspberries in syrup, thawed
- 1 tablespoon cornstarch
- Chocolate Cutouts, if desired, p. 210

Heat oven to 450°F. In medium bowl, combine flour, brown sugar, cocoa and salt; mix well. Using pastry blender or fork, cut in shortening until mixture resembles coarse crumbs. Sprinkle flour mixture with water 1 tablespoon at a time, while tossing and mixing lightly with fork. Add water until dough is just moist enough to hold together.

Shape dough into a ball. Flatten ball; smooth edges. On lightly floured surface, roll ball lightly from center to edge to form 10½-inch circle. Fold pastry in half; place in 9-inch pie pan. Unfold; fit evenly in pan. Do not stretch. Fold edge under to form standing rim; flute. Prick bottom and sides of crust generously with fork. Bake at 450°F. for 8 to

11 minutes or until crust appears dry and flaky. Cool completely.

In medium saucepan, combine sugar and ¼ cup cornstarch. Add milk gradually, stirring over medium heat until mixture boils; boil 1 minute, stirring constantly. Add baking bar and vanilla, stirring until baking bar is melted and mixture is smooth. Pour into large bowl; cover top with plastic wrap. Cool to room temperature.

In small bowl, beat whipping cream with powdered sugar until soft peaks form. Beat cooled baking bar mixture at medium speed until light and fluffy, about 1 minute. Fold whipped cream into mixture. Spoon evenly into cooled, baked pie shell. Refrigerate 2 to 3 hours or until set.

In small saucepan over medium heat, combine raspberries and 1 tablespoon cornstarch. Bring to boil, stirring constantly. Boil 1 minute, stirring constantly. Cool. Serve pie with raspberry sauce. Garnish with Chocolate Cutouts. Store in the refrigerator.

Yield: 8 servings.

NUTRITION PER SERVING:
Calories 500; Protein 6g; Carbohydrate 61g; Fat 27g; Sodium 130mg.

COOK'S NOTE

UNFLAVORED GELATIN

Unflavored gelatin is used to thicken or set a liquid mixture. In recipes, the unflavored gelatin is sprinkled over cold water or liquid and allowed to stand about 2 minutes to soften. The softened gelatin is combined with hot water or a hot liquid. The mixture is then refrigerated to set. Some fresh foods contain an enzyme that prevents the gelatin from setting up. These foods, fresh pineapple, kiwifruit, figs, guava, papaya and gingerroot, can be used successfully with gelatin only after they've been cooked or canned.

CARAMEL CANDY PIE

Caramel candies are melted into a smooth and luscious filling in this winning recipe from the 4th Pillsbury BAKE-OFF® Contest. Caramelized almonds add the finishing touch.

CRUST
    Pastry for One-Crust Pie p. 268

FILLING
  1 **envelope unflavored gelatin**
¼ **cup cold water**
  1 **(14-oz.) pkg. vanilla caramels, unwrapped**
  1 **cup milk**
1½ **cups whipping cream, whipped**

TOPPING
  2 **tablespoons sugar**
¼ **cup slivered almonds**

Prepare and bake pastry as directed for Baked Pie Shell using 9-inch pie pan; cool.

In small bowl, sprinkle gelatin over water; let stand to soften. In medium saucepan, combine caramels and milk. Cook over low heat until caramels are melted and mixture is smooth, stirring occasionally. Stir in softened gelatin. Refrigerate 45 to 60 minutes or until slightly thickened. Fold thickened caramel mixture into whipped cream. Spoon into cooled crust. Refrigerate 2 hours or until set.

Line cookie sheet with foil. In small skillet, combine sugar and almonds. Cook over low heat until sugar is melted and almonds are golden brown, stirring constantly. Immediately spread on foil-lined cookie sheet. Cool completely; break apart. Just before serving, garnish pie with caramelized almonds. Store in refrigerator.

Yield: 8 servings.

NUTRITION PER SERVING:
Calories 530; Protein 6g; Carbohydrate 55g; Fat 32g; Sodium 280mg.

LEMON MERINGUE PIE

Egg whites should be brought to room temperature for fluffy meringue with more volume.

CRUST
>**Pastry for One-Crust Pie p. 268**

FILLING
- 1¼ **cups sugar**
- ⅓ **cup cornstarch**
- ½ **teaspoon salt**
- 1½ **cups cold water**
- 3 **egg yolks**
- 2 **tablespoons margarine or butter**
- 1 **tablespoon grated lemon peel**
- ½ **cup fresh lemon juice**

MERINGUE
- 3 **egg whites**
- ¼ **teaspoon cream of tartar**
- ½ **teaspoon vanilla**
- ¼ **cup sugar**

Prepare and bake pastry as directed for Baked Pie Shell using 9-inch pie pan; cool.

In medium saucepan, combine 1¼ cups sugar, cornstarch and salt; mix well. Gradually stir in cold water until smooth. Cook over medium heat, stirring constantly, until mixture boils; boil 1 minute, stirring constantly. Remove from heat. In small bowl, beat egg yolks; stir about ¼ cup of hot mixture into egg yolks. Gradually stir yolk mixture into hot mixture. Cook over low heat, stirring constantly, until mixture boils. Boil 1 minute, stirring constantly. Remove from heat; stir in margarine, lemon peel and lemon juice. Cool slightly, about 15 minutes. Pour into cooled, baked pie shell.

Heat oven to 350°F. In small deep bowl, beat egg whites, cream of tartar and vanilla at medium speed until soft peaks form, about 1 minute. Add sugar 1 tablespoon at a time, beating at high speed until stiff glossy peaks form and sugar is dissolved. Spoon meringue onto hot filling; spread to edge of crust to seal well and prevent shrinkage. Bake at 350°F. for 12 to 15 minutes or until light golden brown. Cool completely. Refrigerate 3 hours or until filling is set. Store in refrigerator.

Yield: 8 servings.

NUTRITION PER SERVING:
Calories 320; Protein 4g; Carbohydrate 48g; Fat 13g; Sodium 320mg.

LEMON PUFF PEACH PIE

CRUST
- 1 **cup all purpose flour**
- ½ **teaspoon salt**
- ⅓ **cup shortening**
- 3 **to 4 tablespoons milk**

FILLING
- ½ **cup sugar**
- 3 **tablespoons cornstarch**
- ¼ **teaspoon nutmeg**
- 4 **cups sliced peeled peaches**
- ¼ **teaspoon grated lemon peel**

TOPPING
- ½ **cup sugar**
- 1 **tablespoon all purpose flour**
- 1 **tablespoon lemon juice**
- 3 **eggs, separated**
- ¼ **teaspoon grated lemon peel**
- ¼ **teaspoon cream of tartar**

Heat oven to 450°F. In medium bowl, combine 1 cup flour and salt. Using pastry blender or fork, cut in shortening until mixture resembles coarse crumbs. Sprinkle mixture with milk 1 tablespoon at a time, while tossing and mixing lightly with fork. Add milk until dough is moist enough to form a ball when lightly pressed together.

Shape dough into ball. Flatten ball to ½-inch thickness, rounding and smoothing edges. Roll lightly on floured surface from center to edge into 10½-inch circle. Fold pastry in half; place in 9-inch pie pan. Unfold; fit evenly in pan. Do not stretch. Turn edge under to form a standing rim; flute. Prick bottom and sides of pastry generously with fork. Bake at 450°F. for 10 to 12 minutes or until light golden brown; cool.

Reduce oven temperature to 325°F.; place oven rack at lowest position. In medium saucepan, combine ½ cup sugar, cornstarch, nutmeg and peaches. Cook over medium heat until mixture boils and thickens, stirring constantly. Remove from heat. Stir in lemon peel; keep warm while preparing topping.

In small saucepan, combine ½ cup sugar, 1 tablespoon flour, lemon juice and egg yolks; beat until well blended. Cook over medium heat just until mixture comes to a boil, stirring constantly. Remove from heat. Stir in lemon peel; set aside. Cool while preparing egg whites. In small bowl, beat egg whites and cream of tartar until stiff peaks form. Stir about ¼ of egg white mixture into warm egg yolk mixture; fold in remaining egg whites. Spoon peach filling into cooled, baked pie shell. Lightly spoon topping onto peaches; spread to edge of crust to seal well and prevent shrinkage. Bake on lowest oven rack at 325°F. for 25 to 30 minutes or until golden brown. Cool completely. Store in refrigerator.

Yield: 8 servings.

NUTRITION PER SERVING:
Calories 310; Protein 5g; Carbohydrate 49g; Fat 11g; Sodium 160mg.

RHUBARB CREAM PIE

CRUST
Pastry for Filled One-Crust Pie p. 268

FILLING
2   cups diced fresh rhubarb (do not use frozen rhubarb)
3   egg yolks
½   cup half-and-half
1   cup sugar
2   tablespoons all purpose flour
½   teaspoon salt

MERINGUE
3   egg whites
¼   teaspoon cream of tartar
½   teaspoon vanilla
6   tablespoons sugar

Prepare pastry for Filled One-Crust Pie using 9-inch pie pan.

Heat oven to 400°F. Place rhubarb in pastry-lined pan. In small bowl, beat egg yolks until thick and lemon colored. Stir in half-and-half. Add remaining filling ingredients; blend well. Pour egg mixture over rhubarb.

Bake at 400°F. for 10 minutes. Reduce oven temperature to 350°F.; bake an additional 40 minutes.

In small deep bowl, beat egg whites, cream of tartar and vanilla at medium speed until soft peaks form. Gradually add 6 tablespoons sugar 1 tablespoon at a time, beating at high speed until stiff glossy peaks form and sugar is dissolved. Spoon meringue onto hot filling; spread to edge of crust to seal well and prevent shrinkage.

Bake at 350°F. for 15 to 20 minutes or until light golden brown.

Yield: 8 servings.

NUTRITION PER SERVING:
Calories 310; Protein 4g; Carbohydrate 50g; Fat 11g; Sodium 260mg.

SOUTHERN-STYLE LEMON MERINGUE PIE

A layer of preserves makes this pie unique.

CRUST
Pastry for One-Crust Pie p. 268

FILLING
½   cup blackberry or raspberry preserves
1   cup sugar
¼   cup cornstarch
½   teaspoon salt
1⅔ cups water
3   egg yolks
2   tablespoons margarine or butter
1½ teaspoons grated lemon peel
⅓   cup lemon juice

MERINGUE
3   egg whites
¼   teaspoon cream of tartar
6   tablespoons sugar

Prepare and bake pastry as directed for Baked Pie Shell using 9-inch pie pan; cool. Spread preserves in bottom of cooled, baked pie shell.

In medium saucepan, combine 1 cup sugar with cornstarch and salt; mix well. Stir in water; blend until smooth. Cook over medium heat until mixture boils and thickens, stirring constantly. Boil 1 minute, stirring constantly. Remove from heat. In small bowl, beat egg yolks; stir about ¼ cup of hot mixture into egg yolks. Gradually stir yolk mixture into hot mixture. Cook over low heat, stirring constantly, just until mixture begins to bubble. Remove from heat; stir in margarine, lemon peel and lemon juice. Cool slightly, about 15 minutes. Pour over preserves in crust.

Heat oven to 400°F. In small bowl, beat egg whites and cream of tartar until soft peaks form, about 1 minute. Add 6 tablespoons sugar 1 tablespoon at a time, beating at high speed until stiff glossy peaks form and sugar is dissolved. Spoon meringue onto hot filling; spread to edge of crust to seal well and prevent shrinkage.

Bake at 400°F. for 10 to 18 minutes or until light golden brown. Cool completely. Refrigerate 3 hours or until filling is set. Store in refrigerator.

Yield: 8 servings.

NUTRITION PER SERVING:
Calories 390; Protein 4g; Carbohydrate 65g; Fat 13g; Sodium 325mg.

GRAPEFRUIT MERINGUE PIE

In the 1930s Pillsbury had a monthly publication called the Cookery Club Bulletin. This recipe was a favorite published in 1935.

CRUST
    Pastry for One-Crust Pie p. 268

FILLING
  ³/₄ **cup sugar**
  ¹/₄ **cup cornstarch**
   3 **tablespoons all purpose flour**
  ¹/₂ **teaspoon salt**
1¹/₄ **cups cold water**
  ¹/₂ **cup fresh grapefruit juice**
   3 **egg yolks**
   2 **tablespoons margarine or butter**
   1 **teaspoon grated grapefruit peel**

MERINGUE
   3 **egg whites**
  ¹/₄ **teaspoon cream of tartar**
  ¹/₄ **cup sugar**

Prepare and bake pastry as directed for Baked Pie Shell using 9-inch pie pan; cool.

In medium saucepan, combine ³/₄ cup sugar, cornstarch, flour and salt; mix well. Gradually stir in cold water and grapefruit juice until smooth. Cook over medium heat, stirring constantly, until mixture boils; boil 1 minute, stirring constantly. Remove from heat. In small bowl, beat egg yolks; stir about ¹/₄ cup of hot mixture into egg yolks. Gradually stir yolk mixture into hot mixture. Cook over low heat, stirring constantly, until mixture boils. Boil 1 minute, stirring constantly. Remove from heat; stir in margarine and grapefruit peel. Cool slightly, about 15 minutes. Pour into cooled, baked pie shell.

Heat oven to 350°F. In small deep bowl, beat egg whites and cream of tartar at medium speed until soft peaks form, about 1 minute. Add ¹/₄ cup sugar 1 tablespoon at a time, beating at high speed until stiff glossy peaks form and sugar is dissolved. Spoon meringue onto hot filling; spread to edge of crust to seal well and prevent shrinkage. Bake at 350°F. for 12 to 15 minutes or until light golden brown. Cool completely. Refrigerate 3 hours or until filling is set. Store in refrigerator.

Yield: 8 servings.

NUTRITION PER SERVING:
Calories 350; Protein 4g; Carbohydrate 57g; Fat 12g; Sodium 290mg.

MAGIC MERINGUE PIE

This pie features a pineapple filling.

CRUST
    Pastry for One-Crust Pie p. 268

FILLING
  ³/₄ **cup sugar**
   2 **tablespoons all purpose flour**
  ¹/₈ **teaspoon salt**
   1 **cup dairy sour cream**
   1 **tablespoon lemon juice**
   3 **egg yolks**
   1 **(20-oz.) can crushed pineapple, drained, reserving ¹/₂ cup liquid**

MERINGUE
   2 **tablespoons sugar**
   1 **tablespoon cornstarch**
  ¹/₂ **cup water**
   3 **egg whites**
  ¹/₈ **teaspoon salt**
  ¹/₂ **teaspoon vanilla**
   6 **tablespoons sugar**

Prepare and bake pastry as directed for Baked Pie Shell using 9-inch pie pan; cool.

In medium saucepan, combine ³/₄ cup sugar, 2 tablespoons flour and ¹/₈ teaspoon salt; mix well. Stir in sour cream, lemon juice, egg yolks, drained pineapple and reserved liquid. Cook over medium heat until mixture boils and thickens, stirring constantly. Cover surface with plastic wrap. Refrigerate just until cool, about 1 hour. Pour into cooled, baked pie shell.

Heat oven to 350°F. In small saucepan, combine 2 tablespoons sugar and cornstarch; mix well. Gradually stir in water until smooth. Cook over medium heat until mixture boils and thickens, stirring constantly. Cool.

In small bowl, beat egg whites, ¹/₈ teaspoon salt and vanilla at medium speed until soft peaks form. Gradually add cornstarch mixture and 6 tablespoons sugar 1 tablespoon at a time, beating at high speed until stiff peaks form and sugar is dissolved. Spoon meringue onto filling; spread to edge of crust to seal well and prevent shrinkage.

Bake at 350°F. for 10 to 15 minutes or until light golden brown. Cool completely. Store in refrigerator.

Yield: 8 servings.

NUTRITION PER SERVING:
Calories 370; Protein 5g; Carbohydrate 54g; Fat 16g; Sodium 240mg.

CRANBERRY ORANGE FROZEN TART

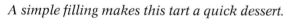

Only 3 ingredients are in the filling!

CRUST
> **Pastry for One-Crust Pie p. 268**

FILLING
- 1 **(14-oz.) can sweetened condensed milk (not evaporated)**
- 1 **(10-oz.) pkg. (1¼ cups) frozen cranberry-orange sauce, thawed**
- 1 **cup frozen whipped topping, thawed**

Prepare and bake pastry as directed for Baked Pie Shell using 10-inch tart pan with removable bottom or 9-inch pie pan; cool.

In medium bowl, combine sweetened condensed milk and cranberry-orange sauce; blend well. Fold in 1 cup whipped topping. Spoon mixture evenly into cooled, baked tart shell. Freeze overnight or until firm. Garnish as desired.

Yield: 12 servings.

NUTRITION PER SERVING:
Calories 250; Protein 3g; Carbohydrate 38g; Fat 9g; Sodium 140mg.

CHERRY BERRY TART

A simple filling makes this tart a quick dessert.

CRUST
> **Pastry for One-Crust Pie p. 268**

FILLING
- 1 **(21-oz.) can cherry fruit pie filling**
- 1 **cup halved strawberries**
- 1 **cup blueberries**

GARNISH
> **Whipped cream, if desired**

Prepare and bake pastry as directed for Baked Pie Shell using 9-inch tart pan with removable bottom or 9-inch pie pan; cool. In large bowl, gently combine all filling ingredients. Spoon into cooled, baked tart shell. Refrigerate at least 1 hour. Remove sides of pan. Garnish with whipped cream.

Yield: 8 servings.

NUTRITION PER SERVING:
Calories 310; Protein 2g; Carbohydrate 50g; Fat 11g; Sodium 170mg.

ZESTY ORANGE PUMPKIN TART

Orange marmalade flavors this elegant variation of pumpkin pie.

CRUST
> **Pastry for Filled One-Crust Pie p. 268**

FILLING
- 1 **(16-oz.) can (2 cups) pumpkin**
- 1 **(12-oz.) can (1½ cups) evaporated milk**
- ½ **cup sugar**
- ⅓ **cup orange marmalade**
- 2 **eggs, slightly beaten**
- 1 **teaspoon pumpkin pie spice**
- ½ **teaspoon salt**

TOPPING
- 1 **cup whipping cream**
- 2 **tablespoons powdered sugar**
- ½ **teaspoon grated orange peel, if desired**

Prepare pastry for Filled One-Crust Pie using 10-inch tart pan with removable bottom or 9-inch pie pan.

Heat oven to 425°F. In large bowl, combine all filling ingredients; blend well. Pour into pastry-lined pan.

Bake at 425°F. for 45 to 55 minutes or until knife inserted in center comes out clean. Cool; remove sides of pan.

In small bowl, beat whipping cream until soft peaks form. Blend in powdered sugar and orange peel; beat until stiff peaks form. Spoon or pipe topping over filling. Store in refrigerator.

Yield: 8 servings.

NUTRITION PER SERVING:
Calories 460; Protein 8g; Carbohydrate 53g; Fat 24g; Sodium 380mg.

Tangy Crescent Nut Tart

This 32nd Pillsbury BAKE-OFF® Contest winner uses refrigerated crescent rolls to form the easy crust for this tangy lemon tart.

CRUST
1 (8-oz.) can refrigerated crescent dinner rolls

FILLING
1 cup sugar
¼ cup all purpose flour
2 to 3 teaspoons grated lemon peel
3 to 4 tablespoons lemon juice
1 teaspoon vanilla
4 eggs
1 cup coconut
1 cup finely chopped hazelnuts (filberts) or walnuts

GARNISH
1 to 2 tablespoons powdered sugar

Heat oven to 350°F. Lightly grease 10-inch tart pan with removable bottom. Separate dough into 8 triangles. Place in greased pan; press in bottom and up sides to form crust. Firmly press perforations to seal.

Bake at 350°F. for 5 minutes. Cool 5 minutes; gently press sides of warm crust to top of pan.

In large bowl, combine sugar, flour, lemon peel, lemon juice, vanilla and eggs; beat 3 minutes at medium speed. Stir in coconut and hazelnuts. Pour filling into partially baked crust.

Bake an additional 25 to 30 minutes or until filling is set and crust is golden brown. Cool completely. Sprinkle with powdered sugar. Store in refrigerator.
Yield: 8 to 12 servings.

TIP:
A 10-inch round pizza pan can be substituted for the tart pan. Bake crust at 350°F. for 5 minutes; bake filled crust an additional 20 to 25 minutes.

NUTRITION PER SERVING:
Calories 230; Protein 5g; Carbohydrate 23g; Fat 14g; Sodium 180mg.

Cherry Cream Cheese Crescent Tarts

Refrigerated crescent rolls form a quick and easy tart shell for these festive hand-held desserts. A fabulous filling of cream cheese, cherries, chocolate and almonds gives them flavor appeal for all ages.

CRUST
2 (8-oz.) cans refrigerated crescent dinner rolls

FILLING
1 (8-oz.) pkg. cream cheese, softened
1 cup powdered sugar
1 egg
½ teaspoon almond extract
½ cup miniature semi-sweet chocolate chips
¼ cup chopped almonds
1 tablespoon finely chopped maraschino cherries, well drained

GLAZE
⅓ cup powdered sugar
1 tablespoon finely chopped maraschino cherries, well drained
2 to 2½ teaspoons maraschino cherry liquid

Heat oven to 350°F. Lightly grease 16 muffin cups. Separate dough into 8 rectangles; firmly press perforations to seal. Press or roll each rectangle into 8x4-inch rectangle; cut in half crosswise to form 16 squares. Place squares in greased muffin cups. Gently press each square in center to cover bottom and sides of cup, leaving corners of dough extended.

In small bowl, combine cream cheese, 1 cup powdered sugar, egg and almond extract; beat well. Stir in remaining filling ingredients. Place about 2 tablespoons filling in each pastry-lined cup.

Bake at 350°F. for 15 to 20 minutes or until golden brown. Cool 5 minutes; remove from muffin cups.

In small bowl, combine all glaze ingredients, adding enough cherry liquid for desired drizzling consistency. Drizzle over warm or cool tarts. Store lightly covered in refrigerator.
Yield: 16 tarts.

NUTRITION PER SERVING:
Calories 240; Protein 4g; Carbohydrate 24g; Fat 14g; Sodium 280mg.

Tangy Crescent Nut Tart

Pear Tart Elegante

A glistening topping of red currant jelly highlights the fruit in this show-off dessert.

CRUST
- ¼ **cup margarine or butter, softened**
- 2 **tablespoons sugar**
-   **Dash salt**
- ½ **teaspoon grated lemon peel**
- ½ **teaspoon vanilla**
- 1 **egg yolk**
- ¾ **cup all purpose flour**
- ¼ **cup finely ground blanched almonds**

FILLING
- 4 **tablespoons red currant jelly**
- ½ **cup all purpose flour**
- 3 **tablespoons sugar**
- ¼ **cup margarine or butter, softened**
- ½ **teaspoon grated lemon peel**
- ½ **teaspoon almond extract**
- 1 **(3-oz.) pkg. cream cheese, softened**
- 1 **egg**
- 5 **canned pear halves, well drained**
- 1 **cup fresh or frozen whole raspberries or strawberries, slightly thawed**

Heat oven to 375°F. In small bowl, combine ¼ cup margarine, 2 tablespoons sugar and salt; beat at medium speed until light and fluffy. Add ½ teaspoon lemon peel, vanilla and egg yolk; beat until smooth. Stir in ¾ cup flour and almonds; blend well. Press mixture in bottom and up sides of 10-inch tart pan or 9-inch springform pan. Bake at 375°F. for 10 minutes; cool.

Brush baked crust with 2 tablespoons of the currant jelly. In small bowl, combine ½ cup flour, 3 tablespoons sugar, ¼ cup margarine, ½ teaspoon grated lemon peel, almond extract, cream cheese and egg; beat 1 minute at medium speed. Pour filling over crust. Arrange pear halves on filling, rounded sides up and narrow ends pointing toward center. If desired, score pears making cuts ⅛-inch deep crosswise at ¼-inch intervals on each side of pear half. Bake at 375°F. for 25 to 35 minutes or until center is set.

In small saucepan, heat remaining 2 tablespoons currant jelly over medium heat until melted. Arrange berries in rows between pear halves. Brush jelly lightly over pears, berries and filling. Garnish as desired.

Yield: 8 servings.

NUTRITION PER SERVING:
Calories 320; Protein 5g; Carbohydrate 35g; Fat 19g; Sodium 195mg.

Caramel Pear Pastry

Pears are ripe when they yield to gentle pressure around the stem. Buy them a few days ahead, if necessary, to allow time for ripening at room temperature. *See Cook's Note p. 139.*

- 1 **(8-oz.) can refrigerated crescent dinner rolls**
- 2 **ripe pears, thinly sliced**
- 1 **tablespoon sugar**
- ¼ **cup firmly packed brown sugar**
- ¼ **cup whipping cream or half-and-half**

Heat oven to 375°F. Unroll dough into 2 long rectangles. On ungreased cookie sheet, overlap long sides ½ inch; firmly press perforations and edges to seal. Press or roll out to form 14x9-inch rectangle. Arrange pear slices in 2 rows lengthwise down center of rectangle leaving 1-inch edge on each side. Fold long sides 1 inch over filling; fold short ends over filling. Pinch slightly to seal corner folds. Sprinkle dough and pears with 1 tablespoon sugar.

Bake at 375°F. for 20 to 30 minutes or until crust is deep golden brown.

Meanwhile, in small saucepan over medium heat bring brown sugar and whipping cream to a boil. Boil gently 5 minutes, stirring constantly. Remove from heat; brush over pears. Serve warm or cool.

Yield: 8 servings.

NUTRITION PER SERVING:
Calories 180; Protein 2g; Carbohydrate 25g; Fat 8g; Sodium 240mg.

APRICOT TEA TART

This apricot and cream cheese tart is topped with an easy lattice crust.

CRUST
> **Pastry for Two-Crust Pie p. 268**

APRICOT FILLING
1½ **cups chopped dried apricots**
½ **cup orange juice**
2 **eggs**
½ **cup sugar**
2 **tablespoons all purpose flour**
½ **cup light corn syrup**
2 **tablespoons margarine or butter, melted**
1 **teaspoon vanilla**

CREAM CHEESE FILLING
1 **(3-oz.) pkg. cream cheese, softened**
¼ **cup sugar**
1 **tablespoon all purpose flour**
⅓ **cup dairy sour cream**
1 **egg**

TOPPING
1 **teaspoon orange juice**
1 **teaspoon sugar**

Prepare pastry for Two-Crust Pie using 10-inch tart pan with removable bottom or 9-inch pie pan.

Heat oven to 375°F. In medium saucepan, combine apricots and ½ cup orange juice; bring to a boil. Reduce heat to low; simmer uncovered for 1 to 2 minutes. Cool slightly. Reserve 1 tablespoonful apricot mixture for cream cheese filling.

Beat 2 eggs in small bowl; reserve 1 teaspoon for topping. Stir remaining beaten eggs, ½ cup sugar, 2 tablespoons flour, corn syrup, margarine and vanilla into apricot mixture in saucepan; mix well. Spoon into pastry-lined pan.

In small bowl, combine all cream cheese filling ingredients and reserved 1 tablespoonful apricot mixture; beat at medium speed until well blended. Spoon over apricot filling. Heat cookie sheet in oven for 10 minutes.

Meanwhile, to make lattice top cut remaining pastry into ½-inch wide strips. Arrange strips in lattice design over filling. Trim and seal edges. In small bowl, combine 1 teaspoon orange juice and reserved 1 teaspoon beaten egg; blend well. Gently brush over lattice crust; sprinkle with 1 teaspoon sugar.

Place tart on preheated cookie sheet. Bake at 375°F. for 45 to 55 minutes or until crust is golden brown. Cool; remove sides of pan. Store in refrigerator.
Yield: 10 to 12 servings.

NUTRITION PER SERVING:
Calories 380; Protein 4g; Carbohydrate 53g; Fat 17g; Sodium 200mg.

COUNTRY RHUBARB TART

An easy shaping of the pastry in this recipe results in the appearance of a tart in a 9-inch pie pan.

CRUST
> **Pastry for Filled One-Crust Pie p. 268**

FILLING
1¼ **cups sugar**
3 **tablespoons all purpose flour**
½ **teaspoon grated orange peel**
3 **eggs, slightly beaten**
½ **cup dairy sour cream**
3½ **cups sliced rhubarb**

TOPPING
¼ **cup sugar**
¼ **cup all purpose flour**
2 **tablespoons margarine or butter, softened**

Prepare pastry for Filled One-Crust Pie. Ease pastry into 9-inch pie pan; gently press toward center to avoid stretching. Press firmly against sides and bottom. Do not flute.

Heat oven to 375°F. In medium bowl, combine 1¼ cups sugar, 3 tablespoons flour and orange peel; stir in eggs and sour cream; mix well. Add rhubarb; toss gently. Spoon filling into pastry-lined pan. Fold edges of pastry over filling, ruffling decoratively.

In small bowl, combine all topping ingredients until crumbly. Sprinkle over filling. Bake at 375°F. for 50 to 60 minutes or until crust is light golden brown. Store in refrigerator.
Yield: 8 servings.

NUTRITION PER SERVING:
Calories 360; Protein 4g; Carbohydrate 53g; Fat 15g; Sodium 220mg.

FRESH FRUIT TARTS

Look for strawberry glaze by the fresh fruit in the produce section of your grocery store. It brings out the natural luster of these fruit-filled tarts.

CRUST
> **Pastry for Two-Crust Pie p. 268**

FILLING
> 5 **cups assorted fresh fruit (blueberries, strawberries, bananas)**
> 1 **(16-oz.) jar strawberry glaze**
> ½ **cup frozen whipped topping, thawed, or whipped cream**

Prepare pastry for Two-Crust Pie. Heat oven to 450°F. Using fluted round cookie cutter, cut five 4-inch circles from each circle of pastry. Fit circles over backs of ungreased muffin cups. Pinch 5 equally spaced pleats around sides of each cup. Prick each pastry generously with fork.

Bake at 450°F. for 9 to 13 minutes or until light golden brown. Cool completely; remove from muffin cups.

In large bowl, combine fruit and strawberry glaze. Refrigerate until thoroughly chilled. Before serving, spoon ½ cup fruit mixture into each cooled tart shell; top with whipped topping.

Yield: 10 tarts.

NUTRITION PER SERVING:
Calories 320; Protein 2g; Carbohydrate 48g; Fat 13g; Sodium 180mg.

COUNTRY FRUIT TART

Now that fresh fruit can be shipped around the world, we can enjoy luscious fruit year-round. Use the fruits suggested or your own combination for a variety of colors and shapes.

CRUST
> **Pastry for One-Crust Pie p. 268**
> **Sugar**

FILLING
> 1 **(3½-oz.) tube almond paste***
> 2 **tablespoons margarine or butter, softened**
> 1½ **to 2 cups small strawberries, raspberries, sliced apricots, nectarines or peaches**
> 2 **to 4 tablespoons apple jelly**
> **Whipped cream, if desired**

Prepare pastry for One-Crust Pie. Place pastry on large ungreased cookie sheet. Using paper pattern or salad plate as guide, cut 8-inch circle from center of pastry; reserve remaining pastry.

Heat oven to 450°F. In small bowl, combine almond paste and margarine; beat until smooth. Spread evenly on pastry circle to within 1 inch of edge. From remaining pastry, cut as many 1-inch circles or decorative shapes as possible, about 35. Moisten uncovered edge of pastry with water. Arrange small circles on edge of pastry, overlapping slightly. Sprinkle with sugar.

Bake at 450°F. for 9 to 11 minutes or until lightly browned. Cool completely on cookie sheet. Place on serving plate. Just before serving, arrange fresh fruit over filling, overlapping cut pieces slightly. In small saucepan, heat jelly just until warm; brush over fruit. Serve with whipped cream.

Yield: 6 to 8 servings.

TIP:
* The following almond paste made in the food processor can be substituted for the 3½-oz. tube almond paste. Place ½ cup toasted whole or slivered almonds in food processor bowl with metal blade. Process until finely ground. Add ⅔ cup powdered sugar and 1 tablespoon water along with the 2 tablespoons margarine from above. Process until smooth. Continue as directed above.

NUTRITION PER SERVING:
Calories 260; Protein 2g; Carbohydrate 27g; Fat 17g; Sodium 230mg.

Fresh Fruit Tarts

FRUIT PIZZA TART

A favorite for summer gatherings.

CRUST
- ¾ cup sugar
- ⅓ cup margarine, softened, or shortening
- ⅓ cup oil
- 1 tablespoon milk
- 1 to 2 teaspoons almond extract
- 1 egg
- 1½ cups all purpose flour
- 1½ teaspoons baking powder
- ¼ teaspoon salt

TOPPING
- 1 (8-oz.) pkg. cream cheese, softened
- ⅓ cup sugar
- ½ teaspoon vanilla
- 1 small peach, peeled and sliced, or 1 cup canned peach slices
- 2 cups strawberry halves
- 1 cup fresh or frozen blueberries (do not thaw)
- ¼ cup orange marmalade
- 1 tablespoon water

Heat oven to 375°F. In large bowl, beat ¾ cup sugar, margarine, oil, milk, almond extract and egg until light and fluffy. Stir in flour, baking powder and salt; blend well. Spread evenly in ungreased 15x10x1-inch baking pan.

Bake at 375°F. for 10 to 12 minutes or until light golden brown. Cool completely.

In small bowl, beat cream cheese, ⅓ cup sugar and vanilla until fluffy. Spread mixture over cooled cookie crust. Arrange fruit over cream cheese. In small bowl, combine orange marmalade and water; blend well. Spoon marmalade mixture over fruit. Refrigerate at least 1 hour before serving. Cut into squares. Store in refrigerator.
Yield: 12 servings.

FOOD PROCESSOR DIRECTIONS:
In food processor bowl with metal blade, combine ¾ cup sugar, margarine, oil, milk, almond extract and egg; process until light and fluffy. Add flour, baking powder and salt. Process using on-off pulses just until flour is well blended. (Do not overprocess or crust will be tough.) Continue as directed above.

NUTRITION PER SERVING:
Calories 330; Protein 4g; Carbohydrate 40g; Fat 19g; Sodium 210mg.

GINGERBREAD TARTS WITH FRUIT AND HONEY CREAM

Enjoy the great taste of gingerbread cookies in these individual tarts.

CRUST
- 3 tablespoons firmly packed brown sugar
- ¼ cup margarine or butter, softened
- 3 tablespoons molasses
- 1 egg
- 1½ cups all purpose flour
- ½ teaspoon ginger
- ½ teaspoon allspice
- ¼ teaspoon salt

FILLING
- 2 small red apples, cut into bite-sized pieces
- 2 kiwifruit, peeled, sliced
- 1 (11-oz.) can mandarin orange segments, drained

TOPPING
- 1 cup whipping cream
- ¼ teaspoon cinnamon
- 2 tablespoons honey

In large bowl, beat brown sugar and margarine until light and fluffy. Add molasses and egg; blend well. Stir in flour, ginger, allspice and salt; mix well. If necessary, refrigerate for easier handling.

Heat oven to 350°F. Invert muffin pan; grease outsides of 10 muffin cups. On lightly floured surface, roll dough to ⅛-inch thickness. Cut dough with floured 4-inch round cookie cutter or knife and paper pattern. Reroll dough scraps for more rounds. Form over backs of greased muffin cups, pleating to fit snugly. Prick each crust generously with fork. Bake at 350°F. for 10 minutes or until firm. Remove from muffin cups; cool on wire rack.

In small bowl, combine all filling ingredients; spoon into cooled tart shells. In small bowl, beat all topping ingredients until soft peaks form. Spoon over fruit.
Yield: 10 to 12 tarts.

NUTRITION PER SERVING:
Calories 240; Protein 3g; Carbohydrate 29g; Fat 12g; Sodium 105mg.

WINTER FRUIT PHYLLO TARTS

These tarts feature a filling of apples and grapes.

PASTRY
- 8 (18x14-inch) frozen phyllo (filo) pastry sheets, thawed
- ¼ cup margarine or butter, melted

FILLING
- ¾ cup sugar
- 1 teaspoon cinnamon
- 2 tablespoons margarine or butter
- ¼ cup water
- 1½ cups thinly sliced peeled apples
- 2 tablespoons cornstarch
- 2 tablespoons water
- ¾ cup seedless green grapes, halved
- ¾ cup seedless red grapes, halved
- ½ teaspoon grated lemon peel
- ¼ cup chopped pecans, toasted, p. 23
  Whipped cream, if desired

Heat oven to 350°F. Grease six 6-oz. custard cups. Brush 1 sheet of phyllo pastry with melted margarine; top with another phyllo dough sheet. Repeat brushing and layering with remaining melted margarine and phyllo.* Cut phyllo stack lengthwise into 6 strips; cut strips into thirds, forming 18 rectangles. Press 3 rectangular stacks into each of 6 greased custard cups, covering entire surface. If desired, trim edges even with custard cup.

Bake at 350°F. for 15 to 20 minutes or until golden brown. Carefully remove from custard cups; cool on wire rack.

In large saucepan, combine sugar, cinnamon, 2 tablespoons margarine and ¼ cup water. Cook over medium heat until bubbly. Add apples. Cover; cook 7 to 10 minutes or just until tender. In small bowl, combine cornstarch and 2 tablespoons water. Stir in about ¼ cup hot syrup from apple mixture; return to saucepan. Cook over medium-high heat until thickened. Fold in green and red grapes and lemon peel. Spoon about ⅓ cup warm or cold fruit mixture into each phyllo cup; sprinkle with pecans. Serve with whipped cream.
Yield: 6 servings.

TIP:
* Phyllo dries out quickly, so tightly wrap unused portion of package and refrigerate or freeze immediately.

NUTRITION PER SERVING:
Calories 340; Protein 2g; Carbohydrate 47g; Fat 18g; Sodium 210mg.

GLAZED DRIED FRUIT TART

This glazed lattice-top tart is fancy enough to serve for special holiday dinners.

CRUST
  Pastry for Two-Crust Pie p. 268

FILLING
- 2 cups water
- 1 cup pitted prunes, cut in half
- ½ cup golden raisins
- 1 (6-oz.) pkg. (1 cup) dried apricots
- ½ cup chopped peeled apple
- ½ cup sugar
- ¼ teaspoon ginger
- ½ cup chopped almonds
- ¼ cup margarine or butter

GLAZE
- ¼ cup apricot preserves

Prepare pastry for Two-Crust Pie using 10-inch tart pan with removable bottom.

Heat oven to 400°F. In medium saucepan, bring water to a boil over high heat. Add prunes, raisins and apricots; reduce heat and simmer 10 minutes. Drain fruits; stir in remaining filling ingredients. Cool 10 minutes; spoon into pastry-lined pan. To make lattice top, cut remaining pastry into ½-inch wide strips. Arrange strips in lattice design over filling. Trim and seal edges.

Bake at 400°F. for 45 to 55 minutes or until golden brown. Cool; remove sides of pan. Melt apricot preserves in small saucepan over low heat; drizzle over tart.
Yield: 8 to 10 servings.

NUTRITION PER SERVING:
Calories 440; Protein 4g; Carbohydrate 63g; Fat 20g; Sodium 210mg.

COOK'S NOTE

WHAT IS PHYLLO OR FILO?

Phyllo or filo is a delicately crisp, layered pastry originally used for Greek and Middle Eastern pastries. The paper-thin dough can be found in the freezer section of the supermarket and is used to make a variety of sweet and savory delicacies. Thaw it as directed and handle it carefully to keep the dough from drying out. See p. 336.

Raspberry Lemon Meringue Tart

This layered tart is scrumptious.

CRUST

Pastry for One-Crust Pie p. 268

RASPBERRY FILLING

- ¼ cup sugar
- 2 tablespoons cornstarch
- 1 (12-oz.) pkg. frozen whole raspberries, thawed, drained, reserving liquid

LEMON FILLING

- 1 cup sugar
- 2 tablespoons cornstarch
- 2 tablespoons all purpose flour
- ¼ teaspoon salt
- 1½ cups water
- 3 egg yolks, beaten
- ⅓ cup lemon juice
- 1 tablespoon grated lemon peel
- 1 tablespoon margarine or butter

MERINGUE

- ⅓ cup sugar
- 1 tablespoon cornstarch
- ⅓ cup water
- 3 egg whites
- ⅛ teaspoon salt

Prepare and bake pastry as directed for Baked Pie Shell using 9-inch tart pan with removable bottom or 9-inch pie pan.

In medium saucepan, combine ¼ cup sugar and 2 tablespoons cornstarch. If necessary, add water to reserved raspberry liquid to measure ½ cup; gradually add liquid to sugar mixture. Cook over medium heat until thickened, stirring constantly. Gently fold in raspberries. Cool. Spread in bottom of cooled, baked pie shell.

In medium saucepan, combine 1 cup sugar, 2 tablespoons cornstarch, flour and ¼ teaspoon salt. Gradually stir in 1½ cups water, stirring until smooth. Over medium heat, bring to a boil; cook and stir an additional 1 minute. Remove filling mixture from heat. Quickly stir about ½ cup hot filling mixture into beaten egg yolks; mix well. Gradually stir egg mixture into hot mixture. Stir in lemon juice and peel. Cook over medium heat about 5 minutes, stirring constantly. Remove from heat. Add margarine; stir until melted. Cool 15 minutes. Carefully pour over raspberry mixture.

Heat oven to 350°F. In small saucepan, combine ⅓ cup sugar and 1 tablespoon cornstarch; mix well. Stir in ⅓ cup water; cook over medium heat until thickened. Cool completely. If desired, place in freezer about 10 minutes. Beat egg whites and ⅛ teaspoon salt until soft peaks form. Add cooled cornstarch mixture, beating at medium speed until stiff peaks form. Gently spread meringue over lemon filling; spread to edges of crust to seal.

Bake at 350°F. for 15 to 20 minutes or until light golden brown. Cool completely before serving, about 2 to 3 hours. Remove sides of pan. Store in refrigerator.

Yield: 8 servings.

NUTRITION PER SERVING:
Calories 400; Protein 4g; Carbohydrate 69g; Fat 12g; Sodium 300mg.

Raspberry Bakewell Tart

This luscious English tart has a press-in-the-pan crust.

CRUST

- 1¼ cups all purpose flour
- 2 tablespoons sugar
- ⅓ cup shortening
- 1 teaspoon vinegar
- 2 to 4 tablespoons cold water

FILLING

- ½ cup raspberry or strawberry preserves
- ⅓ cup sugar
- 3 eggs, separated
- ¾ cup ground almonds
- ½ cup dry bread crumbs
- ½ cup margarine or butter, melted
- 2 teaspoons almond extract
- ¼ cup raspberry or strawberry preserves

Heat oven to 425°F. In medium bowl, combine flour and 2 tablespoons sugar. Using pastry blender or fork, cut in shortening until mixture resembles coarse crumbs. Sprinkle flour mixture with vinegar; add water, 1 tablespoon at a time, while tossing and mixing lightly with fork. Add enough water to form a stiff moist dough. With floured fingers, press dough evenly over bottom and up sides of 10-inch tart pan with removable bottom or 9-inch pie pan.

Bake at 425°F. for 8 to 12 minutes or until crust appears set and light golden brown. Cool slightly.

Reduce oven temperature to 350°F. Spread ½ cup preserves evenly over bottom of crust. In large bowl, mix ⅓ cup sugar and egg yolks until well blended. Stir in almonds, bread crumbs, margarine and almond extract. In small bowl, beat egg whites until stiff peaks form. Gently fold egg whites into filling. Pour into partially baked pastry shell, spreading to edges of crust to cover preserves.

Bake at 350°F. for 30 to 35 minutes or until filling is puffed and golden brown. Cool 30 to 40 minutes; remove sides of tart pan. Place on serving plate. Spread with ¼ cup preserves. Serve warm or cool.
Yield: 10 servings.

NUTRITION PER SERVING:
Calories 370; Protein 5g; Carbohydrate 40g; Fat 21g; Sodium 145mg.

COOK'S NOTE

PIE WEIGHTS

When making a baked pie shell (unfilled before baking), weights can be used to prevent the crust from puffing during baking. First place the crust in the pie pan, taking care not to stretch it. Flute the edge of the crust and prick the bottom with a fork. Line the crust with aluminum foil. Place aluminum or ceramic pie weights (available at kitchen specialty shops) in the foil-lined crust. Dried beans or uncooked rice can be used instead of the weights. Carefully remove the weights when the pastry begins to brown around the edge. Continue baking until the crust is light golden brown.

WALNUT TART WITH RASPBERRY SAUCE

English walnuts are most often used in baking.

CRUST
   Pastry for One-Crust Pie p. 268

FILLING
   1   **cup firmly packed brown sugar**
   2   **eggs**
   ½   **cup all purpose flour**
   ½   **teaspoon baking powder**
   2   **cups chopped walnuts**
   ½   **teaspoon cinnamon**

SAUCE
   1   **(10-oz.) pkg. frozen raspberries in syrup, thawed**
   2   **teaspoons cornstarch**
   1   **teaspoon lemon juice**

Prepare and bake pastry as directed for Baked Pie Shell using 9-inch tart pan with removable bottom.

Reduce oven temperature to 350°F. In medium bowl, beat brown sugar and eggs until fluffy. Add flour, baking powder, walnuts and cinnamon; mix well. Pour into cooled, baked tart shell. Bake at 350°F. for 25 to 35 minutes or until filling is firm.

To prepare sauce, drain raspberries reserving liquid. In small saucepan, combine raspberry liquid and cornstarch; blend well. Cook and stir over medium heat until mixture thickens and boils. Stir in lemon juice and raspberries; cook 1 minute. Cut tart into wedges; serve with warm raspberry sauce. Garnish as desired.
Yield: 8 servings.

MICROWAVE DIRECTIONS:
Prepare tart as directed above. To prepare sauce, drain raspberries reserving liquid. In 4-cup microwave-safe measuring cup, combine raspberry liquid and cornstarch; blend well. Microwave on HIGH for 3 to 4 minutes or until mixture thickens and boils, stirring once halfway through cooking. Stir in lemon juice and raspberries. Microwave on HIGH for 30 seconds or until thoroughly heated.

NUTRITION PER SERVING:
Calories 530; Protein 8g; Carbohydrate 59g; Fat 29g; Sodium 210mg.

FUDGE CROSTATA WITH RASPBERRY SAUCE

~

A beautiful lattice crust bakes into the chocolate fudge filling in this decadent pie. The raspberry sauce adds the finishing touch.

CRUST
    Pastry for Two-Crust Pie p. 268

FILLING
- 1 **(6-oz.) pkg. (1 cup) semi-sweet chocolate chips**
- ½ **cup margarine or butter, softened**
- ⅔ **cup sugar**
- 1 **cup ground almonds**
- 1 **egg**
- 1 **egg, separated**

SAUCE
- 1 **(12-oz.) pkg. frozen whole raspberries, thawed**
- ¾ **cup sugar**
- 1 **teaspoon lemon juice**

GARNISH, if desired
    Sweetened whipped cream
    Chocolate Curls p. 210
    Whole raspberries

Prepare pastry for Two-Crust Pie using 10-inch tart pan with removable bottom or 9-inch pie pan.

Heat oven to 425°F. In small saucepan over low heat, melt chocolate chips and 2 tablespoons of the margarine, stirring constantly until smooth. In medium bowl, beat remaining 6 tablespoons margarine and ⅔ cup sugar until light and fluffy. Add almonds, 1 egg, egg yolk and melted chocolate; blend well. Spread mixture evenly over bottom of pastry-lined pan.

To make lattice top, cut remaining pastry into ½-inch wide strips. Arrange strips in lattice design over chocolate mixture. Trim and seal edges. In small bowl, beat egg white until foamy; gently brush over lattice.

Bake at 425°F. for 10 minutes. Reduce oven temperature to 350°F.; bake an additional 30 to 35 minutes or until crust is golden brown. Cool; remove sides of pan.

In blender container or food processor bowl with metal blade, blend raspberries at highest speed until smooth. Press through strainer to remove seeds; discard seeds. In small saucepan, combine raspberry puree, ¾ cup sugar and lemon juice; mix well. Bring mixture to a boil over medium-low heat. Boil 3 minutes, stirring constantly. Cool.

Garnish pie with whipped cream, Chocolate Curls and whole raspberries. Serve with raspberry sauce. Store in refrigerator.

Yield: 10 to 12 servings.

NUTRITION PER SERVING:
Calories 480; Protein 5g; Carbohydrate 50g; Fat 29g; Sodium 270mg.

MINI GRAPE TARTS

~

These delectable single-serving tarts are topped with colorful red and green grapes.

CRUST
    Pastry for Two-Crust Pie p. 268

FILLING
- ½ **cup whipping cream**
- 1 **(8-oz.) pkg. cream cheese, softened**
- ⅓ **cup sugar**
- 1 **teaspoon grated lemon peel**
- 1½ **cups red and green seedless grapes**
- ¼ **cup apple or currant jelly**

Prepare pastry for Two-Crust Pie. Heat oven to 425°F. Using round cookie cutter, cut five 4-inch circles from each circle of pastry. Fit circles over backs of ungreased muffin cups; press gently to mold over cups. Generously prick bottom of crusts with fork. Bake at 425°F. for 7 to 10 minutes or until light golden brown. Cool completely; remove from muffin cups.

In small bowl, combine whipping cream, cream cheese, sugar and lemon peel; beat until smooth and fluffy. Spoon into cooled tart shells, spreading evenly. Arrange grapes over filling to cover surface. Melt jelly in small saucepan over low heat; brush over grapes. Store in refrigerator. If desired, serve with additional whipped cream.

Yield: 10 tarts.

NUTRITION PER SERVING:
Calories 330; Protein 3g; Carbohydrate 32g; Fat 21g; Sodium 190mg.

Fudge Crostata with Raspberry Sauce

APPLE NUT LATTICE TART

A distinctive lattice top covers a filling of apples, golden raisins and walnuts.

CRUST
   Pastry for Two-Crust Pie p. 268

FILLING
   3 to 3½ cups thinly sliced peeled apples
       (3 to 4 medium)
   ½ cup sugar
   3 tablespoons golden raisins
   3 tablespoons chopped walnuts or pecans
   ½ teaspoon cinnamon
   ¼ to ½ teaspoon grated lemon peel
   2 teaspoons lemon juice
   1 egg yolk, beaten
   1 teaspoon water

GLAZE
   ¼ cup powdered sugar
   1 to 2 teaspoons lemon juice

Prepare pastry for Two-Crust Pie using 10-inch tart pan with removable bottom or 9-inch pie pan.

Heat oven to 400°F. In large bowl, combine apples, sugar, raisins, walnuts, cinnamon, lemon peel and 2 teaspoons lemon juice; toss lightly to coat. Spoon into pastry-lined pan.

To make lattice top, cut remaining pastry into ½-inch wide strips. Arrange strips in lattice design over filling. Trim and seal edges. In small bowl, combine egg yolk and water; gently brush over lattice.

Bake at 400°F. for 40 to 60 minutes or until apples are tender and crust is golden brown. Cool 1 hour.

In small bowl, combine glaze ingredients, adding enough lemon juice for desired drizzling consistency. Drizzle over slightly warm tart. Cool; remove sides of pan.
Yield: 8 servings.

NUTRITION PER SERVING:
Calories 360; Protein 3g; Carbohydrate 49g; Fat 17g; Sodium 270mg.

VARIATION:

APRICOT PEAR LATTICE TART: Substitute 16-oz. can apricot halves and 16-oz. can pear slices, drained, for apples. Substitute ⅓ cup firmly packed brown sugar for ½ cup sugar. Omit glaze; brush baked tart with ⅓ cup apricot preserves, melted.

BAVARIAN APPLE TART

This deep tart, prepared in a springform pan, contains a combination of raisins, almonds and apples in a yogurt custard.

CRUST
   1½ cups all purpose flour
   ½   cup sugar
   ½   cup margarine or butter, softened
   1   egg
   ¼   teaspoon almond extract

FILLING
   ½   cup golden or dark raisins
   ⅓   cup sliced almonds
   2   large apples, peeled, cut into ¼-inch slices
   2   teaspoons cornstarch
   ¼   cup milk
   1   tablespoon lemon juice
   ¼   teaspoon vanilla
   ¼   teaspoon almond extract
   1   (8-oz.) container vanilla yogurt
   1   egg, beaten
   ¼   cup apricot preserves, melted

Heat oven to 375°F. In large bowl, combine flour, sugar and margarine; beat at low speed until well blended. Beat in 1 egg and ¼ teaspoon almond extract until crumbly. Press crumb mixture in bottom and 1½ inches up sides of ungreased 9-inch springform pan. Sprinkle raisins and almonds onto crust. Arrange apple slices over raisins and almonds in desired pattern.

In medium bowl, dissolve cornstarch in milk. Add lemon juice, vanilla, ¼ teaspoon almond extract, yogurt and 1 egg; blend well. Pour over apples.

Bake at 375°F. for 55 to 65 minutes or until apples are tender. Cool 30 minutes; remove sides of pan. Brush preserves over apples. Garnish with whipped cream, if desired. Store in refrigerator.
Yield: 10 to 12 servings.

NUTRITION PER SERVING:
Calories 260; Protein 5g; Carbohydrate 37g; Fat 10g; Sodium 115mg.

CHOCOLATE CARAMEL ALMOND TART

Layers of caramel and chocolate are irresistible!

CRUST
- **Pastry for One-Crust Pie p. 268**

FILLING
- 20 **vanilla caramels, unwrapped**
- 3 **tablespoons whipping cream**
- 3 **tablespoons margarine or butter**
- 1 **cup sifted powdered sugar**
- ³⁄₄ **cup chopped almonds, toasted, p. 23, or unsalted dry roasted peanuts**

GLAZE
- 5 **oz. semi-sweet chocolate, chopped**
- ²⁄₃ **cup whipping cream**

TOPPING
- 1 **cup whipping cream**
- 2 **tablespoons powdered sugar**
- ¹⁄₄ **teaspoon vanilla**
  Almonds, toasted, p. 23

Heat oven to 450°F. Prepare pastry using 9-inch tart pan with removable bottom or 9-inch pie pan; DO NOT TRIM. Fold excess dough along top edge back into pan to form double, thick sides; gently press against sides of pan. Generously prick pastry with fork. Bake at 450°F. for 9 to 11 minutes or until light golden brown. Cool completely.

In small heavy saucepan, combine caramels, 3 tablespoons whipping cream and margarine. Cook over low heat until caramels are melted and mixture is smooth, stirring occasionally. Remove from heat. Beat in 1 cup powdered sugar until well blended. Stir in ³⁄₄ cup almonds. *Immediately* spread over bottom of cooled, baked tart shell.

In another small saucepan over low heat, melt glaze ingredients, stirring constantly until smooth. Pour over caramel mixture. Refrigerate until firm, about 2 hours. Remove sides of pan.

In small bowl, beat 1 cup whipping cream until soft peaks form. Add 2 tablespoons powdered sugar and vanilla; beat until stiff peaks form. Spread half of whipped cream mixture over cooled filling. Spoon or pipe remaining whipped cream mixture to make a decorative border. Sprinkle with toasted almonds. Refrigerate until serving time.* Store in refrigerator.
Yield: 10 to 12 servings.

TIP:
* If tart has been refrigerated more than 4 hours, remove from refrigerator 30 minutes before serving.

NUTRITION PER SERVING:
Calories 430; Protein 4g; Carbohydrate 36g; Fat 31g; Sodium 160mg.

PLUM ALMOND TART

This plum-delicious tart is flavored with lemon and garnished with a sprinkling of powdered sugar, dollops of whipped cream and sliced almonds.

CRUST
- **Pastry for Filled One-Crust Pie p. 268**

FILLING
- ³⁄₄ **cup ground almonds**
- ¹⁄₂ **cup sugar**
- 2 **teaspoons grated lemon peel**
- 1 **egg**
- 2 **(17-oz.) cans whole purple plums, halved, pitted, drained on paper towels**
- 2 **tablespoons margarine or butter**
- 1 **tablespoon sugar**

GARNISH
- **Powdered sugar**
- **Whipped cream**
- **Sliced almonds**

Prepare pastry for Filled One-Crust Pie using 10-inch tart pan with removable bottom.

Heat oven to 350°F. In small bowl, combine ground almonds, ¹⁄₂ cup sugar, lemon peel and egg; mix well. Spread in pastry-lined pan; top with plums, cut side down. Dot plums with margarine; sprinkle with 1 tablespoon sugar.

Bake at 350°F. for 50 to 65 minutes or until deep golden brown. Cool; remove sides of pan. Just before serving, sprinkle with powdered sugar. Garnish with whipped cream and sliced almonds.
Yield: 8 to 10 servings.

NUTRITION PER SERVING:
Calories 310; Protein 4g; Carbohydrate 34g; Fat 18g; Sodium 130mg.

TIN ROOF FUDGE TART

~

Flavors of a popular ice cream treat team up for this tasty pie.

CRUST
   Pastry for One-Crust Pie p. 268
 2 **oz. dark chocolate candy bar or semi-sweet baking chocolate, chopped**
 1 **tablespoon margarine or butter**

PEANUT LAYER
 20 **caramels, unwrapped**
 1/3 **cup whipping cream**
 1½ **cups Spanish peanuts**

MOUSSE LAYER
 8 **oz. dark chocolate candy bar or semi-sweet baking chocolate, chopped**
 2 **tablespoons margarine or butter**
 1 **cup whipping cream**
 2 **teaspoons vanilla**

TOPPING
 5 **caramels, unwrapped**
 3 **tablespoons whipping cream**
 1 **teaspoon margarine or butter**

GARNISH
   Whipped cream, if desired
   Spanish peanuts, if desired

Prepare and bake pastry as directed for Baked Pie Shell using 10-inch tart pan with removable bottom or 9-inch pie pan.

In small, heavy saucepan over very low heat, melt 2 oz. dark chocolate and 1 tablespoon margarine, stirring constantly until smooth. Spread over bottom and sides of cooled, baked tart shell. Refrigerate until chocolate is set.

In medium saucepan over low heat, melt 20 caramels with 1/3 cup whipping cream until mixture is smooth, stirring frequently. Stir in 1½ cups peanuts until well coated; immediately spoon into chocolate-lined tart shell.

In small, heavy saucepan over very low heat, melt 8 oz. dark chocolate and and 2 tablespoons margarine, stirring constantly until smooth. Cool slightly, about 10 minutes. In small bowl, combine 1 cup whipping cream and vanilla; beat until soft peaks form. Fold 1/3 of the whipped cream into chocolate mixture; fold in remaining whipped cream. Spread over peanut layer. Refrigerate 2 hours or until set. Remove sides of pan.

In small saucepan over very low heat, melt all topping ingredients until smooth, stirring frequently. To garnish, pipe or spoon whipped cream around edge of chilled pie. Just before serving, drizzle with topping and sprinkle with peanuts. Store in refrigerator.
Yield: 12 servings.

NUTRITION PER SERVING:
Calories 560; Protein 10g; Carbohydrate 39g; Fat 45g; Sodium 250mg.

COOK'S NOTE

~

LINING TART PANS WITH PARCHMENT PAPER

Parchment paper is grease- and moisture-resistant. It is available in many supermarkets and kitchenware stores.

To line the removable bottom of a tart pan, trace the bottom onto a piece of parchment paper and cut out the parchment piece. Place it in the pan and grease it lightly. Prepare the dessert as directed.

At serving time, slip a pancake turner between the parchment paper and the removable bottom and carefully transfer the dessert to a serving plate.

CREAM PUFFS

This egg-rich dough depends on steam as the leavening agent. Fill the tender puff with your favorite sweet or savory fillings.

- ½ **cup water**
- ¼ **cup margarine or butter**
- ½ **cup all purpose flour**
- ¼ **teaspoon salt**
- 2 **eggs**

Heat oven to 400°F. Grease cookie sheet. In medium saucepan, combine water and margarine; bring to a boil over medium heat. Stir in flour and salt; cook, stirring vigorously, until mixture leaves sides of pan in smooth ball. Remove from heat. Add eggs 1 at a time, beating vigorously after each addition until mixture is smooth and glossy.* Spoon 6 mounds of dough (about ¼ cup each) 3 inches apart onto greased cookie sheet.

Bake at 400°F. for 30 to 40 minutes or until golden brown. Remove from oven; prick puffs with sharp knife to allow steam to escape. Remove from cookie sheet; cool completely. Split; if desired, remove any filaments of soft dough. Fill with ice cream, whipped cream or pudding. If desired, top with chocolate sauce.

Yield: 6 cream puffs.

TIPS:

* An electric mixer at medium speed can be used to beat in eggs 1 at a time. Beat for 1 minute after each addition until smooth and glossy. DO NOT OVERBEAT.

Recipe can be doubled to yield 12 puffs. Bake as directed above.

NUTRITION PER SERVING:
Calories 136; Protein 4g; Carbohydrate 8g; Fat 10g; Sodium 206mg.

VARIATIONS:

ECLAIRS: Pipe or spoon cream puff dough into 12 ovals about 3 to 3½-inches long. Bake as directed above. When cool, fill with prepared vanilla pudding and glaze with **Chocolate Glaze** p. 186.

SNACK CREAM PUFFS: Drop by tablespoons, making 20 small cream puffs. Bake as directed for 13 to 17 minutes.

PRALINE CREAM PUFFS: Prepare and bake 6 cream puffs as directed above. Fill with 2 cups vanilla ice cream. Drizzle with a combination of 1¼ cups warm caramel ice cream topping and ½ cup chopped pecans, toasted, p. 23

FRUIT AND CREAM PASTRY

Phyllo dough, found in your grocer's freezer, makes it possible to easily prepare this many-layered pastry.

- 10 **(18x14-inch) frozen phyllo (filo) pastry sheets, thawed**
- ½ **cup margarine or butter, melted**
- 1 **(3.5-oz.) pkg. instant vanilla pudding and pie filling mix**
- 1 **cup cold milk**
- 1 **cup frozen whipped topping, thawed**
- 1 **cup thinly sliced fresh or canned peaches**
- 1 **cup fresh or frozen blueberries, thawed Powdered sugar**

Heat oven to 375°F. Cover large cookie sheet with foil. Unroll phyllo sheets; do not separate. Cut stack of phyllo sheets in half; cover with plastic wrap or towel. Working with 1 stack of phyllo sheets, place 1 phyllo square on 1 end of foil-lined cookie sheet. Brush with melted margarine. Continue layering and brushing with margarine the remaining 9 squares phyllo dough. Repeat with remaining stack of phyllo sheets, forming 2 pastries.

Bake at 375°F. for 10 to 15 minutes or until golden brown. Cool completely.

In small bowl, combine pudding mix and milk; blend at low speed until smooth. Fold in whipped topping. Carefully remove baked pastries from foil. Place 1 cooled pastry on serving plate. Spread with pudding mixture; arrange fruit on pudding. Top with remaining pastry, pressing gently. Sprinkle with powdered sugar. Refrigerate until serving. Cut into squares.

Yield: 9 servings.

NUTRITION PER SERVING:
Calories 220; Protein 2g; Carbohydrate 23g; Fat 14g; Sodium 230mg.

EASY-METHOD PUFF PASTRY

In contrast to the classic method of using a solid layer of butter, this recipe uses the method of tossing the butter with the flour. Cold butter and ice water are essential to the success of this recipe.

> 4 **cups all purpose flour**
> ½ **teaspoon salt**
> 2 **cups cold butter**
> 1¼ **cups ice water**
> 1 **teaspoon lemon juice**

In large bowl, combine flour and salt. Cut butter into approximately 1x1x½-inch slices; add to flour mixture. Toss until butter is thoroughly coated with flour and slices are separated. In small bowl, combine ice water and lemon juice; pour over flour mixture. Using large spoon, quickly mix together (butter will remain in slices and flour will not be completely moistened).

On lightly floured surface, knead dough 10 to 15 times or until a very rough ball forms. Shape dough into a rectangle (dough will be dry in some areas). Flatten dough slightly, making corners square.

On well floured surface, roll dough to a 15x12-inch rectangle, keeping corners square. Fold dough crosswise into thirds forming a 12x5-inch rectangle. Give dough a quarter turn and repeat folding crosswise into thirds forming a 5x4-inch rectangle. Cover tightly with plastic wrap; refrigerate 20 minutes.

Repeat the rolling, folding, turning and folding steps, forming a 5x4-inch rectangle. Cover tightly with plastic wrap; refrigerate 20 minutes.

Repeat the rolling, folding, turning and folding steps forming a 5x4-inch rectangle. Cover tightly with plastic wrap; refrigerate at least 20 minutes.

To use dough in a recipe, cut dough crosswise in half. Wrap and refrigerate unused portion. Shape and bake puff pastry as directed in the following recipes: **Palmiers** (this page), **Cheesy Pastry Strips** p. 335 and **Patty Shells** p. 335.
Yield: 2 portions

COOK'S NOTE

MAKING PUFF PASTRY

Try these easy tips to create layers of rich buttery pastry.

- For classic puff pastry, use butter. Butter needs to be cold but soft enough to be "moldable." It should not be hard or too soft.
- Dough needs to be chilled to handle it. Don't make puff pastry on a hot humid day.
- To achieve maximum layering, be sure to roll the rectangle to the exact size specified, making sure corners are very square.
- Use a sharp knife to cut straight down through the dough. Always leave the cut edge untreated — don't brush with egg or the edges won't puff. To cut patty shells, flour the cutter each time.
- Line the cookie sheets with parchment paper. Cut the paper to fit the cookie sheet.
- Be sure oven is heated to the proper temperature. To achieve maximum puffing, pastry should go from the refrigerator to a hot oven. Always refrigerate dough while the first sheet is baking.
- If you want to reuse dough scraps, layer them before rerolling. Rolling them into a ball will not allow for puffing during baking.

PALMIERS

A swirl of cinnamon and sugar flavors this rich pastry.

> 1 **portion Easy-Method Puff Pastry (this page)**
> ½ **cup sugar**
> 1 **teaspoon cinnamon**

Line cookie sheets with parchment paper. With sharp knife, cut dough crosswise in half. Cover half of dough with plastic wrap; return to refrigerator.

Heat oven to 375°F. In small bowl, combine sugar and cinnamon; mix well. On lightly floured surface, roll remaining half of dough to 14x10-inch rectangle. Sprinkle with half of the sugar-cinnamon mixture; press lightly into dough. Starting from 2 shortest sides, roll sides to meet in center. With sharp knife, cut into about ⅜-inch slices. Place 2 inches apart on paper-lined cookie sheets.

Bake at 375°F. for 15 to 20 minutes or until golden brown. Remove from paper; cool on wire rack. Repeat with remaining piece of dough and cinnamon sugar mixture. Serve with coffee, tea or as a dessert.

Yield: 56 palmiers.

NUTRITION PER SERVING:
Calories 50; Protein 1g; Carbohydrate 5g; Fat 3g; Sodium 45mg.

PATTY SHELLS

Fill these with fruit yogurt and fresh fruit for a special dessert.

1   portion Easy-Method Puff Pastry p. 334

Line cookie sheets with parchment paper. With sharp knife, cut the portion of dough crosswise in half. Cover half of dough with plastic wrap; return to the refrigerator.

Heat oven to 425°F. On lightly floured surface, roll remaining half of dough into a 12-inch square. Cut dough with floured 3½-inch round-shaped cookie cutter. Do not twist cutter. Dip cutter in flour between cuts. With floured 2½-inch round-shaped cutter, cut into centers of 3½-inch circles by cutting to but not completely through pastry. (This will create center portion to be removed after baking.) Place 2 inches apart on paper-lined cookie sheets.

Bake at 425°F. for 15 to 20 minutes or until golden brown. Remove from paper. Using fork, remove centers from patty shells; cool on wire rack. Repeat with remaining piece of dough.

Yield: 18 patty shells.

TIP:
Three 10-oz. pkg. frozen puff pastry shells can be substituted for recipe.

NUTRITION PER SERVING:
Calories 130; Protein 1g; Carbohydrate 10g; Fat 9g; Sodium 120mg.

CHEESY PASTRY STRIPS

These are a wonderful accompaniment to soup or salad.

1   portion Easy-Method Puff Pastry p. 334
¼   cup grated Parmesan cheese
¾   teaspoon dried basil leaves
¼   teaspoon garlic powder
1   egg, beaten

Line cookie sheets with parchment paper. Heat oven to 425°F. In small bowl, combine Parmesan cheese, basil and garlic powder; mix well. On lightly floured surface, roll dough to 14x10-inch rectangle. Brush with egg; sprinkle with cheese mixture. With sharp knife, cut into two 14x5-inch rectangles. Cut each rectangle into twenty eight 5x½-inch strips. Place strips 2 inches apart on paper-lined cookie sheets.*

Bake at 425°F. for 15 to 20 minutes or until golden brown. Remove from paper; cool on wire rack.

Yield: 56 pastry strips.

TIP:
* Strips of dough can be twisted 3 or 4 times before placing on paper-lined cookie sheets. Press ends of dough down on paper.

NUTRITION PER SERVING:
Calories 50; Protein 1g; Carbohydrate 3g; Fat 4g; Sodium 55mg.

COOK'S NOTE

PURCHASED PUFF PASTRY

Purchased puff pastry can be substituted in these recipes. Be sure to purchase the freshest pastry possible. Thaw the puff pastry in the refrigerator and keep it cold during the preparation of the recipe. Be sure the oven is heated to the proper temperature. To achieve maximum puffing, pastry should go from the refrigerator to a hot oven. Always refrigerate dough while the first sheet is baking.

STEP-BY-STEP FEATURE 〜
How to Handle Phyllo Dough for Strudel

STEP 1. Prepare filling ingredients. After unwrapping the phyllo dough, cover it with plastic wrap. Separate the sheets as you need them, leaving remaining sheets covered.

STEP 2. Working quickly, top the pastry sheets with filling to within 2 inches of edges. Fold the shorter sides of phyllo over filling. Starting with longer side and using plastic wrap to lift, carefully roll up.

APPLE MINCEMEAT STRUDEL

Thaw phyllo in the refrigerator and keep it cold until ready to use. Unused phyllo pastry can be stored tightly wrapped in the refrigerator for up to 1 week, or it can be refrozen.

- 1 **medium apple, chopped**
- 2 **tablespoons brown sugar**
- ½ **teaspoon grated orange peel**
- ¼ **teaspoon cinnamon**
- 1 **cup prepared mincemeat**
- 8 **(18x14-inch) frozen phyllo (filo) pastry sheets, thawed**
- ⅓ **cup margarine or butter, melted**
- 4 **tablespoons dry bread crumbs**

Heat oven to 375°F. Grease cookie sheet. In medium bowl, combine apple, brown sugar, orange peel and cinnamon. Stir in mincemeat; set aside.

Unroll phyllo sheets; cover with plastic wrap or towel. Place 1 phyllo sheet on sheet of plastic wrap; brush with margarine and sprinkle with 1 table-spoon bread crumbs. Repeat layering with remaining phyllo and margarine, sprinkling 1 tablespoon bread crumbs on every other sheet. (Top phyllo sheet should be brushed with marga-rine only.) Spoon mincemeat mixture over phyllo to within 2 inches of edges; press lightly. Fold shorter sides of phyllo up over filling. Starting with longer side and using plastic wrap, lift phyllo and carefully roll up jelly-roll fashion. Place seam side down on greased cookie sheet. Make several cross-wise slits in top of roll. Brush with margarine.

Bake at 375°F. for 20 to 25 minutes or until golden brown. Cool completely. To serve, cut into slices.
Yield: 12 servings.

NUTRITION PER SERVING:
Calories 130; Protein 1g; Carbohydrate 21g; Fat 6g; Sodium 170mg.

Apple Mincemeat Strudel

Mom's Apple Dumplings

For the best results, use firm baking apples. See p. 11 for examples.

SAUCE

1½ cups sugar
1½ cups water
¼ cup red cinnamon candies
¼ teaspoon cinnamon
¼ teaspoon nutmeg

DUMPLINGS

2 cups all purpose flour
2 teaspoons baking powder
1 teaspoon salt
⅔ cup shortening
½ to ⅔ cup cold milk
6 small (2½-inch diameter) baking apples, peeled and cored
3 tablespoons margarine or butter
1 egg white, beaten
1 tablespoon sugar
Half-and-half, if desired

In medium saucepan, combine all sauce ingredients. Bring mixture to a full rolling boil, stirring occasionally. Set aside.

Heat oven to 375°F. In large bowl, combine flour, baking powder and salt. Using pastry blender or fork, cut in shortening until mixture resembles coarse crumbs. Sprinkle flour mixture with milk while tossing and mixing lightly with fork, adding enough milk until soft dough forms. Shape dough into ball. Roll on lightly floured surface into 18x12-inch rectangle. Cut rectangle into 6 squares.* Place an apple in center of each pastry square; dot with margarine. Bring corners of pastry squares up to top of apple; press edges to seal. Repeat with remaining apples. Place in ungreased 13x9-inch pan. Pour sauce in pan evenly around dumplings. Brush dumplings with egg white; sprinkle with 1 tablespoon sugar.

Bake at 375°F. for 40 to 50 minutes or until dumplings are light golden brown and apples are tender. Serve warm or cool with half-and-half.

Yield: 6 dumplings.

TIP:

* If desired, prepare 5 dumplings, reserving remaining pastry square for decorative cutouts. Garnish sealed dumplings with cutouts. Bake as directed above.

Mom's Apple Dumplings

HIGH ALTITUDE:
Above 3500 Feet: No change.

NUTRITION PER SERVING:
Calories 780; Protein 7g; Carbohydrate 114g; Fat 33g; Sodium 580mg.

Pear Dumplings

In this recipe, whole pears are wrapped in dough and baked until golden and tender.

DUMPLINGS

Pastry for Two-Crust Pie p. 268
4 medium, firm, ripe whole pears
1 egg
1 tablespoon milk

SAUCE

½ cup sugar
1 teaspoon cornstarch
1 cup white Zinfandel wine
2 tablespoons margarine or butter
½ to 1 teaspoon cinnamon

Grease cookie sheet. Prepare pastry for Two-Crust Pie. Heat oven to 425°F. Cut four 4½-inch rounds from 1 circle of pastry. Cut remaining pastry into ¾-inch wide strips. Peel pears leaving stem intact. Using apple corer, remove core from bottom half of each pear. Dry surface of pears with paper towels. Place 1 pear in center of pastry round. Press pastry up around base of pear as far as it will go; then attach pastry strips, overlapping each ¼ inch, to completely wrap pear. Press to seal edges. Repeat to wrap remaining pears. Place wrapped pears on greased cookie sheet. In small bowl, beat egg and milk; brush over pastry on each pear.

Bake at 425°F. for 30 to 40 minutes or until golden brown, brushing with egg mixture once halfway through baking.

Meanwhile, in small saucepan combine sugar and cornstarch; mix well. Stir in wine, margarine and cinnamon. Bring to a boil; boil 1 minute, stirring constantly. Reduce heat; simmer until serving time, stirring occasionally. Serve warm dumplings with warm sauce.

Yield: 4 dumplings.

NUTRITION PER SERVING:
Calories 790; Protein 5g; Carbohydrate 96g; Fat 40g; Sodium 740mg.

QUICK BREADS

Quick breads are a welcome addition to breakfast, lunch and dinner. Flaky biscuits fresh from the oven round out a breakfast of fruit and coffee. Enjoy warm herb muffins with soup for a special lunch, or impress dinner guests with a basket of tender golden brown popovers.

Quick breads, like popovers, biscuits, breads and muffins, can be prepared in just minutes because they don't require the time and techniques that yeast breads do. Quick breads are an easy way to deliver fresh-from-the-oven baked goods to meals from everyday to elegant.

Pictured: **Cherry Nut Bread** *p. 379,* **Caramel Biscuit Ring-a-Round** *p. 398,* **Magic Marshmallow Crescent Puffs** *p. 406*

QUICK BREADS

What makes a quick bread quick? No yeast! Quick breads get
their speedy name and preparation time from using fast-acting leavening
agents (baking powder, baking soda or steam) rather than slower-acting yeast.
Some popular quick breads are muffins, popovers, nut bread loaves
and biscuits. They're great for spur-of-the-moment baking.

KINDS OF QUICK BREADS

*The kinds of quick breads can be described by the
thickness or stiffness of their batter or dough.
Here are the most common kinds of quick breads:*

BATTER

There are 2 types of batter for these breads:
- Thin, which can be poured from a mixing
  bowl into a baking pan. (Recipe examples
  include **Perfect Popovers** p. 408 and **Puffed
  Fruit-Topped Pancake** p. 413.)

- Drop, which must be scraped from the
  bowl and then spooned into the baking
  pan. (Recipe examples include **Blueberry
  Orange Drop Biscuits** p. 351, **Lemon
  Poppy Seed Muffins** p. 370 and **Pecan
  Pumpkin Bread** p. 386.)

SOFT DOUGH

The dough for these quick breads is soft,
but firm enough to be handled, patted or
rolled. (Recipe examples include **Cinnamon
Currant Buttermilk Biscuits** p. 350, **Basil
Parmesan Scones** p. 358 and **Norwegian Flat
Bread** p. 410.)

REFRIGERATED DOUGH

These breads are made from convenient, already prepared and packaged dough from the
refrigerator case. The biscuit, crescent or soft
breadstick dough is versatile and can be
shaped, layered and rolled. (Recipe examples
include **Caramel Sticky Buns** p. 405 and
Magic Marshmallow Crescent Puffs p. 406.)

SECRETS FOR SUCCESSFUL QUICK BREADS

*Because quick breads are meant to be stirred
together quickly and then baked, there are just a
few simple secrets to ensure their success:*

SECRETS FOR ALL QUICK BREADS

Use shiny aluminum pans and cookie sheets.
They reflect heat and will produce a golden,
delicate, tender crust. Disposable aluminum
loaf pans also can be used.

Use fresh baking powder and baking soda.
Check the expiration date when purchasing
these ingredients. These leavening agents form
gas bubbles when combined with liquid and
heat, and that's what makes the quick bread
rise. Out-of-date leavenings won't perform as
well. (See p. 8 for directions on how to test
baking powder.)

Avoid overmixing. Overmixing batters and
handling doughs too much will make the
finished quick bread tough.

Serve immediately after baking. Quick breads
such as oven pancakes, popovers and biscuits
are best when they're hot from the oven.

However, loaves, muffins and coffee cakes store well.

Create your own quick bread mix. Stir together the dry ingredients and cut in the shortening, then store the mixture in the refrigerator in a tightly covered container for up to 3 weeks. When ready to bake, allow the mix to come to room temperature, add the liquid ingredients and complete the recipe.

SECRETS FOR MUFFINS

Use regular muffin cups for standard-sized muffins. However, jumbo and mini-muffin pans also are available. You can experiment with different pan sizes, but remember that baking times and yields will vary, depending on the size pan you use.

Grease muffin cups or use paper or foil baking cups as directed in the recipe.

Mix the dry ingredients and liquids just until the dry ingredients are moistened, 12 to 15 strokes. The batter will be lumpy. Mixing the batter until it is smooth will create tough, coarse-textured muffins with unattractive tunnels and pointed (rather than slightly rounded), bumpy tops.

Fill muffin cups as directed in the recipe. If there isn't enough batter to fill all the cups, fill the empty cups with water before baking to protect the pan.

Remove muffins from the pan immediately after baking. This will prevent them from becoming soggy.

SECRETS FOR BISCUITS

Cut in shortening thoroughly. Use a pastry blender or fork to distribute the shortening evenly to give the biscuits a flaky texture.

Knead dough quickly and lightly. Kneading helps make biscuits flaky, but should be done just until the dough is no longer sticky. Kneading also helps distribute the leavening agent.

Roll or pat the dough to an even thickness. Not only will biscuits be more attractive, they will bake more evenly.

Use a floured cutter. To avoid sticking, lightly flour a biscuit cutter or narrow glass or jar. When cutting biscuits, don't twist the cutter.

Brush the tops of the biscuits with butter or milk before baking for a rich brown top.

SECRETS FOR LOAVES

A successful loaf is . . . well shaped, with a thin, golden-brown crust and an even texture (fairly moist with ingredients such as fruit or nuts evenly distributed). A lengthwise crack in the top is common.

Grease loaf pans as directed in the recipe. Ungreased sides allow the batter to climb the sides of the pan during baking and create a rounded top.

Measure accurately. Accurate measurement of dry ingredients and liquids will prevent loaves that are dry on the outside and under-baked on the inside.

Cool loaves completely before slicing them to prevent crumbling. Often, the flavors will mellow and slicing will be easier if the loaf is cooled, tightly wrapped and refrigerated for at least 1 day.

Cut loaves with a thin, sharp knife. Use a light sawing motion to minimize breaking or crumbling of thin slices. An electric knife also can be used.

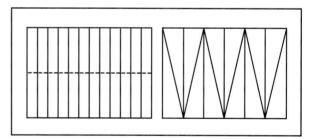

Cutting loaves into slices and wedges

SECRETS FOR SOFT DOUGH QUICK BREADS

Keep handling to a minimum. Handling soft doughs too much can make them tough.

Use the minimum amount of flour when rolling, cutting and shaping. Incorporating too much extra flour into soft doughs can make them tough.

Rub your hands with margarine or butter before shaping the dough. This will help to keep the dough from sticking to your hands.

Grease the pans as directed in the recipe to prevent sticking.

SECRETS FOR REFRIGERATED DOUGH BREADS

Check the "use by" date on the package. Be sure to buy the freshest product and use it before the expiration date.

For maximum freshness, store refrigerated dough products in the main compartment of the refrigerator, not on the door shelves.

Do not freeze unbaked refrigerated dough products.

BAKING AND REHEATING QUICK BREADS IN THE MICROWAVE OVEN

A microwave oven makes preparing some quick breads even quicker, and can be a great way to warm them before serving.

To bake quick breads in the microwave:

- Use microwave-safe baking pans.

- When baking muffins, line each cup with 2 paper baking cups to absorb excess moisture. Remove the second baking cup immediately after baking.

- Follow recipe directions for timing. Set the timer for the shortest time given and then check for doneness. If the recipe requires more cooking time, add it in 30-second increments.

- Remember that foods continue cooking after they are removed from the microwave. The standing time indicated in the recipe is necessary to complete the baking.

To reheat quick breads in the microwave:

- Place slices, rolls or muffins on top of a paper napkin, microwave-safe paper towel or paper plate to absorb moisture. Do not cover them.

- Watch reheating times carefully. Microwave single servings on HIGH for 5 to 10 seconds. Add more time in 10-second increments for additional servings. If the quick bread is frozen, increase the time to 15-second increments.

HOW TO TELL WHEN QUICK BREADS ARE DONE

The length of time quick breads bake varies from muffins to popovers to breads to coffee cakes. But depending on what type of quick bread you're baking, knowing when it's properly done will help ensure that you're serving it at its very best. In general, these are the characteristics to look for:

Muffins are done when . . . the tops are golden brown and a toothpick inserted in the center comes out clean.

Biscuits, coffee cakes and breadsticks are done when . . . they're golden brown.

Popovers are done when . . . they've popped, (at least doubled in volume) and are deep golden brown with a crusty top.

Quick breads or loaves are done when . . . the top is golden brown and a toothpick inserted in the center comes out clean. Also, a lengthwise crack may have developed.

KEEPING QUICK BREADS FRESH AND FLAVORFUL

Many quick breads, such as popovers and oven pancakes, are at the peak of their flavor and appearance immediately after baking and should be served then. Other quick breads are very moist and can become moldy if not refrigerated. Breads, muffins, coffee cakes, rolls and biscuits can be frozen.

Wrap well, then refrigerate. Quick breads lose their freshness and flavor quickly, so place them in tightly covered containers or wrap them tightly in foil or plastic wrap and refrigerate.

To freeze breads, muffins and biscuits:

• Bake, then cool completely.

• Wrap tightly in plastic wrap, plastic bags or foil. Freeze for up to 6 months.

• To thaw, unwrap slightly and thaw at room temperature. Reheat, wrapped in foil, at 350°F. for 15 to 20 minutes. See p. 346 for microwave reheating instructions.

To freeze coffee cakes and rolls:

• Bake, then cool completely.

• Freeze in the pan. Or remove and place on foil-wrapped cardboard; place in a large plastic freezer bag and seal. Freeze up to 1 month.

• To thaw, follow instructions for breads, muffins and biscuits.

• For best results, add icings and glazes just before serving.

SPREADS FOR BREADS

Try these flavorful spreads to enjoy with warm bread, biscuits or muffins.

WHIPPED BUTTERS

In a small bowl, beat ½ cup butter at high speed until light and fluffy. Add 1 of the following and continue beating until well blended:

• ⅛ to ¼ teaspoon garlic powder or 1 to 2 garlic cloves, minced

• ⅛ to ¼ teaspoon dried thyme leaves, finely crushed

• ½ teaspoon grated fresh onion

• ¼ cup grated Parmesan cheese

• ¼ cup honey

• ¼ cup orange marmalade

• 2 tablespoons maple-flavored syrup

• 2 tablespoons orange juice and 1 tablespoon grated orange peel

• 2 tablespoons honey and 2 tablespoons chocolate syrup

WHIPPED CREAM CHEESES

In a small bowl, beat 8-oz. pkg. cream cheese until soft. Gradually beat in 1 of the following until light and fluffy:

• ¼ cup honey

• ¼ cup orange marmalade

• 3 to 4 tablespoons maple-flavored syrup

• 3 to 4 tablespoons orange juice and ½ teaspoon grated orange peel

---

NUTRITION IN THIS CHAPTER

Nutrition per serving means the calculation was done on 1 slice, 1 serving, 1 biscuit, scone, muffin or sweet roll.

STEP-BY-STEP FEATURE ∾
How to Make Baking Powder Biscuits

STEP 1. Using pastry blender, cut shortening into flour mixture until consistency of coarse crumbs. Add milk; stir with fork until soft dough forms.

STEP 2. Dust a rolling pin and smooth surface with flour. Roll out dough to ½-inch thickness. Cut dough with floured 2-inch cutter.

BAKING POWDER BISCUITS

Tossing or kneading biscuit dough lightly helps distribute leavening for even baking and rising. These traditional biscuits are great served with any meal. For variety, try the delicious variations.

- **2 cups all purpose flour**
- **3 teaspoons baking powder**
- **1/2 teaspoon salt**
- **1/2 cup shortening**
- **3/4 to 1 cup milk**

Heat oven to 450°F. In large bowl, combine flour, baking powder and salt. Using pastry blender or fork, cut in shortening until mixture resembles coarse crumbs. Stirring with fork, add enough milk until mixture leaves sides of bowl and forms a soft, moist dough.

On floured surface, toss dough lightly until no longer sticky. Roll or press out to 1/2-inch thickness; cut with floured 2-inch round cutter. Place biscuits on ungreased cookie sheet.

Bake at 450°F. for 8 to 12 minutes or until light golden brown. Serve warm.
Yield: 12 to 14 biscuits.

FOOD PROCESSOR DIRECTIONS:
In food processor bowl with metal blade, combine flour, baking powder and salt. Process with 5 on-off pulses to mix. Add shortening to flour mixture. Process until mixture resembles coarse crumbs. Add 1/2 to 2/3 cup milk; process with on-off pulses just until ball starts to form. On lightly floured surface, roll or press out to 1/2-inch thickness; cut with floured 2-inch round cutter. Continue as directed above.

HIGH ALTITUDE:
Above 3500 Feet: No change.

NUTRITION PER SERVING:
Calories 140; Protein 2g; Carbohydrate 14g; Fat 8g; Sodium 155mg.

(Recipe continued on next page.)

Baking Powder Biscuits

(Recipe continued from previous page.)

VARIATIONS:

BUTTERMILK BISCUITS: Add ¼ teaspoon baking soda to flour. Substitute buttermilk for milk.

CHEESE BISCUITS: Add 4 oz. (1 cup) shredded Cheddar cheese to flour-shortening mixture. Bake on *greased* cookie sheet.

DROP BISCUITS: Increase milk to 1¼ cups. Drop dough by spoonfuls onto *greased* cookie sheets.

SOFT-SIDED BISCUITS: Place biscuits in 9-inch round or square pan or on cookie sheet with sides touching. Bake at 450°F. for 12 to 14 minutes.

SOUTHERN-STYLE BISCUITS: Decrease shortening to ¼ cup.

THIN-CRISPY BISCUITS: Roll dough out to ¼-inch thickness. Cut biscuits with floured 3-inch cutter.

SOUR CREAM DROP BISCUITS

These easy-to-make savory biscuits have a flaky, light texture. Serve them warm from the oven.

- 2 **cups all purpose flour**
- 1 **tablespoon sugar**
- 3 **teaspoons baking powder**
- ½ **teaspoon salt**
- ¼ **cup shortening**
- ⅔ **cup milk**
- ⅔ **cup dairy sour cream**

Heat oven to 450°F. Grease cookie sheet. In medium bowl, combine flour, sugar, baking powder and salt; blend well. Using pastry blender or fork, cut in shortening until mixture is crumbly. In small bowl, combine milk and sour cream. Add all at once, stirring just until moistened. Drop dough by tablespoonfuls onto greased cookie sheet.

Bake at 450°F. for 10 to 12 minutes or until golden brown. Serve warm.

Yield: 12 biscuits.

HIGH ALTITUDE:
Above 3500 Feet: No change.

NUTRITION PER SERVING:
Calories 160; Protein 3g; Carbohydrate 18g; Fat 8g; Sodium 185mg.

CINNAMON CURRANT BUTTERMILK BISCUITS

Serve these anytime with coffee or tea.

BISCUITS
- 2 **cups all purpose flour**
- ¼ **cup sugar**
- 3 **teaspoons baking powder**
- 1 **teaspoon salt**
- 1 **teaspoon cinnamon**
- ¼ **teaspoon baking soda**
- ⅓ **cup shortening**
- ½ **cup dried currants or raisins**
- ¾ **to 1 cup buttermilk**

FROSTING
- ¾ **cup powdered sugar**
- 2 **to 3 teaspoons milk**

Heat oven to 450°F. In large bowl, combine flour, sugar, baking powder, salt, cinnamon and baking soda. Using pastry blender or fork, cut in shortening until mixture resembles coarse crumbs; stir in currants. Stirring with fork, add enough buttermilk until mixture leaves sides of bowl and soft dough forms.

Turn dough out onto floured surface; gently knead dough until no longer sticky. Roll out to ½-inch thickness; cut with floured 2½-inch round cutter. Place biscuits on ungreased cookie sheet with sides touching.

Bake at 450°F. for 10 to 15 minutes or until light golden brown. Cool 5 minutes on wire rack. In small bowl, combine powdered sugar and enough milk for desired frosting consistency. Frost warm biscuits; serve immediately.

Yield: 12 biscuits.

HIGH ALTITUDE:
Above 3500 Feet: No change.

NUTRITION PER SERVING:
Calories 200; Protein 3g; Carbohydrate 33g; Fat 6g; Sodium 300mg.

BLUEBERRY ORANGE DROP BISCUITS

There's no kneading or rolling when making drop biscuits. This fruit-filled version is easy to make and tastes great for breakfast or brunch.

BISCUITS
1½ **cups all purpose flour**
 ½ **cup cornmeal**
 ½ **cup sugar**
 3 **teaspoons baking powder**
 1 **tablespoon grated orange peel**
 ½ **teaspoon salt**
 ½ **cup margarine or butter**
 ⅓ **cup milk**
 1 **egg**
 1 **cup fresh or frozen blueberries (do not thaw)**

TOPPING
 1 **tablespoon sugar**
 1 **tablespoon grated orange peel**

Heat oven to 400°F. In large bowl, combine flour, cornmeal, ½ cup sugar, baking powder, 1 tablespoon orange peel and salt; blend well. Using pastry blender or fork, cut in margarine until mixture is crumbly. Add milk and egg; stir just until moistened. Gently stir in blueberries. To form each biscuit, drop rounded ¼ cup of dough onto large ungreased cookie sheet.

In small bowl, combine topping ingredients. Sprinkle over biscuits. Bake at 400°F. for 11 to 13 minutes or until light golden brown. Serve warm.
Yield: 12 biscuits.

HIGH ALTITUDE:
Above 3500 Feet: Increase flour to 1½ cups plus 1 tablespoon. Bake as directed above.

NUTRITION PER SERVING:
Calories 200; Protein 3g; Carbohydrate 28g; Fat 9g; Sodium 260mg.

CORNMEAL CARROT BISCUITS

Use either white or yellow cornmeal to make these delicious biscuits. White cornmeal is sweeter and lighter than yellow cornmeal and has a milder flavor. Either way, the crunchy texture and slightly sweet flavor of these biscuits makes them a perfect accompaniment to chili.

1¼ **cups all purpose flour**
 ¾ **cup cornmeal**
 ¼ **cup sugar**
 3 **teaspoons baking powder**
 ½ **teaspoon salt**
 ¾ **cup margarine or butter**
 ¾ **cup shredded carrots**
 ½ **cup currants or raisins**
 ⅓ **cup milk**
 1 **egg**

Heat oven to 400°F. In medium bowl, combine flour, cornmeal, sugar, baking powder and salt; blend well. Using pastry blender or fork, cut in margarine until mixture is crumbly. Stir in carrots and currants. Add milk and egg; stir just until moistened. To form each biscuit, drop ¼ cup of dough onto ungreased cookie sheet.

Bake at 400°F. for 10 to 12 minutes or until light golden brown. Serve warm.
Yield: 12 biscuits.

HIGH ALTITUDE:
Above 3500 Feet: Decrease baking powder to 2 teaspoons. Bake at 425°F. for 12 to 15 minutes.

NUTRITION INFORMATION PER SERVING:
Calories 210; Protein 3g; Carbohydrate 22g; Fat 12g; Sodium 310mg.

CARROT AND HERB DINNER BISCUITS

Biscuits are at their best when served warm from the oven and these are no exception. The herb and vegetable flavor is a delicious change of pace.

- 1¼ **cups all purpose flour**
- ¾ **cup cornmeal**
- ¼ **cup sugar**
- 3 **teaspoons baking powder**
- 1 **teaspoon dried basil leaves**
- 1 **teaspoon dried parsley flakes**
- ½ **teaspoon salt**
- ¾ **cup margarine or butter**
- ½ **cup shredded carrots**
- ⅓ **cup milk**
- 1 **egg**

Heat oven to 400°F. In medium bowl, combine flour, cornmeal, sugar, baking powder, basil, parsley flakes and salt; blend well. Using pastry blender or fork, cut in margarine until mixture resembles coarse crumbs. Stir in carrots. Add milk and egg, stirring just until moistened. To form each biscuit, drop ¼ cup of dough onto ungreased cookie sheet.

Bake at 400°F. for 12 to 14 minutes or until light golden brown. Serve warm.
Yield: 12 biscuits.

HIGH ALTITUDE:
Above 3500 Feet: No change.

NUTRITION PER SERVING:
Calories 210; Protein 3g; Carbohydrate 21g; Fat 12g; Sodium 310mg.

CHEDDAR CHIVE DROP BISCUITS

For tender biscuits, stir gently and work quickly. Stirring just until all the dry ingredients are moistened helps keep biscuits from becoming tough.

- 2 **cups all purpose flour**
- 3 **teaspoons baking powder**
- 1 **teaspoon salt**
- ½ **cup shortening**
- 1¼ **cups plain yogurt**
- 4 **oz. (1 cup) shredded Cheddar cheese**
- ¼ **cup chopped fresh chives**

Heat oven to 450°F. Grease cookie sheets. In large bowl, combine flour, baking powder and salt; blend well. Using pastry blender or fork, cut in shortening until mixture resembles coarse crumbs. Add yogurt, cheese and chives; stir just until moistened. Drop dough by generous tablespoonfuls onto greased cookie sheets.

Bake at 450°F. for 9 to 12 minutes or until light golden brown. Serve warm.
Yield: 18 biscuits.

HIGH ALTITUDE:
Above 3500 Feet: No change.

NUTRITION PER SERVING:
Calories 140; Protein 4g; Carbohydrate 12g; Fat 8g; Sodium 220mg.

Carrot and Herb Dinner Biscuits,
Cheddar Chive Drop Biscuits

CURRANT SCONES

The original scones from Scotland were made with oats and griddle-baked. This updated version is made with flour and is slightly sweet. Serve them warm with butter and jam.

  2 **cups all purpose flour**
¼ **cup sugar**
  3 **teaspoons baking powder**
¼ **teaspoon salt**
¼ **cup margarine or butter**
⅔ **cup dried currants**
  1 **(5-oz.) can (⅔ cup) evaporated milk**
  1 **egg**
    Sugar

Heat oven to 400°F. In medium bowl, combine flour, sugar, baking powder and salt; blend well. Using pastry blender or fork, cut in margarine until mixture is crumbly. Stir in currants. In small bowl, combine evaporated milk and egg; add all at once, stirring just until moistened.

On well floured surface, gently knead dough 5 or 6 times. Place on ungreased cookie sheet; press into 8-inch circle, about 1 inch thick. Cut into 8 wedges; do not separate. Sprinkle with sugar.

Bake at 400°F. for 15 to 20 minutes or until golden brown. Cut into wedges; serve warm.

Yield: 8 scones.

HIGH ALTITUDE:
Above 3500 Feet: No change.

NUTRITION PER SERVING:
Calories 250; Protein 6g; Carbohydrate 43g; Fat 7g; Sodium 280mg.

COOK'S NOTE

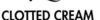

CLOTTED CREAM

Clotted cream, also known as Devonshire cream, is made by gently heating unpasteurized cream until a layer of thick cream forms on the surface. The thickened cream is removed when it has cooled.

SCOTTISH SCONES

In England or Scotland, scones are split in half and served with butter, preserves and clotted cream.

SCONES
1½ **cups all purpose flour**
¾ **cup rolled oats**
¼ **cup firmly packed brown sugar**
  2 **teaspoons baking powder**
½ **teaspoon salt**
½ **teaspoon cinnamon**
½ **cup margarine or butter**
½ **cup milk**

TOPPING
  1 **tablespoon margarine or butter, melted**
  1 **tablespoon sugar**
¼ **teaspoon cinnamon**

Heat oven to 375°F. Lightly grease cookie sheet. In medium bowl, combine flour, oats, brown sugar, baking powder, salt and ½ teaspoon cinnamon; blend well. Using pastry blender or fork, cut in ½ cup margarine until mixture is crumbly. Add milk all at once, stirring just until moistened.

On floured surface, gently knead dough 5 or 6 times. Place on greased cookie sheet; press into 6-inch circle, about 1 inch thick. Brush top of dough with melted margarine. In small bowl, combine sugar and ¼ teaspoon cinnamon; sprinkle over top. Cut dough into 8 wedges; separate slightly.

Bake at 375°F. for 20 to 30 minutes or until golden brown. Serve warm.

Yield: 8 scones.

HIGH ALTITUDE:
Above 3500 Feet: No change.

NUTRITION PER SERVING:
Calories 270; Protein 4g; Carbohydrate 32g; Fat 14g; Sodium 370mg.

WHOLE WHEAT DATE SCONES

Try this updated version of a traditional English teatime biscuit wedge.

1¼ **cups all purpose flour**
¾ **cup whole wheat flour**
2 **tablespoons sugar**
2½ **teaspoons baking powder**
½ **teaspoon salt**
6 **tablespoons margarine or butter**
½ **cup chopped dates**
½ **cup milk**
2 **eggs**

Heat oven to 425°F. Grease cookie sheet. In medium bowl, combine flour, whole wheat flour, sugar, baking powder and salt; mix well. Using pastry blender or fork, cut in margarine until mixture resembles coarse crumbs. Stir in dates. In small bowl, combine milk and eggs; reserve 2 tablespoons. Add remaining egg mixture all at once, stirring just until moistened.

On floured surface, gently knead dough to make a smooth ball. Place on greased cookie sheet. With floured hands, press dough into 8-inch circle. Cut into 8 wedges; do not separate. Brush with reserved egg mixture.

Bake at 425°F. for 13 to 15 minutes or until golden brown. Cut into wedges; serve warm.
Yield: 8 scones.

HIGH ALTITUDE:
Above 3500 Feet: No change.

NUTRITION PER SERVING:
Calories 260; Protein 6g; Carbohydrate 35g; Fat 11g; Sodium 350mg.

MINI-CHIP ORANGE SCONE DROPS

Since they require no kneading, you can make these scone drops even when you're in a time crunch.

SCONES
2 **cups all purpose flour**
⅓ **cup sugar**
2 **teaspoons baking powder**
½ **teaspoon salt**
¼ **teaspoon baking soda**
⅓ **cup margarine or butter**
⅓ **cup orange juice**
⅓ **cup milk**
2 **tablespoons grated orange peel**
½ **cup miniature semi-sweet chocolate chips**

TOPPING
3 **tablespoons sugar**
½ **teaspoon cinnamon**

Heat oven to 375°F. Grease cookie sheets. In large bowl, combine flour, ⅓ cup sugar, baking powder, salt and baking soda; blend well. Using pastry blender or fork, cut in margarine until mixture resembles coarse crumbs. Add orange juice, milk and orange peel; stir just until dry ingredients are moistened. Stir in chocolate chips. Drop by heaping teaspoonfuls 2 inches apart onto greased cookie sheets.

In small bowl, combine topping ingredients; sprinkle over scones. Bake at 375°F. for 8 to 10 minutes or until light golden brown. Immediately remove from cookie sheets. Serve warm.
Yield: 30 scones.

HIGH ALTITUDE:
Above 3500 Feet: No change.

NUTRITION PER SERVING:
Calories 80; Protein 1g; Carbohydrate 12g; Fat 3g; Sodium 90mg.

Bacon Biscuit Wedges

BACON BISCUIT WEDGES

This easy-to-make version of a southern favorite is flavored with bacon.

- 2 **cups all purpose flour**
- ¼ **cup (about 4 slices) crumbled cooked bacon**
- 2 **teaspoons baking powder**
- ½ **teaspoon salt**
- ¼ **cup shortening**
- ⅔ **to 1 cup milk**
- 1 **tablespoon margarine or butter, melted**

Heat oven to 400°F. Grease cookie sheet. In large bowl, combine flour, bacon, baking powder and salt. Using pastry blender or fork, cut in shortening until mixture resembles coarse crumbs. Stirring with fork, add enough milk until mixture leaves sides of bowl and forms a soft, moist dough. On floured surface, gently knead dough 5 or 6 times or until no longer sticky. Shape dough into ball. Place on greased cookie sheet; flatten into 8-inch circle. With sharp knife, score top surface into 8 wedges.

Bake at 400°F. for 21 to 26 minutes or until golden brown. Brush with margarine. Cut into wedges; serve warm.

Yield: 8 biscuit wedges.

HIGH ALTITUDE:
Above 3500 Feet: No change.

NUTRITION PER SERVING:
Calories 220; Protein 5g; Carbohydrate 25g; Fat 10g; Sodium 300mg.

ORANGE PRUNE DROP SCONES

Next time you are looking for a breakfast bread, try these fiber-rich, tender scones.

2¼ cups all purpose flour
½ cup sugar
3 teaspoons baking powder
½ teaspoon salt
2 teaspoons grated orange peel
¼ cup margarine or butter
1 egg
1 to 1¼ cups buttermilk
1 cup finely chopped dried, pitted prunes
Sugar

Heat oven to 375°F. Grease cookie sheet. In large bowl, combine flour, ½ cup sugar, baking powder, salt and orange peel; blend well. Using pastry blender or fork, cut in margarine until mixture is crumbly. Add egg and enough buttermilk until mixture leaves sides of bowl and forms a moist dough. Stir in prunes. To form each scone, drop ¼ cup of dough onto greased cookie sheets. Sprinkle with sugar.

Bake at 375°F. for 13 to 16 minutes or until edges are light golden brown. Serve warm.
Yield: 14 scones.

HIGH ALTITUDE:
Above 3500 Feet: Increase flour to 2½ cups; decrease buttermilk to ¾ to 1 cup. Bake as directed above.

NUTRITION PER SERVING:
Calories 180; Protein 4g; Carbohydrate 31g; Fat 4g; Sodium 210mg.

DOUBLE ORANGE SCONES

Scones are generally richer than biscuits because they contain eggs, cream or milk, and butter. These are highlighted with orange flavor.

2 cups all purpose flour
3 tablespoons sugar
2½ teaspoons baking powder
2 teaspoons grated orange peel
⅓ cup margarine or butter
½ cup chopped canned mandarin orange segments, drained
¼ cup milk
1 egg, slightly beaten
1 tablespoon sugar

Heat oven to 400°F. Lightly grease cookie sheet. In large bowl, combine flour, 3 tablespoons sugar, baking powder and orange peel. Using pastry blender or fork, cut in margarine until mixture resembles coarse crumbs. Add orange segments, milk and egg. With fork, stir just until mixture leaves sides of bowl and soft dough forms.

On floured surface, gently knead dough 10 times. Place on greased cookie sheet; roll or pat into 6-inch circle. Sprinkle dough with 1 tablespoon sugar. Cut dough into 8 wedges; separate slightly.

Bake at 400°F. for 15 to 20 minutes or until golden brown. Serve warm.
Yield: 8 scones.

HIGH ALTITUDE:
Above 3500 Feet: Increase flour to 2¼ cups. Bake as directed above.

NUTRITION PER SERVING:
Calories 220; Protein 4g; Carbohydrate 32g; Fat 9g; Sodium 200mg.

BASIL PARMESAN SCONES

These rich savory scones get their texture from gentle handling and whipping cream rather than butter or shortening.

1¼ to 1½ cups all purpose flour
  3 tablespoons oat bran
  2 tablespoons grated Parmesan cheese
  2 teaspoons baking powder
  1 teaspoon dried basil leaves
  ½ teaspoon salt
  1 cup whipping cream
  1 teaspoon oat bran

Heat oven to 425°F. Grease cookie sheet. In large bowl, combine 1¼ cups flour, 3 tablespoons oat bran, cheese, baking powder, basil and salt; blend well. Reserve 1 teaspoon whipping cream. Add remaining cream to flour mixture, stirring just until soft dough forms. If dough is too wet, stir in flour 1 tablespoon at a time.

On floured surface, gently knead dough to form smooth ball. Place on greased cookie sheet; pat or roll to 6-inch circle. Cut into 8 wedges; do not separate. Brush with reserved 1 teaspoon whipping cream; sprinkle with 1 teaspoon oat bran.

Bake at 425°F. for 15 to 18 minutes or until lightly browned. Cut into wedges; serve warm.
Yield: 8 scones.

HIGH ALTITUDE:
Above 3500 Feet: No change.

NUTRITION PER SERVING:
Calories 200; Protein 4g; Carbohydrate 21g; Fat 12g; Sodium 250mg.

FRESH HERB SCONES

Three popular herbs combine in this savory supper scone.

  2 cups all purpose flour
  ¼ cup chopped fresh parsley
  1 tablespoon sugar
  1 tablespoon chopped fresh thyme or
      1 teaspoon dried thyme leaves
  3 teaspoons baking powder
  1 teaspoon chopped fresh rosemary or
      ¼ teaspoon dried rosemary leaves, crushed
  ½ teaspoon salt
  ⅓ cup margarine or butter
  ½ cup milk
  1 egg, slightly beaten

Heat oven to 400°F. Lightly grease cookie sheet. In large bowl, combine flour, parsley, sugar, thyme, baking powder, rosemary and salt. Using pastry blender or fork, cut in margarine until mixture resembles coarse crumbs. Stir in milk and egg just until moistened.

On floured surface, gently knead dough 10 times. Place on greased cookie sheet; roll or pat dough into 6-inch circle. Cut into 8 wedges; separate slightly.

Bake at 400°F. for 15 to 20 minutes or until golden brown. Cut into wedges; serve warm.
Yield: 8 scones.

HIGH ALTITUDE:
Above 3500 Feet: Decrease baking powder to 2 teaspoons. Bake as directed above.

NUTRITION PER SERVING:
Calories 210; Protein 5g; Carbohydrate 27g; Fat 9g; Sodium 350mg.

POTATO SCONES

Scones can be made in various shapes including rounds, squares, triangles and diamonds.

1¼ **cups all purpose flour**
½ **cup mashed potato flakes**
1 **tablespoon sugar**
2½ **teaspoons baking powder**
½ **teaspoon baking soda**
½ **teaspoon onion salt**
¼ **cup margarine or butter**
½ **cup buttermilk**
1 **egg, slightly beaten**
1 **tablespoon milk**

Heat oven to 375°F. In large bowl, combine flour, potato flakes, sugar, baking powder, baking soda and onion salt; blend well. Using pastry blender or fork, cut in margarine until mixture is crumbly. Add buttermilk and egg; stir just until moistened.

On well floured surface, gently knead dough 5 or 6 times. Place on ungreased cookie sheet; press into 7-inch circle, about 1 inch thick. Brush with milk.

Bake at 375°F. for 15 to 25 minutes or until golden brown. Cut into wedges; serve warm.

Yield: 8 scones.

HIGH ALTITUDE:
Above 3500 Feet: No change.

NUTRITION PER SERVING:
Calories 160; Protein 3g; Carbohydrate 20g; Fat 7g; Sodium 360mg.

BLACK PEPPER AND ONION SCONES

For optimum flavor, use freshly ground black pepper and adjust the level to suit your taste buds.

¾ **cup chopped onions**
¼ **cup margarine or butter**
2 **cups all purpose flour**
2 **tablespoons sugar**
3 **teaspoons baking powder**
½ **teaspoon salt**
½ **to 1 teaspoon coarsely ground black pepper**
½ **cup whipping cream**
1 **egg**
Margarine or butter, melted

Heat oven to 400°F. In small skillet, cook onions in ¼ cup margarine until crisp-tender; set aside. Cool slightly.

In medium bowl, combine flour, sugar, baking powder, salt and pepper; blend well. Add whipping cream, egg and onions; stir just until moistened.

On floured surface, gently knead dough 5 or 6 times. Place on ungreased cookie sheet; press into 8-inch circle, about ½ inch thick. Cut into 8 wedges; separate slightly.

Bake at 400°F. for 12 to 16 minutes or until very light brown. Brush with melted margarine. Cut into wedges; serve warm.

Yield: 8 scones.

HIGH ALTITUDE:
Above 3500 Feet: Decrease baking powder to 2 teaspoons. Bake at 425°F. for 12 to 15 minutes.

NUTRITION PER SERVING:
Calories 240; Protein 4g; Carbohydrate 29g; Fat 12g; Sodium 330mg.

STEP 1. Combine dry ingredients and blueberries; push up sides of bowl to form well. Combine liquid ingredients; pour into well.

STEP 2. Stir just until dry ingredients are moistened (about 12 to 15 strokes). Batter will remain lumpy. Do not overmix.

STEP 3. Lightly grease or line muffin cups with paper baking cups. Fill each cup ⅔ full. Bake at 400°F. for 20 to 25 minutes.

MUFFINS

2 cups all purpose flour
½ cup sugar
3 teaspoons baking powder
½ teaspoon salt
¾ cup milk
⅓ cup oil
1 egg, beaten

Heat oven to 400°F. Grease bottoms only of 12 muffin cups or line with paper baking cups. In medium bowl, combine flour, sugar, baking powder and salt; mix well. In small bowl, combine milk, oil and egg; blend well. Add to dry ingredients all at once; stir just until dry ingredients are moistened (Batter will be lumpy.) Fill greased muffin cups ⅔ full.

Bake at 400°F. for 20 to 25 minutes or until toothpick inserted in center comes out clean. Cool 1 minute before removing from pan. Serve warm. **Yield: 12 muffins.**

MICROWAVE DIRECTIONS:
Prepare muffin batter as directed above. Using 6-cup microwave-safe muffin pan, line each cup with 2 paper baking cups to absorb moisture during cooking. Fill cups ⅔ full. Microwave 6 muffins on HIGH for 2 to 2½ minutes or until toothpick inserted in center comes out clean, rotating pan ½ turn halfway through cooking. Remove muffins from pan and immediately discard outer baking cups. Repeat with remaining batter.

HIGH ALTITUDE:
Above 3500 Feet: No change.

NUTRITION PER SERVING:
Calories 180; Protein 3g; Carbohydrate 25g; Fat 7g; Sodium 180mg.

VARIATIONS:

APPLE MUFFINS: Decrease sugar to ¼ cup. Add 1 teaspoon cinnamon and 1 cup finely chopped, peeled apple to dry ingredients. Substitute apple juice for milk. Bake at 400°F. for 18 to 22 minutes.

BLUEBERRY MUFFINS: Stir 1 cup fresh or frozen blueberries (do not thaw) and 1 teaspoon grated lemon or orange peel into dry ingredients.

(Recipe continued on next page.)

Blueberry Muffins

(Recipe continued from previous page.)

CHOCOLATE CHIP MUFFINS: Add ¾ cup miniature chocolate chips to dry ingredients. Sprinkle tops of muffins before baking with a combination of 3 tablespoons sugar and 2 tablespoons brown sugar.

JAM MUFFINS: Place ½ teaspoon any flavor jam on each muffin before baking; press into batter. If desired, sprinkle with finely chopped nuts.

LEMON MUFFINS: Add 1 tablespoon grated lemon peel to dry ingredients.

ORANGE MUFFINS: Add 1 tablespoon grated orange peel to dry ingredients and substitute orange juice for milk.

STREUSEL-TOPPED MUFFINS: In small bowl, blend ¼ cup firmly packed brown sugar, 1 tablespoon margarine or butter, softened, ½ teaspoon cinnamon and ¼ cup chopped nuts or flaked coconut with fork until crumbly. Sprinkle over muffins before baking.

SUGAR-COATED MUFFINS: Brush tops of hot muffins with 2 tablespoons melted margarine or butter; dip in mixture of ¼ cup sugar and ½ teaspoon cinnamon.

WHOLE WHEAT MUFFINS: Use 1 cup all purpose flour and 1 cup whole wheat flour.

BRAN MUFFINS

A batch of these wholesome refrigerator muffins is great to have on hand for hurried mornings.

2	cups shreds of whole bran cereal
2½	cups buttermilk
½	cup oil
2	eggs
2½	cups all purpose flour
1½	cups sugar
1¼	teaspoons baking soda
1	teaspoon baking powder
½	teaspoon salt
¾	cup raisins, if desired

In large bowl, combine cereal and buttermilk; let stand 5 minutes until cereal is softened. Add oil and eggs; blend well. Stir in flour and remaining ingredients; mix well. Batter can be baked immediately or stored in tightly covered container in refrigerator for up to 2 weeks.

When ready to bake, heat oven to 400°F. Grease desired number of muffin cups or line with paper baking cups. Stir batter; fill greased muffin cups ¾ full.

Bake at 400°F. for 18 to 20 minutes or until toothpick inserted in center comes out clean. Immediately remove from pan. Serve warm.
Yield: 24 to 30 muffins.

MICROWAVE DIRECTIONS:
Prepare muffin batter as directed above. Using 6-cup microwave-safe muffin pan, line each cup with 2 paper baking cups to absorb moisture during cooking. Fill cups ½ full. Microwave on HIGH as directed below or until toothpick inserted in center comes out clean, rotating pan ½ turn halfway through cooking. Remove muffins from pan and immediately discard outer baking cups.

4 muffins - 2 to 2½ minutes
2 muffins - 1¼ to 1¾ minutes

HIGH ALTITUDE:
Above 3500 Feet: Increase flour to 2¾ cups; decrease sugar to 1¼ cups. Bake as directed above.

NUTRITION PER SERVING:
Calories 150; Protein 3g; Carbohydrate 25g; Fat 4g; Sodium 160mg.

Refrigerator Apple Bran Muffins

There are only 4 grams of fat in each muffin.

    2 cups shreds of whole bran cereal
 1½ cups buttermilk
    1 cup unsweetened applesauce
   ½ cup oil
    4 egg whites
    2 cups all purpose flour
   ½ cup whole wheat flour
    1 cup sugar
    1 teaspoon baking powder
    1 teaspoon baking soda
    1 teaspoon cinnamon
    1 teaspoon ginger
   ¼ teaspoon salt
   ½ cup raisins

In large bowl, combine cereal and buttermilk; let stand 5 minutes or until cereal is softened. Add applesauce, oil and egg whites; blend well. Stir in all purpose flour, whole wheat flour and remaining ingredients; mix well. Batter can be baked immediately or stored in tightly covered container in refrigerator for up to 1 week.

When ready to bake, heat oven to 400°F. Grease desired number of muffin cups or line with paper baking cups. Stir batter; fill greased muffin cups ¾ full. Sprinkle with sugar, if desired.

Bake at 400°F. for 15 to 20 minutes or until toothpick inserted in center comes out clean. Immediately remove from pan. Serve warm.
Yield: 30 muffins.

MICROWAVE DIRECTIONS:
Prepare muffin batter as directed above. Using 6-cup microwave-safe muffin pan, line each cup with 2 paper baking cups to absorb moisture during cooking. Fill cups ½ full. Sprinkle with sugar, if desired. Microwave on HIGH as directed below or until toothpick inserted in center comes out clean, rotating pan ½ turn halfway through cooking. Remove muffins from pan and immediately discard outer baking cups.

    6 muffins - 3 to 3½ minutes
    4 muffins - 2½ to 2¾ minutes
    2 muffins - 2 to 2¼ minutes

HIGH ALTITUDE:
Above 3500 Feet: Increase all purpose flour to 2¼ cups. Bake as directed above.

NUTRITION PER SERVING:
Calories 120; Protein 3g; Carbohydrate 21g; Fat 4g; Sodium 125mg.

Refrigerator Sweet Muffins

 4½ cups all purpose flour
    1 cup firmly packed brown sugar
   ½ cup sugar
    4 teaspoons baking powder
    1 teaspoon baking soda
    1 teaspoon salt
    2 cups buttermilk
   ¾ cup oil
 1½ teaspoons vanilla
    3 eggs

In large bowl, combine flour, brown sugar, sugar, baking powder, baking soda and salt; blend well. Add buttermilk, oil, vanilla and eggs; stir just until dry ingredients are moistened. Batter can be baked immediately or stored in tightly covered container in refrigerator for up to 5 days.

When ready to bake, heat oven to 375°F. Grease bottoms only of desired number of muffin cups or line with paper baking cups. Stir batter; fill greased muffin cups ⅔ full.

Bake at 375°F. for 20 to 25 minutes or until toothpick inserted in center comes out clean. Immediately remove from pan. Serve warm.
Yield: 24 muffins.

MICROWAVE DIRECTIONS:
Prepare muffin batter as directed above. Using 6-cup microwave-safe muffin pan, line each cup with 2 paper baking cups to absorb moisture during cooking. Fill cups ½ full. Microwave on HIGH as directed below or until toothpick inserted in center comes out clean, rotating pan ½ turn halfway through cooking. Remove muffins from pan and immediately discard outer baking cups. Cool 1 minute on wire rack before serving.

    6 muffins - 3 to 3½ minutes
    4 muffins - 2½ to 2¾ minutes
    2 muffins - 2 to 2¼ minutes

HIGH ALTITUDE:
Above 3500 Feet: Decrease brown sugar to ¾ cup. Bake as directed above.

NUTRITION PER SERVING:
Calories 210; Protein 4g; Carbohydrate 32g; Fat 8g; Sodium 220mg.

BANANA BRAN MUFFINS

These monster muffins will delight after-school snackers.

- ½ **cup margarine or butter, softened**
- ½ **cup firmly packed brown sugar**
- 1½ **cups (3 medium) mashed ripe bananas**
- ¼ **cup milk**
- 1 **teaspoon vanilla**
- 2 **eggs**
- 1½ **cups all purpose flour**
- ½ **cup unprocessed bran or wheat germ**
- 1 **teaspoon baking powder**
- 1 **teaspoon baking soda**
- ¼ **teaspoon salt**
- 1 **cup chopped walnuts**

Heat oven to 375°F. Grease eight 6-oz. custard cups or 18 muffin cups; place custard cups on 15x10x1-inch baking pan. In large bowl, beat margarine and brown sugar until fluffy. Add bananas, milk, vanilla and eggs; blend well. Stir in flour, bran, baking powder, baking soda and salt just until dry ingredients are moistened; stir in walnuts. Fill greased custard cups ⅔ full.

Bake at 375°F. for 20 to 25 minutes or until toothpick inserted in center comes out clean. Cool 5 minutes; remove from custard cups. Serve warm.
Yield: 8 jumbo or 18 regular-sized muffins.

HIGH ALTITUDE:
Above 3500 Feet: No change.

NUTRITION PER SERVING:
Calories 430; Protein 8g; Carbohydrate 47g; Fat 23g; Sodium 410mg.

BANANA BRAN MUFFINS MAKE-OVER

Now these jumbo muffins are better for you as well as delicious. We've reduced the fat by almost 50 percent.

- ⅓ **cup margarine or butter, softened**
- ½ **cup firmly packed brown sugar**
- 1½ **cups (3 medium) mashed ripe bananas**
- ½ **cup frozen cholesterol-free egg product, thawed, or 2 eggs, slightly beaten**
- ¼ **cup skim milk**
- 1 **teaspoon vanilla**
- ¾ **cup all purpose flour**
- ¾ **cup whole wheat flour**
- ½ **cup unprocessed bran or wheat germ**
- 1 **teaspoon baking powder**
- 1 **teaspoon baking soda**
- 3 **tablespoons chopped walnuts**

Heat oven to 375°F. Grease eight 6-oz. custard cups or 18 muffin cups; place custard cups on 15x10x1-inch baking pan. In large bowl, beat margarine and brown sugar until fluffy. Add bananas, egg product, milk and vanilla; blend well. Stir in all purpose flour, whole wheat flour, wheat germ, baking powder and baking soda just until dry ingredients are moistened. Fill greased custard cups ⅔ full. Sprinkle batter with walnuts.

Bake at 375°F. for 22 to 27 minutes or until toothpick inserted in center comes out clean. Cool 5 minutes; remove from pan. Serve warm.
Yield: 8 jumbo or 18 regular-sized muffins.

HIGH ALTITUDE:
Above 3500 Feet: Increase all purpose flour to 1 cup. Bake as directed above.

NUTRITION PER SERVING:
Calories 310; Protein 7g; Carbohydrate 44g; Fat 12g; Sodium 310mg.

Banana Bran Muffins Make-Over

LEMON POPPY SEED MUFFINS

Enjoy the nutty flavor and crunch of poppy seed combined with the zesty taste of lemonade.

2 cups all purpose flour
¼ cup sugar
1 to 2 tablespoons poppy seed
3 teaspoons baking powder
½ teaspoon salt
½ cup milk
½ cup frozen lemonade concentrate, thawed
⅓ cup margarine or butter, melted
1 egg, slightly beaten

Heat oven to 400°F. Line with paper baking cups or grease bottoms only of 12 muffin cups. In medium bowl, combine flour, sugar, poppy seed, baking powder and salt; mix well. Add milk, lemonade concentrate, margarine and egg, stirring just until dry ingredients are moistened. Fill paper-lined muffin cups ¾ full.

Bake at 400°F. for 15 to 20 minutes or until light golden brown and toothpick inserted in center comes out clean. Immediately remove from pan. Serve warm.
Yield: 12 muffins.

MICROWAVE DIRECTIONS:
Prepare muffin batter as directed above. Using 6-cup microwave-safe muffin pan, line each cup with 2 paper baking cups to absorb moisture during cooking. Fill cups ⅔ full. Microwave 6 muffins on HIGH for 2 to 3 minutes or until toothpick inserted in center comes out clean, rotating pan ½ turn halfway through cooking. Remove muffins from pan and immediately discard outer baking cups. Cool 1 minute on wire rack before serving. Repeat with remaining batter.

HIGH ALTITUDE:
Above 3500 Feet: Increase flour to 2 cups plus 2 tablespoons. Bake as directed above.

NUTRITION PER SERVING:
Calories 180; Protein 3g; Carbohydrate 27g; Fat 7g; Sodium 240mg.

LEMON RASPBERRY STREUSEL MUFFINS

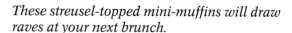

These streusel-topped mini-muffins will draw raves at your next brunch.

MUFFINS
2 cups all purpose flour
½ cup sugar
2 teaspoons baking powder
½ teaspoon baking soda
½ teaspoon salt
1 (8-oz.) container lemon yogurt
½ cup oil
1 teaspoon grated lemon peel
2 eggs
1 cup fresh or frozen raspberries (do not thaw)

TOPPING
⅓ cup sugar
¼ cup all purpose flour
2 tablespoons margarine or butter

Heat oven to 400°F. Grease 36 miniature muffin cups. In large bowl, combine 2 cups flour, ½ cup sugar, baking powder, baking soda and salt; mix well. In small bowl, combine yogurt, oil, lemon peel and eggs; mix well. Add to dry ingredients; stir just until dry ingredients are moistened. Gently stir in raspberries. Fill greased muffin cups ¾ full.

In small bowl, combine ⅓ cup sugar and ¼ cup flour. Using pastry blender or fork, cut in margarine until crumbly. Sprinkle over batter.

Bake at 400°F. for 11 to 13 minutes or until light golden brown and toothpick inserted in center comes out clean. Cool 5 minutes; remove from pan. Serve warm.
Yield: 36 mini-muffins.

TIP:
Recipe can be baked in regular muffin cups. Grease bottoms only of 14 muffin cups or line with paper baking cups. Fill greased muffin cups ¾ full. Bake at 400°F. for 18 to 20 minutes.

HIGH ALTITUDE:
Above 3500 Feet: No change.

NUTRITION PER SERVING:
Calories 90; Protein 1g; Carbohydrate 12g; Fat 4g; Sodium 75mg.

Orange Oat Bran Muffins

There's only whole wheat flour in these hearty muffins, so they will not rise as much as regular muffins. Serve them warm or cool.

- 1 cup oat bran hot cereal, uncooked
- ½ cup firmly packed brown sugar
- ¾ cup skim or lowfat milk
- ¼ cup unsweetened orange juice
- 1 cup whole wheat flour
- 2 teaspoons baking powder
- 1 teaspoon cinnamon
- 1 teaspoon grated orange peel
- ½ teaspoon salt
- ½ cup frozen cholesterol-free egg product, thawed, or 2 eggs, slightly beaten
- ⅓ cup oil
- ½ cup raisins

Heat oven to 400°F. Line with paper baking cups or grease 12 muffin cups. In medium bowl, combine oat bran cereal, brown sugar, milk and orange juice; let stand 10 minutes. Add flour and remaining ingredients; stir just until dry ingredients are moistened. Fill paper-lined muffin cups ¾ full.

Bake at 400°F. for 15 to 18 minutes or until toothpick inserted in center comes out clean. Immediately remove from pan.

Yield: 12 muffins.

MICROWAVE DIRECTIONS:
Prepare muffin batter as directed above. Using 6-cup microwave-safe muffin pan, line each cup with 2 paper baking cups to absorb moisture during cooking. Fill cups ⅔ full. Microwave 6 muffins on HIGH for 2½ to 3½ minutes or until toothpick inserted in center comes out clean, rotating pan ½ turn halfway through cooking. Remove muffins from pan and immediately discard outer baking cups. Cool 1 minute on wire rack before serving. Repeat with remaining batter.

HIGH ALTITUDE:
Above 3500 Feet: Increase flour to 1 cup plus 2 tablespoons. Bake as directed above.

NUTRITION PER SERVING:
Calories 170; Protein 4g; Carbohydrate 24g; Fat 7g; Sodium 150mg.

Orange Date Muffins

The zesty orange flavor in these moist, tender muffins will perk up taste buds.

MUFFINS
- 1½ cups all purpose flour
- ½ cup sugar
- ½ cup chopped dates
- 1 teaspoon baking powder
- 1 teaspoon baking soda
- ½ teaspoon salt
- 1 large orange
- ⅓ cup margarine or butter, melted
- 1 egg

GLAZE
- ½ cup powdered sugar
- ½ teaspoon grated orange peel
- 2 to 3 teaspoons orange juice or milk

Heat oven to 400°F. Grease bottoms only of 12 muffins cups or line with paper baking cups. In large bowl, combine flour, sugar, dates, baking powder, baking soda and salt; mix well. Grate ½ teaspoon peel from orange; reserve for glaze. Cut remainder of unpeeled orange into chunks; remove seeds. Place in food processor bowl with metal blade; process until finely chopped. In small bowl, combine 1 cup of the chopped orange, margarine and egg; blend well. Add to dry ingredients; stir just until dry ingredients are moistened. (Batter will be very stiff.) Divide batter evenly among greased muffin cups.

Bake at 400°F. for 15 to 20 minutes or until toothpick inserted in center comes out clean. Immediately remove from pan.

In small bowl, combine all glaze ingredients, adding enough orange juice for desired drizzling consistency. Drizzle over warm muffins. Serve warm.

Yield: 12 muffins.

HIGH ALTITUDE:
Above 3500 Feet: No change.

NUTRITION PER SERVING:
Calories 180; Protein 2g; Carbohydrate 32g; Fat 6g; Sodium 270mg.

RASPBERRY-FILLED ALMOND MUFFINS

These cake-like muffins are baked in brioche tins for an elegant presentation.

- 2 **cups all purpose flour**
- ⅔ **cup sugar**
- 2 **teaspoons baking powder**
- ½ **teaspoon salt**
- 1 **cup milk**
- ½ **cup margarine or butter, melted**
- 1 **egg, slightly beaten**
- 1 **teaspoon vanilla**
- ½ **teaspoon almond extract**
- 5 **tablespoons raspberry preserves**
- 42 **whole blanched almonds, toasted, p. 23**
- 2 **tablespoons sugar**

Heat oven to 400°F. Grease 14 brioche tins (3½-inch diameter) or muffin cups. In large bowl, combine flour, sugar, baking powder and salt; mix well. Add milk, margarine, egg, vanilla and almond extract; stir just until dry ingredients are moistened. Fill greased brioche tins ½ full. Spoon 1 teaspoon preserves into center of batter. Top with remaining batter, filling brioche tins ¾ full. Top each muffin with 3 whole almonds; lightly press into batter. Sprinkle evenly with 2 tablespoons sugar.

Bake at 400°F. for 12 to 20 minutes or until golden brown. Cool 5 minutes; remove from tins.
Yield: 14 muffins.

HIGH ALTITUDE:
Above 3500 Feet: No change.

NUTRITION PER SERVING:
Calories 240; Protein 4g; Carbohydrate 32g; Fat 11g; Sodium 200mg.

CRAN-APPLE SPICE MUFFINS

Enjoy with a cup of hot tea.

- 2 **cups all purpose flour**
- ½ **cup sugar**
- 1 **teaspoon baking soda**
- 1 **teaspoon cinnamon**
- ½ **teaspoon salt**
- 1 **cup unsweetened applesauce**
- ⅓ **cup oil**
- 1 **egg**
- 1 **cup coarsely chopped fresh or frozen cranberries (do not thaw)***
- ½ **cup chopped pecans**

Heat oven to 350°F. Grease bottoms only of 12 muffin cups or line with paper baking cups. In large bowl, combine flour, sugar, baking soda, cinnamon and salt. In small bowl, combine applesauce, oil and egg; blend well. Add to dry ingredients; stir just until dry ingredients are moistened. Stir in cranberries and pecans. Divide batter evenly in greased muffin cups.

Bake at 350°F. for 25 to 30 minutes or until toothpick inserted in center comes out clean. Cool 2 minutes; remove from pan. Serve warm or cool.
Yield: 12 muffins.

MICROWAVE DIRECTIONS:
Prepare muffin batter as directed above. Using 6-cup microwave-safe muffin pan, line each cup with 2 paper baking cups to absorb moisture during cooking. Fill cups ¾ full. Microwave 6 muffins on HIGH for 2¾ to 3¼ minutes or until toothpick inserted in center comes out clean, rotating pan ½ turn halfway through cooking. Remove muffins from pan and immediately discard outer baking cups. Cool 1 minute on wire rack before serving. Repeat, making 6 additional muffins. With remaining batter, make 3 muffins; microwave 3 muffins on HIGH for 1½ to 2 minutes.
Yield: 15 muffins.

TIP:
* To chop cranberries in food processor, place in food processor bowl with metal blade. Process with 10 on-off pulses or until all berries are chopped.

HIGH ALTITUDE:
Above 3500 Feet: No change.

NUTRITION PER SERVING:
Calories 220; Protein 3g; Carbohydrate 29g; Fat 10g; Sodium 190mg.

Chocolate Chunk Pistachio Muffins

A pocket of raspberry jam is hidden inside each of these indulgent muffins.

- 2 cups all purpose flour
- 3/4 cup sugar
- 2 teaspoons baking powder
- 1/2 teaspoon cinnamon
- 1/4 teaspoon baking soda
- 1/4 teaspoon salt
- 6 oz. sweet baking chocolate, coarsely chopped
- 1/2 cup coarsely chopped pistachios
- 1 cup milk
- 1/2 cup margarine or butter, melted
- 1 teaspoon grated lemon peel
- 1 teaspoon vanilla
- 1 egg, slightly beaten
- 1/3 cup seedless raspberry jam

Heat oven to 375°F. Line with paper baking cups or grease bottoms only of 10 jumbo muffin cups. In large bowl, combine flour, sugar, baking powder, cinnamon, baking soda and salt; mix well. Reserve 1/3 cup of the largest pieces of chopped chocolate; reserve 2 tablespoons of the pistachios. Stir remaining chopped chocolate and pistachios into dry ingredients. In small bowl, combine milk, margarine, lemon peel, vanilla and egg; blend well. Add to dry ingredients all at once; stir just until dry ingredients are moistened.

Fill each paper-lined muffin cup with 2 heaping tablespoonfuls of batter. Spoon rounded teaspoonful of jam in center of batter in each cup. Spoon about 1 heaping tablespoonful of the remaining batter over jam in each cup. Top each with reserved chopped chocolate and pistachios.

Bake at 375°F. for 20 to 25 minutes or until toothpick inserted in center comes out clean. Cool 5 minutes; remove from pan. Serve warm or cool.
Yield: 10 jumbo muffins.

TIP:
For regular-sized muffins, line 20 regular-sized muffin cups with paper baking cups or grease bottoms only. Prepare batter as directed above. Fill each paper-lined muffin cup with 1 tablespoonful of batter. Place rounded 1/2 teaspoonful of jam in center of batter in each cup. Spoon remaining batter evenly over each filled cup, covering jam.

Top each with reserved chopped chocolate and pistachios. Bake at 375°F. for 15 to 20 minutes. Cool 5 minutes; remove from pan.

HIGH ALTITUDE:
Above 3500 Feet: Increase flour to 2 1/4 cups. Bake as directed above.

NUTRITION PER SERVING:
Calories 420; Protein 6g; Carbohydrate 54g; Fat 20g; Sodium 260mg.

Old-Fashioned Rhubarb Muffins

These muffins may have old-fashioned flavor, but they have all-time appeal!

- 2 1/2 cups all purpose flour
- 2/3 cup sugar
- 3 teaspoons baking powder
- 1/2 teaspoon salt
- 1 cup milk
- 1/4 cup oil
- 1/2 teaspoon vanilla
- 1 egg, beaten
- 2 cups finely chopped rhubarb
  Powdered sugar

Heat oven to 400°F. Line 18 muffin cups with paper baking cups. In large bowl, combine flour, sugar, baking powder and salt. Add milk, oil, vanilla and egg; stir just until dry ingredients are moistened. Gently fold in rhubarb. Fill paper-lined muffin cups 2/3 full.

Bake at 400°F. for 20 to 25 minutes or until light golden brown. Immediately remove from pan. Sprinkle warm muffins with powdered sugar. Serve warm.
Yield: 18 muffins.

HIGH ALTITUDE:
Above 3500 Feet: No change.

NUTRITION PER SERVING:
Calories 130; Protein 3g; Carbohydrate 22g; Fat 4g; Sodium 125mg.

Dilly Zucchini Ricotta Muffins

For a summer harvest taste treat, serve these savory muffins warm from the oven!

1½ **cups all purpose flour**
2 **tablespoons sugar**
3 **teaspoons baking powder**
½ **teaspoon salt**
¾ **teaspoon dried dill weed**
¼ **cup milk**
½ **cup margarine or butter, melted**
2 **eggs**
⅔ **cup ricotta cheese**
½ **cup shredded unpeeled zucchini**

Heat oven to 400°F. Line with paper baking cups or grease 12 muffin cups. In large bowl, combine flour, sugar, baking powder, salt and dill weed; mix well. In medium bowl, combine milk, margarine and eggs. Stir in ricotta cheese and zucchini; beat well. Add to dry ingredients, stirring just until moistened. (Batter will be stiff.) Fill paper-lined muffin cups ⅔ full.

Bake at 400°F. for 20 to 25 minutes or until toothpick inserted in center comes out clean. Immediately remove from pan. Serve warm.
Yield: 12 muffins.

HIGH ALTITUDE:
Above 3500 Feet: No change.

NUTRITION PER SERVING:
Calories 170; Protein 5g; Carbohydrate 15g; Fat 10g; Sodium 280mg.

Bacon-Jack Cheese Muffins

2 **cups all purpose flour**
3 **teaspoons sugar**
3 **teaspoons baking powder**
⅛ **to ¼ teaspoon cayenne pepper**
1¼ **cups milk**
2 **tablespoons bacon drippings or oil***
1 **egg**
6 **slices bacon, crisply cooked, crumbled**
3 **oz. (¾ cup) shredded Monterey Jack cheese**

Dilly Zucchini Ricotta Muffins,
Parmesan Herb Muffins p. 376

Heat oven to 400°F. Generously grease 12 muffin cups. In large bowl, combine flour, sugar, baking powder and cayenne pepper; blend well. Add milk, bacon drippings and egg; stir just until dry ingredients are moistened. Stir in bacon and cheese. Fill greased muffin cups ⅔ full.

Bake at 400°F. for 20 to 25 minutes or until golden brown. Cool 1 to 2 minutes before removing from pan. Serve warm.
Yield: 12 muffins.

TIP:
* If using oil, add ¼ teaspoon salt with dry ingredients.

HIGH ALTITUDE:
Above 3500 Feet: No change.

NUTRITION PER SERVING:
Calories 170; Protein 6g; Carbohydrate 18g; Fat 7g; Sodium 230mg.

Onion Rye Muffins

Caraway seed adds special flavor.

¾ **cup chopped onions**
½ **cup margarine or butter**
1¼ **cups all purpose flour**
¾ **cup medium rye flour**
2 **tablespoons sugar**
3 **teaspoons baking powder**
¾ **teaspoon salt**
½ **teaspoon caraway seed, crushed**
½ **cup milk**
2 **eggs**

Heat oven to 400°F. Line with paper baking cups or grease 12 muffin cups. In small skillet, cook onions in margarine until soft; set aside. In large bowl, combine all purpose flour, rye flour, sugar, baking powder, salt and caraway seed; mix well. Add milk, eggs and cooked onion; stir just until dry ingredients are moistened. Fill paper-lined muffin cups ⅔ full.

Bake at 400°F. for 15 to 20 minutes or until toothpick inserted in center comes out clean. Immediately remove from pan. Serve warm.
Yield: 12 muffins.

HIGH ALTITUDE:
Above 3500 Feet: No change.

NUTRITION PER SERVING:
Calories 170; Protein 4g; Carbohydrate 20g; Fat 9g; Sodium 270mg.

MEXICALI CORN MUFFINS

〰

We've added green chiles to corn muffins creating a flavor combination that's hard to beat. They are a great addition to a chili supper.

1¼ **cups all purpose flour**
¾ **cup cornmeal**
2 **tablespoons sugar**
4 **teaspoons baking powder**
½ **teaspoon salt**
¾ **cup milk**
¼ **cup dairy sour cream**
¼ **cup oil**
1 **egg**
1 **(4-oz.) can chopped green chiles, drained**

Heat oven to 400°F. Line with paper baking cups or grease 12 muffin cups. In large bowl, combine flour, cornmeal, sugar, baking powder and salt; mix well. In medium bowl, combine milk, sour cream, oil, egg and chiles; beat well. Add to dry ingredients, stirring just until moistened. Fill paper-lined muffin cups ⅔ full.

Bake at 400°F. for 18 to 22 minutes or until toothpick inserted in center comes out clean. Immediately remove from pan. Serve warm.
Yield: 12 muffins.

MICROWAVE DIRECTIONS:
Prepare muffin batter as directed above. Using 6-cup microwave-safe muffin pan, line each cup with 2 paper baking cups to absorb moisture during cooking. Fill cups ½ full. Microwave 6 muffins on HIGH for 2½ to 3 minutes or until toothpick inserted in center comes out clean, rotating pan ½ turn halfway through cooking. Remove muffins from pan and immediately discard outer baking cups. Cool 1 minute on wire rack before serving. Repeat, making 6 additional muffins. With remaining batter, make 3 muffins; microwave 3 muffins on HIGH for 1½ to 2 minutes. Serve warm.
Yield: 15 muffins.

HIGH ALTITUDE:
Above 3500 Feet: No change.

NUTRITION PER SERVING:
Calories 150; Protein 3g; Carbohydrate 20g; Fat 7g; Sodium 200mg.

PARMESAN HERB MUFFINS

〰

Flecks of parsley and sage flavor these cheesy muffins. Serve them warm with butter.

2 **cups all purpose flour**
1 **tablespoon sugar**
1½ **teaspoons baking powder**
½ **teaspoon baking soda**
½ **teaspoon dried sage leaves, crushed**
½ **cup chopped fresh parsley**
¾ **cup grated Parmesan cheese**
1¼ **cups buttermilk**
¼ **cup margarine or butter, melted**
1 **egg**

Heat oven to 400°F. Grease bottoms only of 12 muffin cups or line with paper baking cups. In large bowl, combine flour, sugar, baking powder, baking soda, sage, parsley and cheese; blend well. Add buttermilk, margarine and egg; stir just until dry ingredients are moistened. Fill greased muffin cups ⅔ full.

Bake at 400°F. for 15 to 20 minutes or until toothpick inserted in center comes out clean. Immediately remove from pan. Serve warm.
Yield: 12 muffins.

MICROWAVE DIRECTIONS:
Prepare muffin batter as directed above. Using 6-cup microwave-safe muffin pan, line each cup with 2 paper baking cups to absorb moisture during cooking. Fill cups ½ full. If desired, sprinkle top of each muffin with *cornflake crumbs*. Microwave 6 muffins on HIGH for 2½ to 3 minutes or until toothpick inserted in center comes out clean, rotating pan ½ turn halfway through cooking. Remove muffins from pan and immediately discard outer baking cups. Cool 1 minute on wire rack before serving. Repeat with remaining batter.

HIGH ALTITUDE:
Above 3500 Feet: No change.

NUTRITION PER SERVING:
Calories 160; Protein 6g; Carbohydrate 19g; Fat 7g; Sodium 280mg.

Raisin, Wheat and Rye Muffins

Sweet spices and raisins flavor these muffins. They are sensational served anytime!

- 1 cup all purpose flour
- ½ cup whole wheat flour
- ½ cup medium rye flour
- ¼ cup sugar
- 3 teaspoons baking powder
- ½ teaspoon salt
- ½ teaspoon cinnamon
- ¼ teaspoon nutmeg
- ½ cup raisins
- 1 cup milk
- ½ cup oil
- 1 egg, slightly beaten

Heat oven to 375°F. Grease bottoms only of 12 muffin cups or line with paper baking cups. In large bowl, combine all purpose flour, whole wheat flour, rye flour, sugar, baking powder, salt, cinnamon, nutmeg and raisins; blend well. Add milk, oil and egg; stir just until dry ingredients are moistened. Fill greased muffin cups ⅔ full.

Bake at 375°F. for 15 to 20 minutes or until very light brown and toothpick inserted in center comes out clean. Immediately remove from pan. Serve warm.

Yield: 12 muffins.

MICROWAVE DIRECTIONS:

Prepare muffin batter as directed above. Using 6-cup microwave-safe muffin pan, line each cup with 2 paper baking cups to absorb moisture during cooking. Fill cups ½ full. Microwave 6 muffins on HIGH for 2 to 2½ minutes or until toothpick inserted in center comes out clean, rotating pan ½ turn halfway through cooking. Remove muffins from pan and immediately discard outer baking cups. Cool 1 minute on wire rack before serving. Repeat, making 6 additional muffins. With remaining batter, make 3 muffins; microwave 3 muffins on HIGH for 1½ to 1¾ minutes, rotating once.

Yield: 15 muffins.

HIGH ALTITUDE:

Above 3500 Feet: Decrease baking powder to 2 teaspoons. Bake at 400°F. for 15 to 20 minutes.

NUTRITION PER SERVING:
Calories 170; Protein 3g; Carbohydrate 17g; Fat 10g; Sodium 220mg.

The Giant's Corn Muffins

These picture perfect muffins were a finalist in the 33rd BAKE-OFF® Contest in 1988.

MUFFINS
- 1 cup cornmeal
- ½ cup all purpose flour
- ½ cup whole wheat flour
- 1 teaspoon baking powder
- 1 teaspoon baking soda
- ½ teaspoon salt
- ¼ teaspoon nutmeg
- 1 cup plain yogurt or buttermilk
- ¼ cup margarine or butter, melted
- 3 tablespoons honey
- 1 egg
- 1 green onion, sliced, including green top
- 1 (11-oz.) can whole kernel corn with red and green peppers, drained

TOPPING
- 1 tablespoon all purpose flour
- 1 tablespoon cornmeal
- 2 teaspoons sugar
  Dash salt
- 4 teaspoons margarine or butter

Heat oven to 400°F. Grease bottoms only of six 6-oz. custard cups or 12 muffin cups; place custard cups on 15x10x1-inch baking pan. In large bowl, combine 1 cup cornmeal, ½ cup all purpose flour, whole wheat flour, baking powder, baking soda, ½ teaspoon salt and nutmeg; blend well. In medium bowl, combine yogurt, ¼ cup margarine, honey, egg, onion and corn; mix well. Add to dry ingredients; stir just until dry ingredients are moistened. Spoon batter evenly into greased custard cups. (Cups will be full.) In small bowl, combine all topping ingredients; mix well. Crumble evenly over muffins.

Bake at 400°F. for 20 to 30 minutes or until toothpick inserted in center comes out clean. Cool 1 minute; remove from custard cups. Serve warm.

Yield: 6 muffins.

HIGH ALTITUDE:

Above 3500 Feet: No change.

NUTRITION PER SERVING:
Calories 380; Protein 9g; Carbohydrate 56g; Fat 13g; Sodium 760mg.

BANANA BREAD

For optimum flavor, use well-ripened bananas to make this family-favorite bread.

- ³/₄ cup sugar
- ¹/₂ cup margarine or butter, softened
- 2 eggs
- 1 cup (2 medium) mashed ripe bananas
- ¹/₃ cup milk
- 1 teaspoon vanilla
- 2 cups all purpose flour
- ¹/₂ cup chopped nuts, if desired
- 1 teaspoon baking soda
- ¹/₂ teaspoon salt

Heat oven to 350°F. Grease bottom only of 9x5 or 8x4-inch loaf pan. In large bowl, beat sugar and margarine until light and fluffy. Beat in eggs. Add bananas, milk and vanilla; blend well. In small bowl, combine flour, nuts, baking soda and salt; mix well. Add to banana mixture; stir just until dry ingredients are moistened. Pour into greased pan.

Bake at 350°F. for 50 to 60 minutes or until tooth-pick inserted in center comes out clean. Cool 5 minutes; remove from pan. Cool completely. Wrap tightly and store in refrigerator.
Yield: 1 (16-slice) loaf.

HIGH ALTITUDE:
Above 3500 Feet: Increase flour to 2 cups plus 1 tablespoon. Bake at 375°F. for 45 to 55 minutes.

NUTRITION PER SERVING:
Calories 190; Protein 3g; Carbohydrate 26g; Fat 9g; Sodium 210mg.

VARIATION:

APPLESAUCE BREAD: Substitute 1 cup apple-sauce for mashed bananas and add ³/₄ teaspoon cinnamon with flour.

NUT BREAD

Try the flavorful variations, too.

- ³/₄ cup sugar
- ¹/₂ cup margarine or butter, softened
- 1 cup buttermilk
- 2 eggs
- 2 cups all purpose flour
- 1 cup chopped nuts
- ¹/₂ teaspoon baking powder
- ¹/₂ teaspoon baking soda
- ¹/₂ teaspoon salt

Heat oven to 350°F. Grease bottom only of 9x5 or 8x4-inch loaf pan. In large bowl, beat sugar and margarine until light and fluffy. Add buttermilk and eggs; blend well. In small bowl, combine flour, nuts, baking powder, baking soda and salt; mix well. Add to buttermilk mixture; stir just until dry ingredients are moistened. Pour into greased pan.

Bake at 350°F. for 55 to 65 minutes or until tooth-pick inserted in center comes out clean. Cool 15 minutes; remove from pan. Cool completely. Wrap tightly and store in refrigerator.
Yield: 1 (16-slice) loaf.

HIGH ALTITUDE:
Above 3500 Feet: Increase flour to 2 cups plus 1 tablespoon. Bake at 375°F. for 50 to 60 minutes.

NUTRITION PER SERVING:
Calories 210; Protein 4g; Carbohydrate 23g; Fat 11g; Sodium 200mg.

VARIATIONS:

DATE BREAD: Prepare batter as directed above, substituting brown sugar for sugar and decreasing nuts to ¹/₂ cup. Stir in 1 cup chopped dates and 1 teaspoon grated orange peel after flour addition.

POCKET OF STREUSEL BREAD: For filling, in small bowl, combine ¹/₂ cup firmly packed brown sugar, ¹/₂ cup chopped walnuts, 1 teaspoon cinnamon and 1 tablespoon margarine or butter, melted; mix well. Prepare batter as directed above, substituting brown sugar for sugar and decreasing nuts to ¹/₂ cup. Spread half of batter in greased and floured 9x5-inch loaf pan. Spoon filling down center of batter and spread to within ¹/₂ inch of all sides. Carefully spoon remaining batter over filling, spreading gently to cover. Bake at 350°F. for 50 to 55 minutes.

CHERRY NUT BREAD

This eye-catching quick bread is perfect for party trays or gift-giving.

- 2 cups all purpose flour
- ⅔ cup sugar
- 2 teaspoons baking powder
- ½ teaspoon salt
- ¾ cup milk
- ½ cup margarine or butter, melted
- 1 teaspoon almond extract
- 2 eggs
- ½ cup slivered almonds
- 1 (10-oz.) jar (¾ cup) maraschino cherries, drained, chopped

Heat oven to 350°F. Grease bottom only of 8x4 or 9x5-inch loaf pan. In large bowl, combine flour, sugar, baking powder and salt; mix well. In small bowl, combine milk, margarine, almond extract and eggs; blend well. Add to flour mixture in large bowl; stir just until dry ingredients are moistened. Stir in almonds and cherries. Pour into greased pan.

For 8x4-inch pan, bake at 350°F. for 65 to 75 minutes or until toothpick inserted in center comes out clean. For 9x5-inch pan, bake 60 to 70 minutes. Cool 10 minutes; remove from pan. Cool completely. Wrap tightly and store in refrigerator.

Yield: 1 (12-slice) loaf.

HIGH ALTITUDE:
Above 3500 Feet: Increase flour to 2¼ cups. For 8x4-inch pan, bake at 375°F. for 55 to 65 minutes. For 9x5-inch pan, bake at 375°F. for 50 to 60 minutes.

NUTRITION PER SERVING:
Calories 250; Protein 5g; Carbohydrate 33g; Fat 12g; Sodium 250mg.

BANANA BLUEBERRY MINI LOAVES

Mini-loaves are an ideal size for singles or small families. For convenience, use the disposable foil mini-loaf pans available in supermarkets.

- 1 cup sugar
- ½ cup oil
- 1 cup (2 medium) mashed ripe bananas
- ½ cup plain yogurt
- 1 teaspoon vanilla
- 2 eggs
- 2 cups all purpose flour
- 1 teaspoon baking soda
- ½ teaspoon salt
- 1 cup fresh or frozen blueberries (do not thaw)

Heat oven to 350°F. Grease and flour bottoms only of three 6x3½-inch loaf pans. In large bowl, beat together sugar and oil. Add bananas, yogurt, vanilla and eggs; blend well. Add flour, baking soda and salt; stir just until dry ingredients are moistened. Gently stir in blueberries. Pour into greased and floured pans.

Bake at 350°F. for 40 to 50 minutes or until toothpick inserted in center comes out clean. Cool 5 minutes; remove from pans. Cool completely. Wrap tightly and store in refrigerator.

Yield: 3 (12-slice) loaves.

TIP:
Recipe can be baked in 9x5-inch loaf pan. Grease and flour bottom only of pan. Bake at 350°F. for 60 to 70 minutes.

HIGH ALTITUDE:
Above 3500 Feet: Increase flour to 2¼ cups. Bake 6x3½-inch pans at 375°F. for 30 to 40 minutes. Bake 9x5-inch pan at 375°F. for 50 to 60 minutes.

NUTRITION PER SERVING:
Calories 90; Protein 1g; Carbohydrate 13g; Fat 4g; Sodium 65mg.

Chocolate Chip Banana Bread

Best when served the next day, this bread is an easy make-ahead. It also can be frozen for later use.

- ¾ **cup sugar**
- ½ **cup margarine or butter, softened**
- 1 **cup (2 medium) mashed ripe bananas**
- ½ **cup dairy sour cream**
- 2 **eggs**
- 2 **cups all purpose flour**
- 1 **teaspoon baking soda**
- ½ **teaspoon salt**
- ¾ **cup miniature semi-sweet chocolate chips**
- ½ **cup chopped nuts**

Heat oven to 350°F. Grease and flour bottom only of one 9x5 or two 8x4-inch loaf pans. In large bowl, combine sugar and margarine; beat until light and fluffy. Add bananas, sour cream and eggs; blend well. Stir in flour, baking soda and salt; blend well. Fold in chocolate chips and nuts. Pour into greased and floured pan.

Bake at 350°F. for 55 to 65 minutes or until tooth-pick inserted in center comes out clean. Cool 15 minutes; remove from pan. Cool completely. Wrap tightly and store in refrigerator.
Yield: 1 (16-slice) loaf.

HIGH ALTITUDE:
Above 3500 Feet: Bake at 375°F. for 50 to 60 minutes.

NUTRITION PER SERVING:
Calories 250; Protein 4g; Carbohydrate 30g; Fat 13g; Sodium 220mg.

Zucchini Orange Bread

This recipe makes 2 loaves.

BREAD
- 4 **eggs**
- 1½ **cups sugar**
- ¾ **cup oil**
- ⅔ **cup orange juice**
- 2 **cups shredded unpeeled zucchini**
- 3¼ **cups all purpose flour**
- 1½ **teaspoons baking powder**
- 1½ **teaspoons baking soda**
- 1 **teaspoon salt**
- 2½ **teaspoons cinnamon**
- ½ **teaspoon cloves**
- 2 **teaspoons grated orange peel**
- ½ **cup chopped nuts, if desired**

GLAZE
- 1 **cup powdered sugar**
- 2 **to 3 teaspoons orange juice**

Heat oven to 350°F. Grease and flour bottoms only of two 8x4 or two 9x5-inch loaf pans. In large bowl, beat eggs until thick and lemon colored; gradually beat in sugar. Stir in oil, ⅔ cup orange juice and zucchini. Stir in remaining bread ingredients; mix well. Pour batter into greased and floured pans.

Bake at 350°F. for 45 to 55 minutes or until tooth-pick inserted in center comes out clean. Cool 10 minutes; remove from pans. Cool slightly.

In small bowl, blend glaze ingredients, adding enough orange juice for desired spreading consistency. Spread over warm loaves. Cool completely. Wrap tightly and store in refrigerator.
Yield: 2 (16-slice) loaves.

HIGH ALTITUDE:
Above 3500 Feet: Increase flour to 3¼ cups plus 3 tablespoons. Bake at 350°F. for 45 to 50 minutes.

NUTRITION PER SERVING:
Calories 170; Protein 2g; Carbohydrate 24g; Fat 7g; Sodium 140mg.

_**Chocolate Chip Banana Bread,
Zucchini Orange Bread**_

SPICY APPLE BREAD

This healthful loaf made with bran cereal is best served the second day.

- 1 cup shreds of whole bran cereal
- 1 cup milk
- ¾ cup sugar
- ½ cup margarine or butter, softened
- 2 eggs
- 1½ cups all purpose flour
- 3 teaspoons baking powder
- ½ teaspoon salt
- ½ teaspoon cinnamon
- ¼ teaspoon allspice
- ¼ teaspoon nutmeg
- 1 cup finely chopped peeled apples

Heat oven to 375°F. Grease bottom only of 8x4 or 9x5-inch loaf pan. In small bowl, combine cereal and milk; let stand 5 minutes.

In large bowl, beat sugar and margarine until light and fluffy. Add eggs and cereal mixture; beat well. Stir in flour, baking powder, salt, cinnamon, allspice and nutmeg; mix well. Fold in apples. Pour batter into greased pan.

Bake at 375°F. for 50 to 60 minutes or until toothpick inserted in center comes out clean. Cool 10 minutes; remove from pan. Cool completely. Wrap tightly and store in refrigerator.

Yield: 1 (16-slice) loaf.

HIGH ALTITUDE:
Above 3500 Feet: No change.

NUTRITION PER SERVING:
Calories 170; Protein 3g; Carbohydrate 23g; Fat 7g; Sodium 255mg.

SWEET CINNAMON QUICK BREAD

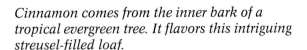

Cinnamon comes from the inner bark of a tropical evergreen tree. It flavors this intriguing streusel-filled loaf.

BREAD
- 2 cups all purpose flour
- 1 cup sugar
- 4 teaspoons baking powder
- 1½ teaspoons cinnamon
- ½ teaspoon salt
- 1 cup buttermilk
- ⅓ cup oil
- 2 teaspoons vanilla
- 2 eggs

STREUSEL
- 2 tablespoons sugar
- 1 teaspoon cinnamon
- 2 teaspoons margarine or butter, softened

Heat oven to 350°F. Grease and flour bottom only of 9x5 or 8x4-inch loaf pan. In large bowl, combine all bread ingredients; beat 3 minutes at medium speed. Pour batter into greased and floured pan.

In small bowl, combine all streusel ingredients until crumbly. Sprinkle over batter; swirl to marble batter and streusel.

Bake at 350°F. for 45 to 55 minutes or until toothpick inserted in center comes out clean. Cool 15 minutes; remove from pan. Cool completely. Wrap tightly and store in refrigerator.

Yield: 1 (12-slice) loaf.

HIGH ALTITUDE:
Above 3500 Feet: Bake at 375°F. for 45 to 50 minutes.

NUTRITION PER SERVING:
Calories 230; Protein 4g; Carbohydrate 36g; Fat 8g; Sodium 230mg.

BUTTERMILK CHOCOLATE BREAD

Tender slices of chocolaty quick bread will satisfy the cravings of the most devoted chocolate lover.

- 1 cup sugar
- ½ cup margarine or butter, softened
- 2 eggs
- 1 cup buttermilk
- 1¾ cups all purpose flour
- ½ cup unsweetened cocoa
- ½ teaspoon baking powder
- ½ teaspoon baking soda
- ½ teaspoon salt
- ⅓ cup chopped nuts

Heat oven to 350°F. Grease bottom only of 8x4 or 9x5-inch loaf pan. In large bowl, combine sugar and margarine; blend well. Add eggs; blend well. Stir in buttermilk. Add flour, cocoa, baking powder, baking soda and salt; stir just until dry ingredients are moistened. Stir in nuts. Pour into greased pan.

Bake at 350°F. for 55 to 65 minutes or until toothpick inserted in center comes out clean. Cool 15 minutes; remove from pan. Cool completely. Wrap tightly and store in refrigerator.

Yield: 1 (12-slice) loaf.

HIGH ALTITUDE:
Above 3500 Feet: Increase flour to 1¾ cups plus 1 tablespoon. Bake at 375°F. for 50 to 55 minutes.

NUTRITION PER SERVING:
Calories 250; Protein 5g; Carbohydrate 32g; Fat 12g; Sodium 300mg.

APRICOT RAISIN BREAD

This rich, fruit-filled loaf is best served chilled.

- 1½ cups all purpose flour
- 1 cup whole wheat flour
- ¾ cup sugar
- 3 teaspoons baking powder
- 1 teaspoon salt
- 1 (6-oz.) pkg. (1 cup) chopped dried apricots
- ½ cup chopped pecans or walnuts
- ½ cup raisins
- ⅓ cup oil
- 1¼ cups milk
- ½ teaspoon almond extract
- 2 eggs, slightly beaten

Heat oven to 350°F. Grease and flour bottom only of 9x5-inch loaf pan. In large bowl, combine all purpose flour, whole wheat flour, sugar, baking powder and salt. Add apricots, pecans and raisins, stirring to coat well. Add oil, milk, almond extract and eggs; stir just until dry ingredients are moistened. Pour into greased and floured pan.

Bake at 350°F. for 55 to 65 minutes or until toothpick inserted in center comes out clean. Cool 10 minutes; remove from pan. Cool completely. Wrap tightly and store in refrigerator.

Yield: 1 (16-slice) loaf.

HIGH ALTITUDE:
Above 3500 Feet: No change.

NUTRITION PER SERVING:
Calories 220; Protein 4g; Carbohydrate 34g; Fat 9g; Sodium 210mg.

HOLIDAY CRANBERRY BREAD

Flavors of orange and cranberry go well together in this festive quick bread.

- 1 cup sugar
- 1 tablespoon grated orange peel
- ¾ cup water
- ⅓ cup orange juice
- 2 tablespoons oil
- 1 egg
- 2 cups all purpose flour
- 1½ teaspoons baking powder
- 1 teaspoon salt
- ½ teaspoon baking soda
- 1 cup halved fresh or frozen whole cranberries (do not thaw)
- 1 cup chopped nuts

Heat oven to 350°F. Grease bottom only of 9x5-inch loaf pan. In large bowl, combine sugar, orange peel, water, orange juice, oil and egg; blend well. Add flour, baking powder, salt and baking soda; stir just until dry ingredients are moistened. Stir in cranberries and nuts. Pour into greased pan.

Bake at 350°F. for 50 to 60 minutes or until toothpick inserted in center comes out clean. Cool 10 minutes; remove from pan. Cool completely. Wrap tightly and store in refrigerator.

Yield: 1 (12-slice) loaf.

HIGH ALTITUDE:
Above 3500 Feet: No change.

NUTRITION PER SERVING:
Calories 240; Protein 4g; Carbohydrate 36g; Fat 9g; Sodium 270mg.

CRANBERRY SURPRISE LOAF

A cream cheese layer highlights this easy-to-make quick bread.

- 2 (3-oz.) pkg. cream cheese, softened
- 1 egg
- 2 cups all purpose flour
- 1 cup sugar
- 1½ teaspoons baking powder
- ½ teaspoon baking soda
- ½ teaspoon salt
- ¾ cup apple juice
- ¼ cup margarine or butter, melted
- 1 egg, beaten
- 1½ cups coarsely chopped fresh cranberries*
- ½ cup chopped nuts

Heat oven to 350°F. Grease and flour bottom only of 9x5-inch loaf pan. In small bowl, beat cream cheese until light and fluffy. Add 1 egg; blend well. Set aside.

In large bowl, combine flour, sugar, baking powder, baking soda and salt. Stir in apple juice, margarine and beaten egg. Fold in cranberries and nuts. Spoon half of batter into greased and floured pan. Spoon cream cheese mixture evenly over batter. Top with remaining batter.

Bake at 350°F. for 65 to 75 minutes or until top springs back when lightly touched in center. Cool 15 minutes; remove from pan. Cool completely. Wrap tightly and store in refrigerator.

Yield: 1 (16-slice) loaf.

TIP:
* To chop cranberries in food processor, add about 2 cups fresh cranberries to food processor bowl with metal blade. Process with 10 on-off pulses or until all berries are coarsely chopped.

HIGH ALTITUDE:
Above 3500 Feet: Increase flour to 2 cups plus 3 tablespoons; decrease sugar to ½ cup. Bake at 375°F. for 55 to 65 minutes.

NUTRITION PER SERVING:
Calories 220; Protein 4g; Carbohydrate 28g; Fat 10g; Sodium 200mg.

Cranberry Surprise Loaf

PECAN PUMPKIN BREAD

This sweetly spiced harvest quick bread is flavored with cinnamon and nutmeg.

- 2½ cups all purpose flour
- 1 cup whole wheat flour
- 3 cups sugar
- 2 teaspoons baking soda
- 1½ teaspoons salt
- 2 teaspoons cinnamon
- 1 teaspoon nutmeg
- 1 cup oil
- ⅔ cup water
- 4 eggs
- 1 (16-oz.) can pumpkin (2 cups)
- 1 cup chopped pecans

Heat oven to 350°F. Grease bottom only of two 9x5-inch loaf pans or three 8x4-inch loaf pans. In large bowl, combine all purpose flour, whole wheat flour, sugar, baking soda, salt, cinnamon and nutmeg; mix well. In medium bowl, combine oil, water, eggs and pumpkin; blend well. Add to flour mixture; beat 1 minute at medium speed. Fold in pecans. Pour batter into greased pans.

Bake at 350°F. for 60 to 70 minutes or until toothpick inserted in center comes out clean. Cool 10 minutes; remove from pans. Cool completely.
Yield: 2 (16-slice) loaves.

HIGH ALTITUDE:
Above 3500 Feet: No change.

NUTRITION PER SERVING:
Calories 230; Protein 3g; Carbohydrate 31g; Fat 10g; Sodium 180mg.

PINEAPPLE PECAN QUICK BREAD

Lemon and pineapple flavor this cake-like bread. It's a great choice for breakfast, brunch or dessert.

BREAD
- 2 cups sugar
- 1 cup margarine or butter, softened
- 4 eggs
- 3 cups all purpose flour
- ½ teaspoon baking powder
- ½ teaspoon baking soda
- ½ teaspoon salt
- 1 cup buttermilk
- 1 to 2 tablespoons grated lemon peel
- ½ teaspoon lemon or pineapple extract
- ½ cup chopped pecans
- 1 (20-oz.) can crushed pineapple, drained, reserving liquid

GLAZE
- ½ cup sugar
- 3 tablespoons reserved pineapple liquid
- ½ teaspoon vanilla

Heat oven to 350°F. Grease and flour bottom only of two 8x4 or two 9x5-inch loaf pans. In large bowl, beat sugar and margarine until light and fluffy. Add eggs 1 at a time, beating well after each addition. Add flour, baking powder, baking soda, salt, buttermilk, lemon peel and lemon extract; mix until smooth. Stir in pecans and pineapple. Pour into greased and floured pans.

Bake at 350°F. for 50 to 65 minutes or until toothpick inserted in center comes out clean. In small bowl, blend all glaze ingredients until smooth; spoon over warm loaves. Cool 10 minutes; remove from pans. Cool completely. Wrap tightly and store in refrigerator.
Yield: 2 (16-slice) loaves.

HIGH ALTITUDE:
Above 3500 Feet: Increase flour to 3 cups plus 3 tablespoons. Bake as directed above.

NUTRITION PER SERVING:
Calories 200; Protein 3g; Carbohydrate 29g; Fat 8g; Sodium 145mg.

EGGNOG QUICK BREAD

This eggnog-flavored quick bread is perfect for the holidays!

- 2 eggs
- 1 cup sugar
- 1 cup dairy eggnog (not canned)
- ½ cup margarine or butter, melted
- 2 teaspoons rum extract
- 1 teaspoon vanilla
- 2¼ cups all purpose flour
- 2 teaspoons baking powder
- ½ teaspoon salt
- ¼ teaspoon nutmeg

Heat oven to 350°F. Grease bottom only of 9x5-inch loaf pan. Beat eggs in large bowl. Add sugar, eggnog, margarine, rum extract and vanilla; blend well. Add flour, baking powder, salt and nutmeg; stir just until dry ingredients are moistened. Pour into greased pan.

Bake at 350°F. for 45 to 50 minutes or until toothpick inserted in center comes out clean. Cool 10 minutes; remove from pan. Cool completely. Wrap tightly and store in refrigerator.

Yield: 1 (16-slice) loaf.

HIGH ALTITUDE:
Above 3500 Feet: No change.

NUTRITION PER SERVING:
Calories 190; Protein 3g; Carbohydrate 28g; Fat 8g; Sodium 190mg.

BROWN BREAD

Serve this sweet, traditional, round-shaped bread with sausage and baked beans.

- 2 cups raisins
  Boiling water
- ½ cup firmly packed brown sugar
- ¼ cup margarine or butter, softened
- 1 cup cornmeal
- ½ cup molasses
- 2 cups buttermilk
- 1 egg
- 3 cups all purpose flour
- 2 teaspoons baking soda

Heat oven to 350°F. Grease and flour bottoms only of two 1-quart casseroles or two 8x4-inch loaf pans. In small bowl, cover raisins with boiling water and let stand 5 minutes; drain.

In large bowl, beat brown sugar and margarine until light and fluffy. Add cornmeal, molasses, buttermilk and egg; blend well. Stir in flour and baking soda. Fold in raisins. Pour batter into greased and floured casseroles.

Bake at 350°F. for 40 to 50 minutes or until toothpick inserted in center comes out clean. Cool 10 minutes; remove from pans. Cool completely. Wrap tightly and store in refrigerator.

Yield: 2 (16-slice) loaves.

HIGH ALTITUDE:
Above 3500 Feet: No change.

NUTRITION PER SERVING:
Calories 130; Protein 3g; Carbohydrate 26g; Fat 2g; Sodium 110mg.

Sour Cream Coffee Cake

Rich, sweet cake-like breads served for breakfast or brunch are called coffee cakes. This version is quick to make and is filled and topped with a nutty brown sugar mixture.

COFFEE CAKE

- ¾ **cup sugar**
- ½ **cup margarine or butter, softened**
- 1 **teaspoon vanilla**
- 3 **eggs**
- 2 **cups all purpose flour**
- 1 **teaspoon baking powder**
- 1 **teaspoon baking soda**
- ⅛ **teaspoon salt**
- 1 **cup dairy sour cream**

FILLING AND TOPPING

- 1¼ **cups firmly packed brown sugar**
- 1 **cup chopped walnuts**
- 2 **teaspoons cinnamon**
- 3 **tablespoons margarine or butter, melted**

Heat oven to 350°F. Grease and lightly flour 10-inch tube pan. In large bowl, beat sugar and ½ cup margarine until light and fluffy. Add vanilla and eggs; mix well. In small bowl, combine flour, baking powder, baking soda and salt. Stir flour mixture and sour cream alternately into sugar mixture, beginning and ending with flour mixture.

In small bowl, combine all filling and topping ingredients; mix well. Spread half of batter in greased pan; sprinkle with half of the brown sugar mixture. Repeat with remaining batter and brown sugar mixture.

Bake at 350°F. for 35 to 40 minutes or until toothpick inserted in center comes out clean. Cool upright in pan 15 minutes. Invert onto large plate or cookie sheet, then invert again onto serving plate, streusel side up.

Yield: 16 servings.

TIP:

Recipe can be baked in greased and floured 13x9-inch pan. Prepare recipe as directed above. Spread half of batter in bottom of pan; sprinkle with half of the brown sugar mixture. Repeat with remaining batter and brown sugar mixture. Bake at 350°F. for 30 to 40 minutes or until toothpick inserted in center comes out clean.

HIGH ALTITUDE:
Above 3500 Feet: No change.

NUTRITION PER SERVING:
Calories 330; Protein 4g; Carbohydrate 40g; Fat 17g; Sodium 225mg.

Apple Streusel Coffee Cake

Leaving the peel on the apples adds color to this delicious coffee cake.

COFFEE CAKE

- 1 **cup all purpose flour**
- 1 **teaspoon baking powder**
- ¼ **teaspoon baking soda**
- ⅛ **teaspoon salt**
- ¼ **cup margarine or butter, softened**
- ½ **cup sugar**
- ¼ **cup frozen cholesterol-free egg product, thawed, or 1 egg**
- 1 **teaspoon vanilla**
- 3 **tablespoons nonfat plain yogurt**
- 2 **cups thinly sliced unpeeled apples**

TOPPING

- ¼ **cup all purpose flour**
- 2 **tablespoons brown sugar**
- ½ **teaspoon cinnamon**
- 2 **tablespoons margarine or butter**

Heat oven to 350°F. Grease 9-inch round cake pan or 8-inch square pan. In small bowl, combine 1 cup flour, baking powder, baking soda and salt; mix well. Set aside.

In large bowl, beat ¼ cup margarine and sugar until light and fluffy. Add egg product and vanilla; blend well. Alternately add dry ingredients and yogurt to sugar mixture, beating well after each addition. Spread batter in greased pan; arrange apple slices over batter.

In small bowl, combine all topping ingredients except margarine. Using pastry blender or fork, cut in 2 tablespoons margarine until crumbly. Sprinkle topping evenly over apples.

Bake at 350°F. for 30 to 35 minutes or until toothpick inserted in center comes out clean. Cool 10 minutes; if desired, remove from pan.

Yield: 8 servings.

HIGH ALTITUDE:
Above 3500 Feet: No change.

NUTRITION PER SERVING:
Calories 230; Protein 3g; Carbohydrate 36g; Fat 9g; Sodium 220mg.

APPLE COFFEE CAKE SUPREME

Savor the down-home goodness of apples in this delicious coffee cake. Baking the cake in a tart pan gives it an elegant look.

COFFEE CAKE
- ½ cup sugar
- 2 eggs
- 1 to 2 teaspoons grated lemon peel
- ½ cup plain yogurt
- 3 tablespoons margarine or butter, melted
- 1⅓ cups all purpose flour
- 2 teaspoons baking powder
- ½ teaspoon salt
- 3 to 4 cups thinly sliced peeled apples
- 2 tablespoons sugar
- ½ to 1 cup sliced almonds

GLAZE
- ⅓ cup sugar
- ⅓ cup margarine or butter, melted
- 1 egg, beaten

Heat oven to 375°F. Grease 10-inch tart pan with removable bottom or 8-inch square pan. In small bowl, beat ½ cup sugar and 2 eggs; stir in lemon peel, yogurt and 3 tablespoons margarine. Add flour, baking powder and salt to egg mixture; blend well. Pour into greased pan. Arrange apple slices on top of dough, overlapping slightly. Sprinkle with 2 tablespoons sugar and almonds.

Bake at 375°F. for 35 to 45 minutes or until golden brown and toothpick inserted in center comes out clean.*

Meanwhile, in small bowl combine all glaze ingredients; blend well. Slowly pour over almonds and allow mixture to soak into hot cake. Broil 5 to 6 inches from heat for 1 to 2 minutes or until bubbly. Serve warm. Store in refrigerator.
Yield: 6 to 8 servings.

TIP:
* If using 8-inch square pan, increase baking time 5 minutes.

HIGH ALTITUDE:
Above 3500 Feet: No change.

NUTRITION PER SERVING:
Calories 400; Protein 8g; Carbohydrate 49g; Fat 21g; Sodium 380mg.

COUNTRY APPLE COFFEE CAKE

Refrigerated flaky biscuits mean quick preparation for this delicious breakfast treat.

COFFEE CAKE
- 2 tablespoons margarine or butter, softened
- 1½ cups chopped peeled apples
- 1 (10-oz.) can refrigerated flaky biscuits
- ⅓ cup firmly packed brown sugar
- ¼ teaspoon cinnamon
- ⅓ cup light corn syrup
- 1 egg
- ½ cup pecan halves or pieces

GLAZE
- ⅓ cup powdered sugar
- ¼ teaspoon vanilla
- 1 to 2 teaspoons milk

Heat oven to 350°F. Using 1 tablespoon of the margarine, generously grease 9-inch round cake pan or 8-inch square pan. Spread 1 cup of the apples in greased pan. Separate dough into 10 biscuits; cut each into quarters. Arrange biscuit pieces, points up, over apples. Top with remaining ½ cup apples. In small bowl, combine remaining 1 tablespoon margarine, brown sugar, cinnamon, corn syrup and egg; beat 2 to 3 minutes or until sugar is partially dissolved. Stir in pecans; spoon over biscuit pieces and apples.

Bake at 350°F. for 35 to 45 minutes or until deep golden brown. Cool 5 minutes. In small bowl, blend all glaze ingredients, adding enough milk for desired drizzling consistency. Drizzle over warm cake. Serve warm or cool. Store in refrigerator.
Yield: 6 to 8 servings.

NUTRITION PER SERVING:
Calories 290; Protein 3g; Carbohydrate 44g; Fat 12g; Sodium 430mg.

QUICK ORANGE COFFEE CAKE

For brunch try this quick streusel-topped coffee cake filled with mandarin orange segments.

COFFEE CAKE
- 2 cups all purpose flour
- ½ cup sugar
- 3 teaspoons baking powder
- ½ teaspoon salt
- 6 tablespoons margarine or butter
- 1 cup milk
- ½ teaspoon vanilla
- 1 egg, slightly beaten

FILLING
- 1 (11-oz.) can mandarin orange segments, well drained

TOPPING
- ¼ cup sugar
- 2 tablespoons all purpose flour
- 2 tablespoons margarine or butter, softened
- ¼ cup chopped nuts
- 1 teaspoon grated orange peel

Heat oven to 350°F. Grease and flour 9-inch square pan. In medium bowl, combine 2 cups flour, ½ cup sugar, baking powder and salt; blend well. Using pastry blender or fork, cut in 6 tablespoons margarine until mixture is crumbly. Add milk, vanilla and egg; mix well. Spread batter in greased pan. Arrange orange segments over batter.

In small bowl, combine all topping ingredients until crumbly; sprinkle over orange segments.

Bake at 350°F. for 35 to 45 minutes or until toothpick inserted in center comes out clean. Cool slightly; cut into squares. Serve warm.

Yield: 9 servings.

HIGH ALTITUDE:
Above 3500 Feet: No change.

NUTRITION PER SERVING:
Calories 320; Protein 5g; Carbohydrate 44g; Fat 14g; Sodium 375mg.

VARIATIONS:

QUICK BLUEBERRY COFFEE CAKE: Substitute 1 cup frozen blueberries, thawed and drained, for mandarin orange segments. For topping, increase sugar to ⅓ cup and flour to ¼ cup. Omit nuts and orange peel; add ¼ teaspoon nutmeg.

QUICK PINEAPPLE-COCONUT COFFEE CAKE: Substitute ½ cup coconut and 8-oz. can crushed pineapple, well drained, for mandarin orange segments. For topping, substitute ¼ cup firmly packed brown sugar for sugar; omit nuts and orange peel.

SKILLET ORANGE COFFEE CAKE

Serve this cinnamon and orange-flavored coffee cake warm right from the skillet.

COFFEE CAKE
- 2¼ cups all purpose flour
- ½ cup sugar
- 3 teaspoons baking powder
- ½ teaspoon salt
- ¾ cup orange juice
- ¼ cup oil
- 2 eggs, beaten

TOPPING
- ¼ cup chopped nuts
- ¼ cup sugar
- 3 teaspoons cinnamon
- 1 tablespoon margarine or butter, softened
- 1 teaspoon grated orange peel

Heat oven to 350°F. Grease 10-inch ovenproof skillet. In large bowl, combine flour, sugar, baking powder and salt; mix well.

In small bowl, combine orange juice, oil and eggs; blend well. Add to dry ingredients all at once; stir just until dry ingredients are moistened. Spread batter evenly in greased skillet.

In small bowl, combine topping ingredients with fork until crumbly. Sprinkle topping evenly over batter.

Bake at 350°F. for 25 to 30 minutes or until toothpick inserted in center comes out clean. Cool 10 minutes. Serve warm.

Yield: 12 servings.

HIGH ALTITUDE:
Above 3500 Feet: Increase flour to 2¼ cups plus 3 tablespoons. Bake as directed above.

NUTRITION PER SERVING:
Calories 220; Protein 4g; Carbohydrate 33g; Fat 8g; Sodium 190mg.

Orange Pineapple Muffin Cake

Whole wheat flour adds texture and wholesomeness to this muffin-like cake.

CAKE
- 1½ cups all purpose flour
- 1 cup whole wheat flour
- ⅓ cup firmly packed brown sugar
- 3 teaspoons baking powder
- ½ teaspoon baking soda
- ¼ teaspoon salt
- 1 (8¼-oz.) can crushed pineapple, drained
- ½ cup orange juice
- ⅓ cup margarine or butter, melted
- ½ to 1 teaspoon grated orange peel
- 1 egg, slightly beaten

GLAZE
- ½ cup powdered sugar
- ½ teaspoon grated orange peel
- 1 to 2 tablespoons orange juice

GARNISH
Fresh orange slices
Mint leaves

Heat oven to 400°F. Grease bottom only of 9-inch springform pan or 9-inch round cake pan. In large bowl, combine all purpose flour, whole wheat flour, brown sugar, baking powder, baking soda and salt; mix well. In medium bowl, combine all remaining cake ingredients; blend well. Add to dry ingredients all at once; stir just until dry ingredients are moistened. Spread dough in greased pan.

Bake at 400°F. for 22 to 27 minutes or until light golden brown and toothpick inserted in center comes out clean. Cool 1 minute; remove from pan.

In small bowl, combine all glaze ingredients, adding enough orange juice for desired drizzling consistency. Drizzle over warm cake. Garnish with orange slices and mint leaves. Serve warm.
Yield: 12 servings.

HIGH ALTITUDE:
Above 3500 Feet: Decrease baking powder to 2 teaspoons. Bake as directed above.

NUTRITION PER SERVING:
Calories 200; Protein 4g; Carbohydrate 34g; Fat 6g; Sodium 230mg.

Orange Rhubarb Coffee Cake

When rhubarb is in season, cut and freeze it in measured packages. Then this fresh spring coffee cake can be baked anytime!

COFFEE CAKE
- ¼ cup margarine or butter, softened
- ¾ cup sugar
- ½ cup orange juice
- 1 egg
- 1¼ cups all purpose flour
- 1½ teaspoons baking powder
- ¼ teaspoon salt
- 2 to 3 teaspoons grated orange peel
- 1½ cups fresh or frozen rhubarb, cut into 1-inch pieces

TOPPING
- 2 tablespoons sugar
- ½ teaspoon cinnamon

Heat oven to 350°F. Grease and flour 9-inch square pan. In large bowl, beat margarine and sugar until light and fluffy. Add orange juice and egg; blend well. Stir in flour, baking powder, salt, orange peel and rhubarb; mix well. Pour into greased and floured pan. In small bowl, combine topping ingredients; sprinkle over cake.

Bake at 350°F. for 35 to 40 minutes or until toothpick inserted in center comes out clean. Serve warm.
Yield: 9 servings.

HIGH ALTITUDE:
Above 3500 Feet: No change.

NUTRITION PER SERVING:
Calories 210; Protein 3g; Carbohydrate 36g; Fat 6g; Sodium 170mg.

Raspberry Cream Cheese Coffee Cake

This indulgent coffee cake is easy to make, and impressive to serve.

2¼ cups all purpose flour
 ¾ cup sugar
 ¾ cup margarine or butter
 ½ teaspoon baking powder
 ½ teaspoon baking soda
 ¼ teaspoon salt
 ¾ cup dairy sour cream
 1 teaspoon almond extract
 1 egg
 1 (8-oz.) pkg. cream cheese, softened
 ¼ cup sugar
 1 egg
 ½ cup raspberry preserves
 ½ cup sliced almonds

Heat oven to 350°F. Grease and flour bottom and sides of 9 or 10-inch springform pan. In large bowl, combine flour and ¾ cup sugar. Using pastry blender or fork, cut in margarine until mixture resembles coarse crumbs. Reserve 1 cup of crumb mixture. To remaining crumb mixture, add baking powder, baking soda, salt, sour cream, almond extract and 1 egg; blend well. Spread batter over bottom and 2 inches up sides of greased and floured pan. (Batter should be about ¼ inch thick on sides.)

In small bowl, combine cream cheese, ¼ cup sugar and 1 egg; blend well. Pour into batter-lined pan. Carefully spoon preserves evenly over cream cheese mixture. In small bowl, combine reserved crumb mixture and sliced almonds. Sprinkle over preserves.

Bake at 350°F. for 45 to 55 minutes or until cream cheese filling is set and crust is deep golden brown. Cool 15 minutes. Remove sides of pan. Serve warm or cool, cut into wedges. Store in refrigerator.
Yield: 16 servings.

HIGH ALTITUDE:
Above 3500 Feet: No change.

NUTRITION PER SERVING:
Calories 320; Protein 5g; Carbohydrate 34g; Fat 18g; Sodium 230mg.

Marbled Raspberry Coffee Cake

This cake, flavored with lemon and swirled with raspberry preserves, is perfect for a Valentine's Day brunch.

COFFEE CAKE
 1 cup all purpose flour
 ½ cup sugar
 1 teaspoon baking powder
 ¼ teaspoon baking soda
 ¼ teaspoon salt
 1 (3-oz.) pkg. cream cheese, softened
 ¼ cup margarine or butter, softened
 ¼ cup milk
 1 teaspoon grated lemon peel
 1 egg
 ¼ cup raspberry preserves

FROSTING
 ½ cup powdered sugar
 1 tablespoon lemon juice
 2 teaspoons margarine or butter, softened
 ¼ cup sliced almonds

Heat oven to 350°F. Grease and flour 8-inch square pan. In small bowl, combine all coffee cake ingredients except preserves; blend at low speed until moistened. Beat 2 minutes at medium speed. Spread batter in greased and floured pan. Spoon preserves by teaspoonfuls over batter. Using knife, swirl preserves over top of batter to marble.

Bake at 350°F. for 25 to 30 minutes or until toothpick inserted in center comes out clean. Cool slightly.

In small bowl, combine all frosting ingredients except almonds; beat until smooth. Frost warm cake; sprinkle with almonds. Serve warm.
Yield: 9 servings.

HIGH ALTITUDE:
Above 3500 Feet: No change.

NUTRITION PER SERVING:
Calories 250; Protein 4g; Carbohydrate 34g; Fat 11g; Sodium 230mg.

Raspberry Cream Cheese Coffee Cake

Raspberry Ripple Crescent Coffee Cake

———— ❧ ————

The cut wedges of this coffee cake show berry pinwheels reminiscent of an Austrian linzer torte.

COFFEE CAKE
- ¾ **cup sugar**
- ¼ **cup margarine or butter, softened**
- 2 **eggs**
- ¾ **cup ground almonds**
- ¼ **cup all purpose flour**
- 1 **teaspoon grated lemon peel**
- 1 **(8-oz.) can refrigerated crescent dinner rolls**
- 8 **teaspoons raspberry preserves**
- ¼ **cup sliced almonds**

GLAZE
- ⅓ **cup powdered sugar**
- 1 **to 2 teaspoons milk**

Heat oven to 375°F. Grease 9-inch round cake pan or 9-inch pie pan. In small bowl, beat sugar, margarine and eggs until smooth. Stir ground almonds, flour and lemon peel into sugar mixture. Set aside.

Separate dough into 8 triangles. Spread 1 teaspoon of the preserves on each triangle. Roll up, starting at shortest side of triangle and rolling to opposite point. Place rolls in greased pan in 2 circles, arranging 5 rolls around outside edge and 3 in center. Pour and carefully spread almond mixture evenly over rolls; sprinkle with almonds.

Bake at 375°F. for 25 to 35 minutes or until deep golden brown and knife inserted in center comes out clean. (If necessary, cover coffee cake with foil during last 5 to 10 minutes of baking to prevent excessive browning.) In small bowl, blend glaze ingredients, adding enough milk for desired drizzling consistency. Drizzle over warm cake. Serve warm.

Yield: 8 servings.

NUTRITION PER SERVING:
Calories 360; Protein 6g; Carbohydrate 44g; Fat 18g; Sodium 320mg.

Fruited Coffee Cake

———— ❧ ————

This fruit-topped coffee cake is a healthful addition to any brunch menu.

- 1 **(8-oz.) pkg. dried fruit, coarsely chopped**
- ½ **cup orange juice**
- 1 **cup all purpose flour**
- 1 **teaspoon baking powder**
- ¼ **teaspoon baking soda**
- ⅛ **teaspoon salt**
- ¼ **cup margarine or butter, softened**
- ½ **cup sugar**
- ¼ **cup frozen cholesterol-free egg product, thawed, or 1 egg**
- 1 **teaspoon vanilla**
- 3 **tablespoons lowfat plain yogurt**
  Powdered sugar

In small saucepan, combine dried fruit and orange juice. Bring to a boil. Reduce heat; simmer 5 minutes or until thickened and fruit is soft, stirring occasionally. Set aside.

Heat oven to 350°F. Grease 9-inch round or 8-inch square pan. In small bowl, combine flour, baking powder, baking soda and salt; mix well. Set aside. In another small bowl, beat margarine and sugar until light and fluffy. Add egg product and vanilla; blend well. Alternately add dry ingredients and yogurt to sugar mixture, beating well after each addition. Spread batter in greased pan; top with fruit mixture.

Bake at 350°F. for 30 to 40 minutes or until toothpick inserted in center comes out clean. (If necessary, cover coffee cake with foil during last 15 to 20 minutes of baking to prevent overbrowning of fruit.) Cool 10 minutes; remove from pan. Sprinkle with powdered sugar. Serve warm.

Yield: 8 servings.

HIGH ALTITUDE:
Above 3500 Feet: Decrease sugar to ⅓ cup. Bake as directed above.

NUTRITION PER SERVING:
Calories 240; Protein 3g; Carbohydrate 45g; Fat 6g; Sodium 530mg.

BLUEBERRY COFFEE CAKE

Blueberries grow wild in many parts of the world. Berries that we rely on from grocery stores are cultivated and are larger than the wild ones. Either type will work well in this fresh berry cake.

COFFEE CAKE
- 2 cups all purpose flour
- 1 cup sugar
- 2 teaspoons baking powder
- 1 teaspoon salt
- 1½ teaspoons grated lemon or orange peel
- ½ cup margarine or butter, softened
- 1 cup milk
- 2 eggs, slightly beaten
- 1 teaspoon vanilla
- 2 cups fresh or frozen blueberries (do not thaw)*

ICING
- 1 cup powdered sugar
- ¼ teaspoon almond extract
- 3 to 5 teaspoons milk

Heat oven to 350°F. Grease 13x9-inch pan. In large bowl, combine flour, sugar, baking powder, salt and lemon peel. Using pastry blender or fork, cut in margarine until mixture resembles coarse crumbs. Add 1 cup milk, eggs and vanilla; stir until well blended. Pour ¾ of batter into greased pan. Top with blueberries. Spoon remaining batter over blueberries.

Bake at 350°F. for 35 to 45 minutes or until toothpick inserted in center comes out clean. Cool 30 minutes.

In small bowl, blend icing ingredients, adding enough milk for desired drizzling consistency. Drizzle over warm cake.
Yield: 12 servings.

TIP:
* Two cups sliced peaches or 3 cups (1 lb.) pitted, halved bing cherries can be substituted for blueberries.

HIGH ALTITUDE:
Above 3500 Feet: Bake at 375°F. for 30 to 35 minutes.

NUTRITION PER SERVING:
Calories 280; Protein 4g; Carbohydrate 47g; Fat 9g; Sodium 340mg.

ONE-STEP TROPICAL COFFEE CAKE

Pineapple yogurt, coconut and cinnamon are teamed together in a deliciously different coffee cake. Serve it warm from the oven.

COFFEE CAKE
- 1½ cups all purpose flour
- 1 cup sugar
- 2 teaspoons baking powder
- ½ teaspoon salt
- 1 (8-oz.) container pineapple or vanilla yogurt
- ½ cup oil
- 2 eggs

TOPPING
- 1 cup coconut
- ⅓ cup sugar
- 1 teaspoon cinnamon

Heat oven to 350°F. Grease 9-inch square or 11x7-inch pan. In large bowl, combine all coffee cake ingredients; stir 70 to 80 strokes until well blended. Pour into greased pan. In small bowl, combine all topping ingredients. Sprinkle over batter.

Bake at 350°F. for 35 to 40 minutes or until toothpick inserted in center comes out clean. Serve warm.
Yield: 9 servings.

HIGH ALTITUDE:
Above 3500 Feet: Decrease sugar to 1 cup minus 2 tablespoons; decrease baking powder to 1½ teaspoons. Bake as directed above.

NUTRITION PER SERVING:
Calories 390; Protein 5g; Carbohydrate 54g; Fat 17g; Sodium 220mg.

BLUEBERRY BRUNCH CAKE

Any flavor fruit pie filling can be used to make this glazed coffee cake.

COFFEE CAKE
  1 cup margarine or butter, softened
1¾ cups sugar
  1 teaspoon vanilla
  4 eggs
  3 cups all purpose flour
1½ teaspoons baking powder
  ½ teaspoon salt
  ¼ teaspoon nutmeg
  1 (21-oz.) can blueberry fruit pie filling

GLAZE
1¼ cups powdered sugar
  1 tablespoon margarine or butter, softened
  2 to 3 tablespoons lemon juice
    Few drops yellow food color

Heat oven to 350°F. Grease and flour 15x10x1-inch baking pan. In large bowl, combine 1 cup margarine, sugar and vanilla. Add eggs 1 at a time, beating well after each addition. By hand, stir in flour, baking powder and salt; mix well. Spread half of batter in greased pan. Stir nutmeg into blueberry filling; spread filling evenly over batter. Drop remaining batter by teaspoonfuls over filling.

Bake at 350°F. for 30 to 40 minutes or until toothpick inserted in center comes out clean and top is golden brown.

In small bowl, blend all glaze ingredients, adding enough lemon juice for desired drizzling consistency. Drizzle over warm cake.

Yield: 24 servings.

HIGH ALTITUDE:
Above 3500 Feet: No change.

NUTRITION PER SERVING:
Calories 250; Protein 3g; Carbohydrate 41g; Fat 10g; Sodium 170mg.

BLUEBERRY MUFFIN CAKE

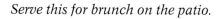

Serve this for brunch on the patio.

TOPPING
  ¼ cup all purpose flour
  ¼ cup sugar
  ½ teaspoon cinnamon
  3 tablespoons margarine or butter

COFFEE CAKE
  2 tablespoons fine dry bread crumbs
  2 cups all purpose flour
  1 cup sugar
  3 teaspoons baking powder
  ½ teaspoon baking soda
  ½ teaspoon salt
  ½ teaspoon cinnamon
  1 cup fresh or frozen blueberries, thawed, drained
  2 eggs
  ⅓ cup orange-flavored liqueur or orange juice
  ¼ cup margarine or butter, melted, cooled
  1 (8-oz.) container dairy sour cream
  1 teaspoon grated orange peel

In small bowl, combine all topping ingredients except margarine; mix well. Using pastry blender or fork, cut in 3 tablespoons margarine until mixture resembles coarse crumbs. Set aside.

Heat oven to 375°F. Grease 10-inch springform pan or 9-inch square pan. Sprinkle with bread crumbs; set aside. In large bowl, combine 2 cups flour, 1 cup sugar, baking powder, baking soda, salt and ½ teaspoon cinnamon; mix well. Stir in blueberries. Beat eggs in medium bowl. Stir in orange liqueur, ¼ cup margarine, sour cream and orange peel. Add to blueberry mixture, stirring just until dry ingredients are moistened. Spoon batter into greased pan; sprinkle with topping.

Bake at 375°F. for 35 to 45 minutes or until toothpick inserted in center comes out clean. Cool 10 minutes; remove sides of pan. Serve warm or cool.

Yield: 12 servings.

HIGH ALTITUDE:
Above 3500 Feet: Decrease baking powder to 2 teaspoons. Bake as directed above.

NUTRITION PER SERVING:
Calories 320; Protein 4g; Carbohydrate 48g; Fat 12g; Sodium 320mg.

Blueberry Muffin Cake

PUMPKIN DATE COFFEE CAKE

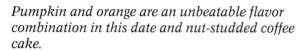

Pumpkin and orange are an unbeatable flavor combination in this date and nut-studded coffee cake.

TOPPING
- ¼ **cup all purpose flour**
- ¼ **cup sugar**
- ½ **teaspoon cinnamon**
- 3 **tablespoons margarine or butter**

COFFEE CAKE
- 2 **cups all purpose flour**
- 1 **cup sugar**
- 3 **teaspoons baking powder**
- 1 **teaspoon pumpkin pie spice**
- ½ **teaspoon baking soda**
- ½ **teaspoon salt**
- 2 **eggs**
- 1 **cup canned pumpkin**
- ⅓ **cup orange juice**
- ¼ **cup margarine or butter, melted, cooled**
- 1 **teaspoon grated orange peel**
- 1 **cup chopped nuts**
- ½ **cup chopped dates**

GLAZE
- ½ **cup powdered sugar**
- 1 **teaspoon grated orange peel**
- 1 **to 2 tablespoons orange juice**

In small bowl, combine all topping ingredients except margarine; mix well. Using pastry blender or fork, cut in 3 tablespoons margarine until mixture resembles coarse crumbs. Set aside.

Heat oven to 375°F. Grease 10-inch tube pan. In large bowl, combine 2 cups flour, 1 cup sugar, baking powder, pumpkin pie spice, baking soda and salt; mix well. Beat eggs in small bowl. Stir in pumpkin, ⅓ cup orange juice, ¼ cup margarine and 1 teaspoon orange peel. Add to dry ingredients, stirring just until dry ingredients are moistened. Stir in nuts and dates. Spoon batter into greased pan; sprinkle with topping.

Bake at 375°F. for 40 to 45 minutes or until toothpick inserted in center comes out clean. Cool 30 minutes; remove from pan.

In small bowl, blend all glaze ingredients, adding enough orange juice for desired drizzling consistency. Drizzle over warm cake. Serve warm or cool. **Yield: 12 servings.**

HIGH ALTITUDE:
Above 3500 Feet: No change.

NUTRITION PER SERVING:
Calories 360; Protein 5g; Carbohydrate 53g; Fat 14g; Sodium 300mg.

CARAMEL BISCUIT RING-A-ROUND

The easiest way to cut the refrigerated biscuits into quarters is to use a kitchen scissors.

- ¾ **cup firmly packed brown sugar**
- ½ **cup chopped nuts**
- ⅓ **cup margarine or butter**
- 2 **tablespoons water**
- 2 **(7.5-oz.) cans refrigerated biscuits**

Heat oven to 400°F. Generously grease 12-cup Bundt® pan. In small saucepan, combine brown sugar, nuts, margarine and water; heat until margarine melts, stirring occasionally. Separate dough into 20 biscuits. Cut each biscuit into quarters; place in large bowl. Pour brown sugar mixture over biscuits; toss lightly to coat evenly. Spoon coated biscuit pieces into greased pan.

Bake at 400°F. for 20 to 30 minutes or until golden brown. Let stand in pan 3 minutes; invert onto serving plate. Serve warm. **Yield: 10 servings.**

NUTRITION PER SERVING:
Calories 260; Protein 4g; Carbohydrate 37g; Fat 11g; Sodium 430mg.

Winter Fruit Coffee Cake

WINTER FRUIT COFFEE CAKE

This coffee cake featuring fresh winter fruits also can be served for dessert with whipped cream.

COFFEE CAKE
- 1½ **cups all purpose flour**
- 2 **teaspoons baking powder**
- ¾ **cup sugar**
- ¼ **cup margarine or butter, softened**
- 2 **eggs**
- ½ **cup buttermilk**
- 2 **teaspoons grated orange peel**
- ½ **cup golden raisins**
- 1 **cup thinly sliced apples**
- 1 **orange, peeled, thinly sliced**

TOPPING
- ¼ **cup sugar**
- ½ **teaspoon cinnamon**
- 2 **tablespoons margarine or butter, melted**
- ½ **cup chopped pecans**

Heat oven to 350°F. Grease and flour 9-inch springform pan. In medium bowl, combine flour and baking powder; set aside. In large bowl, beat ¾ cup sugar and ¼ cup margarine until light and fluffy. Add eggs; blend well. Alternately add dry ingredients and buttermilk to sugar mixture, beating well after each addition. Stir in orange peel and raisins. Pour into greased pan. Arrange apple and orange slices decoratively over top of batter.

In small bowl, combine all topping ingredients; sprinkle over fruit.

Bake at 350°F. for 40 to 50 minutes or until golden brown. Cool 10 minutes; remove sides of pan. Serve warm.
Yield: 8 to 10 servings.

HIGH ALTITUDE:
Above 3500 Feet: No change.

NUTRITION PER SERVING:
Calories 300; Protein 4g; Carbohydrate 45g; Fat 12g; Sodium 170mg.

HONEYCOMB COFFEE CAKE

This scrumptious coffee cake will melt in your mouth as you encounter warm pockets of honey throughout a moist and flaky bread.

- ¼ **cup firmly packed brown sugar**
- 1 **teaspoon cinnamon**
- ¼ **teaspoon mace or nutmeg**
- ¼ **cup margarine or butter, melted**
- 1 **tablespoon lemon juice**
- 1 **(10-oz.) can refrigerated flaky biscuits**
- ¼ **to ⅓ cup graham cracker crumbs (4 to 5 squares)**
- ¼ **cup finely chopped nuts, if desired**
- 2 **to 4 tablespoons honey**

Heat oven to 400°F. Grease 9 or 8-inch round cake pan. In small bowl, combine brown sugar, cinnamon and mace. In another small bowl, combine margarine and lemon juice.

Separate dough into 10 biscuits; cut each into 4 pieces. Place biscuit pieces and graham cracker crumbs in bag; shake to coat. Arrange coated biscuit pieces evenly in greased pan. With small wooden spoon handle, poke a deep hole in each biscuit piece. Sprinkle brown sugar mixture over biscuits; drizzle with margarine mixture. Sprinkle with nuts.

Bake at 400°F. for 12 to 18 minutes or until golden brown. Turn onto wire rack; invert onto serving plate. Fill holes with honey.

Yield: 10 servings.

NUTRITION PER SERVING:
Calories 210; Protein 2g; Carbohydrate 27g; Fat 10g; Sodium 370mg.

ZUCCHINI SPICE COFFEE CAKE

When shredding the zucchini, do not remove the peel. It adds color and texture to this wholesome coffee cake.

COFFEE CAKE
- 1½ **cups all purpose flour**
- 1¼ **cups quick-cooking rolled oats**
- 1 **cup firmly packed brown sugar**
- 1 **teaspoon baking soda**
- 1 **teaspoon cinnamon**
- ½ **teaspoon salt**
- ¼ **teaspoon nutmeg**
- 2 **cups shredded unpeeled zucchini**
- ½ **cup margarine or butter, softened**
- ¼ **cup dairy sour cream**
- 1 **teaspoon vanilla**
- 2 **eggs**

TOPPING
- ¾ **cup sugar**
- ½ **cup all purpose flour**
- ½ **cup quick-cooking rolled oats**
- ½ **teaspoon cinnamon**
- ¼ **cup margarine or butter, softened**

Heat oven to 350°F. Grease and flour 13x9-inch pan. In large bowl, combine all coffee cake ingredients at low speed until moistened; beat 2 minutes at medium speed. Pour into greased pan. In small bowl, combine all topping ingredients until crumbly; sprinkle over batter.

Bake at 350°F. for 30 to 40 minutes or until toothpick inserted in center comes out clean. Serve warm or cool.

Yield: 12 servings.

HIGH ALTITUDE:
Above 3500 Feet: No change.

NUTRITION PER SERVING:
Calories 370; Protein 6g; Carbohydrate 55g; Fat 14g; Sodium 340mg.

OVERNIGHT COFFEE CAKE SWIRL

This delectable coffee cake is refrigerated overnight and baked just before serving.

COFFEE CAKE
- 1 cup all purpose flour
- ¼ cup sugar
- ¼ cup firmly packed brown sugar
- 1 teaspoon baking powder
- ½ teaspoon baking soda
- ¼ teaspoon salt
- ½ cup buttermilk
- ⅓ cup shortening
- 1 egg

TOPPING
- ¼ cup firmly packed brown sugar
- ¼ cup chopped nuts
- ¼ teaspoon nutmeg

Grease and flour 9-inch round or 8-inch square pan. In small bowl, combine all coffee cake ingredients. Blend at low speed until moistened; beat 2 minutes at medium speed. Pour batter into greased and floured pan. In small bowl, combine all topping ingredients; blend well. Sprinkle over batter. Cover; refrigerate overnight.

Heat oven to 350°F. Uncover coffee cake. Bake at 350°F. for 25 to 35 minutes or until toothpick inserted in center comes out clean. Serve warm.

Yield: 8 servings.

HIGH ALTITUDE:
Above 3500 Feet: No change.

NUTRITION PER SERVING:
Calories 250; Protein 3g; Carbohydrate 33g; Fat 12g; Sodium 200mg.

CINNAMON COFFEE CAKE

This moist coffee cake tastes like homemade buttermilk doughnuts that are rolled in sugar and cinnamon — and it's much easier to make!

COFFEE CAKE
- 1¾ cups all purpose flour
- ¾ cup sugar
- 2 teaspoons baking powder
- ¼ teaspoon baking soda
- ¼ teaspoon salt
- ¼ teaspoon nutmeg
- ¾ cup buttermilk
- ⅓ cup margarine or butter, melted
- 1 teaspoon vanilla
- 2 eggs, beaten

TOPPING
- ¼ cup margarine or butter, melted
- 3 tablespoons sugar
- ½ teaspoon cinnamon

Heat oven to 350°F. Grease bottom only of 9-inch square pan. In large bowl, combine all coffee cake ingredients; stir just until dry ingredients are moistened. Spread batter in greased pan.

Bake at 350°F. for 30 to 40 minutes or until toothpick inserted in center comes out clean. Generously pierce hot cake with fork. Brush or drizzle ¼ cup melted margarine over hot cake. In small bowl, combine 3 tablespoons sugar and cinnamon; sprinkle over hot cake. Serve warm.

Yield: 9 servings.

HIGH ALTITUDE:
Above 3500 Feet: Increase flour to 1¾ cups plus 2 tablespoons. Bake as directed above.

NUTRITION PER SERVING:
Calories 300; Protein 5g; Carbohydrate 41g; Fat 13g; Sodium 330mg.

APPLE YOGURT KUCHEN

For baking, use apples such as Rome Beauty, Winesap, Granny Smith or Jonathan. These varieties will retain their shape and remain flavorful during baking.

KUCHEN
- ½ **cup margarine or butter, softened**
- ¼ **cup sugar**
- 1 **teaspoon vanilla**
- 1 **egg**
- 1 **cup all purpose flour**
- ½ **teaspoon baking powder**
- ¼ **teaspoon salt**

FILLING
- ½ **cup vanilla yogurt**
- 1 **egg**
- 1½ **cups thinly sliced peeled apples**
- 3 **tablespoons sugar**
- 1 **teaspoon cinnamon**

Heat oven to 350°F. Grease 9-inch springform pan. In large bowl, beat margarine and ¼ cup sugar until light and fluffy. Add vanilla and 1 egg; beat well. Stir in flour, baking powder and salt; mix well. Spread dough over bottom and 1 inch up sides of pan.

In small bowl, combine yogurt and 1 egg; spread over dough. Arrange sliced apples over filling; sprinkle with 3 tablespoons sugar and cinnamon.

Bake at 350°F. for 35 to 45 minutes or until edges are golden brown. Cool 10 minutes; remove sides of pan. Store in refrigerator.
Yield: 6 to 8 servings.

HIGH ALTITUDE:
Above 3500 Feet: No change.

NUTRITION PER SERVING:
Calories 250; Protein 4g; Carbohydrate 29g; Fat 13g; Sodium 240mg.

PEACH KUCHEN

German in origin, kuchen is traditionally fruit-topped yeast-raised cake. This is a simple quick bread version that uses baking powder for leavening.

- ½ **cup margarine or butter, softened**
- ¼ **cup sugar**
- 1 **teaspoon vanilla**
- 1 **egg**
- 1 **cup all purpose flour**
- ½ **teaspoon baking powder**
- ¼ **teaspoon salt**
- 1 **(29-oz.) can sliced peaches, well drained**
- 3 **tablespoons sugar**
- ½ **to 1 teaspoon cinnamon**

Heat oven to 350°F. Grease 9-inch springform pan. In small bowl, beat margarine and sugar until light and fluffy. Add vanilla and egg; beat well. Add flour, baking powder and salt to margarine mixture; blend well. Spread dough over bottom and 1 inch up sides of pan. Arrange peach slices in spoke fashion over dough. In small bowl, combine sugar and cinnamon; sprinkle over peaches and edges of dough.

Bake at 350°F. for 30 to 35 minutes or until edges are golden brown. Cool 10 minutes; remove sides of pan. Serve warm or cool.
Yield: 8 servings.

HIGH ALTITUDE:
Above 3500 Feet: No change.

NUTRITION PER SERVING:
Calories 240; Protein 3g; Carbohydrate 29g; Fat 12g; Sodium 230mg.

VARIATION:

PEAR CARDAMOM KUCHEN: Add 1 teaspoon cardamom with flour. Substitute 29-oz. can pear halves, well drained, sliced, for peaches. Decrease cinnamon to ⅛ teaspoon and add ½ teaspoon cardamom.

PLUM CUSTARD KUCHEN

This creamy custard-filled coffee cake is outstanding served warm.

KUCHEN
- 1 **cup all purpose flour**
- 1 **tablespoon sugar**
- 1 **teaspoon baking powder**
- ½ **cup butter or margarine**
- 2 **tablespoons whipping cream**
- 1 **egg**

FILLING
- 2½ **cups cut-up or sliced pitted plums (about 6 medium)**
- ½ **cup whipping cream**
- ½ **cup sugar**
- 1 **teaspoon vanilla**
- 1 **egg**

Heat oven to 350°F. In medium bowl, combine flour, 1 tablespoon sugar and baking powder. Using pastry blender or fork, cut in butter until mixture resembles coarse crumbs. Stir in 2 tablespoons whipping cream and 1 egg. Press in bottom of ungreased 9-inch square pan. Arrange plums over batter. Bake at 350°F. for 25 to 30 minutes or until crust is light golden brown.

In medium bowl, combine ½ cup whipping cream, ½ cup sugar, vanilla and 1 egg; beat well. Pour mixture over plums. Bake an additional 20 to 30 minutes or until custard is set. Serve warm or cool. Store in refrigerator.

Yield: 9 servings.

HIGH ALTITUDE:
Above 3500 Feet: No change.

NUTRITION PER SERVING:
Calories 290; Protein 3g; Carbohydrate 30g; Fat 18g; Sodium 160mg.

SCANDINAVIAN KRINGLER

This delectable pastry has a flaky crust.

CRUST
- 1 **cup all purpose flour**
- ½ **cup margarine or butter, chilled**
- 2 **to 3 tablespoons ice water**

TOPPING
- 1 **cup water**
- ½ **cup margarine or butter**
- 1 **cup all purpose flour**
- 3 **eggs**
- ½ **teaspoon almond extract**

FROSTING
- 1 **cup powdered sugar**
- 1 **tablespoon margarine or butter, softened**
- ½ **teaspoon almond extract**
- 2 **to 3 tablespoons milk or cream**
- ¼ **cup sliced almonds or chopped nuts**

Place 1 cup flour in small bowl. Using pastry blender or fork, cut in ½ cup margarine until mixture is crumbly. Sprinkle with ice water 1 tablespoon at a time. Stir with fork just until soft dough forms. Form dough into ball. Divide dough in half. Form each half into 12-inch rope. On ungreased cookie sheet, flatten each rope into 12x3-inch strip.

Heat oven to 350°F. In medium saucepan, bring 1 cup water and ½ cup margarine to a boil. Remove from heat. Immediately stir in 1 cup flour until smooth. Add eggs 1 at a time, beating until smooth after each addition. Stir in ½ teaspoon almond extract. Spoon half of batter over each crust, spreading to within ¼ inch of edges. Bake at 350°F. for 50 to 60 minutes or until golden brown and puffy. Immediately remove from cookie sheet; cool. (Topping will shrink and fall.)

In small bowl, blend all frosting ingredients except almonds, adding enough milk for desired spreading consistency. Spread over cooled kringler. Sprinkle with almonds. Cut into slices to serve.

Yield: 16 to 20 servings.

HIGH ALTITUDE:
Above 3500 Feet: Bake at 375°F. for 50 to 60 minutes.

NUTRITION PER SERVING:
Calories 170; Protein 3g; Carbohydrate 15g; Fat 11g; Sodium 125mg.

CARAMEL STICKY BUNS

Nothing could be easier to make or more tempting to eat than these caramel rolls made with refrigerated biscuit dough.

TOPPING
- ¼ cup margarine or butter, melted
- ¼ cup firmly packed brown sugar
- 2 tablespoons light corn syrup
- ¼ cup chopped pecans

COATING
- 1 tablespoon sugar
- ½ teaspoon cinnamon

BUNS
- 1 (10-oz.) can refrigerated flaky biscuits

Heat oven to 375°F. Grease 12 muffin cups. In small bowl, combine all topping ingredients; mix well. Spoon scant tablespoon topping into each greased muffin cup.

In medium bowl, combine coating ingredients; mix well. Separate dough into 10 biscuits. Cut each biscuit into 6 pieces. Toss pieces in coating mixture. Place 5 coated pieces of dough in each greased muffin cup. Place pan on cookie sheet to guard against spills.

Bake at 375°F. for 15 to 20 minutes or until golden brown. Cool in pan 1 minute; invert onto waxed paper. Serve warm.
Yield: 12 rolls.

NUTRITION PER SERVING:
Calories 150; Protein 2g; Carbohydrate 19g; Fat 8g; Sodium 300mg.

DANISH ALMOND CREAM ROLLS

We've simplified the traditional layering process used to make Danish pastry by using refrigerated crescent rolls. You'll be delighted with the creamy almond filling.

ROLLS
- 2 (3-oz.) pkg. cream cheese, softened
- ½ to 1 teaspoon almond extract
- ½ cup powdered sugar
- ½ cup finely chopped almonds
- 2 (8-oz.) cans refrigerated crescent dinner rolls
- 1 egg white
- 1 teaspoon water
- ¼ cup sliced almonds

GLAZE
- ⅔ cup powdered sugar
- ¼ to ½ teaspoon almond extract
- 3 to 4 teaspoons milk

Heat oven to 350°F. In small bowl, beat cream cheese, ½ teaspoon almond extract and ½ cup powdered sugar until fluffy. Stir in ½ cup chopped almonds.

Separate 1 can of dough into 4 rectangles; firmly press perforations to seal. Press or roll each to form a 7x4-inch rectangle; spread each with about 2 tablespoons of the cream cheese filling to within ¼ inch of edges. Starting at longer side, roll up each rectangle, firmly pinching edges and ends to seal. Gently stretch each roll to 10 inches. Coil each roll into a spiral with the seam on the inside, tucking ends under. Place on ungreased cookie sheets. Repeat with remaining can of dough and cream cheese filling.

In small bowl, combine egg white and water; brush over rolls. Sprinkle with ¼ cup sliced almonds.

Bake at 350°F. for 17 to 23 minutes or until deep golden brown. In small bowl, blend all glaze ingredients, adding enough milk for desired drizzling consistency; drizzle over warm rolls. Serve warm.
Yield: 8 rolls.

NUTRITION PER SERVING:
Calories 410; Protein 8g; Carbohydrate 42g; Fat 24g; Sodium 540mg.

Caramel Sticky Buns

Quick Crescent Cinnamon Crisps

Here's a fast and easy version of the ever popular "elephant ears."

- 1 (8-oz.) can refrigerated crescent dinner rolls
- 2 tablespoons margarine or butter, melted
- ⅓ cup sugar
- 1 teaspoon cinnamon
- ¼ cup finely chopped pecans

Heat oven to 375°F. Unroll dough into 2 long rectangles; firmly press perforations to seal. Brush with margarine. In small bowl, combine sugar and cinnamon; blend well. Sprinkle half of mixture over dough; sprinkle with pecans. Starting at shorter side, roll up each rectangle. Cut each roll crosswise into 4 slices. On ungreased cookie sheet, pat or roll out each slice to a 4-inch circle; sprinkle each with remaining sugar-cinnamon mixture.

Bake at 375°F. for 10 to 15 minutes or until golden brown.
Yield: 8 rolls.

NUTRITION PER SERVING:
Calories 180; Protein 2g; Carbohydrate 20g; Fat 11g; Sodium 260mg.

Cook's Note

CINNAMON

Cinnamon comes from the bark of a tropical evergreen tree. When the bark is dried, it curls and is cut into lengths which are sold as cinnamon sticks. Ground cinnamon is used in baked recipes. Cinnamon sold in bulk at the supermarket or food co-op is less expensive than prepackaged forms.

Magic Marshmallow Crescent Puffs

In 1969, this recipe was the grand prize winner in the 20th Pillsbury BAKE-OFF® Contest. The cinnamon-sugar coated marshmallows melt during baking, forming tender crescent dough puffs with sweet centers.

PUFFS
- ¼ cup sugar
- 2 tablespoons all purpose flour
- 1 teaspoon cinnamon
- 2 (8-oz.) cans refrigerated crescent dinner rolls
- 16 large marshmallows
- ¼ cup margarine or butter, melted

GLAZE
- ½ cup powdered sugar
- ½ teaspoon vanilla
- 2 to 3 teaspoons milk
- ¼ cup chopped nuts, if desired

Heat oven to 375°F. In small bowl, combine sugar, flour and cinnamon. Separate dough into 16 triangles. Dip 1 marshmallow in margarine; roll in sugar mixture. Place marshmallow on wide end of triangle. Roll up starting at wide end of triangle and rolling to opposite point. Completely cover marshmallow with dough; firmly pinch edges to seal. Dip 1 end in remaining margarine; place margarine side down in ungreased large muffin cup or 6-oz. custard cup. Repeat with remaining marshmallows.

Bake at 375°F. for 12 to 15 minutes or until golden brown. (Place foil or cookie sheet on rack below muffin cups to guard against spills.) Immediately remove from muffin cups; cool on wire racks.

In small bowl, blend powdered sugar, vanilla and enough milk for desired drizzling consistency. Drizzle over warm rolls. Sprinkle with nuts.
Yield: 16 rolls.

NUTRITION PER SERVING:
Calories 190; Protein 2g; Carbohydrate 24g; Fat 10g; Sodium 270mg.

Maple Cream Coffee Treat

For breakfast, brunch or dessert, these cream-filled, caramel-topped finger rolls will surely bring rave reviews. Use your favorite nuts or those you might have on hand, such as pecans, almonds or walnuts.

1   cup firmly packed brown sugar
½   cup chopped nuts
⅓   cup maple-flavored syrup or dark corn syrup
¼   cup margarine or butter, melted
1   (8-oz.) pkg. cream cheese, softened
¼   cup powdered sugar
2   tablespoons margarine or butter, softened
½   cup coconut
2   (10-oz.) cans refrigerated flaky biscuits

Heat oven to 350°F. In ungreased 13x9-inch pan, combine brown sugar, nuts, syrup and ¼ cup margarine; spread evenly in bottom of pan.

In small bowl, blend cream cheese, powdered sugar and 2 tablespoons margarine until smooth; stir in coconut.

Separate dough into 20 biscuits. Press or roll each to a 4-inch circle. Spread tablespoonfuls of cream cheese mixture down center of each circle to within ¼ inch of edge. Overlap sides of dough over filling, forming finger-shaped rolls. Arrange rolls, seam side down, in 2 rows of 10 rolls each over brown sugar mixture in pan.

Bake at 350°F. for 25 to 30 minutes or until deep golden brown. Cool 3 to 5 minutes; invert onto foil, waxed paper or serving platter.

Yield: 20 rolls.

NUTRITION PER SERVING:
Calories 250; Protein 3g; Carbohydrate 29g; Fat 14g; Sodium 370mg.

Peanut Butter and Jelly Biscuit Treats

Enjoy these tempting rolls warm from the oven.

ROLLS
1   (10-oz.) can refrigerated flaky biscuits
10   tablespoons peanut butter
8   to 10 tablespoons strawberry preserves

GLAZE
¼   cup powdered sugar
1   to 2 teaspoons milk

Heat oven to 375°F. Separate dough into 10 biscuits; separate each biscuit into 2 layers. Spoon 1 tablespoon peanut butter on center of half of biscuit pieces. Top with remaining biscuit pieces; pinch edges to seal. Place biscuits in ungreased 9-inch round cake pan or 8-inch square pan. With thumb, make imprint in center of each roll; fill each with about 1 tablespoon preserves.

Bake at 375°F. for 23 to 28 minutes or until golden brown. In small bowl, blend powdered sugar and enough milk for desired glaze consistency. Drizzle over warm rolls.

Yield: 10 rolls.

NUTRITION PER SERVING:
Calories 250; Protein 6g; Carbohydrate 31g; Fat 12g; Sodium 370mg.

CORN BREAD

You'll enjoy this version of the all-American quick bread.

- 1 **cup all purpose flour**
- 1 **cup cornmeal**
- 2 **tablespoons sugar**
- 3 **teaspoons baking powder**
- ½ **teaspoon salt**
- 1 **cup milk**
- ¼ **cup oil or melted shortening**
- 1 **egg, slightly beaten**

Heat oven to 425°F. Grease 8 or 9-inch square pan. In medium bowl, combine flour, cornmeal, sugar, baking powder and salt; mix well. Stir in remaining ingredients just until smooth. Pour batter into greased pan. Bake at 425°F. for 18 to 22 minutes or until toothpick inserted in center comes out clean. **Yield: 9 servings.**

HIGH ALTITUDE:
Above 3500 Feet: Decrease baking powder to 2 teaspoons. Bake as directed above.

NUTRITION PER SERVING:
Calories 190; Protein 4g; Carbohydrate 25g; Fat 8g; Sodium 240mg.

VARIATIONS:

BACON CORN BREAD: Cook 4 to 5 slices bacon until crisp; drain on paper towel. Substitute bacon drippings for oil. Sprinkle batter with crumbled bacon before baking.

CORN BREAD RING: Bake in greased 1½-quart (6-cup) ring mold for 15 to 20 minutes. Immediately remove from mold.

CORN MUFFINS: Spoon batter into greased muffin cups and bake 15 to 20 minutes. Immediately remove from muffin cups.
Yield: 12 muffins.

CORN STICKS: Bake in well-greased, hot corn stick pans, filling ⅔ full. Bake 12 to 15 minutes. Immediately remove from pan.
Yield: 18 corn sticks.

MEXICAN CORN BREAD: Prepare batter using 2 eggs, slightly beaten. Stir in 2 oz. (½ cup) shredded Cheddar cheese, ¼ cup chopped green chiles and ¼ cup finely chopped onion. Bake 20 to 25 minutes.

PERFECT POPOVERS

Popovers are a big, puffy, steam-raised quick bread made from an egg-rich batter. They are delicious served plain, with butter and jam, or filled with your favorite sandwich mixture.

- 3 **eggs, room temperature**
- 1¼ **cups milk, room temperature**
- 1¼ **cups all purpose flour**
- ¼ **teaspoon salt**

Heat oven to 450°F. Generously grease 10 popover cups or 6-oz. custard cups.* In small bowl, beat eggs with rotary beater until lemon-colored and foamy. Add milk; blend well. Add flour and salt; beat with rotary beater just until batter is smooth and foamy on top. Pour batter into greased cups, filling about ⅔ full.

Bake at 450°F. for 15 minutes. (DO NOT OPEN OVEN.) Reduce heat to 350°F.; bake an additional 25 to 35 minutes or until popovers are high, hollow and deep golden brown. Remove from oven; insert sharp knife into each popover to allow steam to escape. Remove from pan. Serve warm.
Yield: 10 popovers.

TIP:
* Standard muffin pans can be used. Fill alternating greased cups with batter to prevent sides of popovers from touching.

HIGH ALTITUDE:
Above 3500 Feet: Increase flour to 1¼ cups plus 2 tablespoons. Bake at 450°F. for 15 minutes. Reduce heat to 350°F.; bake an additional 20 to 30 minutes.

NUTRITION PER SERVING:
Calories 90; Protein 4g; Carbohydrate 14g; Fat 2g; Sodium 90mg.

VARIATION:

DILL PARMESAN POPOVERS: Add 2 tablespoons grated Parmesan cheese and 1 teaspoon dried dill weed with flour.

SPOONBREAD

Baked in a casserole and served with a spoon, spoonbread is usually served in place of bread, potatoes or rice.

- 2 cups water
- 1 cup white cornmeal
- 1 teaspoon seasoned salt
- 1 cup buttermilk
- 2 tablespoons margarine or butter, melted
- 2 teaspoons baking powder
- 3 eggs, separated
  Margarine or butter, if desired

Heat oven to 375°F. Grease 2-quart casserole. In medium saucepan, bring water to a boil. Slowly stir in cornmeal and salt. Reduce heat to medium; cook about 5 minutes or until very thick, stirring constantly. Remove from heat; stir in buttermilk. Cool 5 minutes. Gradually beat in 2 tablespoons margarine, baking powder and egg yolks. In small bowl, beat egg whites until stiff but not dry. Fold into cornmeal mixture. Pour batter into greased casserole.

Bake at 375°F. for 40 to 50 minutes or until golden brown and knife inserted near center comes out clean. Serve immediately with margarine.

Yield: 8 (½-cup) servings.

NUTRITION PER SERVING:
Calories 120; Protein 5g; Carbohydrate 14g; Fat 6g; Sodium 370mg.

COOK'S NOTE

HOW TO TEST BAKING POWDER FOR FRESHNESS

The shelf life of baking powder is short, about 6 to 8 months. Check the bottom of the can for it's expiration date. If none is available, determine if yours is active by pouring ⅓ cup hot tap water over 1 teaspoon of baking powder. Watch for active bubbling. If few bubbles result, the baking powder will not leaven your baked product.

PATIO SKILLET BREAD

Try this southern-style version of corn bread baked in a skillet. You'll enjoy the combination of vegetable and herb flavors.

- 1½ cups all purpose flour
- 1½ cups yellow cornmeal
- 2 tablespoons sugar
- 4 teaspoons baking powder
- 2½ teaspoons salt
- ¼ to ½ teaspoon dried sage leaves
- ¼ teaspoon dried thyme leaves
- 1 cup finely chopped celery
- 1 cup finely chopped onions
- 1 (2-oz.) jar chopped pimiento, drained
- 1½ cups milk
- ⅓ cup margarine or butter, melted
- 3 eggs, slightly beaten

Heat oven to 400°F. Line 10-inch ovenproof skillet or 9-inch square pan with foil; grease foil. In large bowl, combine flour, cornmeal, sugar, baking powder, salt, sage, thyme, celery, onions and pimiento; blend well. Add milk, margarine and eggs; stir just until dry ingredients are moistened. Pour into foil-lined skillet. Bake at 400°F. for 30 to 35 minutes or until deep golden brown. Serve immediately. Store in refrigerator.

Yield: 12 servings.

HIGH ALTITUDE:
Above 3500 Feet: No change.

NUTRITION PER SERVING:
Calories 210; Protein 6g; Carbohydrate 29g; Fat 8g; Sodium 640mg.

Norwegian Flat Bread

Serve this thin and crisp cracker-like bread from Norway with butter or cheese. Bite-sized pieces are excellent with your favorite dip.

- 1 **cup buttermilk**
- 2 **tablespoons sugar**
- ½ **teaspoon baking soda**
- 2 **tablespoons margarine or butter, melted**
- 1¾ **to 2 cups whole wheat flour**

Heat oven to 375°F. In large bowl, combine buttermilk, sugar, baking soda and margarine; mix well. Stir in enough flour until dough pulls cleanly away from sides of bowl. (Dough will be soft.) On lightly floured surface, form dough into an 8-inch long roll; cut into 8 pieces. Roll each piece to ⅛-inch thickness.* Place on ungreased cookie sheets.

Bake at 375°F. for 5 to 10 minutes or until light brown. (Watch carefully; bread browns quickly.) Immediately remove from cookie sheets; cool on wire rack. If desired, break into pieces. Store in tightly covered container.
Yield: 8 flat breads.

TIP:
* If crisper flat bread is desired, dough can be rolled thinner. Additional whole wheat flour may need to be added if dough is to be rolled very thin.

HIGH ALTITUDE:
Above 3500 Feet: No change.

NUTRITION PER SERVING:
Calories 150; Protein 5g; Carbohydrate 26g; Fat 3g; Sodium 145mg.

Irish Soda Bread

This traditional Irish loaf has a coarse texture and is flavored with raisins and caraway.

- 2¼ **cups all purpose flour**
- 2 **tablespoons sugar**
- 1 **teaspoon baking powder**
- 1 **teaspoon baking soda**
- ½ **teaspoon salt**
- ¼ **cup margarine or butter**
- ½ **cup raisins**
- 2 **teaspoons caraway seed, if desired**
- 1 **cup buttermilk**
- 1 **tablespoon margarine or butter, melted**

Heat oven to 375°F. Grease 8-inch round cake pan. In large bowl, combine flour, sugar, baking powder, baking soda and salt; blend well. Using pastry blender or fork, cut in ¼ cup margarine until mixture is crumbly. Stir in raisins and caraway seed. Add milk all at once; blend well. On well floured surface, knead dough 5 or 6 times or until no longer sticky. Press dough in greased pan. With sharp knife, cut an "X" ¼ inch deep on top of loaf. Brush with melted margarine.

Bake at 375°F. for 25 to 35 minutes or until golden brown. Immediately remove from pan; cool on wire rack. Serve warm.
Yield: 1 (16-slice) loaf.

HIGH ALTITUDE:
Above 3500 Feet: No change.

NUTRITION PER SERVING:
Calories 120; Protein 2g; Carbohydrate 19g; Fat 4g; Sodium 220mg.

Quick Mix

With this versatile quick bread mix, you can quickly bake biscuits, muffins, coffee cake or banana bread. See recipes that follow.

- 9 **cups all purpose flour**
- 4½ **tablespoons baking powder**
- 4½ **teaspoons salt**
- 1½ **cups shortening**

In large bowl, combine flour, baking powder and salt; mix well. Using pastry blender or fork, cut in shortening until mixture resembles coarse crumbs. Mix can be stored in tightly covered container in refrigerator for up to 4 weeks. To use, stir; dip measuring cup into mix and level off.
Yield: About 10 cups mix.

TIP:
Mix can be measured out ahead of time into 5 equal portions (2 cups each) to save time later and to be assured that each portion is the same measurement.

HIGH ALTITUDE:
Above 3500 Feet: No change.

QUICK MIX BISCUITS

~

Enjoy these warm biscuits with butter and honey.

- **2 cups Quick Mix p. 410**
- **½ cup milk**

Heat oven to 450°F. Dip measuring cup into mix; level off. Place Quick Mix in medium bowl. Add milk; stir with fork just until soft dough forms. Turn dough out onto lightly floured surface; gently knead dough about 10 times or until no longer sticky. Roll or press out to ½-inch thickness; cut with floured 2-inch round cutter. Place on ungreased cookie sheet.

Bake at 450°F. for 10 to 12 minutes or until golden brown. Serve immediately.
Yield: 12 to 15 biscuits.

NUTRITION PER SERVING:
Calories 90; Protein 2g; Carbohydrate 12g; Fat 4g; Sodium 150mg.

QUICK MIX COFFEE CAKE

~

Sugar, cinnamon and nuts top this coffee cake.

TOPPING
- **2 tablespoons sugar**
- **¼ teaspoon cinnamon**
- **¼ cup chopped nuts**

COFFEE CAKE
- **2 cups Quick Mix p. 410**
- **½ cup sugar**
- **⅔ cup milk**
- **2 tablespoons margarine or butter, melted**
- **1 egg, beaten**
- **¼ cup raisins**

Heat oven to 375°F. Grease bottom only of 8-inch square pan. In small bowl, combine topping ingredients; set aside.

Dip measuring cup into mix; level off. In large bowl, combine Quick Mix, ½ cup sugar, milk, margarine and egg; mix well. Stir in raisins. Spread in greased pan; sprinkle with topping.

Bake at 375°F. for 25 to 30 minutes or until toothpick inserted in center comes out clean. Serve warm.
Yield: 9 servings.

NUTRITION PER SERVING:
Calories 280; Protein 5g; Carbohydrate 38g; Fat 12g; Sodium 290mg.

QUICK MIX MUFFINS

~

These muffins go together quickly.

- **2 cups Quick Mix p. 410**
- **2 tablespoons sugar**
- **¾ cup milk**
- **1 egg, beaten**

Heat oven to 400°F. Line with paper baking cups or grease bottoms only of 12 muffin cups. Dip measuring cup into mix; level off. In medium bowl, combine Quick Mix and sugar; mix well. Add milk and egg, stirring just until dry ingredients are moistened. Fill paper-lined muffin cups ⅔ full.

Bake at 400°F. for 20 to 25 minutes or until toothpick inserted in center comes out clean. Serve warm.
Yield: 12 muffins.

NUTRITION PER SERVING:
Calories 130; Protein 3g; Carbohydrate 17g; Fat 6g; Sodium 200mg.

QUICK MIX BANANA BREAD

~

Very ripe bananas work well in quick bread loaves.

- **¾ cup sugar**
- **¼ cup oil**
- **2 eggs**
- **1 cup (2 medium) mashed ripe bananas**
- **2 cups Quick Mix p. 410**
- **½ cup chopped nuts**

Heat oven to 350°F. Grease 9x5-inch loaf pan. In large bowl, combine sugar, oil and eggs; stir in bananas. Dip measuring cup into mix; level off. Add Quick Mix and nuts; stir just until dry ingredients are moistened, about 15 strokes. Pour into greased pan.

Bake at 350°F. for 45 to 55 minutes or until toothpick inserted in center comes out clean. Cool 5 minutes; remove from pan. Cool completely. Wrap tightly and store in refrigerator.
Yield: 1 (16-slice) loaf.

NUTRITION PER SERVING:
Calories 200; Protein 3g; Carbohydrate 24g; Fat 10g; Sodium 150mg.

RASPBERRY NECTARINE PANCAKE PUFF

Serve this warm from the oven, before the pancake loses it's "puff."

PANCAKE
- ½ **cup all purpose flour**
- 1 **tablespoon sugar**
- ¼ **teaspoon salt**
- ½ **cup milk**
- 3 **eggs**
- 2 **tablespoons margarine or butter**

SAUCE
- 1 **(10-oz.) pkg. frozen raspberries in light syrup, thawed**
- ⅓ **cup red currant jelly**
- 1 **tablespoon cornstarch**

FRUIT
- 1½ **cups sliced nectarines or peaches**

Heat oven to 425°F. In medium bowl, combine all pancake ingredients except margarine. Beat with rotary beater until smooth. Place margarine in 10-inch ovenproof, nonstick skillet. Melt in 425°F. oven just until margarine sizzles, about 2 to 3 minutes. Remove skillet from oven; tilt to coat bottom with melted margarine. Immediately pour batter into hot skillet.

Bake at 425°F. for 14 to 18 minutes or until puffed and golden brown.

Meanwhile, drain raspberries; reserve syrup. Set raspberries aside. Add water to syrup to make ¾ cup. In small saucepan, combine syrup, jelly and cornstarch; stir to dissolve cornstarch. Cook and stir over medium heat until thickened and clear. Stir in raspberries. Arrange nectarine slices over pancake; drizzle with some of the raspberry sauce. Cut into wedges. Serve with additional raspberry sauce.

Yield: 4 servings.

HIGH ALTITUDE:
Above 3500 Feet: No change.

NUTRITION PER SERVING:
Calories 350; Protein 9g; Carbohydrate 54g; Fat 11g; Sodium 280mg.

Raspberry Nectarine Pancake Puff

PUFFED FRUIT-TOPPED PANCAKE

This popover-like pancake boasts a delectable fruit topping.

PANCAKE
- ¾ **cup all purpose flour**
- ¼ **cup whole wheat flour**
- ½ **teaspoon grated orange peel**
- ¼ **teaspoon nutmeg**
- ⅛ **teaspoon allspice**
  Dash salt
- 1 **cup milk**
- 3 **eggs**

TOPPING
- 2 **tablespoons margarine or butter**
- 1 **(16-oz.) can sliced pears in lite syrup, drained, reserving ½ cup liquid**
- 1 **(6-oz.) pkg. (1 cup) dried apricots**
- ¼ **cup firmly packed brown sugar**

Heat oven to 450°F. Grease bottom only of 13x9-inch pan. In medium bowl, combine all pancake ingredients. Beat with rotary beater until smooth. Pour into greased pan.

Bake at 450°F. for 15 minutes. (DO NOT OPEN OVEN.) Reduce heat to 350°F.; bake an additional 14 to 17 minutes or until dark golden brown.

Meanwhile, melt margarine in medium skillet over medium heat. Add pear slices, apricots, brown sugar and reserved ½ cup pear liquid. Bring to a boil. Reduce heat to low; simmer 5 to 10 minutes or until apricots are tender, stirring occasionally. Serve pancake immediately with warm fruit topping.

Yield: 6 servings.

TIP:
To microwave topping, place margarine in 1-quart microwave-safe casserole. Microwave on HIGH for 30 to 60 seconds or until melted. Stir in apricots, brown sugar and reserved ½ cup pear liquid; cover tightly. Microwave on HIGH for 4 to 6 minutes or until apricots are tender, stirring once halfway through cooking. Add pear slices; cover tightly. Microwave on HIGH for 1 to 2 minutes or until hot.

HIGH ALTITUDE:
Above 3500 Feet: No change.

NUTRITION PER SERVING:
Calories 330; Protein 8g; Carbohydrate 56g; Fat 8g; Sodium 130mg.

PUFFY SURPRISE OVEN PANCAKES

Serve these tender oven pancakes with your favorite fresh fruit.

   2 eggs
   ½ cup all purpose flour
   ½ cup milk
   2 tablespoons margarine or butter
   4 cups sliced fruit*
   ½ cup firmly packed brown sugar
   1 (8-oz.) container dairy sour cream

Heat oven to 425°F. In medium bowl, beat eggs slightly. Add flour and milk; beat with rotary beater until combined. In oven, melt 1 tablespoon margarine in each of two 9-inch glass pie plates; spread to cover bottom. Pour batter over margarine in pie plates.

Bake at 425°F. for 10 to 15 minutes or until golden brown. (Pancakes will form a well in the center and edges will puff up.) Spoon fruit into center of pancakes. Sprinkle with brown sugar and top with sour cream. Serve immediately.

Yield: 4 servings.

TIP:
* Any of the following fruits can be used: strawberries, bananas, pineapple, raspberries, peaches and blueberries.

HIGH ALTITUDE:
Above 3500 Feet: No change.

NUTRITION PER SERVING:
Calories 490; Protein 9g; Carbohydrate 65g; Fat 22g; Sodium 155mg.

ORANGE OVEN FRENCH TOAST

This recipe is great for large groups and can be easily made ahead. Plan to serve it for your next brunch.

   ½ cup margarine or butter, melted
   ¼ cup honey
   2 teaspoons cinnamon
   6 eggs
   1 cup milk
   1 cup orange juice
   ¼ cup sugar
   2 teaspoons grated orange peel
   ½ teaspoon salt
   ½ teaspoon cinnamon
  16 slices whole wheat or white bread
   2 oranges, sliced

Heat oven to 400°F. In small bowl, combine margarine, honey and 2 teaspoons cinnamon; mix well. Pour mixture evenly into 2 ungreased 15x10x1-inch baking pans. In medium bowl, slightly beat eggs. Add milk, orange juice, sugar, orange peel, salt and ½ teaspoon cinnamon; mix well. Dip bread in egg mixture. Place on margarine mixture in pans. Pour any remaining egg mixture over bread.*

Bake at 400°F. for 10 minutes; turn slices over. Bake an additional 10 minutes or until golden brown. Arrange on serving platter with orange slices.

Yield: 16 slices.

TIP:
* At this point, bread can be covered and refrigerated overnight. Uncover; bake as directed above.

NUTRITION PER SERVING:
Calories 200; Protein 6g; Carbohydrate 24g; Fat 9g; Sodium 300mg.

Crunchy Oven French Toast

CRUNCHY OVEN FRENCH TOAST

~

Minimum last-minute preparation makes this a perfect recipe for company. Make it ahead of time and freeze it for up to 2 weeks.

    3 eggs
    1 cup half-and-half
    2 tablespoons sugar
    1 teaspoon vanilla
  ¼ teaspoon salt
    3 cups cornflakes cereal, crushed to 1 cup
    8 diagonally-cut slices French bread
        (¾ inch thick)
       Strawberry syrup
       Fresh strawberries

Grease 15x10x1-inch baking pan. In shallow bowl, combine eggs, half-and-half, sugar, vanilla and salt; mix well. Place crushed cereal in shallow bowl. Dip bread in egg mixture, making sure all egg mixture is absorbed. Dip bread into crumbs. Place in single layer in greased pan; cover. Freeze 1 to 2 hours or until firm.

Heat oven to 425°F. Bake 15 to 20 minutes or until golden brown, turning once. Serve with syrup and strawberries. Garnish with whipped topping, if desired.

Yield: 8 slices.

NUTRITION PER SERVING:
Calories 200; Protein 6g; Carbohydrate 30g; Fat 6g; Sodium 340mg.

YEAST BREADS

Baking yeast bread is one of those basic skills that people
have mastered throughout the centuries and throughout the world.
Whether you're baking a hearty loaf or a good-morning pan of sweet rolls,
the techniques are simple and easy to learn. Fine-tuning your
yeast bread-baking skills may take a little longer,
but practicing is half the fun!

KINDS OF YEAST BREADS

*These breads all have something in common —
the leavening agent is yeast. Yeast is a
microorganism that is activated with "food"
(sugar and flour), "water" (liquid ingredients)
and warmth. As the yeast grows and multiplies,
it creates gas bubbles that cause bread dough
to rise. Yeast breads can be divided into
2 main categories:*

BATTER

Batter breads could be called short-cut
breads because they don't require kneading.
The dough contains less flour and is stickier.
Instead of kneading, the dough is beaten with
an electric mixer after the first addition of flour,
placed in the pan rather than shaped, and rises
only once, not twice. Batter breads have a
coarse texture and pebbly surface. (Recipe
examples include: **Cornmeal Sesame Batter
Rolls** p. 456 and **English Muffin Batter Bread**
p. 442.)

KNEADED

Kneading dough distributes ingredients
evenly and develops the gluten in flour, which
provides strength, elasticity and structure to the
bread. Kneading gives bread an even texture
and a smooth rounded top. Kneading can be
done by hand, by using a heavy-duty mixer
with bread hooks or with a heavy-duty food
processor. Kneaded breads are usually shaped
and usually require 2 risings. (Recipe examples
include: **Quick Sourdough French Bread**
p. 429, **Sweet Potato Rolls** p. 455 and **Herb
Cheese Pretzels** p. 467.)

SECRETS FOR BAKING
WITH YEAST

*There's a lot of mystique surrounding yeast
because how it is handled will affect the results of
baked goods. Here are some tips that will help
take the mystery out of baking with yeast:*

Check the expiration date on the package.
Outdated yeast won't become active and the
bread won't rise.

**To substitute 1 form of yeast for another form
of yeast, use these equivalents:** One envelope
of active dry yeast equals 2¼ teaspoons of bulk
active dry yeast or ⅓ of a 2-ounce cake of
compressed fresh yeast.

**To substitute fast-acting yeast for regular
yeast, reduce the rise time in the recipe by
about half.**

Test the yeast before beginning. If you're
concerned that your yeast may not be active,
dissolve 1 teaspoon of sugar in ½ cup of warm
water (110 to 115°F.). Slowly sprinkle 1 packet
of yeast into the water. Stir the mixture and set
a timer for 10 minutes. In 3 to 4 minutes, the

yeast should have absorbed enough liquid to activate and will come to the surface.

If at the end of 10 minutes, the yeast has multiplied to the 1-cup mark and has a rounded crown, it's still very active and fresh and can be used in your recipe. Remember to deduct the ½ cup of water used for the test from the total liquid used in the recipe. If the yeast has not multiplied, it will not provide satisfactory results in the recipe. This process is sometimes referred to as "proofing the yeast."

Use a yeast or candy thermometer to accurately determine the temperature of liquids. If the liquid in which the dry yeast is dissolved is too hot, it will kill the yeast cells. If it's too cold, they won't be activated. Use very warm liquid (120 to 130°F.) if the active dry yeast will be added to dry ingredients. If it's to be added to liquid ingredients, use warm liquid (110 to 115°F).

Place dough in a warm spot to rise. Yeast doughs rise or "proof" best when the temperature is 80 to 85°F. To make sure the dough is warm enough:

- Cover the bowl loosely with plastic wrap and/or a cloth towel.

- Place the bowl on a wire rack over a pan of hot water in a draft-free spot.

- OR place the bowl on the top rack of an unheated oven. Put a pan of hot water on the rack below it.

- OR turn the oven on at 400°F. for 1 minute, then turn it off. Place the bowl on the center rack of the oven and close the door.

Test the dough to make sure that it has risen sufficiently. When you think the dough has doubled in size, lightly poke 2 fingers about ½ inch into the dough. If the indentations remain, the dough has risen enough.

SECRETS FOR SUCCESSFUL YEAST BREADS

Although the techniques for making yeast breads are simple, a few "secrets" will ensure that even your first efforts will be attractive and great-tasting.

SECERETS FOR ALL YEAST BREADS
What to do if . . .

- **You forget to add the yeast.** Dissolve it in a small amount of warm liquid and work it into the dough.

- **The dough doesn't rise.** The yeast may have been old, or the liquid may have been too hot or too cold, or you may have added too much salt. Try placing the dough in a warmer spot or waiting longer to give it more time to rise.

- **The dough rises too quickly.** Punch down the dough and let it rise again. If it rises before you're ready to bake it, move the dough to a cooler spot to slow down the action of the yeast.

Use aluminum pans. They give breads and rolls well-browned crusts. Uncoated aluminum pans give the most even browning and uniform results. Dark metal pans and glass pans absorb more heat and will produce a darker crust.

Grease the pan(s) as directed in the recipe.

To make dough a day ahead, cover and refrigerate it up to 24 hours, if desired. The dough is ready to bake when it has doubled in size. If it has not doubled in size in the refrigerator, let it stand at room temperature for 30 to 45 minutes or until it has doubled.

Create a variety of crusts:

- For a crisp crust, gently brush the bread dough with water before baking it.

- For a hard crust, place a pan of water in the bottom of the oven.

- For a shiny crust, beat 1 egg with 1 tablespoon of water and brush it gently on the bread before baking. Sprinkle the bread with sesame or poppy seeds, if desired.

- For a soft, tender crust, gently brush the bread with milk just before baking, or with melted butter just after baking.

Remove the bread from the pan immediately after baking it. Cool the bread on a wire rack to prevent the crust from becoming soggy.

Cool breads away from drafts. This will help prevent the bread from shrinking and the crust from cracking.

Cool breads before slicing them. Slicing a too-warm loaf or coffee cake will cause crumbling and tearing.

Cut breads with a sharp knife or electric knife. Use a back-and-forth sawing motion rather than pressing straight down.

SECRETS FOR BATTER BREADS

Use the same pan for rising and baking. Most batter breads require only 1 rising, so let them rise and bake in the same pan.

Watch for small, unbroken bubbles during rising. Their appearance is an indication that the bread has risen sufficiently. (If large air pockets appear under the baked crust, it is an indication that the dough rose too quickly. Next time proof in a cooler place.)

SECRETS FOR KNEADED BREADS

Practice makes perfect. The more you knead bread, the better technique you'll develop. If a dough is not kneaded enough, the bread will be dry, heavy and have a crumbly texture. Using a dough hook on a standard mixer will result in bread with a slightly lower volume, while a heavy-duty mixer will create loaves with higher volume. Avoid over-kneading the dough. Dough that is kneaded too long (more than 10 minutes) can become dry and coarse because too much flour may be added.

Add flour gradually during kneading. As you knead the dough, add just enough flour so that the dough is no longer sticky. In the recipes, a range is given for the amount of flour because flour can gain or lose moisture depending on weather conditions and how it is stored. Too much flour added during kneading may produce streaks and uneven grain.

Prepare pans while the dough rests. Grease them or leave them ungreased according to the recipe directions.

Shape loaves and rolls to fit the pan. The shaped dough should be large enough so that it will touch the sides of the pan as the dough rises. The pan helps provide support for the dough.

Cover loaves with foil during baking if they become too brown before they're done.

HOW TO TELL WHEN YEAST BREADS ARE DONE

Sound plays a key role in determining if yeast breads are done, so listen carefully!

Yeast breads are done when . . .

- They are golden brown.

- They pull away from the sides of the pan.

- Tapping on the top crust of a loaf produces a hollow sound.

Keeping Yeast Breads Fresh and Flavorful

Breads can become moldy or stale soon after baking. Proper storage is essential in preserving their freshness and flavor.

Cool breads completely before storing.

Store bread in an airtight container in a cool, dry place. Or, wrap it in foil or plastic wrap. Bread should be stored at room temperature no longer than 5 days.

Refrigerate bread to slow the growth of mold. Refrigeration is necessary, especially for moist breads or during hot, humid weather. However, refrigeration won't preserve freshness and can cause bread to dry out. To store bread for a longer period of time, freeze it.

To freeze bread, see the chart on p. 25.

To freeze rolls:

- Bake and cool completely.

- Place the rolls on foil-wrapped cardboard and seal in a large plastic freezer bag. Label and date the bag.

- Freeze for up to 1 month.

Use stale bread for croutons or crumbs.

Using Bread Flour

Bread flour is made from the finest hard spring wheat available, and contains more protein strength than all purpose flour. Its higher protein content gives the dough more structure and allows it to have more elasticity, resulting in loaves with better texture and higher volume.

Bread flour performs well in all yeast bread baking.

Bread flour can be directly substituted in any traditional bread recipe calling for all purpose flour. When substituting bread flour for all purpose flour, knead the dough for 10 to 15 minutes, let it rest 15 minutes before shaping, and allow for a slightly longer rise time.

Store bread flour in an airtight container in a cool, dry place. Bread flour should be used within 18 to 24 months of purchase.

Baking with a Bread Machine

Bread machines that mix, knead and bake bread have become popular appliances. Here are a few tips for making the most of your bread machine:

- **Read and follow manufacturer's directions.**

- **Use only recipes specifically developed for your bread machine.**

- **Always use bread flour.**

- **For a whole grain loaf, whole grain flour can be substituted for up to half of the bread flour.** The volume of a whole grain loaf will be less than a regular loaf.

- **Measure ingredients accurately.** This should be done with all baked recipes, but it is especially important when using these appliances.

- **Bring ingredients to room temperature before placing them in the machine.** However, don't use perishable ingredients such as yogurt, eggs or milk if you're using the delayed-time bake cycle. The ingredients can spoil before baking begins.

NUTRITION IN THIS CHAPTER

Nutrition per serving means the calculation was done on 1 slice, 1 serving, 1 roll, 1 bread stick or 1 pretzel.

STEP-BY-STEP FEATURE ～
How to Make Yeast Bread

STEP 1. To knead dough, push dough down and away with heels of hands. Give dough a quarter turn. Repeat until dough is smooth and elastic.

STEP 2. Let dough rise until doubled in size. To test for doubled size, poke 2 fingers into dough. It is doubled when indentations remain.

STEP 3. Roll dough to 14x7-inch rectangle. Starting with 7-inch side, roll up. Pinch edges and ends to seal. Place, seam side down, in pan.

DELICIOUS WHITE BREAD

Use this basic recipe with its many variations to bake your family favorites.

> 5 **to 6 cups all purpose flour**
> 3 **tablespoons sugar**
> 2 **teaspoons salt**
> 2 **pkg. active dry yeast**
> 2 **cups water**
> ¼ **cup oil or shortening**
> 1 **tablespoon margarine or butter, melted**

In large bowl, combine 2 cups flour, sugar, salt and yeast; blend well. In small saucepan, heat water and oil until very warm (120 to 130°F.). Add warm liquid to flour mixture. Blend at low speed until moistened; beat 3 minutes at medium speed. By hand, stir in an additional 2½ to 3 cups flour until dough pulls cleanly away from sides of bowl.

On floured surface, knead in ½ to 1 cup flour until dough is smooth and elastic, about 5 minutes. Place dough in greased bowl; cover loosely with plastic wrap and cloth towel. Let rise in warm place (80 to 85°F.) until light and doubled in size, 45 to 60 minutes.

Grease two 8x4 or two 9x5-inch loaf pans. Punch down dough several times to remove all air bubbles. Divide dough into 2 parts; shape into loaves. Place in greased pans. Cover; let rise in warm place until dough fills pans and tops of loaves are about 1 inch above pan edges, 30 to 35 minutes.

Heat oven to 375°F. Uncover dough. Bake 40 to 50 minutes or until loaves sound hollow when lightly tapped. Immediately remove from pans; cool on wire racks. Brush with melted margarine.
Yield: 2 (18-slice) loaves.

HIGH ALTITUDE:
Above 3500 Feet: No change.

NUTRITION PER SERVING:
Calories 100; Protein 2g; Carbohydrate 17g; Fat 2g; Sodium 125mg.

(Recipe continued on next page.)

Delicious White Bread

(Recipe continued from previous page.)

VARIATIONS:

BREAD STICKS: After first rise time, punch down dough. Divide dough in half. Cut each half into 32 pieces; shape each into 8-inch long breadstick. Place on greased cookie sheets. Brush with beaten egg white; sprinkle with sesame seed. Cover; let rise in warm place about 30 minutes or until doubled in size. Bake at 400°F. for about 14 minutes. **Yield: 64 bread sticks.**

BUTTER-TOPPED MINI-LOAVES: Prepare dough as directed above. After allowing dough to rest, divide into 12 pieces. Shape each piece into a 7-inch oblong loaf; taper ends. Place loaves 3 inches apart on greased cookie sheets. Cover; let rise in warm place until doubled in size, about 45 minutes. Make ¼-inch deep slit down center of each loaf; drizzle with 1 teaspoon melted butter. Sprinkle with sesame seed or poppy seed, if desired. Bake at 375°F. for 20 to 25 minutes or until loaves sound hollow when lightly tapped. **Yield: 12 mini-loaves.**

CINNAMON SWIRL BREAD: Divide dough into 2 parts. Roll each to 14x7-inch rectangle of dough. Brush each with melted margarine or butter; sprinkle each with mixture of ¼ cup sugar and 1 teaspoon cinnamon. Starting with 7-inch side, roll up. Seal edges and place seam side down in greased loaf pans. Let rise and bake as directed above. **Yield: 2 (18-slice) loaves.**

HAMBURGER BUNS: After first rise time, punch down dough. Divide dough in half; shape each half into eight 2-inch balls. If desired, flatten slightly. Place on greased cookie sheets. Let rise in warm place about 30 minutes. Bake at 400°F. for about 15 minutes. **Yield: 16 buns.**

RAISIN BREAD: Add ½ teaspoon cinnamon with the salt and stir in 1 cup raisins after beating step. Shape and bake as directed above. **Yield: 2 (18-slice) loaves.**

WHOLE WHEAT BREAD

The nut-like flavor of whole wheat comes through in these flavorful loaves.

2	pkg. active dry yeast
¼	cup warm water
½	cup firmly packed brown sugar or honey
3	teaspoons salt
2½	cups hot water
¼	cup margarine or butter
4½	cups whole wheat flour
2¾	to 3¾ cups all purpose flour

In small bowl, dissolve yeast in warm water (105 to 115°F.). In large bowl, combine brown sugar, salt, hot water and margarine; cool slightly. To cooled mixture, add 3 cups whole wheat flour. Blend at low speed until moistened; beat 3 minutes at medium speed. Add remaining whole wheat flour and dissolved yeast; mix well. By hand, stir in an additional 2¼ to 2¾ cups all purpose flour until dough pulls cleanly away from sides of bowl.

On floured surface, knead in ½ to 1 cup all purpose flour until dough is smooth and elastic, about 10 to 15 minutes. Place dough in greased bowl; cover loosely with plastic wrap and cloth towel. Let rise in warm place (80 to 85°F.) until light and doubled in size, about 30 to 45 minutes.

Generously grease two 8x4 or 9x5-inch loaf pans. Punch down dough several times to remove all air bubbles. Divide dough into 2 parts; shape into loaves. Place in greased pans. Cover; let rise in warm place until light and doubled in size, about 30 to 45 minutes.

Heat oven to 375°F. Uncover dough. Bake 30 minutes. Reduce oven temperature to 350°F.; bake an additional 10 to 15 minutes or until loaves sound hollow when lightly tapped. Immediately remove from pans; cool on wire racks. **Yield: 2 (16-slice) loaves.**

HIGH ALTITUDE:
Above 3500 Feet: No change.

NUTRITION PER SERVING:
Calories 140; Protein 4g; Carbohydrate 27g; Fat 2g; Sodium 220mg.

RYE BREAD

Dense and hearty, this classic bread makes wonderful sandwiches or provides a satisfying accompaniment to robust soups.

- 2 **pkg. active dry yeast**
- 1 **cup warm water**
- 1 **cup warm milk**
- ½ **cup molasses**
- ¼ **cup shortening, melted**
- 2 **teaspoons salt**
- 3 **to 3½ cups all purpose flour**
- 3 **cups medium rye flour**
- 1 **tablespoon water**
- 1 **egg yolk**

In small bowl, dissolve yeast in warm water (105 to 115°F.). In large bowl, combine warm milk (105 to 115°F.), molasses, shortening and salt; blend well. Add dissolved yeast. Add 2 cups all purpose flour. Blend at low speed until moistened. Beat 3 minutes at medium speed. By hand, stir in 3 cups rye flour and an additional ¾ to 1 cup all purpose flour until dough pulls cleanly away from sides of bowl.

On floured surface, knead in ¼ to ½ cup all purpose flour until dough is smooth and elastic, about 5 minutes. Place dough in greased bowl; cover loosely with plastic wrap and cloth towel. Let rise in warm place (80 to 85°F.) until light and doubled in size, about 45 to 60 minutes.

Grease 2 cookie sheets. Punch down dough several times to remove all air bubbles. Divide dough into 2 parts; shape into balls. Shape dough into two 12-inch oblong loaves; round ends. Place on greased cookie sheets. With sharp knife, make four ¼-inch deep diagonal slashes on top of each loaf. Cover; let rise in warm place until doubled in size, about 20 to 30 minutes.

Heat oven to 350°F. Uncover dough. Combine water and egg yolk; brush on loaves. Bake at 350°F. for 35 to 45 minutes or until loaves sound hollow when lightly tapped. Immediately remove from pans; cool on wire racks.
Yield: 2 (22-slice) loaves.

HIGH ALTITUDE:
Above 3500 Feet: Decrease first rise time by 15 to 30 minutes. Decrease second rise time by 10 minutes. Bake as directed above.

NUTRITION PER SERVING:
Calories 80; Protein 2g; Carbohydrate 17g; Fat 1g; Sodium 175mg.

BUTTERMILK BREAD

Serve this simply delicious bread with butter and jam.

- 5 **to 6 cups all purpose flour**
- ¼ **cup sugar**
- 2 **teaspoons salt**
- ½ **teaspoon baking soda**
- 2 **pkg. active dry yeast**
- 1½ **cups buttermilk**
- ½ **cup water**
- ½ **cup margarine or butter**
- 1 **tablespoon margarine or butter, melted**

In large bowl, combine 2 cups flour, sugar, salt, baking soda and yeast; blend well. In small saucepan, heat buttermilk, water and ½ cup margarine until very warm (120 to 130°F.). (Mixture will look curdled.) Add warm liquid to flour mixture. Blend at low speed until moistened; beat 3 minutes at medium speed. By hand, stir in an additional 2½ to 3 cups flour until dough pulls cleanly away from sides of bowl.

On floured surface, knead in ½ to 1 cup flour until dough is smooth and elastic, about 10 minutes. Place dough in greased bowl; cover loosely with plastic wrap and cloth towel. Let rise in warm place (80 to 85°F.) until light and doubled in size, 30 to 45 minutes.

Grease two 8x4 or 9x5-inch loaf pans. Punch down dough several times to remove all air bubbles. Divide dough into 4 parts; shape into balls. Shape into 4 rolls by rolling out each ball into a 10x7-inch rectangle. Starting with shorter side, roll up; pinch edges firmly to seal. Place 2 rolls side by side, seam side down, in each greased pan. Cover; let rise in warm place until dough fills pans and tops of loaves are about 1 inch above pan edges, 15 to 30 minutes.

Heat oven to 375°F. Uncover dough. Bake 30 to 40 minutes or until loaves sound hollow when lightly tapped. Immediately remove from pans; brush with 1 tablespoon melted margarine. Cool on wire racks.
Yield: 2 (14-slice) loaves.

HIGH ALTITUDE:
Above 3500 Feet: No change.

NUTRITION PER SERVING:
Calories 140; Protein 3g; Carbohydrate 22g; Fat 4g; Sodium 230mg.

VIENNA BREAD

Vienna bread traditionally is an oval yeast bread with a crisp, shiny crust. You will be pleased with this sesame seed-topped version.

1 pkg. active dry yeast
1 cup warm water
5½ to 6 cups all purpose flour
3 tablespoons sugar
1 cup milk
2 tablespoons oil
2 teaspoons salt
1 egg white, slightly beaten
   Sesame seed

In large bowl, dissolve yeast in warm water (105 to 115°F.). Stir in 2 cups flour and sugar. Cover; let rise in warm place (80 to 85°F.) for 1 hour.

In small saucepan, heat milk and oil until warm (105 to 115°F.). Add warm liquid to flour mixture. Stir in salt and an additional 2½ to 2¾ cups flour until dough pulls cleanly away from sides of bowl.

On floured surface, knead in 1 to 1¼ cups flour until dough is smooth and elastic, 8 to 10 minutes. Place dough in greased bowl; cover loosely with plastic wrap and cloth towel. Let rise in warm place until light and doubled in size, about 1 to 1¼ hours. Punch down dough. Cover; let rise a second time until light and doubled in size, about 50 to 60 minutes.

Generously grease large cookie sheet. Punch down dough several times to remove all air bubbles. Divide dough into 2 parts. Shape into two 14-inch oblong loaves. Place loaves on greased cookie sheet. With scissors, cut five 1-inch deep slits on tops of loaves. Cover; let rise in warm place until light and doubled in size, about 30 to 40 minutes.

Heat oven to 350°F. Uncover dough. Brush tops and sides of loaves with beaten egg white; sprinkle with sesame seed. Bake 40 to 50 minutes or until loaves sound hollow when lightly tapped. Immediately remove from cookie sheet; cool on wire racks.
Yield: 2 (18-slice) loaves.

HIGH ALTITUDE:
Above 3500 Feet: No change.

NUTRITION PER SERVING:
Calories 90; Protein 3g; Carbohydrate 17g; Fat 1g; Sodium 125mg.

FRENCH BREAD BRAIDS

French bread is a light, crusty yeast-raised bread made with water instead of milk. This braided version of the classic is a welcome addition to any meal.

4¾ to 5¾ cups all purpose flour
3 teaspoons salt
1 tablespoon sugar
2 pkg. active dry yeast
2 cups water
2 tablespoons shortening
1 tablespoon water
1 egg white

In large bowl, combine 3 cups flour, salt, sugar and yeast; blend well. In small saucepan, heat 2 cups water and shortening until very warm (120 to 130°F.). Add warm liquid to flour mixture. Blend at low speed until moistened; beat 3 minutes at medium speed. By hand, stir in an additional 1½ to 2¼ cups flour to form a stiff dough.

On floured surface, knead in ¼ to ½ cup flour until dough is smooth and elastic, about 8 minutes. Place dough in greased bowl; cover loosely with plastic wrap and cloth towel. Let rise in warm place (80 to 85°F.) until light and doubled in size, about 1 hour.

Grease large cookie sheet. Punch down dough several times to remove all air bubbles. Divide dough in half; divide each half into 3 equal parts. Roll each part into 14-inch rope. Braid 3 ropes together; seal ends. Place on greased cookie sheet. Repeat with other half of dough. In small bowl, combine 1 tablespoon water and egg white; beat slightly. Carefully brush over loaves. Cover loosely with greased plastic wrap and cloth towel; let rise in warm place until light and doubled in size, 20 to 30 minutes.

Heat oven to 375°F. Uncover dough. Brush loaves again with egg white mixture. Bake 25 to 30 minutes or until golden brown. Immediately remove from cookie sheet; cool on wire racks.
Yield: 2 (18-slice) loaves.

HIGH ALTITUDE:
Above 3500 Feet: No change.

NUTRITION PER SERVING:
Calories 80; Protein 2g; Carbohydrate 16g; Fat 1g; Sodium 180mg.

CHALLAH

This rich egg bread is a Jewish tradition. It is served on the Sabbath and holidays.

4½ to 5½ cups all purpose flour
  2 tablespoons sugar
  1 teaspoon salt
  2 pkg. active dry yeast
  1 cup water
 ⅓ cup margarine or butter
  4 eggs
  1 egg white
  1 tablespoon water
    Poppy seed

In large bowl, combine 2 cups flour, sugar, salt and yeast; blend well. In small saucepan, heat 1 cup water and margarine until very warm (120 to 130°F.). Add warm liquid and 4 eggs to flour mixture. Blend at low speed until moistened; beat 3 minutes at medium speed. By hand, stir in an additional 2 to 2½ cups flour until dough pulls cleanly away from sides of bowl.

On floured surface, knead in ½ to 1 cup flour until dough is smooth and elastic, about 5 minutes. Place dough in greased bowl; cover loosely with plastic wrap and cloth towel. Let rise in warm place (80 to 85°F.) until light and doubled in size, about 35 to 45 minutes.

Grease large cookie sheet. Punch down dough several times to remove all air bubbles. Divide dough in half; divide each half into 3 equal parts. Roll each part into 14-inch rope. Braid 3 ropes together; seal ends. Place on greased cookie sheet. Repeat with other half of dough. Cover; let rise in warm place until doubled in size, about 15 to 25 minutes.

Heat oven to 400°F. Uncover dough. Bake 10 minutes. Brush with mixture of egg white and 1 tablespoon water; sprinkle with poppy seed. Return to oven; bake an additional 5 to 10 minutes or until loaves sound hollow when lightly tapped. Immediately remove from cookie sheet; cool on wire racks.

Yield: 2 (15-slice) loaves.

HIGH ALTITUDE:
Above 3500 Feet: Decrease each rise time by 10 to 15 minutes.

NUTRITION PER SERVING:
Calories 120; Protein 4g; Carbohydrate 20g; Fat 3g; Sodium 105mg.

GOLDEN PARTY LOAVES

Carrots add color, texture and flavor to these party perfect mini-loaves.

4½ to 5½ cups all purpose flour
1½ cups finely shredded carrots
  1 teaspoon salt
  1 pkg. active dry yeast
 ¾ cup apricot nectar
 ½ cup plain yogurt
 ¼ cup honey
 ¼ cup margarine or butter
  1 egg
    Margarine or butter, softened

In large bowl, combine 2 cups flour, carrots, salt and yeast; blend well. In small saucepan, heat apricot nectar, yogurt, honey and ¼ cup margarine until very warm (120 to 130°F.). Add warm liquid and egg to flour mixture. Blend at low speed until moistened; beat 3 minutes at medium speed. By hand, stir in an additional 2 to 2½ cups flour to form a stiff dough.

On floured surface, knead in ½ to 1 cup flour until dough is smooth and elastic, about 5 minutes. Place dough in greased bowl; cover loosely with plastic wrap and cloth towel. Let rise in warm place (80 to 85°F.) until light and doubled in size, about 1 hour.

Grease and flour two 9x5 or 8x4-inch loaf pans. Punch down dough several times to remove all air bubbles. Divide dough in half. Work dough with hands to remove large air bubbles. Divide each half into thirds. Shape each third into a small loaf. Spread sides of loaves with softened margarine. Place 3 loaves crosswise in greased and floured pans. Repeat with remaining dough. Cover; let rise in warm place until light and doubled in size, about 45 minutes.

Heat oven to 375°F. Uncover dough. Bake 30 to 35 minutes or until deep golden brown and loaves sound hollow when lightly tapped. Immediately remove from pans; cool on wire racks. Brush warm loaves with softened margarine.

Yield: 6 (7-slice) mini-loaves.

HIGH ALTITUDE:
Above 3500 Feet: No change.

NUTRITION PER SERVING:
Calories 90; Protein 2g; Carbohydrate 16g; Fat 2g; Sodium 70mg.

QUICK SOURDOUGH FRENCH BREAD

In this recipe, we've kept the traditional sourdough flavor but streamlined the method using fast-acting yeast, sour cream and vinegar.

- 4 to 5 cups all purpose flour
- 2 tablespoons wheat germ
- 1 tablespoon sugar
- 2 teaspoons salt
- ½ teaspoon ginger
- 2 pkg. fast-acting dry yeast
- 1 cup very warm water
- 1 cup dairy sour cream, room temperature
- 2 tablespoons vinegar
- 1 egg white
- 1 tablespoon water
- 2 teaspoons poppy seed

In large bowl, combine 1½ cups flour, wheat germ, sugar, salt, ginger and yeast; blend well. Add 1 cup very warm water (120 to 130°F.), sour cream and vinegar to flour mixture. Blend at low speed until moistened; beat 3 minutes at medium speed. By hand, stir in an additional 2 to 2½ cups flour until dough pulls cleanly away from sides of bowl.

On floured surface, knead in ½ to 1 cup flour until dough is smooth and elastic, about 3 minutes. Place dough in greased bowl; cover loosely with plastic wrap and cloth towel. Let rise in warm place (80 to 85°F.) until light and doubled in size, 25 to 30 minutes.

Grease large cookie sheet. Punch down dough several times to remove all air bubbles. Divide dough in half; roll each half into 14x8-inch rectangle. Starting with 14-inch side, roll up; pinch edges firmly to seal. Place, seam side down, on greased cookie sheet; taper ends to a point. With sharp knife, make five ¼-inch deep diagonal slashes on top of each loaf. Cover; let rise in warm place until light and doubled in size, about 15 minutes.

Heat oven to 375°F. Uncover dough. Bake 25 minutes. In small bowl, beat egg white and 1 tablespoon water. Brush top of loaves with egg white mixture. Sprinkle with poppy seed. Bake an additional 5 to 10 minutes or until golden brown and loaves sound hollow when lightly tapped. Immediately remove from cookie sheet; cool on wire racks.

Yield: 2 (17-slice) loaves.

HIGH ALTITUDE:
Above 3500 Feet: No change.

NUTRITION PER SERVING:
Calories 90; Protein 3g; Carbohydrate 16g; Fat 2g; Sodium 130mg.

COOK'S NOTE

YEAST

Yeast is a living single-cell organism used for making bread. Healthy yeast cells feed on sugar or starch in a moist environment, causing fermentation which produces carbon dioxide and alcohol that leaven the bread. During baking, the yeast cells finally reach a temperature that kills them, the bread sets in its risen form, the alcohol evaporates and carbon dioxide is driven off. To determine if your yeast is fresh, refer to Secrets for Baking with Yeast p. 418.

Quick Sourdough French Bread

Sourdough Bread

This delicious bread has a slightly sour, tangy flavor created by using a yeast or sourdough starter as the leavener. Since the starter takes 5 days to develop, you'll need to plan ahead to make this bread.

STARTER
- 1 pkg. active dry yeast
- 2 cups warm water
- 3½ cups all purpose flour
- 1 tablespoon sugar or honey

BREAD
- 1 cup starter
- 5½ to 6 cups all purpose flour
- ¼ cup sugar
- 1 tablespoon salt
- 1²⁄₃ cups warm water
- ⅓ cup oil

In large nonmetal bowl, dissolve yeast in 2 cups warm water (105 to 115°F.); let stand 5 minutes. Add 3½ cups flour and 1 tablespoon sugar; blend well. Cover loosely with plastic wrap and cloth towel. Let stand in warm place (80 to 85°F.) for 5 days, stirring at least once each day. When the starter is ready for use, it is bubbly and may have a yellow liquid layer on top. Stir well before using.*

Place 1 cup starter in large bowl.** Add 2 cups flour, ¼ cup sugar, salt, 1²⁄₃ cups warm water (105 to 115°F.) and oil; blend well. Stir in 2½ to 2¾ cups flour until dough pulls cleanly away from sides of bowl.

On floured surface, knead in remaining 1 to 1¼ cups flour until dough is smooth and elastic, about 5 minutes. Place dough in greased bowl; cover loosely with plastic wrap and cloth towel. Let rise in warm place 8 to 10 hours or overnight.

Grease 3 cookie sheets or 9-inch round cake pans.*** Uncover dough. Punch down dough several times to remove air bubbles. Divide dough into 3 parts. Work dough with hands to remove all air bubbles. Shape into round loaves. Place on greased cookie sheets. Cover; let rise in warm place until doubled in size, 2 to 3 hours.

Heat oven to 400°F. With sharp knife, make three ¼-inch deep slits on top of each loaf. Bake 20 to 25 minutes or until loaves sound hollow when lightly tapped. Immediately remove from cookie sheets; cool on wire racks.
Yield: 3 (16-slice) loaves.

TIPS:
* If starter will not be used immediately, cover and refrigerate until ready to use. Return to room temperature before using.

** If desired, starter can be replenished for future use. After removing 1 cup starter, add to remaining starter 1 cup flour, ⅔ cup warm water (105 to 115°F.) and 1 teaspoon sugar or honey; blend well. Cover loosely with plastic wrap and cloth towel. Let stand in warm place (80 to 85°F.) 10 to 12 hours or overnight. The starter will become bubbly and rise. Stir, cover and store in refrigerator. Repeat this process each time the starter is used. If starter is used once a week, it will remain active. If not used, stir in 1 teaspoon sugar or honey weekly.

*** Three 8x4-inch loaf pans can be used. Bake at 400°F. for 25 to 30 minutes.

HIGH ALTITUDE:
Above 3500 Feet: No change.

NUTRITION PER SERVING:
Calories 100; Protein 3g; Carbohydrate 18g; Fat 2g; Sodium 135mg.

Cook's Note

YEAST STARTER

Before yeast was commercially available, yeast starters were used as the leavening agent for making breads. The starters were made with a combination of flour, water, sugar and airborne yeast. The airborne yeast served as the catalyst for the starter. The starter was put in a warm place until the yeast fermented and the mixture became foamy. A portion of this starter was used to leaven a batch of bread, and the remaining starter was "fed" with flour, water and sugar to be kept "alive" for future baking. Today yeast starters are often used for sourdough bread.

OAT BRAN FRENCH BREAD

You'll enjoy this updated, contemporary version of French bread.

2¼ to 2¾ cups all purpose flour
⅓ cup oat bran hot cereal, uncooked
1 pkg. active dry yeast
1 teaspoon salt
1 cup water
1 tablespoon honey
1 tablespoon cornmeal
½ teaspoon cornstarch
¼ cup water

In large bowl, combine 1 cup flour, cereal, yeast and salt; blend well. In small saucepan, heat 1 cup water and honey until very warm (120 to 130°F.). Add warm liquid to flour mixture. Blend at low speed until moistened; beat 3 minutes at medium speed. By hand, stir in an additional 1 to 1¼ cups flour to form a stiff dough.

On floured surface, knead in ¼ to ½ cup flour until dough is smooth and elastic, about 5 minutes. Place dough in greased bowl; cover loosely with plastic wrap and cloth towel. Let rise in warm place (80 to 85°F.), about 30 minutes.

Grease cookie sheet; sprinkle with cornmeal. Punch down dough several times to remove all air bubbles. Shape dough by rolling back and forth on counter into a 15-inch long loaf. Place on greased cookie sheet. Cover; let rise in warm place until almost doubled in size, about 15 minutes.

Heat oven to 400°F. In small saucepan, combine cornstarch and ¼ cup water; mix well. Bring to a boil; cook until mixture is thickened and clear. Remove from heat; cool, stirring occasionally. Uncover dough. With very sharp knife, cut four ½-inch deep diagonal slashes on top of loaf. Brush loaf with thin layer of cornstarch mixture. Bake at 400°F. for 10 minutes. Brush with cornstarch mixture again. Bake an additional 15 to 20 minutes or until golden brown and loaf sounds hollow when lightly tapped. Immediately remove from cookie sheet; cool on wire rack.
Yield: 1 (15-slice) loaf.

FOOD PROCESSOR DIRECTIONS:
Grease cookie sheet; sprinkle with cornmeal. Sprinkle yeast over ¼ *cup water heated to 105 to 115°F.* Stir in honey. Let stand until foamy, about 5 minutes. In food processor bowl with metal blade, combine 2¼ cups flour, cereal and salt; process to blend. Stir ⅔ cup water heated to 105 to 115°F. into yeast mixture. With motor running, pour yeast mixture through feed tube in a steady stream as fast as flour absorbs it. When dough forms a ball, stop machine. Dough should feel slightly sticky. If dough is too wet, add flour by tablespoons with motor running; if too dry, add water by teaspoons until well blended. Knead by processing continuously for 45 seconds. Continue as directed above.

TIP:
A French bread pan can be substituted for a cookie sheet. Grease pan; sprinkle with cornmeal. To shape bread, divide dough in half. Gently elongate each half by rolling back and forth to 1 inch shorter than length of pan. Place in greased pan. Continue as directed above.

HIGH ALTITUDE:
Above 3500 Feet: No change.

NUTRITION PER SERVING:
Calories 90; Protein 3g; Carbohydrate 19g; Fat 0g; Sodium 140mg.

SPEEDY CARAWAY RYE BREAD

This bread can be ready to serve in less than 2 hours.

      3 **to 4 cups all purpose flour**
      1 **tablespoon caraway seed**
      2 **teaspoons salt**
  1½ **teaspoons onion powder**
      3 **pkg. active dry yeast**
  2¼ **cups water**
      3 **tablespoons brown sugar**
      3 **tablespoons margarine or butter**
  2½ **cups medium rye flour**
         Egg white, beaten
         Coarse salt, if desired

In large bowl, combine 2 cups all purpose flour, caraway seed, salt, onion powder and yeast; blend well. In small saucepan, heat water, brown sugar and margarine until very warm (120 to 130°F.). Add warm liquid to flour mixture. Blend at low speed until moistened; beat 3 minutes at medium speed. Stir in rye flour and an additional ¾ to 1½ cups all purpose flour until dough pulls cleanly away from sides of bowl.

On floured surface, knead in ¼ to ½ cup all purpose flour until dough is smooth and elastic, about 5 minutes. Place dough in greased bowl; cover loosely with plastic wrap and cloth towel. Place bowl in pan of warm water (about 95°F.); let rise 15 minutes.

Grease large cookie sheet. Punch down dough several times to remove all air bubbles. Divide dough into 2 parts; shape into two 12-inch oblong loaves. Place on greased cookie sheet. With sharp knife, make ⅛-inch deep slash down center of each loaf. Brush with egg white. Cover; let rise in warm place 15 minutes.

Heat oven to 375°F. Uncover dough. Sprinkle loaves with coarse salt, if desired. Bake 25 to 35 minutes or until loaves sound hollow when lightly tapped. Immediately remove from cookie sheet; cool on wire racks.
Yield: 2 (16-slice) loaves.

HIGH ALTITUDE:
Above 3500 Feet: No change.

NUTRITION PER SERVING:
Calories 90; Protein 3g; Carbohydrate 16g; Fat 1g; Sodium 150mg.

SPEEDY WHOLE WHEAT BREAD

Toasted sesame seed tops these quick-to-prepare round loaves.

  2½ **to 3 cups all purpose flour**
      3 **tablespoons sesame seed, toasted, p. 23**
      2 **teaspoons salt**
      3 **pkg. active dry yeast**
  2¼ **cups water**
      ¼ **cup honey**
      3 **tablespoons margarine or butter**
      3 **cups whole wheat flour**
      1 **egg white, beaten**
         Sesame seed, toasted, p. 23

In large bowl, combine 2 cups all purpose flour, 3 tablespoons sesame seed, salt and yeast; blend well. In small saucepan, heat water, honey and margarine until very warm (120 to 130°F.). Add warm liquid to flour mixture. Blend at low speed until moistened; beat 3 minutes at medium speed. By hand, stir in whole wheat flour and an additional ¼ to ½ cup all purpose flour until dough pulls cleanly away from sides of bowl.

On floured surface, knead in ¼ to ½ cup all purpose flour until dough is smooth and elastic, about 5 to 8 minutes. Place dough in greased bowl; cover loosely with plastic wrap and cloth towel. Place bowl in pan of warm water (about 95°F.); let rise 15 minutes.

Grease large cookie sheet or 15x10x1-inch baking pan. Punch down dough several times to remove all air bubbles. Divide dough into 2 parts; shape into round balls. Place 3 inches apart on greased cookie sheet. With sharp knife, make three ⅛-inch deep slashes on top of each loaf. Carefully brush loaves with egg white; sprinkle with sesame seed. Cover; let rise in warm place until light and doubled in size, about 15 minutes.

Heat oven to 375°F. Uncover dough. Bake 25 to 35 minutes or until loaves sound hollow when lightly tapped. Immediately remove from cookie sheet; cool on wire racks.
Yield: 2 (16-slice) loaves.

HIGH ALTITUDE:
Above 3500 Feet: No change.

NUTRITION PER SERVING:
Calories 110; Protein 3g; Carbohydrate 19g; Fat 2g; Sodium 150mg.

SPEEDY WHITE BREAD

These homey loaves are filled with old-fashioned goodness — and we've streamlined the method for convenience.

  5 to 6 cups all purpose flour
  3 tablespoons sugar
2¼ teaspoons salt
  3 pkg. active dry yeast
2¼ cups water
  3 tablespoons margarine or butter

In large bowl, combine 2 cups flour, sugar, salt and yeast; blend well. In small saucepan, heat water and margarine until very warm (120 to 130°F.). Add warm liquid to flour mixture. Blend at low speed until moistened; beat 3 minutes at medium speed. Stir in an additional 2½ to 3 cups flour until dough pulls cleanly away from sides of bowl.

On floured surface, knead in ½ to 1 cup flour until dough is smooth and elastic, about 5 minutes. Place dough in greased bowl; cover loosely with plastic wrap and cloth towel. Place bowl in pan of warm water (about 95°F.); let rise 15 minutes.

Grease large cookie sheet. Punch down dough several times to remove all air bubbles. Divide dough into 2 parts; shape into round balls. Place on greased cookie sheet. With sharp knife, slash ¼-inch deep lattice design on top of each loaf. Cover; let rise in warm place 15 minutes.

Heat oven to 400°F. Uncover dough. Bake 20 to 30 minutes or until loaves sound hollow when lightly tapped. Immediately remove from cookie sheet; cool on wire racks.
Yield: 2 (16-slice) loaves.

HIGH ALTITUDE:
Above 3500 Feet: Bake at 375°F. for 25 to 30 minutes.

NUTRITION PER SERVING:
Calories 110; Protein 3g; Carbohydrate 21g; Fat 1g; Sodium 165mg.

COOK'S NOTE

BRAIDING BREAD DOUGH

For ease in braiding, place the strips of dough side by side on a greased cookie sheet. Braid from the center to the ends. Press and pinch the ends of the strips together; tuck ends under to seal.

TWO-TONE RYE TWIST LOAVES

2½ cups all purpose flour
2½ cups medium rye flour
  1 tablespoon salt
  1 tablespoon grated orange peel
  2 pkg. active dry yeast
  2 cups milk
¼ cup molasses
¼ cup margarine or butter
  2 teaspoons unsweetened cocoa
  1 to 2 teaspoons anise seed
  1 teaspoon instant coffee granules or crystals
  1 to 1½ cups all purpose flour

In large bowl, combine 2½ cups each all purpose and rye flour; mix well. In another large bowl, combine 2 cups of the flour mixture, salt, orange peel and yeast; blend well. In medium saucepan, heat milk, molasses and margarine until very warm (120 to 130°F.). Add warm liquid to flour-yeast mixture. Blend at low speed until moistened; beat 3 minutes at medium speed. Pour half of batter into another bowl; set aside. To remaining batter, stir in cocoa, anise seed, instant coffee and 1 to 1½ cups flour mixture to form a stiff dough. On floured surface, knead in ½ to 1 cup flour mixture until dough is smooth and elastic, about 5 minutes.

To reserved batter, stir in remaining flour mixture and ½ to ¾ cup all purpose flour to make a stiff dough. On floured surface, knead in ½ to ¾ cup additional all purpose flour until dough is smooth and elastic, about 5 minutes. Place doughs in greased bowls; cover loosely with plastic wrap and cloth towels. Let rise in warm place (80 to 85°F.) until light and doubled in size, about 1 hour.

Grease 2 cookie sheets. Punch down doughs. Divide each dough into 2 parts. Roll each part into 14-inch rope. For each loaf, twist a dark and a light rope together, pinching ends to seal. Place on greased cookie sheets. Cover; let rise until doubled in size, about 1 hour.

Heat oven to 350°F. Uncover dough. Bake 25 to 30 minutes or until loaves sound hollow when lightly tapped. Immediately remove from cookie sheets; cool on wire racks.
Yield: 2 (12-slice) loaves.

HIGH ALTITUDE:
Above 3500 Feet: No change.

NUTRITION PER SERVING:
Calories 150; Protein 4g; Carbohydrate 28g; Fat 3g; Sodium 300mg.

THREE GRAIN BREAD

A healthy, hearty loaf — great for sandwiches!

3½ to 4 cups all purpose flour
1¾ cups medium rye flour
1¾ cups whole wheat flour
2 teaspoons salt
3 pkg. active dry yeast
1¾ cups milk
¾ cup water
⅔ cup honey
3 tablespoons margarine or butter
2 tablespoons molasses
½ cup shelled sunflower seeds
¼ cup wheat germ
¼ cup shreds of whole bran cereal

Combine 2 cups all purpose flour, the rye flour and whole wheat flour. In large bowl, combine 3 cups flour mixture, salt and yeast. In small saucepan, heat milk, water, honey, margarine and molasses until very warm (120 to 130°F.). Add warm liquid to flour mixture. Blend at low speed until moistened; beat 3 minutes at medium speed. By hand, stir in sunflower nuts, wheat germ, bran cereal, remaining flour mixture and an additional 1¼ to 1½ cups all purpose flour until dough pulls cleanly away from sides of bowl.

On floured surface, knead in ¼ to ½ cup all purpose flour until smooth and elastic, about 5 minutes. Place dough in greased bowl; cover loosely with plastic wrap and cloth towel. Let rise in warm place (80 to 85°F.) until light and doubled in size, about 45 minutes.

Grease two 8x4-inch loaf pans. Punch down dough several times to remove all air bubbles. Divide dough into 2 parts; shape into loaves. Place in greased pans. Cover; let rise in warm place until dough fills pans and tops of loaves are about 1 inch above pan edges, about 20 to 30 minutes.

Heat oven to 350°F. Uncover dough. Bake 40 to 45 minutes or until loaves sound hollow when lightly tapped. Immediately remove from pans; cool on wire racks.
Yield: 2 (16-slice) loaves.

HIGH ALTITUDE:
Above 3500 Feet: No change.

NUTRITION PER SERVING:
Calories 150; Protein 4g; Carbohydrate 29g; Fat 2g;
Sodium 160mg.

CRACKED WHEAT RAISIN BREAD

Try this wholesome bread toasted — it's great!

1½ cups cracked wheat
1 cup raisins
½ cup firmly packed brown sugar
2 teaspoons salt
3 tablespoons margarine or butter
2 cups boiling water
2 pkg. active dry yeast
⅔ cup warm water
5 to 6 cups all purpose flour
Beaten egg

In large bowl, combine cracked wheat, raisins, brown sugar, salt, margarine and 2 cups boiling water. Mix well and allow to cool to 105 to 115°F. In small bowl, dissolve yeast in warm water (105 to 115°F.). Add to cooled cracked wheat mixture. Add 2 cups flour to cracked wheat mixture. Blend at low speed until moistened; beat 2 minutes at medium speed. By hand, stir in an additional 2½ to 3 cups flour until dough pulls cleanly away from sides of bowl.

On floured surface, knead in ½ to 1 cup flour until dough is smooth and elastic, about 10 minutes. Place dough in greased bowl; cover loosely with plastic wrap and cloth towel. Let rise in warm place (80 to 85°F.) until light and doubled in size, about 45 to 60 minutes.

Grease large cookie sheet. Punch down dough several times to remove all air bubbles. Divide dough into 2 parts; shape into balls. Place on greased cookie sheet. Cover; let rise in warm place until light and doubled in size, about 45 to 60 minutes.

Heat oven to 350°F. Uncover dough. With sharp knife, slash a ½-inch deep lattice design on top of each loaf. Brush with beaten egg. Bake at 350°F. for 35 to 45 minutes or until loaves sound hollow when lightly tapped. Immediately remove from cookie sheet; cool on wire racks.
Yield: 2 (20-slice) loaves.

HIGH ALTITUDE:
Above 3500 Feet: No change.

NUTRITION PER SERVING:
Calories 110; Protein 3g; Carbohydrate 23g; Fat 1g;
Sodium 120mg.

Cracked Wheat Raisin Bread

SWISS BRAIDED RAISIN LOAF

Swiss cheese and raisins are featured in this pretty braided loaf.

3½ to 4 cups all purpose flour
1 tablespoon sugar
1 teaspoon salt
2 pkg. active dry yeast
⅔ cup milk
⅓ cup margarine or butter
3 eggs
½ to 1 cup golden raisins or dark raisins
2 oz. (½ cup) shredded Swiss cheese
   Margarine or butter, melted

In large bowl, combine 1½ cups flour, sugar, salt and yeast; blend well. In small saucepan, heat milk and margarine until very warm (120 to 130°F.). Add warm liquid and eggs to flour mixture. Blend at low speed until moistened; beat 3 minutes at medium speed. By hand, stir in raisins, cheese and an additional 1½ to 1¾ cups flour until dough pulls cleanly away from sides of bowl.

On floured surface, knead in ½ to ¾ cup flour until dough is smooth and elastic, about 5 minutes. Place dough in greased bowl; cover loosely with plastic wrap and cloth towel. Let rise in warm place (80 to 85°F.) until light and doubled in size, about 45 to 55 minutes.

Grease large cookie sheet. Punch down dough several times to remove all air bubbles. Divide dough into 4 parts. Roll each part into 20-inch rope. Place the 4 ropes, side by side, on greased cookie sheet, pinching together at 1 end to seal. Braid by weaving far right rope over and under other ropes to far left, then weave next far right rope over and under; repeat until ropes are completely braided. Pinch ends together and tuck both ends under to seal. Cover; let rise in warm place until light and doubled in size, about 30 minutes.

Heat oven to 375°F. Uncover dough. Bake 20 to 30 minutes or until golden brown and loaf sounds hollow when lightly tapped. Immediately remove from cookie sheet; cool on wire rack. While warm, brush with melted margarine.

Yield: 1 (17-slice) loaf.

HIGH ALTITUDE:
Above 3500 Feet: No change.

NUTRITION PER SERVING:
Calories 210; Protein 6g; Carbohydrate 31g; Fat 7g; Sodium 230mg.

WHOLE WHEAT RAISIN LOAF

If you like whole wheat bread, you'll enjoy this raisin-studded, slightly sweet loaf. Serve it toasted with your favorite jam.

3 to 3¾ cups all purpose flour
½ cup sugar
3 teaspoons salt
1 teaspoon cinnamon
½ teaspoon nutmeg
2 pkg. active dry yeast
2 cups milk
¾ cup water
¼ cup oil
4 cups whole wheat flour
1 cup rolled oats
1 cup raisins
   Margarine or butter, melted
   Sugar, if desired

In large bowl, combine 1½ cups all purpose flour, ½ cup sugar, salt, cinnamon, nutmeg and yeast; blend well. In small saucepan, heat milk, water and ¼ cup oil until very warm (120 to 130°F.). Add warm liquid to flour mixture. Blend at low speed until moistened; beat 3 minutes at medium speed. By hand, stir in whole wheat flour, rolled oats, raisins and an additional 1 to 1½ cups all purpose flour until dough pulls cleanly away from sides of bowl.

On floured surface, knead in ½ to ¾ cup all purpose flour until dough is smooth and elastic, about 5 minutes. Place dough in greased bowl; cover loosely with plastic wrap and cloth towel. Let rise in warm place (80 to 85°F.) until light and doubled in size, about 20 to 30 minutes.

Grease two 9x5 or 8x4-inch loaf pans. Punch down dough several times to remove all air bubbles. Divide dough into 2 parts; shape into loaves. Place in greased pans; brush tops with oil. Cover; let rise in warm place until light and doubled in size, 30 to 45 minutes.

Heat oven to 375°F. Uncover dough. Bake 40 to 50 minutes or until deep golden brown and loaves sound hollow when lightly tapped. Cover with foil last 10 minutes of baking if necessary to avoid excessive browning. Immediately remove from pans; cool on wire racks. Brush tops of loaves with margarine; sprinkle with sugar.

Yield: 2 (16-slice) loaves.

Above 3500 Feet: No change.

NUTRITION PER SERVING:
Calories 170; Protein 5g; Carbohydrate 32g; Fat 3g; Sodium 210mg.

WHOLE WHEAT BUBBLE LOAF

This pull-apart loaf is great to serve with any meal. It has terrific nutty whole wheat flavor.

2	to 2½ cups all purpose flour
2	tablespoons sugar
1½	teaspoons salt
1	pkg. active dry yeast
1¼	cups milk
2	tablespoons margarine or butter
1	egg
1½	cups whole wheat flour
¼	cup margarine or butter, melted
4	teaspoons sesame seed

In large bowl, combine 1 cup all purpose flour, sugar, salt and yeast; blend well. In small saucepan, heat milk and 2 tablespoons margarine until very warm (120 to 130°F.). Add warm liquid and egg to flour mixture. Blend at low speed until moistened; beat 3 minutes at medium speed. By hand, stir in whole wheat flour until dough pulls cleanly away from sides of bowl.

On floured surface, knead in 1 to 1½ cups all purpose flour until dough is smooth and elastic, about 5 minutes. Place in greased bowl; cover loosely with plastic wrap and cloth towel. Let rise in warm place (80 to 85°F.) until light and doubled in size, about 45 to 60 minutes.

Generously grease one 2-quart deep casserole. Punch down dough several times to remove all air bubbles. Using sharp knife or scissors, cut dough into 30 to 40 walnut-size pieces. Place half of dough pieces in greased casserole. Drizzle with 2 tablespoons melted margarine; sprinkle with 2 teaspoons sesame seed. Repeat with remaining dough pieces, margarine and sesame seed. Cover; let rise in warm place until light and doubled in size, about 30 to 45 minutes.

Heat oven to 400°F. Uncover dough. Bake 25 to 35 minutes or until loaf sounds hollow when lightly tapped. Cool 5 minutes; remove from casserole. Pull apart to serve.
Yield: 1 loaf; 20 servings.

HIGH ALTITUDE:
Above 3500 Feet: Decrease first rise time to 30 to 45 minutes.

NUTRITION PER SERVING:
Calories 140; Protein 4g; Carbohydrate 21g; Fat 5g; Sodium 210mg.

COOK'S NOTE

WHOLE WHEAT FLOUR

Whole wheat or graham flour is milled from the entire wheat kernel. It has a higher nutritional value and contains more fiber than other flours. Baked products made with whole wheat flour will have a heavier, more compact texture. Because whole wheat flour has less baking strength than all purpose flour, it should be used in combination with all purpose or bread flour.

HI-PROTEIN HONEY WHEAT BREAD

This wholesome bread is delicious by itself or for sandwiches. In this recipe, use creamed cottage cheese, which has cream added to it.

   4 to 5 cups all purpose flour
   2 teaspoons salt
   2 pkg. active dry yeast
   1 cup water
   ½ cup honey
   ¼ cup margarine or butter
   1 cup creamed cottage cheese
   2 eggs
   1 cup whole wheat flour
   ½ cup rolled oats
   1 cup chopped nuts

In large bowl, combine 2 cups all purpose flour, salt and yeast; blend well. In medium saucepan, heat water, honey, margarine and cottage cheese until very warm (120 to 130°F.). (Margarine does not need to melt completely.) Add warm liquid and eggs to flour mixture. Blend at low speed until moistened; beat 3 minutes at medium speed. By hand, stir in whole wheat flour, oats, nuts and enough all purpose flour to form a soft dough.

On floured surface, knead dough until smooth and elastic, about 10 minutes. Place in greased bowl; cover loosely with plastic wrap and cloth towel. Let rise in warm place (80 to 85°F.) until light and doubled in size, about 1 hour.

Generously grease two 8x4 or 9x5-inch loaf pans or two 8 or 9-inch round cake pans. Punch down dough. Divide dough into 2 parts; shape into loaves. Place in greased pans. Cover; let rise in warm place until light and doubled in size, about 1 hour.

Heat oven to 375°F. Uncover dough. Bake 35 to 40 minutes or until loaves sound hollow when lightly tapped. Immediately remove from pans; cool on wire racks. For softer crusts, brush tops of loaves with melted margarine, if desired.
Yield: 2 (16-slice) loaves.

HIGH ALTITUDE:
Above 3500 Feet: No change.

NUTRITION PER SERVING:
Calories 150; Protein 5g; Carbohydrate 22g; Fat 5g; Sodium 170mg.

HONEY GRANOLA BREAD

Whole wheat flour, honey and granola make this a tasty sandwich bread for the school lunch box.

   5 to 5½ cups all purpose flour
   1 cup granola cereal
   2 teaspoons salt
   2 pkg. active dry yeast
 1½ cups water
   1 cup plain yogurt
   ½ cup honey
   ¼ cup oil or shortening
   2 eggs
   2 cups whole wheat flour

In large bowl, combine 3 cups all purpose flour, granola, salt and yeast; blend well. In medium saucepan, heat water, yogurt, honey and oil until very warm (120 to 130°F.). Add warm liquid and eggs to flour mixture. Blend at low speed until moistened; beat 3 minutes at medium speed. By hand, stir in whole wheat flour and an additional 1 cup all purpose flour to form a stiff dough.

On floured surface, knead in 1 to 1½ cups all purpose flour until dough is smooth and elastic, about 10 minutes. Place dough in greased bowl; cover loosely with plastic wrap and cloth towel. Let rise in warm place (80 to 85°F.) until light and doubled in size, about 1 hour.

Generously grease two 9x5 or 8x4-inch loaf pans. Punch down dough several times to remove all air bubbles. Divide dough into 2 parts; shape into loaves. Place in greased pans. Cover; let rise in warm place until light and doubled in size, 30 to 45 minutes.

Heat oven to 350°F. Uncover dough. Bake 30 to 40 minutes or until loaves sound hollow when lightly tapped. Immediately remove from pans; cool on wire racks. If desired, brush loaves with melted margarine.
Yield: 2 (17-slice) loaves.

HIGH ALTITUDE:
Above 3500 Feet: Bake at 350°F. for 40 to 50 minutes.

NUTRITION PER SERVING:
Calories 150; Protein 4g; Carbohydrate 27g; Fat 3g; Sodium 135mg.

TOASTED OAT BREAD

Rolled oats are sprinkled over the dough before baking.

BREAD
5½ to 6 cups all purpose flour
  1 cup rolled oats, toasted*
½ cup sugar
  2 teaspoons salt
  2 pkg. active dry yeast
  2 cups milk
¼ cup margarine or butter
  1 egg

TOPPING
  1 tablespoon water
  1 egg white
  1 tablespoon rolled oats

In large bowl, combine 2 cups flour, 1 cup rolled oats, sugar, salt and yeast; blend well. In small saucepan, heat milk and margarine until very warm (120 to 130°F.). Add warm liquid and egg to flour mixture. Blend at low speed until moistened; beat 3 minutes at medium speed. By hand, stir in an additional 3¼ to 3½ cups flour until dough pulls cleanly away from sides of bowl.

On floured surface, knead in ¼ to ½ cup flour until dough is smooth and elastic, about 5 minutes. Place dough in greased bowl; cover loosely with plastic wrap and cloth towel. Let rise in warm place (80 to 85°F.) until light and doubled in size, about 30 to 45 minutes.

Grease two 8x4 or 9x5-inch loaf pans. Punch down dough several times to remove all air bubbles. Divide dough into 2 parts; shape into loaves. Place in greased pans. Cover; let rise in warm place until dough fills pans and tops of loaves are about 1 inch above pan edges, about 20 to 30 minutes.

Heat oven to 375°F. Uncover dough. In small bowl, combine water and egg white; beat slightly. Carefully brush on loaves; sprinkle with 1 tablespoon rolled oats.

Bake at 375°F. for 25 to 35 minutes or until loaves sound hollow when lightly tapped. Cover with foil during last 10 minutes of baking if necessary to avoid excessive browning. Immediately remove from pans; cool on wire racks.
Yield: 2 (16-slice) loaves.

TIP:
* To toast rolled oats, spread on 15x10x1-inch baking pan; place in oven at 375°F. for 10 to 15 minutes or until light brown. (Oats brown rapidly.)

HIGH ALTITUDE:
Above 3500 Feet: No change.

NUTRITION PER SERVING:
Calories 130; Protein 4g; Carbohydrate 24g; Fat 2g; Sodium 160mg.

COOK'S NOTE

BUTTER CUTOUTS

Slice chilled butter about ¼ inch thick. Cut out small shapes with canape cutters or small cookie cutters. (Open top cutters are necessary to push out the shapes; simple shapes work best.) Refrigerate until served. Arrange the cutouts on individual bread and butter plates, on a butter serving plate or on a bed of crushed ice in a shallow bowl. (Margarine does not work well for cutouts.)

EASY CHEESE BATTER BREAD

Batter breads are among the simplest to prepare because they aren't kneaded or shaped. This moist version is even better the second day.

2½ **cups all purpose flour**
2 **teaspoons sugar**
1½ **teaspoons salt**
1 **pkg. active dry yeast**
4 **oz. (1 cup) shredded Cheddar cheese**
¾ **cup milk**
½ **cup margarine or butter**
3 **eggs**

In large bowl, combine 1½ cups flour, sugar, salt and yeast; blend well. Stir in cheese. In small saucepan, heat milk and margarine until very warm (120 to 130°F.). Add warm liquid and eggs to flour mixture. Blend at low speed until moistened; beat 3 minutes at medium speed. By hand, stir in remaining 1 cup flour. Cover loosely with plastic wrap and cloth towel. Let rise in warm place (80 to 85°F.) until light and doubled in size, 45 to 60 minutes.

Generously grease 1½ or 2-quart casserole or 9x5-inch loaf pan. Stir down dough to remove all air bubbles. Turn into greased casserole. Cover; let rise in warm place until light and doubled in size, 20 to 25 minutes.

Heat oven to 350°F. Uncover dough. Bake 40 to 45 minutes or until deep golden brown. Immediately remove from casserole; cool on wire rack.

Yield: 1 (18-slice) loaf.

HIGH ALTITUDE:
Above 3500 Feet: Bake at 375°F. for 40 to 45 minutes.

NUTRITION PER SERVING:
Calories 150; Protein 5g; Carbohydrate 15g; Fat 8g; Sodium 290mg.

ITALIAN CHEESE BREAD RING

Try this exceptional cheese-filled loaf whenever you're in the mood for something special. It's almost like a sandwich in a loaf!

BREAD
4½ **to 5¼ cups all purpose flour**
¼ **cup sugar**
1½ **teaspoons salt**
2 **pkg. active dry yeast**
1 **cup milk**
1 **cup water**
½ **cup margarine or butter**
2 **eggs**
2 **tablespoons sesame seed**

FILLING
4 **oz. (1 cup) shredded mozzarella cheese**
½ **teaspoon dried Italian seasoning**
¼ **teaspoon garlic powder**
¼ **cup margarine or butter, softened**

In large bowl, combine 2½ cups flour, sugar, salt and yeast; blend well. In small saucepan, heat milk, water and ½ cup margarine until very warm (120 to 130°F.). Add warm liquid and eggs to flour mixture. Blend at low speed until moistened; beat 3 minutes at medium speed. By hand, stir in remaining 2 to 2¾ cups all purpose flour to form a stiff batter.

Generously grease 12-cup Bundt® or 10-inch tube pan; sprinkle with sesame seed. In small bowl, combine all filling ingredients; mix well. Spoon half of batter into greased pan; spoon filling mixture evenly over batter to within ½ inch of sides of pan. Spoon remaining batter over filling. Cover loosely with plastic wrap and cloth towel. Let rise in warm place (80 to 85°F.) until light and doubled in size, about 30 minutes.

Heat oven to 350°F. Uncover dough. Bake 30 to 40 minutes or until golden brown and loaf sounds hollow when lightly tapped. Immediately remove from pan; cool on wire rack. Serve warm or cool.

Yield: 1 (24-slice) loaf.

HIGH ALTITUDE:
Above 3500 Feet: No change.

NUTRITION PER SERVING:
Calories 190; Protein 5g; Carbohydrate 24g; Fat 8g; Sodium 240mg.

Italian Cheese Bread Ring

Austrian Almond Loaf

This round loaf is topped with a glaze.

BREAD
- 1/3 cup margarine or butter
- 1 cup chopped almonds
- 3 1/4 cups all purpose flour
- 1/2 cup sugar
- 1/2 cup mashed potato flakes
- 1 to 2 teaspoons anise seed or 1 teaspoon cinnamon
- 1 teaspoon salt
- 1 pkg. active dry yeast
- 1 cup lemon yogurt or dairy sour cream
- 1/2 cup water
- 2 eggs, reserving 1 teaspoon egg white
- 2 tablespoons coarse sugar or crushed sugar cubes

GLAZE
- 1/2 cup powdered sugar
- 1/4 teaspoon almond extract
- 3 to 4 teaspoons milk

In small skillet over medium heat, cook margarine and almonds until almonds are light golden brown, stirring constantly. Set aside. In large bowl, combine 1 cup flour, sugar, potato flakes, anise seed, salt and yeast; blend well. In small saucepan, heat yogurt and water until very warm (120 to 130°F.). Add warm liquid and eggs to flour mixture. Blend at low speed until moistened; beat 3 minutes at medium speed. By hand, stir in remaining 2 1/4 cups flour and 1 cup of the almond mixture to form a soft dough. Cover loosely with plastic wrap and cloth towel. Let rise in warm place (80 to 85°F.) until light and doubled in size, about 1 hour.

Generously grease 2 or 2 1/2-quart casserole. Stir down dough; spoon into greased casserole. Cover; let rise in warm place until light and doubled in size, about 1 hour.

Heat oven to 350°F. Uncover dough. In small bowl, beat reserved 1 teaspoon egg white; brush over top of loaf. Sprinkle with coarse sugar. Bake at 350°F. for 35 to 45 minutes or until loaf sounds hollow when lightly tapped. Immediately remove from casserole; cool on wire rack about 30 minutes.

In small bowl, blend remaining almond mixture, powdered sugar, almond extract and enough milk for desired drizzling consistency. Drizzle over warm loaf.

Yield: 1 (16-slice) loaf.

HIGH ALTITUDE:
Above 3500 Feet: Bake at 350°F. for 40 to 50 minutes.

NUTRITION PER SERVING:
Calories 260; Protein 7g; Carbohydrate 38g; Fat 9g; Sodium 200mg.

English Muffin Batter Bread

This coarse-textured bread is delicious toasted.

- 4 to 4 1/2 cups all purpose flour
- 1/4 cup sugar
- 2 teaspoons salt
- 2 pkg. active dry yeast
- 1 1/4 cups water
- 1/2 cup oil
- 2 eggs
- Cornmeal

In large bowl, combine 1 1/2 cups flour, sugar, salt and yeast. In small saucepan, heat water and oil until very warm (120 to 130°F.). Add warm liquid and eggs to flour mixture. Blend at low speed until moistened; beat 2 minutes at medium speed. By hand, stir in remaining 2 1/2 to 3 cups flour to form a stiff batter. Cover loosely with plastic wrap and cloth towel. Let rise in warm place (80 to 85°F.) until light and doubled in size, about 45 to 60 minutes.

Grease two 8x4-inch loaf pans; sprinkle with cornmeal. Stir batter vigorously 30 seconds; spoon into greased pans. Cover; let rise in warm place until doubled in size, about 30 to 45 minutes.

Heat oven to 375°F. Uncover dough. Bake 20 to 30 minutes or until loaves sound hollow when lightly tapped. Immediately remove from pans; cool on wire racks.

Yield: 2 (12-slice) loaves.

HIGH ALTITUDE:
Above 3500 Feet: No change.

NUTRITION PER SERVING:
Calories 140; Protein 3g; Carbohydrate 20g; Fat 5g; Sodium 180mg.

HEARTY PUMPERNICKEL BATTER BREAD

This no-knead batter bread has authentic, robust pumpernickel flavor.

1	pkg. active dry yeast
1¼	cups warm water
1	tablespoon sugar
1	teaspoon salt
¾	teaspoon onion powder
½	teaspoon instant coffee granules or crystals
2	tablespoons oil
2	tablespoons molasses
1	oz. unsweetened chocolate, melted
1½	cups all purpose flour
1	cup medium rye flour
1	teaspoon caraway seed

In large bowl, dissolve yeast in warm water (105 to 115°F.). Add sugar, salt, onion powder, instant coffee, oil, molasses and chocolate; blend well. Add 1 cup all purpose flour to yeast mixture. Blend at low speed until moistened; beat 3 minutes at medium speed. By hand, stir in remaining all purpose flour, rye flour and caraway seed to form a stiff batter. Cover loosely with plastic wrap and cloth towel. Let rise in warm place (80 to 85°F.) until light and doubled in size, about 45 minutes.

Generously grease 8x4 or 9x5-inch loaf pan. Stir down dough to remove all air bubbles. Turn into greased pan. Cover with greased plastic wrap; let rise in warm place until light and doubled in size, about 30 to 45 minutes.

Heat oven to 375°F. Uncover dough. Bake 28 to 35 minutes or until deep golden brown and loaf sounds hollow when lightly tapped. Immediately remove from pan; cool on wire rack.

Yield: 1 (16-slice) loaf.

HIGH ALTITUDE:
Above 3500 Feet: Increase all purpose flour to 1¾ cups. Bake as directed above.

NUTRITION PER SERVING:
Calories 100; Protein 2g; Carbohydrate 16g; Fat 3g; Sodium 135mg.

NO-KNEAD GERMAN RYE BREAD

Caraway seed adds distinctive flavor to these round loaves.

3	tablespoons instant minced onion
3	teaspoons garlic salt
3	teaspoons caraway seed
1	teaspoon dried celery flakes
1	(12-oz.) can beer
2	cups bran flakes cereal
2	pkg. active dry yeast
½	cup warm water
⅓	cup corn syrup
¼	cup oil
2	eggs
3	to 4 cups all purpose flour
⅔	cup instant nonfat dry milk
½	cup medium rye flour

In small saucepan, combine onion, garlic salt, caraway seed, celery flakes and beer; bring to a boil. Remove from heat. In large bowl, combine beer mixture and cereal; mix well. Cool to lukewarm. In small bowl, dissolve yeast in warm water (105 to 115°F.). Add yeast mixture, corn syrup, oil and eggs to cereal mixture; mix well. Add 1½ cups all purpose flour, dry milk and rye flour to cereal mixture. Blend at low speed until moistened; beat 3 minutes at medium speed. By hand, stir in remaining 1½ to 2½ cups all purpose flour to form a stiff batter. Cover loosely with plastic wrap and cloth towel. Let rise in warm place (80 to 85°F.) until light and doubled in size, 45 to 60 minutes.

Generously grease two 1½-quart casseroles or two 8x4-inch loaf pans. Stir down dough to remove all air bubbles. Divide dough in half. Turn into greased casseroles. Cover; let rise in warm place until light and doubled in size, 45 to 60 minutes.

Heat oven to 350°F. Uncover dough. Bake 25 to 35 minutes or until deep golden brown and loaves sound hollow when lightly tapped. Immediately remove from casseroles; cool on wire racks.

Yield: 2 (16-slice) loaves.

HIGH ALTITUDE:
Above 3500 Feet: No change.

NUTRITION PER SERVING:
Calories 110; Protein 3g; Carbohydrate 19g; Fat 2g; Sodium 210mg.

Dilly Casserole Bread

DILLY CASSEROLE BREAD

❦

The next time you want to impress family or friends, bake them a loaf of this easy bread. It is a BAKE-OFF® Contest grand prize winner and one of Pillsbury's most requested recipes.

- 2 **to 2⅔ cups all purpose flour**
- 2 **tablespoons sugar**
- 2 **to 3 teaspoons instant minced onion**
- 2 **teaspoons dill seed**
- 1 **teaspoon salt**
- ¼ **teaspoon baking soda**
- 1 **pkg. active dry yeast**
- ¼ **cup water**
- 1 **tablespoon margarine or butter**
- 1 **cup creamed cottage cheese**
- 1 **egg**
- 2 **teaspoons margarine or butter, melted**
- ¼ **teaspoon coarse salt, if desired**

In large bowl, combine 1 cup flour, sugar, onion, dill seed, 1 teaspoon salt, baking soda and yeast; blend well. In small saucepan, heat water, 1 tablespoon margarine and cottage cheese until very warm (120 to 130°F.). Add warm liquid and egg to flour mixture. Blend at low speed until moistened; beat 3 minutes at medium speed. By hand, stir in remaining 1 to 1⅔ cups flour to form a stiff batter. Cover loosely with plastic wrap and cloth towel. Let rise in warm place (80 to 85°F.) until light and doubled in size, 45 to 60 minutes.

Generously grease 1½ or 2-quart casserole. Stir down dough to remove all air bubbles. Turn into greased casserole. Cover; let rise in warm place until light and doubled in size, 30 to 45 minutes.

Heat oven to 350°F. Uncover dough. Bake 30 to 40 minutes or until deep golden brown and loaf sounds hollow when lightly tapped. Immediately remove from casserole; cool on wire rack. Brush warm loaf with melted margarine; sprinkle with coarse salt.
Yield: 1 (18-slice) loaf.

FOOD PROCESSOR DIRECTIONS:

In small bowl, soften yeast in ¼ cup warm water (105 to 115°F.). In food processor bowl with metal blade, combine 2 cups flour, sugar, onion, dill seed, 1 teaspoon salt, baking soda and 1 tablespoon margarine. Cover; process 5 seconds. Add cottage cheese and egg. Cover; process about 10 seconds or until blended. With machine running, pour yeast mixture through feed tube. Continue processing until blended, about 20 seconds or until mixture pulls away from sides of bowl and forms a ball, adding additional flour if necessary. Carefully scrape dough from blade and bowl; place in lightly greased bowl. Cover loosely with plastic wrap and cloth towel. Let rise in warm place (80 to 85°F.) until light and doubled in size, 45 to 60 minutes. Continue as directed above.

HIGH ALTITUDE:

Above 3500 Feet: Bake at 375°F. for 35 to 40 minutes.

NUTRITION PER SERVING:

Calories 100; Protein 4g; Carbohydrate 16g; Fat 2g; Sodium 125mg.

SAVORY BUBBLE LOAF

This loaf is best served warm from the oven.

BREAD
- 3 **to 3½ cups all purpose flour**
- 2 **tablespoons sugar**
- 1 **teaspoon salt**
- 1 **pkg. active dry yeast**
- 1¼ **cups milk**
- 2 **tablespoons oil**
- 1 **egg**
- ⅓ **cup margarine or butter, melted**

TOPPING
- 2 **tablespoons grated Parmesan cheese**
- 1 **tablespoon sesame seed**
- ½ **to 1 teaspoon garlic salt**
- ½ **teaspoon paprika**

In large bowl, combine 1½ cups flour, sugar, salt and yeast; blend well. In small saucepan, heat milk and oil until very warm (120 to 130°F.). Add warm liquid and egg to flour mixture. Blend at low speed until moistened; beat 3 minutes at medium speed. By hand, stir in an additional 1¼ to 1½ cups flour until dough pulls cleanly away from sides of bowl.

On floured surface, knead in ¼ to ½ cup flour until dough is smooth and elastic, about 2 minutes. Place dough in greased bowl; cover loosely with plastic wrap and cloth towel. Let rise in warm place (80 to 85°F.) until light and doubled in size, about 45 to 60 minutes.

Punch down dough several times to remove all air bubbles. Divide dough into 16 equal pieces; shape into balls. Dip each into melted margarine. Place half of balls in ungreased 12-cup Bundt® pan, forming 1 layer. Combine topping ingredients; sprinkle half over layer of balls. Form second layer with remaining balls. Pour any remaining margarine over balls. Sprinkle with remaining topping. Cover; let rise in warm place until light and doubled in size, about 30 to 45 minutes.

Heat oven to 375°F. Uncover dough. Bake 25 to 30 minutes or until golden brown and loaf sounds hollow when lightly tapped. Cool 5 minutes; remove from pan. Serve warm.

Yield: 1 (16-slice) loaf.

HIGH ALTITUDE:

Above 3500 Feet: No change.

NUTRITION PER SERVING:

Calories 180; Protein 4g; Carbohydrate 24g; Fat 7g; Sodium 315mg.

COOK'S NOTE

MILK IN YEAST BREADS

Milk can be used in place of water when baking bread. It will give the bread a browner crust, a yellower grain and a sweeter flavor.

DANISH SESAME BRAN BREAD

Sesame seed highlights these loaves.

- 1 **cup boiling water**
- 1 **cup yellow cornmeal**
- 2½ **to 3 cups all purpose flour**
- 3 **cups whole wheat flour**
- ½ **cup shreds of whole bran cereal**
- ½ **cup sesame seed, toasted, p. 23**
- 2 **teaspoons salt**
- 2 **pkg. active dry yeast**
- 1 **cup milk**
- ¼ **cup oil**
- ¼ **cup molasses**
- ¼ **cup honey**
- ½ **cup plain yogurt, room temperature**

In small bowl, combine 1 cup boiling water and cornmeal. In large bowl, combine 1 cup all purpose flour, 1 cup whole wheat flour, cereal, sesame seed, salt and yeast; blend well. In small saucepan, heat milk, oil, molasses and honey until very warm (120 to 130°F.). (Mixture will look curdled.) Add warm liquid, cornmeal mixture and yogurt to flour mixture. Blend at low speed until moistened; beat 3 minutes at medium speed. By hand, stir in remaining 2 cups whole wheat flour and about ½ cup all purpose flour until dough pulls cleanly away from sides of bowl.

On floured surface, knead in 1 to 1½ cups all purpose flour until dough is smooth and elastic, about 8 minutes. Place in greased bowl; cover loosely with plastic wrap and cloth towel. Let rise in warm place (80 to 85°F.) until light and doubled in size, about 1 to 1½ hours.

Grease two 9x5 or 8x4-inch loaf pans. Punch down dough several times to remove all air bubbles. Divide dough into 2 parts; shape into loaves. Place in greased pans. Cover; let rise in warm place until dough fills pans and tops of loaves are about 1 inch above pan edges, about 45 to 60 minutes.

Heat oven to 350°F. Uncover dough. Bake 30 to 40 minutes or until golden brown and loaves sound hollow when lightly tapped. Immediately remove from pans; cool on wire racks.

Yield: 2 (14-slice) loaves.

HIGH ALTITUDE:
Above 3500 Feet: No change.

NUTRITION PER SERVING:
Calories 160; Protein 5g; Carbohydrate 29g; Fat 4g; Sodium 170mg.

ONION LOVER'S TWIST

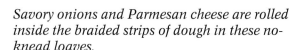

Savory onions and Parmesan cheese are rolled inside the braided strips of dough in these no-knead loaves.

BREAD
- 3½ **to 4½ cups all purpose flour**
- ¼ **cup sugar**
- 1½ **teaspoons salt**
- 1 **pkg. active dry yeast**
- ¾ **cup water**
- ½ **cup milk**
- ¼ **cup margarine or butter**
- 1 **egg**

FILLING
- ¼ **cup margarine or butter**
- 1 **cup finely chopped onions or ¼ cup instant minced onion**
- 1 **tablespoon grated Parmesan cheese**
- 1 **tablespoon sesame or poppy seed**
- ½ **to 1 teaspoon garlic salt**
- 1 **teaspoon paprika**

In large bowl, combine 2 cups flour, sugar, salt and yeast; blend well. In small saucepan, heat water, milk and ¼ cup margarine until very warm (120 to 130°F.). Add warm liquid and egg to flour mixture. Blend at low speed until moistened; beat 3 minutes at medium speed. By hand, stir in remaining 1½ to 2½ cups flour to form a soft dough. Cover loosely with plastic wrap and cloth towel. Let rise in warm place (80 to 85°F.) until light and doubled in size, 45 to 60 minutes.

Grease large cookie sheet. Melt ¼ cup margarine in small saucepan; stir in remaining filling ingredients. Set aside. Stir down dough to remove all air bubbles. On floured surface, toss dough until no longer sticky. Roll dough into 18x12-inch rectangle; spread with filling. Cut rectangle in half crosswise to make two 12x9-inch rectangles. Cut each rectangle into three 9x4-inch strips. Starting with 9-inch side, roll up each strip; pinch edges and ends to seal. On greased cookie sheet, braid 3 rolls together; pinch ends to seal. Repeat with remaining 3 rolls for second loaf. Cover; let rise in warm place until light and doubled in size, 25 to 30 minutes.

Heat oven to 350°F. Uncover dough. Bake 27 to 35 minutes or until golden brown and loaves sound hollow when lightly tapped. Immediately remove from cookie sheet; cool on wire racks.

Yield: 2 (16-slice) loaves.

Above 3500 Feet: No change.

NUTRITION PER SERVING:
Calories 100; Protein 2g; Carbohydrate 16g; Fat 3g;
Sodium 200mg.

HAWAIIAN POTATO BREAD

*Spread slices of this pineapple-flavored loaf with
butter and pineapple preserves. Serve them with
coffee or tea.*

BREAD
- 5 to 6 cups all purpose flour
- 2 teaspoons salt
- 2 pkg. active dry yeast
- 1 cup pineapple juice
- 1½ cups water
- ¼ cup margarine or butter
- 2 eggs
- 2 cups mashed potato flakes

TOPPING
- 1 tablespoon margarine or butter, melted
- ¼ cup sugar
- 3 tablespoons all purpose flour
- ¼ teaspoon nutmeg

In large bowl, combine 1½ cups flour, salt and
yeast; blend well. In medium saucepan, heat pineapple juice, water and ¼ cup margarine until very
warm (120 to 130°F.). Add warm liquid and eggs to
flour mixture. Blend at low speed until moistened;
beat 4 minutes at medium speed. Add potato flakes,
beating only until thoroughly moistened. Stir in an
additional 3 to 3½ cups flour until dough pulls
cleanly away from sides of bowl.

On floured surface, knead in ½ to 1 cup flour until
dough is smooth and elastic, about 10 minutes.
Place dough in greased bowl; cover loosely with
plastic wrap and cloth towel. Let rise in warm place
(80 to 85°F.) until light and doubled in size, about
1 hour.

Grease two 8 or 9-inch round cake pans. Punch
down dough several times to remove all air bubbles. With floured hands, divide dough into 2 parts;
shape into 2 round loaves. Place in greased pans.
Cover; let rise in warm place until light and doubled in size, about 30 to 45 minutes.

Heat oven to 350°F. Uncover dough. Brush loaves
with melted margarine. Combine remaining topping ingredients until crumbly; sprinkle evenly over
loaves. Bake at 350°F. for 35 to 45 minutes or until
loaves sound hollow when lightly tapped. Immediately remove from pans by loosening sides and
placing loaves on wire racks; cool.
Yield: 2 (24-slice) loaves.

HIGH ALTITUDE:
Above 3500 Feet: Decrease first rise time to 40 to
45 minutes.

NUTRITION PER SERVING:
Calories 90; Protein 2g; Carbohydrate 16g; Fat 2g;
Sodium 110mg.

COOK'S NOTE

USING POTATO FLAKES IN RECIPES
To measure potato flakes, lightly pour them
into a measuring cup and level them off
with the straight edge of a spatula or knife.

BRAIDED HOLIDAY STOLLEN

Stollen, Germany's traditional Christmas bread, is a rich, dried fruit-filled loaf. This tempting bread can be decorated with candied cherries.

BREAD
5½ to 6½ cups all purpose flour
1 cup sugar
1 teaspoon salt
2 pkg. active dry yeast
1 cup water
1 cup milk
1 cup margarine or butter
2 eggs
1½ cups golden raisins
1½ cups slivered almonds

FROSTING
½ cup powdered sugar
2 teaspoons milk

In large bowl, combine 2 cups flour, sugar, salt and yeast; blend well. In small saucepan, heat water, 1 cup milk and margarine until very warm (120 to 130°F.). Add warm liquid and eggs to flour mixture. Blend at low speed until moistened; beat 2 minutes at medium speed. By hand, stir in raisins, almonds and remaining 3½ to 4½ cups flour until dough pulls away from sides of bowl. Cover tightly and refrigerate overnight.

Grease 3 cookie sheets. Remove dough from refrigerator. On lightly floured surface, divide dough into 3 equal parts. Divide each part into 3 pieces. Roll each piece into a rope 16 inches long. Place 3 ropes lengthwise on each greased cookie sheet. Braid ropes loosely from center to each end. Pinch ends together; tuck under to seal. Cover loosely with plastic wrap and cloth towel. Let rise in warm place (80 to 85°F.) until doubled in size, about 1½ to 2 hours.

Heat oven to 350°F. Uncover dough. Bake 25 to 35 minutes or until light golden brown.* Immediately remove from cookie sheets; cool on wire racks. In small bowl, combine frosting ingredients. Drizzle over cooled loaves.
Yield: 3 (16-slice) loaves.

TIP:
* If baking only 1 loaf at a time, cover and refrigerate remaining loaves until ready to bake. If baking 2 loaves, alternate cookie sheet positions halfway through baking.

HIGH ALTITUDE:
Above 3500 Feet: No change.

NUTRITION PER SERVING:
Calories 160; Protein 3g; Carbohydrate 23g; Fat 7g; Sodium 95mg.

JULEKAKE

Scandinavian for "Christmas cake," Julekake is a fragrant yeast loaf flavored with fruits and sweet spices. This recipe makes 3 loaves.

BREAD
5½ to 6½ cups all purpose flour
½ cup sugar
1 teaspoon salt
1 teaspoon cardamom
½ teaspoon cinnamon
2 pkg. active dry yeast
1 cup milk
½ cup water
⅔ cup margarine or butter
3 eggs
½ cup candied green cherries, halved
½ cup candied red cherries, halved
½ cup raisins

GLAZE
1½ cups powdered sugar
¼ teaspoon almond extract
2 to 3 tablespoons milk

In large bowl, combine 2 cups flour, sugar, salt, cardamom, cinnamon and yeast; blend well. In small saucepan, heat 1 cup milk, water and margarine until very warm (120 to 130°F.). Add warm liquid and eggs to flour mixture. Blend at low speed until moistened; beat 3 minutes at medium speed. By hand, stir in an additional 3 to 3½ cups flour, cherries and raisins to form a soft dough.

On floured surface, knead in ½ to 1 cup flour until smooth and elastic, about 8 minutes. Place dough in greased bowl; cover loosely with plastic wrap and cloth towel. Let rise in warm place (80 to 85°F.) until light and doubled in size, about 55 to 60 minutes.

Grease 2 large cookie sheets. Punch down dough several times to remove all air bubbles. Divide dough into 3 equal parts; shape into round balls. Place on greased cookie sheets; flatten slightly.

Cover; let rise in warm place until light and doubled in size, about 45 minutes.

Heat oven to 350°F. Uncover dough. Bake 30 to 35 minutes or until golden brown. Immediately remove from cookie sheets; cool on wire racks. In small bowl, combine all glaze ingredients, adding enough milk for desired drizzling consistency. Drizzle over cooled loaves. Garnish as desired.

Yield: 3 (16-slice) loaves.

HIGH ALTITUDE:
Above 3500 Feet: No change.

NUTRITION PER SERVING:
Calories 130; Protein 2g; Carbohydrate 22g; Fat 3g; Sodium 80mg.

RICH CHOCOLATE YEAST BREAD

A cinnamon-nut filling is surrounded by rich chocolate dough in this indulgent bread.

BREAD
  1 cup milk
  ½ cup water
  2 pkg. active dry yeast
  6 to 7 cups all purpose flour
  ½ cup sugar
  ¼ cup unsweetened cocoa
  2 teaspoons salt
  3 eggs
  ½ cup margarine or butter, melted
  ½ cup dairy sour cream
  2 teaspoons vanilla

FILLING
  ⅓ cup sugar
  1 teaspoon cinnamon
  2 tablespoons margarine or butter, softened
  ¼ cup chopped pecans

GLAZE
  1 cup powdered sugar
  3 tablespoons unsweetened cocoa
  2 tablespoons margarine or butter, softened
  1 teaspoon vanilla
  2 tablespoons milk

In small saucepan, heat 1 cup milk and water until warm (105 to 115°F.). Dissolve yeast in liquid. In large bowl, combine 2 cups flour, ½ cup sugar, ¼ cup cocoa and salt; blend well. Add warm liquid, eggs, melted margarine, sour cream and 2 teaspoons vanilla to flour mixture. Blend at low speed until moistened; beat 3 minutes at medium speed. By hand, stir in 3 cups additional flour to form a stiff dough.

On floured surface, knead in 1 to 2 cups flour until dough is smooth and elastic, about 10 minutes. Place dough in greased bowl; cover loosely with plastic wrap and cloth towel. Let rise in warm place (80 to 85°F.) until light and doubled in size, about 1 to 1½ hours.

Grease 2 cookie sheets. Punch down dough several times to remove all air bubbles. Divide dough into 2 equal parts; shape into balls. In small bowl, combine ⅓ cup sugar and cinnamon.

On lightly floured surface, roll each half into a 12x9-inch rectangle. Spread each rectangle with 1 tablespoon margarine; sprinkle each with half of the sugar-cinnamon mixture and 2 tablespoons of the pecans. Starting with longer side, roll up tightly, pressing edges and ends to seal. Place each roll, seam side down, on greased cookie sheet, joining ends to form circle; pinch to seal. With scissors or sharp knife, make cuts at 1½-inch intervals to within ½ inch of inside of ring. Turn each slice on side, cut side up. Cover; let rise in warm place until light and doubled in size, about 1 to 1½ hours.

Heat oven to 350°F. Uncover dough. Bake 25 to 30 minutes or until loaves sound hollow when lightly tapped. Immediately remove from cookie sheets; cool on wire racks. In small bowl, combine all glaze ingredients; mix until smooth. Spoon glaze over cooled loaves.

Yield: 2 (12-slice) loaves.

HIGH ALTITUDE:
Above 3500 Feet: No change.

NUTRITION PER SERVING:
Calories 290; Protein 7g; Carbohydrate 44g; Fat 10g; Sodium 265mg.

Basic Dinner Rolls

Each variation uses half of the dough so you can try 2 different shapings.

5³⁄₄ to 6³⁄₄ cups all purpose flour
¼ cup sugar
2 teaspoons salt
2 pkg. active dry yeast
1 cup water
1 cup milk
½ cup margarine or butter
1 egg
Melted margarine or butter, if desired

In large bowl, combine 2 cups flour, sugar, salt and yeast; blend well. In small saucepan, heat water, milk and ½ cup margarine until very warm (120 to 130°F.). Add warm liquid and egg to flour mixture. Blend at low speed until moistened; beat 3 minutes at medium speed. By hand, stir in an additional 2½ to 3 cups flour until dough pulls cleanly away from sides of bowl.

On floured surface, knead in 1¼ to 1³⁄₄ cups flour until dough is smooth and elastic, about 8 to 10 minutes. Place dough in greased bowl; cover loosely with plastic wrap and cloth towel. Let rise in warm place (80 to 85°F.) until light and doubled in size, about 45 to 60 minutes.

Punch down dough several times to remove all air bubbles. Divide dough in half. To make **Pan Rolls**, lightly grease two 13x9-inch pans. Divide each half of dough into 16 equal pieces. Shape each into a ball, pulling edges under to make a smooth top. Place balls, smooth side up, in greased pans. Cover; let rise in warm place until light and doubled in size, about 20 to 30 minutes.

Heat oven to 400°F. Uncover dough. Bake at 400°F. for 16 to 20 minutes or until golden brown. Remove rolls from pans immediately; cool on wire racks. Brush with melted margarine.
Yield: 32 rolls

TIP:
To make dough a day ahead, after first rise time, punch down dough, cover and refrigerate dough overnight. Shape dough as directed in recipe; let rise a second time until light and doubled in size, about 25 to 35 minutes.

HIGH ALTITUDE:
Above 3500 Feet: No change.

NUTRITION PER SERVING:
Calories 280; Protein 7g; Carbohydrate 46g; Fat 8g; Sodium 360mg.

VARIATIONS:

BOW KNOT ROLLS: Lightly grease cookie sheets. Using half of dough, divide dough into 16 equal pieces. On lightly floured surface, roll each piece into a 9-inch rope. Tie each into a loose knot. Place 2 to 3 inches apart on greased cookie sheets. After rising, bake 12 to 15 minutes or until golden brown.
Yield: 16 rolls.

CLOVERLEAF ROLLS: Lightly grease 12 muffin cups. Using half of dough, divide dough into 12 equal pieces; divide each into thirds. Shape each into a ball, pulling edges under to make a smooth top. Place 3 balls, smooth side up, in each greased muffin cup. After rising, bake 14 to 18 minutes or until golden brown.
Yield: 12 rolls.

CRESCENT ROLLS: Lightly grease cookie sheets. Using half of dough, divide dough in half again; shape each half into a ball. On lightly floured surface, roll each ball into a 12-inch circle. Spread each with 1 tablespoon softened margarine or butter. Cut each circle into 12 wedges. Beginning at wide end of wedge, roll toward point. Place, point side down, 2 to 3 inches apart on greased cookie sheets. Curve ends to form a crescent shape. After rising, bake 12 to 15 minutes or until golden brown.
Yield: 24 rolls.

CROWN ROLLS: Lightly grease 12 muffin cups. Using half of dough, divide dough into 12 equal pieces. Shape each into a ball, pulling edges under to make a smooth top. Place 1 ball, smooth side up, in each greased muffin cup. Using kitchen shears dipped in flour, cut balls of dough into quarters almost to bottom. After rising, bake 14 to 18 minutes or until golden brown.
Yield: 12 rolls.

SWIRL ROLLS: Lightly grease cookie sheets. Using half of dough, divide dough into 16 equal pieces. On lightly floured surface, roll each piece into an 8-inch rope. Beginning at center, make a loose swirl or coil with each rope; tuck end under. Place 2 to 3 inches apart on greased cookie sheets. After rising, bake 12 to 15 minutes or until golden brown.
Yield: 16 rolls.

HOW TO SHAPE DINNER ROLLS

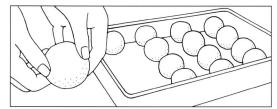

Pan Rolls

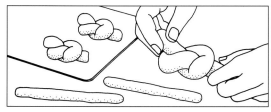

Bow Knot Rolls

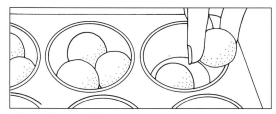

Cloverleaf Rolls

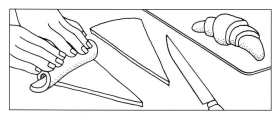

Crescent Rolls

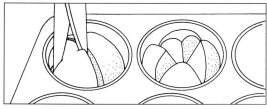

Crown Rolls

Swirl Rolls

OATS 'N WHEAT DINNER ROLLS

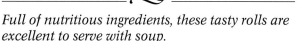

Full of nutritious ingredients, these tasty rolls are excellent to serve with soup.

ROLLS
1¾ to 2¾ cups all purpose flour
⅓ cup rolled oats
¼ cup sugar
1 teaspoon salt
1 pkg. active dry yeast
1 cup milk
3 tablespoons margarine or butter
1 egg
¾ cup whole wheat flour

TOPPING
1 egg white
1 tablespoon water
1 tablespoon rolled oats

In large bowl, combine 1 cup all purpose flour, ⅓ cup rolled oats, sugar, salt and yeast; blend well. In small saucepan, heat milk and margarine until very warm (120 to 130°F.). Add warm liquid and egg to flour mixture. Blend at low speed until moistened; beat 2 minutes at medium speed. By hand, stir in whole wheat flour and an additional ½ to 1¼ cups all purpose flour until dough pulls cleanly away from sides of bowl.

On floured surface, knead in ¼ to ½ cup all purpose flour until dough is smooth and elastic, about 5 minutes. Place dough in greased bowl; cover loosely with plastic wrap and cloth towel. Let rise in warm place (80 to 85°F.) until light and doubled in size, about 1 hour.

Grease 9-inch square pan. Punch down dough several times to remove all air bubbles. Divide dough into 16 pieces; shape into balls. Place in greased pan. Cover; let rise in warm place until light and doubled in size, about 35 to 45 minutes.

Heat oven to 375°F. Uncover dough. In small bowl, combine egg white and water; beat slightly. Carefully brush over rolls; sprinkle with 1 tablespoon rolled oats. Bake at 375°F. for 20 to 30 minutes or until golden brown. Immediately remove from pan. Serve warm.
Yield: 16 rolls.

HIGH ALTITUDE:
Above 3500 Feet: No change.

NUTRITION PER SERVING:
Calories 150; Protein 5g; Carbohydrate 26g; Fat 3g; Sodium 170mg.

ROSEMARY FRENCH ROLLS

Fast-acting yeast shortens the rise time in this recipe.

- **2 to 2½ cups all purpose flour**
- **1 teaspoon sugar**
- **1 teaspoon salt**
- **1 pkg. fast-acting yeast**
- **1 cup water**
- **1 egg white, beaten**
- **3 teaspoons dried rosemary leaves, crushed**

In large bowl, combine 1 cup flour, sugar, salt and yeast; mix well. In small saucepan, heat water until very warm (120 to 130°F.). Add warm water to flour mixture. Blend at low speed until moistened; beat 2 minutes at medium speed. By hand, stir in an additional ½ to 1 cup flour until dough pulls cleanly away from sides of bowl.

On floured surface, knead in ½ cup flour until dough is smooth and elastic, about 5 minutes. Place dough in greased bowl; cover loosely with plastic wrap. Let rise in warm place (80 to 85°F.) until light and doubled in size, about 30 minutes.

Grease large cookie sheet. Punch down dough several times to remove all air bubbles. Divide dough into 12 pieces; shape into balls. Place on greased cookie sheet. Cover with greased plastic wrap. Let rise in warm place until doubled in size, about 15 minutes.

Place shallow pan half full of hot water on lower oven rack. Heat oven to 425°F. Uncover dough. Brush rolls with egg white; sprinkle with rosemary. Bake at 425°F. for 14 to 21 minutes or until light golden brown. Immediately remove from cookie sheet; cool on wire rack.
Yield: 12 rolls.

FOOD PROCESSOR DIRECTIONS:
Grease large cookie sheet. In food processor bowl with metal blade, combine 2½ cups flour, sugar, salt and yeast. Cover; process 5 seconds. With machine running, pour hot water through feed tube; continue processing until dough forms a ball. (If dough does not form a ball, add additional flour 1 tablespoon at a time.) Process an additional 40 to 60 seconds. Do not knead dough; place in greased bowl and continue as directed above.

HIGH ALTITUDE:
Above 3500 Feet: No change.

Rosemary French Rolls

NUTRITION PER SERVING:
Calories 100; Protein 3g; Carbohydrate 21g; Fat 0g; Sodium 180mg.

SWEET POTATO ROLLS

Sweet potatoes add a southern twist to these wonderful dinner rolls.

- **3¾ to 4 cups all purpose flour**
- **¼ cup sugar**
- **1 teaspoon salt**
- **1 pkg. active dry yeast**
- **1 cup milk**
- **¼ cup margarine or butter**
- **¾ cup mashed canned sweet potatoes**
- **1 egg**
- **Melted margarine or butter, if desired**

In large bowl, combine 1 cup flour, sugar, salt and yeast; blend well. In small saucepan, heat milk and margarine until very warm (120 to 130°F.). Add warm liquid, sweet potatoes and egg to flour mixture. Blend at low speed until moistened; beat 2 minutes at medium speed. By hand, stir in remaining 2¾ to 3 cups flour to form a soft dough. (Dough will be somewhat sticky.)

On floured surface, knead dough until smooth and elastic, about 2 minutes. Place dough in greased bowl; cover loosely with plastic wrap and cloth towel. Let rise in warm place (80 to 85°F.) until light and doubled in size, about 45 to 55 minutes.

Grease 2 large cookie sheets. Punch down dough several times to remove all air bubbles. On floured surface, toss dough lightly until no longer sticky. Divide dough into 18 pieces; shape into balls. Place 2 inches apart on greased cookie sheets. Cover; let rise in warm place until light and doubled in size, about 30 to 40 minutes.

Heat oven to 375°F. Uncover dough. Bake 15 to 20 minutes or until golden brown. Immediately remove from cookie sheets; cool on wire racks. Brush with melted margarine.
Yield: 18 rolls.

HIGH ALTITUDE:
Above 3500 Feet: No change.

NUTRITION PER SERVING:
Calories 170; Protein 4g; Carbohydrate 28g; Fat 4g; Sodium 170mg.

CORNMEAL SESAME BATTER ROLLS

Batter breads are not kneaded. The dough rises in the baking pan, then it is baked. These tender cornmeal rolls are a welcome addition to any meal.

- 1¾ to 2 cups all purpose flour
- ½ cup cornmeal
- 1 tablespoon sugar
- 1 teaspoon salt
- 1 pkg. active dry yeast
- 1 cup milk
- ¼ cup margarine or butter
- 1 egg
  Sesame seed

In large bowl, combine 1 cup flour, cornmeal, sugar, salt and yeast; blend well. In small saucepan, heat milk and margarine until very warm (120 to 130°F.). Add warm liquid and egg to flour mixture. Blend at low speed until moistened; beat 2 minutes at medium speed. By hand, stir in ¾ to 1 cup flour to form a stiff batter. Cover; let rise in warm place (80 to 85°F.) until light and doubled in size, about 45 minutes.

Generously grease 12 muffin cups. Stir down batter; spoon into greased muffin cups. Sprinkle with sesame seed. Cover loosely with greased plastic wrap and cloth towel. Let rise in warm place until light and doubled in size, about 30 minutes.

Heat oven to 400°F. Uncover dough. Bake 10 to 15 minutes or until golden brown. Immediately remove from pan; cool on wire racks.
Yield: 12 rolls.

HIGH ALTITUDE:
Above 3500 Feet: No change.

NUTRITION PER SERVING:
Calories 150; Protein 4g; Carbohydrate 22g; Fat 5g; Sodium 240mg.

HALF-TIME SPOON ROLLS

No kneading, no rolling, no shaping!

- 3 to 3½ cups all purpose flour
- ¼ cup sugar
- 1 teaspoon salt
- 1 pkg. active dry yeast
- ¾ cup milk
- ¾ cup water
- ⅓ cup margarine or butter
- 1 egg

In large bowl, combine 1½ cups flour, sugar, salt and yeast; blend well. In small saucepan, heat milk, water and margarine until very warm (120 to 130°F.). Add warm liquid and egg to flour mixture. Blend at low speed until moistened; beat 3 minutes at medium speed. By hand, stir in remaining 1½ to 2 cups flour to form a stiff batter. Cover loosely with plastic wrap and cloth towel. Let rise in warm place (80 to 85°F.) until light and doubled in size, about 45 to 50 minutes.

Grease 18 muffin cups. Stir down dough to remove all air bubbles. Spoon into greased muffin cups, filling about ⅔ full. Cover loosely with greased plastic wrap and cloth towel. Let rise in warm place until light and doubled in size, about 25 to 35 minutes.

Heat oven to 400°F. Uncover dough. Bake 15 to 20 minutes or until golden brown. Immediately remove from pan; cool on wire racks.
Yield: 18 rolls.

HIGH ALTITUDE:
Above 3500 Feet: No change.

NUTRITION PER SERVING:
Calories 140; Protein 3g; Carbohydrate 22g; Fat 4g; Sodium 170mg.

GOLDEN HONEY ROLLS

These dinner rolls boast a honey glaze that adds a touch of sweetness.

ROLLS
3½ cups all purpose flour
1 teaspoon salt
1 pkg. active dry yeast
1 cup milk
½ cup oil
2 tablespoons honey
2 eggs, reserving 1 egg white for topping

TOPPING
⅓ cup sugar or powdered sugar
2 tablespoons margarine or butter, softened
1 tablespoon honey
   Reserved egg white

In large bowl, combine 1½ cups flour, salt and yeast; blend well. In small saucepan, heat milk, oil and 2 tablespoons honey until very warm (120 to 130°F.). Add warm liquid, 1 egg and 1 egg yolk to flour mixture. Blend at low speed until moistened; beat 3 minutes at medium speed. By hand, stir in remaining 2 cups flour to form a soft dough. Cover loosely with plastic wrap and cloth towel. Let rise in warm place (80 to 85°F.) until light and doubled in size, about 45 to 60 minutes.

Generously grease two 8 or 9-inch round cake or pie pans. Punch down dough several times to remove all air bubbles. On floured surface, toss dough lightly until no longer sticky. Divide dough into 20 pieces; shape into balls. Place in greased pans.

In small bowl, combine all topping ingredients; drizzle half over rolls. Cover; let rise in warm place until light and doubled in size, about 20 to 30 minutes.

Heat oven to 350°F. Uncover dough. Drizzle remaining topping over rolls. Bake at 350°F. for 25 to 30 minutes or until golden brown. Immediately remove from pans; cool on wire racks.
Yield: 20 rolls.

HIGH ALTITUDE:
Above 3500 Feet: Bake at 375°F. for 25 to 30 minutes.

NUTRITION PER SERVING:
Calories 170; Protein 3g; Carbohydrate 23g; Fat 8g; Sodium 130mg.

LIGHT RYE ROLLS

There are several types of rye flour but the most common is medium rye flour. It is available in most supermarkets and gives these rolls their characteristic flavor.

1 to 1¼ cups all purpose flour
2 tablespoons sugar
1 teaspoon caraway seed, if desired
1 teaspoon salt
1 pkg. active dry yeast
1 cup milk
2 tablespoons shortening
1 egg
1 cup medium rye flour
   Margarine or butter, melted

Grease 12 muffin cups. In large bowl, combine ¾ cup all purpose flour, sugar, caraway seed, salt and yeast; blend well. In small saucepan, heat milk and shortening until very warm (120 to 130°F.). Add warm liquid and egg to flour mixture. Blend at low speed until moistened; beat 3 minutes at medium speed. By hand, stir in rye flour and an additional ¼ to ½ cup all purpose flour to form a stiff batter. Spoon into greased muffin cups, filling about ⅔ full. Let rise, uncovered, in warm place (80 to 85°F.) until light, about 15 to 25 minutes.

Heat oven to 400°F. Bake 12 to 15 minutes or until light golden brown. Immediately remove from pan; brush with melted margarine. Serve warm.
Yield: 12 rolls.

HIGH ALTITUDE:
Above 3500 Feet: No change.

NUTRITION PER SERVING:
Calories 120; Protein 4g; Carbohydrate 19g; Fat 3g; Sodium 190mg.

HERBED OATMEAL PAN BREAD

A unique shaping method highlights these herb topped rolls.

BREAD
   2 **cups water**
   1 **cup rolled oats**
   3 **tablespoons margarine or butter**
3¾ **to 4¾ cups all purpose flour**
   ¼ **cup sugar**
   2 **teaspoons salt**
   2 **pkg. active dry yeast**
   1 **egg**

HERB BUTTER
   1 **tablespoon grated Parmesan cheese**
   ½ **teaspoon dried basil leaves**
   ¼ **teaspoon dried oregano leaves**
   ¼ **teaspoon garlic powder**
   6 **tablespoons margarine or butter, melted**

Bring water to a boil in medium saucepan; stir in rolled oats. Remove from heat; stir in 3 tablespoons margarine. Cool to 120 to 130°F. In large bowl, combine 1½ cups flour, sugar, salt and yeast; blend well. Add rolled oats mixture and egg. Blend at low speed until moistened; beat 3 minutes at medium speed. By hand, stir in an additional 1¾ cups to 2½ cups flour to form stiff dough.

On floured surface, knead in ½ to ¾ cup flour until dough is smooth and elastic, about 5 minutes. Shape dough into ball; cover with large bowl. Let rest 15 minutes. Grease 13x9-inch baking pan. Punch down dough several times to remove all air bubbles; press into greased pan. Using very sharp knife, cut diagonal lines 1½ inches apart, cutting completely through dough. Repeat in opposite direction creating diamond pattern. Cover loosely with greased plastic wrap and cloth towel.* Let rise in warm place (80 to 85°F.) until light and doubled in size, about 45 minutes.

Heat oven to 375°F. Uncover dough. Redefine cuts by poking tip of knife into cuts until knife hits bottom of pan; do not pull knife through dough. In small bowl, combine Parmesan cheese, basil, oregano and garlic powder; mix well. Set aside. Spoon 4 tablespoons of the butter over cut dough.

Bake at 375°F. for 15 minutes. Brush remaining 2 tablespoons of butter over bread. Sprinkle with Parmesan cheese-herb mixture. Bake for an additional 10 to 15 minutes or until golden brown. Serve warm or cool.
Yield: 16 rolls.

TIPS:
* To bake at a later time, at this point let stand at room temperature for 20 minutes. Remove cloth towel. Refrigerate 2 to 24 hours. Remove plastic wrap from dough; let stand at room temperature 30 minutes. Bake as directed above.

Two 8 or 9-inch square pans or one 8-inch and one 9-inch square pan can be substituted for 13x9-inch pan. When using 2 square pans, one pan can be baked and the other pan refrigerated for baking the next day.

HIGH ALTITUDE:
Above 3500 Feet: No change.

NUTRITION PER SERVING:
Calories 240; Protein 6g; Carbohydrate 35g; Fat 8g; Sodium 350mg.

COOK'S NOTES

ROLLED OATS

Rolled oats can be purchased in 3 varieties: old-fashioned, quick-cooking and instant. Old-fashioned rolled oats are whole oats that have been hulled, steamed and flattened by rollers into flakes. Quick-cooking rolled oats have been cut into smaller pieces before rolling, yielding thinner flakes that cook more quickly. Instant oats have been cut into even smaller pieces, precooked and dried so that they cook very fast.

Old-fashioned and quick-cooking rolled oats usually can be used interchangeably in our recipes unless we specify a variety. However, old-fashioned rolled oats will result in a firmer textured end product. Instant oats are not usually used for baking; most instant oat products include sugar, salt or flavorings and are meant to be used primarily as breakfast cereal.

Herbed Oatmeal Pan Bread

POTATO CHIVE ROLLS

These light and tender dinner rolls are mildly flavored with sour cream and chives.

4½ to 5 cups all purpose flour
  1 cup mashed potato flakes
  1 tablespoon sugar
  3 to 4 teaspoons chopped fresh or freeze-dried chives
  2 teaspoons salt
  2 pkg. active dry yeast
  2 cups milk
  ½ cup dairy sour cream
  2 eggs

In large bowl, combine 1½ cups flour, potato flakes, sugar, chives, salt and yeast; blend well. In small saucepan, heat milk and sour cream until very warm (120 to 130°F.). Add warm liquid and eggs to flour mixture. Blend at low speed until moistened; beat 3 minutes at medium speed. By hand, stir in remaining 3 to 3½ cups flour to form a stiff dough. Cover loosely with plastic wrap and cloth towel. Let rise in warm place (80 to 85°F.) until light and doubled in size, about 45 to 55 minutes.

Generously grease 13x9-inch pan. On floured surface, knead dough gently until no longer sticky. Divide dough into 24 pieces; shape into balls. Place in greased pan. Cover; let rise in warm place until light and doubled in size, 30 to 35 minutes.

Heat oven to 375°F. Uncover dough. Bake 25 to 35 minutes or until golden brown. Remove from pan immediately; cool on wire rack. If desired, lightly dust tops of rolls with flour.

Yield: 24 rolls.

HIGH ALTITUDE:
Above 3500 Feet: No change.

NUTRITION PER SERVING:
Calories 130; Protein 4g; Carbohydrate 24g; Fat 2g; Sodium 200mg.

WHOLE WHEAT PARTY BUNS

The goodness of whole wheat makes these dinner rolls delicious anytime.

3¾ to 4¼ cups all purpose flour
  3 cups whole wheat flour
  ½ cup sugar
  2 teaspoons salt
  2 pkg. active dry yeast
  2 cups water
  ¾ cup shortening or oil
  2 tablespoons molasses
  2 eggs, beaten

In large bowl, combine 2 cups all purpose flour, 1 cup whole wheat flour, sugar, salt and yeast; blend well. In small saucepan, heat water, shortening and molasses until very warm (120 to 130°F.). Add warm liquid to flour mixture; blend at low speed until moistened. Add eggs; beat 3 minutes at medium speed. By hand, stir in remaining whole wheat flour and enough all purpose flour (about 1¼ cups) to make a stiff dough.

On floured surface, knead in ½ to 1 cup all purpose flour until dough is smooth and elastic, about 5 minutes. Place in greased bowl; cover loosely with plastic wrap and cloth towel. Let rise in warm place (80 to 85°F.) until light and doubled in size, about 45 to 60 minutes.

Generously grease two 15x10x1-inch baking pans or cookie sheets. Punch down dough. Divide into 36 pieces; shape into balls. Arrange 18 balls in each greased pan. Cover; let rise in warm place (80 to 85°F.) until doubled in size, about 30 to 45 minutes.

Heat oven to 375°F. Uncover dough. Bake 15 to 20 minutes or until golden brown. If desired, brush with melted butter. Remove from pans immediately; cool on wire racks. Serve warm or cool.

Yield: 36 rolls.

HIGH ALTITUDE :
Above 3500 Feet: No change.

NUTRITION PER SERVING:
Calories 140; Protein 3g; Carbohydrate 22g; Fat 5g; Sodium 125mg.

FLAKY BUTTER BRIOCHES

~

A brioche is a tender French roll, rich in butter and eggs, distinguished by its top knot.

4¼ to 4¾ cups all purpose flour
⅓ cup sugar
1 teaspoon salt
2 pkg. active dry yeast
1¼ cups milk
½ cup butter or margarine
3 eggs

In large bowl, combine 2 cups flour, sugar, salt and yeast; blend well. In small saucepan, heat milk and butter until very warm (120 to 130°F.). Add warm liquid and 2 of the eggs to flour mixture. Blend at low speed until moistened; beat 3 minutes at medium speed. By hand, stir in an additional 2 to 2¼ cups flour until dough pulls cleanly away from sides of bowl.

Generously grease 24 individual brioche pans or muffin cups. On floured surface, knead in ¼ to ½ cup flour until dough is smooth, about 2 to 3 minutes. Divide dough into 4 equal parts. Shape 3 dough parts into 8 balls each. Place 1 ball in each greased pan. Shape remaining dough into 24 small balls. With finger, make a deep indentation in center of each large ball. Place 1 small ball in each indentation, pressing down slightly. Cover; let rise in warm place (80 to 85°F.) until light and doubled in size, about 45 minutes.

Heat oven to 350°F. Uncover dough. Beat remaining egg; carefully brush over rolls. Bake at 350°F. for 15 to 20 minutes or until golden brown. Immediately remove from pans; cool on wire racks.
Yield: 24 rolls.

HIGH ALTITUDE:
Above 3500 Feet: No change.

NUTRITION PER SERVING:
Calories 150; Protein 4g; Carbohydrate 23g; Fat 5g; Sodium 140mg.

BUTTERHORN CRESCENTS

~

Serve these impressive looking rolls for your next dinner party.

1 pkg. active dry yeast
1 cup warm milk
3¾ cups all purpose flour
1 teaspoon salt
1 cup butter or margarine
¼ cup sugar
1 egg

In small bowl, dissolve yeast in warm milk (105 to 115°F.). In large bowl, combine flour and salt. Using pastry blender or fork, cut in butter until mixture is crumbly. Beat sugar and egg together; add yeast mixture and sugar-egg mixture to flour mixture, mixing well. (Dough will be stiff.) Cover; refrigerate overnight.

Divide dough into 3 parts. On lightly floured surface, roll each part into a 12-inch circle; cut each circle into 12 wedges. Roll up starting with wide end. Place, point side down, on ungreased cookie sheets. Curve ends to form a crescent shape. Cover loosely with plastic wrap and cloth towel. Let rise in warm place (80 to 85°F.) until light and doubled in size, about 30 to 45 minutes.

Heat oven to 375°F. Uncover dough. Bake 10 to 15 minutes or until light golden brown. Immediately remove from cookie sheets; cool on wire racks.
Yield: 36 rolls.

HIGH ALTITUDE :
Above 3500 Feet: No change.

NUTRITION PER SERVING:
Calories 100; Protein 2g; Carbohydrate 12g; Fat 6g; Sodium 115mg.

VARIATION:

FROSTED BUTTERHORN CRESCENTS:
In small bowl, combine 2 cups powdered sugar, ½ teaspoon almond extract and 2 to 3 tablespoons milk, adding enough milk for desired spreading consistency. Spread over cooled rolls.

Basic Pizza Crust

If you make pizza often, you may want to double this recipe. The crusts can be prebaked and frozen for tasty homemade pizza anytime.

2¼ to 2¾ cups all purpose flour
  1 teaspoon sugar
  1 teaspoon salt
  1 pkg. fast-acting yeast
  1 cup water
  2 tablespoons olive oil or oil

In large bowl, combine 1½ cups flour, sugar, salt and yeast; mix well. In small saucepan, heat water until very hot (120 to 130°F.). Add warm water and oil to flour mixture. Blend at low speed until well moistened; beat 2 minutes at medium speed. By hand, stir in an additional ½ to ¾ cup flour until dough pulls cleanly away from sides of bowl.

On floured surface, knead in ¼ to ½ cup flour until dough is smooth and elastic, about 3 to 5 minutes. Cover loosely with plastic wrap and cloth towel. Let rise in warm place (80 to 85°F.) until light and doubled in size, about 30 minutes.

Place oven rack at lowest position; heat oven to 425°F. Grease two 12-inch pizza pans. Punch down dough several times to remove air bubbles. Divide dough in half; press into greased pizza pans. Bake at 425°F. on lowest oven rack for 15 minutes. Top as desired with favorite pizza toppings. Bake an additional 15 to 20 minutes or until crust is golden brown and toppings are thoroughly heated. **Yield: 2 crusts; 8 servings each.**

FOOD PROCESSOR DIRECTIONS:
In food processor bowl with metal blade, combine 2¼ cups flour, sugar, salt and yeast. Cover; process 5 seconds. With machine running, pour 1 cup water heated to 120 to 130°F. and oil through feed tube; continue processing until dough forms a ball. (If dough does not form a ball, add an additional ½ cup flour, 1 tablespoon at a time.) Process an additional 40 to 60 seconds. Cover; let rise. Continue as directed above.

TIP:
To freeze 1 pizza crust, prepare as directed above. Grease 12-inch pizza pan. Press half of dough in greased pan. Bake at 425°F. for 15 minutes. Cool. Place in moisture-proof freezer bag. Freeze for up to 2 months. Thaw before using and top with favorite pizza toppings. Bake at 425°F. on lowest oven rack for 18 to 22 minutes or until crust is golden brown and toppings are thoroughly heated.

HIGH ALTITUDE:
Above 3500 Feet: No change.

NUTRITION PER SERVING:
Calories 100; Protein 2g,; Carbohydrates 17g; Fat 2g; Sodium 135mg.

Cornmeal Bread Sticks

The use of fast-acting yeast and the food processor will save you time in the preparation of these bread sticks.

1¾ to 2¼ cups all purpose flour
  1 cup cornmeal
  ¼ cup sugar
  1 teaspoon salt
  1 pkg. fast-acting dry yeast
  1 cup water
  ¼ cup margarine or butter
    Margarine or butter, melted
    Cornmeal

In large bowl, combine 1 cup flour, 1 cup cornmeal, sugar, salt and yeast; blend well. In small saucepan, heat water and ¼ cup margarine until very warm (120 to 130°F.). Add warm liquid to flour mixture. Blend at low speed until moistened; beat 2 minutes at medium speed. By hand, stir in an additional ½ to 1 cup flour until dough pulls cleanly away from sides of bowl.

On floured surface, knead in ¼ cup flour until dough is smooth and elastic, about 2 minutes. Place in greased bowl; cover loosely with plastic wrap and cloth towel. Let rise in warm place (80 to 85°F.) until light and doubled in size, about 10 minutes.

Grease 2 large cookie sheets; sprinkle with cornmeal. Punch down dough several times to remove all air bubbles. Divide dough into 24 parts; roll each into 10-inch rope. Place on greased cookie sheets. Cover; let rise in warm place until light and doubled in size, about 10 minutes.

Heat oven to 375°F. Uncover dough. Carefully brush sticks with melted margarine; sprinkle with cornmeal. Bake at 375°F. for 12 to 16 minutes or until bottoms are golden brown. Immediately remove from pans; cool on wire racks.

Yield: 24 bread sticks.

FOOD PROCESSOR DIRECTIONS:
In food processor bowl with metal blade, combine 1¼ cups flour, 1 cup cornmeal, sugar, salt, yeast and ¼ cup margarine. Cover; process 5 seconds. With machine running, pour 1 cup water heated to 120 to 130°F. through feed tube; continue processing until blended, about 20 seconds. Add ½ to 1 cup flour; process 10 to 20 seconds longer or until stiff dough forms. With rubber scraper, carefully pull dough from blade and bowl; place in lightly greased bowl. Continue as directed above.

HIGH ALTITUDE:
Above 3500 Feet: No change.

NUTRITION PER SERVING:
Calories 110; Protein 2g; Carbohydrate 17g; Fat 4g; Sodium 130mg.

COOK'S NOTE

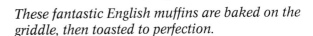

CORNMEAL

By definition, cornmeal is ground dried corn kernels. Commercial cornmeal has the tough outer hull (bran) or the corn kernel steamed away in the milling process. Once the germ is removed, the endosperm is ground by steel rollers into granules. The granules are separated by size; the largest are grits, the medium size are used as cornmeal and the small ones are used as corn flour.

The color of cornmeal can be yellow, white or blue depending on the variety of corn. All are generally interchangeable in recipes. However, when blue cornmeal is used in baking, it turns grayish blue. Much of the blue cornmeal available is grown organically without chemicals or fertilizers in New Mexico. It is abundant in the Southwest and is sold in specialty stores or in food co-ops.

EASY ENGLISH MUFFINS

These fantastic English muffins are baked on the griddle, then toasted to perfection.

2 pkg. active dry yeast
2 cups warm water
5 to 6 cups all purpose flour
1 tablespoon sugar
3 teaspoons salt
½ cup shortening
  Cornmeal
  Margarine or butter

In large bowl, dissolve yeast in warm water (105 to 115°F.). Add 3 cups flour, sugar, salt and shortening to yeast mixture, stirring by hand until moistened. Stir vigorously by hand until smooth. Gradually add remaining 2 to 3 cups flour to form a stiff dough, beating well after each addition. On floured surface, gently knead dough 5 to 6 times until no longer sticky. Roll dough to ¼ to ⅜-inch thickness; cut with floured 3 to 4-inch round cutter. Sprinkle cornmeal evenly over 2 ungreased cookie sheets. Place cut-out dough on cornmeal; sprinkle with additional cornmeal. Cover loosely with plastic wrap and cloth towel. Let rise in warm place until light, about 30 to 45 minutes.

Heat griddle to 350°F. With wide spatula, invert dough onto ungreased griddle. Bake 5 to 6 minutes on each side or until light golden brown; cool. Split in half and toast before serving. Spread with margarine.

Yield: 18 to 26 muffins.

HIGH ALTITUDE:
Above 3500 Feet: No change.

NUTRITION PER SERVING:
Calories 149; Protein 3g; Carbohydrate 23g; Fat 4g; Sodium 250mg.

HERB FOCACCIA

This large, flat, round Italian bread is topped with olive oil and rosemary.

3½ **cups all purpose flour**
1 **teaspoon sugar**
1 **teaspoon salt**
1 **pkg. fast-acting yeast**
1 **cup water**
2 **tablespoons oil**
1 **egg**
3 **to 4 tablespoons olive oil**
1 **teaspoon dried rosemary or basil leaves, crushed**

Grease cookie sheet. In large bowl, combine 1 cup flour, sugar, salt and yeast; mix well. In small saucepan, heat water and oil until very warm (120 to 130°F.). Add warm liquid and egg to flour mixture. Blend at low speed until moistened; beat 2 minutes at medium speed. By hand, stir in an additional 1¾ cups flour until dough pulls away from sides of bowl. On floured surface, knead in ¾ cup flour until dough is smooth and elastic, about 5 minutes. Cover with large bowl; let rest 5 minutes.

Place dough on greased cookie sheet. Roll or press to 12-inch circle. Cover loosely with greased plastic wrap and cloth towel. Let rise in warm place (80 to 85°F.) until light and doubled in size, about 30 minutes.

Heat oven to 400°F. Uncover dough. With fingers or handle of wooden spoon, poke holes in dough at 1 inch intervals. Drizzle 3 to 4 tablespoons olive oil over top of dough. Sprinkle evenly with rosemary.

Bake at 400°F. for 17 to 27 minutes or until golden brown. Immediately remove from cookie sheet; cool on wire rack.
Yield: 1 (16-slice) loaf.

TIPS:
For two smaller loaves, grease 2 cookie sheets. Divide dough in half. Roll or press each half into an 8-inch circle. Continue as directed above. Bake for 10 to 20 minutes.

To freeze focaccia, wrap in plastic wrap or foil and store up to 3 months in freezer.

HIGH ALTITUDE:
Above 3500 Feet: No change.

NUTRITION PER SERVING:
Calories 150; Protein 3g; Carbohydrate 21g; Fat 6g; Sodium 140mg.

ITALIAN BREAD STICKS

These garlic-flavored sticks of bread are a perfect accompaniment to Italian entrees.

1 **pkg. active dry yeast**
⅔ **cup warm water**
2 **to 2¼ cups all purpose flour**
1½ **teaspoons sugar**
1 **teaspoon garlic salt**
¼ **cup shortening**
1 **tablespoon water**
1 **egg white**
 Sesame or poppy seed

In large bowl, dissolve yeast in ⅔ cup warm water (105 to 115°F.). Add 1 cup flour, sugar, garlic salt and shortening. Blend at low speed until moistened; beat 3 minutes at medium speed. By hand, stir in an additional 1 to 1¼ cups flour to form a soft dough.

Place dough in greased bowl; cover loosely with plastic wrap and cloth towel. Let rise in warm place (80 to 85°F.) until light and doubled in size, about 30 to 40 minutes.

Grease 15x10x1-inch baking pan. On lightly floured surface, knead dough about 10 times, or until no longer sticky. Roll into 15x10-inch rectangle; place in greased pan. Starting with 10-inch side, cut dough into 12 strips. Cut strips in half forming 24 sticks. Combine 1 tablespoon water and egg white; blend well. Brush on sticks; sprinkle with sesame seed. Cover; let rise in warm place, about 15 to 20 minutes.

Heat oven to 375°F. Uncover dough. Bake 18 to 22 minutes or until golden brown. Immediately remove from pan; cool on wire rack.
Yield: 24 bread sticks.

TIP:
For softer bread sticks, dough can be baked in greased 13x9-inch pan. Cut into 20 bread sticks.

HIGH ALTITUDE:
Above 3500 Feet: No change.

NUTRITION PER SERVING:
Calories 60; Protein 1g; Carbohydrate 9g; Fat 2g; Sodium 80mg.

Herb Focaccia, Italian Bread Sticks

CHEWY BREAD RINGS

These will remind you of bagels in flavor and texture, but they are much easier to make.

2½ to 3½ cups all purpose flour
2 teaspoons sugar
1 teaspoon salt
1 pkg. active dry yeast
¾ cup water
½ cup milk
2 teaspoons oil
1 egg, beaten
 Poppy seed, sesame seed or caraway seed, if desired
 Water

In large bowl, combine 1½ cups flour, sugar, salt and yeast. In small saucepan, heat water, milk and oil until very warm (120 to 130°F.). Add warm liquid to flour mixture. Blend at low speed until moistened; beat 2 minutes at medium speed. By hand, stir in an additional ¾ to 1½ cups flour until dough pulls cleanly away from sides of bowl.

On floured surface, knead in ¼ to ½ cup flour until dough is smooth and elastic, about 5 minutes. Place dough in greased bowl; cover loosely with plastic wrap and cloth towel. Let rise in warm place (80 to 85°F.) until light and doubled in size, about 40 to 50 minutes.

Grease 2 cookie sheets. Punch down dough several times to remove all air bubbles. Divide dough into 18 pieces. Roll each into 8-inch rope. Form rings, overlapping ends; press to seal. Place on greased cookie sheets. Cover; let rise in warm place until light and doubled in size, about 15 to 25 minutes.

Heat oven to 400°F. Uncover dough. Gently brush rings with egg; sprinkle with poppy seed. Place 13x9-inch pan of hot water on lowest oven rack. Place cookie sheet on middle oven rack over baking pan. Bake at 400°F. for 18 to 22 minutes or until golden brown and rings sound hollow when lightly tapped. Remove from oven; immediately brush with water. Cool on cookie sheet.
Yield: 18 bread rings.

HIGH ALTITUDE:
Above 3500 Feet: No change.

NUTRITION PER SERVING:
Calories 100; Protein 3g; Carbohydrate 19g; Fat 1g; Sodium 125mg.

BAGEL STICKS

The bagel sticks are cooked in water before baking.

3½ to 4½ cups all purpose flour
2 tablespoons sugar
½ teaspoon salt
2 pkg. active dry yeast
1½ cups water
1 egg, separated
2 quarts water
1 tablespoon sugar
1 tablespoon water
2 tablespoons sesame seed

In large bowl, combine 1½ cups flour, 2 tablespoons sugar, salt and yeast; blend well. In small saucepan, heat 1½ cups water until hot (120 to 130°F.). Add hot water and egg white to flour mixture. Blend at low speed until moistened; beat 3 minutes at medium speed. By hand, stir in 1¾ to 2¼ cups flour to form a stiff dough.

On floured surface, knead in ¼ to ¾ cup flour until dough is smooth and elastic, about 7 minutes. Place dough in greased bowl; cover loosely with plastic wrap and cloth towel. Let rise in warm place (80 to 85°F.) until light and doubled in size, about 30 minutes.

Grease 2 cookie sheets. Punch down dough several times to remove all air bubbles. Divide dough into 16 equal pieces; shape into 6-inch sticks. Place on greased cookie sheets. Cover loosely with greased plastic wrap and cloth towel; let rise in warm place until light and doubled in size, about 10 minutes.

Heat oven to 375°F. In Dutch oven, or large kettle combine 2 quarts water and 1 tablespoon sugar. Bring to a boil. Cook 2 bagel sticks at a time in boiling water for 30 seconds, turning once; drain with slotted spoon. Return to greased cookie sheets. In small bowl, combine egg yolk and 1 tablespoon water. Brush over bagel sticks; sprinkle with sesame seed. Bake at 375°F. for 20 to 24 minutes or until light golden brown. Immediately remove from cookie sheets.
Yield: 16 sticks.

HIGH ALTITUDE:
Above 3500 Feet: No change.

NUTRITION PER SERVING:
Calories 150; Protein 5g; Carbohydrate 29g; Fat 1g; Sodium 75mg.

SOFT PRETZELS

Enjoy these with mustard.

3 to 3½ cups all purpose flour
1 tablespoon sugar
1 teaspoon salt
1 pkg. active dry yeast
1 cup water
1 tablespoon shortening
6 cups water
¼ cup baking soda
1 tablespoon water
1 egg white
   Coarse salt or sesame seed

In large bowl, combine 1 cup flour, sugar, salt and yeast; blend well. In small saucepan, heat 1 cup water and shortening until very warm (120 to 130°F.). Add warm liquid to flour mixture. Blend at low speed until moistened; beat 3 minutes at medium speed. Stir in an additional 1½ to 1¾ cups flour until dough pulls cleanly away from sides of bowl.

On floured surface, knead in ½ to ¾ cup flour until dough is smooth and elastic, about 5 minutes. Place dough in greased bowl; cover loosely with plastic wrap and cloth towel. Let rise in warm place (80 to 85°F.) until light and doubled in size, about 45 to 60 minutes.

Grease cookie sheets. Punch down dough several times to remove all air bubbles. Shape dough into ball. Divide dough into 12 pieces. Roll each into 16-inch rope; form pretzel shape. Place on greased cookie sheets. Cover; let rise in warm place until light, about 15 to 20 minutes.

Heat oven to 400°F. In large non-aluminum saucepan, combine 6 cups water and baking soda; bring to a boil. Drop pretzels in water that is just boiling, one at a time, cooking 5 seconds on each side. Remove from water with slotted spoon; place on greased cookie sheet. Combine 1 tablespoon water and egg white; brush on pretzels. Sprinkle with coarse salt.

Bake at 400°F. for 8 to 10 minutes or until golden brown. Immediately remove from cookie sheet; cool on wire racks. Serve warm.
Yield: 12 pretzels.

HIGH ALTITUDE:
Above 3500 Feet: No change.

NUTRITION PER SERVING:
Calories 140; Protein 5g; Carbohydrate 27g; Fat 1g; Sodium 185mg.

HERB CHEESE PRETZELS

A flavorful soft pretzel — perfect to serve with soup or salad.

2 cups all purpose flour
2 teaspoons sugar
1 pkg. active dry yeast
1 teaspoon salt
½ teaspoon Italian seasoning
¼ teaspoon onion powder
¼ teaspoon garlic powder
1½ cups water
3 tablespoons oil
2 tablespoons grated Parmesan cheese
3 oz. (¾ cup) shredded Cheddar cheese
1½ to 2 cups whole wheat flour
1 tablespoon water
1 egg white

In large bowl, combine all purpose flour, sugar, yeast, salt, Italian seasoning, onion powder and garlic powder. In small saucepan, heat 1½ cups water and oil until very warm (120 to 130°F.). Add warm mixture to flour mixture. Blend at low speed until moistened; beat 3 minutes at medium speed. Add Parmesan cheese and Cheddar cheese. Stir in 1½ to 2 cups whole wheat flour until dough pulls cleanly away from sides of bowl.

On floured surface, knead dough until smooth and elastic, about 3 to 5 minutes. Place dough in greased bowl; cover loosely with plastic wrap and cloth towel. Let rise in warm place (80 to 85°F.) about 30 minutes.

Heat oven to 400°F. Generously grease 2 cookie sheets. Punch down dough several times to remove all air bubbles. Divide dough into 12 pieces. Roll each piece into a pencil-shaped 20-inch rope; tie in loose pretzel shape. Place on greased cookie sheets. In small bowl, combine 1 tablespoon water and egg white; blend well. Brush over pretzels.

Bake for 20 to 25 minutes or until golden brown. Immediately remove from cookie sheets; cool on wire racks.
Yield: 12 pretzels.

HIGH ALTITUDE:
Above 3500 Feet: Bake at 400°F. for 15 to 20 minutes.

NUTRITION PER SERVING:
Calories 210; Protein 8g; Carbohydrate 31g; Fat 7g; Sodium 250mg.

REFRIGERATED COFFEE CAKE DOUGH

This easy no-knead dough is made ahead and refrigerated, then shaped into any of the following coffee cakes. By changing the shape and adding your favorite filling, you can create your own specialties.

3¾ **to 4 cups all purpose flour**
 ¼ **cup sugar**
 1 **teaspoon salt**
 2 **pkg. active dry yeast**
 1 **cup milk**
 ¼ **cup water**
 ½ **cup margarine or butter**
 2 **eggs**

In large bowl, combine 1½ cups flour, sugar, salt and yeast; blend well. In small saucepan, heat milk, water and margarine until very warm (120 to 130°F.). Add warm liquid and eggs to flour mixture. Blend at low speed until moistened; beat 3 minutes at medium speed. By hand, stir in 2¼ to 2½ cups flour to make a stiff dough. Cover tightly; refrigerate overnight. Shape and bake as directed in the following recipes.

HIGH ALTITUDE:
Above 3500 Feet: No change.

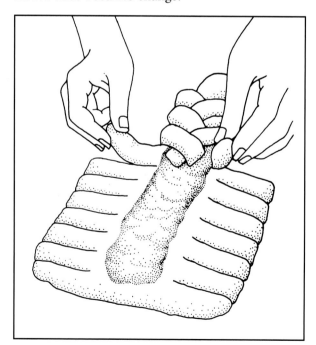

Making an easy braid

PINEAPPLE NUT COFFEE CAKE

This coffee cake features a braided look that is easy to create.

COFFEE CAKES
 ¼ **cup sugar**
 1 **tablespoon cornstarch**
 1 **(8¼-oz.) can crushed pineapple, undrained**
 2 **tablespoons margarine or butter**
 ½ **cup chopped nuts**
 ½ **cup raisins, if desired**
 1 **recipe Refrigerated Coffee Cake Dough (this page)**

TOPPING
 ¼ **cup sugar**
 2 **tablespoons all purpose flour**
 1 **tablespoon margarine or butter, softened**

In small saucepan, combine ¼ cup sugar, cornstarch and pineapple; blend well. Cook over medium heat until thickened, stirring constantly, about 3 minutes. Remove from heat; stir in 2 tablespoons margarine, nuts and raisins. Cool. Set aside.

Grease 2 cookie sheets. Turn dough onto lightly floured surface; divide in half. Roll half of dough into 12x6-inch rectangle; place on greased cookie sheet. Spread half of prepared filling lengthwise down center ⅓ of rectangle. Cut 1-inch wide strips on each side of rectangle just to edge of filling. To give braided appearance, fold strips of dough at an angle across filling, alternating from side to side as shown in diagram. Repeat with second half of dough. Cover loosely with plastic wrap and cloth towel. Let rise in warm place (80 to 85°F.) until light and doubled in size, about 30 to 40 minutes.

Heat oven to 375°F. Uncover dough. In small bowl, combine all topping ingredients; blend well. Sprinkle half of mixture on top of each coffee cake. Bake at 375°F. for 20 to 25 minutes or until golden brown. Immediately remove from cookie sheets; cool on wire racks.
Yield: 2 (12-slice) coffee cakes.

NUTRITION PER SERVING:
Calories 200; Protein 4g; Carbohydrate 29g; Fat 8g; Sodium 160mg.

STREUSEL COFFEE CAKE

There's no special shaping required for this easy coffee cake.

- 1 **recipe Refrigerated Coffee Cake Dough p. 468**
- ½ **cup all purpose flour**
- ⅓ **cup firmly packed brown sugar**
- 1 **teaspoon cinnamon**
- ¼ **cup margarine or butter**
- ½ **cup chopped nuts**

Grease 13x9-inch pan. Press dough in greased pan. Cover loosely with plastic wrap and cloth towel. Let rise in warm place (80 to 85°F.) until light and doubled in size, about 45 to 60 minutes.

In small bowl, combine flour, brown sugar and cinnamon; mix well. Using pastry blender or fork, cut in margarine until mixture is crumbly. Stir in nuts. Set aside.

Heat oven to 375°F. Uncover dough. Sprinkle brown sugar mixture over dough. Bake at 375°F. for 20 to 25 minutes or until golden brown. Serve warm.

Yield: 15 servings.

NUTRITION PER SERVING:
Calories 190; Protein 4g; Carbohydrate 25g; Fat 9g; Sodium 150mg.

FRESH APPLE COFFEE CAKE

Rows of apples sprinkled with cinnamon and sugar top this wonderful bread.

- 1 **recipe Refrigerated Coffee Cake Dough p. 468**
- 4 **cups sliced peeled apples**
- ¾ **cup sugar**
- 3 **tablespoons all purpose flour**
- ½ **teaspoon cinnamon**
- 2 **tablespoons margarine or butter**
- ½ **cup powdered sugar**
- 3 **to 4 teaspoons milk**

Generously grease 13x9-inch pan. Press dough in greased pan. Arrange apple slices in rows on top of dough. In small bowl, combine sugar, flour and cinnamon; mix well. Using pastry blender or fork, cut in margarine until mixture is crumbly. Sprinkle

evenly over apples. Cover loosely with plastic wrap and cloth towel. Let rise in warm place (80 to 85°F.) until light and doubled in size, about 40 to 45 minutes.

Heat oven to 375°F. Uncover dough. Bake 30 to 40 minutes or until golden brown around edges and apples are tender. In small bowl, blend powdered sugar and enough milk for desired drizzling consistency. Drizzle over warm coffee cake. Serve warm.

Yield: 15 servings.

NUTRITION PER SERVING:
Calories 310; Protein 6g; Carbohydrate 51g; Fat 9g; Sodium 250mg.

FANNED PRUNE COFFEE CAKE

Use a kitchen shears to cut the slices for this beautiful coffee cake.

- 2 **cups cooked chopped prunes**
- 3 **tablespoons sugar**
- 2 **tablespoons lemon juice**
- 1 **recipe Refrigerated Coffee Cake Dough p. 468**
- ¼ **cup honey**
- 2 **tablespoons margarine or butter, melted**

In medium saucepan, combine prunes, sugar and lemon juice; bring to a boil. Boil 1 minute, stirring occasionally; cool. Grease 2 cookie sheets. On lightly floured surface, divide dough in half. Roll half into 18x9-inch rectangle. Spread half of prepared filling crosswise on two-thirds of dough. Fold dough over half of filling. Fold again, forming 3 layers of dough and 2 layers of filling. Seal edges well. Place on greased cookie sheet. With scissors or sharp knife, make 8 cuts at 1-inch intervals, to within 1 inch of opposite side. Separate strips slightly; twist so filling shows. Repeat with second half of dough. Cover loosely with plastic wrap and cloth towel. Let rise in warm place (80 to 85°F.) until light and doubled in size, about 30 to 40 minutes.

Heat oven to 375°F. Uncover dough. Bake 15 to 25 minutes or until golden brown. In small bowl, combine honey and margarine. Brush mixture over hot coffee cakes to glaze. Serve warm.

Yield: 2 (16-slice) coffee cakes.

NUTRITION PER SERVING:
Calories 140; Protein 3g; Carbohydrate 22g; Fat 4g; Sodium 120mg.

APRICOT COFFEE CAKE

A tea ring shape shows off the apricot filling.

- 1 (6-oz.) pkg. (1 cup) dried apricots, finely chopped
- 1 cup water
- 3 tablespoons brown sugar
- 2 teaspoons orange juice
- ¼ cup chopped nuts
- 1 recipe Refrigerated Coffee Cake Dough p. 468
- 1 cup powdered sugar, if desired
- 2 to 3 tablespoons milk, if desired

In small saucepan, combine apricots and water. Cook over medium heat, stirring occasionally, until water is absorbed and apricots are soft, about 20 to 25 minutes. Add brown sugar, orange juice and nuts; cool.

Grease 2 cookie sheets. On lightly floured surface, divide dough in half. Roll half of dough into 18x12-inch rectangle; spread with half of filling. Starting with 18-inch side, roll up tightly, pressing edges to seal. Place seam side down on greased cookie sheet. Join ends to form ring; pinch ends to seal. With scissors or sharp knife, cut from outside edge of ring to within ½ inch of inside of ring, making cuts 1 inch apart. Repeat with second half of dough. Cover loosely with plastic wrap and cloth towel. Let rise in warm place (80 to 85°F.) until light and doubled in size, about 30 to 40 minutes.

Heat oven to 375°F. Uncover dough. Bake 20 to 25 minutes or until golden brown. Immediately remove from cookie sheets; cool on wire racks. In small bowl, combine powdered sugar and enough milk for desired drizzling consistency. Drizzle over warm coffee cakes.

Yield: 2 (16-slice) coffee cakes.

NUTRITION PER SERVING:
Calories 140; Protein 3g; Carbohydrate 24g; Fat 4g; Sodium 115mg.

TROPICAL TREAT COFFEE CAKE

Peach or apricot preserves, coconut and nuts top this special coffee cake.

- 1 recipe Refrigerated Coffee Cake Dough p. 468
- 1 (10-oz.) jar peach or apricot preserves
- 2 tablespoons margarine or butter, melted
- ½ cup coconut
- ¼ cup chopped nuts, if desired

Grease 13x9-inch pan. Press dough in greased pan. In small bowl, combine preserves and margarine; spread over dough. Sprinkle with coconut and nuts. Cover loosely with greased plastic wrap and cloth towel. Let rise in warm place (80 to 85°F.) until light and doubled in size, about 40 to 45 minutes.

Heat oven to 375°F. Uncover dough. Bake 30 to 40 minutes or until golden brown around edges. Serve warm.

Yield: 15 servings.

NUTRITION PER SERVING:
Calories 200; Protein 3g; Carbohydrate 31g; Fat 7g; Sodium 135mg.

BUTTER ALMOND COFFEE CAKE

Serve this buttery almond delicacy warm or cool. It's indescribable!

TOPPING
- ⅓ cup butter or margarine, melted
- ½ cup sliced almonds
- ½ cup sugar
- 2 tablespoons light corn syrup
- ½ teaspoon almond extract

COFFEE CAKE
- 1¾ to 2 cups all purpose flour
- ¼ cup sugar
- ½ teaspoon salt
- 1 pkg. active dry yeast
- ½ cup milk
- ¼ cup butter or margarine
- 1 egg

Grease 8 or 9-inch square pan. In small bowl, combine all topping ingredients; blend well. Spread evenly in bottom of greased pan; set aside.

In large bowl, combine 1 cup flour, ¼ cup sugar, salt and yeast; blend well. In small saucepan, heat milk and ¼ cup butter until very warm (120 to 130°F.). Add warm liquid and egg to flour mixture. Blend at low speed until moistened; beat 3 minutes at medium speed. By hand, stir in an additional ¾ to 1 cup flour to make a stiff batter. Spoon evenly over topping mixture in pan. Cover loosely with plastic wrap and cloth towel. Let rise in warm place (80 to 85°F.) until light and doubled in size, about 1½ hours.

Heat oven to 375°F. Uncover dough. Bake 20 to 25 minutes or until golden brown. Immediately turn onto serving platter or foil.

Yield: 9 servings.

HIGH ALTITUDE:
Above 3500 Feet: No change.

NUTRITION PER SERVING:
Calories 340; Protein 5g; Carbohydrate 43g; Fat 16g; Sodium 280mg.

Orange Butter Coffee Cake

Enjoy the aroma of yeast dough when you bake this delightful coffee cake — it has a mouthwatering orange and coconut filling and glaze.

COFFEE CAKE
- 1 pkg. active dry yeast
- ¼ cup warm water
- 2¾ to 3 cups all purpose flour
- ¼ cup sugar
- 1 teaspoon salt
- ⅔ cup dairy sour cream
- 6 tablespoons butter or margarine, melted
- 2 eggs

FILLING
- ¾ cup sugar
- ¾ cup coconut, toasted, p. 23
- 2 tablespoons grated orange peel
- 2 tablespoons butter or margarine, melted

GLAZE
- ¾ cup sugar
- ⅓ cup dairy sour cream
- ¼ cup butter or margarine
- 3 tablespoons orange juice
- ¼ cup coconut, toasted, p. 23

In large bowl, dissolve yeast in warm water (105 to 115°F.). Add 1¾ cups flour and remaining coffee cake ingredients to yeast mixture. Beat 2 minutes at medium speed. By hand, stir in remaining 1 to 1¼ cups flour to form a soft dough. Cover with plastic wrap and cloth towel. Let rise in warm place (80 to 85°F.) until light and doubled in size, about 45 to 60 minutes.

Generously grease 13x9-inch pan. In small bowl, combine all filling ingredients except butter; set aside. On floured surface, knead dough about 15 times. Divide dough in half; roll half of dough into 12-inch circle. Brush with 1 tablespoon of the melted butter. Sprinkle with half of filling mixture. Cut into 12 wedges. Roll up each wedge starting with wide end. Repeat with second half of dough. Place rolls, point side down, in 3 lengthwise rows in greased pan. Cover; let rise in warm place until light and doubled in size, about 45 to 60 minutes.

Heat oven to 350°F. Uncover dough. Bake 25 to 30 minutes or until golden brown. Leave in pan. Meanwhile, in small saucepan combine all glaze ingredients except coconut. Bring to a boil; boil 3 minutes, stirring occasionally. Pour glaze over warm coffee cake. Sprinkle with ¼ cup toasted coconut.

Yield: 24 servings.

HIGH ALTITUDE:
Above 3500 Feet: Bake at 350°F. for 20 to 25 minutes.

NUTRITION PER SERVING:
Calories 220; Protein 3g; Carbohydrate 29g; Fat 10g; Sodium 160mg.

Cook's Note

SOUR CREAM

Sour cream lasts longer if you turn the original container, tightly sealed, upside down in the refrigerator. This prevents air from filling the top.

STEP-BY-STEP FEATURE ❧
How to Shape Tannenbaum Coffee Cakes

STEP 1. Roll half of the dough into a triangle with two 15-inch sides and a 12-inch base. Brush with melted margarine; sprinkle with filling.

STEP 2. Fold 15-inch sides of triangle toward center, covering filling. Press all seams to seal. Invert, seam side down, onto greased pan.

STEP 3. Make 12 slits (1 inch apart) along outside edges to within ½ inch of center of dough. Twist each strip so cut side is up to show filling.

TANNENBAUM COFFEE CAKES

Tannenbaum, the German word for pine tree, is a fitting name for these Christmas tree-shaped loaves.

COFFEE CAKES
- 5 to 6 cups all purpose flour
- ½ cup sugar
- 2 teaspoons salt
- 2 pkg. active dry yeast
- 1½ cups milk
- ½ cup margarine or butter
- 2 eggs

FILLING
- ¼ cup margarine or butter, melted
- 1 cup sugar
- ½ cup chopped nuts
- 1 tablespoon cinnamon

TOPPING
- 1 cup powdered sugar
- 2 to 3 tablespoons milk
- Candied cherries

In large bowl, combine 2 cups flour, ½ cup sugar, salt and yeast; blend well. In medium saucepan, heat 1½ cups milk and ½ cup margarine until very warm (120 to 130°F.). Add warm liquid and eggs to flour mixture. Blend at low speed until moistened; beat 3 minutes at medium speed. By hand, stir in an additional 2 to 2½ cups flour to form a stiff dough.

On floured surface, knead in 1 to 1½ cups flour until dough is smooth and elastic, about 5 to 8 minutes. Place dough in greased bowl; cover loosely with plastic wrap and cloth towel. Let rise in warm place (80 to 85°F.) until light and doubled in size, about 1 to 1¼ hours.

Generously grease two 15x10x1-inch baking pans. Punch down dough several times to remove all air bubbles. Divide dough into 2 parts. On lightly floured surface, roll one part into a triangle with two 15-inch sides and a 12-inch base.* Brush with 1 tablespoon of the melted margarine. In small bowl, combine 2 tablespoons melted margarine, 1 cup sugar, nuts and cinnamon; mix well. Sprinkle ½ of filling mixture evenly over dough.

(Recipe continued on next page.)

Tannenbaum Coffee Cakes

(Recipes continued from previous page.)

To shape tree, starting at top point of dough triangle, fold 15-inch sides to meet in center, pressing all seams to seal. Invert, seam side down, onto greased pan. With scissors or sharp knife, make 12 slits about 1 inch apart along each long outside edge of tree, cutting to within ½ inch of center of dough. Starting at bottom of tree, twist each strip so cut side is up to show filling. Cover; let rise in warm place until light and doubled in size, about 30 to 40 minutes. Repeat with remaining dough and filling.

Heat oven to 350°F. Uncover dough. Bake 20 to 30 minutes or until golden brown. Cool 5 minutes; remove from pans. Cool on wire racks. In small bowl, blend powdered sugar and enough milk for desired drizzling consistency. Drizzle over coffee cakes. Garnish with candied cherries.

Yield: 2 (24-slice) coffee cakes.

TIP:
* For easier shaping of each coffee cake, roll dough on lightly floured cookie sheet. When ready to place on baking pan, invert baking pan over tree on cookie sheet. Invert again; remove cookie sheet.

HIGH ALTITUDE:
Above 3500 Feet: No change.

NUTRITION PER SERVING:
Calories 140; Protein 2g; Carbohydrate 22g; Fat 4g; Sodium 130mg.

POTICA

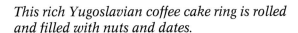

This rich Yugoslavian coffee cake ring is rolled and filled with nuts and dates.

COFFEE CAKE
- 1 pkg. active dry yeast
- ½ cup warm water
- 2 cups all purpose flour
- 2 tablespoons sugar
- ¼ teaspoon salt
- ½ cup margarine or butter
- 1 egg

FILLING
- ¼ cup sugar
- ¼ teaspoon cinnamon
- ¼ cup milk
- ¼ cup honey
- ½ cup ground walnuts
- ½ cup chopped dates

In small bowl, dissolve yeast in warm water (105 to 115°F.). In large bowl, combine flour, 2 tablespoons sugar and salt. With pastry blender or fork, cut in margarine until mixture is crumbly. Add yeast mixture and egg to flour mixture; mix well. Cover tightly and refrigerate overnight.

In large saucepan, combine all filling ingredients. Bring to a boil, stirring constantly. Remove from heat; cool 10 minutes. Set aside.

Grease 6½-cup ring mold. On well floured surface, toss dough until no longer sticky. Roll dough into 20x10-inch rectangle; spread filling evenly over dough. Starting with 20-inch side, roll up tightly, pressing edges to seal. Place seam side down in greased ring mold. Pinch ends to seal. Cover; let rise in warm place (80 to 85°F.) until light and doubled in size, about 1 to 2 hours.

Heat oven to 350°F. Uncover dough. Bake 30 to 40 minutes or until light golden brown. Immediately remove from pan; cool on wire rack.

Yield: 1 (16-slice) coffee cake.

HIGH ALTITUDE:
Above 3500 Feet: No change.

NUTRITION PER SERVING:
Calories 190; Protein 3g; Carbohydrate 26g; Fat 8g; Sodium 105mg.

RUM PECAN RING

Pretty shaping plus an irresistible nut filling make this coffee cake a winner!

COFFEE CAKE
- 3 to 3¼ cups all purpose flour
- ¼ cup sugar
- ½ teaspoon salt
- 1 pkg. active dry yeast
- 1 cup milk
- ½ cup margarine or butter
- 1 egg

FILLING
- ⅔ cup firmly packed brown sugar
- ¼ cup margarine or butter, softened
- ½ cup ground pecans
- ½ teaspoon rum extract

GLAZE
- 1 cup powdered sugar
- ¼ teaspoon rum extract
- 3 to 5 teaspoons milk
  Pecan halves

In large bowl, combine 1½ cups flour, sugar, salt and yeast; mix well. In medium saucepan, heat 1 cup milk and ½ cup margarine until very warm (120 to 130°F.). Add warm liquid and egg to flour mixture. Blend at low speed until moistened; beat 3 minutes at medium speed. By hand, gradually stir in remaining flour until dough pulls cleanly away from sides of bowl.

On floured surface, knead dough until smooth and elastic, about 3 to 5 minutes. Place dough in greased bowl; cover loosely with plastic wrap and cloth towel. Let rise in warm place (80 to 85°F.) until light and doubled in size, about 50 to 60 minutes.

To prepare filling, in small bowl, combine brown sugar and ¼ cup margarine. Stir in ground pecans and ½ teaspoon rum extract.

Grease large cookie sheet. Punch down dough several times to remove all air bubbles. Turn dough onto lightly floured surface. Roll dough into 18x12-inch rectangle. Spread with filling to within ½ inch of edges. Starting with 18-inch side, roll up tightly, pressing edges to seal. Place seam side down on greased cookie sheet. Join ends to form ring; pinch ends to seal. With scissors or sharp knife, cut from outside edge of ring to within ½ inch of inside of ring, making cuts 2 inches apart. Using wooden spoon handle, crease middle of each 2-inch section until dough fans out on either side of crease. Cover; let rise in warm place until light and doubled in size, about 30 to 40 minutes.

Heat oven to 350°F. Uncover dough. Bake 25 to 35 minutes or until golden brown. Immediately remove from cookie sheet; cool on wire rack. In small bowl, blend all glaze ingredients except pecans, adding enough milk for desired drizzling consistency. Drizzle over ring. Garnish with pecan halves.
Yield: 16 servings.

HIGH ALTITUDE:
Above 3500 Feet: No change.

NUTRITION PER SERVING:
Calories 280; Protein 4g; Carbohydrate 41g; Fat 12g; Sodium 180mg.

RICH DANISH RING

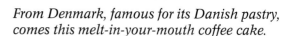

From Denmark, famous for its Danish pastry, comes this melt-in-your-mouth coffee cake.

COFFEE CAKE
- 1 pkg. active dry yeast
- 1 cup warm milk
- 3½ cups all purpose flour
- ½ cup sugar
- 1 teaspoon salt
- ½ cup margarine or butter
- 2 eggs, slightly beaten

FILLING
- ¼ cup margarine or butter, softened
- ½ cup raisins or dried currants, if desired
  Powdered sugar

In small bowl, dissolve yeast in warm milk (105 to 115°F.). In large bowl, combine flour, sugar and salt; blend well. Using pastry blender or fork, cut in ½ cup margarine until mixture is crumbly. Add yeast mixture and eggs; stir well. Cover loosely with plastic wrap and cloth towel. Let rise in warm place (80 to 85°F.) until light and doubled in size, about 1 hour.

Grease 12-cup Bundt® pan or 10-inch tube pan. On well floured surface, toss dough lightly until no longer sticky. Roll dough into 20x10-inch rectangle; spread with ¼ cup margarine and raisins. Starting with 20-inch side, roll up tightly, pressing edges to seal. Place, seam side down, in greased pan. Join ends to form ring; pinch ends to seal. Cover; let rise in warm place until light and doubled in size, about 45 to 50 minutes.

Heat oven to 350°F. Uncover dough. Bake 40 to 50 minutes or until golden brown. Immediately remove from pan; cool on wire rack. Sprinkle with powdered sugar.
Yield: 16 servings.

HIGH ALTITUDE:
Above 3500 Feet: No change.

NUTRITION PER SERVING:
Calories 230; Protein 4g; Carbohydrate 32g; Fat 10g; Sodium 255mg.

CINNAMON ROLLS

Everyone's favorite!

½ recipe Basic Sweet Roll Dough p. 482
¼ cup margarine or butter, softened
½ cup sugar or firmly packed brown sugar
2 teaspoons cinnamon
¾ cup powdered sugar
1 tablespoon margarine or butter, softened
¼ teaspoon vanilla
1 to 2 tablespoons milk

Generously grease 13x9-inch pan. On lightly floured surface, roll out dough into 18x12-inch rectangle. Spread with ¼ cup margarine. In small bowl, combine sugar and cinnamon; blend well. Sprinkle over dough. Starting with 18-inch side, roll up tightly, pressing edges to seal. Cut into 18 slices; place slices, cut side down, in greased pan. Cover; let rise in warm place until light and doubled in size, about 35 to 45 minutes.

Heat oven to 375°F. Uncover dough. Bake 25 to 30 minutes or until golden brown. Immediately remove from pan; place on wire racks. In small bowl, blend powdered sugar, 1 tablespoon margarine, vanilla and enough milk for desired drizzling consistency. Drizzle over warm rolls. Serve warm.
Yield: 18 rolls.

NUTRITION PER SERVING:
Calories 200; Protein 3g; Carbohydrate 33g; Fat 6g; Sodium 190mg.

─── *RECIPE MAKE-OVER* ───

LIGHT CINNAMON ROLLS

We've kept the flavor, but reduced the fat and calories in these luscious rolls.

ROLLS
3½ cups all purpose flour
1 teaspoon sugar
1 teaspoon salt
1 pkg. fast-acting yeast
1 cup water
2 tablespoons reduced-calorie margarine or regular margarine
2 egg whites

2 tablespoons apple juice
⅓ cup sugar or firmly packed brown sugar
2 teaspoons cinnamon

GLAZE
¼ cup powdered sugar
2 to 3 teaspoons skim milk

In large bowl, combine 1 cup of the flour, 1 teaspoon sugar, salt and yeast; blend well. In small saucepan, heat water and margarine until very warm (120 to 130°F.). Add warm liquid and egg whites to flour mixture. Blend at low speed until moistened; beat 2 minutes at medium speed. By hand, stir in an additional 1¾ cups flour until dough pulls cleanly away from sides of bowl. On floured surface, knead in ¾ cup flour until dough is smooth and elastic, about 5 minutes. Cover with large bowl; let rest 5 minutes.

Grease two 9 or 8-inch square pans. On lightly floured surface, roll dough into 18x10-inch rectangle. Brush with apple juice. In small bowl, combine ⅓ cup sugar and cinnamon; mix well. Sprinkle evenly over dough. Starting with 18-inch side, roll up tightly, pressing edges to seal. Cut into 18 slices; place cut side down in greased pans. Cover; let rise in warm place (80 to 85°F.) until light and doubled in size, about 30 minutes.

Heat oven to 375°F. Uncover dough. Bake 25 to 30 minutes or until light golden brown. In small bowl, blend powdered sugar and enough milk for desired glaze consistency. Drizzle over warm rolls. Serve warm.
Yield: 18 rolls.

HIGH ALTITUDE:
Above 3500 Feet: No change.

NUTRITION PER SERVING:
Calories 120; Protein 3g; Carbohydrate 25g; Fat 1g; Sodium 135mg.

WHOLE WHEAT CARAMEL ROLLS

These sensational whole wheat rolls form their own caramel topping as they bake.

- 1 to 2 cups all purpose flour
- 1 cup whole wheat flour
- 3 tablespoons sugar
- 1 teaspoon salt
- 1 pkg. active dry yeast
- ¾ cup milk
- ¼ cup water
- 2 tablespoons shortening
- 1 cup firmly packed brown sugar
- ⅓ cup margarine or butter, melted
- ½ cup chopped nuts

In large bowl, combine ½ cup all purpose flour, whole wheat flour, sugar, salt and yeast; blend well. In small saucepan, heat milk, water and shortening until very warm (120 to 130°F.). Add warm liquid to flour mixture. Stir by hand until moistened. Stir in an additional ¼ to ¾ cup all purpose flour to form a stiff dough.

On floured surface, knead in ¼ to ¾ cup all purpose flour until dough is smooth and elastic, about 5 minutes. Place dough in greased bowl; cover loosely with plastic wrap and cloth towel. Let rise in warm place (80 to 85°F.) until light and doubled in size, about 1¼ hours.

Grease 9-inch square pan. Punch down dough several times to remove all air bubbles. On lightly floured surface, roll into 16x12-inch rectangle. In small bowl, combine brown sugar and margarine; blend well. Spread evenly over dough; sprinkle with nuts. Starting with 16-inch side, roll up tightly, pressing edge to seal. Cut into 16 slices; place cut side down in greased pan. Cover; let rise in warm place until light and doubled in size, about 45 to 60 minutes.

Heat oven to 350°F. Uncover dough. Bake 25 to 30 minutes or until golden brown. Cool 2 minutes; turn onto serving plate or foil.

Yield: 16 rolls.

HIGH ALTITUDE :
Above 3500 Feet: Bake at 375°F. for 25 to 30 minutes.

NUTRITION PER SERVING:
Calories 210; Protein 3g; Carbohydrate 31g; Fat 8g; Sodium 190mg.

ONE-RISE CARAMEL ROLLS

Wonderfully gooey through and through, these rolls are at their best served warm.

TOPPING
- 1 cup firmly packed brown sugar
- 1 cup whipping cream (do not substitute)

ROLLS
- 3½ cups all purpose flour
- ¼ cup sugar
- 1 teaspoon salt
- 1 pkg. active dry yeast
- 1 cup water
- 2 tablespoons margarine or butter
- 1 egg

FILLING
- ½ cup sugar
- 2 teaspoons cinnamon
- ½ cup margarine or butter, softened

In ungreased 13x9-inch pan, combine topping ingredients. Set aside.

In large bowl, combine 1½ cups flour, ¼ cup sugar, salt and yeast; blend well. In small saucepan, heat water and 2 tablespoons margarine until very warm (120 to 130°F.). Add warm liquid and egg to flour mixture. Blend at low speed until moistened; beat 3 minutes at medium speed. By hand, stir in remaining 2 cups flour to form a stiff dough.

On floured surface, knead 2 to 3 minutes. Press or roll dough into 15x7-inch rectangle. In small bowl, combine filling ingredients; spread over dough. Starting with 15-inch side, roll up tightly, pressing edges to seal. Cut into 15 rolls; place, cut side down, over topping in pan. Cover; let rise in warm place (80 to 85°F.) until light and doubled in size, about 35 to 45 minutes.

Heat oven to 400°F. Uncover dough. Bake 20 to 25 minutes or until golden brown. Cool in pan 10 to 15 minutes. Invert onto serving platter or foil.
Yield: 15 rolls.

HIGH ALTITUDE:
Above 3500 Feet: No change.

NUTRITION PER SERVING:
Calories 340; Protein 5g; Carbohydrate 49g; Fat 14g; Sodium 250mg.

Jumbo Pineapple Caramel Rolls

────── ∾ ──────

Be ready for a pineapple and caramel treat when you make these giant sweet rolls.

ROLLS
- 1 (8-oz.) can crushed pineapple in its own juice, drained, reserving liquid
  Water
- 2 tablespoons margarine or butter
- 2½ to 3 cups all purpose flour
- 1 teaspoon salt
- 1 pkg. active dry yeast
- 1 egg
- 1 cup mashed potato flakes

TOPPING
- ¼ cup margarine or butter
- ½ cup firmly packed brown sugar
- 2 tablespoons corn syrup
  Reserved crushed pineapple
- ½ cup coconut, if desired

FILLING
- 2 tablespoons margarine or butter, softened
- ¼ cup firmly packed brown sugar
- ½ teaspoon cinnamon

Measure out ⅓ cup pineapple liquid; add water to measure 1¼ cups. Reserve crushed pineapple. In small saucepan, heat liquid and 2 tablespoons margarine until very warm (120 to 130°F.). In large bowl, combine 1½ cups flour, salt and yeast. Add warm liquid and egg. Blend at low speed until moistened; beat 3 minutes at medium speed. Add potato flakes, beating just until moistened. By hand, stir in an additional ½ to ¾ cup flour until dough pulls cleanly away from sides of bowl.

On floured surface, knead in ½ to ¾ cup flour until dough is smooth and elastic, about 5 minutes. Place dough in greased bowl; cover loosely with plastic wrap and cloth towel. Let rise in warm place (80 to 85°F.) until light and doubled in size, about 45 to 60 minutes.

To prepare topping, melt ¼ cup margarine in 13x9-inch pan. Stir in remaining topping ingredients. Set aside.

Punch down dough. On floured surface, roll dough into 16x10-inch rectangle. Spread with 2 tablespoons margarine. In small bowl, combine ¼ cup brown sugar and cinnamon; sprinkle evenly over dough. Starting with 16-inch side, roll up tightly, pressing edges to seal. Cut into 12 slices; place, cut side down, over topping in pan. Cover; let rise in warm place until doubled in size, about 30 to 45 minutes.

Heat oven to 375°F. Uncover dough. Bake 25 to 30 minutes or until golden brown. Immediately invert onto serving platter or foil.
Yield: 12 rolls.

HIGH ALTITUDE:
Above 3500 Feet: No change.

NUTRITION PER SERVING:
Calories 300; Protein 5g; Carbohydrate 48g; Fat 10g; Sodium 280mg.

Cook's Note

────── ∾ ──────

BUTTER BALLS
Using the large end of a melon baller dipped in hot water, cut balls out of hard butter, then refrigerate them. For best results, use a 1-pound block of butter.

QUICK PRALINE ROLLS

Yeast and baking powder give these rolls a biscuit-like texture.

FILLING
 ¾ **cup firmly packed brown sugar**
 ⅓ **cup margarine or butter, softened**
 ½ **cup chopped walnuts**

ROLLS
1¾ **to 2¾ cups all purpose flour**
 2 **tablespoons sugar**
 1 **teaspoon baking powder**
 ½ **teaspoon salt**
 1 **pkg. active dry yeast**
 ⅓ **cup milk**
 ¼ **cup water**
 ⅓ **cup margarine or butter**
 1 **egg**
 ¼ **cup chopped walnuts**

In small bowl, combine brown sugar and ⅓ cup margarine; beat until light and fluffy. Stir in ½ cup nuts; set aside.

In large bowl, combine 1 cup flour, sugar, baking powder, salt and yeast; blend well. In small saucepan, heat milk, water and ⅓ cup margarine until very warm (120 to 130°F.). Add warm liquid and egg to flour mixture. Blend at low speed until moistened; beat 3 minutes at medium speed. By hand, stir in remaining ¾ to 1¾ cups flour to form a soft dough.

Grease cookie sheet. On floured surface, toss dough until no longer sticky. Roll into 15x10-inch rectangle; spread with half of filling mixture. Starting with 15-inch side, roll up tightly, pressing edges to seal. Cut into 15 slices. Place cut side down on greased cookie sheet; flatten to ½ inch. Spread tops of rolls with remaining filling. Sprinkle with ¼ cup nuts. Cover loosely with greased plastic wrap and cloth towel. Let rise in warm place (80 to 85°F.) until light, about 45 minutes.

Heat oven to 400°F. Uncover dough. Bake 10 to 12 minutes or until light golden brown. Immediately remove from cookie sheet; place on wire racks. Serve warm.
Yield: 15 rolls.

HIGH ALTITUDE :
Above 3500 Feet: No change.

NUTRITION PER SERVING:
Calories 260; Protein 4g; Carbohydrate 32g; Fat 13g; Sodium 200mg.

ORANGE GLORY ROLLS

These scrumptious marmalade-topped rolls will melt in your mouth!

TOPPING
 ¾ **cup orange marmalade**
 1 **tablespoon margarine or butter**

ROLLS
4¼ **to 5¼ cups all purpose flour**
 ½ **cup sugar**
 1 **teaspoon salt**
 2 **pkg. active dry yeast**
 1 **cup milk**
 ½ **cup water**
 ¼ **cup margarine or butter**
 2 **eggs**
 2 **tablespoons margarine or butter, softened**

Generously grease 24 muffin cups. In small saucepan, combine topping ingredients. Cook over low heat until melted, stirring frequently. Place heaping teaspoonful of topping in each greased muffin cup; set aside.

In large bowl, combine 1½ cups flour, sugar, salt and yeast; blend well. In small saucepan, heat milk, water and ¼ cup margarine until very warm (120 to 130°F.). Add warm liquid and eggs to flour mixture. Blend at low speed until moistened; beat 2 minutes at medium speed. By hand, stir in remaining 2¾ to 3¾ cups flour to form a stiff dough.

On floured surface, toss dough until no longer sticky. Divide dough in half. Roll half into 12x10-inch rectangle; spread with 1 tablespoon of the softened margarine. Starting with 12-inch side, roll up tightly, pressing edges to seal. Cut into 12 slices; place cut side down over marmalade mixture in muffin cups. Repeat with second half of dough. Cover loosely with plastic wrap and cloth towel. Let rise in warm place (80 to 85°F.) until light and doubled in size, about 35 to 45 minutes.

Heat oven to 375°F. Uncover dough. Bake 15 to 20 minutes or until light golden brown. (Place foil or cookie sheet on rack below pan during baking to guard against spills.) Immediately invert onto foil or waxed paper.
Yield: 24 rolls.

HIGH ALTITUDE :
Above 3500 Feet: No change.

NUTRITION PER SERVING:
Calories 180; Protein 4g; Carbohydrate 33g; Fat 4g; Sodium 140mg.

GLAZED CHEESECAKE ROLLS

These feather-light yeast rolls have a lemon-flavored cheesecake filling.

ROLLS
- 1 pkg. active dry yeast
- ¼ cup warm water
- 1 teaspoon sugar
- 3½ to 4½ cups all purpose flour
- ⅓ cup sugar
- ½ teaspoon salt
- ½ cup water
- ½ cup margarine or butter
- 2 eggs
- 2 tablespoons margarine or butter, melted

FILLING
- 2 tablespoons sugar
- 1 tablespoon all purpose flour
- ¼ cup dairy sour cream
- 1 (3-oz.) pkg. cream cheese, softened
- 1 tablespoon lemon juice
- ¼ teaspoon vanilla
- 1 egg white

GLAZE
- 2 cups powdered sugar
- 1 tablespoon margarine or butter, softened
- ½ teaspoon vanilla
- 3 to 4 tablespoons milk

Dissolve yeast in ¼ cup warm water (105 to 115°F.); add 1 teaspoon sugar. Let stand 10 minutes. In large bowl, blend 1½ cups flour, ⅓ cup sugar and salt. In small saucepan, heat ½ cup water and ½ cup margarine until very warm (120 to 130°F.). Add warm liquid, yeast mixture and eggs to flour mixture. Blend at low speed until moistened; beat 2 minutes at medium speed. By hand, stir in an additional 1 to 1½ cups flour to form a soft, sticky batter. Cover loosely with plastic wrap and cloth towel. Let rise in warm place (80 to 85°F.) until light and doubled in size, about 1 hour.

On floured surface, knead in 1 to 1½ cups flour until dough is smooth and elastic, about 5 minutes.

Grease 2 cookie sheets. With floured hands, divide dough into 16 parts; shape each into smooth ball. Place 3 inches apart on greased cookie sheets. Brush with melted margarine. Cover; let rise in warm place until light and doubled in size, about 1 hour.

Heat oven to 375°F. In small bowl, blend all filling ingredients until smooth. Uncover dough. With thumb, make 1½-inch deep indentation in center of each roll; fill with 1 tablespoon filling.

Bake at 375°F. for 10 to 15 minutes or until light golden brown. Immediately remove from cookie sheets; cool slightly on wire racks. In small bowl, combine all glaze ingredients, adding enough milk for desired drizzling consistency. Drizzle glaze over warm rolls. Store in refrigerator.

Yield: 16 rolls.

HIGH ALTITUDE:
Above 3500 Feet: No change.

NUTRITION PER SERVING:
Calories 290; Protein 5g; Carbohydrate 40g; Fat 12g; Sodium 190mg.

COOK'S NOTES

ENRICHED FLOUR

Flour is enriched to restore the natural iron and B vitamins that are lost in the milling process. Enrichment causes no change in the flour's taste, color, texture, quality or caloric value.

RASPBERRY SWEET ROLLS

What could be more inviting than a tender sweet roll filled with preserves, then topped with a creamy glaze?

ROLLS

3½ to 4 cups all purpose flour
 ½ cup sugar
 1 teaspoon salt
 2 pkg. active dry yeast
 1 cup milk
 ½ cup margarine or butter
 2 eggs

TOPPING

 ¼ cup margarine or butter, melted
 ½ cup red raspberry preserves

GLAZE

 1 cup powdered sugar
 2 to 3 tablespoons milk

In large bowl, combine 1½ cups flour, sugar, salt and yeast; blend well. In small saucepan, heat 1 cup milk and ½ cup margarine until very warm (120 to 130°F.). Add warm liquid and eggs to flour mixture. Blend at low speed until moistened; beat 3 minutes at medium speed. By hand, stir in an additional 1¾ to 2 cups flour until dough pulls cleanly away from sides of bowl.

On floured surface, knead in ¼ to ½ cup flour until dough is smooth and elastic, about 3 to 5 minutes. Place dough in greased bowl; cover loosely with plastic wrap and cloth towel. Let rise in warm place (80 to 85°F.) until light and doubled in size, about 45 to 60 minutes.

Grease 3 cookie sheets. Punch down dough several times to remove all air bubbles. Turn dough onto lightly floured surface; divide into 24 pieces. Roll each piece into 15-inch rope. On greased cookie sheet, loosely coil each rope into a circle, tucking ends under. Cover; let rise in warm place until light and doubled in size, about 15 to 20 minutes.

Heat oven to 350°F. Uncover dough. Carefully brush rolls with half of the melted margarine. Make deep thumbprint in center of each roll; fill with 1 teaspoon preserves.

Bake at 350°F. for 10 to 20 minutes or until golden brown. Immediately remove from pan; brush a second time with half of the melted margarine. Cool slightly on wire rack.

In small bowl, blend powdered sugar and enough milk for desired drizzling consistency. Drizzle over warm rolls.

Yield: 24 rolls.

HIGH ALTITUDE:
Above 3500 Feet: No change.

NUTRITION PER SERVING:
Calories 190; Protein 3g; Carbohydrate 30g; Fat 7g; Sodium 170mg.

Raspberry Sweet Rolls

SUGAR 'N SPICE PUFFS

The delicious taste of a raised doughnut comes to mind when you eat this tender fluffy sweet roll.

ROLLS

3¼ to 3½ cups all purpose flour
1 cup rolled oats
½ cup sugar
1¼ teaspoons salt
1 teaspoon grated orange peel
1 pkg. active dry yeast
1 cup milk
½ cup water
¼ cup dairy sour cream
3 tablespoons shortening or oil
1 egg

TOPPING

¾ cup sugar
2 teaspoons cinnamon
½ cup margarine or butter, melted

In large bowl, combine 1½ cups flour, ½ cup oats, ¼ cup sugar, salt, orange peel and yeast; blend well. In medium saucepan, heat milk, water, sour cream and shortening until very warm (120 to 130°F.). Add warm liquid and egg to flour mixture. Blend at low speed until moistened; beat 3 minutes at medium speed. By hand, stir in ½ cup oats and 1½ cups flour to form a stiff dough.

On floured surface, knead in remaining ¼ to ½ cup flour until smooth and elastic, about 5 minutes. Place in greased bowl; cover loosely with plastic wrap and cloth towel. Let rise in warm place (80 to 85°F.) until light and doubled in size, about 1 hour.

Generously grease 18 muffin cups. Punch down dough; shape into ball. Divide dough into 18 pieces; shape into balls. Place in greased muffin cups. Cover; let rise in warm place until light and doubled in size, about 45 minutes.

Heat oven to 375°F. Uncover dough. Bake 15 to 20 minutes or until golden brown. Cool 5 minutes; remove from muffin cups. In small bowl, combine ¾ cup sugar and cinnamon. Roll warm rolls in melted margarine, then in cinnamon-sugar mixture. **Yield: 18 rolls.**

HIGH ALTITUDE :
Above 3500 Feet: No change.

NUTRITION PER SERVING:
Calories 240; Protein 5g; Carbohydrate 35g; Fat 9g; Sodium 225mg.

OVERNIGHT MINI SWEET ROLLS

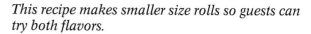

This recipe makes smaller size rolls so guests can try both flavors.

ROLLS

3 to 3¾ cups all purpose flour
¼ cup sugar
½ teaspoon salt
1 pkg. active dry yeast
1 cup milk
¼ cup margarine or butter
1 egg

BLUEBERRY FILLING

¼ cup all purpose flour
¼ cup sugar
½ teaspoon cinnamon
3 tablespoons margarine or butter
¾ cup fresh blueberries

CHERRY FILLING

1 (3½-oz.) tube almond paste
1 tablespoon margarine or butter, softened
1 tablespoon light corn syrup
1 (6-oz.) jar maraschino cherries, drained, halved

In large bowl, combine 1½ cups flour, ¼ cup sugar, salt and yeast; blend well. In small saucepan, heat milk and ¼ cup margarine until very warm (120 to 130°F.). Add warm liquid and egg to flour mixture. Blend at low speed until moistened; beat 2 minutes at medium speed. By hand, stir in an additional 1¼ to 1¾ cups flour until dough pulls cleanly away from sides of bowl.

On floured surface, knead in ¼ to ½ cup flour until dough is smooth and elastic, about 5 minutes. Place in greased bowl; cover loosely with plastic wrap and cloth towel. Let rise in warm place (80 to 85°F.) until light and doubled in size, about 45 minutes.

Grease two 9-inch round pans. Punch down dough several times to remove all air bubbles. Divide dough in half. On lightly floured surface, roll out half of dough into 16x6-inch rectangle. In small bowl, combine all blueberry filling ingredients except blueberries; mix well. Sprinkle evenly over dough; top with blueberries. Starting with 16-inch side, roll up tightly, pressing edges to seal. Cut into 16 slices; place cut side down in 1 greased pan. Cover with greased plastic wrap; refrigerate overnight.

On lightly floured surface, roll out remaining half of dough into 16x6-inch rectangle. In small bowl, combine all cherry filling ingredients except cherries; beat well. Spread evenly over dough; top with cherries. Starting with 16-inch side, roll up tightly, pressing edges to seal. Cut into 16 slices; place cut side down in other greased pan. Cover with greased plastic wrap; refrigerate overnight.

When ready to bake, let rolls stand at room temperature 1 hour. Heat oven to 375°F. Uncover rolls. Bake 22 to 27 minutes or until deep golden brown. Immediately remove from pan; cool on wire racks. If desired, drizzle with powdered sugar glaze.*

Yield: 32 rolls.

TIP:

* To make powdered sugar glaze, in small bowl combine 1 cup powdered sugar and enough water for desired drizzling consistency (about 4 to 6 teaspoons); blend well.

HIGH ALTITUDE :

Above 3500 Feet: No change.

NUTRITION PER SERVING:
Calories 130; Protein 3g; Carbohydrate 19g; Fat 4g; Sodium 65mg.

PEANUT BUTTER AND JELLY ROLLS

A peanut lover's dream — chopped peanuts are swirled into a peanut butter dough and topped with peanut butter frosting.

ROLLS
4½ to 5 cups all purpose flour
½ cup sugar
2 teaspoons salt
2 pkg. active dry yeast
2 cups milk
½ cup peanut butter

FILLING
1 cup chopped peanuts
6 tablespoons grape jelly

GLAZE
1 cup powdered sugar
2 tablespoons peanut butter
1 to 2 tablespoons milk

In large bowl, combine 2 cups flour, sugar, salt and yeast; blend well. In small saucepan, heat 2 cups milk until very warm (120 to 130°F.). Add warm milk and ½ cup peanut butter to flour mixture. Blend at low speed until moistened; beat 3 minutes at medium speed. By hand, stir in an additional 2 to 2¼ cups flour until dough pulls cleanly away from sides of bowl.

On floured surface, knead in ½ to ¾ cup flour until dough is smooth and elastic, about 5 minutes. Place dough in greased bowl; cover loosely with plastic wrap and cloth towel. Let rise in warm place (80 to 85°F.) until light and doubled in size, about 1 hour.

Grease two 9-inch square or round cake pans. Punch down dough several times to remove all air bubbles. Shape into ball. Roll into 18x12-inch rectangle; sprinkle with peanuts. Starting with 18-inch side, roll up tightly, pressing edges to seal. Cut into 18 slices; place in greased pans. Make deep thumbprint in center of each roll; fill each with 1 teaspoon grape jelly. Cover; let rise in warm place until light and doubled in size, about 30 to 45 minutes.

Heat oven to 350°F. Uncover dough. Bake 25 to 35 minutes or until golden brown. Cool in pans about 5 minutes. Carefully remove from pans; cool on wire racks.

In small bowl, blend all glaze ingredients, adding enough milk for desired drizzling consistency. Drizzle over rolls.

Yield: 18 rolls.

HIGH ALTITUDE :
Above 3500 Feet: No change.

NUTRITION PER SERVING:
Calories 320; Protein 10g; Carbohydrate 48g; Fat 10g; Sodium 305mg.

BEEHIVE BUNS

These honey-flavored raisin buns are shaped like miniature beehives. Serve them warm with butter.

ROLLS
- 2 cups whole wheat flour
- 2 pkg. active dry yeast
- 1 teaspoon salt
- 1 cup raisins
- 1 cup very hot water
- 1 cup milk
- ⅓ cup honey
- ⅓ cup margarine or butter
- 2 eggs
- 2 to 3¼ cups all purpose flour

GLAZE
- 3 tablespoons honey
- 3 tablespoons margarine or butter
- 1¼ cups powdered sugar
- 1 teaspoon vanilla

In large bowl, combine whole wheat flour, yeast and salt; set aside. Cover raisins with water for 1 minute; drain. In small saucepan, heat milk, ⅓ cup honey and ⅓ cup margarine until very warm (120 to 130°F.). Add warm mixture to flour mixture. Beat in eggs 1 at a time; stir in drained raisins. By hand, stir in 1½ to 2 cups of the all purpose flour until dough pulls cleanly away from sides of bowl.

On floured surface, knead in remaining ½ to 1¼ cups of the all purpose flour until dough is smooth and elastic, about 5 minutes. Place dough in greased bowl; cover loosely with plastic wrap and cloth towel. Let rise in warm place (80 to 85°F.) until light and doubled in size, about 45 to 60 minutes.

Grease 24 muffin cups. Punch down dough several times to remove all air bubbles. Divide dough into 24 pieces. (Cover dough pieces with inverted bowl to prevent drying out.) Using 1 piece of dough at a time, roll to form 10 to 12-inch rope. Coil rope in muffin cup, tucking end into top center to form beehive shape. Repeat with remaining pieces. Cover; let rise in warm place until light and doubled in size, about 30 to 45 minutes.

Heat oven to 350°F. Uncover dough. Bake 15 to 20 minutes or until golden brown. Immediately remove from muffin cups; place on wire racks. In small saucepan, heat 3 tablespoons each honey and margarine. Stir in powdered sugar and vanilla until smooth. Drizzle over warm rolls.
Yield: 24 rolls.

HIGH ALTITUDE:
Above 3500 Feet: No change.

NUTRITION PER SERVING:
Calories 210; Protein 4g; Carbohydrate 37g; Fat 5g; Sodium 150mg.

STREUSEL PUMPKIN SWEET ROLLS

For convenience, follow our easy tip to prepare these rolls, refrigerate overnight, then pop them in the oven in the morning.

ROLLS
- 4¾ to 5¾ cups all purpose flour
- ½ cup sugar
- 2 teaspoons grated lemon peel
- 1½ teaspoons salt
- 1 pkg. active dry yeast
- 1¼ cups milk
- 1 cup canned pumpkin
- ½ cup margarine or butter

CRUMB TOPPING
- 1½ cups all purpose flour
- 1 cup firmly packed brown sugar
- 1 teaspoon cinnamon
- ½ teaspoon allspice
- ¾ cup margarine or butter
- ½ cup chopped nuts

GLAZE
- 1 cup powdered sugar
- ½ teaspoon vanilla
- 1 to 2 tablespoons milk

In large bowl, combine 1½ cups flour, sugar, lemon peel, salt and yeast; mix well. In small saucepan, heat 1¼ cups milk, pumpkin and ½ cup margarine until very warm (120 to 130°F.). Add warm mixture to flour mixture. Blend at low speed until moistened; beat 3 minutes at medium speed. By hand, stir in an additional 2½ to 3 cups flour until dough pulls cleanly away from sides of bowl.

Streusel Pumpkin Sweet Rolls

On floured surface, knead in ¾ to 1¼ cups flour until dough is smooth and elastic, about 5 to 8 minutes. Place dough in greased bowl; cover loosely with plastic wrap and cloth towel. Let rise in warm place (80 to 85°F.) until light and doubled in size, about 1 hour.

Grease 15x10x1-inch baking pan.* In medium bowl, combine 1½ cups flour, brown sugar, cinnamon and allspice. With fork or pastry blender, cut in ¾ cup margarine until mixture is crumbly. Punch dough down several times to remove all air bubbles. On lightly floured surface, roll into 20x15-inch rectangle. Spoon 2½ cups of the crumb topping evenly over dough; sprinkle with nuts. Starting with 20-inch side, roll up tightly, pressing edges to seal. Cut into 20 slices; place cut side down in greased pan. Cover loosely with plastic wrap and cloth towel.** Let rise in warm place until light and doubled in size, about 45 minutes.

Heat oven to 350°F. Uncover dough. Sprinkle with remaining crumb topping. Bake at 350°F. for 35 to 50 minutes or until golden brown.

In small bowl, blend all glaze ingredients, adding enough milk for desired drizzling consistency. Drizzle over warm rolls.
Yield: 20 rolls.

TIPS:
* Rolls can be baked in two 13x9-inch baking pans. Decrease baking time to 25 to 35 minutes. Place on separate oven racks and stagger for more even heat distribution.

** At this point, dough can be refrigerated overnight. Dough may rise in the refrigerator. If necessary, let dough stand at room temperature until almost double original size. Bake as directed above.

HIGH ALTITUDE :
Above 3500 Feet: No change.

NUTRITION PER SERVING:
Calories 380; Protein 6g; Carbohydrate 59g; Fat 14g; Sodium 310mg.

DELICIOUS HOT CROSS BUNS

These cinnamon-flavored, currant-filled rolls had their origin in England and were traditionally served on Good Friday.

ROLLS
4 to 4½ cups all purpose flour
⅓ cup sugar
½ teaspoon salt
½ teaspoon cinnamon
2 pkg. active dry yeast
¾ cup milk
½ cup oil
3 eggs
½ cup dried currants or raisins
1 egg white, beaten

FROSTING*
1½ cups powdered sugar
2 tablespoons margarine or butter, softened
½ teaspoon vanilla
1 to 2 tablespoons milk

In large bowl, combine 1½ cups flour, sugar, salt, cinnamon and yeast; blend well. In small saucepan, heat ¾ cup milk and oil until very warm (120 to 130°F.). Add warm liquid and eggs to flour mixture. Blend at low speed until moistened; beat 3 minutes at medium speed. By hand, stir in currants and an additional 2¼ to 2½ cups flour until dough pulls cleanly away from sides of bowl.

On floured surface, knead in ¼ to ½ cup flour until dough is smooth and elastic, about 5 minutes. Place dough in greased bowl; cover loosely with plastic wrap and cloth towel. Let rise in warm place (80 to 85°F.) until light and doubled in size, about 30 to 45 minutes.

Grease 15x10x1-inch baking pan. Punch down dough several times to remove all air bubbles. Divide dough into 35 parts; shape into balls. Place in greased pan; brush with egg white. Cover; let rise in warm place until light and doubled in size, about 20 to 30 minutes.

Heat oven to 375°F. Uncover dough. Bake 15 to 20 minutes or until golden brown. Cool slightly. In small bowl, combine all frosting ingredients, adding enough milk for desired piping consistency; beat well. Using decorating bag or spoon, make crosses on each roll.
Yield: 35 rolls.

TIP:
* If frosting is not desired, before brushing with egg white, carefully cut cross on each roll with sharp knife.

HIGH ALTITUDE:
Above 3500 Feet: No change.

NUTRITION PER SERVING:
Calories 140; Protein 3g; Carbohydrate 21g; Fat 4g; Sodium 50mg.

COOK'S NOTE

RAISINS AND DRIED CURRANTS

Raisins are grapes that are harvested and sun-dried for 3 to 5 weeks. Golden raisins, known for their amber color and moist texture, are not sun-dried and are sent for processing immediately after harvest. Golden raisins are dipped in hot water and treated with sulfur dioxide to retain color, then dried in dehydrators. Most raisins come from Thompson seedless grapes, but Muscat and Sultana varieties are also used. Most grapes for raisins are grown in California.

Dried currants resemble tiny, dark raisins. They are dried, seedless Zante grapes. Dried currants are often used interchanegably with raisins.

LUCIA BUNS

These delicately saffron-flavored rolls are served in Sweden on December 13, St. Lucia Day.

ROLLS
- ¾ **cup milk**
- ½ **teaspoon dried saffron threads or cardamom**
- 1 **pkg. active dry yeast**
- ¼ **cup warm water**
- 3¾ **to 4¾ cups all purpose flour**
- ½ **cup margarine or butter, softened**
- ½ **cup sugar**
- 1 **teaspoon salt**
- 2 **eggs**
- 40 **raisins (2 tablespoons)**

GLAZE
- 1 **egg**
- 1 **tablespoon water**

In small saucepan, heat milk and saffron until milk is bright yellow; cool. In large bowl, dissolve yeast in warm water (105 to 115°F.). Strain milk into yeast mixture. Add 1½ cups flour, margarine, sugar, salt and 2 eggs to yeast mixture. Blend at low speed until moistened; beat 3 minutes at medium speed. By hand, stir in an additional 2 to 2¾ cups flour until dough pulls cleanly away from sides of bowl.

On floured surface, knead in ¼ to ½ cup flour until dough is smooth and elastic, about 5 minutes. Place dough in greased bowl; cover loosely with plastic wrap and cloth towel. Let rise in warm place (80 to 85°F.) until light, about 2 hours. (Dough does not double in size.)

Lightly grease 2 cookie sheets. Punch down dough several times to remove all air bubbles. Divide dough into 20 equal pieces. Roll each piece to make a 10-inch rope; shape into "S." Repeat with remaining dough. Place on greased cookie sheets. Cover with greased plastic wrap and cloth towel. Let rise in warm place until light, about 30 to 45 minutes.

Heat oven to 375°F. Uncover dough. Firmly press 1 raisin into center of each coil of each "S." Combine glaze ingredients; brush carefully over rolls. Bake at 375°F. for 10 to 15 minutes or until light golden brown. Immediately remove from cookie sheets; cool on wire racks.
Yield: 20 rolls.

HIGH ALTITUDE :
Above 3500 Feet: No change.

NUTRITION PER SERVING:
Calories 180; Protein 4g; Carbohydrate 28g; Fat 6g; Sodium 180mg.

VARIATION:

LUCIA COFFEE CAKES: Prepare dough as directed above. When ready to shape dough, divide dough in half. Cut each half into 9 equal pieces. Roll each piece into a 7-inch rope. Curl one end of each of 8 of the ropes into a coil. Arrange in a sunburst pattern on greased cookie sheet, fitting the uncurled ends together. Coil the 9th rope and place in the center of sunburst. Repeat with remaining half of dough. Cover with greased plastic wrap and cloth towel. Let rise in warm place until light, about 1 hour. Heat oven to 375°F. Firmly press 1 raisin in center of each coil. Combine glaze ingredients; brush carefully over coffee cakes. Bake at 375°F. for 15 to 20 minutes or until light golden brown. Immediately remove from cookie sheets; cool on wire racks.
Yield: 2 (16-slice) coffee cakes.

NUTRITION INFORMATION

NUTRITION INFORMATION

Pillsbury provides information for each recipe as a guideline for making food choices. Recipe analysis is based on the most current nutritional values available from the United States Department of Agriculture (USDA) and food manufacturers. For each recipe, you'll find calories per serving, plus grams of protein, carbohydrate and fat, and milligrams of sodium.

CALCULATING NUTRITION INFORMATION:

The recipe nutrition calculations are based on:

- a single unit (1 cookie), or the largest number of servings when a range is given (1/10 of recipe when 8 to 10 servings are listed).

- the first ingredient listed when an option is given.

- the larger amount of an ingredient when a range is given.

- 'if desired' or garnishing ingredients when they are included in the ingredient listing.

USING NUTRITION INFORMATION:

The amount of nutrients a person needs is determined by one's age, sex, size and activity level. The following are general guidelines to use for evaluating daily food intake. These numbers will increase or decrease according to individual needs.

Calories:	2350
Protein:	45 to 65 grams
Carbohydrates:	325 grams
Fat:	75 grams or less
Sodium:	2400 milligrams

REDUCING FAT IN BAKED GOODS

Ingredients high in fat, such as margarine, butter, shortening, oil, whipping cream, cream cheese, sour cream and chocolate, add flavor to recipes but also add calories and grams of fat to our diet. In addition to enhancing flavor, fat makes pastry flaky, cakes moist and tender, and cookies crisp. Decreasing fat in a baked item can create a drier, coarser, denser texture and reduce overall flavor. If you would like to try reducing the fat in baked recipes, here are some suggestions:

- Reduce the amount of margarine, butter, shortening or oil in a recipe by ¼ to ⅓.

- Substitute skim milk for 2% or whole milk.

- Substitute lowfat yogurt, light sour cream and light cream cheese in place of the regular products. Although nonfat counter-parts are available, they are not always as successful in baked recipes.

- Limit the use of nuts. For example, sprinkle 2 table-spoons chopped nuts over a frosted cake instead of adding ½ cup of them to the batter.

- Use cholesterol-free, fat-free egg product or egg whites in place of whole eggs in recipes.

- Use evaporated skimmed milk instead of whipping cream in dessert sauces.

- Substitute or add flavorings and/or seasonings to replace the flavor lost from fat. For example, add chocolate and rum flavoring to a cocoa sauce for more intense flavor.

- Serve lowfat baked items such as muffins and coffee cakes warm from the oven. The texture change is not as noticeable when they're eaten warm.

- See our Recipe Make-Overs section in the Index, p. 511.

INDEX

MW = Microwave Option

G

H

I – K

L

EQUIVALENT MEASURES AND WEIGHTS

Dash	=	less than ⅛ teaspoon
3 teaspoons	=	1 tablespoon
2 tablespoons	=	⅛ cup or 1 fluid ounce
4 tablespoons	=	¼ cup
5⅓ tablespoons	=	⅓ cup
8 tablespoons	=	½ cup
12 tablespoons	=	¾ cup
16 tablespoons	=	1 cup
1 cup	=	8 fluid ounces
1 liter	=	1.06 quarts
2 cups	=	1 pint or 16 fluid ounces
4 cups	=	1 quart
2 pints	=	1 quart or 32 fluid ounces
4 quarts	=	1 gallon
8 quarts	=	1 peck
4 pecks	=	1 bushel
16 ounces	=	1 pound
1 ounce	=	28.35 grams

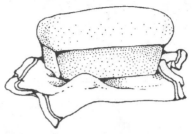

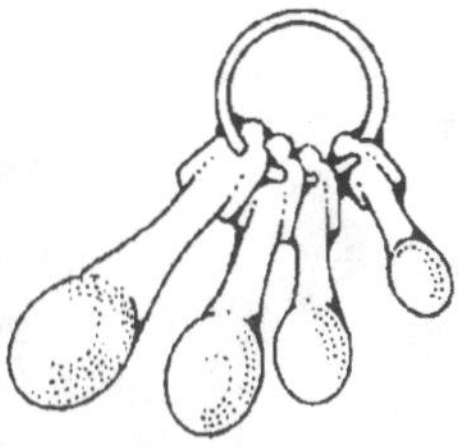

EMERGENCY SUBSTITUTIONS

Ingredient	Substitute
Active dry yeast, 1 package	2¼ teaspoons dry or ⅓ cake compressed yeast, crumbled
Baking powder, 1 teaspoon	¼ teaspoon baking soda plus ½ teaspoon cream of tartar
Buttermilk, 1 cup	1 tablespoon vinegar or lemon juice plus enough milk to make 1 cup
Cake flour, 1 cup	1 cup all purpose flour minus 2 tablespoons
Cornstarch, 1 tablespoon	2 tablespoons flour
Dairy sour cream, 1 cup	1 cup plain yogurt
Flour (for thickening), 1 tablespoon	1½ teaspoons cornstarch
Half-and-half, 1 cup	⅞ cup (¾ cup plus 2 tablespoons) milk plus 3 tablespoons margarine or butter
Honey, 1 cup	1¼ cups sugar plus ¼ cup liquid
Lemon, 1 medium (fresh juice)	2 to 3 tablespoons bottled lemon juice
Orange, 1 medium (fresh juice)	¼ to ⅓ cup orange juice
Yogurt (plain), 1 cup	1 cup dairy sour cream
Self rising flour, 1 cup	1 cup all purpose flour plus 1½ teaspoons baking powder and ½ teaspoon salt
Semi-sweet chocolate, 1 ounce	1 ounce unsweetened chocolate plus 1 tablespoon sugar OR 3 tablespoons semi-sweet chocolate chips
Semi-sweet chocolate chips (for melting), ½ cup	3 ounces semi-sweet chocolate
Unsweetened chocolate, 1 ounce	3 tablespoons unsweetened cocoa plus 1 tablespoon shortening or margarine